EUROPEAN WRITERS
The Twentieth Century

EUROPEAN WRITERS
The Twentieth Century

GEORGE STADE

EDITOR IN CHIEF

Volume 11

WALTER BENJAMIN

TO

YURI OLESHA

CHARLES SCRIBNER'S SONS / NEW YORK

Copyright © 1990 Charles Scribner's Sons

Library of Congress Cataloging-in-Publication Data
(Revised for volumes 10–11)

European writers.

Vols. 5– . Jacques Barzun, editor, George Stade, editor in chief.
Vols. 8– . George Stade, editor in chief.
Includes bibliographies.
Contents: v. 1–2. The Middle Ages and the Renaissance:
Prudentius to Medieval Drama. Petrarch to Renaissance
Short Fiction—v. 3–4. The Age of Reason and the
Enlightenment: René Descartes to Montesquieu.
Voltaire to André Chénier.—v. 5–7. The Romantic
Century: Goethe to Pushkin. Hugo to Fontane.
Baudelaire to the Well-Made Play—v. 8–9. The
Twentieth Century: Sigmund Freud to Paul Valéry.
Pío Baroja to Franz Kafka. v. 10–11. Yevgeny Zamyatin
to Pär Lagerkvist. Walter Benjamin to Yuri Olesha.
  1. European literature—History and criticism—
Addresses, essays, lectures. I. Jackson, W.T.H.
(William Thomas Hobdell), 1915–1983. II. Stade,
George.   III. Barzun, Jacques.
PN501.E9 1983   809'.894   83–16333

ISBN 0–684–16594–5 (v. 1–2)   ISBN 0–684–18924–0 (v. 9)
ISBN 0–684–17914–8 (v. 3–4)   ISBN 0–684–17916–4 (v. 10)
ISBN 0–684–17915–6 (v. 5–7)   ISBN 0–684–18798–1 (v. 11)
ISBN 0–684–18923–2 (v. 8)

The following pamphlets in the Columbia University Press Series "Columbia
Essays on Modern Writers" have been reprinted in this volume by special
arrangement with Columbia University Press, the publisher:

Esslin, Martin: *Bertolt Brecht.* Copyright © 1969 Columbia University Press.
Hayman, David: *Louis-Ferdinand Céline.* Copyright © 1965 Columbia University Press.
Matthews, J. H.: *André Breton.* Copyright © 1967 Columbia University Press.

The paper in this book meets the guidelines for permanence and durability of
the Committee on Production Guidelines for Book Longevity of the
Council on Library Resources

LIST OF SUBJECTS

Volume 10

LIST OF SUBJECTS
Volume 11

CONTRIBUTORS TO VOLUME 11

JOSEPHINE V. ARNOLD
Staunton, Virgina
HENRY DE MONTHERLANT

JARED BECKER
Columbia University
EUGENIO MONTALE

RALPH BOGERT
Harvard University
MIROSLAV KRLEŽA

MARTIN ESSLIN
Stanford University
BERTOLT BRECHT

GREGORY FREIDIN
Stanford University
ISAAC BABEL

DAVID T. HABERLY
University of Virginia
JOSÉ MARIA FERREIRA DE CASTRO

WILLIAM E. HARKINS
Columbia University
YURI OLESHA

DAVID HAYMAN
University of Wisconsin at Madison
LOUIS FERDINAND CÉLINE

VIDA T. JOHNSON
Tufts University
IVO ANDRIĆ

J. MARIN KING
Boston University
MARINA TSVETAEVA

HELENA LEWIS
Center for European Studies, Harvard University
LOUIS ARAGON

SYLVÈRE LOTRINGER
Columbia University
ANTONIN ARTAUD

J. H. MATTHEWS †
Syracuse University
ANDRÉ BRETON

JEFFREY MEYERS
University of Colorado at Boulder
GUISEPPE TOMASI DI LAMPEDUSA

GEORGE C. SCHOOLFIELD
Yale University
EDITH SÖDERGRAN

HENNING K. SEHMSDORF
University of Washington at Seatt
TARJEI VESAAS

ROBERT M. STEIN
State University of New York at Purchase
WALTER BENJAMIN

VICTOR TERRAS
Brown University
VLADIMIR MAYAKOVSKY

LARS G. WARME
University of Washington at Seattle
VILHELM MOBERG

ARNOLD WEINSTEIN
Columbia University
FEDERICO GARCÍA LORCA

DAVID WILLINGER
The City College and Graduate Center of the *City University of New York*
MICHEL DE GHELDERODE

EUROPEAN WRITERS
The Twentieth Century

WALTER BENJAMIN

(1892–1940)

WALTER BENJAMIN ASPIRED to be the greatest literary critic of his time. Among other things this meant single-handedly reinventing criticism as a serious literary enterprise. His work was known only to a small number of readers during his short life. Yet his friends and admirers read like a roll call of the German artistic and intellectual elite of the early twentieth century—including poets Hugo von Hofmannsthal and Bertolt Brecht, philosophers Ernst Bloch and Theodor Adorno, and critics and scholars Gershom Scholem and Siegfried Kracauer—and his impact on them was profound and lasting. Benjamin published only three books, two of which were academic: his doctoral dissertation and his *Ursprung des deutschen Trauerspiels* (*The Origin of German Tragic Drama*, 1928), a second dissertation required by the German university system as a prerequisite to teaching. The third, *Einbahnstraße* (*One-Way Street*, 1928), is a collection of aphorisms, dreams, descriptions, and slogans in the manner of a montage. Benjamin did not continue his university career, however, and the rest of his critical work consists of short essays, sketches, occasional pieces, reviews, and various commissioned work. Published for the most part in newspapers and literary reviews, his writings became unobtainable during the period of National Socialism, when Benjamin's already obscure star seemed to fade entirely from view. The publication in 1955 of *Schriften* (Writings), a two-volume collection of essays, reviews, and personal writings, marked the beginning of an astonishing Benjamin renaissance in Germany. Since the publication in 1968 of a small selection of his essays in English translation, there has been an explosion of interest in his life and work both within and without academic circles; at last count the bibliography of books and articles about him numbers well over four hundred entries, and there is no sign of a slowdown in its growth.

Benjamin's work is scattered among a variety of publications for various audiences and is prompted by quite different occasions. Nevertheless, certain overriding concerns are apparent throughout his writings. Language, the epistemological status of the work of art, the nature of symbolic and allegorical literature, and the task of the critic—these themes are variously present in all his work. Above all there is Benjamin's own situation as a modernist critic of modernism, a displaced European secular Jew on the eve of the most barbaric anti-Semitic outrage in human history, a Marxist of extreme unconventionality, a writer of uncommon power and beauty. Benjamin divided his own critical interests into three periods, marked by three love affairs; scholars see his life as divided by the influence of three friendships; the early period up to the failure of his academic plans was influenced by his friendship with the young Gershom (then still Gerhard) Scholem, a student of mathematics and philosophy and an anarchist and unconventional Zionist who later became the premier scholar of the cabala and Jewish mysticism; the middle period consisted of his commitment to Marxism and his friendship with Brecht; and the final period of exile and work was problematically connected to the Frankfurt Institut für Sozialforschung (Institute for Social Research, known as the Frankfurt School) and his friendship with Adorno.

Benjamin was born (15 July 1892) into a fairly wealthy, middle-class Jewish family in Berlin. His father, Emil, was an auctioneer and dealer in antiques and collectibles, and his mother Paula, née Schönfleiss, was related to the Heine family. Benjamin was seized with the passion for collecting that possessed him throughout his life and that he wrote about frequently. Educated at a progressive secondary school in Berlin and then at Freiburg, Berlin, and Munich, he became for a time a leader in heterodox circles of the German youth movement, the widespread organization of hiking and athletic associations based on an ideology of spontaneity and the moral solidarity of youth. His earliest writings, celebrations of the spirit of youth and polemics over the internal politics of the various factions of the student associations, were published in movement journals. The outbreak of World War I was traumatic for the youth movement, which all but collapsed over the imposition of military conscription and the issue of war resistance. Disgusted by what he saw as false patriotism and deeply stirred by the romantic double suicide of his friends the poet Fritz Heinle and Rika Seligsohn, Benjamin resigned from the movement and cut all his ties with movement friends. He avoided conscription and managed to go to neutral Switzerland.

In 1920 at the University of Bern he was awarded a doctorate summa cum laude in the faculty of philosophy. His dissertation, *Der Begriff der Kunstkritik in der deutschen Romantik* (The Concept of Art Criticism in German Romanticism, 1920), has unfortunately not yet been translated into English. An investigation of the work of Friedrich von Schlegel and the critical fragments of Novalis, the dissertation is the first substantial piece of Benjamin's criticism, and it carries the seeds of much of his future work. Among his earliest critical work are several papers important for understanding his development: the critical pieces "Zwei Gedichte von Friedrich Hölderlin" ("Two Poems of Friedrich Hölderlin," 1915) and "*Der Idiot* von Dostojewskii" ("*The Idiot* of Dostoyevski," 1917), the Sorelian essay "Zur Kritik der Gewalt" ("Critique of Violence," 1921), and the essay on language "Über Sprache überhaupt und über die Sprache des Menschen" ("On Language as Such and on the Human Language," 1916) set much of his critical agenda. His earliest masterpiece is "Die Aufgabe des Übersetzers" ("The Task of the Translator," 1923), an introduction to his translation of poems from Charles Baudelaire's *Tableaux Parisiens* (Parisian Scenes). This phase of Benjamin's work reaches a first conclusion in the great essay on Johann Wolfgang von Goethe's 1809 work *Die Wahlverwandtschaften* (*Elective Affinities*), published in 1924 by Hugo von Hofmannsthal in his journal *Neue Deutsche Beiträge*. (Unfortunately, this piece, among the most important of Benjamin's works, is not yet available in English translation.) His first period culminates in *The Origin of German Tragic Drama.*

His work then radically changed direction. Benjamin became a working journalist, reviewer, and translator. For the rest of his life, he worked out an uncompromising set of ideas on history, society, and the work of art. His later criticism is continuous with the efforts of the earlier work, but these efforts were then transformed by the concepts, methods, and political stance of Marxist analysis.

THE EARLY WORK

Benjamin's modernism consists first of all in a criticism based on the text as an autonomous entity. In this it can be seen as continuous with impulses that lead away from the traditional academic practice of literary study based either on philology, which starts from the assumption that the stages of language preserved in literary texts are documents significant for their disclosure of a nation's cultural development, or on "empirical" literary history, which is the attempt to document and classify literary production, to trace lines of influence and development of genres—to arrange, as it were, taxonomic tables of the genera and species of national literatures. In his move to an analysis of the text in its own right Benjamin was not alone. His work is a direct development of the celebration of art that surfaced in the nineteenth century as "art for art's sake." The French late Romantics and symbolists and especially Oscar Wilde in England carried the idea of art for art's sake over into criticism, and the critical essay became paradoxically enshrined as the purest form of art: art is the antithesis of life, and if art is valuable because it has no connection with life, what could be more valuable than writing that draws its whole being from art, that emerges from the sphere of art and returns only to the sphere of art? The critical essay serves no material purpose; it has nothing to do with academic research and still less to do with Sunday book reviewing. Criticism as art is strictly useless, just as all expression, always ultimately self-expression, is useless.

The exultant tone of the celebrants of pure art is no accident. We tend now to see the movement as the expression in positive language of a social crisis in the arts—the marginalization of the artist's role and the restriction of the artist's sphere of significant activity on the one hand and the growth of the art market and mass culture on the other. The freedom of *la bohème* is a joyous embrace of what in other terms is called alienation, depersonalization, and the fragmentation of social life. Pure art and pure criticism are signs of social disintegration in the guise of the celebration of freedom.

Benjamin's early criticism is pure criticism.

It is not intended to help an uninitiated reader understand a difficult text, nor does it intend to contribute to the knowledge of specialists. The critical activity is carried on for its own sake and consists solely in the encounter between the critic and the text. Critical interpretation is expression. Nevertheless, even as pure criticism Benjamin's critical activity contains a dimension that is as crucial as it is difficult to name. It is, first of all, a criticism practiced at the borders of criticism; it is criticism always about to become something else. That something else has the appearance of philosophy, but it is not in any strict sense philosophy. Rather, its impulse is what underlies philosophical speculation, particularly what underlies metaphysics. Benjamin encounters a text in order to approach the sphere where meaning arises as transparent and self-evident. This sphere has a name in traditional Western thinking: it is the mind of God, and its investigation is theology. Yet Benjamin's criticism, if it is theological, is not by any means in the service of a creed, and if it is religious, it is not founded upon belief. If Benjamin reasons theologically, if he is drawn in his reading to theological argument, and if his most striking formulations are made in theological language, it is because theology is the domain where meaning was last seen to arise as transparent and self-evident. Benjamin does not attempt to rescue theology; Benjamin's attempt is to rescue meaning for criticism.

The turn toward theology is not personal and idiosyncratic. Contemporary with the beginnings of Benjamin's critical activity, some of those who became Europe's most formidable thinkers were similarly engaged in theological argument. One need only think of Martin Heidegger, whose earliest work, centered on the Middle Ages, was the starting point of his general reconstruction of metaphysics for the twentieth century, or of the young György Lukács, or of Bloch, whose *Geist der Utopie* (*Spirit of Utopia*, 1918) was written in the language of an apocalyptic messianism. For a 1962 reissue of his *Theorie des Romans* (*The-*

ory of the Novel, 1920), Lukács wrote a self-critical preface in which he connected the theoretical position of the book with the work of Benjamin and Bloch and suggested that they all arose from the same historical situation, a mood of political and social despair occasioned by the outbreak of World War I and the collapse of all political opposition to the disgrace of patriotic war fever. The urgency of the intellectuals' attempts to find a sphere of meaning and to assert it for knowledge is a measure of the depth of despair.

Benjamin grew up in an upper-middle-class family in a comfortable Jewish neighborhood in Berlin. Like many others, his family was entirely assimilated; they thought of themselves as Germans who happened to be Jewish, celebrated Christmas as a national holiday, and lived in the manner appropriate to their comfortably wealthy urban milieu. There is no biographical evidence of Jewish education or experience of Jewish ritual in Benjamin's upbringing, yet his theology is entirely Jewish. It is especially related to cabalistic and other forms of heterodox Judaism.

Benjamin's attraction to the heterodox, the castoff, is a permanent part of his psychological makeup. Yet the cabalistic writings supplied him with a set of vitally fruitful ideas concerning language, text, and history. The connection in the writings runs roughly as follows: the language of the sacred text, the Torah, continually reveals the presence of God, but this presence is always revealed as a "not yet"; the full presence of God is made manifest in the continual discrepancy between what is revealed and what is still to be revealed, between the expressed and the not yet expressed, hence the necessity for the continuing interpretation of the text that in its own enduring life, tradition, constitutes all meaning. The order of this perpetual revelation is precisely what history is. Since meaning is never fully present but is always still in the process of coming into being, revelation is never complete within history. Its completion rather marks the end of history. The coming of the Messiah is a violent interruption; it destroys all that there is. In history redemption is always negative: redemption is different from what is, it is later than what is, and it destroys what is. The language of the sacred text, in this light, has a dual meaning: it reveals by expressing the expressible, and in so doing it symbolizes the presence of the inexpressible, a presence knowable now only through its absence, only through its being not yet present. And among some cabalists this duality is indicated by the idea that at the end of time the Torah that we now possess will be replaced by the "Torah of Redemption," a Torah in which word and meaning, language and truth, are one, and all is fully expressed to a redeemed mankind living in the full knowledge of truth.

Benjamin's earliest works at the borders of criticism are explorations in the philosophy of language. The essay "On Language as Such and on the Human Language" was written in 1916, and Benjamin refers back to it throughout his later writings. The basis for his exploration of language is the problem of knowledge. In the early essay Benjamin proceeds from the contrast between what he calls the inadequate "bourgeois theory of language"—the idea that language is a structure of conventional signs through which a speaker communicates information to a listener (or a writer to a reader)—and what he calls the fundamental insight of the philosophy of language, the theological conception that the world of nature is permeated with language, that everything participates in it in some way, and that human language is a special and privileged case of "language as such." Information is communicated *through* language, but what is communicated *in* language is the very fact of communication. What is communicated by things is their own communicability, and that is precisely what we have knowledge of: we know of the world what it has communicated to us through its own communicability. This knowledge is then manifested in the uniquely human act of naming the things of the world, and in so doing, the silent communication of things is given a voice. Human language differs from all other language only and decisively in that it is speech: in human speech the fact of communicability itself is communicated.

The essay is an extended commentary on the creation myth in Genesis. Benjamin reads the text structurally, noting that in the narrative of the creation of nature there is a repetition of the rhythm "Let there be" / "He created" / "He called." He also notes the exception of the creation of man: God did not create man from the word, and He did not name him. In the creation of nature language begins and ends the act. Man, made in the divine image, mirrors the divine creativity in human knowledge. Yet even in the paradise of Adamic naming there is an abyss between the human and the divine: the word of God is unlimited and creative; human naming is limited and reflective.

And there is yet another abyss. At the heart of the essay is a moving description of human isolation and ignorance and of a world grown mute in sadness (sad because it is mute, and more importantly, mute because it mourns its sadness). Benjamin uses the myth of the fall and the ensuing confusion of tongues to express the abyss that opens between the essential totality of the natural and human world in language on the one hand and the stark factuality of isolation and silence on the other. The attempt to know good and evil in a world originally named as all good introduces a factitious knowledge as the parody of real knowledge, and a corresponding degraded language mediately communicating only in conventional signs—the transformation of the knowing/naming word to what Kierkegaard called *Geschwätz,* or "empty talking"—as a parody of authentic language.

The full force of the essay lies precisely in its power to suspend the vision of the totality of language, meaning, and name over the abyss of silence and mourning. Here is the locus of critical activity, a place of infinite danger and infinite necessity, and it manifests itself in two modes—translation and criticism—precisely because the diverse human languages, which include not only such entities as English and German but also the languages of dance, music, and other artistic forms, still contain, though only in degraded form, knowledge of things.

The essay "The Task of the Translator" was written initially as the preface to a set of translations from Baudelaire's *Tableaux Parisiens,* Benjamin's first engagement with the poet whose work was to occupy a central place in his thinking throughout his life. The essay examines the constellation of language, text, and history by developing the idea of history as the medium within which the literary text is situated. The essay begins to define the task of the translator by means of a negative characterization of the nature of the literary text. The stance is typical of pure criticism: "A consideration of the receiver never proves fruitful for the understanding of a work of art or an art form. . . . For no poem is for its reader, no image for its beholder, no symphony for the community of its listeners."

Just as a literary text is not for its reader, a translation is not for an audience that does not understand the language of the original. Rather, the act of translation (and the necessity of translation) depends on an intrinsic property of the original—its *translatability*—a property that for Benjamin is strictly independent from the question of whether someone has been able to translate it. To explain this apparent paradox, Benjamin makes use of a beautiful analogy that he had originally formed in his essay on Dostoevsky's *Idiot:* we may call someone an unforgettable person even if everyone has forgotten him. If the essence of the person requires that he not be forgotten, the fact that people have forgotten him does not make the statement false; rather, it shows us a true state of affairs that the world has left unfulfilled, a demand with which the world has not complied. The force of the comparison lies in its precise definition of the realm of meaning in experience as a necessity, and therefore as a demand leveled on the future. Experience is an opening of possibilities demanding the fulfillment of meaning. Translatability is an idea. It is made manifest in the work, and it has nothing to do with the work's content, with the merely contingent fact that a literary work contains information that it passes on to its reader; a bad translation is "the inexact, repetitive communication of an inessential message." This fundamental distinction between what is communicated through language (information, content) and what is communicated in it (communicability, translatability) is carried over from the essay on language.

Translatability is one aspect of the text's life in history—this means a text has antecedents, comes into being at a particular moment, and continues to live for later generations. Elements in it that were once fresh become old and worn, tendencies that lay hidden come to light, qualities that were unimportant become most important of all. Moreover, the language of the original text is similarly a living entity. Between the moment of the original and the translation, the language of the original—perhaps even because of the linguistic force of the original text—has become something other than it was. Translation can in no way be in the service of the original. The fact that translation comes later than the original is part of its essence. It marks the moment when the text outgrows the intimacy of its original relationship to its own language. Translation is one form of the continuing life of the text: from the perspective of the text, translatability is a mark of the continuing possibility of its life in language; from the perspective of language, translatability marks the essential relationship of all languages.

A translation is thus a point of intersection between two languages, each living and changing, and at this point of intersection the relationship of the text to each language is antithetical. For the original language the text is a moment of culmination. The literary work of art thus happens once and once only; on that rests its uniqueness and unreproducibility. For the new language the text is a moment of renewal. The act of translation needs to be done again and again; on that rests the fact that a translation can never itself be translated and the fact that a translation into one language represents the possibility of translation into all others.

What, then, is the task of the translator? The literary text is a privileged object because it is, in the sense of the essay on language, a language, a site of continuous revelation. Its being is a mode of the presentation of meaning, and this mode is irony. The literary text by its necessarily partial presentation of meaning is itself a symbol of the fully present meaning that it does not attain, a symbol of pure language "which no longer means anything, but is, as expressionless and creative Word, that which is meant in all languages." The task of the translator, then, is to break through the limitations of his own language by finding in it the echo of the original, and thus to liberate in his own tongue that pure language—"that which is meant in all languages"—from its imprisonment in the literary text of another.

What is decisive in Benjamin's further development is not the messianic standpoint, but the sense of history as the arena in which the text unfolds its truth, an idea which the messianic standpoint enables. The text is not a passive thing remaining unchanged from what it was when it first came into being; it is a life in a process of constant development, of revealing its truth. The task of the translator is not in the service of the text; it is in the service of the further revelation of the truth that the text contains. In this, the task of the translator is the task of the critic.

In the idea of the historical development of the text Benjamin has taken the presuppositions of pure art and of pure criticism as art and transformed them almost beyond recognition. The fin de siècle writers had raised criticism to the level of art by asserting its connections to art alone. Benjamin preserves the status of criticism as a literary genre by demonstrating its direct relation to the object of literary value: criticism is the presentation of the truth of the work of art, a truth made evident in the work of art's intention to mean.

To rescue meaning for criticism meant the return to the sources of the great privileging of the work of art whose last unfolding began with the movement of art for art's sake. In this regard, Lukács signals his own return to the tradition of Hegel, Goethe, and Romanticism. Benjamin had only the slightest acquaintance with Hegel. His tradition was Hölderlin and Goethe, and his dissertation, written while he was in virtual exile in Switzerland during the war, was an investigation of the concept of criticism in the work of the early German Romantics Schlegel and Novalis. Their work is decisive for Benjamin precisely insofar as it indicates the possibility of a rigorous and pure literary criticism in the service of meaning.

The dissertation is not a piece of pure research. It is Benjamin's attempt, through research, to clarify his own position as literary critic. The critical theory of the early Romantics as Benjamin presents it contains several elements that he makes his own. The first is the notion of the literary work as a mode—along with philosophy and religion—of the coming into being of truth. But unlike Hegel, who saw the work of art as only a very limited step in the unfolding of truth, the Romantics endowed art with the highest privilege. This privileging of the work of art, however, was actually a means of asserting the ultimate value of criticism. Benjamin begins with a consideration of Johann Gottlieb Fichte's epistemological notion of reflection, the movement of *Geist*—which is both mind and spirit, that is, both the subjective and objective side of mental activity—from lower to higher orders of intention. This is the logical movement from having an immediate thought to making that thought the object of thinking: this thinking "the thought of the thought" is called mediation, through which the Absolute, the totality of the real, is progressively revealed as immediately present knowledge. Fichte saw the ego as the object of this second order of reflection (the thought of the thought), which he called form. Schlegel recognized aesthetic form as a possible object of second-order reflection, and in so doing grounded both the work of art and criticism within a general system of epistemology.

For the Romantics the work of art is the occasion for the critic to ascend to ever-higher levels of knowledge and self-knowledge in pursuit of ultimate, absolute truth. This version of the task of criticism, the task of furthering what was begun in the text by "reflection of its reflection," is directly related to what the Romantics called "immanent criticism." The idea of "immanent criticism," a hallmark of the Romantic theory of art, which plays a crucial role in such further elaborations of this theory as the Anglo-American New Criticism (with its acknowledged roots in the critical thought of Samuel Taylor Coleridge and therefore of Schlegel), is often mistakenly taken to imply the critic's self-effacement before the work, or the critic's reading without consideration of factors external to the text. The latter implication brings with it the pedagogical method of virtually all contemporary English and modern language departments in American universities—instruction in "close reading" of texts after some brief lectures on historical backgrounds and literary influences. Immanent criticism, as the Romantics used the term, has particularly to do with judging aesthetic worth and is part of the reaction against the neoclassic attempt to devise a canon of rules of form for judging works of art—rules such as the famous unities of time, place, and action by which good tragedy was distinguished from bad. For the Romantics, no work of art is to be judged by anything outside itself; the work generates its own form and therefore its own idea, and through it provides its own criteria for judgment.

The most important result of this formulation, however, is the shift of criticism completely away from the question of judging literary works. Ultimately for the Romantics the only criterion the work of art can provide is its recognizability *as* a work of art in the possibility of its own criticism, "because there is no measure, no criterion for the presence of reflection other than the possibility of its fruitful unfolding which *is* criticism." If it can be fruitfully criticized, it is a work of art; if not, not. There is no middle ground. "Criticism is as it were an experiment on the work of art, through which its reflection is awakened, through which it is brought to consciousness and to the knowledge of itself." We can easily recognize in this characterization Benjamin's idea of translatability. The idea of immanent criticism does not carry with it the obligation for the critic to submit to the text. Rather it is a condition of the text's being that it submit to criticism.

GOETHE'S ELECTIVE AFFINITIES

Benjamin carries forward the Romantic idea of criticism as culmination, completion, and systematization of what the work of art has begun. Thus, far from being in the service of the text, criticism is rather the activity through which the text reaches its end. Like translation, criticism is a mode of textual development, part of the continuing life in history that all literary texts possess. In Benjamin's essay "Goethes *Wahlverwandtschaften*" ("Goethe's *Elective Affinities*") we can see the full seriousness and the far-reaching consequences of his return to the Romantics. Benjamin's choice of Goethe as his subject is itself an homage and a challenge to his Romantic precursors: Schlegel had begun his critical activity with an essay on Goethe's *Wilhelm Meisters Lehr- und Wanderjahre* (*The Apprenticeship and Travels of Wilhelm Meister*, 1796).

Benjamin's essay is in three parts, each of which begins with a general theoretical exposition before examining the text of Goethe's novel. In an outline of the essay Benjamin titled the three sections "Mythos als These" (The Mythic as Thesis), "Erlösung als Antithese" (Redemption as Antithesis), and "Hoffnung als Synthese" (Hope as Synthesis). In the first part

a distinction is made between commentary and criticism: the aim of commentary is to clarify the "material-content," the subject matter of the literary text; the aim of criticism is to reveal the text's "truth-content." When a work first appears, interest in its significance is inextricably bound up with interest in its subject matter. For the author and for contemporary readers the work's truth is indistinguishable from its contents. In the course of its life the work becomes strange, obsolete, foreign, and even irrelevant for later generations, but not in its significance. It is because of the truth it contains that the work continues to be read. Extracting this truth is the business of criticism. However, since the truth of the work is entangled in its material content, or to put it another way, since the material content is the historical form of the appearance of the work's truth, criticism must begin as commentary. As in Benjamin's idea of translation, the literary work is neither a once-and-for-all occurrence absolutely embedded in the conditions of its own composition, nor is it a magical, transcendent object timelessly communicating timeless truths to the ages. The work has a history, and the way a text continues to live is part of its significance.

Goethe's *Elective Affinities* is a novel about a married couple, Eduard and Charlotte, and a pair of houseguests, Charlotte's young ward and Eduard's best friend. Eduard and Charlotte each find themselves inexorably drawn to the corresponding guest, and the result is the collapse of the marriage and ultimately the death of the young ward, Ottilie. In conversation Goethe had indicated that the subject of the novel was the tragic conflict between the competing demands of the emotional and moral life (*sinnliche und sittliche Leben*), and critics have generally followed the author's lead, discussing the novel in terms of the conflicts between love and marriage, inner freedom and social conformity, passion and reason, and so forth, and seeing in Ottilie's death a kind of transfiguration in which the tragic conflict is resolved in a higher, spiritual realm.

WALTER BENJAMIN

Benjamin's commentary is entirely different from the traditional interpretation. He begins by noting that the novel is not about marriage at all. Rather, the novel contains varieties of the dissolution of marriages. Marriage has no power in the novel, neither moral nor social, neither in the lives of Eduard and Charlotte nor in the lives of their friends the Baron and Baroness, who openly live together while each is married to someone else. The thrust of this observation is ultimately to assert that the polar opposition between the emotional and the moral life is made possible by a more essential content of the novel. In the language of the novel and in its structuring of events, the moral and emotional life are in fact not in conflict. Both are expressions of the same power, which lies elsewhere and which is revealed in the text in omens, presences, mysterious attractions, unavoidable encounters, the power of inanimate objects. The real content of the novel is the mythic world, the world of nature perceived as raw power. The mode of its perception is the symbol, and Benjamin spends much of part 1 cataloguing the symbolic weight that objects in the novel take on. In the unraveling of the marriage, the world of nature makes its power felt as guilt in the protagonists, and concomitantly, the world itself appears guilty. The world in this appearance is held together as fate. Benjamin sees the real content of the novel to be its principle of structure, fatality, for fate is the structure of the mythic world. If the characters in the novel are guilty, their guilt is presented solely in terms of the structure of myth; their guilt is fated and thus fatal, a guilt that must be exorcised by the sacrifice of an innocent (Ottilie). The conventional reading of the novel, which enshrines Ottilie as a saint and thus finds a justification for her death, reveals itself as being in total complicity with the ideology inscribed in the novel's structure. The unmasking of this complicity is the impulse for Benjamin's polemic in the second part of the essay against Friedrich Gundolf's massive biography of Goethe (1916).

Part 2 has both a negative and positive aim.

The first is the demolition of Gundolf's reading of Goethe's life and work. A polemic is essentially leveled against the tradition of literary study of Goethe in particular and ultimately of literary study itself, with Gundolf as its representative. Benjamin's positive aim is to elaborate the structure of Goethe's novel, and he proceeds by analyzing the correspondences between the novel and the novella embedded within it, the story of the eccentric neighbors that lies at the novel's center. Out of this emerges a new opposition between the fatal world of myth and the world where decision is possible.

The argument with Gundolf centers on the relation between the life of the artist and his work. As Benjamin sees it, traditional criticism proceeds from the fallacious assumption that the work is a reflection of the life of the artist, that the emotional power of the work of art directly corresponds to the emotional experience of the artist, which is its source. Thus the traditional critical method becomes a version of "empathy": the critic feels his way into the work of art and simultaneously into the artist's life; the work becomes the medium through which the emotional experience of the artist is directly transmitted to the reader, who in turn reproduces it within himself. The effect of this assumption is the creation of a myth of the artist as the heroic bearer of experience for the rest of humanity. The artist is a hero of feeling. And like the mythic hero, the artist is neither a unique nor an individual human being, but rather a type who symbolizes, through his role as proxy for all humanity, the moral norm: "For he [the hero] is not alone before his God, but the representative of all humanity before its gods. In the moral sphere of mythic nature, all is symbolic representation, from the patriotic 'one for all' to the sacrificial death of the redeemer." The hero is thus fully symbolic, like all mythic forms, and the motif of the hero's task, whether it be Orpheus' descent to Hades or the twelve tasks of Hercules, is the expression of the symbolic character of the hero's life. In the myth of the artist, the task is the creation of the work of art, and the artist's principal creation becomes, in this way of thinking, his own life.

For Benjamin the artist's life is not an open book. He characterizes biography, in a formulation that Sigmund Freud would have fully appreciated, as "the archive of the self-undecodable documents of the self's existence." This argument moves in territory quite different from the discussion of the "intentional fallacy" by the American New Critics. Benjamin does not exclude biographical inquiry from criticism. Rather, he argues for a far more indirect, overdetermined relationship between the author's life and art.

Among the various results of the myth of the artist, Benjamin sees one as central to the criticism of *Elective Affinities.* The critical biography, itself mythic, is trapped inside the myth of the novel. As the novel's shadow it brings darkness out of light, merely reproducing the novel's content without being able to reach a determination about its significance. In the first part of the essay, Benjamin shows the material content of the novel to be the mythic world and the aesthetic means of its representation to be the symbol. In the novel, events become portents, and houses, clothes, elements of the landscape, and various inanimate objects become charged with the appearance of embodied meaning. When he turns to Goethe's life, Benjamin presents a complex set of attitudes, experiences, and events that discloses Goethe's sense of the power of nature and his reaction to it, which was a reaction of fear—as Benjamin analyzes it, fear of death in the first instance and, as its corollary, fear of life. In mid-life Goethe attempts to master this fear by simultaneously submitting to it and protesting against that submission. The composition of *Elective Affinities* is not a logical outcome of Goethe's experience—the novel is not "deducible" from the life. It is one mode of this experience. Its intention is as much to hide as to reveal its biographical significance, not only from its reader but from its writer as well.

The rest of the second part furthers Benjamin's argument by examining the connections between the embedded novella and the novel. Benjamin sees the novella as forming a structural antithesis to its frame. The oppositions range from the smallest details—for example, where water in the novel is always still and deep, in the novella it is rushing and shallow—to the largest elements of action. The characters in the novella make decisions and take action, whereas in the novel they passively submit to fate as to a natural power. As a result, the novel embodies in its center a vision of everything it has excluded to make its form possible. The world of action, decision, accountability, and reconciliation in community opposes the mythic world of fate and inexorable sacrifice. In this opposition the mythic world is revealed as appearance.

The conclusion of the essay is a radical interrogation of the symbol that constitutes myth. Benjamin returns to the figure of Ottilie, and performs a critical tour de force in which Ottilie, whose sacrifice is demanded by the myth, is shown to be the point in the total structure of the novel at which the myth unravels. As her character develops its full symbolic weight, she becomes first a figure for beauty, which exists only as appearance, then a figure for appearance itself as opposed to truth, and ultimately a revelation of the mythic content of the novel as beautiful appearance that is not truth but is instead the representation of what lies beyond its own possibilities of expression, the expressionless without which there is no symbol. The truth-content of *Elective Affinities* is glimpsed in figure precisely at the point at which the novel reveals its own principles of structure, the point at which the conditions of symbolic art become part of the work's own content. In this glimpse the work points the way out of the prison of its own myth. The way out is criticism.

Criticism is not judgment in the conventional sense; it wants to be a last judgment. In criticism of this sort, the work is annihilated because in disclosing its structure, criticism reveals that its aesthetic power rests on a necessary inadequacy. Insofar as *Elective Affinities* makes this inadequacy its own content, it serves as the perfect object of Benjamin's critical program—the release of truth from its fetters in the work.

At the time of the composition of the essay, Benjamin was planning the publication of a journal that he hoped would rival the great critical journal of the early Romantics, *The Athenaeum*. "Angelus Novus," as the journal was to be called, never got beyond the planning stage. It was to be edited by a small group of like-minded friends in close collaboration and was to contain only pieces that reflected their shared sense of truth. Its audience was conceived as consisting of kindred spirits. The name of the journal was taken from a watercolor by Paul Klee that Benjamin owned and that he associated with the "new angels" of Talmudic legend (these are constantly created only to sing a hymn of praise to God before reverting to nothingness—a figure for Benjamin of the momentariness of the appearance of truth). Criticism would not be relegated to the "back of the book" but would be interspersed with fiction, poetry, and translation throughout. Benjamin planned to publish his essay on the task of the translator in the first issue, along with fiction by S. J. Agnon, then a little-known writer whom Scholem had recruited for the journal, poems by the brothers Wolf and Fritz Heinle, an essay on the Carnival by an older friend, the theologian Florens Christian Rang, and a piece by Scholem on Jewish questions. No doubt the Goethe essay was conceived with this journal in mind. Like the journal, the essay envisioned neither a professionally academic nor a mass audience for its readership. We may say, then, that the social form of Benjamin's early work, which was conceived during and in the aftermath of the war, was expressed in the idea of a "private newspaper" or small-circulation journal. Such a journal fills the space inhabited by a free bourgeois intelligentsia, a social formation that was fast disappearing from European society in the early twentieth century. Before the first issue of "Angelus Novus" appeared, the publisher backed out in the face of the economic inflation of the early 1920's. Benjamin cast around for a publisher for the Goethe essay until finally it was accepted by Hofmannsthal's *Neue Deutsche Beiträge,* a magazine very like "Angelus Novus" in intention and audience. Hofmannsthal was overwhelmed by the essay.

Although Benjamin was aware that publication in such a journal was not directly in his academic interests, it spurred him to continue his studies in pursuit of an academic career, a career that Scholem says was always his "clear-cut ambition." Benjamin, already married during the war and the father of a child, lived in Heidelberg when he wrote the Goethe essay. Then, with the onset of the inflation, he moved with his family to his parents' house in Berlin. This was not unusual among the upper middle class at the time, but tension and difficulties between the two families were not unusual either, and Benjamin decided that he must get himself and his family out of his parents' house at all costs. To achieve this goal he considered various possibilities, including the antiquarian book trade and working in a bank. Although it necessitated prolonged parental support and therefore was the occasion for further difficulties, entry into the German university was likely for a middle-class intellectual with family money, and although the career path there for a Jew was hard, it was possible.

THE ORIGIN OF THE GERMAN TRAGIC DRAMA

Benjamin had already made inquiries about a possible position at Heidelberg, but this was ruled out after the habilitation there of Karl Mannheim. One Jew was enough. In 1923 Benjamin applied to Frankfurt in *Germanistik* (German literature and linguistics), thinking at first to continue his studies of Goethe, but finally proposing to work on the German baroque. The result was his *Origin of the German*

Tragic Drama, an extraordinary book completed in two extremely event-filled years that included runaway inflation and the collapse of his parents' financial stability, the deaths of two of his closest friends, the unraveling of his marriage, a fateful love affair, and finally "a vital freeing and an intensive insight into the relevance of a radical communism" and consideration of "the political practice of communism, not as a theoretical problem but first of all as a binding commitment." Benjamin finished the work and submitted it to the *Germanistik* department. The professors found it unsuited to the tradition of their studies and transferred it to the philosophy department. There it met with hostility. With no desire to teach general aesthetics in a philosophy department, Benjamin withdrew the book from consideration before it could be officially rejected. Thus ended his ambition for an academic career. The book was ultimately published in 1928 by the firm of Rowohlt. It received a handful of dismissively hostile reviews in academic journals. The book inspired some of its early readers, notably Adorno, who directed a seminar on it, ironically, in Frankfurt, where he had recently become a *Privatdozent* (unsalaried university lecturer); but it was not until the Benjamin revival of the 1950's and 1960's that it achieved widespread recognition.

His experiences during the years of the book's composition led to a complete transformation of Benjamin's life and work. Although Benjamin referred to the book as definitively marking the end of a period of his life, we may see it as both a culmination of his early work and an indication of the work's future direction. The point of transition is marked by Benjamin's emphasis on history: just as symbolic art, which as myth is the material content of *Elective Affinities,* becomes the essential object of Benjamin's criticism in the Goethe essay, so in his study of the baroque play's history, the material content of the *Trauerspiel* becomes the critical center of Benjamin's presentation. (*Trauerspiel,* literally "mourning-play," is usually rendered as "tragedy" in English translations. Benjamin, however, reserves tragedy—*Tragödie* in German—for Greek drama and insists on the independence of the *Trauerspiel* as a genre. Since there is no English word for this, I will simply refer to the genre as *Trauerspiel.*)

The *Trauerspiel* book studies a genre that Benjamin treats as a single work. Its aim is the critical presentation of the baroque *Trauerspiel* as a totality that Benjamin, following the Romantics, calls an Idea. "Ideas are to things as constellations are to stars." Concepts (*Begriffe*), as etymology makes plain, are the way things are grasped: in a concept phenomena are possessed as knowledge. In an Idea, as Benjamin's analogy suggests, phenomena are revealed as in a map. What the map reveals are sets of possible interrelationships among phenomena of the greatest individual diversity. In this light the idea of genre, which attempts to define the significance of the particular way literary phenomena are interrelated, exists in a separate world from individual texts: nothing is more false than the conventional determination of genre as an average or set of common properties, arrived at by surveying the elements of a number of texts and then arranging what they have in common into an "abstract type" of, say, tragedy—a sort of wardrobe chest filled with flawed heroes, turns, recognitions, kings, hubris, oracles, falls from high places, pity, fear, an occasional chorus, and some queens. Such a notion is not only the basis for the innumerable school exercises concerning the nature of tragedy in *Oedipus, Macbeth,* and *Death of a Salesman;* it is also the justification for the kind of academic literary history that considers the history of the Renaissance sonnet, for example, from its first flowering in Petrarch to its high point—or decadence, depending on the historian's taste—in John Donne. As the latter example indicates, a kind of teleology or naive evolutionism follows literary history as its shadow. As a constellation or map, genre is more significantly revealed by a consideration of extremes than by a construction of the average.

Viewed this way a genre may have a temporal and a spatial dispersion—various of its bordering elements come into view at different times and different places. Accordingly, in discussing the German baroque *Trauerspiel,* Benjamin also considers the plays of Pedro Calderón and William Shakespeare, the Viennese operetta, and the Sturm und Drang tragedy of fate. But such a view by no means entails an evolutionary or developmental structure for the genre. Rather, the connection between the structure of the genre and its historical dispersion is complex and problematic and is itself part of the critical effort of presentation.

The book is highly crafted. Two main sections are each divided into three parts, and the whole is prefaced by an articulation of critical theory. Benjamin originally planned a conclusion to match the introduction, in which he intended to return to the theoretical question of criticism, reconsidered in light of the central critical investigation. He never wrote the conclusion, and the introduction as we now have it is notorious for its density and impenetrability. In a letter Benjamin commented, only half jokingly, that it could be understood only by someone acquainted with the cabalistic teaching that every statement contains at least forty-nine levels of meaning. He seriously recommended that it be read only after completion of the book.

The first main section, "Trauerspiel und Tragödie" ("*Trauerspiel* and Tragedy"), moves primarily by means of commentary toward the development of a critical contrast between tragedy and *Trauerspiel* as generic ideas. The second main section, "Allegorie und Trauerspiel" ("Allegory and *Trauerspiel*") develops the opposition between allegory and symbol as modes, and discusses allegory not as baroque ornamentation but as the essential mode of the discourse of the *Trauerspiel.* Benjamin links the two sections by discussing the baroque development of the Renaissance theory of melancholy, for just as the melancholy prince is an essential part of the material content of the *Trauerspiel,* allegory is the mode of perception of the world from the point of view of melancholia.

The *Trauerspiel* book is a stylistic showpiece. Its prose is polished, aphoristic, discontinuous, brilliant; the book achieves a tight, definite structure from a mosaic of quotations, digressions, tightly reasoned argument, and suggestive parallels. It is based on extensive, thorough, and manifestly careful scholarship, and it illuminates the baroque age as virtually no other work of criticism has done. Although it contains—or rather in its very excellence is—an implicit, devastating critique of the trivial practice and impoverished theory of much of what then passed (and alas still passes) for the academic study of literature, there is nothing omitted from or committed in the book that should have led to its rejection.

The book illuminates the baroque *Trauerspiel* and the baroque age. Yet its critical function is not to conserve. Benjamin has more at stake than to renew appreciation for a group of plays—the plays of Daniel Casper von Lohenstein, Martin Opitz, and Andreas Gryphius—that had long since ceased being produced and were not even much read by specialists in other areas of the baroque or in theater history. Not that baroque art was unknown. In academic circles Heinrich Wölfflin's great work on Renaissance and baroque art had sparked much interest in the period. Moreover, the rise of expressionist art had provoked new interest in the work of the baroque masters. Nevertheless, the period was usually viewed as a decadence, a mannered falling off from the greatness of the Renaissance. Baroque plays were treated with disdain: in the standard works of literary history, they were seen either as decadent reworkings of Renaissance forms, as unsuccessful attempts to write classical tragedy, or as weak forerunners of the rise of Romantic drama in the age of Friedrich von Schiller and Goethe. Benjamin does not mount a polemic against any of this, yet his book undermines all the assumptions on which such a view of the baroque is based.

Alois Riegl's *Spätrömische Kunstindustrie*

(The Late Roman Art Industry, 1901) is fundamental to Benjamin's way of thinking about the baroque. Riegl took the Romantic notion of the autonomy of the work of art to its logical conclusion by folding back the realm of art into social history. Art is the expression of the will of its makers and its audience; changes in artistic techniques, methods, and intentions are the result of changes in the way people see the world. There is no history of art; there is only the history of people with changing needs and changing ways of fulfilling them. Riegl develops these ideas by a close consideration of a period of artistic production, the Christian and pagan art of the late Roman empire that was uniformly despised by art historians of his time and was discussed as if the artists were attempting to execute works in the manner of their predecessors without being able to succeed. Riegl on the other hand was able to account for the extreme features characteristic of this art—erosion of bodily contours, geometric patterning, drilled eyeholes, radical distortions of perspective, rigidity, and expressionlessness—by considering the spiritual situation of the period. Benjamin similarly chooses a period whose works were treated either as decadent extensions of an earlier period or primitive beginnings of a later one, but were never seen as having expressive value in themselves. Like Riegl, he works from a set of assumptions and with a set of critical techniques that together deny all possibility of an uncritical history of art. A look at some of the book's main lines of argument leads to a sense of its real critical accomplishment and of the significance of the work for Benjamin's later development.

The *Trauerspiel* as a genre, as Benjamin sees it, is the particular organization of its content—history itself—and therefore it comes into being only at a determinate point in history. The Reformation and Counter-Reformation view of history is a necessary condition for the existence of *Trauerspiel*. And that view of history is itself the product of real historical experience. History, not as an abstract idea but as a real field of human action and human attitudes, becomes the subject of Benjamin's inquiry. At the same time Benjamin is permanently concerned with the work of art as a historically transcendent object. As much as it is embedded in the historical moment that made its production possible and as much as it freezes that moment within itself, the significance of the work of art is nevertheless not exhausted by the historicity of its origin. It has something about it that grants it continued life, that allows it to function as a work of art for later generations: if the plays of Lohenstein have fallen into obscurity, the great trauerspiels of Shakespeare and Calderón have not.

The serious play of the baroque period is typically considered as a tragedy, but the second section of the first part is devoted primarily to contrasting the baroque play with tragedy as its antithesis. For this Benjamin relies primarily on the discussion of tragedy and "meta-ethical man" in Franz Rosenzweig's *Der Stern der Erlösung* (*Star of Redemption*). Published in 1921, this book had a great and permanent impact on Benjamin's thinking. In an article for *Literarische Welt*, "Bücher, die lebendig geblieben sind" (Books That Have Stayed Alive), written in 1929, Benjamin cites Rosenzweig's book, along with Riegl's work and Lukács's *Geschichte und Klassenbewußtsein* (*History and Class Consciousness*, 1923), as among the books that ought not to be housed merely in specialists' libraries, which he describes as "a particular form of being forgotten." For Rosenzweig and Benjamin the decisive fact about tragedy is that it can no longer be written. The genre is determined by a particular historical and social situation; it is inseparable from the Greek sense of *agon*, competition as the dominant motive of Greek life, and from its emergence from the cult. The fundamental stance of the tragic hero is defiance, and the fundamental expression of the hero's defiance is silence. In unrelenting defiance the hero's death is an ironic atonement; it is a sacrificial offering to the old gods that affirms law while also undermining the old laws that demand his sacrifice.

The death of the hero is the scene of the birth of a new law for the community, a law that can only come into being by his death. And language is always the possession of the community, while the hero is possessed of nothing but self. Hence the hero is silent, for the words that need to be spoken to justify his death are not his and are not yet possessed by the community. The community that comes after transforms the hero's silence into words.

The hero of the *Trauerspiel* is on the other hand a victim of fate. He does not stand on the threshold of a new world but is merely one more example of the world's subjection to death. Here Benjamin discusses fate in the terms he worked out in the Goethe essay. But to these terms he adds a significant difference— the historical development of Counter-Reformation theology. Within this theological field fate is the expression of creatureliness, guilt is the condition of original sin, for which the creature is not individually responsible yet for which he is entirely culpable and to which mourning and lamentation are the adequate response. In this field human life is driven solely by passion, and the world that stands over against it takes on a characteristically threatening shape. The threat is visible most significantly in inanimate objects, which become charged with threatening meaning: unlike the tragedy, the baroque *Trauerspiel* is a theater of props, and the stage property—one may think of Macbeth's dagger—like the innumerable ghosts, witches, and demonic apparitions that populate the dramas, is simultaneously the repository of creaturely guilt and its avenger.

Intimately related to the creaturely sense of fatality is the fact of repetition in the *Trauerspiel.* The same events occur again and again from play to play; within plays the plots are embellished with subplots that mirror the main action; and above all, in the center of the plays there is often another play that again repeats the external action. Another aspect of this sense of repetition is the endlessness, the inconclusiveness, of the drama. After *Hamlet* one could conceivably write a *Fortinbras,* Benjamin notes, just as he might well have noted the tendency of the English history plays to form ever larger cycles. Tragedy ends with a decision; in the *Trauerspiel* the action is simply adjourned among wreckage and a pile of corpses, ready to be taken up again in another play.

If the Catholic sense of the value of the world was necessary for the full development of fatality in the *Trauerspiel,* it is precisely the Lutheran antinomian devaluation of the world that produces one of the *Trauerspiel*'s most important elements—the empty world: "that excessive reaction which finally struck good works absolutely, and not just their serviceable and penitential character, out of the field. Every worth was taken from human behavior. Something new emerged: an empty world." The baroque reaction to the emptiness of the world was dual: on the one hand withdrawal and distaste for life and on the other hand mourning, "the state of mind in which feeling revives the empty world in the form of a mask, in order to have a riddling pleasure in its look." From this standpoint all the world is a stage, a mere play that in all its pomp and ostentation is nothing but an empty show. It is contemplated endlessly, however; precisely because it lacks any natural relationship to us, the face of the world seems to be "a sign of an enigmatic wisdom." Stoic withdrawal in the baroque age becomes pathological. In the *Trauerspiel* the prince is a melancholic, the baroque version of what we now call the clinically depressive.

In the last section of part 1, Benjamin sets forth the baroque theory of melancholia. He brings together material from emblem books, paintings, and medical and astrological treatises to portray the physio-psychological type of the melancholic—the withdrawn, contemplative, depressed, invalid prince, endlessly ruminative, indecisive, cold, sick of life. This is the melancholy of the medieval medical books. To it the baroque adds the Renaissance emphasis on melancholy and its astrological connection to Saturn as the basis for intellectual ascent: the devoted contemplation of the things

1717

of the world is the first step up the Neoplatonic ladder to truth. In the baroque the melancholic becomes the *penseroso,* the intellectual attempting to rescue truth from its confines in a dead world, yet himself always threatened with the abyss of madness that opens at his feet. His speculative mode is allegory.

Part 2 constitutes a significant rehabilitation of allegorical art. This rehabilitation is the result not only of Benjamin's scholarly immersion in the baroque texts nor of those aspects of his sensibility that allowed him to respond to the power of these texts. Allegory had already reemerged in modernism. Benjamin, significantly, sees Baudelaire as an allegorist, and certainly the expressionists and the Dada and surrealist artists were fundamentally allegorists, not symbolic artists. What Benjamin has done, then, is to discover a critical language adequate to modern art as well as to lay bare the impulses and procedures of modern art that the lack of such a discourse had veiled.

The section starts by describing as false the traditional assertion that symbol reveals the general through the particular whereas allegory attempts to signify the general by a particular. Benjamin opposes this with a more adequate distinction. The symbol is an instantaneous shining forth of a transcendent significance in immanent appearance. It is a totality, existing entirely in itself—whole, clear, instant, permanent, self-subsistent. The symbol is the visual representation of moral perfection—hence, beauty is the ultimate symbol. The Romantic idea of Greek sculpture as the perfect aesthetic object—in which the god is represented as the beautiful human body— unites the symbol with the demands of art— that the artistic work be whole, organic, and beautiful and that organic beauty be the radiant symbol of moral/divine perfection.

As against the instantaneousness of the symbol, allegory is a form of expression like writing, and unfolds violently in time in a dialectical movement. It exists in the sphere where significance is necessarily different from embodiment. Hence, where the symbol is unified, allegory is dispersed; where the symbol is clear, allegory is enigmatic; where the symbol is necessary, allegory is arbitrary; where the symbol is individual, allegory is a profusion of images. In allegory, anything can signify anything else. No detail, no element of the world is valuable in itself, but since any element of the world may signify, it draws to itself an enormous value by virtue of its signifying possibility. And since each element is organically separate from the others and able to enter into unlimited relationships with others, the world is a dispersion, a heap of fragments that nevertheless, as allegory, signify. Historical events are deposited as potentially legible. Benjamin's metaphor for this perspective is the ruin in the landscape:

> In the trauerspiel, when history wanders into the theater, it does so as script. "History" stands on the face of nature written in the hieroglyphs of transitoriness. The allegorical physiognomy of natural history, which is placed on the stage in the trauerspiel, is actually present as a ruin. With this, history has merged mentally into the setting. And thus formed, history is expressed not as the process of an eternal life, but rather as the occasion of unstoppable decay. Thus allegory makes itself known as beyond beauty. Allegories are in the realm of thoughts what ruins are in the realm of things.
>
> (*Gesammelte Schriften* 1.1.353–354)

Symbol is the imitation of a nature shaped by God; allegory is the representation of fallen nature in inexorable decay and subject to death.

Allegory, then, is nature under the contemplative gaze of the melancholic. It is a pile of images that can be read and reread, that are nothing in themselves but that always promise to point beyond themselves to a realm where meaning is whole. Thus the old metaphor of the world as a book here receives its most extreme form: the world is a book in an unknown language or in an unknown script. The object is

> . . . incapable of emanating any significance or sense of its own; it acquires only the significance

which the allegorist lends it. He places significance within it, and stands behind it; not a psychological but an ontological state of affairs. In his hands the object becomes something different; through it he speaks of something different, and for him it becomes a key to the territory of buried knowledge. He honors it as the emblem of this. This constitutes the character of allegory as script.

(*Gesammelte Schriften* 1.1.359)

Hence also the paradoxical being of the allegorist: he has supreme mastery over the world, yet the world that he masters is dead.

Considered this way, allegory accounts for a wide variety of stylistic features of the baroque play. The variety is brought together in the allegorical tension between meaning and image. Benjamin discusses, for example, the tendency toward double titles in the plays, one title indicating the plot and the other providing commentary on the plot's significance. Similarly, the choric interludes break the steady development of action with commentary, often delivered by personified virtues or vices. In the plays speech itself, which is often composed of a chain of maxims, works like captions in the emblem books and offers commentary rather than furthering the drama. But speech itself is a substance that, like every substance in the plays, is subject to allegorical treatment: its elements become fragmented, and the fragments become occasions for endless reflection and interpretation. From this Benjamin derives the stylistic features often condemned in the baroque as bombast and strained metaphor. He notes the stylistic tendency toward the coupling, sometimes in bizarre forms, of abstract and concrete words as yet another manifestation of the same allegorical impulse. Similarly he notes the disjunction between sound and meaning—that is, between the spoken and written status of the baroque text—in the employment of the alexandrine line, with its principles of formally logical balance and its simultaneously violent diction and sound.

Only in allegory could the *Trauerspiel* assimilate "as its content the material which contemporary conditions provide it." This material is history theologically conceived as the world of natural guilt, a conception that provides the answer to the most important specific question about the content of the *Trauerspiel:* the significance of scenes of incredible cruelty in the plays. The answer has been prepared by Benjamin's distinction between the symbolic and the allegorical. If the purely symbolic is the beautiful human body, which in its form, proportion, and presence manifests the significance of life, then the essential allegorical emblem is the corpse, dissected and contemplated piece by piece.

The allegorical effort is so desperate and so extreme because the abyss that opens at the feet of the allegorist is the material world itself, the wreckage of history taken as the pure object of knowledge. The depressive madness that threatens to engulf the melancholic visionary results from the infinity of the quest for absolute knowledge of the world. And the figure for this madness is Satan, who tempts with absolute knowledge of the material world and mocks the attempt to achieve this knowledge with a laughter that proclaims the triumph of dead matter over mind. Yet allegory discovers a limit and reaches its end in taking its most extreme objects as emblems:

It is precisely in the vision of the madness of destruction in which everything earthly collapses into a field of wreckage that the limit and not the ideal of allegorical immersion is revealed. The desperate confusion of Golgotha, which is the schema of allegorical figures to be read in the thousands of engravings and descriptions of the time, is not only the image of the desolation of human existence. In it, transitoriness is not signified by allegory; rather transitoriness itself in its own significance is presented as allegory. As the allegory of resurrection. . . . This breaks the code of the most fragmented, the most defunct, the most dispersed. Thus, to be sure, allegory loses everything which it called its own: the secret, privileged knowledge, the arbitrary rule in the realm of dead things, the supposed infinity of the empty hope. All this disappeared with that *one* reversal, in which allegorical immersion has to empty out the last phantasmagoria of objectivity, and entirely on its own, rediscovers itself not playfully in the earthly world of things but seriously under heaven. This is the essence of melancholy immersion: its last objects, in which it thinks completely to convince itself of depravity, reverse themselves in allegory, and they fill and disavow the void in which they are presented, so that finally, thought does not faithfully rest in the contemplation of bones but faithlessly leaps up to resurrection.

(*Gesammelte Schriften* 1.1.405–406)

At its limit allegory undoes itself, and just as the world the allegorist contemplates reveals itself to be the image of the world constructed by allegorical contemplation, so the possibility of its redemption comes into view in the distance:

Allegory exits empty-handed. Absolute Evil, which cherishes itself as enduring profundity, exists only in allegory—it is uniquely and merely allegory—and it signifies something other than what it is. Indeed, it signifies precisely the nothingness of what it represents. The absolute vices, as the tyrants and intriguers show, are allegories. They are not real, and they have what they seem to have only for the subjective view of melancholy. They are this view, which its results negate, because they signify only its blindness.

(*Gesammelte Schriften* 1.1.406)

From this perspective the value of the German *Trauerspiel* becomes clear: "In the spirit of allegory [the German *Trauerspiel*] is conceived from the outset as wreckage and as fragment. If other forms shine beautifully as on the first day, this form holds the image of the beautiful to the last."

It is no accident that in the years when Benjamin composed the book on the *Trauerspiel*, a writer as different from him as T. S. Eliot envisioned history as "a heap of broken images," or that in the same years other great modernist writers saw their tasks as unmasking the false appearance of social order, revealing the world

as a junk heap, and endlessly contemplating the shards of experience in the hope of its redemption. Benjamin's allusion to the knowledge of the impermanence of life as a fact staring humanity of the baroque age in the face is a key. In 1923 Benjamin's dear friend Scholem emigrated to a new life in Palestine, and Zionist emigration was always a possibility Benjamin entertained for himself. At the time Scholem left, Benjamin was studying Hebrew, as he did at various times in his life, but never with success. In the 1930's, in exile in Paris, Benjamin again thought of emigrating to Palestine; the other possibility was radical communism. Only complacency, the dream of a contented life as a middle-class citizen, was ruled out. As a going-away present Benjamin gave Scholem a beautifully hand-written scroll of his own composing, entitled "Reise durch die deutsche Inflation" ("A Tour Through the German Inflation"). Its first section begins:

In the treasury of phrases with which the lifestyle of the German bourgeoisie, welded together of stupidity and cowardice, daily betrays itself, the phrase about the impending catastrophe— "things can't go on like this any longer"—is especially remarkable. The helpless fixation on the ideas of certainty and property ownership of the past decades keeps the man in the street from realizing the really remarkable stabilities of a new sort on which the present situation is based. Because the relative stabilization of the prewar years pleased him, he thinks that he has to see each event which dispossesses him as unstable. But stable conditions need not always be pleasant conditions, and before the war there were classes for whom stabilized conditions meant stabilized misery.

(*Gesammelte Schriften* 4.1.94)

And the section ends:

Middle European society lives like the inhabitants of a completely encircled city whose provisions and gunpowder are running out and who, according to human measures, can hardly expect rescue. A situation, in which unconditional surrender, willingly or unwillingly, must be most seriously considered. But the dumb, uncertain power, which middle Europe feels against itself, does not negotiate. So nothing remains but to direct the gaze, in the perpetual expectation of the final onslaught, on nothing but the extraordinary which alone can still rescue. This necessary circumstance of tense, uncomplaining attention could, since we are in a mysterious contact with the powers besieging us, actually accomplish the miracle. On the other hand, the expectation that things can't go on like this any longer, one day may learn that for the suffering of an individual, as for a society, the only limit beyond which things cannot go is annihilation.

(*Gesammelte Schriften* 4.1.95)

Even if the objects toward which he has directed his gaze are of the past, Benjamin's criticism is always contemporary. The *Trauerspiel* as an object of critical attention derives its significance from the contemporary actuality of allegory as an aesthetic mode and a mode of knowledge. And Benjamin's ability to make the past speak is based as much on his clarity about his own historical moment as it is on his capacity as a scholar to sink into alien material. Much of the force of the analysis of the *Trauerspiel* is won from the insight that history is the content of the form and that allegory is the mode in which history appears as a text. But it is a text in a state of emergency. History is a city under siege. Can a critic's gaze rescue a besieged city?

THE LATER WORK

The failure of Benjamin's academic plans brought to a head the intellectual and emotional process that had begun as early as 1924, when Benjamin, a frequent traveler, was working on the *Trauerspiel* book on the island of Capri, where he could live cheaply among a circle of German intellectuals. Bloch was there working on a long review of Lukács's *History and Class Consciousness*, which had just been published. Bloch's intense excitement over the book was a spur to Benjamin, as was his chance encounter with Asja Lacis, a Lithuanian stage director who was part of the avant-garde movement to fuse new art with revolutionary political action. Lacis had worked with Brecht, in the development of proletarian theater, and with children's theater. Benjamin's dedication to his collection of aphorisms and sketches *One-Way Street,* which reads "This street is called Asja-Lacis Street, after the engineer who broke it through in the author," expresses that the result of their encounter was a total and extreme radicalization. In 1924 Benjamin considered his joining the Communist party to be only a matter of time.

In December 1926 he went to Moscow for a two-month stay, partly to see the revolution, partly to see Lacis. More important was his attempt there to enter the ranks of the Communist intellectuals. Benjamin proposed to write the entry on Goethe for the *Great Soviet Encyclopedia* and to become a correspondent on German affairs for Russian periodicals; the long article was turned down. Benjamin's trip was partly financed by a contract for an article for Martin Buber's periodical *Die Kreatur.* The article, "Moscow," is one of several city portraits written by Benjamin. It is remarkable for its precision of observation and evocative power of detail. The influence of surrealist art is paramount, and Benjamin reaches for effects of description more easily arrived at in film. While in Moscow he kept a diary that details his activities, his sadly comic lack of progress in the affair with Lacis, and his deliberations about joining the German Communist party. That he never did join says more about the internal history of the party and about such events as the infamous Hitler-Stalin pact than about Benjamin's political commitment. It is significant, however, that almost all of Benjamin's contacts in Moscow, including Lacis herself (who wound up spending some ten years in a prison camp), either were or became members of the opposition to Stalinist rule.

The results of Benjamin's political resolve for his work are manifold. One of the first is that he became a free-lance journalist. He was regularly published in the literary section of the *Frankfurter Zeitung,* a prestigious liberal-left newspaper of the 1920's, and he accepted a position as a regular contributor to a new literary magazine, *Die Literarische Welt* (Literary World), which the book publisher Rowohlt had just established. Benjamin was offered a standing quarterly article on literary developments in France as well as a place for reviews and miscellaneous articles. He also became a professional literary translator. He translated some of the poetry of Saint-John Perse, and with Franz Hessel as collaborator, he did the German translation of Marcel Proust's *À la recherche du temps perdu* (*Remembrance of Things Past,* 1913–1927) for Rowohlt. Nazi censorship brought the latter project to nought. There seems to be no surviving trace of the manuscript.

Until Nazi censorship made publication in Germany impossible, Benjamin made his living by such writing. Afterward, in exile in Paris, he established a relationship with the Institute for Social Research, an endowed, independently Marxist, quasi-academic study group with headquarters in Frankfurt and then, in exile, in New York. Under the leadership of Max Horkheimer and Friedrich Pollack, and with such members as Adorno, Herbert Marcuse, Erich Fromm, and Leo Löwenthal, the Institute and its journal, the *Zeitschrift für Sozialforschung* (Journal of Social Research), attempted a reformulation of Marxist theory to probe the crisis in culture and society signified by the rise of totalitarianism. The *Zeitschrift* became Benjamin's only significant publishing outlet in the years before his suicide, and the institute provided his principal financial support.

Benjamin's move to journalism necessitated a change in the style of his writing and in the objects of his critical attention—a shift that corresponded to changes motivated by his own political commitments. This was largely a move from the past to the present—Benjamin now wrote on the surrealists, Proust, the Vien-

nese satirist Karl Kraus, Franz Kafka—and a shift toward a much more open style, direct statement, and unconcealed political engagement. In a letter to Scholem, he indicated his desire as a critic to comment on texts that were themselves political and, in their absence, to "spin a politics out of himself." In content, however, the later work is directly continuous with the earlier. Myth, history, language, and the epistemological status and function of the work of art stand as before at the center of his work.

In 1929 Benjamin met Brecht. Their friendship became close, artistically and critically fruitful, and lasting. During Benjamin's life their relationship was a source of irritation and sometimes outrage to his friends; since his death it has become the center of fierce critical battles. Benjamin was steadfast in defending Brecht and their friendship. In a letter of 1933 he referred to his connection with Brecht's artistic production as "one of the most important and most reinforced points in my whole position." Some of his most significant critical pieces, notably the essay "Autor als Produzent" ("The Author as Producer"), and much of his writing on film are directly indebted to Brecht's influence. The possibility of Benjamin's influence on Brecht has not been studied at all, however. But it is significant in this connection that the first critical formulations about epic theater and the "alienation effect" were Benjamin's, and that Brecht's theoretical writing on these topics came later. Brecht and Benjamin planned to publish a journal of radical criticism and the arts, "Krisis und Kritik" (Crisis and Criticism), with Benjamin chiefly responsible for the theory and direction of criticism, but political events made such a publication in Germany impossible. Upon hearing of Benjamin's death in 1940, Brecht is said to have remarked that this was the first loss to German literature that Hitler had caused. He wrote three extraordinarily beautiful commemorative poems: "An Walter Benjamin, der sich auf der Flucht vor Hitler entleibte"; "Zum Freitod des Flüchtling W. B."; and "Die Verlustliste" (To Walter Benjamin, Who Took His Life While Fleeing Hitler; On the Voluntary Death of the Fugitive W. B.; List of Damages; 1941). The friendship has tended to be explained away: Rolf Tidemann, Adorno's student and the editor of Benjamin's complete works, treats it as a psychological symptom; Hannah Arendt, who knew Benjamin in Paris, wrote of his attraction to Brecht's "plumpes Denken" (crude thinking), as if he needed a remedy for his own dialectical subtlety, and the notion of *plumpes Denken* is duly repeated by most American writers on Benjamin whenever Brecht's name comes up. Whatever the psychological truth—friendship, like love, being tricky psychological business—such explanations fail to take seriously the one decisive point: Brecht and Benjamin were natural political allies. Such a failure of critical insight is no accident. It corresponds to the predicament of many lovers of the theater who find Brecht's politics reprehensible but can't do without his plays. Explaining away Benjamin's friendship with Brecht is an attempt to hold onto Benjamin's criticism without its radical content.

There is an unresolved tension in Marxist theory that surfaces with particular urgency in discussion of the necessity of the proletarian revolution. On the one hand there is the sense, reinforced by the articulation of social theory in terms drawn from Hegelian logic, that socialism is the logically necessary result of the contradictions of capitalism. The internal development of capitalism leads inexorably and progressively to the revolution; because capitalism, like all stages of "prehistory," carries with it the seeds of its own destruction, it will destroy itself, perhaps in the violent convulsion of revolution, perhaps in a peaceful transition to a classless and stateless society. From this standpoint, then, a whole array of political positions is possible, ranging from moderate democratic-socialism to aggressive revolutionary organization. The positions are united in agreement about the inevitability of socialism. On the other hand—and here are located such

disparate types as Vladimir Lenin, Antonio Gramsci, Brecht, and Benjamin—there is the sense that capitalism knows no progress except the progress of its own power, a progress that may lead to utter annihilation. The revolution is necessary in this sense not as a logical necessity, brought about by the inexorable working out of contradictions, but as the only hope. Such a position is messianic. The dialectical overthrow of capitalism is not the fulfillment of history. It is its radical negation, the cancellation of a history whose continuity is nothing but the continuity of oppression, where, as Benjamin describes it, "the rulers are the heirs of those who conquered before them" and where "whoever has emerged victorious marches to this day in the triumphal procession in which the present rulers step over those who are lying prostrate."

The overtly messianic position raises practical questions about the role of the radical middle-class intellectual. Historically, intellectuals (such as Lenin and Leon Trotsky) formed the party leadership and saw their role as organizing and radicalizing the proletariat, who would themselves bring about the revolution. Benjamin, on the other hand, attempted to root his political activity in his own sphere: he wrote as a disaffected and disenfranchised middle-class intellectual for middle-class intellectuals. In a 1930 review of Kracauer's *Die Angestellten* (White-Collar Workers), Benjamin asks why it is that the intellectual who is necessarily "proletarianized" by the conditions of his employment never turns into a proletarian. He suggests that part of the answer lies in the relationship of the intellectual to his upbringing *within* culture even if his economic position makes him undeniably an outsider. Benjamin's work during the 1930's consists of a coherent, if fragmentary, exploration and development of this paradoxical position. He characterized it as writing about art in such a way that its results could not be used by the enemy.

Benjamin's journalism embraces a variety of subjects, but always attempts to clarify the social and historical position of the middle-class readership. The rest of Benjamin's work during this decade centers on a project that he intended to be his masterwork. The "Passagen-arbeit" (Arcades Project), as he called it, never came to completion, and at his death he left hundreds of pages of notes, sketches, and plans. Besides this, there are a set of essays on Baudelaire, extracted from the project and published separately under the title *Charles Baudelaire, Ein Lyriker im Zeitalter des Hochkapitalismus* (*Charles Baudelaire, A Lyric Poet in the Era of High Capitalism,* 1969); the essay "Das Kunstwerk im Zeitalter seiner technischen Reproduzierbarkeit" (The Work of Art in the Age of Its Technological Reproducibility, 1935, translated as "The Work of Art in the Age of Mechanical Reproduction"); the essay "Der Erzähler" ("The Storyteller," 1936), a reworking of material originally set forth in his review of Alfred Döblin's *Berlin Alexanderplatz* (1929); an essay on Kafka ("Franz Kafka," 1934), and "Über den Begriff der Geschichte" (On the Concept of History, published in translation as "Theses on the Philosophy of History," 1940). This material was all either designed originally for the Arcades Project or is allied to it in theoretical perspective. Named for the arcades of Paris—the construction of walkways through a block of buildings that were then lined with shops, cafés, and restaurants—Benjamin's project was to be nothing less than a complete rewriting of the history of the nineteenth century. The method, it is clear, is similar to that of the book on the *Trauerspiel,* the arrangement of the material and commentary into a constellation or map. The perspective, however, is dialectical materialism as Benjamin understood it, and this entailed a critique of the notion of progress and a critique of the notion of culture.

Benjamin starts with the famous distinction Marx draws in *Zur Kritik der Politischeu Ökonomie* (*The Critique of Political Economy,* 1859) between the economic structure of society as the real foundation (*Unterbau*) of social existence, and the "legal and political superstructure" (*Überbau*) that rises on top of it and "to which correspond definite forms of social consciousness." The crux of Marx's passage is as follows:

> The changes in the economic foundation lead sooner or later to the transformation of the whole immense superstructure. In studying such transformations it is always necessary to distinguish between the material transformation of the economic conditions of production, which can be determined with the precision of natural science, and the legal, political, religious, artistic or philosophic—in short ideological forms in which men become conscious of this conflict and fight it out. Just as one does not judge an individual by what he thinks about himself, so one cannot judge such a period of transformation by its consciousness, but, on the contrary, this consciousness must be explained from the contradictions of material life, from the conflict existing between the social forces of production and the relations of production.
>
> (Karl Marx, *Early Writings* [1975], p. 426)

This statement, Marx's guiding principle in all his studies, is ambiguous at its most important moment. What is the precise relationship between the economic foundation and the "whole immense superstructure"? For most nineteenth- and early twentieth-century Marxists the answer is some variant of logical causation or of the notion that the superstructure *reflects* the base. All cultural being is in either case merely epiphenomenal. Law, art, religion, philosophy have a shadow existence, and since Marx also introduces the idea of "false consciousness," they are like images in a funhouse mirror.

Benjamin makes only a slight alteration in the idea of reflection, but it is an alteration with profound consequences. He carries forward the central idea of his earlier writing and proposes that the superstructure is the sphere in which the foundation of society comes to expression, just as "an overfull stomach may reach expression—yet not be reflected—in the content of a dream. The collective first expresses the conditions of its life; those conditions find their expression in a dream and their significance upon awakening." The sphere of culture becomes in this way a text analogous to the work of art, a center of collective reflection whose significance is to be drawn out in criticism. From this standpoint, historical knowledge is the result of what we might call critical history. It always occurs as a moment of awakening: at a particular moment in the present when a moment of past experience becomes knowable. The past thus becomes "citable," and full awakening (a messianic idea of revolution) would constitute the complete citability of the past. The critical historian thus turns his gaze to the detritus of the past, for the canonical past is nothing but the victory celebration of the conquerors. The forgotten, the discarded, the castoff, the marginal—at any instant a piece of the wreckage of history may reveal its significance and flare up as a momentary awakening in the present. In this light the continuum of history is a myth, and progress is its doctrine. ("History is a nightmare from which I am trying to awaken," says James Joyce's Stephen Dedalus.) The revolutionary task of the critic is the dissolution of the myth and therefore of its power over the present.

Baudelaire is a key figure for Benjamin precisely because his artistic production stands at the threshold of industrial capitalism. His work is in the sphere of art what Marx's is in the sphere of critical philosophy. Baudelaire writes lyric poetry at the very moment when the times are least propitious for the lyric—that is, when the configuration of the literary marketplace is fast relegating the lyric and the lyricist to economic marginality, and when the experiences of modernity seem least capable of being registered in lyric forms. His poetry stands at the beginning of a process that ends in Stéphane Mallarmé's aesthetic of pure art, poetry with no material content whatsoever. Baudelaire desired to be read one day as a classic poet, and his achievement of that status occurred faster than he could have imagined. It occurred precisely because of the ways in which his work registered the experience of modernity:

> Baudelaire's poetry is not esoteric. The social experiences whose precipitate is to be found in his work are, to be sure, nowhere gained from the production process—least of all in its most advanced form, the industrial process—but all of them are present as extensive detours. But these lie in his works exposed in the light of day. The most important of these detours are the experiences of the neurasthenic, of the big-city dweller, and of the customer.
>
> (*Gesammelte Schriften* 1.1.1169)

When Benjamin proposed to extract the material on Baudelaire from the Arcades Project, he had in mind a three-part book very like the Goethe essay in structure: a first part, "Baudelaire as Allegorist," would develop the theory of allegory begun in the book on the *Trauerspiel*; a second part, "The Paris of the Second Empire in Baudelaire," would consist primarily of commentary and articulate the multiple connections between the social setting of Baudelaire's poetry and its material content or subject matter; a third part, "The Commodity as a Subject of Poetry," would develop the connections between the "fetishized commodity," as already discussed by Marx and Lukács, and the work of art. The first and third parts exist only in fragments. The second part was submitted to the *Zeitschrift für Sozialforschung*, where it received a long critique by Adorno and was rejected. Benjamin rewrote it, and it was published in 1939 in the *Zeitschrift* as "Über einige Motive bei Baudelaire" ("Some Motifs in Baudelaire"). The original version was first published in 1969.

Adorno objected to what was most characteristic of Benjamin's work in this period, and indeed to what had always been his characteristic strength—the way he brings widely disparate material from widely disparate areas of experience into immediate unity. Thus Benjamin's discussion of Baudelaire's "Vin des chiffoniers" ("Ragpickers' Wine") takes off from a presentation of the particular atmosphere of revolt in the professional conspiratorial circles of the Paris *bohème,* and it includes an account of the style, ideology, and demeanor of Louis Blanqui, the barricade chief; the erection of the barricades during the July revolution; the wine tax and the tax-free wine sold outside city limits, called *vin de la barrière;* the appearance of ragpickers and the discussion about them by the first investigators of pauperism; and Baudelaire's satanism and its peculiar ambivalences. All this leads to a thorough discussion of the emergence of literary sections in newspapers, changes in subscription policy, the rise of the serialized novel, advertising—in short, the whole formation of the literary market and Baudelaire's place in it. And all this in some ten pages! Benjamin connected his compressed, allusive style to the photomontage and to the synthetic images of the surrealist artists. His intent was to break the false appearance of history as a continuum—to read historical detail as a ruin in the landscape of history whose significance springs to light only as it achieves legibility.

Adorno objected that material from the base was brought into connection with superstructural manifestations without sufficient mediation, that only via mediation through the *whole* cultural sphere could such analysis escape the falsifications of "vulgar Marxism." This objection arises less from defects in Benjamin's analytic method than from a fundamental difference of intent between Benjamin's work and the program of the Frankfurt Institute.

In brief, the writers of the Frankfurt Institute were engaged in what has come to be called "ideology critique," an attempt to unmask the power interests served by "false consciousness" by understanding the precise way in which the superstructure as a whole can absorb and deflect energies that would otherwise constitute revolutionary challenges to bourgeois hegemony. Adorno's 1938 essay "Über den Fetischcharakter in der Musik und die Regression des Hörers" ("On the Fetish-Character in Music and the Regression of Listening") is an excellent example of this type of analysis. It

investigates the way the popular music industry and the aesthetic nature of jazz both become comprehensible as elements of social control. The essay is both influenced by Benjamin and is an overt argument against the thrust of his work. It represents a position that Adorno continually tried to get Benjamin to accept. Benjamin greatly admired Adorno's work but shared neither his aim nor his political standpoint. His relation to both the present and past was otherwise, and while Adorno pursued a politics of unmasking that became ever further removed from the possibility of any action, Benjamin—and here the connection to Brecht is essential—saw his work as directly connected to the awakening of political activism.

For Benjamin the present appears in the past as the latent content of a dream, a content that comes to expression only subject to all the conditions of distortion, displacement, condensation, and negation that Freud unveiled. His historical criticism is dream interpretation, a modern mode of allegorical reading in which the past is made to deliver up its present significance. And just as dream interpretation is a method for curing the neurotic patient, Benjamin's criticism wants to release the present from the trauma of its origins. This is the basis of literary criticism as political praxis. Art is inseparable from its cultic origins, and it carries these origins with it in the form of tradition, or of the religion of pure art. Their ultimate expression is what Benjamin calls the aura that surrounds the work of art. And the significance of the aura becomes clear precisely at the moment of its disappearance, a disappearance made possible by the capacity for art to be mechanically reproduced. Still photography and the sound film accomplish within the realm of art what Benjamin's criticism intends in the realm of history. Freeing art from its cultic origins creates the conditions for art's entry into the sphere of politics. It also creates the conditions for a critical understanding of tradition. Such an understanding contributes to the positive political awakening that is otherwise felt negatively as a crisis in tradition or as the modern sickness of tradition.

In his review of Döblin's *Berlin Alexanderplatz* and in his essays on Nicolai Leskov ("The Storyteller") and Kafka, Benjamin develops a notion of tradition that has caused much misunderstanding in American academic circles. The source of the misunderstanding is that Benjamin admires the art of the three great writers immensely while at the same time he rejoices in the transformation of conditions that has made their art obsolete. To call Döblin, Leskov, and Kafka storytellers is to increase their distance from modern life. At the same time it makes visible the great, exceptional beauty of their work. The traditional appears in Benjamin's descriptions as a thing of great beauty; the modern appears in alienated form. Yet Benjamin is no conservator of the cultural treasures of the past, and it is only in the modern that Benjamin sees a chance for survival.

> What the materialist historian surveys as "cultural-goods," come of a lineage which he cannot contemplate without horror. They owe their existence not only to the striving of the great geniuses who created them, but also to the nameless drudgery of their contemporaries. There is never a document of culture that is not at the same time a document of barbarism. And just as it is not free from barbarism, neither is the process of transmission by which it goes from one person to another. The historical materialist distances himself from this process according to the measure of his ability. He sees it as his task to rub history against the grain.
>
> (*Gesammelte Schriften* 1.2.696)

Benjamin discusses tradition in terms of a bipolar opposition. At the one pole cluster experience (*Erfahrung* in German), memory, storytelling, counsel, wisdom, the figure of the sage; at the other are the lived moment (*Erlebnis*), remembrance, the novel, information, verification, the figure of the writer. The relation of the two poles can be understood historically: the story comes from the long ago or the far away, whereas the novel emerges from the here and now. Thus the peasant who lives on the same plot of ground as his ancestors or the merchant trader who has seen the world are prime types of storytellers. The amalgam of the two types took place within the artisan culture of the Middle Ages: the traveling apprentice becomes a settled master craftsman who passes his experience along to the next generation of apprentices. A story is told to convey counsel (not accidentally an old-fashioned sounding idea), either embodied in a moral or embedded directly within the telling, and it is listened to always in company, if only in the company of the storyteller, so that it may be remembered and retold. Even a written story emerges from the oral tradition and can reenter it by being told. And an event capable of such telling constitutes experience. If storytelling is dying out—and Benjamin notes the phenomenon of World War I veterans who returned silent—it is the result of the decline of experience:

> And no wonder. For never was experience more fundamentally given the lie than strategic experience by tactical warfare, economic experience by inflation, bodily experience by mechanized war, ethical experience by the power brokers. A generation which had been taken to school in horse-drawn carriages stood under an open sky in a landscape in which nothing remained unchanged except for the sky, and under it, in a force field of destructive streams and explosions, the tiny, fragile human body.
>
> (*Gesammelte Schriften* 2.2.439)

Proust's sense that to experience even one's own life had become merely a matter of chance is the great witness to this decline. Yet this sense is part of a long process. With the dissolution of artisan culture in the rise of middle-class capitalism, the conditions of experience change radically. No longer does the wisdom of the long ago and far away suffice as the experience of reality: it is replaced by the necessity for information about the near at hand. The newspaper replaces the sage.

The negative side of the decline of experience is precisely the growing impossibility of wisdom: storytelling, says Benjamin, is the "epic side of truth," and here he has in mind Lukács's idea of epic as being formed of actions that fully present meaning. The epic side of truth is, in other words, the condition of truth's capacity to be transmitted. This transmitability constitutes tradition. The story is the form in which action enters collective experience—the form of its entry into tradition—and the storyteller is a sage precisely because, as the conveyer of experience, he has counsel for all conceivable situations. In these terms Kafka's incredible beauty and overwhelming significance lie, in a manner of speaking, in a choice to forgo truth in order to preserve its transmitability—although the individual Kafka had no choice at all. Kafka's stories thus appear to be either parables derived from a long-forgotten doctrine or parables waiting for the emergence of a new doctrine—a doctrine that will, in any case, emerge only when it is too late to be of any use.

> Kafka's world, frequently so high-spirited and interlaced with angels, is the exact complement of his era which is preparing to do away with the inhabitants of this planet on a considerable scale. The experience which corresponds to that of Kafka, the private individual, will probably not become accessible to the masses until they are being done away with.
>
> (*Briefe,* p. 762)

The positive side of the decline of experience is that it prepares the political grounds for what Benjamin sees as the only hope against mass destruction. This again is the grounds for Benjamin's estimate of the artistic significance of Brecht: his poetry is in a completely *disenchanted* language. It is an art stripped of its cultic origins and therefore an art become newly useful. The technological development of photography and the sound film point the direction for a similarly new utility for art. No longer the vehicle for the transmission of experience, art in the age of mechanical reproduction is instead the sphere in which humanity learns to live the shock of the moment. Technological production and reproduction change the whole realm of art and in the change reveal the significance of certain previously veiled properties of artworks. Benjamin calls the nexus of these properties the aura. The aura is "the unique appearance of a distance, no matter how close the thing actually is." It is dependent on the work's unique existence, its irreplaceability, and its originality. The aura is inseparable from the concept of authenticity and also from tradition, which is the form in which the authentic is transmitted. Mechanical reproducibility calls into question the whole realm of the authentic in art: there is no single authentic print of a movie; enlargements and filtration bring out new rather than "inauthentic" aspects of a photographic negative; and sound recording and radio transmission eliminate the unique existence of a musical performance. By substituting a plurality of objects for a single authentic work and by reducing or even eliminating the distance between the object and the receiver, mechanical reproduction "detaches the reproduced object from the domain of tradition." Put negatively, this is "a tremendous shattering of tradition which is the reverse side of the contemporary crisis and the renewal of mankind."

Art stripped of its aura meets its receiver more than halfway. It acquires the capacity to provide necessary information about the lived moment. Thus the camera becomes an instrument of knowledge that by means of the close-up or of slow motion reveals aspects of nature previously unavailable to knowledge. In decreasing the distance from the spectator, such art also abolishes the distinction between the ordinary receiver and the critic. Benjamin notes the contrast between the public's mass revulsion from Pablo Picasso and its progressive acceptance of Charlie Chaplin. In its immediacy non-auratic art renders its audience spontaneously critical, like the spectators at a sporting event, and it tends ultimately to abolish the distinction between art and audience entirely: in the documentary newsreel the audience becomes itself the subject matter of the film. The differentiation between artist, spectator, and critic, and the arduous process that criticism had become, can all be overcome within the sphere of the new art precisely because the technological nature of the new art itself unties the mythic knot in the thought of the world, present from its origins and preserved in the sphere of art in the aura.

These are only tendencies. Their realization or actualization is dependent on the real social transformation that they themselves indicate. In the absence of such transformations, the new art is pressed violently into the service of the myth. Benjamin's diagnosis is acute:

> Imperialistic war is a rebellion of technology which collects, in "human material," the claims to which society has denied its natural material. Instead of channeling rivers, society directs a human stream into a bed of trenches; instead of dropping seeds from airplanes, it drops fire bombs over cities; and in gas warfare it finds a new way to do away with the aura. "*Fiat ars—pereat mundus*" [Let there be art—let the world perish] says Fascism and . . . expects war to supply the artistic gratification of a sense perception altered by technology. This is without doubt the consummation of "*l'art pour l'art*" [art for art's sake]. Humanity, which once in Homer's time was an object of contemplation for the Olympian gods, now is one for itself. Its self-alienation has reached a level where it experiences its own destruction as an aesthetic pleasure of the first order.
>
> (*Gesammelte Schriften* 1.2.507–508)

In 1940 Benjamin, along with a party of fellow refugees, was turned back after attempting to cross the Spanish border from France. The journey had been hard, and he was in poor health. That night he committed suicide. He is buried in the cemetery at Port Bou. The location of his grave is unknown.

Selected Bibliography

EDITIONS

Der Begriff der Kunstkritik in der deutschen Romantik. Inaugural-Dissertation der Philosophischen Fakultät der Universität Bern zur Erlangung der Doktorwürde. Vorgelegt von Walter Benjamin aus Berlin. Berlin, 1920.
Einbahnstraße. Berlin, 1928.
Ursprung des deutschen Trauerspiels. Berlin, 1928.

COLLECTED WORKS

Gesammelte Schriften. Edited by Rolf Tiedemann and Hermann Schweppenhäuser. 6 vols. Frankfurt, 1974–1985.

SELECTED WORKS

Schriften. Edited by Theodor Adorno. 2 vols. Frankfurt, 1955.
Illuminationen. Ausgewählte Schriften 1. Edited by Siegfried Unseld. Frankfurt, 1961.
Angelus Novus. Ausgewählte Schriften 2. Frankfurt, 1966.
Charles Baudelaire. Ein Lyriker im Zeitalter des Hochkapitalismus. Edited by Rolf Tiedemann. Frankfurt, 1969.
Versuche über Brecht. Exp. ed. Frankfurt, 1978.

CORRESPONDENCE

Briefe. Edited by Theodor Adorno and Gershom Scholem. 2 vols. Frankfurt, 1966.
Briefwechsel: 1933–1940. Edited by Gershom Scholem. Frankfurt, 1980. (Benjamin's correspondence with Gershom Scholem.)

TRANSLATIONS

Charles Baudelaire: A Lyric Poet in the Era of High Capitalism. Translated by Harry Zohn. London, 1973.
Illuminations. Edited by Hannah Arendt. Translated by Harry Zohn. New York, 1968.
Moscow Diary. Edited by Gary Smith. Translated by Richard Sieburth. Cambridge, 1986.
One-Way Street and Other Writings. Translated by Edmund Jephcott and Kingsley Shorter. London, 1979.

The Origin of German Tragic Drama. Translated by John Osborne. London, 1977.

Reflections. Edited by Peter Demetz. Translated by Edmund Jephcott. New York, 1978.

Understanding Brecht. Translated by Anna Bostok. London, 1973.

BIOGRAPHICAL AND CRITICAL STUDIES

Buck-Morss, Susan. *The Origin of Negative Dialectics: Theodor W. Adorno, Walter Benjamin and the Frankfurt Institute.* New York, 1977.

Jameson, Fredric. *Marxism and Form.* Princeton, N.J., 1971.

Jay, Martin. *The Dialectical Imagination: A History of the Frankfurt School and the Institute for Social Research, 1923–1950.* Boston, 1973.

Lacis, Asja. *Revolutionär im Beruf: Berichte über proletarisches Theater, über Meyerhold, Brecht, Benjamin, und Piscator.* Munich, 1971.

Roberts, Julian. *Walter Benjamin.* Atlantic Highlands, N.J., 1983.

Rosen, Charles. "Walter Benjamin and His Ruins." *New York Review of Books* 27 October 1977; 17 November 1977.

Salzinger, Helmut. *Swinging Benjamin.* Frankfurt, 1973.

Scholem, Gershom. *Walter Benjamin: The Story of a Friendship.* Translated by Harry Zohn. Philadelphia, 1981.

———. *Walter Benjamin und sein Engle.* Frankfurt, 1983.

Sontag, Susan. "Walter Benjamin: The Last Intellectual." *New York Review of Books* 12 October 1978.

Tiedemann, Rolf. *Studien zur Philosophie Walter Benjamins.* Frankfurt, 1973.

Unseld, Siegfried, ed. *Zur Aktualität Walter Benjamins.* Frankfurt, 1972.

Witte, Bernd. *Walter Benjamin: Der Intellecktuelle als Kritiker.* Stuttgart, 1976.

Wolin, Richard. *Walter Benjamin: An Aesthetic of Redemption.* New York, 1982.

ROBERT M. STEIN

MARINA TSVETAEVA

(1892–1941)

WHEN THE RUSSIAN Revolution of February 1917 broke out, Marina Tsvetaeva was living in Moscow with her husband, Sergei Efron, and their four-year-old daughter, Ariadna. The family occupied a spacious apartment imaginatively laid out on three levels of a stuccoed building typical of the domestic architecture of mid-nineteenth-century Moscow. Compact and massive, the building turned its symmetrical front facade toward Borisogleb Lane, one of the many picturesque streets that crisscross the central Moscow district known as the Arbat, a quarter populated by artists, musicians, writers, and by the educated, often politically active, segment of Russian society known as the intelligentsia. Through her family and her chosen vocation, Tsvetaeva was linked with the creative intelligentsia; thus, the Borisogleb apartment was an apt physical setting and, ultimately, also a symbol for the poet's ancestry and destiny.

Equally significant was Tsvetaeva's chronological location. For the first decades of the twentieth century, which heightened political activity among parties from Left to Right, also accelerated an extraordinary cultural revival. The prerevolutionary years in Russia had brought forth the music of Igor Stravinsky and Alexander Scriabin (Scriabin lived across the courtyard from Tsvetaeva), had fostered the painting, architecture, and graphic design of Léon Bakst, Natalya Goncharova, Mikhail Larionov, Vladimir Tatlin, and Kasimir Malevich,

had witnessed the debuts of theatrical innovators like Vsevolod Meyerhold and Yevgeny Vakhtangov, and had exported to Paris and beyond the multi-media spectacles of Sergei Diaghilev's Ballets Russes.

No less remarkable and abundant was the resurgence of Russian literature. A new literary age was underway, begun in the 1890's under the aegis of symbolism. Influenced by philosophies of aestheticism and idealism, symbolism restored to Russian verse-making its high standards of craftsmanship, its influence on the other arts, and its avid, disputatious readership. The vitality of symbolism was evident in the range and number of its practitioners, which included prose writers, theoreticians, critics, and even classical scholars, as well as major poets like Innokenty Annensky, Vyacheslav Ivanov, Konstantin Bal'mont, Valery Bryusov, and Alexander Blok.

Equally, and paradoxically so, symbolism showed its importance in the strength and talent of the next, younger generation of poets, who revolted against symbolist metaphysics while appropriating its technical know-how, its polemical bent, and at least some of its readers. This was the generation of 1910, the year in which Tsvetaeva published her first collection of poetry. Its poets issued manifestos under the names of acmeism and futurism, and by 1917 the poets Nikolai Gumilov, Anna Akhmatova, Boris Pasternak, Osip Mandelshtam, and Vladimir Mayakovsky had emerged in the final wave of the renascence that came to be known as Russia's Silver Age of Poetry. Tsvetaeva belongs to this epoch and her life offers a small but appropriate material token of her place in Russian literature, for, just as the word *hand* became Tsvetaeva's favored metonym for the poet, the silver bracelets Tsvetaeva wore even in the worst periods of poverty became her personal, sartorial signature.

MOSCOW:
CHILDHOOD, YOUTH, AND MARRIAGE

Within walking distance of the Borisogleb apartment was the house where Tsvetaeva spent her childhood. Again, architecture seems to acquire symbolic value. The house in which Tsvetaeva spent her childhood and adolescence was a large private house with a poplar-lined, enclosed yard and court located on Three Ponds Lane. This house, like the one on Borisogleb, was a typically Muscovite, middle-class dwelling, and the external similarities between the houses of Tsvetaeva's childhood and of her early married life betoken myriad inner continuities.

The Three Ponds house had come into the family through the first marriage of the poet's father, Ivan Vladimirovich Tsvetaev. He had studied classical languages, had won a university gold medal, and had gone to Italy to research his doctoral dissertation on a Latin dialect. Later, however, he studied the classical period under a different aspect when he assumed a professorship of art history at Moscow University and began what was to become his life's work, the building of a museum to house reproductions of classical sculpture. Ivan Vladimirovich married Varvara Dmitrievna Ilovaiskaia, the daughter of a historian and well-known political conservative. The house that had been part of Varvara Dmitrievna's dowry passed to her children Valeriya and Andrey when she died soon after Andrey's birth.

Ivan Vladimirovich married again. His second wife, Mariia Aleksandrovna, née Meyn, was born of Polish and Baltic German forebears and had had a serious musical education, which had fostered her hopes of having a career as a pianist. Instead, she married Professor Tsvetaev, her senior by twenty years, motivated by her father's strictures against an early and unsuitable attachment and by an innate bent for self-sacrifice. Their daughter Marina was born on 26 September 1892 and a second daughter named Anastasiya (or Asya) in 1894. The girls' earliest memories rang with the sounds of their mother's piano. Soon Asya's uncertain notes and Marina's precociously skillful octaves were added to the music of Beethoven, Schumann, and the popular Russian songs or "romances" that filled the large formal reception room.

Familial harmony was far less in evidence. Ivan Vladimirovich's oldest child, Valeriya, waged her brand of adolescent warfare against the new, and to her mind intrusive, stepmother. Little Marina soon came to resent her role as wunderkind and began to hate piano practice; very early she sensed that her inborn gift was not for the music of pianos but for the music of poems. Ivan Vladimirovich remained unaware of any domestic problems and, it would seem, equally unaware of his young wife's passionate temperament. He devoted himself wholly to his new museum, raising funds, ordering reproductions in the ateliers of Italy, prospecting in the Urals for marble suitable for the museum's columns and facing, meeting with architects and builders, and gradually expanding both the size of the building and the scope of its acquisitions.

In the fall of 1902, just when Marina turned ten, Mariia Aleksandrovna became ill with tuberculosis. For the next three years the mother and her two daughters lived abroad. Mariia Aleksandrovna sought a cure in the milder climate of Italy, while Marina and Asya spent the academic year in boarding schools, first a pleasant French school, more like an enlarged family, in Switzerland, then in a discipline-minded, hateful German school that underfed its students, thereby unknowingly preparing the Russian sisters for their hungry years in revolutionary Moscow.

In 1905 mother and daughters returned to Russia. They were living in Yalta when the Revolution of 1905 ushered in a period of political liberalization and optimism and stimulated further the already intense activity in the arts. For a time, the idealistic young Marina was infected by Russia's revolutionary fervor.

But a drastic change soon shook the family. Mariia Aleksandrovna died from tuberculosis in July 1906. During the next five years Tsvetaeva was largely on her own as she tried to fill the void left by her mother's death. She had received a bitter maternal legacy, for her mother had poisoned the child's love by demanding unreasonable hours of piano practice to compensate for her own frustrated musical career and by showing a truly perverse preference for her stepson and the musically ungifted Asya. Marina's worth had always been on trial—the trial of the keyboard and the metronome. Still, as long as her mother was alive Marina knew whom to please and how. Now she had to find a new focus for her intense inner strivings.

Marina was fourteen when her mother died and she should have resumed regular schooling with other girls her age. She did enroll in secondary schools in Moscow but always had to leave; she was not interested in the regular gymnasiia (the Russian secondary school) curriculum, only in literature and languages, and she received unsatisfactory grades.

Asya adjusted better to school and to her orphaned life. Except for the two sisters and the somewhat transient housekeepers, the house at Three Ponds was now populated only by servants. Valeriya and Andrey, the legal heir to the house, had gone on their own ways for the time. In this middle-class, very Victorian-seeming household, the two sisters were both sequestered and unsupervised, a situation created mainly by the frequent absence of their elderly father, whose selflessness in labor for the museum was as profound as his neglect of his daughters. In these circumstances everything depended on one's circle of friends. But the dedicated Ivan Vladimirovich sought out art collectors and patrons, not peer contacts for his children.

The sisters began on their own to acquire friends. Two of Asya's schoolmates visited the house and, in 1909, another regular visitor appeared. This was a man belonging to an older generation, a symbolist poet and critic named Lev Kobylinskii who wrote under the pen name Ellis. Thanks to Ellis the door of the Three Ponds house now opened just a crack onto the bohemian world of literary Moscow.

Through Ellis, Marina met a young translator and classicist named Vladimir Nilender. Their first avowals of love were followed quickly by permanent separation, and when Tsvetaeva published her first collection of poetry, *Vechernii al'bom* (Evening Album), late in 1910 she used the volume to send several cryptic messages to Nilender. Although printed privately *Vechernii al'bom* was reviewed by several important critics. A second collection, *Volshebnyi fonar'* (The Magic Lantern), followed in 1912.

The two collections heralded the most important genre in the youthful poet's future work. Tsvetaeva is first of all a lyricist, not only because the sheer volume and quality of her lyric poetry is remarkable (they comprise three hefty volumes), but also because her lyrical voice remains audible even in her narrative poetry, her prose, and her letters. The first two collections of 1910 and 1912 indicate their subject matter in their titles; the poems present scenes of a childhood and youth passed quietly in the nursery, study, and reception hall of a middle-class home in Moscow. The viewpoint is intimate, but never trivial or banal, despite the youth of the author.

The word *album* in the first title refers to a real album in which the young poet wrote her poems. But the collection can also be compared to the tabletop, parlor albums containing drawings, photos, and postcards that were a main means of female self-expression among the nineteenth century bourgeoisie. Indeed the collections are full of picturelike poems. The young poet, moreover, displays her mastery of the iambs, trochees, anapests, dactylls, and amphibracs used in nineteenth-century Russian poetry and also her inventiveness in devising stanza forms. Both traits of versification persist in her later poetry alongside two characteristic innovations: inter-stanzaic enjambments and the logaoedic line, that is, a line that contains nontraditional sequences of stressed and unstressed syllables that are repeated and thereby become a regular pattern within a stanza or an entire poem.

Meanwhile, however, another literary visitor had appeared in the Three Ponds house, the poet and painter Maksimilian Voloshin, a man whose massive physical presence (he was corpulent, tall, and curly-headed) betokened his considerable impact on Tsvetaeva's life and career. Voloshin had been one of those who had reviewed *Vechernii al'bom*. When he called on Marina, at her invitation, in 1911, the older and younger poets took an immediate liking to one another and became lifelong friends. Voloshin, moreover, became Tsvetaeva's first sincere literary advocate. He drew her away from Maria Bashkirtseva and Edmond Rostand, whom the young Marina idolized, toward the French symbolists and the novelists of the nineteenth and, eventually, those of the eighteenth century. He took the fledgling poet to the publishing offices of Musaget, a kind of literary club-cum-press where she met poets from the second generation of Russian symbolists, including the marvelously eccentric Andrey Bely and several adherents of the newer acmeist movement. Now Tsvetaeva had her first real encounter with the ferment of contemporary literature.

During the summer Voloshin and his eccentric mother—the woman wore cropped hair and balloon pants—invited Tsvetaeva to a remote Crimean village called Koktebel' where the Voloshin villa had become an artists' and writers' spring and summer colony. Here, in May 1911, she met Sergei Efron, a man one year younger than herself whose complicated family background included a Jewish father of radically anti-tsarist views and a mother who belonged to the Russian nobility and who was likewise an opponent of the tsarist government.

Efron and Tsvetaeva returned together to Moscow that fall, thoroughly involved with one another. Efron dedicated his debut collection of short stories to Tsvetaeva. She dedicated her second collection, *Volshebnyi fonar'* to him. They were married in 1912. The bride was nineteen, the groom eighteen. A photograph shows a husky, chubby-faced, and determined-looking Tsvetaeva standing next to a slender, somewhat spectral young man with the round, encircled, and unfocused eyes of an icon.

The couple bought a house in the merchant's quarter—Tsvetaeva had inherited a large sum of money from her mother's side of the family—and there she gave birth to her daughter Ariadna late in 1912. In 1913 she published a selection of poems from her first two collections entitled, appropriately, *Iz dvukh knig* (From Two Books). A year later, in 1914, the family moved to the Borisogleb house in the Arbat. The house was well furnished and there was a rather sizeable staff of servants, including a valet, a nurse for little Ariadna, and a cook. During the summers Efron and Tsvetaeva returned to Koktebel' by the sea where they had first met and where they continued to enjoy the company of people who shared their literary interests. Tsvetaeva now dressed elegantly and had become fashionably slender.

By the middle of 1916 Marina was pregnant with a second child. Meanwhile she had completed the poems that would form a new collection entitled *Iunosheskie stixi* (Youthful Verses, written in 1913–1915, published in 1976). By early 1917, she completed yet another collection, entitled *Versty I* (Mileposts I, 1922) and containing poems dating from the year 1916.

All this was perhaps the usual course of things for a financially independent young couple devoted to each other and to literature, but there were serious disruptions, both personal and global. Tsvetaeva's father had lived to see the tsar's brother inaugurate his museum and died not long afterward in 1913. World War I broke out in 1914, and several of Tsvetaeva's associates had premonitions that the guns of August would find an echo deep inside Russia and destroy it. Tsvetaeva did not seem to share these fears; by late 1914 she was involved in an inner war of passions that fully engaged her attention and threatened to disrupt her married family life.

These passions were aroused by Sofiia Parnok, a poet who had already published two collections but whose most important work as poet and critic still lay in the future. Sofiia Parnok was not only a poet; she was a mature, self-assured woman, the first female to reciprocate Tsvetaeva's adult, sexual love. A cycle of poems grew out of their affair and so too a cycle of passions, indeed, something of a vicious cycle. In this love affair sexual ecstasy alternated with girlish escapades and moments of indifference lived side by side with fierce struggles for conquest. Tsvetaeva, less than three years into a marriage to which she would remain faithful to the end, found herself passionately and possessively in love with a woman. An unhappy outcome was perhaps predictable. Parnok was some dozen years older than Tsvetaeva and she was the more experienced of the two. Moreover, she valued her liberty of choice as the privilege of a sexuality that, though it was accepted in artistic circles, had provoked the wrath of the Parnok family. Tsvetaeva's letters show that she was painfully torn between her love for her husband and her love for Parnok. Few passions would bring Tsvetaeva this much pain, but the pattern of this affair was to reassert itself in the future: a struggle to possess or to be possessed, an abrupt ending of the affair followed by a period of intense creativity and reevaluation.

The end of the love affair followed soon after a visit to St. Petersburg in December 1915 and early January 1916, a trip made possible by and taken with Parnok. Parnok contributed her work to the St. Petersburg literary journal *Se-vernye zapiski* (Northern Annals). She introduced Tsvetaeva to the journal's two publishers, who began to print Tsvetaeva's poems regularly and invited her to the capital. The main event of the stay was a literary gathering in a private home where Tsvetaeva met Sergey Esenin, the renowned poet of rural Russia, and Mikhail Kuzmin, the founder, *avant la lettre* of acemism. She also had a second encounter with the poet Osip Mandelshtam. The poets had met in Koktebel'; now they heard each other recite and each understood the importance of the other's poetic gift. All told, the literary evening was not only a meeting between poets, but also between Moscow, which Tsvetaeva was proudly conscious of representing, and St. Petersburg, which was represented by Kuzmin and Mandelshtam, and, in Tsvetaeva's vision of it, by Anna Akhmatova, although she did not actually attend the gathering.

Parnok, too, was absent from that evening, and a quarrel ensued. Early in 1916, back in Moscow, Parnok ended her affair with Tsvetaeva. Tsvetaeva never forgave her; no other love and parting was to leave such permanent bitterness in her as this one. No doubt, in yielding to her sudden passion for Parnok, Tsvetaeva had felt she was risking a great deal, especially her marriage. To be rejected angered her and hurt her considerable and very fragile pride.

From St. Petersburg the poet Mandelshtam followed Tsvetaeva to Moscow to continue and deepen their acquaintance. He returned several times in 1916, clearly transfixed by Tsvetaeva's person and talent. Tsvetaeva walked Mandelshtam through Moscow and shared her native city's history and culture with her fellow poet, who until then had remained entirely Petersburgian, that is, oriented toward Europe and "European Russia." In presenting Moscow to Mandelshtam, Tsvetaeva's consciousness of her Moscovite identity deepened—or rather her several pseudo-identities, since she saw herself in many of the city's past and present denizens—and so too did her awareness of her place in the new poetry now being created in the old and the new capitals of Russia. The city walks enriched Mandelshtam too. This mutually enriching encounter led each poet to celebrate the friendship by writing poems to the other.

Tsvetaeva extended her dialogue with St. Petersburg and that city's poetic tradition in yet another way: she read intensively in the work of two Petersburg poets, Alexander Blok, the greatest symbolist of the younger, turn-of-the-century generation, and Anna Akhmatova, a new voice of the 1910 generation of acmeists and the first major female voice to be heard in the history of Russian poetry. Again, Tsvetaeva was discovering and articulating her sense of identity. Whereas Blok, an older, male poet, became an object of veneration (a status she never accorded to anyone else except Rainer Maria Rilke), Akhmatova was a supremely female poet in her themes and psychology, and in defining herself vis à vis this persona of Akhmatova, Tsvetaeva became fully aware of the nonfemale in her own poetic practice and heritage.

Still other encounters, including an important love affair with one Nikodim Plutser-Sarna, about whom little is known, enriched the year 1916. Judging from the poems that grew out of this watershed year, the poems that comprise the collection *Versty I*, all these encounters, passions, and affections tended toward the single effect of intensifying Tsvetaeva's sense of herself as a product of Moscow, as the heir to the many figures, male and female, linked with the city's history. For example, she liked to put herself in the persona of Marina Mnishek, the Polish-born (Tsvetaeva's ancestry was also partly Polish) wife of the first False Dmitry. All these ideas found expression in *Versty I*.

This collection displays a new range in the rapidly developing poet and three hallmarks of Tsvetaeva's mature style emerge. First, Tsvetaeva dates each of her poems and publishes them, with few exceptions, in strictly chronological order. *Versty I* forms a diary in verse for the year 1916. Second, she includes in the collection cycles of poems that fall into fairly regular chronological sequence among the single poems, evidence that certain themes now receive sustained expression and variation and that the poet's reach has become more extensive. One such cycle announces the theme of *Versty I*, the "Stikhi o Moskve" ("Poems on Moscow"). Two cycles are dedicated to poets—again a trait betokening the future—the "Stikhi k Akhmatovoi" ("Poems to Akhmatova") and the "Stikhi k Bloku" ("Poems to Blok"), which will reappear, amplified by additional poems commemorating Blok's death, in a later, separate volume of 1922. Third, she reveals in the *Versty I* collection her gift as a dramatist—her ability to don verbal masks, to speak as an invented character, to merge the dramatic and the lyric in monologues, dialogues, choruses, and one-sided perorations.

The book of poems from the year 1916 is, moreover, curiously saturated with a sense of what can only be called watchfulness; indeed, the theme of insomnia closes the collection. There is something touching and prophetic here, as if Tsvetaeva wanted to preserve the old Moscow—and with it the old Russia—the Moscow of her birth, her childhood, her marriage, her father's museum, her motherhood, and her first achievements and fame as a poet, to preserve it by celebrating in verse the city's final year before the two revolutions of 1917.

REVOLUTION AND CIVIL WAR

The revolution of February 1917 established the provisional government and brought to Russia the first liberal and democratic regime in its history. The tempos of political and cultural life accelerated. But World War I was still being fought, Russian losses were heavy, and by October 1917 the Bolshevik faction of the Social Democratic party, led by Vladimir Lenin, was able to use the Petrograd soviet, a left-wing body claiming to represent soldiers and workers, as an operational center to first undermine and then overthrow the provisional government.

During the weeks before and after the October Revolution when the Bolsheviks seized power, Tsvetaeva traveled twice across Russia from Moscow to Feodosia in the Crimea, a large town not far from Max Voloshin's Koktebel' villa. She planned to join her sister in Feodosia, bringing her daughter Ariadna and her second daughter, the baby Irina, born in April 1917.

But the civil war broke out, and in late November Tsvetaeva found herself alone with her children in Moscow; the war had blocked her way to the Crimea, to her sister and Voloshin, and to her husband, Efron, who, newly graduated as an officer from a Moscow military school, had gone to join the White Russian Army to fight against the new Bolshevik regime.

Now began Tsvetaeva's five-year struggle to survive the cold, the hunger, and the political terror of a different sort of Moscow, one ruled theoretically by something called the dictatorship of the proletariat, but actually dominated by bureaucrats, Cheka men (members of the secret police), and eventually, by profiteers and black marketeers.

Until the end of 1917, Tsvetaeva and her family had occupied the spacious apartment at Borisogleb; there, they had been amply supplied with money and servants. Now the family's capital and its income were confiscated. Tsvetaeva had always worked hard at her writing table, but she had no official job and was, therefore, not entitled to a government ration card under the new regime. The city rapidly degenerated. Even running water was not available on the upper floors of the Borisogleb house. Tsvetaeva rented out parts of the Borisogleb apartment to a variety of transient tenants and moved with her children up into the attic rooms to save on increasingly scarce fuel. After a winter or two, even the stairway bannisters were used as firewood. To get food, Tsvetaeva bartered away everything, even her clothes; she was left with one sacklike dress, a leather belt, and a tsarist army field pouch, which she defiantly sported even at public poetry readings held under the aegis of the new Red government.

Into this modern hell of cold, deprivation, and anxiety, relief came time and again, like so many beneficent lightning bolts darting from a dark, immobile thundercloud. A top Cheka man, tenanted at Borisogleb, helped get Tsvetaeva an office job that entitled her to food rations. She was also helped by a woman living downstairs, by the wife of a cobbler living next door, by the actress and poet Vera Zviagintseva, and by other friends and admirers of her poetry. Ariadna, too, found a friend who took the child out to the country for better food. But Tsvetaeva's second child, little Irina, who was sickly from birth, did not survive the terrible winters; she died in February 1920 before reaching her third year.

As sometimes happens, hardships strengthened loyalties among old friends and brought rapidly formed, intense new friendships. Tsvetaeva thrived whenever she was surrounded by friendship and loyalty, and her productivity during the five years after the 1917 Bolshevik revolution is, especially considering her material circumstances, utterly astonishing. She kept a prose journal that chronicles her life in Moscow, her various encounters on her train trips to the Crimea, her misadventures in bartering for food, and her five months as a filing clerk in the Commissariat of Nationalities, headed by—Tsvetaeva did not know it—one Joseph Stalin. These accounts were later collectively entitled *Zemnye primety* (Earthbound Omens). They were published as separate sketches years later, when Tsvetaeva had emigrated, but they never were printed in the two-volume edition Tsvetaeva hoped for. Instead they appeared in the various journals founded in Berlin, Prague, and Paris by journalists, critics, and scholars who had left Russia.

Ever loyal to her husband and sharing his loyalty to the tsar and to liberalized, prerevolutionary Russia, she also became the chronicler in verse of the White Army fighting on the civil war's Crimean front. These poems formed a long cycle entitled *Lebedinyi stan* (*The Demesne of the Swans,* written in 1917–1920), some of them, again, published in emigration, but published as a whole only in 1957.

As the months of cold and hunger in Moscow wore on, a new acquaintance with the poet Pavel Antokolskii brought Tsvetaeva into the circle of authors and actors associated with an experimental theater project, an offspring of the well-known Moscow Art Theater known as Vakhtangov's Third Studio. In 1918–1919 she wrote six plays in verse, all designed for the Third Studio but never staged there. Five of the plays were set in the eighteenth century, an epoch to which her friend Max Voloshin had drawn her attention. Under Voloshin's influence, she had read Casanova's memoirs and the exploits of Cagliostro. Now, as events in Russia seemed to parallel the course of the French Revolution with its left-wing extreme in the Reign of Terror and its rightist opposition in the Vendée, the glittery life of eighteenth-century aristocrats acquired a dimension of glamour, pathos, and at times, even heroism that served to rekindle Tsvetaeva's youthful romanticism.

Far more important than these early plays was Tsvetaeva's debut in a new genre known in Russian as the *poema*. As its name suggests, the term *poema* designates a long poem, traditionally a poem having a narrative structure and primarily narrative contents. In the hands of twentieth century poets, the genre began to change and came to include lyrical as well as narratives themes, including themes from the poet's autobiography. Such long narratives in verse were to become some of Tsvetaeva's most important works; their experimental craftsmanship, technical brilliance, and passionately held worldview entitle them to be ranked among the supreme achievements of the genre.

A significant early *poema* based on themes from Russian folklore is entitled "Tsar'-devitsa" (The Tsar Maiden, 1922). "Tsar'-devitsa," subtitled "A Fairy-tale Poem," is Tsve-

taeva's leap into sublime comedy. Its humor and pathos spring from the contrast she draws between the two main protagonists. The Tsar Maiden is an Amazon, a soldiering woman of huge physique who enjoys only her sword, her war horse, and the sounds of battle; she is, however, conquered immediately by the sounds of the male protagonist's music. He is her exact opposite, a maidenly tsarevich, slight of physique and devoted to his musical art. These extreme contrasts between the poem's heroes are matched by other contrasts among character types and events. An important element of the plot, for instance, is the lust of the Tsarevich's young stepmother for her stepson. Tsvetaeva borrowed her heroes, the Tsar Maiden and the Tsarevich, from two Russian folktales found in a collection well known to all Russians by the name of its collector Afanas'ev. But she had the striking idea of combining the folk elements with a plot from Greek classical mythology, the story of Phaedra and Hippolytus, a story that reappears in her later plays and poems. The scope of her sources is matched by the breathtaking, almost delerium-producing gyre of images and associations. Thus, for example, the Tsar Maiden announces that her father is fire, her mother is water, her brother is the wind, her sister is the storm, and she is a demon incarnate. Of all Tsvetaeva's works, this long poem boasts the most unabashed display of feeling and impulse. The poem is full of sudden shifts in feeling, from pathos to hilarity, from suspense to vast peacefulness.

Meanwhile, Tsvetaeva produced two new collections of shorter poems. A second volume entitled *Versty* (Mileposts, 1921), which has come to be known as *Versty II* to distinguish it from the earlier 1916 poems bearing the same title, and *Psikheia* (Psyche, 1923), which gathers poems sharing the various themes of romanticism.

A third collection from the postrevolutionary years is one of Tsvetaeva's most important. Entitled *Remeslo* (Craft, 1923) it contains almost all the poems Tsvetaeva wrote from April 1921 through April 1922 arranged in chronological order. Again, as in the first *Versty,* a full year is chronicled in verse. Again important cycles dominate the book, most remarkable among them "Khanskii Polon" ("Prisoner of the Khan"). In it, Tsvetaeva presents analogies to the present situation of Russia drawn from the period known as the Tatar Yoke, the twelfth-century invasions of Russia by Mongol hordes from the East. Appropriately, she draws some of her imagery from a great epic poem, "Slovo o polku Igoreve," known in English as "The Igor Tale," that came from this period. The devoted and superb Tsvetaeva scholar Viktoriia Shveitser has summarized *Remeslo* as "the beginning of the mature, tragic Tsvetaeva. This is a book of farewells: to youth, to the Muse, to the White Movement, to Russia. This is Tsvetaeva's lyrical diary on the threshold of a new life and at the same time an interpretation of what had happened in Russia." The collection concludes with a *poema* called "Pereulochki" ("Sidestreets") based, like the "Tsar'-devitsa," on themes from Russian folktales.

For four years after the second 1917 revolution Tsvetaeva had no word about her husband, who was fighting on the southern front. Then the civil war ended, the White Army retreated in defeat through the Crimea, and Tsvetaeva received the welcome news of her husband's survival in July 1921, brought to Moscow by the novelist and memoirist Ilya Ehrenburg. She now prepared to leave Russia. In May of 1922 she and Ariadna joined Sergei Efron in Berlin.

Oddly enough, the months before Tsvetaeva's emigration saw the sudden reappearance of her work inside the Soviet Union, where a temporary period of quasi-liberalization was under way. After four years during which none of her writings had appeared, a privately owned press brought out *Versty II* in 1921. She was also published officially by the government-controlled press, then going through a period of vacillation before censorship was imposed. A state-owned and run publishing house printed "Tsar'-devitsa" and *Versty I* in 1922, the very year Tsvetaeva left the Soviet Union.

Tsvetaeva's work, moreover, had preceded her into emigration where intense literary activity, including the founding of new journals and newspapers, flourished among Russians newly arrived in the various European capitals. Thus, when Tsvetaeva reached Berlin she was soon lionized in that city's literary circles. Her friend Ehrenburg had already arranged the publication of a small volume of poems entitled *Razluka* (Separation, 1922), containing an early, quasi-autobiographical *poema* entitled "Na krasnom kone" ("On a Red Steed"), and the publication of a new, enlarged cycle of lyrics about Tsvetaeva's best-beloved symbolist poet, *Stikhi k Bloku* (Poems to Blok, 1922). Tsvetaeva now arranged to publish her epoch-making collection *Remeslo,* a second edition of "Tsar'-devitsa," and *Psikheia,* containing poems culled from earlier collections and over fifty new poems.

She also laid the ground for future work through her friendship with the symbolist poet and novelist Andrey Bely, then living in Berlin and considering whether to choose emigration. New poetry collections brought Tsvetaeva an opportunity to renew and deepen her acquaintance with her contemporary and fellow Moscovite Boris Pasternak, a poet who was to become extremely important to Tsvetaeva in myriad ways.

After a few months in Berlin, the family moved to Prague in Czechoslovakia, then one of the main centers of Russian culture and scholarship outside Russia. Tsvetaeva was to spend seventeen years in emigration, first in Czechoslovakia, then in France. The patterns of her émigré life began to take shape as soon as the family reached Prague. Here and in Paris Tsvetaeva and Ariadna lived not in the city centers but in villages or *banlieu* settlements that surrounded the capitals. Sergei Efron spent his days and some nights in Prague; he was not available for domestic chores and he earned virtually no money, a pattern that continued in Paris until the mid 1930's when he earned money, unbeknownst to his wife, as a Soviet agent. However primitive the village living conditions were—in her first suburban village Tsvetaeva had to haul water from the local well—Tsvetaeva found solace and freedom through the proximity of hills and forests. She became and remained a passionate walker.

She needed some kind of enjoyment, for heavy domestic burdens fell primarily on her and on the very young but loyal Ariadna. Tsvetaeva not only cooked, cleaned, washed, shopped, and mended, but also provided the financial support of her family, which, in February 1925, was enlarged by the birth of a son, Georgy, known by his nickname "Moor." For income Tsvetaeva had three sources: a monthly stipend from the Czech government, whose president Thomas Masaryk had the wisdom and generosity to foster Russian culture in emigration; gifts from friends and admirers; and payments for the publication of her works. The opportunity and the pressing need to publish actively brought Tsvetaeva into contact with the editors of the new émigré newspapers and journals. Her relations with the publishers were sometimes excellent, especially when the editors' tastes were subtle and in advance of the general émigré reader; in Paris a journal was even founded by one of the best literary critics of the day and named *Versty* (Mileposts) in her honor. But as time passed and Tsvetaeva ventured into literary criticism, her outspokenness made enemies of influential critics belonging to an older, somewhat more conservative school, while other critics proved unable to appreciate Tsvetaeva's ever-changing poetic technique. Alas for her, one of Tsvetaeva's greatest gifts was for satire and invective, and there were targets aplenty among the extraordinarily diverse, but sometimes pompous, literary world of the emigration.

A fourth hallmark of Tsvetaeva's émigré period was the importance and volume of her letters. From 1922 on Tsvetaeva's correspon-dence became both a personal lifeline linking her with loyal friends—especially women friends who aided her materially as well as emotionally—and a valuable extension of her literary art into a new literary genre. Some of her letters contain what is tantamount to short essays on such serious topics as the nature and destiny of art, while others serve to explain some of her most difficult poetic works by pointing to specific borrowings from folklore or providing hints as to sources in her autobiography. All the letters reveal Tsvetaeva as an immensely, often infuriatingly, complicated human being as well as a superbly talented artist; virtually none of the letters are impersonal or routine, and Tsvetaeva's correspondence takes its place alongside the best exemplars of epistolary art of any period. Thus, for example, the Prague years produced an important group of letters written in the summer of 1923 to a young critic in Paris, one Alexander Bakhrakh. In the same year Tsvetaeva and Boris Pasternak began to exchange letters. Their correspondence documents the lives of two artists who struggled to sustain their art and their personal integrity under very difficult conditions and who succeeded in reaching one another through the barriers created by the division of Russian culture into its Soviet and émigré domains, an achievement of which Tsvetaeva was particularly proud. The importance of Tsvetaeva's correspondence with women friends is exemplified by her letters to her fellow émigrés Olga Kolbasina-Chernova and Vera Nikolaevna Bunina, wife of the Nobel laureate Ivan Bunin, and to her Czech friend from Prague, Anna Teskovà.

The Prague years were rich in poetic achievement. Individual poems and lyric cycles written in Berlin and Prague show Tsvetaeva continuing to conquer new techniques and to explore new subject matter. Especially characteristic are her poems to other poets like Boris Pasternak, and the poems placed in the mouth of heroes and heroines from Greek mythology and from Shakespeare (Orpheus and Eurydice, Phaedra and Hippolytus, Hamlet and Ophelia). These poems appeared as a collection under the title *Posle Rossii* (After Russia) five years later in Paris in 1928. Tsvetaeva's lyric power is deepened by a new, classical solemnity. Her outpouring of sustained cycles displays an expanded thematic and vocal range, a range that encompasses the nocturnal secrecy of the twenty-three poems written in Berlin in 1922, the pantheistic exaltation of "Derev'ia" ("Trees"), the stoic renunciation of "Provoda" ("Cables") and "Dvoe" ("Pairs"), and the tragic, proud credo of "Poety" ("Poets").

Prague witnessed and partly inspired two of Tsvetaeva's greatest long poems (*poemy*): the lyric-narrative diptych "Poema gory" ("The Poem of the Mountain") and "Poema kontsa" ("The Poem of the End"), both poems written in 1924 and published separately in 1926: the first in the Paris-based *Versty,* the second in an almanac called *Kovcheg* (The Ark) produced in Prague. The two poems celebrate and then lament a love that was born on the hills of the city, wandered its streets, and came to an end near the bridges that span Prague's Vltava river, a river that both divides and unites the capital and the protagonists of the poems. The mountain of "The Poem of the Mountain" (in real life a hill in the city on which Tsvetaeva lived for a brief period) becomes the spatial setting and symbol for the lovers' happiness and for the power that lifts them above the mundane. The river that figures in "The Poem of the End" takes on multifarious meanings: it is associated with the classical river Lethe and the heroine's urge to live as a shade somewhere between death and life; it stands for time and change, and also for poetry itself, which will absorb the protagonists' griefs and bear them away into the common stream of suffering, of personal forgetfulness, and of universal recollection through art.

These two poems are part of an impressive group of major works, major both in length and in originality. In 1923 she completed a long epic-romantic *poema, Molodets,* published in 1924. The title can be translated into English as "The Swain" or "The Country Gallant." This is the third *poema* based on Russian folklore, the story of a vampire who enraptures a village maiden named Marusya. The folktale's structure becomes a vehicle for two of Tsvetaeva's favorite themes: fidelity, evinced in Marusya's refusal to reveal her connection with the vampire, and transcendence, embodied in the ending to the *poema* when Marusya abandons her earthbound life and unites with the vampire's unearthly power.

In 1923 Tsvetaeva turned again to writing drama; now, however, she took her story material not from the eighteenth century but from the Greek myths linked to Theseus. The play *Tezei: Ariadna* (Theseus-Ariadne, 1924) was the first in a planned triology of verse tragedies, collectively entitled *Gnev Afrodity* (Aphrodite's Rage). The second play was completed in 1927; this was the *Fedra* (Phaedra). Tsvetaeva never wrote the last play in the trilogy and the first two were published separately in different journals based in Paris, in 1927 and 1928.

These plays and several poems later published in *Posle Rossii* represent that portion of the poet's mature work known as "the Greek Tsvetaeva"; it comprises some of the poet's greatest achievements both in stanzaic and metrical forms and in the philosophical depth of her questions and meditations. Thus, Tsvetaeva's legacy has enriched not only the considerable production of art, music, and literature based on Russian and European folklore, but also the intellectual and artistic achievements of Russian philosophy and philosophic poetry whose exponents include the nineteenth-century poets Fyodor Tyutchev and Yevgeny Baratynsky, and the twentieth-century philosophers Nikolay Berdyaev and Lev Shestov.

In 1925 she produced another long poem that many consider to be Tsvetaeva's masterpiece, *Krysolov* (The Pied Piper) published serially in the Prague journal *Volia Rossii* (Russia's Freedom) in 1925–1926. As the title suggests, the *poema* is based on the story of the pied piper of Hamelin, but the poem's subtitle, "A lyrical satire," reveals what is more essential to the work's power and originality, namely, the lyrical "I" that orchestrates the work, for the retold legend is only the spark that ignited in Tsvetaeva an extraordinary explosion of political and ethical satire fueled to white heat by the poet's rhythmic, stanzaic, and verbal virtuosity. The poem strides from a world of Gogolian pettiness to an envisioned world of Goethean harmony: this is the path along which the pied piper, betrayed by the bourgeois citizenry, leads the town's children.

By now Tsvetaeva was actively corresponding with Boris Pasternak. He wrote an enthusiastic letter praising her *Krysolov*. Pasternak's insights are relevant not only to this *poema* but to all Tsvetaeva's work. Pasternak writes:

In *Krysolov*, notwithstanding your inherent gift for composition, as displayed with such masterly skill and diversity in the folktale poems [Pasternak refers here to "Tsar'-devitsa" and to "Molodets"], notwithstanding the tendency of all your cycles of verse to become long poems, and notwithstanding the superb composition of The Pied Piper itself (the concept of the entire poem concentrated in the image of the rats!! The social rebirth of the rats!!—an idea startlingly simple, a manifestation of genius, like the appearance of Minerva)—notwithstanding all this, the poetic originality of the fabric is so great that *probably* it rips apart the cohesive forces of compositional unity, for this is precisely the effect of the poem. What you have accomplished speaks with the tongue of *potential,* as happens so often with great poets in their youth, or with self-made men of genius—at the beginning. Yours is an astonishingly youthful thing, giving glimpses of extraordinary puissance. The impression of poetic raw material, or, more simply, of raw poetry, so completely outweighs all its other virtues that it would be better to declare this aspect the core of the work and call it madness through and through.

At the end of 1925 Tsvetaeva and her family, including the new baby Moor-Georgy, moved to Paris, carried there in part by the momentum of Tsvetaeva's current literary productivity and by the prominence of Paris as the new center of Russian culture in emigration. Not only had Tsvetaeva's new works been published, including collections such as *Razluka* and *Remeslo,* the new, full-length play *Tezei: Ariadna,* and the remarkable *poemy* based on themes borrowed from Russian and German folklore, but Tsvetaeva's poetry also continued, for a time, to be available in the Soviet Union, where poets whose work and judgment she respected, among them Pasternak, could read her work and comment on it.

"Russian" Paris welcomed Tsvetaeva as a celebrity. On 6 February 1926 she gave a triumphal poetry recital to a large auditorium overflowing with eager listeners. But this popularity soon subsided when, in April of the same year, Tsvetaeva provoked quite another strong reaction, this time of indignation, with her essay "Poet o kritike" (A Poet on Criticism). Published in the journal *Blagonamerennyi* (The Loyalist), the essay not only discussed the theory and significance of criticism (a bold new step in Tsvetaeva's literary career), it also took to task practicing critics of varied political and literary persuasions represented in the émigré press. The essay elicited a storm of controversy; it permanently alienated several influential writers and forced editors (who of course had the power to accept or reject Tsvetaeva's writings in the future) into the difficult role of mediating violent reactions against the poet who had suddenly revealed herself as an upstart critic.

Tsvetaeva's supporters had to calm the storm in her absence from Paris, however. As it happened, just when some of the émigré community in Paris was unleashing its hostility for what was, rightly, judged to be a slap in the face by a newcomer to the Russian literary community in Paris, Tsvetaeva had found quite a different community consisting entirely of poets, one that meant more to her than any quantity of critics, hostile or friendly. In May of 1926 Tsvetaeva began corresponding with the poet Rainer Maria Rilke. Rilke, in turn, had received a letter from Boris Pasternak. During the summer of 1926 a three-way correspondence brought the three poets together and prompted them to begin sending one another poetry as well as letters. Much of this has been translated into English in the volume *Letters, Summer 1926* (see bibliography).

These months were for Tsvetaeva a sublime summer. Soon Tsvetaeva began writing new works inspired by these intense epistolary encounters with Rilke, whom she revered, and with Pasternak, who had suddenly become a passionate devotée of both Tsvetaeva herself and her work. Once again, an intense emotional experience inspired Tsvetaeva to turn to the *poema*. And again, she extended the boundaries of that form, this time in the direction of radically new imagery. At the end of May she wrote "S moria" ("From the Sea," 1926), which describes a dream meeting with Pasternak. Her next *poema*, "Popytka komnaty" ("An Attempt to Build a Room," 1926), ventures into surrealism; it is addressed to Rilke and Pasternak and deals with the spiritual unity poets achieve across physical separation. The two *poemy* were published separately in two émigré journals in 1928. Rilke, meanwhile, wrote and sent to Tsvetaeva his "Elegie an Marina Zwetajewa-Efron," written in June 1926.

Rilke died in December 1926. In February 1927 Tsvetaeva lamented his death in yet another *poema* called "Novogodnee" ("New Year's Greetings"), which is an epitaph and an elegy on Rilke and an exploration into the metaphysics of space and time.

Among the poems linked with Rilke and Pasternak is a satirical *poema* entitled "Poema lestnitsy" ("The Poem of the Staircase," 1926) that can be compared with the earlier *Krysolov* in its philosophy and its technical brilliance. The poem depicts a staircase in an ugly, working-class neighborhood; during the night the various material objects belonging to the people who traverse the staircase, metonyms for exploited nature and for the excesses of industrial civilization, revolt against their pseudo-creators. In the poem's last section, the staircase, a mock edifice of upwardly spiraling materialism, is destroyed by fire, a climax that, as the scholar Simon Karlinsky pointed out, has a certain prophetic overtone today.

In 1928 Tsvetaeva's last new collection appeared, the remarkable *Posle Rossii*. She continued to write new lyrics including remarkable cycles of lyrical and satirical poems, but she now began to have difficulty getting new poems printed. Editors complained about the obscurity and incomprehensibility of the newest poetry, and certainly, the pace of Tsvetaeva's innovations startles and challenges even those readers of today who are more accustomed to the bold experiments of the avantgarde.

EMIGRATION: THE 1930'S

Tsvetaeva's final decade in emigration, the 1930's, evinced important changes in her worldview, her literary work, and in her family's life in Paris and its suburbs.

One of Tsvetaeva's favorite visions was that of another world beyond this one, a world where mundane categories and limitations would fall away. The images she created for this world include the "masculine heaven" and the "Spartan brotherhood." The terms do not mean a world populated only by men (although it is certainly significant that Tsvetaeva chose these words over words designating women) but one characterized by strength and the renunciation of material comfort. Here the word "possession" would refer not to an owned object but to the higher power that inspires and transports—quite literally *enraptures* each individual.

The opposite world was the one epitomized in her *Krysolov*—the smug, respectable town of Hamelin. Tsvetaeva saw moderation as her enemy and as the enemy of poetry; the "golden" mean was made of lead, not gold. To moderation and measure, Tsvetaeva opposed measurelessness—that reach beyond apparent limits so evident in her approach to genre, stanza, meter, and sound textures in poetry.

For a good part of her life, Tsvetaeva's fate had brought some elements of this paradisal vision within her reach. She had often been able to experience what an ideal life might be like. Before 1917 she had been freed by inherited wealth from gross material cares and drudgery. During the years of the civil war and war communism, she had known what it was to live by the spirit, and not only because she was forced to do without adequate food and clothing, but also because she was increasingly aware that work, courage, and maternal passion were also life-giving. Then in the summer of 1926 she had enjoyed a Parnassus-by-post, the purely temporal, nonphysical paradise shared with Rilke and Pasternak. Just as her walks in Prague's hills had strengthened Tsvetaeva's physical endurance and freed her spirit, these epochal extremes of plenty and deprivation had a similar effect in the long run.

After the 1928 publication of her collection *Posle Rossii,* Tsvetaeva paused and began to look more closely at the historical era in which she was living, the era her contemporary Mandelshtam named (after a species of fierce dog), "the wolfkiller." As if in answer the era soon turned, bared its fangs, and attacked.

Tsvetaeva now wrote fewer poems; her imagery changed, becoming more physical, even corporeal. She turned largely to prose—which happened also to be more saleable to émigré magazines—and used it as a vehicle of philosophical and personal exploration. She focused on three topics, all bound up with poetry: first, the problems of the poet in relation to history, ethics, and the populace of nonpoets; second, the lives and personalities of her gifted contemporaries, mainly poets; third, her own childhood and family history. In following this trajectory from the general and abstract to the specific and personal, Tsvetaeva sought evidence to answer her questions: Does the poet live mainly within a given historical epoch or both within and outside it? Are the standards of art analogous to ethical standards? What forces generate and sustain poets and poetry?

Of course, Tsvetaeva was not the first to pose these questions. Within the Russian tradition, not to speak of wider contexts, the works of Tolstoy and Dostoevsky have long been known for their probing into the moral, psychological, and philosophical bases of existence as well as for their unmatched artistry in fiction. Tsvetaeva's essays, sketches, and literary criticism of the 1930's place her in this important Russian tradition.

In the mid 1920's Tsvetaeva had published two prose works on Bal'mont and Bryusov, "Bal'montu" ("To Balmont," 1925) and "Geroi truda" ("A Hero of Labor," 1925), two poets belonging to the first symbolist generation active in Russia at the turn of the century. In the late 1920's, Tsvetaeva turned again to studies in the lives and works of forebears and contemporaries. Her first prose works after 1928 are devoted to Rilke, to the painter and scenic designer Natalya Goncharova, and to Mandelshtam. The prose on Rilke, "Neskolko pisem R. M. Rilke" ("A Few Letters of Rilke's," 1929) flows out of and forms a prose companion piece to Tsvetaeva's longer poems of 1926–1927, especially the elegy on the poet's death, "Novogodnee."

The prose on Goncharova represents Tsvetaeva's only attempt at a monograph, "Natal'ia Goncharova: zhizn'i tvorchestvo" ("Natalya Goncharova: Life and Work," 1928). Although Tsvetaeva approached this work with enthusiasm—she interviewed the painter and visited her studio in Paris—the form of the monograph was somewhat uncongenial; she found it impossible to avoid digressing away from visual and into verbal art. The result is an uneven work in which the best passages are the digressions: fascinating, elliptical, and difficult glimpses into Tsvetaeva's metaphysics of creativity.

The prose on Mandelshtam, "Istoriia odnogo posviashcheniia" ("The History of a Dedication," written in 1931, published in 1964), depicts the meetings between Tsvetaeva and Mandelshtam in the summer of 1916. Here too Tsvetaeva digresses, this time into stories about her own childhood attempts at writing poetry. It is the digressions in both the prose on Goncharova and on Mandelshtam that anticipate the themes and style of Tsvetaeva's greatest prose achievements.

Outstanding among these are two essays on literary art, examined in the light of history, ethics, and moral philosophy: "Poet i vremia" ("The Poet and Time," 1932) and "Iskusstvo pri svete sovesti" ("Art in the Light of Conscience," 1932). To art Tsvetaeva ascribes a power and authority that stand above the individual will. Paradoxically, she uses religious imagery to emphasize her central assertion that the hierarchies of artistic creation are *not* the same as moral categories, nor are they a substitute for morality or religion.

The meaning and value of historical truth, primarily though not invariably vested in demonstrable facts, had been Tsvetaeva's concerns in her first prose works, the sketches set in the years of revolution and civil war. In these early works, fidelity to history impelled her to turn frequently to diary forms and fragmented sketches. During the 1930's, Tsvetaeva became fascinated by the interplay of history and mythology: she saw myth as a force constantly exerting itself on and shaping history. The result of this force was not, in Tsvetaeva's vision of it, distortion but clarification, for history and biography (understood as history on an individual scale) are either remembered and transmitted by a whole people or written and shaped by single individuals. Myth uses a people's or an individual's selective memory—Tsvetaeva envisioned the poet's role as analogous to that of a *volk*—to shape and reshape recognizable stories. Thus, history conforms to the patterns established by the myth of the eternal return.

The results of this view are evident in Tsvetaeva's prose works depicting other poets, a genre known as the literary portrait. The first of these is devoted to her friend Max Voloshin, poet and painter, and has the odd-sounding title "Zhivoe o zhivom" ("A Living Word About a Living Man," 1933). Her method here is typical of both her literary portraits and her longer autobiographical prose works of the 1930's; the raw historical, biographical, and autobiographical data are shaped into a narrative, propelled not by a central, chronologically sequential plot, but instead by the linking and variation of several key images. At the center of Voloshin's portrait, for example, stands not so much Voloshin in his everyday physical self and personality (a feature noted immediately by Tsvetaeva's émigré reviewers) as Tsvetaeva's images for Voloshin: the solar and terrestrial spheres filled with fire, the mountain creature who combines the animate goat-man and the inanimate stone profile embedded in the mountain's face. Here and in subsequent prose works, myth enters wherever mere facts must be shaped—imaged—to attain permanence.

Often, however, facts proved to be so apt, so eloquent, as to acquire mythic significance in their own right. Tsvetaeva seized on this kind of data and underlined its force in juxtapositions. Moreover, she saw herself—and rightly so—as the defender or restorer of accurate pictures, as the champion of a vanishing past, especially the past of her childhood and youth, from which she had been torn away by violent political change. Her portraits of Mandelshtam and Voloshin, for example, had an initial negative motivation; publications in the émigré and in the Soviet press had distorted the truth about these men as she knew it.

A more positive inspiration to write on Andrey Bely, her acquaintance in Moscow and Berlin, came from a work written by Tsvetaeva's fellow émigré and poet Vsevolod Khodasevich. Tsvetaeva admired Khodasevich's prose work and wanted to follow his example by writing her own eyewitness account. The result was "Plennyi dukh" ("A Captive Spirit," 1934). Again, as in the piece on Voloshin, images and associations grew out of accurately remembered details. Indeed, the very eccentricity of both Voloshin and Bely seemed of itself to bring the legendary, the mythic, into the workaday world. Tsvetaeva selected images for each poet not to embellish what was odd and unusual but to seek out what eternally recurred. Analogy, simile, and metaphor are no longer devices or technique; they attain the status of facts, for they express the deep truth of each poet's inner being.

In her autobiographical prose Tsvetaeva achieves this same deft poising of detail between fact and legend. The publication history of this prose is extremely complicated and unfortunately tends mainly to obscure the poet's aims and originality. To earn money Tsvetaeva wrote what might be publishable. She even lapsed—the word is not too strong, given the mature Tsvetaeva's drive toward longer, concentric works—into writing feuilletons, that is, very short, deft sketches suitable for daily newspapers. But both her letters and the imagery of the autobiographical prose show that Tsvetaeva's talent for sustained, major works constantly asserted itself. Just as the lyrics of the 1920's tended toward unification in cycles, so too the autobiographical prose strove almost of itself toward a single, long work. The ultimate result was a family chronicle (again the Russian tradition emerges) combined with the etiological myth of a poet's birth and rebirth into poetry.

The feuilleton form proved appropriate for what Tsvetaeva had to say about her father and his museum. She wrote a series of sketches grouped under the general title "Otets i ego muzei" ("My Father and His Museum," 1933). But these sketches were only the prelude to the real autobiography.

This prose masterwork consists of four pieces written in a sequence that corresponds to the time frame of the poet's early childhood. The first work, "Dom u Starogo Pimena" ("The House at Old Pimen's," 1933) is the "grandfather" chapter of Tsvetaeva's autobiography; in it she juxtaposes grandfathers from the paternal and maternal sides. She envisages the paternal grandfather, moreover, as a frightening Chronos-figure, a near monster who devours his progeny, primarily female children. The second part, "Mat' i muzyka" ("Mother and Music," 1934) depicts the parental generation,

in the person of Tsvetaeva's mother. Again Tsvetaeva turns the *realia* of her childhood into legendary images. Here the piano on which the mother forces her child to practice becomes both a life-threatening and an alluring presence: the piano with its music is a river that innundates and nearly drowns the child poet; it is also a black mirror in which the future poet sees the first, dark intimation of her future.

In the third work, "Chert" ("The Devil," 1934) Tsvetaeva abruptly refers to her childself as "an orphan," a word that brings together the biographical and the mythical: Marina's mother did actually die and the poet-to-be's destiny did set her apart from the ordinary human family. The Devil is a comic figure whose mission is to save the young Marina from the historical fate of women in her and her mother's generation, the fate of mismatches in marriage and early death. In effect, the Devil is a substitute bridegroom, a beneficent demon (in the classical sense of the Greek *daemon*) who choses the child as his bride. He has links with the tragic, Byronic demon of Lermontov in that poet's *poema* "Demon" (1841), but also with the ludicrous rural devils of Gogol's stories. In becoming betrothed to this Devil, little Marina pledges herself forever to literature. Thus, the union of the child and the Devil, adumbrated in the prose work's one-line epigraph, saves the child from a fatal, secular marriage, and binds her to the sacred vocation of the poet.

The final work in the four-part sequence, "Moi Pushkin" ("My Pushkin," 1937), named for Alexander Pushkin, presents a young poet coming to awareness of her gift and of the poet's tragic status in the mundane world of history and contingency. These prose pieces, published separately in émigré journals and newspapers, form four chapters in an innovative autobiographical work. Tsvetaeva presents many vivid and authentic details of middle-class life in nineteenth-century Moscow. But the story does not follow conventional patterns. Chronology is pulled apart; it is imagery and myth that bring every recollection, every detail into a coherent narrative. In fact Tsvetaeva's myth-making imagery is so consistent and goes so far beyond what is usually termed "classical allusions" that the term "mythobiography" would be more appropriate for Tsvetaeva's prose than the term "autobiography." Myth is the main framework and driving force of the story; yet myth and history are dynamically interrelated: the story of the young poet proves by example that myth will always emerge and be recognizable even through the most chaotic events of history.

During this decade of prose writing, Tsvetaeva did not cease writing poetry. Her style becomes stronger and some of her late poems, written between 1926 and 1939, approach a precision and clarity linked in the history of Russian verse with the poet Pushkin, the very poet depicted in Tsvetaeva's prose autobiography as the archetype for all poets.

Her tendency to write cycles of lyrics rather than isolated poems and her choice of subjects are also consistent with her achievements in prose. Poems of this period include cycles devoted to Mayakovsky, to Pushkin, to Voloshin, and, perhaps the most telling theme, to her writing table. Tsvetaeva's loyalties were not distributed according to political criteria. Rather she praised contemporaries for their poetry or for their personal worth. The disapproval of some critics and readers in the émigré community did not cause her loyalties to flag: she praised the poet Mayakovsky, who supported the Bolshevik regime and was disliked by many émigrés, and she continued to express her love for her first literary friend Voloshin.

The political events of the 1930's intruded more and more into Tsvetaeva's life in Paris. Her refusal to condemn everything Soviet incurred the suspicion and even hostility of some editors, and that at a time when the number of periodicals in which her work could be published was diminishing. Politics entered her domestic as well as her professional life. Her husband became a Soviet sympathizer and began working for an agency of the Soviet government in 1934. Efron drew both children to his newfound point of view. The beloved Ariadna, so long her mother's main support, returned to the Soviet Union in 1937, and Georgy-Moor began begging persistently to go back. In the same year an investigation into a murder committed in September near Lausanne, Switzerland, revealed that Efron was working for the Soviet secret police and was implicated in political assassinations. Efron escaped to the Soviet Union, leaving his wife and son to bear the consequences of his political activities.

Tsvetaeva found herself not only deprived of outlets for her writing and therefore all means of livelihood, she was also socially isolated—even ostracized—by some émigrés. Sergei and Ariadna were gone; Moor wanted to follow. In her letters Tsvetaeva clearly stated that she did not want to return to Russia—she had an idea of what life there was like. But she gave in and left France in June 1939.

In the Soviet Union, some old friends, including Pasternak, welcomed her and tried to help, but there was little they could do. She was given translating jobs, but allotments of housing and food were subject to decisions from above and were thus unreliable. In the eyes of officialdom and so too of many fellow writers, she was not a great poet, but rather the wife of a former White Army officer and an émigré who had lived for nearly two decades in the West.

Her family's fate was worse than anything she had feared. In August 1939, police arrived and took Ariadna away to prison. Efron was also arrested and later shot. Her sister Anastasiya was sent to Siberia.

World War II started just two months after her arrival in the Soviet Union. (She had protested the Nazi invasion of Czechoslovakia, her first refuge after leaving Russia, by writing the cycle "Stikhi k Chekhii" ["Poems to Czechoslovakia"] in 1939.) When the German offensive threatened Moscow in the summer of 1941, she was evacuated to the small town of Elabuga in the Tatar Autonomous Republic. Moor accompanied her. For his safety she had left Moscow. But far from her native city, without family or close friends, Tsvetaeva committed suicide on 31 August 1941.

TSVETAEVA IN PERSPECTIVE

As chance, or perhaps culture, would have it, the first women poets of major talent appeared in America and Russia. Chronologically, Emily Dickinson precedes by far her sisters of the steppes, yet her reputation grew during approximately the same decades as Tsvetaeva's; only by the mid twentieth century, it seems, was the world ready to acknowledge revolutions in poetics led by women.

Tsvetaeva's nearly exact contemporary was Anna Akhmatova. Like Dostoevsky and Tolstoy, Akhmatova and Tsvetaeva seem to have been born close together for the sake of comparisons and contrasts. Akhmatova is associated with Petersburg; Tsvetaeva with Moscow. Akhmatova endured the terrible 1930's inside the Soviet Union and survived the war and the Leningrad blockade; Tsvetaeva suffered the trials of exile, returned to her homeland, and found herself and her loved ones caught in Stalin's merciless machine of terror. Akhmatova's talent was recognized almost immediately; Tsvetaeva had early admirers but has gained in-depth critical attention and a wide public only during the last three decades.

Tsvetaeva defies the stereotypes long associated with poetry written by women. Her subject matter was wide-ranging and often distinctly nonfeminine. She admired soldiers—of both sexes—and celebrated the trappings and vicissitudes of battle. She seized eagerly and easily the public roles of satirist and moralist. Her forms and voice were not modest; she reveled in hyperbole and exulted in sustained, even massive forms; her gift was like a whirlpool, turning in ever-widening circles and pulling the most varied themes and devices into its churning depths.

The sound of Tsvetaeva's voice carried and the sounds of Russian carried her poetry everywhere, from the most basic to the most remote resources of the language. In versification she stands out as both a master and an innovator, and that in an era burgeoning with experimenters in meter and the sound texture of verse. Significantly, she first caught the ear of other poets, and among them were the greatest talents of this century.

Today, that peer recognition is sustained by the poet Joseph Brodsky, foremost among Tsvetaeva's many champions. Tsvetaeva now enjoys wide popular appeal both within the Soviet Union and among the new waves of émigrés. Her poetry has few equals in its diversity and range and in the sheer volume of her output. Her prose claims almost as high a place as her verse. Interestingly enough, Tsvetaeva's life has won her as much esteem as has her work. In an era when so many languished or fell silent in exile, and so many others capitulated to their oppressors, Tsvetaeva wrote and lived as if isolation and suffering were the very nectar and ambrosia of her godless, ungodly age.

Tsvetaeva takes her rightful place among Russia's greatest poets. She was entirely conscious of her gift and her mission. Perhaps that is why poets and poetry itself are the dominant themes in her work, a preference she shares with her great contemporaries. And it is other poets who have most eloquently defined Tsvetaeva's particular genius. Thus, Pasternak's praise of her first mature collection, *Versty,* applies to all her poetry. "I was immediately tamed," he wrote, "by the lyrical power of Tsvetaeva's form, which had become her very flesh and blood, which had strong lungs, had a tight, concentrated hold, which did not gasp for breath between lines but encompassed without a break in rhythm whole sequences of stanzas, all developing their innate elements."

More recently, Joseph Brodsky has written of Tsvetaeva's place in her epoch and in Russian literature:

Represented on a graph, Tsvetaeva's work would

exhibit a curve—or rather, a straight line—rising at almost a right angle because of her constant effort to raise the pitch a note higher, an idea higher (or, more precisely, an octave and act of faith higher). She always carried everything she had to say to its conceivable and expressible end. In both her poetry and her prose, nothing remains hanging or leaves a feeling of ambivalence. Tsvetaeva is the unique case in which the paramount spiritual experience of an epoch—the sense of ambivalence, of contradictoriness in the nature of human existence—served not as the object of expression but as its means, the means by which it was transformed into the material of art.

Selected Bibliography

Tsvetaeva's many prose works were never collected during her lifetime but were published separately in émigré journals and newspapers based in various European cities. The two-volume collected prose published by Russica in New York in 1979 is cited in the bibliography under "Prose" as *Izbrannaia proza v dvukh tomakh 1917–1939*. Those prose works that have been translated into English are in the volume *A Captive Spirit: Selected Prose*, cited in the bibliography under "Translations."

EDITIONS

INDIVIDUAL WORKS

POETRY
Vechernii al'bom. Moscow, 1910.
Volshebnyi fonar'. Moscow, 1912.
Iz dvukh knig. Moscow, 1913.
Versty. Moscow, 1921.
Razluka. Moscow, Berlin, 1922.
Stikhi k Bloku. Berlin, 1922.
Tsar'-Devitsa. Moscow, 1922.
Versty I. 1922.
Psikheia. Berlin, 1923.
Remeslo. Moscow, Berlin, 1923.
Molodets. Prague, 1924.
Posle Rossii. Paris, 1928.
Lebedinyi stan. Munich, 1957.
Lebedinyi stan. Perekop. Edited by G. Struve. Paris, 1971.

Iunosheskie stixi. 1976.
Krysolov. Letchworth Herts, England, 1978.

PLAYS
Konets Kazanovy. Moscow, 1922.
Metel'. Priklucheniie. Ariadna. Letchworth Herts, England, 1978.

PROSE
Proza. New York, 1953.
Mat' i muzyka. Letchworth Herts, England, 1977.
Izbrannaia proza v dvukh tomakh 1917–1937. 2 vols. New York, 1979.
Mon frère féminin. Paris, 1979.

COLLECTED WORKS
Izbrannoe. Edited by V. Orlov. Moscow, 1961.
Izbrannye proizvedeniia. Edited by Ariadna Efron and Anna Saakiants. Moscow, Leningrad, 1965.
Moi Pushkin. Edited by Ariadna Efron and Anna Saakiants. Moscow, 1967.
Nesobrannye proizvedeniia. Munich, 1971.
Neizdannoe: Stikhi. Teatr. Proza. Paris, 1976.
Stikhotvoreniia i poemy. Edited by Anna Saakiants. Leningrad, 1979.
Sochineniia v dvukh tomakh. Moscow, 1980–1981.
Stikhotvoreniia i poemy. 4 vols. New York, 1980–1983.

CORRESPONDENCE

Pis'ma k Anne Teskovoj. Prague, 1969.
Neizdannye pis'ma. Edited by Gleb and Nikita Struve. Paris, 1972.

TRANSLATIONS

Boris Pasternak, Maria Tsvetayeva, Rainer Maria Rilke: Letters, Summer 1926. Translated by Margaret Wettlin and Walter Arndt. New York, 1983.
A Captive Spirit: Selected Prose. Translated by J. Marin King. Ann Arbor, Mich., 1980. Includes "A Living Word About a Living Man (Voloshin)," "A Captive Spirit," "An Otherworldly Evening," "My Father and His Museum," "Charlottenburg," "The Uniform," "The Laurel Wreath," "The Opening of the Museum," "The Intended," "The Tower of Ivy," "The House at Old Pimen's," "Mother and Music," "The Devil," "My Pushkin," "Two Forest Kings," and "Pushkin and Pugachev."

The Demesne of the Swans. Translated by Robin Kemball. Ann Arbor, Mich., 1980.

Marina Tsvetayeva: Selected Poems. Translated by David McDuff. Newcastle-upon-Tyne, England, 1987.

Selected Poems of Marina Tsvetayeva. Translated by Elaine Feinstein. New and enlarged edition. New York, 1987.

Three Russian Women Poets: Anna Akhmatova, Marina Tsvetayeva, Bella Akhmadulina. Translated by Mary Maddock. Trumansburg, N.Y., 1983.

BIOGRAPHICAL AND CRITICAL STUDIES

Feinstein, Elaine. *A Captive Lion: The Life of Marina Tsvetayeva.* New York, 1987.

Karlinsky, Simon. *Marina Cvetaeva: Her Life and Art.* Berkeley, Calif., 1966.

———. *Marina Tsvetaeva: The Woman, Her World and Her Poetry.* Cambridge, England, 1985.

Lossky, Véronique. *Marina Tsvétaeva: Un itinéraire poétique.* Malakoff, France, 1987.

Saakjanc, Anna. *Marina Tsvetaeva: Stranitsy zhizni i tvorchestva (1910–1922).* Moscow, 1986.

Shveitser, Viktoriia. *Byt i bytie Mariny Tsvetaevoi.* Fontenay-aux-Roses, France, 1988.

Tsvetaeva, Anastasiia. *Vospominaniia.* Moscow, 1971; 3d ed. Moscow, 1983.

J. MARIN KING

IVO ANDRIĆ

1892–1975

EARLY LIFE, PROSE POEMS, AND SHORT STORIES

WHEN IVO ANDRIĆ was awarded the Nobel Prize for literature in 1961, the greatest living Yugoslav writer finally received global recognition. His countrymen had long ago enshrined him and given him every conceivable literary honor. In fact, Andrić's literary career at home, which began in the 1910's, was marked by early and universal agreement on his monumental talent. Six decades of literary productivity generated numerous critical books and articles by Yugoslav scholars. Yet outside of his native country Andrić was not well known until the Nobel Prize award. Since 1961, however, his works have been translated into many languages, and his most famous novel, *Na Drini ćuprija* (*The Bridge on the Drina*, 1945), has become a part of high school and university curricula in world literature courses in many countries. Although Andrić is the best-known Yugoslav writer, he still remains relatively unknown in the United States. To date only three novels, *The Bridge on the Drina, Travnička hronika* (*Bosnian Chronicle,* or *Bosnian Story,* 1945), and *Gospodjica* (*The Woman from Sarajevo,* 1945); the novella *Prokleta avlija* (*Devil's Yard,* 1954); and a handful of his best stories have been translated into English. While admittedly this list does represent a substantial portion of Andrić's best

fiction, the English reader is still denied first-hand knowledge of the richness and variety of his whole *oeuvre*: the latest Yugoslav edition of Andrić's collected works, for example, comprises seventeen volumes of short stories, novels, lyrical and prose poems, literary and meditative essays, critical reviews, travel sketches, and aphoristic meditations.

Ivo Andrić was born in Travnik in Bosnia, on 10 October 1892. He came from a Catholic family of modest means. At the time of Andrić's birth, Bosnia was a crossroads of Eastern and Western cultural, religious, and political influences. Populated largely by Southern Slavs who spoke various dialects of the same Serbo-Croatian language, Bosnia was for centuries the frontier where the Ottoman and the Austro-Hungarian empires clashed. Under administrative rule of the Ottoman Turks until 1878 (when the Austrians took over), Bosnia had its own powerful indigenous aristocracy consisting of Slavs who had converted to Islam. These native "Turks" (as they were called) lived in an uneasy truce with their Christian Slavic brothers, both Catholic and Orthodox. There was also a sizeable group of Sephardic Jews who had drifted to Bosnia in the sixteenth and seventeeth centuries. Bosnia was truly a place where East met West, where Muslim, Christian, and Jewish religions and cultures clashed and intermingled. Over four hundred years of Turkish rule gave Bosnia a decidedly "eastern" flavor, one still visible today in its buildings, native dress, and artifacts.

By the time of Andrić's birth, Travnik, the former seat of the Turkish vizier, had lost its political significance. Although the town plays a significant role in several of Andrić's literary works, Andrić had almost no personal recollection of it from these early years. He always considered Višegrad, another ancient Bosnian town picturesquely situated on the river Drina, to be his real hometown. There, after his father's death from tuberculosis at the age of thirty-two, Andrić was raised by an aunt and uncle while his mother went to work. In both his memoiristic and his fictional writing the Višegrad childhood emerges as a crucial time in the formation of the writer's worldview. Here Andrić became acquainted with his Bosnian heritage. He avidly listened to tales and legends told by the old-timers at the local meeting place on the Drina bridge. A favorite teacher introduced him to books, and Andrić became a lifelong, passionate admirer of the written word. After a generally happy, although at times lonely childhood in Višegrad, Andrić received a scholarship to attend the gymnasium in Sarajevo. In 1903, Andrić moved to this Bosnian center of cultural and political activity and lived there until his graduation in 1911. Here he seriously entered the world of books, both as a student and a fledgling writer whose first publication, in 1911, was a mournful poem.

An idealistic and patriotic young man, Andrić allied himself in Sarajevo with the Young Bosnia movement, which espoused the independence and unity of Southern Slavs and freedom from foreign domination. In 1912, Andrić enrolled in the university at Zagreb, the capital city of neighboring Croatia, where his interests both in literature and in the fate of his countrymen deepened. He spent the years immediately preceding World War I abroad, studying first in Vienna and then in Kraków (Poland). In 1914, when a radical member of the Young Bosnia movement shot Archduke Ferdinand of Austria, the act which precipitated World War I, Andrić hurried home. Almost immediately upon his arrival, he was arrested for his connection with Young Bosnia. He was imprisoned for less than a year, but was interned in a village near Travnik for two more years, although he had not been involved in any actions against the government.

The prison experience made a strong physical and psychological impression on the sensitive young man. The recurring themes of loneliness, fear, and alienation that are found in much of Andrić's writing have often been attributed to this period of his life. At the end of 1917, he returned to the University of Zagreb, but ill health and his family's dire financial situation forced him to abandon his studies in his last year at the university. He did not give up his literary work, however; in fact, writing and editing now provided a meager income. The occasional poems, reviews, and essays that appeared in *Književni jug* (The Literary South), a journal that Andrić helped to found, were followed by two collections of meditative prose poems, *Ex Ponto* (1918) and *Nemiri* (Anxieties, 1920). These two publications, along with his first short story, "Put Alije Djerzeleza" ("The Journey of Ali Djerzelez"), established Andrić as a major writer in the Kingdom of Serbs, Croats, and Slovenes, a newly created country commonly known as Yugoslavia.

Ex Ponto and *Nemiri* are both characterized by a subjective, often melancholy tone and represent a highly personal outpouring of the author's reflections on life. Although well received by a society that now found itself questioning the world's very existence in the aftermath of World War I, these two early collections pale in comparison with Andrić's more distanced and less autobiographical prose. In stories and novels primarily set in his native Bosnia, Andrić explores the human condition as well as his own cultural heritage and identity. As Andre Esterling, a member of the Swedish Academy of Sciences, pointed out in 1961, Andrić was awarded the Nobel Prize for literature for the epic force with which he presented the history of his land. The works singled out by the Nobel Prize committee were the major novels *The Bridge on the Drina* and *Bosnian Chronicle,* the novella, *Devil's Yard,* and a short story, "Pismo is 1920 godine" (The Letter from the Year 1920, 1946.)

The Bosnian setting predominates in three of Andrić's four novels and one unified cycle of stories, as well as in more than 80 out of some 140 short stories and fragments. It is with Bosnia that Andrić both began and ended his career as a prose writer. The first complete short story, "Put Alije Djerzeleza," was published in 1920, although two fragments, "Djerzelez u hanu" (Djerzelez at the Inn) and "Djerzelez na putu" (Djerzelez on the Road) had appeared, in issues of *Kniževni jug,* in 1918 and 1919, respectively. This untraditional story of a foolish, love-smitten Muslim folk hero was the first in a long series of stories reflecting Andrić's unique visions of Bosnia. Indeed, at the time of his death in March 1975, Andrić was still working on a new Bosnian novel titled *Omerpaša Latas* (Omerpasha Latas, 1976).

Andrić explains his preoccupation with Bosnia for almost sixty years by observing that a man writes about his homeland for the simple reason that he knows it best. Every time he visited Bosnia, he was reminded of what he called the "eastern" idea that a man is always indebted to his homeland. He stated his case most eloquently in a meditative essay entitled "Staze" (Pathways, 1940):

> And on all the roads and pathways which I have traveled later in life, I have lived only from that impoverished joy, from my Višegrad concept of the richness and beauty of the created world. For beneath all the roads of the earth, there has always run that jagged Višegrad path, seen and felt only by me, from the day I left it until today. In fact, I have always measured my step and adjusted my pace according to it. Throughout my life it has not abandoned me.
>
> (10:10)[1]

[1] All quotations from Andrić's writings are from the 1976–1981 edition of his collected works, *Sabrana dela Ive Andrića.*

The steep, rocky path of Andrić's Bosnian hometown was his constant inspiration and companion, the measure of all things in life. Hence it is not surprising that the setting of many of his short stories and of the chronicle-novel *The Bridge on the Drina* is Višegrad. Travnik is immortalized in *Bosnian Chronicle* and in "Priča o vezirovom slonu" ("The Vizier's Elephant," 1947). Sarajevo is the setting for numerous fragments and short stories and the unfinished novel *Omerpaša Latas,* and one of the settings, along with Belgrade, of the novel *The Woman from Sarajevo.* Thus each of the cities that played an important role in his life is immortalized in a novel.

It is noteworthy that Andrić began writing stories about Bosnia only after it was no longer his domicile. His last stay of any length was during the wartime internment, from 1915 to 1917. Although he was now gaining recognition as a major new literary talent in neighboring Zagreb, Andrić felt that he could not adequately support his aging relatives as a writer. In 1919 he joined the civil service and moved permanently to Belgrade, the capital of Yugoslavia. Ironically, from 1921 to 1941, while he was establishing his reputation at home as a writer of Bosnian stories, he was far from Bosnia, serving in the diplomatic service in various European cities. His experiences abroad are recorded primarily in his nonfiction works—travel sketches, meditative essays, and the collection of personal, aphoristic reflections entitled *Znakovi pored puta* (Signs by the Roadside, 1976).

The Bosnia of Andrić's fiction is not a real setting in which the writer continued to live and create, but a complex historical and mythical entity. While working abroad, Andrić carried out archival research on Bosnian history both for his doctoral dissertation and for his fictional writings. In 1924 he received his doctorate in history from the University of Graz (Austria) for a study of cultural and spiritual life in Bosnia under Turkish rule. In this dissertation as well as in many of the early stories written between the two world wars Andrić subscribes to the view that the Turkish "yoke" was solely responsible for Bosnia's decline from the sixteenth to the nineteenth century. Yet, even though Christianity suffered a setback under the Turks, very important cultural activity was nonetheless carried on by the Franciscan order. Two of Andrić's most successful characters, Fra (Brother) Marko and Fra Petar, appear in a number of stories that record the day-to-day struggle of the Catholic monasteries against the Muslims (i.e., both the local Bosnians and the foreign Turks).

Brother Marko, a character who never quite acquires the proper monastic contemplative demeanor, is a hearty Bosnian peasant who tills the fields and tries to protect his monastery from the whims of Turkish soldiers and officials. Although he holds the conventional view of Muslims as infidels and bitter enemies, in the story "U musafirhani" (At the Monastery Inn, 1923) he not only tries to convert one such Turk and save him from perdition, but genuinely comes to care for the dying man. Even though the man spits on the cross and dies unrepentant, Brother Marko thinks: "Saved or not saved: he had taken care of him and come to love him like a brother" (10:21). The point of the story is in its delicate irony. The simple, kindhearted Brother Marko is not aware of the contradictory nature of his emotions and his religious views. In fact, he is often bewildered by the evil he sees around him, and like many of Andrić's characters he finds the borderline between good and evil, between God's domain and that of the devil, difficult to draw.

Some literary scholars have argued that in his doctoral dissertation Andrić had already presented the real-life, historical prototype for Brother Petar, the wise, widely traveled, erudite monk who is the narrator and protagonist of several of Andrić's Bosnian stories: "Trup" (The Torso, 1937), "Čaša" (The Goblet, 1940), "U vodenici" (In the Mill, 1941), "Šala u Samsarinom hanu" (The Joke in Samsara's Inn, 1946), and, most significantly, the novella *Devil's Yard*. In the Brother Petar stories An-

drić presents one aspect of the cultural activity for which his dissertation commends the Franciscans. In telling his stories to a young monk, Brother Petar is literally passing on his knowledge, experience, and wisdom to the next generation. The frame of all the stories is the same. The ailing, bedridden Brother Petar is reminded of events in the past by some object in his cell or by some recent incident. He proceeds to tell stories of violence, of Turkish oppression, but of survival as well. His lessons from the past give the listener in the story— and the reader as well—some perspective on the hardships of the present. Critics have observed that Andrić's stories about the Catholic monks embody the passions and struggles of the Bosnian people under Turkish rule. But these stories, suffused with humor and irony, also attest to the universal indomitability of the human spirit, which manages to survive in the most hostile circumstances. Brother Marko's simpleminded, brute resistance to the Turks ends in his death. But the message of Andrić's stories is not pessimistic. The memory of Brother Marko, combined with the instructive stories woven by the physically weak but morally strong Brother Petar, will continue to provide spiritual support to the besieged monks.

Like his storyteller, Brother Petar, Andrić himself passes on the history of his people. As a young man writing to his professor, Andrić revealed the nature of his fascination with Bosnia and its past and foreshadowed his role as a writer:

> It saddens me to think that with every passing day our strange old Bosnia is dying out and that there is no one to record and preserve the dark beauty of that former life. . . . And it saddens me to think that a verse dies with every old woman and a story is buried with every monk.

In his self-appointed role as the preserver of Bosnia's past, Andrić is both an "objective" historian and a "subjective" folk storyteller. The delicate balance and tension created by two seemingly contradictory viewpoints combined with a a fluid narrative style make most of Andrić's tales highly suspenseful. His stories and novels are replete with fascinating, verifiable historical and ethnographic details. They are filled as well with folk tales and legends embodying the spirit of his culture. Through history and myth Andrić weaves spellbinding tales of passion, violence, depravity, revenge, and occasionally, of honor, faith, and sacrifice. Clearly Bosnia's "dark beauty" haunts Andrić. In story after story written in the 1920's and 1930's, a specific historical setting is imperceptibly transformed into a morbid, mythical environment, characterized by inexplicable, bizarre events and enigmatic, monumental characters. In particular, bloodcurdling violence and decadent sensuality create the exotic, "eastern" atmosphere that unifies these stories into what could be called a Bosnian cycle. Although most stories were first published individually, Andrić himself recognized their cohesiveness by combining the best into three highly acclaimed collections (*Pripovetke* [Stories], 1924, 1931, and 1936).

Two of the earliest stories, "Za logorovanja ("In the Camp," 1922) and "Mustafa Madžar" ("Mustapha Magyar," 1923), present monstrous crimes committed during war. Throughout his fiction Andrić uses times of crisis as a moral prism through which the complex human personality is broken up into its constituent positive and negative elements. "In the Camp" offers a strikingly graphic description of the violent rape-murder of a Bosnian girl by a mullah, a Muslim prayer leader in the Turkish pasha's army. In "Mustapha Magyar," Andrić presents a similar event, the wartime rape of four Russian boys by marauding Turkish soldiers. Here the focus of the story is not the violent crime itself but the resulting spiritual suffering of one soldier, Mustapha Magyar. A Muslim folk hero, he is stripped of his heroic stature and emerges as a complex, tortured being driven insane by the memory of his heinous deed and the realization of evil's existence in himself and in the world. Unlike the repugnant, demented mullah of "In the Camp," the character of Mustapha Magyar at once fascinates and repels. The reader follows with mixed emotions, even with sympathy, the detailed process of the disintegration of Mustapha's mind, and is relieved when Mustapha finally finds peace in death.

Unhealthy passions take many forms in Andrić's Bosnia and are not only found in individuals but are latent in whole communities. They predominate in such early stories as "The Journey of Ali Djerzelez," "Ćorkan i Švabica" (Ćorkan and the German Girl, 1921), "Ljubav u kasabi" (Love in a Country Town, 1923), "Čudo u Olovu" (The Miracle in Olovo, 1926), "Mara milosnica" ("The Pasha's Concubine," 1926), "Smrt u Sinanovoj tekiji" (Death in the Sinan Tekke, 1932), "Olujaci" (The Village of Olujaci, 1934), and "Anikina vremena" ("Anika's Times," 1931). The catalyst is typically a beautiful woman who causes a temporary sensual madness. Andrić's first published story, "The Journey of Ali Djerzelez," already records the hero's feverish search for an ideal woman. Djerzelez is repeatedly smitten by feminine beauty and reaches for it like a man possessed. In "Ćorkan i Švabica" not only the town fool, Ćorkan, but all the men are similarly mesmerized by a pretty circus performer.

While in "Ćorkan i Švabica" an exotic stranger causes a collective sensual delirium in the town, in "Anika's Times" a local girl develops into an unusual beauty and similarly wreaks havoc in the community. Spurned by the man she loves, Anika becomes a prostitute and avenges herself on the whole town by subjugating all the men, even the most virtuous, to her whims. She battles the spiritual and secular authorities and wins when both the priest's son and the Turkish official succumb to her charms. Although Anika's spell is temporary, many years later the local priest, a descendant of Anika's worshiper, is literally driven insane by the same sensual fever that had afflicted the entire town in Anika's time. In Andrić's fiction, history inevitably repeats itself.

In these early Bosnian stories, the outcome is often violent and almost always tragic. Although physical passion may temporarily be satisfied, love is always unrequited. Djerzelez fails in his every attempt to possess his ideal woman and has to settle for the favors of a prostitute. Ćorkan is savagely beaten for his role in the public wooing of the German circus performer. The love affair of the young Jewish girl and the Austrian officer in "Ljubav u kasabi" ends in scandal and the girl's suicide. The Christian concubine of a Turkish pasha dies of shame and guilt after he abandons her ("The Pasha's Concubine"). Although successful in her revenge, the temptress Anika nevertheless rushes toward self-destruction by orchestrating her own murder. She summons the two people who hate her the most, her brother and her would-be lover, knowing full well that one will kill her. But after Anika's murder, the town heals quickly. While the resolution is always tragic for the individual, in each story the community as a whole survives and returns to normalcy.

Violence and cruelty are not only associated with extraordinary events or with instances of individual or mass derangement but are a common denominator, the most basic fact of life in Andrić's Bosnia. A Turkish official tortures a Catholic monk and an Orthodox priest in "U zindanu" (In the Jail, 1924). An Austrian official tortures a Serbian rebel in "Žedj" ("Thirst," 1934). Brothers by nationality and language, but enemies by religion, the Muslim and Orthodox Bosnians destroy each other with abandon in "Veletovci" (The People of Veletovo, 1928). In fact, these early stories end with the shockingly violent death of Andrić's most memorable characters: Mustapha Magyar, Fra Marko, Anika, and the unforgettable, nameless women ("In the Camp," "Olujaci") who are raped, murdered, or burned alive. Is this inhuman cruelty conditioned by the times that Andrić depicts, war-torn Bosnia in the eighteenth

and nineteenth centuries? The shocking atrocities, physical disfigurements, and tortures cannot be interpreted simply as a reflection of a specific historical moment. They reflect the writer's subjective view of Bosnia's troubled Eastern heritage as well as his more universal recognition of the existence of evil in the world.

Brother Petar narrates "Trup" (The Torso, 1937), the most mesmerizing of Andrić's tales of terrifying oriental revenge. As a prisoner in Turkey, Brother Petar is called to repair a clock at the estate of a wealthy Turk. There he sees a mysterious, barely human figure, a faceless torso, and hears its story from one of the servants. For this is the infamous Čelebi Hafiz ("Fiery Hafiz"), the conqueror of Syria who mercilessly destroyed everything in his path. Only once in his life did he take pity on a woman prisoner, sparing her life after apparently killing her whole family. Eventually she became his wife and his most trusted companion. But she plotted her revenge carefully, and when the moment arrived she was not satisfied with simply killing him. Under her orders, his arms and legs were broken, and just before she herself was felled by Hafiz' rescuers, she disfigured his face with a burning torch. Hafiz survived only as a torso without limbs or a face, because, as Brother Petar states, it is impossible to kill a "Turk," a Muslim in Fra Petar's parlance. Hafiz' mutilated body is symbolic of "Turkish" barbarity, but it stands even more as a disconcerting affirmation of the dark side of human nature. Yet even here man's potential for violence is offset by his ability to persevere.

In these early stories the mystifying protagonists are inextricably tied to Andrić's mythic environment. Not surprisingly, they are primarily divided into two groups: victims and tormentors. With the exception of the positive figures of the Catholic monks, and occasional heroic warriors (both Muslim and Christian), the male protagonists are generally either decadent sensualists or deranged tormentors, or both. They can be complex incarnations of evil: educated and refined, yet brutal and savage.

Their lives ruled by secret vices, these degenerates reflect the physical and spiritual deterioration of a decaying society.

Women, for the most part, are unreachable ideals, victims of men's passions, or conscious and unconscious temptresses, but rarely true aggressors. Often nameless, they have unforgettable symbolic roles. The girl from Trebinje who becomes the mute victim of the mullah's perverse passion ("In the Camp") is reflected more than ten years later in the unidentified woman from Mostar who is monstrously burned alive by her crazed husband in "Olujaci." "The Pasha's Concubine" presents a series of mostly passive women who are spiritually or physically abused by men. The central character, Mara, is herself a victim whose physical trauma becomes a spiritual one. She is tormented by the shame that she feels and is made to feel by the community for being the concubine of a heathen Turk to whom she is strangely attached. Abandoned by the powerful, dissolute pasha, scorned by the Christian community and even rejected by the Catholic priest, Mara seeks refuge in insanity and dies shortly after giving birth to a stillborn child. Death is the only escape from the unrelenting torment of her world.

Particularly in the monks' stories, such as "U musafirhani," "Kod kazana" ("By the Brandy Still," 1930), "U vodenici," and "Napast" (Trouble, 1933), women are not passive but active forces, temptresses who lead men to sin. Again, they are often unnamed and function as catalysts rather than fully developed characters. To the celibate monks from whose viewpoint the stories are told, they are traditional symbols of sinful temptation. In one of Andrić's best stories, "Smrt u Sinanovoj tekiji" (Death in the Sinan Tekke, 1932), the memory of two unknown women poisons the last moments in the otherwise pure life of a dervish, the Muslim equivalent of the celibate monk. Alidede is surrounded by his admiring students as he lies dying of a heart attack. While they are trying to imagine the holy thoughts passing through Alidede's mind, he himself is vividly recalling the only two shameful experiences in his life: as a young boy seeing the naked body of a drowned woman, and as a young monk stunned by the appearance at the monastery gates of a disheveled woman pursued by attackers. In both cases Alidede is immobilized by what he sees and cannot act. Although these two women are clearly victims, for Alidede they represent that temptation of the flesh that he had so painstakingly avoided throughout his life. The often-quoted passage from Alidede's dying thoughts exposes woman's pivotal role in Andrić's fiction: "I had forgotten that woman stands like a gate, at the exit as well as at the entrance to this world" (6:206). Two important early stories that do not belong to the Bosnian tales also present women in highly symbolic roles: the fantasy ideal figure in "Jelena, žena koje nema" (Jelena, the Woman Who Was Not, 1934) and also the threatening, even emasculating dream figure in "Žena od slonove kosti" (The Woman Made of Ivory, 1921).

While often highly schematic, Andrić's most complex and sensitive portrayals are those of women. The story "Thirst" explores the thoughts and emotions of a woman forced to deal firsthand with the cruelties of war. Andrić uses this character as a center of consciousness, and all events are refracted through her mind. The protagonist, once again a nameless woman, is the wife of the Austrian commandant in a small Bosnian town. She spends an endless night listening to the groans of a tortured prisoner lodged in the basement of her house. Her anguish is vividly recorded, and the story is a delicate study of the female psyche.

Both temptress and victim, Anika is Andrić's most fascinating female character. She is a monumental, inexplicable presence, commanding in her majestic, self-contained beauty. Anika is an alien and alienated being, one typical of Andrić's early protagonists. Many are loners, misfits in their communities, or outsiders, foreigners in a hostile environment. Their sense of alienation and bewilderment underscores the fragility of their existence. These memorable creations (Mustapha Magyar, Ali Djerzelez, Brother Marko, Čelebi Hafiz, Anika, Mara, and many others) gain monumental stature by functioning outside of society's rules. Their physical characteristics, their virtues, vices, and torments are of mythic proportions. Like many classical or folk heroes, they seem to suffer from a tragic flaw that is never fully explained, biographically, socially, or psychologically. Thus, the enigmatic characters themselves become spiritual extensions of Andrić's mythical environment. In fact, Bosnia itself attains the status of an autonomous being and becomes Andrić's most important protagonist. From a realistic setting, in story after story, Bosnia is transformed into a powerful myth. Andrić is the self-appointed preserver of its complex essence, its "dark beauty."

Through the Bosnian stories and legends, Andrić explores both his own cultural heritage and the good-evil dichotomy of human existence. Accused by critics of being a pessimistic writer, Andrić nevertheless exhibits a deep faith in the survival of communities, in nature, and in man's creations. Nature itself embodies the human conflicts: most of the small towns nestled in the rugged Bosnian mountains have both a dark and a light side. This constricting topography of the countryside is opposed to the expansive vistas that open before Andrić's most important protagonists, such as Brother Marko and Ćorkan, in moments of ecstatic well-being, of dreamlike transcendence over the harsh reality of their lives. The opposition of dream and reality ("san i java") is a hallmark of many Andrić stories. Ecstasy, endurance, and the survival of mankind and its creations are positive counterweights to the oppressively negative portrayal of individual fates. Andrić's most famous symbol of beauty and permanence is a man-made structure. The bridge first makes its appearance in the story "Most na Žepi" ("The Bridge on the Žepa," 1925); it is a precursor to the most acclaimed of Andrić's

Bosnian bridges, that of *The Bridge on the Drina.*

Still, the bridges notwithstanding, Andrić's stories written between the two world wars have a predominantly dark tonality that is most powerfully articulated in the stories about Bosnia. Here instinct and biological and cultural determinants reign supreme. As literary critics have noted, these mesmerizing tales are permeated by a unique combination of Catholic mysticism and eastern sensuality and fatalism. Even the occasional humorous stories—primarily those about the Catholic monks and the wonderfully bumbling Brother Marko—are more likely to be ironic, grotesque, and tragicomic than downright funny. While reading Andrić, one may chuckle but never guffaw. Throughout, the reader is most likely to be mystified and enthralled.

WORLD WAR II AND THE NOVELS

The end of World War II was a creative milestone for Andrić, just as the end of World War I had been. The year 1918 had seen the publication of Andrić's first short story and first collection of prose poetry, while 1945 was marked by the almost simultaneous appearance of all three of Andrić's completed novels: *The Bridge on the Drina, Bosnian Chronicle,* and *The Woman from Sarajevo.* Andrić himself later stated that the two wars were the only genuine illnesses he had to endure in his lifetime. Both periods were spent in enforced isolation: the first war in prison and internment and the second under virtual house arrest in Nazi-occupied Belgrade. In April 1941, Andrić's successful twenty-year career as a diplomat terminated abruptly with the German attack on Yugoslavia. At that time Andrić was the Yugoslav ambassador to Germany. After the breakdown of diplomatic relations between Germany and Yugoslavia, he resigned from the service but was kept under surveillance throughout the war by the new collaborationist government in Belgrade. Diplomacy's loss, however, was literature's gain. These years of hardship were the most intensively creative period of Andrić's life. Surrounded by the destruction and privation of war, he completed each novel in less than a year. None of these works, however, appeared during the war; Andrić did not allow them to be published under the Nazi occupation. At war's end, *The Bridge on the Drina* was, in fact, the first publication of Prosveta, a newly created state publishing house in now-socialist Yugoslavia.

Appearing within a short span of time in 1945, Andrić's three novels, particularly *The Bridge on the Drina* and *Bosnian Chronicle*, created a literary sensation. These two historical novels represent some of the highest achievements of Yugoslav literature and are masterpieces of twentieth-century European fiction as well. Although written quickly, they were conceptualized and researched over many years. As was true of most of Andrić's early stories, here, too, Bosnia itself remains the major presence. In *The Bridge on the Drina*, Andrić uses local legends and stories as he intertwines a realistic geographical and historical setting with multilayered mythologizing. At first glance the novel is a chronicle of events in the life of the town of Višegrad over a period of four hundred years. The structure of the work is episodic. Each historical period is remembered for one significant event in the life of the community, which is presented either as historical fact or, more often, as it is transposed into local tales and legends. But *The Bridge on the Drina* is not a true chronicle. The events are not related in a purely chronological order but rather in cyclical fashion. The novel opens in some undefined present from whose vantage point the events of the past are narrated. The end of each chapter underscores the distance of that past time frame and thus reminds the reader of both the past and the present. In fact, the passing of time and the nature of memory, which captures that process, become the unifying underlying themes of the novel.

The most pervasive image in the novel is the bridge itself. As the title implies, it is the main protagonist around which the novel is tightly structured. All human events take place either on or near the bridge. The novel is the story of the bridge at Višegrad and the community around it from the founding of the bridge in the sixteenth century to its partial destruction in 1914 at the beginning of World War I. The very first chapter ends with a statement by the omniscient narrator, whose wise voice soon becomes familiar:

> Certainly, one thing is clear. Between the lives of the townspeople and this bridge exists a close, centuries-old bond. Their fates are so intertwined that they could not be imagined or told separately. Thus the story of the founding and the fate of the bridge is at the same time the story of the life of the town and that of its people, from generation to generation, just as through all the storytelling about the town stretches the line of the stone bridge with eleven arches, with its gate, like a crown, in the middle.
>
> (1:20)

Every chapter underscores the importance of the bridge. It is there that the townspeople have learned to deal with life's misfortunes:

> So at the gate, between the sky, the river and the hills, generation after generation learned not to mourn too much what the muddy waters had borne away. They absorbed the unconscious philosophy of the town: that life was an incomprehensible miracle since it was constantly wasted and spent and still it lasted and stood firm "like the bridge on the Drina."
>
> (1:94)

Each episode in the novel is the story of an individual tragedy or communal hardship, of natural disasters or sociohistorical unrests. Each demonstrates some change, loss, or destruction that, in the end, is always contrasted to that concrete symbol of beauty, permanence, and endurance, the bridge itself:

> Everything appeared as an exciting and new game on that ancient bridge that glistened in the

moonlight of those July nights, clean, young, and unalterable, perfectly beautiful and strong, stronger than all that time could bring and that people could imagine or accomplish.

(1:291)

In sharp contrast to the enduring, serene loveliness of the bridge are the transitory, tortuous lives of the town's inhabitants. But then, the magnificent bridge itself was engendered in violence. The famous Turkish vizier who built it, Mehmed Pasha Sokoli, did so in order to bridge a chasm, a deep black line he felt in his soul. As a ten-year-old boy he had been forcibly torn from Bosnia and taken to Istanbul, in one of the notorious Turkish customs of blood tribute exacted from subject populations. His last memory is of the local road broken in two by the river Drina. Although Mehmed Pasha becomes a powerful Turkish vizier, this memory persists, and one of his last good deeds is to give his native town a bridge. Ironically, Mehmed Pasha himself is felled by an assassin's knife as the black line takes on a final, concrete form. He never experiences the healing power of his creation.

The novel, however, does not begin with this psycho-historical interpretation of the founding of the bridge. Instead, the omniscient narrator in the guise of a local chronicler relates all the tales and legends associated with the building and the life of the bridge. These tales are numerous and mostly violent. The children are frightened of the black Arab who supposedly lives in the bridge. The narrator later describes, with seeming historical veracity, how the architect's servant, an Arab, was accidentally crushed by a falling stone and "built" into the bridge. The bridge claims another human sacrifice, the poor Bosnian peasant Radisav. Radisav, one of the underfed and overworked laborers, tries to stop the bridge work by pulling apart at night what has been done by day. The local legend makes Radisav into a Christian heroic warrior who stood up to the Turkish vizier but was betrayed by his servant and killed by the vizier's men. Again, the "real"

story is quite different. The simple, meek Radisav was quietly caught on one of his nightly forays. The most powerful scene in the novel is the naturalistic description of the grisly traditional Turkish torture to which Radisav is subjected. As an example to the whole town, he is publicly impaled alive on a sharpened wooden pole and left to die in slow torment. Although he maintains a basic human dignity in his suffering, Radisav is not a valiant hero but a weak mortal. Yet his sacrifice serves as a focus for the Christian population's feelings of hatred and resistance to the Muslim Turks. Although in this novel the clash between East and West, Christian and Muslim is not the major theme, it is the ever-present reality of Bosnian life. Mehmed Pasha's "black line" symbolizes, on an individual level, that same irreconcilable conflict.

Andrić offers multilayered truths: psychological, historical, legendary. At first glance, this is a realistic historical novel with objective, detailed narration, interspersed with facts and dates, and a causal sequence of events. The omniscient narrator can even divine the thoughts and feelings of the characters. He is also a local storyteller who offers folk wisdom and legends, which are juxtaposed in an ironic fashion to the historical truth. The complexity of Andrić's novel (as of many of his short stories) is that his realism is deceptive. History, folk tales, and legends are intertwined on a deeper level. As the Yugoslav critic Petar Džadžić notes in *Hrastova greda u kamenoj kapiji* (The Oak Beam in the Stone Bridge, 1983), a dual system of motivation exists in this novel: mythic as well as realistic, or more precisely, mythic developments in a realistic geographical and sociohistorical setting. For example, in many cultures, legends about the construction of great works involve two sacrifices, a "black" and a "white" one. Thus the story of the two human sacrifices, the black Arab and the white Radisav, are not only presented as historically verifiable events or as local legends, but exist on a deeper, more profound third level of universal myth. As seen in the early stories, and in this novel as well, Andrić's characters are often archetypes with inherited physical, emotional, and spiritual traits, and Bosnia itself is given a universal mythic dimension.

All the novel's themes function on a broadly universal level as well. The beauty, permanence, and endurance of man's creations is contrasted with the transitoriness of individual human life. As in the early stories, death is the predictable resolution to most human dilemmas. But the community pulls together and, like the bridge, survives all natural and man-made disasters. Even individuals endure in songs, tales, and legends. In one of the novel's best episodes, the wealthy, beautiful, and proud Fata, who takes her own life, is immortalized in death. Fata is pledged by her father to marry a man she has publicly rejected and whose village she has sworn not to enter. In order not to go back on either her own or her father's word, Fata sets off for the wedding, but at the halfway point, on the bridge over the Drina, she stops her horse and quickly jumps into the raging water below. Her defiant gesture is unforgettable. Fata remains forever alive in a haunting Bosnian song and in Andrić's masterful psychological portrait.

Two other protagonists are inextricably linked with the bridge and its fate. The innkeeper Lotika, the intelligent, energetic matriarch of an extended Jewish family, has a total breakdown in the last days of the bridge, during the chaotic times of war. She sees the whole civilized world vanishing before her and sees herself and her family sinking back to the poverty she had all her life struggled to conquer. Her collapse adds to the inevitable catacylsmic finale of the novel. But even more closely related to the bridge is the fate of Alihodža, the last descendant of the original caretakers of the inn built next to the bridge by Mehmed Pasha. Alihodža's presentiments of disaster are realized when he has a fatal heart attack after seeing the bridge severed in two by Austrian dynamite. The novel ends with the outbreak of World War I.

There has been much critical discussion of the novel's final message. On the one hand, the ending seems pessimistic. The harmonious unity of the bridge, which had inspired and supported the community, has been destroyed, and Alihodža is expiring in the street. The future seems bleak. Perhaps this gloomy outlook reflected Andrić's mood in the darkest period of World War II, during which the novel was written. But Alihodža's dying thoughts also offer hope for the future and affirm Andrić's refusal to give in to despair. Alihodža clearly acts as the author's mouthpiece as he voices the novel's basically optimistic message of survival:

> But one thing could not be: it could not be that great, wise, and kindhearted men who for the love of God raise lasting buildings, so that the world would be more beautiful and men live in it better and more easily, will disappear completely and for all time. If they were to vanish, it would mean that God's love was extinguished and had disappeared from the world. That could not be.
>
> (1:395)

Bosnian Chronicle deals once again with Bosnian history, but its scope, perspective, and thematic focus are different. It presents not four hundred years, but only seven years of "consular times" at the beginning of the nineteenth century in Travnik, the seat of the Turkish sultan's representative in Bosnia. Based on comprehensive archival research, primarily on the correspondences of the French and Austrian consuls, this realistic novel is openly grounded in historical data. The French consul's real name, Davide, is thinly disguised as Daville, and his assistant Desfosses, who actually wrote a book on Bosnia, is correctly named. The legendary plane is absent; it is here replaced by detailed sociohistorical analysis and psychological portraiture.

Unlike the episodic *Bridge on the Drina*, this novel has continuity of both action and character and the unifying theme of alienation. *Bosnian Chronicle* is framed by the arrival and departure of the French consul, Daville, and much of the novel's action is filtered through his consciousness. Although there are several protagonists (Turkish pashas, Austrian consuls, the French consul's assistant, Desfosses, and the Levantines, men of mixed cultural heritage who work for the foreigners), they are all united by the fact of being outsiders in this closed community. Bosnia is a land of physical and spiritual exile for these unhappy transients. Daville's first ride through the town is accompanied by hisses, spitting, and a wall of "oriental" hatred. The memory of this tormenting experience is a searing, black line, the one he shares with another outsider who cannot bridge the distance between East and West: Mehmed Pasha in *The Bridge on the Drina.*

The Eastern and Western foreigners, the Christian consuls as well as the Muslim viziers and even the Levantines, voice a similar despair about Bosnian backwardness. The characters' reflections create a refrain that brings the theme of cultural conflict between East and West to the forefront of the novel. Implicitly present in Andrić's earlier fiction, this theme is now fully explored. Bosnia is a crossroads where Catholic and Orthodox Christians, Muslims and Jews coexist in constant tense hatred and uneasy accommodation. Thus the land itself engenders feelings of distrust, hopelessness, and alienation. Yet paradoxically it also inspires highly sensitive visionaries such as the philosophical Levantine Dr. Giovanni Mario Cologna. In one of the most poetic statements in the novel, Cologna tries to explain life in a land between the East and the West:

No one knows what it means to be born and to live on the edge between two worlds, knowing and understanding both, yet unable to help them understand each other, or draw closer, loving and hating both, wavering and stumbling one's whole life, having two homelands and yet none, being at home everywhere and remaining always a foreigner; in short, living crucified, but as victim and tormentor simultaneously. . . . That is the lot of the Levantine because he is *poussière humaine,* human dust, which passes tortuously between East and West, belonging to neither and pulverized by both. These are people who know many languages, but have none of their own, who know two faiths, but are not firm in either. These are victims of the fatal division of mankind into Christians and non-Christians.

(2:315–316)

But then Doctor Cologna abandons all geographical landmarks in his final description of a metaphysical "third world" and its weary inhabitants:

These are people from a spiritual and physical border, from the black and bloody line which through some weighty, absurd misunderstanding was drawn between people, God's creatures, between whom there should not and must not be boundaries. This is the edge of the sea and the shore doomed to eternal movement and unrest. This is the "third world" on which has descended the whole curse following the division of the earth into two worlds. This is . . .

(2:316)

As his voice trails off, Cologna is no longer speaking of Bosnia, of the Levant, of the crossroads of East and West, but of the tentativeness of human existence everywhere. Andrić's tendency to universalize his Bosnia is ever-present. In this novel he gives a metaphysical rather than a mythic significance to the concrete geographical and historical Bosnian setting.

Bosnian Chronicle follows the constant daily struggle that is Daville's life in Bosnia. A representative of the Napoleonic Empire, Daville is pitted not only against the local Bosnians and their Turkish vizier but also against the Austrian consul who quickly arrives to preserve the interests of the Austro-Hungarian Empire. His occasional diplomatic victories are short-lived not only because of the passive Bosnian morass, but because distant events are threatening the very existence of Napoleon's empire. In fact, the alienation and instability the foreigners feel inside Bosnia is universalized as both the West and the East are in turmoil at the beginning of the nineteenth century. Thus the psychological traumas and philosophical ruminations of Cologna and many other characters have a sound historical basis. Typically for Andrić, the whole novel operates on more than one level, ranging from the specifically historical and realistic to the more universally psychological, metaphysical, and existential.

Unlike *The Bridge on the Drina, Bosnian Chronicle* does not have a counterweight to all the spiritual and political instability. Daville's happy family life is a temporary haven that has only individual meaning and does not extend to other characters. At first glance, art might seem to be a solution, as all major protagonists seek refuge in writing. But the Austrian consul's hardly artistic, methodical descriptions of Bosnia are fated to gather dust in some distant archive. And Daville's stilted epic *Alexandriade* will remain incomplete because of the defeat of its real-life prototype, Napoleon. However, the French consul's energetic young assistant, Desfosses, the only character who manages to withstand Bosnia's depressing influence, does write a book filled with useful ethnographic observations. He is the only person to leave Bosnia with the optimistic belief that things can change, but even he does not have the last word. That is left to Daville himself, and to the townfolk.

As Daville prepares for departure, he is both mourning the passing of the Napoleonic era and feeling the full force of the "oriental poison" that had devastated his life in Bosnia. He sees his diplomatic mission as a personal and professional failure. But the novel does not end with gloomy reflections on a turbulent historical reality. As he had done more tentatively in *The Bridge on the Drina,* Andrić here offers an unquestionably heartening solution: survival and hope for the future. While sorting his papers and contemplating a new life in France, Daville himself begins to feel his energy and his faith returning:

And that mechanical task was accompanied by a vague but persistent thought like an obstinately recurring melody: still, somewhere there must exist that "right road" that he had all his life sought in vain. It exists, and man will someday find it and open it to all men. He himself did not know how, when, or where, but someday his children would find it, or his children's children, or even more distant generations. Like an unheard inner melody this thought lightened his labor.

(2:512–513)

The main text of the novel ends with these highly optimistic words for the future.

As he had done at the end of *The Bridge on the Drina,* Andrić here uses a major character's reflections to present his most closely held ideas. Daville underscores Andrić's basic faith in a better future for mankind and the perseverance of the human spirit in the most trying circumstances. Moreover, Andrić's longstanding theme of communal continuity and survival frames the novel. In the prologue the townspeople discussed the arrival of the consuls with apprehension. In the novel's epilogue they are quietly relishing their victory: the consuls' imminent departure and the town's return to normalcy.

The Woman from Sarajevo, the third and last novel that Andrić completed during World War II, has a much narrower scope and a different focus. It is a psychological portrait of a warped human being, the miser Rajka Radaković, whose every thought and gesture is aimed toward saving. Her father's bankruptcy leaves an indelible mark on Rajka, and she sacrifices her personal life in a vain attempt to undo his loss. Basically an unsympathetic character, this spinster acquires a tragic dimension in Andrić's penetrating portrayal. Although the novel has admittedly neither the epic scope of the *Bridge on the Drina* nor the historical intuitiveness of *Bosnian Chronicle,* it is unfortunate that its complexity has escaped most literary critics; it has been undeservedly neglected.

IVO ANDRIĆ

POSTWAR STORIES (1945–1975)

After the publication of the three novels in 1945, Andrić returned to shorter fictional forms and to nonfiction in the immediate postwar period. In fact, boundaries between stories, essays, and political tracts are sometimes blurred. Andrić continued to write stories set in Bosnia, ones that now received a new set of emphases and functions different from the earlier Bosnian tales and novels. The new stories are characterized by minimal plots and frequent absence of action. The striking dynamism of narration found in early Andrić is replaced by a more static narrative structure in "Pismo is 1920 godine," one of his earliest and most important postwar stories. Instead of weaving a Bosnian legend, here Andrić polemicizes and explicates the objective social and material conditions of Bosnia.

The story opens with a standard framing device—a chance meeting of two childhood friends. As often happens when two old friends meet after a long separation, they have very little to say to one another. But the strained encounter has two results: it leads the narrator to rethink his childhood, to remember how under the tutelage of this friend he discovered the world of books. The narrator's disappointment when he discovers that his idealistic friend has become an embittered man places this story in the cycle of childhood tales beginning with "Deca" (Children, 1935) in which Andrić reflects a child's perception of a mysterious adult world.

The second result of the encounter and the main focus of "Pismo is 1920 godine" is the letter which the friend, Max Lewenfeld, subsequently writes to the narrator in order to fill in what was left unsaid in their brief meeting. Max, an Austrian raised in Bosnia, has decided to leave his adopted country forever. In the course of explaining the reasons for his decision, he gives a sociopsychological portrait of that country. His basic premise is that "Bosnia is a land of hatred and fear" (9:180). He reiter-ates and analyzes in detail the complexities of the Bosnian psyche:

> Yes, Bosnia is a land of hatred. That is Bosnia. And by a strange paradox, which is really not even so strange, but could perhaps easily be explained through more careful analysis, one could also say that there are few lands with so much firm faith, so much exalted strength of character, so much tenderness and passion, so much depth of feeling, loyalty, and unswerving devotion, so much thirst for truth. But in the opaque depths beneath all that are hidden storms of hatred, whole hurricanes of compressed and pent-up hates that ripen and await their moment. Between your loves and your hatred the relation is the same as between your high mountains and the thousandfold greater and heavier unseen geologic strata on which they rest. And so you are condemned to live on top of deep layers of explosives that from time to time are ignited by the sparks of those very loves and of your cruel and fiery sensitivity. Perhaps your greatest misfortune is precisely that you do not even suspect how much hatred there is in your loves and ecstasies, your traditions and pieties.
>
> (9:181–182)

In this passage Andrić finally provides an explanation for the mystifying psychological and physical traumas of his early protagonists. Fear and hatred are motivating forces that lead to physical destruction and murder in "Mustapha Magyar," "Olujaci," "Anika's Times," and "Trup." Yet these powerful negative emotions have an energizing positive pole in the human psyche. Thus they exist side by side with a heightened awareness of beauty and a longing for an ideal, transcendent existence in "The Journey of Alija Djerzelez," "Ćorkan i Švabica," "Anika's Times," "U musafirhani," and "Ćorkanova smrt" (Corkan's Death, 1935), and, of course, in *Bosnian Chronicle*.

The virulent hatred and this spiritual and psychological dichotomy are rooted in deep religious and cultural discord among Orthodox and Catholic Christians, Muslims, and Jews. As Max further elaborates, their different time-keeping systems capture the quintessence of Bosnian life and demonstrate, forcefully and openly, its insoluble conflicts:

> Whoever spends a sleepless night in his Sarajevo bed can hear the town's nocturnal voices. The clock on the Catholic cathedral strikes ponderously and reliably: two in the morning. More than a minute passes (exactly seventy-five seconds—I have counted them myself), and only then the clock from the Orthodox church sounds in a somewhat weaker but penetrating voice; it strikes its own two-in-the-morning. Shortly thereafter the bell tower of the bey's mosque strikes a hoarse, distant note, marking eleven o'clock in ghostly Turkish time, according to the strange calculations of distant, foreign lands! The Jews do not have a clock that strikes, and God only knows what time it is for them, what time in Sephardic and what time in Ashkenazy calculations. Thus even at night, when everyone is asleep, still awake in the counting of those late empty hours is the difference that divides those sleeping people, those people who, when awake, rejoice and grieve, entertain and fast, according to four separate and discordant calendars, all sending their prayers to the same heaven in four different church languages. And that difference is—sometimes visibly and openly, sometimes invisibly and treacherously—always similar to hatred and frequently identical with it.

(9:184–185)

While reading Max's lengthy exposition on Bosnia, the reader begins to interpret the complex vision of its virtues and vices as Andrić's own. Max acts as the author's mouthpiece and the letter is an eloquent articulation of Andrić's conflicting feelings about his homeland. "Pismo is 1920 godine" has been called an explanatory footnote, a postscript to Andrić's Bosnian fiction. Although Andrić does not totally abandon Bosnia in his new stories, he certainly demythologizes it. Andrić's exploration of his favorite subject is no longer mythical or metaphysical, but sociological and analytical. His thematic focus shifts from a mesmerizing hatred, violence, and sensuality

to communal passivity and cowardice, a concomitant of decaying societies. Evil as an inexplicable metaphysical condition becomes an explainable social problem. Tragic, monumental heroes become simple everyday folk. Andrić not only dissects the negative elements in Bosnia's cultural history; he also begins to focus on the positive traits of individual members of this community, on their courage, integrity, and—what is most important—their sense of social responsibility.

"The Vizier's Elephant," one of the best stories of the immediate postwar period, explores the social dynamics of a typical crisis situation in Bosnia—the arrival of a new ruler. The whole community of Travnik is paralyzed by fear after the new vizier, Jelaludin Pasha, in order to crush all potential resistance, lures the community leaders to a meeting at which they are unceremoniously executed. Although a brutal act is the catalyst for the story, the central interest is the community's response. The slaughter of the beys frightens the townspeople into total silence. All agree that the new vizier is so evil that no words can possibly describe him. The town transfers its fearful hatred of the vizier to an equally alien being, the vizier's pet elephant. Since it cannot openly oppose the vizier, the community resorts stealthily to poisoning the animal.

Only under the protective cover of night and the influence of alcohol do the townspeople dare voice their feelings about the vizier's troublesome beast. On one such occasion the town braggart decides that he will lodge a complaint with the vizier. He finds eager followers among his drunken friends. The following morning, in sober daylight, one by one the brave volunteers abandon their dangerous task. Only one, a young tradesman, Alyo, actually walks up to the gate of the vizier's residence. When he realizes that he will have to face the pasha alone, Alyo, too, loses his nerve. Accosted by the guards at the gate, he simply pretends to be headed to another destination. He then climbs a hill above the town, where he is able to think clearly about this turn of events and its broader social and ethical implications. In a moment of rare insight Alyo recognizes the ignoble and cowardly existence that he and his countrymen lead and will continue to lead until someone stands up to the tyrants of this world. The instructive nature of Alyo's thoughts is highly reminiscent of Max's comments in "Pismo is 1920 godine." Although doubly camouflaged in this story by an omniscient third-person narrator as well as the character of Alyo, Andrić's moralizing voice is clearly heard in this somewhat awkward passage that noticeably retards the plot's development. The openly didactic narrator is typical for the immediate postwar period (1946–1950), but fortunately is not to be found often in Andrić's subsequent fiction.

In "The Vizier's Elephant" the crisis passes, this particular evil ruler is removed, and his elephant is finally successfully poisoned. Community life is once again stabilized, as is typical in most of the earlier stories and novels. But in the postwar period, the theme of continuity and survival becomes more pronounced and extends from the community to its individual members. In the earlier work, violence most often results in death, and the individual, whether good or evil, victim or aggressor, perishes. Now the heroes no longer have to die. In this story, while the evil ruler is forced to commit suicide, Alyo, the simple townsman, escapes the potentially serious consequences of his action and survives to lead a socially useful life.

The didactic narrator, the upbeat ending, and the theme of social responsibility characterize most stories of the immediate postwar period. They can be explained by the sociopolitical conditions of postwar Yugoslavia and Andrić's new, active role. At the end of World War II the Socialist Federated Republic of Yugoslavia was created under the leadership of Tito, a Communist guerrilla leader who had fought with the Allies against Germany. This was a time of political involvement for writers under the brief but strong influence of Soviet socialist realism. Having had no official function or affiliation during World War II, Andrić now stepped very actively into the role of a socially engaged professional writer. Elected president of the Writer's Union, he plunged into the cultural life of the country, lecturing to students, writers, and workers, visiting schools, factories, and construction sites in an effort to lend a hand in the physical as well as political reconstruction of his country. For him, by nature a reclusive individual, this was an uncharacteristic and at times difficult role. Although he remained a very private person until the end of his life, he took his responsibilities as a leading Yugoslav writer very seriously.

In the late 1940's Andrić's shortlived attempt to be socially and politically current in his fictional writing, to break with his sometimes obsessive preoccupation with the Bosnian past, resulted in a number of unremarkable short stories set mostly in the present. Typical for this period is a very uneven collection titled *Nove pripovetke* (New Stories, 1948), which contains, besides the memorable "Pismo is 1920 godine," sensitive psychological portraits and childhood stories alongside several forgettable, strongly didactic stories. Not surprisingly, World War II and its aftermath are the frequent subjects of stories written in the late 1940's.

"Zeko" ("Zeko," in *Nove pripovetke*), the longest and perhaps most typical story of the period, explicitly treats the problem of collaboration and resistance during the war and links it to the broader concepts of personal integrity and social responsibility. In this story these concepts are inextricably linked to the hero's struggle to become a man. The protagonist is a meek, henpecked clerk, as his nickname, Zeko ("rabbit"), indicates. He is also a man of talent whose potential is not realized until he is forced to take sides in the war. Disgusted by his wife's and son's fearful, aggrandizing selfishness, Zeko becomes aware of the suffering around him. His moral and spiritual odyssey is completed when he joins the Communist resistance movement against the Nazis. Although Zeko himself dies on a mission, the story ends on a highly optimistic note. The narrator predicts the imminent liberation of the city and the success of the revolutionary resistance movement. The sentimental ending and the caricatured portraits of Zeko's hysterical, shrewish wife and spoiled, good-for-nothing son relegate this story, along with almost all the others in the same collection, to Andrić's least successful literary endeavors.

Despite the openly didactic nature of many postwar stories, some are rescued from mediocrity by Andrić's keen insight into the human psyche and the universally shared wartime emotion, fear. With the accuracy and immediacy of an eyewitness, Andrić describes the bombings and the resulting physical and spiritual destruction of war. The better stories leave aside optimistic didactic conclusions and social responsibility and instead focus on the human toll in fear, suffering, and inner turmoil. By far the most successful story of the spiritual agony of the war, "Bife Titanik" ("Bar Titanic," 1950), examines the war's dehumanizing effect in what at first seems to be a typical confrontation between good and evil, victim and oppressor. But the story is suffused with irony. The title itself is a clue to the hopelessness inherent in the large-scale annihilation of war. It is, of course, ironic that the name associated with a great ship disaster is given to a small, back-street bar run by an impoverished, powerless Jew. In this setting the nightime arrest of the proprietor, Mento Papo, by a recent Nazi collaborator, the *ustasha* Stephen Kovíc, is not the expected clash between hapless victim and cruel oppressor but a grotesque and finally tragic confrontation of the fears, hopes, and misery shared in equal measure by the two men.

Andrić is at his best not in portrayals of positive, idealized heroes but in his depiction of tragic, alienated beings. Both the Jew and the Nazi collaborator in "Bar Titanic" are social failures, outsiders, and finally victims. The happy-go-lucky Jew, who lives in sin with a Catholic woman and deals with shady people, is scorned and then abandoned by the respectable Jewish community. The ungainly, slow-witted Stephen Kovíc, who fails in all attempts to earn the attention, if not the respect, of his community, puts on the Nazi uniform and demeanor as a final test of his power and as compensation for his personal weakness. But he once again sees himself being cheated by fate. During his harsh interrogation of a Jew, it becomes clear that the cowering little man in front of him is not the evil, rich Jew of his imagination. This man not only has no money, but he seems to mock Kovíc even as he begs for a reprieve so that he can try to raise an appropriate payoff for his Nazi tormentor. Both men suspect that their predicament will end with the death of the Jew, that the Nazi collaborator must kill him, because that is his duty. But Stephen Kovíc must also prove himself different from his victim. Precisely at the moment that he sees his own reflection in the pitiful Jew, Stephen Kovíc pulls the trigger. In their final dance of death, he becomes a frenzied beast cornering his flailing prey. Both men emerge as victims dehumanized by their fear and desperation, by deadly forces outside of their control.

The message that is repeatedly conveyed by Andrić's wartime stories is that giving in to fear dehumanizes man and is a kind of living death. The issues of cowardice and personal integrity are ones that Andrić himself had to face in occupied Belgrade, where he was subject to air attacks by enemy and allies alike. Once, when asked by a friend why he had not sought safety outside the city during the bombings, Andrić replied that all the people fleeing the bombing had someone or something to save. But he had only had his life, and it would have been undignified to run only in order to save himself. A Yugoslav journalist remembered accidentally encountering Andrić in 1944 during the battle for Belgrade. While seeking shelter from the bombing, he discovered a man sitting at a table in the hallway of a strange house. Totally oblivious to the raging battle, the man, who turned out to be Ivo Andrić, was quietly reading. In the ensuing conversation, Andrić told the journalist that he had two goals during the war: to stay alive and to remain a human being. Facing one's own fear and humanity is thus not surprisingly a frequent theme in the stories written in the decade following the war's end.

The emphasis in most of the best postwar stories, as in "Bar Titanic," is not on broad social and political issues of wartime conflict but on accompanying spiritual repercussions for individuals and human relationships. Even after he abandoned his timely exploration of the war theme, Andrić continued to focus on the inner world of his heroes. Andrić had always reflected his characters' thoughts and feelings and the conflict between the subjective inner world and the objective exterior reality, as is seen in such early stories as "Mustapha Magyar," "Thirst," and "Death in the Sinan Tekke," as well as in the first of a number of autobiographical prison stories, "Zanos i stradanje Tome Galusa" (The Ecstasy and Suffering of Thomas Galus, 1931). But often the inner reality he portrayed was subordinated to action and atmosphere. Now the stories become almost plotless, focusing as they do on a realistic description of a single, seemingly insignificant event or a cryptic psychological portrait. The best stories of the 1950's—"Žena na kamenu" ("Woman on the Rock," 1954), "Igra" (The Game, 1956), "Panorama" (1957), and "Letovanje na jugu" ("A Summer in the South," 1959)—all focus on personal reflections or observations of an unseen, inner existence.

Andrić continued to write about women with an occasional uncanny insight into the female psyche. The woman on the rock, in the story of that title, is a middle-aged opera singer trying to come to grips with the realization that her lithe, elegant body is beginning to show signs of aging. While she is sunbathing at the seacoast, she remembers her first feelings of womanly power. As a fifteen-year-old, sitting high on a fence with one leg raised, she lets an elderly, poor worker feast his eyes on her bare legs. Both the girl and the old man are trans-

ported in a timeless moment of sensual ecstasy. Now, many years later, the woman is angered by the memories that contrast so sharply with her present sense of mortality. As she gracefully dives into the water, in communion with the sun and the sea, she is able to shake off her fears and to revive her former feelings of effortless well-being. Although the story is narrated in the third person, with several generalizing interruptions in the first person plural, it reads as an interior monologue. The woman is used throughout as a center of consciousness, and her thoughts and feelings are vividly recorded. A very high level of identification and empathy is thus created between reader and character. The later Andrić is at his best in such delicate, subtly nuanced portraits.

In exploring the nature of unseen but real actions and feelings, Andrić continues to write stories about childhood fears, hopes, and dreams. Like the prison stories, these create a loose cycle. Written over a period of more than thirty years, they attest to the durability of Andrić's imagery. "Panorama," thematically the richest of these stories, is told by a middle-aged engineer whom Andrić often uses as a "frame" narrator. He remembers the exotic beauty of the "panorama," a traveling show that lured him as a young boy with its colorful pictures of far-off people and places. The power of his imagination is so strong that the people in the picture show come alive as the story of their lives is told. It is the memory of the panorama and the beautiful story he created around it which guide the narrator through life's vicissitudes.

In his later writings, Andrić resolves more and more openly the tension between internal and external existence by removing the distinction between illusion and reality. Only within this context can one understand the fantastic story "A Summer in the South." The familiar feelings of ecstasy and transcendence, which in the early stories represented only a momentary respite from life's tribulations, are now fully and permanently realized. An Austrian professor vacationing with his wife in a small seaside town in Yugoslavia is constantly daydreaming, seeing himself disappear into the light of the warm southern sun. One morning he walks off into that light, and when his wife comes back as usual from her morning shopping, he is nowhere to be found. And he is never found. The wife goes back to Vienna, and the professor remains the talk of the town. No rational explanation is offered for the professor's disappearance in an otherwise realistic story. But the professor's growing detachment from the concrete reality surrounding him, and his powerful sense of well-being in contact with nature, with the sun and the sea, are so vividly detailed that the distinction between dream and reality is totally obliterated. Andrić's story is an eloquent statement on the power of the human spirit and imagination in union with nature. Whether interpreted as fantastic realism or pantheistic allegory, "A Summer in the South" is one of Andrić's most heartening stories. For the Austrian professor manages to find what all of Andrić's protagonists rarely glimpse but continue to reach for: that other side of life, that unseen yet magnificently beautiful existence. Andrić's most optimistic stories date to this period of the late 1950's. They are often imbued with a similar lyrical pantheism, a worship of nature, the sun, the sea, and the open horizon.

"A Summer in the South" was one of the best stories in the last major work published during Andrić's lifetime, *Lica* (Faces, 1960). This mixed collection of new and old stories is unusual in that it was Andrić's first attempt to unify his stories with an introductory essay ("Lica") that provided the title. Although the first-person narrator who describes the indelible imprint of diverse human faces on his memory is not identified, the reader nonetheless recognizes the voice of the author. In the stories that ensue, the narrative viewpoint does not remain constant, and the elusive figure of the narrator-writer is absent in many stories. The stories themselves are uneven in aesthetic value, quite disparate in substance, and do not

form a compositional whole. The critical response to *Lica* was mixed. Some literary critics intimated that it did not measure up to his best historical-mythic prose, while others recognized a continuing refinement of his contemporary short story. Both views have merit and are not mutually exclusive.

The last of Andrić's works to receive justifiable universal critical acclaim was the 1954 novella *Devil's Yard,* the last major piece of Andrić's Bosnian fiction to be published during his lifetime and perhaps his greatest work. This novella marks the final appearance of Andrić's oldest narrator, Brother Petar. It is Andrić's most complex literary construct, possessed of the compactness and elegance of poetry. *Devil's Yard* incorporates all of Andrić's thematic dualities and conflicts: reality and illusion, innocence and guilt, freedom and imprisonment, attack and defense, individual identity and archetype, life and death, good and evil, and most importantly, history and myth, reality and legend. Finally, it is Andrić's most intricate story within a story, an exploration of the nature of storytelling itself. Andrić was never to publish anything that would rival this work in thematic and structural intricacy. After 1960, during the last fifteen years of his life, Andrić published little other than a handful of fragments of his last unfinished novel, *Omerpaša Latas.*

In the 1950's and 1960's Andrić continued his many professional activities, crisscrossing Yugoslavia and traveling abroad as cultural ambassador. His literary fame spread as his works, primarily his novels, were translated into many languages. In 1958, at the age of sixty-six, Andrić married Milica Babić, a costume designer at the National Theater in Belgrade, to whom he had been devoted for many years. Until his wife's death ten years later, the 1960's were a time of personal happiness and professional recognition, culminating in the Nobel Prize award. By 1970, failing health forced Andrić to curtail his missions abroad and to reduce his public participation significantly. After a lengthy hospitalization, he died in 1975 at the age of eighty-two. His funeral was attended by some ten thousand of his countrymen. He was a beloved writer and a national institution. Just as he had donated much of his Nobel Prize money toward the acquisition of books for schools and libraries all over Yugoslavia, Andrić left his sizable estate to his country. On the basis of an oral testament, Andrić's royalties went to a foundation set up in his name, and almost all of his original manuscripts and correspondence were given to the Serbian Academy of Arts and Sciences.

It was noteworthy that in the last fifteen years of his life, during the time of his highest professional recognition, Andrić published very little. Was he stung by the critics' mixed reception of his last collection of stories, or had he begun to doubt his own creative ability? In the very last years, did his artistic vision and powers of concentration simply diminish with declining health? Characteristically, Andrić himself provided no answers. For this highly revered public persona remained a personal enigma. Andrić rarely granted long interviews, and when he did he divulged very little about his private life or current writing. In the last years, he was particularly wary of discussing his unfinished novel. He was prescient in his concern that he would never complete it. According to his lifelong friend, secretary, and assistant, Vera Stojić, Andrić had serious writing difficulties with this work.

Behind Andrić's well-known and highly revered public persona was a reclusive, enigmatic individual whom no one really knew. Even his fellow writers and friends repeatedly commented that no one penetrated the polite, affable exterior of an excellent listener, a highly cultured man interested in everything in life. But what he himself really thought and felt was a mystery to all. Critics have respected Andrić's desire for privacy even after his death and have never probed deeply into his personal life. For example, in view of the pivotal role of women and the mostly tragic nature of male-female relations in his fiction, it would seem obvious that Andrić's personal feelings about and relations with women have not been adequately examined. Nevertheless, critics have continued to search for the private Andrić in his works. For Andrić's writing toward the end of his life does become more openly, though still guardedly, autobiographical. Two brief stories in particular, "Legenda o pobuni" (The Legend about the Rebellion, 1971) and "Slepac" (The Blind Man, 1975), seem to bare Andrić's final thoughts and feelings. Andrić had a long-standing tendency to cloak anything personal in allegory, symbol, and myth. But in these poignant visions of human existence, personal details and feelings emerge clearly through the allegory.

In "Legenda o pobuni" man's fear of dying takes on a concrete form: it is a whirlpool into which the good angels are drawn after an apocalyptic confrontation with their enemies. What begins as an old man's recollection of a legend he heard as a young boy (again the childhood theme) ends as a terrifying realization that the whole history of mankind is precisely this process of falling into a bottomless abyss. The recurring nightmare caused by a legend heard long ago is at least momentarily obliterated by the vision of the sun's rays on the sea. As they have been for all of Andrić's characters, these positive visions of nature are the only salvation for the old man. This story also has clear autobiographical elements. Andrić loved the Adriatic sea, and although his main residence continued to be in Belgrade he spent much time in the last years of his life at the seacoast. The story is also narrated in the first person by Lazar, a character Andrić often used as his alter ego.

"Slepac" is an allegory of the artist's life. An unnamed first-person narrator (Andrić himself?) recalls a childhood story of a blind man who moves through life with ease because he is guided by an inner light in the shape of a golden calf. He knows that the light that gives meaning to his life has to remain his secret. But in a dark moment the blind man reveals that secret, and the light disappears forever. As the narrator tells us, in human existence the growth of man's power and will is always accompanied by the potential for suffering and ruin. Having lost his beacon, the blind man disappears too. Perhaps he exists in some world where there is no light or darkness, but no one can say, because nothing reaches us from there. The final sentence ("Even the story fades and ends here") points to Andrić's unceasing concern with the artist's storytelling. At this point in time, Andrić clearly knew that he was dying, but, typically, in his last publication he shied away from the confessional mode and instead cloaked his deepest feelings in poignant allegory.

Although in "Slepac" Andrić denies any traditional religious possibilities of the afterlife, in a final poem written in 1973, but published only posthumously, he tempers that disbelief:

> No gods nor prayers!
> And yet it happens that I occasionally hear
> Something in me like a prayerful whisper.
> That is my old and eternally living desire
> Appearing from somewhere in the depths
> And in a soft voice asking for a little space
> In one of the endless gardens of paradise,
> Where I might finally find
> What I have here always sought in vain:
> Breadth and space, an open vista,
> A little unfettered breathing.
>
> (11:243)

In this succinct and undeniably personal expression of his life's search Andrić both echoes the strivings of his fictional characters and recognizes them as his own. But Andrić rarely expressed himself in lyrical poetry. A modest volume of poems written over a period of sixty years was published posthumously under the title *Šta sanjam i šta mi se dogadja* (What I Dream and What Happens to Me, 1976). Highly personal, melancholy, at times self-absorbed, these lyrics only occasionally reach the artistic heights of the prose Andrić continued to write to the very end of his life.

POSTHUMOUS PUBLICATIONS

The posthumous publication in 1976 of the short-story collection *Kuća na osami* (The House on Its Own), the unfinished novel *Omerpaša Latas,* and a collection of aphoristic reflections entitled *Znakovi pored puta* (Signs by the Roadside) attests to the continuing productivity and evolution in Andrić's writing. It is now clear that Andrić's prodigious talent had not been exhausted. Of greatest interest to Andrić scholars may in fact be not his last fiction but the writer's memorabilia, collected in *Znakovi pored puta.* This, the longest of Andrić's works, consists of numerous pithy observations of places, events, and individuals and profound reflections on human existence, on history, art, and literature written in a period of almost fifty years. Many texts, however, are dated 1973 and thus, in large measure, do represent Andrić's latest work.

Disliking diaries and memoirs, Andrić here created a kind of writer's laboratory, one where ideas for fictional works first appear in the form of astute personal and general commentary. Throughout his career, Andrić wrote elegant essays on literature and art and lyrical reflections on his many travels. *Znakovi pored puta* represents a splendid poetic condensation and the stylistic apex of the "nonfictional" writings. But particularly in Andrić's last works it becomes increasingly difficult to make distinctions of genre, or fiction and nonfiction. In *Kuća na osami,* for example, he uses a first-person narrator who he wants us to believe is the writer himself. In one of the stories in this collection Andrić places in the mouth of a character a direct quote from his Nobel Prize acceptance speech. In analyzing Andrić's *oeuvre* scholars have increasingly paid attention to what Andrić himself observed about his works: that all his life he was writing one and the same work, whether it was called a story, an essay, or a poem. Thus it is not surprising that both *Kuća na osami* and *Omerpaša Latas* are retrospectives of Andrić's earliest characters and thematics, and at the same time syntheses and further developments of his dominant imagery, narrative techniques, and, in the case of *Kuća na osami,* even compositional structure.

While offering a panoramic view of Andrić's most enduring character types, in its composition *Kuća na osami,* which was written between 1972 and 1974, fundamentally differs from Andrić's previous collections of stories. It is a unified whole, a unified cycle with a primary setting or frame and a single narrator who connects all the stories. Andrić's previous collections had all been "open" cycles, with no formal links between the stories. Only the last collection, *Lica,* can be seen as a less successful precursor to *Kuća na osami.* Although the introduction to each collection presents a narrator "attacked" by visions of human faces, in *Lica* the narrator disappears and the stories remain unconnected. In *Kuća na osami* the narrator proceeds to establish himself as the writer who in the seclusion of his Bosnian house is assailed by faces from his literary past. For he is visited not by real people, but by ghosts of his characters who insistently intrude upon him. They come back from the dead to expose the tragedy of complex lives often hidden behind banal external appearances.

Each story, then, is a revelation or a reevaluation of a human life. The theme of reconciliation that permeates the work is introduced in the very beginning. The primary setting, "the house on its own," physically embodies Bosnia's cultural diversity, but here the mix of Eastern and Western architectural details is quite charming. The house seems to be a workable testament to their forced accommodation. In *Kuća na osami,* as well as in *Omerpaša Latas,* the predominance of the Bosnian setting confirms the durability and significance of that historical, mythic, and metaphysical landscape which informs Andrić's best fiction. Thus it is not surprising to meet again those alienated beings who inhabit this setting. The eleven stories themselves are a series of finely nuanced portraits of a motley crew of dreamers, inveterate liars and drunkards, recluses, libertines, ruthless rulers and social outcasts,

tormentors and victims. For each one life was a physical or spiritual imprisonment from which they have been willingly or forcibly liberated.

The second story, "Alipaša" (Ali Pasha), presents a nineteenth-century historical figure, a haughty vizier who is taken prisoner by Omerpaša Latas, the Turkish sultan's emissary to Bosnia. Alipaša's last days as a disgraced prisoner are marked by an epiphany that reveals to him the eternal truths of human existence. Paradoxically, in his degradation Alipaša attains a grandeur he had never possessed as an undisputed ruler. The unifying thematic focus of the stories is an inner, previously hidden existence, characterized by fear, pain, and anguish, punctuated at times by moments of ecstatic transcendence. A concomitant theme, escape from these imaginary or real torments, is most successfully presented in "Robinja" (The Slave Girl). In this most memorable story of the cycle the girl, a Christian prisoner captured in a Turkish raid, is caged and waiting to be sold. In a twist of a frequent scenario in the early Andrić stories, a wasted libertine is now openly bargaining for her robust beauty. But the healthy peasant girl takes her own life in a gruesome gesture of self-will. She obliterates her spiritual agony in sharp physical pain as she slowly and methodically presses her head between the wooden bars of her cage. The oblivion she finds is awesome in its immediacy and finality as the reader follows her thoughts into oblivion. This story is one of Andrić's most powerful realizations of his long-standing metaphor of both Bosnia and physical existence itself as a prison. In death the slave girl manages a successful escape. Andrić's writing has always proffered mesmerizing and paradoxical forms of deliverance from an agonizing reality.

The unfinished novel *Omerpaša Latas* holds out the tantalizing promise of a masterpiece. As is true of all of Andrić's longer fiction, the conception or actual beginning of the work is difficult to date. Omerpaša's name appears as early as 1924 in Andrić's doctoral dissertation. The novel's first published fragment is dated 1950, and over the next twenty years Andrić published some fifteen short fragments of the novel. Although impossible to date accurately, much of the text of the posthumously published novel was written in the last years of Andrić's life. Whereas Andrić originally conceived a vast chronicle of Sarajevo, he narrowed its scope to focus on one brief but turbulent period in Bosnian history, the brutal military campaign from 1850 through 1852 of Omerpaša Latas. This Christian renegade was the Ottoman Turkish military commander sent from Istanbul to reassert control over the rebellious Bosnian beys. The brief published fragments are a series of unconnected individual portraits or events portraying Omerpaša's campaign of terror. Full of seemingly realistic historical details, they amply demonstrate Andrić's descriptive skills but only suggest the rich thematic content of the posthumously published novel.

The novel *Omerpaša Latas* shares much of its thematics and composition with the earlier work *Bosnian Chronicle*. (Even in its unfinished state, the novel was published in the order in which Andrić had left his unpaginated manuscript.) It is framed by the arrival and departure from Sarajevo of Omerpaša's army, a dazzling, powerful body of clean, well-fed soldiers and animals. With its loud, discordant military music and opulent, exotic officers' uniforms, Omerpaša's army seemed like a mirage to the poor Bosnian populace. The conflict of illusion and reality, one of the novel's major themes, is thus immediately introduced. Much of the novel explores the inner workings of Omerpaša's entourage, just as the novel *Bosnian Chronicle* had examined the households of the French, Austrian, and Turkish emissaries. Once again the foreigners' perceptions of Bosnia as a prison are a constant refrain, with the accompanying familiar motifs of alienation and isolation. But beginning with Omerpaša himself, Andrić now focuses not on contrasting representatives of the East and the West but on the Christian converts to Islam, those foreigners who carry the irreconcilable differences within their souls. Omerpaša, the cold, arrogant Ottoman aristocrat, is also Mićo Latas, a Catholic Croatian peasant, a renegade from Austria-Hungary and a convert to Islam. This cultural and psychological schizophrenia forms the thematic nexus of the novel.

As Omerpaša's private and public lives are scrutinized, the inner workings of his colorful household are revealed. As it now stands, the novel is a gallery of striking individual portraits reminiscent of Andrić's early, monumental protagonists. Each of these eccentrics has an obsession that is typically sensual in nature. The somnolent, corpulent Ahmetaga is a refined epicure who finds ecstasy in eating. Yet he is disgusted by Omerpaša's insatiable sexual appetite. In the process of his reincarnation as Omerpaša, Mićo Latas repudiated his name, family, religion, and country and destroyed all human feelings. His resulting inhuman quest for power is displayed in his cruelty as well as in his deviant sexuality. In the mesmerizing figure of Omerpaša, Andrić synthesizes the instinctual morbid eroticism of his early stories and the contemporary psychological exploration of alienation begun in the *Bosnian Chronicle.* Psychologically bared, Omerpaša still retains a mythic monumentality. As in his other two major novels, the mythic and psychological dimensions coexist with the historical. Here Andrić also examines the political and social implications of the phenomenon of the Bosnian "Turks'" conversion to Islam. Was Omerpaša's metamorphosis, as that of many of his hired mercenaries, fake, merely a case of convenient mimicry? Or was it real? Omerpaša continues to fascinate on all levels of interpretation.

The elusive search for beauty, often in the form of a woman, is a major theme that permeates the novel. For Andrić's protagonists, beginning with his first hero, Ali Djerzelez, woman is a fatal, mysterious creature, unattainable in either her physical or spiritual totality. Djerzelez is the first to ask the question which Andrić repeatedly raises, but never answers: "Why is the path to a woman so circuitous and mysterious?" (7:32). The actual attempt to possess her reintroduces the same gamut of relationships—from idealized longing to vicious rape—that is found in the early stories. A young local man literally loses his mind in the search for the lovely smile of a young girl whose uncovered face he has accidentally seen. Hired by Omerpaša to paint his official portrait, the artist Karas is inevitably drawn to Omerpaša's beautiful wife. As always, imaginary moments of rapture in reality result in rejection and despair. In thinking about the beauty of women, Karas repeats Ali Dzerzelez' words. In Omerpaša's household, the sudden infatuation of a quiet, respectable man for an attractive girl of easy virtue results in a murder-suicide. A marauding band of Omerpaša's soldiers brutally rapes a half-mad gypsy girl.

Bosnia itself is now implicated in all this madness. The landscape embodies the sexual fever as the Bosnian hills shimmer in the shape of a giant nude female body. In *Omerpaša Latas,* Andrić evokes his early legendary Bosnian environment with its monumental characters and their tragic flaws and bizarre passions. But in recreating his powerful myth of Bosnia's "dark beauty," Andrić is also reinterpreting it in modern psychological and existential terms by completely internalizing its cultural schizophrenia in the landscape itself as well as in his protagonists.

LEGENDS AND STORYTELLING

An overview of Andrić's literary work leaves the reader with an appreciation of its variety and evolution as well as with the realization of a fundamental uniformity of Andrić's artistic vision. His genius lies in his ability to fascinate the reader with yet another permutation of the same basic story.

In his Nobel Prize acceptance speech (1961) Andrić identified what gave cohesiveness to his works when he spoke of storytelling and legends: the purpose of all storytelling, as in the tales of Scheherazade, is to cheat death.

And all stories are, in fact, just variations on a few basic legends of mankind. Andrić had written about legends many years earlier in his imaginary "Razgovor s Gojom" (Conversation with Goya, 1935), a polemical essay about the nature of art and the role of the artist. In this essay the famous Spanish artist Goya clearly expresses Andrić's own views as he reflects on the meaning of life:

> I came to one negative conclusion: that our individual thought in all its effort does not mean much and cannot achieve anything; and a second, positive conclusion: that we must listen closely to legends, those traces of collective human endeavor through the centuries, and that in them, as much as possible, we must decipher the meaning of our destiny.
>
> (12:24–25)

Now, more than twenty-five years later, speaking finally in his own voice, Andrić eloquently connects storytelling with legends:

> In thousands of different languages, in the most diverse life conditions, from century to century, from ancient patriarchal storytelling in huts, around the fire, to the works of modern storytellers appearing at this moment from publishing houses in great world centers, the tale of man's destiny unfolds, told, without end or break, by man to man. The means and forms of that storytelling change with time and circumstance, but the need for stories and storytelling remains, and the story flows on and there is no end to storytelling.
>
> (12:66)

This universal function of storytelling in its transmission of folktales and legends becomes Andrić's most essential theme. It increasingly permeates and unifies his best works. It is highly significant that for his first protagonist Andrić chooses a Muslim folk hero, the legendary Ali Djerzelez, but presents him not in typical heroic fashion. When Djerzelez Alija descends from his horse, he is a short, bowlegged man, the butt of his friends' jokes. Yet his strong emotions, his capacity for anger and love, give him a unique monumentality. From the beginning Andrić builds his fiction on legends and folk stories refracted through the ironic distancing of his own imagination. Andrić's early stories, although usually told by some omniscient third-person narrator, often make reference to the lore that the Bosnians pass on from generation to generation. They are firmly grounded in such stories and legends.

In *The Bridge on the Drina* Andrić explores the nature of Bosnian legends even more closely. Like Andrić himself, the townspeople grow up around the bridge listening to tales and legends in which "imagination and reality, dream and waking, are strangely and inextricably mixed and interwoven" (12:12). One cannot miss the irony in the conflicting legends that the Christian and Muslim children hear. For the Christian children a series of gigantic paired marks which appear beside the bridge are the hoofprints of Šarac, the horse of their most famous folk hero, Prince Marko. For the Muslim children, they belong to the winged steed of their hero, Ali Djerzelez. Both the Christians and the Muslims are firmly convinced of the truthfulness of their tales. And Andrić demonstrates in his chronicle-novel how such tales have the power of truth. They are the preservers of each cultural tradition, and whether they actually ever happened is irrelevant. After the local tales are told, then the historical events are revealed. In *The Bridge on the Drina* Andrić's narrator appears in two guises: as a local storyteller and as a historical chronicler. But Andrić does not yet begin to expose the nature of his own, the artist's, storytelling.

Increasingly in the postwar period, Andrić openly explores the nature of tales and legends, as in this frequently quoted beginning of "The Vizier's Elephant":

Bosnian towns and cities abound with stories. In these, most frequently, *made-up* tales, in the guise of unlikely events and under the mask of frequently fabricated names, is concealed the

real and unacknowledged history of that region, of living people and generations long since passed. These are the oriental lies described by the Turkish proverb as "truer than any truth."

(5:41; original emphasis)

Andrić calls attention to the dual nature of the tale, which paradoxically operates as both truth and fiction. The story ends with the narrator's comment: "The people suffer, whisper, and protect themselves, if by no other means, than through stories that perpetuate their unclear yet indestructible desire for justice, for a different life and better times" (5:87). Fabricated or not, tales and legends play a vital role in society as repositories of the people's hopes as well as a defense mechanism against life's misfortunes. On an aesthetic plane the tale is more beautiful than reality. On an ethical level it has more value for the community. While recognizing its fictional nature, Andrić presents his story not as individual literary construct but rather as an organic communal creation.

Several stories of the late 1940's and the 1950's are precisely about Bosnian storytellers. The protagonists of "Razgovor" (The Conversation, 1948), "Proba" (The Rehearsal, 1951), and "Lov na tetreba" (The Grouse Hunt, 1959) mesmerize their appreciative audiences with fantastic tales. The stories may be sad or humorous, pathetic or ludicrous, yet they all accomplish their aim brilliantly. They allow the listeners to transcend the mundane and often harsh reality of their lives. Moreover, in "Proba" the monk who regales his friends with comic impersonations is an artist whose creative efforts transform his surroundings as well as his listeners. The peals of laughter that sweep over the assembled group break down the walls of the room. The dark town wedged between steep hills disappears, and before them opens a magnificent vista of the whole world, burning in the flame of laughter. In recognizing the metamorphic power of Brother Serafin's storytelling, Andrić begins to identify the creative role of the storyteller with that the artist. But not until his last completed work, *Kuća na osami,* does Andrić identify himself as that artist and the writer of all these stories.

The novella *Devil's Yard* and the collection of stories *Kuća na osami,* two works separated by almost twenty years, deal most thoroughly with storytelling and the nature of truth and fiction, or history and legend. In the earlier work, Andrić weaves a suspenseful tale through the use of myriad storytellers who offer differing glimpses of the main protagonist, Ćamil, their fellow prisoner in the notorious Turkish prison, the Devil's Yard. A lonely, sensitive young man, unhappy in love and with a tragic family background, Ćamil steeps himself in history books. He is drawn to the figure of Džemsultan, who many years earlier unsuccessfully fought a war of succession with his brother and died a disillusioned prisoner, a pawn in the hands of Western enemies. Ćamil's delusion is considered dangerous by the authorities, since a similar fraternal battle is being waged by the current Turkish sultan. He is arrested and probably killed, although his fate remains shrouded in mystery. Ćamil's fateful words, "I am he," in which he identifies himself with Džem, are the cause of his demise. These words have a strong symbolic meaning since they embody both the power of speech as well as myth. For as Andrić's narrator points out, Džem's story is archetypal, a replaying of the ancient tale of two warring brothers. Critics have recognized Thomas Mann's "formula of myth" in Ćamil's words. There is something essentially mystical as well as mythical in the totality of this identification: Christ, too, spoke these words in the garden of Gethsemane. As in *The Bridge on the Drina,* Andrić operates on the level of universal myth, which, like the local legends, is "truer than the truth."

Although the tale of Džem-Ćamil is the central thematic core of *Devil's Yard,* the process by which it is told is equally significant. The primary narrator seems to be Brother Petar, who, on his deathbed, tells this tale of Ćamil from his personal recollections. But beginning with the young monk who hears

Brother Petar's story and remembers it after his death, and extending to the prisoners, the garrulous Haim, Zaim, and Ćamil himself, concentric circles of storytelling are created. Mendacious, partial, onesided, or brilliantly intuitive, taken all together these stories demonstrate the profound complexity of truth. Andrić masterfully orchestrates his narrators, and his voice is always clearly heard, as in these thoughts of Brother Petar:

> What would we know of others' minds and souls, or of other people, and therefore of ourselves, [what would we know] of other ways of life and regions we have never seen nor will ever see, were it not for people such as these who have the need to tell, in speech or in writing, what they have seen and heard and what they have thought or experienced as a result? Little, very little. And if their accounts are incomplete, colored by personal needs and desires, or even inaccurate, we have reason and experience and can judge and compare them, accept or reject them, in part or whole. Thus, something of human truth always remains for those who patiently listen or read.
>
> (4:54)

Not only do storytellers pass on universal knowledge from which truth can be gleaned, but this primal drive to communicate affirms man's very existence. Its absence is equated with death in the end of *Devil's Yard:*

> And so it ends. There is nothing more. Only a grave among the invisible monks' graves, lost like a flake in the snowy mound that spreads like an ocean and transforms everything into a cold desert without name and sign. No more stories or storytelling. As if there were no world left worth the effort of seeing, walking, breathing. No more Istanbul or Devil's Yard. . . . There is nothing. Only the snow and the simple fact that men die and are returned to the earth.
>
> (4:119)

While recognizing the brilliance of this work, some critics have found it to be Andrić's darkest and most fatalistic. But the story does not end on this pessimistic note. The young man who is here contemplating Brother Petar's death is pulled out of his reverie and brought back to life by the voices, insistent, alive, that are recording the monk's possessions. As long as man speaks, he lives. As long as he speaks, truth will be told. No wonder that very early in *Devil's Yard* the unidentified, omniscient narrator comments: "It's best to let each man speak freely" (5:13).

Although the fundamental complexity of storytelling is fully brought out in *Devil's Yard,* Andrić himself remains doubly hidden behind a generalizing narrator, as well as his circle of identified "local" storytellers, particularly Brother Petar. Although storytellers die and there are no more stories, what does remain, besides voices which will continue to speak, is this written text that preserves and exposes the truth. As Brother Petar noted, one should read as well as listen, for storytellers write as well as speak. But Andrić does not break the spell of his own storytelling and does not reveal himself to be the most masterful storyteller of all.

Only some twenty years later, in *Kuća na osami,* does Andrić delve into the writer's memory and explore the art of storytelling in a self-conscious manner. Memory and storytelling, in fact, become the main thematic links of this cycle. At the outset the first-person narrator is established as the storyteller who relates recollections, or true occurrences. However, he is then also exposed as the writer himself who is dealing with purely imaginary characters, whose ghosts actually haunt him. Andrić's artistry lies in his ability to combine these two seemingly contradictory intentions in the voice of a single narrator-writer who openly stands for the author himself.

In *Kuća na osami,* Andrić uses the device of storytelling to make a final declaration, to sum up both his life and his art. He calls up fictional characters from his literary past in order to settle accounts with them, to give them their due and let them speak. Andrić will once again repeat the refrain of *Devil's Yard,* that everyone should be allowed to speak freely. Incomplete stories are filled in, and those never

told are at last recounted. But Andrić is not only exorcising visions of the "real" people who filled his universe. He is making a final settlement with all the places (the sea, cities, streets, even houses) that crowd an old man's mind and will not let him rest. *Kuća na osami* is an act of literary as well as autobiographical reminiscence, exorcism and reconciliation through the cathartic and metamorphic process of storytelling.

Andrić writes his own epitaph when he describes Ibrahim-efendija ("effendi") Skaro, a recluse who becomes a spellbinding storyteller, in a story simply titled "Priča" (Story). Andrić himself shares his Bosnian background and his hermetic personality with this figure:

> And thus his life passed in stories, as if it were all a story. . . . He did not live. . . . Instead of that so-called real life, whose blow he felt in his mother's womb, he created for himself another reality composed of stories. It is as if he protected himself from everything that really happened from day to day with these stories about what could have been but never was, what was often truer and more beautiful than all that really happened. Thus he escaped life and cheated fate. And now for almost fifty years he has been lying in the cemetery on the Alifakovac. But he still lives sometime and somewhere as a story.
>
> (15:91)

Ibrahim-efendija is buried on the same street that "the house on its own" stands on.

Andrić writes his final testament from the spiritual isolation of the artist embodied in the physical remoteness of that Bosnian house. He finally admits that he is that Bosnian storyteller, that continuator of myths, who tells the "oriental" tales that are truer than truth, the young boy who sat mesmerized on the bridge at Višegrad listening to the old-timers, and the young man who wanted to preserve the "dark beauty" of the Bosnian past. One is reminded once again of that bare and rocky path in Višegrad that guided Andrić throughout his life and that he immortalized in his art.

IVO ANDRIĆ

Selected Bibliography

EDITIONS

INDIVIDUAL WORKS

POETIC PROSE
Ex Ponto. Zagreb, 1918.
Nemiri. Zagreb, 1920.

STORIES
"Put Alije Djerzeleza." Belgrade, 1920.
Pripovetke. Belgrade, 1924. Contains "U musafir-hani" (At the Monastery Inn), "U zindanu" (In the Jail), "Ćorkan i Švabica" (Ćorkan and the German Girl), "Za logorovanja" ("In the Camp"), "Mustafa Madžar" ("Mustapha Magyar"), "Dan u Rimu" (A Day in Rome), "Rzavski bregovi" (The Rzav Hills), "Ljubav u kasabi" (Love in a Country Town), "Noć u Alhambri" (Night at the Alhambra).
Pripovetke. Belgrade, 1931. Contains "Mara mi-losnica" ("The Pasha's Concubine"), "Ispovijed" ("Confession"), "Čudo u Olovu" (The Miracle in Olovu), "Kod kazana" ("By the Brandy Still"), "Most na Žepi" ("The Bridge on the Žepa"), "Ani-kina vremena" ("Anika's Times").
Pripovetke. Belgrade, 1936. Contains "Svadba" (The Wedding), "Smrt u Sinanovoj tekiji" (Death in the Sinan Tekke), "Napast" (Trouble), "Olujaci" (The Village of Olujaci), "Žedj" ("Thirst"), "Mila i Pre-lac" (Mila and Prelac).
Nove pripovetke. Belgrade, 1948. Contains "Priča o kmetu Simanu" (The Story of the Serf Siman), "Zmija" ("The Snake"), "Deca" (Children), "Knjiga" (The Book), "Susedi" (Neighbors), "San" (The Dream), "Zlostavljanje" (Persecution), "Pismo is 1920 godine" (The Letter from 1920), "Ćilim" (The Carpet), "Zeko" ("Zeko"), "Snopići" (Bundles of Wood), "Dedin dnevnik" (Grandfa-ther's Diary).
Panorama. Belgrade, 1958. Includes "Panorama," and "Žena na kamenu" ("Woman on the Rock").
Lica. Zagreb, 1960. Includes "Lica" and "Letovanje na jugu" ("A Summer in the South").
Kuća na osami. Belgrade, 1976.

NOVELS
Na Drini ćuprija. Belgrade, 1945.
Gospodjica. Sarajevo, 1945.
Travnička hronika. Belgrade, 1945.

Prokleta avlija. Novi Sad, 1954. Novella.
Omerpaša Latas. Belgrade, 1976.

POETRY
Šta sanjam i šta mi se dogadja. Belgrade, 1976.

COLLECTED WORKS

Sabrana dela Ive Andrića. 10 vols. Belgrade, Zagreb, Sarajevo, Ljubljana, 1963.
Sabrana dela Ive Andrića. 17 vols. Belgrade, 1976–1981.

TRANSLATIONS

Bosnian Chronicle. Translated by Joseph Hitrec. New York, 1963.
Bosnian Story. Translated by Kenneth Johnstone. London, 1959. Rev. ed., London, 1979.
The Bridge on the Drina. Translated by Lovett F. Edwards. New York, 1959.
Devil's Yard. Translated by Kenneth Johnstone. New York, 1962.
Letters. Translated, edited, and with an introduction by Želimir B. Juričić. Toronto, 1984.
The Pasha's Concubine and Other Tales. Translated by Joseph Hitrec. New York, 1962.
The Vizier's Elephant: Three Novellas. Translated by Drenka Willen. New York, 1962. Contains "The Vizier's Elephant," "Anika's Times," and "Zeko."
The Woman from Sarajevo. Translated by Joseph Hitrec. New York, 1965.

BIOGRAPHICAL AND CRITICAL STUDIES

IN SERBO-CROATIAN

Bandić, Miloš. *Zagonetka vedrine.* Novi Sad, 1963.
Džadžić, Petar. *O Prokletoj avliji.* Belgrade, 1975.
———. *Hrastova greda u kamenoj kapiji.* Belgrade, 1983.
Filipović, Vuk. *Delo Ive Andrića.* Pristina, Yugosla-via, 1976.
Isaković, Antonije, ed. *Zbornik radova o Ivi Andricu.* Belgrade, 1979.
Jandrić, Ljubo. *Sa Ivo Andrićem.* Belgrade, 1977.
Karaulac, Miroslav. *Rani Andrić.* Belgrade and Sara-jevo, 1980.
Koljević, Svetozar, ed. *Delo Ive Andrića u kontekstu evropski književnosti i kulture.* Belgrade, 1981.

IVO ANDRIĆ

Leovac, Slavko. *Pripovedać Ivo Andrić.* Novi Sad, 1979.

Milanovic, Branko, ed. *Ivo Andrić u svjetlu kritike.* Sarajevo, 1977.

Palavestra, Predrag. *Skriveni pesnik.* Belgrade, 1981.

Popović, Radovan. *Životopis Ive Andrića.* Belgrade, 1980.

Tartalja, Ivo. *Pripovedačeva estetika.* Belgrad, 1979.

Vucković, Radovan. *Velika sinteza o Ivi Andriću.* Sarajevo, 1974.

IN ENGLISH

Hawkesworth, Celia. *Ivo Andrić: Bridge Between East and West.* Dover, N.H., 1984.

Hawkesworth, E. C. *Ivo Andrić* (Proceedings of a Symposium Held at the School of Slavonic and East European Studies, 10–12 July 1984). London, 1985.

Johnson, Vidosava Taranovski. "Ivo Andrić: The Development of the Bosnian Stories." Ph.D. diss., Harvard University, 1977.

Juričić, Želimir B. *The Man and the Artist: Essays on Ivo Andrić.* Lanham, Md., 1986.

Loud, John Fiske, "'Zanos' in the Early Stories of Ivo Andrić." Ph.D. diss., Harvard University, 1971.

Peterson, Lorna. "The Development of Narrative Technique in Ivo Andrić." Ph.D. diss., Yale University, 1973.

BIBLIOGRAPHY

Lukić, Radomir, ed. *Ivo Andrić. Bibliografija dela, prevoda i literature.* Belgrade, 1974.

VIDA T. JOHNSON

EDITH SÖDERGRAN

(1892–1923)

DESCRIBING EDITH SÖDERGRAN to W. H. Auden, Gunnar Ekelöf wrote:

> She is a very great poet, as far as I can judge in Akhmatova's class or even beyond, a young Swedish woman in the *diaspora,* one of our Byzantines, brave and loving as your Emily Brontë. It is a pity that such a rare bird should be buried for the world in a grave over which the war has passed several times. She belongs to the world although her language might seem an Old Aeolian dialect.
>
> (Quoted in Leif Sjöberg, *A Reader's Guide to Gunnar Ekelöf's* A Mölna Elegy [New York, 1973], p. 47)

In the summer of 1938 Ekelöf had made a trip to the Karelian Isthmus, then a part of the Republic of Finland, but incorporated into the Soviet Union in 1940 and again in 1944. He had been invited to Terijoki, a seaside resort close to the Soviet border, by Elmer Diktonius, the Finnish "modernist" lyricist who had been entrusted with the editing of Södergran's hitherto unpublished poems, *Landet som icke är* (The Land That Is Not, 1925). Diktonius took young Ekelöf inland to the little town of Raivola (Russian: Rodzino), where Södergran's mother still lived; this excursion impelled Ekelöf to write essays on Södergran's personality and work and ultimately to try to introduce her work to Auden. In the essays, Ekelöf argued that only a person who had seen her native landscape could fully understand her poetry: "It is a landscape with great lines, forming the background of her poetry. . . . The railroad runs straight, mile upon mile, along a cleared strip a hundred meters wide, in which the little Finnish locomotives seem to strive in vain against the landscape's monotony and melancholy." About Södergran herself he continued: "[She] cannot be called Swedish. Her very language, with its turns of phrase, archaically stiff and learned in its grammar, betrays a lack of contact with the mother tongue and its organic development. Nor is she Finnish, she is a stranger—yet her alien quality is somehow very Nordic."

These statements by Ekelöf—one of Sweden's great poetic voices—may be initially confusing to the foreign reader. Like Johan Ludvig Runeberg, Finland's preeminent nineteenth-century poet and the author of its national anthem, Södergran belonged to Finland's Swedish-speaking minority, a group resembling the Anglo-Irish and the "Prague Germans" in the wealth of its contributions to literature. Her works have thus become at least as much a property of Sweden as they are of her homeland. But even among Finland's Swedish speakers she was an outsider; on the last of her visits to Helsinki, in September 1917, she impressed another young poet, Jarl Hemmer, as having "intellectual roots different from ours; she knew little of Swedish lyric poetry," and he detected an exotic accent in her speech. She was unusual in other ways, too: "She found us [Finland-Swedes] to be stiff, reserved, impersonal. . . . She was too much of a special personality, too greatly filled with her own lonely exaltation, to be able to enter into any sort of profitable exchange with the rest of us." In the poem "Vadär mitt hemland . . ." ("What Is My Homeland . . .") from 1918 she asked, "What is my homeland? Is it distant Finland, strewn with stars?"

Nevertheless, Södergran's bloodlines were as unimpeachably "Finland-Swedish" as Hemmer's own. Her father, Matts Södergran, came from the Swedish-speaking coastal population of the province of Ostrobothnia in western Finland. Like other poor Ostrobothnians, many of whom immigrated to America, Matts Södergran decided to make his fortune away from home; styling himself an "engineer," he found work in Russia. (Finland had been a semi-autonomous grand duchy of the czars since the War of 1808–1809, when it had passed from Swedish to Russian control.) At St. Petersburg in 1882, Matts Södergran was hired by the firm of Alfred Nobel, in whose employ he traveled extensively; in Smolensk, he married the daughter of a Russian merchant, only to lose her to tuberculosis. After this episode (in the course of which Södergran may have caught the disease), he left Nobel for a wood-processing firm, settling in Raivola, some twenty-five miles northwest of St. Petersburg on the railroad line to Viipuri (Viborg), the capital of Karelia. Raivola was known for its larch forests, planted by Peter the Great to provide timber for his fleet. Here, or in St. Petersburg, he found a second wife, Helena Lovisa Holmroos.

Like Matts Södergran, Helena's father, Gabriel, was an expatriate Swedish speaker of humble origins, and like Södergran he had gone to Russia in the hope of turning his technical skills to good account. An iron-master, he made a considerable fortune and married a woman from a background as simple as his own had been, the daughter of a cotter from the Turku (Åbo) skerries. With some social ambitions, the couple sent their daughter Helena to one of St. Petersburg's elegant girls' schools, the Annenschule, where the language of instruction was German (it served the Russian capital's sizable and prosperous German minority). Then a calamity took place: in 1884 Helena gave birth to an illegitimate child (who lived only a few days), and no doubt her parents were relieved when in 1890 Matts Södergran asked for her hand. She was twenty-nine, a voracious reader; he was forty-five, quite without intellectual pretensions. The union produced one child, Edith Irene, born on 4 April 1892. The little family lived at Raivola, in a villa that the generous Gabriel Holmroos had purchased for his daughter. Helena could overlook Matts Södergran's financial improvidence because of the substantial inheritance she received from her parents; she was probably more irritated by his Ostrobothnian dialect, a painful contrast to her excessively correct Swedish, a language she knew as much from books as from practical use.

When Edith was ten, her mother took an apartment in St. Petersburg for the sake of the girl's education, while Matts stayed in Raivola. The school chosen was, as in Helena's case, a German one, Die deutsche Hauptschule zu Sankt Petri. The result of her schooling (which also included training in French, Russian, and English) was an international viewpoint rather than a Scandinavian one. Yet it confronted her with a crisis about her linguistic identity; dependent on her parents for a "Swedish" milieu, she chose German as her first literary instrument, and shortly before her death she still claimed that it was her "best language."

At the outset of the Winter War between the Soviet Union and Finland in December 1939, Helena Södergran, blind, and with her husband and daughter dead, was evacuated from the Karelian Isthmus; among the possessions she took with her was an oilcloth notebook that the adolescent Edith Södergran had filled with poetry between January 1907 and the summer of 1909. In 1961 the notebook, entitled *Edith Södergran's dikter 1907–1909* (Edith Södergran's Poems 1907–1909), was published. It contains 238 poems and demonstrates the girl's multilingualism: the majority of the poems are in German, but twenty-six are in Swedish, five in French, and one in Russian. The German poems are imitative of Heinrich Heine (and of Heine's tone, hovering between pathos and satire) and of the turn-of-the-century German verse she knew from popular anthologies—lyrics describing enchanted gardens, somnolent ponds bordered with reeds, skiffs that float aimlessly, all imbued with a vague longing or melancholy. Many of the notebook entries have to do with classroom reactions: her crush on her French teacher, Henri Cottier, and her affection for her companions "Claudia" ("Her eyes come from a fairy tale, / She's soft and cool and fair: / And she's the husband, I'm the wife, / We are a happy pair," she writes in an untitled poem of 1907) and "Paula" ("Your hot eyes run lightly over me . . . / My glance must avoid you, anxiously," she writes in the poem "In meinem Herzen" ["In My Heart"]). At the same time, Södergran tried her first self-portraits in poems about the illness or death of a young girl, about a girl who becomes a princess in a fairy-tale world, and about her own identity as a poet. She is the object of an autopsy ("My lungs will be as black / As earth that's soaked with blood"); she is the entrancing being "with cool eyes" and a "mocking smile" who scorns her husbands and suitors; and she is chosen by the "fair god of song" and realizes that poets have a way to be immortal ("Going into eternity, / Only our songs survive").

She also sees herself as a freedom fighter, a bringer of revolution: "Die Zukunft" ("The Future") is embodied in a heroine who strides through a "blood-drenched land" where she is surrounded by the masses, who ask "for bread and for counsel." Södergran was quite aware of the revolutionary fervor sweeping over Russia, and she caricatures a terrified Nicholas II, hidden in the Winter Palace, a tyrant who cannot sleep, in "Wenn sich die Sonne neigt" ("When the Sun Goes Down"):

Next day, he puts his imperial name
To death-decrees in reams,
But how the people will hang him is
The stuff of his next night's dreams.

She was fascinated by St. Petersburg itself ("I love the greenish Neva"), seeing it as a place of ominous allure; "creeping mist" lies over "hidden horror," and "shadows of men and women" slip along the city's streets. Her St. Petersburg verses, however, like those about her school involvements, are less polished than the German poems about her summers in Raivola; at her Finnish home she was occasionally able to write poems that outdo their German *Jugendstil* models in quiet mellifluousness, making Raivola seem lush and southern. In an untitled poem of 1908 she writes of lying in a boat and enjoying the pleasant melancholy of the world she has created:

Slumbering silently, the water lilies
Shine in their whiteness against the dark deep,
And vapors of dampness emerge from the water,
And all is but dreaming and resting and sleep.

The Swedish verses in the notebook have been called "exceedingly weak from an artistic standpoint" by her principal biographer, Gunnar Tideström. Her first Swedish poem, "Sommarminnen" ("Summer Memories") is simply a catalogue of twenty-three "summer objects"—"a lake with forest-clad edges, [and] reeds and sand and water's splash and ducks" and so forth—and may fairly be dismissed as an exercise in vocabulary expansion; in Swedish, too, she seems to be more prone to sentimentality—after all, this was her mother tongue, or, as Søren Kierkegaard would have said, the language of her heart. Notably, she allows herself liberties in Swedish that she does not attempt in German: she quickly abandons rhyme, depending on the force of her images to carry the poem along. And in 1908 she writes what Tideström calls the first genuinely Södergranian poem, with its view of the division of life into "low" and "high" and of human emotions into "happiness" and "sorrow"—the latter being a pain that ennobles the sufferer:

> Happiness is a butterfly
> That flutters low over the field,
> But sorrow is a bird
> With great strong black wings.
> They bear one high above life
> Which flows along below, sunlit and green.
> The bird of sorrow flies high
> To a place where the angels of pain keep watch
> Over the couch of death.

In the Swedish verse, too, the schoolgirl passion for "Claudia" and "Paula" vanishes, while that for Cottier changes. In a poem of October 1908 he is led through a series of rooms and is found wanting. The first is filled with flowers speaking the language of love, but the beloved teacher says in French, "Je n'aime pas les parfums" (I do not love perfumes), and passes on to a second chamber, where "emptiness, tiredness, and despair dwell." A third room, roofless and without walls, has scenery that constantly changes—evergreens on a winter night, traffic-filled streets, sparrows twittering, horses eating, "battles roaring," the voices of happy children—but the variety is too much for Cottier, and a wind catches his coattails, suddenly and comically, making them flap around his "warlike form." In a fourth room, a door "covered with white cloths" leads to a final chamber; he tries to force his way in, but something holds him back, and he goes away, half embarrassed. The Cottier of the dream is able to understand neither love nor despair—neither the phantasmagoria of the poet's mind nor the threat of illness and death under which she lives.

The last of the German poems in the notebook says: "I do not know to whom to bring my songs, / I do not know in whose language to write." The direct cause of Södergran's decision to make Swedish her literary language is unknown; visiting relatives in Helsinki in 1908, she had met the philologist Hugo Berg-roth, who advised her to abandon German for her "native tongue," of which he was an impas-sioned advocate. Another contributing factor must have been the milieu into which her illness forced her. In October 1907 her father had died of tuberculosis, and in 1909 she was diagnosed as having the disease; removed from school, she was sent to Nummela, a sanatorium west of Helsinki, where her father had been treated. There the prevailing language was Swedish; the staff itself and most of the patients were Finland-Swedes. Furthermore, she began to study some Swedish-language literature as a part of her preparation for the university entrance examinations—certainly she read Runeberg and Zacharias Topelius, the great figures of national romanticism, and she quite possibly read other Swedish verse from Finland that was much in vogue: the reflective work of Hjalmar Procopé and the lurid verse of Bertel Gripenberg.

The Finnish hospital's director evidently suggested that Södergran move from Nummela to a sanatorium in the Swiss Grisons; in the autumn of 1911 the Södergrans set out for the continent, and after a short stay in Arosa they moved on to Davos-Dorf. The milieu was intellectually stimulating: a well-equipped reading room at Dr. Ludwig von Muralt's sanatorium contained journals from all over Europe; a friendship with an Australian girl inspired Södergran to read Algernon Charles Swinburne in the original, as well as Shakespeare and Charles Dickens; and she read all of Dante's *Inferno*. After mother and daughter had taken an Italian trip in the spring of 1913, they returned to Raivola for a summer stay that was interrupted seven times by journeys to Nummela for a treatment called "insufflation," which consisted of filling the patient's lungs with nitrogen gas. A second full winter at Davos brought about no improvement in the young woman's condition, and when the Södergrans were back in Finland in the spring of 1914, she was packed off to Nummela again. This time she ran away and returned to Raivola, leaving a note behind: "I have such a terrible, superstitious horror of Nummela. When I visited my father [here] . . . , I felt this boundless terror, this terrible revulsion in the presence of death. . . ."

The summer on the eve of the war was not wholly given over to sickness and fear; Södergran—now twenty-two—confessed to the family's housekeeper that she had a sweetheart. The man in question was a Russian physician at Terijoki, married and sixteen years Södergran's senior. The romance appears to have lasted until the following year, when the doctor was ordered to Russia proper for service in a military hospital. Södergran's health grew steadily worse after her lover's departure, and by the beginning of 1916 she fell into a severe depression requiring psychiatric care. At the same time she began to think of collecting and publishing some of her poems. On one of her excursions to Helsinki she showed her poems to a respected poet, Arvid Mörne, and, encouraged, she approached the new—and, she hoped, venturesome—publishing house of Holger Schildt. Her first letter, written in January 1916, went unanswered; a second, written in May, received the attention of Runar Schildt, the distinguished novella writer who served as a reader for his cousin Holger. He recommended publication saying, ". . . for all [the poems'] oddities, one gets a sense . . . of something absolutely genuine." Södergran renounced all royalties, perhaps because she regarded the book's appearance as a life-sustaining event.

Dikter (Poems), issued for the Christmas market in 1916, was the largest and most heterogeneous of Södergran's books, containing sixty-four poems; it would have been even larger if Runar Schildt had not omitted a handful of weak items and, more important, if Södergran had not held back sixteen other poems that were published only after her death. The poems have a single major landscape, Raivola, around which three strands of thematically related lyrics are woven: reflections on the enigma of the poet's self, the tale of unhappy love, and a set of instructions for endurance. As in the oilcloth notebook, the Karelian setting is made green and soft, a place that provides

companionship; in her loneliness and desire for companionship, the poet makes the garden and trees speak. Obviously, these lyrics contain much of the stock-in-trade of the continental European lyric of neoromanticism: wandering clouds, lonely girls, languor mixed with anticipation or apprehension—a sense of waiting for a seasonal change, for an erotic experience, for an end of the fragile idyll. Some of the poetry revels in a dreamy atmosphere, as in "Nocturne":

Shadows fall across the pathway,
Gently, at the water's edge, the bushes weep,
Black giants by the beach's silver keep their watch.

Elsewhere, as in "Den sörjande trädgaården" ("The Garden in Lament"), there is an almost arch blending of childlike naïveté with adult bitterness:

Oh, that windows see
And walls remember, that a garden can stand and
    lament,
And a tree can turn and ask: Who has not come and
    what is not well,
Why is the emptiness heavy, saying nothing?

If Södergran had filled the entire volume with such musical and melancholy lyrics (regular in rhythm, sometimes adorned with the occasional rhymes favored by the *Jugendstil*), there would have been little question about its wholehearted acceptance by Swedish Finland's literary critics, since established poets had been busily cultivating magic gardens as, for example, Gripenberg had done in his *Gallergrinden* (The Grillwork Gate) of 1905. Similarly, Södergran's fairy-tale mode was scarcely upsetting; here she worked in the tradition of the beloved Topelius, Finland's blander and sweeter version of Hans Christian Andersen. What disturbed the early audiences of *Dikter* was Södergran's mythologizing of herself—a development of the several roles the adolescent had played in the oilcloth notebook. Revolting against her gentle pleasure in her garden life, she grows impatient, chafing at her captivity. The poem "Jag" ("I") begins with an oppressive view of an existence lived, as it were, beneath the sea; suddenly, the ocean depths turn into a forest, and the speaker—in one of the invalid Södergran's frequent outbursts of imaginary athletic ability—decides to try to climb to the treetops. There, she keeps a lookout for the distant world (of St. Petersburg?) that she regards as her spiritual homeland:

> I am a stranger in this land,
> Which lies beneath the pressing sea,
> The sun looks in with swirling beams,
> And the air flows between my hands.
> They told me I was born in imprisonment—
>
> . . . .
>
> I lie in ambush here at the foot of the murmuring
>   tree,
> How can I climb up the slippery trunks?
> Up there, the swaying crowns meet,
> I will sit there and hold watch
> For the smoke of my homeland's chimneys. . . .

Other poems of imprisonment do not have quite the same suggestive power, the same brilliant metamorphoses, and can become almost banal: a bird sits imprisoned "in a golden cage / In a white castle by a deep blue sea" ("En fången fågel" ["A Captive Bird"]), and "the last flower of autumn," standing as a sentinel against "the wind of the North," knows that her "calix has no other seed than death's" ("Hös · - tens sista blomina" ["The Last Flower of Au- · tumn"]).

For Södergran the captivity in which she found herself was not just that of the enchanted garden or of physical illness; her body also tormented her with its desires: "Till Eros" ("To Eros," in *Landet som icke är*) is surely not a joyous acceptance of the god's power. (Not surprisingly, she did not send it to Schildt for publication.) In it she rails against what she sees as an expulsion from the sweet realm of childhood and, worse, as a forced initiation into humiliating slavery:

> See, I am bound, both hands and feet,
> Feel, I am compelled in all my thoughts.
> Eros, you cruelest of all the gods,
> I do not flee. I do not wait.
> I only suffer like an animal.

Brutally frank for its time and milieu, the poem may owe something to Freud, who was already well known to readers of Swedish in Finland through Gustaf Mattsson's journalistic presentation of his theories: the word *tvungen* (compelled) may allude to Freud's *Zwangsvorstellung* (obsession or obsessive thought). But a superficial knowledge of the Freudian vocabulary was not necessary for Södergran; she could be—and often was—an unblushing observer of herself.

Even as she depicted herself as a prisoner, Södergran developed a second line of poetic life in which her personae are free and happy girls. In "Skogens ljusa dotter" ("The Forest's Bright Daughter"), a wedding is prepared; the daughter is to marry, and all nature rejoices at the report. But in another of Södergran's surprises, no groom appears in this epithalamium, and the girl is "free from longing," though she herself "awakens all desires." (Perhaps she is a descendant of the elusive and androgynous Tintomara in the novel *Drottningens juvelsmycke* [The Queen's Diadem, 1833] by C. J. L. Almqvist, an author Södergran is known to have admired.) In another of the *Dikter*, Södergran employs figures from Greek mythology; the speaker of "Violetta skymningar" ("Violet Twilights") is a member of what seems to be an Amazon band: "I bear violet twilights within me from my primeval time, / Naked maidens playing with galloping centaurs. . . ." Mere men get their comeuppance in a series of definitions (a favorite structural device for Södergran):

> Man has not come, has never been, shall never
>   be . . .
> Man is a false mirror the sun's daughter, enraged,
>   casts against the cliff's wall,

Man is a lie, whom white children do not
   understand,
Man is a spoiled fruit that proud lips scorn.

Beyond this catalogue of images, the poem combines other and more important elements that are predictive of the way Södergran later developed her mythic patterns: her dream of a band of sisters (here described as "warriors, heroines, riders" and "tiger spots, taut strings, stars without dizziness") and her proposal that the proper husband for such maidens is the sun itself.

"Violet Twilights" may have been intended to annoy male readers; its companion, "Vierge moderne" ("Modern Virgin")—Södergran had the two poems placed close together near the beginning of her book—provides another catalogue of challenging definitions: "I am no woman. I am a neuter"; "I am a net for all greedy fish"; "I am a toast to all women's honor"; "I am the whispering of the blood in the man's ear"; "I am fire and water, honorably joined, on conditions of freedom." No wonder that the poem, despite some of its contradictions (but contradictoriness, Södergran implies, is a prime quality of her modern virgin), has won a large feminist following in Scandinavia. Taken not as a manifesto but as a part of Södergran's intensely personal work, its resemblance to many other lyrics by her hand is notable: she forever tells herself what she *is* or what she *must be.* Before all else, Södergran is a poet of self-injunction.

During that September 1917 visit to Helsinki, Södergran surprised Hemmer and his friends by the magnitude of the questions she put to them: "Does life have a meaning?" and "Do you think one can be happy?" Beneath these formulations lay her knowledge that she had very little time in which to find the happiness she sought. Her medical predicament, so often addressed overtly or implicitly in her poetry, is the source of the opening of "Den speglande brunnen" ("The Mirroring Well"): "Fate said: white you shall live, or red you shall die."

Her physicians had given her the choice either to live longer, in a circumscribed and inactive existence, or to throw herself into life, and die. Thus "white" means "chastity" or "asceticism" and refers to the first option, and "red" means "passion," of whatever nature, and refers to the second. The speaker of the poem, seated at the edge of a well, decides to follow her heart's dictates: "Red I shall live," she decides, in defiance of her fate. But matters do not turn out as expected: against her own decision she is assigned to the contemplative world of the mirroring well, and "happiness is far away," in the realm of normal human activity, represented by a young woman sewing a child's blanket, a man building a hut in the forest. As for the speaker, the redness she had thought she chose lies only in the aesthetically pleasing decorations of her limited world:

Here red roses grow around bottomless wells,
Here fair days mirror their smiling features,
And great flowers lose their fairest petals. . . .

There is no escaping her imprisonment, and her attempts to do so end in idle contemplation or catastrophe.

Much attention has been concentrated on those of the *Dikter* that tell of attempts to break free from the enchanted garden or the mirroring well by means of love. The book's opening poem, "Jag såg en träd" ("I Saw a Tree"), immediately announces the theme of erotic disappointment:

I saw a woman who, smiling and painted,
Cast dice for her happiness
And saw that she had lost.

The most frequently translated of all Södergran's poems, the four-part suite "Dagen svalnar" ("The Day Is Cooling"), recounts again the affair with the Russian physician. The speaker invites her lover to take what she possesses—warmth, a hand, a white arm, "my slender shoulders' longing." Yet a disharmony immediately becomes apparent; the head of the lover, resting on her breast, is "heavy," and—once he has "cast [his] love's red rose into [her] white womb" (Södergran is at once sentimental and outspoken about what has happened)—the man turns out to be "a ruler with cold eyes," with a "heavy hand on [her] light arm." She regrets the loss of her "ringing maiden laughter, [her] woman's freedom with head held high." The sweeping anaphoras of part 4 list and chastise the man's small and selfish expectations and his reaction:

> You sought a flower
> and found a fruit.
> You sought a spring
> and found a sea.
> You sought a woman
> and found a soul—
> You are disappointed.

The condemnations of a man apparently incapable of appreciating the woman's richness and totality come thick and fast in the poems: her life has become meaningless since the day "I saw a white-clad woman / In my beloved's arm"; her "longing" has followed a "glad cuckoo"—a biting reference to the notoriously faithless bird whose name in Swedish, *gök*, can also mean a dandified man; and she hurls a curse at the lover: "If my child does not live, it will be his." If the outwardly directed insults seem excessive (but memorable), so does the self-contempt: "filth [lies] in joy's short spring," Södergran writes, and in "Två vägar" ("Two Paths") the speaker enjoins herself to abandon her old way:

> Your way is filthy,
> There men wait with lustful glances,
> The word "happiness" is heard upon all lips.

The other path of "purity," however, is no better: along it children play with the poppy, the flower of sleep and death, and women mourn "and speak of sorrows." At the path's end a "pale saint" stands, his or her foot on a dead dragon's neck—the dragon of sexuality, slain at a terrible cost. The several attempts to construct an alliance of women against men ("We women, we women, are nearer to the brown earth") are undercut by the speaker's belief that she has made herself unworthy of membership by succumbing to lust: "I have fever like a sick plant, / I sweat sweetness like a sticky leaf" are lines in "Sjuka dagar" ("Sick Days," in *Landet som icke är*), one of the poems not submitted to Schildt. These attempts are also vitiated by her awareness of her own seductiveness: in "Avsked" ("Departure") she takes an embarrassed farewell of her "sisters," as she beseeches them to hold her back, and she lists her alluring attributes, which seem to make her less human than she was before:

> I have nothing left of myself but my black hair,
> My two long braids, which glide like snakes.
> My lips have become burning coal. . . .

A similar self-analysis characterizes what may be the finest of all her love poems, which is entitled—with ambiguous straightforwardness—simply "Kärlek" ("Love"):

> My soul was a bright blue dress of the sky's color;
> I left it on a rock beside the sea,
> And naked I came unto you and resembled a
> woman.
> And as a woman I sat at your table
> And drank a toast with wine and breathed in the
> smell of some roses.
> You found that I was beautiful and resembled
> something you had seen in a dream,
> I forgot everything, I forgot my childhood and my
> homeland,
> I only knew that your caresses held me captive,
> And smiling you took a mirror and bade me see
> myself.
> I saw that my shoulders were made of dust and
> crumbled,
> I saw that my beauty was sick and had no will
> save—to disappear.
> Oh, hold me closed so tightly in your arms that I
> need nothing.

The implications of the poem are manifold: the sense of a loss of personal freedom—of physical and emotional fragility and of uncertainty about personal identity—is inserted into a trite scene of seduction: the dinner, the wine, the roses, the flattery, the surrender—and then the awful realization, at the sight in the mirror, of her own physical decay, a realization at which she can only cry out for the embrace of a lover vastly distrusted, a lover she has seen through.

There is good textual evidence that as Södergran reflected on her love affair, she began to find consolation by casting herself in the role of an abandoned Ariadne (in classical mythology, Ariadne was abandoned by Theseus and later saved by Dionysus). As a close reader of Friedrich Nietzsche, she knew his "Klage der Ariadne" ("Ariadne's Lament"), and although she does not explicitly identify herself as Ariadne until the poem "Dionysos," in *Rosenaltaret* (The Rose Altar, 1919), the poems contain repeated references to a lonely woman on a rocky shore or a lonely island, and to a lover who has sailed away. In "Två stranddikter" ("Two Beach-Poems") she even experiences, like Ariadne on Naxos, "silence without echo, / Loneliness without mirror," and in "Den låga stranden" ("The Low Beach") she finds herself wholly cut off from the world ("The light birds high in the air / Do not fly for me, / But the heavy stones on the low beach rest for me"), and her lover has left her "trembling with tears / On an island that is called winter." There is an impressive and dignified pathos in these numerous laments that nicely counterbalances the equally numerous (and probably earlier) poems of vague, moonlit melancholy. Still, it seems that the genuinely original poems of the collection—remember Runar Schildt's words about absolute originality—are those such as "I" or "Love" where, depending neither on classical myth nor on neo-Romantic practice, Södergran gives her own creative imagination full play. This is surely the case with such a poem as "Helvetet" ("Hell"), placed near the end of the *Dikter* as a part of a series of "defini-tions" of "Skönhet" ("Beauty"), "Livet" ("Life"), "Smärtan" ("Pain"), among others. It opens with scornful praise—"Oh, how splendid hell is"—and continues the mock eulogy by saying that in hell (logically enough) "No one speaks of death" and everything is meaningful ("No one says an empty word")—hell is eternal, and torment gives import to every outcry. As in heaven, "No one grows ill and no one grows tired." The "true" paradoxes are interlarded, however, with the formulas of a terrifying and traditional Christian sermon: "No one has drunk, and no one has slept / And no one rests and no one sits still." The double onslaught of paradoxical praise and of old-fashioned hellfire and brimstone leads first to the reader's wry amusement and then to the realization that Södergran speaks in the cruelest fashion about her own captivity in illness. Not wishing to end with black humor, though, she followed "Hell" in the *Dikter* with "Den väntande själen" ("The Waiting Soul"), which once more describes the companionship Raivola's nature has given her, and with "Pain," in which, rather sententiously, she announces that "happiness" does not cause poetic production, while "pain" does:

Do you know pain? . . .
She gives songs and dreams,
She gives us a thousand kisses that all are empty,
She gives us the only kiss that is real.

It is regrettable that Södergran did not close her collection with another poem bearing a single-word title, "Ingenting" ("Nothing"), from among the sheaf she held back:

Be calm, my child, for there is nothing,
And all is as you see: the woods, the smoke, and the
flight of the rails.
Somewhere far away in a distant land
There is a bluer sky and a wall with roses
Or a palm and a milder wind—
And that is all.
There is nothing more than snow on the fir tree's
branch,

There is nothing to kiss with warm lips,
And all lips grow cool with time.

But you say, my child, that your heart is mighty,
And that to live in vain is less than to die.
What would you want of death? Do you know the
 repugnance his clothes spread,
And nothing is more loathsome than to die by your
 own hand.
We should love life's hours of sickness
And narrow years of longing
As the brief moments when the desert blooms.

Some critics have taken the poem as an imaginary conversation between a mother and a child at a lonely railroad station in Karelia where the "bluer sky" and "the wall with roses" are the travel posters on the station's walls and the rails—like those of the line through Raivola, as Ekelöf observed—run off into infinity, or nothingness. However, the mother and child—its replies can only be inferred—are simply the two voices of Södergran's constant internal dialogue (as in the poems where she speaks to a "sister" or "sisters"). At first the "speaking" voice seems to devalue existence, to turn it into nothing, whether existence be the bare realities of the station or the illusory pleasures of a land far away. Then the younger voice apparently retorts that it possesses emotions so mighty that death—suicide—would be preferable to enduring them in solitude. The experienced voice makes its reply: whatever life gives us should be cherished. "Nothing" is meant to speak against abandonment of the world, and it tells how to value life's pain in a far more persuasive fashion than in such apodictic poems as "Pain" itself.

The critical reception of *Dikter* was mixed; the claim that it was received "with indifference or ridicule" (made in the introduction to one of the English translations of Södergran's works) is incorrect. Some provincial reviewers made fun of what they took to be Södergran's casting of herself in the role of an Amazon or a much-desired "bright daughter of the forest," and they found some of her imagery incomprehensible or simply comical; but the major

Swedish-language newspapers and journals were enthusiastic or at least respectful. Erik Grotenfelt, himself a young writer of considerable stature, spoke of a "cause for rejoicing" and "a new direction we have not seen before," and the aesthetician Hans Ruin thought her strength lay in her "original imagination." The occasional unfriendly voices, though, sounded louder to Södergran than the favorable majority opinion, and on Christmas Night 1916 she wrote "Jungfruns död" ("The Death of the Maiden"), in which a fragile and perceptive girl simply vanishes, leaving her shoes behind in a field of lilies of the valley. Södergran appears to have stopped writing for a few months; perhaps perceiving that political upheaval was imminent, mother and daughter paid their last visit to St. Petersburg in March 1917, just after the abdication of Nicholas II, and in September they made their last trip to Helsinki.

The victory of the Bolsheviks in the October Revolution took place almost simultaneously with the calling of a general strike in Finland in which the tension between bourgeois and socialist elements led to political murder and to skirmishes between the former's Defense Corps and the latter's Red Guard. On 6 December 1917, the Finnish diet declared the former grand duchy's independence. This event unhappily led to a widening of the gap between the Right and Left; the bourgeois faction was particularly nervous about the presence of large numbers of Russian troops in the country (who, it was feared, would try to support the Finnish Left), and a militia was created, to be commanded by a former cavalry general in the tsarist army, C. G. Mannerheim. Meanwhile, radical socialist elements prepared a coup that was carried out at the end of January. A civil war began in which the White Army held central and northern Finland, while the Reds occupied the more industrialized south, including the major cities of Helsinki, Turku, and Viipuri. The Södergrans found themselves behind the Red lines, but although they were members of a privileged class and speakers of a minority language, they were not harmed during the months in which the Reds controlled Raivola; in late April 1918 the village was taken by White troops—fortuitously, by soldiers from Matts Södergran's home province of Ostrobothnia. Shortly thereafter the war ended with the surrender of the Red Guard and the flight of its leadership to Russia; the Whites—taking revenge for instances of Red terrorism—carried out mass executions of many Red prisoners, confining others to concentration camps.

The war and its aftermath brought about a new wave of poetic excitement, or even exaltation, in Södergran—stemming not so much from the White victory (although she and her mother soon realized that they had lost their fortune when the Bolsheviks came to power in St. Petersburg) as from her belief that she witnessed a watershed in world history. At the same time, her reading of Nietzsche led to a notion that she had been chosen to spread certain aspects of his teachings by means of her verse; she called September 1918 her holy month of inspiration, in imitation of Nietzsche's "holy January" of 1882, described in *Die fröhliche Wissenschaft* (*The Joyful Wisdom,* 1882). She wrote that she had "suddenly felt with unfailing certainty that a stronger hand had seized [my] pen." All the same, she permitted herself to include poetry composed in 1916, 1917, and the first months of 1918 in her next collection, *Septemberlyran* (The September Lyre), which she mailed to Schildt in October 1918, insisting that all the poems be dated so that her readers could see what had been done before her "rebirth" and what after. The manuscript—written on paper from an old school notebook—contained fifty-one poems. Of these, some were held over until her next book, *Rosenaltaret* (1919); others, including some of the most interesting, were omitted, remaining unpublished until they entered Diktonius's collection; while still others did not come out in print until Tideström published his critical edition in 1949. These omissions took place with Södergran's permission; she had told Runar Schildt to leave out whatever poems he thought "weaker" or liable to

"cause offense by their presumptuousness." (After he had done so, she complained bitterly about his choices.) She had also made the unusual request, which was impossible to fulfill, that the book be kept out of the hands of the provincial press and the "broad public." To be sure, she challenged her readers with her introductory statement to the little volume, which contained such statements as: "That my poetry is poesy, no one can deny: I will not assert that it is verse"; and "My self-assurance rests on the fact that I have discovered my dimensions. It is unfitting for me to make myself smaller than I am." Not content, she next sent an open letter to the newspaper *Dagens Press* (Daily Press) that was printed on 31 December 1918, in which she proclaimed that

> This book is not intended for the public, scarcely even for higher intellectual circles, but only for those few individuals standing closest to the boundary of the future. . . . What makes many of these poems precious is that they come from an individual of a new sort. . . . I sacrifice every atom of my strength to my lofty goal, I live the life of a saint, I lose myself in the highest productions of the human spirit, I avoid all influences of a baser kind. . . . I hope that I shall not be alone with the greatness I have to bring.

Sensing good copy, journalists were happy to attack the book; in a *causerie* in *Dagens Press,* the poems were called "thirty-one laughter pills," and in the country's largest Swedish-language paper, *Hufvudstadsbladet* (Capital City Paper), the columnist "Jumbo" wrote about "Nietzsche-crazed womenfolk." When the poet and painter Ragnar Ekelund came to Södergran's defense, praising her "ruthless honesty," "Jumbo" retorted that Södergran had perhaps been "infected with the intellectual disease that in the political arena is called Bolshevism." Södergran attracted other champions: in one of his last pieces of writing before he committed suicide, consumed by guilt at having participated in the courts-martial of Red prisoners, Grotenfelt praised her once again, concluding that her poetry was a spontaneous reaction to the events that had just shaken Finland; and a paid public announcement in *Hufvudstadsbladet,* signed by Runar Schildt and Mörne, among others, said that the undersigned wished "openly and without hesitation, to join the band of lunatics who perceive in Edith Södergran's poetry an artist's devoted striving." Hoping for greater newspaper sales, "Jumbo" asked a psychiatrist for an opinion on *Septemberlyran* but could get only guarded statements about "an unusual capacity for associative thought" and "a special realm of the imagination." Also, *Dagens Press* brought out a complete and balanced review of the book by a young woman named Hagar Olsson, who found "purity and elevation of soul" in it, although she chided the poet for having degraded herself and her art by the open letter to the press. Södergran began a correspondence with her reviewer, sending her some new poems together with the text of a second open letter to *Dagens Press,* which she asked Olsson to transmit to the paper's editors. Olsson advised against its publication, not least because it was extremely difficult to understand: it began with an episode from Nietzsche's *Also sprach Zarathustra* (*Thus Spoke Zarathustra,* 1883–1885) in which a young herdsman bites off the head of a snake that has crept into his mouth and laughs about the experience. Södergran identified herself with the herdsman: "With the support of Nietzsche's authority, I repeat that I am an individual of a new kind." Södergran persisted, and this letter too was published. Hoping to put an end to the long debate, Olsson wrote another article in which she argued that Södergran did not suffer from "individual megalomania" but rather viewed herself as "a mere instrument or medium" of a higher power—like Angelus Silesius, the German mystic of the baroque. Having found out about Södergran's physical condition, Olsson also alluded to the "earnestness of death" that was the poet's constant companion.

In her opening letter to Olsson, Södergran dismissed a good number of the poems in *Sep-temberlyran* as "belonging to a transitional stage" or as being simply "banal." Several of them could have readily found a place in the *Dikter;* more mood music is made, and the story of the unhappy love affair is repeated: in the poem "Upptäckt" ("Discovery") she says baldly, "Your hand is lust, / my hand is longing," and in "Vad är i morgon?" ("What is Tomorrow?") she uses especially "feminine" imagery (threads, yarn, dress) in her threats of dealing her lover a final humiliation: "I shall smile and twist silken threads around my finger. / And I'll hide your fate's little yarnball in the folds of my dress." Also, there are her reactions to what she perceived as the bad treatment the *Dikter* had received; in "Tjuren" ("The Bull") she pretends that her "character" is a tormenting red cloth, and in "Grimace d'artiste" she proclaims that she has nothing left but her "shining cloak" and her "red undauntedness" as she sets forth on a quest into "shabby lands." (Schildt did not include the poem in the printing, perhaps because he was aware of how irritating the word "red," too often employed, could be in post–civil war Finland.) Repeatedly, theatrical gestures of departure, of contemptuous abandonment of an unworthy audience, are made: "Grimace d'artiste" ends, "My rising pride takes the lyre beneath its arm / And bows farewell."

The poet's presentation of herself shifts; wistfulness gives way to exaltation, and the frail girl becomes the prophetess, albeit a prophetess terribly aware of her own mortality. The oldest poem in the collection, "Triumf att finnas till" ("Triumph of Existing"), written sometime in 1916, presages the development. It begins: "What do I fear? I am a part of infinity, / I am a part of the cosmos' great strength," and the poet, unafraid, will be nourished on Zarathustra's favorite food, honey. "A star of the first magnitude that is extinguished last," she—again like Zarathustra—will accept her eventual obliteration as a part of the natural order of things. "O mina solbrandsfärgade toppar" ("Oh My Sun-flame-colored Tops") is filled with a Nietzschean striving for the heights, an awareness of being elect, and a contempt for those below. The climax of the poem—written in the spring of 1918 but placed first in the book's printing—is, as so often with Södergran, a self-admonition: her "longing" and her "will" are urged onward and upward. Then a band of imaginary followers is summoned: "Rise up, bold warriors, / Light and merry as devils bearing arms!"—an allusion to Nietzsche's call for "deviltry" in order to bring about a general housecleaning of the world. By unhappy chance the line about the devils was printed with wide-spaced letters, and the designer of the book's jacket devised an imp as its logo, both calling unnecessary attention to the line and trivializing Nietzsche's concept, while Södergran had intended the poem, and the book as a whole, as a cry for radical if unspecified change.

For Södergran the change came, or appeared to come, to Finland with the civil war; "Världen babar i blod" ("The World Bathes in Blood") views war as the instrument of transformation: "The world bathes in blood so that God may live" and "God wishes to create afresh / . . . therefore he girds himself in a belt of lightning bolts . . . ." (Like Nietzsche, her *vade mecum,* Södergran had a gift for quasi-biblical turns of phrase.) Poems from the spring of 1918 try in various ways to deal with the conflict as it spread through Finland: "Stormen" ("The Storm"), for example, has been thought to depict the approach of the White Army under Mannerheim's leadership: "Where will he strike, / The man come from the heights." As so often in Södergran's poetry, such proclamatory verse is less fascinating than the poems of private experience: "Aftonvandring" ("Evening Promenade") stammers with excitement as the speaker announces that she is proof against sudden death:

Is there death for me, annihilation.—No.
Death is in Helsinki—he captures sparks on the
    roofs.
I walk across the square with my future in my hand.

The poem baffled Schildt, who left it out; ap-

parently Södergran is thinking here of the capture of Finland's capital by a German expeditionary force on 14 April 1918 and concludes that—bearing "all the time's golden stars on [her] dark velvet dress"—she is exempt from being snuffed out by violence, although less important human lives are extinguished as though by the spark catcher on a chimney. A related kind of selfish rejoicing can be found in "Månens hemlighet" ("The Moon's Secret"), about which Södergran confided to Olsson that it had "a sneaking desire for the smell of corpses." Olof Enckell wrote that it smacked of decadence. In its brevity it expresses neither horror nor satisfaction at the execution of Red prisoners, but rather an aesthetic appreciation:

The moon knows . . . that blood shall be shed here
    tonight.
On copper paths across the lake a certainty goes
    forth:
Corpses shall lie among the alders on a wondrously
    beautiful beach.
The moon shall cast its most beautiful light upon
    the strange beach.
The wind shall go forth as a reveille-horn through
    the firs.
How beautiful the earth is in this lonely hour.

Or, in "Visan från molnet" ("The Song from the Cloud"), which alludes to the Red stragglers who engaged in partisan warfare around Raivola ("Farewell, green forests of my youth. / Monsters lurk there"), the value lies not in the passing comment upon a detail of the realities of 1918, but in the special poetic vision. Once again the poet is on high, borne aloft by an eagle: "White, in sun that blinds, inaccessibly happy, waving farewell." Yet the behavior of the singer on the cloud is startling and humorous: "Down onto the earth drips quick-silver-mocking laughter— / Out of it grows tickle-grass and explosive flowers." Again, Schildt omitted the poem; he may have been put off by its technical puns. With the line "my day-light-sure intuitions, my flash-light-quick certainties," Södergran, an amateur photographer, thought of taking pictures by natural light and with flashbulbs; and as the daughter of Nobel's sometime engineer, she had some notion about explosives: "quick-silver-mocking laughter" refers to the "detonating quicksilver" commonly used in those days for explosives.

The playful visionary Södergran also is at work in "Landskap i solnedgång" ("Landscape in Sunset"). That which is "high"—sun and clouds—will transform and triumph over the "low," the earth. The poem begins with a procession of sunlit clouds:

> See in the sunset
> Swimming fire-islands proceeding
> Imperially over cream-green seas.
> Islands in flame! Islands like torches!
> Islands in victory procession!

Södergran suggests that the "islands" are ships in a naval engagement, attacked by a treacherous enemy:

> Up from the depths flashes black a forest,
> Crafty, envious . . .
> Poor strips of forest in pale mists
> Are seized, lifted up—join themselves to majesty.

Carefully she observes lighting effects: as the sun sinks, elements of the dark foe defect, joining the clouds in the sun's colors. The battle, described in terms straight from the pages of boys' adventure books or popular military history (with terms such as "proceeding imperially," "flashing" as of cannons, and "falling into line, triumph upon triumph"), is closed with another gesture of theatricality: "The day goes throning to its end . . . / Invisible hands cut off the threads of light."

The reader, aware that Södergran here renders a mock heroic painting of an heroic scene ("Gloria! Victory! / Kneel, lion-monsters, / In the worlds' dark corners"), smiles and at the same time is captivated by the grandeur of it all. In "Förhoppning" ("Hope"), another of the omitted poems, Södergran blends humor with grandeur as she speaks of her poetic calling. She becomes a baker, meaning to create one of

the architectonic wonders for which the St. Petersburg *confiseries* were famed:

> I wish to be unconstrained—
> Therefore I scorn noble styles.
> I roll up my sleeves.
> The poem's dough is fermenting . . .
> Oh, there's one worry—
> Not to be able to bake cathedrals . . .
> Loftiness of the forms—
> Persistent longing's goal.
> Child of the present—
> Does your spirit not have its proper crust?
> Before I die
> I'll bake a cathedral.

In the introduction to *Septemberlyran,* Södergran emphasizes the importance of relaxation in creation, of working with sleeves rolled up, unconstrained: "I let my instinct build up what my intellect, in an expectant attitude, observes." She expresses concern about her inability to join her gift for verbal and image association to the complexity of structure and elevation of tone she believes are necessary for the great poetic edifice. Here, she jokes about the problem: a cathedral of pastry would be the object of "constant longing" for any child with its nose pressed against a tea-room window— not just for herself, the "child of the present."

The *Septemberlyran* poems themselves—of which eighteen were written in that month— are all attempts at "noble styles." This group, of which she was so proud, sustains an unrelieved elevation of tone (often emphasized by an artificial or even tortured syntax) that Södergran deemed suitable, or even necessary, for the importance of her message: she orders the whole of mankind to follow Zarathustra's way ("Mankind, / Do not collect gold or jewels . . . / Give your children a beauty human eyes have not seen"), and she demands that it give its children "a strength to break open heaven's gates" in a quest for "the power of kings." To be sure, the poems praise lightness and grace— requirements readily connected with Nietzsche's admiration of the dance and his demand for a "gaiety of the spirit": the goddess in "Gryningen" ("The Dawn"), for all her self-proclaimed mercilessness in the making of a new world (a world never clearly defined), says that her winds must run "lightly, lightly over the sea"; and the suppliant of "Den skönaste guden" ("The Fairest God") offers a heart "light as a bird" to the deity in order that she may be carried aloft to meet him. The "god" or "God" approached in these poems, the pretentiousness of which often contravenes their demands for grace, is not in fact a deity of any formal religion but simply the poet's own calling, which has to be substantiated again and again. If the poet believes in this calling, in the ability to ascend to the heights, then she is safe; in "Sorglöshet" ("Lightheartedness") she echoes Psalm 23: "If I am his true child—naught can befall me."

A keen commentator on Finland's culture, Johannes Salminen, has observed that in the revolutionary poet Södergran there runs a strong current of traditionalism or even epigonalism: the time-honored symbol of the poetic vocation, the lyre, is used five times in the September poems, and it appears twice elsewhere in the collection, as well as in its title. At her German school Södergran had been introduced to the literature of German idealism: like Friedrich Gottlieb Klopstock, Friedrich von Schiller, and Friedrich Hölderlin, she readily assumed the attitude of a *vates* (inspired prophetic bard) in the belief that her gift must be employed for the edification of humanity:

> Where then is the lyre
> Of silver and ivory
> The gods once lent
> To the mortals' race?

In "Revanche" ("Revenge") she claims that with her lyre the poet will "sing down the stars from the sky"; and in "Villkoret" ("The Stipulation"), it is argued that the poet must have not only a calling but also a cause:

> Though for me the lyre is the earth's loftiest thing,
> If I stayed true to it [alone],
> I should not set a soul aflame.

Outcries of self-questioning ("If I am a liar—may accursed spirits bury my lyre / In rotting sulphur pools") are mingled with self-praise: in "Min lyra" ("My Lyre") she announces that she will cast herself "lightheartedly" onto the strings of her "blessed giant lyre, / . . . strung with sun, fairy-tale-like, hanging from the clouds." Does the splendor of these visions make up for the almost obsessive monotony of their theme and language? A contemporary poet from Finland, Tua Försstrom, has expressed her skepticism both about the often abstract rhetoric and about the patent contempt for humankind expressed by "Nietzsche's first child in tears of gladness," Södergran's term for herself in "Vid Nietzsches grav" ("At Nietzsche's Grave"), which she regarded as the capstone of her September poems.

The inordinacy of her diction seems wholly appropriate for the long poem "Fragment" ("Fragment"), which closed the original printing of *Septemberlyran*: it is one of the great visionary poems from the north. "Fragment" opens with memories of the St. Petersburg of her childhood and youth ("Petersburg, Petersburg / From your battlements flutters my childhood's enchanted banner"), in the time before "the deep wounds, before the mighty scars." Then it passes on to a dream of the new Finland's capital—or of Suomenlinna (Sveaborg), the great fortress at the entrance of Helsinki's harbor that had become the new nation's symbol:

> In Helsinki, does our marvelous citadel not rise out
>   of the sea?
> Do not sentries stand there, with red and blue
>   banners the world has not seen?
> Do they not stand, leaning on their spears, looking
>   out over the sea
> With the granite of fate in their features of stone?

Next, the scene moves to the Engadine, to Switzerland's Alps, where "Zarathustra waits for chosen guests." The Swiss idyll is destroyed by the tempest, and the old peasant farms are amazed but accept the storm:

Whence does this beauty come to us? . . .
Beauty's restless, demanding, greedy spirit . . .
Tearing down our flowers of many colors. Smashing
　　the window pane where the geraniums stand.
No longer do idyllic paths lead to homes that have
　　lasted hundreds of years.

In their long speech the farms—another of Södergran's speaking objects—assume the role of the whole of humanity, ready to accept the change and die: " 'Perishing, we bless you, incomprehensible night of stars.' " The poem ends with a prediction that in the great storm's aftermath mankind will be united with the cosmos: "Stream through us, eternal winds, / Heaven's honey, blessing of the whole!"

It was Edith Södergran's good fortune that her tormentors in the press did not try to squeeze a political interpretation out of her mighty winds of change, for what she proclaimed was the Nietzsche-inspired "festival of beauty," the festival of Dionysian exaltation that had been the aim of German poets and artists some twenty years earlier—see, for example, the "festivals of beauty" announced by Harald Malcorn, the central figure in Rainer Maria Rilke's partly autobiographical *Die Letzten* (*The Last Ones,* 1900) or the manifesto of Peter Behrens, *Feste des Lebens und der Kunst* (*Festival of Life and of Art,* 1900). Again, the presence of a cultural time lag in Södergran cannot be denied; but the intensity of her expression is such that it can dazzle even the most historically minded of literary critics, and the grandeur is leavened, as so often in her best work, by childlike playfulness. Beauty has lain dead a thousand years, in a glass coffin like Snow White's; Lilliputian humanity has "wandered along the bridge of her nose" and has "trampled on her eyelids."

Only four months after *Septemberlyran* appeared Södergran completed her next book, *Rosenaltaret,* a second presentation of her message about a beauty that will somehow redeem the world. It is doubtful that she would have finished it so quickly and confidently had it not been for the encouragement Olsson's friendship gave her. Yet after her friend's death, Olsson expressed only a tepid liking for the book, apart from a section that flattered her: "Save for the beautifully lyrical 'Fantastique,' it did not have much to offer that was new." Olsson was right about the resumption of an already familiar theme; in the book's first part the exhortations continue, and the tone becomes more strident. The poet's voice is now completely that of the priestess, "guarding the future's fire" and bringing "not Christ's dwindling empire" but a religion whose altar is crowned with "a mountain of roses," the most beautiful of flowers. She tries to make converts; "strong people" are told to follow "the stars' unwritten laws," and "human beings" are told to bow down "before the gods." In "Det fasansfulla tåget" ("The Terrible Procession"), a strange anthem for her new army of Dionysian fighters for beauty, the marchers are ordered to be of good cheer:

Bravery is the highest thing . . .
God's realm stands on our strong side.
Unfurl the redness of your heart.

The last of these lines, so easily misinterpreted, is probably, again, what caused Schildt to leave the poem out of the collection; but *Rosenaltaret* contained more than enough other (and less dangerously colored) announcements of what she wanted: she promises to kindle her torches in the Alps and on the tundras, saying, "Without beauty, mankind cannot live for a second."

In her isolation the priestess can be assailed by doubts ("My feebler hands grasp the cup of suffering / And lift it to paler lips") and by an enormous sense of longing. Seven poems in the first, proclamatory section of *Rosenaltaret* have "heart" as their central word, replacing the lyre. This heart has to find its own identity, and the quest has been an overwhelmingly long one:

On foot
I had to walk through the solar systems

Before I found the first thread of my red attire.
I already have a sense of myself.
Somewhere in space my heart hangs,
Sparks fly from it, shaking the air,
To other boundless hearts.

This untitled poem does more than merely suggest the enormous difficulty of a trek through space (on foot!). The poet seeks the crimson garment that is so often a sign of poetic election for Södergran, and she also seeks the comradeship of kindred spirits. Other "heart" poems try to explore the requirements and hardships placed upon the poet-priestess. In "my heart" there dwell "giants with dark countenances" who someday will step forth and summon pain, the giver of poetic inspiration ("Lidandets kalk" ["The Chalice of Suffering"]); and the "heart," in order to endure the rigors of the sublime calling, must be of stone ("This hardness is necessary for every mountain climber," Nietzsche's Zarathustra says), yet the hardness must simultaneously be overcome—a hammer must be brought to "hew out my soul, / So that she may find words that have never lain upon the tongue of man."

In her imagination the poet may turn herself into a martyr of her cause, as in "Martyren" ("The Martyr"), which closes the first section of *Rosenaltaret:* "Lightly he takes on his shoulders / The victim's many-colored coat." This description of an *auto-da-fé* was written when the newspaper campaign against *Septemberlyran* was at its height. Or the poet may bear the mark of Cain: in "Särtecknet" ("The Special Mark") in *Septemberlyran* she had had a "blackish-red mark" upon her dress to distinguish her, even as she had had "golden stars" on her dress in "Evening Promenade"; now—in "Verktygets klagan" ("The Tool's Lament")—the mark is on her forehead:

> Oh, to be the richest one!
> To have it written on your forehead
> To play fate's strange game
> At necessity's behest.

And the "chosen one," the owner of the mighty heart, also bears another sign, the rose; if the heart is the birthplace of poetry, the rose is beauty itself. The matter is stated at length in the programmatic "Skönhetens stod" ("The Statue of Beauty"): "When shall I arise, light as a feather, / To fetch the rose, the single one that never dies." All the doubts about her aesthetic religion are dispelled in the finale of *Rosenaltaret,* "Rosor" ("Roses"):

> The world is mine.
> Wherever I go,
> I cast roses to all.
> The artist loves each marble ear that understands
>   his words.

Rosenaltaret also has a more personal side, "Fantastique," the poems addressed to her critical champion Olsson. The tone of the "sister-cycle" is not so far removed from that of the schoolgirl verse to Paula and Claudia: in "Spring Mystery," the very presence of the beloved gives nature a special enchantment ("the violets in the shadow smell of delicious fulfillment"), and secrets will be exchanged in "the most delicious corner" of the forest. As in the case of the man from Terijoki, a love story is told, although the means of expression are less subtle: "My sister . . . / Has she betrayed me?" (The melodramatic answer is risible: "No, a thousand times no. . . .") Södergran grew frantic at the thought of what her friend might be up to in the capital (Olsson was engaged to the author Eklund at the time), and some hard questions are put to the distant object of her affection: "What dreams of lust can you dream / On tired beds?" Still, however flawed the cycle is by its exaggerations ("Are the gods playing thus with us?") and by its frequent banalities (the white silken dress of the beloved, left behind, is asked: "Do you remember her rosy limbs?"), it is invaluable for an understanding of Södergran's personality—the emotional excesses (which could also give rise to great poetry) and the possessiveness that made Södergran try to transform her friend into a mirror image of herself, both in the appearance she ascribes to Olsson (she becomes the fairy-tale princess that Södergran herself had been in the *Dikter*) and in her attempt to shape Olsson's thought. In "Syster, min syster" ("Sister, My Sister"), which Södergran held back from publication, she mocks Olsson for her new-found Christian enthusiasms: "When you saw God, you drew away from human beings."

In the strength of its passion, "Fantastique" is related to the handful of poems that form the last section of the book—except for the coda, "Roses." They present other comments on Södergran's isolation: "Dionysos" provides the key to the Ariadne patterns discerned in the *Dikter* (as the "supplicant woman" clambers up into the chariot of the god), "Fragment av on stämning" ("Fragment of a Mood") is a lament for the "son of the highlands," the late Dr. von Muralt; "Offrets timme" ("The Hour of the Sacrifice") is a bitter attack on the renegade from the cause of beauty, Olsson ("In your hand the rose is dead, / The wind does not touch your cheek"); and "Scherzo" once again enters the realm of visionary playfulness in which the poet is happiest and most at home— it tells about a dream of dancing on a tightrope of stars, stretched out across space. The dancer sits on the rope, exhausted after her performance—or the perilous creation of art. The threatening abyss below her is time itself, into which she may fall and be swallowed up; this is a "danger for tiring dancer's feet," a "danger for weakening climber's arms." Then she is encouraged to continue by a toast she receives from "the sea-king" (the sea of space); it is not clear whether the king or the dancer herself utters the injunctions with which the poem ends: the audience of the performance is told not to move.

> But let the dancer go
> Forth on midnight toes
> And fall on her knees and stretch out her arms
> And kiss the fair one.

Thus the dancer is encouraged to resume the difficult and dangerous task of poetic creation;

another Nietzschean metaphor, that of the poet as tightrope walker, is discernible here.

Little attention was paid to *Rosenaltaret* in Finland's press; the public had grown tired of the Södergran sensation. Meanwhile Södergran was at work on new poems that, she wrote to Olsson, she found "boring and with the color of action; they're almost all concerned with planets and stars." These poems, under the subtitle "Planeterna stiga" ("The Planets Ascend"), constitute the first part of *Framtidens skugga* (The Shadow of the Future, 1920), a manuscript of which she sent to Schildt in November 1919. (At the same time she included a sheaf of aphorisms; unimaginatively dubbed *Brokiga iakttagelser* [Manifold Observations] by the publisher, they were published separately at Christmas 1919. Mostly platitudinous, they contain much admiration for "great men" and emphasize "Life's three great gifts, poverty, loneliness, and suffering.") The book of poems was held back by Schildt until November 1920, when they came out in an augmented form. The first version had closed with the deeply pessimistic poems "Materialism" and "Hamlet"; but sometime early in 1920, Södergran wrote the eight poems that became the book's finale, and in them she espoused a more tranquil view of her fate. She had discovered a new spiritual counselor, the Austrian anthroposophist Rudolf Steiner, to whose works she had been introduced by a retired schoolteacher living in Raivola. Steiner taught her to embrace the Goethean concept of death as a natural part of the great chain of being (*Stirb und werde*, meaning "Die and become"), and he also demanded of her (so she thought) that she have an "absolutely healthy spiritual life" in which discipline of her emotions would play a very large part, a cure very difficult and even stultifying for Södergran, with her leaning toward brilliantly illogical associations of words, moods, and images.

Initially *Framtidens skugga* repeats much that *Rosenaltaret* says, but still more aggressively and shrilly. In "Skaparegestalter" ("Figures of Creation"), as the planets ascend, a "band of riders on loose saddles"—recalling the "blessed rider on the purple saddle" in *Thus Spoke Zarathustra*—are told what to do:

> Force, force
> The son of mankind,
> Form, form
> Mankind's huge mass into a joy for the gods.

In the misleadingly titled "Tolerans" ("Tolerance"), a "star with a redder shine" will drive its fellows out of the way, and a hand, following its own law, "will topple what others preserve, / A victor approaches, inaudible lips pronounce the forcer's name." The message of "Makt" ("Power") is unmistakable:

> I am the strength that commands . . .
> I follow no law.
> I am a law unto myself.
> I am the being that takes.

As usual the bald proclamations of arrogant strength—recalling Södergran's admiration for Napoleon—are coupled with niggling worries about whether or not the poet has indeed been chosen mercilessly to transform the world. At the end of the suite all doubts are put aside; in "Planeterna" ("The Planets") the pitiless sword—the favorite word now, replacing "lyre" and "heart"—is changed into pitiless planets, roving through space, "Swifter, bolder, more merciless." Almost sinister implications lie in these lyrics; they inevitably conjure up thoughts of the ruthless leaders about to appear in postwar Europe, proclaiming their right to "force" mankind in accordance with their own concept of a "new world." Had Södergran lived, her reaction to Mussolini, Hitler, or Stalin would have demanded close attention. But her proclamations are of course both innocent and pathetic, made by a young woman impoverished and mortally ill, writing in a small language—a minority language in her own nation—in an obscure corner of northern Europe.

The middle section, called "Framtidens skugga" like the book itself, implies that the shadow is but a first sign of the bliss that will someday fall to mankind's lot; but the title may also have an ominous secondary note. Writing to Olsson in the summer of 1919, Södergran alluded to the title of her work in progress and then added, after complaining that she had not received a letter from her beloved: "I suffer quietly cruelly intensely." The urgency of her outcry is emphasized by the omission of commas. A poem bearing the same name as the section and the book announces bravely that the speaker will accept a death in ecstasy, transfixed by the sun ("bored through by light I shall die"—a patently sexual image); drawing upon Zarathustra's thoughts about his own passing, like "a star, ready and mature at its zenith, glowing, pierced, blessed by destructive arrows of the sun," she writes more and more feverishly about her own blissful love-death: in "Solen" ("The Sun") she says, "The sun has kissed me, / . . . someday I shall spin myself into the sun like a fly in amber"; and in "Sällhet" ("Bliss") she again describes her death in terms of physical pleasure: "For very bliss I shall bite into my shroud, / My foot will curl with bliss in my white shoes" (Amid white veils and red roses, she is laid out on her bier in funereal attire). The celebration of Eros as a means of making death acceptable leads to a hymn to eroticism itself, "Du store Eros" ("Thou Great Eros"); now eroticism was no longer the degrading force it had been in the *Dikter*, but was a sustaining factor for the sick woman: "This lightning bolt is all-powerful, / The lightning does what it will with the children of man." (In the despairing letter to Olsson of July 1919, she spoke of her fear that she could no longer write; in August, though, she felt a return of creative power, saying that she had been filled with "an almost unendurable electricity . . . as if I lay in the arms of Eros himself the whole time.") Briefly she thought of giving her new collection another and franker title, "Köttets mysterier" (Mysteries of the

Flesh), which hints at the autoeroticism she now associated with the ability to write.

The third part of *Framtidens skugga* opens with and bears the title of a long poem, "Alv-drottningens spira" ("The Elf-Queen's Wand"), a piece of unconscious pornography and surely the most bizarre of Södergran's erotic poems. A dead girl is stimulated by a male figure, whom she instructs in what to do:

> Your tears will fall between my feet,
> They will trickle between my knees,
> As though they should cause an awakening unto
> life.

Tears are a surrogate for semen. The lover is also told to undress her, his hand wet with tears: "You disrobe me, / The silk falls from my shoulders." In this retelling of the story of Snow White, the man's protracted efforts are in vain; abruptly, another way to bring the talkative dead girl to life materializes. A "blue tower" appears in the lover's garden; elves dance around it, and the elf queen stands on its battlements. These little beings (who are female, for the queen's command is "Girls, hurry!") reproach the male lover for having abandoned his efforts to rouse his "bride," and the elf queen summons a cat named Elektrus to "purr" the dead girl back to life—an attempt at which the cat seems to succeed. In the erotic poems that follow the poet speaks of being grasped "by electric hands" and of being seized by "a thundering waterfall of pleasure." These experiences in turn give her a new message to proclaim—the joys of her own body, which give rise to poetry:

> As long as this fragile thing lives,
> You shall feel its might.
> I shall save the world.
> Therefore the blood of Eros rushes in my lips.

She describes "ecstasy" in terms that clearly combine the moment of poetic inspiration with a sexual experience: "Through my lips streams the heat of a god, / All my atoms are parted and are afire. . . ."

Looking back, Hagar Olsson thought that these fits of self-induced ecstasy had been more than her friend could bear, and they are in fact followed by "Materialism" and "Hamlet," which bespeak horror of death and disgust at life itself. The former poem speaks bluntly: "I am a chemical mass. I know [it] so well, / I do not believe in illusion and soul." A brief thought of playing "the game of games"—subscribing to the Christian message of an afterlife ("Game of games, you taste good, you have a wonderful aroma")—is abandoned: "There is no soul and never has been a soul. / It is illusion, illusion, illusion and a mere game." The awful plainness of the language and the scorn in the last line's repetition bear witness to the latest crisis Södergran had entered. "Hamlet," then, is based on the passage at the opening of *Die Geburt der Tragödie* (*The Birth of Tragedy*, 1872), in which Nietzsche compares the "Dionysian man" to Shakespeare's Dane; both have "understood and are sickened by action . . . [and] now the human being perceives everywhere the horror and absurdity of existence." Södergran begins the poem with a farewell to life, by no means as theatrical as in some of the earlier poems of departure: "My mortal heart wishes nothing. / Here lies the whole earth. You turn away revulsed." As elsewhere in her poems, Södergran, haranguing herself, switches from one mode of address to another: an implied third person ("my mortal heart") becomes a second person ("you"), and then a first person, "I." Thinking of Hamlet's soliloquy and of the "undiscover'd country," she continues:

> There is no choice for me,
> Truth, I follow you into the land of mists.
> Truth, truth, do you dwell there in a mortuary amidst
> snakes and dust?

Hamlet has a choice, to decide whether or not to continue his life; Södergran, doomed, does not, and soon the "truth" of death ("truth" is repeated five times in the poem) will overtake her. She still sees death as final—the decay of the flesh, and no more: "Truth, do you dwell there, where there is everything I detest?" Nevertheless, "Hamlet" does not end with flat statements, as in the case of "Materialism"; instead, it concludes with questions: "Truth, do sorrowful lanterns light your way?"

After writing "Hamlet," Södergran read Olsson's lyrical and biblical novel *Kvinnan och nåden* (The Woman and Grace, 1919), with its message of life emerging from death: "When some day the night is past, new hearts shall arise from our graves . . . . Like flowers they shall sprout on the pile of dust we have left behind." She connected this message with the "healthy mysticism" of Goethe's *Stirb und werde.* Telling Olsson that when she had finished the book there was "such an aroma within [her] of hyacinths, lilies of the valley, and young birch leaves," she responded with "Hyacinten" ("The Hyacinth"), which describes how, in the midst of withered brown blossoms from the year past, the new blooms come: "I am a hyacinth, a hyacinth that cannot die." Thus she found a comforting new way to deal with the thought of death, alongside her ideas about the sun-marriage and the electric hour: "I am triumphant as life itself," she wrote in "Fyra små dikter" ("Four Small Poems"). She believed that if she was to become the hyacinth or the bride of the sun, she must do away with her sense of individual worth, Nietzsche's *principium individuationis.* In "Animalisk hymn" ("Animalian Hymn"), her favorite pronoun, "I," does not appear: "The red sun . . . is alike toward all. / We rejoice in the sun like children."

On 9 March 1920, about two months before Södergran sent the eight hopeful poems to Schildt, she wrote to Olsson that in consequence of the "limitless devotion" that had suddenly erupted within her, she would "abandon everything, art too, because it is unholy." One of these eight poems, "Beslut" ("Decision"), says much the same thing: "You will never write poetry again." The artist's spirit has entered a higher and uncommunicative realm,

and in "Blixtens trängtan" ("The Lightning's Pining") she continues the transformation:

I am eagle.
That is my confession.
Not a poet
. . . for me there is naught else than circling in the eagle's flight.

(Both "Decision" and "The Lightning's Pining" echo Zarathustra's "Das Lied der Schwermut" ["Song of Melancholy"] about the futility of the poet's calling: "*Only* a fool! *Only* a poet!") The urge to create and to communicate died hard; in "Den stora trädgården" ("The Great Garden") Södergran dreams once more about gathering her "siblings" around her: "From our silent garden / We shall give the world a new life." A month later she called her garden poem "antiquated," and added once again that she believed her career as a poet was over. The last poem in *Framtidens skugga,* "Stjärnan" ("The Star"), would seem to bear her out: "Where shall I get the heavy hand that grasps the sword?" the speaker asks the star, which replies: "That which is your own, that which is your own will give you the power." But by November of 1920, Södergran looked for strength outside herself: "Grace exists only in the Gospels . . . I have no words for how I love Christ." The anti-Christian and Nietzschean Södergran had suddenly been converted, by her own reading in the New Testament, to a belief in salvation by Jesus.

During 1921 and 1922 Södergran's life became steadily emptier: to make ends meet, mother and daughter moved out of their villa into a drafty summer house; Olsson made very few appearances (she feared tubercular infection); *Framtidens skugga* got a cold critical reception; and Schildt forgot to send the author's small fee. Some of the family's lace was sold, and whenever her health allowed, Södergran made pin money by taking pictures of soldiers from the Raivola detachment with their fiancées. Perhaps the brightest spot in these years was a visit in March 1922 from young

Diktonius, who wrote the first of his several tributes to Södergran for a new little magazine called *Ultra:* "In a little hovel beside a wood Russian church in the Karelian borderland there lives a young woman. With a little, red-cheeked lady who is her mother, and a black dog who is her friend." In Raivola, Diktonius and Södergran discussed a new and unselfish project: she was at work on a volume of German translations of contemporary poetry from Swedish Finland (and also a German rendering of Olsson's *The Woman and Grace*). She attempted to find a German publisher for it but did not succeed, although she was quite willing to underwrite the printing with five thousand marks she had received from Finland's Swedish Author's Union. Most of the manuscript was burned sometime during the last winter of her life; her mother recalled that "she took the [notebooks] and placed them in the fire. She sacrificed them to God."

Södergran contributed to the bilingual *Ultra,* where Olsson was the Swedish-language editor, but her entries were few: translations of two Russian poems (by Igor Severyanin) and one from the French (by Edmond Fleg), some aphorisms on nature, and, most important, four original poems: "Zigenerskan" ("The Gypsy Woman"), "Min barndoms träd" ("My Childhood's Trees"), "Hemkomst" ("Homecoming"), and "Månen" ("The Moon"). They are in a simple style quite unlike that of the collections built around Nietzsche's texts. Eventually Diktonius included them, together with six other poems presumably from Södergran's last year, in *Landet som icke är.* Actually "The Gypsy Woman" belonged to an earlier creative period, although it presaged Södergran's final style; its manuscript is dated February 1920, which would place its composition directly prior to Södergran's decision to "abandon art, too, for it is unholy." Perhaps Södergran decided to leave it out of *Framtidens skugga* because she thought its tenor was not lofty enough or because the poem's message— to continue in the calling, either the gypsy woman's of fortune-telling or the poet's of liter-

ary creation—contradicted her own desire to give up literature: in it she writes, "These heedless hands will do their task in the gloomily fire-flame-colored night." The publication of "The Gypsy Woman" was one more sign of her decision to resume literary creation. And as an early critic, Erik Kihlman, remarked, it returned in its color and naturalness to the *Dikter* of 1916, even though it contained one remnant from the long Nietzschean period, the thought of being elect: "There is but one such pair of hands in all the world."

Several other "new" or "late" poems (in *Ultra* and *Landet som icke är*) address Södergran's return from her long excursion to the heights and into the cosmos. In "My Childhood's Trees" the poet is reproached by the forest of Raivola:

What has become of you . . . ?
When you were a child, you carried on long talks
 with us,
Your glance was wise.

They tell her how to understand her life: "The key to all secrets lies in the grass on the raspberry hill"—a hill that, visitors to Raivola observed, lay close to the fence of the little community's church cemetery. The trees may suggest that the poet accepts the truth already stated in "The Hyacinth," that the passage from life into death is an inevitable part of nature's plan. "Homecoming" is at once less scolding and brighter: the trees and the grass welcome the prodigal, and she tells them: "Now I turn my back on everything that lies behind me: / My only companions become the woods and the beach and the lake." The word "now"—an indication of the immediacy of the change— occurs in five lines, among them: "Now I drink wisdom from the sap-filled crown of the firs," and "Now I drink power from the smallest and frailest of grass-blades." Nature has become her protector, and nature in its turn is under the protection of God—as Södergran had said in her recent aphorisms.

Rediscovering nature, Södergran had also rediscovered Holy Scripture. "The truth exists only in the New Testament, and nowhere else in the world," she wrote to Olsson on 24 May 1921, noting that she had just looked at 2 Corinthians on "God's surpassing clarity." This biblical verse became the theme of "O himmelska klarhet" ("Oh Heavenly Clarity") from September 1922. "God is hidden in the smallest flower, / And the very things proclaim his name"; and the "heart of man" does not know how close it dwells to the Father in nature—although children, to be sure, speaking "the language of the creation," have known it. "Novembermorgon" ("November Morning") emphasizes simplicity of spirit once again; this time the beach, the "water's edge," speaks:

See, here you have walked as a child . . .
And I am forever the same . . .
Say, where have you wandered in foreign lands
Learning your bungler's habits?

God—"who has made the scales fall from your eyes"—should be praised, and, more surprisingly, books should be burned, a patent reference to Nietzsche:

Now the fir and the heather are your teachers.
Bring the false prophets hither, the books that lie,
In the dell by the water we'll light a merrily
    flickering pyre.

The solution is as drastic—almost comically drastic—as that of "My Childhood's Trees," in which the trees threaten to strike the girl, whose spirit is asleep, on her forehead, and it helps to give the poem an unmistakably Södergranian tone, naive and playful in its earnestness. The new canon of simplicity and happiness is rounded off by a poem that lacks a title, telling somewhat saccharinely about God as the only being in the world that "has time"—time to answer the prayers of flowers, ants, and bees, and time to observe the little old woman who meets her cat by the well. The Almighty had "brought them together / And wished them this wonderful friendship for fourteen years."

An additional strophe to the poem exists, which begins by describing a redstart that God helps to escape from the cat's claws. This last strophe was for some reason omitted by Diktonius from the first printing in *Landet som icke är*, but Tideström included it in his standard edition of 1949. After the redstart's precipitous flight "from the ash tree by the well," there are four more lines:

But in a dark dream a little worm saw
That the moon-sickle cut its being into two parts:
The one was nothing,
The other was everything and God Himself.

The worm (or Job's "son of man, that is a worm"?) is aware that, even though the redstart has escaped, death will someday come, dividing it into a "chemical mass" and a soul—God's emanation and so a part of God, immortal. The certainty of her own death bore in more and more closely on Södergran. In the ballad-like "Kyrkogårdsfantasi" ("Churchyard Phantasy"), a woman, her child in her arms, hurries to join her dead husband, who calls to her from the cemetery; in the much more convincing "The Moon," an attempt is made to beautify death, even while recognizing the terror it brings. Death will come as surely as the moon does; all the flowers know "a secret"—that "the moon's circling around our earth / Is the path of death" and that "the moon spins its fairytale net / Around all our lives." In her "Tankar om naturen" ("Thoughts on Nature"), Södergran wrote about the "dying children of nature" who "love death" and long for it; in this poem the moon's sickle, the sickle that had cut the worm in two, "cuts down flowers in nights of late autumn," and "all flowers wait for the moon's kiss in endless longing." Death has been romanticized, made palatable once more.

Olsson wrote that "The Moon," "Landet som icke är" ("The Land That Is Not"), and "Ankomst i Hades" ("Arrival in Hades") are the deathbed poems, over which "the shadow of her passing lies." The connection of "The Moon" to "The Land That Is Not" is readily evident; in the latter,

> The moon tells me in silver runes
> About the land that is not,
> The land where all our wishing is fulfilled,
> The land where all our chains fall,
> The land where we cool our bloodied forehead
> In the moon's dew.

This first strophe, with its hints of church hymns about the glories of the afterlife, can be taken as a statement of the acceptance of these helpful beliefs; yet it can also be read as an ironic catalogue of the promises of the land that is not. The second strophe has caused much argument about the identity of the "beloved" who "walks there with a glittering crown." Olsson was quite sure it was Christ himself, Olof Lagercrantz suggested it was death as a bringer of release from suffering, Kihlman thought it was "love itself, forever sought," and a Danish critic, Finn Stein Larsen, proposed that it might be the embodiment of the "power of poetic creation," calling attention to the answer sent out to the "child of man" in the poem's last line: "And an answer came: I am the one you love and forever will love." Larsen's proposal, that the ultimate object of Södergran's love was poetry itself, may be supported by the evidence of "Scherzo" cited above: there the poet walks the tightrope of creation in the presence of the "sea-king," "the fair one." All these commentators overlook the negating effect of the refrain line in the poem; the beloved dwells in "the land that is not."

"Arrival in Hades" was written shortly before Södergran died and may be a return to her beginnings; it has extremely simple and regular prosody and occasional rhymes, reminiscent of the style she used in the earliest *Dikter*, while the imagery likewise suggests the German turn of the century and its most popular painter, Arnold Böcklin, who painted *Self Portrait* (1872) and *The Isle of the Dead* (1886):

> See, here is the shore of eternity,
> And here the stream rushes along,

> And death plays in the bushes
> His same and monotonous song.

The spokeswoman of a band of the dead at the edge of an unnamed Styx continues, "We are come from far away," and wonders why death's song has fallen silent; having heard it from childhood, she longs for even it to resume. A final and quite empty consolation, she tells it what it will show her in its realm, those wonders she knows have existed only in her poetic imagination:

> The wreath which never adorned my forehead
> I silently put at your foot.
> You shall show me a wondrous land
> Where high the palmtrees grow,
> And where among rows of columns
> The waves of longing go.

Olsson left Finland in March 1923 and was on the Riviera when she learned about Edith's passing from Helena Södergran: she had died on 24 June, Midsummer's Day. A farewell to her distant friend was scribbled on the inside of a notebook cover: "Have you forgotten me Hagar aren't we bound together in life and death Out of my [heart?] there ascends a spring of reverence [,] in my moment of purity I call upon you Lord [for] my dearest child in the loveliest of the pure moments I remember Hagar." She was buried in the cemetery of the Russian church; her grave—the Author's Union had had a monument by Wäinö Aaltonen placed there on the tenth anniversary of her death—disappeared during the Winter War (1939–1940).

Because of the air of tragic loneliness surrounding her, Södergran has become the object of a cult; poems, plays, and novels have been written about her fate. Of the poets to come out of Finland, she—next to Runeberg, the patriotic bard—has had far and away the largest impact on the rest of Scandinavia. Outside the north she has slowly become known: there are two more or less complete translations of her verse into English, as well as two books of selections, and there are two translations of her collected works into French, one into German, and one into Russian. Certain elements in her production have made her, understandably, a favorite of feminist critics (and of feminist propagandists); and others have claimed her on much less solid grounds: the Soviet Union has celebrated her as a voice in that nation's multilingual poetic chorus, and although she was never in her father's home province, the local patriotism of Swedish-speaking Ostrobothnians has led to the formation of an Edith Södergran Society. To literary historians she reveals a good number of derivative qualities—as has been shown, from German verse of the turn of the century, from Nietzsche, and (a matter much debated but still little explored) from the Russian poets of the so-called Silver Age and beyond: Konstantin Balmont, Alexander Blok, Valery Bryusov, and Severyanin. Nonetheless, she has a special originality, an unmistakable tone: in her constant awareness of her doom, in her fey humor (she particularly admired Severyanin's "frivolity"), in her visionary flights, and in her sometimes gauche frankness about herself. Her special mark, perhaps, is the sheer intensity of her oeuvre; there are clumsy poems, turgid poems, purely sentimental poems, but nothing that is the product of indifference, nothing that is a mere exercise. How she would rank if she had written in a major language cannot be determined; important as her liberating example once was for the technically backward lyric of Scandinavia (in her abandonment of regular rhythm, for example), her "innovations" hardly seem remarkable if measured against the chronological development of, say, English, French, or German literature. Had she continued writing in German, she might well occupy a position as the owner of a singular but not particularly flexible voice, something like that of Else Lasker-Schüler. (Södergran knew Lasker-Schüler's earlier poetry and found it "celestially splendid.") Or maybe, as Ekelöf wrote, she is in truth "a very great poet" who overcame the relative narrowness of her thematology by her emotional strength and by her ability to express that strength in unforgettable formulations.

Selected Bibliography

EDITIONS

INDIVIDUAL WORKS
Dikter. Helsinki, 1916.
Septemberlyran. Helsinki, 1918.
Brokiga iakttagelser. Helsinki, 1919.
Rosenaltaret. Helsinki, 1919.
Framtidens skugga. Helsinki, 1920.
Landet som icke är. Helsinki, 1925.

COLLECTED WORKS
Samlade dikter. Edited by Gunnar Tideström. Stockholm, 1949.
Edith Södergrans dikter 1907–1909: I: Inledning och Kommentar; II: Texten. Edited by Olof Enckell. Helsinki, 1961.

CORRESPONDENCE

Ediths brev: Brev från Edith Södergran till Hagar Olsson. Med kommentar av Hagar Olsson. Stockholm, 1955.

TRANSLATIONS

The Collected Poems of Edith Södergran. Translated by Martin Allwood, in collaboration with Cate Ewing and Robert Lyng. Mullsjö, 1980.
Complete Poems. Translated by David McDuff. Newcastle-on-Tyne, 1984.
Feindliche Sterne: Gesammelte Gedichte. Translated by Karl R. Kern and Marguerite Schlüter. Wiesbaden and Munich, 1977.
Love & Solitude: Selected Poems 1916–1923. Translated by Stina Katchadourian. San Francisco, 1981; expanded ed. 1985. With Swedish texts.
Poèmes complets. Translated by Régis Boyer. Paris, 1973.
Poèmes du pays qui n'est pas. Translated by Pierre Naert. Paris, 1954.
We Women: Selected Poems of Edith Södergran. Translated by Samuel Charters. Berkeley, Calif., 1977.

EDITH SÖDERGRAN

BIOGRAPHICAL AND CRITICAL STUDIES

Björck, Staffan. "Att baka katedraler." In his *Lyriska läsövningar.* Lund, 1961.

Boyer, Régis. "Les structures de l'imaginaire chez Edith Södergran, génie baroque." *Études Germaniques* 26:524–549 (1971).

Brunner, Ernst. *Till fots genom solsystemen: En studie i Edith Södergrans expressionism.* Stockholm, 1985.

Ekelöf, Gunnar. "Edith Södergran studier." *Svenska Akademiens Handlingar* 75:3–26 (1967).

Enckell, Olof. *Esteticism och Nietzscheanism i Edith Södergrans lyrik.* Helsinki, 1949.

———. "Edith Södergran och den estetiska idealismen." *Historiska och litteraturhistoriska studier* 33:82–99 (1958).

Espmark, Kjell. "The Translation of the Soul: A Principal Feature in Finland-Swedish Modernism." *Scandinavica* 15:5–27 (1976).

Fages, Loup de. *Edith Södergran.* Paris, 1970.

Fernandez, Jocelyne. "Présence rimbaldienne d'une Vierge moderne: Ou Edith Södergran et la critique étrangère." *Scandinavica* 15:105–121 (1976).

Forsström, Tua. "Den heta villan (Edith Södergran)." In *Författare om författare: 24 finlandssvenska diktarporträtt.* Edited by Merete Mozzarella et al. Helsinki, 1980.

Jänicke, Gisbert. *Edith Södergran: Diktare pa två språk.* Helsinki, 1984.

Julén, Björn. "Den speglande brunnen." In his *Tjugo diktanalyser från Södergran till Tranströmer.* Stockholm, 1963.

Lagercrantz, Olof. "Lekarnas lek." In his *Svenska lyriker.* Stockholm, 1961.

Larsen, Finn Stein. "Et grundmønster i Edith Södergrans første digtning." *Edda* 58:298–309 (1958).

———. "Edith Södergran." In *Fremmede digtere i det 20. århundrede.* 3 vols. Edited by Sven Møller Kristenson. Copenhagen, 1967. II: 169–183.

Lundström, Göran. "Edith Södergrans förhållande till rysk poesi." *Poesi* 3:43–50 (1950).

Nag, Martin. "Russiske impulser hos Edith Södergran." *Ordet: Tidskrift for fri sprogutvikling* 22: 196–212 (1971).

Salminen, Johannes. "Så har jag åter fot mot jord." In *Levande och död tradition.* Helsinki, 1963.

Schoolfield, George C. *Edith Södergran: Modernist Poet in Finland.* Westport and London, 1984.

Tideström, Gunnar. *Edith Södergran.* Stockholm 1949.

Tottie, Thomas. "Edith Södergran och förlaget." *Bonniers Litterära Magasin* 26:241–251 (1957).

Wrede, Johan. "Illusion-utopi-realism: Edith Södergran, Hagar Olsson och Finland omkring 1920." *Finsk tidskrift* 195–196:273–282 (1974).

———. "The Birth of Finland-Swedish Modernism." *Scandinavica* 15:73–103 (1976).

GEORGE C. SCHOOLFIELD

MIROSLAV KRLEŽA

(1893–1981)

MIROSLAV KRLEŽA IS a dramatist, novelist, poet, essayist, and cultural figure of exceptional magnitude. Publishing the equivalent of one book for each of his more than sixty-five years of literary activity, this immensely productive, polygraphic Yugoslav writer produced a monumental oeuvre of universal significance. In quantity of output, creative energy, personal magnetism, and cultural exuberance Krleža can be compared to such literary giants as Balzac and Hugo. He reached the peak of his artistic and critical powers in the decade preceding World War II and became the most important author produced by the Croatian nation, the most many-sided and prolific contemporary writer in the Serbo-Croatian language, and the most culturally and politically influential Yugoslav intellectual of the twentieth century. Creating within Central European and South Slavic literary traditions, he exerted an influence on several generations of writers in Yugoslavia comparable to that exercised by André Gide at about the same time in France.

Outside Yugoslavia, Krleža is known for his poetic and polemical *engagement* and for his repeated interventions in favor of a more humanistic orientation in Communist praxis. In much of his work, he is a satirical modernist with a varied artistic temperament. Literary critics have drawn parallels between his technique of social criticism and that of Orwell, Galsworthy, Gorky, and Mann, even as they have noted in him a dislike of literalized reality very much like that of Mayakovsky, Kafka, and Céline. In its density and complexity his style has been compared to that of Proust, Joyce, and Faulkner. He is thematically concerned with the contradictions of modern existence, especially as man is confronted with social ideologies. In this regard, the philosophical influences on him of Schopenhauer, Nietzsche, and Dostoevsky are strong. Within the broad spectrum of European literature, critics regard him as a precursor of existentialism and of the literature of the absurd. His early prose anticipated works by Sartre and Camus, and in a general way the novels of Beckett. He was most accomplished as an avant-garde dramatist, and he brought about a revolution on the Yugoslav stage with his many innovative works. He wrote one of the first plays of the modern "popular" theater that was to engross Romain Rolland, Bertolt Brecht, Ödön von Horváth, and Peter Weiss. He is also a master of psychological dialogue, but his handling of philosophical and ideological topics shows he has a much broader intellect than most writers of the Norwegian school. In Yugoslavia and much of Europe his name is accorded the same recognition as Chekhov, Ibsen, and Strindberg. He has been widely translated and was a candidate for the Nobel Prize more than once.

MIROSLAV KRLEŽA

BACKGROUND, LIFE, SIGNIFICANCE

In terms of nationality and culture, Krleža is a Croat whose historical heritage reaches back to the foundations of the Roman Empire through its Illyrian provinces east of the Adriatic—Dalmatia and Pannonia. In respect to modern political and philosophical traditions, he belongs to Central Europe, where his writings have been received with particular interest, largely due to Yugoslavia's crucial position between East and West. Krleža was an "Agramer," from *Agram,* the German name for his native Zagreb, a thousand-year-old cultural site and capital of the Kingdom of Croatia under the Austrian emperor. In the nineteenth century, Zagreb became the center of the movement for the creation of Yugoslavia and later of the political opposition within the Kingdom of Yugoslavia, as well as of the illegal Communist movement in the interwar period. During World War II it served as the governing city of the fascist Independent State of Croatia; after the war, it became one of the republican capitals in the Yugoslav federation.

Raised and educated in the Austro-Hungarian empire, of which Croatia was a part, Krleža spoke and wrote German and Hungarian fluently. The ethnic diversity and supranational dimensions of this social and political setting form the basis of the universality of his writings, which transcend geographical and historical limitations. His tableau of characters and themes reveals that he shares cultural values with several leading intellectuals of Austria-Hungary who wrote about the moral and aesthetic contradictions of Habsburg society as the empire declined under the Dual Monarchy. Over and above the external divisions of language, nationality, and ideology, a common spirit of social critique links Kafka's Prague, Robert Musil's Vienna, György Lukács's Budapest, and Italo Svevo's Trieste with Krleža's Zagreb. Krleža's literary program and stylistic technique were most similar to those of his Austrian contemporary, the social satirist Karl Kraus. In Austria and

Hungary today, Krleža is considered almost a national writer. His multivolume historical novel, which appeared during the sixties, was published in book form in Hungarian translation before it appeared as a single work in the original Serbo-Croatian, and a recent collection of his works was published in Budapest in an edition three times larger than his Yugoslav editions. In 1962, Stiasny Verlag in Graz began to publish Krleža's collected works in German translation, and in 1968 he received the Herder Prize, the highest Austrian state award for literature.

Along with Ivo Andrić, Miloš Crnjanski, and Augustin Ujević, Krleža belongs to the generation of Yugoslav writers that matured on the eve of World War I and whose writings elevated Yugoslav literature to world-class status during the 1920's and 1930's. At the same time, he stands out as the writer most actively and consistently committed to the idea of social and political change. Like Gorky in Russia, he was the "harbinger of the revolution" in Yugoslavia—the proscribed and indexed critic of Austro-Hungarian feudalism, of the provincial nobility and bourgeoisie, of capitalism, and of the Yugoslav monarchy. His early education in military schools of the empire, the results of warfare he witnessed as a soldier in the emperor's army, and the material plight of the common people transformed him into an anti-war activist and supporter of the social democrats. His radical pacifist and social views soon led him to embrace Marxism and the workers' cause, and he became an early advocate of communism in his country. His first books of poetry and fiction plays were published while he was simultaneously engaged in an ambitious program to publicize his political ideas. Soon after the first Yugoslav state was established in 1918, Krleža drew attention as an outspoken critic of the authoritarian policies of the new royalist government. This was the beginning of an almost constant battle with administration officials and the censor's pen. Between the two world wars, authorities shut down three of the four literary journals he established, confiscated many of his books, banned him from making some speeches, and prohibited the staging of some of his plays. Nevertheless, because of the broad appeal and effectiveness of his writing Krleža emerged as the most influential Yugoslav writer between the wars. In this period he wrote sixteen plays, six collections of lyric verse, five novels, four volumes of stories, a cycle of six long narrative poems, and a book of poetic ballads. He also gained a reputation for his many essays on problems of art, history, politics, literature, philosophy, and military strategy. He was recognized as a formidable polemicist, an accomplished literary critic, and the author of an early travelogue about Soviet Russia that was to become a classic. By 1939 he had published more than forty books and proven himself to be a superb stylist and a writer of ebullient temperament and encyclopedic erudition. He was particularly esteemed as an important voice in socially committed literature, one that constantly denounced the ills of bourgeois society.

Krleža, however, was a Communist of his own making, and his most dangerous opponents did not come from the establishment on the right. Beginning in the late 1920's, he became increasingly critical of cultural policies sponsored by leftist elements that mandated conformity of all progressive writers to a fixed ideological line. He played an active part in the skirmishes on the left, advocating a liberal, autonomous role for creative expression in the social struggle. He sympathized with expressionism in art and literature and defended the work of the Serbian surrealists, who were attacked and ostracized by party ideologues. During the 1930's he became disillusioned with Stalin's policies toward the arts, and it may be said that even before World War II, Krleža was almost single-handedly responsible for the demise of socialist realism as an artistic doctrine in Yugoslavia. In 1933 he took a clear stand, publishing an aesthetic credo in which he maintained that the ego was as essential to authentic creative expression as so-

cial conscience. The Yugoslav exponents of literary Stalinism soon mounted a campaign against what they considered his "revisionistic" Marxism, and even the head of the underground Communist party, Josip Broz Tito, chastized him for helping the "Trotskyists." At the height of this clash on the left, Krleža founded his most independent liberal journal, and in 1939, in a scathing 160-page essay written with the compelling urgency of Émile Zola's "J'Accuse," he made his personal declaration of war on the stupefied ideological thinking of the Communists. This polemic, perhaps the best refutation of the totalitarian manipulation of the arts ever written, led to his virtual expulsion from the ranks of the leftist movement on the eve of World War II.

During the next five years, under suspicion by both the Left and the Right, Krleža published nothing. Under the Nazi occupation his life was threatened, his works confiscated, and he was under house arrest most of the time. Immediately after the war and the socialist revolution, he took an active part in cultural and political life and soon recouped his prewar status as the leading spokesman for the intellectual vanguard. This was due largely to his earlier literary prestige and to his longstanding personal ties with Tito. The Tito-Krleža relationship, especially after Yugoslavia's break with Stalin in 1948, can be compared to the one between André Malraux and Charles de Gaulle. Krleža was elected to the Yugoslav Academy of Arts and Sciences and became its vice president. He was also an official in literary organizations and in the party. In 1952, in an important speech to the Congress of Yugoslav Writers, he proclaimed in flamboyant terms the bankruptcy of socialist realism, reaffirmed his liberal beliefs through a unique interpretation of Baudelaire and modern art, and defined the role Yugoslav writers would play in European literature.

As the doyen of Yugoslav letters during the last thirty years of his life, Krleža published new editions of his earlier writings, wrote many new works, and continued to express himself in independent ways. In this period he wrote a third act for an important prewar play, completed the third volume of an earlier novel, a new opera-length drama, a mammoth six-volume novel, and a film scenario based on one of his short stories. He also founded the Yugoslav Lexicographic Institute. As its director for three decades, he masterminded the most comprehensive series of bibliographies and encyclopedias ever published in Eastern Europe. While working as editor in chief of these reference works, he published more than six hundred pages of historical and cultural essays based on the editorial annotations he wrote for the vast number of article entries that passed before his eyes. During this period several notable books of his memoirs came out, along with six books of essays.

The five volumes of his diary that appeared during the last years of his life have been read and studied less as autobiographical testimony than as innovative literary texts in their own right. Nor did Krleža's creative and independent spirit wane with old age. In spite of his supranational convictions and the international influence of his writings, he insisted on the political and cultural integrity of his own Croatian heritage and literary language. He received much official recognition and himself became a state cultural institution. When he died at the age of eighty-eight, he was still at the center of literary activity in his country and was honored as a national asset. Even though with time some of his political involvements appeared more complex and controversial, he remained a model of the creative intellectual supremely engaged all his life in the emancipation of the individual from the hierarchies and drudgeries imposed by society.

GENESIS OF A WRITER

Krleža was born into a middle-class civil servant's family with roots in the semiurbanized Croatian working class. The superstitious, antiquated *biedermeier* mentality still alive in the provinces of the empire during the last decade of the nineteenth century was preserved in the family by his half-Hungarian grandmother. This domestic atmosphere would serve as the basis of Krleža's sensitivity to the local Kajkavian dialect and of his personal study of the old Croatian literature written in it. His formal education, though, stressed a command of Latin, German, and Hungarian. He used his knowledge of all four of these literatures when he began to contribute to the newer tradition of a fifth literature at the beginning of this century—by writing in the modern literary language of his nation, Serbo-Croatian.

His first lessons were in Zagreb's Old Town at the parish school within the shadow of the cathedral. As a small boy, he participated in a paschal passion based on an eight-century-old tradition of Latin liturgical plays in Zagreb. Later, in his first published prose piece, "Fragmenti" (Fragments), Krleža refers to his early iconoclastic aesthetic attitude, depicting how he smashed the little wooden altar his parents had set up for him in his room: "In the little boy's soul a great big picture was growing, a picture of how he would build a big, big theater out of that same wood." His thespian talents were first realized in children's plays he wrote and enacted when he was eleven. While attending the classical gymnasium, he dramatized a scene from The *Iliad* and wrote dialogues on themes extolling the glory of Croatian knights and town nobles from a mythical past. The title of one of these, "Krvava noć na Grebengradu" (A Bloody Night in Grebengrad), evokes a sense of legend about medieval Zagreb. In another sketch named after the historical ship *Bellerophon,* he portrays the defeated Napoleon on his way to Saint Helena.

At the age of fifteen Krleža was sent to military school in Hungary where German was the formal medium of training and Hungarian the language of local life. There he was exposed to political reality in the form of Magyar resentment of Austrian imperialism and to modern European culture through literature and art. He translated Ibsen, in whom he found the idea of

1810

permanent revolution, and Sándor Petőfi, the great lyric poet and hero of the Hungarian rebellion of 1848. At eighteen, he received a scholarship to the elite Ludoviceum military academy in Budapest, where he tempered the regimented life by reading Nietzsche and thinking about the long-sought South Slavic unity. At the end of his first year there the First Balkan War broke out, and Krleža made a clandestine trip to Belgrade where he tried to enlist in the Serbian army. However, he was regarded more as a possible agent of Vienna than as a fellow Slav and comrade-in-arms. Sobered by the xenophobia of Serbia, a nation he had formerly regarded as a fraternal "Piedmont of the Balkans," he returned to Budapest. There he matured intellectually and underwent an aesthetic conversion while reading works of the Hungarian poet Endre Ady and those of Baudelaire, Schopenhauer, and Nietzsche. As a cadet-officer, he wrote satirical classroom compositions, "stylistic exercises" as he called them, for which he received a severe reprimand and penalty. The disillusionment of his youthful idealism, his alienation from the contending nationalisms of Central Europe, and the cultural displacement he felt as a trainee for the Austro-Hungarian army led him to break with the life of the barracks, into which, he later wrote, he had fallen while still a child and in which he had spent his life from the time of the annexation of Bosnia in 1908 until the Second Balkan War in 1913. That year he made another attempt to join the Serbian army, but was arrested, accused of espionage, and sent back to the empire, where he was expelled from the academy.

In 1914 Krleža returned to Zagreb and published his first works in various literary journals: the autobiographical sketch *Fragmenti*; a prose poem, *Zaratustra i mladić* (Zarathustra and the Youth); and two plays, *Legenda* (A Legend) and *Maskerata* (Mascherata, A Carnival Poem). He tried to break into the Zagreb theater, offering six other plays to the dramaturge of the National Theater. Two of these, *Saloma* (Salomé) and *Sodoma* (Sodom), were based on biblical themes, while four, *Leševi* (Corpses), *GospoDica Lili* (Miss Lily), *Utopija* (Utopia), and *Kraljevo* (The Kermess) dealt with contemporary social issues. All these were praised for being well written but were rejected as "unstageable." Krleža preserved and published only two of them: *Kraljevo* in 1918 and *Saloma* in 1963.

At this time he was also capturing the landscape of the city's parks and sylvan environs in a series of long, lyrical tone poems in free verse that eventually comprised a cycle of "symphonies." They show the stylistic influence of symbolism, but incorporate the philosophical dialectics of Nietzsche. The descriptive mood of the best known of them, *Pan* (1917), is reminiscent of Stéphane Mallarmé's "L'Après-midi d'un faune," but the dramatic line evolves out of a Dionysian-Apollonian tension, a struggle between pagan and evangelical views of the world. The poem presents Slavic peasants as the followers of the daemon Pan, a primitive deity who represents the unfettered, clairvoyant expression of instinctual creativity. The faun uses his panpipes to compete with and finally defeat the rigidly dogmatic ritual of institutional spirituality, represented by the death-oriented mystery of the mass played on an organ. The concluding lines show the lucid, lyrical, and spontaneous shepherd's song victorious over the piously solemn fortissimo of a gloomy and bombastic *Te Deum.* At the turning point, the dance of colors and the laughter of the sky infuse the peasant worshipers' souls, while the melody of the organ grows desperate:

> *Oblici su nebeski prozirni i svijetli*
> *i dršću kopna, zemlje, ko koralji na plimi.*
> *Na globu se Bezdan crveno bukteć dimi*
> *u sjeni Neba, svijetla Vječnost bruja,*
> *Aleluja, Aleluja!*
>
> (16:35)[1]

The sky's shapes are transparent and light
and earths, lands, tremble like coral in the tide.

[1] All quotations from Krleža's writings are from the 1953–1972 edition of his collected works: *Sabrana djela Miroslava Krleže,* 27 vols. (Zagreb, 1953–1972).

On the globe, a blazing red Abyss smokes
in Heaven's shadow, bright Eternity hums,
Hallelujah, Hallelujah!

Then, Pan's pipes overcome the voice of the organ:

> O, svijetlo jesenje Nebo, Magije Boja i Svijetla!
> Ta vani luduje dan, neviDen, svečano divan:
> sveto zlatno popodne teče mu s mirisne usne.
> Ja ću vam pjevati pjesmu,
> i savjest će Vaša da usne,
> ko zaborav na strave ove gnusne,
> što se kao mòra u hladnoj crkvi zgusne.
>
> (16:35)

Oh bright autumn Sky, Magic of Colors and Lights!
Out there the day is in a frenzy, unequalled,
  gloriously magnificent:
the sacred golden afternoon flows from its fragrant
  lip.
I will sing you a song,
and your conscience will fall asleep,
oblivious of these loathsome terrors,
that cluster in the cold church like a nightmare.

This work is Krleža's poetic acknowledgment of *The Birth of Tragedy from the Spirit of Music,* Nietzsche's reinterpretation of the place of the Judeo-Christian aesthetic tradition in reference to the art of the classical world. Krleža chooses to concentrate on the dramatic moment of transition between the ancient and modern worlds when Pan achieves complete expression—and then dies. The other five "symphonies" in the cycle paint a stark reality in which the earthly emotion of man, now left without Pan, is gradually overcome by darkness and enchained by a dogmatic faith. In 1916 Krleža's *Podnevna simfonija* (Midday Symphony), his first published verse, appeared. This was followed by *Pan* and *Tri simfonije* (Three Symphonies), both printed as separate books in 1917. Critics praised these works as masterpieces of poetic language, and the next year he published two collections of his shorter wartime lyric poems, *Pjesme I* (Poems I) and *Pjesme II* (Poems II).

As early as 1914, the year Austria declared war on Serbia, Krleža felt acutely the irrelevance of fin-de-siècle aesthetic canons emulated by the local cultural establishment: "Our dilettantes come from Vienna waving their banners of Schnitzler and proclaiming Hermann Bahr to be a 'revolution.' " After he was recruited into the Austro-Hungarian army as a noncommissioned officer in 1915, he not only was faced again with daily life in the barracks but was surrounded everywhere by signs of internecine insanity. Though he never directly saw battle, his experiences in military camps, on the Galician front, and in army hospital wards during the war prompted him to go beyond Nietzsche's philosophy in search of thematic material from the bloody reality of the present: "Not Zarathustra, but the Twenty-Fifth Home Guards Unit in Krajiška Street!" (11–12:155). It was then that he conceived of and began writing the stories that would become his stark antiwar cycle *Hrvatski bog Mars* (The Croatian God Mars, 1922). At the time of the Russian Revolution, he wrote a drama dedicated to Lenin in which Columbus figured as an idealistic visionary leading the common man to a "New World." Though none of the plays he wrote were accepted for the stage at this time, the ones he published—*Hrvatska rapsodija* (Croatian Rhapsody, 1918), *Cristoval Colon* (Christopher Columbus, 1918), *Michelangelo Buonarroti* (1919)—earned him a reputation as an important young dramatist.

In the last years of the war, Krleža plied his pen in accordance with his growing political and social conscience. He worked on a committee to assist war orphans, and contributed articles, often anonymous or signed with a pseudonym, to social democratic journals. Some of them about the impoverished lower class, in which he called for aid to the hungry and destitute of Zagreb, were confiscated by the authorities. In spite of censorship, he managed to publish some eighty reports in the local press in which he expertly analyzed the tactics employed on the battlefield and assessed, sometimes in biting satire, the course of the war and the way in which it was conducted. His association with other progressives of his generation, some of whom had been violently opposed to the old order even before the war, brought about a significant shift in his political thinking, in tune with the revolutionary atmosphere that spread over Europe after the war ended, especially in Russia, Bavaria, and Hungary. An antiwar movement formed among the masses in Croatia, where many peasants deserted from the Austro-Hungarian army in the aftermath of the conflict. Still in uniform, they formed armed groups in the countryside, the "green cadres" about whom Krleža wrote, and for a time, even after the creation of the new Yugoslavia, their movement continued to resist all state violence. For Krleža, this revolt reflected the desire for social revolution that had not been satisfied by the policies of the social democrats, who had compromised with the monarchists. He was disillusioned by the actions of the Croatian coalition with the Serbs, which helped establish a royalist government that included even former Austrian officers in its army. He joined the radical opposition as it grew into the Yugoslav Communist party in 1919, encouraged by leftist victories in the local elections.

LITERARY ACTIVISM AND AFFIRMATION

At the beginning of that year, he pursued his literary activism in earnest by establishing *Plamen* (The Flame), the first leftist literary and sociopolitical journal in the Balkans. On its pages he published two powerful political essays, a literary form he would use masterfully over the next half century. In one of these, "Hrvatska književna laž" (The Croatian Literary Lie), Krleža attacked the nineteenth-century nationalistic ideology that was based on the royalist mythology of Croatia's cultural past, and he condemned as a lie the notion that the nation's modern literature was "national" in any democratic sense. The second article, "Eppur si muove," took its title from Galileo's defiant reply to the Inquisition about the earth: "Nevertheless, it moves." It was an analysis of the cultural and material history of Eastern Europe vis-à-vis the West in which Lenin's signing of the Treaty of Brest-Litovsk was interpreted as a momentous turn in the history of mankind. The mood of revolutionary pathos Krleža evoked through the poetic rhetoric of utopian faith was intended to castigate the bourgeois and monarchist structure of the new state—now called the Kingdom of Serbs, Croats, and Slovenes—in all its social and cultural forms. Although the authorities shut down *Plamen* after only six months and arrested Krleža, he did not cease his political activities. In 1920 he gave many speeches on behalf of the socialist cause in the course of the parliamentary election campaign. At the end of the year, after the leftists were successful in the elections, the Communist party was banned by government decree. *Galicija* (Galicia), the first of Krleža's plays to be accepted for performance in the National Theater in Zagreb, had been scheduled to premiere on the very day this order was issued. The performance was cancelled, ostensibly by "a general strike and communist disturbances," and the play was not put on in Zagreb until after World War II. The Zagreb press accused Krleža of trying to start a coup d'état in the theater, while in Belgrade the campaign of state misinformation against the leftists resulted in a press report that the performance had taken place but that the public had rejected the play by this "communist writer."

The period from 1918 to 1923 was a time of intensive creativity for Krleža. Besides his journalistic writings, his own purely fictional works also appeared in the pages of *Plamen*, including a long antimilitaristic poem, "Ulica u jesenje jutro" (A Street on an Autumn Morning, 1919). In that same year, he published his third and fourth books of poetry,

Pjesme III (Poems III) and *Lirika* (Lyric Poems). His reputation as a writer of prose fiction was established by 1921, after he published several stories about bourgeois life—"Hodorlahomor veliki" (Hodorlahomor the Great), "Veliki meštar sviju hulja" (Grand Master of All Scoundrels), "Mlada misa Alojza Tičeka" (The First Mass of Alojz Tiček)—and five antiwar stories from the *Hrvatski bog Mars* cycle. His first substantial work of prose fiction, the novel *Tri kavalira gospoDice Melanije* (Miss Melany's Three Suitors), appeared in 1922, followed by a short novel, *Vraži otok* (Devil's Island), in 1923. He continued his work on drama, publishing *Galicija* (subtitled "Kroaten Lager") and the new plays *Golgota* (Golgotha) and *Adam i Eva* (Adam and Eve), all in 1922, and completing *Vučjak* (The Village of Vučjak) the next year.

In 1923 Krleža founded his second journal, *Književna republika* (Literary Republic). This marked a change in his literary attitude. In the first issue he editorialized about the emotionally romantic nature of his earlier journalistic work and defined a program for himself that owed less to Nietzsche than to Marx: he would no longer be anarchic and temperamental, but rationally focused along a systematic line of literary-political action. Accordingly, he published a series of texts by theoreticians on the Left and devoted a whole issue of the journal to Lenin. It included a picture of a bust of the revolutionary leader made especially for Krleža by the great sculptor Ivan Meštrović, one that portrays Lenin as a demonic Nietzschean titan. At this time, Russian readers were introduced to Krleža in the pages of Mayakovsky's journal *LEF.* In 1925, he traveled through Eastern Europe and to Moscow. The fruit of this journey, a book of travel essays entitled *Izlet u Rusiju* (An Excursion to Russia), was published in 1926. In this remarkable work about his visit to the Soviet Union, written a year after Lenin's death, Krleža gave Yugoslav readers the first eyewitness account of the social realities and the life of the intelligentsia under the new system in Russia. He framed his observations in a

personal creative style that was nostalgic, subjective, and sometimes pessimistic, as he accomplished a literary desacralization of the Kremlin and the mythical "soul" of Mother Russia. This record of his impressions reflects the influence of Proust, and in *Književna republika* a year after his excursion he published a lengthy essay, "O Marcelu Proustu" (About Marcel Proust), in which he offers an appreciative analysis of the writer's style, as well as thoughtful comparisons of French and Russian authors. During the next four years, Krleža published major critical essays on Goya, Grosz, Shaw, Mann, Gide, Hofmannsthal, and Rilke. One of the chief areas of his nonfiction writing at the time was polemics, but most of his attention was taken up with political essays. In his journal, he continued the persuasive negative criticism of the national cultural establishment he had begun in *Plamen,* but now, with less nihilistic invective, he presented an informed synthesis of historical, sociological, and ideological factors. In 1937, when this series of essays on bourgeois culture was published as a book, *Deset krvavih godina* (Ten Years of Blood), the courts ordered its confiscation.

The most significant accomplishment in Krleža's literary biography during the 1920's was the recognition of his plays. The brilliant staging of several of them caused a public sensation year after year: *Galicija* in 1920, *Golgota* in 1922 (which was praised by Konstantin Stanislavsky and members of the Moscow Art Theater visiting Zagreb), *Vučjak* in 1923, and *Michelangelo Buonarroti* and *Adam i Eva* in 1925. In spite of the acclaim and award he finally received as a playwright, he was totally revising his dramaturgic ideas at this time. A new stage in his literary development would coincide with fundamental changes in the political life of the country as well as in Krleža's personal views of the relation between art and life.

The authorities accused Krleža of spreading leftist propaganda, an illegal activity in Yugoslavia at the time, and *Književna republika* was suppressed in 1927. He continued his political writing in other journals, even after the dissolution of the national parliament and the beginning of autocratic rule by the king in Belgrade. At the same time, his aesthetic reevaluation led him to fault his earlier plays as "quantitative"—full of mass scenes, overt phantasmagoric action, and heavy rhetorical speech. He abandoned his experiment with expressionism and retreated into a sober dramaturgic articulation of Ibsenesque analytics. The result of this revision of artistic principles was his best known and most ambitious literary project, the Glembay cycle. This series of eleven prose pieces and three plays—*Gospoda Glembajevi* (The Noble Glembays, 1928), *U agoniji* (In Agony, 1931), and *Leda* (1932)— deals with the origin and degeneration of a fictional high-bourgeois family from Zagreb's old "Austrianized" society. The staging of the first two of these plays in 1929 met with great success. Subsequent performances throughout Yugoslavia and abroad brought the author critical acclaim, but also denunciation.

Though Krleža was now recognized as one of Yugoslavia's most talented writers, some in the press reproached him for having betrayed the spirit of his earlier work and regarded his new plays, in spite of their delicately crafted dialogue, as immoral and calculated to cause a scandal through the use of overly "dramatic" stage effects. The antagonism that Krleža's writing had provoked from the beginning became acute with the appearance of the Glembay plays. After the closing down of his journal, Krleža was less involved in the growing debate among the Marxists over the relationship between politics and literature. Deprived of an independent forum in which to present his own leftist views of art, he concentrated his polemical energies against conservative aesthetic prejudices in the literary establishment, even those held by activists within "progressive" political circles. This came to a head in 1930 on the eve of the premiere of *Leda,* when Krleža gave a public lecture about the reviews of his plays. He used his critics' own words to demonstrate their cultural illiteracy. The ensuing campaign against him in the press, which focused both on his writing and his private life, reached contradictory proportions: the bourgeois press argued that he had betrayed his socialist ideals, while the social democrats accused him of defiling bourgeois society's most sacred images, especially those of womanhood and marriage. This controversy culminated in 1932 with the appearance of Krleža's book of polemics, *Moj obračun s njima* (Settling Accounts). In it he sarcastically debunked the critics. This uncompromising stand spelled the end of his battle for modern theatrical principles and to the influence of his dramatic texts in the theater, even though he was already considered to be his nation's most important dramatist. During the previous decade eight of his plays had been enthusiastically received, with each new premiere the major event of the theatrical season. But between 1930 and 1945 not one of his plays was staged in Zagreb.

By the 1930's Krleža had established himself as an exceptionally productive and original writer. Along with many other works, he had written his "symphonic" cycle of long melodious poems treating impressionistic motifs in an experimentally elegiac manner; a series of dramatic "legends" presenting symbolist themes in a neonaturalistic way; three expressionistic plays dealing with misplaced intellectuals caught up in war and the pettiness of provincial life; two books of macabre stories about army recruits and prostitutes who end their lives in the syphilis wards of military hospitals and in the gutters of an urban landscape; a fictional social critique of the family chronicle à la Mann and Galsworthy consisting of a set of stories and a trilogy of plays about the final years of a bourgeois banking dynasty; and a quasi-Proustian novel that treats in Freudian undertones the cultural self-search of a neurasthenic prodigy from Central Europe who had become a painter in Paris. This last work, *Povratak Filipa Latinovicza (The Return of Philip Latinovicz),* was written in 1932, when Krleža was traveling abroad during a lull in his polemical battles. That year, the prestigious publishing house Minerva revealed its plan to publish the thirty-nine-year-old author's collected works in eighteen volumes. This undertaking, which integrated his earlier books and the many pieces he had written for journals into a programmatic summa of his first twenty years of writing, distinguished him as the leading writer in Yugoslavia.

AN INDEPENDENT AESTHETIC CREDO

By the time Krleža returned to Zagreb from Paris, the critics' attacks against him were in full swing. In the spring of 1933 he responded by announcing his intention to give a public lecture about the national literary tradition and contemporary writing. A poster campaign ensued in which nationalists, quoting Krleža's earlier slander of the cultural past, called for a "settling of accounts with stinking communism" and encouraged citizens to disrupt the talk. After a group of leading liberal artists and intellectuals countered by posting their defense of Krleža, the police intervened to avoid violence and prevented him from speaking.

By this time Krleža was particularly esteemed by the Communist Left as an important voice in socially committed literature. He constantly denounced bourgeois society, and his synecdoche for it became its standard metaphorical designation. He dubbed it the "civilization of the top hat," a society where the capitalist mentality was personified by *homo cylindriacus*. He had shown himself to be a man with a powerful critical talent, one that seemed to be enlisted on the side of Marxist principles. His influence on several generations of writers and cultural workers, especially the generation that reached maturity just before World War II, was immense. He was an activist writer who appeared to be faithful to the spirit of historical and dialectical materialism. Yet his faith in the letter of that ideology met its greatest challenge when his artistic reputation was at its apogee.

Krleža had begun to focus on the danger of utilitarianism in literature a decade earlier, when there was an increasing proletarianization and then a centralization of leftist criticism at the expense of creative writing. He emerged as the one writer with the creative stamina necessary to sustain the artistic imagination against the growing barrage of aesthetic and social demands. Already by the end of the 1920's, after his "Leninist years" and the propagandist efforts of *Književna republika* were behind him, he had grown beyond his earlier preoccupation with ideological doctrines. He had subsumed the revolutionary mood of 1917 and was intent on addressing social and political issues in his creative work proper. In spite of the Marxist critique of society that his writing implied, his actual literary technique was ironic, complex, and pessimistic. He was preoccupied with the psyches of spiritually aberrant individuals, describing their unconstructive actions in satirical, gloomy, and sometimes morbid terms and emphasizing man's solipsistic existence as reflected in a rationally void world. All this was antithetical to the proletarian, positive, and progressive principles of those orthodox leftists who considered themselves the literary apologists of a vanguardist party, a dialectical philosophy, and a revolutionary dogma.

Beginning in 1928 Krleža's works came under increasing attack from leftist ideologues, and between 1929 and 1931 articles disapproving of his writing appeared in the Zagreb and Belgrade organs of the Soviet-sponsored International Organization of Revolutionary Writers. He was criticized for being too willing to debate the means and goals of committed literature and for manifesting a skeptical and unegalitarian viewpoint that kept him out of step with the movement of contemporary socialist thought. In the early 1930's his critics were disturbed by the pessimism that seemed to glare at them out of his fictional literature. In their view, this mood of Krleža's writing appeared more and more to vitiate the powerful, purposeful thrust of the political essays he was writing at the same time. Those critics who were more kindly disposed toward him detected a spirit of reforming social commitment in his imaginative pieces; they saw him as the initiator of a line of socially tendentious literature and as the writer who best represented the breadth and versatility of leftist art. But in the eyes of the more extreme dialectical critics, his stature was diminished by his negativistic "strayings." His most severe critics saw his literary style and philosophical views as completely outdated. They asserted that he had not progressed ideologically or creatively since 1917 and that the development of "socialist literature" had had no effect on him. He was judged to be a master only of the literature of doubt. He could convey a sense of despair, resignation, and capitulation to life, but he was incapable of issuing the kind of rousing summons to mankind they wished to see. Whereas he had been eloquently useful in the 1920's, now he had nothing to offer the brave new generation on the Left.

By the 1930's Krleža found himself unable to accept the growing demands made of him to subordinate his individual artistic inclinations to a collectivist imperative. It was impossible for him to separate his compulsive drive to blast backward social views from his personal penchant for expressing doubts darkly. In his first lyric verse, he had shown that these two strains overlapped, and that in a single poem, as in his "Jesenja noć" (Autumn Night, 1919), he could express both harsh expressionistic defiance:

> *Cvrči cvrčak.*
> *Duša moja strši, kô popaljen trčak*
> (26:92)

A cricket chirps.
My soul juts out like a scorched beetle

and solemn, symbolist privatism:

> *Sada,*
> *kad odlijeću laste,*

osjećam Jesen, gdje se u meni otkriva—
i raste.

(26:93)

Now,
when the swallows are flying away,
I feel the Autumn unfolding in me—
and growing.

In 1933 he published an essay in which he defended the mood of pessimism in his earlier wartime poetry as legitimate, even for the socially conscious "revolutionary" writer. It was precisely at the point where he first began to be criticized openly on the Left that his already tenuous ties with the cultural power-holders on the Right were completely severed. He was attacked by a group of conservatives who accused him of being a Bolshevist and "negator of Croatian national sentiment." Ironically, Krleža's fifteen-year assault on the royalist and clerical forces in Yugoslavia culminated in his final break with the nationalists at the very moment when he was most estranged from the internationalist movement. As his sensitivity to the pressure on all sides grew, his fundamental philosophy emerged as an urbane skepticism modified by the unrelieved need for ideological commitment.

In 1933 Krleža came out with his most important aesthetic manifesto, published in the form of an essay written as a "foreword" to *Podravski motivi* (Scenes From the Drava Region), a book of illustrations by the artist Krsto Hegedušić depicting the Croatian peasant underclass. In it Krleža's debt to Nietzsche, Darwin, and Freud is apparent as he presents a conception of committed art quite different from the ideas of the young proponents of socialist literature. Stating that any group that acts to limit artistic expression in the name of a social imperative is harmful to man's spirit, he says that Nikolay Chernyshevsky was "not much different from the eighth-century iconoclasts" and asserts that the necessary relationship between art and society is not determined by ideological conviction. He claims that creativity is contingent on a dialectical clash between the individual and the collective and that authentic art results from life's instinctual negation of material culture. Consequently, art is both autonomous and engaged: though it cannot result from decree, it is instrumental in opposing the old order. Nevertheless, Krleža sees the creative act in evolutionary rather than revolutionary terms, as a product of man's awareness of his mortality and his will to project himself beyond death. He portrays this projection as a continuum running from the cave paintings of Altamira to George Grosz's caricatures of Weimar German society. Soon after this essay appeared, he was attacked in an anonymous article, "Quo vadis Krleža?" one of the first attempts to challenge his literary reputation directly in the name of the proletarian cause. It criticized him for his "aristocratic indifference," pessimism, and "egocentrism" and accused him of "deviating to the right."

That year he went to Belgrade and established his third journal, *Danas* (Today), together with the prominent Serbian surrealist Marko Ristić and several other independent leftist writers. After the preceding seven years involved in numerous polemical disputes, he now planned a literary forum in which he could present his own views. The vehicle for this was *Danas,* which was conceived as a socially enlightening, quality journal with an ambitious format, complete with a separately published quarterly index and lexicon of "names, books, events, phenomena, and concepts." It was to be the Communist intellectuals' answer to the growing fascist threat in Europe, a medium for addressing problems of culture and politics, of analyzing the international social crisis and the general state of civilization. It also aimed to present the situation in Yugoslavia in a series of high-caliber essays on social and ideological issues, such as farm debt, social security, domestic echoes of fascism, and the relation between Marxism and psychoanalysis. Many pages were devoted to Marxist ideology and problems of Soviet culture, especially film and literature. The appearance of *Danas* in the capital in 1934 provoked fear in reactionary circles and Krleža was once more condemned for spreading Communist propaganda. After five issues, authorities stopped the publication of his journal.

However, *Danas* was Krleža's double-edged sword, for in it he also settled accounts with some of his enemies on the Left. In an article called "Najnovija anatema moje malenkosti" (The Latest Anathema of My Insignificance), published in the first issue of the journal, he derided the amateurish methods of the anonymous author of "Quo vadis Krleža?" pointing out sarcastically that according to the Christian legend, the question used as the title of that article had been asked by the guilty one. As an intuitively ironic, inciting polemicist and consummate stylist, he was able to turn these attacks against him to his own use. He ridiculed what he called the "verbalism" of his detractors, who turned out much criticism but no original works that would exemplify their notions of what socialist literature was supposed to be. From this point, his critics began to perceive him as an ideological rebel who saw man's social conceptions as reflections of his innate creative talent, not his needs or his convictions. Krleža's "subjectivism" and Ristić's "surrealism" were seen as the worst kinds of deviation from the leftist literary doctrine then known in Yugoslavia as "new realism." The silencing of *Danas* signaled an end to that period of Krleža's active participation in public literary life. He was now boycotted by the press and publishers, his works prohibited or seized. His essays from that time were collected and published as *Evropa danas* (Europe Today) in 1935. From then until 1938, he wrote neither as a polemicist nor a publicist, but devoted himself to imaginative literature.

CONFLICT WITH THE LITERARY LEFT AND RIGHT

At this critical point in his literary development, Krleža relied on virtual solitude for inspiration, just as he had some four years earlier when he withdrew into privacy after being deprived of a forum for his writing. Then, in 1931, he turned to the beating of his heart and wrote:

Ti mi se javljaš mudrim polutihim glasom
u grlu, prstu, radosti i suzi,
kad sjaju svijetla i u mračnoj tuzi
tvog glasa glas se glasa glasnim glasom.
(26:345)

You talk to me with wise, half-quiet voice
in throat, finger, joy and tear,
when lights glow and in the dark sorrow
of your voice your voice voices with vociferous voice.

It was this tenebrous pathos of his creative writing (often wrongly considered nihilistic and decadent), as much as his intolerance of intellectual laxity on all sides, that brought Krleža to a point of confrontation with all dogmatists on the literary scene. Elements of pessimism and negation were the most controversial aspects of his expression, though they were essential to his affirmation of art. This principle is best seen in his most exceptional work, *Balade Petrice Kerempuha* (The Ballads of Petrica Kerempuh), which he wrote at this time and published in 1936. In this collection of thirty-four ribald and tragic poems, a Breughelesque panorama of Croatian history, he achieves a virtuoso reconstruction of the pithy local language of past centuries. He distills his knowledge of the old Kajkavian literature of northern Croatia and of the present-day vernacular in the person of Petrica Kerempuh, the traditional figure of a wily peasant and itinerant jack-of-all-trades, who exercises his rustic wit, plays jokes, and sings laments on the fate of the common man. He relates this Croatian Till Eulenspiegel to a fatalistic, pre-Enlightenment faith in Providence and a sense of mystery and futility ruling human destiny. In his songs full of gallows humor, Kerempuh is the folk *raissoneur*, embodying the native's resistance to oppression and his coarse-grained, resilient, and resigned perseverence in the face of personal tragedy:

Na galgama tri galženjaka,
tri tata, tri obešenjaka,
pod njimi čarni potepuh
tamburu svira Kerempuh.
(10:9)

Three gallows-birds on the gallows,
three thieves, three hung high
under them a vagabond in black
strums his strings, Kerempuh.

It is indicative of Krleža's insistence on the unprescribed individuality of the creative process that his literary response in these critical years of ideological struggle took the form of an imaginative and linguistic tour de force.

Because the basis of his *Balade* is an antiquated regional dialect instead of the standard modern literary language, Krleža might seem to have withdrawn from present reality and the social struggle. Yet his intention was just the opposite: to locate and speak with the voice of the downtrodden. He does this by merging the literary sources of the sixteenth, seventeenth, and eighteenth centuries and the living local speech into an idiom that could convey to the twentieth-century reader a sense of the crisis of the human social condition. The result was a product capable of the kind of crudely lyrical, ironic attitude found in François Villon's ballads:

A koga vraga cmizdriš,
zamusana mužača,
kaj su ti sinu dali tatski ogerlič?
Na galge dojde samo fini fičfirič,
naj sliniti, smardljiva bedača.

Još su ga mogli nabiti na ketača,
z goročim kleštram popokati mu nokte.
Od sega tega občuval je dragi nam Bog te
i rešil te za navek tega čarvendača!
(10:108)

What the devil are you sobbing for,
you shabby hick woman,
that they gave your son a thief's necklace?
Only the finest featherbrain makes it to the gallows,
don't snivel, you stinking ninny.

Why, they could have stretched him on the rack,
plucked out his nails with burning tongs.
Our dear Lord spared you all that
and rid you of that red-throat bird forever.

The allusion in the last line to the son's political identity (more than merely that of a dandy run afoul of the law) relates the entire poetic cycle to the specific contemporary context in a global way. Krleža's songs treat a variety of topics in a wide range of forms. Speaking of feudal families and peasant uprisings, he encapsulates the entire historical experience of a humble people. In the final ballad, "Planetarijom" (Planetarium), he provides a vast, fantastic astrological overview predicting the events and fate of almost the whole national past, assuming the pleb's point of view and conjuring up and chronicling the sense of oppression and revolt beginning with the Croatian jacquerie of the 1500's.

The collection was printed in the style of old baroque manuscripts, with elaborate initials, illustrations, and Latin titles referring to ritualistic expression—wake, lamentation, prayer, psalm—and complete with the author's fifty-page glossary of words, places, and names. In this work, Krleža created a folk liturgy *sui generis* written in the ultimate Aesopian manner. The fact that it did not receive even a line of mention in leftist journals at the time is a sign of the writer's distance from their baldly dogmatic socialist literary doctrine. The ideologues thought he had simply retreated to neighboring Slovenia (where he had gone in fact to find a publisher) and was writing obscure dialectical poems. But while they were deploring the fascist atrocities of the Spanish Civil War at that time in tendentious works such as Radovan Zogorić's poem about a vengeful "Don Quixote in a Bomber," Krleža reacted to that tragedy by focusing his attention more universally and more potently on the suffering of the people. In doing so, he created a Yugoslav literary equivalent to Pablo Picasso's painting *Guernica*. The *Balade* constitutes Krleža's supreme work of committed art.

The years 1937 through 1939 were ones of intense creativity and of growing political isolation for Krleža. After the earlier censorship, which caused the discontinuation of the Minerva edition after only nine volumes, these three years saw an ambitious project by him to put out a new edition of his writings, including a bibliography of his works from 1914 to 1937. A new collection of poems, *Pjesme u tmini* (Poems in the Dark, 1937), was published, along with two volumes of essays, *Deset krvavih godina* (1937) and *Eppur si muove: Studijei osvrti* (1938). Both of these were banned, but not before they were sold out and a second edition was planned. Krleža was also the target of censorship on the stage. In 1938, the minister of culture personally intervened to stop the performance in Belgrade of his play *U logoru* (In the Camp), a new version of his ill-fated earlier play *Galicija*. But during this period, he fared no better with the self-appointed "ministers" of socialist culture. By 1937, Milovan Đilas and other party ideologues emerged to spearhead the growing criticism of him. In 1938, Krleža published *Na rubu pameti (On the Edge of Reason)*, a novel that directly reflected the realities of the clash. In a prison cell, the anonymous intellectual hero of this roman à clef argues with a Stalinist "engineer" against the herd instinct, the bleating after a dogma to follow, and finally ends up in the Sistine Chapel alone with his vision of personal revolt and the inspiration provided by Michelangelo's *Last Judgment*.

In 1938 and 1939 Krleža published the first and second parts of a grand new novel conceived in three volumes, *Banket u Blitvi* (Banquet in Blithuania), set in a fictional East European totalitarian state. This novel, which has a subtext of allusion to Poland and other countries, may be considered Krleža's allegory for the state of Europe on the eve of World War II. Through the internal monologues of prelates, generals, poets, and politicians, he portrays men as sordid marionettes drawn along by the capricious play of political forces.

By the time the conflict on the Left reached

its height in 1939, Krleža had stopped playing ideological chess with the dialectical materialists and undertook to orchestrate the stillbirth of socialist realism in Yugoslavia by shifting the debate onto polemical grounds (where he had proven himself superior) through the establishment of a new journal, *Pečat* (The Stamp). The uncompromising invective of his opening editorial was stronger than any of his earlier cautionary criticism of the Left. He denounced the doctrinaire allegiances of the socialist literati, stamping them "pseudo-leftist phrasemongers" and accusing them of being no better than their clerical counterparts in wanting to take art back to the antediluvian cave era. He made it clear that he no longer intended to debate the principles of socialist art in general terms. He directly confronted the would-be arbiters of leftist literature, travestying their sentimental "lemonade" lines of poetry and charging them with a lack of talent and critical integrity. The purpose of his challenge was to draw out his opponents, and he did this on the level of stylistic criticism by actually using their names and by printing long passages from their works, only in order to expose their literary ineptitude in concrete analyses of the texts. The reaction to *Pečat* came in the form of personal incrimination by Tito, in an article published in the official party organ, accusing Krleža's close associates of "Trotskyism," the ultimate Communist anathema of the time. After this attack, Krleža's voice lost its direct influence on the development of leftist literary aesthetics, and he stood virtually alone.

In his "Dijalektički antibarbarus" (The Dialectical Antibarbarian), a defiant article that occupied most of one issue of *Pečat*, Krleža fired a final salvo at the unliterary tactics of the dogmatists. In the thirty-eight sections of this mammoth essay, Krleža demonstrated the absurd proportions to which the conflict on the Left had grown. Pulling out all stops, he crafted a pastiche of "dialectical seminars" and parodied "revolutionary" poems into a gigantic feuilleton caricaturizing the mainstream of socialist hack writing. This was his final contribution to the conflict. He was officially condemned by name in an anthology of articles published by party ideologues who aimed to silence the spirit of *pečatovština,* the term inspired by Krleža's journal and signifying his unorthodox, rebellious leftist affiliation. He ceased publishing *Pečat* at the end of 1939.

BETWEEN AUTONOMY AND COMMITMENT

It was due to Krleža's virtual expulsion from the party on the eve of the war, as well as to his preeminent public literary reputation, that he did not meet the fate of almost all other Yugoslav leftist intellectuals during the war: execution if caught living under the Nazi occupation, or escape to Tito's partisans in the mountains. All publication or possession of his works was forbidden, and he was arrested three times. For a while he was hidden in a sanitorium, but most of the time he remained isolated and uneasy at home in Zagreb.

During these five dangerous years, he wrote much that would be published later. Besides writing a long philosophical play and a memoir of childhood containing a major aesthetic statement, he continued his preoccupation with philosophical problems of creative expression by studying the development of thought and imagination in the history of Western medical theory and by writing a long essay on Paracelsus. During the war he also demonstrated his concern for the restoration of reason in times of bloodshed and tyrannical ideologies by writing "O Erazmu Rotterdamskom" (On Erasmus of Rotterdam, published in 1953), a sympathetic study of Desiderius Erasmus in which he portrayed the independent-minded humanist as an intellectual rebel and archetypal spiritual refugee from the human folly of those who would reform man's spirit through dogma.

A poem he wrote in the middle of this five-year period, "Evropa godine tisuću devet stotina četrdeset i druge" (Europe in Nineteen-Hundred Forty-Two), suggests that this was a time of intense introspection and reevaluation for him. Far removed from the struggle for survival and the revolution in Yugoslavia, he calls for those who are incapable of being heroes of battle to "say so with a loud silence." And he reaffirms his earlier commitment to defining an autonomous yet functional place for art in life:

—Mi danas nijesmo više što bijasmo kô djeca,
mi danas znamo jedno, a to je što znamo:
poezija da nije zlatna ribica
u kristalnome loncu tihe, lirske sobe,
ni tamjan slatkih riječi u gubici krvnika . . .
(26:539–540)

—Today we are no longer what we were as children,
today we know one thing, and that is:
we know that poetry is not a goldfish
in the crystal bowl of a quiet, lyrical room,
nor the incense of sweet words in the jaws of an
    executioner . . .

Krleža's own aesthetic stance lies between the extremes given in this definition. The basic contrast here is between words that are divorced from life and words that tyrannize it. Already in the long poems of his symphonic cycle *Simfonije* he had identified this dichotomy: the use of art only for its own sake, here and now, and art used for the sake of a promise in the hereafter. And in his essays on art, he had designated these, respectively, as *larpulartizam* (from *l'art pour l'art*, Théophile Gautier's post-Baudelairean elitist slogan) and *kampanilizam* (from *campanile*, the omnipresent symbol of the parochialization of the spirit by the Church of Rome). Krleža conceived of these as the extreme axes of a dualistic universe in which solipsism and dogma complement each other even as they are in constant conflict. Behind these antinomic concepts stand man the guilt-free primitive, the painter of goldfish and player of panpipes on the one hand, and man the priest, the arbiter of guilt and toller of the bell for the *propaganda fide* on the other.

The aesthetic problem of this Nietzschean opposition is embodied here in Krleža's language as a tension between the legacies of Jean-Jacques Rousseau and Ignatius of Loyola.

In the development of his philosophy of art and in his practice of literary art, Krleža defines his position in relation to both of these forces. He is a direct heir to their artistic manifestation in the literary traditions of his nation. He was decisively influenced by the finely forged autotelic art of the Croatian Moderna, the modernist movement at the beginning of the twentieth century (best seen in the work of Antun Gustav Matoš, the most prominent Croatian poet living during Krleža's youth). And he was also influenced by the long tradition of conceit-ridden propagandistic art derived from the Jesuit baroque, as old as the work of Ivan Gundulić and the seventeenth-century Counter-Reformation. For Krleža, then, these are the Yugoslav reflexes, the indigenous national sources of the impressionistic, lyrical "goldfish" and the "sweet words" of salvation offered at the inquisitor's censer. Both these factors must be taken into account in order to understand the extent to which Krleža's caustic literary style had a paradoxical reception among his critics. During the last days of royalist Yugoslavia in 1940, a supporter of the regime declared that, "In the last ten years Krleža's writing has converted more people to Marxism than the words of Marx himself." But in 1971, a Bosnian priest writing in socialist Yugoslavia stated that "Krleža has contributed more to the credibility and dignity of the Catholic church in Croatia than those who have condemned him." Possibly Krleža's own answer to this contradiction lies in the definition of the purpose of poetry that he offers in Baudelairean imagery in the final lines of his wartime poem on Europe in 1942:

jer dostojanstvo stiha nije dah ni dim,
već rt rapira u gnjilom truplu zločina!
(26:540)

For the dignity of verse is neither breath nor smoke,
but the point of a rapier in the fetid corpse of crime!

IN SERVICE AGAINST DOGMA

Soon after the end of that criminal war, Krleža began to participate in the cultural life of socialist Yugoslavia, helping establish and edit *Republika* (The Republic) in 1945, one of the most important new literary journals. In an article in its first issue, he condemned the recent years of armed conflict by giving his own characteristic twist to the Latin adage "Inter arma silent musae," stating that the power of literature lies in helping mankind not to forget, even if no art is created in times of violence: "When men flick their tails like dogs, the muses are silent." The first issue also included a new dramatic text by Krleža, *Krokodilina ili razgovor o istini* (Crocodile Song; or, A Talk About Truth), in which the devil shows up at the end of the war to foil the outdated mouthings of bourgeois reactionaries. First he speaks as an intelligent advocate for himself in the guise of one of the interlocutors, and then he turns into a vexatious fly that escapes from the visionary state of the future evoked on the stage. Partly didactic and partly fantastic, this work fell far short of satisfying the demands of the socialist, realist literary aesthetics of the day. Krleža's darkly erudite and experimentally ambiguous postwar literary debut could only provoke the suspicion of the party, and the play was never performed or reprinted.

Yet prewar experience had shown the ideologues that it was important to include Krleža in the new echelons of power, and the next year he was elected to the Yugoslav Academy of Arts and Sciences. In the years that followed, he engaged his literary imagination in writing a few prose feuilletons about contemporary life, but then turned to public life. In 1947 he visited Hungary as part of a government cultural delegation. In the prose sketch he wrote about this trip, "Iz knjige 'Izlet u Madžarsku 1947' " (From the Book "Excursion to Hungary 1947"), which describes his military education there thirty-five years earlier, he initiated what would become an important new area of literary creativity for him. Though several of his earlier books were published then, they were not popular in terms of the prevailing socialist ideology. His prewar works, especially his most "realistic"—like the Glembay cycle and his antiwar stories—did not offer the "positive" heroes or reflect the social "reality" called for by those in power. Whether or not the publishing of some of his books and the performance of one of his plays were actually suppressed right after the war, as he later complained, certainly his works were not especially favored. Nor could they provoke any public discussion at a time when literary ideology was a conditioned reflex to the call for socialist romanticization in the treatment of life.

In 1948, in his capacity as the vice president of the Academy, Krleža joined the public reply to the condemnation of Yugoslavia by the Soviet-led Communist Information Bureau, siding with Tito in his opposition to Stalin. From a position of official power and responsibility, he continued his active contributions by writing on topics of literary history and participating in the ongoing debate over the role of art in society. In 1950, after organizing a highly successful exhibit of medieval art of the Yugoslav peoples in Paris, he conceived of a monumental undertaking that would result in the first comprehensive encyclopedia of Yugoslavia. When he returned to Zagreb, he founded the Lexicographic Institute and became chief editor of a project that was to produce a battery of reference works—ten different multivolume encyclopedias—during the next quarter century. He continued his varied activities by participating in discussions of political issues, as well as writing essays on Serbian and Macedonian frescoes, the heretical church art of medieval Bosnia, and the old gold and silver masterpieces from church treasuries in Dalmatia.

The planning for the Yugoslav encyclopedia was a political as well as a scientific venture, and in a key essay on the problems of synthesizing the manifold cultural heritage of the Yugoslavs, Krleža indicated that, without being glorified or mythicized, the richness and grandeur of the past could be demonstrated and balanced against the "revolutionary" present. Such a panoramic survey could show how nations and cultures last, while ideologies and political movements are transitory. Even then, at a time when history seemed to focus on the party and Tito's revolution, Krleža was beginning a personal program to relativize recent events and the new power structure.

At the Congress of Writers in 1952, Krleža gave a now-famous speech in which he made a studied metaphorical declaration for freedom of expression on the Left. Stressing the writer's obligation to society, he defined the interdependence of creativity and culture in terms of the immediate, grave historical circumstances: the independent, if precarious, course of Yugoslavia after Tito's break with Stalin. At the same time, he rejected as detrimental to the creative process any duty imposed on a writer. He attacked the sacrosanct dogma preached by Andrey Zhdanov and Mikhail Gerasimov, the main Soviet spokesmen for artistic puritanism, asserting that Stalin's program of socialist realism had actually turned into a systematic kind of "aesthetic Caligula-ism." He drew on a pantheon of examples—from Shakespeare and Baudelaire to Chagall, Matisse, and Picasso—to illustrate his thesis that it is individual temperament, not social or political conviction, that produces effective and moving art. And he stressed that artistic expression cannot be ideologically harnessed to political action.

The very fact that Krleža made the keynote speech at a congress intended to reorient Yugoslav arts and letters was an indication that his earlier work and views were now officially approved. This was confirmed later that year when he received a national award for his life's work. He spoke at a moment when he was riding the crest of the times. Events in Yugoslavia seemed to have fully caught up with his earlier prewar actions. Only seven years after emerging from his wartime Erasmian withdrawal, Krleža spoke from a position of absolute preeminence. Also in 1952, he gave another crucial speech, "Kako stoje stvari" (How Things Stand), to the officers of the Yugoslav army. It

was a devastating criticism of Stalinism as the "blind bureaucratic manipulation" of a police state. (He referred to this speech later on the occasions of the Hungarian Uprising of 1956 and the Prague Spring of 1968.)

But these speeches were not only a symbolic vindication of all that Krleža had stood for before the war. They signaled a shift in aesthetics that was a challenge to new writers who, now that they had an officially sanctioned creative freedom, were left alone to seek creative achievement. The publication that same year of Krleža's introspective memoir, *Djetinjstvo u Agramu godine 1902–3* (Childhood in Agram 1902–1903), exemplified his answer to the crude ideological schemes that had been formulated along the lines of dialectical materialism and the theory of art as an imitation of life. His analysis of his own childhood, which he wrote during World War II, destroys these schemes through an implicit ridicule of them. In meditating on his early years, even drawing an analogy between his own youth and that of Saint Augustine, he presents an impressionistic picture of his surroundings, stressing the role of instinct and intuition and making a parallel between the spontaneous, pre–socially conscious state of childhood and the artistic state of mind. This work heralded a new form of writing in the development of his literary art.

REDISCOVERY OF A DRAMATURGIC MASTER

The postwar publication of Krleža's collected works began in 1953, when the first of a projected thirty-six volumes was issued. Even before many of the previously banned works were reissued in this edition, his earliest plays were discovered for the stage. The successful premiere of the early *Kristofor Kolumbo* (originally *Cristoval Colon*) in Belgrade in 1955 opened Yugoslav theaters to all those first pieces that had been considered "unstageable." From its inception in 1913 Krleža conceived of this cycle of legends as a "Hebrew pentology," with his *Saloma* as a prelude. In each play of this series he proposed to deal with a monumental figure of Western civilization. He intended to dispute the models inherited from the literature of modernism by focusing not on the moment of ecstasy but on the moment of crisis in the earthly lives of his five heroes: Christ, Michelangelo, Columbus, Kant, Goya. Instead of illuminating the traditional aspects of mystical inspiration associated with these spiritual titans, he aimed at portraying their psychological self-awareness and their inner sense of personal mortality. In the first work of the cycle, *Legenda* (A Legend), which bears the subtitle *Novozavjetna fantazija u tri slike* (A New Testament Fantasy in Three Scenes), Krleža chooses to focus on Christ in the garden of Gethsemane at the moment when he renounces his love for Mary Magdalene and lifts his face upward with cries for support. The response comes not from on high, but from within, in the form of an internal voice: the shadow of doubt. The entire play is really an interior monologue elaborated as a discussion between Christ and his alter ego, his infernal spiritual dimension. Krleža's Christ carries on a dialogue with his own earthly shade about the future problems of the church, the historical institution that will result from the decision taken at this moment in the garden. Instead of positing the destruction of the sacred myth, Krleža humanizes it, extracting from it his own dialectic and developing an original form of dramatic conflict for the central legend of Christianity by locating new points of tension in it.

Kristofor Kolumbo was finished at the time of the Russian Revolution. The basic conflict centers on the contradiction between man as an individual carrying the lofty ideals of a personal egotistical vision and man as a mortal social being mired in the here and now. In this play, which is really an expressionistic dramatic scenario, we see not the revolution realized, but an eschatology of revolution. It is a tragedy not of faith but of doubt. The poetic vision is expressed as doubt in the possibility that eschatological thought can ever be actu-

ally realized in terms of human history. The play ends with the Admiral, a solipsistic titan who represents the Nietzschean *Übermensch* (overman), defying the doubts of the mutinous weaker masses (the ship's crew) and following his personal vision of a New World—alone:

> *The Admiral, tied to the mast, looks at the mob in silence. Suddenly he twitches and begins to twist and struggle to break free, shouting at the top of his voice:* "It's a lie, people! It's all a lie, what you say! All of your vice-admirals and your continents and your close-knit majority with its mainstream beliefs!" *Then his wounds break open and blood runs down the mast in red streams.*
>
> (9:167)

This scene does not depict the omniscient helmsman of a successful revolution here on earth, but the death of an idealist crucified on the cross of his own vision. (Krleža originally dedicated this play to Lenin, but later removed his name.) Here individual ideology is shown as a negation of the will of the masses resulting in the Admiral's self-destruction. Thus Krleža presents the idea that the eschatological vision of total revolution cannot be realized, that social order is a compromise between the cave and the stars. Man's ideals are metastasized in the present. For the idealist, the "path to paradise" is a perilous tightwire suspended in the here-and-now between Olduvai Gorge and Alpha Centauri. Krleža's Columbus, like his Christ and his Michelangelo, is an example of an expressionist protagonist, an incarnation of the myth of the messiah-martyr as the carrier of a heretical conscience. He appears not in the classical mold of Greek tragedy as Prometheus, but in the Judeo-Christian tradition as Lucifer. This figure of spritual apostasy, of ideological rebellion, often portrayed as an artist or other soul in social revolt, is one of the most frequently occurring and fascinating in Krleža's opus. His original idea of a "pentology" never materialized, and the eight plays that eventually comprised the final edition of his visionary legends contained only three of his legendary heroes: Christ, Michelangelo, and Columbus.

The most farsighted of Krleža's early plays is *Kraljevo*, written in 1915 but rejected by the director of drama at the National Theater on the grounds that it was completely impossible to produce on the stage. In fact, this is one of the first works of the so-called popular theater. Instead of the stage being a place where representatives of the middle class present their problems, it becomes a theatrical meeting place where the people interact en masse to explain their lives from their own points of view. Thus, there is no classical protagonist.

Kraljevo is set at the beginning of the century in Zagreb. In the dramatist's imagination, this is where the national psyche is exposed. As the crowd moves through a fair, the attention centers on the collective scene more than on individual movements. In his elaborate stage instructions, Krleža presents this mass soul dynamically and synaesthetically as a "miracle of life." At the moment the curtain rises, "the rhythm of colors, lines, planes, and tones must be so intense that nothing can be made out separately. A chaos of undefined shapes swirl in the scene. Streams of color gush forth, great cascades of sound fall with a roar, the elementary miracle of life dances on the stage" (9:201). Various scenes then take place within the hum and bustle of the fair: a quarrel between a policeman and a peasant; petit-bourgeois revelers toasting one another and swearing; prostitutes resting at a table, talking and complaining about life; a pack of black dogs that bound into the fairgrounds as a bad omen. Then two characters appear to focus the play: Janez and Štijef, two dead men who had committed suicide because of unhappy love affairs and then returned to this world to see once more the women who caused their tragedy. In the dialogue between these two, Janez reveals that he has come back from the dead to see his old mistress Anka (who had humiliated him) in order to win her back. She refuses him, and the bodies of all those driven by Woman to their deaths gather to sing a hymn of despairing lovers, "Ave victrix Eva." The dead men want Anka to join in a *danse macabre* with them, but she flees just before the cock crows, and Janez falls dead again. The festivities continue on into the night.

The presence of the two dead men make this an antidrama. Their actions suggest that those who are unreal shadows lost in the limbo between life and death are in fact the most alive. These sad clowns, men who have taken their own lives, thus live out the dramaturgic conception: as heroes of a theater existence, the dead are more real than the living, their tragic fate overpowers illusion. At the point where the notion of the collective and the sense of the individual intersect, the play becomes a confrontation between nature and the supernatural, the sensible and the incoherent, life and illusion.

Thus, the fantasy of *Kraljevo* demands nothing less than a fuller conception of reality. When it was finally staged in the postwar period (first by the Belgrade Drama Theater, to great success), modern theater expression proved that what had been considered to be technical impossibilities posed by the vivid imagination of a young playwright (who was only twenty-two when he wrote the play) were actually obstacles erected by a traditional way of regarding the world and the theater. Before World War II the mature Krleža had been famous for his psychological realism (especially in the Glembay cycle), but the renewed interest in his earlier plays in 1955 marked the beginning of a reevaluation of his dramatic texts. Young new directors were attracted to the ideological rebellion implicit in his "legend" plays and during the next few years four of them were staged for the first time. These and the premieres of three other new plays written by Krleža after World War II, together with the numerous performances of his entire interwar dramatic repertoire, made him the most respected and most performed playwright in Yugoslavia.

MIROSLAV KRLEŽA

POSTWAR MASTERPIECES

The appearance of *Davni dani* (Distant Days) in 1956 was a landmark in the development of Krleža's prose style. This book of reflections about the period from 1914 to 1921, edited in the post-Stalinist atmosphere of growing aesthetic pluralism in Yugoslavia, is a work of auto-creation and auto-interpretation. It is far from a pure document; historical skepticism prevents it from being treated as a completely authentic diary. (Additional material from those years was added later.) Instead, it is an original amalgam of autobiographical notes, erudite cultural essays and lyrical prose. The result is an intentionally crafted and revised testament to the belief that freedom of artistic expression comes largely through self-concern and that the recognition of a writer's doubts, dilemmas, and dark thoughts plays an essential role in the formation of an antidogmatic intellect. An entry for 12 February 1916 reads:

> A person can lean over his darknesses as if over abysses. To test the depth of his abysses, a person can toss a pebble of his own doubts into himself from above in order to hear how deep that doubting question mark of his will roll, where and what sort of dark recesses of his own thoughts that little pebble will plumb. Unfortunately, a person will learn nothing except about the anxiety that is there and that tells us the same thing over and over: that everything is cramped and dark.
>
> (11–12:82)

The publication of this book testifies to the virtual victory of modernism in Yugoslavia during the 1950's. In Krleža, this process began during World War I with his assimilation of Baudelaire and Nietzsche. As is evident from his later writing, he developed into the Marxist apologist for these writers. *Davni dani* confirmed his unusual ability to achieve autobiographical distance by combining complete lyrical subjectivity and conventional memoir-istic propriety into a fictional confession that is a profession of artistic autonomy.

In 1958 Krleža published a new version of his Glembay play, *U agoniji*. This sublime, low-keyed drama with a classic existential triangle reminiscent of Strindberg, originally written in two acts with a predominantly psychological approach, now gained new sociological and satirical depth by the modification of the second act and the addition of a third. The sparring between a lawyer and a police investigator helps reveal the dubious social foundations and hypocritical morality of bourgeois civilization and transforms what had been the intimate personal drama of the sensitive Laura into the general tragedy of a society giving its last gasp.

In 1959 Krleža produced his longest and most complex experiment for the stage, a new five-act play, *Aretej ili Legenda o Svetoj Ancili, Rajskoj Ptici* (Aretaeus; or, The Legend of Saint Ancilla, the Bird of Paradise). This is an intellectual tragedy in which many of the author's artistic and political themes meet. The fictional motivation is the survival of the individual's right to his personal dream in times dominated by dogma, polemics, and ideological tendentiousness. Krleža draws on the legend about Aretaeus of Cappadocia, the second-century Greek physician and writer at the palatine court in Rome who rebelled against the intrigues of assassination, torture, and corruption around him. Through a play of the fantastic (the subtitle is *Fantazija u pet slika*, "A Fantasy in Five Scenes"), Aretaeus appears in Europe in 1938, where he is drawn into the vortex of events caused by the onset of modern-day totalitarianism adequate to the excesses of his own age. From this sense of scenic simultaneity of two bloodthirsty epochs, Krleža constructs a parable of what has remained primitive and violent in man throughout history. In what became the most famous aphorism from a play full of Socratic dialogues and learned observations, one of the characters states the author's hypothesis as he reprimands the eternally anthropoidal in man: "The essential thing is not that we telephone one another, but that it is still the ape in us that is doing the telephoning!"

This fantastic rendezvous of ancient Rome with twentieth-century Europe is the setting not only for a play about political terror (Krleža conceived of the play in 1938) but also for a philosophical drama about the predicament of the human spirit and thought. As he does elsewhere, Krleža takes what is an essential and productive theme and expands it. Here, he carries the baroque notion of the illusion of reality (Calderón's *La vida es sueño*) to completion: Life is a dream—and the other way around. The result is a kind of ironic truth that can only be achieved in the oneiric state that encompasses the play. Thus, when Aretaeus appears in today's world dressed as a Roman, he is taken as someone who has run away from a circus. Yet his presence in the twentieth century, even when he marvels at its material accomplishments, keeps a tragic pressure on the performance, causing each actor and spectator to wonder, "Who am I?" And when Aretaeus turns to all those watching, who in his eyes are dressed in fantastic fashion, and asks, "Whose slaves are you?" his words resound like a rhetorical judgment of a modern world in which everything has changed except the brutal relations between men.

After the successful staging of *Aretej* throughout Yugoslavia, it was apparent that the new postwar artistic method Krleža had chosen appealed to a broad audience, even as a four-hour, scenically avant-garde intellectual play. In 1961 he was a candidate along with Ivo Andrić for the Nobel Prize, and his reputation as a writer of international stature was apparent. In 1960 Jean-Paul Sartre came to Zagreb and was welcomed by Krleža at the Academy. From this meeting dates the now-famous apocryphal statement attributed to the French writer that, if he had known that Krleža had already written *Povratak Filipa Latinovicza* in 1932, he would never have taken it into

his head to write *La nausée*. Between 1961 and 1967 a collection of Krleža's essays appeared in six volumes, showing him to be a profound and wide-ranging interpreter of European art, science, and intellectual history. In 1962 he helped establish a new literary journal, *Forum*, put out under the auspices of the Academy, in which he would publish much during the sixties and seventies. He became one of the journal's five editors, a group whose collaboration dated from the times of his prewar "renegade" leftist journal *Pečat*. The new journal was launched with a spate of more than seven hundred pages of new prose text by Krleža in its first issues. The first of these issues comprised the third volume of his prewar novel, *Banket u Blitvi*, his allegorical catastrophist tract about the sanguinary nature of totalitarian systems in general, full of concrete allusions to the Central European and Baltic states, as well as to the dictatorship of monarchist Yugoslavia. This last volume is the conclusion of his grotesque political satire of the era of secret police regimes, purges, and coups d'état. In it he recaptures and refines his earlier mastery of internal monologue through a lyrical psychological portrayal of the principal figure, the vacillating intellectual Nielsen.

In 1962 Krleža began to publish the first parts of his most voluminous single work, *Zastave* (Banners), which took fifteen years to complete. This novel spans the time between 1912 and 1923, a decade covering the disruption and dissolution of the Habsburg Empire and contemporaneous with the author's years of maturation. During World War I, he had foreseen "a novel about Croatian civilization, one of the novels within the framework of a large decorative *panneau*—'Österreich-Ungarn in Wort und Bild.'" Half a century later his contribution to that work appeared as this six-volume epic. In a panoramic coverage that combines typical settings of Zagreb, Budapest, Vienna, and Belgrade, he creates a Pannonian-Danubian overview of Central European and Balkan societies in turmoil when the old bourgeois-imperial world of Austria-Hungary declined and died, radical national and international youth movements were born, new states were created amidst the noise of revolutions and the shuffling of political forces, and a reorientation of ideas and ideals of intellectuals took place. All these elements form the fabric in which a father and son are caught up and clash. The minister Emerički is loyal and servile to the state; young Kamilo, a student and lawyer, is rebellious and idealistic and seeks change. The antithesis between cataclysm, destruction, and the death of the historical order on the one hand, and the apocalyptic formation and foment of political ideas and ideologies on the other, forms the dialectic of a novel in which allegiances and causes are symbolized by the "banners."

In *Zastave*, Krleža deals with the conflict of generations, but without using a "genealogical" approach. Similarly, he evokes the end of an epoch in the solemn spirit of a requiem, but without being nostalgically "atmospheric." He does not show the diminished glory, but only the ruin of Austria as it lies "in state." Neither does he iterate the promise of the future in the mouth of his idealistic hero. Kamilo's state is one of disorientation, search, commitment. Krleža achieves this balance by avoiding a narrative that is made "belletristic," whether through philosophical, psychological, or poetic means. Instead of relying on techniques of plotting and character development along lines of sequence or coincidence that would emphasize some causal nexus, some hint either of determination or chance—instead of composing a grand epic harmony through the mixing of events and personalities—he produces a book in which the currents of happenings and actions are neither those of providential destiny nor individual will. They are, rather, the currents of historical occurrences and the interpersonal reactions to them. The only orders Krleža follows are those of the intellectual life of his hero and of the institutional death of the empire. Political drama and historical chronicle are interrelated through internal monologue and the communication of occasion. (Krleža draws on his dramaturgic talent here by using the telephone as a neutral medium that links minds with events, as he does with the telephoning "gorilla" elsewhere in his works.) The result is an epic of synthetic historical realism that possesses the existential fluidity and simultaneity of a Proustian "search for lost time."

Zastave represents a new phase in Krleža's fictional art, one in which an objective sense of history is conveyed from a personal perspective. His vision is a result of his own chronological distance and his psychological preoccupation with the early years of the twentieth century—days long gone, yet so immediate. This is his only work of prose fiction not written more or less proximate to the subject matter. He remembers vividly, with a virtuoso command of all the intricate titles and forms of address used by the bureaucracy and aristocracy of that improbable Dual Monarchy. What he remembers, fifty years later, has now become history. This factor alone probably accounts for the almost immediate translation of the novel into Hungarian and its controversial reception in Hungary as a roman à clef describing the intimate lives of leading intellectuals there. Although in the book's characters many critics have seen, among others, the figures of the renowned sociologist Oszkár Jászi and his wife, the famous poetess Anna Lesznai, Krleža vehemently denied any such direct correlation. In fact, for the first time, he created a work from the point of view less of contention with the world than acceptance of it. The novel is not constructed through the typical Krležian antithesis of ideologies, but through a synthesis of chronicle and memoir. Nevertheless, everything in it is fictionalized; there is no question of regarding the work as an autobiographical key. Conceived and written largely during the sixties, *Zastave* is Krleža's avant-garde answer to the professed crisis of the novel and to Sartre's notion of the *anti-roman.* In it he creates possibly his only truly positive hero, but one whose future is, at the end, punctuated by a large question mark.

HONORS AND THE VANTAGE OF AGE

The year 1963 was marked by the publication of celebratory volumes honoring Krleža's seventieth birthday and definitive bibliographies of his fifty years of literary work (almost twelve hundred entries) and critical studies of his work (seventeen hundred). Stiasny Verlag in Graz, Austria announced a project to publish his "collected works" in German. That year he published his *Saloma,* the play that he had intended to be the prelude to his cycle of legends and that had been rejected by the National Theater half a century earlier. It is a witty parody of the elliptical, sophisticated drawing-room conversation of fin-de-siècle drama in which he degrades the biblical legend as presented in Oscar Wilde's play and popularized by Max Reinhardt and Richard Strauss. In Krleža's version, John the Baptist head twice, the first time in Salomé's luxurious lap:

> Without a word John kneels in front of Salomé and kisses her sandals in the same way one kisses the slippers of martyrs. A nocturnal scene. Moonlight. Crickets. Salomé leans toward the Prophet and lyrically, brokenheartedly raises his head up into her lap.
>
> (9:295)

The publication of this impressionistic dramatic scherzo on the struggle between the sexes (one of his most "decadent" texts) in the same year that he was feted by the Academy as a prime mover of "socialist culture" was proof of Krleža's determination not to perform an ideological auto-da-fé against his first, pre-Marxist literary creations.

In 1964 Krleža was elected to the Central Committee of the Croatian League of Communists and made an official visit to Budapest,

where he was shown an edition of his works printed in 150,000 copies. At the Academy of Arts and Sciences there, he left the only recording in existence of him reading his own works—in Hungarian translation. He continued his official duties, visiting the Soviet Union with Tito in 1965, but in 1967, after signing the controversial "Declaration Concerning the Name and Status of the Croatian Literary Language" (which he claimed he thought of as a purely "nominal" constitutional issue), he lost his official post in the party hierarchy. In 1969 *Razgovori s Miroslavom Krležom* (Conversations with Miroslav Krleža) was published, in which he responded to the censorious dogmatic mentality displayed by many of his countrymen, paraphrasing the words of Maupassant—"Comme la République était belle sous l'Empire!"—from the ironic vantage point of one who had lived to see the less-than-perfect materialization of his youthful ideals: "Comme le socialisme était beau sous le capitalisme." And he defined his notion of the paradoxical relationship between the artist and society:

> For a writer to be worthy of his craft, he must have the possibility of being a *dissident* to some extent, even of being a *defeatist* in relation to the state and its institutions, in relation to the nation and its authorities. He is a "prodigal son" who returns to his father's hearth only in order to leave it again. Negation is his most familiar way of accepting the world.
>
> (Matvejević, *Razgovori*, 1969, p. 32)

In 1970 Krleža published his last play, a film scenario, *Put u raj* (The Path to Paradise), in which it is possible to see the evolution his dialectic of "legends" had undergone over the years. The play is modeled on the dialogic form of church drama (the hero is the counterpart of Saint Bernard in the medieval mystery). Here, however, the eschatological theme is fully developed in favor of the ironic mode. The visionary has assumed an air of superiority toward his fantasies. This play is a dramatization of Krleža's story "Cvrčak pod vodopadom" ("The

Cricket Beneath the Waterfall"), published in 1937.

In that work, he had posited the image of man in ironic revolt against the stagnant, parochial mentality that infects all social strata. They all reflect the chaotic Pannonian mind of the teeming masses ready to worship brute, rational ideologies. In the midst of the clash on the Left, Krleža opposes to all social classes his idle dreamers and singing poets, who by virtue of their bringing notes of sunlight into the dark, ammonia-laden atmosphere, represent revolt. They are the seekers, the prodigals, the neurotic agents, vagabonds, and intellectuals who live in a reality of fantasy. They form a spiritual clan of all those referred to by average, talentless people as poets, individualists, schizoids, and misfits. The poet, the dreamer, the seeker is the one who remains innermost an idealist. Krleža symbolizes the dreamer in man as a cricket; the dreamless world, against which the cricket revolts, as the water falling into a provincial cloaca. His cricket is the Pannonian equivalent of Don Quixote in the West. It is his metaphor for a small but lyrically pure voice singing in a backwater on the periphery of Europe. To be a heroic dreamer in the East "means to be a cricket who sings and never ceases singing in the pissoir of a tavern on the edge of town." In such a place, Krleža sets his poet chirping "beneath the waterfall of that stinking tar-covered cliff where pieces of citron float and ammonia stings the nostrils like in a laboratory, there, at the bottom of this human stench . . . " (8:613).

In *Put u raj*, it is apparent from the ironic tone in which the hero Bernardo speaks to his phantoms that he is fully conscious of the futile meaning of his "legendary" personality. This scenario indicates the development of Krleža's aesthetics after 1917, in a period when he was concerned with defining the relationship of art and the individual to revolution and society. Somewhere during the conflict on the Left, the carrier of eschatological irony ceased to be the externalized, confronting conscience and became the conscience that has rebelled and then been internalized once more. In this, Krleža's last dramatic work, the ironic conscience is carried by a hero who, as the author openly declares, has become a quixotic "cricket," the socially heretical artist.

During the 1970's Krleža published more of his autobiographical texts, the last truly creative literary work to come out during his life. The appearance of his *Dnevnik* (Diary) in 1977, a five-volume collection of his memoiristic prose, was a manifestation of what he had always been: a creative writer with expressly self-analytical, egocentric inclinations. From the beginning of his literary career, he wrote much about himself, continuously interpreting his artistic and nonartistic activities and repeating his own views—even interpolating earlier texts into new ones—to demonstrate either the consistency of his thought, or its development. He constantly revised and emended his texts, and some of the diary, which covers the period from 1914 to 1969, is based on what he wrote later. His fiction and nonfiction writings alike were always oriented toward the writer's own self, but it was the *literary* self. Several thousand pages of his diaries, chronicling the intellectual events and artistic aspirations of his life, have been published. Yet there is no focus in them on the many intimate facts, details, and involvements of his life. This is due largely to his own intervention, as Krleža continually directs attention away from the social peripeteia of his personal life and toward the thoughts and ideas contained in his works. He knew that dogmatically inclined minds on all sides sought to diminish his ethical stature, just as he was aware that the bohemian spirits with whom he associated wanted to exaggerate his image as an aesthete. But through his memoiristic texts, which are the essential breviary for understanding all of his work, he accomplishes two things: resistance to those who would seek scandal in him, and deflection of those who would make a public spectacle of him. All his books were, fundamentally and foremost, part of his independent portrait of the writer vis-à-vis society.

In this larger sense of his *opera omnia*, for which he received the Premio Mediterraneo in 1978, his autobiographical texts possess an artistic value of their own and make up one of the most important forms of his literary statement about the world. In them, he records his actual dreams, and it is not possible in every case to distinguish the dream from the daily reality. They are another proof that, for the consummate master of what Krleža himself referred to as "the literary medium," art and life, literature and reality, are no more separable than are the writer and society. To the end, Krleža maintained the same instinctual faith in the power of literature that he expresses in the last sentence of *Banket u Blitvi,* where he specifies the printed word as the single thing that remains for man in his struggle to refine his behavior and to define himself as *homo politicus:* "A box of lead letters. It isn't much, but it's the only thing man has invented up to now as a weapon to defend his human pride." Krleža's stance toward his calling as a writer was ethical. It was a life-long position he had defined early in his career, one he had expressed in 1919 in the poem "Riječ mati Čina" (The Word is Mother of the Deed):

> Riječ je trudna žena, što kolose raCa,
> cvile njeni nervi i utroba se njena puna krvi kida,
> kroz Riječ sijeva sviju stvari os.
> Riječ je trudna žena,
> i Čin,
> taj krvavi kolos,
> je tihe Riječi sin.
>
> (26:131)

> The Word is a pregnant woman who gives birth to
>   giants,
> nerves crying out, womb writhing full of blood,
> through the Word flashes the axis of all things.
> The Word is a pregnant woman,
> and the Deed,
> that bloody colossus,
> is son of the quiet Word.

Selected Bibliography

FIRST EDITIONS

INDIVIDUAL WORKS

POETRY

Pan. Zagreb, 1917.
Tri simfonije. Zagreb, 1917.
Pjesme I. Zagreb, 1918.
Pjesme II. Zagreb, 1918.
Pjesme III. Zagreb, 1919.
Lirika. Zagreb, 1919.
Knjiga pjesama. Belgrade, 1931.
Knjiga lirike. Zagreb, 1932.
Simfonije. Zagreb, 1933.
Balade Petrice Kerempuha. Ljubljana, 1936.
Pjesme u tmini. Zagreb, 1937.

PROSE

Tri kavalira gospođice Melanije. Zagreb, 1920.
Magyar Királyi honvéd novela. Zagreb, 1921.
Hrvatski bog Mars. Zagreb, 1922.
Novele. Koprivnica, 1923.
Vražji otok. Zagreb, 1924.
Izlet u Rusiju. Zagreb, 1926.
Povratak Filipa Latinovicza. Zagreb, 1932.
Hiljadu i jedna smrt. Zagreb, 1933.
Novele. Zagreb, 1937.
Banket u Blitvi. 2 vols. Zagreb, 1938–1939.
Knjiga proze. Zagreb, 1938.
Na rubu pameti. Zagreb, 1938.
Djetinjstvo u Agramu godine 1902–3. Zagreb, 1952.
Davni dani. Zagreb, 1956.
Banket u Blitvi. Vol. 3. Zagreb, 1964.
Zastave. 4 vols. Zagreb, 1967.
Dnevnik. 5 vols. Sarajevo, 1977.

ESSAYS, POLEMICS, CRITICISM

Eseji. Zagreb, 1932.
Moj obračun s njima. Zagreb, 1932.
Podravski motivi. Zagreb, 1933. With Kristo Hegedušić.
Evropa danas. Zagreb, 1935.
Deset krvavih godina. Zagreb, 1937.
Eppur si muove: Studije i osvrti. Zagreb, 1938.
Dijalektički antibarbarus. Zagreb, 1939.
Knjiga studija i putopisa. Zagreb, 1939.
Račić. Zagreb, 1947.

MIROSLAV KRLEŽA

Goya. Zagreb, 1948.

O Marinu Držiću. Belgrade, 1949.

Govor na Kongresu književnika u Ljubljani. Zagreb, 1952.

Pijana noć. Zagreb, 1952.

O Erazmu Rotterdamskom. Zagreb, 1953.

O nekim problemima Enciklopedije. Zagreb, 1953.

Kalendar jedne bitke godine 1942. Zagreb, 1953.

Kako stoje stvari. Zagreb, 1953.

Kalendar jedne parlamentarne komedije. Zagreb, 1953.

O parlamentarizmu i demokraciji kod nas. Zagreb, 1953.

Eseji. Belgrade, 1958.

Eseji. 6 vols. Zagreb, 1961–1967.

Panorama pogleda, pojava i pojmova. 5 vols. Sarajevo, 1975.

Iz naše književne krčme. Sarajevo, 1983.

Ratne teme. Sarajevo, 1983.

Sa urednčkog stola. Sarajevo, 1983.

PLAYS

Hrvatska rapsodija. Zagreb, 1918. Includes *Hrvatska rapsodija, Kraljevo,* and *Cristoval Colon.*

U predvečerje. Plamen 1:26–35 (1919).

Galicija (Kroaten-Lager). *Kritika* 3:99–108, 154–164, 217–218 (1922).

Vučjak. Koprivnica, 1923.

Gospoda Glembajevi. Zagreb, 1928.

U agoniji. Belgrade, 1931.

Glembajevi. Zagreb, 1932. Includes *Gospoda Glembajevi, U agoniji,* and *Leda.*

Legende. Zagreb, 1933. Includes *Legenda, Michelangelo Buonarotti, Kristofor Kolumbo, Maskerata, Kraljevo,* and *Adam i Eva.*

U logoru; Vučjak. Zagreb, 1934.

Golgota. Zagreb, 1937.

Glembajevi. 2 vols. Zagreb, 1945. Includes *Gospoda Glembaji, U agoniji,* and *Leda.*

Krokodilina ili razgovor o istini. Republika 1:226–240 (1945).

Aretej. Novi Sad, 1963.

Put u raj. Zagreb, 1970.

Drame. 5 vols. Sarajevo, 1981. Includes *Galicija* and *Saloma.*

COLLECTED WORKS

Sabrana djela Miroslava Krleže. 3 vols. Koprivnica, 1923–1926.

Miroslav Krleža. Sabrana djela. 9 vols. Zagreb, 1932–1934.

Djela Miroslava Krleže. 11 vols. Zagreb, 1937–1939.

Sabrana djela Miroslava Krleže. 27 vols. Zagreb, 1953–1972.

Sabrana djela Miroslava Krleže. Sarajevo, 1980–.

TRANSLATIONS

The Return of Philip Latinovicz. Trans. Zora G. Depolo. New York, 1969.

The Cricket Beneath the Waterfall and Other Stories. New York, 1972.

On the Edge of Reason. Trans. Zora G. Depolo. New York: Vangard, 1976.

CRITICAL STUDIES

COLLECTIONS

Baur, R. S., ed. *Miroslav Krleža zum 80. Geburtstag.* Munich, 1973.

Durić, Vojislav, ed. *Miroslav Krleža.* Belgrade, 1967.

Frangeš, Ivo, and Aleksandar Flaker, eds. *Krležin zbornik.* Zagreb, 1964.

Krolo, Ivan, and Marijan Matković, eds. *Miroslav Krleža 1973.* Zagreb, 1975.

Matković, Marijan, ed. *Zbornik o Miroslavu Krleži.* Zagreb, 1963.

MONOGRAPHS

Arapović, Boris. *Miroslav Krležas den Kroatiske guden Mars: Tillhomsthistoria, stil, genre.* Stockholm, 1984.

Bogdanović, Milan. *O Krleži.* Belgrade, 1956.

Bori, Imre. *Miroslav Krleža.* Újvidék, 1976.

Čengić, Enes. *Krleža.* Zagreb, 1982.

Donat, Branimir. *O pjesničkom teatru Miroslava Krleže.* Zagreb, 1970.

Engelsfeld, Mladen. *Interpretacija Krležina romana Povratak Filipa Latinovicza.* Zagreb, 1975.

Lasić, Stanko. *Struktura Krležinih Zastava.* Zagreb, 1975.

———. *Krleža: Kronologija života i rada.* Zagreb, 1982.

———. *Mladi Krleža i njegovi kritičari: 1914–1924.* Zagreb, 1987.

Lauer, Reinhard. *Miroslav Krleža und der deutsche Expressionismus.* Göttingen, 1984.

Leitner, Andreas. *Die Gestalt des Künstlers bei Miroslav Krleža.* Heidelberg, 1986.

Matković, Marijan. *La vie et l'oeuvre de Miroslav Krleža.* Paris, 1977.

Matvejević, Predrag. *Razgovori s Miroslavom Krležom.* Zagreb, 1969.

———. *Stari i novi razgovori s Krležom.* Zagreb, 1982.

Očak, Ivan. *Krleža—Partija.* Zagreb, 1982.

Ristić, Marko. *Krleža.* Zagreb, 1954.

Spiró, György. *Miroslav Krleža.* Budapest, 1982.

Vaupotić, Miroslav. *Siva boja smrti.* Zagreb, 1974.

Vučetić, Šime. *Krležino književno djelo.* Sarajevo, 1958; Zagreb, 1982.

Wierzbicki, Jan. *Miroslav Krleža.* Warsaw, 1975; Zagreb, 1980.

Zelmanović, Đorđe. *Kadet Krleža. Školovanje Miroslavia Krleže u mađarskim vojnin učilištima.* Zagreb, 1987.

Žmegač, Viktor. *Krležini evropski obzori. Djelo u Komparativnom kontekstu.* Zagreb, 1986.

BIBLIOGRAPHIES

Kapetanić, Davor. "Bibliografija djela Miroslava Krleže." In *Zbornik o Miroslavu Krleži,* edited by Marijan Matković. Zagreb, 1963. Pp. 601–773.

———. "Bibliografija Miroslava Krleže." *Revija* 5:80–133 (1968).

———. "Literatura o Miroslavu Krleži, 1914–1963." In *Miroslav Krleža,* edited by Vojislav Đurić. Belgrade, 1967. Pp. 335–451.

Tešić, Gojko M. "Bibliografija o Miroslavu Krleži 1968–1973." *Književna istorija* 6:351–434 (1973).

———. Literatura o Miroslavu Krleži 1973." In *Miroslav Krleža 1973,* edited by Ivan Krolo and Marijan Matković. Zagreb, 1975. Pp. 627–672.

Krleža's manuscripts and a collection of his personal letters are held in the archives of the Zavod za književnost i teatrologiju JAZU (The Institute for Literature and Theater of the Yugoslav Academy of Arts and Sciences) in Zagreb.

RALPH BOGERT

VLADIMIR MAYAKOVSKY

(1893–1930)

INTRODUCTION

AS BORIS PASTERNAK once observed, Vladimir Mayakovsky chose to make his life a spectacle, insisting that his life and his poetry were one. He was by his own choice always in the public eye, not only as a poet but also as a popular cartoonist, as a propagandist and ad-man, as a filmmaker and actor, and as a world traveler and journalist. Hence his biography is more directly relevant to an understanding of his poetry than is true in the case of most modern poets.

Vladimir Vladimirovich Mayakovsky was born on 19 July 1893 in Bagdadi (now named Mayakovsky in his honor), a village in western Georgia. "Volodya" remained close to his mother and two older sisters all his life, but his father, a forester in the government service, died in 1906. The family moved to Moscow after his father's death. Young Mayakovsky attended secondary school in Moscow, but as early as 1908 he got involved in the revolutionary underground, was arrested three times, and never graduated. He had an exceptional talent for drawing and in 1911 enrolled in the Moscow Institute of Painting, Sculpture, and Architecture, where he was immediately caught up in the ferment of modernist art. An older fellow student, the painter and poet David Burlyuk, discovered Mayakovsky's poetic gift, and soon Mayakovsky was a signatory and contributor to the futurist manifestos *Poshche-china obshchestvennomu vkusu* (A Slap in the Face of Public Taste, December 1912) and *Sadok sudei, II* (A Trap for Judges, II, February 1913). The group of which Mayakovsky found himself a member initially called itself Gileya (Hylaea) after the Greek name of the region on the Black Sea that was the home of the Burlyuk family. Benedikt Livshits, a member of the group, invented the name to signal the futurists' admiration for the savage freedom of the Scythian horsemen who had once lived there. Mayakovsky, however, did not share the archaist and primitivist tendencies of some of the other futurists, notably Velemir Khlebnikov, the most imaginative and original poet of the group. The futurist group to which Mayakovsky belonged was soon labeled "cubo-futurist" to distinguish it from the "ego-futurists" led by Igor Severyanin, and some other avant-garde groups such as those associated with *Mezonin poezii* (The Mezzanine of Poetry) and *Tsentrifuga* (Centrifuge).

When Burlyuk took the futurist show of modernist "happenings" on the road in the winter of 1913, Mayakovsky was its star. He also began to publish competent essays on modern art and film. In December 1913 Mayakovsky's play *Vladimir Mayakovskii: Tragediya* (*Vladimir Mayakovsky: A Tragedy*) was performed twice at the Luna Park Theater in St. Petersburg, alternating with the even more notorious *Pobeda nad solntsem* (*Victory over the Sun*, 1913) by the futurists Aleksei Kruchenykh and Khlebnikov. Mayakovsky directed his play and also played the lead. Both futurist extravaganzas met with a mixture of puzzlement and derision. (Costumes for Mayakovsky's play were designed by Pavel Filonov, who became one of Russia's great modern painters, and the sets for *Victory over the Sun* were by Kazimir Malevich.)

The outbreak of World War I caused the futurists to disband. They were to be reunited only by the revolution of 1917. In 1915 Mayakovsky met Lilya Brik, the great love of his life. She was two years older than he and married to Osip Maksimovich Brik (1888–1945), who became a good friend of Mayakovsky's, publishing his works and eventually collaborating with him in various literary ventures. The first complete edition of Mayakovsky's first *poema* (the Russian term for a narrative poem several hundred lines or more in length), *Oblako v shtanakh* (A Cloud in Trousers, 1915), bears the dedication "To you, Lilya." However, most of it was written before Mayakovsky had met Lilya. His next *poema, Fleita-pozvonochnik* (The Backbone Flute, 1915), is a candid expression of the poet's love, jealousy, and suffering (Lilya was rather cold to him during all the years of their *ménage à trois*).

Mayakovsky's reaction to the horrors of war, the lengthy *poema Voina i mir* (War and the World, 1918) and the *poema Chelovek* (Man, 1918), Mayakovsky's blasphemous self-apotheosis, could only be published after the Revolution. The Russian avant-garde, and hence the futurists, led by Mayakovsky, welcomed the October Revolution, believing that the new regime would create a favorable ambience for progressive art. As early as the winter of 1918 the Moscow futurists published their "Decree No. 1 on the Democratization of Art," and Mayakovsky created a steady stream of aggressively revolutionary poetry. From 1919 to 1921 his principal outlet was the display windows of the Soviet Telegraph Agency (ROSTA), for which he wrote versified comments on recent events, illustrated by his own cartoons. This strictly utilitarian work—Mayakovsky's topics ranged from the Soviet war effort to the need to boil water before drinking it—was often technically brilliant, featuring ingenious rhymes, clever puns, and spirited parody of literary classics.

Mayakovsky's play *Misteriya-buff: Geroicheskoe, epicheskoe i satiricheskoe izobrazhenie nashei epokhi* (*Mystery-Bouffe: A Heroic, Epic, and Satirical Representation of Our Epoch*, 1918) was staged at the Petrograd Musical Theater to celebrate the first anniversary of the October Revolution. Directed by the great Vsevolod Meyerhold and featuring amateur actors (Mayakovsky himself played one major and two minor roles), it was decidedly a "happening," and repeat performances in 1920 and 1921 were even closer to the genre of the public spectacle. The 1921 performance, which employed 350 actors and dancers, was staged in a circus before the delegates of the Third Congress of the Comintern. In 1918 Mayakovsky also started his career as a filmmaker; he wrote scenarios for several films in which he also played the lead. *Zakovannyi fil'moi* (Fettered by Film, 1918), in which Lilya Brik was his leading lady, featured some clever gags, the key one being that the object of the hero's love, a movie star, remains forever elusive because she can materialize only on screen. Mayakovsky also drew the poster advertising the film: a bust of Lilya Brik, emaciated and with no breasts, growing from a giant heart, her thin arms fettered by a snakelike roll of film.

Mayakovsky's revolutionary *poema 150,-000,000* (1920–1921) was not well received, least of all where it counted, with the Bolshevik leadership, Lenin and Trotsky in particular. The former found Mayakovsky's revolutionary fantasy "absurd, stupid, monstrously stupid and pretentious." Mayakovsky nevertheless continued in the good graces of the party (which he never joined), and with the beginning of the New Economic Policy (NEP) period in 1921, he established himself as the regime's principal versifying propagandist and satirist. In the following years many of his pieces appeared in *Izvestiya* (News), the organ of the Soviet government, or *Komsomolskaya pravda* (Komsomol Truth), the organ of the Young Communist League; his poems usually referred directly to headlines or editorials in the same or in a recent issue of the paper. They covered every conceivable topic, from condemnations of Western capitalism (and its "lackeys," such as the British Labour Party) to denunciations of church holidays because they cause drunkenness and absenteeism. When the time came in 1928, Mayakovsky duly supported Stalin's Five Year Plan and, of course, the collectivization of agriculture. Mayakovsky's frequent personal appearances throughout the Soviet Union, as well as his radio addresses, were also attuned to the Soviet government's position on current issues. In addition he found time to write didactic poems for children and a good deal of strictly utilitarian verse, including advertising copy and propaganda slogans.

One of the rewards of Mayakovsky's loyal support of the Soviet regime was a passport, the subject of one of his most famous poems, "Stikhi o sovetskom pasporte" (Verses on My Soviet Passport, 1929), which allowed him to travel frequently to the West. He often visited France, where Lilya Brik's younger sister Elsa Triolet (who later married Louis Aragon) was his hostess and where he developed contacts with French intellectuals, especially with artists (Braque, Léger, Picasso, and others), on whose work he reported competently. In 1925 Mayakovsky spent three months in the United States, having arrived there via Cuba and Mexico. He gave talks and poetry readings in several major cities, did a lot of sightseeing (Coney Island, Broadway, a World Series baseball game), and busily took notes. His American travelogue *Moe otkrytie Ameriki* (My Discovery of America, 1925–1926) is lively and perceptive, and his dozen or so poems on American themes are among his best. They are all impeccably orthodox in their political outlook.

In 1923 Mayakovsky and his friends founded a journal, *Lef* (short for *Levyi front,* "Left Front"), which was to be an organ of the Russian and international avant-garde. Among its contributors were major poets and writers such as Pasternak and Isaak Babel, painters such as Aleksandr Rodchenko, filmmakers such as Sergei Eisenstein, and literary theorists such as Osip Brik and Viktor Shklovsky. In comparison with other loyal Communist groups such as Pereval and the Onguardists (later RAPP, the Russian Association of Proletarian Writers) and their journals, *Krasnaya nov'* (Red Virgin Soil) and *Na postu* (On Guard), *Lef* was distinguished not by its political views but by its aesthetics. While the other groups of the left favored conservative mimetic art, *Lef* advocated a modern form to accompany revolutionary content. The artists and writers of *Lef* sought to express their ideas in sharply focused and overstated images rather than to seek a compromise between revolutionary zeal and conventional realism. In retrospect *Lef* was far superior in quality to its competitors, but it never sold well, had to suspend publication in 1925, tried a new start as *Novyi Lef* (New *Lef*) in 1927, and finally ceased publication in 1930, by which time Mayakovsky had already abandoned it.

During those years Mayakovsky produced a huge number of shorter poems (many of which were not all that short, sixty lines or more being not uncommon) and several major verse epics. The most interesting of these, *Pro eto* (About That, 1923), was the feature attraction of the first issue of *Lef.* The first year of Stalin's Five Year Plan, 1928, found Mayakovsky as busy and successful as ever. In the fall of that year he brought back from Paris a brand new Renault car. He felt that an explanation was in order and wrote a poem, "Otvet na budushchie spletni" (An Answer to Future Gossip, 1928), to justify his possession. He felt that his automobile, his trips to the West, his custom tailored suits and clean shirts were all a legitimate part of what he stood for: economic and cultural progress through hard work. Also in the fall of 1928, Mayakovsky fell in love with Tatyana Yakovlev, a beautiful Russian émigré. He was again inclined to "squander some lines on lyrics," as he put it in his poem "Pis'mo tovarishchu Kostrovu iz Parizha o sushchnosti lyubvi" (A Letter to Comrade Kostrov from Paris, on the Nature of Love, 1928). Kostrov, editor of *Komsomolskaya pravda,* who had commissioned some political poems, must have been puzzled, but he did print the poem.

But there were reverses also. A film based on a scenario by Mayakovsky, *Dekabryukhov i Oktyabryukhov* (Dekabryukhov and Oktyabryukhov), shown in Kiev in May and in Moscow in September of 1928, drew scathing reviews and was soon withdrawn. Two of Mayakovsky's earlier film scenarios had been rejected. *Lef* was on its last legs, and Mayakovsky abandoned it in September 1928. In two public lectures entitled "Levei LEFa!" (To the Left of *Lef!* 1928), he justified his step by suggesting that the time had come to jettison narrow "sectarian" groupings and to join the broad mainstream of Soviet life, reflected in periodicals of mass circulation.

On 13 February 1929 Mayakovsky's satirical play *Klop* (The Bedbug, 1929), which was a rewrite of a film scenario earlier rejected by the Soviet film agency Sovkino, was staged at Meyerhold's theater in Moscow. The music was by Dimitry Shostakovich, and Rodchenko created some of the sets. It was a popular success but received mixed reviews. The day after the first night of *The Bedbug,* Mayakovsky went abroad again to sign a contract for a German translation of his works and to arrange for the staging of *The Bedbug* in Prague (this did not work out). He then went on to France, where he continued his courtship of Tatyana Yakovlev.

Upon his return to Russia in May, Mayakovsky immediately plunged back into the usual whirlpool of his varied activities. In September he tried to launch a new group, *Ref* (Revolutionary Front), to supersede *Lef,* but it never got off the ground. Also in September he was denied a passport and soon received word that Tatyana had married a French diplomat, a Vicomte du Plessix (the American

writer Francine du Plessix is their daughter). Suddenly Mayakovsky's fortunes were in decline. The Leningrad opening of his new play, *Banya* (*The Bathhouse,* 1930), on 30 January 1930 was a disaster. The night after the Leningrad debacle Mayakovsky read his last great poem, "Vo ves' golos" (At the Top of My Voice, 1930), at the opening of his exhibition "Twenty Years of Work" at the Writers' Club in Moscow. The exhibition featured documentary evidence of his early revolutionary activities; manuscripts, drafts, and notebooks; his early works, with illustrations and cover designs by artists such as Larionov, Malevich, and Lisitsky; a selection of Mayakovsky's cartoons, posters, and advertising copy; many photographs of Mayakovsky in film roles, and so on; and various other memorabilia. The exhibition was well attended, but some important literary functionaries were conspicuously absent.

When *The Bathhouse* opened at Meyerhold's theater on 16 March, the stage and theater were decorated with numerous posters to drive home the message of the play. One of these read: "You can't / wash away at once / the whole swarm of bureaucrats. // There just aren't enough / bathhouses / or soap. // And besides, bureaucrats get help from the pen / of critics / like Ermilov." V. V. Ermilov, a member of RAPP, protested, and his organization pressured Meyerhold into removing the poster. Mayakovsky grudgingly agreed to have it taken down. In his suicide note written a month later, he said that he regretted that he had. Opening night in Moscow was not the disaster it had been in Leningrad, but reviews were every bit as bad. The new generation of Soviet critics and a good part of the audience, too, lacked the capacity for suspension of disbelief needed to appreciate Mayakovsky's futuristic grotesque. Mayakovsky put up a spirited defense of his play in a series of public discussions and immediately went to work on a new play, *Moskva gorit (1905)* (*Moscow on Fire [1905]: A Mass Spectacle with Songs and Words,* 1930). The spectacle had been commissioned to celebrate the twenty-fifth anniversary of the revolution of 1905. It was performed at the Moscow Circus a mere week after Mayakovsky's death.

At 10:15 A.M. on 14 April 1930, Mayakovsky shot himself through the heart in his Moscow office, shortly after Veronika Polonsky, a young actress who had been with him that morning, had left. He left a note that gave no reason for his suicide, except that he "had no other choice." Of the individuals mentioned in it, the Briks, who had been abroad at the time of Mayakovsky's suicide, became executors of his posthumous papers; Polonsky could give no explanation for her lover's suicide; and the critic Ermilov prospered for many years as a faithful servant of the Party. The suicide had the effect of a bombshell. It was then and still is the subject of much speculation. The suicide theme appears often in Mayakovsky's poetry, and Lilya Brik suggested that his poetic threats of suicide were a reflection of genuine and deep depressions.

THE EARLY POETRY (1912–1916)

When Russian futurism took the stage in 1912 it had to coexist with several other schools, some of them modernist and some not. Symbolism, with a decadent and a mystic branch, had been in existence for over a decade, but its leading poets, Alexander Blok and Andrey Bely, were only a few years older than some of the futurists. The acmeists, who, like the futurists, were challenging symbolism, belonged to the same generation as the futurists. In the futurist manifesto *Poshchechina obshchestvennomu vkusu,* the symbolists Fyodor Sologub, Mikhail Kuzmin, Konstantin Balmont, and Valery Bryusov were listed among those to be "thrown overboard from the ship of contemporary life." The futurist aesthetic was in fact an antithesis to that of symbolism. Also, the mystic symbolists, such as Bely and Vyacheslav Ivanov, were god-seekers with a passionate involvement in metaphysics, while the futurists' outlook was oriented toward this world. The symbolists (and the acmeists, too) were oriented toward world literature in a historical perspective, while the futurists' stance was either one of archaic and ahistorical primitivism or of antihistorical modern urbanism. The symbolists were sophisticated intellectuals, obsessed with a premonition of Russia's impending relapse into barbarism, metaphorically an "Invasion of the Huns" (the title of a poem by Bryusov, 1905). Mayakovsky, in one of his early poems, "Nate!" (There! 1914), accepted this challenge, calling himself a "rude Hun," and his fellow futurists pointedly cultivated an Asiatic and "barbarian" orientation. The symbolists, with some exceptions, adhered to an organic aesthetic, while the futurists embraced a formalist aesthetic, seeing the material of which the work of art is made (language, in the case of poetry) as the artist's point of departure. This made art a skillful manipulation of that material and the work of art a product of that skill.

The futurists, and Mayakovsky in particular, cultivated an aggressive humanism, with man the adversary and conqueror of nature. The futurists' feud with the sun, symbol of nature's power, was an expression of this attitude. The futurist spectacle *Victory over the Sun* was one of many treatments of this theme. "Picking quarrels with the Sun," presented as a stage in a poet's progress in Pasternak's poem "So they start" (1919), was a frequent preoccupation of the young Mayakovsky.

Symbolism was oriented mainly toward music. The futurists, including Mayakovsky, had a background in the visual arts. Cubist painting stimulated them to break down their material, language, into its constituent elements (sounds and word roots) and to reconstitute it in new arrangements. The futurists approached poetry in terms of "the word as such" (*samovitoe slovo*), "surface texture" (*faktura,* a term relating to the texture of canvas), and "displacement" (*sdvig,* a term denoting the deformation of figures in cubist painting).

The basic traits of Russian futurism and of Mayakovsky's early poetry have parallels in various modernist styles of painting as well as other art forms, and may be explained in part by their influence. The cosmic themes and imagery so prominent in Mayakovsky's early poetry may be perceived as a materialized—some would say "vulgarized"—version of the cosmic and theosophic visions of symbolist poets such as Vyacheslav Ivanov and painters such as Kandinsky and Malevich. The primitivism of Mikhail Larionov and others who painted in the manner of a child or sign painter had some equivalents in futurist poetry, Mayakovsky's in particular, for instance in his "Vyveskam" (To Signs, 1913), a versified medley of signs (for a fish market, funeral parlor, and so on.)

Some of Mayakovsky's early poems are patterned after cubist paintings, presenting sharply deformed cityscapes. In the poem "Iz ulitsy v ulitsu" (From Street to Street, 1913), the familiar is artfully defamiliarized, as one recognizes a moving streetcar in the lines "a magician / pulling / a pair of tracks / from a streetcar's jaws" and a streetcorner at night: "A bald lantern / voluptuously takes off / a street's / black stockings." One of the futurists, Livshits, later said that in this kind of poetry "the word, having gotten all too close to painting, ceased having sound." Some of the futurists, such as Burlyuk and Vasily Kamensky, enhanced the visual quality of their poems by using typographical arrangements symbolic of their meaning. Mayakovsky employed the graphic aspect of his medium sparingly, though in his earliest poetry he used such "gimmicks" as interspersing a description of an automobile ride with shreds of signs whirling by: for example, the word "post" abruptly appears and after a full line is followed by the next word on the sign—"office." He also left it to other futurists, such as Kruchenykh and Ilya Zdanevich, to explore poetic composition based on the sounds rather than the meaningful morphemes of the Russian language.

In some ways Mayakovsky's early lyrics are "expressionist" more than "cubist," featuring bold outlines, loud colors, sudden transitions, and a hatred of the pretty and sentimental—all of which led to pointedly "unaesthetic" imagery. The main subjects of Mayakovsky's early poetry are savagely distorted cityscapes depicting "Adishche goroda" ("The Hell of the City," 1913) in its fearsome ugliness and macabre absurdity. In "Koe-chto po povodu dirizhera" (The Case of the Bandleader, 1915), the bandleader lets his trumpet slap a bearded patron's "stuffed mug with a handful of brassy tears," while his trombones and bassoons bowl over other patrons, one of whom "dies with his cheek dipped in gravy," whereupon the bandleader sticks his trumpet into the corpse's teeth and listens to the wails resounding in the victim's bloated belly. In the morning, when the owner of the nightclub brings the bandleader his termination notice, he finds him "turned blue hanging from the chandelier, / swinging and turning bluer."

All his life Mayakovsky liked to parody the poetry of others, but he never admitted to anybody's specific influence on his own poetry. He shared this attitude with the futurists as a group who vigorously, although not altogether convincingly, denied that the Italian futurist Filippo Tommaso Marinetti (1876–1944) had anything to do with their movement. Marinetti's first manifesto, of 20 February 1909, had appeared in the Petersburg newspaper *Vecher* (Evening) on 8 March of that year, and a good deal more had already been reported on Franco-Italian futurism by various Russian sources when Marinetti himself visited Moscow and Petersburg in the winter of 1914. However, after his second Petersburg lecture on 4 February 1914, a group of Russian futurists, Mayakovsky among them, published a declaration to the effect that their group had nothing in common with Italian futurism save the name. This was hardly true. The Russian futurists had little of Marinetti's aggressive nationalism and none of his militarism, but they shared his uncompromising hatred of *passéisme* and his urbanism and enthusiasm for modern technology and speed. His misogyny had explicit parallels in *Victory over the Sun* and some other futurist works, though not so much in Mayakovsky. But then, Mayakovsky's farfetched metaphors and fractured trains of images bear a distinct resemblance to Marinetti's "wireless imagination," which arbitrarily passes from one region of time and space to another. Also, Mayakovsky's early poetry is written mostly in rhymed free rhythms, a manner that Marinetti also cultivated.

Mayakovsky knew modern French poetry (in translation): Arthur Rimbaud, Paul Verlaine, Émile Verhaeren and Guillaume Apollinaire. But ironically it was the naive religious poetry of Francis Jammes that found a real echo in a couple of Mayakovsky's early poems. Mayakovsky's poem "Poslushaite!" (Listen! 1913) features this striking variant of the argument for the existence of God "from design": "Is it not true that if stars are lit, // this means that somebody needs them?" This is apparently an echo of "Prayer for a Star" by Jammes, much as Mayakovsky's line "I like to watch how children die" in "Neskol'ko slov obo mne samom" (A Few Words About Myself, 1913) is a jibe at "Prayer That the Child Won't Die." Walt Whitman was much admired by the Russian avant-garde. When Mayakovsky describes the glories of American capitalism in "150,000,000," he sees "a hall full of / all kinds of Lincolns, Whitmans, Edisons." When Mayakovsky makes Vladimir Mayakovsky, "handsome, twenty-two years old," the persona of his *poema Oblako v shtanakh,* this reminds one of Whitman's "Song of Myself," begun by the poet when he was "now thirty-seven years old in perfect health." There are other similarities besides the huge egos of both poets: a fancy for hyperbole and paradoxic imagery, a penchant for personification and metamorphosis, use of free verse (then as now, a rarity in Russia), and, in general, a certain robust rambunctiousness.

The young Mayakovsky often saw himself as a martyred saint or as Jesus Christ himself, albeit rarely without a touch of travesty. A connection between this theme and the Nietzschean archetype of the suffering god is not unlikely. Nietzsche was a major influence in Russian symbolism, and Mayakovsky, while ostensibly disdainful of his symbolist *confrères,* attentively followed their work. Altogether, for a young man of little formal education, Mayakovsky was remarkably literate. The imagery of his early poetry covers the whole range of Russian and Western civilization.

The young Mayakovsky's aesthetic was diametrically opposed to the utilitarian theory and practice of his postrevolutionary writings. In the essay "Zhivopis' segodyashnego dnya" (The Painting of Today, 1914) he declared:

> It was not so long ago, either, that nobody so much as dreamed of art as an end in itself. Doubled up under the load of the concern for dumb animal existence and the struggle for survival, we forced even the artist to join us in our screams for bread and justice.
>
> (*Polnoe sobranie sochinenii* 1:286)

He suggested that there were other and better ways to fulfill the mimetic, didactic, and moral goals of man and that art ought to be left alone to pursue its "only and eternal goal: free play of man's cognitive faculties." He made the same point more drastically in another essay of 1914, "Shtatskaya shrapnel" (A Civilian Shrapnel): "While, as a Russian, I hold sacred our soldiers' every effort to snatch away one inch of soil from the enemy, I must also think [as an artist] that the whole war was thought up for the sole purpose of enabling someone to write one good poem."

A competent art critic, the young Mayakovsky enthusiastically embraced the modern art of his day. Apparently alluding to Henri Matisse's panneau *The Dance,* he said: "Instead of paintings that are camels or other such beasts of burden, serving the conveyance of 'the rational meaning of the subject matter,' we ought to have paintings that are merry barefooted dancers, whirling about in a passionate and brightly colored dance." To the young Mayakovsky art meant essentially the realization of a new vision of the world, achieved through deformation, dislocation, and deconstruction:

At once, I blotched the map of humdrum life
by splashing some paint on it from a glass;
I displayed, on a dish of fish-jelly,
the ocean's slanting cheekbones.
On the scales of a tin fish,
I read the call of new lips.
But you,
could you
play a nocturne
on the flute of a drainpipe?
        ("A vy mogli by?" [But Could You? 1913])

In another essay of 1914, "Bez belykh flagov" (No White Flags), Mayakovsky drew a line between himself, a futurist, and the symbolist "decadents" who also asserted that the poetic word was an end in itself. They were, he said, like the ancient Egyptians, who knew that you could produce electric sparks by stroking a dry black cat but who never learned how to use this knowledge to run streetcars and light up cities. Only the futurists, he said, had the strength and courage to bring the word under a master innovator's conscious control.

Mayakovsky's prerevolutionary poetry features a great deal of fractured construction, cubist dissection of objects into their constituent elements, and other forms of defamiliarization, thus creating a new, fantastic world that, upon closer scrutiny, is still that of empirical reality. Some of the early poems read like a rebus or charade; consider the poem "Port" (Seaport, 1912):

Bedsheets of water under her belly
torn into waves by a white tooth.
The wail of sirens, as though the brass of pipes
were pouring out their love and lechery.
Lifeboats in the cradles of their berths
snuggling up to the teats of their iron mothers.
In the steamers' ears gone deaf,
there burned the earrings of anchors.

While Mayakovsky shared the aesthetic, the themes, and most of the techniques of his poetry with the other futurists, his verse soon showed an ingredient that theirs lacked: Mayakovsky's huge and idiosyncratic ego. The first-person singular, which so dominates his early poetry, is often a kind of cosmic "I," the poet-creator challenging the Creator: "In a second // I shall meet // the monarch of the heavens— // and I shall simply kill the Sun!" ("Ya i Napoleon" [I and Napoleon, 1915]). A concomitant trait is the persona's alienation, which is as hyperbolic as its ego. In a poem of 1916 characteristically entitled "Sebe lyubimomu, posvyashchaet eti stroki avtor" (To Himself, Beloved by Him, the Author Dedicates These Lines), Mayakovsky exclaims: "If I were // little, // like the Great Ocean, // I'd rise to my tiptoes on its waves // and I'd be the tide fondling the moon. // Where could I find myself a beloved //such as myself?" Hyperbolic alienation causes hyperbolic suffering, and the theme of such suffering permeates the young Mayakovsky's poetry. In a poem entitled "Ko vsemu" (To All, 1916), the poet imagines himself to be "a white bull with his neck festering under the yoke and a swarm of flies" or "a moose with his antlers caught in some wires, his bloodshot eyes bulging."

Mayakovsky's first *poema, Oblako v shtanakh,* features all of these themes. Its title is explained in a prologue:

If you want me to,
I'll be mad with flesh,
but, like the sky changing its hue,
if you want me to,
I shall be irreproachably tender,
not a man, but a cloud in trousers.

In *Oblako v shtanakh* the cosmos, God and a whole arsenal of religious symbols, the history of mankind, recent news headlines, and so forth all serve one purpose: to provide metaphors for the love and suffering of Vladimir Mayakovsky (identified by name in the text). The cause of his anguish is a young lady named Mariya who, however, makes only a brief appearance to announce that she is getting married. The whole drift of the poem is toward a cosmic Golgotha. Mayakovsky, who will "use the sun for a monocle" and before whom "all earth will spread herself like a woman, her flesh fidgeting," also imagines himself as "the spat-upon man of Golgotha" and likens himself to "a dog licking the hand that beats it." The poem contains much gratuitously blasphemous imagery, but it includes a strain of what might be genuine pain and self-pity: "And while my voice // shouts bawdy words, // hour after hour, // all day long, // maybe, Jesus Christ is sniffing // the forget-me-nots of my soul." Mayakovsky's imagery is interesting and unpredictable throughout this poem, though somewhat strained. His rhymed free verse is fresh and vigorous; his rhymes are ingenious, and there is a great deal of inner rhyme, assonance, and alliteration to enhance the rhythm.

Mayakovsky's next *poema, Fleita-pozvonochnik* (The Backbone Flute, 1915), is a shorter, tighter, and more intense version of *Oblako v shtanakh.* Its title is also explained in a prologue: "Today I shall play the flute // on my own backbone." The object of the poet's love and despair is now Lilya, though she is not named in the text, and his feelings for her are unequivocally *odi et amo* (I hate and love):

> Where can I go with such hell within me!
> What heavenly Hoffmann
> dreamed you up, accursed one?!
> (*Polnoe sobranie sochinenii* 1:200)

The metaphor of the diabolic *femme fatale* is promptly realized, as we hear that if one made the sign of the cross over her marital couch, "there surely would be a smell of burnt wool, // and a devil's flesh would go up in sulfurous smoke." But there follows a quick transition to the cosmos as the poet implores God, "that almighty inquisitor," to "tie him to comets, as to horses' tails, // and whirl him into space, // rending him against the jags of stars," or to "string him up, the criminal, // using the Milky Way for a gallows."

Mayakovsky's next two major verse epics, *Voina i mir* and *Chelovek,* saw print only after the Revolution, but their poetics is still purely

futurist. In *Voina i mir* a world ablaze becomes an extension of Mayakovsky (still identified by name!) who, in a series of conceits, sees himself as victim and tormentor alike. It is he who "stands on the place of execution, // gasping for his last // breath of air," but it is also he "who carried // a beheaded babe // to the idol's altar." Mayakovsky's self-identification with victims as well as perpetrators of horrors eventually dovetails into the theme of resurrection and new life:

> Let me bleed to death, hacked to pieces,
> but with my blood I shall eat away
> the name of "murdered"
> with which man is branded.
> (*Polnoe sobranie sochinenii* 1:230)

The poem ends in a celebration of universal love and brotherhood.

Chelovek is a polyphonic composition with a plot, in which several leitmotivs are set off against each other in a lyrical "minor" and a satirical "major" key. The plot structure is provided by the travesty of an Orthodox saint's life: The Nativity of Mayakovsky—The Life of Mayakovsky—The Passion of Mayakovsky—The Ascension of Mayakovsky—Mayakovsky in Heaven—The Return of Mayakovsky—Mayakovsky to the Aeons. The text is saturated with quotations, usually in free variations, from biblical and liturgical texts. The more clearly liturgic (in travesty, of course) prologue and epilogue are composed in a liturgic prose recitative. The *vita* itself alternates between rhymed free verse, close to the "spoken verse" (*skazovyi stikh*) of Russian folklore, and iambic passages of a driving staccato rhythm. The satire and boutade are all in the former, the lyric passages almost all in the latter form. *Chelovek* is the most euphonically orchestrated of Mayakovsky's longer poems, featuring a great wealth of inner rhyme, complex and extended alliteration patterns, assonance and vowel modulation, and sound symbolism.

The main theme of *Chelovek* is the metaphysical anguish of the poet, who appears as

Christ, martyr, dandy, or clown, and his painful alienation in an absurd and hostile world, a world in which he either finds himself a prisoner, "the globe of the Earth // chained to his feet," "locked // into a senseless tale // forever" or is pursued by "Him, the Sovereign of All, // my invincible adversary." "He" is not identified, but it was "He" who "ordered the late Phidias // to make him some buxom broads //from marble," it was "He" whose "nimble cook, // God, // created pheasant meat for him // from clay," and it is "He" who has "legions of Galileos // scurrying about the stars through the eyes of telescopes" to find him "the most priceless of females." Soviet critics have identified "Him" with "capitalism," but it is more likely that "He" is the side of man that insists that day-to-day living (*byt*) *is* life. It was *byt* that of all things Mayakovsky most hated, feared, and despised.

"Mayakovsky's Ascension" is dominated by the suicide motif: a bullet, a razor, poison at a drugstore counter. In the end Mayakovsky conquers the laws of physics and levitates himself around the drugstore counter, through the ceiling, and up into the sky. "Mayakovsky's Return" finds the earth changed due to the presence of multitudes of tunnels, superhighways, and airplanes, but it is still run by "Him." In the last section, "Mayakovsky to the Aeons," the poet returns to his old apartment on Zhukovsky Street to learn that "it has been Mayakovsky Street for a thousand years: // here he shot himself at the door of his beloved." He walks up the stairs to join his beloved and to get even at last with "Him." But in what used to be his bedroom he finds one Nikolaev, a civil engineer, and his wife, "a stranger, // stark naked, // the corners of her mouth twitching." The poem then reaches a powerful finale in two iambic quatrains:

All will perish.
All will come to naught.
And he
who is the mover of life will burn out the last ray
of the last suns over planets cast into darkness.
  And only
my pain

is sharper, as I stand,
engulfed by fire,
on the everburning pyre
of an unthinkable love.

MAYAKOVSKY AND THE REVOLUTION (1917–1922)

In the first few years after the Revolution avant-garde artists such as cubists, suprematists, constructivists, and others, collectively called "futurists," hoped that the Soviet regime would welcome them as allies. Poets and musicians went into the factories to perform before audiences of workers, and artists displayed their paintings in the streets and squares and drew propaganda posters. Mass spectacles with audience participation were staged. Mayakovsky was right in the thick of these activities. The Moscow cubo-futurists Burlyuk, Kamensky, and Mayakovsky were again functioning as a group. Between the fall of 1917 and April 1918 they gave frequent poetry readings at their own café of poets. The first (and only) issue of the *Gazeta futuristov* (Futurist Gazette), dated 15 March 1918, contained manifestos, essays, and poetry, all professing the futurists' solidarity with the working class and declaring that the social revolution was unthinkable without a cultural revolution that would sweep away the old art and replace it with a new art—futurism.

In the winter of 1918 Osip Brik founded a literary society called Iskusstvo Molodykh (IMO, Art of the Young), among whose members were the cubo-futurists Mayakovsky, Burlyuk, Kamensky, Khlebnikov, Kruchenykh, and also Pasternak and Nikolai Aseev, who had belonged to the *Centrifuge* group, as well as the formalist critics and theorists Boris Eikhenbaum, Shklovsky, and Roman Jakobson. In the summer of 1918 the entire IMO group was invited to join the Department of Fine Arts (IZO) of the People's Commissariat of Public Education, headed by A. V. Lunacharsky. Mayakovsky could now publish his work in *Is-*

kusstvo kommuny (Art of the Commune), an organ of IZO. Among its other contributors were Brik, Shklovsky, and the artists Kandinsky, Chagall, Ivan Pougny, and Malevich. But in May 1919 the publishing branch of the Commissariat of Public Education was transferred to the State Publishing House (Gosizdat), and henceforth Mayakovsky had to deal with that agency, which was at best lukewarm in its support of futurism. A resolution of the Communist Party on the Proletarian Culture (*Proletkul't*) movement, dated 1 December 1920, confirmed what had been clear even earlier, namely that the Soviet authorities by no means sought the support of futurism, but, on the contrary, considered it harmful.

The main reason for this was the conservatism of Lenin and other party leaders in matters of art and literature. Another was that the ultramodern style of the avant-garde met with no enthusiastic response from the proletarian masses. The avant-garde was promoting the creation of a radically new environment of functionally designed objects ("constructivism"), and its poets dealt with language in an analogous way. The Soviet public, meanwhile, preferred traditional forms in art and literature. A third reason was that Mayakovsky and his friends could never live down the label of "bourgeois decadents" and were never quite trusted by the activists of the Revolution. In fact, though, Mayakovsky's ideology was impeccable. There was no more tireless propagandist of the Revolution, nor did he ever shun even the most mundane and trivial hack work. In his cartoons and rhymes the capitalist West was presented as an ugly bourgeois with a huge belly and a giant cigar. The Soviet regime's internal enemies, such as "whiteguardists," Mensheviks, priests, kulaks, and "speculators," were cast as hideous monsters, wholly devoid of a human face. On the positive side Mayakovsky proclaimed the poet's solidarity with the worker, as in "Poet rabochii" (The Poet-Worker, 1918): "Who will ever // accuse us of idleness? // We grind the brain with the file of language. // Who is superior: the poet

// or the technician // who // leads people toward material welfare? // Both are. // Hearts are no different from motors. // The soul is nothing but a cleverly constructed machine. // We are equals."

Such a functional approach to poetry was quite compatible with the formalist and constructivist aspect of the futurist aesthetic. Mayakovsky utopian and cosmic strain, however, also persisted in his revolutionary poetry. He saw himself as a torchbearer of "a different revolution, // the third revolution // of the spirit" ("Chetvertyi internatsional" [The Fourth International, 1922]). Much like the poets of the Proletarian Culture movement, he perceived the Revolution as a cosmic event, and depicted it as such in his play *Mystery-Bouffe,* in his revolutionary epic *150, 000, 000,* and in many other poems.

The range of Mayakovsky's poetry expanded as he became a poet of the Revolution. A whole series of his poems, such as "Prikaz po armii iskusstva" (Order to the Army of the Arts, 1918) or "Tretii internatsional" (The Third International, 1920), were versified tracts on the poet's role in the Revolution, a communist *ars poetica.* These years also produced the first of Mayakovsky's revolutionary marches, "Nash marsh" (Our March, 1918) and "Levyi marsh" (Left March, 1918). In the satirical genre Mayakovsky's battle against a new Soviet philistinism began early. "O dryani" (On Trash, 1920) is a good example. There were some relapses into a prerevolutionary futurist manner. "Neobychainoe priklyuchenie, byvshee s Vladimirom Mayakovskim letom na dache" (An Extraordinary Adventure, Which Happened to Vladimir Mayakovsky in the Summer, While on Vacation, 1920), a ballad in iambic quatrains, features a visit that the Sun pays to Vladimir Mayakovsky one summer day. The two chat and discover they have much in common. They make a pact to cast light, each after his own fashion, into the gray trash of this world, dispelling "the wall of shadows, // the prison of nights."

But the vast bulk of Mayakovsky's poetry of

those years was pure propaganda, in particular the many hundreds of cartoons and jingles that appeared in the windows of the Soviet Telegraph Agency (ROSTA) from 1919 to 1922. Some of these were witty and even literate. Heinrich Heine's "Grenadiers" became three beaten White Russian generals. Goethe's "The Flea" became a ballad about King George of England and his trained flea, Denikin, a White Russian general. Marshal Pilsudski of Poland became the "dashing merchant" of a nineteenth-century ballad by I. S. Nikitin, and so on.

Mayakovsky's revolutionary epic *150,000,000* is a mixture of utopia, satire, and the grotesque. Like the preceding verse epics, it contains echoes of the Bible, Orthodox liturgy, and world literature. It also reintroduces familiar constructivist and cosmic themes, adding those of class struggle and world revolution. The plot features a mythic Armageddon in which the giant Ivan, a symbol of 150,000,000 starving, freezing, and desperate Russians, meets an—equally mythical—Woodrow Wilson, all-powerful ruler of Chicago and the capitalist world. The departure of the 150,000,000 is highlighted by a rousing revolutionary march whose effect is based entirely on rhythm and sound modulation, as forms of the verb *bit'* (to beat) and the noun *baraban* (drum) are combined with other words containing the same sounds, such as *bar* (bar) and *rab* (slave) to create the impression of an unstoppable tide of humanity.

Chicago is a place of incredible splendor, wealth, and technological miracles. It also consistently alliterates with various words that include the "ch" sound. It is ruled by an enormously fat Wilson whose "clothes are so fine, // as if there weren't any at all, // made of the most delicate poetic languor, // with underpants // which are no underpants, but a sonnet, // yards from their *Onegin*." As the 150,000,000 march on Chicago, having crossed the Atlantic Ocean, all humanity, the animal world, then inanimate objects, and finally the whole universe take sides. Race horses join Wilson, dray horses join Ivan, and similarly limousines and trucks, decadent and futurist poets, and even heavenly bodies

> Line up with those beaver collars,
>   Generals Constellations,
> Line up with the coveralls,
>   millions of the Milky Way!
>   (*Polnoe sobranie
>   sochinenii* 2:149)

When the battle is joined trucks pursue billionaires' wives, table legs spear capitalists, and Rockefeller is garrotted by his own collar. Wilson sends into battle economic ruin, famine, lice, and epidemics, and when these have been defeated by the appropriate Soviet agencies, he sends forth his last army, "the poisonous army of ideas: // democratism, / humanism, // and all those / other 'isms.'" Philosophers, professors, priests, and writers all take their turn trying to stop Ivan. They fail. The classics of literature vainly seek refuge in their "Collected Works," protected by Maxim Gorky. The futurists rout the culture of the past, "scattering its shreds in the wind, like confetti."

Then, suddenly, Wilson is reduced to ashes and "the squadron of the past goes down to the bottom of the sea." The epilogue features a utopian peace festival with visiting Martians, the Sahara Desert turned into a garden of Eden, and a celebration of humans, animals, and things of the past that "in spite of everything, did their job, / in spite of everything, put in some work."

The imagination of *150,000,000* is that of an animated cartoon. Realized metaphor is its key device, coupled with travesty, meaning that the relation between signifier and signified is arbitrarily distorted. The work succeeds in fusing futurist poetics, revolutionary enthusiasm, and Mayakovsky's declamatory style to produce a work of questionable propaganda value (note Lenin's negative reaction, mentioned earlier), but of indubitable poetic freshness and vigor.

VLADIMIR MAYAKOVSKY

THE SOVIET POET (1923–1930)

Pro eto (About That, 1923) belongs to the same genre as *Oblako v shtanakh* and *Fleita-pozvonochik*. Like these, and like a shorter piece, "Lyublyu" (I Love, 1922), it deals with the ups and downs (mostly the latter) of the poet's romance with Lilya Brik, which it reflects in a kaleidoscope of moods ranging from high pathos to the uproariously grotesque. Like the earlier poems it mixes the personal with the literary, being saturated with literary parody and literary allusions. The title of part 1, "Ballada redingskoi tyur'my" (The Ballad of Reading Gaol), alludes to Mayakovsky's "prison term" served at his flat in Lyubyansky Passage after Lilya had banished him from her presence. When Mayakovsky walks up the stairs to her place, he feels "just like / Raskolnikov / after the murder, // when he came back to ring the bell." The suicide theme shows up in conjunction with allusions to Mikhail Lermontov's last, fatal duel.

Mayakovsky's versification is brilliantly adapted to the emotion of the moment, as when the excited one-step rhythm of a drunken Christmas party is interrupted by the flowing iambs of the poet's lyric effusion of despair. In spite of its length (1,800 lines) the poem is distinctly lyrical, its rhythm dominated by the fluid lilt of iambs, anapests, and amphibrachs. An inserted "romance" echoes the trochaic pentameter of Lermontov's famous poem "Vykhozhu odin ya na dorogu" (Alone I Walk Out on the Road, 1841).

The "that" of the poem's title is of course "love." After a half-teasing, half-ardent prologue, love's trials and tribulations take Mayakovsky through a series of fantastic journeys and surrealist metamorphoses to his "last death," when he is shot to pieces and only a red rag remains of him, flying over the Kremlin, and "the Great She-Bear [Ursa Major] takes to troubadouring, to make herself queen of poets"—a punning allusion to one of the earlier metamorphoses, one that finds the poet floating down the Neva river as a bear on an ice floe.

The epilogue is a petition to the chemist of A.D. 3000 to resurrect the poet, who feels confident that "the thirtieth century / will overtake the droves // of heartrending trivia, // to make up for the lack of love today // with the starriness of countless nights." The moral of the poem, duly noted by Soviet critics, is that in the society of the future "love, the servant of marriage, lust, and bread," will be no more, but that instead, "upon the first outcry: / 'Comrade!' // the whole / Earth will turn around in response."

Aside from a few deviations such as *Pro eto*, the aesthetic of *Lef*, to which Mayakovsky was inextricably bound, was rationalist, formalist, and utilitarian. Its ideals were precision, intensity, and purposefulness. Poetry was held to be a tool serving the purpose of organizing life better, that is, more rationally. Mayakovsky expressed this view frequently, for instance in "Domoi" (Homeward Bound, 1925):

> I consider
>   myself a Soviet
>   factory,
> Engaged in the manufacture of happiness.
> I don't want
>   to be plucked,
> like some flower in a meadow,
>   for relaxation after work.
> I want
>   the State Planning Commission
>   to sweat in debate
> over my assignment
>   for each year.

The aesthetic of *Lef* also wanted the personal element, the inner life, and psychology removed from art. It wanted art to be factual and functional. All this was by no means the official view, nor was it that of all left-wing theorists. Rather, Gorky and Lunacharsky, for example, felt that "revolutionary romanticism" was on the whole a good thing. Mayakovsky bitterly attacked Gorky and his opinions in a lengthy versified diatribe, "Pis'mo pisatelya Vladimira Vladimirovicha Mayakovskogo pisatelyu Alekseyu Maksimovichu Gor'komu" (Letter from the Writer Vladimir Vladimirovich Mayakovsky to the Writer Aleksei Maksimovich Gorky, 1927). The theorists of RAPP and Pereval favored psychological realism and in fact branded Mayakovsky a "scribbler of odes" (*odopisets*). The notion that Mayakovsky's poetry of the 1920's was in fact a return to the didactic and allegorical poetry of classicism and its principle, *instruire en divertissant* ("to instruct by entertaining"), was taken up later by Andrei Sinyavsky in his essay "On Socialist Realism" (1959).

Mayakovsky scoffed at "objective" literature and prided himself on his ideological commitment. Also, he wanted his poetry to be topical. Yet while he was ready to write "to order" ("social commission," it was called), he demanded a free hand as far as the form of his work was concerned. In his essay "Kak delat' stikhi" ("How to Make Verse," 1926), which gives a brilliant account of how "Sergeyu Eseninu" (To Sergei Esenin, 1926) was made, Mayakovsky conceded that "social commission" should supersede the poet's private persona, but he also made a plea for professionalism in poetry, which, he establishes, is "production, difficult, very complicated, but production."

Mayakovsky's repertoire of utilitarian poetry was huge. His didactic pieces covered every imaginable aspect of Soviet life. He campaigned against absenteeism, church holidays, drunkenness, swearing, anti-Semitism, jaywalking, and many other things. He denounced nepotism and corruption, hooliganism, prostitution, and various other evils. He encouraged housewives to quit their kitchens and opt for factory cafeterias, peasants to plant more beets, carrots, and turnips, and every citizen to open a savings account. He faithfully echoed the party line in foreign affairs. He was a tireless activist of antireligious propaganda and an enthusiastic cheerleader of Stalin's Five Year Plan. He wrote a number of pieces for children, all properly didactic. Also, he produced a great deal of outright commercial art and verse, as well as public service messages on such subjects as the fuel crisis, prompt pay-

ment of taxes, hygiene, the confiscation of church property, government bond issues and lotteries, and so forth. Needless to say Mayakovsky was always available when some congratulatory verses were needed to celebrate a party congress, Aviation Day, or a youth festival—much in the same way as court poets had celebrated royal birthdays, weddings, and anniversaries.

In addition to a huge mass of occasional poetry Mayakovsky also produced several major propaganda epics, of which *Vladimir Il'ich Lenin* (*Vladimir Ilyich Lenin*, 1924) and *Khorosho! Oktyabr'skaya poema* (Good! A Poem of October, 1927) are officially considered his most important works. Both fall well within the genre of the historical-didactic epic. They are carefully, sometimes brilliantly versified (Mayakovsky finds rhymes for "Marx," "publicism," "capitalist," and even "surplus value"), feature some judiciously applied sound symbolism, and abound in ingenious conceits. Their manner, as variable as that of the earlier verse epics, ranges from the solemnly panegyric to the soberly prosaic, from hymn and invocation to instruction and reportage, from literary parody to folksy satire and anecdote. On the whole the intellectual level presumed in the audience is that of a gathering of party cadres taking a refresher course in Marxism-Leninism. Neither work was an immediate success. Phrases in *Vladimir Ilyich Lenin* such as "I want / to make it shine again, // that noblest of words, / the PARTY" were perceived as cerebral, affected, and insincere, even by devoted Communists. It was only considerably later that Soviet critics began to find that the poem was "characterized by a monumental power of socio-historical generalization and philosophic harmony." In spite of more than a few flashes of brilliance, both *Vladimir Ilyich Lenin* and *Khorosho!* were stillborn works, later promoted to classics for their political virtues.

Much of Mayakovsky's most interesting poetry—and prose, too—was the product of his frequent trips abroad. He enjoyed Paris, America, and the West in general, but was still looking primarily for targets for his communist propaganda. The beauties of Western culture held no attraction for him. "Stikhi o krasotakh arkhitektury" (Verses on the Beauties of Architecture, 1928) is a ballad about a building in Paris that collapsed, killing thirty workers. In a poem entitled "Notre Dame" (1925), Mayakovsky reflects on what will happen to the cathedral when "the workers have stormed the Prefecture across the square." It is too dark for a workers' club but might serve as a movie theater and would certainly provide a great façade for neon signs. In "Black and White" (the title is in English, 1925) the beauty of tropical nature in Cuba is merely a backdrop for the familiar propaganda line: greedy, brutal, and lecherous white capitalists exploiting and abusing hard-working but naive colored people who are ready for Comintern leadership "to translate / racial hatred / into class hatred" ("Svidetel'stvuyu" [I Testify, 1926]).

Mayakovsky's cycle *Stikhi ob Amerike* (Verses About America, 1925–1926), consisting of some twenty poems, most of them over one hundred lines long, shares the ideological edge of his other poems of that period, but is also interesting and provocative. Mayakovsky's American cityscapes—"Brodvey" (Broadway, 1925), "Bruklinskii most" (Brooklyn Bridge, 1925), and "Baryshnova i Vul'vort" (The Miss and Woolworth's, 1925)—are masterful. Mayakovsky obviously liked and admired America. In a prose sketch of Chicago he quotes Carl Sandburg's poem copiously and expatiates on the city's industrial might with some enthusiasm. Although he did not know English, he incorporated many English words into his American poems and found rhymes for "avenue," "street," "Coolidge," "chewing gum," "money," "dollar," "business," "subway," "elevator," "Maxwell House coffee," and even "good to the last drop." But he never neglected to put down the way of life that so impressed him, attacking what he saw as America's philistinism, social injustice, and hypocrisy.

The best poems of Mayakovsky's America cycle return once again to the themes of his futurist verse. In "Bruklinskii most" the poet assumes the point of view of an archaeologist of the distant future to whom this marvel of technology will appear as no more than a promise of greater things to come. He also recognizes in the Brooklyn Bridge something kindred to his own art:

> My own visions
>   arose in it, alive—
> the struggle
>   for construction
>   instead of style,
> austere calculation
>   of bolts
>   and steel.

"Kemp 'Nit gedaige' " (Camp "Nit Gedaige," 1925), whose trochaic hexameter produces what is perhaps Mayakovsky's most irresistible rhythmic composition, tells about the New York Young Communists (*komsomol'tsy*) at their summer camp on the Hudson, "whose song / makes / the Hudson flow into the Moscow river." However, its real subject is the futurist dream to master the flow of time.

It is difficult to separate what our own Western view tends to see as Mayakovsky's "real poetry" from his "propaganda poetry." However, some poems of the 1920's that deal with "the poet's / place / in the work force" ("Razgovor s fininspektorom o poezii" [Conversation with a Tax Collector, on Poetry, 1926,]) are generally recognized by Western critics to be among his best. "Sergeyu Eseninu," a response to the poet Sergei Esenin's suicide note, ends in the lines, "In this life, to die is nothing new, // but to live isn't any newer, either." The poem bitterly complains about the pettiness and philistinism of the literary establishment and scoffs at the suggestion that Esenin's suicide was caused by insufficient "linkage" with the working class, but in the end it has no better way to respond to Esenin's lines than this:

> As for merriment,
>   our planet

is poorly equipped.
One must
   extract
    joy
      from days to come.
In this life
  to die
    is not difficult.
To make life
    is considerably more difficult.

The poem addressed to the tax collector, occasioned by Mayakovsky's very real income tax troubles, is an amusing potpourri of half-ironic, half-serious observations on the poet, the creative process, and the social role of poetry. Mayakovsky's last major poem, "Vo ves' golos: Pervoe vstuplenie v poemu" (At the Top of My Voice: A First Prelude to a *Poema,* 1930), was his *Exegi monumentum,* a summing-up. There was a Russian precedent for a poet, still young and seemingly at the height of his career, to write such a poem. Aleksandr Pushkin had done so, also at only thirty-six years of age and only months before his death. In Mayakovsky's case it must be considered that he had earlier viewed himself from the vantage point of future generations in *Chelovek* and *Pro eto,* and the suicide theme had recurred frequently in his poetry almost from the beginning. "Vo ves' golos" is technically Mayakovsky's finest poem, showing his command of rhythm and sound patterns at its most virtuosic. Its imagery is apt and expressive, its rhetoric vigorous. Mayakovsky wants to be remembered as a humble craftsman who served the Revolution and the building of a socialist society. He wants his poetry to reach posterity "much as an aqueduct, / built by / the slaves of Rome," carries water, and he prides himself on his loyalty to the party:

When I appear
  before the C[entral] C[ontrol] C[ommission]
    of those bright years
      of the future,
I shall raise
  as my Bolshevik Party membership card

all hundred volumes
  of my
    pro-Party books.

There is another theme that is raised only in this last poem. Mayakovsky plaintively declares that, in order to become the activist he was, he had "stepped on the throat of / his own songs," refusing "to scribble / romances // which would have been more profitable / and more glamorous." Neither assertion is to his credit. The first suggests what Mayakovsky's critics had claimed all along, that he had made himself into a literary hack, while the second is patently disingenuous, for Mayakovsky collected more worldly fame and material rewards for his work than any Russian poet of his generation. The whole poem, with all its brilliance, smacks of the aging prima donna wallowing in self-pity.

THE PLAYS

Mayakovsky's first play, *Vladimir Mayakovsky: A Tragedy,* is really an extended lyric monologue with a number of personalized props and foils, such as "a man without a head," "a man without one leg and one eye," "an old man with dry black cats, several thousand years old," and so forth. In many of its details *Vladimir Mayakovsky* is a futurist manifesto, like its sister piece, Kruchenykh and Khlebnikov's *Victory over the Sun.* It, too, challenges the sun, as the old man with the cats exclaims, "We shall pin suns to our lasses' dresses, / we shall forge silver brooches from the stars." It advertises the universal trans-rational language of *zaum'* (trans–sense): "And you will / grow lips // for immense kisses / and a language / native to all nations." Its key device is "realized metaphor," which turns objects into articulate subjects and abstractions into objects. Much of all this amounts to no more and no less than puns and language games. Vladimir Mayakovsky's monologues are a blend of confession, lyric effusion, flight of a surrealist imagination, and outright *épatage* (baiting), all of it propelled mostly by rather transparent rhetorical devices. The flashes of real poetry amount to a kind of poetic self-immolation: "How could you understand, // why I // calmly, // through a thunderstorm of ridicule, // carry my soul on a dish // to the dinner of years to come?"

While *Vladimir Mayakovsky* is in many ways a juvenile and amateurish piece, Mayakovsky's propaganda spectacle *Mystery-Bouffe* shows him at his professional best. It is in many details still a cubo-futurist work, featuring a great deal of blatant sound symbolism and sound patterning, whimsical imagery, and a chaotic confusion of semantic levels. The list of *dramatis personae* includes allegorical figures; ethnic and social types; political caricatures; saints, angels, devils (all in travesty, of course); personified machines, things, even foodstuffs—and much more. In the play seven "clean couples" (royalty, capitalists, and so on) and seven "dirty couples" (proletarians) build an ark to save themselves from the great flood of the Revolution, which has even the North Pole awash. As the ark sails along the "dirty ones" throw the "clean ones" overboard. They then visit hell, which is not nearly as bad as hell on earth under capitalism, and heaven, where the old Christ is replaced by a new one who promises paradise on earth, not in heaven. Having returned to earth, the "dirty ones" fight economic ruin and other threats to the young Soviet regime. In the end a "dirty" machinist takes over Sabaoth's lightning bolts (an allegory of Lenin's electrification project), and the victory march of the "dirty ones" takes them "up solar scales, up the stairs of rainbows," and on to a conquest of outer space.

Mystery-Bouffe follows the model of a medieval morality play in being set on earth, in hell, and in heaven. Like a morality play it mixes indoctrination with folksy humor and grotesque satire. Of course it makes a travesty of the various biblical themes that it introduces. But even more than that *Mystery-Bouffe* is a political comedy in the manner of Aristophanes, using also the modes of the barker, of the ditty, and of the gibes and jeering of a carnival parade.

Mayakovsky's plays *The Bedbug* and *The Bathhouse* were written for Meyerhold's theater and were emphatic assertions of the principles that guided Mayakovsky and Meyerhold in their production of *Mystery-Bouffe.* Their basic notion was that the theater should not engage in any simulations of "real life" but should instead create autonomous structures through which statements about "real life" could be made. Mayakovsky's plays were well suited to Meyerhold's theater of overstatement and the grotesque and to his nimble, puppetlike actors. Also, Mayakovsky and Meyerhold were in agreement that the stage ought to be "an arena dispensing political slogans."

The Bedbug: A Fantastic Comedy in Nine Pictures has two parts. The first is a Soviet version of Molière's *Le bourgeois gentilhomme* (*The Would-be Gentleman,* 1670). Prisypkin, a proletarian, has decided not to postpone reaping the fruits of the Revolution but rather to enjoy the finer things in life now. Though still spouting Communist slogans, he has ditched his proletarian girl and is engaged to be married to Elzevira Davidovna Renaissance, manicurist in her parents' flourishing beauty salon. At the wedding party the drunken guests start a brawl, and a blazing oil stove is overturned. The Renaissance salon goes up in flames, and the whole wedding party perishes. It being winter, the site of the fire soon resembles a skating rink.

The second part is set fifty years later, in 1979. Prisypkin's body has been discovered, frozen solid, and has been referred to the Institute of Human Resurrection. Resurrected with Prisypkin is a bedbug inside his shirt collar, and Prisypkin, who soon finds that he is a total stranger in the new world, tearfully greets the familiar bedbug. The worst fears of those who had opposed Prisypkin's resurrection materialize. His guitar strumming and crooning infect hundreds of young citizens with an extinct disease, love. Hundreds of other citizens are hospitalized with acute poisoning by a fermented beverage called "beer," which had been prepared for Prisypkin to ease his transition to a useful new life. Additional hundreds of citizens are suffering horrible contortions while locked in a tight embrace: Prisypkin has taught them to do the foxtrot. But all these disconcerting developments are forgotten when the discovery of an animal species long thought to be extinct is announced: the bedbug is captured and taken in triumph to the local zoo. In the final scene Prisypkin also finds himself in a cage at the zoo, whose main attraction he will be. A crowd has gathered to hear the director explain that Prisypkin has been determined to be a specimen of *philistinus vulgaris,* a "terrible humanoid simulator and most amazing parasite" whose lifestyle is strikingly similar to that of the other parasite, *bedbugus normalis.* In the end Prisypkin addresses the crowd: "Citizens! Brothers! My own pals! Friends! Where you all from? How many of you? When were you all unfrozen? Why am I alone in my cage? Brothers, pals, come join me! Why must I suffer so?! Citizens!" The crowd, frightened and dumbfounded, is assured by the director that "the creature is suffering from hallucinations."

The Bedbug is an ambiguous play. Each of its many apt and vivid details is anchored in Soviet reality, but each allows for a negative as well as a positive interpretation. The inane but sanitized banality of 1979 may be seen as a desirable alternative to the dirty if lively vulgarity of 1929. The bland smugness of Mayakovsky's mechanized utopia may be perceived as the only possible solution to man's problems. Or it may all be the other way around. Ideology aside, *The Bedbug* is a great comedy. Racy, brazen, and with a sharp satirical bite, its dialogue never flags. It is full of clever gags and provocative fancy. The action is lively from beginning to end.

The Bathhouse: A Drama in Six Acts, with Circus and Fireworks is a spectacle more than a play. It is explicitly an allegory (the title suggests that it will give a bath to all that is dirty in Soviet life). What little plot there is is provided by a time machine that transports one into A.D. 2030, the age of communism, or vice versa. The time machine explodes—literally—into a world that is anything but ready for communism, a world of bureaucrats and careerists, of smug vulgarity and meaningless slogans. As in the earlier plays much of the action is generated by various realized metaphors, such as the train of time that carries its passengers into the communist future. Bureaucrats, foreign capitalists, and their assorted lackeys are thrown off the train, and the main villain of the play is "run over by Time."

The Bathhouse has its moments, as in the truly rousing "March of Time," and the satire has not lost its cutting edge even in today's Soviet Union. But the train into the future has little going for it except that it leaves behind the banal absurdity of the present. The only message conveyed by *The Bathhouse* is that of the intellectual and emotional bankruptcy of Stalin's Russia.

Mayakovsky's last play, *Moscow on Fire (1905): A Heroic Melomime / A Mass Spectacle with Songs and Words,* had been commissioned for the celebration of the twenty-fifth anniversary of the Revolution of 1905. It was performed by five hundred participants at the Moscow Circus on 21 April 1930, a week after Mayakovsky's death. It is Mayakovsky's most avant-gardist dramatic work, discounting his film scenarios. There is no plot. Instead, there is a rapid-fire sequence of partly concurrent attractions: scenes from the Revolution of 1905 with no pretense at all to historical veracity, antireligious and anti-tsarist satire, proclamations shouted by teams of barkers, slogans of the Five Year Plan and the collectivization of agriculture, a lot of shooting and fireworks, clowns cracking antireligious and anti-tsarist jokes, and so forth. A huge film screen was used, allowing even assorted enemies of the Soviet Union, such as Premiers MacDonald and Tardieu, Marshal Pilsudski, and the pope, to make appearances and to be finally routed by an exploding bomb scattering proclamations all over the place. A rousing march of the victorious workers ended the spectacle.

SUMMARY

Mayakovsky is the most versatile and virtuosic versifier in all Russian poetry. His verse is declamatory; hence he printed it "stairway fashion," moving one space down after each pause:

Comrade tax collector:
          Pardon the intrusion.
Thank you . . .
       don't bother . . .
            I'll stand.

This graphic pattern often conceals a syllabotonic or accentual meter.

Mayakovsky used meter and rhythm as an expressive device rather than as a rigid form of his verse. He was a skillful parodist of the meters and rhythms of earlier Russian poets, such as Pushkin and Lermontov. His poetry features every form of Russian verse, including conventional syllabotonic verse at the one extreme, and free verse at the other, that is, lines with a random number of syllables and stresses. Mayakovsky's verses are always rhymed but are rarely stanzaically structured.

Much of Mayakovsky's poetry is in free verse. But even here, his rhythm is distinctly that of verse, not of prose. This is accomplished by a high rate of alliteration, assonance, and inner rhyme, as well as by emphatic stresses and pauses that would not appear in ordinary discourse (so-called accentological estrangement). Often Mayakovsky's apparent "free verse" is really stress verse; the number of stresses in successive lines is a constant, while the number of unstressed syllables is free, a form common in twentieth-century Russian poetry. Mayakovsky also wrote many trochaic and iambic poems; most of his propaganda jingles belong to this category. He was a master of the ditty (*chastushka,* a quatrain of rhymed trochaic tetrameters with a "punch line"). A specialty of his were "free iambs" and "free trochees," iambic and trochaic lines with more or less frequent irregularities. One will recognize in some of Mayakovsky best-known poems, printed "stairway fashion" though they are, familiar syllabotonic meters, such as an iambic tetrameter in "Neobychainoe priklyuchenie, byvshee s Vladimirom Mayakovskim letom na dache," an iambic pentameter in "Vo ves' golos," and a trochaic hexameter (with caesura) in "Kemp 'Nit Gedaige.'" Ternary meters, usually in a "free" version, appear particularly in Mayakovsky's longer poems, such as *Pro eto* (anapests and amphibrachs), "Pis'mo tovarishchu Kostrovo iz Parizha o sushchnosti lyubvi" (amphibrachs).

Mayakovsky was a virtuoso of rhyme. His rhymes are not only original and ingenious but often semantically active as well, for instance in the second episode of *Khorosho!,* where a series of epiphoric rhymes (the last word of a line rhyming with the first word of the following line) is symbolic of the chain reaction of revolutionary unrest gripping the country. Mayakovsky excelled in various trick rhymes, such as compound and punning rhymes, and in intricate rhyme patterns. In a poem addressing an international congress of Young Communists, "Privet, KIM" (Greetings, KIM, 1928), every second line either ends in KIM or rhymes with KIM. In a lengthy "Nota Kitayu" (A Note to China, 1929), every rhyme responds to a case form of *Kitai* (China). In another lengthy poem, "Lenintsy" (Leninists, 1930), a similar game is played with Lenin's patronymic, Ilyich.

Mayakovsky's rhymes differ significantly from those of earlier Russian poetry. In the latter rhyme is created by repetition of the last stressed vowel of a line and the vowels and consonants following it, for example, *móre: góre.* In Mayakovsky's verse the correspondence to the right of the last stress is only approximate, while a correspondence to the left of it is actively pursued; for example, vy*delkoi* *stáli: doklády Stálin; Bruklinskii móst: vlyublen i óstr.*

Mayakovsky, who systematically broke most of the conventional strictures of poetic form, cultivated the free forms of sound patterning, such as alliteration, assonance, inner rhyme, vowel modulation, and sound symbolism. He was also a tireless inventor of puns, some witty, some not, and he had an acute sense of what his friend Jakobson later called "the poetry of grammar," that is, foregrounding and contrasting grammatical forms for poetic effect. For example, in the lengthy poem "Komsomol'skaya" (The Young Communist, 1924), the refrain "Lenin / lived, // Lenin / lives, // Lenin / will live" rhymes with the preceding lines not only phonetically, but even conceptually: the past is still there in the present and grows into the future, and so on throughout the poem.

In spite of a professed hostility to the literature of the past, Mayakovsky incorporated into his poetry innumerable quotes from and allusions to many Russian and foreign poets and writers. Pushkin, Lermontov, Gogol, Nekrasov, Tolstoy, Dostoevsky, Blok, Esenin, Goethe, Hugo, Maupassant, Verlaine, Wilde, Whitman, Longfellow, Marinetti, and many others are referred to directly or indirectly. Of course the art and poetry of the past are treated strictly as material. In "Yubileinoe" (Anniversary Poem, 1924, written on the occasion of the 125th anniversary of Pushkin's birth), Mayakovsky hustles Pushkin off his pedestal and home to his own flat for a friendly chat. The host does all the talking, in a tone of condescending light banter, pointedly misquoting Pushkin all along. He suggests that Pushkin would have made a good editorial assistant on the staff of *Lef* and intimates that soon enough they will be almost neighbors in the encyclopedia, separated only by Nekrasov—and so on, in the same vein.

Mayakovsky's frequent use of religious imagery and of biblical and liturgical language is brazenly blasphemous in his prerevolutionary works and coldly sarcastic in his atheist propaganda of the Soviet period. In the early poetry the poet's persona appears an a usurper of God's power or as Christ's rival. In the later poetry God and Christ are simply declared to be silly superstitions. However, Mayakovsky uses sublime imagery and "high-style" rhetoric when professing his humanist metaphysics. Passages such as the following from *Pro eto* are not uncommon: "I can see, / see clearly, down to details. // Air to air, / like stone to stone, // unassailable to putrefaction and crumbling, // bursting into brilliance, / towering across the ages, // the workshop of human resurrection."

The range of Mayakovsky's imagery is extremely broad, and his conceits are usually original and often bold. He described his peculiar imagination aptly in *Fleita-pozvonochnik*: "I strung out my soul across a chasm, like a cable, // juggling words, I am swaying over it." Mayakovsky's imagery is inclined toward hyperbole, the grotesque, and violence. He rather likes the image of a bomb, for example. His description of a Western customs officer taking Mayakovsky's Soviet passport is typical of his style: "He takes it / like a bomb, / he takes it / like a porcupine, // like a double-edged / razor, // he takes it / like a snake / two meters long, // rattling her / twenty fangs."

Lawrence L. Stahlberger has established a pattern of archetypal images in Mayakovsky, particularly images of "bondage," "eternal recurrence," and "cosmic alienation." Examples of these are found in all of the *poemy*, from *Oblako v shtanakh* to *Pro eto*, and in many of the shorter poems as well. Stahlberger also detects in Mayakovsky a dominant tendency to present the poet's persona as a martyr, a dandy, or a clown, often all three together. Mayakovsky played these roles in life, too.

Mayakovsky's verbal range is as broad as that of his imagery, extending over the whole lexicon of the Russian language, from pompous archaisms to modern slang. His general tendency is to abolish the social and generic boundaries of language: he uses "book words" in poems addressed to the proletariat and vulgarisms (replaced by ellipses in the Academy edition of his works!) in "Vo ves' golas," a poem close to the genre of the ode. But he can use words discriminatingly, aptly, and wittily when he so chooses. Mayakovsky's poetry contains a very large number of neologisms, which are, however, well within the rules of normal creative speech. He never indulged in the creation of "trans-sense" neologisms, as some of the other futurists did.

Mayakovsky's poetic persona is a contradictory one. The most self-assertive of all Russian poets, he became the bard of an anti-individualist society. He performed this *tour de force* by converting the individual titanism of his prerevolutionary poetry into the collective revolutionary titanism that marked the first decade of Soviet power. A contradiction that affects all of Mayakovsky's poetry is that he combines a predilection for palpable and specific imagery with a vague and simplistic treatment of his psychological and social content. More precisely, the details of his language and imagery are concrete and objective, while his content is pointedly subjective in his prerevolutionary poetry and heavily slanted, often simply insincere, in his postrevolutionary civic poetry.

Mayakovsky's futurist rebellion against God leads directly to an adversary relationship with nature. In the early poetry this amounts mainly to an assertion of the poet's freedom and self-will. Later it is channeled into the revolutionary scheme to "remake the world." Mayakovsky's rebellion finds its most poignant expression in his perception of time and in the many time metaphors of his poetry. His whole life and much of his poetry were a frantic struggle against time's inertia. Mayakovsky loathed *today* with its routine of day-to-day living and was aware of *yesterday* only inasmuch as it meant something odious that no longer existed. It was an onrushing *tomorrow* that gave a content to his life and to his poetry. Time for him was not so much the bringer of the future as that which delayed it, a sentiment he expressed in *150,000,000:*

> In savage destruction,
> we shall sweep away the old,

> announcing, in a thunderous voice,
> a new myth to the world.
> We shall kick to pieces
> the fence of time.

Mayakovsky lived in an epoch of history when nothing was permanent or sacred, and he helped to make it that way. His cosmic nihilism rather easily adapted itself to the secular chiliasm of the Revolution. The dream of both was to escape from the burden of history and the travails of day-to-day living into a future of mechanical things that could be manipulated at will. As Stahlberger has pointed out, Mayakovsky chose neither God nor animal as his ideal of man, but rather the machine.

More often than not time the destroyer is Mayakovsky's ally. He greeted the cosmic flood of the Revolution with genuine exultation, and *Mystery-Bouffe* is one of his more cheerful works. In an endless chain of conceits throughout his poetry, Mayakovsky gloats at the sight of time sweeping away, running over, and wiping out "the old." His favorite conceit is the Promethean one of Soviet man grabbing time by the throat and thrusting it forward:

> Enough
>   of your crawling,
>   time-the-snake,
> Enough
>   of your digging,
>   time-the-mole,
> Thrust of workers'
>   shock brigades,
> Fling
>   time
>   forward.
>   ("Zastrel'shchiki"
>   [Shock Workers, 1929])

In Mayakovsky's ethics, too, there may be observed a certain continuity between the cubo-futurist and the Soviet propagandist. The amoralism of the former became the ruthlessness of the latter. To the former, religious and ethical values were raw material for his artistic imagination. The latter filled the void of his

1855

moral nihilism with an unquestioning loyalty to the Soviet regime. Mayakovsky the propagandist seconded every falsehood, cruelty, and meanness of the Soviet regime with apparent gusto. Kicking a prostrate enemy, such as religion, Mensheviks, or Social Revolutionaries, was well within his code of ethics, as was repeating the brazen lies of the Soviet government about the sinister doings of Western spies and saboteurs, denouncing Russian Baptists as forming a front for dollar imperialism, or presenting F. E. Dzerzhinsky, the infamous head of the Cheka, as a role model.

An assessment of Mayakovsky the poet cannot be based on a separation of his "personal" and his "civic" poetry. A good deal of his propaganda poetry is technically superior to his prerevolutionary verse. What also makes it difficult to assess Mayakovsky's true worth are his flamboyant personality, his histrionic talents and brilliant delivery of his poetry (preserved in recordings), and his spirited and ingenious defense of his own works. The fact that he was always in the public eye contributed to his great stature among his contemporaries. He was not the originator of the ideas and devices of Russian futurism (Burlyuk, Khlebnikov, and Kruchenykh were), but it was he who represented futurism before the public.

The poet Osip Mandelshtam, a perceptive critic, saw Mayakovsky's greatest merit "in his having used the powerful resources of visual education to educate the masses." And Pasternak related that Mayakovsky once said to him: "You and I are different. You like lightning in the sky, and I like it in an electric iron." Didactic poetry was nothing new, of course, but didactic poetry about the construction of a hydroelectric plant was. It was also new that a poet of indubitable talent would devote almost his entire energy to the production of utilitarian pieces. Mayakovsky saw this as a return of poetry to its proper social role.

Mayakovsky influenced more Russian poets than any other twentieth-century poet. There are several reasons for this. Like Pushkin he had a "galaxy" of his own. Some major poets, such as Kamensky, Aseev, and Semyon Kirsanov, belonged to it and helped to preserve his fame after his death. Since Mayakovsky was never in disgrace with Soviet authorities but was in fact warmly praised by Stalin himself, his poetry remained accessible at a time when that of Pasternak, Mandelshtam, Anna Akhmatova, Marina Tsvetaeva, and others was not. Thus, when Soviet literature returned to life during the "thaw" after Stalin's death, young poets, such as Evgeny Evtushenko, Boris Slutsky, Robert Rozhdestvensky, Leonid Martynov, and others, tended to write their poetry in the style of Mayakovsky.

Mayakovsky has exerted a strong attraction on poets of the leftist avant-garde all over the world. Bertolt Brecht, Johannes R. Becher, Paul Eluard, Louis Aragon, Pablo Neruda, Wladyslaw Broniewski, S.K. Neumann, and many others have expressed their appreciation of Mayakovsky's art and have credited him with some influence on their own work.

Selected Bibliography

EDITIONS

Vladimir Mayakovskii: Tragediya v dvukh deistviyakh a prologom i epilogom. Moscow, 1914.

Fleita-pozvonochnik. St. Petersburg, 1915.

Oblako v shtanakh: Tetraptikh. St. Petersburg, 1915. Uncensored edition. Petrograd, 1918.

Chelovek. Petrograd, 1918.

Misteriya-buff: Geroicheskoe, epicheskoe i satiricheskoe izobrazhenie nashei epokhi, sdelannoe Vladimirom Mayakovskim. 3 deistviya, 5 kartin. Petrograd, 1918.

Voina i mir. Petrograd, 1918.

150, 000, 000. Moscow, 1920–1921.

Pro eto. Moscow and Leningrad, 1923.

Vladimir Il'ich Lenin: Poema. Leningrad and Moscow, 1924.

Stikhi ob Amerike. Moscow, 1925–1926.

Khorosho! Oktyabr'skaya poema. Moscow and Leningrad, 1927.

Klop: Feericheskaya komediya. Devyat' kartin. Moscow and Leningrad, 1929.

Banya: Drama v 6-ti deistviyakh s tsirkom i feier-verkom. Moscow and Leningrad, 1930.

COLLECTED WORKS

Sochineniya. 8 vols. Edited by N. N. Aseev, L. V. Maiakovskaia, et al. Moscow and Leningrad, 1929–1931.

Polnoe sobranie sochinenii. Complete collected works. 13 vols. Edited by V. A. Katanyan. Moscow, 1955–1961.

Sobranie sochinenii. 12 vols. Moscow, 1978.

TRANSLATIONS

For translations of individual pieces in anthologies see Richard C. Lewanski, comp., *The Literatures of the World in English Translation: A Bibliography*, 2. *The Slavic Literatures.* New York, 1967 Pp. 302–304.

The Bedbug and Selected Poetry. Edited by Patricia Blake. Translated by Max Hayward and George Reavey. New York, 1960.

The Complete Plays. Translated by Guy Daniels. Introduction by Robert Payne. New York, 1968.

Electric Iron. Translated by Jack Hirshman and Victor Erlich. Berkeley, Calif., 1971.

How Are Verses Made? Translated by G. M. Hyde. London, 1970.

How To Make Verse. Willimantic, Conn., 1985.

Mayakovsky. Translated and edited by Herbert Marshall. New York, 1965.

Mayakovsky and His Poetry. Compiled and translated by Herbert Marshall. 3rd ed. Bombay, 1955.

Mystery-Bouffe. In *Masterpieces of the Russian Drama.* Edited by George Rapall Noyes. New York and London, 1933.

Selected Poetry. Translated by Dorian Rottenberg. Moscow, 1972.

"Two Mayakovsky Scenarios." Introduction by Peter Wollen. *Screen* 12:122–149 (Winter 1971–1972).

Vladimir Ilyich Lenin. Translated by Dorian Rottenberg. Moscow, 1976.

Vladimir Mayakovsky: A Tragedy. Translated by A. Briggs. Oxford, 1979.

BIOGRAPHICAL AND CRITICAL STUDIES

Barooshian, Vahan D. *Brik and Mayakovsky.* The Hague, 1978.

———. *Russian Cubo-Futurism 1910–1930: A Study in Avant-Gardism.* The Hague, 1974.

Bowlt, John E. *Russian Art of the Avant-Garde: Theory and Criticism, 1902–1934.* New York, 1976.

Brown, Edward J. *Mayakovsky: A Poet in the Revolution.* Princeton, N. J., 1973.

Charters, Anna, and Samuel Charters. *I Love: The Story of Vladimir Mayakovsky and Lili Brik.* New York, 1979.

Erlich, Victor. "The Dead Hand of the Future: The Predicament of Vladimir Mayakovsky." *Slavic Review* 21:432–440 (1962).

Eventov, Isaak. *Mayakovskii-plakatist.* Leningrad, 1940.

Everts-Grigat, Senta. *V. V. Majakovskij, "Pro eto": Übersetzung und Interpretation.* Munich, 1975.

Gasparov, Mikhail. *Sovremennyi russkii stikh: Metrika i ritmika.* Moscow, 1974. Much of this study deals with Mayakovsky's versification.

Humesky, Assya. *Mayakovskij and His Neologisms.* New York, 1964.

Jakobson, Roman. *Noveishaya russkaya poeziya.* Prague, 1921.

———. "On a Generation That Squandered Its Poets." In *Major Soviet Writers: Essays in Criticism.* Edited by Edward J. Brown. London, Oxford, and New York, 1973. Pp. 7–32.

Jangfeldt, Bengt. *Majakovskij and Futurism. 1917–1921.* Stockholm, 1976.

Jangfeldt, Bengt, and Nils Åke Nilsson, eds. *Vladimir Majakovskij: Memoirs and Essays.* Stockholm, 1975.

Kamensky, Vasilii. *Zhizn' s Mayakovskim.* Munich, 1974.

Katanyan, Viktor. *Mayakovsky: Literaturnaya khronika.* 4th rev. ed. Moscow, 1961.

Kemrad, Semyon. *Mayakovskii v Amerike.* Moscow, 1970.

Khardzhiev, Nikolai, and Vladimir Trenin. *Poeticheskaya kul'tura Mayakovskogo.* Moscow, 1970.

Livshits, Benedikt. *The One and a Half-Eyed Archer.* Translated by John E. Bowlt. Newtonville, Mass., 1977.

Markov, Vladimir. *Russian Futurism: A History.* Berkeley, Calif., 1968.

Mitchell, Stanley. "Marinetti and Mayakovsky: Futurism, Fascism, Communism." *Screen* 12: 152–160 (Winter 1971–1972).

Moser, Charles A. "Mayakovsky and America." *Russian Review* 25:242–256 (1966).

Pertsov, Viktor. *Mayakovskii: Zhizn' i tvorchestvo.* 3rd ed. 3 vols. Moscow, 1976.

Proffer, Ellendea, and Carl L. Proffer, eds. *The Ardis*

Anthology of Russian Futurism. Ann Arbor, Mich., 1980.

Shklovsky, Victor. *Mayakovsky and His Circle.* Edited and translated by Lily Feiler. New York, 1972.

Shtokmar, Mikhail. *Rifma Mayakovskogo.* Moscow, 1958.

Stahlberger, Lawrence L. *The Symbolic System of Majakovskij.* The Hague, 1964.

Stapanian, Juliette R. *Mayakovsky's Cubo-Futurist Vision.* College Station, Tex., 1985.

Stephan, Halina. *"Lef" and the Left Front of the Arts.* Munich, 1981.

Vinokur, Grigorii. *Mayakovskii: Novator yazyka.* Moscow, 1943.

Williams, Robert C. *Artists in Revolution: Portraits of the Russian Avant-Garde, 1905–1925.* Bloomington, Ind., 1977.

Woroszylski, Boleslaw. *The Life of Mayakovsky.* Translated from the Polish by Boleslaw Taborski. New York, 1971.

BIBLIOGRAPHIES

Darring, Gerald. "Mayakovsky: A Bibliography of Criticism (1912–1930)," *Russian Literature Triquarterly* 2:510–529 (1972).

Laufer, Yu. M. *Bibliograficheskie posobiya po Mayakovskomu.* Moscow, 1955.

Metchenko, A. I., ed. *Satira V. V. Mayakovskogo: Rekomendatel'nyi ukazatel' literatury.* Compiled by Yu S. Zubov. Moscow, 1955.

Muratova, K. D., ed. *Istoriya russkoi literatury kontsa XIX – nachala XX veka: Bibliograficheskii ukazatel'.* Moscow, 1963.

Zubov, Yu. S., comp. *V. V. Mayakovskii: Kratkii rekomendatel'nyi ukazatel' literatury.* Moscow, 1955.

VICTOR TERRAS

LOUIS-FERDINAND CÉLINE

(1894–1961)

HIS REAL NAME was Louis-Ferdinand Destouches. Born in 1894, he was the son of a petty insurance clerk and a crippled lace merchant. It was paranoid angst that led him to write under the pen name Céline, but that name was also his tribute to a much-loved grandmother, a strong-willed woman who served as a model for his many portraits of sympathetic but crusty old ladies.

Writing was, Céline thought, a fine way for a poor doctor with a facile pen to make some extra cash. It was also a necessary procedure, a way to lance the boil of rage. His first novel, *Voyage au bout de la nuit* (*Journey to the End of the Night*, 1932), was an immediate success, almost winning him the Prix Goncourt. (His consolation was the less prestigious Prix Renaudot.) Critics compared him to François Rabelais and François Villon, to James Joyce and Marcel Proust. He has since been called the liberator of the French language, and his volatile suprarealist prose, together with his frantic, hallucinatory vision, has been a potent influence on writers as diverse as Jean-Paul Sartre, Raymond Queneau, Henry Miller, Jack Kerouac, William Burroughs, J. P. Donleavy, Kurt Vonnegut, and Philippe Sollers. Packed with exclamations of anguish and anger unsurpassed in the literature of any language or any century, exploding into the raucous laughter of the pit, dealing with specific emblems of distress in an outlaw's language so rich in affective resonances that it engages even the least

willing reader, his books are models for the literature of the absurd and the late modernist parables of exclusion. His half-invented language, a versatile compound of argot neologisms and impolite French, is perhaps the saltiest and richest since the poets of the Pléiade put their idiom through the Latin wringer and the French Academy began to fix its diction. Yet, until very recently, he was among the least recognized writers of his generation.

Céline's harsh style and sordid perspective, his reputation as a World War II collaborationist, and his outrageous anti-Semitic and racist pronouncements were largely to blame for this neglect. The rise of the New Novel and late modernist fiction, the triumph of poststructuralist criticism and Lacanian psychoanalysis, and the drive to understand rather than bury the wartime experience have restored interest in his work, most of which is now available in good English translations.

Although Céline is not a difficult author, history has shown that he is easily misunderstood. But this should not cause surprise. His particular brand of misanthropy and paranoia (incipient and advanced) puts other rebellious authors in the shade. The anger of Voltaire, the voluptuous satanism of Baudelaire, the cries of the adolescent Rimbaud—"Je suis négre"—and even the ecstatic evil-lust of Lautréamont seem thin and shopworn next to the volleys of expletives, the exuberant apocalypses, the comic turbulence of Céline at his best. In the nineteenth century, only the neglected pamphleteer and novelist of the left Jules Valles approximated his anarchistic verve. The first volume of Valles's autobiographical trilogy, his *L'Étudiant* (first published in 1879 as *Jacques Vingtras*), was perhaps as important to the development of Céline's presentation of his own youth, to say nothing of his later manner, as any single influence could be. Like Valles, a Caliban haunted by the face of Ariel, Céline was no poseur. His anger, his intransigence, his misery, his hatred were all as real and incredible as the crippling wound he received during World War I. A friend of his youth, trying to explode the myths spread by the author himself, describes the writer at twenty as already "haunted by curiosity, changeable, a faker, irascible, a mythomaniac, and a genius!" Céline himself wrote in 1933, "I guess I have been humiliated so abominably, and so stupidly for so long by so many people that I have finally succumbed to the disease of pride."

Céline is a difficult subject, but not because his books are difficult. They are, more accurately, astounding. It is rather that his life as a man and as an author—two lives that can be neither joined nor separated—is full of contradictions and surprises. He lived that life much as he wrote his books, confusing the creation and the creator in a manner ironically reminiscent of Oscar Wilde and Alfred Jarry, treating his public much as William Faulkner treated his—providing it with a medley of fact and fiction designed to satisfy its demands and perpetuate a mask in which even he appears to have had considerable faith.

LIFE

Louis-Ferdinand Destouches (who, unlike his hero, preferred to be called simply Louis) was born in the unpromising Paris suburb of Courbevoie on 27 May 1894 and raised in his mother's lace shop in the depressing Passage Choiseul near the Palais Royal. His paternal grandfather, a teacher of rhetoric at a secondary school in Le Havre, held a liberal arts degree, and his father held a degree in literature from which he was never able to profit. According to his biographer, François Gibault, Céline was "raised by bourgeois in a popular milieu according to aristocratic principles and under proletarian financial constraints." Thanks to his parents' fears and commercial ambitions, his education was a curious mix of the formal and the informal involving long stays in Germany and England, where he was to learn the languages "needed" for a career in commerce. Although he eventually completed his training as a doctor, in a profound sense he was self-educated. Perhaps he was right to believe that his literary gifts were inherited from Breton and Flemish forebears—people who were, after all, the storytellers and fantasts of western Europe.

In his second novel, *Mort à credit* (*Death on the Installment Plan,* 1936), he describes, however hyperbolically, his childhood in the gaslit alley, his early education (omitting the German years), his introduction to commerce, his sojourn in a British boarding school (a conflation of two actual schools), and his eventual enlistment in the cavalry. It has been noted that the novel distorts the facts and chronology of those early years, paints the existence of the Destouches family in murky colors, exaggerates even the bitterness and rage of his father. But then, Céline saw fit to arrange reality according to aesthetic patterns that pleased him, and his judgment has been repeatedly vindicated. In a curious way, his honesty or truth-to-impression inhibited his accuracy. "For me," he wrote Milton Hindus, "real objective life is impossible, *unbearable.* It drives me mad—makes me furious it's so ghastly. So I transpose it as I go along, without breaking my stride." His vision, which accentuates and vitalizes accumulations of detail and lends life to banal objects while highlighting human distress, contributes a measure of truth denied the works of more "objective" writers. Céline, as J. H. Mathews insists and few today would deny, was no naturalist. His literary life glows incandescent with the possible as an extension of the real. In his own words, it is a "delirium," not a slice of life.

In 1912, after passing his first *baccalauréat* examination, he enlisted for three years in the cavalry. The notebook he kept at the time gives us a faithful account of his initiation into that life. His unfinished novel, *Casse-pipe* (1949), which he drafted during World War II, gives us an impressionistic one. Taken together, these accounts flesh out the truncated version given in the opening pages of *Journey to the End of the Night,* a fanciful and bitterly comic, pacifist blast. In November 1914, having volunteered for a dangerous mission at Poelkapelle in Flanders, he received wounds that earned him a medal and a pension for 75 percent disability. These wounds partially paralyzed his right arm and impaired his hearing, causing migraines and perhaps a permanent buzzing in his ears. The war, the wounds, the pension, and his deteriorating health were to become leading motifs in his later novels, where the writer's vertiginous style is attributed by turns to a (fictive) trepanation and malarial fever.

After his recovery he was sent to London where he performed minor consular duties, contracted a first unsuccessful marriage, and stored up details for his third novel, *Guignol's Band* (1944). Later, in 1916, he accepted a job with a trading company in Africa, where he caught malaria and dysentery, maladies that haunted him for the rest of his life. Back in Paris in 1917, while working for Henry de Graffigny (a pseudonym for Raoul Marquis), the principal model for Courtial des Pereires, the tragic buffoon of *Death on the Installment Plan,* he passed his second *baccalauréat*. The period between 1918 and 1924 is not covered in any of the novels, though it is alluded to in *Journey to the End of the Night.* During those years he worked for the Rockefeller Foundation

in Brittany (1918), studied medicine at Rennes, where he married Edith Follet, the daughter of the medical school director (1919), had a daughter of his own, Colette (1920), and completed his medical degree (1924). Finally, fed up with a stable and sedentary middle-class existence, he abandoned his family to work for the League of Nations in Zurich.

Céline's literary career began informally in 1924 with the publication of his doctoral thesis, *La vie et l'oeuvre de Philippe-Ignace Semmelweis* (*The Life and Work of Semmelweis*), on the life of Dr. Semmelweis, the unsung crusader for the prevention of puerperal fever through sterile obstetrical techniques. But it was not until 1928, after his departure from the League of Nations, under whose auspices he traveled to Africa and America, that Céline began writing seriously. The product of his disappointment and rage, his satirical play *L'Église* (The Church, 1933), describes the League years and his initial experience as a doctor in the working-class suburb of Clichy. Out of this failure grew *Journey to the End of the Night,* written in his spare time and acclaimed by critics both left and right in spite of its clear anarchistic implications. It is characteristic of Céline, the dealer in paradox, that he attributed all of his later miseries to this single and singular success, and that, throughout his life, he remained a doctor to the poor. The charitable and conscientious but acerbic doctor, who loved animals, children, and dancers and treated his impoverished patients with gentleness, contrasts strangely with the misanthrope who poured vitriol into the pages of his massive novels and political pamphlets. Still, there linger in his books an underlying concern for humanity and a genuine, if misfocused, dedication to France.

In 1936, Céline published *Death on the Installment Plan,* which, although critics found it disappointing, many now consider to be his best novel. That same year, in order to spend the royalties due him from the translation of *Journey to the End of the Night* made by Elsa

Triolet and Louis Aragon, Céline traveled to Russia. The trip shocked him into writing the first of his polemical pamphlets, the anticommunist tirade *Mea Culpa* (1936). This, his only contact with the Orient, may also have given birth to his obsessive belief that the yellow race would soon overrun Europe and absorb a white race weakened by war and decadence. In 1937, he published the first of his anti-Semitic and pacifist pamphlets, *Bagatelles pour un massacre,* a book so extravagantly virulent that André Gide mistook it for another Célinean farce. It was followed in 1938 by *L'École des cadavres.* Paradoxically, the first of these thunderclaps of paratactic rage, which earned him the support of the fascist as well as the royalist press and resulted in his postwar exile and imprisonment, contains three of his most delicately beautiful ballet scenarios: "La naissance d'une fée," "Voyou Paul, brave Virginie," and "Van Bagaden." Céline whose art transforms words into gestures, loved the mute and gratuitous expression of the dance and the physical beauty of the dancers, out of which he claimed he could "shape a sort of artificial paradise on earth." The scenarios present the writer at his most engaging, employing as they do realistic fantasy rather than fantastic realism.

Almost as much has been written about Céline's anti-Semitism as about his novels. Jean-Paul Sartre suggests that it derived from a fundamentally catastrophic vision of the world and a Manichaean obsession, a tendency to lash out at the "evil" while turning his back on the "good." Some, like François Gibault and Philippe Muray, trace it partly to the anti-Dreyfusard, promilitary, and generally anti-Semitic attitudes of his father. Most relate it to his paranoid temperament. Céline himself speaks of bitter experiences with Jews in positions of power (at the League, in the medical world) and pretends that his anti-Semitism is an aspect of his pacifism. It is certain that his circle of friends, especially those in the Action Français group, reinforced his phobias, as did his early contact with nazism. Whatever its

causes, anti-Semitism provided him with a happy focus for his despair for just so long as he could meaningfully consider the Jew (and a Judaized Europe) as the root of all evil. By directing his hatred and fear and indulging his paranoia, however, he temporarily wasted the vitality that could otherwise have gone into his novels. The monolithic and monotonous hatred of the pamphlets is, from a literary point of view, a poor substitute for the more diversified disgust of the novels.

Virulence in Céline's books is a verbal manifestation of his obsessive dread of violence in addition to his fascination with destruction. For such a man, words are acts; as Céline told an interviewer, the reader experiences in his books a rape of conscience. (It is perhaps symptomatic of the Célinean mode that this attitude toward the reader is a staple of farce.) Like Semmelweis, the prophet of hygiene, the writer was the agent of his own destruction. "We should in the service of truth," Céline wrote, "note Semmelweis' great fault: he was brutal in everything he did and above all brutal toward himself." It is worth noting that the two moments in his life that supplied the least grist for his mill were superficially the longest pastoral periods. He was unable to give a satisfactory fictional account of the middle-class stability he abandoned to join the League of Nations or of the "good" years between 1932 and 1938, when he was, however tentatively, in the literary spotlight.

During the war years, 1939 to 1944, Céline served briefly as a ship's doctor and was involved in a marine disaster; he drove an ambulance during the exodus from Paris (an event evoked in the overture to *Guignol's Band*); later he served in two dispensaries. (He had lost his previous position after the publication of his pamphlets thanks to his Jewish colleagues, whom he offended and by whom he was attacked.) In 1943, his second wife having long since divorced him, he married the dancer Lucette Almanzor, his mistress since 1940. As Lili in the later novels, Lucette is the model of stability and gentleness, a buffer against a world in tatters where Céline perceived universal hatred and disgust. During the German occupation, he associated with collaborationists, was supported by certain of the Germans, and had connections with Vichy. He also published letters to the press and prided himself on his credentials as a "racist." Still, his contact with Germans was minimal, and as the war progressed, his attitude concerning their future was pessimistic. Early on, he smelled defeat: "An army that can't draw revolution in its wake, in a war like this, is sunk. Washed up, the Fritzies." According to his friend Lucien Rebatet, he "was constantly pursued by the demon of persecution, which inspired him to dream up fabulous systems in the hope of outwitting his numerous imaginary enemies." Nevertheless, he remained in Paris until 1944, writing the two parts of *Guignol's Band* and drafting *Casse-pipe,* most of which was lost when his apartment was looted during the Liberation. He left for Denmark only after his nightmare visions materialized and the BBC began denouncing him as a traitor.

After eight months of wandering in the disintegrating Reich, the Célines and their cat Bébert arrived in Copenhagen, where he had cached some gold, in March 1945. As Merlin Thomas notes, this period of pilgrimage is covered more or less chronologically by *Nord* (*North,* 1960), the first half of *Rigodon* (*Rigadoon,* 1969), *D'un château l'autre* (*Castle to Castle,* 1957), and the second half of *Rigadoon.* Less than a year after his safe arrival, he was to be confined to a cell on death row where he remained for fourteen months under threat of extradition to France. Paroled in 1947, he spent nearly five years in a primitive hut by the Baltic Sea. It was there that he wrote *Féerie pour une autre fois I* (Masque for Some Tomorrow, 1952) and its sequel *Normance: Féerie pour une autre fois II* (1954) while awaiting the French amnesty. In 1951, he returned to France and settled in Meudon (on the Seine near Paris). There he continued to write until his death on 1 July 1961, immediately after the "completion" of *Rigadoon.*

WORKS

Céline's last sixteen years resemble the plot of one of his early books. Appropriately, he wrote five novels to describe them. By this point in his career as a novelist, it was impossible to mask his inimitable voice and useless to adopt another name; so he abandoned his fictional persona, Bardamu. Now, as Ferdinand Destouches, he depicted himself as the obsessed and hallucinating "chronicler" of the historic events in which he participated "with article 75 [for treason] pinned to [his] tail." In the early novels, the narrator has suffered the experiences he describes, but he remains, despite the force of his rhetoric, simply a man who has been around, one who has learned the score and somehow made the best of a bad deal. By contrast, Destouches is a sufferer glorying in his misery, a besmirched scapegoat groaning under the weight of the world's misery—but intransigent, refusing to accept either blame or defeat. This astonishing voice continually puts obstacles in the way of our affection, making us share his visceral responses even when we find his laments overblown and his situation in good measure self-induced.

In Europe in general, and increasingly in France, Céline's reputation has prospered of late. His major work is now out in the prestigious Pléiade edition; criticism of the most sophisticated sort abounds (see especially Philippe Muray's *Céline* and Julia Kristeva's *Pouvoirs de l'horreur* [*Powers of Horror*]), and as well as the fine three-volume work by François Gibault, a second biography is being written by Frédéric Vitoux. At the insistence of Lucette Destouches, the pamphlets, including the critique of the French war effort, *Les beaux draps* (A Nice Mess, 1941), are out of print even in France. American translations exist of all the novels except both parts of *Féerie* and the posthumously published *Pont de Londres* (London Bridge, 1964), the second part of *Guignol's Band.*

If we omit the lost army novel, *Casse-pipe,*

Céline's work is divided into four novelistic sequences, two of which belong to the postwar period. But it would be accurate to think of the pamphlets, which fall between the first two pairs of novels, as an intermediary sequence and note that despite the seeming uniformity of his discourse, Céline's methods did evolve. Indeed, the evolution of his work, viewed with considerable hindsight, is quite startling. This is true even within the first sequence, *Journey to the End of the Night* and *Death on the Installment Plan.* As Céline himself recognized, despite its hectic pace, its harsh tone, and its outsider's perspective, his first novel did not make a radical break with the naturalism of his predecessors. The real break came with *Death,* where, influenced perhaps by the practice of Jules Valles, he innovated a staccato, paratactic rhythm and began to break up his discourse with the famous "three dots," while casting his narrative more fully in the "spoken" idiom. There followed the pamplets, which built upon those procedures in an obsessive, grinding way to produce the effect of a prolonged volcanic disturbance. The style of the pamphlets informed the overture of *Guignol's Band,* but otherwise, the main departure in that novel and its sequel is suggested by its title, which refers most directly to a farcical puppet show. Indeed, it is the commedia del l'arte format and cast of characters, already implicit in *Death,* that gives the brilliant wartime sequence its distinctive coloration, that and the grotesque violence and bloodletting characteristic of the Grand Guignol. The greater sea change occurred between the *Guignol* sequence and *Féerie,* parts 1 and 2, a sequence Céline clearly associated with his literary rebirth. These astonishing volumes, as the most advanced products of his formal experimentation, achieve a fusion of the styles and procedures of the early fiction with that of the pamphlets. No wonder that, quite beyond their self-serving attack on the sensibilities of postwar France, they proved critically indigestible in 1952 and 1954. It is only recently that they have begun to receive the critical attention they merit and to find in the work of contemporary novelists (for example, Robert Coover's *Gerald's Party* [1986]) significant creative echoes.

Pressure from the critics and an unresponsive public, reinforced by the advice of a publisher anxious to rehabilitate a valuable property, soon led Céline to revert to earlier formulas (although with fresh twists and a new emphasis). His next book was the seriously intended mock interview *Entretiens avec le Professeur Y* (Conversations with Professor Y, 1955), in which he abandoned the pose of literary naïf to outline and defend his methods of composition. This was followed in 1957 by *Castle to Castle,* where, after a mere hundred pages of divagation on his life as an impoverished doctor in Meudon, he takes us by way of a Stygian hallucination to Sigmaringen and the Vichy government in exile. The narrative becomes almost limpid; the action is controlled by the character of the historical events despite liberties taken with facts and chronology and despite the frequent asides. Critics were enchanted; the book sold. Encouraged, Céline tried to recover more of his past glory. In *North,* which recounts his wanderings prior to Sigmaringen, he resumes something approximating the picaresque format of his early books, recovering as well, in his depiction of numerous minor characters, the aura of Guignol and the commedia. Despite his age and his altered condition, health, and reputation, he tries once again to play the resilient Bardamu of the prewar and wartime works. The social commentary, theorizing, and grumbling have been integrated into, or at least subordinated to, a coherent adventure sequence. Thus, shortly before his death, he once again tasted critical and popular success. *North* was followed by a less remarkable book, *Rigadoon,* a road novel as ragged as its harried protagonists, purporting to tell how the Destoucheses finally got to Denmark, availing themselves of a series of inadequate and dangerous modes of transportation. Its publication was delayed until 1969, when Céline's readership was guaranteed.

Sensibility and fervor aren't worth much

"without a great deal of anarchy," Céline wrote a Belgian friend in 1933. "Not on principle, mind you, but because we live in a cockeyed world. All the light is in the forbidden places—alas!" Earlier he had written Léon Daudet to the same effect: "You must know the superb *Festival of Folly* by Breughel, the one in Vienna. For me, that's the whole story. . . . I'd like to be able to understand something else. I can't." (This was before the advent of the Russian critic Mikhail Bakhtin and his theory of the "carnivalesque.") Pieter Breughel and later Hieronymus Bosch: Céline repeatedly claimed them as ancestors, proud as he was of his fraction of Flemish blood. Like them, he believed that truth can be approximated only by exaggerating and reversing experience. Well in advance of his time, Céline devoted himself entirely to the rediscovery of the true farcical impulse and, hence, to the formal tradition that best expresses the age of revolutions, gas chambers, and the atom bomb. He did so because the upside-down universe was in his blood and he could not bear to inspect a quotidian life from which he never completely escaped: "I've always had a horrible fear of the future, of the humiliations it will bring. From what I know of the past . . ." This anxiety and terror, along with a terrible tenderness, are perhaps the true sources of his literary vision. From them he derives his subject matter, his characters, his catastrophic humor, and his style. Nothing is strong enough to express them, so "you have to blacken everything and yourself along with it." Already in September 1933, less than a year after its publication, Céline wrote of his *Journey:* "I find the whole thing so flat and dull that it turns my stomach. It's funny that all this clowning manages to seduce the reader." For all the power he assigns to the *word,* the apocalypse can't be achieved by writing about it; the inevitable movement, as Allen Thiher has noted, is toward further delirium.

"The critics object to my speaking *argot,*" Céline remarked to Robert Poulet. "It isn't *argot* at all! It's a special language that suits me. I've got the secret recipe." Céline's coherence is largely a function of this language, the essential qualities of which he altered very little after *Death on the Installment Plan.* We may notice a progression from the clear, forceful, conventional, but relatively informal French of *Semmelweis* to *L'Église,* in which Céline uses popular speech only in Parisian scenes and even so makes every possible concession to the cultivated ear. Even in *Journey* the style was, as he put it, "too literary," so he aimed in his second novel at a "calculated and subtle" simplicity.

Céline has been compared to Joyce (whom he read without understanding) as a liberator of the literary idiom, but his language is radically different and infinitely less varied, an emotive rather than an evocative tool, an instrument of seduction. He was not interested in density or nuance of meaning, but simply, although such effects are not easily achieved or sustained, in the direct and forceful communication of sensation, or, as he puts it, of "delirium." The result is a language spoken by no Frenchman but capable of conveying "pure sentiments" with the artless immediacy of the spoken language, complete with the inevitable gestures. The "pure sentiments" of which Céline speaks are the forbidden ones that "all of us share but no one dares to express." To convey them, he concocted a savant mixture of puns, neologisms, obscenity, and finally, argot, thereby developing an increasingly disjunct but surprisingly literate and resonant style. The result is a vehicle capable of carrying everything, a tidal wave—or, to use his own tongue-in-cheek expression, a "metro emotif" (emotive subway) that sucks the outer world into its dark maw and spews it out again reconstituted.

Argot is perhaps the most startling component of that "style," along with, after *Death,* the three points of suspension that follow sentences and often phrases. These can be used to produce an explosive stutter, but by their spacing they can also indicate and reinforce the appropriate rhythm. Spoken mainly by people on the fringe, be they workers, criminals, students, prostitutes, or vagabonds, argot is closer to gypsy cant than to our slang. It is a limited language if a language at all, an ageless corpus of frequently ugly and obscene synonyms for parts of the anatomy and animal functions and for clandestine or quite ordinary acts, objects, or attitudes. Céline called it a language of hate and used it sparingly, as a condiment, for fear he might otherwise dull its literary edge. This is the main ingredient, along with the peculiar rhythms of French speech, that is missing from even the best of the English translations, those by Ralph Manheim.

Although he failed in his single attempt to write a play, Céline's novels show a fine dramatic sense. Even his landscape, the street scene or room, is animated, poised to spring or ready to crumble engulfing mobs of squirming beings. Sentence after sentence strikes with the impact of a foul gesture whose ugliness turns on itself in rhetorical heat, a blend of fear, disgust, and repressed affection:

> As well as it can, the city conceals those mobs of dirty feet in its long electric sewers. They surface only on Sundays. Then, when they'll be out, better not show yourself. Just to see them having a good time, that's enough to kill your taste for joy permanently. Around the subway station, close to the battlements, crackles, endemic, a lingering odor of wars, whiffs of half-burned, badly cooked villages, aborted revolutions, failed businesses.

And so on, building up momentum, expanding the possible, adding images and paradoxes, this descriptive sequence from the opening of the second half of *Journey* swells its flow until checked by some innocuous anticlimax, a trickle only, left to dirty the stream of memory. Clearly, a Céline landscape is not composed of buildings and foliage alone. Interested, as was Flaubert before him, in perceptions of motion, in revealing verbal gestures rather than objects frozen in space, he fills his scenes with pullulating details or with the crowd, a nameless multitude, a roar, a rush that could eventuate

in something like the mob of eager inventors that supports the semicharlatan Courtial des Pereires in *Death* and eventually, storming his shop, reduces everything to rubble.

In later years, Céline invented two terms, "lacework" and "emotive subway," to describe his technique. He told Robert Poulet that the writer should leave accurate reporting to the press and omit "even from his imaginings" the insipid details of what the reader already knows. In his own work this results in lacunae, in the missing transitions appropriate to parataxis. He establishes "the basic outline, the landmarks: and surrounding them, [leaves] holes." There are two aspects to the "emotive subway" described at length in his interview with Professor Y. Unable to choose between surface reality and subterranean truth, the author has decided to draw the surface down with him helter-skelter into a subway of his own invention, one that makes no stops and that, accommodating all experience, transports it on rails that are not straight. These bent rails with which he approximates emotive truth are like the stick in the water to which he compares his "realistic" discourse. "If you want it to *look* straight, you have to break it slightly—or *bend* it, you might say," he wrote Milton Hindus,

> When you put one end in, a normally straight stick looks bent—and the same with language. On the page, the liveliest dialogue taken down word for word seems flat, complicated, heavy. . . .
>
> To reproduce the effect of spontaneous spoken life on the page, you have to bend language in every way—in its rhythm and cadence, in its words. A kind of poetry weaves the best spell: the impression, the fascination, the dynamism.

The omissions—"not everything can be transposed"—the inclusions, and the distortions characterize the vision of a man who wished "to lay back the flesh" of his subject matter. As mentioned above, the conventions that best suit this vision are those of traditional farce, but a farce that accents its dark potential or darkens its joy.

Céline's titles reflect both his emotional commitment to inverted values and his awareness of the ambivalent potential of traditional figures of fun. The *journey through accustomed darkness toward the unattainable light* and the *piecemeal purchase of death* suggest an irony that turns back on itself, a hilarity of horror, a tender brutality. "As for me," Céline told Robert Poulet, "death is part of me. And, *it makes me laugh!* That's what you mustn't forget: that my *danse macabre* pleases me, like an immense farce. . . . Believe me, the world is funny, death is funny; that's why my books are funny, and why, fundamentally, I am full of joy." The sort of joy expressed here is ambiguous, like that of the danse macabre itself or exposing the grin of the candy skulls sold in Mexico on the day of the dead. Céline's sideshow is like an apocalypse by Bosch.

A third title, *Guignol's Band,* suggests the quality of Ferdinand's experience in the underworld of French expatriates in wartime London: the pimps and whores, dope smugglers, pushers and addicts, charlatans, and lost souls. Deliberately anglicized, it refers first to the guttersnipe hero of a postrevolutionary Lyonnais puppet show, a figure who dresses like a silk worker and speaks the popular dialect. Like young Ferdinand, he is ignorant and naive, but skeptical and unscrupulous, a perfect butt gifted with unnatural powers of survival. If we add to this the fact that all the members of the "band" derive their traits from the commedia tradition and that the title suggests the hyperrealistic mayhem of Grand Guignol, the double thrust is evident.

A more complex and bitter comic irony operates in the titles *Féerie pour une autre fois* and *Castle to Castle.* Both titles have pleasantly fantastic and elegant overtones. In addition to being a splendid spectacle, a *féerie* is a fairy romp or festival. Yet, for two-thirds of that novel, the spectacle is spun from the mind of the ailing and hallucinating Destouches, a sort of black magician who conjures up complications born of his suffering, monsters of thought with immense exploding anuses. The last third

is seemingly in a lighter vein. There we witness the *féerique* (or commedia-like) exploits of the sculptor Jules, a Punch-like amputee who possesses the power to fascinate beauty and mobilize destruction. The pleasure domes of *Castle to Castle* may formerly have been asylums for the great or the princely mansions of the fairy tales, but they are now dark with suspicion, rage, and discontent. They reek of the urine and offal of refugee "traitors" and witness acts of folly and brutality.

A movie buff from childhood, Céline envisaged a film version of *Journey to the End of the Night;* he spoke of his novels' filmic potential to Milton Hindus, saying that his characters are "almost never realized completely. They are sketched, and from the sketch you can go in the direction of the objective, that is the moving picture, or the subjective, that is the novel." (It is curious to note how limited Céline's cinematic imagination was and that it took a vision as powerful as Jean-Luc Godard's to translate his novelistic vision into the powerfully evocative *Pierrot le fou* [1965].) In effect, with the possible exception of Bardamu-Destouches seen as narrator/protagonist and of Courtial des Pereires, Céline's people are all figures of fun, stereotypes of one sort or another. With the emphasis on the unsavory and morose, the normal is presented hyperbolically as in a nightmare, its hidden motives hanging out. The distance between the acceptable and the odd, the beautiful and the grotesque, is often spanned by a comma or by three points. A hair in a mole can render an otherwise pleasing face decidedly unpleasant, while a few strategically located boils can dissolve any amount of dignity. In Céline's descriptions the hair becomes a mass of bristles of extraordinary length and thickness, the boils a corrupt, erupting mess.

In *Journey,* the Henrouilles are a perfectly ordinary couple embodying middle-class virtues while struggling to defend their little piece of property against the encroaching city. They expose themselves to Ferdinand as grasping, small-minded hypocrites whose single ambition is to rid themselves of an embarrassing relative, Mother Henrouille, the crone who lives in a dirty shack in their backyard. Bardamu, by recording their vicious behavior, attacks the sordid motives underlying upward mobility. Conversely, the colonial sergeant whom he meets during his stay in the Congo appears to be no more than a petty profiteer who systematically bilks his ignorant black charges. In him we discover one of Céline's rare "good" characters when we learn that all the money is going to support a niece in France whom the sergeant does not even know.

Céline's cast of characters is as conventional as it is natural to his vision. The thieves, profiteers, pimps, and others who constellate his pages are staples of low comedy and ribald satire. Their normal prey is the bourgeois of any stripe. There is seldom any need to present members of either group in depth simply because they are all socioliterary bywords. To achieve startling effects, Céline had only to alter the conventions underlying his choices, attacking our conditioned responses. From the raw materials of harlotry and age he could fashion Mère Vitruve, the old whore who has to scout in the dark. Even while turning her into just another of his poor crones, he was able to expose her many vices with sympathy. Frequently, a single cliché is subjected in the course of several books to different readings, all of which defamiliarize it. The legless man is a conventional object of pity and disgust; yet the vicious Jules in *Féerie* is a remarkably self-reliant and resilient clown. On the other hand, the legless baron in *North* is a positive menace, a suffering Punch whose death goes unmourned.

Readers of the first two books will recognize in the gory suicide of Courtial des Pereires, who shoots his brains out in *Death on the Installment Plan,* an echo of the equally bloody end of Ferdinand's alter ego Robinson, shot in the belly at the end of *Journey.* Brains and guts are clearly opposite equivalents. The beautiful and giving American whore, Molly, one of the few pleasant characters in *Journey,* becomes in

Death a healthy, big-nosed, stupid animal. In *North*, the syphilitic whores from Berlin are loathsome harpies capable of beating an old man to a pulp. The fat and energetic SS doctor Haubolt in *North,* with his epicurean tastes and animal laugh, proves a genial host and useful protector for the Destouches clan, but earlier, in *Guignol's Band,* Céline created a less satisfactory protector in the fat, slothful pawnbroker Van Claben, whose head is smashed open in a dope orgy. If we think of Céline's characters and situations as so many Tinker Toy creations with interchangeable parts, it is clear that the author has discovered the source of the endless vitality that animates painters of the grotesque.

If, like their creator, they travel constantly either in body or in spirit, Céline's heroes and their doubles or antitypes seldom have coherent goals. Generally, the lessons they learn cannot be communicated even among pariahs. The first of these Cassandras was certainly the Austro-Hungarian doctor Semmelweis, whose intemperate battle against ignorance and pride made him a pariah and then a madman. Céline is kinder to his other alter egos, providing them with surrogate scapegoats, generally not forcing them to go the whole distance if only because those who do go never survive to tell their tale. "When the cardiac arteries snap one by one," he writes in the overture to *Death,* "it's not your ordinary harp. . . . Too bad nobody ever comes back from angina pectoris. There'd be wisdom and insight to spare."

Ferdinand Bardamu or Ferdinand Destouches, the semiautobiographical protagonist of nine novels (and three pamphlets), wears many masks over a single and stable identity. He rehearses all sorts of comic roles to become less like Everyman, a limited creature seeking the center, than like Every-comic-man, a fantastical outcast who wears the brand of Cain as a battle scar. Although effectively interwoven, the conventions he embodies are quite transparently dictated by the author's attempts to "fix" his image at a given moment and in relation to given circumstances that must take precedence over character. Ferdinand tends to learn from experience, but since as protagonist he is constantly being acted upon and reacting, his vision is seldom sufficient. To supplement it, Céline adds a second, more reflective, and retrospectively and discursively more violent Ferdinand to serve as our narrator and guide: the voice of the text. Inevitably, this first person, evaluating past misfortune, adds density and depth to the portrait, creating, even in the first novel, a stereopticon effect. This is enhanced in most instances by the doubles and mentors who mirror and complete the hero's experience.

Generally, Ferdinand stands within a moral context to which he does not subscribe but against which he is unable to rebel. By contrast, his double is a complete outsider, inflexible and vulnerable, a sort of demented visionary like Robinson in *Journey,* Courtial in *Death,* or Le Vigan in *North.* Céline was sincere when he said to his secretary in 1933, "Bardamu? He's not me, he's my double. But so is Robinson." The same may be said for the protagonists of the other books, if we bear in mind Céline's changing vision and altered concerns, but the relationship is clearest in that first novel, perhaps because the author had not yet begun defining his narrator as a character in his own right, one whose experience is in some sense distinct from that of his hero and whose vision is frequently hallucinated (even though the hallucinations are not uniform in their intensity).

Nevertheless, *Journey* is already "life seen from the other side." In the first half of that book the hero is adrift on a great exegetical voyage through the domain of human folly, absurdity, and meanness of spirit. Minimal though it is, there is already an overture. The first chapter states the novel's themes and even establishes the fantastic tone. Bardamu, a cynical and anarchistic medical student conversing with a colleague in a café, begins by systematically exposing and exploding various shibboleths: race ("nothing but a great clot of mangy louts like me, blear-eyed, lousy, shiver-

ing, who've landed here, chased by hunger, plague, tumors, and cold, come beaten from the four corners of the globe"), love ("the infinite available to a poodle"), patriotism, work, war, and wealth. Unexpectedly, this potential Ivan Karamazov becomes a Candide, falling into step with a passing regiment and marching till the music stops: " 'Well,' I said to myself when I saw what was going on, 'the lark is over. I'd better reconsider.' I was ready to leave. Too late! They'd shut the gate quietly behind us, those civilians. We were caught, like rats." What follows illustrates the validity of his original position.

There has seldom been a less dedicated quest hero than Ferdinand, whose major goal is peace and an end to misery, but in a world so disorganized, so frenetic, so devoid of any sense of justice or proportion, the simple fact of his quest represents a movement upstream. With no philosophy to let him down, no Cunégonde to retrieve, he survives war, patriotic fever, a trip to Africa—where he catches malaria and is sold into slavery—and a voyage to America, where he experiences New York and Detroit. By turns an indomitable Charlot, a desperate Pierrot, a sly trickster, and a sensitive observer, Bardamu provides a hilarious foil for the norm to which his existence is tangential: "The war, finally it was everything you couldn't understand. It couldn't go on. Something had happened to those people, something extraordinary. That hadn't touched me. If it had, I'm sure I would have noticed." The quality of his vagabondage is unmotivated frenzy; its logic is ambiguous and fantastic, like his job as a louse counter in the port of New York.

Sequences follow each other like fast-paced skits in a hectic evening of vaudeville designed to exploit the talents of a single, versatile clown. Some of these skits are grotesque and hallucinatory; others are frantic, sordid, absurd, comic, or simply pathetic. There is, for example, the trip to Africa, during which the irrational hostility of the other passengers and their threats of personal violence lead to Ferdinand's deliberate self-abasement. For Milton Hindus this pure and avowed fabrication is evidence of a deep-seated and early paranoia, but Céline's satirical intent is clear from a statement that echoes the theme of Joseph Conrad's *Heart of Darkness* (1902): "In the cold European climate, under the chaste neo-classical greys of the North, except in times of carnage, we're barely aware of the swarming cruelty of our brothers, but their rottenness breaks the surface as soon as they're tickled by the ignoble fever of the tropics." Given the cramped social and colonial context, it is only logical that Ferdinand should play the comic pharmakos. In another episode Bardamu flickers before our eyes in a dumb show reminiscent of the early Charlie Chaplin films. The scene is a New York cafeteria: "That dining area was so clean, so well lit, you felt you were floating on the polished tiles like a fly in a bowl of milk." Intimidated, he overloads his tray and carries it "as though crossing an operating theatre" to an "immaculately washed little table" only to find that he can't hide his feet: "They projected out in every direction." Finally, he takes off after a bus girl before the eyes of the astonished diners: "She'd looked at me, the little darling, too bad for her. I'd had enough of being lonely! No more dreaming! Sympathy! Human contact!" The sequence ends with his eviction "like a dog that's forgotten himself. It was just as it should be, I had no complaints."

The first half of *Journey* ends abruptly with Ferdinand's departure from Detroit, where he has discovered the mechanical universe of Ford and the selfless goodness of Molly, a whore who threatens for a while to lead him toward a settled inversion of middle-class life. Regretfully, he abandons her when his quest takes on an absurd and terrible urgency, an almost mystical aura. Perhaps, in Ferdinand's experience with Molly, as well as in Robinson's affair with the love-crazed Madelon, Céline paid his last respects to the terrors and joys of his marriage to Edith Follet in Rennes.

In Detroit, Ferdinand intuits the nature of the bottom end of the night when he sees the charmen returning home from work. They are wan, tired people drifting toward "imprecise compartments, little streets of ill-defined houses." Among these people Ferdinand rediscovers his opposite and double Robinson, the clandestine man who appeared first as a deserter in the World War I sequence and reappeared at intervals thereafter. Robinson's fate is always to get there first, although his means of locomotion and his motivation are seemingly different from Ferdinand's.

Bardamu is basically a hostage to the morality that so distresses him. His instinct for survival is stronger than his terror of conformity and the social trap. Robinson survives by spitting on morality. He is a *débrouillard,* a trickster, a *pícaro* who invariably does precisely what Ferdinand refuses to do. His role in the first half of the novel is mechanical. He appears repeatedly and unheralded but several steps ahead of Bardamu and always in the know. We might compare him to Conrad's Kurtz, whose function is in part to venture further into the darkness than Marlow, fleshing out his quest and maintaining the mystery. But Céline's project is larger than Conrad's was, more expansive, more overtly destructive. His Marlow is far less amenable to social controls, as his radical discourse makes clear. Thus Robinson becomes in the first half of *Journey* one of the few constants in a world gone awry, one of the saints of the night. If, when we see him in Detroit, his mask has begun to chip and molder, misery has enhanced its disturbing appeal.

Without identity papers, wanted by the police, Robinson has been cleaning offices and toilets: "His step was ponderous but with a touch of true nobility, as though he had just completed a dangerous and somehow sacred mission in town. That was the style, as it happens, of those night chars. . . . Fatigue and solitude elicits the divinity in men." Later, when he is saying good-bye to Molly, Ferdinand reflects, "Perhaps in life that is all we're looking for, just that, the greatest possible distress so as to become ourselves before dying."

The world's error and redemption through suffering and debasement are fitting themes for a French Dostoevsky whose god has gone underground. Bardamu of the gentle pessimistic murmur expresses Céline at his rarest. The mood is calibrated to convince. But such sadness is reserved for those moments when the narrator has wiped the spittle from his lips.

The catastrophic events, exotic contexts, and delirium of Ferdinand's travel cede place to the fauna of the Paris street and the suburban quagmire into which he sinks after obtaining his M.D. in two paragraphs and six days on page 239 of *Voyage:* "To have returned from the Other World isn't everything! You pick up the thread of life where you left it hanging, uncertain, sticky. It's waiting for you." The change of pace, though less startling than similar shifts in the later novels, gives us pause, especially since this curious subhuman monotony, this litany of the sorrows of the mean streets, fills most of the book's remaining pages. If Bardamu, as a vagabond, suffered from his sense of alienation, he nevertheless kicked feebly against the pricks. As doctor to the poor in the dreary suburb of Rancy, he watches, helpless, as a thousand small evils and petty injustices accumulate to draw him gradually toward accommodation to the alien culture into which he was born. The big world of the voyages, the wars, the love affairs has been replaced by its little equivalent. The Parisian suburbs so carefully and, despite the inevitable hyperboles, so accurately depicted breed not success but varying degrees of failure:

> The sky of Rancy, it's like the sky of Detroit, a sooty ooze drenches the plain as far as Levallois. A jumble of hovels fixed to the ground by black filth. The short and tall chimneys resemble from afar those thick posts stuck in the slime by the sea. There we are, in the midst of it.

It follows that Bardamu, for all his efforts, is even more out of place here than elsewhere—even less the actor, more the observer. In the end he prefers not to capitulate to the moral jungle represented by "good people" like the Henrouilles and the spiritual swamp that snuffs out the light of little Bébert, the concierge's nephew. He abandons his none-too-lucrative private practice and retreats to the inverted world of the asylum, where inmates' demands do not threaten his peace of mind. There, he gradually acquires authority and equanimity in a fool's paradise.

Success of a sort is reserved in this half of the book for Robinson, who returns to haunt Ferdinand, becoming increasingly intransigent. By the simple expedient of doing precisely the opposite of what Ferdinand does, he arrives at the bottom of the heap, and, with a supreme act of self-assertion, becomes truly himself "before [and through] death." To justify the inverted splendor of Robinson's end and to establish his heroes in a moral perspective, Céline develops throughout the novel the image of the carnival: the play world, society's palliative device shaped from the detritus of its terrors and frustrations. Appropriately, Robinson finds death at the hands of a lovesick girl after a visit to a fair. He has refused life, and his refusal forces Ferdinand to reexamine his conscience. Sancho Panza has been won over to the position of Don Quixote. Kurtz has traveled the road for Marlow. The parallels point up distinctions. Céline has neither the equanimity of a Cervantes nor the painful high seriousness of a Conrad, but what he lacks in faith and tenderness he makes up for in force and integrity.

Throughout his career, Céline thought of himself as a doctor first and a writer second. His books, which at first brought him exceptionally high royalties, were written, he insisted, to supplement his meager earnings as a doctor to the poor. Nevertheless, he took great pleasure in his gifts, seeing himself as a natural (Breton) storyteller and a poet in prose and showing pride in his rhetorical skills. No doubt he was truly dedicated to medicine, but one suspects that his double commitment was rooted in his misanthropy and paranoia. From the start, he felt his books would endanger and perhaps destroy him. Paradoxically, even after he had been pursued and imprisoned for his pamphlets and wartime associations, he considered *Journey* his most damaging book: "It's for *Journey* they're out to get me. I'll shout it from the scaffold! That's the unsettled account, between 'Them' and me! So deep . . . unutterable . . . Of all my books, the only really wicked one, it's *Journey*." Wrong in the eyes of history perhaps, but from his perspective, the logic of this statement is sound. The book's horrendous farce, balanced and focused by the pseudonaturalistic melodrama of its second half, constitutes an attack on contemporary mores, an assault more vicious than anything in Voltaire or Swift. It is the most satirical of all the books, although its sting is often cushioned by the literary effects. While the objects or groups attacked in the later volumes are specific and limited (Jews, Freemasons, communists, publishers, self-righteous fellow countrymen, and Danish prisons) and the attacks direct and outrageous, nothing compares with the sweeping indictment, the terrible logic, and the deadly accuracy of the portraits of war, patriotic fervor, colonialism, industrialism, and middle-class morality in *Journey.*

The precision of Céline's distorted vision is illustrated by his treatment of Ford's mass production methods; not only did he incorporate a description of them in his novel, he also wrote and published a factual account of observations made during his postwar mission. The two accounts are remarkably similar, but in the novel Céline (who had surely seen Chaplin's 1936 film *Modern Times*) provides a more intimate point of view, extends possibility, animates machines, robotizes men, and moves us in the direction of a pointed but perversely tender satire:

> The wriggling little cart with its load of scrap metal struggles to make its way among the machines. Out of the way! Hop! so that it can lunge again, the little hysteric [. . .] Depressing sight, the workers bending over, anxious to give the utmost pleasure to their machines, to pass them the calibrated screws and again more

screws, rather than have done with it forever, with the stink of oil, the racket that burns your ears.

Although a number of critics have noted his negativism, few have been disturbed by Céline's satirical assaults. Until recently, most would have agreed with Eliseo Vivas, who admires the consistency of the hatred that informs the book and describes the writer as a "magnificently gifted paranoid." At the same time Vivas insists that "neither audacity nor love nor malice are creative of epic destruction, they are impotent. Resentment and self-hatred trims all size to its own scale, perceives nothing but what is emotionally and morally congruous with it." Ironically, the key word here is "impotent," since it is precisely at the poetic conveyance of the impact of frustration and impotence that Céline excels. The concept of glory is as alien to his vision as it is to the mode in which he operates. Ferdinand's relative success in the world is a measure of his failure to see the fruitlessness of success and the inaccessability of the tolerable existence. Robinson's ignoble death and senseless life are incompatible with any sort of grandeur.

The view of life in these novels should not be confused with life itself. Here Céline is ahead of the moralizing critics who will necessarily find in his work an affront to human dignity. True, he means what he says: the world is horrible; we fail to see the horror because our vision is blunted by habit; we are courting corruption and waltzing toward the abyss. But his message relates principally to his fears rather than to his knowledge, and his overstatement surely serves to mute the humming in his ears. After all, the grotesque is a necessary counter to the sublime, and considerably less dangerous. We will probably never be as seasick in life as we are vicariously when reading the fantastic account of the Channel crossing in *Death.* Céline is a purge for the very fanaticism he espouses.

Events conspired to make *Death on the Installment Plan* Céline's most characteristic and most readable book, arguably his strongest and most balanced production. Written in the full glow of a literary triumph at a time when he was fully aware of the destructive potential of his new weapon, it was conceived before he began to court personal catastrophe with his pamphlets, before he began to suspect that his power could be turned back on him. The result is a cruel, a brutal, and explosive book, a gargantuan burst of hilarity and rage. But the rage, hysteria, and hallucination are all controlled and masterfully timed. Although the language, the punctuation, the rhythmic shifts, and the syntax suggest a sustained howl of frustration and animosity, there is little of the redundancy that mars many of the later books. Although they are used in the first novel, it is in *Death* that the famous three points of suspension become unavoidable . . . punctuation for the sustained stutter of progressive rage . . . argot and neologisms . . . fragments of speech . . . apocalypses roaring across pages . . . vitalizing the Rabelaisian catalogs . . . illuminating them . . . turning them into molten emotion and the fear of the human crowd . . . the violent mob latent in every individual. The pace is swift, the action varied, the motifs and themes consistent without being obtrusive. This second novel, although less satirical, has all the first one had but with greater intensity and more bite. It makes fewer concessions to literary prejudices and harks back more directly, through the intermediaries Jules Valles and Henri Barbusse, to the carnivalesque tradition of Aristophanes, Petronius, Rabelais, and Ben Jonson. The French critics, disappointed and bewildered by these further developments, reacted negatively. Céline, the scourger, felt victimized. Even his publisher, Denoël, found the apparent lack of restraint, especially in sexual matters, disturbing. Blanks were left for self-censored passages. The first American edition omitted several chunks of lurid obscenity that would probably pass muster today, but only barely.

The novel records the youth of Bardamu, his apprenticeship to sorrow, exposing the forces that eventually drove him to enlist in the cav-

alry. Céline's narrator, whose situation is established in the first nine chapters (a double overture), is a more experienced version of Dr. Bardamu, one who has survived and already recorded the dawn of the end of the night. Now, to relieve the tedium and squalor of his suburban existence, he writes a curious romance, the product of childhood musings, "Le roi Krogold" (Krogold the king). Impossibly high in tone, funny only by inadvertence, and featuring a brutal, vengeful hero, the tale forms a counterpoint to the life he leads at the clinic among the poor of Paris. The reader is aware of the double enchantment being worked. The poor magic of the tale is drawn off by the apparently naturalistic surface of the novel, and reality becomes a part of an extravagant but meaningless allegory peopled with creatures of fancy. Everything tends to point up the moral: man kills his life finding ways to enjoy dying.

The overture, foreshadowing the catastrophic rhythm of the whole book, builds toward a fabulous climax in the Bois de Boulogne, where Bardamu has gone with a young whore he suspects of spreading gossip about him. The outing, which he begins peacefully enough by telling her some of "Krogold," ends when he loses control and in a hallucinatory rage assaults her before a heterogeneous mob dredged from his fancy and thundered upon the page like an avalanche of fallen humanity:

Once at the Arc de Triomphe, the whole crowd was in attack formation. All of them took out after Mireille. There were corpses everywhere. The remainder tore at their organs. The English woman heaved her car above her head, at arm's length. Hurray! Hurray! She slams it into the autobus [. . .] Mireille's dress flew up. The old English lady hops on her, chumps on her breasts, it trickles, it pours, red everywhere. . . . We totter, we creep together, suffocate. . . . It was hell.

He wakes up in his room, feverish, still raving.

By the end of the book we have learned to expect these explosive sneezes through which Céline mimes an unattainable finality. Nothing in *Journey* has prepared us for this degree of fury and joy. This is a new sort of narrator, committed to a far more open and direct form of expression, a true delirium. If similar sequences in Henry Miller and William Burroughs and even the "Circe" chapter of *Ulysses* (1922) seem labored by comparison, it is worth noting that even at his most hallucinatory, Céline neither completely abandons his objective base (resembling Picasso in this) nor crams his books with symbolic significance.

The overture, like the opening chapter of *Journey,* states the themes of the book within a more or less coherent narrative frame. Beyond that, it establishes the character and situation of the narrator, describes his physical and spiritual position, and justifies what follows as both the product and the cause of his delirium and persecution mania. This strategy later became one of Céline's favorites, but at this point he appears to be writing an outrageous parody of Marcel Proust's "Overture" in *Remembrance of Things Past* (1913–1927). What follows are to be the reminiscences of a sick and tormented man of an impoverished and harassed childhood and adolescence, reminiscences born of hallucination brought on by fever. We are to take them for a very special and immediate kind of truth.

The nominal hero of this novel is the boy, Ferdinand, who from his unlicked and unwiped beginnings protects his identity and nurses his vices by feigning stupidity and incompetence. It is his fate to fail at everything he tries but somehow to rise from the ashes of others' destruction, from his mother's struggles to maintain a moribund lace business, from the total collapse of Meanwell College and the suicide of Nora Merrywin, from his father's growing awareness of inadequacy, and, finally, from the total failure and suicide of Courtial des Pereires. The boy figures principally as a glass through which the narrator can see himself and with the aid of which he can measure the forces that contribute to his present condition.

Beginning in the dreary Passage de Bérésinas, where his crippled mother struggles to sell and repair a commodity that is as completely out of vogue as the family morality, he exposes sequentially the family's cramped existence, the frustrations and failures of his father, Auguste, and his own failure to hold jobs in the face of misunderstandings and brutal exploitation. Release comes when he is sent to England, to the seedy Meanwell College. There, he deliberately fails to learn English but enjoys an Edenic peace as the companion of a cretinous boy, becoming the admirer and eventual seducee of the master's beautiful wife, Nora. This period of complete insouciance prepares him to leave the Passage, where his father's mindless rages and the endless economies and precautions symbolized by his mother's trade have deformed his childhood. After a fight that rocks the Passage, a thunderous belch of frustration, Auguste disowns him, and Ferdinand is apprenticed to his scrupulous and plodding father's opposite number, the genial fraud and mythomaniac Courtial.

Living by his wits and for his whims, Courtial is a fantastic jack-of-all-trades. Inventor, writer of manuals, editor, and above all huckster, he has shored up his ego with tangible accomplishments. The rhetorical gifts Auguste wastes on his rages, Courtial pours into his manuscripts and lectures. A born teacher, he pretends that even the tattered balloon, the emblematic windbag with which he barnstorms at local fairs, is "instructive." Bound by his responsibilities, Auguste, who has a genuine passion for the sea, wastes his life at a job he hates with a hatred that poisons his otherwise exemplary home life. Courtial, on the other hand, lives his dreams and gradually ruins himself with gambling and women. He finishes the job with alcohol and birdshot, while his wife, a splendid version of Punch's Judy, does her best to keep things going and to tear down Courtial's mask of phony industry.

Ferdinand's role is once again that of Sancho Panza. A loyal servant, he brings to his new situation the morality he thinks he has discarded. While assuming the inventor's responsibilities, however, he gradually acquires his ability to dream. But beyond this, from Courtial's childishness and buffoonery he lowers his defenses, learns compassion. Some time after Courtial's death, having returned to Paris weakened by fever, the boy sees his master projected before him on the facades of the houses, beside his bench, standing in front of him. Recalling his lectures and losing all self-control, he begins to rave in Courtial's stead:

> That's what it is the presence of death . . . It's when you talk for them . . . Suddenly, I straightened up . . . I stopped resisting . . . I was about to let out one terrible scream . . . Let myself go but good . . . I'd lifted my eyes to the sky . . . so as not to see the buildings . . . They made me feel so sad . . . I saw his head all over the walls . . . against the windows . . . in the dark . . .

In the end, unlike Sancho, Ferdinand attempts to shed his past, to become his own man and complete the education begun in the Passage des Bérésinas.

Death on the Installment Plan is in most respects a sounder and more original novel than its predecessor. Although neither realistic nor truly autobiographical, it motivates the narrator's delirium through the self-portraiture in its overture, establishing a coherent structure, a well-motivated narrative posture, and a unified tone. The language is clearly more versatile than that of *Journey*, approaching Céline's goals: the spoken idiom and an antiliterary style. Since the units of time and action are larger, there is more room for character development. However, the focus is still on grotesque or hyperbolically rendered traits. More than ever, we experience their outlandish gestures, but unlike the bald caricatures and sentimental cliches of *Journey*, the outlandish puppets of this book often have faces behind their masks. Consequently, we detect as we never will again the narrator's furtive sympathy for the flayed clown.

Take, for example, the treatment of Irène Perreire's farewell in the following scene, which occurs in the village of Blême, where Courtial has recently ended his life. It should be noted that Ferdinand is wearing a coat "made mostly of string," that the ugly "old crone" is wearing trousers. As the train pulled out,

> [she] stood in the carriage door with Dodule's little mutt . . . She signaled "good-bye"! . . . I gestured in response! . . . Just then the train started . . . she was taken by a fit of distress . . . Ah! something terrible! . . . She was making atrocious grimaces from the door of her compartment . . . And then she gurgled "rrah! rrah!" like someone being choked . . . like some sort of animal . . .
>
> "Ferdinand! Ferdinand!" she was still able to holler . . . like that across the station . . . Above all the racket . . . The train rushed into the tunnel . . . We never saw each other again! . . .

Here the traits of the mad clown are drawn less from Chaplin or the nineteenth-century Pierrot with his sad stasis than from the paintings of Breughel and Bosch.

The mixture of wild action and strong emotion within an absurd context is typical of Céline's later work, but nowhere else does he achieve a pathos so genuine because seemingly so much against the grain. In later books the characters become increasingly aspects of the dream landscape, replacing in effect the foreign lands described in *Journey*. They are gesticulating dolls whose humanity is submerged by the speaker's rhetoric and personality. This progressive dehumanization is most evident in the handling of important deaths, moving from the pathos of Robinson's murder/suicide to the horror of Courtial's exploded head to the hallucinated violence of van Claben's killing to the establishment of the Halles porter Normance's bloody corpse as the centerpiece of *Normance*. All of these events are projections of Céline's obsession with head wounds; all derive from or contribute to the narrator's identity.

Robinson's death, though quickly pressed into the service of theme, is thoroughly human and deeply moving. Pariah and madman, schemer and misanthrope, failure though he is, Robinson is more the *pícaro* and the saint than the contorted grotesque. We have been party to his dreams and frustrations in the book's first half, and later we have witnessed his failure to kill the indomitable old Henrouille, his blindness, and his eventual cure. He has dreamed of achieving minimal security, but when it finally comes (accompanied by the love of an attractive woman), he runs back to his former life and eventually induces his own death. Although potentially terrible, his end is not gory; although potentially base, within the inverted scheme of the novel it is treated as the justification of his life. His corpse is neatly and promptly disposed of.

Courtial's end comes early one winter morning on the road in front of a farm. His decline, though potentially pathetic, has been played as low comedy. So it is obscenely proper that his tremendously inflated brain should be ventilated with bird shot after it has ceased to provide the family with food (and sustain his self-respect). When Ferdinand and Irene discover him, he has become a thing:

> He was all shrunk, the old man . . . shriveled up in his frock coat . . . And then, well, it was really him! . . . But the head was just a massacre! . . . He'd blown it to bits . . . He had practically no skull left [. . .] The double-barrel of the shotgun had entered through his mouth, rammed on through . . . It'd skewered the whole pudding . . . All that rotten meat, hamburger! . . . in little shreds, in clots [. . .] He'd lost his peepers . . . They'd just clean popped out . . .

What follows—their efforts to free his remains from the frozen road, the vigil, the inquest—is a dance of death, a grotesquerie beyond anything produced by the medieval imagination and far beyond the imaginings of a Baudelaire, Rimbaud, or Goya. Yet Courtial emerges as pathetically human, a sack of vices but lovable and beyond disgust. Like Robinson, he has been a good teacher.

This can hardly be said of the pawnbroker Titus van Claben, who briefly entertains the scapegrace Ferdinand and his friend Borokrom in part 1 of *Guignol's Band,* and whose corpse is the focus of the conclusion of part 2. Van Claben is an impossibly gross figure, slothful, lecherous, sensual, and greedy. Mammon personified, he has amassed a huge store of gold and booty while unaccountably retaining a love for good music. Céline reduces him to a revolting puppet, a beturbaned mock pasha enthroned on his bed and served by a demented slattern and broken-down musician. Van Claben silently suffers an animal's death during a dope orgy that rivals anything in Burrough's *Naked Lunch* (1959). When Ferdinand and Borokrom imagine he is stuffing himself with gold coins, they try to make him vomit, lifting his enormous bulk by the feet and dropping him on his head down a stairway. Finally, his skull split, he is unceremoniously dumped into the cellar. Painful pleasure is the essence of all Grand Guignol. Here, the catastrophic act is reduced to a side effect in an emotional riot. For the first time, the author has transferred rather than shared his horrific sense of injury. Paradoxically, he gives the wound to the only Jew in his fiction, a displacement brilliantly interpreted by Philippe Muray.

In 1947, after leaving his Danish cell, Céline created yet another surrogate corpse. Reworking the murder of van Claben for *Normance,* devising some rather ponderous allegorical implications for the trepanation, he turned it into a public event, loading it onto the conscience of all France. The scene is the lobby of the Destouches's apartment house, where the residents have gathered to wait out the Royal Air Force bombardment of Montmartre, an event Céline suggests occurred in 1944. The central figure and victim is a huge, slothful, debilitated market porter named Normance. In the course of one riotous sequence, his head, used as a battering ram against a locked door, is smashed open and wrapped in a towel, turban fashion. He bleeds to death silently amidst the confusion of the raid, while the other tenants drink stolen liquor. A metaphor for Céline's France, the body of the dying giant lies in the lobby until it can be unceremoniously dumped down the elevator shaft into the cellars that honeycomb the hill of martyrs. Nothing about this circumstance is calculated to arouse our sympathy. Normance is a mute presence and a symbol, never a character. Yet Céline clearly but ironically intends to identify Normance/France with his tormented narrator, Dr. Destouches. In the overture, it is Destouches who has fallen down the shaft of the disused elevator, injuring his head. During the frenetic narrative that follows as a consequence of that fall and a projection of the doctor's anxieties, Destouches, conscious of the distrust and suspicion of his neighbors, remains active and sober. While the others go to pieces, he alone looks after Normance's ailing wife. Finally, after the raid, overcome by his fears, he tries to hide by rolling in the flood of clotted gore that has gushed from the porter's skull. The wound has become terrifyingly immediate in this fantastic context.

In 1944, eight years after the publication of *Death on the Installment Plan* and three years before he began to write *Normance,* Céline published part 1 of *Guignol's Band.* Following as it did the shapeless bombast of the pamphlets, *Guignol* appears at first glance to be the most gratuitous of his novels, a series of loosely connected adventures, each a stylistic tour de force, each culminating in a verbal explosion. In addition there is the antagonistic narrative pose. The narrator is reliving the experience of World War I London from the perspective of the present one, tossing his "unreadable" slop in the faces of those who will surely reject it.

The tactic is a time-honored one, the clown's gambit designed to lure an audience into a garden of forbidden delights and unnamable distress. We find it in the introduction to Rabelais's *Gargantua* (1532), in Baudelaire's address "Au lecteur" (1857), and in dozens of other irreverent works. But no previous clown has been so deliberately, so outrageously offensive. *Guignol*'s overture clearly suggests the rhetorical stance of Céline the pamphle-

teer, but here the tactic is subtler: the attack is accomplished by exposing the French reader to events from the recent past, the horrendous exodus from Paris that accompanied the collapse of the French army. Indeed, we may see it as a pendant to the attack on the army made in *Les beaux draps,* the last of the pamphlets. But here Céline and the reader are united in the center of the action as potential victims to reconstitute outrage and carnage on the page as an extension of Grand Guignol. It is only after that softening-up procedure that the narrator launches into his address to the reader, compounding (but strangely mitigating) the clownish offense. The comic thrust is inescapable, as is its conventional nature: "Readers, friends, less than friends, enemies, critics!" What follows in the novel proper is darkly obsessive fun, rhetorical hysteria carefully distanced in time and space as well as by its locus on the absolute fringe of society.

The main protagonist is the recently trepanned Ferdinand, released both from the war ("75 percent disabled") and from all morality, loose in the garish *Beggar's Opera* atmosphere of the London underworld, in which he functions as pimp, leech, and smuggler. This is a world of objects, gestures, and people presented in a breathless prose with an exuberance formerly reserved for the hate pamphlets but with a narrative vigor carried over from the novels. Written in the depths of the war and occupation by an anxious man who was losing his faith in the power of the thousand-year Reich to maintain itself and protect him, it is a curiously vital and perversely joyous book full of memorable profiles and fabulous events. There is the vengeful, boisterous Cascade, chief of the pimping brotherhood; there is Dr. Clodovitz with Punch's nose and unnumbered troubles, a vaguely sympathetic clown; there is Carmen, the whore with the lacerated buttock; and then there is Borokrom, the piano-playing bomber and dope smuggler, "a real angel on the skids." And of course, as centerpiece there is van Claben's demise. The end of the book ushers in another avatar of Courtial or rather of

Courtial's commedia persona, the learned fool. Part illuminated mystic, part half-mad inventor, and part confidence man, Sosthene will have a major role as Ferdinand's protector in the next volume.

The manuscript for *Le Pont de Londres* was left in Paris at the time of the Destouches's hasty departure for Denmark. There are signs, especially in the unintentionally hilarious bits of broken English, that the writer had not really completed his revisions. We also have Céline's own word that he planned a third volume to complete the London cycle. Still, the second volume is a wonderful gift. Without it *Guignol's Band* was both inconclusive and a bit wispy; with it we have a substantial comic masterwork, Céline in a new mode and his best form.

The novel continues with Ferdinand playing the sorcerer's apprentice to Sosthene, who, in partnership with a demented colonel, is intent on inventing a better gas mask. Throughout the book there is a counterpoint to that enterprise with its explosive consequences and the courtship, flirtation, and seduction by Ferdinand/ Pierrot of one of Céline's most delightful female creations, the Columbine-like Virginie, the colonel's lovely niece. Aside from the fairy creatures of the ballets, Virginie is the freshest thing in all of Céline's oeuvre. Indeed, she is straight out of the pastoral universe of *Paul et Virginie,* and the romantic interlude comments both on the lost potential for innocence in the corrupt London environment of World War I but also in the modern world in general. Combining the traits of the ballet dancers seen obliquely in *Normance* with those of Destouches's wife, Lili, in the postwar trilogy, she manages to turn the rogue Ferdinand into a perversely naive urban shepherd.

Parental opposition to this affair eventually leads the two lovers to attempt to elope with the connivance of Ferdinand's underworld cronies from part 1. Their escapade ends, appropriately enough, in the bar of a man named Prospero. Along the way we are exposed to a splen-

did battery of effects and three major dramatic movements, each culminating in a masterful explosion: the catastrophic failure of the gas mask experiment; the trip to town during which Ferdinand and Virginie are escorted to a nightclub called Touit-Touit (or Tweet-Tweet) by an apparently dead crook named Mille Pattes (or Centipede); and the reappearance of the rotting corpse of van Claben at Prospero's. These extended sequences provide Céline with opportunities to innovate verbal pyrotechnics in the Guignol tradition. All of his characters are stereotypes, but each of them is given a variety of comic/grotesque turns illuminated by deft prose gestures and ample delirium.

A ghoulish presence, a Grand Guignol and puppet show staple, Mille Pattes's appearance discomforts Ferdinand almost beyond measure and leaves the reader at a loss to rationalize what follows. How much of this is actually hallucinated by Ferdinand? Is the ghost as real for Virginie as he is for Ferdinand? It is raining in Hyde Park when this figure worthy of H. P. Lovecraft materializes, startling Virginie, who accepts his cadaverous presence, terrifying Ferdinand, who knows Mille Pattes to be dead:

> Where did he come from this comic valentine? . . . when everybody else has gone . . . Just like that in the downpour? . . . Why'd he approach us? . . . He speaks in a white voice . . . His voice quavers . . . I eyeball him hard . . . There's something about him . . . come to think of it . . . I recognize him . . . or do I? . . . He looks at me too . . . I'm not sure . . . He's there, upright! . . . in front of us there, in the cloudburst . . . it's pouring off him! . . . cascading . . . seems not to notice [. . .] He puts out his hand . . . I'm not going to holler . . . scream . . . I take that hand . . . it's cold . . . freezing even . . . and hard . . . like wood . . . But he's not trembling . . . He's quite calm . . . He's dressed all in black . . . Me, I palpitate . . . I want to say something!

Typically, the episode builds from its eerie opening through countless comic twists far beyond what the reader feels able to endure to a thunderous climax and the usual anticlimax in tiny steps, each like a tensed bit of spring steel. But what sets this novel off from the earlier work is a curious cinematic impact. It is almost as though, like the movie cartoonist, Céline has found a way to reduce motion to visual frames that the reader's eye will animate. This is Céline at his most visual and perhaps his most relaxed, despite the tension of the times. It is not hard to fathom why he never returned to complete the *Guignol* series after the war and his incarceration.

As Céline's first postwar novel, *Féerie pour une autre fois,* part 1, demonstrates how far he could push the form—on the one hand toward the frantic monologue, on the other toward the farcical set piece, *Normance,* part 2 of *Féerie,* shows how far he could extend a single moment of desperate slapstick violence. In a very real sense these are the true post-pamphlet novels: narratives of self-serving and propagandistic self-exculpation that somehow work better than they should. Or perhaps it is a matter of perspective. Thirty-five years after their publication, in the wake of the "postmodern" decomposition of narrative, they represent Céline's strongest contribution to narrative technique. Not surprisingly, they have had a strong and continuing underground influence.

Féerie, part 1, Céline's *de profundis,* may be his strangest and most personal novel. Two-thirds of it takes place (if a plotless and angry meditation can be said to "take place") in a dismal cell in the death house of a Danish prison. The voice of Dr. Destouches is dark, cruelly ironic, defiant, venomous, an underground voice hurling confused echoes of his hatred, disgust, pain, and despair out through the tiny window. There is next to no narrative development though the novel begins in pre-Liberation Paris with Destouches's recollection of a visit paid him by the wife and son of an old friend, a woman who "hardly ever comes to see me" but has come this time despite "alerts, metro breakdowns, and barricaded streets." This is a fine opening for a novel of suspense that never materializes.

True, Céline evokes the suspicion, opportunism, and distrust of the moment, his own uneasiness in the face of BBC denunciations. But we never learn what prompted the visit or what transpired. Instead, this event becomes, like Proust's famous good-night kiss, the thread guiding us through the labyrinth of this monumental reverie, this reconstitution of time present. By a curious process, a gradual sedimentary sifting and sinking, we share the prison experience, not as it is lived but rather as it operates upon the consciousness of a pariah who sees himself as innocent, patriotic, maligned, and persecuted. The big events, the cross-examinations, the hospital confinements, the visits of Destouches's wife and of the vindictive French consul, are conveyed piecemeal through the prisoner's groans and mumblings interspersed with curses and harsh laughter. From this description *Féerie* may sound like a recipe for novelistic disaster, but the voice in question is amazingly versatile, capable of rapid shifts of pace, mood, and subject matter. His monologue is unmatched verbal vaudeville, albeit frequently dark, as befits the context. (One thinks of Samuel Beckett's Unnamable.) Many of the prisoner's words are affronts to his potential readers and their beliefs, which he attacks less with satire than with vituperation; yet, whatever our sympathies, we are with him, sharing his discomforts and maladies, his hallucinations, among hated foreigners, jackels, lackeys.

Unexpectedly, in the last third of *Féerie,* the howls and groans are replaced by Destouches's recollection of a happy gargoyle, a puckish sculptor. Jules is an amputee (a "mutilé de guerre" like Destouches/Céline), a Punch/Harlequin who trundles his legless torso about Montmartre at horrendous speeds in a little wagon, drinking anything available and soiling his cart by pissing freely. (As so often happens, there is a living model for this evil sprite: Céline's sidekick and friendly antagonist, the artist Gen Paul, a "free spirit" who lost one of his legs and lived amidst impossible clutter with a succession of women.) Capitalizing on his disability, Jules is a frantic womanizer who spirits Lili's young ballet students to his studio, where they willingly pose in the nude.

Jules is one of Céline's great comic creations and another of his alter egos, volatile, unpredictable, abusive, capable of erecting impenetrable verbal shields against friend and enemy alike. Free of purpose and principles but compounded of vice and malice, he proves as seductive to the reader as he was to those who sheltered him. While Destouches's voice transmits despair, the hilarious and mute antics of Jules are made to suggest insouciance and to symbolize the twisted values of the world that has condemned the narrator. In order to clinch this point, Céline ends *Féerie* with an absurd seduction. Over her husband's objections, Lili poses nude for the little voyeur under a lurid green light. If the effect is traumatic—a symbolic cuckolding of the voyeuristic husband by his voyeuristic alter ego—the scene is appropriately farcical, with Destouches cast as a morose, jealous Pantaloon to Lili's Columbine and Jules's Harlequin. But we are not allowed to forget the moral implications that take us full circle back to the death cell and the question of the moral choices made by the French during the Occupation.

The crippled clown continues to play the role of evil genius in *Normance.* From atop the Moulin de la Galette he appears to be directing the Royal Air Force bombers as he scuttles dizzily and thirstily around a teetering platform while his fellow tenants cower under the table in the lobby of the house on rue Girardon. After the bombardment, Jules is brought down, Normance is tossed into the catacomb, and Destouches is saved from the mob he believes is after his collaborationist skin. The family then climbs through the shattered building to the fifth floor. There, the dream effect is accentuated by the appearance of the actor Norbert, who is waiting in a virtually undamaged room placidly oblivious to a corpse in his bathtub, which also contains a stock of liquor. He is expecting the heads of state with whom he plans to parley. The scene and the book end with this giant absurdity.

In *Féerie pour une autre fois* image and action are subordinated to the flux of ideas; humor derives almost entirely from the rhetoric. In *Normance* language is the servant of action. The underdeveloped characters, the jerky movements, the collisions, the spills and explosions, the crazy animation of the furniture, all the improbable behavior of the Keystone Cops and Harold Lloyd, are captured in a prose that approximates the rhythm of arterial bleeding. But if inspiration is taken from the silent flickers, the subject matter is truly grotesque and sick in the tradition of Sade, Lautréamont, and Rimbaud. The real force is the narrator's mind and vision, distorted by injuries and anxieties. His raucous laughter provides us with a matrix for life, dulls the edge of asocial horror.

Céline, who hoped, as he told Robert Poulet, to make his version of the "truth shine through absurdities," had always been interested in the divine marquis. Like Sade, he took pleasure in pointing up unpleasant and asocial morals, but his *Normance* was as much a protest against violence as a sadomasochistic frolic. Perhaps, after all, our interest in Céline's work comes in part from such complex interleaving of motives. The verbal stick with which we and our world are beaten is also the instrument that turns the world against the author and, paradoxically, a sign of his concern both for that world and for his own real and critical skin. Hatred is an expression of love on the part of a man who fears to turn the other cheek. For all of this, even though, like so much contemporary fiction, its effects are tenacious and even brilliant, *Normance* is far too long for its content. Critics may well be right to judge it a novelistic failure, but it is best seen as a failure in terms of its timing and proportions rather than of its conception. Perhaps that is why it has become a novelist's novel.

We may read the two volumes of *Féerie* as a retrospective meditation on the Occupation—as seen from the pit—and a reflection on the mounting tension that led to flight. The next three novels are, by contrast, the "chronicle" of defeat, retreat, and exile written from a postmortal position. The struggling doctor who narrates *Castle to Castle, North,* and *Rigadoon* is a modern Dante returned from death after having passed through the hell he attempts to depict. We begin from a static present, in Meudon, where Destouches, Lili, and their numerous pets lead a precarious existence. As in *Féerie,* the opening pages of *Castle* contain a long and initially tedious lament. But here the tone is relatively serene. The past is past and Destouches will not live to see the future. The aging victim has donned a new mask, one with two faces: one bitterly petulant, the other resigned. On the one hand, complaints and curses mingle, scapegoats abound. The doctor feels exploited by publishers, betrayed by friends, threatened by neighbors. On the other hand, he lives quietly and writes, only in the hope of providing the improvident Lili with an inheritance. In a frenzied world, this bitter/resigned Candide cultivates his verbal cabbage patch. His voice seems calm and mature, his dual face/mask composed. Even his most heated prose understates the horror. Finally, during a visit to his only patient, he has a vision. He sees Charon's ferry in the guise of an ancient *bateau mouche* skippered by the actor Le Vigan (an avatar of Norbert) returned from exile in Argentina. Unnerved and, as usual in Céline's novels, feverish, the doctor flees this apparition.

During a severe malarial attack he and we are transported back to 1944 and eventually to the Hohenzollern castle of Sigmaringen, where the Germans have established a Vichy government in exile. A fantastic amalgam of styles and splendors, the castle serves as a fairy palace of disaster for the heterogeneous mass of human refuse following their puppet leaders. In town the undernourished and frightened refugees fill the air with flatulence, fight among themselves, and foment revolts, while Petain and his followers in the castle live in regal splendor in full knowledge of the catastrophe to come. The air overheard is completely dominated by the Americans and the Royal Air Force.

As official doctor to the government, Destouches occupies a cubbyhole subject to flooding from the nearby water closet, itself the social center of their hotel. His daily rounds, filled with vignettes of misery, violence, folly, and resignation, provide a framework for this mosaic of degradation and collapse. In one of the last episodes, pursuing the dream of escaping to Denmark, he makes a fantastic and pointless trip to the icy north to witness the burial of a high official dead at the hands of a German quack surgeon. The delegation travels in a railway car opulently furnished by Kaiser Wilhelm for a shah's visit during the pre–World War I days. Threatened by enemy planes, deprived of food and heat, wrapped in draperies installed to shade and cool a king, they reach their destination ten days late but in time to participate in a snowy funeral before a closed coffin. With the *Horst Wessel Lied* and the *Marseillaise* ringing in their ears, their minds on food, warmth, and the retreat from Moscow, they retrain for Sigmaringen. The whole trip is typically gothic, and Céline, exploiting its grotesque and comic potential, makes it the emblem of the decaying splendor of Vichy.

In *Castle to Castle* Céline pours his spleen on the heads of publishers intent on improving his image and correcting his style. The fruits of their efforts are apparent in *North,* the most conventionally literary and coherent of the postwar books. Readers, though not burdened by the usual overture, may approach this fairly sympathetic rendering of the collapse at the center of the Third Reich with some misgivings; for the exacerbated tone of the earlier books provided much more distance for the observer than does the tense and resigned tone of *North,* its uncluttered plot and well-paced narrative. For once, however, we participate in a world of reversed values from the perspective of a pariah whose sympathies are nearer to ours than to those of the alien world he describes.

The events treated in *North* antedate Sigmaringen. But, though Germany is still being softened up for invasion, Céline reads the bombing of Berlin as terminal, equating it ironically with Richard Wagner's *Götterdämmerung* (1874). Orchestrating his book like a Wagnerian opera, he uses the ceaseless roar of planes and the seismic tremors caused by the bombs as background music. Against this cataclysm (Céline, incidentally, called Hitler a cataclysmic clown), the author projects three stages of the Destouches's pilgrimage, three false paradises, each more perilous than the preceding one. As hotel doctor in Baden-Baden, he watches with distaste the behavior of the rich international set, witnesses their revels on the night of the attempt on Hitler's life, the eve of their expulsion from this garden. Traveling to Berlin, the little clan, which includes their paranoid friend Le Vigan, ferrets out a colleague, the SS man Hauboldt, whose medical headquarters is a sort of mock Venusberg beneath the ruined splendors of a Berlin garden. Hauboldt proves a generous if unpredictable host. The last of Céline's fat giants, he is at once a guide to the ruins and the genie of the lamp, intervening when the going gets too rough.

Against Destouches's better judgment, Hauboldt relocates the little group on the estate of a senile Prussian noble ironically named Schertz (German, "joke"). There, in an openly hostile environment but in relative safety, they wait out the bombing of Berlin (and the destruction of Hauboldt's garden retreat). Krantzlin, the Schertzes' eighteenth-century estate, with its French park and thatched village, is situated on the edge of the hungry steppe in the midst of a population of half-assimilated Poles and a complex of dangerous undesirables. The principal concern of this long section of the novel is the decay of the Schertz family and its estates, formerly a bulwark against the "yellow" tide. Within a context suggestive of fairy tale and myth, against the Wagnerian backdrop, the Schertzes act out a shadow play, a bizarre tragicomedy culminating in two deaths and multiple exiles. The perpetually hungry Destouches, ill-lodged and deprived of ration cards, divide their time between hunting for food and making themselves inconspicuous in a human landscape dotted with traps and pitfalls, real and imaginary. The world has turned savage and animal; all of the "higher" joys have turned to dust. The well-stocked Schertz library is valued for its collection of Paul de Kock; delicacies are stored in Hauboldt's secret cabinet, but bread is practically unobtainable. The slightly overripe vamp Isis Schertz plots to poison her ailing husband, a vindictive Punch; rutting whores rage like bacchantes on the steppe. Here, as elsewhere, Céline's effects are cumulative; the fragments of experience and facets of action, developed separately, are forced into a contracting context until the inevitable explosion sends them all skyward or toward some unnamed abyss.

In the late 1950's, with his fate assured for the first time since the beginning of the war, Céline, the writer as outcast elder statesman, could relax, lick his wounds, and contemplate past chaos. *North* shows him at what might be called the height of his technical powers, less insistent about the damage done his own ego, more objective, if still obsessed. Like the early masterpieces, it is full of brilliant technical turns, unified, but rich in detail and incident, abounding in dramatic sequences, lavish in its use of atmosphere, full of comic tension, irony, and surprise. Not unexpectedly, the tighter control of means, the slightly strained allegory, and the detachment make this penultimate book more coherent and readable (in Roland Barthes's sense), hence more acceptable to critics. But they also result in diminished force. The "impersonal" Céline, clownish historian of the collapse of the Nazi dream, proves less interesting than the hectic maniac who recorded personal catastrophes in the more "writerly" volumes of the *Féerie* sequence. The aging clown, rehearsing the capers that once made his fortune, often loses points to the ingenuous/explosive Bardamu.

If this is true of the relatively successful *North,* it is doubly so for its sequel, *Rigadoon.* Posthumously published in 1969, the book was allegedly complete at the time of the writer's death, a fact that should give it a certain cachet. But we may question whether this rambling account of travels in war-torn Germany on rails about to be demolished and unpredictable trains among a ragtag group of refugees was indeed finished. Repetitious, poorly timed, lacking variety, detail, and vigor, it reads like an early draft rather than a polished production. All that can be said for it is that it gives us one last glimpse of Céline's infamous wit and rhetorical vigor and that it takes us to the end of the night. There we will await the coming of the "Chinese," who will get no further than Cognac, where, the anti-alcoholic Céline says, "they'll end up, the dread yellow peril, happy drunk in the cellars."

Once read, a Céline novel cannot be forgotten. His gloomy humor, his bombast, his buffoonery, his verbal energy, and his excesses all stick like burrs to the consciousness. However, one must have read the entire canon to be aware of how brilliantly he tested the frontiers of farce, forcing the gates of the imagination. For him, writing was always a means of expressing a mature frenzy upon which history and experience could make but few marks. True, he saw himself by turns as a clinician and a destroyer, a moralist and a clown. Above all, he was a stylist who could "resensitize the language so that it pulses more than it reasons." (Like D. H. Lawrence, he saw reason as the enemy, the source of decadence in art and experience.) But his work stands unified like a huge altarpiece celebrating in many panels the last judgment in terms of the community of outcasts (or innocents) created by contemporary dislocations.

Perhaps unfairly, Céline's fame rests on two books, but his place in literary history has a broader base. He is the black magician of hilarity and rage, the perverse mirror of twentieth-century energy—a force so dynamic and diverse that it leads inevitably to overproduction and suicide. His vision supplements in our time that of Kafka and Beckett, putting a real gun in the hand of the metaphorical fool, substituting explosion for restraint. He stands next to Proust as a painter of a moribund society, next to Joyce as a liberator of language. His rhetoric, however much skill it conceals, is as natural as his breath and may have been even more necessary.

Selected Bibliography

EDITIONS

INDIVIDUAL WORKS

La vie et l'oeuvre de Philippe-Ignace Semmelweis. Paris, 1924.
Voyage au bout de la nuit. Paris, 1932.
L'Église. Paris, 1933.
Mea culpa suivi de "Semmelweis." Paris, 1936.
Mort à credit. Paris, 1936.
Bagatelles pour un massacre. Paris, 1937. Includes three of the ballets: "La naissance d'une fée," "Voyou Paul, brave Virginie," and "Van Bagaden."
L'École des cadavres. Paris, 1938.
Les beaux draps. Paris, 1941.
Guignol's Band. Paris, 1944.
Casse-pipe. Paris, 1952.
Féerie pour une autre fois I. Paris, 1952.
Normance: Féerie pour une autre fois II. Paris, 1954.
Entretiens avec le professeur Y. Paris, 1955.
Ballets sans musique, sans personne, sans rien. Paris, 1957.
D'un château l'autre. Paris, 1957.
Nord. Paris, 1960.
Pont de Londres: Guignol's Band II. Paris, 1964.
Rigodon. Paris, 1969.

COLLECTED WORKS

Oeuvres de Céline. 9 vols. Edited by Frederic Vitoux. Paris, 1981.

LOUIS-FERDINAND CÉLINE

LETTERS, DOCUMENTS, INTERVIEWS, AND MEMOIRS

Cahiers Celine 1–6 (1976–1980).

Les cahiers de l'Herne 3 (1963) and 5 (1965).

"Excerpts from Letters to Milton Hindus." *The Texas Quarterly* 5/4 (1962).

Lettres à des amis. Edited by Colin W. Nettlebeck. Paris, 1979.

Lettres à son avocat. Paris, 1984.

Lettres à Tixier-Vignancour. Edited by Frédéric Monnier. Paris, 1985.

Lettres et premiers écrits d'Afrique 1916–1917. Edited by Jean-Pierre Dauphin. Paris, 1978.

Poulet, Robert. *Entretiens familiers avec L.-F. Céline.* Paris, 1958.

TRANSLATIONS

Castle to Castle. Translated by Ralph Manheim. New York, 1968.

Death on the Installment Plan. Translated by Ralph Manheim. New York, 1966.

"From *Casse-pipe.*" Translated by J. Fuchs. In *The Iowa Review* 3/2 (Spring 1972).

Guignol's Band. Translated by Bernard Frechtman and Jack T. Nile. New York, 1954.

Journey to the End of the Night. Translated by John H. P. Marks. New York, 1934.

Journey to the End of the Night. Translated by Ralph Manheim. New York, 1983.

Mea Culpa and The Life and Work of Semmelweis. Translated by Robert Allerton Parker. Boston, 1937.

North. Translated by Ralph Manheim. New York, 1971.

"The Notebook of Cavalryman Destouches." Translated by David Hayman. In *The Iowa Review* 3/2 (Spring 1972). A translation of *Casse-pipe.*

Rigadoon. Translated by Ralph Manheim. New York, 1974.

BIOGRAPHICAL AND CRITICAL STUDIES

Aebersold, Denise. *Céline, un demystificateur mythomane.* Paris, 1978.

Brée, Germaine, and Margaret Guiton. *The French Novel from Gide to Camus.* New York, 1962.

Buckley, William K., ed. *Critical Essays on Louis-Ferdinand Céline.* Boston, 1989.

Burns, Wayne, et al. *Understanding Céline: Essays.* Seattle, 1984.

Chesneau, Albert. *Essai de psychocritique de L.-F. Céline.* Paris, 1971.

Dauphin, Jean-Pierre, ed. *L.-F. Céline.* Paris, 1974–1979.

Dauphin, Jean-Pierre, and Henri Godard, eds. *Céline: Actes du Colloque internationale de Paris, July 1979.* Paris, 1979.

Gibault, François. *Céline: Le temps des espérances 1894–1932.* Paris, 1977. *Céline: Delires et persécutions 1932–1944.* Paris, 1985. *Céline: Cavalier de l'apocalypse 1944–1961.* Paris, 1981.

Hanrez, Marc. *Céline.* Paris, 1961.

Hindus, Milton. *The Crippled Giant.* New York, 1950. A new and expanded edition, including the Hindus-Céline correspondence. Hanover, N.H., 1986.

Hauptman, Robert. *The Pathological Vision: Jean Genet, L. F. Céline, and Tennessee Williams.* New York, 1984.

Knapp, Bettina L. *Céline, Man of Hate.* Tuscaloosa, Ala., 1974.

Kristeva, Julia. *Powers of Horror.* Translated by Leon S. Roudiez. New York, 1982.

Mathews, J. H.. *The Inner Dream: Céline as Novelist.* Syracuse, N.Y. 1978.

McCarthy, Patrick. *Céline: A Critical Biography.* London, 1975.

Muray, Philippe. *L'Opium des lettres.* Paris, 1979.

———. *Céline.* Paris, 1981.

Ostrovsky, Erika. *Voyeur voyant: A Portrait of Louis-Ferdinand Céline.* New York, 1971.

Thiher, Allen. *Céline: The Novel as Delirium.* New Brunswick, N.J., 1972.

Thomas, Merlin. *Louis-Ferdinand Céline.* New York, 1979.

O'Connell, David. *L.-F. Céline.* Boston, 1976.

Richard, Jean-Pierre. *La nausée de Céline.* Montpellier, 1973.

Vandromme, Pol. *Du Coté de Céline: Lili.* Brussels, 1983.

Vitoux, Frédéric. *Louis-Ferdinand Céline: Misère et parole.* Paris, 1973.

BIBLIOGRAPHIES

Bibliography des écrits de L.-F. Céline, 1918–1984. Edited by Jean-Pierre Dauphin and Pascal Fouché. Paris, 1985.

A Half-Century of Céline: An Annotated Bibliography. Edited by Stanford Luce and William K. Buckley. New York, 1983.

DAVID HAYMAN

ISAAC BABEL

(1894–1941?)

ISAAC BABEL WAS perhaps the first Soviet prose writer to achieve a truly stellar stature in Russia, to enjoy a wide-ranging international reputation as grand master of the short story, and to continue to influence—through his own work as well as through criticism and scholarship—literature produced in our own day. All this acclaim notwithstanding, Babel, whom contemporaries remember as a man with a penchant for mystification, remains one of the more enigmatic figures of Russian modernism. Even the corpus of his writings is uncertain and may never be firmly established. The works by which he wished to be known, however, indeed his best-known works, have gone through thirty-five editions in the Soviet Union alone and, beginning in 1926, have been translated into all the major European tongues. In contrast to this renown, Babel's "authorized" legacy is quite compact. Begun and finished, for the most part, between 1921 and 1926, it consists of three major story cycles, two plays, and several pieces of short fiction—all fitting comfortably into an average-sized volume. Together they account for approximately half of Babel's extant output: movie scripts, early short fiction, journalistic sketches, one translation, and a few later stories that remained unpublished in Babel's lifetime (they were considered offensive either to the party or to the censor's sense of public delicacy).

His most famous work, the cycle of short stories and vignettes *Konarmiia (Red Cavalry)*, was first published in a separate edition in 1926. It dealt with the experiences of the Russo-Polish War of 1920 as seen through the bespectacled eyes of a Russian Jewish intellectual working, as Babel himself had, for the newspaper of the Red Cossack army. This autobiographical aura was critical to the success and popularity of the cycle. The thirty-three jewel-like pieces, strung together to form the first edition of *Red Cavalry*, were composed in a short period of time, between the summer of 1923 and the beginning of 1925, and together constitute Babel's longest work of fiction (two more pieces would be added subsequently). They also represent his most innovative and daring technical accomplishment. For the first time in Russian letters at least, the opulence and subtlety of modernism lent themselves to the expression of the cruelest and basest sensibility. An instant success, *Red Cavalry* met with virtually universal acclaim as the first true masterpiece of Russia's postrevolutionary prose fiction; it had generated a critical response that had exceeded Babel's own output even before the appearance of the separate edition. Clearly he touched the raw nerve of contemporary culture.

Another cycle, *Odesskie rasskazy (Odessa Tales)*, contains four novellas: "Korol'" ("The King," 1921), "Kak eto delalos' v Odesse" ("The Way It Used to Be Done in Odessa," 1923), "Otets" ("The Father," 1924), and "Liubka Kozak" ("Liubka the Cossack," 1924). Although completed between 1921 and 1923, for a long time the cycle was believed to have preceded *Red Cavalry.* United, like the stories of *Red Cavalry,* by their protagonists, the setting, and the narrator, *Odessa Tales* presented a larger-than-life, Rabelaisian picture of the city's Jewish underworld, whose members go about their carnivalesque business, meting out poetic justice to the melancholy powers of prudery, capital, and the local police. Inherently theatrical, *Odessa Tales* had an easy time crossing over into film and drama. In 1925 and 1926, Babel wrote a script based on the story cycle, naming it *Benia Krik* after the chief protagonist of the Odessa stories. By contrast with *Odessa Tales,* where the action takes place in the years 1905 to 1907 and the king of the Odessa gangsters reigns unchallenged, the script stretches to include the 1917 revolution and the civil war. It ends with a close-up of the back of Benia Krik's head as it is being shattered—deservedly, we are supposed to think—by a Red executioner's bullet. Perhaps by coincidence, the characters in the script fall without exception into two groups: the traders and the criminals are Jews (like the author of the script and the film director), whereas the proletarian revolutionary activists, who finish off the gangs, are ethnic Russians. Produced in 1926, the film ran into brief trouble with the censors but was released in January 1927 to enjoy considerable popularity.

Also in 1927, Babel completed his first play, *Zakat* (*Sunset,* 1928). Thematically different, it was in other respects closely related to the *Odessa Tales;* from this common milieu derives some of the most comical dialogue known to Russian theater. As the title suggests, *Sunset* offered a melancholy meditation on the passage of time as revealed through a bloody conflict between a brutal father who refuses to act his age and his children, who do not hesitate to use force in order to age him. Although the younger generation prevails and the play ends with the children's triumph, theirs is a Pyrrhic victory, and not only because it anticipates their eventual defeat at the hands of their own children. The small Jewish, bourgeois, and criminal world in which such a victory possessed some relative value would soon be ground up by the revolution and the new Soviet state. Babel's contemporaries understood this without any prompting from the playwright. In print, the play made for good reading; on stage, the response was mixed. In Odessa *Sunset* played to packed audiences in two theaters simultaneously (in Yiddish and in Russian), but the Moscow production of 1928, staged while Babel was in Paris, ended in disaster, largely, it seems, because the director tuned it to a crudely ethnic and anecdotal key.

Babel began work on the book *Istoriia moei golubiatni* (*The Story of My Dovecote*), his other major tetraptych, in 1925, when two of the stories were published, but did not complete the other two until five years later. An episodic fictional chronicle of the author's childhood years, the four stories combine into a portrait of the artist not as a young man, but rather as a studious Jewish boy poised at the edge of adolescence. Less exuberant in their style, the four novellas have more in common with the more traditional autobiographical fiction of Leo Tolstoy and Maxim Gorky than with the more probing explorations of the consciousness of a gifted child found in *The Noise of Time* by Osip Mandelshtam, *The Childhood of Luvers* by Boris Pasternak, and, earlier, *Kotik Letaev* by Andrey Bely. Indeed, the cycle appears to have been aimed at a wider audience, one that possessed only limited patience and little taste for modernism. Nevertheless, crafted as skillfully as anything that Babel ever wrote, *The Story of My Dovecote* must be counted among the minor masterpieces of short fiction.

After *Sunset* came out in February 1928, Babel published very little that had not appeared previously, although editions of his writings, revised and expanded to include a most recent story or two, kept being issued with what was surely an enviable regularity. Close to thirty separate editions, among them a volume of collected works, rolled off the presses during the decade following the publication of *Red Cavalry*. One work not related to the three cycles, the play *Mariia* (*Maria*, 1935), represented a rather uninspired attempt to appease Babel's official "creditors"—the high cultural and, it seems, political establishment that had allowed the "silent" author to continue maintaining a remarkably high profile. With its pathos directed against the remnant of the aristocracy and the unscrupulous Jewish bourgeoisie under the New Economic Policy (NEP, 1921–1928), the play arrived long after the NEP, with all of its remnants, had been obliterated in the Stalinist revolution. Babel worked too slowly, political winds were changing fast, and the play misfired, although it may have earned him a brief respite—just for trying—from the intense official pressure to produce.

In the 1930's Babel devoted much of his energy to film, random journalistic work, and almost compulsive travel, roaming ceaselessly across the Soviet Union, ostensibly in search of new material for his work in progress. Throughout this period he assured his family and friends in correspondence as well as in conversation that he was working on a major project—a novel, perhaps. In 1925 he told Dmitrii Furmanov, a fellow writer, he was considering a novel about the Cheka. Possibly some echoes of this project may be discerned in the rumors, circulating in Russia in the late 1920's and reported in the émigré press, that the Cheka had stopped the publication of a new piece by Babel. According to several memoirists, including Ilya Ehrenburg, in the late 1920's and early 1930's Babel was working on a novel, "Kolia Topuz," in which a con man successfully reforms himself through work in socialist construction. During the period of the first Five-Year Plan (1928–1932), when the prison population engaged in forced labor was rapidly expanding, such topics were in the air. Babel's patron and protector, Gorky, at the time the most important figure in Soviet culture, actively encouraged fellow writers to explore this subject. Whether Babel tried his hand at it or merely wished to appear to is a question that will most likely remain unanswered.

His tendency to subtitle his stories as part of a larger work in progress—a consistent practice beginning with *Odessa Tales*—confuses matters further. "V shchelochku" ("Through the Crack"), an odd piece about a scene observed by the narrator through a peephole in a bordello, was published in 1923 and came, according to its subtitle, "From the Book *Etchings*." It has no acknowledged companions in the published Babel, although it resembles his two stories published by Gorky in 1916. Some fifteen years later, "Gapa Guzhva" (1931, in *The Lonely Years*), a story about a Ukrainian village whore caught up in the collectivization of agriculture, was published as "The First Chapter of *Velikaia Krinitsa*." Its companion piece, "Kolyvushka," published posthumously in 1963, also in *The Lonely Years*, and yet to appear in the Soviet Union, bore a slightly different subtitle: "From the Book *Velikaia Staritsa*." There are no traces of other chapters. In response to the harsh criticism of *Mariia*, Babel declared that he was revising the play as part of a trilogy covering the period 1920 to 1935. But in the words of the Soviet commentator on the play, "No materials testifying to Babel's continued work on the trilogy have been preserved." When Babel was arrested on 15 May 1939, all the papers that were with him at his dacha in Peredelkino were confiscated. Now they are presumed lost, destroyed together with a portion of the NKVD (as the KGB was known in the 1930's) archive in 1941, when the seizure of Moscow by the German armies seemed imminent. For years, Antonina Pirozhkova, the writer's widow, had been pressing the KGB to reveal the fate of Babel's papers only to be informed in 1988 that the KGB possessed no record of Babel's papers. Thus we may never know whether Babel was writing for the drawer or trying to produce literature that could be officially accepted. Nor will we ever know whether any of his efforts, if indeed there were such efforts, led to substantial results.

The only extant manuscript of an unfinished work of fiction, *Evreika* (The Jewess, 1979), lends credence to the claims that Babel had indeed tried his hand at a different genre and a different thematic material. A third-person narrative with an unmarked, "objective" style, it tells the story of a recently widowed woman who leaves her decaying shtetl for Moscow to settle there with her only son. He insists on this move and she follows him, but apprehensively; for as she puts it, the capital already has too many Jews. A civil war hero, a decorated Red Army commander, and a student at a military academy, her son belongs to the new Soviet elite, and yet, he also acknowledges, if only to himself, the unease he feels in his new prestigious surroundings. The manuscript breaks off just as the narrative reaches its first potential conflict: the more cultivated neighbors are beginning to complain about the smell of his mother's Jewish cooking. It is a bitter but fitting irony that the unfinished novella was finally published in the Soviet Union in 1988, not in the original Russian, but in Yiddish, in Yiddish-language journal *Sovietish Heimland.* The fate of the work itself has remained enigmatic. Did Babel abandon this project for reasons of censorship or for fear that its publication might damage his reputation? Or could it be that he simply failed to sustain the narrative style that seems alien to the rest of his known fiction? Or did he complete *Evreika* only to lose it once and for all in the incinerators of the Lubyanka prison?

We do know, however, that with the exception of *Mariia,* the unfinished *Evreika,* and two or three later stories, Babel's major fiction is all of a piece. The three cycles share the same narrator, although they emphasize his different facets, and we continue to encounter him in the later stories, which, accordingly, borrow their settings, or sets, from *Red Cavalry, The Story of My Dovecote,* and *Odessa Tales.* Even the two novellas dealing with the collectivization— both third-person narratives—recall with such pungency and vividness the style of *Red Cavalry* that a knowing reader of Babel would find the absence of that bungling and humane *intelligent*—who failed to acquire the hoped-for "simplest of human skills," the ability to

kill—at least conspicuous and at most profoundly telling. It is this narrator who represents the chief protagonist of what has reached us of Babel's fiction. The author's mask, he came with time to be identified with the name of Isaac Babel, blending into one the man, the character, and the persona that straddled the two—the writer.

For an author whose best-known works were composed and published during a six-year period (1921–1928), the spectacular renown enjoyed during the remaining eleven virtually barren years and a remarkable posthumous fame must be considered, on a par with his texts, as part of his literary career. A member of the post–World War I generation of European and American writers, he developed, not unlike Ernest Hemingway and F. Scott Fitzgerald, a charismatic public persona that could appeal, often justifiably, to different facets of the European and American literary taste. To some Babel appeared first and foremost as an artist whose genius, forged in the revolution, transcended the boundaries of ethnicity and class; others, for whom the aesthetic criterion took pride of place, admired him as an avant-gardist who reinvigorated Russian prose and elevated the short story, a humbler genre, to the lofty heights of great art. And those of his readers who felt disillusioned with the Russian Revolution or never accepted its promise could focus their attention on Babel's meager output in the 1930's and, after 1939, his disappearance in the Gulag, citing them as evidence for the incompatibility of true art and Communist totalitarianism.

Babel's posthumous "rehabilitation," the official clearing of his name of all charges in 1954, and the subsequent reissuing of his work in the Soviet Union at the time of de-Stalinization made him an attractive symbolic figure to the less orthodox members of the Soviet cultural elite. They eagerly promoted his name and his writings, eliciting protest from the die-hard Stalinists whose interference made it easier for the champions of Babel to dissociate themselves retrospectively from the worst brutalities of the Soviet state. But in identifying with this "martyred" star of Soviet literature (and by implication with the more tolerant 1920's, when Babel made his spectacular debut), these advocates tended to magnify the author's tragic demise while underplaying his—and by implication, their own—loyalty to the regime during the period of worst terror.

An analogous revision of the writer's legacy, if on a smaller scale, took place among the intellectuals of the Left in the West in the late 1950's and 1960's. With new editions of his writings running off the presses throughout Western Europe and the United States, Babel's name was once again coming into vogue—even as more and more evidence testified to the catastrophic scale of the Stalinist purges. In the United States in particular, where the later, post-McCarthy fashion for Babel had been anticipated at least as early as 1947, according to Raymond Rosenthal, the figure of the writer was recruited to perform a multiple duty by such influential critics as Lionel Trilling and Irving Howe. Presented as a symbolic distillation of beauty and truth (Russian authors victimized by the regime seem to lend themselves naturally to such treatment), Babel served as a powerful indictment of Stalinism and at the same time as a man committed to the promise of Bolshevism. He provided a vindication for the long-standing fascination with the Russian Revolution on the part of the intellectual Left. Moreover, at a time when the exclusively political and Manichaean formulas for political engagement were losing their appeal, Babel turned into an exemplary case of the ambivalences and ambiguities faced by an intellectual—and a Jewish one, too—whose identification with the "people's cause" is tested most rudely by his supposed beneficiaries.

As a Russian Jew who in his writings thematized the advantages and liabilities of this double designation, Babel attracted a substantial Jewish readership both in his own country and abroad, and especially in the United States. For this audience, too, and with special poignancy after World War II, he served not only as a storyteller and playwright, but as a powerful symbolic figure whose life reproduced the recent history of the Jews of Europe, with all their accomplishments and tragic fate. Because there is no more consensus regarding this history than that of modern Europe or Russia, Babel has been alternately called upon to provide evidence for the failure or success, or merely the complexity, of the attempts made by Diaspora Jews to identify with the political or cultural agenda of their native country. More recently, Babel's biography and his writings, in which Jewish characters often assert themselves with vigor and militancy, provided a stimulus for a new sense of collective identity among the Jews of the Soviet Union—an unanticipated consequence of the coming together of de-Stalinization, awareness of the Holocaust, and Israel's 1967 victory in the Six-Day War.

Babel's writings, which made his effectiveness as a symbolic figure possible in the first place, have influenced the course of literary history in a significant and productive way. As in the history of political and aesthetic sensibility, Babel's achievement in this area possesses an exemplary character. He was one of the first major Jewish writers, along with Franz Kafka, to develop and practice a particular literary idiom in the language of the dominant culture, the idiom that has come to be associated with the experience of the assimilated, modern European Jew. Some of his more perceptive compatriots understood this at once. A. Z. Lezhnev, a well-known critic and a member of the editorial board of the influential *Pechat' i revolutsiia* (Press and Revolution), wrote in 1926:

> Babel is the first Jew who entered Russian literature as a Russian writer, at least the first prose writer. Up until now we only had Jewish writers attached to Russian literature. . . . [Their work] was interesting for the reader curious about the ethnographic details rather than art. It is only in Babel's hands that the life of [the Jews of] Odessa has acquired aesthetic value. . . . *Odessa Tales* and "The Story of My Dovecote" prove that he is

capable of transcending the limitations of anecdotal or ethnographic tendencies.

(p. 85)

Judging by his impact on such an accomplished and mature author as Osip Mandelshtam (*The Egyptian Stamp,* 1928), on a score of lesser and younger writers who began in his shadow, and, most remarkable, on Jewish-American writers like Philip Roth and Grace Paley, Babel established the foundation for what might have emerged as a Jewish Russian literature had it not been for the Great Russian chauvinism of the Soviet state.

Equally important, the exemplary character of Babel's achievement goes beyond the properly Jewish theme to encompass other forms of what sociologists call the phenomenon of cultural marginality. A member of the intelligentsia, a Jew, and because of this doubly different from his fictional setting, Babel's author-narrator rejected some aspects of his Jewish heritage and combined others, openly and skillfully, with powerful strands in his adopted milieu. In the process he produced a master script for future writers who, whether Jewish or not, wished to play the role of the other at the very center, and not the margins, of their country's culture.

A protagonist in the drama of his own making (although he had to share the directing with the times), Isaac Babel not only produced some of the best short fiction of this century, he also performed the role of a "marginal" writer with consummate skill. Indeed, he was able to maintain the illusion of authorship during those years when, by his own sardonic admission made from the stage of the First Congress of Soviet Writers, he was practicing "silence—the most difficult of all literary genres." Thus the oeuvre alone, especially its "authoritative" version, cannot account with sufficient fullness for the whole complex of ideas, texts, and events that have come to be associated with Babel's name. His background, the cultural tradition that he entered when he embarked on a career of literary authorship, the expectations of the more powerful segment of the reading public, his fiction, and his strategy for achieving and maintaining a high literary profile—all have contributed to the formation of what constitutes Babel's legacy for us.

Isaac Emmanuilovich Babel or, according to the records of the Odessa rabbinate, Isaac Manievich Bobel, was born to Man' Yitzkhovich and Feiga Bobel in the city of Odessa on 30 June 1894. His only sibling, Meri (after her emigration to Belgium, Madame Marie Chapochnikoff), was born in 1900. Even these two facts, which should be as innocuous as any birth certificate, are hard to disentangle from the two sets of narratives we associate with Isaac Babel. One of them, his own fiction, follows the autobiographical convention and centers on the narrator whose biographical attributes identify him (apparently) with the author himself. The other set is harder to circumscribe: simply put, it consists of what the reading public knows about the history of culture, politics, and society in modern Russia, including the history of Russia's Jews.

The two narratives impart a specific meaning to the fact that Babel's family was Jewish, secular, and, at the time of his birth, well on its way toward joining the middle class. Although lacking in systematic education, the parents identified with the Haskalah, the Jewish Enlightenment movement that had accepted Russian as the language of emancipation. And so it was embraced in the Babel household, functioning as the intergenerational lingua franca, with Yiddish reserved for the parents as their private tongue. Obviously, the culture of the shtetl and the ghetto, inseparable from Yiddish, was still very much their culture. Born and raised in an enclosed, small, homogeneous community which they later fled, Babel's family nevertheless experienced it as an irreducible place of origin, one where they had once wholly belonged, and one whose spiritual and emotional resources were still accessible to them. By contrast, their children, who were expected to make the final break with this culture, would never be part of either that or any other undivided world. With his wife and daughter living in France, his mother and sister in Belgium, another wife and another daughter in Russia, scores of relatives in Odessa and Kiev, and his own career as a Soviet writer now reaching for the stars, now descending into silence, Babel was the mobile (or homeless) man of the twentieth century par excellence.

Mobility had already distinguished his parents' generation. The comfortable financial position his father achieved early in his son's life placed the family in a distinct minority among the subjects of the Russian empire. It belonged to an even more distinct minority among Russia's Jews, who had to contend with the official and informal, but officially sponsored, anti-Semitism as well as severe legal disabilities. The latter included the prohibition to dwell outside the Pale of Settlement, specially designated urban areas in Russia's southwest, and rigid restrictions on access to education. "In Odessa, there is a very poor, populous and suffering Jewish ghetto, a very self-satisfied bourgeoisie, and a very pogromist city council," wrote Babel in 1917 about the city of his birth, fully aware of the misery and humiliation he was spared because his parents belonged to the second, fortunate category.

To be born in Odessa, or rather to have lived there in the years 1905 to 1915, was another stroke of luck Babel frequently acknowledged. The revolution of 1905, although it failed to destroy the old regime, immensely strengthened civil society, creating in the urban centers of Russia a heady atmosphere replete with political debate, strikes and demonstrations, a pluralistic press, and a thriving market for art and literature. Under these conditions, no matter how hostile the official policy, the Jewish community of Odessa was too large (in 1900, a third of Odessa's half a million citizens were Jewish), too well organized, and too varied to be kept in a state of hopeless oppression. On this count alone, Odessa was unique. As Simon Markish tells us in his essay on Babel, the city resembled Jewish communities in turn-of-the-century America more than it did those in Russia. The effect of the government policy regarding Jews was further limited by the heterogeneity of the city population, the rest of which constituted a mélange of ethnic Russians, Ukrainians, Poles, Greeks, and, in addition, small but culturally important enclaves of French, German, and English merchants. The pungent, freewheeling atmosphere of a major port city and industrial center, the remarkable ethnic mix, and a considerable, heavily Jewish bourgeoisie supporting a network of secondary schools, newspapers and journals, several theaters, an opera company, and a university provided an Odessa Jew in search of a worldly fortune with an opportunity to breach the isolation of third-class citizenship and the ghetto milieu. Surmounting the legal and social obstacles would have been much harder in a smaller, less cosmopolitan place and would have involved more painful compromises with the official policies in St. Petersburg or Moscow, the two capitals kept largely free of Jews.

Equally important, in a country that was growing weary of the old regime—symbolized by the aristocratic, decorous, northern St. Petersburg—the thoroughly middle-class, southern Odessa could be seen as one of the sources of the country's social and cultural rebirth. True, a Petersburg snob was likely to turn his nose up at this "very awful city," but the growing contribution to Russian culture by the provincial artists and writers gave substance to Babel's prediction in "Moi listki: Odessa" ("My Notes: Odessa," 1917) that the spirit of Odessa, bright, merry, and bourgeois, would soon be challenging the dominant Petersburg sensibility, its Dostoevskian moodiness, classical splendor, and imperial chill:

A man from Odessa is the opposite of a Petrogradian. It is becoming an axiom that Odessans do well in Petrograd. They make money. Because they are brunets, plump blondes fall in love with them. . . . This, one might say, begins to sound too much like a joke. No, sir. Something more profound is involved here. The point is simply that these brunets are bringing with them a little sun and a little levity.

Apart from the gentlemen who bring with them a little sun and a lot of canned sardines with interesting labels, I think there must arrive—and soon—the fertile, invigorating influence of the Russian South, the Russian Odessa, perhaps *(qui sais?)*, the only city in Russia where our national and so badly needed Maupassant can emerge.

("Moi listki: Odessa," *Zabytyi Babel'*, pp. 48ff.)

Babel's optimism was, in part, borne out by the history of Russian literature and society in the 1920's. As soon as the imperial center ceased to hold, the provincial intelligentsia quickly stepped in to fill the vacancy, with the "men of Odessa" marching stylishly in the forefront. Some of the better-known writers and poets of the postrevolutionary decade, indeed, the "classics" of Soviet literature, including Valentin Kataev, Konstantin Paustovsky, Illia Ilf, Eduard Bagritsky, and, of course, Babel himself, came from Odessa. What was happening in literature paralleled the postrevolutionary reshuffling of the empire's social and demographic deck. Together with the limited free enterprise permitted under the New Economic Policy, these changes may well have imparted to Petrograd or Moscow some of the Levantine commercial atmosphere of Odessa during its most thriving period, inaugurated by the 1905 revolution and brought to a close by World War I.

This was the Odessa Babel knew and liked best, and credit for the city's reputation as the Russian Marseille, which is how some imagined it in its halcyon days, must go to *Odessa Tales.* Conceived in the austere world of 1920 and 1921, these tales paint a picture of the city as Babel remembered or wished to remember it during his school years, 1905 to 1911. But books have their own fate, and in the imagination of Babel's readers, this cycle of four stories has forever transformed Odessa, or, more precisely, its Jewish ghetto, with its underworld, into a romantic *pays de Cocagne,* historically the first Jewish or, for that matter, Russian Jew-

ish or, simply, Russian version of such a place.

Few facts are available on which to base a reconstruction of Babel's childhood or family. His own autobiographical writings have often proved to be misleading sources, as least when compared to the recollections of his sister, to those of two Odessa poets who had some contact with his family, and to his own, only partially published, correspondence. A writer, above all a writer with a cultivated public persona, he was more concerned with following the spirit of the truth than its letter. He admitted as much in a 1931 note to his mother that accompanied his autobiographical fiction: "All the stories are from the childhood years, with lies added, of course, and much that is altered." More important, by modifying the facts of his childhood, Babel was not simply exercising the prerogative of a writer of fiction; he was, it seems, carrying out a deliberate strategy—one with significant consequences for an author with a high public profile. "When the book is finished, then it will become clear why I needed all that," he ended the explanation, suggesting, cryptically, that the four stories were only a part of a larger cycle. Indeed, a 1937 story, "Di Grasso," would have fitted neatly with the earlier four, whereas most of the stories that appeared in the 1930's fill the "autobiographical" gap between childhood years and *Red Cavalry.*

Given Babel's talent for cyclization, it would appear that he had in mind a larger autobiographical frame designed to incorporate his known and future work, enclosing the entire life span of the boy who grew up to be the author-narrator of *Red Cavalry* and, finally, a major Soviet writer. The great success enjoyed by the autobiographical fiction of Gorky and its elevation to the status of a national epic in the 1930's lend support to this conjecture. Furthermore, in the early 1930's, when Babel's output was diminishing, such a master frame would have helped to allay the pressure to produce, permitting him to present his past achievement, perhaps even the writings he had previously suppressed, in a fresh, more contemporary light. Far from being opportunistic, this strategy would make use of the essential attributes of Babel's art, its apparent autobiographical character. The other, no less significant properties of his writings, especially *Red Cavalry*—their modernistic fragmentariness and the delirious mixture of pathos and baseness for which the broad reading public and the cultural bureaucracy were losing tolerance—these "outmoded" properties would have lost their prominence, after they were integrated into a more coherent, epic narrative frame.

How early did Babel decide to pursue this strategy? The pressure to follow the ragged and fragmented vision of the post–civil war literature with the Apollonian gaze of an epic masterpiece was already noticeable in the middle 1920's. An epic, it was felt, was needed to certify the revolution as a fait accompli, to transform it from the event of an overwhelming immediate experience into a holiday that all would happily celebrate. Treated in this way, the revolution would be wrapped in the magical aura of Origin, conferring legitimacy on the status quo and constituting the present as a natural order. Some writers, among them Yevgeny Zamyatin, actively resisted this sort of program, but many, if not most, went along with it out of either conviction, opportunism, or sheer exhaustion with the revolutionary flux. This need for a revolutionary epic intensified as the 1920's progressed and became a key issue in the broader political project of nation- and citizenship-building under the new Stalinist order. Babel, whose friendship was appreciated among the discerning members of the Soviet elite, was sensitive to the literary as well as political trends and eager to stay in the forefront of the emerging Soviet Russian literature. This ambition can be seen clearly in many statements both public and private in which he expressed his desire for a new style and a different genre.

"Istoriya moey golubyatni" ("The Story of My Dovecote"), which bore a meaningful dedication to Gorky and gave its name to the entire childhood cycle, was published in 1925. It was also during this time that Babel was trying to make up his mind on the future of *Red Cavalry*—whether to freeze the cycle in its present form or to expand it until the number of pieces approached fifty (his original plan). That he published it as a separate edition in 1926 shows the project to have been essentially completed. Babel was ready or, better, was compelled to go on to other things if he wished to remain among the key players in Soviet Russian literature. The anxiety of falling behind, indicative of Babel's own ambition, was typical among the Russian literati of the time. The 1920's and early 1930's were a period when neither the reading public nor the cultural establishment, neither the printing nor the distribution of literature, had yet to be stabilized or, rather, Stalinized—that is to say, reach the stage when publishing became strictly regimented and the reading public atomized. True, the inclusion of "Argamak" (1924–1930) in the 1933 and subsequent editions of *Red Cavalry* and the publication in 1937 of "Potselui" ("The Kiss"), a story clearly associated with it, changed the élan of the book, but these were two master strokes meant to ease the incorporation of *Red Cavalry* into the larger autobiographical framework.

The romantic tradition of playing art and life against one another has had a particularly welcome reception in Russia. With the tremendous growth in educated readership and literary commerce by the 1900's, it virtually set the tone for the literary world for the rest of the twentieth century. Indeed, such authors as Alexander Blok, Vladimir Mayakovsky, Mandelshtam, Gorky, Pasternak, Marina Tsvetaeva, not to mention Tolstoy and Dostoevsky, are remembered as much for their gesture as for their art. The phenomenon of literary celebrity did not become an object of systematic study until shortly after the death of Blok in 1921, when the formalist critics attempted to come to terms intellectually with the passing of the foremost figure among the Russian modernists. Using Blok's career as a paradigmatic case, they persuasively demonstrated the tendency of an author's life, whether fictional or real, toward a powerful symbolic transformation in the eyes of his readership. Some of the best writings of Yurii Tynianov (on Blok and Khlebnikov), Boris Eikhenbaum (on Blok and Tolstoy), and Roman Jakobson (on Mayakovsky), and Boris Tomashevskii's work on the typology of authorship, were devoted to charting this aspect of Russian literary culture. According to the formalists a single contingent fact in an author's biography could acquire in the eye of the devoted public the fateful necessity of an event in a fictional narrative and at the same time retain the undeniable materiality of a lived experience. The life of an author therefore had the potential of being at once symbolic and real: a biographical detail could function as a "literary fact" (Tynianov's paradoxical coinage); the biography as a whole could become transformed into what we now call myth and its protagonist-author into an object of veneration among the reading and sometimes even nonreading public.

Needless to say, this complex phenomenon had its own history. Literary expression began to play a pivotal role in the formation of the self-image of the Russian intelligentsia in the middle decades of the nineteenth century, when the educated classes grew progressively alienated from the institutions of the autocratic state. Combined with the primacy of the artist in the ideology of European modernism and its corollary, the crisis of faith, this aspect of Russia's cultural history helps explain the facility with which the figure of a Russian writer could acquire the charismatic aura of a secular saint. Indeed, it was (and to a lesser extent still is) a matter of general belief that a writer had his or her hand on the pulse of the nation, which the reader could feel only by keeping his or her hand on the writer's pulse.

Babel was very much part of this tradition, indeed, one of its more masterful vehicles in this century. As a member of the Russian intelligentsia, he was its product; as a writer, he paid tribute to it all his life. This is why in order to bring his fictional construct into a sharper relief and to gain a better understanding of his literary project as a whole, it is important, where possible, to juxtapose the author's own narrative account with historical testimony, including memoirs, documents, and correspondence. Almost everything written on Babel has been done with the awareness of these two interdependent paths, however often writers may have conflated them, as did Lionel Trilling in his influential 1956 essay, or kept them too far apart, treading softly on one and marching merrily along the other.

Soon after Babel's birth, most likely for business reasons, the family moved to Nikolaev, a small port town about a hundred miles northwest of Odessa, where in the course of ten years his father had established himself as a representative of an overseas manufacturer of agricultural equipment. When in Nikolaev, the boy had a dovecote to keep, a yard to play in, and a garden to pick fruit from, and he witnessed a pogrom that happily did not directly affect the Babel household or diminish its fortune. It was also in Nikolaev that at the age of nine or ten he began to attend the Count Witte Commercial School, an institution that did not discriminate on the basis of religion. We do not know whether Babel ever tried to enroll in the less liberal but far more prestigious gymnasium, but his fictional alter ego in "The Story of My Dovecote" does, and more. That boy nearly loses his mind from the pressure of preparing for the entrance examination, which he, a Jew, has to pass with distinction; and having passed and having been admitted, he finds himself in the middle of a pogrom and nearly loses his life.

In 1905 Babel's family was affluent enough to return to Odessa, where all of the son's childhood distractions, save for the school and, perhaps, an occasional pogrom, were replaced by tutors—in French, English, German, in the "hated" violin, and, until the age of sixteen, in Hebrew, the Bible, and the Talmud. The mix of the subjects is significant, for some have tended to imagine the young Babel as a rather stereotypical Jewish youth immersed in the traditional scriptural studies until the age of fifteen, when he discovered secular learning, sex, and Maupassant. As with many images of Babel, this one can be traced to the author's own self-presentation, which in 1926, when the "Avtobiografiia" ("Autobiography") was published, may have been perceived as a fresh conceptualization of the experience of an assimilated Jew. In fact, it may stand at the origins of what by now has become a cliché:

> I was born in 1894 in Odessa, in the Moldavanka, the son of a tradesman Jew. On father's insistence, I studied Hebrew, the Bible, the Talmud till the age of sixteen. Life at home was hard, because I was forced to study a multitude of subjects. Resting I did at school.

Thus begins Babel's "Autobiography." The items are carefully selected to produce the highest contrast with the author's present position as a famous Russian writer. The oppressive "ghetto" Jewishness is emphasized through detailed enumeration whereas the cosmopolitan nature of Babel's home education is represented as an indiscriminate agglomeration of anonymous disciplines. But emancipation was not long in coming. By the end of this opening paragraph, the typical product of the traditional ghetto milieu was fluent enough in French to produce what would appear as competent French fiction: "At the age of fifteen, I began writing stories in French. I wrote them for two years and then stopped: my *paysans* and all sorts of authorial meditations came out colorless; only the dialogue was a success."

The educational fervor, befitting a middle-class family on its way up, was matched by the residence on the second or third floor of an imposing building that stood at the intersection of Post and Richelieu, two of the city's more fashionable avenues. The new address contrasted sharply with their former home in the Moldavanka, the humble Jewish neighborhood where the author was born. Two decades

later, he would headquarter his fictional family there after its move from Nikolaev to Odessa ("V podvale" ["In the Basement," 1931], and "Pervaia liubov'" ["First Love," 1925]). Of course, in fiction, what this "populous and suffering Jewish ghetto" ("Odessa," 1917) lacked in life's comforts—and the script *Benia Krik* paints a horrific picture of Jewish poverty—it made up in the local color that Babel had been applying unsparingly beginning with the first story of the Odessa cycle, "The King," in 1921.

Even a cursory comparison of the biographical details with the autobiographical fiction published between 1925 and 1932 reveals a certain tactic: the author's bourgeois background was an acceptable part of the constructed biography only if it was *bourgeois manqué*. A number of Babel scholars have suggested that the author tried to "proletarianize" his fictional background in order to curry favor with the class-conscious Bolshevik regime. In the 1920's, however, this sort of humbling could yield no more than small change, especially coming from a "fellow traveler" and not a "proletarian" writer. It did, however, make perfect narrative sense: it echoed the tried-and-true "bourgeois" novelistic convention according to which heroes were to be cultivated not in a well-endowed hothouse, but in the open—and preferably on top of a social compost heap. Babel must receive credit for producing a stunningly effective Jewish version of this plot motif, which, after the Soviet climate had turned inhospitable, migrated to New York and Hollywood, where it continued to enjoy a thriving career.

In keeping with this principle, Babel's fictional parents have been completely ruined in a pogrom. In addition to this misfortune, their son has become severely ill, forcing them to move to Odessa in search of a qualified medical cure. Their only child, he has developed a nervous condition in reaction, it seems, to a triple shock caused by the violence, the scene of his father's self-abasement before a cossack officer, and the unexpected proximity of the luscious bosom and hips incautiously paraded by the family's Russian neighbor, Galina. She is the first woman to steal the boy's heart and is kind enough to offer temporary refuge to the Babel family ("First Love"). From the reader's perspective, the story provides a "realistic" (in psychoanalytic terms) motivation for the sensibility Kirill Vasilievich Liutov (meaning literally "the vicious one") displays in *Red Cavalry*. But in the sense of Babel's emerging bildungsroman, it was not the child who, as the saying goes, was father to the man. Rather, it was the man who was fathering his own childhood.

According to family lore, Babel's grandmother played an important role in his upbringing. Babel's sister remembers her as quarrelsome. She was excessively strict with her granddaughter and equally indulgent with her grandson. Babel left a portrait of her in a 1915 unfinished story entitled "U babushki" ("At Grandmother's"), which was to be part of a cycle, *Detstvo* (Childhood). He spent Saturdays at her frightfully overheated home, doing his homework and receiving tutors while she sat and watched. At regular intervals she would interrupt her vigil in order to indulge them both in largely recreational eating. If the story is to be trusted, this formidable woman was rather informal about observing the Sabbath, but worshiped ardently and with complete devotion her grandson's secular education. Illiterate herself, she was in a sense a child of the Enlightenment and believed fervently in knowledge as the sole means of conquering the world. And that, in its turn, was the only end she thought worth pursuing: " 'Study,' she says suddenly with great force; 'you will achieve everything—wealth, fame. You must know everything. Do not trust people. Do not have friends. Do not give them your money. Do not give them your heart.' "

Some of the elements making up Babel's poetics are already present here: hyperbole, in the mountains of food; contrast, in the difference between the grandmother's own illiteracy and the studiousness of her charge; and even sadomasochistic sensuality, in the overwhelming

excitement the boy feels as he reads and re-reads the famous "whipping scene" in Ivan Turgenev's "First Love" (1859). As in the later stories, a key metaphor here becomes thematized—unfolded to produce its own minor narrative, a mini-myth. Consider the story's physical ambience: the atmosphere of the grandmother's room was literally stifling and that of the household in which the boy grew up was figuratively so. By now a cliché, this figure of speech can still provide fictional motivation for young men in a hurry to take flight from their nests—Jewish young men, and also Southern young men, in North American fiction, and Irish ones in English fiction. However, the air at the grandmother's was not only stifling, it was also intolerably hot. This atmospheric item, placed in a suggestive context, begins to translate into desire, a tightly wound spring of desire typical for a narrative of sexual frustration. Babel would have it uncoil spectacularly in the numerous episodes of sexual violence and abandon in *Red Cavalry, Odessa Tales,* and "First Love"—episodes that powerfully stir the narrator destined only to observe and never (or almost never) to participate. "At Grandmother's" displays parts of this narrative machinery operating still at a relatively low idle:

> I was then reading Turgenev's "First Love." I liked everything about it: clear words, descriptions, the dialogue, but it was that scene when Vladimir's father hits Zinaida on the cheek with his whip that would cause in me an extraordinary turmoil. I would hear the swishing of the whip; its pliant, leather body, sharply, painfully, would light into me. I would be gripped by an ineffable anxiety. At that point I would have to abandon the reading and pace the room. But Grandma sat motionless, and even the air, hot and stupefying, was motionless as though it knew that I was studying and was not to be disturbed.
> (*Literaturnoe nasledstvo,* vol. 74 [1965], p. 486)

However much it anticipates the later Babel, "At Grandmother's" would not have fit the master autobiography without major revisions, for it offered no visible escape route nor any palpable future. The material of the story lacked variety, and its virtual uniformity tended to dominate the story unchallenged, depriving the episodes of relative scale. Under such conditions, hyperbole and contrast were prevented from growing into a Babelian grotesque, and the slightly bizarre sensuality was kept from evolving into something more orgiastic. Even the proverbial detachment of Babel's narrator, so unsettling in his later work and already detectable here, might appear quite natural, given the soporific monotony of the milieu. What seems to be entirely absent but what would distinguish the later stories beginning with "The King" is excess—whether in emotional intensity or affectless detachment—excess born of an unclouded Nietzschean admiration for the beauty and power of life that exists, if not beyond, then to the side of the "accursed" worries about good and evil.

"The Story of My Dovecote" provides an instructive contrast. There a Jewish boy who has finally earned his acceptance by the state and become a student at an elite school runs into a pogrom. The rewards for his efforts, four long-coveted pigeons, are taken away from him and are literally smashed against his head, but this is done by a man whose hands are touched by leprosy, a man who has no legs. These details of the grotesque, one might say excessive, deficiency (absence of legs) and overabundant presence (can there be just the right amount of leprosy?), provide an aesthetic escape hatch, which at first is too narrow to notice but soon becomes as wide as the doors of the church:

> I was lying on the ground and the entrails of a smashed bird were dripping down my temple. They were flowing down my cheeks, in small rivulets, dripping and blinding me. The tender intestine of a pigeon was crawling across my forehead and I was closing the other, still unstuck eye in order not to see the world lying about me. This world was small and horrifying.
>
> (*Izbrannoe* [Moscow, 1966], p. 217)

Still, the boy gets up. Walking home, he finds his attention drawn to the sight of a young peasant lad smashing the window frames of the house belonging to a certain Kharitos Efrussi. Mentioned only in passing, the address is significant because it transforms the pogrom into an all-too-visible hand of poetic justice. This hand not only punishes Jewish boys who play successfully by the rules of the hated empire, but also takes revenge on the Jewish merchant Efrussi, who does not, and who used bribes the previous year to place his son in the gymnasium at the expense of the more deserving protagonist. Once the economy of vengeance has been established, the reader can begin to enjoy vicariously—through the eyes of the narrator—the sight of the unrestrained natural beauty and pure strength displayed unabashedly by the pogromist:

> He was bashing at the frame with a wooden mallet, swinging with his whole body and, when he sighed, he smiled all around with an amiable smile of intoxication, sweat and spiritual strength. The entire street was filled with the cracking, snapping, and singing of the breaking wood. The fellow kept on bashing just to bend his body, just to break into sweat, and to shout the words of an unknown, non-Russian language. He was shouting them and singing, and tearing from the inside of his blue eyes.
>
> (p. 218)

A dozen or so years later, this Slavic version of Nietzsche's *blonde Bestie* would be riding with (or against, it does not matter) Budennyi's cavalry, followed by the narrator's admiring gaze.

Like his formidable mother, Man' (or more urbanely, Emmanuel) Babel placed great value on education and the worldly accomplishments it was bound to facilitate. He enforced his convictions with the vigor and excess of a self-made man, creating for his male offspring a studious and extremely tense household. "Resting I did at school," was how Babel qualified his home academic program. Babel's father—moody, sarcastic, and given to memorable fits of anger—was not averse to literary composition and penned satires in Hebrew or Yiddish aimed at the failings of his relatives and friends. In his son's fiction, with its uncon-cealed oedipal economy, he played the role of a weak man who cared more about property than dignity, as in the following from "First Love":

> Ahead of them, at the corner of Fish Street, the pogromists were smashing our shop, throwing out boxes with nails, tools, and my new portrait in the gymnasium uniform.
>
> "Look," said my father, and did not get up from his knees, "they are taking my sweat and blood, Captain, why . . ."
>
> The officer mumbled something, saluted with his lemon glove and touched the bridle, but the horse did not move. Father was crawling around it on his knees, rubbing himself against its short, kindly, slightly shaggy legs.
>
> "Yes, sir," said the Captain, pulled at the bridle, and was off; the Cossacks followed. . . .
>
> "Lousy kopecks," mother said as father and I were entering the room, "your life, and children, and our unhappy happiness—you have given up everything for them. . . . Lousy kopecks.
>
> (p. 223)

Because such a character was unworthy of being cast as a closet writer (an anticipation of the author's own vocation), Babel pressed the cherished gift into the hands of an exorbitantly colorful maternal grandfather, Levi-Yitzkhok— a ragtag type stitched together from patches of a bohemian fantasy, Dickensian and Rabe-laisian characters, and, perhaps, a boyhood wish ("In the Basement"). A different picture emerges from Babel's letters, in which he could treat his father's memory with conciliation and generosity, even if tinged ever so slightly with the feelings that posthumous effusiveness and forgiveness had not completely effaced:

> When I go through moments of despair, I think of Papa. What he expected and wanted from us was success, not complaining. . . . Remembering him I feel a surge of strength, and I urge myself forward. Everything I promised him, *not in words but in thought,* I shall carry out because I have a sacred respect for his memory [emphasis added].
>
> (*Lonely Years,* p. 87)

As far as his public persona was concerned, Babel's father was a well-respected business-man who radiated so much dignity and hon-esty that his neighbors felt honored to be shar-ing a building with him.

We know considerably less about Babel's mother, except that she was given to worry, a trait to which her son's correspondence pro-vides repeated testimony. "I think that you and Mama are suffering from an anxiety mania that is becoming pathological," reads one of Babel's letters to his sister, in an oft-repeated episto-lary expression of filial exasperation. In an-other, Babel castigates his mother for a "weak-ness of character," an especially vexing trait that he believed he had inherited from her. The glimpse afforded by her daughter's reminis-cences is less conflicted, if bland: "Mother was kind, had a gentle character, often had to humor father when he was upset; he was quick to anger. Mother ran the household and brought up the children. She taught my brother to read." In his fiction, Babel sketched her as a woman capable of grand emotions, disillu-sioned in marriage ("our unhappy happiness"), nobly ashamed of her husband's acquisitive-ness, and eager to make up for these misfor-tunes by loving her son much too much ("First Love").

As for Babel's sister, she was denied the role of a protagonist in the family's ambitious script. In her brother's stories she appears not at all except in the plural of the reference in "First Love" to the children that the fictional father had ignored in his capitalist pursuits. It is tempting to think that in acknowledgment of her conspicuous absence, Babel paid her an ironic tribute in naming after her the lead char-acter, who, in turn, gave her name to the play *Mariia*. Like his sister in his fiction, Mariia never steps out onto the stage but, remaining invisible, exerts a crucial influence on all the other dramatis personae.

However complicated Babel's relationship with his parents and sister, the bonds estab-lished in his youth remained powerful throughout his life. They were strong enough for him to accept financial responsibility for his mother and sister after they emigrated to Belgium in 1925 (a little over a year after his father's death); and, more remarkable, he corresponded with them regularly throughout the worst years of terror in the 1930's, insisting, from all indications sincerely, that they join him in the Soviet Union. His last letter to them was postmarked 10 May 1939, antedating his arrest by only five days. Perhaps the clearest echo of Babel's attachment to his mother and sister, so evident in his correspondence, can be found in the unfinished *Evreika,* in which his nostalgia for his family and his desire to reunite and share a household with them found fictional fulfillment.

A man of broad and varied education, Babel had bypassed the gymnasium and the university, the two elite, although not exclusive, educational institutions of the Russian empire. In 1906 his parents enrolled him in the second grade of the Nicholas I Odessa Commercial School No. 1. According to their charter, schools of this type prepared young men for careers in business or industry, or if they wished to continue their studies, for admission to specialized colleges and polytechnics. By contrast with the gymnasium's classical curriculum, commercial schools emphasized "practical knowledge," such as sciences and modern languages. The shibboleth of the higher stratum in the empire's educational system, the study of ancient tongues, was excluded from the curriculum of the commercial schools, an exclusion that made it more difficult for their graduates to go on to a university.

Notwithstanding the obvious liability, some schools of this type, among them the famous Tenishev, had a good academic reputation and were popular. They were also less regimented (Jews, for example, were freely admitted), and they tended to have a more varied student body whose members, as in the case of Babel's class,

were distinguished by the impurity of their pedigree, "the sons of foreign merchants, Jewish brokers, titled Polish nobility, Old Believers, and a lot of superannuated billiard players." (The order of Babel's listing may give some idea of the social hierarchy at the empire's outer fringe.) Many "progressive" families, including the aristocratic Nabokovs, the academic Struves, and the well-off Mandelshtams, found this sort of schooling preferable to the "conservative" gymnasium education.

Whether Babel's parents enrolled their son in a commercial school as a matter of choice or for reasons of necessity cannot be determined with certainty. What we know, however, is that Babel completed the course of study two years ahead of his contemporaries, earning the highest grades in such subjects as Russian literature, Russian grammar, German, French, English, commercial geography, law, history, and political economy. It may be tempting to see some residue of bitterness in Babel about being sent to the commercial school in "The Story of My Dovecote," in which the boy protagonist succeeds, under his father's relentless pressure, in being admitted to a gymnasium. But Babel had sufficient narrative reasons for giving his plot a different spin: the admission in the story's first movement serves as a perfect counterpoint for the denouement of the second movement, the pogrom.

Three of Babel's lifelong attachments can be traced to his years at the commercial school: the first to Russian literature; the second to France (encouraged by his French teacher, Mr. Vadon); and the third to Odessa. None of these should be taken for granted. The fact that an ambitious young man, a Jew, chose a career in Russian letters indicates that opportunities in this area existed even for a Jew and that pursuit of a writer's career was deemed significant enough to satisfy what surely must have been an intense desire for fame and attainment. Russian literature, the literature of Dostoevsky and Tolstoy, Anton Chekhov and Nikolai Chernyshevsky, Gorky and Blok, served the intelligentsia as a symbol of everything worthy and magnificent in the country's culture, and for an educated Russian Jew it was surely one of the ultimate elective affinities. Nor was there anything self-evident in Babel's identification with Odessa. He lived there continuously for only six out of his forty-five years (while studying at the commercial school) and returned to it only briefly in the years after the revolution. Indeed, few writers raised in the provinces grow up to identify with the city of their birth.

Equally significant, among the three languages he learned well at the commercial school, only French happened to become a point of identification for Babel. Even if he made the selection under the influence of an exceptionally gifted teacher, the choice cannot be regarded as accidental, as it fell on the supremely cosmopolitan language, one associated with a nobility of manner and spirit, literary high culture, and diplomatic intercourse. It was a significant move in Babel's strategy of self-presentation to point out that he began to write Russian fiction only after he had tried his hand at producing stories in French under the tutelage of his French teacher. Mr. Vadon was not merely French, he was a native of Brittany, a provincial man, like Babel himself. Babel displayed this attribute prominently during the years when he was lionized in Petrograd and Moscow. It was also around that time that Vladimir Shklovskii, who pronounced Babel the best contemporary author, praised him for "having seen Russia the way a French writer accompanying Napoleon's army could." Emphatic, cultivated identification with what was outside Russia proper served to give Babel the reputation of being a writer who could penetrate to the very heart of things.

Yet neither Odessa nor France would have played a role in Babel's legacy if he had not developed a style in which the two became mutually reinforcing. The southern port city of Odessa made more palpable the riper aspects of French cultural heritage, while *les lettres françaises* enabled Babel to transform the prosaic "dusty Odessa," as Alexandr Pushkin

once referred to it, into a mythic metropolis that he would later on serve up to his readers, exhausted by the years of war and revolution and starved for color and abundance, in a pungent Rabelaisian sauce. In fact, it would not be an exaggeration to say that Odessa became a meaningful entity on the literary map only after Babel had put it there, and Babel thought about putting it there only after he had been able to see in it a city that bore some resemblance to Nikolai Gogol's frivolous Ukraine, but situated to the west of it, halfway between the Mediterranean of romantic fiction (Shklovskii pointed to Gustave Flaubert's *Salammbô* [1863]) and the *Cocagne* of the French popular tradition and François Rabelais. Indeed, no native son of Odessa in Babel's generation has produced a picture of the city that owes a greater debt to the Gallic carnivalesque.

Even more important, although Babel had in his possession all the necessary ingredients as early as 1917 (see "My Notes: Odessa"), the particular style emerged only after the civil war, when he returned to his native city after a stint as a war correspondent in Budennyi's cavalry army. The experience of the revolution combined with the ability to see beauty in the exercise of power unrestrained by the notions of good and evil—this is what enabled Babel to produce a feast for the mind's eye rather than a series of rough and wordy collage portraits of desolate and ravaged Russia à la Boris Pilniak or Vsevolod Ivanov. Both *Red Cavalry* and *Odessa Tales* embodied the simple twentieth-century discovery—it had been prophesied before, most notably by Nietzsche—that power could be justified by form, not by the measure of evil or goodness, but by the criteria that discriminated against the sick, the weak, and the ugly. What made Babel's version of the superman particularly moving and ethically acceptable to people who identified with the oppressed was his success at endowing lowly characters with all the attributes of life's supreme masters. Hitherto they had been depicted as the humiliated and the wronged, whose credo, in Nietzsche's terms, never went beyond the hissing *ressentiment* of the down-trodden. In Babel's work these people acquire a joyful Gargantuan stature. A Jew can "pick a fight in the streets and stammer on paper, be a tiger, a lion, a cat, spend a night with a Russian woman and leave her satisfied" ("The Way It Used to Be Done in Odessa"). A soldier elevated by the revolution to the rank of division commander can make one wonder at the "beauty of his giant body" (a phrase from "My First Goose"):

> He stood up and, with the crimson of his breeches, the tilted red little cap, the medals nailed into his chest, cleaved the hut in two like a battle flag cleaving the heaven. He exuded the smell of perfume and the cloying coolness of soap. His long legs resembled young women sheathed up to the shoulders in the shining riding boots.
>
> (p. 53)

Like his Jewish counterpart, the gangster boss Benia Krik, this cossack general "stammered on paper." His irresistible vitality is unaware of civilization's restraint, as the narrator discovers while watching him finish writing out an order:

> "With the destruction of which" [the enemy], continued the division commander, and messed up the entire sheet, "I charge the above Chesnokov up to and including the capital penalty, whom I will blow away on the spot, which you, Comrade Chesnokov, having worked with me at the front for more than a month, cannot doubt."
>
> The Division Commander signed the order with a curlicue, tossed it to his orderlies, and turned to me, his gray eyes dancing with merriment.
>
> ("Moi pervyi gus" ["My First Goose," 1924], p. 53)

Already Dostoevsky had acknowledged the supreme seductiveness of the combination of power and beauty (as in the handsome Stavrogin in *The Possessed* [1871–1872]), and the idea animated the writings of Babel's immediate predecessors, foremost among them Gorky, Blok, and Nikolai Gumilev. But Babel was the first one to surround with a deceptively ethical aura the cruel truth that even the most brutal power could be made palatable if it was beautifully attired.

After graduating from the commercial school in 1911 and finding himself unable to enter the University of Odessa because of the quota for Jews, Babel was sent to Kiev to enroll in economics at the Kiev Commercial Institute. It was in Kiev that he met his future wife, Evgeniia Gronfein. She came from a much richer and far more cultivated family than his own, and Babel appreciated the intellectual and artistic atmosphere that existed in her household, and especially the ease that came with the family's inherited wealth and well-established social status. Her father, an importer of agricultural equipment, had done business with Babel's father and was happy to receive his partner's son in his house, although not happy enough to favor his daughter's interest in the aspiring economist. From both the testimony of Nathalie Babel, the writer's daughter, and his own correspondence, we know that the future in-laws saw in Babel a provincial upstart, an opinion that Mrs. Gronfein was to change only when he became a famous and well-connected Soviet writer.

An echo, and only an echo, of Babel's experience at the Gronfeins may be heard in "Guy de Maupassant" (1932), a story about an aspiring writer who is hired by the wife of a Jewish banker to help her translate the complete Maupassant. Like the Gronfeins, Raisa Bendersky, the banker's wife, is a native of Kiev; she also happens to bear the first name of Babel's sister-in-law. Mrs. Bendersky possesses the "ravishing body" of a Kievan Jewess, literary pretensions supported by a genuine artistic sensitivity, and a bottle of 1883 Muscadet, her husband's favorite and most intoxicating vintage. Predictably, the writer, by contrast with Mr. Bendersky, is poor as a church mouse but has imagination, energy, talent, and style. While working on "L'Aveu" he finds himself reenacting clumsily, together with the banker's wife and in the banker's absence, the novella's artlessly seductive plot. Another glimpse of Babel's Kievan period (1911–1915) is afforded by his daughter's biographical sketch (*The Lonely Years*), which outlines a complementary picture. Aware of his weakness for the bourgeois opulence and self-indulgence displayed in the Gronfein household, Babel responded by cultivating a heroic stance of life-affirming asceticism. Nathalie Babel writes:

> My mother refused to wear the furs and pretty dresses her parents gave her. My father, to harden himself, would walk bareheaded in the dead of winter without an overcoat, dressed only in jacket. These Spartan efforts ended abruptly one day when my parents were walking, in their usual costume, and a woman stopped, and, apparently mesmerized by what she saw, pointed at my father and shouted, "A madman!" Thirty years later my mother was still mortified when she remembered this incident. Nor had she forgotten her astonishment when her fiancé took her out to tea for the first time and she watched him gobble down cake after cake with dizzying speed. At the Gronfeins, he refused everything but tea. The explanation was simple. "When I start eating cake, I can't stop," he said. "So it's better for me not to start at all."
>
> (p. xvii)

It was also while in Kiev that Babel made his debut in print. "Staryi Shloime" ("Old Shloime," 1913) tells the story of one Jewish family's response to forced resettlement: the younger generation decides to convert rather than be uprooted, but the old man, who discerns the truth through the fog of senility, hangs himself. Written in a sentimental key and in the third person (both uncharacteristic for the later Babel), the three-page story belongs wholly to the genre of bleak "socially aware" Russian prose, including its Jewish variety, in which government oppression and calls for liberation follow one another with the same unimaginative inevitability as night follows day. Nothing about "Old Shloime," not even its violent outcome, is unexpected, and the protest implied by the story is so grimly conventional that instead of challenging the

status quo, which was apparently the intention, it tends to do the opposite, implicitly affirming the present as part of the order of things. However, what is significant about "Old Shloime," as well as the far more sophisticated "At Grandmother's," is a lack of hesitation on Babel's part to engage openly the Jewish theme. One would look in vain in the pre-1917 Mandelshtam or Pasternak, roughly Babel's contemporaries, for overt signs of such identification.

In October 1915, the Kiev Commercial Institute was evacuated to Saratov, a town in the provincial heartland of Russia, where Babel remained until graduation in May 1916. Only two years had passed after the publication of "Old Shloime," but "At Grandmother's," completed in Saratov, displayed a different literary sensibility. The protagonist himself narrates the story, and his voice, still hesitant but growing hollow with distance, presents the most intimate milieu, that of his childhood, as a strange world, driven by forces unacknowledged and unmatched by conventional narrative patterns:

> It was quiet, spectrally quiet; not a sound could be heard. At that moment, everything seemed extraordinary, and I wished to flee from it all, and I wanted to stay here forever. The darkening room, Grandma's yellow eyes, her slight frame wrapped in a shawl, hunched over and keeping silent in the corner, the heated air, the closed door, and the stroke of the whip, and that piercing swishing sound—only now I understand how strange it all was and how full of meaning.
>
> (*Literaturnoe nasledstvo*, vol. 74 [1965], p. 487)

At the end of 1915, Babel completed his course work at the commercial institute, but before taking the final examinations, he transferred his credits to the law faculty of the Petrograd Psychoneurological Institute. This was a private establishment with the rank of a university that, among other things, qualified its Jewish students for temporary residence in the capital. Living in Petrograd illegally for months at a time, Babel was finally enrolled as a fourth-year student on 10 October 1916, and received his residence permit a few days later. The permit was to expire on 15 February 1917, timed perfectly, as fate would have it, to coincide with the expiration of the issuing body. Although the "Autobiography" creates the impression that he abandoned all plans for a respectable business or professional career as soon as he moved to Petrograd, the record shows otherwise. A certain amount of hesitation is evident in his decision to proceed with qualifying examinations at the commercial institute in the spring of 1916. He did well, receiving "excellent" in political economy, general accounting, and urban and rural economics with statistical analysis, "good" in commercial law, and "satisfactory" in economic geography. On the basis of this performance, he was informed more than a year later, he had been awarded the degree of candidate of economic sciences of the second rank. Such academic diligence, especially in a nonphilological field, was considered unbecoming by the author, whose loyalty could not be divided between material matters and the essential world of art. From the reader's view the clutter of factual detail might have obscured the bohemian and heroic persona that Babel was cultivating during the publication of *Red Cavalry.*

Whether or not he took seriously his law studies at the Psychoneurological Institute, Babel pursued his literary interests with concentration. In a matter of months after his arrival in Petrograd, a short period for a beginner—even a talented one—without connections, his persistence paid off. At first, he wrote in his "Autobiography," setting up another situation of high contrast, the Petrograd editors gave him the cold shoulder, suggesting that his future was in the retail trade. Then, in 1916, a sudden success: he was discovered by Gorky, who published two of his stories, "Ilia Isaakovich i Margareta Prokofievna" ("Ilia Isaakovich and Margarita Prokofievna") and "Mama, Rimma, i Alla" ("Mother, Rimma, and Alla"), in the November issue of *Letopis'* (The Chronicle), a prominent left-wing journal edited by the grand man of letters himself.

The stories are masterly, vintage Babel in subject matter as well as style. Similar to his later writing, they invite the reader to an unblinking examination of the detritus of existence, rewarding the reader who is not too fastidious to persevere with the pleasurable jolt of discovering a shining, if slightly oversized, human pearl. Written in the third person, they project a consciousness (based on the self-image of the Russian intelligentsia) that incongruously combines detached perspectivalism with a delicately muted appeal to a sentimental heart. In the first story, a plump prostitute with a penchant for squeezing her pimples in view of her clients gives grudging refuge to a Jewish businessman without a residence permit who eats herring for supper and has a habit of airing his toes before climbing into bed. As the story winds to a close, each, it turns out, possesses a heart of gold and is capable of striking up a fleeting and touchingly disinterested friendship. The ending of the second story surprises the reader with a lightning glimpse of the emotional treasure concealed under the grimly incautious romances of two adolescent girls and the insidious pressures of middle-class poverty crushing their aging mother. Pointing to the other shore, where the view of human misery and ugliness was unclouded by conventional compassion, Babel was ready to make the crossing.

Throughout his career Babel emphasized Gorky's recognition of his talent to the exclusion of all others, treating it virtually as a divine sanction to practice his art and later invoking it as a talisman for protection. The publication of the two novellas, however, did not pass unnoticed, which shows that in the literary world of Petrograd, Babel had more than one friend. "The stories are simple, full of observation and a sense of measure," wrote a critic on the staff of *Zhurnal zhurnalov* (Review of Reviews), "qualities that are not as ordinary as one might think. In effect, to learn literary technique means to acquire a sense of measure and an awareness of scale. Here Babel has a gift." This recognition led to an invitation to contribute a regular column to this journal and a productive association with Gorky's postrevolutionary anti-Leninist newspaper *Novaia zhizn'* (New Life). The first carried Babel's name on its masthead in October–February 1916–1917: "Bab-El' [and later, I. Babel]: Moi listki" ("Bab-El: My Notes"). The second published Babel's "Dnevnik" (*Diary*), a series of sketches about revolutionary Petrograd, from February to November 1918. These writings stand halfway between Babel's fiction and ordinary reportage, and although not as distinguished as Babel's stories, they firmly established him as a professional writer.

Like most of his contemporaries among the intelligentsia, indeed, like the entire country, Babel led a peripatetic existence during the years of revolution and civil war. In the spring of 1917, he joined the Russian army at the Rumanian front, resurfacing in Petrograd early in 1918 as a reporter for Gorky's *Novaia zhizn'*. His "Diary," published regularly until the closing of the newspaper by the Bolsheviks at the end of 1918, followed the general direction of Gorky's critical stance, combining pleas for greater humanity with dispassionate observations of the daily cruelties brought about by the revolution and exacerbated by the ruthlessness of the Bolshevik regime. "To hoist a rifle and shoot one another—on occasion, this may not be so stupid, but this is not the whole revolution," Babel wrote in 1918 on the subject of a new maternity hospital. He concluded in a typical *Novaia zhizn'* fashion with a defense of the noble institution of motherhood: "Who knows, maybe this is not the revolution at all? Children must be born under good conditions. And this—I know for certain—is the real revolution."

This early collaboration with Gorky found only a partial acknowledgment in Babel's official self-portrait. A mention of *Novaia zhizn'* (in 1918, Babel also wrote for *Zhizn' iskusstva* [Life of Art]) is nowhere to be found. What must have felt as an honor for a beginning writer turned out to be, in retrospect, a politically imprudent association. In addition

(and it is difficult to determine which was a more decisive factor), dwelling on a regular literary employment could dull the luster of Babel's cultivated reputation as an extraordinary author who bore the mark of election visible only to the genius of Gorky and who was, as it were, disgorged complete on the literary scene by the revolution itself. He writes in his "Autobiography":

> To this day, I pronounce the name of Alexei Maximovich [Gorky] with piety. He published my first stories in the November issue of *Letopis'*, 1916 . . . , he taught me remarkably important things, and when it turned out that two or three tolerable youthful works of mine were merely an accident, that nothing was coming out of my literary efforts, and that I wrote remarkably badly—Alexei Maximovich told me to go into apprenticeship among the people.
>
> And for seven years—from 1917 to 1924—I have been apprenticing among the people. During this time I served as a soldier at the Rumanian front, in the Cheka, in the People's Commissariat of Enlightenment, in the food requisitioning teams of 1918, in the Northern Army against Iudenich, in the First Cavalry Army, in the Executive Committee of the Odessa Guberniia, in the 7th Soviet Printing House in Odessa, did reporting in Petrograd and Tiflis, etc. And only in 1923 did I learn to express my thoughts clearly and concisely. Then I once again began to compose fiction.
>
> (*Izbrannoe* [Moscow, 1966], p. 23)

There is a certain irony in the fact that this humble "apprenticeship among the people," the phrase serving as title for the second volume of Gorky's autobiographical trilogy, consisted of writing essays and sketches for several newspapers, chief among them Gorky's *Novaia zhizn'*. The chronology of events, too, is intentionally jumbled, with the Petrograd reporting of 1917 and 1918 sandwiched between the items referring to 1920 and 1922. Such stories as "Khodia: Iz knigi *Petersburg 1918*," ("The Chinaman: From the Book *Petersburg 1918*," 1923), an anecdote that possibly planted the seed of Yury Olesha's "Envy," and the hilariously anti-Dostoevskian "Iisusov grekh" ("The Sin of Jesus," 1923), were passed over in silence. Some significant events were omitted, among them Babel's marriage to Evgeniia Gronfein in 1919—an absence that, like his failure to mention the hard-earned degree in economics, served to magnify his commitment to the writer's vocation. Otherwise he would not have been able to write, as he did in "Guy de Maupassant":

> When I was only twenty, I said to myself: I'd rather starve, go to jail, have no home of my own than do accounts ten hours a day. There isn't any special valiancy in this vow, but I have not broken it, nor ever will. The wisdom of my ancestors was sitting in my head: we are born in order to enjoy working, fighting, loving—that's what we are born for, and nothing else.
>
> (p. 271)

Still, however distorted factually, the account conveys the spirit of the truth. A one-time employee of the Cheka and a member of the food requisitioning teams, Isaac Babel must have had a hard time subsisting exclusively on a vegetarian diet. It is tempting to imagine that these experiences as well as his participation in the revolution and the civil war had made him a very different writer. His most astute and least sentimental admirer, Victor Shklovskii, appears to have thought as much:

> Russian literature is as gray as a siskin, it needs raspberry-colored riding breeches and leather shoes the color of heavenly azure.
>
> It also needs that which prompted Babel to leave his Chinamen to their own devices and to join *Red Cavalry*.
>
> Literary protagonists, maidens, old men and young lads and all the situations have been worn thin. What literature needs is concreteness and to be cross-fertilized *with the new style of life* [emphasis added].
>
> ("Isaac Babel: A Critical Romance" [1924], in Bloom, p. 14)

In June 1920, soon after Babel had returned to Odessa, he published four short novellas adapted from a popular collection of war anecdotes by Gaston Vidal, *Figures et anecdotes de la grand guerre* (1918). A short step separates the "ridiculous" fare of Vidal from the true sublime of *Red Cavalry*, reminding one of Anna Akhmatova's poetic apostrophe to the pious reader: "If only you knew from what trash poetry emerges, unaware of shame." In the staccato precision and the brevity of the adaptations, Babel easily eclipsed the wordy braggadoccio of the original, but the narrative play with the grotesqueries of life and death lacked sufficient seriousness and was still redolent of the officers' mess and the cheap thrills of the wartime middle-brow periodicals. In retrospect, however, it is apparent that the four pieces represented a crucial exercise in the verbal orientation toward a new consciousness, the source of Babel's future esteem. This was a mind-set steeled by the brutality and misshapen absurdity of life that, in the experience of contemporaries, had no precedent before 1914 or, for the Russian intelligentsia at large, until the beginning of the civil war in 1918. Exotic, alien to the Russian reader (existential curiosities at the western front), Vidal's material, if he still had any, relieved Babel of the compulsion to balance the senseless cruelty of war with sentimental appeals.

A whole new horizon opened up when he decided to interpose between the author and the events the figure of Gaston Vidal, whose voice was borrowed, as it were, for the main narrative. Drawing such a clear distinction between the narrator and the author further obviated the necessity for an explicit judgment. Perhaps the most important discovery was made in "Dezertir" ("The Deserter"), a story about an officer who has just offered a shell-shocked young soldier a choice between the firing squad, with its eternal shame, and suicide with honor. When the deserter proves unable to shoot himself, the officer, who does "not take offense at small things," obligingly pulls the trigger. In a postscript added to the story, the author-narrator removes the mask of the Frenchman and repeats Vidal's characterization of the officer verbatim, demonstrating that the same statement, no matter how trite, can generate a new and profound meaning when uttered by a different speaker:

> Gaston Vidal writes about this incident in his book. The soldier was actually called Bauji. Whether the name Gémier I have given the Captain is the right one, I cannot really say. Vidal's story is dedicated to a certain Firmin Gémier "in token of deep respect." I think this dedication gives the game away. Of course, the Captain was called Gémier. And then Vidal tells us that the Captain was a patriot, a soldier, a good father, and not a man to take offense at small things. That's something if a man doesn't take offense at small things.
>
> (*You Must Know Something*, p. 85)

This "discovery" of the interdependence of the voice and statement, and, therefore, of the relativity of meaning, helps account for Babel's mastery over the overwhelming material in *Red Cavalry*—for his skill in shifting nimbly from one to another voice. The device of narrating in marked voices, which the Russians term *skaz* if the voice happens to be speaking substandard Russian, was used widely in postrevolutionary prose, a literary and linguistic tribute to the post-1917 social leveling and the saturation of the urban bastions of the intelligentsia culture by members of the semiliterate lower classes and provincial milieu. However, it was contemporary poetry that served Babel as the ultimate model for his narrative technique. Many poets, especially Blok, Mandelshtam, Sergei Esenin, and Mayakovsky, were masters at weaving the voice of the other into the fabric of their verse. What distinguished their use of the voice of the other from *skaz* was the dominant presence of the dramatically complete figure of the poet. Even if merely implied, this chief protagonist whom the reader identified with the author functioned as the central referent in much the same way as a star's gravitational pull defines the course of the orbiting planet.

In *Odessa Tales* and *Red Cavalry*, the function of this Poet (with the capital *P*) would be performed by the man from Odessa, a Jew and a Russian *intelligent* who had "autumn in his heart and spectacles on his nose" but wished to look at life as a green promenade for "women and horses" and was possessed by a still greater desire to retain the intellectual's central position in the country's culture, the position from which the revolution had threatened to displace him. This narrator would be the first to walk into the verbal ambush of the changing world. Camouflaged from the reader's unaided eye, the author would be moving behind the narrator, maintaining a safe distance for himself (but not necessarily the reader), yet staying close enough to keep the narrator in full sight. If in "The Deserter" Babel went out of the way to emphasize this distance, in *Red Cavalry*, more sure of his craft, he caused it to emerge imperceptibly and grow from story to story.

Kirill Liutov, the compassionate, humane—all too humane—narrator, cannot grant his mortally wounded comrade the last wish: to be put out of his misery before the attacking Poles take him prisoner ("Smert' Dolgusheva" ["The Death of Dolgushev," 1923). But the author, who remains invisible, can and does—through his emissary, a wild, violent, and only slightly "Red" cossack, Afon'ka Bida. In a sense, Babel reveals the nature of his authorial pathos in the ostensibly autobiographical "Guy de Maupassant," in which the young narrator—more Babel than Liutov—flings down the gauntlet before the venerable ghost of Tolstoy. Drunk on wine bought with his first honorarium, he launches into a monologue:

> "He got scared, your Count [Tolstoy], he lost his nerve . . . . His religion is—fear. . . . Scared by the cold, by old age, the Count made himself a shirt out of faith. . . ."
>
> "And then what?" Kazantsev asked me, his birdlike head swaying from side to side.

The question remained unanswered, because the response—only in part to Tolstoy's *The Cossacks* (1863)—had been provided in *Red Cavalry*. There the narrator would play the role of a latter-day Count Tolstoy, a distant relative of the noble protagonist of *The Cossacks* and a spiritual heir to the vegetarian humanism of the late Tolstoy. But the author, who had learned from Nietzsche, not Dostoevsky, about the tragic sense of life and the beauty of power, and who had experienced both, would know no fear, accepting calmly and with majesty all the gifts from the Pandora's box of life. In the adaptations from Gaston Vidal, Babel's author functions as a Russian voice conveying a Frenchman's witness to the carnage at the western front. In *Odessa Tales* and *Red Cavalry*, Babel constructed a "foreign" author, foreign in his sensibility, watching with cool curiosity a Russian Jewish intellectual as he picks his way through a minefield of daily life in a cossack army fighting for the "world revolution" and—the overused, bland pathos is spiced up with irony—"a pickled cuke" ("Konkin," 1924).

The spectacular acclaim Babel enjoyed during the publication of *Red Cavalry* and *Odessa Tales* helps us to understand why his later writing was dominated by the figure of the autobiographical narrator-protagonist. The intelligentsia, who were sympathetic to the Revolution but shocked and disoriented by the catastrophic events of the preceding decade, embraced his stories as the first true masterpiece of the new era. What they saw in them was above all a new language, a new way of speaking about the world, that made it possible to assimilate revolutionary change without compromising their moral and, even more important, aesthetic sense. "Babel knows about the necessity of cruelty," wrote the influential critic A. Lezhnev in his 1926 essay,

> no less than those who criticize him. In his work, it is justified ("Salt," "The Death of Dolgushev"), justified with the revolutionary pathos. His cavalrymen are no brutes; otherwise *Red Cavalry* would have amounted to a libel of the Cavalry Army. But the justification of cruelty—in a strange and conflicting way—exists side by the side with his rejection of it. This contradiction cannot be resolved.
>
> (p. 85)

Instead of trying to solve this paradox by conceptual manipulation, Babel opted for a mimetic construct, inventing an exemplary, aesthetically convincing model of the self. As Lezhnev's analysis implied, this model, if internalized, would help one become reconciled to the brutal and unsightly way that power was exercised in the good revolution. But not everyone was able to discern in Babel's art a complex truth and a positive spirit.

The most sophisticated among Babel's detractors accused him of the cardinal sin of the intelligentsia: apologizing for the revolution by appealing to abstract moral principles. That Babel's "bourgeois humanism" was no longer moving sluggishly through the veins of a typical "intelligentsia" hero but was pulsating mightily through the hearts of muscular protagonists—that fact made Babel's stance particularly pernicious. The most impressive bill of particulars, entitled "Poeziia banditizma" (The Poetry of Banditry, 1924), was drawn by V. Veshnev (Vl. Przhetslavskii), a critic associated with the Komsomol journal *Molodaia gvardiia* (Young Guard). Trying to dispel Babel's considerable mystique, Veshnev cautioned youthful readers to be wary of what he believed to be Babel's insidious moral economy:

> For the most part, Babel depicts the greatest cruelties of our civil war. But these cruelties are presented in the light of total justification of those who perpetrated them. . . . Babel approached the revolution with a moral yardstick. This is damning enough. Revolution is not subject to morality. On the contrary, morality is subject to the revolution.
>
> (p. 276)

Paying homage to Babel's craft, Veshnev saw the greatest danger precisely in the effectiveness of his fiction, implying that Babel made the acceptance of the revolution a matter of not ideological or even moral choice, but aesthetic judgment: "The bandit stories with their poetry of anarchism are written simply, transparently, and seductively. They can and they will enjoy ideological success. Are we going to be pleased by this?" Apparently Veshnev was not pleased, but his prediction turned out to be correct. The stories were successful and, what is more, they soon achieved the reputation of the foremost masterpieces of Soviet fiction and maintained this status, despite repeated assaults, throughout the 1930's.

Whatever one might say, the cultural sphere of the revolution belonged to the intelligentsia, and Babel fulfilled, in the Marxist critical parlance of the day, the social command of this "pseudo-class"; he endowed, according to N. Stepanov, the experience of the revolution and the civil war with a heroic and romantic aura. Many were called to the task, but Babel alone was chosen, not least because he had managed to continue looking at the world through the traditional perspective of the Russian intelligentsia, that established in the masterpieces of Russia's literary art. Wrote Ia. Benni (Ia. Cherniak) in 1924:

> Writers are compulsively drawn to the plots and events of the revolution that lie about at every corner. They grab at and burn their fingers on the still smoldering logs. There is neither enough strength nor aesthetic stability. And how can there be enough to enable one to clear away the fiery ashes and, burning with memories, to touch the smoldering and bloody years. . . .
>
> [Intentional] propaganda destroys art, depriving it altogether of its true effectiveness as a tool of mobilization. . . . The revolution in the soul of contemporary reader is much more terrifying, more profound, and its voice is softer than the thunderous sighs of the so-called revolutionary art. . . .
>
> What overwhelms in Babel's stories is their truthfulness, a strange echo of the familiar Ukrainian laughter of the "little Gogol," conjoined with the great intensity of the justification of sacrifice.
>
> (p. 136)

Benni comes the heart of the matter when he seeks an explanation for the effectiveness of Babel's art and locates it in the "autobiographi-cal" basis of his writings. Nothing could be more convincing, according to him, than the individual experience of an *intelligent,* mediated though it might be by the invention of fiction:

> Babel's stories are heroic stories. Their biographical, even autobiographical, truthfulness, which at once determines the reader's trust in the artist and his writings, constitutes their sole foundation. Literary mastery, rich and colorful language, even the invention itself, emerge out of this biographical truth as naturally as grass and flowers on a meadow.
>
> (p. 139)

A writer who was able to justify the revolution morally and aesthetically, who made this justification the matter of self-sacrifice, Babel was likewise credited with the invention of the new linguistic culture. "In the art of using live language, Babel is successfully catching up with the classics," wrote a Marxist literary critic, Georgii Gorbachev, offering what counted, perhaps, as the highest praise for a contemporary writer. He continued in an awkward but, for this reason, more telling manner:

> Babel's work with the language serves the cognition of life, development of technique, aesthetic expressiveness, the cause of the creation of a [new] linguistic culture, which is so important for us, for language represents the most important tool of the enlightenment and communication among the masses, which have entered a period of great cultural and social ferment.
>
> (p. 275)

As in an echo chamber, the praise continued to amplify Babel's achievement until *Red Cavalry* was declared by V. Polonskii to "constitute, alone, a factor determining the development of our art" and a "token of the urban, industrial future of Soviet Russia." The editor of *Krasnaia nov',* Alexander Voronskii, a pivotal figure in the literary life of the 1920's, stated clearly and simply that "Babel was strengthening the association of literature with the Soviet republic and the Communist party." Coming from the man whom the party had commissioned to win the intelligentsia to the cause of the Bolshevik Revolution, this was high praise indeed. No wonder Babel dismissed his pre-1917 literary efforts as insignificant, declaring in the "Autobiography" that his career had commenced in 1923 and 1924, when the trend-setting avant-garde *LEF* and *Krasnaia nov'* (Red Virgin Soil), the most prestigious and weighty of contemporary journals, began publishing stories from his two major cycles.

Controversy was an unwelcome part of Babel's celebrity; *Red Cavalry* was centered on events in the immediate past and had a strong documentary flavor. Not only could the places of action be located on the map of the Polish campaign, but many actors in *Red Cavalry* retained their prototypes' names. (These would be altered only in the later editions.) However, perhaps because it was risky, this strategy contributed to Babel's success. Even when the notable verity of his civil war cycle impinged on the self-image of Commander of the First Cavalry Army Semyon Budennyi, it was the author, not the warrior, who came out the winner. Unlike his more urbane comrades-in-arms (Kliment Voroshilov, for one), who patronized the arts and knew the value of being made part of Babel's canvas, this semi-educated warrior could not make sense out of Babel's unconventional expression and failed to appreciate his admiration for the mighty barbarians of the revolutionary war. Affronted by the lurid detail in *Red Cavalry* and exploited by the enemies of Voronskii's journal, he accused Babel in print of vicious libel of the heroes of the First Cavalry Army. The verbal charge, which bore the title "Babizm Babelia iz 'kraznoi novi'" ("Floozy-ism of Babel from *Krasnaia nov'*"), a clumsy pun on the Russian *baba* (a common condescending term for a woman), succeeded only in bestowing on Budennyi himself a reputation as a comical Goliath. When another opportunity arose in 1928, after the fall of Voron-

skii, Budennyi once again stepped into the fray—only to be snubbed in *Pravda* by Gorky himself. The great man of letters, an undisputed authority on culture at the time, explained to the general with barely concealed exasperation that in a backward country like Russia, it was not the business of undereducated men to meddle in matters concerning enlightenment. Any subsequent attempts to reignite the controversy had little chance of success after Stalin pronounced his laconic verdict: "There is nothing wrong with *Red Cavalry.*"

It is not easy to walk away from a gold mine that has yielded a great treasure, no matter how scant the present return may be. Babel's gold mine was his invention of a new theme and style, and he was either unwilling or unable to surrender them, even at the risk of becoming a prisoner of his uncommonly good fortune. The theme was that of an emancipated Jewish intellectual who was trying to integrate himself into a world that was his by claim of reason but that could offer him only a dangerous and palpably very alien way of life. Like the narrator of *Red Cavalry*, Liutov, this character wishes to learn to accept the vibrant brutality and the baseness of existence (the Dionysian element) and to transfix it in the cool, contemplative beauty that, according to Nietzsche, was the gift of Apollonian art (the theme received a narrative development in "Pan Apolek," 1923). Together with his nonfictional contemporaries, Liutov had seen humanistic values pulverized in World War I, and he found the conventional, ultimately Christian ethic unacceptable. To do otherwise was for him tantamount to the loss of sight—symbolic castration—a motif that runs throughout Babel's fiction, especially *Red Cavalry* ("Perekhod cherez Zbruch" ["Crossing the Zbruch," 1924], "Gedali" [1924], "Liniia i tsvet" ["Line and Color," 1923]).

Indeed, the spirit of the Antichrist is in Liutov's blood. He is described in "Kostel v Novograde" ("The Novograde Cathedral," 1923): "I see you from here, the treasonous monk in lilac habit, the plumpness of your hands, your soul, tender and merciless, like a cat's soul, I see the wounds of your god, oozing semen, the fragrant poison intoxicating virgins."

The more astute among Babel's sympathetic readers recognized in his writings the ethos of Nietzsche, although they avoided pronouncing his name, preferring such code words as "paganism," "nature," and "life." The style was such that it undermined any discourse that could be defined as dominant. "Babel speaks in one voice about the stars and the clap," wrote Shklovskii in 1924 in his essay on Babel, giving what to this day is, perhaps, the sharpest and, certainly, most concise formulation of the Babelian style. That theme and that style, with only slight variations, Babel continued to practice well into the 1930's.

The four novellas of 1937 and 1938, which were his last fiction to appear in Soviet journals in his lifetime, do not suggest that his writing was likely to change. "Sud" ("The Trial," published in *Ogonek,* vol. 23 [1938]) tells the story of a deracinated White officer who is being convicted of petty fraud by an indifferent French court. Written in a staccato style, thematically it belongs to the genre of exposing the ills of the capitalist West that is practiced by Soviet writers wishing to justify their travels beyond the Soviet borders. Babel, who belonged to a handful of well-traveled authors, must have felt a particular sense of obligation. He had three long sojourns in France between 1928 and 1935, the briefest lasting several months. He had a wife and a daughter in France and a mother and a sister in Belgium, and he had to contend with persistent rumors about his alleged intention to emigrate. "The Trial" was also one of the few third-person stories Babel ever wrote; he ordinarily eschewed the objective authority associated with this narrative stance. But the other three return once again, whether ostensibly or by implication, to the narrator of *Red Cavalry.*

"The Kiss," the only story about Liutov's successful seduction, ends in the narrator cruelly betraying the woman that he has won by displays of sentimental humanity. "The Kiss" could easily have been integrated into yet another edition of the civil war cycle (the last one came out in 1932), but the central motif of the story represented, if anything, a sign of the more recent times. "Sulak" (1937), named after a peasant rebel killed in the story, fills a chronological gap in the Liutov "epic," placing the bespectacled narrator in the Ukraine in 1928, at the beginning of the collectivization drive. He is accompanying a Cheka officer ordered to seek out, arrest, and, if need be, destroy Sulak. The story is as grotesquely brutal as anything in *Red Cavalry.* Published, as chance would have it, in the journal *Molodoi kolkhoznik* (Young Collective Farmer), "Sulak" must have been especially appreciated by the young inhabitants of the terrorized countryside.

"Di Grasso," the fourth story, belongs thematically to the childhood cycle. Seen against the background of the Great Terror, and one of the writer's last stories, it begs to be interpreted as Babel's literary testament: a retrospective allegory of his life in art. The story is set in the familiar Rabelaisian Odessa of the early 1910's and told in the first person—in the voice of a man and writer sharing with his readers a formative episode from his bygone youth. A boy of fourteen, he becomes involved with a gang of scalpers who do a lively business, exploiting the Odessans' weakness for the performing arts. Incautiously, he chooses to obtain the start-up capital by pawning his father's watch with the head scalper, an unscrupulous man who thinks nothing of keeping both the watch and the money. The boy, on the contrary, is terrified by the prospect of facing his father's Jehovah-like wrath. What saves him is the sudden popularity of a visiting Sicilian actor, the tragedian Di Grasso, and not only the money he is able to make by scalping tickets to Di Grasso's performances, but quite literally his art. Night after night, in a spirited interpretation of his role, Di Grasso leaps into the air, flies across the stage, kills his wealthy rival with his bare teeth, and proceeds to drink the enemy's blood, growling and shooting fiery glances at the enraptured audience as the curtain slowly descends on the crime of the heart. This extraordinary display of the power of passion so moves the scalper's wife that she forces her husband to return the watch to the boy, who has already arranged to flee Odessa aboard an English steamer. The story ends with the boy— delivered from his misfortune by the orgiastic art of Di Grasso—transfixed by a sudden experience of an Apollonian epiphany:

> Clutching the timepiece, I was left alone and suddenly, with the kind of clarity I had never experienced before, I saw the towering pillars of the City Hall, the illuminated foliage of the boulevard, the bronze head of Pushkin under the pale gleam of the moon—for the first time, I saw what surrounded me as it really was: quiet and ineffably beautiful.

> (*Izbrannoe* [Moscow, 1966], p. 301)

Babel's predicament in the 1930's was not unlike that of the boy in "Di Grasso." He, too, was living on borrowed time, hoping for a deliverance through an artistic miracle. Confronted with the choice between the materialist Scylla of the West, with art at the mercy of scalpers, and the revolutionary Charybdis, presided over by the father figure Stalin, he chose not to emigrate (and he had plenty of opportunities to do so) but to remain in Russia, which he continued to see through the eye of his art. By no means blind to the Stalinist repression, he continued to measure the social and political experience of his country, so massively tragic and irreducibly complex, with the aesthetic formula according to which unbridled and violent passion revealed the real world—"quiet and ineffably beautiful." Whether or not Babel ever intended "Di Grasso" to be interpreted in this manner, many of his contemporaries among the intelligentsia, desperate for a rationalization of the Great Terror, could hardly have misread the story's subtle appeal.

It must have seemed for a while that Babel would be spared the fate of millions of his contemporaries who disappeared in the massive waves of arrests in 1937 and 1938. This was not to be. Babel's turn came on 16 May 1939, when he was arrested on unspecified charges at his country home in Peredelkino. Until recently, the circumstances of Babel's arrest and death have been shrouded in mystery. Now we know (Arkady Vaksberg, "Protsessy" [The Trials]) that a warrant for his arrest was issued thirty-five days after he had been taken into custody, that he was charged with belonging to a secret Trotskyist organization since 1927 and, since 1934, serving both French and Austrian intelligence. The litany of fantastic charges contained in the verdict suggests the actual motive for Babel's arrest: his association with Gladun-Khaiutina, a longtime Odessa friend and colleague at the editorial offices of *SSSR na stroike* (USSR in Construction), who also happened to be the wife of the recently deposed head of the secret police, Nikolai Yezhov (he was last seen in public on 31 January 1939). Babel's verdict read in part: "Having been organizationally associated in his anti-Soviet activity with the wife of an enemy of the people Yezhov—Gladun-Khaiutuna—Babel was drawn by the latter into anti-Soviet conspiratorial terrorist activity, shared the goal and tasks of this organization, including terrorist acts . . . against the leaders of the Communist party of the Soviet Union and Soviet government." Even Babel's famous *Red Cavalry* became an item in the writer's indictment as a "description of all the cruelties and inconsistencies of the civil war, emphasizing only the sensational and rough episodes." In the course of seventy-two hours of continuous interrogation (the "conveyor belt," as it is known in the language of the Gulag), Babel, who at first denied all the charges, finally relented and "confessed" to having been recruited into the spy network by Ilya Ehrenburg and to having provided André Malraux with, of all things, secrets of Soviet aviation. The latter charge must have been suggested by the film script that he had just completed: it dealt with uncovering saboteurs among the Soviet dirigible designers (Falen, pp. 231ff.).

The list of Babel's co-conspirators read like a who's who of Soviet culture. In addition to Ehrenburg, it included such writers as Valentin Kataev, Leonid Leonov, Yury Olesha, Lydia Seifullina, and Vsevolod Ivanov; filmmakers S. Eisenstein and G. Alexandrov; actors S. Mikhoels and L. Utesov, and even one polar explorer, the academician Otto Shmit. As Vaksberg suggests, the NKVD must have been planning a large-scale show trial involving the flower of the Soviet intelligentsia. But plans changed and the operation had to be mopped up. On four separate occasions, in October and November 1939, and finally in January 1940, Babel wrote appeals renouncing the testimony he was forced to give under torture, pleaded to have witnesses called, and asked for an attorney. On 26 January these appeals reached the chairman of the Military Collegium of the Supreme Court, V. Ul'rikh, who responded to them by signing the death warrant. A day later, Babel was shot. Fourteen years later, in a posthumous review of his case by the same Military Collegium, Babel was cleared of all charges "for lack of any basis" in the original indictment.

At the time of his arrest, Babel was forty-five —"the middle of life's way" for a prose writer, with a lot more to tell us about what happened to Liutov as he was trying to integrate himself into the new world of Soviet Russia. But whereas Babel, man and writer, could be arrested and executed, the theme and the style he invented found their own separate fate. The Soviet soil may have been increasingly inhospitable, but in a more temperate climate, grafted to the English language, they emerged in the American version of the narrator "with the autumn in his heart, spectacles on his nose," and, as Philip Roth expanded the formula in his *The Ghost Writer* (1979), "an erect penis." Victor Shklovskii, who better than anybody understood the intensely "writerly" *(scriptible)* nature of Babel's art, had anticipated this turn of phrase when he cautioned the readers not to identify the narrator type with the writer himself: "Babel is not like that: he does not stammer. He is brave, I even think that he 'can spend the night with a Russian woman, and a Russian woman would be satisfied.' Because a Russian woman likes a good tale." As do all Russian and non-Russian men and women. They now can satisfy their desire for a good Babelian narrative in Philip Roth and—marvel of marvels, considering the hairy-chested machismo of Babel's characters—in the stories of Grace Paley. Even American television is known to make use of the themes and styles invented by Isaac Babel, as it did in the PBS series *Gustav Mahler,* where the Austrian composer, perhaps in deference to the expectations of the Babel-touting audience, was forced into living the childhood of Babel's narrator in "Probuzhdenie" ("The Awakening," 1931). We have not heard the last of Isaac Babel.

Selected Bibliography

EDITIONS

INDIVIDUAL WORKS

Liubka Kozak: Rasskazy. Moscow, 1925.
Rasskazy. Moscow, 1925.
Benia Krik: Kinopovest'. Moscow, 1926.
Bluzhdaiushchie zvezdy: Kinostsenarii. Moscow, 1926.
Istoriia moei golubiatni: Rasskazy. Moscow, Leningrad, 1926.
Konarmiia. Moscow, 1926.
Zakat. Moscow, 1928.
Odesskie rasskazy. Moscow, 1931.
Mariia. Moscow, 1935.
Bezhin lug (vtoroi variant). In Sergei Eizenstein, *Izbrannye proizvedeniia,* 6 vols. Vol. 6. Moscow, 1971.
Evreika. Moscow, 1987.

COLLECTED WORKS

Rasskazy. Moscow, 1936.
Izbrannoe. Introduction by I. G. Erenburg. Moscow, 1957.
Izbrannoe. Introduction by L. Poliak. Moscow, 1966.
Izbrannoe. Kemerovo, 1966.
Zabytyi Babel': Sbornik maloizvestnykh proizve-

denii I. Babelia. Compiled and edited by Nikolas Stroud. Ann Arbor, Mich., 1979.

Evreika, god za godom. Literaturnyi ezhegodnik 4. Moscow, 1988.

Izbrannye proizvedeniia. 2 vols. Introduction by G. Belaia. Moscow, 1988.

MEMOIRS AND DOCUMENTS

Annenkov, Iurii. *Dnevnik moikh vstrech.* New York, 1966.

Anonymous. "Vyderzhki iz pisem I. E. Babelia k materi i sestre (1925–1939)." *Vozdushnye puti* 3 (1963).

Ehrenburg, Il'ia. *Liudi, gody, zhizn'.* In *Sobranie sochinenii,* vols. 8–9. Moscow, 1966. Translated as *Men, Years, Life* by Tatiana Shebunina and Yvonne Kapp. London, 1962–1963.

"Gor'kii—I. E. Babel' [Correspondence]." *Literaturnoe nasledstvo* 70. Moscow, 1963.

Ivanova, T. "Isaak Emanuilovich Babel'." In *Moi sovremenniki, kakimi ia ikh znala: Ocherki.* Moscow, 1984.

Nikulin, L. "Isaak Babel'." In *Gody nashei zhizni: Vospominaniia i portrety.* Moscow, 1966.

Paustovskii, K. *Povest' o zhizni.* 2 vols. Moscow, 1966. Translated as *Years of Hope (The Story of My Life)* by Manya Harari and Andrew Thompson. New York, 1968.

Pirozhkova, A., and N. Turgeneva, eds. *Babel': Vospominaniia sovremennikov.* Moscow, 1972.

———, and I. Smirin. "I. Babel': Novye materialy." *Literaturnoe nasledstvo* 74. Moscow, 1965.

Sinkó, Ervin. *Roman eines Romans: Moskauer Tagebuch.* Cologne, 1962.

Solajczyk, J. "Polzki epizod w biografii Izaaka E. Babla." *Zeszyty naukowe wyzszej szkoly pedagogicznej im. Powstancow slaskich w Opolu. Filologia rosyjska.* 9 (A). Opole, 1972.

Souvarine, Boris. *Souvenirs sur Isaak Babel, Panait Istrati, Pierre Pascal; suivi de Lettre à Alexandre Soljenitsine.* Paris, 1985.

Vaksberg, A. "Protsessy." *Literaturnaia gazeta* (4 May 1988).

TRANSLATIONS

Benya Krik: A Film-Novel. Translated by Ivor Montagu and S. S. Nalbandov. London, 1935.

Benya Krik the Gangster and Other Stories. Edited by Avrahm Yarmolinsky. New York, 1948.

The Collected Stories. Introduction by Lionel Trilling. Edited and translated by Walter Morison. New York, 1955.

The Forgotten Prose. Edited and translated by Nicholas Stroud. Ann Arbor, Mich., 1978.

The Lonely Years: 1925–1939. Edited by Nathalie Babel. Translated by Max Hayward and Andrew R. MacAndrew. New York, 1964. Unpublished stories and private correspondence.

Red Cavalry. Translated by John Harland. London, 1929. Translated by Nadia Helstein. London, New York, 1929.

Sunset. Translated by Raymond Rosenthal and Mirra Ginsburg. *Noonday* 3. New York, 1960.

You Must Know Everything: Stories, 1915–1937. Edited by Nathalie Babel. Translated by Max Hayward. New York, 1966.

BIOGRAPHICAL AND CRITICAL STUDIES

Baak, J. J. van. *The Place of Space in Narration: A Semiotic Approach to the Problem of Literary Space. With an Analysis of the Role of Space in Isaak Babel's "Konarmija." Studies in Slavic Literature and Poetics* 3. Amsterdam, 1983.

I. Babel': Vospominaniia sovremennikov. Moscow, 1972.

Benni, Ia. (Ia. Cherniak). "Isaak Babel'." *Pechat' i revoliutsiia* 3 (1924).

Bloom, Harold, ed. *Isaac Babel.* New York, 1987.

———, ed. *Modern Critical Views: Isaac Babel.* Introduction by Bloom. New York, 1987. This anthology of Babel criticism and scholarship (twenty items) is the most comprehensive collection of its kind in any language.

Bydennyi, S. "Babizm Babelia iz *Krasnoi novi.*" *Oktiabr'* 3 (1924).

———. "Otkrytoe pis'mo Maksimu Gor'komu." *Pravda* (26 October 1928).

Carden, Patricia. *The Art of Isaac Babel.* Ithaca, N.Y., 1972.

Eastman, M. *Writers in Uniform: A Study of Literature and Bureaucratism.* New York, 1934.

Ehre, M. *Isaac Babel.* Boston, 1986.

Falen, James E. *Isaac Babel, Russian Master of the Short Story.* Knoxville, Tenn., 1974. Includes comprehensive bibliography.

Freidin, G. "Fat Tuesday in Odessa: Isaac Babel's 'Di Grasso' as Testament and Manifesto." *The Russian Review* 40/2 (April 1981).

Gorbachev, Georgii. "O tvorchestve Babelia i po povodu nego." *Zvezda* 4 (1925).

Gor'kii, M. "Otvet Budennomu." *Pravda* (27 November 1928).

Hallett, R. W. *Isaac Babel.* New York, 1973.

Howe, Irving. "The Right to Write Badly." *The New Republic* (4 July 1955).

———. "The Genius of Isaac Babel." *New York Review of Books* (20 August 1964).

Hyman, Stanley Edgar. "Identities of Isaac Babel." *Hudson Review* 8/4 (1956).

———. "New Voices of Isaac Babel." *New Leader* (20 July 1964).

Jovanovic, M. *Umetnost Isaka Babelja.* Belgrade, 1975.

Kaun, A. "Babel: Voice of New Russia." *Menorah Journal* 15 (November 1928).

Lelevich, G. "Babel'." *Na postu* 1 (1924).

Levin, F. *Babel'.* Moscow, 1972.

Lezhnev, A. Z. "Babel'." *Pechat i revoliutsiia* 6 (1926).

Luck, C. D. *The Field of Honor: An Analysis of Isaac Babel's Cycle "On the Field of Honor" (Na pole chesti) with Reference to Gaston Vidal's "Figures et anecdotes de la Grand Guerre."* Birmingham Slavonic Monographs No. 18. Birmingham, 1987. The study contains the original text of Babel's cycle *On the Field of Honor.*

Luplow, Carol. *Isaac Babel's "Red Cavalry."* Ann Arbor, Mich. 1982.

Maguire, Robert A. *Red Virgin Soil: Soviet Literature in the 1920's.* Princeton, 1968.

Marcus, Steven. "The Stories of Isaac Babel." *Partisan Review* 22/3 (1955).

Markish, Simon. "The Example of Isaac Babel." *Commentary* 64 (1977).

Mendelson, Danuta. *Metaphor in Babel's Short Stories.* Ann Arbor, Mich., 1982.

Meney, L. *L'Art du recit chez Isaac Babel.* Quebec, 1983.

Mirsky, D. S. "I. Babel: Rasskazy." *Sovremennye zapiski* 26 (1925).

———. "Babel." *Nation* (23 January 1926).

Morsbach, P. *Isaak Babel auf der sowietischen Buhne.* Munich, 1983.

Osinskii, N. "Literaturnyi god." *Pravda* (1 January 1926).

Polonskii, Viach. "Kritičeskie zametki Babele." *Novyi mir* 1 (1927).

Pozner, Vladimir. *Panorama de la littérature russe contemporaine.* Paris, 1929.

Rosenthal, Raymond. "The Fate of Isaac Babel: A Child of the Russian Emancipation." *Commentary* 3 (February 1947).

Shklovskii, Victor. "I. Babel': Kriticheskii roman." *Lef* 2/6 (1924). Translated as "Isaac Babel: A Critical Romance" in Edward J. Brown, ed., *Major Soviet Writers.* London, 1973.

Sicher, E. *Style and Structure in the Prose of Isaac Babel.* Columbus, Ohio, 1986.

Sinyavsky, A. "Isaac Babel." In Edward J. Brown, ed., *Major Soviet Writers.* London, 1973.

Spektor, Iu. "Molodoi Babel'." *Voprosy literatury* 7 (1982).

Stepanov, Nik. "Novella Babelia." In *Mastera sovremennoi literatury II: I. E. Babel',* edited by B. V. Kazanskii and Iu. N. Tyniainov. Leningrad, 1928.

Stora-Sándor, Judith. *Isaac Babel': L'Homme et l'oeuvre.* Paris, 1968.

Strelets (M. Stoliarov). "Dvulikii Ianus." *Rossiia* 5 (1925).

Terras, V. "Line and Color: The Structure of I. Babel's Short Stories in *Red Cavalry.*" *Studies in Short Fiction* 3/2 (1966).

Trilling, Lionel. "The Fate of Isaac Babel." *London Magazine* 7 (1956).

Veshnev, V. (V. Przhetslavskii). "Poeziia banditizma (I. Babel')." *Molodaia gvardiia* 7–8 (1924).

Voronskii, A. "Babel', Seifullina." *Krasnaia nov'* 5 (1924).

GREGORY FREIDIN

HENRY DE MONTHERLANT

(1895–1972)

THE FRENCH WRITER Henry-Marie-Joseph-Frédéric-Expédite Millon de Montherlant was born in Paris on 20 April 1895 and not on 21 April 1896, as he claimed for most of his life. He chose 21 April because it was the date of the founding of Rome. At the age of ten he read a French translation of Henryk Sienkiewicz's novel *Quo Vadis?* (1896), which inspired him with a passionate and enduring attachment to the ancient Romans and their history. Why he made himself a year younger is anybody's guess. It has been suggested that it was either a question of vanity or a way of postponing his eligibility for active service in World War I.

Both of Montherlant's parents belonged to the class of minor nobility. They were quite conscious of the station in life to which it had pleased God to call them and brought up their son accordingly. His mother refused to allow him to serve as an altar boy because he would have been obliged to don vestments worn by other, doubtless humbler, youths. His parents' snobbishness nearly prevented him from taking the examination for his baccalaureate because they found it intolerable that their son should be examined by persons of unknown extraction. Fortunately, the son was clever enough to get around the idiosyncrasies of his upbringing, although his parents surely contributed to the aloofness for which Montherlant was known throughout his adult life.

His father was a distant man who had little to do with his son and even less with his wife. After Henry's birth, which brought on a hemorrhage that nearly cost her her life, Madame de Montherlant divided the remainder of her days between her bed and her chaise longue. Her husband would sit on the edge of her bed every evening for fifteen minutes, without saying a word, after which he would get up and leave the room. The example of his parents' marriage left its mark on the young Montherlant, as did his mother's obsessive love for him. As an invalid, she had nothing to give to her husband or to society, and so she concentrated her affections on her son. Although he loved her in his own way, he struggled against her possessiveness by refusing to demonstrate or accept affection. He was to claim over and over again in his writings that he disliked being kissed or touched and that he preferred to love rather than be loved.

This preference for active rather than passive emotion found expression in a wild enthusiasm for the bullring. In 1909, in the course of a pilgrimage to Lourdes with his grandmother, Montherlant saw his first bullfight in Bayonne. It was an experience that completely overwhelmed him and may well have been the most violent passion of his life. He not only studied manuals about bullfighting; he also secretly took lessons and actually fought young bulls in both France and Spain at the age of sixteen. The intensity of his feelings for bulls and the art of bullfighting found its way into many aspects of his thought and most specifically into two of his novels, *Les bestiaires* (The Gladiators, translated as *The Matador*, 1926) and *Le chaos et la nuit* (*Chaos and Night*, 1963), and a play, *Pasiphaé* (1936).

Montherlant's love for the bullring did not in any way interfere with his education, but another attachment did. In January 1911 he enrolled as a student at the École Sainte-Croix de Neuilly, against the better judgment of his father, who wanted his son to go to a Jesuit school. Monsieur de Montherlant was obliged to yield to his son's preference for Sainte-Croix because the boy, who had recently undergone an operation for removal of his appendix, kept reopening his wound until he managed to obtain his father's consent. This would seem a rather drastic method for getting one's own way, but for Montherlant no other school would do. A beloved friend and comrade from a previous educational establishment had also enrolled at Sainte-Croix and Henry did not wish to be separated from him.

The relatively brief period, fifteen months, during which Montherlant was a student at Sainte-Croix seems to have been the happiest time of his life. His sudden dismissal from the school in March of 1912 was a terrible blow from which he never recovered psychologically. He was sent away because of what appeared to be a suspiciously close relationship with the younger boy on whose account Montherlant had insisted upon going to Sainte-Croix. His experiences at the school and the circumstances surrounding his dismissal were later to serve as the subject of a play, *La ville dont le prince est un enfant* (The City Whose Prince Is a Child, translated as *The Fire That Consumes*, 1951), and a novel, *Les garçons* (*The Boys*, 1969).

Montherlant continued his preparation for the baccalaureate with private tutors and passed the examination in the fall of 1912. Between 1913 and 1915 he made a desultory attempt to study law at the Institut Catholique in Paris, while at the same time working for his uncle's insurance firm. Neither of these activities held any interest for him. He preferred the newly discovered pleasures of society. He subsequently reproached himself for wasting his time at parties and dances, but claimed to have gone out in order to please his dying mother. She wanted him to have his good times, but most particularly to find an heiress and settle down. With the death of his father in 1914, followed by the death of his mother a year later, Montherlant was left with no parents to please. He had wished to volunteer for the army in 1914, at the outbreak of World War I. However, his mother had begged him to wait until after her death. He waited dutifully until a month after her demise to present himself for active service, but was refused because of an enlarged heart. Montherlant returned to the home that he shared with his uncles and his maternal grandmother, a remarkable woman with whom he had a close and extremely frank relationship.

During the first three years of the war, Montherlant spent much of his time reading such authors as Friedrich Nietzsche, Marcus Aurelius, Seneca, Blaise Pascal, Victor Hugo, Gabriele D'Annunzio, Gustave Flaubert, Johann Wolfgang von Goethe, and Maurice Barrès. He went often to the Louvre, since he was something of an artist himself, and also joined a sports club, through which he was to become seriously involved in athletic activities for a number of years.

At this time Montherlant was not only developing into a young man of many interests; he was also becoming a serious writer. He had been composing stories and sketches from his childhood onward. After his expulsion from Sainte-Croix, Montherlant began a novel entitled *Thrasylle* (Thrasyllus), which tells of an idyll between two young boys in ancient Greece. The manuscript was never published in his lifetime. It finally appeared in 1983. In 1914 he wrote the first versions of *The Fire That Consumes* and *The Boys*. At the end of that same year he wrote his first play, *L'Exil* (The Exile, 1929), the subject of which is a mother's refusal to let her son go off to war.

By 1917 the French army was willing to overlook Montherlant's physical deficiencies. He was drafted into the auxiliary branch of the armed forces. This meant that he would not serve in combat units but could perform other tasks that would free those men more fit to go to the front. Montherlant never wanted to let on that he had a heart problem. He feared that he would be considered a coward for not doing his duty. He wanted the experience of combat, of being wounded, of actually killing a man. On the other hand, his letters to his grandmother express a certain ambivalence concerning the risks of war. The budding writer clearly desired some firsthand knowledge, but the young man held back from the threat of death. He did finally succeed in getting near the front lines and even managed to get the sort of wound he had hoped for: some shell fragments that would neither kill nor incapacitate, but would serve to demonstrate to one and all that he had indeed risked his life for his country. The wound did have its ironic aspect, however, since the shell that reached him did not come from enemy fire: Montherlant was hit accidentally in the course of artillery practice by French troops.

Released from military service in August of 1919, Montherlant began to cast about for something to do. He had no inclination whatsoever to return to his uncle's insurance office. Life was pleasant for him in postwar Paris. He was in no hurry to confine himself to unpalatable tasks. However, his family, especially his grandmother, felt that he should find work of some kind so as not to waste his talents, as some of the other men in her household had done, notably Montherlant's uncles, whose story he would relate in the novel *Les célibataires* (*The Bachelors,* 1934). At last an ideal situation presented itself: he became the general secretary of an organization to raise funds for a war memorial. He worked at this job for several years, all the while continuing to write for himself and for various newspapers.

In 1920 Montherlant published his first book, a volume of essays entitled *La relève du matin* (The Changing of the Guard, portions translated in *Selected Essays*). After being refused by eleven Parisian publishers, the book was printed at Montherlant's own expense. It was an immediate success and was quickly reissued by another publisher. *La relève du matin* was awarded the Montyon Prize by the Académie française. Montherlant received letters of praise from such authors as Paul Claudel and François Mauriac. The volume of essays was followed in 1922 by his first novel, *Le songe* (*The Dream),* which incorporated his experiences in the war, and *Les olympiques* (The Olympians, portions translated in *Selected Essays*), a collection of essays, short narratives, and poems glorifying sports, published in 1924.

After the death of his grandmother in 1923, Montherlant decided to rid himself of the family home, with its accumulated belongings of several generations, and to head for the southern countries, which had long attracted him. He traveled to various points on the Mediterranean with only two suitcases, one for his clothes and the other for his manuscripts. While in Spain, Montherlant wrote *The Matador,* a novel dealing largely with the art of bullfighting in both its physical and emotional aspects. It was published in 1926 with a dedication to Gaston Doumergue, the French president who was the first to authorize the killing of bulls during bullfights held in France. Although Montherlant's previous publications had brought him a certain amount of recognition, *The Matador* was the book that made him famous.

He returned briefly to Paris in 1926 to move his stored belongings into an apartment. Montherlant kept that apartment for thirteen years without ever unpacking his trunks. His possessions remained exactly where the movers had left them. Resuming his peripatetic existence, he proceeded to North Africa by way of Spain. For the next few years, he was to shuttle between France and North Africa, always taking the long way through Spain because of an unfortunate tendency toward seasickness. He lived for varying periods in Morocco, Algeria, and Tunisia. Some of the writings that date from his years of wandering are *Pasiphaé,* a play about the mythological heroine's love for a young bull; essays; poems; and the lengthy manuscript of *La rose de sable* (The Desert Rose, 1968), a novel on French colonialism in Morocco. He also continued to read extensively and to take notes on characters and situations that were to appear in later works.

Returning to Paris in 1932, Montherlant asked two of his friends to read the manuscript of *La rose de sable.* He was uncertain about publishing a novel that was critical of France's colonial policies. He finally decided not to publish the book because the political climate of the 1930's was a tense and difficult one that would sooner or later lead to war. It would be wrong, he felt, to openly find fault with his country at that time. Setting aside *La rose de sable,* Montherlant wrote what is probably his best-known novel, *The Bachelors,* which appeared in 1934. In that same year he was awarded the Gran Prix de Littérature by the Académie française. Montherlant sent all the prize money, ten thousand francs, to General Henri-Honoré Giraud, the French commander in chief in Morocco, with instructions to divide the money equally between the victorious French soldiers and the Moroccan troops they had conquered, because both sides were only doing their duty. General Giraud did not know what to make of such a bizarre request and simply handed the money over to the Red Cross. Montherlant was also awarded the Northcliffe-Heineman Prize for Literature for *The Bachelors.* He gave away that prize money too, this time to the London hospitals. He refused a third award, which consisted of twenty thousand francs plus a free sojourn of one month in Tunisia, on the condition that he write a work specifically concerning that French colony. Realizing that he would be under an obligation to write a favorable piece, he declined the offer. Montherlant liked to maintain his independence at all costs. In 1935 he published another collection of essays,

Service inutile (Useless Service, portions translated in *Selected Essays*), which has an important introduction that helps the reader to follow the evolution of his thought between 1925 and 1935.

While staying in Paris, Montherlant met a young woman whom he seriously considered marrying. He had experienced a similar élan about ten years earlier, out of a desire to regularize his life and to have a home and children. In neither case could he bring himself to take the final step. His very real hesitations and difficulties concerning women and marriage are dealt with at length in the series of four novels subsumed under the title of *Les jeunes filles* (The Girls). The first volume, also titled *Les jeunes filles,* appeared in 1936. It was followed later that same year by *Pitié pour les femmes* (Pity for Women). The last two volumes, *Le démon du bien* (The Demon of Good, translated as *The Hippogriff*) and *Les lépreuses* (The Lepers), appeared in 1937 and 1939 respectively. This tetralogy attained a widespread and distinctly scandalous notoriety because of the flagrant, relentless misogyny expressed in its many hundreds of pages.

Montherlant continued to disturb his readers in a series of essays published in 1938 under the title of *L'Equinoxe de septembre* (The September Equinox, portions translated in *Selected Essays*), wherein he voiced his opposition to the Munich Accords and to the notion of "peace at any price." He also wrote articles that were hostile to the Italian campaign in Ethiopia. Working as a war correspondent for *Marianne,* a weekly publication, he was able to penetrate the war zone in May and June of 1940. Therefore he had the opportunity to observe the retreat of the French army at first hand. In 1941, about a year after the armistice, Montherlant published *Le solstice de juin* (The Summer Solstice), which should be read in conjunction with *L'Equinoxe de septembre.* In *Le solstice de juin* Montherlant made statements that were not flattering to his country, implying that it had allowed itself to be defeated by the Germans. On the other hand, he wrote that the wheel turns, that everything revolves, that destinies rise and fall, thereby indicating that France would one day be great again. Both sides were troubled by the implications of these essays. The Germans banned the book and only relented on the recommendation of Montherlant's German translator, K. H. Bremer, who happened to be the assistant director of the German Institute in Paris. The book continued to be banned in Belgium and Holland throughout the Occupation.

In 1941 Montherlant was approached by Jean-Louis Vaudoyer, the chief administrator of France's national theater, the Comédie-Française, to translate a Spanish play for him. On examining the text, *Reinar después de morir* (To Reign After Death, 1630), by Luis Vélez de Guevara, Montherlant decided that he was not interested in translating it, but that he would be willing to use it as a basis for a play of his own. That is how his most famous play, *La reine morte* (The Dead Queen, translated as *Queen After Death*, 1942), was created. It was produced at the Comédie-Française in December 1942. The success of the play was so great that the Germans were willing to sponsor a series of performances in their prison camps. Montherlant refused. He also refused to take part in a meeting of European writers in Weimar. In general, Montherlant attempted to keep his distance from the Germans. Nonetheless, when the war ended, he was called to account for the views expressed in *Le solstice de juin*, as well as for other articles written during the occupation. His dossier was examined by the Bureau of Special Services, which found nothing in particular, and by the Committee for the Purification of Arts and Letters, which came up with a token condemnation, a retroactive suspension of publication for one year.

For the remainder of the war and on into the next two decades, Montherlant continued to write plays, some more successful than others, and some downright failures. His best-known plays are *Queen After Death, Le maître de Santiago* (*The Master of Santiago*, 1947), and *Port-Royal* (1954).

Perhaps because of his continuing involvement with the theater, and perhaps also because his wanderlust had subsided, Montherlant remained in Paris for the rest of his days in an apartment on the Quai Voltaire. In 1960 he was invited by two members of the Académie française to become a candidate for the chair recently vacated by André Siegfried. Montherlant agreed to do so on the condition that he be exempted from the round of activities usually expected and even required of a candidate. By this time his celebrity was such that his conditions were accepted. He was elected by twenty-four out of twenty-nine votes. Although he had disdained to solicit support, once elected he became an active member of the Académie, scrupulously fulfilling the obligations of his position.

In the last ten years of his life Montherlant published four novels: *Chaos and Night, La rose de sable, The Boys,* and *Un assassin est mon maître* (An Assassin Is My Master, 1971). This great burst of literary activity occurred during a period of increasing ill health. Montherlant, who had so openly admired bodies that were physically fit (*Les olympiques*) and beautiful in their strength and courage (*The Matador*), was gradually growing more and more infirm. In 1968 he lost the sight of one eye. Fearing blindness and dependence, he committed suicide in thorough fashion by swallowing cyanide, then shooting himself in the temple, on 21 September 1972, the September equinox. His body was cremated and the ashes scattered about the Temple of Virile Fortune in the Roman Forum. What more fitting resting place for a man who had dedicated his life and most of his literary work to the cult of "l'ordre mâle" (the male order)?

Montherlant's literary universe is indeed a masculine one, despite the fact that his tetralogy *The Girls* constitutes a fairly large percentage of his novelistic production. Women are present throughout his works, but are seen only from bizarre angles. It is as though the mask that Montherlant donned to hide himself from public scrutiny also obscured his own vision of the palpable world. Montherlant's deception concerning the date of his birth is particularly telling because he misled his readers not only about his age but also about his own highly specialized inclinations. It was not until 1977, when Roger Peyrefitte, one of Montherlant's old friends, published his *Propos secrets* (Secret Remarks) that the public at large became aware that Montherlant had been a lifelong pederast. From the earliest days of his celebrity, Montherlant had jealously guarded his private life. The reaction to Peyrefitte's avowal included surprise and even shock for some. For others, Peyrefitte provided corroborating evidence for their own awareness, through Montherlant's writings, of his manifestly disturbed and complex sexuality. To judge by the comments of more than one critic and journalist, Montherlant's secret became less and less of a secret as time wore on. Despite the hints and whispers that circulated throughout the Parisian literary world, no critic actually confronted the problem directly—or, usually, even indirectly—in Montherlant's lifetime.

Since an important segment of Montherlant's work deals with women, and since *The Girls,* which was a sensational best-seller in its time, may well have caused him to be regarded as the foremost misogynist of the western world, the revelation of his pederasty assumes an importance that it otherwise would not have had. On the one hand, Montherlant was extremely closemouthed about his personal life; on the other hand, he went out of his way to give the impression that he was a persistent and dedicated womanizer. This carefully projected image of a skirt-chasing misogynist has been a source of more than a little confusion, particularly for female readers.

The publication in 1983 of Montherlant and Roger Peyrefitte's correspondence with an introduction entitled "Les après-midi de deux faunes" (The Afternoons of Two Fauns) is a truly explosive literary bombshell, splattering its fragments over much of Montherlant's work.

Of course, readers should not allow the knowledge of the compulsive aspect of his pedophilia to mar their appreciation of his writings. Peyrefitte, a fellow pederast, states in the preface to the correspondence that readers should be grateful to him for making public what he felt to be the very source of Montherlant's genius. Pierre Sipriot, coeditor of the correspondence, concludes in his own separate preface that the letters are improper, but that it would be too bad if such exploits were to remain unknown.

The gratitude of present and future readers has yet to be assessed. What we can now be certain of is that a great deal of sexual transposition occurs throughout all of Montherlant's writings and that everything dealing with seemingly specific sexual identity has to be reexamined. What is the reason behind Montherlant's personal and literary mystifications? We must look to the French laws for the answer. In his preface to the correspondence Pierre Sipriot informs us that according to a law passed on 27 August 1942, during the German occupation of France, persons found guilty of committing homosexual acts with minors were to be sentenced to anywhere from six months to three years in prison. A minor was defined as anyone under the age of twenty-one. As late as 1977 this law was denounced as discriminatory toward homosexuals. Heterosexual men were considered guilty of corrupting a minor only if the girl in question was under fifteen. It was not until the law of 4 August 1982 that fifteen became the age of consent for both males and females with regard to sexual acts.

With these legal considerations in mind it is clear that Montherlant, as an extremely active pedophile, was in perpetual danger of running afoul of the law. Even in his letters to Peyrefitte, adolescent boys are referred to as young girls; masculine pronouns become feminine pronouns; boys' names are changed to girls' names. This was done not only to fool the censor, since many of the letters made available in the correspondence were written in the early years of World War II, but also because Montherlant genuinely believed that what he liked in young boys was their feminine aspect. Therefore, he could argue that his feelings for them were basically heterosexual. It is this kind of self-justification that helps to throw light on some of the more oblique and contradictory aspects of *The Girls.*

In the opening pages of the tetralogy we read with disbelief a line informing us that one of the horrors of war, to which not nearly enough attention has been paid, is that women are spared. For more than six hundred pages Montherlant wields his pen as though it were an ax, ever ready to bludgeon the foe whose name is woman. The hero of *The Girls* is a writer, Pierre Costals, who in simpler times might have been described as a confirmed bachelor. He is a man for whom marriage, or anything resembling ties with women, is a perversion of masculine nature to be avoided at all costs. Yet this same man spends all his leisure time and even some of his working hours either chasing after, or writing to, women of every size and description. He cannot confine himself to one because he claims to be tantalized by them all. Meanwhile, he does nothing but vilify this same sex, which he claims to need physically but to despise intellectually and emotionally. For Costals a woman is inferior in every possible way: in her heart, in her mind, in her soul. She is a slug, a succubus, a vampire. She will cling to a man unshakably and unashamedly in order to drain him of his very substance. Women want a man's time, money, and attention, all in the name of something called love, which they and they alone have invented. According to Costals, love does not exist. He will admit only to a feeling of affection mingled with desire in his attraction to women. But the attraction is always accompanied by repulsion. He does not seem to be able to stop himself from expressing utter contempt for these beings whom he will scarcely recognize as fellow creatures.

It is impossible, for reasons of space and credibility, to give more than a sketchy indication of the extent and magnitude of Costals' vituperations against women. Multiple examples are found on nearly every page in each of the four volumes. He lashes out at them in every possible way. He hates their dress, their makeup, their intelligence or lack thereof, their ignorance, their dependence, their weakness, their soft and flabby bodies, their greediness, their gluttony, their laziness, their intrusiveness, their immorality, and worst of all, their need for marriage. This list could be prolonged, but as it stands, the reader will have some sense of just how much hostility toward women is found in *The Girls* and of how excessive it is.

Costals despises women but cannot do without them. Although he complains bitterly about their demands and expectations, he is the one who will not leave them alone. What is a creator without his creatures? For the three principal female characters in *The Girls,* Costals is a godlike male whose will must be done. He has a spiritual relationship with one young woman, an intellectual relationship with another, and a sensual relationship with a third, thereby manifesting himself in his tripartite aspect, but always, and unfailingly, with inferiors. He will never put his superiority to the test by pitting himself against an equal. Indeed, it becomes increasingly evident that Costals does not have any equals, least of all among women. However, the god business is a lonely one, and there are moments when Costals dreams of embraces more worthy of him. What an experience it would be, he muses, to wrestle with strength rather than weakness. A victory over feeble creatures is no victory at all. In the lucid aftermath of sexual appeasement, Costals concedes that he has humbled himself out of vanity, for the sake of libidinous exploits, and believes that he is worth more than the sum of his actions.

Here Costals pleads with us to understand why he persists in dealing with the sex he despises. He seriously considers marriage with a particular young woman, Solange Dandillot, because he wants to experience life in all its variety. He makes it clear that he does not wish to spend the rest of his days as an outsider. This is the very predicament shared by Montherlant at the time he was writing *The Girls.* He, too, was grappling with the idea of marriage in the hope of leading a so-called normal existence. He, too, tried and failed.

In a few scattered moments of calm, when both Montherlant and his hero (since their voices do alternate in the narrative) seem to step back and assume reflective attitudes toward women, the reader is told that women are what men have made them. They are artificial, ignorant, and weak because men like them that way. Women are obliged to please men, for marriage, they believe, is their only acceptable destiny. Women are therefore dependent on men for everything. They cannot generate their own happiness, as men can. As a result they have no self-esteem and no dignity. Men and women, for Montherlant and for his hero, are two distinct and separate races who cannot understand each other and should never have anything to do with one another. But nature, for the survival of the species, forces them to come together and form a couple, to the everlasting unhappiness of the male, and consequently of the female as well. In acknowledging this fundamental incompatibility, Costals and Montherlant decide against marriage. Neither one can bear to share a jealously guarded private life with a woman, regardless of what a heterosexual society expects from a man. The relentlessly expressed rage against women in *The Girls* can now be understood as the fury of the male who is part of a biological system that depends upon the X chromosome. The very fact that women exist is a personal affront to hero and author alike. If society could do without this plague of womankind, how free and pure the males would be. There would be no need for homosexuals to hide or for pederasts to dissimulate. In a telling phrase in which Costals uses the word *angel,* giving it a feminine article rather than the generally accepted masculine one, he asks himself why pure spirits should be represented as masculine. He answers his own question by concluding that in so doing, we thereby recognize the unavowed pederasty of humankind.

If Montherlant could have conspired with fate to mold things nearer to his heart's desire, he would have changed the world or changed himself. Since he could do neither, he created and embraced a philosophy of living for which he became well known, a philosophy set forth in 1927 in an essay entitled "Syncrétisme et alternance" (Systole and Diastole). Here again we find the image of an angel as a symbol of the finer traits in one's character. Montherlant tells us that we must allow both the angel and the beast residing within us to manifest themselves in our behavior. We have the needs of a beast as well as those of an angel, and we should not deny these needs. We should give vent to both, not at the same time, of course, but alternately. There is a time for moral and intellectual concerns and a time for the claims of the flesh. According to Montherlant, it would be a healthy thing for all of us if we recognized these contradictory needs instead of denying them. By admitting to ourselves that our animal nature must be appeased, and by consciously setting out to do so, we can then calmly attend to our more reputable activities without having to be ashamed of anything we have done before and are quite likely to do again. After all, nature is responsible for the contradictions within us, as it is responsible for all the other contradictions in the world. It is therefore useless to struggle against natural impulses, however contradictory they may be. Let us yield to them and thereby experience all the wealth that life has to offer.

With this system of systole and diastole, Montherlant offered a seductive scheme for living that could and did attract numerous readers, even as it repelled many others, who were and are unwilling to admit that both good and evil have claims upon us that must be respected equally. For English readers this philosophy inevitably calls to mind the familiar Dr. Jekyll and Mr. Hyde story, in which, as we all know, Robert Louis Stevenson's hero comes to a bad end. Mr. Hyde's indiscretions eventually destroy Dr. Jekyll. But Montherlant's own indiscretions, that is to say, the hours he daily gave over to the beast within himself, did not apparently harm him. For decades he systematically divided his time between writing in the morning and early afternoon and pederastic expeditions in the late afternoon and early evening, yielding ineluctably to impulses he could not control. He did actually have numerous brushes with the law, but was never prosecuted because his fame protected him.

Montherlant was to justify and finally reconcile the angel and the beast with the publication of *The Boys* in the last few years of his life. He had started working on this book as early as 1914, took it up again in 1929, then in 1947, producing the finished version between 1965 and 1967. His play on the same subject, *The Fire That Consumes,* which was published in 1951 but not produced on the stage until 1967, is a more selective and refined version of the events that transpired in *The Boys.* Montherlant also worked on the play over many years before it finally appeared. Both the novel and the play deal with the circumstances that led to his expulsion from the École Sainte-Croix de Neuilly. His experience at Sainte-Croix, and what he felt to be an unjustified dismissal, marked him as nothing else ever would again.

The subject of *The Boys* and *The Fire That Consumes* is the love of a sixteen-year-old boy for another boy who is two years younger and attends the same school. The play treats only the emotional attachment, keeps the relationship on an extremely elevated plane, and is largely concerned with demonstrating the high-mindedness and purity of the attachment. One of the teachers, a priest, who himself loves the younger boy and is responsible for putting an end to the friendship of the two boys, as well as for the dismissal of the elder, is the only personage whose motives have a hint of impurity about them. The novel fleshes out, so to speak, what retrospectively appears to be the mere outline of a story in the play. It provides a wealth of emotional and psychological detail.

Beyond that, and of far more interest, *The Boys* paints a portrait of passion as experienced by the very young, and, moreover, by the very young of the same sex.

In 1944 Roger Peyrefitte, Montherlant's erstwhile friend and correspondent, published *Les amitiés particulières* (Special Friendships), a novel about intense friendships among adolescents in a Catholic boys' school. Montherlant was somewhat disturbed when he learned about the contents of the book because he felt that his friend had robbed him of a theme that he himself had been working on for a long time. In his *Propos secrets* Peyrefitte states that he had reproached Montherlant for not writing about pederasty, blaming him for doing nothing to further the cause that was at the very center of life and thought for both of them. Peyrefitte's *Les amitiés particulières* may well have served as a challenge to Montherlant, who knew that he could do better, and did.

The Boys is not just one more book about fun and games in a boys' school. In this novel Montherlant frees himself at last from his self-imposed restrictions. He re-creates the unisexual world that had always been his ideal. There is no transposition of sexes as there often is in his other writing and in his correspondence with Peyrefitte. He can at last talk about himself and the sex he loves best without having to pander to the requirements of a heterosexual society. The rage against women is largely gone. What is left of it is an ongoing duel of wits with a mother who wants all of her son's love and is continually frustrated by his elaborate attempts to elude her tentacular grasp. School is, for Alban de Bricoule, the young hero of *The Boys,* a private world that his mother cannot enter. His love for his young friend Serge is a deeply passionate and sexual feeling that his mother cannot share.

The love between Serge and Alban is played out against the larger background of a highly organized pederastic order known as "La Protection" (The Protectorate). Not all the pupils belong to this special order, only a select but fairly sizable number. The order consists of two groups: the protectors and their protégés. The protectors are boys from the upper division of the school, largely sixteen- and seventeen-year-olds. The protégés are selected from the lower division, where the pupils are several years younger. The protectorate has its code of conduct, consisting of rigorous rules and responsibilities. It is a new kind of chivalry from which women are necessarily excluded.

In *Le solstice de juin* the first essay, entitled "Les chevaleries" (The Knighthoods), describes the founding of a similar order by Montherlant in 1919, after his release from the army. He also alludes to a group he had belonged to at Sainte-Croix called "La Famille" (The Family), which was persecuted and finally disbanded by the administrators of the college. The Montherlant-Peyrefitte correspondence contains numerous references to "L'Ordre" (The Order), leaving no doubt whatsoever concerning its pederastic nature. The order mentioned in the correspondence is not an existing organization, but rather one which the writers have conjured up to refer to men like themselves. In *Le solstice de juin* the order manifests itself as a morally superior code of ethics; in *The Boys* it appears as a passionately exalted ideal; in the correspondence it is an excuse for self-mockery and occasional self-disgust. Once again the angel and the beast receive their tributes.

None of Montherlant's real or imaginary groups seemed able to hold together. Society was clearly not ready for them (or, alternatively, they were not ready for society). For both the author and his protagonist, Alban, the dismissal from school was an expulsion from a youthful paradise. With school days ended, where could a young man who felt isolated because of special needs go to find companionship? Two obvious possibilities are war and sports. As we know, Montherlant participated in both. His two early novels, *The Dream* and *Les olympiques,* reflect his continuing interest in the activities of the male order. Alban is the hero of *The Dream,* as well as of *The Matador*

and *The Boys.* The novels, read in the order in which they were written, do not parallel Alban's growing into maturity. If one wishes to read them in that way, one should first read *The Matador,* then *The Dream,* and finally *The Boys.* However, it is not necessary to do so. The three works may be read in any sequence without confusion or diminishment. Each narrative serves to portray a different set of masculine adventures, yet each provides a focus for the reactions of a passionate, sensitive nature in the midst of circumstances that often reflect the more coarse and brutal aspects of the masculine experience. Montherlant's evocation of the consequences of battle in *The Dream* can withstand comparisons with any similar portrayals. He reveals that war can be a source not only of horror but of plenitude as well. Alban's compassion for the wounded German soldiers arouses in him the overwhelming need to resurrect his Christian impulses. He prays for his own lost friend, who may also be wounded and abandoned in some unknown battlefield. As he prays he forgets himself, and in so doing, the years of painful exile from the profoundly shared experience of the protectorate are obliterated.

In *The Dream* Montherlant mixes war, love, and sports in a curiously bisexual manner, introducing that which was, in the 1920's, a new phenomenon: the athletic female. Later on, in *Les olympiques,* he designates the women who participate seriously in sports as persons belonging to a new sex because their appearance differs radically from that of other females. Alban is attracted to two young women. The more feminine of the two satisfies his sexual requirements, while the other, who is boyish-looking and athletic, fulfills his emotional and spiritual needs. For once, Montherlant's hero does not express contempt for the woman he takes to bed, as Costals does afterward, indefatigably, in *The Girls.* Alban expresses only gratitude toward Douce for calming his body's desires. He reserves his more complex intellectual demands for the athletic and virginal

Dominique. He loves her but refuses her body when she offers it to him. To touch her would be to defile her purity. What is odd here is that Montherlant also regarded adolescent boys, those who had not yet sprouted a beard, as a sort of third sex. Yet, as we know through Montherlant's letters to Peyrefitte, he relentlessly sought out this so-called other sex for both emotional and carnal satisfaction. What the author has done in *The Dream* is to personify, in the characters of Douce and Dominique, the dual nature of his own concept of desire: sexual attraction to the feminine aspect of humanity and idealized love for the boyish, that which is neither wholly male nor female.

According to Montherlant, the athletic world can liberate us from the trap of sexual stereotypes. It can cleanse us of the impurities that cling to our own sexual and social identities. In *Les olympiques* he issues a clarion call to youth to come and purify itself in the sports stadium. In his opinion, physical training produces its most astonishing results in the bodies of women. He describes what a revelation it was for him when for the first time he laid eyes on a group of girls who had undergone athletic training. He had never seen women who looked like that and did not even know that it was possible for them to resemble anything other than the vain coquettes he had been accustomed to encountering in daily life. These women athletes, as representatives of a new sex, are not regarded by Montherlant as inferiors. In dealing with them, he feels he is dealing with equals. He also notes with wonder and awe that in a sports club it is possible for the male and female members to actually become friends. They can experience a pure camaraderie that has nothing to do with physical desire. Montherlant states that men have carefully avoided familiarity with women. They have wanted women to remain mysterious because to take away the mystery would be to endanger the propagation of the species. Montherlant believes that this attitude is wrong and that women who accept it do so because they have no confidence in themselves.

On the theme of equality, Montherlant makes the subversive statement that not only sexual but also class distinctions cease to matter on the playing fields. It did not trouble Montherlant, the son of a count, to engage in a sport with the son of his concierge. His readers, however, were troubled and even shocked by his defiance of class differences and also by what they perceived to be his immodest portrayals of athletes. Television has accustomed us to the sight of grunting, sweating, half-naked athletes of both sexes. We are also indifferent to the class origins of these same athletes, as they are themselves. But all this was new to the French public of the 1920's. Montherlant was openly criticized in the newspapers for his lack of propriety. He was incensed by these criticisms, not just because of their narrow-mindedness, but also because he felt that his countrymen had been entirely too quick to forget, with regard to the class problem, that the sons of the peasantry and the proletariat fought side by side with the sons of the aristocracy and the bourgeoisie in World War I, and that both of the latter groups had been more than happy to have the assistance of their humbler brethren.

Pierre Sipriot in his *Montherlant sans masque* (Montherlant Unmasked, 1982) gives an extraordinary assessment of the influence that *Les olympiques* had upon the development of youth movements, beginning with the decade of its publication and carrying through to the student uprisings of the 1960's. By emphasizing sports, Montherlant also emphasized youth. Everyone recognizes that high achievement in sports is normally reserved for the young. Except for rare instances, the elderly are disqualified. As the elders proved to be inept in sports, the young came to think of them as incompetent in other matters. Little did the students who were barricading the Quai Voltaire in Paris during the revolt of May 1968 realize, according to Sipriot, that the old man who could not get past them to reach his apartment was one of those whose writings had helped to make their movement possible.

One movement that Montherlant might have helped to advance, but consciously did not, was that of anticolonialism. In his novel *La rose de sable* Montherlant was openly opposed to French colonialist activities in North Africa. Yet he chose not to publish this work because, as he later claimed, he did not wish to be critical of his country at a time when it was being threatened by fascist governments. He had begun the narrative in 1930 in Algiers. After spending two long, hard years on it, he returned to France with the intention of publishing it. But in view of existing political conditions, he thought better of it and set the manuscript aside. During the next few years he published extracts from the novel in various periodicals. *La rose de sable* appeared in 1938 in a limited, noncommercial edition of sixty-five copies that were distributed to friends in France and other countries, doubtless to safeguard the book in the very likely event of war. This edition was published with another title, *Mission providentielle* (Providential Mission), and under the pseudonym of François Lazerge. The part of the novel containing the love story between the young officer Auligny and Ram, the Arab girl, was published separately in 1954 and was entitled *L'Histoire d'amour de "La rose de sable"* (translated as *Desert Love*). The complete story, with its original title, was finally issued in a deluxe edition in 1967 and in an edition available to the public at large in 1968, just four years before Montherlant's death and at a time when France no longer had any colonies in North Africa.

The appearance of *La rose de sable* in its entirety provoked a heated critical debate. Certain critics felt that the book should have been published when it was first written in order to alert the French people to what was really going on in North Africa. As an eyewitness to the mistreatment and exploitation of the Arabs, Montherlant could have played a valuable role in the awakening of a national conscience.

Some critics, assuming a more practical attitude, pointed out that by refusing to publish the book in the early 1930's, Montherlant did a disservice to both his fame and his purse by not making his voice heard on what was then a highly topical subject. Other critics defended him for not taking advantage of a burning contemporary issue in order to advance his literary career. His disinterestedness was applauded on the one hand, while his unwillingness to oppose his country's official policy was considered regrettable. Was the author a patriot or a coward? The critics still disagree. In treating the issue of whether a literary work is to be regarded as a work of art or a political act, Montherlant pointed out that both motives influence writing, but that works created primarily as political acts run the very serious risk of being mistaken in their assumptions and of being quickly forgotten. To further bolster his own position Montherlant referred to a critic who had stated unequivocally that an author has the right to publish his own work whenever he chooses and that no one else can make that decision for him. With that pronouncement one should consider the question closed.

La rose de sable is far from being just a protest against French colonialism. It is a novel about parents and children, masters and servants, soldiers and civilians, lovers and beloved, art and life. Montherlant's narrative contains many moving figures, changes of scenery, and significant shifts in moral perspective. Here for the first and only time the author moves away from the narrower focus of his other novels. We journey with Auligny from France, the mother country, to the cities and desert outposts of the colonies. We also follow the young lieutenant in his inner journey of spiritual transformation. At the outset of the novel Auligny believes wholeheartedly in the civilizing mission of France. He is represented as an average young man from a bourgeois family, a person who never questions anything and always tries to do what is expected of him, insofar as his mediocre abilities permit. During the early part of his sojourn in Morocco, he accepts the French opinion that Arabs are childlike inferiors who must be treated as such, regardless of their age or situation in life. As the narrative evolves, Auligny's attitude toward the Arabs is gradually modified until he finally comes to love them, ultimately refusing to take up arms against them.

Auligny's love for an Arab girl helps to render him more sensitive to the debasement of the Arabs by their French masters. The love story serves as a vital link between the affective and political awakenings in the novel. However, the relationship between Auligny and his Arab mistress is, as always in Montherlant's writings, an unusual one. The girl is fourteen years old. She is called Rahma, but as soon as Auligny learns her name, he changes it to the more masculine Ram. Her physical appearance is that of an early adolescent. This places her in the category of that other, or third, sex that Montherlant found so delightful. Once again we come upon an example of what appears to be sexual transposition. It was not the custom in North Africa for girls living with their families, as was the case with Ram, to agree to become any man's mistress. Prostitutes, who lived on the fringes of society, were the only women who would sell themselves. Early on in the novel, in discussing bedouin poetry, Montherlant informs us that in certain regions of North Africa, especially Tunisia and Morocco, women were considered necessary only for reproductive purposes, and that all sentimental feelings among Arab men were reserved for young boys. As Auligny's affection for Ram deepens and becomes more complex, he begins to realize that he relates to her not just as a lover but also as a father. He likes the fact that she is not his equal and that she is still a child. He concludes that when Arab men do manage to care for women, they are actually attracted to the child in them. Children are for the Arabs a third sex. This is the sex they really love. That, according to Montherlant, explains why Moslem brides are often extremely young and why, once married, they are treated mor-

ally and legally as children in the home and in society.

Since Moslem women are regarded as property, Auligny, in a fraternal gesture, offers Ram to his friend Guiscart, who out of perverseness refuses to take advantage of the lieutenant's magnanimity. Guiscart, a painter, is a precursor of the writer Costals in *The Girls,* with many of the same habits and attitudes. He, too, stalks the streets in search of women, with the same compulsive feelings of attraction and repulsion toward them. Guiscart's opinion of the women he goes to bed with is succinctly and devastatingly summarized in the following words: "Formerly, I only hated them afterward. Now I hate them before, during, and after." Guiscart is represented ironically, as is Costals. But their words draw blood nonetheless. The compassion expressed in *La rose de sable* for the condition of the Arabs does not even remotely extend itself to women, who must be bludgeoned, in one way or another (in this case by Guiscart), whether they need it or not.

The only one of Montherlant's novels having nothing to do with women is *The Bachelors,* which is probably his best. Here we have a simple story, remarkable for its unity of structure and harmony of tone. There are no discordant notes to irritate either the reader or writer. For Montherlant, to introduce women into a narrative is to introduce disharmony. In *The Bachelors* there is no need for women, because it is a tale of three men who have never known what to do with them. The bachelors, two brothers and their nephew, are among the last representatives of a noble caste, unable to adapt to the modern world. Although one brother, Octave, is wealthy and the other brother, Elie, and the nephew, Léon, are poor, all three are misfits. Octave has money by mere chance, not ability. Less fortunate than Octave, Elie and Léon are misfits of the most helpless variety imaginable. They are not only incapable of working to support themselves; they are incapable of any sustained activity whatsoever. They cannot survive without regular material assistance. The younger, Léon, who is still physically capable of helping himself, is morally unable to do so and dies as a result of abandonment and neglect.

What on the surface appears to be the story of three grown men caught in the machinery of a changing society is actually a tale of three children who never matured mentally, emotionally, or sexually. This is the tragedy of children trapped in aging bodies, of the needs, desires, and outlook of the third sex blocked and frustrated by the suffocating mask of the years. *The Bachelors* is an elegy dedicated to all the unadaptable souls whose very existence society is loath to acknowledge. In this novel Montherlant, the champion of machismo, has shown a compassion for human frailty that has scarcely been equaled in western literature.

Throughout Montherlant's writings we discern, either alternately or side by side, the themes of weakness and of strength, of the call to life and the call to death. We find perhaps the best illustration of the workings of these themes in juxtaposing his early novel *The Matador* with one of his late novels, *Chaos and Night*. The highlight of each of these narratives is a scene in the bullring. *The Matador* recounts the adventures of the young Alban de Bricoule during the summer before he enrolls at the École Notre-Dame du Parc, the school in *The Boys*. He goes to Spain because of his love for bulls, manages to acquire some training in the art of bullfighting, and is actually invited to enter the ring and take on a bull or two, including a particularly nasty one known as "the bad angel." Out of youthful pride and high spirits, and despite his very real fear, Alban accepts the invitation, prepared to do his best. By taking on this most virile of challenges, he hopes to affirm his manhood publicly. His performance in the ring is insufficient until he confronts "the bad angel." Despite his inexperience, Alban succeeds in outdoing himself. His triumph over the dangerous beast is the author's tribute to youth, to courage, and to life.

Montherlant writes in *Chaos and Night* that life and death exist side by side, but are oblivious to one another. But, at the inevitable moment of recognition, each is perceived by the other as some sort of joke. In the bullring, life and death coexist in a spectacular manner that is evident to all. Both participants and spectators wait to see which one will make a mockery of the other. When the elderly Celestino, the central personage in *Chaos and Night*, goes back to Spain and sees his first bullfight in twenty years, he finds to his horror that his perceptions have changed completely. For him a bullfight is no longer a demonstration of virile mastery or of an exuberant life force; it has become an ineluctable dance of death. Celestino sees the bull as a victim. The role assigned to the animal is that of dupe. The bull who is thrust into the arena is like a man who is thrust into life. Both can be dangerous, yet both are helpless in the face of unavoidable death. Bull and man have become interchangeable for Celestino. His pity for the bull's fate and for his own, since Celestino knows that he is old and will soon die, overwhelms him to the point that he is obliged to leave the stands before the performance is over. He returns to his hotel room in Madrid to engage in his own final struggle with death.

Celestino is an exile from the Spanish Civil War who spends the last twenty years of his life in Paris, seeing only his daughter and other Spanish friends, never participating in any aspect of French life. He is an exile in every respect. He exists as though he were suspended in time, constantly reliving the war and maintaining a pugnacious attitude toward all things, even to the point of flinging regular challenges to the pigeons and to automobiles in the streets. The one forward movement in his life is the inexorable aging process. *Chaos and Night* is, in fact, a novel about old age and death. Celestino is sixty-seven, approximately the same age as Montherlant as he wrote the novel. At that time in his life Montherlant was becoming more and more aware of his infirmities, as was Celestino. The latter lives with a daughter who is growing older and more distant. He feels that he can no longer depend on her to provide the care he will eventually need.

He therefore arranges to have a storeroom in his apartment remodeled into a bedroom for the nurse whose services he may require at any moment. He refers to it as the bedchamber of his fiancée, the fiancée being none other than death.

From this point onward Celestino is caught between the horror of living and the horror of dying. He can speak to no one about his fears because he is aware that the subject of death is a taboo in France. At this juncture the author expresses immense pity for all the elderly, whom nature has condemned to imminent death, and who, like his hero, must bear this intolerable burden alone. Celestino sinks slowly, silently toward the abyss. He is recalled from the brink of the precipice by a telegram announcing the death of his sister in Madrid. He is invited by his brother-in-law to go back there to claim his inheritance. Celestino is well aware that, as a former member of the Republican army, he will run a serious risk by returning to a Spain still ruled by Franco. Despite the risk, he elects to travel to his homeland, even though his presence there is not indispensable. He is afraid, but since he lives in a constant state of fear anyway, he feels he has nothing to lose. Realizing that there are two types of fear, one good and one bad, Celestino chooses the good fear that is born of audacity rather than the bad one stemming from passivity. The good fear has a galvanizing effect on him. It makes him feel young again and thereby helps to keep death at bay.

By returning to Spain, Celestino does in fact shorten his days. As he had feared, the police do indeed come to arrest him, but they find him in his hotel room, already dead. Celestino dies because the Spain he remembered no longer exists: the cause he fought for has gone up in smoke; even the bullring has become merely a place of meaningless sacrifice. There is nothing left for him but to die as the bull dies, to go directly from chaos into night.

With Celestino, Montherlant depicts one more character who cannot adapt to existing conditions. In his last novel, *Un assassin est mon maître,* the hero, Exupère, does make an attempt to understand himself through the culture of his day. But this effort at what would now be called self-help involves him in concepts that he only partly understands and therefore misuses to his own detriment and eventual destruction. Exupère's manual for self-knowledge is Freud's *A General Introduction to Psychoanalysis* (1910). In describing his hero's reaction to this book, Montherlant embarks on a delightfully ironic portrayal of the uses and abuses of psychoanalysis. Freud's celebrated work is a revelation for Exupère; it changes his life completely. He has the book rebound and takes it everywhere with him. It becomes, in effect, his bible. Exupère goes so far as to refuse to read any other book on the subject of psychoanalysis because to do so would be a profanation.

How does Exupère come to read *A General Introduction to Psychoanalysis* in the first place? In relating the background to his character's obsession, Montherlant seems to take a good deal of satisfaction in pointing out the weaknesses of a society that encourages dependence and discourages individuals from developing the virtues of self-reliance. At the outbreak of World War I, Exupère is of an age to be called into military service. He is a timorous soul who feels no patriotic enthusiasm and no particular interest in humanity. He cares about his books and his eventual career and determines to do his utmost to avoid the army. Aware that there is nothing physically wrong with him, he feels that it will be difficult to feign illness. However, it strikes him that he did have a few little nervous habits. Therefore, he hits upon the notion of a possible nervous illness and goes to a fashionable psychiatrist for an official diagnosis. The psychiatrist examines his patient, lets drop a few significant words such as "hyperemotionalism" and "paranoia," then obligingly signs a certificate that will exempt Exupère from military service.

Now that Exupère's mental state has been professionally diagnosed and named for all the world to see, he becomes attracted to the idea of psychoanalysis and actually ends up believing in the disorder that he has invented. Freud's *General Introduction to Psychoanalysis* confirms him in his obsession. Exupère decides that he, too, should be psychoanalyzed, but he is uncertain as to how to go about it. He worries over the fact that he never dreams and will therefore have no dreams to describe to a potential analyst, who will naturally expect him to do so. Furthermore, Exupère has never been in love with his mother and can dredge up no trace of hostility whatever toward his father. With no dreams and no Oedipus complex, what can he possibly find to speak of on an analyst's couch? Even if he could think of something, he has no money to pay for the treatment. He carefully broaches the subject with his mother, who categorically refuses to give him a centime. She is not about to pay some stranger to listen to her son ramble on about indecent things. This refusal confirms his suspicion that he hates his mother, and so he learns something definite about himself after all, without even having to go near an analyst's office. Besides, he has his precious volume of Freud to consult whenever he needs to know about the inner workings of his psyche.

Having read about the strong link between attraction and repulsion, Exupère decides to go to Algeria to work as a librarian because he hates that country. Thinking that there must be a subconscious reason for that hatred, he moves heaven and earth to get there in order to find out what that reason might be. Once again he goes to see a doctor, and has himself diagnosed as pretubercular. As such he must be transferred from his post in Paris to a job in a warmer climate. Another roundabout reason for going to Algeria is that Exupère is sexually attracted to Jewish women, but is at the same time anti-Semitic. Having heard that there are a lot of Jewish women in that colony, he feels that it would be easier for him to satisfy his libido in French territory rather than in some alien land farther east.

Exupère succeeds in obtaining a position as archivist at a library in Oran. Arriving on the continent of Africa with his precious volume of Freud in his suitcase, he notes that the place is just as bad as he feared it would be. Almost immediately, he does everything possible to be transferred to another library, in Algiers, a much larger, more interesting city than the provincial Oran. Once again he obtains a transfer; once again he hates the place he has so eagerly solicited. Everyone and everything disappoints Exupère, including the Jewish women, who are neither so available nor so desirable as he has hoped. We follow the unfortunate protagonist as he gradually disintegrates, mentally and emotionally, in the face of his colleagues, his social connections, and his own conflicting desires. The ghastly Algerian summer as experienced by Exupère becomes a metaphor for inactivity, inadaptation, and a total inability to come to terms with his life.

In a last violent spurt of energy, he begs to be sent back to France. Algeria has become unbearable. If he stays there, he knows he will die. His request is granted, on the condition that he will agree to report to a hospital in France before assuming his new post. As the boat taking him back to France pulls away from the shore, Exupère, characteristically, no longer wishes to leave. Now that he is not obliged to stay there, he truly believes that he has been happy in Algiers. As the sound of the ship's siren bursts out above the water, Exupère screams wildly along with it, in one long cry heard by no one else at all. He knows that he will never be able to resolve the contradictions within himself and that he is sailing toward his own ultimate self-destruction.

Montherlant expressed over and over again in his writings the belief that people are full of contradictory impulses and that each of us is made up of many different selves that are often, if not always, in contradiction with one another. He illustrates this so thoroughly that the contrary impulses described in some of his characters often turn into a kind of predictable monomania. Such individuals as Costals and

Guiscart are so obsessed with their internal contradictions that they develop into caricatures of their own contrariness.

This notion of the conflicting selves has held a prominent place in Montherlant's theater. Yet, on examining the plays, one is struck less by a sense of inner conflict and much more by the prevalence of idées fixes that seem to function as the real motivating force in the conduct of the principal personages. They appear to be settled into a type of rigidity that cannot (and will not) modify itself, regardless of the disastrous consequences. The tragedy, when there is one, does not arise from the antagonism between the different aspects of the self, but rather from the fact that the self must be true to its contradictions at all costs. A character will sacrifice not only others but also, and primarily, himself in order to avoid an unconflicted decision. The two most interesting works from this point of view are *Pasiphaé* and *Don Juan* (1958). These have never been ranked among Montherlant's better plays. Beginning in 1942 and for more than a quarter of a century, his widespread celebrity as a playwright was built upon such stately, classical productions as *Queen After Death, The Master of Santiago, Le cardinal d'Espagne* (The Spanish Cardinal, 1960), and *Port-Royal.* These plays have a somewhat static grandiloquence for contemporary audiences, whereas *Pasiphaé* and *Don Juan* provide more stimulating experiences. Montherlant himself stated that one day *Don Juan* would be considered his best play. That day has not yet arrived, but one can certainly present a good case for the work.

Don Juan is a wry, sardonic elaboration of a very private joke that Montherlant, the closet pederast, was playing upon a heterosexual audience. It made no sense to Parisian spectators, who came to view one more example of the theater of grandeur. What they saw instead was the seamy underside of one of the great western myths. Here the adventures of that most fabulous of seducers are paced not to the echoes of Mozartean strains, but rather to the thud of falling chamber pots. Montherlant's Don Juan is old, broken-down, and touchingly pathetic. He knows that he is getting to be too decrepit to walk the streets in search of the next sexual adventure, which, if he can only manage to hold on, might be just around the corner. The subtitle that Montherlant gave to the play is "La mort qui fait le trottoir" (Death Who Walks the Streets). Don Juan, the great lover, has become an old prostitute whose ultimate client is death. In the face of certain destruction the hero remains true to his obsession.

In *Pasiphaé* Montherlant takes on another myth, this time from the ancient world, to treat a subject of personal fascination: the bull. Pasiphaé's sexual obsession (the term actually occurs in one of her speeches) with a forbidden love object is also a public enactment of the author's covert longings. The heroine's debilitating struggle against an uncontrollable desire takes on a tragic resonance when we recognize that her words apply to all those who cannot conform to the sexual mores and habits of the world around them. She asks why it is that a woman is supposed to love men only. Who imposed such limitations? Where were the so-called rules written down? As the daughter of the Sun, Pasiphaé knows that she is an exceptional person and should not, therefore, be bound to love as others do. She does not herself believe that it is wrong to love a bull, but she fears the horror in the faces of the persons who might find out about her amorous activities. She envies the fact that women with normal desires can express their sentiments openly, without fear of evil tongues. Even the woman who is in love with the worst of reprobates need not be ashamed of her feelings. Yet Pasiphaé would not, even if she could, confine herself to the platitudinous amours that would be acceptable to her society. Recognizing the fact that she is different, she wallows in that difference, despite the certainty that it will consume her.

Both Pasiphaé and Don Juan persist in their

obsessions and accept the dangers that such conduct inevitably courts. Exposure is not the only danger. Isolation—the temptation to retreat from the world—is another. The mad queen in *Le cardinal d'Espagne* is the most extreme of Montherlant's characters in this regard. She renounces the world entirely because of an obsessive love for her dead husband. Her erotic deprivation is so intense that she denies every other bodily need as well. She lives in seclusion and extreme discomfort, unwilling to wash, eating like an animal, refusing every action or reaction that might recall her to a life that has no meaning for her. She has a son, but will not emerge from seclusion to see him. All that which is not obsession does not exist, not even children, the blood of our blood. Children in Montherlant's plays often serve as objects to be obliterated when they stand in the way of a personal conflict. In *Queen After Death* a dying king puts to death an undesirable daughter-in-law, pregnant with his grandchild, for reasons of state. The king knows that he is dying and that, therefore, those same reasons of state will soon be pointless. Despite, or perhaps because of this contradiction, the young woman and the fetus are destroyed.

Another child is sacrificed to her father's rigid requirements in *The Master of Santiago.* A son is emotionally abandoned in *Fils de personne* (No Man's Son, 1943), then indirectly sent to his death in the sequel, *Demain il fera jour* (Tomorrow Is Another Day, translated as *Tomorrow the Dawn*, 1949), by a father who cannot reconcile the needs of his ego with the demands of paternity. Children are used, abused, and ultimately denied. Alvaro, in *The Master of Santiago,* refers to his daughter as a being who only exists because of one of his moments of weakness. In *Queen After Death* the old king, Ferrante, gives utterance to thoughts that are echoed both in *No Man's Son* and, later on, in *Chaos and Night.* We find reiterated in these three works the conviction that our children are everything to us until their early teens, at which time they inevitably begin to disappoint us and go on to become our enemies. The implication, most pointedly expressed by Ferrante, is that our children will destroy us unless we destroy them first. Here we find again the continuing theme of the delightful young child or adolescent who is pleasing because he or she seems to belong to a third, nonthreatening sex. Once the child reaches physical maturity, with clearly defined sexual characteristics, he or she becomes an unworthy and menacing object, to be mistrusted, avoided, and somehow neutralized.

The dangers that can befall posterity are set forth in a seriocomic vein in Montherlant's play *Brocéliande* (1956). Here the author focuses on a character, Persilès, who is mediocre in every respect. In his late fifties he learns that he is a descendant of King Louis IX, or Saint Louis. Once Persilès discovers that in his veins flows the blood of one of France's most famous kings, his conduct toward others begins to change. He takes on a royal manner that is simultaneously amusing and irritating. The knowledge of a remote royal paternity stretching back over seven hundred years confers upon Persilès a sense of importance he has never before experienced. He feels that he has been elevated above the common herd. Unfortunately for him, his condescending attitude also extends to his wife, who finds his pretensions unbearable. She avenges herself by letting her husband know that he is not, as he thinks, unique. He is only one of about fifteen thousand other descendants of the great Saint Louis. Thrust rudely back into mediocrity, Persilès commits suicide, preferring death to faceless anonymity. In this play the principal character is both uplifted and destroyed by a very distant father. It would have been far better for him to have been fatherless, like the boy in *No Man's Son.* In that play the father is disappointed by the mediocrity of his offspring. In *Brocéliande* Persilès is cast down by the mediocrity of his ancestry. It appears that antagonism between generations cannot be avoided.

The root cause is probably procreation itself. The father in *No Man's Son,* Georges Carrion, reproaches his son, Gillou, for being the son of woman. For Georges, this means that the boy has been contaminated by his mother's weakness. Because he has been reared by a woman, Gillou does not measure up to his father's ideals. Georges proceeds to distance himself from a son who is unworthy of him. He also contrives to discredit the boy's mother by accusing her of putting her own interests ahead of her son's. Gillou now belongs to no one. This play is an oblique reproach to nature for having conferred upon women the honor and burden of perpetuating the human race. Montherlant seems to be asking, in the manner of Pasiphaé, where it is written that human beings can reproduce themselves in only one way. Like Alvaro in *The Master of Santiago,* Montherlant feels that commerce with woman is a momentary weakness that nature imposes upon man. By accepting the sacrifice of her woman's life to join him in his retreat from the world (he to a monastery and she to a convent), Alvaro sees to it that his daughter will not repeat his own moment of sexual weakness. In *Queen After Death* the king has put to death the woman who is bearing his son's child. Man's dependence on woman must be combated. Her importance must be negated. Her very existence must be questioned and, when possible, obliterated.

Montherlant does all of these things most extensively and thoroughly in *The Girls.* With respect to the specific matter of procreation, Costals poses conditions to his prospective fiancée that are virtually unthinkable for a civilized person. He will marry Solange only if she agrees not to have children. If she should become pregnant, she must consent to an abortion. If she should allow the fetus to come to term, she must be a party to infanticide. To the horror of Costals and of the reader and, one suspects, to the hidden amusement of the author, that degenerate young woman consents to all conditions without blinking an eye. Costals thereby reaffirms the wretched inferiority of women, who will do anything—even become accomplices to unspeakable crimes—in order to get men to marry them. John Cruickshank in

his book *Montherlant* (1964) states that however irritating his views on women may be, "their value (and therefore their defense) lies in the fact that they boldly express what most men feel on occasions but normally try to conceal from themselves as well as from others. . . . It is because his readers find his revelations uncomfortably true that they react so violently against them."

This aspect of uncomfortable truth may perhaps enter into the reaction of male readers, but it scarcely accounts for the reaction of female readers. Their anger is aroused because whenever he writes about women, the author is transformed into a raving monomaniac who pretends to sit in judgment upon a lesser breed. Women are outraged because a self-appointed demiurge wishes to eliminate them from his universe. Montherlant tries to keep himself from being ripped to pieces by a female audience, which he has single-handedly transformed into a host of furies, by throwing them a bone to gnaw on in the final pages of *The Lepers,* the fourth and last novel of the tetralogy. Here Costals, in one of his usual contradictory postures, realizing that he has gone too far in his prolonged vituperations, turns around and states that he is just as capable of defending women as he is of denouncing them. But the furies were not deceived. They still smelled blood and were unwilling to abandon their prey. Simone de Beauvoir, in *Le deuxième sexe* (*The Second Sex,* 1949), includes a chapter on Montherlant that rakes him over the coals in no uncertain terms. What Montherlant could not do to defend himself against the righteous anger of women, his friend, Roger Peyrefitte, and his biographer, Pierre Sipriot, did for him. An attitude that is unforgivable in a heterosexual male can be accepted, given what we now know about Montherlant's sexuality, in a spirit of comprehension and even compassion. The author's rage against women was never meant for them; it was meant for himself.

Montherlant was a maverick, a loner, belonging to no school, completely outside the main currents of twentieth-century literature.

Some of his works were considered subversive, others conventional, some scandalous, others respectable. The bourgeois public applauded his theater when it set forth grandiose themes and stately characters. Such plays also found favor because they continued a classical tradition, a source of pride to the French, who needed to hold their heads a bit higher during the difficult years of the German occupation and the postwar period. The comic plays were failures because of their all-too-common touch. According to his biographer Henri Perruchot, Montherlant's timing was always wrong. His books usually appeared when the subject they treated was felt to be passé. He published *The Dream,* a novel dealing largely with World War I, in 1922, when everyone was tired of the war. He refused to publish *La rose de sable* at a time when it might have interested his public. He wrote *L'Equinoxe de septembre,* a document in favor of war with Germany, in a year when everyone was clamoring for peace. His *Le solstice de juin,* which was not favorable to the Vichy government, appeared at the very moment when that government was fully entrenched. He wrote a play about Don Juan when the theme was considered old hat. Moreover, Montherlant's writings give no indication whatever that such movements as Dada, surrealism, existentialism, or any other "ism" ever took place.

Despite this unfortunate sense of timing, which seems to have put off critics and readers alike, Montherlant was nonetheless an extraordinarily popular and successful writer. Not only was *The Girls* a best-seller, but over three million paperback copies of his books were sold in his lifetime. One must conclude, therefore, that his timing was sometimes right. *Les olympiques* appeared when sports were becoming popular and the Olympic Games were beginning to attract worldwide attention. *The Girls,* by focusing on women for good or ill, obliged a nation that had not yet granted women the vote to give some thought to the status of a good half of its population.

Montherlant also taught a generation caught between the horrors of two world wars that life was the only thing that matters and that it must be experienced to the fullest. He claimed that a richly expressed sensuality was good and should require no apologies. He believed that everyone was right, always, and that we should strive to accept others, accept ourselves, accept the arbitrariness and variability of human existence. These ideas, which constitute an art of living, are found repeatedly throughout Montherlant's writings. The reader can also find in his work what can only be called an art of dying. For Montherlant it is equally important for an individual to learn how to approach life and how and when to approach death. Although it is inevitable, death need not be met passively. The author tells us that we can issue a challenge to death; we can choose the weapons and the ground where our meeting with death shall occur. When life becomes impossible, we can decide how to escape from it. It is preferable for the decision to be a conscious one, as it was for Persilès, but an unconscious one will serve the purpose almost as well. For example, Auligny, by espousing the cause of the Arabs, follows his own path to annihilation, as does Celestino by returning to his native Spain.

Montherlant carefully selected his own time and place for quitting the arena. He put an end to his life after leaving a short note to his heir and legal executor, Jean-Claude Barat, in which he stated in the simplest possible language: "Je deviens aveugle. Je me tue" (I am going blind. I am going to kill myself). Montherlant's close friend Gabriel Matzneff wrote in an article in the Paris newspaper *Le monde* dated 3 September 1982, almost exactly ten years after the author's suicide, that Montherlant had always had a real horror of being helpless and dependent. He had often told Matzneff that he did not want to become a vegetable in his old age. He was incapable of imagining himself blind and in a wheelchair. Indeed, he saw to it that he would never reach that state.

Whatever we may think of suicide, we cannot help but respect the decision made by a seventy-seven-year-old man at four o'clock in the afternoon during the September equinox.

We know where Montherlant's ashes have been scattered, but what has become of his literary remains since 1972? Montherlant himself did not believe that his work would survive him. Toward the end of his life, he was aware that young people were no longer reading his books. His last four novels, all written along traditional narrative lines, appeared at a time when the *nouveau roman* (new novel) was in full swing. Once again he remained outside contemporary trends. According to Pierre de Boisdeffre, in an article appearing in *Le monde* on 2 September 1973, a year after the author's suicide, Montherlant believed that a certain set of conditions was necessary to maintain a writer's reputation after his death. First of all, the writer had to be supported by a powerful literary coterie. Second, he had to have the backing of the Sorbonne and of literary historians. Last but not least, for a work to remain in the public eye, the author had to have heirs who were simultaneously greedy and socially well connected. Montherlant was aware that not even one of these conditions would operate in his favor.

His fears have proved justified. Montherlant is best known both in France and elsewhere for a few of his plays, for some random notions gleaned from his essays, and for little else, with the possible exception of *The Bachelors* and *The Girls.* He has been omitted from university reading lists and neglected by contemporary literary critics and by recent historians of twentieth-century literature. Known largely for his misogyny, he is detested by feminists and often cast aside by academics of both sexes, who feel uncomfortable with regard to his virulent opinions and his unabashed espousal of a dubious sexual hedonism. It is true that Montherlant annoys, angers, and irritates his readers, not just by scattered remarks, but often throughout long passages and repeti-

tively, to the point of exasperation and even violent outrage. We must agree with Cruickshank, who finds the effect of Montherlant upon his readers to be "bracing and disturbing." He forces us to react to those aspects of his work that make us uncomfortable and to think about our reasons for feeling that way. We are so often troubled by what he says that we continue to read and to reflect on what we have read in the hope of finding answers to the questions he has raised. More importantly, we are challenged to find answers to the responses that his questions have drawn out of us. The interaction between Montherlant and his readers can be intense, unsettling, and at times unrelenting. He is the writer we love to hate and hate to love. Montherlant's mastery of his craft is an impressive example of the triumph of art over life. He deliberately persists in antagonizing us. We pull away in an attempt to disassociate ourselves from this troublesome, cantankerous writer with whom we appear to have little in common, when suddenly we are plunged back into a scene that overwhelms us with its poignancy and profound humanity. Our hostility fades away and we yield, in spite of ourselves, to the spell of an artist who knows how to make us savor the inconsistencies of creation.

For example, both the opening and closing pages of *The Dream* distress us by the boundless arrogance, not to mention bad taste, displayed toward women. Alban's placid mistress, Douce, is scarcely more than an animal for the cocky young hero. After a night of love, he refuses to wash his hands so that he may carry away with him, on the train that takes him off to war, the intimate scent of the cowlike creature he has left behind. Douce never appears in the narrative. All we know of her is that she completely fulfills Alban's sexual needs and makes no other demands on him. Dominique, his intellectual love, does make demands on him by asking for more than he is willing to give. He sacrifices her to his own questionable sense of purity. The young man rationalizes this sacrifice in the most appalling manner. He believes that by withholding himself physically from this woman who desires him, he is acting as the instrument of some kind of large-scale justice. Firmly convinced that the only kind of suffering that is worthwhile is physical suffering, he feels it is only right that those who have been spared this agony, such as women, who do not go into battle, must somehow redress the balance through some type of spiritual anguish. It is possible that God exacts a certain amount of suffering from His creatures. Therefore, by inflicting pain on Dominique, Alban may well have spared someone worth far more than she, that is to say, a soldier, any soldier at all.

Montherlant's hero has managed to convince himself that in dumping an old girlfriend, he is carrying out a divine mission. As readers, we can only regard this as megalomania. Yet sandwiched between these perplexing extravagances we find beautifully eloquent pages on the comradeship arising between men in time of war and deeply moving descriptions of the wounded, the dying, and the dead as they are brought back from the field of battle. Most stirring of all are the passages dealing with the wounded German prisoners. Montherlant makes us see and feel the horror experienced by Alban when he discovers that vital treatment is deliberately being withheld from the suffering Germans by their French captors. He speaks to a French doctor in the hope of drawing the latter's attention to the plight of the wounded enemy soldiers. The doctor stares in seeming incomprehension, then bursts out laughing, after which he tells the young man to mind his own business. Alban, aware at that moment that mankind is his business, heads directly into the crowd of wounded Germans to see if there is anything at all he can do to assist them in their utter abandonment. But there is, in fact, very little he can do. He has no medicines, no food or water, nothing to give but his compassion. He manages to prop up the dangling heads of one or two men who have been thrown onto stretchers every which way. One helpless prisoner tries to give Alban a gold ring from his finger in order to pay for an assistance that the young Frenchman is powerless to provide. What he does do for a dying soldier is to take down his name and address, promising to write to his mother in Germany to inform her of her son's death. Alban clasps the prisoner's hand, transmitting thereby a last bit of human warmth. When Alban tries to withdraw his hand, the young German clings to it with all that remains of strength and life, begging not to be abandoned. Crazed by sudden fear of the dying man, Alban wrenches himself free of that macabre grasp and walks away. On turning back for a last look, he can see that the young German is weeping.

At this juncture, Montherlant, his hero, and his audience have become one in their pity for the helpless, senseless misery of this world. This moment of communion is a profound one for the reader. Yet once again, Montherlant's real pity seems to be reserved for men only; women need not apply. However much we may be troubled by this attitude, we continue onward in fascination through the alternately moving and exasperating riches of the Montherlantian universe. We review Celestino's last colorful and sonorous fantasy about the loudspeakers of death; the flight of the geese toward a warm and beckoning light, as seen through the dying eyes of Léon de Coantré; the ailing Madame de Bricoule's bitter knowledge that her relationship with her son has been her greatest failure. Such gripping scenes as these, as well as Celestino's humorous jousting with pigeons and automobiles, Alban's helplessly amusing quest for a ticket to a bullfight, Costals' quixotic cavalcade through Paris in search of a not-too-repulsive movie, and even the machinations of that sly old Don Juan, whom not even falling chamber pots can dissuade from his appointed rounds, manage to convince us that Montherlant himself is a wily seducer who teases, insults, moves, and charms, pushes us away and drags us back, in a constant alternation of systole and diastole, the very pulse of life itself.

1936

Selected Bibliography

EDITIONS

INDIVIDUAL WORKS

ESSAYS AND NOTEBOOKS

La relève du matin. Paris, 1920.
Chant funèbre pour les morts de Verdun. Paris, 1924.
Aux fontaines du désir. Paris, 1927.
Mors et vita. Paris, 1932.
Service inutile. Paris, 1935.
L'Equinoxe de septembre. Paris, 1938.
Le solstice de juin. Paris, 1941.
Un voyageur solitaire est un diable. Paris, 1945.
Textes sous une occupation. Paris, 1953.
Carnets, 1930–1944. Paris, 1957.
Va jouer avec cette poussière. Paris, 1966.
Le treizième César. Paris, 1970.
La marée du soir. Paris, 1972.
La tragédie sans masque. Paris, 1972.
Mais aimons-nous ceux que nous aimons? Paris, 1973.
Tous feux éteints. Paris, 1975.

NOVELS

Le songe. Paris, 1922.
Première olympique: Le paradis à l'ombre des épées. Paris, 1924.
Deuxième olympique: Les onze devant la porte dorée. Paris, 1924.
Les bestiaires. Paris, 1926.
La petite infante de Castille. Paris, 1929.
Les célibataires. Paris, 1934.
Les jeunes filles. Paris, 1936.
Pitié pour les femmes. Paris, 1936.
Le démon du bien. Paris, 1937.
Les olympiques. Paris, 1938.
Les lépreuses. Paris, 1939.
L'Histoire d'amour de "La rose de sable." Paris, 1954.
Le chaos et la nuit. Paris, 1963.
La rose de sable. Paris, 1968.
Les garçons. Paris, 1969.
Un assassin est mon maître. Paris, 1971.
Thrasylle. Paris, 1983.
Moustique. Paris, 1986.

POEMS

Encore un instant de bonheur. Paris, 1934.

PLAYS

L'Exil. Paris, 1929.
Pasiphaé. Tunis, 1936.
La reine morte. Paris, 1942.
Fils de personne. Paris, 1943.
Un incompris. Paris, 1944.
Malatesta. Lausanne, 1946.
Le maître de Santiago. Paris, 1947.
Demain il fera jour. Paris, 1949.
Celles qu'on prend dans ses bras. Paris, 1950.
La ville dont le prince est un enfant. Paris, 1951.
Port-Royal. Paris, 1954.
Brocéliande. Paris, 1956.
Don Juan. Paris, 1958.
Le cardinal d'Espagne. Paris, 1960.
La guerre civile. Paris, 1965.

COLLECTED WORKS

Théâtre. Preface by Jacques de Laprade. Paris, 1958.
Romans et oeuvres de fiction nonthéâtrales. Preface by Roger Secrétain. Vol. I. Paris, 1959.
Essais. Preface by Pierre Sipriot. Paris, 1963.
Romans. Preface by Michel Raimond. Vol. II. Paris, 1982.

CORRESPONDENCE

Montherlant, Henry de, and Peyrefitte, Roger. *Correspondance.* Paris, 1983.

TRANSLATIONS

The Bachelors. Translated by Terence Kilmartin. New York, 1960.
The Boys. Translated by Terence Kilmartin. London, 1974.
Chaos and Night. Translated by Terence Kilmartin. New York, 1964.
Desert Love. Translated by Alec Brown. London, 1957; New York, 1958. Translation of *L'Histoire d'amour de "La rose de sable."*
The Dream. Translated by Terence Kilmartin. New York, 1963.
The Fire That Consumes. Translated by Vivian Cox with Bernard Miles. San Francisco, 1980.
The Girls: A Tetralogy of Novels. Translated by Terence Kilmartin. New York, 1968. Includes *The Girls, Pity for Women, The Hippogriff,* and *The Lepers.*
The Master of Santiago and Four Other Plays. Translated by Jonathan Griffin. New York, 1951. In-

cludes *Queen After Death, No Man's Son, Malatesta,* and *Tomorrow the Dawn.*

The Matador. Translated by Peter Wiles. London, 1957.

Selected Essays. Translated by John Weightman. New York, 1960. Includes portions of *La relève du matin, Les olympiques, L'Equinoxe de septembre,* and *Service inutile.*

BIOGRAPHICAL AND CRITICAL STUDIES

Arx, Paule d'. *La femme dans le théâtre de Montherlant.* Paris, 1973.

Batchelor, John. *Existence and Imagination: The Theatre of Henry de Montherlant.* St. Lucia, 1967.

Beauvoir, Simone de. *Le deuxième sexe.* Paris, 1949. Translated as *The Second Sex* by H. M. Parshley. New York, 1953.

Beer, Jean de. *Montherlant, ou l'homme encombré de Dieu.* Paris, 1963.

Becker, Lucille. *Henry de Montherlant: A Critical Biography.* Carbondale, Ill., 1970.

Blanc, André. *Montherlant, un pessimisme heureux.* Paris, 1968.

———, ed. *Les critiques de notre temps et Montherlant.* Paris, 1973.

Cruickshank, John. *Montherlant.* London, 1964.

Debrie-Panel, Nicole. *Montherlant: L'art et l'amour.* Lyon, 1960.

Duroisin, Pierre. *Montherlant et l'antiquité.* Paris, 1987.

Faure-Biguet, J.-N. *Les enfances de Montherlant. Montherlant, homme de la Renaissance.* 2 vols. Paris, 1948.

Golsan, Richard Joseph. *"Service inutile": A Study of the Tragic in the Theatre of Henry de Montherlant.* 1988.

Guicharnaud, Jacques. *Modern French Theater from Giraudoux to Beckett.* New Haven, 1961.

Johnson, Robert B. *Henry de Montherlant.* New York, 1968.

Krémer, Jean-Pierre. *Le desir dans l'oeuvre de Montherlant.* Paris, 1987.

Laprade, Jacques de. *Le théâtre de Montherlant.* Paris, 1950.

Mohrt, Michel. *Montherlant, "homme libre."* Paris, 1943.

Perruchot, Henri. *Montherlant.* Paris, 1969.

Peyrefitte, Roger. *Propos secrets.* Paris, 1977.

Raimond, Michel. *Les romans de Montherlant.* Paris, 1982.

Robichez, Jacques. *Le théâtre de Montherlant.* Paris, 1973.

Saint-Robert, Philippe de. *Montherlant le séparé.* Paris, 1969.

Sandelion, Jeanne. *Montherlant et les femmes.* Paris, 1950.

Sipriot, Pierre. *Montherlant.* Paris, 1975.

———. *Montherlant sans masque.* Paris, 1982.

JOSEPHINE V. ARNOLD

ANDRÉ BRETON

(1896–1966)

BORN IN 1896 AT TINCHEBRAY (Orne), France, André Breton embarked upon pre-medical studies at the age of seventeen only to discover that medicine was to be, for him, but "an alibi." His true vocation was poetry.

Breton's first models were a curious medley of poets. Clearly, he did not yet know what kind of poems he wished to write. It is true of course that, considered in retrospect, his admiration for certain aspects of the work of J. K. Huysmans and for Gustave Moreau takes on anticipatory significance: "The discovery of the Gustave Moreau museum, when I was sixteen," Breton wrote in 1961, "conditioned for always my way of loving." We cannot but notice, though, that the young Breton respected at the same time Mallarmé, Viélé-Griffin, and Jean Royère. Among his first publications was a sonnet printed in *La Phalange,* beneath a dedication to Paul Valéry. Yet, although Breton hardly knew the work of Rimbaud, one may detect in him a restlessness regarding the nature of poetry which soon made him attach particular meaning to Rimbaud's gesture of turning his back upon literature, as well as to Valéry's prolonged silence from the year 1892.

Called to service in World War I, Breton found himself precipitated into a mode of existence from which he received a psychological jolt severe enough to make him readily responsive to two new attractions, which were to take him from the path of symbolism: Guillaume Apollinaire and Jacques Vaché. Prophet of modernity, acutely sensitive to new developments in art and literature, Apollinaire helped to show Breton where he might satisfy his thirst for something new. Meanwhile Vaché, whom Breton met in Nantes in 1916, exercised no less significant an influence upon him: his iconoclasm, displayed in a destructive form of humor he called *umour,* combined with a contempt for literature which fascinated Breton. "But for him," Breton later remarked, "I would have been a poet."

Mistrustful by now of the conventions of established literary forms that seemed to debase the title of poet to the point that he felt compelled to reject it, Breton found himself better prepared, as the war progressed, to accept a new influence, that of total revolt against all literary and artistic pretension, stridently expressed in the first two numbers of a review called *Dada,* which he read in Apollinaire's apartment.

Breton was already acquainted with Louis Aragon and Philippe Soupault. Together they had founded a magazine ironically entitled *Littérature.* Appearing for the first time in March 1919, *Littérature* serialized in its first four issues the *Poésies* of Lautréamont, copied by Breton from the only known copy, in the French National Library. Yet while the inclusion in *Littérature* of Lautréamont's text is a fact of signal importance for those concerned to trace the direction which Breton's evolution as a writer was beginning to take, the presence in the magazine of material signed by André Gide, Valéry, Jean Giraudoux, and Drieu La Rochelle is proof enough that regard for tradition still counted for Breton and his friends. An example of integral revolt was still needed to release them from remaining traces of respect for convention. Such an example was supplied by a group of writers and artists in Zurich whose activities were mirrored in the review *Dada.* When Tristan Tzara, a leading dadaist and author of a celebrated Dada manifesto dating from 1918, arrived in Paris, he was greeted, Breton has recalled, "like a Messiah."

Breton's participation in dadaist activities in Paris beginning in 1919 helped to liberate him from residual influences which would have impeded the full development of his poetic independence. For a while, in fact, Breton's fidelity to dadaism could not be challenged. Gradually, however, he reached the conclusion that dadaist practice limited its ambition to a destructive program, precluding the possibility of advance beyond negation. What is more, he was alarmed as early as August 1920 by the sympathetic tone Jacques Rivière adopted when discussing Dada in *La nouvelle revue française.* Dada, it appeared, was not only ceasing to progress beyond limited success; it was in imminent danger of becoming respectable and of being assimilated to literature.

After his withdrawal from dadaism in 1922, Breton attached increased importance to various experiments in writing in which he had participated even while playing a role in Dada's resistance to convention. There is evidence of this experimentation in *Littérature,* despite its having become the organ of dadaism in Paris. Reflection upon the material in question—the most impressive single text was *Les champs magnétiques (The Magnetic Fields),* published by Breton and Soupault in *Littérature* at the end of 1919—induced Breton to consider the nature of the results obtainable by methods so far used only haphazardly. This effort culminated in October 1924 in the *Manifeste du surréalisme (Manifesto of Surrealism),* which motivated several ex-dadaists and some new allies to rally around Breton.

Consideration of the full consequences of the assertion of liberty that Breton made in the name of surrealism is impractical in the present context. It is sufficient to say of the first *Manifesto of Surrealism,* as of the second manifesto (which appeared originally in *La révolution surréaliste* [December 1929]) that its author neither condescends to engage in discussion nor aims at persuasion. From the moment when surrealism became articulate, jibes about the weakness of its program and about the instability of its foundation in reason or philosophical argument left its defenders unperturbed. Typical of their attitude is the complete disregard for adverse criticism evidenced in Breton's manifestos. In these texts, with a logic for which he has been given too little credit, he makes an impassioned appeal to those human impulses which come from a predisposition to cast off the restrictions of the rational universe. Breton consistently addressed himself only to those eager to accept surrealism's invitation to explore directions in which reason places no trust. The sources of the vitality of the surrealist spirit lie here, as does the origin of the attraction exercised for four decades by Breton's published works and magnetic personality.

Nevertheless, the rank of leader of the surrealist group was not an entirely enviable one. Natural as it may seem to critics to select Breton as an exemplary surrealist figure, repeated reference to his work as simply a convenient source of information on surrealist attitudes has the unfortunate effect of reducing his status to that of theoretician. The result has been relative neglect of the creative elements in his writing. All too frequently, critics ignore the fact that Breton practiced surrealism as ably as he preached it, and that no assessment of his contribution to surrealism will be complete until his achievements as a poet have been established.

While it may seem to limit the significance of what Breton had to say, a narrower focus than is usually employed commends itself, to the extent that it allows us to resist, so far as possible, the temptation to read *through* the prose works of Breton, rather than to relate them to the state of mind in which his poetry was produced. Then these essays can be seen to cast light upon the poetic sensibility of their author and to make possible a better understanding as much of the nature of his poetic effort as of the impulses and aspirations that gave it life. As Breton himself wrote in his preface to Max Ernst's *La femme 100 têtes,* "The particular truth of each of us is a game of solitaire in which one must, from all others, and without ever having seen them, seize the elements in flight." It is to *Nadja* (1928), to *Les vases communicants* (*Communicating Vessels,* 1932), to *L'Amour fou* (*Mad Love,* 1937), and to *Arcane 17* (1944) that we must first look for the rules of the game of solitaire that Breton, as poet, played for over forty years.

In 1926 Breton's *Légitime défense* declared, in the name of the surrealists, "It seems to us that revolt alone is creative." The following year the antirational stress of the *Manifesto* was confirmed by his *Introduction au discours sur le peu de réalité.* Meanwhile, Breton was facing the problem of applying surrealist principles to the practice and evaluation of painting, in a series of articles written for the magazine *La révolution surréaliste,* which replaced *Littérature* in 1924. These articles were published separately in a volume entitled *Le surréalisme et la peinture* (*Surrealism and Painting*) in February 1928.

Well before 1928, in other words, surrealism had become for Breton the only possible answer to the problem of man's relationship to a world where everything conspires to frustrate his desires. If we consider the implications of the direction Breton's thought was taking in the mid-twenties, it is fair to conclude that he was in some danger of finding his situation difficult. Rejecting as valueless the purely realistic depiction of the world, Breton nonetheless required the satisfaction of needs which, if definitively alienated from reality, must end in

frustration. At the same time, of course, in continued aversion to literature, Breton esteemed the act of writing, and even more that of publishing, to be pure vanity. Thus it is permissible to ask, firstly, why he wrote *Nadja* and, secondly, why he published it in May 1928.

In *Nadja,* Breton gives attention to a succession of unexpected incidents, curious coincidences, and inexplicable occurrences he has witnessed—events that "do not permit our return to reasoned activity except, in most cases, if we appeal to the instinct of self-preservation." In the perspective of the preoccupations thus betrayed in the early pages of his book, it must have seemed to Breton a notable sign of the beneficent intervention of chance in human affairs when, in 1926, he met a young woman calling herself Nadja, "because in Russian that's the beginning of the word hope, and only the beginning."

The fascination of the unrelated events assembled in the early pages of *Nadja* is brought into focus when Breton gives attention to the mystery of Nadja, "free from all earthly bonds, so little does she belong, but marvelously, to life." Anticipating one of the major themes of *Arcane 17,* Breton borrows from Celtic mythology the figure of Melusina to render the strange attraction of Nadja. As the incarnation of Melusina, Nadja represents the union of opposites, and hence the reconciliation of the world of desire with that of reality. She is for Breton a figure of interrogation. He does not omit to note, therefore, that when she arrived in Paris for the first time, it was the illuminated sign of the Sphinx Hotel on the Boulevard Magenta that induced her to take a room there. Meeting her the day after presenting her with a copy of *Les pas perdus* (1924), he notices that she has the book open to a text recounting a meeting which, within a few moments of one another, he, Aragon, and André Derain each had with an unknown woman. The significance of the enigmatic question that the sight of this woman is enough to pose is made explicit when, in *Nadja,* Breton refers to "this veritable Sphinx beneath the features of a charming young woman." The theme of interrogation becomes completely identified with the role of the marvelous in human life when Breton describes himself as appearing before Nadja "like man dumbfounded at the feet of the Sphinx."

What, then, is the nature of the question raised by Breton's encounter with the Sphinx? In a footnote to the 1963 edition of *Nadja,* Breton himself wonders what he could have been seeking and, faced with the inconclusiveness of his own text, admits that at the time the book was written surrealism was still seeking its way.

What might be taken for the weakness of Breton's position is really its strength. Breton was a man who, without fear of ridicule, could mention in *Nadja* one of his cherished wishes—that of meeting a beautiful, naked woman at night in a wood—and then observe, "or rather, such a wish no longer meaning anything, once expressed, I regret to an incredible degree not having encountered her." This was a man who admitted that at one time he would leave open his hotel room door in the hope of awaking to find by his side a woman he had not chosen. Just as gladly as he would have accepted such a companion, Breton (then thirty years old) accepted Nadja. Concerned with gathering evidence of what the surrealists were already calling "daily magic," Breton could not resist the attraction of this "inspiring creature," whom he found able to release in him that sense of the marvelous to which surrealism attaches so much importance. Without difficulty he realized that, whatever the nature of the question his meetings with Nadja would answer, he must continue to see her: "And what if I no longer saw her? *I no longer would know. I would have deserved therefore not to know."*

An essential clue to the nature of the knowledge Breton aspired to attain through contact with Nadja is provided in his admission, "While close to her I am closer to the things that are close to her." The usefulness of this clue is confirmed by the function of the photographs reproduced in *Nadja.*

Breton's meetings with Nadja took place in Paris. However, as a study of his text confirms, his aim in utilizing photographs of certain Paris landmarks is not to attain an impression of greater realism. The first sentence of *Nadja* is "Qui suis-je?"—meaning simultaneously "Who am I following?" and "Who am I?" Soon Breton is asking "Whom do I haunt?" and reflecting upon the verb *haunt:* "It gives me to understand that what I regard as the objective, more or less deliberate manifestations of my existence are only what passes within the limits of this life from an activity the true extent of which is quite unknown to me." The illustrations in *Nadja* relate to these manifestations. In a foreword written in 1962, Breton speaks of the battle which takes place within man between subjectivity and objectivity, noting that the latter is usually the victor. The incidents reported in *Nadja* appear to mark a welcome reversal of this depressing trend. They are noteworthy instances of privileged insight in which, as Pierre Mabille puts it in his *Le miroir du merveilleux,* "an extraordinary complicity is established between the needs of the heart, between the processes of thought and the laws of a universe we wrongly believed to be mechanical, anonymous and indifferent." Such moments constitute the primary material of *Nadja,* whose author's sense of privilege comes from his conviction that, through contact with certain manifestations of objective reality, he can hope to discover the true nature of his own subjectivity: *who* he is.

Nadja rejects the idea of the reconquest of the self and defends the view that the self exists not in the past but in the future, as a potentiality to be explored with every chance of infinite progress toward discovery and understanding. Breton shows himself to be less interested in recognition (*la reconnaissance*) than in cognition (*la connaissance*). He has in view "a general aptitude that would be special to me, and is not given to me." Hence the complete uselessness of merely attempting to copy the real with exactitude. Not until one has undertaken a search for more than is given, through the confrontation of the subjective with the objective, can the latter take on its true meaning, as the photographs of *Nadja* take their significance from the emotions associated with them in the text. Accordingly, Breton sees himself as he sees Huysmans:

> The object of those perpetual solicitations that seem to come from without and to immobilize us for a few seconds before one of those fortuitous arrangements, of a more or less new character, to which it seems that, by thoroughly questioning ourselves, we should find in us the secret.

In the final analysis, what Breton finds in his meetings with Nadja is the occasion for self-discovery: the solution to the riddle of the Sphinx becomes man himself. If the answer to human needs comes from within, though, it is not to be found by turning one's back upon reality. This is a major discovery to which *Nadja* testifies. Meeting Nadja constitutes for Breton proof that the marvelous is innate in the real, thus offering support to a theory of immanence according to which "surreality is contained in reality itself, and is neither superior nor exterior to it. And conversely, because the container is also the content. It is almost a matter of communicating vessels between container and content."

Meanwhile, unfortunately, Nadja had been committed to an asylum, leaving Breton with the guilty feeling that perhaps he had not helped her as much as he might have. The ambiguity of Breton's position cannot escape notice: although genuinely concerned for Nadja's fate, Breton had retained a particular interest in the kind of liberation that madness grants the imagination, ever since he had observed insanity during the war while attached to the Second Army Psychiatric Center at Saint-Dizier. One wonders if his encounter with Nadja did not provide the necessary impetus for the inclusion in *L'Immaculée conception* (1930) of a section entitled "Les possessions," five essays simulating various states of insanity, which the public is asked to judge on their *poetic* merit. Be that as it may, two years later,

in November 1932, *Communicating Vessels* appeared, demonstrating what progress in his search for liberation Breton's acquaintance with Nadja had made possible.

Communicating Vessels described Breton's state of mind in mid 1931. Intellectually, he was feeling acutely the indifference of a public too ready to identify surrealism's defense of revolution with a debased form of romanticism. His frustration was aggravated by a deep sense of emotional disturbance resulting from the loss of the woman he loved. Breton had reached the point of questioning the vitality of surrealist action. It would have been understandable, under the circumstances, if he had turned away from the problems to which surrealism lent urgency, and had fallen back upon some kind of evasion. At first glance, indeed, it would seem that *Communicating Vessels*, concerned as it is with the "communicating vessels" of dreaming and waking experience, reflects such an inclination to escape and to resort to substitutes. But nothing could be further from the truth than the assumption that this work betrays surrealist principles.

Communicating Vessels clearly states Breton's wish to have us understand that surrealism has attempted to "place a conductor between the all too dissociated worlds of waking and dreaming, of external reality and internal reality, of reason and madness, of the calm of knowledge and of love, of life for life's sake and of revolution." Far from relinquishing positions so far gained, Breton intended his new book to move forward from an assertion that is fundamental to surrealist theory: that surrealism is capable of resolving, to the individual's satisfaction, certain antinomies generally regarded as basic to human existence.

As was his custom, Breton faced the artistic problems that commanded his attention from the standpoint of personal experience. In this instance, he analyzed several of his own dreams, to which incidents occurring in April 1931 lend special significance. Basing his conclusions upon the postulation that every reader will be struck by the analogy of what he recounts with the dream state as it is generally conceived, Breton asks us to notice "how strangely the exigency of desire searching for the *object* of its realization arranges the exterior data, selfishly tending to retain of these only that which may serve its cause." The point at issue presents no novelty to those who have noticed how selective are the details supporting the conclusions drawn in *Nadja;* those unmoved by the surrealist manifestos or by *Nadja* will be equally indifferent to what *Communicating Vessels* has to say. For now it becomes Breton's intention to present an argument which, "by means of the dream, attempts to prosecute materialist knowledge," taking as its point of departure the conviction that "the world of the dream and the real world are one and the same."

Communicating Vessels maintains Breton's emphasis upon the role of the subjective element in man's exploration of objective reality for the purpose of extending knowledge. It gives a glimpse of the means available to make dreams "serve a greater understanding of the dreamer's fundamental aspirations, as well as a more accurate appreciation of his immediate needs." At the same time, by categorically dismissing the idea that man should retreat into dreams in order to escape the pressure of reality, Breton is able to stress another aspect of the surrealist program.

In *Communicating Vessels,* Breton writes of those who "have considered once and for all that after so many interpretations of the world it was time to go on to its transformation." The conclusions already reached in *Nadja* about the relationship that subjectivity must bear to objectivity lead increasingly, in Breton's subsequent publications, to emphasis on the need for transforming the latter. The immediate consequences of this emphasis were twofold. On the one hand, Breton published *Communicating Vessels* in order to draw attention, through an examination of those processes of the mind on which reflection exercises least influence, to the existence of a "capillary tissue" capable of "ensuring the constant ex-

change which must take place in thought between the internal and external worlds." On the other hand, he published *Position politique du surréalisme* (1935).

Breton, approaching all matters from the surrealist standpoint, saw no conflict between the privately motivated curiosity that impelled him to write *Communicating Vessels* and a sense of public responsibility that resulted in his delivering the lectures collected in *Position politique du surréalisme.* The demonstration Breton took it upon himself to provide, in *Communicating Vessels*, of the interpenetration of dream and reality, of the inner and outer worlds, constituted a necessary advance from the *Second Manifesto,* where Breton reveals his increasing awareness of the social and moral consequences of surrealism's defense of the principle of integral freedom.

Breton writes in *Communicating Vessels:* "Thus we arrive at conceiving a synthetic attitude in which the need to transform the world radically finds itself reconciled with the need to interpret it as completely as possible." At no time in the history of surrealism has it been possible to question the sincerity of a complementary declaration, which Breton made in 1930 and published in *Point du jour* (1934): "We persist, here, in wishing to deduce revolutionary duty from the most general human duty, from human duty such as, in the place we occupy, it is given to us to conceive it."

The theoretical positions defended by the surrealists were mapped once again in a lecture Breton gave in Brussels and published under the title *Qu'est-ce que le surréalisme?* (*What Is Surrealism?*, 1934). At the same time the surrealist outlook was defined in two other texts, which Breton wrote with Paul Éluard: *Notes sur la poésie* (1936), reprinted from the last number of *La révolution surréaliste* (December 1929), and the catalogue of the 1938 International Surrealist Exhibition, *Dictionnaire abrégé du surréalisme.* To those interested in identifying Breton's independent contribution to surrealist theory and in understanding his literary personality, however, the most significant of his publications during the second half of the decade preceding World War II was *Mad Love.*

In *Point du jour,* Breton spoke for all the surrealists when he asserted, "There is no solution outside love." Yet after reading in *Communicating Vessels* that love needs to be "rebuilt" and reestablished on its "true basis," one may feel a little disappointed when in *Mad Love* one comes upon the statement: "Never was there any forbidden fruit. Temptation alone is divine." Does the reinvention of love mean no more than the promotion of sexual freedom in disdain for moral reprobation? Hardly. Breton has in view quite a different form of liberation, for which those who know his *Position politique du surréalisme* are partly prepared.

Although he does not consider love to be an instrument of political revolt, Breton does see in the repressive forces that oppose the love experience the very social pressures which need to be combated on the political plane if man is to attain full liberty. In his mind, the right to love and the need to guarantee all men independence of action go together, since both postulate the transformation of the world.

Of necessity, discussion of "mad love" obliges Breton to face the problem of the conflict resulting from the opposition which social conditions offer an individual's love for another. Even so, social protest is not the primary theme of *Mad Love.* The demands of love are to be met within the social framework, it is true, but only by "abandoning ordinary logical paths." What calls for explanation, therefore, is the sentence with which Breton brought *Nadja* to a close and which he was to repeat in 1942, in an essay on Max Ernst: "Beauty will be CONVULSIVE or will not exist."

Mad Love reveals that the meaning of the adjective "convulsive" is to be sought by examining the relationship between a person in love and the object of his or her passion. The presence of convulsive love is guaranteed, Breton claims, by what he calls "circumstantial magic." Hence the care taken in *Mad Love* to identify the characteristics Breton feels are attributable to certain unusual circumstances recalled in his book. These circumstances are brought together by the element he regards as their common denominator—desire. In *Mad Love* desire is seen to have its own devious, strange ways of seeking out and taking possession of its object. Thus Breton here makes the discovery that "Tournesol," which he wrote in 1923, was a prophetic poem, forecasting events, which did not take place until 1934, that culminated in his marriage with Jacqueline Lamba the following year. He speaks too of visiting the flea market with Alberto Giacometti and of finding a mask and wooden spoon. Then he explains how the mask appeared to "take its place" in Giacometti's personal search (by suggesting the features necessary to complete a sculpture he had been unable to finish) and how the spoon answered some quite unconscious needs of his own.

Throughout *Mad Love* we may trace Breton's preoccupation with a familiar question: the problem of the relationship of objectivity to subjectivity. His examination of the question advances a step in this work, thanks to his increased awareness of the role of chance in human affairs.

Between desire and its objectively represented object stands beneficent chance, to which Breton owed his meeting with Nadja. Chance now seemed to be embodied in found objects (*objets trouvés*), as Breton concluded that the find (*la trouvaille*) exercises a remarkable magnetism because it is capable of revealing in us desires of which we have remained ignorant. In a footnote in *Mad Love* referring readers to *Communicating Vessels,* Breton reminds us that the *trouvaille* has the same function as the dream "in that it liberates the individual from paralyzing affective scruples, comforts him and allows him to understand that the obstacle which he might have believed insurmountable has been passed."

The effect of the find is similar to that of the electric storm: lightning is released, and unexpected illumination results. The *trouvaille* induces reconsideration of a question that was of fundamental importance for Breton ever since his *Introduction au discours sur le peu de réalité* testified to his belief that the merit attaching to objective reality may vary from zero to infinity. The find that proves to correspond to a previously inarticulate desire illuminates reality in a way which Breton considered especially revealing. So long as the find relates to the individual's inner needs, its role is analogous to that of love, since love sheds light on the real to the extent that it determines subjective responsiveness to the outside world. Above all, love is the supreme form of desire, capable of the kind of transformation that the adjective "convulsive" suggests: a violent disturbance takes place that affects the relationship of people to society. Thus the attention given to love in *Mad Love* carries forward the inquiry undertaken in Breton's previous essays, as he now asserts that only by adducing evidence of the close connection of the real to the imaginative can one hope to strike a new blow against the unfounded distinction between the subjective and the objective.

In this sense, we may speak of Breton as a writer who used his own experience in order to probe and evaluate problems that he felt were significant for all people. He examined events from his own life not in order to discover what separated him from others, but rather to uncover what linked his desires with theirs. In *Mad Love*, Breton accumulated proof of "irrationality close at hand," basing his evidence upon the experience he was best able to record with fidelity—his own. He expressed continued confidence in the rewards obtainable by unwavering willingness to accept all that chance may place in one's path: "Indépendamment de ce qui arrive, n'arrive pas, c'est l'attente qui est magnifique." It is characteristic of Breton that he should use the word *attente* here simultaneously as "waiting" and "expectation."

Each of the essays written before World War II was intended to assume the significance of a human document, as Breton used the term: a testimony to human aspirations that stand outside the materialistic world. Each essay

reveals Breton's attention to what he termed "the beginning of a contact, dazzling above all, between man and the world of things," and confirms his interest in defining "the law governing these mysterious exchanges between the material and the mental." In stressing on every occasion the revelatory nature of the incidents that claim his attention, he sought justification for the statement made in *Mad Love:* "The greatest weakness of contemporary thought seems to me to reside in the extravagant overestimation of the known compared with what remains to be known."

In 1939 Breton was recalled to military service. The collapse of the French Army occurred when he was in the Free Zone, and after he was demobilized in 1940, he wrote the long poem *Fata Morgana* as well as his *Anthologie de l'humour noir.* Finally, he made his way in the following year via Martinique to the United States.

Breton's period of residence in the United States was marked by two important statements on surrealism: a lecture delivered at Yale University in 1942, "Situation du surréalisme entre les deux guerres" (published in 1945), and "Prolégomènes à un troisième manifeste du surréalisme ou non" (*Prolegomena to a Third Manifesto of Surrealism or Else,* 1942; published in 1946). From this period dates also the essay *Arcane 17,* which appeared in New York two years later.

Arcane 17 displays Breton's concern for pressing personal problems. The stress of his circumstance—exile from France at the time when news reports told of the Allies' advance upon Paris—led him to give his essay an orientation and emphasis that would today seem dated. However, far from being outmoded, *Arcane 17* marks the culmination of certain themes that run through the essays written during the 1920's and 1930's.

A framework for *Arcane 17* is provided by Breton's logbook of a trip made off the Gaspé Peninsula in 1944. It is true that the thoughts that accompany passages describing the Gulf of St. Lawrence find their point of departure in the news of the Allies' advance through France, but when raising the question of "resistance" and "liberation," Breton characteristically rejected the popular interpretations placed on these words in occupied France and chose to discuss freedom and rebellion in relation neither to private nor to national destiny. Faithful to the principles that had governed his life for two decades, he undertook to evaluate man's situation in the perspective that surrealism recommends.

Breton gives attention to those permanent elements of civilization that remain untouched by such disruptive circumstances as war brings. Among the constants that must be acknowledged in man's thought, Breton gives prominence to the aspiration toward freedom. This is not merely freedom from alien domination but a permanent state of rebellion that, he claims, "carries its justification within itself, quite independently of the chance it has of modifying or not modifying the state of affairs that determines it."

So far as Breton was concerned, recent events in France proved conclusively that liberation is a meaningless concept so long as it implies anything les than "a dynamic state." This is why, in *Arcane 17*, he admits to being dissatisfied when he provisionally defines liberty "by opposition to all forms of servitude and constraint." Such a definition, he argues, tends to represent liberty as a state—"that is to say in immobility." And this, he declares, anticipating intuitively the conclusions to which the spectacle of postwar France would bring him in *La lampe dans l'horloge* (1948), leads inevitably to its ruination. Man's aspirations toward liberty, on the contrary, should be able to "recreate themselves ceaselessly." This means that liberty must be conceived not as a state but as *"a vital force"* entailing "a continual progression": liberty stands for the affirmation of what man can be rather than of what he is.

Arcane 17 expands conclusions earlier expressed in *Mad Love* which amply demonstrated the incompatibility of social demands and the full development and satisfaction of human desire. Basically, poetry and love are, in Breton's eyes, antisocial activities, interrelated assertions of a principle of liberty much farther-reaching in its effects than the postulation of political self-determination alone would entail. Love, poetry, and art are presented in *Arcane 17* as the principal means by which man's confidence can be renewed and by which his thought can be enabled to "take to the open sea once again."

It is therefore entirely appropriate that throughout *Arcane 17* runs the lyrical theme of Breton's love for Elisa, whom he met in 1943 and married in 1945. Love nourishes protest against what Breton calls "opacity," which he considered to be man's greatest enemy because it is the product of inculcated respect for conventional opinions. Beyond question, his attachment to Elisa reinforced Breton's belief that only love, "the true panacea," is capable of fusing existence and essence in complete harmony. Thus *Arcane 17* reveals the growing influence of the social philosopher Charles Fourier. Breton's insistence upon words like "panacea" and "regeneration" indicate that he turns to love for more than an example of passion untrammeled by social controls. Woman finally reaches her full stature in Breton's writing when, rejecting the idea of Christian redemption, he asks of love the solution to man's most serious problems: "The great malediction is raised, and it is in human love that all the regenerative power of the world resides."

Here, too, Breton gives prominence to a profoundly surrealist theme as he casts woman in the role of mediatrix. Breton shows woman releasing man from opacity when he once more evokes the figure of Melusina, taking care to emphasize that he does not intend the "childwoman" to be esteemed in opposition to the mature woman. In Melusina seems to reside "in a state of absolute transparency the *other* prism of vision which we obstinately refuse to take into account, because it obeys very different laws, which masculine despotism must prevent at all cost from being divulged."

Convinced that man's thinking has brought

nothing but suffering, Breton is persuaded that it is time to look at last to woman for guidance. He sees Melusina as "always woman lost, the one who sings to the imagination of man, but, after what trials for her and for him, she must also be woman found once more." He judges her to be perpetually attractive to poets since, as child-woman, she is able to dissipate the best-organized systems: "Nothing has been able to make her subject to them or understood by them."

Breton's admiration for Melusina is completely consistent with his conviction that it is imperative to release human life and thought from the oppressive weight of time. She represents the very personification of revolt and liberty as, synthesizing the themes of his essay, Breton brings it to a close with a passage in which his calm confidence in the vitality of the principle of liberty finds full expression:

> It is revolt itself, revolt alone that is creative of light. And this light can know only three paths: poetry, liberty, and love which must inspire the same ardor and converge, so as to make of it the very cup of eternal youth, on the darker and most illuminable point of the human heart.

Those who persist in defending the view that surrealism's period of activity was confined to the years between the two world wars believe themselves entitled to draw support from at least two facts. First, it is clear that, thanks to the dispersion of the French surrealist group in 1940 and the absence of its major figures during the Occupation, by 1945 surrealism had lost the initiative in France. Breton returned to Paris in 1946 to find that the existentialism of Jean-Paul Sartre now commanded the attention of French youth. Despite a major international surrealist exhibition in Paris in 1947, it was several years before distracting considerations like the surrealists' abstention from participation in the Resistance ceased to cloud judgment upon the contribution surrealism continued to be capable of making. Second, after the war the fortunes of the elder surrealists entered a new phase. These writers, who in the past had so often had to publish privately, now found their work being reprinted by commercial houses. Surrealism was achieving a form of consecration that was not entirely advantageous, since it tended to assume the character of an interment.

In the case of André Breton, especially, the reprinting of the manifestos in 1946 and of *Arcane 17* in 1947, together with the appearance of a representative selection of his poetry (*Poèmes*, 1948), appeared to support the view that here was a writer who had outlived his productive period. *Ode à Charles Fourier* (written in 1945), it is true, was published in 1947, while two other poetic texts, both privately printed, have appeared since. But the twenty years following his return to France would have offered little proof of active interest in the ideas he had defended for so long had Breton not made an impressive contribution as an art critic.

It may be tempting to see in the author of *L'Art magique* (1957, written with the help of Gérard Legrand), of the "prose parallels" that accompanied Joan Miró's *Constellations* in 1959, and above all of the greatly expanded edition of *Surrealism and Painting* (1965) a writer whose critical personality set him apart from the person to whom we owe some of the most significant of the surrealist essays. In reality, one would be guilty of a grave misunderstanding in doing so, since Breton himself made no distinction between those of his writings in which he explored the meaning of his own life and those in which he examined pictorial evidence of the experience of others. His observations on art confirm attitudes expressed in his essays and complete our understanding of his outlook.

In July 1938 the question of the relationship of art to politics, which *Position politique du surréalisme* had shown to be rooted in Breton's deep concern for the revolutionary role of art, was posed with great clarity in the manifesto

Pour un art révolutionnaire indépendant, which Breton wrote in collaboration with Leon Trotsky during a visit to Mexico. That same year Breton praised the painter Frida Kahlo de Rivera because her work seemed to

> stand at the point of intersection of the political (philosophical) line and the artistic line, from which we wish that these lines become unified in one revolutionary consciousness, without, for that reason, the essentially different motives which belong to them being merged.

In the following year, in a note on André Masson, Breton assured his readers that the surrealists continued to believe that art must be above all "love rather than hate or pity," insisting that "the problem is no longer as it used to be that of knowing whether a picture 'stands up' for example in a corn field, but if it stands up next to a daily newspaper, open or closed, which is a jungle."

At no time do Breton's articles on painting neglect to stress the need for a "revision of values" and the necessity to measure the appropriateness of artistic means to this end. Breton questions the usefulness of the work of any painter whose eye "limits itself to the passive role of a mirror" and, in a text on Arshile Gorky, asserts in 1945 that the painter's eye is capable of serving as a *fil conducteur* between things apparently unrelated. This return to the image of the clew and of the conductor, familiar to those who have read *Communicating Vessels* and the poem "Vigilance" (1932), is proof enough of consistency in Breton's thought and of his conviction, so clearly imaged in the 1928 version of *Surrealism and Painting,* that it is a grave mistake to equate art with imitation.

Breton advises that we replace the exterior model with an interior model, "resolutely giving representation precedence over perception" on the understanding that "nothing around us is object to us, all is subject." Thus, discussion of artists and their techniques provides the occasion to emphasize once again the fact that the true object of discussion is reality itself. Speaking of the sculpture of Maria, Breton reaffirms in 1947 what Nadja had taught him earlier: "It is, one can never repeat often enough, the universe that must be interrogated first about man, and not man about the universe."

If Breton's art criticism could provide no more than confirmation of what we have learned already, it would hardly be worth mentioning. It happens, though, that his observations on painting are guaranteed special value by the contribution they make to explaining his poetry.

Unfortunately, reference to the language of painting is such a commonplace of critical jargon that one might easily fail to notice, on first contact with Breton's articles, that he really does consider painting to be a language. Inattention to this fact results in concealment of another, which must be taken into account before we can appreciate how indicative these writings on art are of the attitude Breton adopts toward poetry. For him, poetry and painting are truly but two forms of one and the same language, placed at the disposal of those inspired to surrealist expression. Opening the 1928 version of *Surrealism and Painting,* we encounter characteristic references to the technique of pictorial automatism as the vehicle that allows Roberto Matta, Esteban Frances, and Onslow Ford to set out to conquer "a new morphology that will exhaust in the most concrete language the whole process by which the psychic has its echo in the physical." Speaking of the work of Yves Tanguy, Breton talks of "sensorial verbs," which he claims "demand not to be conjugated like others," adding: "To this necessity astonishing participles make their response: already seen, already heard, never seen, etc." Breton concludes characteristically: "To see, to hear is nothing. To recognize (or not to recognize) is everything. Between what I recognize and what I do not recognize is I."

We can be sure, of course, that being in the beginning less confident of the suitability of painting than of poetry to surrealism's aims, Breton was inclined at first to seek as many points of contact as possible between the two media, to bring them closer together by treating the former as he would the latter. But it is evident too that as the years went by Breton became convinced of his right to make the same demands upon the painter as upon the poet. By 1939 he could describe the work of Masson as "plastic metaphor in its pure state" and could insist, "I mean literally untranslatable." In an essay on recent trends in surrealist painting written in the same year, he returned to the case of Tanguy and described the elements typical of his painting as "the words of a language which we do not yet understand, but which soon we shall read and speak, about which we are going to discover that it is the language best suited to new exchanges." A note on Rufino Tamayo dating from 1950 makes explicit what is hinted here when Breton admits to his concern for painting as "universal language." We are reminded of the remark he made in 1928 to the effect that in Ernst's collages, disparate elements are "seeking to discover for themselves new affinities." We are reminded too of his comment on Miró: "No one comes close to associating as he does the unassociable, to breaking without discrimination that which we do not dare to wish to see broken." Breton consistently places his trust in those painters in whose work "the key to the mental prison can be found only in breaking those paltry means of cognition: it lies in the free, unlimited play of *analogies*."

Once alerted to Breton's practice of estimating the efficacy of the language of painting as he does that of poetry, we can detect in his art criticism many indications that help to set his approach to poetry in perspective. Identifying the "great enigma"—the permanent cause of the conflict between man and the world—as the "impossibility of justifying everything by the logical," he asks, "How can one call to account the artist, the man of science, for the voices chosen for its satisfaction by the imperious human need to form *against* exterior things

other exterior things, in which all the resistance offered by the inner being is at once abdicated and included?" Implied here is "the proposal of an absolutely virgin visual organization," which Breton saw early in his career as corresponding, in the Ernst collages of 1920, to what Lautréamont and Rimbaud desired in poetry:

> The exterior object broke with its habitual field of action, its constituent parts became so to speak emancipated, in such a way as to bear with other elements entirely new relationships, escaping the principle of reality but nevertheless having consequences on the plane of the real (upsetting the notion of relationship).

Hence the celebrated maxim: "It is thus impossible for me to consider a picture otherwise than as a window about which my first concern is to know what it looks out upon."

Works of art, Breton believed, should resemble the poems Apollinaire wrote just before World War I; each should be "an event." Art must draw its justification, he remarked in 1939, "solely from its revelatory power." Almost twenty years later, he reaffirmed in 1958 his preference for painting that seeks to be "a recreation of the world in terms of the inner necessity experienced by the artist." Thus everything Breton wrote about painting and poetry is designed to marshal evidence in support of two statements made in the 1928 version of *Surrealism and Painting*:

> The essential discovery of surrealism is, in fact, that, without preconceived intention, the pen which runs in writing, or the pencil which runs in drawing, spins an infinitely precious substance of which not all perhaps is material for exchange but which, at least, appears charged with what the poet or painter then has within him by way of emotion.

But, Breton urges, once the stage of emotion for emotion's sake is passed, we should not forget that "at this period, it is reality itself that is at stake." Close attention to the verse he wrote persuades us that when he spoke of Ernst's dream as "a dream of *mediation*," Breton was identifying in the painter an ambition that gave direction to his own effort in poetry.

In 1919 Breton began to give attention to the phrases which, without his knowing why, would run through his head just before he fell asleep. These phrases, which impressed him by their striking imagery yet syntactical correctness, seemed to be "poetic elements of the first order." The careful consideration they commanded from Breton can be explained by his state of mind at the time. As he later explained in his first surrealist manifesto, "At that time I had just attempted the poetic adventure with the minimum of luck, that is, my aspirations were the same as today. But I had faith in slowness of elaboration to save me from useless contacts, from contacts which I disapproved of greatly." When he was writing the final poems of his first verse collection, *Mont de piété* (1919), Breton's youthful faith in deliberation, his effort to exploit the interplay of words and the spaces surrounding them on the page—the associations they were capable of stimulating—led him (to take but one example) to spend six months writing "Forêt-noire," a poem only thirty words long. At this period his method still owed much to the example of Mallarmé. However, this example was ceasing to promise the kind of success that by now Breton was seeking. Hence his decision to undertake with Soupault to reproduce, by the deliberate exclusion of all extraneous thoughts and ideas, the state in which the proximity of sleep released new and exciting poetic elements. The immediate result was the series of texts published as *The Magnetic Fields,* reprinted in book form from *Littérature* in 1920. The long-term consequences of this effort were estimated only when, after he and Soupault had baptized their method *surréalisme* out of respect for Apollinaire, Breton wrote his *Manifeste du surréalisme* and considered the implications of automatism, which relegates the poet's function to that of "modest recording instrument."

When, as Breton did, the poet holds literature in contempt, when, distinguishing poetic accomplishment from the practice of literature, he seeks in poetry a valid solution to the problems of human existence, he can feel only indifference for verse that reveals the cardinal sin of care for form. For Breton, form as external to poetry was always an unwelcome limitation—through rhyme, rhythm, or any other restrictive device—upon poetic content. Just as he tired of imitating Mallarmé, so he very soon divested himself of his admiration of Valéry, in accordance with his growing belief that precedence over every other consideration must be given to the attainment and presentation of what he called poetic intuition.

Breton subscribed without question to the opinion that poetic excellence can only be the result of spontaneity. To be a poet, in his opinion, is to be the privileged beneficiary of insights that the poet's duty is to capture in words. Hence his eagerness to examine the revelations made possible by exercising the technique of automatic writing.

The well-known definition supplied in the first surrealist manifesto introduced surrealism as "pure psychic automatism by which we propose to express, either verbally, or in writing, or in any other manner the real functioning of thought," and it presented automatic expression as "thought dictated in the absence of all control exercised by reason." Critics are only too ready to demonstrate the weakness inherent in the postulations upon which surrealism rests and to show how unsound is the declaration that surrealism stands on "the belief in the superior reality of certain forms of association heretofore neglected, in the omnipotence of the dream, in the disinterested play of thought"; such critics are generally so busy telling one another that surrealist poetry is not feasible that they have little or no time to notice that this poetry exists and that Breton was one of its leading practitioners.

Literary critics take pains to dismiss the

validity of automatism as a poetic method without admitting that no one has judged with greater penetration than André Breton the weaknesses inherent in the automatic method. They would do well to note that, although admitting that automatism must produce its share of "dross," Breton never repudiated its contribution to his own poetry. A letter addressed to Jean Gaulmier establishes his position with clarity:

> I take care not to reread the texts of *Poisson soluble,* no doubt because the manner in which they were obtained prevents my passing calm judgment upon them, because 'looked at coolly' they would soon overwhelm me with their weaknesses—which, deep down, does not stop me from remaining *jealously faithful to the spirit that controls them.*

This spirit counts far more than the results first obtained by the exercise of automatism. In this sense, therefore, Julien Gracq very properly stressed the value of *Poisson soluble* when he spoke of its contents as "poems that are an invitation to poetry." The technique to which *Poisson soluble* owes its existence is one that redefined poetry at a time when, discouraged with results obtained by imitating other poets, Breton was seeking a poetic mode promising satisfaction of increasingly urgent needs.

What is important for us is not to assess the first texts that Breton owed to automatism so much as to appreciate the fact that the automatic method opened up perspectives where the prospect had previously seemed depressingly uninviting. Initiated by automatic practice, Breton became confirmed in his belief that innovation in poetic language was an imminent possibility as well as a pressing necessity.

Here we see the reason for a striking change in language that becomes noticeable when, turning from his prose works, one begins to read Breton's poetry. It is apparent that once he began to write verse he willingly abandoned the remarkably persuasive style that distinguishes his prose. The author to whom we are indebted for *Arcane 17* is also the writer who once declared that the function of language is not to communicate and who made public his lack of concern for that elementary characteristic of language, its "power of immediate exchange." In his *Introduction au discours sur le peu de réalité,* Breton invites us to address our critical faculties to the laws presiding over verbal arrangements and asks, "Does not the mediocrity of our universe depend upon our power of enunciation?"

The special power he attributed to poetic enunciation accounts for Breton's sharp reproval of all who purport to explain the poetic image. As early as September 1924 his *Introduction au discours* dismissed as impertinent explanations provided in a recent anthology: "What Saint-Pol-Roux wished to say," he proclaimed, "you can be sure he said." Breton instinctively resisted the pretension of the language of reason to elucidate that of poetry. Meanwhile, in his own poetry linguistic experimentation, whatever degree of unconscious motivation is involved in its use, is an expression of revolt against a universe that has ceased to accord with man's desires. Hence his unyielding resistance to attempts that may be made to explain the results of such experimentation. The poetic image, as he assessed its vitality, not only denies explanation; it defies it. "Let us not forget," he warned, "that only a certain practical necessity prevents us from granting poetic testimony a value equal to that granted, for example, the testimony of an explorer." Undermining practical necessity, Breton the poet reserved for himself the role, rights, and privileges of an explorer.

To the extent that the practice of poetry becomes an exploratory venture, the pleasure it provides is that of the *trouvaille,* which plays the same part in a Breton poem as found objects do in the events discussed in *Mad Love.* In both cases the find expresses concretely the externalization of desires and assumes consequently the value of revelation, becoming the "marvelous precipitate of desire" capable of enlarging the universe. This surely is why an article entitled "Les mots sans rides" (Words Without Wrinkles), reprinted in *Les pas perdus,* spoke out boldly for innovation in poetic language and pointed to the striking verbal effects for which Robert Desnos and Marcel Duchamp were responsible. Breton might have cited just as pertinently other young poets, first associated with Dada and then affiliated with surrealism, who were expressing their opposition to literary forms they regarded as outdated through iconoclastic humor, anti-aesthetic images, vulgarity, and mocking word-play. Yet, during the period when Desnos was at work on *Rrose Sélavy, L'Aumonyme,* and *Langage cuit,* when Roger Vitrac was preparing *Peau-Asie* and Éluard was engaged in composing his *Exemples,* Breton himself was writing less revolutionary poetic texts: *Clair de terre* (1923).

When reading *Clair de terre,* we comprehend that of all the young surrealists Breton had the greatest need to liberate himself from early literary influences. Today the poems in this volume appear self-conscious, contrived, and generally lacking in the spontaneity their author was soon to advocate. Breton was inclined still to rely on conventional comparisons and somewhat labored grammatical constructions. As yet, certainly, his use of phrases built upon the word *comme* ("like") gave no foretaste of the contribution he later demanded of the word after he came to the conclusion that it performs the same grammatical function as a verb, being capable of making something happen between the words it brings together.

Clair de terre, of course, antedated the first surrealist manifesto. Before Breton could find his way as a poet, he first had to discover that "language has been given man so that he may make surrealist use of it." Soon, however, two volumes of poetry that he helped to write in 1930 (*Ralentir travaux* and *L'Immaculée conception*) bore witness to his eagerness to test the surrealist capabilities of language. Then, in 1931, his poem "L'Union libre," published anonymously under the imprint "Editions surréalistes," inaugurated a period of poetic productivity marked by the publication of *Le revolver à cheveux blancs* (The White-Haired Revolver, 1932) and *L'Air de l'eau* (1934).

By highlighting the constant exchange taking place in thought between "the internal and external worlds" and by emphasizing that the demands of love are to be met by "abandoning ordinary logical paths," *Communicating Vessels* indicated the theoretical basis upon which the poem "L'Union libre" was built.

In "L'Union libre" a succession of images displays in their arrangement no more order than might be expected from the freely associative method to which they owe their existence and presentation. Clearly, justification for the poetic method utilized in this poem is not to be found in the realm of the logical and rational. For an understanding of this text we must refer to *Communicating Vessels,* where Breton writes:

> The spirit is marvelously prompt to seize the faintest rapport that can exist between two objects selected by chance and the poets know they can always, without fear of deceit, say that the one is *like* the other: the only hierarchy that may be established among poets can rest solely upon the greater or lesser liberty which they demonstrate in this respect.

A footnote clarifies: "To compare two subjects as distant as possible one from the other, or, by any other method, to bring them face to face, remains the highest task to which poetry can aspire."

Reading "L'Union libre," we see how this conception of poetry leads in Breton's verse, through circumstantial magic and the creation of convulsive beauty, to the formulation of the exigency of desire, which works analogously to the dream in its search for "the *object* of its realization" in such a way as to "arrange" the exterior data borrowed from objective reality. The clew in "L'Union libre" is the poet's love for his wife, which provides the contact between him and the world of things in such a manner as to make explicit Breton's meaning when he declared that nothing around us is object; all is subject. The result is a text drawing its strength from *l'amour fou* and typical of Breton's surrealist poetry in its most striking form. One arresting image ("My wife with the tongue of a stabbed host") is set off by a line of disarming banality ("With the tongue of a doll that opens and closes its eyes"). Then the latter verse, in which the poetic charge is low, appears to suggest other lines that do not occur until later in the poem, when Breton speaks of "the movement of clockwork and despair" and writes:

> My wife with hips of a skiff
> With hips of luster and of arrow-feathers
> And of shafts of white peacock plumes
> Of imperceptible swaying.

If admissible at all, such relationships between individual verses have to be established by the reader himself. Given the method of "free union" according to which the images accumulate, one cannot demand of the poet a deliberate pattern of imagery. "L'Union libre" is the product of a hypnotic state in which the invocation of automatism is instinctive. Taking as an example the verse "Ma femme aux mollets de moelle de sureau" ("My wife with calves of elder pith"), we notice how an obscure relationship exists audibly between *mollets* and *moelle,* even though it is not rationally explicable. The result is a line in which sound association of the kind first practiced by Raymond Roussel produces a statement that, however irrational it may be, articulates a desire to which Breton's *Introduction au discours sur le peu de réalité* had confessed: "The idea of a bed of stones or of feathers is equally unbearable to me: What do you expect; I can sleep only on a bed of elder pith."

It is worth pausing here, because the verse quoted above exemplifies an essential feature of Breton's poetic art. Echoing Apollinaire's maxim, he asserts in *Mad Love:* "Surprise must be sought for itself, unconditionally." Surprise, for Breton, exists "in the intrication in a single object of the natural and the supernatural, in

the emotion of holding the lyre-bird and at the same time feeling it escape." To those who read hurriedly, these words might seem to authorize the very kind of verbal contrivance that Breton abjured once the potentiality of surrealism was revealed to him. In reality, however, Breton is expressing his confidence in the ability of language to surprise the poet himself before it surprises his readers. He is referring to the verbal *trouvaille,* which has the effect of bringing to the poet's attention, with the shock of surprise, elements of his own thought and feeling previously imprisoned within the unconscious.

There seems no reason to doubt that here we touch upon the reason for Breton's protest, in an article reprinted in *La clé des champs* (1953), against those who qualify poets as visionaries: "The great peots are 'auditives,' not visionaries. In them vision, the 'illumination,' is, in any case, not the *cause* but the *effect.*" While this observation embodies a tendentious definition of poetry, it does indicate both the nature of Breton's poetic ambition and the method by which he sought to fulfill it. When, during a lecture in Prague on 29 March 1935, he followed Hegel's lead in placing poetry above all the other arts as the only universal art, he cited also Lautréamont, borrowing as the surrealists frequently do his phrase "poetry must be made by all," and adding *"poetry must be heard by all."*

The gravity that has contributed to making Breton one of the most remarkable prose stylists France has known in this century ruled out, from the beginning, all possibility of levity in his verse. One misses the joyous destructiveness which gave the early verse of Aragon its brilliance, just as one misses the inner turbulence which left its mark on the poems of Antonin Artaud. Time has confirmed the conclusion which in the 1920's might have seemed premature: Breton's poetic tone takes its place between Benjamin Péret's violence and Éluard's artful simplicity.

As a poet, Breton speaks with authoritative tones. So much so, indeed, that a malicious observer might be inclined to attribute special importance to his respect for Victor Hugo. From the moment when Breton's poetry began to evidence self-assurance, it was characterized by a tone which has done much to lend support to accusations that he assumed the role of pontiff. Breton's unshakable conviction that his was a privileged voice underlies many of his statements which lend themselves to misinterpretation. It is displayed even better in an innate respect for language patterns and an intuitive command of their capabilities. These qualities would strike a discordant note of harmony in the calculated cacophony of early surrealist writing, were it not that Breton possessed to an uncanny degree the power to persuade us that mediation is, in his case, not a self-imposed role but a natural gift. In a way that sets his verse notably apart from that of his companions in the surrealist venture, Breton undertook to give language in his poetry the function surrealism attributes to it: "To make cognition take a long step." In a manner totally consistent with the preoccupations which provide his essays with their dominant themes, he sought to face the fundamental problem of perception and representation, observing attentively along the way how words "make love."

In 1932 "L'Union libre" was followed by Breton's first collection of truly surrealist verse, *Le revolver à cheveux blancs*. Breton prefaced this volume with the unequivocal statement, "Imagination is not a gift but an object of conquest par excellence." He declared too that it does not have to "humiliate itself before life" because the imaginary is "that which tends to become real." Anyone who questions Breton's firm belief in this surrealist-inspired principle will neither understand his poetry nor comprehend why it was written.

The poems of *Le revolver à cheveux blancs* clearly express confidence in the ultimate supremacy of the subjective over the objective. We are introduced to a universe created by the exercise of poetic imagination of a remarkable nature. This is a universe of anticipated and wished-for experience in which Breton never once doubts that his role is that of revelator. Reconciliation of desire with the world of reality is shown to be an act of conquest, not of resigned acceptance, as the poet becomes an explorer who seeks and finds "more than is given." Like the eye of the painter Gorky, praised by Breton for providing a *fil conducteur* between things apparently unconnected with one another, the imagination of the poet supplies a guiding thread through the labyrinthine ways of the unforeseen and the hoped-for. In such a universe as the imagination brings within his purview, chronological time is among the first elements of the rational world to lose their power. Present and future exist contemporaneously because no distinction need be made any longer between what is and what the imagination gives assurances will be. Dismissal of clock time is thus a token of the ever-widening influence of the imagined, which tends progressively to take the place of the real. Absence of time sequence is the prophetic sign of the metamorphosis of reality in response to the imperious command of desire.

In the fluid time vacuum of Breton's poetry, we are conscious of flux, of a world changing so rapidly that we barely have the opportunity to identify an object before it is transformed into another with such facility as to dispose of any preconceptions we may retain regarding an ordered world.

Of each of his poems in *Le revolver à cheveux blancs* Breton might say, as he does of one of them, that they represent a descent "à l'intérieur de ma pensée." Thought, here, is of course not reasoned observation. Rather, it is an intuitive exploration of feelings and aspirations made possible only when the poet, having discovered that "the bars are on the inside of the cage," has found a way to force them apart and to escape inward, often under the enticement of a vision of feminine beauty, half-Ariadne, half-Melusina. Now he comes to see that all the external manifestations we call real are but the elements from which the imagination must and will reconstruct the world. Acknowledging no outside authority and acting as "caretaker" of a world that no one has seen before, he enjoys the liberty to "chase away before [him] real appearances." Absence and presence are "in connivance," as he expresses his revolt against the "consent" which the rational world extorts.

Like those of *Le revolver,* the poems of *L'Air de l'eau,* which succeeded them in 1934, record moments in which the facade of the real crumbles to uncover the surreal. They offer examples of prescience of a kind that disposes of the "great interdiction" which Breton is sure that poetry can remove. On the voyage of discovery that is the poem, Breton sees things that can be rendered only in a language which ignores the ordered classifications of a world all too familiar. Here a woman passes "with the sound of flowers," there female singing voices "have the color of sand on tender and dangerous shores." Phrases of this type, and the texts from which they come, project the theory of immanence upon which Breton's surrealism rests, attesting to the vision that is granted man once "the bars of the spectacle are twisted marvelously," and he becomes aware of the splitting of "the frightful mental milestones."

The impact of the poet's vision of liberation is not diminished by its brevity. On the contrary, the excitement communicated in a poem like "Au beau demi-jour de 1934" comes largely from the intensity of Breton's sense of release, accompanied by the realization that conventional reality constantly threatens to efface what has been glimpsed momentarily. The more we read his verse, the more we perceive that it is the fugitive, fragile quality of the imaginative revelation that gives his poetry its special mood. These elements produce their effect in conjunction with the poet's expressions of joy at having received a revelation for which there is no substitute in the world of everyday reality. What he stresses above all is the privilege of penetrating appearances: "I have only a transparent body," he writes, "within which transparent doves hurl them-

selves upon a transparent dagger held by a transparent hand." Divesting himself of the constrictive feeling of the duality of body and soul, he animates a universe all his own: "*I am the unreal breath of this garden.*"

Even more than in *Le revolver,* Breton associates his sense of penetration in *L'Air de l'eau* with the experience of love. Woman is at once mediatrix and initiator as, anticipating the prose texts of *Mad Love,* new poems celebrate in love "this rushing together of systems considered separately as subjective" which

Sets off a series of very real phenomena
That take part in the formation of a distinct world
Of a kind to bring shame on what we would perceive
Without it.

Such is the wonder released in the poet, such is his excitement at the spectacle of a new world which shames the old, that we cannot expect him to express his feelings in language elaborated for use in the world he delights in leaving behind. Breton's is the language of the new, a lyricism nurtured by the creative play of analogies, as he sings of "marvelous infiltrations" which, no longer content to exist side by side with the conventional, in the end replace it altogether.

Here should be noted that place reserved in Breton's poetry for coincidence, the coming together of the imagined with the real in a manner similar to that of Ernst's collages, which Ernst himself defined as "the coupling of two realities, irreconcilable in appearance, upon a plane which apparently does not suit them." Where Ernst speaks of the coupling of disparate realities, Breton talks of words that make love. For both artists the ambition is the same: to invoke the generative principle so that something new can be born. This is why in his poem *Fata Morgana* Breton calls coincidences "veritable beacons in the night of meaning" and love "that promise which goes beyond our comprehension."

After *Fata Morgana* Breton wrote the long

poem *Ode à Charles Fourier,* during a period of travel that permitted him to see Nevada, Arizona, and New Mexico and to come in contact with the Pueblo Indians. Until 1940, Fourier had interested Breton simply from the point of view of social reform. Now, taking with him on his journey west five volumes of Fourier's works, viewing current events from the standpoint which enabled him to write *Arcane 17,* Breton turned away from the horror of the world about him to affirm his hope in the future of mankind as predicted by the nineteenth-century utopians. Among these he was particularly impressed by Fourier, who foresaw the reign of harmony: "I salute you from the Petrified Forest of human culture / Where nothing is standing any more." The instability of the modern world did nothing to shake Breton's confidence. On the contrary, *Ode à Charles Fourier* affirms his belief that, if the improvement of man's destiny will be effected slowly, "the real lever nevertheless will remain irrational belief in advance toward an Edenic future."

Ode à Charles Fourier was Breton's last major poetic work. So dramatic is the change noticeable in the form and content of the *Ode* that its publication raises questions that cannot be ignored. Does Breton's return to a more conventional poetic form prove his dissatisfaction with the modes he had practiced for twenty years in defiance of conventionality? Does his surrender of the opportunity for further discoveries released in coincidences by the use of verbal automatism constitute an admission of failure, which should be taken into account when estimating his achievements in *Le revolver à cheveux blancs* and *L'Air de l'eau?*

Ode à Charles Fourier stands alone in Breton's work as a philosophical poem. Its origins, which have been examined in detail by Jean Gaulmier (1961), need not be recalled here. We know from Breton's own statements during an interview with Aimé Patri in March 1948 that the poem took its point of departure in automatism, finding its unity in the personality of Fou-

rier and in his work, "the greatest constructive work ever elaborated on the basis of unrestrained desire." While apparently seeming to indulge in occasional verse, Breton proposed to "kill" occasional verse. And so in a letter to Gaulmier dating from 1957, he indicated that his intention in writing his ode was partly critical. He added:

> I permitted myself the luxury of an infraction of my own principles (to affranchise poetry at all cost from the controls that feed upon it) and I wished to give this infraction of my own principles the meaning of voluntary elective sacrifice to the memory of Fourier, the most recent person who seemed to be worthy of it.

Just as this letter is a tribute to its author's admiration for Fourier, so it is equally an acknowledgment of his continued respect for automatism, which, Gérald Schaeffer has demonstrated, makes a noteworthy contribution to *Ode à Charles Fourier.*

Despite Breton's deliberate control of automatism in his ode, we may detect in it characteristic features of his verse that result from the poet's search for a universal language. Such a language, Breton maintains, does not have to satisfy the requirements of reason. It bypasses these so as to set off resonances at levels of sensibility common to all, where reason does not make its influence felt. Breton's central assumption is that the inner demands to which the poet must be responsive at all times, although personal to him, are universal in significance: in seeking the *key to the mental prison* in order to escape the "principle of reality," he is impelled by his "dream of mediation" to make available to all men the means to liberate themselves.

Escape takes the form of a new understanding of how the external world relates to subjective desire. Analogy substitutes for causal explanations of "the spontaneous, extra-lucid, insolent relationship which is established in certain conditions between this thing and that, which common sense would prevent us from bringing face to face." Thus the poet must be above all the "master of the image" because the image is "the generative element par excellence of that world which in place of the old we intend to make our own."

Here lies Breton's justification for rejecting literary modes that he considers serve no better purpose than to impose on the spirit a discipline inappropriate to it. Only the image, he observes, "gives me the measure of possible liberation, and this liberation is so complete that it frightens me." In the use of the poetic image man takes possession of a power that is proof against all resistance.

"In the final analysis," Breton comments, "everything depends upon our power of voluntary hallucination." The fascinating spectacle of the freedom granted by states that the reasoning world qualifies as insane gives the word "hallucination" special value for Breton. At the same time the qualifying adjective "voluntary" makes it plain that the form of hallucination that commands his admiration is not the uncontrolled liberty of the mind unhinged, refusing to come to terms with the real. Rather, he advocates the poet's deliberate surrender to hallucinatory experience made possible by willing abandon of the control exercised by reason over habitual thought. In his exciting rearrangement of elements that habit would persuade us to view in a conventional order, the poet must safeguard himself against the danger of vainly pursuing private obsession. For he must be an explorer bold enough to advance into the interior of thought, beyond the peripheral regions over which reason reigns, and he must report his findings through poetic statement. His poem signposts his journey without giving any guarantee that those who care to follow behind will find their experience enriched by what he can show them.

We must not forget in this connection that *L'Immaculée conception* invites us to take inspiration from the spaces between the lines and that Éluard has written that poems always have big white margins, "margins of silence"—

a silence which clearly we ourselves must break. And so Breton's reference to the function of language as "not to communicate" would be misinterpreted, if viewed as authority for incomprehensibility. Breton shuns commonplace communication, in which meaningless banalities are exchanged by persons indifferent to the pressing need to transform the world. Such a form of communication must be replaced with another, aimed at promoting a perception of reality that owes more to inner vision than to external contingency.

Perhaps what impresses most about André Breton's work is its unity, ensured by more than forty years of fidelity to surrealism. Breton spoke for surrealism in such resounding tones that even today those who find it all too easy to disregard the contribution to surrealist theory of Aragon, Éluard, Mabille, and Péret consider Breton to be surrealism's only spokesman. They tend to forget that he never spoke as a mere theorist. Any discoveries he shares with us he first made for himself, and what he has to tell us he first had to learn for himself. His essays are statements of poetic aspiration to which his verses lend full meaning. Both essay and poem serve to express a view of existence that projects a special faith and hope. Whatever text of Breton's we open, we find the same beliefs, the same determination to surmount obstacles that to many of us seem insurmountable. Casting off the pessimistic conclusions to which immediate circumstance would reduce us, Breton's work offers the promise, at least, of a serene vision of striking optimism, sufficient in itself to guarantee Breton a special place among twentieth-century French writers. In 1948 he brought his selected poems to a close with "Sur la route de San Romano." Fittingly, this poem ends with three lines that sum up a whole lifetime of poetic effort, set it in perspective, and ensure it our respect:

The poetic embrace like the embrace of the flesh
While it lasts
Protects against any glimpse of the misery of the
world.

1958

Selected Bibliography

EDITIONS

INDIVIDUAL WORKS

Mont dé piété. Paris, 1919.
Clair de terre. Paris, 1923.
Les pas perdus. Paris, 1924.
Manifeste du surréalisme; Poisson soluble. Paris, 1924.
Introduction au discours sur le peu de réalité. Paris, 1927.
Nadja. Paris, 1928; revised edition, Paris, 1963.
Le surréalisme et la peinture. Paris, 1928; enlarged edition, New York, 1945.
Second manifeste du surréalisme. Paris, 1930.
L'Union libre. Paris, 1931.
Le revolver à cheveux blancs. Paris, 1932.
Les vases communicants. Paris, 1932.
L'Air de l'eau. Paris, 1934.
Point du jour. Paris, 1934.
Qu'est-ce que le surréalisme? Brussels, 1934.
Position politique du surréalisme. Paris, 1935.
L'Amour fou. Paris, 1937.
Anthologie de l'humour noir. Paris, 1940; enlarged edition, 1950.
Arcane 17. New York, 1944.
Situation du surréalisme entre les deux guerres. Paris, 1945.
Les manifestes du surréalisme suivis de prolégomènes à un troisième manifeste du surréalisme ou non. Paris, 1946.
Ode à Charles Fourier. Paris, 1947.
La lampe dans l'horloge. Paris, 1948.
Poèmes. Paris, 1948.
Entretiens 1913–1952. Paris, 1952.
La clé des champs. Paris, 1953.
Adieu ne plaise. Alès, 1954.
Les manifestes du surréalisme suivis de Prolégomènes à un troisième manifeste du surréalisme ou non; Du Surréalisme en ses oeuvres vives; et d'Ephémérides surréalistes. Paris, 1955.
Le la. Alès, 1961.
Manifestes du surréalisme. Paris, 1962. Includes *Manifeste du surréalisme, Second manifeste, Prolégomènes à un troisième manifeste du surréalisme ou non, Position politique du surréalisme* [extracts], *Poisson soluble, Lettre aux voyantes, Du surréalisme en ses oeuvres vives;* 2d rev.ed., Paris, 1963.
Perspective cavalière. Paris, 1970.

COLLABORATIVE WORKS

Les champs magnétiques (with Philippe Soupault). Paris, 1920.
L'Imaculée conception (with Paul Éluard). Paris, 1930; reprinted Paris, 1961.
Ralentir travaux (with René Char and Paul Éluard). Paris, 1930.
Notes sur la poésie (with Paul Éluard). Paris, 1936.
Pour un art révolutionnaire indépendant (with Leon Trotsky, though Diego Rivera's name appears on the cover). Mexico, 1938.
First Papers of Surrealism (with Marcel Duchamp). New York, 1942.
Martinique, charmeuse de serpents (with André Masson). Paris, 1948.
L'Art magique (with Gérard Legrand). Paris, 1957.

COLLECTED WORKS

Oeuvres complètes. Vol. 1. Edited by Marguerite Bonnet. Paris, 1988–.

MODERN EDITIONS

INDIVIDUAL WORKS

L'Amour fou. Paris, 1975.
Arcane 17. Paris, 1971.
Les champs magnétiques (with Philippe Soupault). Paris, 1988.
Clair de terre. Paris, 1966.
L'Immaculée conception (with Paul Éluard). Paris, 1987.
Manifestes du surréalisme. Paris, 1988.
Les pas perdus. Paris, 1979.
Point du jour. Paris, 1970.
Position politique du surréalisme. Paris, 1970.
Le surréalisme et la peinture. Enlarged edition. Paris, 1965.

TRANSLATIONS

Arcane 17. New York, 1945.
Communicating Vessels. Translated by Mary Ann Caws. Lincoln, Nebr., 1988.
If You Please. Translated by George E. Wellwarth. In *Modern French Theater,* edited by Michael Benedikt. New York, 1964.
Mad Love. Translated by Mary Ann Caws. Lincoln, Nebr., 1987.
The Magnetic Fields. Translated by David Gascoyne. London, 1985.
Manifestoes of Surrealism. Translated by Richard

Seaver and Helen R. Lane. Ann Arbor, Mich., 1967.

Nadja. Translated by Richard Howard. New York, 1960.

Ode to Charles Fourier. Translated by Kenneth White. London, 1969.

Poems of André Breton: A Bilingual Anthology. Translated and edited by Jean-Pierre Cauvin and Mary Ann Caws. Austin, Texas, 1982.

Prolegomena to a Third Manifesto of Surrealism or Else. VVV 1:18–26 (June 1942).

Selected Poems. Translated by Kenneth White. London, 1969.

Surrealism and Painting. Translated by S. W. Taylor. New York, 1972.

What Is Surrealism? Translated by David Gascoyne. London, 1936.

BIOGRAPHICAL AND CRITICAL STUDIES

Alexandrian, Sarane. *André Breton par lui-même.* Paris, 1971.

Audouin, Philippe. *Breton.* Paris, 1970.

Balakian, Anna. *André Breton: Magus of Surrealism.* New York, 1971.

Bédouin, Jean-Louis. *André Breton.* Paris, 1950.

Bonnet, Marguerite. *André Breton: Naissance de l'aventure surréaliste.* Paris, 1975.

Browder, Clifford. *André Breton: Arbiter of Surrealism.* Geneva, 1967.

Carrouges, Michel. *André Breton and the Basic Concepts of Surrealism.* Tuscaloosa, Ala., 1974.

Caws, Mary Ann. *Surrealism and the Literary Imagination: A Study of Breton and Bachelard.* The Hague, 1966.

———. *André Breton.* New York, 1971.

Crastre, Victor. *André Breton.* Paris, 1952.

Durozoi, Gérard and Bernard Lercherbonnier. *André Breton: L'Écriture surréaliste.* Paris, 1974.

Eigeldinger, Marc, ed. *André Breton: Essais et témoignages.* Neuchâtel, 1950.

Gaulmier, Jean. Commentary in André Breton, *Ode à Charles Fourier.* Paris, 1961. Pp. 78–97.

Gracq, Julien. *André Breton: Quelques aspects de l'écrivain.* Paris, 1948.

Lenk, Elisabeth. *Der springende Narziss: André Bretons poetischer Materialismus.* Munich, 1971.

Matthews, J. H. *Surrealism, Insanity, and Poetry.* Syracuse, N.Y., 1982.

———. *André Breton: Sketch for an Early Portrait.* Amsterdam and Philadelphia, 1986.

Mauriac, Claude. *André Breton.* Paris, 1949.

Sheringham, Michael. *André Breton: A Bibliography.* London, 1972.

Vielwahr, André. *Sous le signe des contradictions: André Breton de 1913 à 1924.* Paris, 1980.

J. H. MATTHEWS

ANTONIN ARTAUD

(1896–1948)

> "Blessed be all illness. . . . "
> —*Cahiers de Rodez,* 1945

THE CENTURY HAD hardly begun when young Antonin Artaud (christened Antoine), five years old, suffered a near-fatal attack of meningitis. What happened then he may not have remembered consciously, but the experience clearly had an impact on his life and his writing.

The beginning is sudden, even startlingly so. As often happens with fulminating onsets, the child went to bed perfectly well and was found unconscious the next morning. Esther, the domestic, remembers him saying when she took him to his room the night before: "How funny, I see two staircases." Vomiting, severe headache, and shivering first appeared, followed in a few hours by stiffness of the neck and rigidity of the limbs. Soon the young "Antonin" (his father, a shipbuilder, was already called Antoine) went into convulsions.

The child emitted high-pitched cries; his tongue became furry and dry; soon red spots appeared on the surface of his trunk. His body was tender to the touch; his joints and limbs were painful. As the membrane covering the brain and spinal cord got even more inflamed, the brain became swollen with pus. The size of his head increased. Within a few days the child's mental state progressed from malaise and nausea to drowsiness, confusion, stupor, and coma.

In many similar cases of meningitis the patient died within a week of onset. Vascular collapse can lead to shock. The heart suddenly gives up. After the first week, if the patient lives, the disease gradually abates; the rigidity disappears and the temperature becomes normal. But other complications may arise. The disease may pass into a chronic state with great debilitation; in a young child, the head becomes markedly retracted and the body greatly bent forward. In the chronic stage the child may become blind or deaf. Some survivors bear residual signs of cranial nerve damage and hydrocephalus, and show noticeable mental deterioration or even permanent cerebral disorder.

Meningitis had no known cure at the time of Artaud's illness. Syphilis, suspected by some to have existed in the Artaud family, is cited as a rare cause of meningitis.

The young Artaud never quite recovered from this sudden onslaught. His body had been snatched away from him by a malicious power; his health remained fragile and he had to be nursed at home. Like Heliogabalus, the Roman emperor whom Artaud later wrote about, he was brought up surrounded and cared for by women. (His father, a cultivated and erudite man, remained distant from his children and had no direct influence on Artaud's early life.)

The disease went into remission for the remainder of Artaud's childhood, but struck again when he was nineteen. Besides an occasional facial tic and a contraction of the tongue accompanied by light stammering, the young

1961

man suffered from intense headaches and erratic pains. He later told one of his doctors:

My condition, which had worsened since last year, has suddenly become absolutely MADDENING . . . I fell back into a total absence of thought, a near-impossibility of speaking that made me incapable of formulating the simplest thing. I could only speak with a stammer, a terrible mumbling. And I fell into a COLOSSAL anguish that held me for entire days and from dark to dawn in the thralls of a veritable suffocation. I was choking. The pressure was physical. It was a real *aspiration* of my sensibility! My limbs were getting limp, it took me hours to recover the feeling of an arm, a hand.

(Letter to Dr. Toulouse, 11 January 1930, in *Oeuvres complètes,* supplement to vol. 1, 1970).

In 1919 Artaud resorted to taking laudanum, to which he remained addicted for the rest of his life. "I only stopped once a year or once every two years, and never for more than fifteen days," he declared in 1935, in an effort to be admitted to a hospital. Opium, he declared, dissolved his irrepressible states of anguish "like water dissolves sugar"; it also made him "cowardly and less scrupulous." "There's a sort of denutrition of all moral values within me," he admitted. "It destroys the mind's resilience, while at the same time casting a pall over the nervous symptoms. And the nervous symptoms continue unabated while the mind rots." Artaud was hopelessly caught in what William Burroughs has since called the "algebra of need." He couldn't do without drugs, but they blocked his mind, impeded his work, and made him "almost completely impotent."

Although one of the myths about Artaud is that he was a derelict living on the edges of poverty, he was actually brought up in a fairly affluent family engaged in Mediterranean trading. After a mediocre schooling, he was sent to various private sanatoriums in the south of France (near his family's home in Marseilles) and in Switzerland. Artaud experienced both world wars entirely from within the confines of mental institutions: in his own way, he shared the wars' madness. The young Artaud came out of this ordeal outwardly untouched but with a body "twisted and cut off, and a sawed-off brain." At least he managed to survive. Of the nine children his mother bore—Euphrasia Nalpas was a devout Catholic from Smyrna—half were stillborn. Only three survived past childhood. "Childhood," Artaud reminisced, "is like death."

It is no wonder that death and rebirth are at the heart of Artaud's writing. Nor is it surprising that the physicality of pain plays such an overwhelming part in his work. It would be simplistic, however, to consider Artaud's convulsive and paroxysmal outlook on life as the direct expression of his biographical circumstances, or even worse, as a mere symptom of his illness. Dr. Gaston Ferdière, director of the Rodez asylum where Artaud was to spend the last period of his life, once assured me that Artaud was an "authentic madman." The painter André Masson was even closer to the truth when he saw in his friend's extremist attitude a deliberate dare to his destiny. "You should never forget one thing," Masson wrote, "Artaud upped the ante even on his impasses; with him *prestige* always came first."

Young Artaud's staunch upbringing in the Catholic Church loomed very large in his resolution. As a child, Artaud was deeply attached to his devout mother and to his equally devout sister, Marie-Ange, who, like Friedrich Nietzsche's sister, remained the jealous defender of her brother's orthodoxy. "I've always seen him rosary in hand," she recalled. "I often found him kneeling and praying fervently. Despite what people continue to invent about his character, he was a true believer." (Perhaps because of his close relationship with his mother and sister, Artaud developed an ambivalent equation between sexuality and religion.) The young Antoine-Marie-Joseph (with these patrons, he could only—and would—become Jesus Christ) attended Catholic school and even considered entering the priesthood—a desire he was to deny vehemently during his later anticlerical period.

Artaud's attitude toward religion remained a matter of angry controversy among friends and followers. There is no doubt, though, that he first experienced suffering and self-denial in the context of deep religious fervor. "I am a man who has suffered much from the mind," he declared to Jacques Rivière, "and as such I have the *right* to speak." Artaud bore his curse like a cross, daring God to answer his claims and his followers to emulate his fate.

Artaud transcended purely literary boundaries because he set an example. To talk about Nietzsche, Georges Bataille said, you have to become Nietzsche. This is even truer for Artaud, whose work operates by contagion, abolishing the reader's critical distance. "What you mistook for my works," he declares in *Le pèsenerfs* (*The Nerve Meter*, 1925), "were merely the waste products of myself." Artaud is probably the first modern writer to explode the idea of literature as a discrete activity. His writings, now collected in some twenty-five volumes, are, in his words, the "scrapings of my soul"; his letters, aphorisms, fragments, manifestos, diaries, dreams, visions, and ravings are always tightly woven into the texture of his life. Comedian and martyr, Artaud kept backing up his works with his wounds, prompting his readers to identify completely with him. It is difficult to read Artaud without becoming Artaud—or an Artaud clone. William Burroughs once said that an artist creates out of need, not willpower. Artaud took on his disembodied existence as a challenge. "Where others present their works," he wrote in his preface to *L'Ombilic des limbes* (*The Umbilicus of Limbo*, 1925), "I claim to do no more than show my mind."

Artaud left Marseilles in 1920. At twenty-four he had shown no special aptitude for business and, for lack of a better solution, his family invited him to try his luck in Paris. For a few years he did his best to establish a career in the theater, consorting with the most famous directors of his day, Aurélian-Marie, Lugné-Poe and Jacques Copeau, and eventually joining Charles Dullin's L'Atelier, a newly formed theatrical ensemble, in 1921. There he met Génica Athanasiou, an actor—like himself—of Greek origin, with whom he struck up an intense and impossible relationship, the only romantic relationship he would ever have. (It ended six years later in recrimination and bitterness.) Artaud was a formidable but highly awkward actor. He was so trapped in his body that he moved it around like a machine, reenacting in his mind a dark tragedy of his own—and paying little attention to what was happening onstage. He was strikingly handsome and charismatic, but he had no place of his own and little regard for personal hygiene. His feet smelled and his fellow actors avoided him offstage as much as possible.

Artaud also wrote art criticism and, most important to him, lyrical poetry. His introduction to literature came through Dr. Edouard Toulouse, a renowned psychiatrist who had offered to look after him (as a friend of the family and a psychiatrist) at the Sainte-Anne asylum and to welcome him in his own home in Paris. Dr. Toulouse, a physician-poet of the type Artaud would encounter throughout his life, specialized in intellectual geniuses. He recognized at once the exceptional quality of Artaud's mind and involved him with his small literary magazine. He supervised his reading, sent him to exhibitions, and acquainted him with the tightly knit Parisian literary world.

If Artaud had any doubts as to where his true strength lay, his encounter with Rivière, the powerful editor of the sacrosanct *Nouvelle revue française* (it was then backed by established writers like André Gide and Paul Valéry) put him on the right track once and for all. In 1923 Artaud was twenty-seven years old and acutely conscious of being unknown and undecided. He couldn't choose, however, between writing, painting, and acting. Outwardly at least, he seemed intent upon pursuing a traditional literary career—in many ways a path more conservative than that of many of his contemporaries. He addressed his poems to Jacques Rivière, who in spite of his classical taste had recently shown some interest in young French writers like André Breton and Louis Aragon. Rivière politely declined the opportunity to publish Artaud's work (unsolicited material was rarely accepted by established magazines, but he read his poetry thoroughly enough to be struck by the discrepancy between the traditional verse structure of the poems and their awkward and skewed imagery. This, to Rivière, was a fault. Somewhat patronizingly he assured the would-be poet that with a little patience, he would "succeed in writing poems that are perfectly coherent and harmonious."

This piece of advice hardly answered Artaud's urgent desire to "exist *literarily*" for fear of not existing at all. After several months of silence, Artaud tried another angle. Instead of seeking Rivière's literary judgment "on some poems which I did not value," he decided to interest him in his "psychic anomaly." What followed was a superb literary and psychological confrontation between the two men, carried out in a stunning correspondence. With admirable finesse Artaud lay himself down on the couch as a model of tortured consciousness, successively adopting a number of roles—the aspiring young writer, the poetic visionary, the mental patient—and spelling out his symptoms with an almost hallucinatory precision. There is something, he wrote, "which destroys my thought; something which does not prevent me from being what I might be, but which leaves me, so to speak, in suspension. Something furtive which robs me of the words *that I have found.*" Artaud asked Rivière if he was willing to save him from his mental limbo by recognizing that his brain and his soul exist and—here Artaud addressed the publisher— "deserve a certain place."

Rivière was too sensitive to matters of style not to recognize in Artaud's writing, which he found "tormented, wavering, collapsing, as if sucked in here and there by secret whirlpools," the proof of this surprising "mental erosion." One senses that he was already secretly being drawn into Artaud's mental maelstrom. Abandoning all pretense of judging him as a poet—

or of curing him as a patient—Rivière finally acknowledged the unusual nature of the demand; the true subject, he realized, was not the poetry, but Artaud himself. The contrast that he noted between "the extraordinary precision of your self-diagnosis and the vagueness, or at least the formlessness, of your creative efforts" convinced him to publish, in lieu of Artaud's poems, their correspondence from 1923 and 1924 in the *Nouvelle revue française* in September 1924. (The letters were published in a separate volume in 1927.)

From this point on Artaud abandoned literature in favor of a frenetic dialogue about its absolute impossibility. Artaud himself and the minutiae of his daily struggles to remain alive and articulate himself are the subject of Artaud's writings. The letters that Artaud addressed to Rivière manifest a kind of unintentional realization of the surrealist movement's writing program. The surrealists (who were just beginning to emerge from their Dada phase) rejected conventional fictional forms in favor of a more translucent autobiographical prose that could openly explore the movement of the unconscious. When Rivière, fine-tuning his project, suggested giving their letters "an appearance of fiction," Artaud instantly reacted in a manner that showed how close he already was to surrealism's ethos. Why turn into an "epistolary novel," he retorted, what is "the cry of life itself"?

In his letter of 25 May 1924, Artaud went even further. The "horrible sickness of the mind" he complained of was all too real, but it also seemed to afflict "the whole age, as witness Tristan Tzara, André Breton, Pierre Reverdy. . . . What, then," Artaud wondered, "is the source of the trouble, is it really the atmosphere of the age, a miracle floating in the air, a cosmic and evil anomaly, or the discovery of a new world, an actual expansion of reality?" Artaud's mental erosion—whatever its specific causes—at this point took on a wider cultural significance. Artaud himself universalized his dilemma by declaring his unease to be paradigmatic, an attunement to the atmosphere of

1964

the age rather than a "morbid personal phenomenon." Seeking a more public forum, he became increasingly involved with the surrealist group and the theater.

"I am not as mad as you'd think."
—Letter to Louis Jouvet, 1931

In 1920 Artaud arrived in a Paris that was welcoming the young people who had escaped or avoided the massacre of World War I and were thronging to the capital of the artistic world. While French "patriots" kept noisily celebrating their victory and showing their contempt for anything foreign, artists and writers from all over the world—Amedeo Modigliani, Joan Miró, Pablo Picasso, Juan Gris, Chaim Soutine, Tsvgovharu Foujita, Francis Picabia, and the Americans Man Ray and Gertrude Stein—were gathering in Montparnasse, which was quickly becoming a prodigious melting pot of cultures, the laboratory of modernity. Like Artaud, most lived under strenuous conditions, eager to assert themselves on the French cultural scene. News of the Zurich Dada movement, scandalous and anarchist, was creating excitement throughout Europe, and when Dada impresario Tristan Tzara arrived in Paris in January 1920, he was welcomed by Breton, Aragon, and Philippe Soupault as the prophet of a new age. And, by all accounts this period *was* a new age.

New technological developments were irrevocably transforming Europe's perceptual landscape, now readily accessible through mass transit and communications. Local cultures were no longer fixed points of reference to their inhabitants. Although societies were liberated from dogmatic traditions that had remained fixed for centuries, this new freedom had its price in the deterritorialization, rootlessness, and anomie that are being described by philosophers in the 1980's. Artaud was to sense this dilemma fifty years ago, after his nostalgic and spiritual voyage to the peyote-smoking Indians of the Tarahumara.

The art of the twentieth century directly paralleled the epoch's technology and could probably best be captured in one word: "abstraction," the separation of thought from object. As is often the case, painters were the first to name and promote this tendency, but the effects of abstraction were felt everywhere: disembodied voices were heard over the radio; free-floating cinematic images reproduced life without any material support; newfound speed created ubiquity by bridging distances. If one were to extend this notion of abstraction philosophically, now ideas preceded, or even superseded, reality. Material form, the technology of the new media taught, had become redundant. Marcel Duchamp dramatically announced this new state of things by renouncing the physical act of painting in favor of framing "readymade" objects. And in Geneva, an obscure Indo-European language specialist, Ferdinand de Saussure, began to separate signs from the things they represented, turning the study of humanity into an abstract science, semiotics.

Artists worked out these realizations in various ways. Italian futurism glorified the coming of the mechanical age with odes to technology and war, written with a cinematic energy and telegraphic speed. The dadaists took an opposite approach, looking back to the ritualistic performances of primitive African cultures and trying to transcend rational language altogether by producing gibberish poems, collaged texts, and rhythmic manifestos. On a more cerebral plane, Guillaume Apollinaire composed exquisite "concrete" poetry and Man Ray took photographs without a camera. But throughout the art world there was a convergence of the conventions of primitive art with the new tendency toward cubist representation.

This search for primitivism was partly nostalgic, inspired by the dematerialization and deterritorialization of European culture in the early twentieth century. But while the Judeo-Christian tradition was losing its symbolic impact, avant-garde thinkers of this period embraced new theories and cultural ideologies. Russia's Bolshevik Revolution was three years old at the beginning of the decade, and the pre-Stalinist period offered the promise of changing not only the aesthetics but also the social relations of the world. The work of Sigmund Freud was discovered first by artists, who saw psychoanalysis as a key to drawing upon the unconscious. Everyone read Nietzsche avidly and dreamt about the *Übermensch*. There was a sense that this period was the dawn of another Renaissance.

It is impossible to tell in what way Artaud's illnesses attuned him so intimately to this radically disrupted world, but one thing is certain: his well-monitored psychosis was an echo chamber of the new age. In 1923 Artaud met the painter André Masson, an ex-patient of Dr. Toulouse. Through this acquaintance, Artaud became a frequent visitor to Masson's atelier in the rue Blomet, where painters and poets met nightly to engage in passionate literary discussions. They read Arthur Rimbaud and the German Romantics, discovered the Marquis de Sade and Le Comte de Lautréamont, and debated about Nietzsche and Dada. Breton's new review, *Littérature* (so named by Valéry in defiance of literature) was beginning to circulate.

In 1924 Breton, impressed by the *Correspondance,* invited Artaud to join the nascent Centrale surréaliste. Artaud was, Breton and the other members quickly realized—first in awe, then with a growing irritation—a "natural." Artaud's reality was already surreal. For the surrealists, their investigations of dreams and irrationality and their first attempts at "automatic writing" were daring experiments flaunted in the face of the literary world. For Artaud they were the only way he could live.

The coming months were the most exhilarating of Artaud's life, his first—and last—experience of a congenial artistic community. Impressed by his dark aura and contagious furor, Breton put Artaud in charge of the Centrale surréaliste, which Artaud instantly turned into a hotbed of insurrection. The new "dictator," as Aragon hailed him publicly, wrote every word of the third issue of *La révolution surréaliste*

himself, and dedicated it to "the end of the Christian era." In his "Adresse au Dalaï-Lama" (Address to the Dalai-Lama), Artaud condemned decadence; in the "Lettre aux médicin-chefs des asiles de fous" (Letter to the Head-Psychiatrists of Nut Houses), he denounced the "social dictatorship" that masqueraded as sanity; in the "Adresse au Pape" (Letter to the Pope), he declared a holy war on "you, Pope, dog." In all these texts he introduced a level of violence, passion, and wildness that the surrealists had thus far only theoretically aspired to.

Like Jean-Paul Marat (whom he impersonated in Abel Gance's *Napoléon,* 1926–1927) Artaud's mysticism and verbal maximalism soon crossed with the surrealists, especially as they were discovering radical politics through their opposition to the bloody war France was waging in Morocco. "War, be it in Morocco or elsewhere," declared Artaud, "is for me a question of the flesh." However hard he tried to accommodate his friends' involvement, Artaud could not help feeling unveiled contempt for their new Communist party membership and their rechristened surrealist magazine, *Le surréalisme au service de la révolution* (Surrealism at the Service of the Revolution). "Marxism," he wrote in *Point final,* his second pamphlet against the surrealists, "is the last rotten fruit of Western mentality." Only an "integral idealism," he warned, could fulfill the true aspirations of the surrealist revolution. Always careful to retain the power to define the movement's parameters, Breton, the pope of surrealism, withdrew the editorship of the magazine from Artaud, excommunicating him in "Au grand jour" (In the Open, 1927), calling him mad, cowardly, and dictatorial.

Actually Artaud's differences with the surrealists were present all along. In his correspondence with Riviére, Artaud mentioned Tzara, Breton, and Reverdy as symptomatic of the new age. But in their cases, he pointed out, "The soul is not physiologically damaged, it is not damaged substantially." Artaud's public reply to Breton, "A la grande nuit, ou le bluff surréaliste" ("In Total Darkness, or The Surrealist

Bluff," 1927), was curiously restrained. Instead of responding with further insults, Artaud wrote: "I have too much contempt for life to think that any change in the realm of appearances could improve my detestable condition. What separates me from the surrealists is that they love life as much as I despise it."

Artaud's answer to the first surrealist questionnaire—"Enquête—Le suicide est-il une solution?" ("Inquiry—Is Suicide a Solution?" 1925)—was immediate and blunt. "No," he replied, "suicide is still a hypothesis. I claim the right to doubt suicide as I do all the rest of reality. . . . Suicide is merely the fabulous and remote victory of men who think well. . . . Before I commit suicide I want to be assured of being. I want to be sure of my own death." *L'Art et le mort* (*Art and Death*, 1927) provides a paroxysmal answer to the question on suicide. To be sure of his death, Artaud, step by step, makes it come alive.

Artaud was never able to regard his own unconscious as a playground for surrealistic imagery. The separation that he experienced between his affections and his intelligence was too painful; he didn't feel free to use either as a source of literary conceits. His own mental experience was so immediate that his texts lack surrealistic whimsy and irony. They are located in the twilight and terror of a world in agony. For Artaud the most unbearable nightmare was not the possibility of an end of the self, or of the world—that was what he longed for. Estranged from emotions and thoughts that he hardly dared call his own, Artaud lived at the mercy of his lucidity. From as far back as he could remember, his best ally—his mind—had also been his worst enemy: "It is not that I actually thought when I was six years old," he wrote, "but I believe that I had the desire, the piercing perception to do so." In defiance of his own abstraction, Artaud turned himself into a methodical intellectual monster. Like an invalid checking the strength of each limb, he carefully checked each thought as if he had never thought before, as if no one had ever thought anything before. This didn't make Artaud es-

pecially easy to deal with, as his only lover, Génica Athanasiou, soon realized.

Artaud's despair was so extreme that it often seemed to cancel itself out. Although he appeared tense and tormented, isolated in the abysses of his own mind—he was "carrying about him a panorama of a gothic novel punctuated with lightning," said Breton—he was also a master of black humor. This humor is so integral to his work that no one seems to notice it. Artaud's work does offer the "greatest *quantity* of suffering in the history of literature," as Susan Sontag has written in her introduction to *Antonin Artaud: Selected Writings* (1976), but his excesses are completely provocative. If we, despite his urging that we do so, can avoid seeing Artaud as a victim, we can appreciate the brutal humor that he levies against himself and society.

Writing on the Marx Brothers in 1932, Artaud remarked that humor had lost "its sense of integral liberation, [of] tearing away every reality in the spirit." His own sense of humor was so corrosive that only his closest friends realized that his ravings and provocations were meant to test their integrity. Like Franz Kafka, Artaud took everything at face value. "You think I am a parasite," grins Gregor Samsa, and he turns into a cockroach; "You think I am a madman," shrieks Artaud, and he turns into Artaud. (But what does this turn us into?)

Language is essentially metaphorical, but Kafka and Artaud, both acrobats of language, act as if it told the truth—implicitly making an extravagant claim. Just as water boils into steam, images turn to paradox; written language becomes a land of *metamorphosis* where the perverse twists of meaning are recognized and used to question the culture.

For Artaud, letters were the literary form ideally suited to his tasks of confession, introspection, and sarcasm. In "À un ami" (To a Friend, 1931), Artaud meditated obsessively on the nature of thought, imagining the "thousand internal impressions, the thousand intimate creases whose melody, whose texture make up through unconscious associations thought, and in some sense its hazardous progression." He wanted to know, he insisted, pinning down his elusive object,

> at what time this so-called thought first prompt-ed the spirit to recognize that there was some-thing in store, then induced it to react in an infor-mal and abstract fashion, then at what time the spirit passed its contents to the personality, itself informal or formal, then to the nervous personal-ity seen through the self, and at what point this personality in turn abandoned the generality to go into the specifics, into some kind of physical realization in order—through a series of refrac-tions from nerves to spirit, spirit to self, self to person, person to spirit, spirit to nerves, nerves to synaptic consistency and continuity, to that power nerves have of arresting a thought long enough for words to fit in with their color and consistency, thus satisfying the needs of the mind, through that series of operations whose stages can be roughly delineated although they constitute the most active circulation within one's being—to *bring out* a thought formulated in such a way that it lasts and so efficient that it has an impact!!!

These strange synaptic contortions betray a poignant lyricism. We can imagine Artaud tip-toeing through his own mind to track down the frail passage of his thoughts. But the impact of this realization on the reader may be quite dif-ferent. Like those in a medical manual, his de-scriptions are intimidating. How could anyone blindly trust the natural flow of his or her own thoughts after such a mind-blowing dissec-tion? The maniacal minutiae of his investiga-tion, finally, come through with a devastating self-irony. As in Alain Robbe-Grillet's novels, excessive description turns us into *total* ab-straction. At the same time Artaud's hyperreal-ism bluntly called the surrealists' bluff. Breton's faith in historical materialism, he im-plied, was not material enough since it didn't acknowledge the fact that the mind is also mat-ter (or, as Yvonne Rainer phrased it, "the mind is a muscle"). If revolution occurred in the realm of the spirit, as the surrealists claimed, then "integral idealism" was the only possible materialist philosophy.

Most of the texts collected in *The Umbilicus of Limbo* and *The Nerve Meter* operate in the same way. Although they deal explicitly with dreams, paintings, dramas, and so on, they all address one central subject: the reality of the mind as refracted through the multiple facets of the writer's life. These books, neither of which received much attention at the time, are among the most astute that Artaud ever wrote.

In *The Umbilicus of Limbo* Artaud de-scribes the Renaissance painter Paolo Uccello "struggling in the middle of a vast mental web in which he has lost all the pathways of his soul, and even the form and suspension of his reality." This essay, "Paul les Oiseaux ou la place de l'amour" ("Paul the Birds, or the Place of Love"), is less a work of art criticism than Artaud's first scripted drama enacting the conflicts within his own mind. In this essay, Paolo Uccello represents himself, Artaud, and the "insectlike" André Masson, all three men sharing a total detachment from their bodies. Lost in speculation, Uccello, inventor of per-spective, hardly notices that his wife, Selvag-gia, is dying of hunger. What is the "place of love," wonders Artaud (thinking of Génica) for someone like Uccello—or himself or Masson—who is "caught like a fly in painting, in *his* painting, which consequently is layered"?

Artaud's text is certainly layered as well. It's written on a variety of planes that intersect only through our intuitive apprehension. When Uc-cello looks at fellow artists Filippo Brunel-leschi the architect and Donatello the sculptor as exemplars of certain tendencies within him-self, his quest is not merely aesthetic. Artaud sees himself in Uccello, probing his own mind/body schism through descriptions of the two artists: Donatello, who exalts the soul, and Brunelleschi, who celebrates the body. One is a saint, the other a pervert; one aspires to tran-scendent human love, the other thinks only of fornication. But where does Uccello stand in relation to the flesh? (In "Position de la chair" ["Situation of the Flesh," 1925], Artaud answers this question directly, in his own name, not through a "fictional" character.) Like Uccello, Artaud is groping for a body and a mind that could really be his own. He addresses the painter like an alter ego, begging him to wrench himself away from his hideous abstraction to join him, Artaud, "beyond time," where their answers can crisscross and their ideas "fuse into one." Leave your tongue, Paolo Uccello, exhorts the writer, "leave your tongue, my tongue, shit, who's speaking, where are you?" Artaud sensed his own sexuality to be, like Uccello's "glazed and mercurial, and as cold as ether." He wished he could be reborn somewhere else where love could have a "place." Could he manage to "feed" Génica even though he, like Uccello, had "nothing under his robe"? Was he capable of human compassion while struggling to understand the nature of what is called "myself"?

Artaud's *Lettres à Génica Athanasiou* (Paris, 1969) (some of which are included anonymously in *The Nerve Meter*) testifies to the intensity of this dilemma. Génica refused to condone his drug addiction although Artaud insisted it was the only way he could live without physical pain. He berated her with characteristic misogyny—"You judge with your sex, not with your mind"—although this was the same diatribe he used against his former surrealist friends. By the time Artaud's second text on Uccello, "Uccello le poil" ("Uccello the Hair"), dedicated to Génica, appeared in 1926, they had already broken up.

Artaud was unable to find a position for himself in Uccello's mental schema without shattering its unity. Detached from his body, he experienced a cubism of the mind. "Uccello the Hair" shows us the other side of the coin, a condition as fluid and arborescent as the first was glazed and stratified. Artaud hallucinates, envisioning Uccello in a maze of lines; his beard, wrinkles, eyelashes, the vegetation in his ear are part of the foliage in the natural world. From the circulation of branches to the network of veins, "everything is turning, everything is vibratile." Just as opium dissolves pain, lines dissolve perspective.

Artaud used Uccello to investigate his own spiritual impasse, and the amazing insight this provides sets a prodigious example for literary criticism. Actually Artaud does not criticize anything. His first essay on the theater, "L'Évolution du décors" ("The Evolution of Décor," 1924), is illustrative of this approach; perhaps we can better understand Artaud's critical methodology through his dramaturgic theories. The reader, wrote Artaud, is like a stage director. He or she must interpret the text musically (not just intellectually), giving it breath and energy, like an actor with his own body. This kind of reading is not a commentary; it is an act and an art. The director/reader must set logic aside to establish a "magnetic intercommunication" with the spirit of the author. Artaud opposes here the conventions of the French literary theater, which remained subservient to the author and myopically dependent on the letter of the text. "All language is garbage," Artaud pithily proclaims.

Artaud did not want the theater to renounce the text altogether—this is a common misreading—and he certainly did not want it to simply imitate life. His approach was more radical; signs or written words or play scripts should not be dead "dictionary-language." They should act directly on the soul. (Artaud's later experiments with glossolalia were the ultimate form of his new semiosis.) Interpreting a text is not a rational exercise, but a "drama of possession." The reader's "magnetic intercommunication" with the text should be active and creative, but never parasitical. Readers of Artaud who have tried to ape his suffering or use his drug addiction to condone their own have become "inert copies," like the two-dimensional stage actors Artaud criticizes, failing to discover in themselves the "other reality dangerous and typical" that Artaud strove to uncover.

1969

Clearly, Artaud's own reading was no sedentary activity. When he "read" Uccello—or Abélard, Masson, Heliogabalus, Gérard de Nerval, Jacques Villon, Vincent van Gogh, or Charles Baudelaire—he engaged in strange exorcistic dialogues, capturing the essences of these artists in order to relive the particular traumas of their spiritual awakenings. Artaud identified with original thinkers who, like him, went "off the track." Their relations with the cultures in which they lived were necessarily adversarial, and they achieved no worldly success. Artaud wrote in 1933 that the theater should stage men "taken as the emanation of forces and from the point of view of the events and the historical fate in which they played a part." By identifying with other individuals in cultural history one recognizes one's genealogy and the fatality and potential that it holds.

Uccello stood at the threshold of a new world. His deployment of perspective, in retrospect, seemed to Artaud to fit perfectly into the philosophical void of the late Middle Ages, when saints and demons had lost their power over the imagination. Perspective allowed the observer's eye to replace the eye of God. In order for perspective to render three-dimensional space, the viewer's eye must coincide with the vanishing point of the picture's frame. Aware of its arbitrary effectiveness, Uccello was loath to accept his construction as true depth or a new realism. Instead, he wondered, what would happen if several center points were introduced within a single painting? What would that say about the nature of reality and the reality of representation? And what would happen to the viewers' sense of themselves if, instead of assuming center-stage positions, they had to encompass simultaneously several contradictory perceptions? Like a scientist testing the truth of a new abstraction by reformulating its parameters, Uccello demonstrated that the unity of the perception he had discovered (and hence the perception of subjectivity) was an illusion. Like artists who would follow him hundreds of years later, Uccello transformed the orderly space of perspective into a pattern of conflicting lines, thereby revealing the true flatness of the canvas.

Like all great artists, Artaud only wrote about himself. But his work is not autobiographical in any traditional sense. How could it be, if the self was the "unthinkable problem"? Artaud didn't write "about" his life; he wrote himself *into* life. "I feel sometimes that I am not writing," he told Anaïs Nin, "but describing the struggles with writing, the struggles of birth." Like photographic paper exposed to a changing light, Artaud's writing exposes the different stages of his mind as it struggles to come into being. Painters can paint endlessly the same subject and yet each time produce an altogether different artwork. Artaud's writing registers the fleeting pulses of his mind and the distant tremors of his culture with seismographic accuracy. It is this sustained effort that gives his work, apparently so disconnected, its prodigious unity. There is a magic in Artaud's style, instantly recognizable, and yet impossible to account for in purely stylistic terms. Only a new literary seismology could describe the pitch, intensity, rhythm, pattern, consistency, and the singular feel of Artaud's language.

Artaud's mental dramas—all his texts, whether dramatic or not, could be described that way—are immediately perceptible in his writing. Like Abélard, the unhappy twelfth-century monk who fell in love with Héloïse and whom Artaud wrote about in "Héloïse et Abélard" (1925), Artaud was endlessly trying to "stabilize his atoms" in the hope of "enjoying" (possessing) his mind. If he could only smoothly "glide from one state to the next," Artaud wrote, his mind wouldn't be "reduced to a series of ascents and descents." He would be centered "on one point," and the question of loving (whether Abélard's loving Héloïse or his loving) would become simple.

I have shed so many corpses from myself, that I have become the antidote to the plague.
—*Cahiers de Rodez, 1945*

1970

The years between 1925 and 1935 were the most intensely prolific of Artaud's career. During these years he continued to work as a movie actor—although mostly to earn a living. He had become interested in the emotional properties of cinema. Film, he discovered, was like morphine: its images affected the brain directly. Most of Artaud's later ideas on theater (his rejection of plot and so on) are foreshadowed in these incisive observations on the cinema. Artaud wrote several film scripts. One of them, *La coquille et le clergyman* (*The Seashell and the Clergyman*, 1927), was produced and directed by Germaine Dulac, whom he quickly denounced for betraying his intentions (she had turned Artaud's "subjective images" into a dream sequence).

Despairing of the talkies—which he called a bland "substitute for verbal theater"—Artaud turned toward the theater to give his ideas about language, ritual, and culture a social and communicable form. In 1926 Artaud created the Théâtre Alfred Jarry with Robert Aron and Roger Vitrac, a young dramatist who had just been dismissed from the surrealist circle by Breton. (This association contributed to Artaud's estrangement from the group.) The surrealists continued to alternatively support and disrupt Artaud's efforts, and their polemics spilled over into the public sphere. Another poet-psychiatrist, Dr. René Allendy, provided some financial backing for the theater—and eventually professional help to Artaud.

The Théâtre Alfred Jarry mobilized all of Artaud's energies. At this point he really saw the possibility of making an artistic and career breakthrough. The company presented three productions, including Artaud's own surrealist spoof "Le jet de sang" ("The Spurt of Blood," 1925), but the success he anticipated kept evading him. His attempt in 1932 to mobilize the *Nouvelle Revue Française* behind his "theater of cruelty" also failed. Even *Les Cenci* (*The Cenci*, 1935), Artaud's most ambitious creation, which he produced, directed, and starred in, ended in disaster despite its initial success. *The Cenci*, a twentieth-century update

of an Elizabethan tragedy, revolves around the themes of incest, violence, and imperial misrule. One can readily understand Artaud's attraction to this kind of drama: its violence is so raw and so close to primal emotions that it defies theatrical naturalism. The play also embodies everything missing from our culture: ritual, impetuousness, selfless passion. *The Cenci*, in fact, is so violent in a baroque way that it reads today as a kind of black comedy.

Despite his practical failures, Artaud experimented enough in the cinema and the theater to formulate, between 1931 and 1936, ideas that revolutionized the theater for decades to come. For the most part these ideas would only be discussed after World War II; Artaud had the greatest influence upon directors Jerzy Grotowski, Peter Brook, Julian Beck, and Judith Malina, who all matured artistically in the 1960's. Today Artaud is best known for his theories of the theater. Yet few people realize how much these theories related to his total life experience. In 1933 Allendy invited Artaud to deliver a lecture at the Sorbonne on "Le théâtre et la peste" ("The Theater and the Plague"). Artaud researched his subject carefully in medical and history books, but in a sense he didn't have to; he knew intimately what "a powerful state of physical disorganization" was and what it entailed. His conception of the plague tells a lot about how he thought of his own illness. (In 1927 Artaud had written to Gance, "I have the plague in the soul of my nerves, and I suffer from it.")

In his lecture, Artaud described the plague as a fundamental disorder of secretive glands. The disease worked its way into the entrails, filling veins and arteries with its dark and sticky substance before erupting into monstrous boils. But the transmission of the illness remained mysterious, and Artaud made a bold suggestion: the plague does not spread by contact but operates from a distance, selecting its organism by virtue of a "mysterious affinity." The plague affected the brain and the lungs, both of which manifest human will, consciousness, thought. Like Heliogabalus, whose love for disorder was "merely the application of a metaphysical and superior idea of order," the plague is a spiritual energy that seizes the body and makes it react in a paroxysm before disappearing as if by magic.

The theater, Artaud asserted, is just like this. Just as the plague attacks a human body, theater attacks a social body that has become vulnerable because it stands divorced from organic life. This conceit was actually a perverse reversal of Saint Augustine's anathema on the theater, in which he compared the theater to "a plague corrupting souls" in *The City of God.* Artaud demanded from the theater the same purifying experience that his illness was to him, a spiritual antidote to the "mal blanc" (the French phrase "mal blanc" designates both a blister and a broader notion of Western decay). Artaud's lecture, which he read as if "in agony," scandalized his audience, who left the room laughing and hissing. But for Artaud his "act" was the very soul of teaching. "They always want to hear *about,*" he told his friend Anaïs Nin. "I want to give them the experience itself, the plague itself, so they will be terrified, and awaken. They do not realize *they are dead.*"

Throughout *Le théâtre et son double* (*The Theater and Its Double,* 1938)—the collection of essays that includes this lecture—Artaud invokes different measures that could alchemically transform the theater into the "real spectacle of life." First and foremost, the theater must shake itself free from the superstition of the written text and the stifling claims of the classics. "Enough with masterpieces," Artaud exclaimed, denouncing the tyranny of the author and the sterility of criticism. Since the Renaissance the theater had fallen prey to description and psychology, turning the stage into a verbal abstraction. The theater had to be reinvented anew, Artaud believed, by treating everything on the stage, *language included,* in the most concrete fashion. Taking precedence over the author, the director must become a creator in his or her own right, assuming total control over the scenic space by every possible means: dance, music, mime, intonation, decor,

lighting. Only by emphasizing the physicality of its signs and the energy of its images could the theater regain its occult and fabulous power. Reality, for Artaud, is not rational or reassuring; instead it is dangerous and inhuman, and it is the responsibility of the theater to match in kind the cruelty of the universe. *Cruelty:* the term stands out in the imagination because it connotes blood, revenge, and barbarity. For Artaud it also involved the idea of an implacable necessity pushing conflicts to their ineluctable outcome. The theater of cruelty is a radical kind of catharsis in which images as absolute as the flailing arms of victims being burned at the stake touch audiences to the depths of the unconscious. In a sense, Artaud grafted a frightening medieval religiosity onto the popular comedic conventions of the Elizabethan stage. Yet this catharsis is never like a modern "happening," improvised or out of hand, nor is it reckless or sadistic. Through his studies of Balinese dance, Artaud had come to admire the rote precision of authentic ritual. The scenic structure of his theater was deliberate and compressed. Excessive, passionate, convulsive—but thoroughly exacting—his theater of cruelty manifested the existence of a superior cosmic necessity.

Another "magical agent" that Artaud invokes in *The Theater and Its Double* is metaphysics. Like cruelty and the plague, it is a "double" of the theater, a dark force capable of giving the culture back its shadow. In 1931, watching the Balinese dancers moving upon the stage like perfectly oiled automatons, Artaud sensed that they incarnated "another scene" upon the stage—another scene as obscure and threatening as E. T. A. Hoffmann's doppelgängers. In both cases the existence of some absolute evil was being displayed with dispassionate objectivity. The metaphysical scope of eastern theater with its strict impersonality and gestural hieroglyphics led Artaud into studies of esoteric doctrines, astrology, the cabala, and tarot—all disciplines that value concrete visual symbols more than modern logical discourse.

Artaud's involvement with gnostic cosmogonies and syncretic systems led him in 1933 to write a book on Heliogabalus (*Héliogabale, ou l'anarchiste couronné* [*Heliogabalus; or, The Anarchist Crowned,* 1934]), the pagan emperor who, in the third century, attempted to impose the cult of the sun on Rome "to punish the Latin world for no longer believing in its myths or in any myths." It is not the mad caesar's biography per se that Artaud was interested in, although the kinship he felt with him is not to be doubted. Heliogabalus, like Artaud, was so permeated with "a disturbing taste for disease and discomfort" that he dedicated himself to "the pursuit of disease on the largest possible scale." (The Solar Emperor's perverse eroticism, however, ran so counter to Artaud's increasing asceticism, that he would eventually denounce the text in 1944.) What *Heliogabalus* gave Artaud was a rare opportunity to use murder, derision, and excesses of all kinds to dramatize the malicious principle that, he felt, ravaged his organism and played havoc with the whole universe. Although it wasn't written for the stage, *Heliogabalus, or The Anarchist Crowned* remains by far the best example of Artaud's theater of cruelty.

It was at this moment of Artaud's clearest theoretical formulations that he found himself most dependent on the approval of Paris' artistic and literary worlds. He had a vision that demanded a major transformation of consciousness in the world, but he was penniless and addicted and all he had behind him was a string of commercial flops. Nin, who knew him at the time, sensed that his life was on such a downward spiral that all he could hope for was "a revolution, a catastrophe, a disaster that would put an end to his unbearable existence." The failure of *The Cenci* was the last straw. Artaud decided to find, as he wrote in *Heliogabalus,* "a people where the theater wasn't on the stage, but in life." He left for Mexico, where he hoped "a new idea of man [was] being born."

Artaud's trip to Mexico was motivated by an immense misunderstanding, which he managed, against all odds, to turn into a mystical experience. Artaud had been fascinated by ancient American religions and Aztec civilization since his youth. More recently, he had acquired some knowledge of the Popol Vuh and read about Mexican gods in the Codices. In 1933—the year in which he wrote *Heliogabalus*—he began to write a play script called "La conquête du Mexique" (The Conquest of Mexico), which he meant to be the first production of his theater of cruelty. The metaphysical fund of old pre-Cortésian religions, he believed, was still alive: "It wouldn't take much to light up the fires again."

Upon arriving, however, Artaud found the country in the aftermath of a social revolution. Mexicans were more preoccupied with Marxism and European culture than with their own native traditions. Replaying his bitter political quarrel with the surrealists on foreign ground, Artaud vainly exhorted Mexican youths to renounce materialist "idolatry" for the total metaphysics of their "red" (that is, Indian) roots. But to them he was just an obscure and misguided French poet. He did not speak Spanish, and his behavior was so idiosyncratic that he soon came to be known as "the mad Frenchman." He spent a lot of time looking for drugs. For a few months Artaud survived the best he could (terribly, actually) in Mexico City, giving lectures and writing newspaper articles that a few acquaintances translated for him on the spot. His closest friend, a surrealist poet whom he had met briefly in Paris, Luís Cardoza y Aragon, told me that Artaud had little contact in Mexico with his intellectual contemporaries. The only Mexican artists flourishing at the time were the mural painters Diego Rivera, David Siqueiros, and José Clemente, all of whose work Artaud despised for its European formalism. "Today's painting," Artaud wrote, "lacks an infusion of mythical blood." At any rate no Mexican intellectual in the 1930's shared his conviction that revolution was to be found in "the eternal culture" of Mexico.

Paradoxically Artaud ignored the wealth of pre-Columbian art and the extraordinary Aztec cosmogonic sculptures that could be reached so easily from Mexico City. He had not come all the way from the Latin Quarter to visit tourist sites; he had already decided what he was going to find. In an open letter to the governors of the states of Mexico, Artaud proclaimed that "rites and sacred dances of the Indians are the best possible forms of theater and the only ones that can't be denied." After years of frustration, he was impatient to see "the *real* drama come true."

And it did. Artaud had heard of the Tarahumara, a North Mexican tribe isolated in the volcanic region of the Sierra Madre who had eluded missionaries and were adepts of peyote. When Artaud set out on the difficult voyage into the mountains, he was already suffering from acute withdrawal symptoms. After a few weeks of maneuvering between the Indians and local authorities, he finally managed to secure permission to participate in the curative rite of the peyote enacted during the dance of the Tutuguri. What actually happened there we only know about from Artaud's *D'un voyage au pays des Tarahumaras* (A Voyage to the Land of the Tarahumara, 1945, translated as *Peyote Dance*), a collection of texts written between 1936 and 1948.

It would be misleading to read the Tarahumara cycle as a homogeneous narrative, especially since the order of the fragments as they were published is widely at variance with the chronology of their composition. The first text of the volume, "Le rite du peyote chez les Tarahumaras" ("The Rite of the Peyote Among the Tarahumara") was written in the Rodez asylum in 1943; "La montagne des signes" ("The Mountain of Signs"), which follows, was written in Mexico in 1936, as were the three texts on the Tarahumara later added at the end of the volume; the third piece, "La danse du peyotl" ("The Peyote Dance"), was written in 1937 in Paris; and "Tutuguri," the last text, was completed (in its second version) only three weeks before his death. These dates are important; although the various fragments of his text deal with the same event, in each essay readers find

themselves in a different world. More than any other work, Artaud's Mexican cycle reveals that his only subject was his mind.

The texts written in Mexico, especially "The Mountain of Signs," are unparalleled in Artaud's work for their limpidity. They are as perfectly poised and vibrant as a wide-eyed stare. Entering the land of the Tarahumara, Artaud felt as if he were seeing for the first time; he saw human forms carved into the rock, a giant statue of death, trees burned in the shapes of the cross, numbers, circles, and triangles, all intelligent signs directly evolved from the earth. These forms seemed to speak to him in the syncretic language of principles. The secret science lost after the Renaissance, Artaud believed, was being born in the Mexico highlands out of stones and chaos. Nature was alive, and thinking.

Written once he was back in Paris, "The Peyote Dance" speaks an altogether different language. Like Artaud's daily life, the essay seemed to him like a "dislocated assemblage," a piece of "damaged geology," friable, full of crevices, a vast landscape of ice "on the verge of breaking up." And the head, Artaud writes, "can no longer control its whirls, the head feels all the swirling energies of the earth below, which throw it into a panic, keeping it from standing erect." This was how Artaud felt when he returned to a Paris where nothing had changed, except for the worse. He was addicted to drugs again, laudanum, heroin, and cocaine, and moving from hospital to hospital in the hope of being cured. His engagement to Cécile Schramme, an affluent Belgian artist, broke up after he gave a scandalous lecture, "La décomposition de Paris" (The Decomposition of Paris), in Brussels in 1937. He was obsessed with cabalistic signs, astrology, and numerology, and quickly mastered the tarot and spent days interpreting cards. His *Les nouvelles révélations de l'être* (*The New Revelations of Being,* 1937) a work based on the tarot, was published anonymously. Artaud now refused to sign his name because soon, he said, he wouldn't need it anyway.

Artaud exaggerated and exacerbated his madness, although he may have lost his ability to discern when he was playing it for effect. Refusing his friends' help, he begged in the street and slept in public parks. He believed he had a mission. "I *know* now not only from intuition," he wrote to Jean Paulhan, "but by precise, even mathematical Ways, that sensational events are in the offing, which this ordeal announced."

As Artaud's "Peyote Dance" of 1937 tells us, the ecstatic vision of the Tarahumara had turned into a nightmare. The giant rocks whose wondrous geometry Artaud once admired were now menaces that prevented him from entering the "terrible" mountain. Writing during one of his many rehabilitations, Artaud suffered from an acute withdrawal that reminded him of the twenty-eight days he spent in northern Mexico waiting for the magic cure. Around him sorcerers performed an abject comedy, some "on crutches, others like sawed-off puppets." And Artaud lay among them like a "broken robot," incapable of penetrating their mysterious ceremony. His earlier assertions were now replaced by questions: "What is the singular word, the lost word that the Master of Peyote communicates to them?" Was it worth going through this agony only "to bring back a collection of outworn imageries from which the Age, true to its own system, would at most derive ideas for advertisements and models for clothing designers"? His receptivity had turned into vengeful lucidity. What was there for him to do but wish for "the first fruits of the fire in view of a conflagration that would soon be generalized"?

After nine months in Paris spent living completely on the edge, Artaud went on the road again. This time he left for Dublin carrying a strange knotted cane that he found and attributed to Saint Patrick. "I am going to fulfill my destiny," he wrote Breton. Artaud had no money and spoke no English. The letters he sent from Ireland were filled with fantasies of revenge and apocalyptic prophecies. What happened during the next six weeks remains, for the most part, a mystery. He is known to have registered at various guest houses and to have left without paying the bill. He was put in jail after picking a fight at a monastery and finally deported on the *Washington.* He claimed that while on board he was treated brutally by the sailors. He arrived in Le Havre "very agitated" and was immediately sent in a straitjacket to a mental hospital, Quatre-Mares, in Rouen. It took him nine years to regain his freedom. Doctors at the hospital diagnosed him as having paranoid delusions and transferred him in 1938 first to the psychiatric ward of Sotteville-lès-Rouen, then to the famous asylum of Sainte-Anne in Paris. *The Theater and Its Double* had just been published. Marthe Robert, a literary critic and close friend of Artaud, told me that "Artaud should never have left the Latin Quarter. We understood his idiosyncrasies. With us he would have been safe."

In 1939, declared incurable, Artaud was transferred to the drug-addict ward of Ville-Evrard, where he would remain for four years. The early 1940's were terrible years for the insane. Paris was occupied by the Germans, and Artaud's friends had scattered. Asylums throughout France were being turned into death camps. Artaud would probably have died at Ville-Evrard like thousands of undernourished patients if Robert Desnos hadn't managed, in 1943, to have him transferred farther south to the Rodez asylum in Aveyron, then in the French free zone. (Desnos himself died in a concentration camp one year later.)

The Rodez asylum was directed by Dr. Gaston Ferdière, another psychiatrist-poet whom Artaud had briefly met among the surrealist entourage. Starved and prostrated but moderately famous, Artaud was given special treatment. A few months later he was given a series of electroshocks, which seem to have brought him somewhat back to his senses. (Artaud's electroshock therapy, which he later angrily denounced, remains at the center of an endless controversy. Dr. Ferdière maintains that it was the only treatment then available, and saved Artaud from remaining "a vegetable.") At Ville-Evrard Artaud had adopted his mother's maiden name, calling himself Antonin Nalpas; he believed he was a reincarnation of Saint Hippolytus and Jesus Christ. After the first round of shocks, his "double personality," as Dr. Ferdière called it, disappeared. Artaud returned to his earlier Catholicism, but with a fanaticism that shocked both Ferdière's assistant, Dr. Jacques Latremolière, who was himself staunchly religious, and Frère Julien, the local priest. Artaud's religious outlook was fiercely Manichaean. Persecuted by demons, he abhorred anything sexual.

In spite of his supplications, Artaud received a second series of shocks. A few weeks later his health seemed to improve. He started writing again, translated poems from English with Frère Julien's help, and rediscovered drawing and painting, which he pursued assiduously until his death. (His drawings and paintings are now collected in one volume, *Antonin Artaud: Dessins et portraits* [1986].) But his hallucinations apparently returned and in 1944 he received a third and maybe a fourth round of shocks. Each treatment left him disoriented and deadened for weeks on end. It was in late 1943 or early 1944 that Artaud wrote "The Rite of the Peyote Among the Tarahumara" at the request of Henri Parisot of Editions Fontaine.

Thematically this text overlaps with "The Peyote Dance." He describes once again his initiation into peyote, but with neither the deep disarray of the earlier Parisian version nor the visionary conviction of the Mexican one. It is simply—and sometimes blandly—evangelical. (In an aside Artaud apologized, as if at confession, for the bizarre gestures he had made until "a few weeks ago," exorcizing demons, whistling, chanting, spitting in public, "like some patients suffering from *religious mania.*" "These are merely the residue of regrettable habits I had developed under beliefs that didn't exist," he wrote.) "The Peyote Dance" was written in the voice of a religious fanatic; "The Rite of the Peyote" was written, as Artaud

himself later noted, "in the stupid mental condition of the *convert.*"

Artaud's conversion was striking. Now he described the peyote sorcerers as "priests of the *Master of all things,*" God and His Verb (i.e., Jesus Christ). Just as Artaud now claimed that the Tarahumara Indians paid little attention to their bodies (Artaud actually saw some of them masturbating publicly, throwing furious glances in his direction), so his language in "The Rite of the Peyote" seems disembodied, less spiritual than spirited. CIGURI, or peyote (which is God, Artaud claims), makes "the idea of matter" in the Indians' bodies *volatile.* (Capital letters abound in Artaud's treatment of religious essences.) The "crude purgation" he earlier described in earthy terms and the sorcerer spitting abundantly "the thickest and most compact gobs" reappear, but the rite is not crude anymore—instead it is curiously abstracted. In one striking formula, Artaud depicts the Indian "priest" spitting, "not saliva but his breath." Artaud describes his approach to the land of the Tarahumara more prosaically and hence less accurately here than in any of the other Mexican texts because for Artaud, at this point, reality lies elsewhere. The vision has turned inside. Syncretic signs, triangles, numbers, letters, the whole alphabet, are now received "hands folded," like the Christian host.

Who could have guessed that Artaud would bounce back from this period of astounding orthodoxy with his creativity intact and with a "holy" rage against all religions? In a sense, Artaud's conversion finally led him to touch base with reality again. Although after September 1945 he furiously rejected as "fetid spiritual assimilations" the supplement to the texts on the Tarahumara he had written in January 1944, one senses that by then he was already regaining his strength. His language is tighter and his mood more aggressively combative. The letters "J-E" (I, in French, or JEsus) that he saw earlier, surging among the flames in a mystic revelation once again became the central question. Cornered by madness—and by dependency on his caretakers—into reassuming his childhood ties, even considering for a while becoming a priest, Artaud now had no choice but to fight, once and for all, the enemy within.

The war at first took on purely Christian tones, but it quickly moved beyond metaphysical mysticism to concentrate on the "abject eroticism" with which evil kept tempting him. Artaud found in Catharist asceticism, a strain of medieval Manichaeism still alive in the region, a way of exceeding Catholicism. "The world," he proclaimed, "will only be cured of its madness and delirium when it renounces the principle of its intimate sexuality." But on 1 April 1945, "this so-called Sunday of the Passion," Artaud suddenly renounced the Catholic faith. Throwing "out of the window communion, eucharist, god and his christ" (and all the capital letters), he decided to be himself, "that is, simply Antonin Artaud, an unbeliever irreligious by nature and soul who never hated anything more than god and his religions, whether they come from christ, Jehovah, or Brahma."

Artaud was cured of his faith but not of the religious impulse. Actually its madness becomes his cure. In a clinically typical delirium, Artaud reshuffled the whole universe in order, he said, to preserve his "intentions of purity." Each night, as Artaud wrote, he imagined that an army of succubi and incubi who were also living people from all races and nations would come to overwhelm his consciousness and submit his body to obscene manipulations. Artaud's sexual organs were the prime targets of a cosmic conspiracy led by "the vampire with the beard." The aristocracy of religious leaders, scientists, doctors, capitalists, and magicians had manipulated the masses with the humbug of eroticism, Artaud asserted, pressing with all their weight on the few "arch-individuals" who, like Artaud, refused to submit to sex. Priests, police, and psychiatrists, all agents provocateurs, had locked him up in

asylums; they were afraid that his ideas, if published, would explode human consciousness and disrupt the rigged theater of reality. Actually the apocalypse had already begun; "the order of the beard" (that is, god's creatures) kept sucking him dry of his life and sexual substance in order to maintain a semblance of reality and prevent him from "putting a stop to this chaos."

What sounded at first like paranoid delirium at this point took on a truth of its own. It could be said that Artaud invented a system of political and religious bewitchment of cosmic dimension in order to account for what remained for him inadmissible: that he, Artaud, would be, like anyone else, submitted to the abjection of his sexuality. Accumulating concrete instances of the world-wide conspiracy that threatened his corporeal integrity, Artaud managed, though, to make us suspend our disbelief and to convince us, if not of the reality of his persecution, at least of the reality of his suffering and the authenticity of his vision. By setting himself up as a propitiatory victim, Artaud turned his delirium into a revelation. As Jacques Lacan himself recognized, delirium is not just passive. It is the direct translation of the unconscious into a creative activity that has a bearing on reality. It was from his paranoid delirium that Artaud derived a formidable insight into other poets' predicament— Lautréamont, Gérard de Nerval, Edgar Allan Poe, Baudelaire, Rimbaud, Nietzsche, all poisoned, imprisoned, paralyzed, bewitched, "suicided" by society, as he claims in *Suppôts et supplications* (1978). In his preface Artaud warns his readers against the "universal spiritual laziness" that denies delirium any reality; he actually made an active attempt on his part to shrug off "the evil spirits, who are the authentic bourgeoisie of life."

Like the rest of his work, Artaud's delirium at Rodez was both real and forced, especially when replayed in letters to his friends, which were intended for publication. By forcing his madness, Artaud managed to cast doubt on what is taken for sanity. One month before leaving the asylum Artaud wrote to Arthur Adamov: "I have found other means of action that don't concern the law, or will make it laugh. It is *concrete absolute humor,* but humor all the same." Artaud's humor is rarely recognized. And this is hardly surprising: his humor is imperceptible. It is for Artaud (as it was for Jonathan Swift) the weapon of the weak and the oppressed, people who are in no position to confront authority openly. Instead of resisting the law, Artaud takes its injunctions literally, thus bringing out its latent absurdity. Instead of questioning God's existence, Artaud simply puts himself in his place, ridiculing him through his own derisive claim to be Jesus Christ. This humor, "hallucinating and terrible," which "reveals an atrocious illness over a profile of absolute beauty," is the cruel humor of madness, already celebrated by the Marx Brothers, of whom Artaud had written in 1932, "One finds there some sort of intellectual freedom where the unconscious of all the characters, repressed by customs and conventions, takes its revenge, and ours as well." Delirium too is "monkey business," to quote a Marx Brothers title.

The biggest "monkey" of all, for Artaud, was god, who keeps "rigging the soul of this world." For centuries, Artaud asserted, he had been martyred because he denied god's existence and was himself suspected of being god—and so is he, Artaud goes on, imperturbable, "because god's real name is Artaud." Once crucified on Golgotha, he had been forced to take the identity of a "stuttering cripple neurotically obsessed with his self." To counter society's obsession with family, Artaud built himself a fabulous biography populated by his own version of the Holy Family, six "daughters of the heart" (some dead, like his own grandmothers or Yvonne Allendy; some alive, like Cecile Schramme or Anie Besnard; and some invented, like Ana Corbin) whom he keeps invoking tenderly and paternally. In poignant passages, he described the ordeal of his imaginary daughters in the hands of the police,

medicine, and religion. Their warm company helped him exorcise his solitude and deprivation, giving him the courage to be reborn without a father or mother, out of his own works.

A few elements of this prodigious spiritual adventure surface in the *Lettres de Rodez* (1946), in which Artaud kept begging his friends to take him out of Rodez. They also appear in larger fragments in *Suppôts et supplications,* which he rewrote in 1947 and 1948, but which was only published in 1978. This three-part book, like the *Umbilicus,* is made of short texts and letters; more than any previous work, it exposes the suffering body of Artaud "breathlessly straddling the culture." The letters to his friends provide "the bridge of a true correspondence" between the fragmentations of the first part and the violent interjections of the last. But it is in Artaud's private notes—started in February 1945 and comprising some three thousand pages of intense meditation as Artaud struggles to regain his own self—that the scope and depth of his bewildering enterprise is revealed. The *Cahiers de Rodez* (The Rodez Notebooks, published between 1981 and 1985 in the *Oeuvres complètes*) are a direct transcription of the mental ordeal Artaud went through before he could finally leave Rodez in May 1946—not as a victim but, as his literary executor Paule Thévenin writes, "as a conqueror."

After nine years spent in asylums, the "conqueror" was in terrible shape. With his collapsed jaw, a ravaged face, untrimmed hair, his wasted body floating inside a worn-out coat, Artaud was the double of his former self and the spitting image of his thoughts. At fifty, the *poète maudit* looked like an eighty-year-old bum, yet Paule Thévenin, meeting him for the first time, found him "royal."

Paris, just freed from German occupation, had changed, too. Food was rationed, the surrealists were still in exile, and St. Germaindes-Prés had replaced Montparnasse as the cultural center of Paris. A new generation of friends and devotees, mobilized by the dramatist Arthur Adamov and Marthe Robert, who had visited Artaud in Rodez, actively sought ways of securing Artaud's financial independence, which was the first condition Dr. Ferdière imposed upon his release. A prestigious benefit performance and an auction of works by countless artists and writers were organized to take care of this.

Artaud found a home (fulfilling Ferdière's second condition) in the private clinic of Dr. Adrille Delmas in Ivry, a Parisian suburb, from which he could come and go as he pleased. Artaud covered the walls of his room with haunting drawings and, ax in hand, nailed his poetry to tree stumps. Whenever he could, he dictated his poems, testing their rhythms carefully, often adding and improvising in the process.

Artaud wrote feverishly wherever he went, in buses, in cabs, in cafés, in bed. He went out with children's notebooks stuffed into his pockets. He was often seen in St. Germain-des-Prés gouging holes into the tables of fashionable literary cafés with his pocketknife, resting in friends' apartments, or procuring drugs, which he continued to consume in enormous quantities. His drug habit, condoned by his friends, became the subject of bitter quarrels between them and Artaud's family and psychiatrists, all of whom continued to fight amongst themselves long after Artaud's death (which, during these years in Paris, was imminent).

Although freed from mental institutions and religious dogma, Artaud was still prey to countless fantasies. He believed a certain Mr. Artaud was crucified two thousand years ago, and not Jesus Christ, an impostor. He also believed that he had been knifed by a pimp in Marseilles in 1917 after leading a rebellion. These fantasies and his public persona were cultivated with sovereign disregard for bourgeois sensibilities. Artaud grunted, chanted, and gesticulated obscenely while walking down the street. Every so often he screwed his knife on the top of his head in a kind of self-administered acupuncture. But what were these harmless eccentricities compared to the "formidable suction, the formidable tentacular oppression of a kind of civic magic" that, Artaud argued, "suicided" van Gogh and kept "sucking my life." In "Le retour d'Artaud le mômo" ("The Return of Artaud, le Mômo," 1947), a poem of rage and self-deprecation (a *mômo* is a village idiot, and suggests a mummy), this suction is described more explicitly and ontologically. The poem addresses in scatological terms the scandal of his uncalled-for conception "between the ass and the shirt," that is, the scandal of being born with a sex. Artaud's old demons, sexuality and spirituality, were still there, conspiring in "the foul butt-end of Christian orgies" (from "La culture indienne" ["Indian Culture," 1947]). Since his return from Rodez, however, his indictment of society had become more strident, compounded by an intense aversion to psychiatry, which, with its "ridiculous terminology," masqueraded as a science.

Artaud's *Van Gogh, le suicidé de la societé* (*Van Gogh, the Man Suicided by Society*, 1947) was prompted by the diagnosis of the artist as a "degenerative psychopath" ventured by a psychiatrist after the van Gogh exhibition at the Orangerie. Artaud reacted immediately and violently. Even "Dr. L.," the now famous Jacques Lacan, who flirted for a while with surrealism, is portrayed as an "erotomaniac" and a "rotten bastard." Reliving his own experience through van Gogh, Artaud gave a step-by-step analysis of the ways psychiatrists managed insidiously (and not just through straight electroshocks) to "cut off at its root that impulse of rebellious vindication which is at the origin of genius."

The first part of *Van Gogh, the Man Suicided by Society* actually echoes Artaud's "Letter to the Head Psychiatrists of Nut Houses," which he wrote at the height of his surrealist involvement. And in some way, through van Gogh (as Georges Bataille did through de Sade), Artaud settled his accounts with Breton, with whom he had resumed his friendship in the early 1930's. Breton always celebrated madness but detested madmen (and madwomen), eventually abandoning Nadja, his medium, to the hands of psychiatrists. Artaud never seems to have forgiven Breton for having failed him in 1937, when he was sent in a straitjacket to the asylum. One of Artaud's most obdurate obsessions (which he even recounted later *as a fact* to Breton himself) is that Breton was killed by a machine gun in Le Havre, trying to save his friend from the hands of the police—a chilling instance of Artaud's macabre humor. True to himself, Breton had treated Artaud like Nadja.

In *Van Gogh, the Man Suicided by Society* Artaud superimposes his philosophical differences with Breton upon the rivalry between van Gogh and his contemporary Paul Gauguin. Gauguin, who sought a Jungian panorama of myth and symbol through his painting, told his friend van Gogh that he should try painting from memory. Van Gogh couldn't. His only access to infinity was through immediate experience. "I believe," Artaud wrote,

> that Gauguin thought that the artist must look for symbol, for myth, must enlarge the things of life to the magnitude of myth,
>
> whereas van Gogh thought that one must know how to deduce myth from the most ordinary things of life.
>
> In which I think he was bloody well right,
>
> For reality is frighteningly superior to all fiction, all fable, all divinity, all surreality.
>
> All you need is the genius to know how to interpret it.
>
> (*Antonin Artaud: Selected Writings*, p. 491)

For Artaud, real genius lay not in the construction of a symbolic world, but in the ability to look at life so spontaneously, directly, and clearly that one discovered an animation in things and in the relation between things far more lucid and arresting than surrealism's phantasmagoric haze of dreams and symbols. It is precisely van Gogh's *form* of vision that was most threatening to society. And society, as we know, did not treat van Gogh kindly. Artaud went a little further. "Worming its way" inside van Gogh's body, society managed to erase the "superior lucidity" he had just achieved. In this light van Gogh's self-mutilation makes perfect sense: van Gogh cooked his hand, severed his ear, and shot himself in the stomach not out of guilt or surrealistic madness, but to reclaim his own body. Van Gogh's "madness" is the opposite of irrationality; it is "direct logic," in Artaud's perception.

Just as Artaud, dismissing metaphors, immersed himself in the physicality of writing, van Gogh heroically stuck to his easel and to direct contact with nature, refusing to transcend painting through dream imagery or mannerism. Artaud's magnificent essay on van Gogh (the only one, by the way, for which he ever got a prize—the Prix Sainte-Beuve, in 1948) was his final effort at self-realization through appreciation of an alter-ego artist, and he achieved more clarity and a more tangible and frightening sense of the social world surrounding the individual than ever before.

Artaud wanted to be reborn of *himself*, not of the "execration of Father-Mother," nor of religion's black magic. In his post-1945 drawings he was obsessed with what his "new body" might look like, a strangely tangled amalgam of man and machine. These "anatomical reconstructions," as he called them, are as rigid as Incan statues or primitive totems and as intricately sketched as diagrams. (One recognizes here the two poles brought out through Uccello's painting.) The new "machines of being," as Artaud titled them, are encased in womblike boxes, coffins, or sarcophagi, with mechanical parts or detached organs flying in all directions. Like Artaud's portraits and self-portraits, they are also bombarded with molecules, which could be minuscule craters on lunar surfaces or extreme close-ups of human skin. For Freud, this exploded panorama was characteristic of schizophrenia. For Artaud, it constituted "a slow genesic nightmare gradually becoming clear."

The vision of a "glorious body" emerging from frenzied machinery haunted Artaud's last years. In *Van Gogh* he wrote, "The body under the skin is an overheated factory, / and, outside, / the patient shines, / he shimmers, / from

1980

all his pores, / burst open." The feeling of an imminent rebirth recurs in the last series of texts Artaud wrote on the Tarahumara. In "Une note sur le peyotl" ("A Note on Peyote," written in May 1947), he claimed that taking the drug he understood that "I invented life, that it was my function and raison d'être." The "ABOLITION OF THE CROSS" can be read as this kind of invention, and is certainly what Artaud accomplishes in "Tutuguri, The Rite of the Black Sun" (a first version of the February 1948 work written in October 1947). The poem opens with a stunning vision that welds van Gogh's whirling sunflowers—in French, *tournesols,* "not suns, but whirling soils"—to the galloping figure of "the last sun, / the first man, / the black horse with a / naked man, / stark naked / and *virgin* / riding it."

Artaud completed a longer version of "Tutuguri" three weeks before his death. This version shows the naked, truncated man holding not the cross, but a horseshoe like the jaws of a yoke, "slashed in a gash of his blood." As happened to van Gogh, the "anatomical logic" is catching up with Artaud. "I am loaded," he wrote his editor, "with a bloody experience that I didn't have in 1936. This bloody experience is that I've just had here three attacks which left me *bathing* in my blood, a full pool of blood, from which the 'Tutuguri' here enclosed comes."

Pour en finir avec le jugement de dieu (*To Have Done with the Judgment of God,* 1947), Artaud's last work, recapitulates all the attempts he made over the last decade— through theater and poetry, through his mystical experience in Mexico, through madness and religion—to reinvent his life and cure a culture "trembling on the brink of an abyss." "It is a time to try anything," Artaud had proclaimed in *The Cenci,* and he did so all along, but never with such scathing, insane violence, scatological revulsion, and prophetic power as we see in this radio play commissioned by the French government radio station. The fate of the program actually confirmed Artaud's worst suspicions of conspiracy and persecution.

Alerted by the press, Wladimir Porshe, director of the French radio, vetoed the broadcast "to protect the public" from obscenity, but perhaps also from the violent anti-Americanism it propounded. Artaud's last attempt ended in disaster.

Fortunately a tape of the program remains, and it is an extraordinary document. Recorded by Artaud with Roger Blin, Maria Casares, and Paule Thévenin, *To Have Done with the Judgment of God* is a virtuosic tirade that glides effortlessly from sarcasm to prophecy, revulsion and rage to serenity and humor. Childlike singsong builds into shrieks and strings of rhythmic glossolalia. Using xylophones, drums, kettledrums, and gongs, Artaud invents a music that is somewhere between oriental music and the ritual chants of North American Indians. Mixing metaphysical satire and fragments of pop philosophy, the play is written in a carnivalesque mode, taking the reader from the abomination of God's creation to intimations of a "novel, strange and radiant Epiphany."

It begins with a flat description of the fate of the contemporary world. With startling foresight—this, after all, is postwar 1947 in a Paris recently liberated by the Allies—Artaud depicts a world divided by permanent war between two mammoths, the United States and Russia. Artaud scathingly ridicules the "American Way," with its ethos of productivity and competition, and sees within it the germs of modern destruction. America will cheerfully create "test-tube soldiers" through artificial insemination to safeguard its synthesized products and atomic bomb. This end-game civilization is contrasted with the universe of the American Indians, those "people who eat off the bare earth the delirium [peyote] from which they were born . . . and who kill the sun to establish the kingdom of black night."

Reformulating the mechanics of the Tutuguri ritual as contemporary industry, Artaud suggests that the "insane manufacture" of a self-destructing civilization could be avoided if belief in the divine origins of man were ritually exorcised. "Do you know what the Americans and the Russians use to make their atoms?" Artaud asks. "They make them with the microbes of god."

Artaud's *To Have Done with the Judgment of God* is an updated version of the Good News of God's death that Nietzsche brought to the world. But even though god has died, it doesn't mean that he has disappeared. God survives as an abstraction in people's minds that fuels their obsession with the flesh. God isn't an outside presence anymore, according to Artaud, but he still manipulates people from inside through guilt or sexuality. Humanity is then doubly at war, and a cleansing operation is needed to again lay bare in the human body the abject nature of the creator.

The theater of cruelty, a modern counterpart to primitive rituals, is thus meant to cure people of their crippling spirituality. Violently, but methodically, as with a surgeon's knife, god must be located and removed from the human body. But first the invisible must be revealed in its true form. The search for god's hidden place leads to "The Pursuit of Fecality" (a subtitle of one of the work's sections). Parodying René Descartes' *cogito ergo sum,* Artaud crudely asks, "Is god a being? / If he is one, he is shit. / And if he is not one/ he *is* not. / And he is not, / Except as the void that approaches with all its forms"—from crab lice to black holes. In the most sacrilegious piece, which is also the most hilarious, "The Question Arises of . . . ," Artaud, pressing his point, challenges god to prove his existence by letting out "a big fart."

Exit god.

It is now man who will be "emasculated." But emasculated of what? Of the tyranny of his organs, tongue, anus, glans, all the "infinum within" that bars him from the "infinite outside." The entire range of human energy, Artaud argues, has become narrowly focused on sexual anima instead of reaching for "all the wandering wealth" of the universe. Man can be freed from his organs, however, only by pulling them out of his anatomy:

Man is sick because he is badly constructed. We must decide to strip him bare in order to scrape off this animalcule that itches him mortally,

> god,
>
> and with god
>
> his organs.

For tie me up if you wish, but there is nothing more useless than an organ. When you will have made him a body without organs, then you will have delivered him from all his automatisms and restored him to his true freedom.

(*Antonin Artaud: Selected Writings,* pp. 570–571)

Humanity's true freedom lies in an explosive affirmation: This is my body! "Let's make the human anatomy dance," Artaud exclaims, echoing Nietzsche, "downward and upward, / from back to front and / front to back, / but much more so from back backwards, / than from back downwards."

"Grammar never was anything more for me than black humor."
—*Cahiers de Rodez,* 1946

Defending his radio play one month before his death, Artaud asserted that he devised "a language specially conceived to be understood by any laborer or shopkeeper and capable of bringing through bodily emission the highest metaphysical truths." Artaud was always concerned with "bodily emission," starting with the system of breathing he invented in "Un athlétisme affectif" ("An Emotional Athleticism"), a 1935 essay included in *The Theater and its Double.* Passions, he maintained, are material and they are localized in the body. "The secret," he wrote, "was to exacerbate these points like a musculature that is being flayed. The rest is achieved by screams."

Even more than he wished for an emotional cinema that could act directly on the brain, Artaud dreamed of an emotional language that would be liberated from syntax and the abstraction of concepts. He had begun to grasp the principle of this new language as early as 1943, while making his therapeutic "translation" of Lewis Carroll's *Through the Looking Glass* (1872). The choice of text was excellent, though perhaps not what Dr. Ferdière had in mind, because Artaud's subtitle, "An Anti-Grammatical Attempt *Against* Lewis Carroll," announces what separates him from the original. In September 1945 Artaud expressed his distrust of Carroll's successful virtuosity, contrasting it with poems born out of suffering. Like the anus, Artaud writes, creation "is always terror and I can't tolerate that one loses an excrement without tearing oneself away at the thought of losing one's soul." One is reminded here of his 1925 statement that "all writing is garbage." Writing is a nerve meter, a seismograph of the soul. But in order to bare "the sexual flesh of the glottis," it is necessary to invent a language unlike anything else, the meaning of which everyone could re-create for him- or herself. Echoing the Leibnizian dream of a universal language, Artaud bases it not on abstractions, but on pure rhythmical instinct. Unlike James Joyce's portmanteau words, this new language, which Roman Jakobson coined "glossolalia," is not fabricated syllable after syllable but all at once, in a spontaneous outburst: "tara ta ta kardu dali / e ter ter de zitera / e koperdo ritera / e co reperdo kali."

Glossolalia starts appearing in the Rodez notebooks after 1945, the year Artaud renounced Catholicism. Soon the dark gutturality of glossolalia resounds in all his major texts and genesic drawings. Both show the writer's obstinate desire to "leave his tongue," turning language and representation into a "glorious body," a "crowned" body without grammatical organs and, like van Gogh's paintings, without drama, plot, or narrative. Born out of breathing and grounded in the sphincter, this athletic language is Artaud's biggest attempt to put language in motion and emotion in language, as in this passage from *To Have Done with the Judgment of God:* "Then it dances / by chunks of / KHA, KHA / infinitely more arid / but more organic." (The Ka is the Egyptian spirit that lives inside the body like a double and survives in embalmed bodies.)

In a 1946 letter to Breton, Artaud argued that he had "never been mad or sick in the head." Breton knew better, but Artaud was absolutely right. The madness was not his own. Instead of papering over cultural anomie with dreamlike images, Artaud gave his own body to the grind. He turned himself into its propitiatory victim, hoping to reveal through his ordeal that it was the world, and not him, that was being dispossessed of its reality—an extreme example of "absolute concrete humor." Artaud was simple enough to take everything—including language—literally. Metaphors would have saved him from the truth.

Artaud told Breton that "the world had put its veto in the sphincter of his ass." Everyone in their right mind would have assumed, as Breton did, that it was just another of Artaud's flights into delirium or another instance of his weird obsession with anality. But he was right. On 4 March 1948 Artaud died of cancer of the rectum. Direct logic, right to the end.

In spite of its Christian overtones, Artaud's suffering was not just a dubious exercise in self-mortification. Like Edgar Allan Poe, Gérard de Nerval, Nietzsche, Lautréamont, and van Gogh, Artaud didn't choose his madness, but lucidly recognized its deeper sanity, or at least its possible curative power. Like these great exemplars of the heroic period of literary modernism, as Sontag dubs them, Artaud had to assume the role of *poète maudit* in order to remain a true poet. Like them, though, he was well aware, as he wrote in the preface to *The Theatre and Its Double,* that "what is infernal and truly *maudit* in these times lies with those who keep lingering over artistic forms instead of signaling wildly in the distance as victims on the stakes."

To the postmodern sensibility imbued with hyperreal images and disembodied information, there may be something deeply embarrassing, grotesque, or even obscene in Artaud's paroxysmal posturing. Of the theater of cruelty, it seems, Artaud was the foremost actor and ultimate casualty. We've become so used to seeing open wounds on our mental screens that it may be hard to believe that flashing them in the flesh, relentlessly, as Artaud did, would ever succeed in forcing the evil out from this world. Artaud had to signal all the more vociferously that the fire—and the stakes— were no longer visible. His gothic world of electroshocks and redeeming stigmata already belongs to another age, the humanistic era of death camps, death squads, and deadly plagues. As Artaud himself foreshadowed in *To Have Done with the Judgment of God,* we've learned how to manufacture death as well as life. Whether or not the culture can be cured of such an insidious sickness is uncertain. As Marcel Proust said of Swann's love, the disease is so much a part of our reality as to be utterly *inoperable.* It might be easier at this point to celebrate madness in our dead cultural heroes than to expose ourselves to the impossible truths they disclosed.

Selected Bibliography

EDITIONS

INDIVIDUAL WORKS
Bilboquet. Paris, 1923.
Tric Trac du ciel. Paris, 1923.
L'Ombilic des limbes. Paris, 1925.
Le pèse-nerfs. Paris, 1925. A second edition (Marseilles, 1927) includes *Fragments d'un journal d'enfer.*
Correspondance avec Jacques Rivière. Paris, 1927. These letters were first published in the *Nouvelle Revue Française,* no. 132 (1 September 1924), under the title "Une correspondance."
L'Art et la mort. Paris, 1927.
Héliogabale, ou l'anarchiste couronné. Paris, 1934.
Les nouvelles révélations de l'être. Paris, 1937.
Le théâtre et son double. Paris, 1938.
D'un voyage au pays des Tarahumaras. Paris, 1945.
Lettres de Rodez. Paris, 1946.
Artaud le mômo. Paris, 1947.
Ci-gît, précédé de "La culture indienne." Paris, 1947.
Van Gogh, le suicidé de la société. Paris, 1947.
Pour en finir avec le jugement de dieu. Paris, 1948.

Suppôts et supplications. Paris, 1978.
Antonin Artaud: Dessins et portraits. Edited by Paule Therenin and Jacques Derrida. Munich and Paris, 1986.

COLLECTED WORKS
Oeuvres complètes. Edited by Paule Thévenin. 23 vols. Paris, 1956–1988. Several volumes forthcoming.
Lettres à Génica Athanasiou. Paris, 1969.
Nouveau écrits de Rodez. Edited by Pierre Chaleix. Paris, 1977.

TRANSLATIONS

Antonin Artaud Anthology. Edited by Jack Hirshman. San Francisco, 1965.
Antonin Artaud: Collected Works. 4 vols. Translated by Victor Corti. London, 1968–1974.
Antonin Artaud: Four Texts. Translated by Clayton Eshleman and Norman Glass. Los Angeles, 1982.
Antonin Artaud: Selected Writings. Edited by Susan Sontag. Introduction by Susan Sontag. Translated by Helen Weaver. New York, 1976.
The Cenci. Translated by Simon Watson-Taylor. London, 1969.
Chanson. Translated by James Arnold and Clayton Eshleman. New York, 1985.
Peyote Dance. Translated by Helen Weaver. New York, 1976. A translation of *D'Un voyage au pays des Tarahumaras.*
Theatre and Its Double. Translated by Mary Caroline Richards. New York, 1958.

BIOGRAPHICAL AND CRITICAL STUDIES

Blanchot, Maurice. "Artaud," in *Le livre à venir.* Paris, 1959.
———. "La cruelle raison poétique." In *L'Entretien infini.* Paris, 1969.
Deleuze, Gilles, and Felix Guattari. *Anti-Oedipus: Capitalism and Schizophrenia.* Translated by Robert Hurley, Mark Seem, and Helen R. Lave. New York, 1977.
Derrida, Jacques, *Writing & Difference.* Translated by Alan Bass. Chicago, 1978.
Foucault, Michel, *Madness and Civilization.* Translated by Richard Howard. New York, 1965.
Greene, Naomi. *Antonin Artaud: Poet Without Words.* New York, 1970.

Knapp, Bettina. *Antonin Artaud: Man of Vision.* Preface by Anaïs Nin. New York, 1969.

Kristeva, Julia. "Le sujet en procès." In *Polylogue.* Paris, 1977.

Laporte, René. "Antonin Artaud ou la pensée au supplice. *Le nouveau commerce* 12 (1968).

Maeder, Thomas. *Antonin Artaud.* Paris, 1978.

Sellin, Eric. *The Dramatic Concepts of Antonin Artaud.* Chicago, 1968.

Sollers, Philippe. "La pensée émet des signes." In *Logiques.* Paris, 1968.

——— , ed. *Artaud.* Paris, 1973.

SYLVÈRE LOTRINGER

EUGENIO MONTALE

(1896–1981)

EUGENIO MONTALE WAS a backward youth, kept from school as a child because of ill health, and shielded well into manhood from the necessity of earning a living by his comfortably well-off Genoese family. His father was a successful businessman and expected this youngest son to follow his older brothers into a useful occupation, but Eugenio preferred to spend his time at the local library reading Italian literature and philosophy, absorbing the works of the French symbolist poets, and teaching himself English and Spanish by deciphering John Keats and Miguel de Cervantes. His own interest in being a writer was slow to blossom. For a while he contemplated a career in bel canto, studying with an ancient maestro named Ernesto Sivori. His professional aspirations as a baritone were ultimately cut short by Sivori's death, though the pupil's passion for music did not decline so much as it shifted direction, resurfacing in early verse that was written to imitate Claude Debussy, or in many later references to opera woven into his poetry.

Given his youthful cultivation of bel canto and his later taste for painting, it is easy to understand why Montale should have had a special affinity for the dilettante-artist, a figure regularly found in his verse and sketches. This eccentric type is first of all a nostalgic re-creation of the privileged circumstances in which Montale himself grew up. But the poet also comes to conceive of the dilettante as a token for individualism and the autonomy of the artist. As the century wore on and mass movements like fascism sought to mobilize culture to serve political ends, the hapless dabblers and dandies scattered throughout Montale's writings gained greater stature. They were no longer just amiable eccentrics (as Montale the young baritone might have seemed), but independent, thinking souls who kept faith in human decency while the masses were driven to unreason and violence.

In 1917 Montale was called to serve as an officer in World War I. His years in the military at least broke some of the intellectual isolation he felt in his provincial existence. During training, he met Sergio Solmi, who would be a lifelong friend and sympathetic critic; he also associated with a group of aspiring writers, among whom Francesco Meriano stood out. Meriano wanted to create a magazine called *Trotyl,* named after an explosive. As the title suggests, it was to be a futurist enterprise, an enthusiastic espousal of the razing of the old order—in literature and in society—to its foundations. This was the plan of action formulated by the futurists in the decade before the war, and now in the great conflict those destructive impulses were realized. Montale frequented and corresponded with Meriano's set, but finally the futurist poetics and politics of the group repelled him. Opposing the position of much of the Italian avant-garde, Montale registered the mass slaughter and social disruptions that accompanied World War I with no sense of excitement at the dawning of a new age. Unlike Giuseppe Ungaretti, an Italian modernist whose poetic voice first came to full strength in verse about the conflict, Montale wrote about his wartime experiences only sparingly, and always in muted tones and with melancholy.

His glancing encounter with a fringe of futurism was part of a poetic coming-of-age that included as its central struggle a grappling with two contrary influences, Gabriele D'Annunzio and the so-called twilight poets (*poeti crepuscolari*). D'Annunzio had been a child prodigy and in his twenties was the darling of Roman literary magazines that pioneered ideas of mass culture in a nation just then emerging from mass illiteracy. Fortified in the 1890's by a reading of Nietzsche and the popular success of his novels translated into French, D'Annunzio formulated a vision of the artist-as-superman, a figure who would shape not only the artistic tastes but also the political direction of the populace by the force of his imagination and the splendor of his words. Heir to ideas of decadence that he garnered especially from his contacts with French culture of the late nineteenth century, the Italian writer nevertheless turned these images of decline into implicit calls for a revival of what he eventually termed the "Latin spirit." The united Italy, according to blueprints offered in his fiction, poetry, and drama, was to reclaim its long-lost heritage as cultural and imperial power. D'Annunzio's lyric voice was so enchanting (especially at its apex, demonstrated in *Alcyone,* published in 1903) and his self-promotion so canny that he did indeed assume an unprecedented cultural and political importance for the nation. A play of his that addressed the question of Italian minorities in Austro-Hungary created an international incident; and after a career as a World War I daredevil flier, his leadership of a coup d'état aimed at forcibly annexing the Adriatic port of Fiume to Italy made him for a time a popular hero before whom the parliamentary democracy trembled

and faltered. Moreover, D'Annunzio's example exercised a potent influence on Benito Mussolini, and the growing fascist movement sought to appropriate the poet's methods and following.

D'Annunzio had his detractors, and in fact when Montale was demobilized and returned to Genoa in 1919, he began to frequent a café patronized by the anti-D'Annunzians. (The admirers of the poet-condottiere gathered at a rival establishment.) But the deeper testimony to Montale's rejection of his elder contemporary's example was worked out in his first collection of verse, *Ossi di seppia (Cuttlefish Bones,* 1925), derived from writings that date chiefly from the end of the war to the mid-1920's. The younger writer contests D'Annunzio on poetic grounds, refusing his sublime and mellifluous voice, and subverting some typically D'Annunzian commonplaces, such as a glorious, burgeoning nature and an identification between the lyrical speaker and the gods and heroes of antiquity. Obviously, countering D'Annunzio is both a poetic and a political enterprise, and thus the failure of vitalism and the anomie of Montale's persona in *Cuttlefish Bones* express not just a distaste for a previous literary model, but also an incipient antifascism. As will be seen, this antifascism is crystallized in Montale's associations with his editor, Piero Gobetti, and with Benedetto Croce's intellectual resistance to the new regime. But even before his public embrace of antifascism in 1925, Montale worked through a refusal of D'Annunzio that is at once literary and closely connected to polemics between fascism and its opponents.

Montale was not in the first generation of poets to resist D'Annunzio's example. Shortly after the turn of the century, an assortment of writers eventually dubbed the twilight poets (presumably because of their shared sense of being all too wan in the wake of D'Annunzio's brightness) came to prominence. Their sometimes whimsical verse seemed the antithesis of their elder's serious claim to the sublime, and they were wont to parody celebrated pieces by their predecessor, such as "La pioggia nel pineto" ("The Rain in the Pine Wood," dated 1903), with mockingly bathetic imitations. Guido Gozzano was the most representative figure of this disgruntled generation; the critic Croce took him to be so, and Montale also gravitated toward him, though without much patience for the more flippant manifestations of the twilight poets' deflation of D'Annunzio. Montale empathized with the weak and wan lyrical speakers of Gozzano's verse, and he devised analogous alter egos in his own poetry. A will-o'-the-wisp female character in Gozzano also captured his attention, and a facsimile of that personage can be found in Montale's verse of the late 1920's and early 1930's, surrounded, however, with a more relentlessly elegiac imagery than the original. Finally, the linguistic lessons of the twilight generation influenced Montale. After the incredibly rich musicality of D'Annunzio, after his claim to produce discourse rivaling the Wagnerian orchestra, the successor poets strove for a more colloquial register. Montale also felt the need to severely trim this overinflated language, although once again he did not simply follow the twilight poets, endorsing all their parodies, but instead insisted on what he called a "countereloquence" of his own—a new, sparer sublime. On several occasions he gave credit to Gozzano's generation for having been the first to reject the overpowering voice and persona of D'Annunzio (which he compared to the inescapable influence of Victor Hugo on nineteenth-century French letters). But it is also evident that the twilight writers had not finished the task of exorcising their predecessor as far as Montale was concerned. Furthermore, by the time the Genoese poet came to maturity, much of D'Annunzio's reputation had gotten entangled with the question of fascism, and so it was natural that Montale's reading of his elder contained more political undertones than did the earlier generation's.

As formative and complicated as his relationship to D'Annunzio and the twilight poets is Montale's connection to Benedetto Croce and Piero Gobetti. Their different eminence should be noted immediately in linking these two names, for even in Montale's youth Croce was a monumental figure in Italian culture, a protean aesthetician, critic, historian, and political force, whereas Gobetti was just beginning to develop as a political activist and publisher of modern writing. Like so many Italian intellectuals who came of age in the first half of the twentieth century, Montale assimilated Crocean aesthetics as a primary influence. Notebooks that the poet kept when he was twenty show him struck by the ideas put forth by the philosopher of art in his *Aesthetics* (1902), while a lengthy article that Montale published in 1962 on the same book attests to the lifelong hold that Crocean thinking exerted on him. It is easy to see why: Croce's separation of art from erudition and from moral or political discourse, together with his emphasis on the intuition rather than the rationality of the artist, seemed to bring his theory in line with the most important trends in modern British and French poetry, from Samuel Taylor Coleridge and Charles Baudelaire onward— and this was exactly the current with which the young Montale identified.

The problem was that Croce the practical critic soon began to reject most modern poets (Arthur Rimbaud and Stéphane Mallarmé in France; D'Annunzio, Giovanni Pascoli, and Ungaretti in Italy), eventually accusing them of being the bearers of a noxious breakdown in artistic forms as well as a decline of humanity and reason that foreshadowed and sometimes (as in the case of futurism) even abetted the rise of fascism and Nazism. In common with other artists and intellectuals of his generation, Montale reacted with dismay at this wholesale condemnation of modern writing. After the fall of the fascist regime one of the preoccupations of his poetry and essays was to defend the moderns and defuse Croce's attack.

Nevertheless, Montale did not find all of Croce's antifascism unpalatable. Although he defended much modern writing (including, implicitly, his own) from the critic's invective, he did accept the general outlines of the historian and political commentator's thinking on fascism itself. Indeed, at the beginning of the twenty-year fascist period, the poet underwent the same wavering about the new movement as his elder and far more influential contemporary. Croce the politician at first wondered whether fascism was not a healthy antidote to a leftist-induced chaos wracking the nation after World War I. Likewise, Montale expressed admiration for his old comrade-in-arms Meriano when, in 1922, he made a name for himself as a member of the fascist shock troops then warring with Italian leftists. (After the regime as well Montale commented that fascism initially had not seemed so fearsome as the simultaneous Bolshevik threat to the nation.) Only in 1925, three years after Mussolini seized power, did Croce forcefully constitute himself as an opponent of the regime. He issued a manifesto denouncing a fascist-promoted cultural organization, arguing—quite coherently with his aesthetics—that art and science should not and could not be contaminated by practical, political concerns. Montale signed this document and made its thesis his own, for he steadily maintained the independence of art from utilitarian ends throughout his career, even when the times had radically changed and it was a post–World War II leftism, rather than fascism, that issued its appeal for the commitment of art to political goals. Yet paradoxically the poet's own writing is continually plagued by the question of the connection between art and the historical moment. Despite his repeated assertions of poetry's independence, Montale frequently writes verse that is political just because it speaks of the necessity of poetry remaining above the political fray. And some of his most impassioned lyrics are written out of scorn for the mass movements that sought to recruit art to serve political ends.

By 1925 Montale had also come in contact with another influential antifascist, the editor Piero Gobetti. This relationship was much more personal than the one with Croce. Go-betti, though scarcely past his teens, had already made a name for himself as an Italian promoter of modern European writing (his magazines carried early notices of James Joyce, Bertolt Brecht, Marcel Proust, and Paul Valéry). Even more important for Gobetti, however, was the modernization of Italian society; he always attempted to integrate his cultural promotion into this wider goal. His vision called for an alliance of liberal intellectuals and a progressive proletariat, a project summed up in the title of his review *Rivoluzione liberale* (The Liberal Revolution). Harassed and censored by personal order of Mussolini, Gobetti had to abandon his native Turin in 1925 for exile in Paris, where he died the following year, evidently from the aftereffects of one of the fascist beatings he had received. (Montale reported being the one to see him off at the train station.) It was Gobetti who published the poet's first collection of verse, *Cuttlefish Bones,* as well as his first important statement of poetics, "Stile e tradizione" ("Style and Tradition"), both of which appeared in 1925. In the postfascist years Montale wrote reverently of Gobetti's moral example, although on close inspection one sees that the editor's enthusiasm for contemporary literature appealed to the poet more than his plans for a union of the working class and the intelligentsia. Montale tended to gloss over or even distort the second aspect of his friend's thinking, and with only a brief relenting, his own politics remained an embittered elitism, antagonistic to the mass of men both during and after the fascist regime.

In 1927 Montale finally escaped from the cocoon of his family. He left behind both Genoa and his parents' villa at Monterosso, on the rugged Ligurian riviera, where he had spent twenty-odd summers. (This isolated coastal resort provided most of the backdrop for the poems in *Cuttlefish Bones.*) Moving to Florence, he worked first for the publishing house Bemporad (at a lowly job, writing copy for an almanac), then won the post of chief librarian at the Gabinetto Vieusseux, a venerable archive frequented in the nineteenth century by such men of letters as Feodor Dostoyeski and Giacomo Leopardi. The story goes that Montale was chosen for the position at the Vieusseux by an old-line mayor who disdained the other candidates because they were all members of the Fascist party. Ironically, as the poet recounted in a postwar sketch included in his *La farfalla di Dinard* (*The Butterfly of Dinard,* 1956), a decade later he was removed from the job by a new city administration zealously dedicated to rooting out civil servants without party affiliation.

The late 1920's and the 1930's saw a gradual growth of Montale's influence, especially among Florentine artists and intellectuals who felt steadily less enthusiasm for fascist Italy. Among this circle of friends were the novelists Elio Vittorini and Vasco Pratolini, and the poet Salvatore Quasimodo, all of whom would write against the regime with increasing openness as fascism tottered toward its disastrous end in World War II. But Montale's antifascism, expressed in subtle, allusive verse, did not appeal to other intellectuals, for example Silvio Guarnieri and Giaime Pintor, both of whom criticized the poet for what they felt was his all-too-passive resistance to an ever-greater evil. Unlike Pintor, who was an early casualty in the armed partisan combat against the regime, Montale never picked up a gun to fight fascism. He always remained a man of letters, not a man of action, and humbly acknowledged that personal destiny by identifying himself in his verse with figures like the mouse of the first part of "Botta e risposta" (Thrust and Parry, dated 1961, published 1971).

While Montale was becoming a focal point for the disaffected intelligentsia of fascist Italy, recognition also came to him from abroad. A translation of his poem "Arsenio" (the title is a distortion of his own first name Eugenio) appeared in T. S. Eliot's *Criterion* in 1928, and his verse received notices in the London *Times Literary Supplement* (1934) and, in the United States, in the *Saturday Review of Literature* (1936). This last piece was written by Irma Brandeis, an American scholar and teacher whose encounter with Montale in Florence in 1933 had great consequences for the poet's life and work. At the time Montale was already the companion of Drusilla Tanzi, the wife of an art critic named Matteo Marangoni. Sharing quarters with the couple in the late 1920's, the poet had developed an affection for this sharp-witted, sardonic woman whom he nicknamed "Mosca" (the fly). Eventually she became his wife, although judging from the poems he dedicated to her after her death in 1963, their relationship was founded not so much on romance as on a shared irony toward pretense and convention. Irma Brandeis, however, inspired Montale with an entirely different passion. Translated into his verse of the 1930's and 1940's under the name "Clizia" (of Dantesque and Ovidian origin), her figure stands at the center of both love lyrics and antifascist political allegories. These allegories marked a decisive turning away from the fading, weak female character, variously called Arletta or Annetta, who is evidently an imitation of a twilight type and can frequently be glimpsed in the poet's verse of the late 1920's and early 1930's. It is likely that Brandeis helped to move Montale to redirect his poetry toward a new political purpose. (In "L'Eroismo" ["Heroism"], a poem dated 1975, the poet reports that she urged him to join the antifascist forces fighting in Spain, a suggestion to which the "mouse" clearly could not respond.) At any rate, his cryptic political parables, published in the collection he dedicated to Brandeis, *Le occasioni* (*The Occasions,* 1939), were followed four years later by *Finisterre* (Land's End, 1943), a small book brought out in Switzerland because its epigraph about wicked princes seemed too obvious a reference to the totalitarian states that were terrorizing Europe. Meanwhile Brandeis had returned to North America, where she worked for the Italian broadcast division of the Office of War Information and began to teach at the New School for Social Research. At one point in the 1930's Montale himself had considered immigrating to the United States to take a job at a university, but that would have meant abandoning Mosca, and he apparently could not bring himself to break that bond.

As one can see, the female characters in the poet's verse are apt to be complex mixtures of private and public concerns. Love lyrics and political meditations coincide in the Clizia cycle, and that formula is repeated with variations in Montale's postwar poetry, even as a new personage, whom he calls the "fox-woman" (la volpe), enters his world. A cipher for Maria Luisa Spaziani, a young writer Montale met in the late 1940's, the fox-woman becomes the poet's vehicle for describing a postfascist Italy that, to his mind, quickly dissipates the hopes aroused by the toppling of the regime. After the liberation Montale joined the Action Party, an amalgam of liberal intellectuals from which came Italy's first, albeit short-lived postwar government. Very soon, however, the Action Party withered as the Christian Democrats and the Communists occupied dominant positions in the nation's political life. For these two mass organizations the poet shows the highest scorn in his verse. Thus the poems to the fox-woman are often tinged with a disillusionment occasioned, paradoxically enough, as the absolutely clear moral choices presented by fascism gave way to what Montale saw as the compromise and cynicism of postwar politics.

Closely connected to his political analysis of the late 1940's is Montale's defense of modern writing. Impugned by Croce as the symptom of an intellectual and moral dissolution that led to fascism, modernism was also attacked in the postwar years because it seemed to propose an ideal of art-for-art's-sake. To a new wave of committed artists, modernism's individualistic styles and preoccupation with psychological depths looked suspiciously like the intelligentsia's betrayal of its social responsibilities. In a letter of 1946 to his critic friend Gianfranco Contini, Montale describes a conference at which the complicated metrical devices of his verse were cited by some partici-

pants as proof that his chief characteristic as a writer during the regime had been aestheticism rather than opposition to the totalitarian state. In short, postwar proponents of a socially activist art and an accessible style found Montale's difficult allegories against fascism to be dubious exercises. But in his essays of the late 1940's, as well as in several of the poems dedicated to the fox-woman, he replies by defending modernist writers and by decrying leftist calls to commitment as the prelude to another totalitarian manipulation of culture.

In 1948 Montale ended a decade of freelancing by accepting a job with the Corriere della Sera, a Milanese daily with a reputation for moderate politics and sophisticated cultural criticism. He got this position in part because he had produced under deadline pressure a long analytical piece on Gandhi's assassination. But one may assume that Montale's appreciation of the Indian leader's principle of nonviolent resistance was an act of empathy rather than just reportage. During the next twenty-five years the poet wrote regularly for the paper, contributing book reviews and semi-autobiographical sketches, eventually collected in The Butterfly of Dinard. The publication of this somewhat whimsical volume in 1956 coincided with the release of La bufera e altro (The Storm and Other Things), which contained the high tragedy of Finisterre as well as the pieces devoted to the fox-woman.

Much of the last phase of Montale's work may be understood by considering the polyvalent title of his next collection, Satura (1971). The word's significance fluctuates between "satire" and "miscellany." The first definition spells a fall into farce from the tragic register of the earlier poetry, while the second sums up the worldview that underlies this impulse to parody. Montale mocks any attempt to systematize human history, preferring to see the saga of the species as a miscellaneous assortment of unconnected, bewildering events. He turns his satire toward such varied targets as the leftist image of man's inevitable progress toward a better society, and the idealist scheme of an orderly historical development guided by a half-human, half-transcendental "spirit." Visions of trash and offal recur in this last verse, as tokens of the poet's lack of esteem for the neat systems proposed by the various ideologues to explain human experience. Basically the late Montale raises his earlier and fairly localized dissidence to a universal principle. Instead of the malaise of the Florentine intellectual before fascism's recruitment of culture, or the postwar artist's dismay at leftist appeals to subordinate poetry to political ends, the poet of the 1960's and 1970's expresses a grand anomie, a disaffection for every ordering of reality. It would be a savagely gloomy view— a picture of the world as pure chaos—if he did not also conceive a kind of unspoken solidarity among the few lost souls who cannot conform, who do not join any of the vast marches of history. These are the people who "look back" as the crowd surges forward—to use an image from *Cuttlefish Bones* that was celebrated among antifascist admirers of the poet and is resuscitated by him in *Satura*'s "Gli uomini che si voltano" ("Men Who Turn Back," dated 1969). Dilettantes, like the reclusive musicologist who appears in "Botta e risposta," also win the poet's sympathy, not just for their entertainingly quixotic pursuits, but because he feels that they too have let the crowds pass them by and so have not forfeited their independence. Montale's chief heroes are not active resisters, but quiet, almost hapless nonconformists. Thus when he refers to poetry in his 1975 Nobel Prize address as "an absolutely useless product," he intends by that label not just self-satire, but also a belief in the dilettante, the apparently useless putterer whose reluctance to subordinate his art to the practical, utilitarian ends of causes and movements redeems him in Montale's eyes.

CUTTLEFISH BONES

"I limoni" ("The Lemon Trees"), one of the first poems in *Cuttlefish Bones*, begins by drawing a sharp distinction between exalted "poets laureate" and the modest lyrical speaker. The narrator formulates this difference in somewhat humorous terms: the laurel-crowned bards, he says, surround themselves with august vegetation, while he himself prefers grassy ditches, common canebrakes, and lemon trees. This poem in praise of lemons is one of many essays at poetic self-definition in Montale's first collection. With its unpretentious, sometimes conversational language and its shunning of the lofty laurel, the piece recalls the twilight attempts to counter D'Annunzio's often magniloquent verse and fabulous themes. Not by chance does "The Lemon Trees" show a poet searching vainly for divinities in nature and eventually taking comfort instead in a glimpse at golden lemons in a wintry courtyard. D'Annunzio's most famous poems, collected in *Alcyone*, abound with nymphs and gods, conjured up by a writer who felt it his destiny to resurrect the power of classical art in modern times. The humbler dimensions of nature and the artist in "The Lemon Trees," and indeed in many pieces of *Cuttlefish Bones*, constitute an implicit reply to D'Annunzio.

But Montale's more important account of artistic self-definition comes in the suite of nine poems entitled "Mediterraneo" ("Mediterranean"). With the rugged Ligurian coast as his backdrop, the lyrical speaker tells a story of struggle between the landsman (himself) and a powerful, tumultuous sea. Many times the contest is phrased as a combat that pits the stripling writer against an overwhelming predecessor. The sea produces music (song) and is even likened in one metaphor to the resounding page of a book. As for the landsman-poet, he sometimes approaches the great expanse of water with ecstasy, inspired by its majesty; at other moments, however, he grows dejected and feels its vastness as a humiliating, annihilating force. He hopefully imagines that at least a portion of the sea's magical voice will be transmitted to the syllables he composes. But soon afterward he concedes his inability to capture the watery element's music. Then he sees himself the creator of only worn phrases and halting rhythms.

On occasion the sea is also incarnated as an overbearing father, and then the struggle with the lyrical speaker takes on Oedipal significance. Moreover, the child's rancor toward his parent in "Mediterranean" brings Montale's fable very close to the terms in which the twilight generation's relationship to D'Annunzio manifested itself. As Edoardo Sanguineti wrote in his study "Da D'Annunzio a Gozzano" (From D'Annunzio to Gozzano, 1961), the younger writers seemed to conceive themselves as puny offspring of an immensely gifted sire; their creative energies were spent resisting his mighty example, and they never completely overcame their sense of inferiority. "Mediterranean" also involves a weak child striving against a parent whose great voice cannot be equaled—in fact, who nearly obliterates the progeny. Ultimately, however, Montale's strategy in confronting his predecessor diverges from that of the twilight company, for while the latter generally remain hobbled by their own self-deprecation (as Sanguineti shows), the poet of "Mediterranean" escapes from his abjection. For the nine pieces conclude with a passionate assertion of the lyrical speaker's independent identity. Instead of leaving him debilitated, capable of producing only lamentation, not song, the final lines of the suite raise him up by seizing as his own the low, panting voice of the sea at midday, and by equating him with the spark on the tip of a burning brand. These are not august attributes, but of course the author of "Mediterranean" does not take himself to be a poet laureate. Nevertheless, they do bespeak a resilient individuality (a spark is the absolute contrary of water) and simultaneously lay claim to a poetic voice that, for all its muted, harsh sound, is offered as no less valid than the sea's mightiest roar. One can see why "Style and Tradition," Montale's manifesto on poetry published the same year as *Cuttlefish Bones,* should have alluded slightingly to the twilight poets. Without the strength to emerge from beneath D'Annunzio's

overwhelming influence, they remained, in his judgment, pathetic complainers. (He later modified this severe opinion and indeed paid homage to some of the twilight themes, especially in the Arletta cycle.) "Mediterranean" ends with a quite different response to the predecessor; a countereloquence springs up in Montale's verse, and the father can no longer stifle the son.

For samples of the poet's countereloquence, one can turn to the section of *Cuttlefish Bones* that gave its name to the entire book. These twenty-two succinct pieces form the heart of the collection, and among them are several of Montale's best-known works. Like "Mediterranean," they contain flashes of an ecstatic contemplation of nature, as when the lyrical speaker exults at the glorious midday, or at the equally solar sunflower. But there can be no doubt that the prevailing spirit of these spare poems is aridity and negation. To the onlooker in one piece, children dancing in a dry streambed appear as emblems of life bursting from the scorched earth. Yet their innocent exuberance only serves to remind him of his own distance from such felicity. The narrator of this and most of the poems in the sequence counts himself among the parched souls of the world—spirits whose vitality and self-assurance have withered. (The adjective *arso* [parched] and its noun form *arsura* play a key role in *Cuttlefish Bones;* the word even furnishes the root for the name of the poet's alter ego, Arsenio.) Montale also devises auditory correlatives for the sense of barrenness and throttled possibilities that pervades these pieces. Taking a lesson from Dante's harsh rhymes in canto 32 of the *Inferno,* he gathers deliberately unmelodious sounds into his lines, such as the double *z* or the palatal *gli.* Irregular rhyming patterns and oddly off-center internal rhymes add to the dissonance of this poetry, so novel for the Italian ear accustomed to an easy mellifluousness.

In his essay "Eugenio Montale poeta fisico e metafisico" (Eugenio Montale as Physical and Metaphysical Poet, 1934), Pietro Pancrazi offered one of the most popular early diagnoses of *Cuttlefish Bones*. According to the critic, two complementary aspects could be discerned in this verse: the evocation of a landscape, and an incisive, idiosyncratic philosophical commentary on the physical features. This analysis accurately describes pieces like the very early "Meriggiare pallido e assorto" ("To Spend the Noontide, Pale and Absorbed," written in 1916), whose forbidding orchard wall topped by shards of glass becomes the image of what the narrator calls life's *travaglio* (travail). The same technique operates in "Spesso il male di vivere ho incontrato" ("Ofttimes Have I Met the Grief of Living," undated), where the opening line's generalization is followed by a series of stark and painful images, expressed with words that are appropriately grating in sound. But when one thinks of Montale as a metaphysical writer, one poem above all others in *Cuttlefish Bones* must come to mind. "Forse un mattino, andando in un'aria di vetro" ("Perhaps Some Morning, Walking in a Vitreous, Clear Air," undated) portrays the lyrical speaker looking back as he walks along one day and sees a miraculous and terrifying emptiness. When he returns to a usual state of mind, perceiving all the common objects in a normal way, he feels himself alienated from those around him who never seem to suffer from such visions of the void. This piece indeed raises the quintessentially metaphysical problem of the real world's existence. And as Gianfranco Contini asserted in his essay "Montale e *La bufera*" (Montale and *The Storm*, 1956), there is no more fundamental question for the poetry of *Cuttlefish Bones* than this doubt about the reality of the real world.

Nevertheless, the metaphysical doubts that Montale entertained—and more broadly speaking, all of the existential anguish of his first collection—also need to be seen as attitudes that directly contradict the fascist mentality as it was being expressed in the 1920's. When the poet signed Croce's antifascist manifesto in 1925, for instance, he put his name to a denunciation of a fascist document that proclaimed praxis, not theory, to be the idol of the new movement. Fascism took an unequivocal position on the same metaphysical issue that troubled Montale. Unlike the poet, it put its conviction squarely in the material world and was determined to act on that reality without any of what it regarded as the traditional intellectual's squeamishness about approaching practical matters. Moreover, the fascist ethos emphasized optimism and self-confidence; to be an actor in the real world obviously meant suppressing doubts and hesitations.

When Montale's poem speaks of "gli uomini che non si voltano" (the men who do not look back), contrasting them with his troubled persona, it does not take much effort to see that these blithe characters are near-kin to the new, confident man described in the fascist manifesto. Indeed one suspects that several depictions in *Cuttlefish Bones* of the afflicted narrator out of step with unfeeling others reflect the situation of the dissenter in a regime that aims at erasing malaise and mocks the questioning, uncertain spirit. For example, "So l'ora in cui la faccia più impassibile" ("I Know the Hour When the Most Impassive Face") presents a solitary character who suffers "una pena invisibile" (an invisible pain), while the crowd in the street continues to hurry past, seeing nothing. (It is no coincidence that this same antithesis between the blind and the perceptive should also play a large role in the more explicit allegories about fascism and its opponents that the poet elaborates in the late 1930's and early 1940's.) And lastly, "Non chiederci la parola che squadri da ogni lato" ("Do Not Ask Us for the Word Which Can Give a Shape"), perhaps the most quoted poem in *Cuttlefish Bones*, offers a similar juxtaposition of a profoundly skeptical speaker and a man unhampered by qualms. Although the first-person narrator denies his capacity to give definition to the world or to his formless self, the central stanza of the poem paints a confident man, "agli altri ed a se stesso amico" (friend to himself and others). The closing lines of the piece, moreover, contain powerful negations, or rather a paradoxical assertion that the only thing that can be affirmed is "ciò che *non* siamo, ciò che *non* vogliamo" (what we are *not,* and what we do *not* want). These words were often read as an anti-fascist statement by Montale's admirers. Vasco Pratolini, for instance, used them as the epigraph for his novel *Il quartiere* (The Neighborhood, translated as *The Naked Streets,* 1945), a book that pointed directly toward armed resistance to the regime. Montale's lines, however, have more in common with a passive refusal of fascism, a disaffection that is more typical of the circles in which he moved in the late 1920's and the 1930's than it is representative of the partisan struggle.

The focus of *Cuttlefish Bones* eventually shifts from the paired themes of landscape and metaphysics, and Montale begins to experiment with a device that will be central to all his subsequent poetry: the dialogue with a female interlocutor. The poet also invents a persona for himself in the latter part of the collection. Arsenio, who appears in the poem of the same title, seems to summarize the anxieties and incapacities of the book's metaphysician-narrator, while also pointing toward a salvation—of a completely unorthodox sort—that Montale's successive writing will insistently develop. The setting for "Arsenio" is a picturesque seaside resort about to be invested by a summer thunderstorm. Attracted by the meteorological wonder that looms on the horizon, the protagonist descends shoreward, passing hotels, carriage horses, and palms. But his real interest is a metaphysical one, for the coming tempest disrupts the monotonous hours and so gives him hope of a revelation, an entrance into another dimension. Rain begins to fall, and this climactic juncture in the poem is rendered doubly pregnant because the encounter between water and the "parched one," Arsenio, suggests the archetypal moment of joyful rebirth. But instead, Montale's protagonist meets only disappointment. The ordinary world catches him up again as all his extraordinary sensations dissolve. Especially bitter is the poem's close, which speaks of the character

pitched from great hopes into a "ghiacciata moltitudine di morti" (icy multitude of the dead). This is a hellish vision worthy of Dante, and perhaps adds another emblem of alienation to *Cuttlefish Bones*'s collection of jaundiced looks at the mass of people.

"Arsenio" deals with an unhappy quest for revelation that in part recalls the fruitless search for a glimpse at divine things in "The Lemon Trees." But the theme takes a new and rather interesting twist in the six poems that make up the penultimate section of the book. Here Montale's lyrical speaker contemplates a weak, insubstantial female and articulates what the poet himself once termed (in a 1954 interview with Ferdinando Camon) the "hypothesis of grace." A burgeoning April garden in which the woman is represented as a plant raises high expectations in "Crisalide" ("Chrysalis"). Yet the miracle of renewal soon palls, and the narrator looks instead to the horizon, where he sights a "barca di salvezza" (vessel of salvation). In the somewhat jumbled imagery of the poem, this token of grace is finally occluded by a contrary metaphor, an immovable wall, and the lyrical speaker can only finish by praying for his companion's release from a joyless imprisonment.

While "Chrysalis" merely ends in gloom, the pieces that close the suite of poems are entirely permeated by desolation. The female presences in "Delta" and "Incontro" ("Encounter") are ghostly figures in hallucinatory landscapes borrowed in part from Dante's *Inferno.* Exploring these eerie places, the narrator seeks sustenance from the woman, and must content himself with very little comfort. He strains to commune with her, but her spirit has no staying power. This evanescent character, later identified by the poet with the name Arletta, derives from the twilight canon; she bears signs of the consumption that is the classic malady of that current (Gozzano, incidentally, died of this debilitating disease), and, in the second place, she embodies the pallid decline that the post-D'Annunzio generation embraced as its fate. The somber Arletta cycle stretches well into Montale's next collection, *The Occasions,* where its hold is broken abruptly, though not definitively, by the arrival of Clizia's powerful angelic visage and rather straightforward function as antifascist standard-bearer. It would be easy, in fact, to connect Arletta's continuance in the poet's verse of the late 1920's and early 1930's with an increasing despair and withdrawal as fascism consolidated its hegemony. Significantly, Croce's 1928 *Storia d'Italia* (*A History of Italy*) chooses Gozzano's twilight debilitation and skepticism as a counterpoint to D'Annunzian bellicosity in a chronicle that veils its criticism of the regime very thinly. Montale's *Cuttlefish Bones* labors to controvert the magnificent bard's example, and predictably enough it is the twilight generation that supplies him with models of disheartenment when D'Annunzio's triumphalism has been crudely translated into a new fascist epoch.

THE OCCASIONS

In a letter of 2 June 1926 to his old friend Solmi, Montale spoke of feeling himself more and more an "outcast" (he used the English word) in fascist Italy, and also remarked bitterly on the "incredible delirium" with which people were now greeting the Duce. These two perceptions furnish a rather precise anticipation of the next season in the poet's writing. *The Occasions* is fraught with the narrator's sense of isolation, no doubt connected to what Montale described in a post-regime retrospective, "Intenzioni (Intervista immaginaria)" ("Intentions [Imaginary Interview]," 1946), as his endeavor to live in the Florence of the 1930's with the detachment of a Robert Browning—in short, as a foreign writer who could devote himself to his art and ignore the distasteful politics of the country in which he sojourned. But as the 1930's wore on, the poet's verse also focuses on the mass of men, furiously possessed and blind to reason. Against their frenzies he sets a small band, often under the aegis of Clizia, who remain immune to the general madness.

The poems of *The Occasions* that date from the late 1920's and early 1930's frequently revolve around memory, whether they call up recollections of a childhood summer on the Ligurian coast ("Vecchi versi" ["Old Verses"]), or draw on characters from opera to create a memento-in-poetry ("Keepsake," a title Montale gives in English). But the theme of nostalgia takes on a slightly different cast in the pieces "Carnevale di Gerti" ("Gerti's Carnival") and "Dora Markus" (a poem named for its protagonist). Gerti yearns for her native land and stages a melancholy carnival party with gifts for her faraway friends. Empathizing with this homesickness, the narrator wonders if there can be any means of exit from the oppressive present (in this meditation he bears a resemblance to the metaphysician-speaker of "Arsenio"). But the poem concludes with a sad return to a dreary here-and-now, an unhappy submission to fate that the speaker wishes to share with the woman.

In common with "Gerti's Carnival," the first part of "Dora Markus" summons up nostalgic, dreamy visions of a homeland only to acknowledge their inability to provide real comfort. But "Dora Markus" is an oddity, for Montale joined to its first section, dated 1926, a second part written in 1939. In the later segment, the existential anguish of the female protagonist is overshadowed by a malevolent external force, "una fede feroce" (a ferocious faith), ominously occupied with brewing poison. A note appended to *The Occasions* in postwar editions explained that Dora, like the character Liuba who is the subject of another piece in the collection, was Jewish. This unobtrusive annotation is precious, for it allows one to see how the poet passes from the more or less ahistorical metaphysical terms of his writing of the late 1920's to the unmistakably historical dimensions of the poetry written in the years just before World War II. The second section of "Dora Markus" rewrites, as it were, the inner malaise of the first part, endowing it with a concrete exterior cause, the "ferocious faith" that one inevitably identifies with Nazism and fascism. (Montale's use of the word "faith" to describe the nefarious political phenomena is not accident, as will presently be seen.)

In annotating "Dora Markus," the poet also alludes to the imperfect melding of its two halves. Yet in fact the entire middle zone (chronologically speaking) of *The Occasions* exhibits notable splices and discontinuities that on closer inspection prove to be merely the outward signs of a deeply significant mutation in Montale's subject matter. This shift is due chiefly to the arrival of Clizia in his verse, and the elaboration of her role as an angel of resistance to dreadful mass movements. Perhaps the most conspicuous example of this transition in outlook occurs in the two poems "Stanze" ("Stanzas," dated 1927–1929), an Arletta piece, and "Nuove stanze" ("New Stanzas," dated 1939), a work in which Clizia makes one of her most striking appearances. "Stanzas," like "Encounter" in *Cuttlefish Bones,* presents an insubstantial female figure marked by consumption and vainly sought by a narrator who hopes for a consolatory message. Her ghostly manifestations all slip past, tantalizing but never satisfying, and at the close of the piece an "amara oscurità" (bitter darkness) descends upon the speaker. This twilight story is radically revised in "New Stanzas," whose very title suggests a will to alter the previous course. In the poem of 1939, Montale employs a game of chess and cigarette smoke as props with which to enact a parable of the terrible war machine menacing the keepers of the good. The chessboard's mock war maneuvers pale beside the real savagery embodied in a sinister troop of men in the outside world, and when a gust of wind disrupts smoke spiraling over the chess game from the woman's cigarette, one imagines this to be an indication that she is as frail as Arletta. But the disparity between her strength and the power of the fierce demons is only apparent. She turns "occhi d'acciaio" (steely eyes) toward their burning mirror—and

this fearsome engine of war cannot defeat her gaze.

"New Stanzas" completely reverses the passivity and defeat of its twilight predecessor. Far from leaving the narrator in gloom, the later poem offers him an alliance with an undaunted antagonist of evil whose glance is lightning. Indeed Clizia has wrought a remarkable change in this verse of the 1930's, and the alteration looms even larger when one remembers that in 1932 Montale published a provisional version of his second collection, drawing the title from "La casa dei doganieri" ("The Coastguard Station," dated 1930), an Arletta piece in much the same spirit as "Stanza"; but the expanded, definitive editions of the book in the postwar years will bear a dedication to "I. B."—Irma Brandeis, the inspiration for Clizia.

Still another reflection of the changing course of *The Occasions* comes in a sequence of twenty short pieces, the "Mottetti" ("Motets"), that stand at the center of the book. These are true love poems, written in praise of a woman whom the narrator loses, regains, and loses again. But the tragedy of separation is not just a private affair, for the forces that intervene to part the lovers gradually become something very similar to the "ferocious faith" of "Dora Markus" or the devilish plotters of "New Stanzas." At first the narrator's beloved has more of the twilight characteristics than Clizia's. Thus the third motet shows the woman confined to a sanatorium, as the speaker meanwhile manages to survive the crackling grenades of World War I. (*The Occasions* are replete with auditory effects, especially threatening or unnerving sounds.) In this twilight piece, the message is passive endurance; but in the very next poem, composed about 1939, or five years later, the narrator represents his survival of World War I as much more purposeful. Indeed the later piece contains a strong affirmation, for the speaker asserts that he now knows that he was meant to meet his beloved, and must have been saved for that reason. For Montale's previously negativistic persona, this is a departure almost as marked as the invention of the powerful female protagonist of "New Stanzas."

The grim arms of World War I referred to in these two motets, together with the diabolical "burning mirror" of "New Stanzas," are part of a systematic line of development in Montale's imagery. For him machinery provides a key metaphor for the increasingly inhuman and war-bent regime of the late 1930's. In the fifth motet, for example, the narrator bids farewell to the woman, and the train station where they separate suggests an unsettling vision of human beings enslaved by a terrifying machine. The rumble of the train supplants the human good-byes, while the most prominent characters in the scene are "automatons," robots that, as the poem notes, seem to have gained the upper hand. The same antagonism between the rumbling train and all that is human recurs in the fifteenth motet, where the machine's rigid schedule contrasts with the woman's humane presence. All of these expressions of antipathy for mechanical devices put Montale in direct opposition to futurism's passionate admiration for modern technology, a theme that became an important part of fascist propaganda as well. Croce's *Storia d'Europa nel secolo decimonono* (*The History of Europe in the Nineteenth Century,* 1932), on the other hand, spoke of the baneful influence of technical progress, and, in the oblique terms made necessary by censorship, linked the contemporary fascination for potent machines with the rise of an inhuman regime. Certainly the poet concurs with this opinion when he represents machine-age man as a sinister force and uses him to typify the somber close of the 1930's.

The automatons of the fifth motet are closely related to an image from "New Stanzas" that has not yet been mentioned: the chessboard pawns, which are blinded by the "burning mirror." Both of these metaphors summon up the mass of men, and give a version of the multitude as unflattering as the ones found in *Cuttlefish Bones.* Two other Clizia poems of 1939

also dwell contemptuously on the many, seen as blind to reason and poor in humanity. "Palio," named after the traditional and often tumultuous horse race run at Siena, portrays the woman against the backdrop of an excited, noisy crowd. The poet, however, injects ominous notes into his account of the colorful spectacle, juxtaposing the public's thrilled roar to a disquieting, if cryptic, "balbuzie dei dannati" (stammering of the damned). Meanwhile Clizia looks heavenward above the mob and her hands hold a seal that the narrator recognizes as a private token of resistance to the general delirium. Just as in "New Stanzas," the poet here proposes a dichotomy between the few who keep their humanity, and the masses who seem so readily swayed to collective madness.

When she looks toward heaven, the woman of "Palio" gives a preview of an important evolution to come in Montale's myth of Clizia. Already the twelfth motet had endowed her figure with wings, and this startling transformation into an angel will be continued and fortified in the verse of the 1940's. The poet intends no conventional religiosity by this development, and in fact the Clizia poem that immediately precedes "New Stanzas" in *The Occasions* violently derides the traditional Catholicism of rural Italy. The "Elegia di Pico Farnese" ("Elegy of Pico Farnese"), like "Palio," sets the unreasoning many against the enlightened few. Scornfully the narrator of the piece denounces pilgrims making votive offerings at a paleo-Christian shrine in the village of Pico Farnese. Their superstitions are a sign of mental sloth for him, and an implied comparison connects them to satyrlike creatures that evidently signify instinctual, rather than rational, beings. But Clizia, in angelic guise, appears in spirit to counter the base and ignorant crowd. Her emblems are lightning and an eye, both obviously symbols of the illumination or intelligence that the pilgrims lack.

One may wonder why, in the midst of allegories clearly directed against fascism, Montale should turn his attention to abusing primitive Catholicism. The two objects of his assaults, however, are not as distinct to his and others' minds as they may appear. Opponents of the regime were quick to note similarities between fascist and Catholic predilections for public ritual and the orchestration of the multitude's emotions. Croce's antifascist manifesto bitterly lamented that the new movement seemed to think of itself as a religion or a gospel. Montale follows much the same logic when he abominates church and a militant state indiscriminately; thus his description of Nazism and fascism as a "fierce faith" in "Dora Markus." If the Clizia poems of 1939 stage a concerted attack on traditional religion, popular festivities, and the scheming warmongers and pawns of the regime, that should come as no surprise. All three pieces denounce a malleable people and the malevolent powers (as Montale believes) that lead them astray.

War and peace are also very much on the mind of the narrator in the later verse of *The Occasions.* "Eastbourne" inserts in its portrayal of an English holiday lines about handicapped World War I veterans, followed by the somber reflection that evil was not banished, but relentlessly reviving. Another holiday, this time in France, supplies the pretext for "Barche sulla Marna" ("Boats on the Marne"). Although the poem does not explicitly refer to the immense battles of World War I fought on the river's banks, the boat ride does move the lyrical speaker to imagine a future of peace and good works, as if in reply to the sad history of the place. But he calls this vision a "dream," and thus, like many other poems of the late 1930's in the collection, this one leaves the reader with a chilly sensation of the coming apocalypse. As Montale wrote in "Intentions (Imaginary Interview)," it did not require much imagination to prophesy catastrophe in those years. Storms figure conspicuously as metaphors in the poet's verse of this period, foretelling the dominant image and even the eventual title of his third collection. A hailstorm massacres flowers in the fourteenth motet, while the

seventeenth piece of the series finishes with a menacing slate sky soon to be overrun by gaunt horses. (Perhaps Montale refers here to the biblical horsemen of the apocalypse.) Against these frightening tempests the narrator continues to project the sustaining figure of Clizia, although she seldom appears so powerful as she was in "New Stanzas." The last poem of *The Occasions,* "Notizie dall'Amiata" ("News from Amiata," dated 1938), is, in fact, quite disconsolate; here gloomy weather frames a lonely narrator writing letters to the faraway woman. Yet a "filo di pietà" (thin stream of mercy) emerges at the last moment in this three-part composition, and to that slender hope the narrator attaches himself.

THE STORM AND OTHER THINGS

Although almost all of the fifteen poems of *Finisterre* had been previously printed in Italian periodicals, when Montale set an epigraph about persecutor-princes to the brief collection in 1943, it became unpublishable in fascist Italy and had to be exported to Switzerland, where it appeared in a small edition. These facts about the Swiss publication of what was to become the first section in *The Storm and Other Things* are significant because they reveal the poet halfway between the obscure allegories of the late 1930's and early 1940's (which were indeed uncensored during fascism), and the more direct allusions to the world that characterize certain parts of his postwar writing. The fall of the regime permitted an explosive liberation of pent-up artistic expression in Italy. But to an even greater degree than contemporaries like Quasimodo and Vittorini, Montale remained intensely ambivalent about a new literature that would respond to immediate concerns, to the politics of the moment. So it is that in *The Storm and Other Things* he balances between an allegiance to a timeless, universal poetry and the postwar impulse to use art for a more explicit commentary on the times than was ever permitted to the antifascist during the regime. Representative of this ambivalence are two small segments of the book set side by side and yet standing at odds. The first, called "Dopo" ("Afterward"), includes pieces bearing dates laden with wartime meaning (11 September 1943, the day Mussolini was installed by the Nazis as the head of a puppet government in northern Italy). The second, "Intermezzo," seems completely abstracted from contemporary tumult, and even contains an Arletta poem (retrieved from an old notebook, as the poet's gloss confides). Thus, in the sequence of *The Storm and Other Things,* Arletta, Montale's vehicle for depicting private anguish, paradoxically faces some of the book's most public writing.

This same tension between withdrawal and engagement also informs many of the poems to Clizia and to her successor, the fox-woman, each of whom is the subject of major cycles of verse in the collection. In his postwar "Intentions (Imaginary Interview)," for example, Montale characterized *Finisterre* as a portrait of an angel projected against the backdrop of a "cosmic and terrestrial war." He means to leave the nature of the conflict ambiguous: in part it is a particular war provoked by a particular dictatorship, but he also insists on seeing the battle as an eternal struggle between good and evil. So the poet allows *Finisterre* to refer to immediate events, while also preserving for it a measure of universality.

These poems of the early war years include some of Montale's most haunting works. Vivid renderings of Armageddon alternate with depictions of a woman who sometimes dwindles and grows distant, other times waxes strong and angel-like, promising to bring salvation to the beleaguered. As in *The Occasions,* acoustic effects are exploited as tellingly as visual imagery to convey the terror of this apocalypse. The storm that gives the piece its title, "La bufera," raises an infernal din of blasts, ratcheting, and throbbing, evoked in one of the most extraordinary variations on the poet's habitual repertory of harsh, unmusical sounds. Clizia, meanwhile, is shown at the close of the poem

waving farewell and disappearing into the dark—a vignette that establishes the pessimistic tone of many of these pieces, and also doubtless alludes to the departure of Montale's real-life beloved for North America.

In poems like "Lungomare" (Seaside Promenade) and "Serenata indiana" ("Indian Serenade"), the individual appears compromised, even overwhelmed, by sinister forces. "Gli orecchini" ("The Earrings") spreads the gloom further by repeating the motif, worked out at the end of *The Occasions,* of vicious mechanical devices (this time droning propeller blades) that devour human lives. The steely Clizia seems to have lost all her strength. Yet by the close of *Finisterre* Montale injects new elements into her mythology, transforming her into a peculiarly sacred emblem. The tendency to model Clizia after an angel was already present in the verse of the late 1930's, but now the poet lends theological substance, so to speak, to his invention. In "Il ventaglio" ("The Fan"), even as the gaping earth swallows up more victims, her angel plumage begins to glow and the narrator can announce that "il giorno è forse salvo" (the day is perhaps saved). This redemptive power will henceforth be the chief of Clizia's faculties. "La frangia dei capelli . . . " (The Strands of Hair . . .), for instance, evokes her beautiful, pale bangs as a sign of heaven, superimposes them upon the dawn (an obvious symbol of hope), and makes them serve as a token of forgiveness.

The woman's vocation as a savior comes to fruition in poems published after the Liberation, in particular "Iride" ("Rainbow") and "La primavera hitleriana" ("Hitler Spring"). In the first of these, she acts as a double of Christ; her works (of compassion, one understands) replicate the works of Jesus. The poem, moreover, mingles Christian and Judaic images. A shroud imprinted with bloody, tormented features (doubtless Montale has in mind the Shroud of Turin, with its supposed death mask of Christ) summons up the scene of the Crucifixion, while the woman is said to be from Canaan, the Hebrew homeland, and her name,

"Iris," may be connected to the rainbow that God gives as an emblem of his covenant with Noah in Genesis. Glimpses of this mixture of the two faiths were visible in the poems dedicated to Jewish characters in *The Occasions,* but nowhere is the fusion more evident than in "Rainbow." The poet's intent scarcely requires elaboration: Christians and Jews had been savagely sundered by the Nazis and fascists, but Montale unites the two traditions in his praise of Clizia.

"Hitler Spring," completed in 1946, offers the most generous redemption of all these poems, and also marks a high point in the poet's brief postwar social activism. Hitler and Mussolini's encounter in Florence on the eve of the war furnishes the point of departure for this meditation, which begins on the descriptive, apocalyptic register but then moves to some important moral summations. No one can escape guilt for the evils committed in the wake of that fateful meeting, asserts the narrator. Even the apparently innocent have a share in the blame. This equal division of culpability contrasts with the Clizia poems of the late 1930's, which left a small band morally unblemished while making the masses accomplices or worse. From his new vantage point as the politically committed writer, a member of the Action Party, Montale may have felt the need to soften his previous antipopular viewpoint. Indeed, having judged the responsibilities general, "Hitler Spring" also grants mercy to all, for Clizia returns, once again as a christlike figure, sacrificing herself for the redemption of everyone.

But the empathy with the populace implied in this poem has a very short life. Only a year later, already disgruntled at the failure of the Action Party's idealistic, intellectual brand of politics, the poet falls back into upbraiding the multitude, whereas only a few, still presided over by Clizia, keep their faith intact. Such is the scheme of "L'Ombra della magnolia" ("The Shade of the Magnolia," 1947), in which an abrupt chill in the air, a figure close to the meteorological metaphors used to political ef-

fect by Montale in the 1930's, ushers in a new season of struggles for another tiny group of dissidents. Umberto Carpi has observed that such a swift return to disaffection after World War II was inevitable for someone like Montale, who had no sympathy for either of the mass movements, the Christian Democrats and the Communists, who quickly divided up the political life of Italy in an acrimonious contest that followed soon after the Liberation. This polarization affects much of the rest of the verse in *The Storm and Other Things,* leading the poet to refuse what he considers the unappetizing calls to political commitment, though provoking him as well to occasional outbursts against the two monolithic political foes.

Clizia's grave angelic presence now fades from Montale's verse—although like Arletta, she will intermittently reappear through the last stage of his writing. The vacuum left by her departure is filled when the poet contrives a new creature, whom he calls the fox-woman. He designs her, in part, to be an antithesis to Clizia, more profane than sacred, more earthly than divine. In "Nubi color magenta" ("Magenta-Colored Clouds") he gives her the role of the courtesan Thaïs, allotting to the narrator the part of Paphnuce, a desert hermit who lacks the holiness to resist the woman's sensual charms. This story of the perversely bewitching female had also been told in *Thaïs* (1890), a novel by Anatole France, one of the most popular writers associated with turn-of-the-century "decadent" culture. The poems to the fox-woman, however, contain allusions not just to France's tale, but also to other elements from the repertory of those late-nineteenth-century writers who were lumped together, at least by critics like Croce, under the rubric "decadent." "Per un 'Omaggio a Rimbaud'" ("For an 'Homage to Rimbaud,'" dated 1950) and "Da un lago svizzero" ("From a Swiss Lake," dated 1949) both invoke the literary tradition attacked with renewed vehemence by Croce in the postwar years as being the cultural harbinger of fascism. In an essay of 1945, "Il fascismo e la letteratura" ("Fascism and Literature"), as well as in a piece from the following year, "Esiste un decadentismo in Italia?" ("Is There an Italian Decadence?"), Montale maintained that invectives like Croce's were ill founded, for the influence of the decadents in Italy had been mostly benign. He did distance himself from the most unrestrained iconoclasm of the decadents (one example of this being, in his view, the enfant terrible Rimbaud); yet even this extremism, according to the poet, had left important literary contributions in its wake. Montale's gingerly embrace of the decadents is reflected in "For an 'Homage to Rimbaud,'" which portrays the hectic course of the French prodigy, but urges the woman not to follow it. (Interestingly, a journal kept by the poet in 1917 and published in 1982 as the *Quaderno genovese,* shows him enamored of Rimbaud's poetry. When he cautions the fox-woman, Montale in effect may be criticizing his own youthful enthusiasm as well.) "From a Swiss Lake" exploits a decadent image with less qualification. Its opening runs: "Mia volpe un giorno fui anch'io il 'poeta / assassinato'" (My fox, I too was one day the "assassinated poet"). Here Montale takes up an ancient etymology linking "assassin" and "hashish," which both Rimbaud and his predecessor Baudelaire had employed in speaking of the modern writer's experimentation with altered states of consciousness. The fox-woman indeed inspires her admirer with something akin to a delirium of the sense, not just in "From a Swiss Lake," but in other poems as well. A sometimes reserved, sometimes warmer tribute to decadent practice thus emerges from the fox-woman cycle. Perhaps the most surprising reference to decadent thematics comes in "Anniversario" ("Anniversary"). Like "The Shade of the Magnolia," this composition represents the poet removed once more from the mass of men, insulating himself from the all-too-crass postwar politics. Kneeling to the fox-woman as though she were a deity, the poem's narrator ends by picturing himself as God, a god separated from men. The decadents, Baudelaire and Rimbaud in particular, also see their creativity as bringing them near to godliness. For Montale, usually so modest in personifying himself in his verse, "Anniversary" constitutes an exceptional moment of hauteur. But if one observes the anger with which he retreats from what he regards as the base aftermath of fascism, and if one considers the empathy with which he depicts the decadents in the late 1940's, this self-apotheosis becomes more comprehensible. The decadent artist was apt to see himself above and beyond ordinary human society, an attitude that suits Montale very well in these years.

Rounding out *The Storm and Other Things* are "Piccolo testamento" ("Little Testament," dated 1953) and "Il sogno del prigioniero" ("The Prisoner's Dream," dated 1954), two poems that more or less summarize the poet's stance toward the postfascist world. The first acidly declines to put faith in either red or black "clerics"—an easily decipherable insult directed toward what Montale holds to be his nation's equally dogmatic Communist and Christian Democratic parties. Instead the narrator vows fidelity to humble emblems similar to those that sustained the speaker in the verse written during the fascist era. "The Prisoner's Dream," on the other hand, does not rely on historically identifiable images in describing the grotesque torments and fortitude of a prisoner of conscience. In this finale Montale thus insists again on a timeless art, and with no very optimistic intent, for to universalize this prisoner's experience implies not only a general praise of resisters, but also that the horrific regimes that the poet has witnessed in his lifetime are likely to spring up again in other, future forms.

SATURA *AND LAST POEMS*

In his old age Montale grew astonishingly productive. Whereas a decade and a half separated *Cuttlefish Bones* from *The Occasions,* and another fifteen years were required to assemble *The Storm and Other Things,* the poet published no fewer than three volumes of verse in the 1970's, and still more new works were brought out in the 1980 critical edition prepared by Gianfranco Contini and Rosanna Bettarini. The compositions from the winter of the poet's life tend to be less assuming than his earlier writing. Rather than being elegiac or tragic, as the Arletta and Clizia cycles were, they are often satirical and even farcical. Continuities between the old and the new Montale do exist, however. His preferred political themes resurface in other guises, especially his disaffection toward mainstream thinking, which now involves him in sardonic forays against various systematizations of history. On the level of language, he persists in contesting the Italian tradition of a mellifluous sublime, for he rejects conventionally lovely language and frequently draws awkward modern jargon into his verse as though to challenge himself once more to absorb ungainly linguistic material and generate a countereloquence.

Close to the preoccupations of *The Storm and Other Things* are pieces scattered through *Satura* but united by the general title "Botta e risposta." The first two parts of the sequence begin with epistles in verse from Asolo and Ascona, respectively—two resorts known as haunts of decadent artists. As one might expect, each of these poems implies a defense of decadent culture, particularly against charges of its treasonous evasion of civic responsibilities. In reply to these accusations, Montale proposes the insulation of the poet from the here-and-now as the only creditable position. But while he speaks again of the artist's necessary remove from the times, he does not indulge in the arrogant selfishness of "Anniversary." Instead of deifying the narrator, the first part of "Botta e risposta" only equates him with a timid mouse. In the fox-woman's cycle the poet toyed with the exalted sense of self common to many decadents. But here he returns to self-deprecation, bringing himself back into conformity with the many uncertain, anguished personae of his early verse.

Ironically, the justification of the writer's disengagement from the times in the first piece of "Botta e risposta" also involves a revisitation of those times. As has often been his lot, Montale remains curiously divided between his ideal of an art independent from the immediate and an irresistible urge to address that present. Using the figure of the Augean stables to stand for fascism, the poem's speaker conveys his helpless disgust toward the regime. Moreover, he refrains from celebrating the Hercules who drained the filth, but rather depicts the postwar world as another, only slightly less noisome, maelstrom of ordure. Thus the hostility toward post-Liberation society already vented in *The Storm and Other Things* finds another acerbic expression.

The offal in this poem, meanwhile, seems to have inspired many other images of waste products in Montale's last verse. Refuse serves as a vehicle for his distaste at the muddled postwar world, but its significance also widens to become the poet's basic emblem for history. In "Dialogo" (Dialogue, dated 1968) he asserts that history is not a system, but only a "flea market"—in other words, a hodgepodge. By rejecting the idea of any orderly historical process, Montale prepares himself to ridicule the premises of such diverse optimistic worldviews as Marxism and Crocean idealism. In "Piove" (It's Raining, dated 1969) he scornfully defines leftists as "teologi in tuta" (theologians in coveralls), a barb that recalls the "red clerics" of "Little Testament," while also making the point that communism, as far as the poet is concerned, relies on a reductive and unconvincing view of historical evolution. "Cielo e terra" (Heaven and Earth, dated 1969), in a similarly jocular maneuver, takes the partly human, partly transcendental spirit held by idealist philosophy to be the prime mover of history and compares it to a boomerang hurtling back and forth between heaven and earth.

These two diatribes both belong to the cycle dedicated to Mosca, whose pungent skepticism, portrayed in the two sets of "Xenia" poems, make her a fit mascot for the poet's cynicism in *Satura.* Wary of the representatives of orthodox religion, she substitutes for conventional faith a quirky collection of appeals to Saint Anthony for lost umbrellas and prayers for the departed—a patchwork kindly accepted by the priest after her death as sufficient. Her last moments, furthermore, are not cause for any grand summing-up, but only evoke disconnected, inconsequential memories—a personal history with no more informing order than Montale allows to the history of the entire species in *Satura.* Even poetry is demystified under her tutelage: she understands that any notion of poetry as registering a totality—making sense of it all—is merely foolish. In her skeptical view, art apparently is not the vehicle of great truths. Moreover, while the fox-woman brought out a heady egoism in her companion, Mosca can be found laughing till the tears come at a pompous testimonial dinner given in his honor in Portugal. She deflates this solemn ceremony in much the same way that Montale himself in his last verse goes about demolishing the dignified and rational constructions of positive-minded men. At the close of the "Xenia" suites, the poet produces a particularly vivid picture of the world in disorder. This melancholy piece describes the depredations of the flood that ruined so many of Florence's treasures in 1966. Then the muddy, destructive inundation recalls to the narrator's mind the equally wanton tide of historical events through which he somehow survived. Both the local disaster and the larger catastrophes are incredible, beyond comprehension. Facing these vagaries, the poet borrows a bit of stoicism from the woman, but that is all. He seems to imply that one cannot hope to understand such a random world.

Playing on her nickname, Montale addresses Mosca in the second piece of the "Xenia" series as the "povero insetto che ali / avevi solo nella fantasia" (poor little insect, whose only wings were imaginary). One remembers Clizia's winged angel of resistance

and realizes how stunted and pathetic things have become in the last season of the poet's verse. Yet he has not completely abandoned his taste for the noble and the miraculous if he continues, even in *Satura,* to create angelic presences and discover other loves worth commemorating. It is just that these late manifestations of admiration and ardor are couched in less splendid terms than were his great poems dedicated to Clizia. Typical is the case of "L'angelo nero" ("The Black Angel," dated 1968), where the sooty, urchinlike being of the title hovers by humble ovens and street vendors' braziers but nevertheless excites the narrator to joyful prayers and invocations. This "mini-angel," as Montale calls the creature, using the prefix popularized in the late 1960's, has flashes of the divine, despite its reduced dimensions.

After the Mosca cycle, the most conspicuous sequence in *Satura* is "Dopo una fuga" ("After a Flight," dated 1969). The love poems of this suite revolve around the poet's quest for a quasi-religious sign of hope from the woman, a familiar theme in his verse. But this time the pursuit is set against the chaos of modern days. A babel of languages, deafening sirens, and gods and demons indistinguishable from each other summon up this jumble. The young woman briefly seems to point the way of escape from the confusion; the narrator looks to her for comfort and revelation, much as Montale's earlier personae looked to Clizia or Arletta. He even compares her to Cordelia and himself to Lear, reaching for the highest tragedy in order to portray their strange communion. But the poet of this late verse cannot muster such a lofty genre. Mercilessly he dissects his passion, revealing its farcical aspects. But after all, he says, as though to ease his disappointment, people are no longer supposed to emote over such trivialities as romance—an observation that joins *Satura*'s chorus of assertions about the bathos of present times. Like the "mini-angel," the woman of "After a Flight" shines in her own way, and yet in comparison to the celebrated inspirers of Montale's earlier poetry, she must appear as something of a melancholy afterimage.

Perhaps just because the contemporary world leaves him so frequently disgruntled, Montale resuscitates Clizia and Arletta with increasing frequency in his last writings, collected in *Altri versi e poesie disperse* (translated as *Otherwise: Last and First Poems of Eugenio Montale,* 1981). In his final reckoning, these two characters have by far the most significance. It is not that he has resolved all the mysteries attached to them, however; in fact, the continuing uncertainties that he connects with them are probably a chief part of their attraction. Clizia, since she was a key figure in the poet's antifascism, often spurs political questions when she resurfaces in his verse. In "Quartetto" ("Foursome," dated 1979) a forty-year-old photograph of her with the poet at Siena's Palio emerges from a drawer. This souvenir calls to mind both the mad crowd—a crucial political image in *The Occasions*—and metaphysical questions about time and being. One might say that the tension between politics and metaphysics that resides at the center of Montale's mature thinking is brought back by this recollection of Clizia. Politics in truth remains something not quite palatable for the poet. The report that Clizia showed leftist tendencies, mentioned in the poem "Nel '38" ("In '38," dated 1978), does not meet with an enthusiastic reception from her admirer. But he does not overly concern himself with such worldly issues; it is enough that Clizia still arouses him to a "faith" that will endure into a world beyond the present one. That is the conclusion of "Ho tanta fede in te" ("I Have Such Faith in You"), a poem remarkable for the later Montale in that it points past the contemporary muddle—evoked as an "immenso cascame" (immense rubbish heap)—to a realm of purity. Here, as in the past, Clizia possesses the extraordinary capacity to lift the poet's vision above the present horrors to a higher, peaceable zone. (Not by coincidence, this same piece

refers to Dante's *Divine Comedy,* the object of Irma Brandeis's scholarship, and certainly suggestive for Montale as he invents an angelic woman who uplifts her loving admirer.)

The final poem in *Altri versi,* the last collection published by the poet, is devoted to Arletta. (Its title, "Ah," gives an almost whispered version of the first sound of her name.) She is not entangled in the political questions that Clizia inevitably raises. Instead she appears as the fragile memory tenderly cultivated by the poet almost in defiance of the various bits of real news about her life that filter to him through the many years after their brief meeting when she was a child. The most ethereal and insubstantial figure in his verse thus maintains a peculiarly strong hold on the poet, occupying, in fact, the very last page of his works. This allegiance is not hard to understand: Montale rarely saw himself in any other mode beside those of alienation and disaffection; Arletta's remove from the real world is his most wistful embodiment of a desire to escape the cruel here-and-now.

As Montale himself said in "Intentions (Imaginary Interview)," his early readers found his poetry difficult to situate. It was quite distinct from radical elements of the avant-garde such as futurism, but it also had little in common with contemporary Italian writing that looked back to the early nineteenth century and naively sought to imitate Giacomo Leopardi's poetry or Alessandro Manzoni's prose. If Montale felt any affinities for his contemporaries, they were apt to be for such foreign exemplars of "high modernism" as T. S. Eliot and Paul Valéry. (He published essays about both these writers.) Toward his immediate surroundings in the Italian cultural landscape—especially D'Annunzio and the twilight poets—there was a diffidence that nevertheless could itself become material for his verse. As his ambivalent relationship to these sources has grown clearer, we can better appreciate the way in which Montale referred precisely to his own literary coming of age when he said in "Intentions (Imaginary Interview)" that a poet's language is "an historicized language . . . valid to the degree that it opposes or differentiates itself from other languages."

It has also been difficult to assess the political aspects of the poet's work. While some of his verse published during the fascist era was seized as a token of at least passive resistance to the regime, influential critics like Contini chose to emphasize the timelessness of Montale's malaise, from which his poetry could be seen emerging only after 1945. But this view turns out to be inadequate, first because Montale's reactions to writers like D'Annunzio and the twilight poets could scarcely avoid the political implications that hung over their work in the 1920's, and secondly because by the mid 1930's Irma Brandeis had given the poet a powerful inspiration to create political allegories. The compositions about Europe's totalitarian madness that appear in the latter part of *The Occasions* (and are continued in *The Storm and Other Things*) constitute a great body of political art. Yet the political meaning of these poems cannot be divorced from the fact that most of them were oblique enough to be published in Italy during the fascist regime. Not surprisingly, Montale in the postwar years repeatedly felt compelled to confront the question of a work of art's relation to the world; this was a chief concern, for example, in his revisitation of decadent culture, a theme that runs from the poems devoted to the fox-woman to the verse of "Botta e risposta." Obviously the answers he offers are not those of a Pablo Neruda or a Bertolt Brecht. The direct intervention of art into politics is not for him. Instead, with a mixture of pride and humility, he maintains that elusiveness and marginality (being "on the edge," as one critic has described it) are the artist's best—and perhaps only conceivable—position vis-à-vis the times. Such an affirmation is bound to be provocative, and if for no other reason than this provocation, we may be grateful to Montale for bestowing upon us his poetry.

Selected Bibliography

EDITIONS

INDIVIDUAL WORKS
Ossi di seppia. Turin, 1925.
La casa dei doganieri e altri versi. Florence, 1932.
Le occasioni. Turin, 1939.
Finisterre. Lugano, 1943.
La bufera e altro. Venice, 1956.
La farfalla di Dinard. Vicenza, 1956.
Auto da fé: Cronache in due tempi. Milan, 1966.
Satura (1962–1970). Milan, 1971.
Diario del '71 e del '72. Milan, 1973.
Quaderno di quattro anni. Milan, 1978.

COLLECTED WORKS
Sulla poesia. Edited by Giorgio Zampa. Milan, 1976.
L'Opera in versi. Edited by Rosanna Bettarini and Gianfranco Contini. Turin, 1980. A critical edition of the poetry.
Altri versi e poesie disperse. Milan, 1981.
Quaderno genovese. Edited by L. Barile. Milan, 1982. A journal kept by Montale in 1917.
Tutte le poesie. Edited by Giorgio Zampa. Milan, 1984.

TRANSLATIONS

The Butterfly of Dinard. Translated by Ghanshyam Singh. Lexington, Ky., 1971.
It Depends: A Poet's Notebook. Translated by Ghanshyam Singh. Manchester, 1978.
"Mediterranean," in *Pequod* 2 (Winter 1977). A special issue devoted to translations of Montale's work.
New Poems: A Selection from "Satura" and "Diario del '71 e del '72." Translated by Ghanshyam Singh. New York, 1976.
The Occasions. Translated by William Arrowsmith. New York, 1987.
Otherwise: Last and First Poems of Eugenio Montale. Translated by Jonathan Galassi. New York, 1984. A translation of *Altri versi e poesie disperse.*
Provisional Conclusions: A Selection of the Poetry of Eugenio Montale. Translated by Edith Farnsworth. Chicago, 1970.
The Second Life of Art: Selected Essays of Eugenio Montale. Translated and edited by Jonathan

Galassi. New York, 1982. Contains the essays "Aesthetics and Criticism," "Intentions (Imaginary Interview)," "Fascism and Literature," "Is There an Italian Decadence?" "Style and Tradition," as well as pieces on T. S. Eliot and Paul Valéry.

Selected Essays. Translated and introduced by Ghanshyam Singh. Manchester, 1978.

Selected Poems. Translated by Glauco Cambon et al. New York, 1965.

Selected Poems. Translated by George Kay. Baltimore, 1969.

The Storm and Other Poems. Translated by Charles Wright. Oberlin, 1978.

The Storm and Other Things. Translated by William Arrowsmith. New York, 1985.

BIOGRAPHICAL AND CRITICAL STUDIES

Almansi, Guido, and Bruce Merry. *Eugenio Montale: The Private Language of Poetry.* Edinburgh, 1977.

Atti del convegno internazionale: La poesia di Eugenio Montale (Milano/Genova 12–15 sett. 1982). Milan, 1983.

Avalle, D'Arco Silvio. *Tre saggi su Montale.* Turin, 1970.

Becker, Jared. *Eugenio Montale.* Boston, 1986.

Brandeis, Irma. "Eugenio Montale." *Saturday Review of Literature* (18 July 1936).

Cambon, Glauco. *Eugenio Montale's Poetry: A Dream in Reason's Presence.* Princeton, 1982.

Camon, Ferdinando. "Montale," in his *Il mestiere di poeta.* Milan, 1954.

Carpi, Umberto. *Montale dopo il fascismo dalla "Bufera" a "Satura."* Padua, 1971.

Cima, Annalisa, and Cesare Segre, eds. *Profilo di un autore: Eugenio Montale.* Milan, 1977.

Contini, Gianfranco. *Una lunga fedeltà: Scritti su Eugenio Montale.* Naples, 1978. Contains essays published from 1933 to 1973.

Corti, Maria, and Maria Antonietta Grignani, eds. *Autografi di Montale.* Turin, 1976.

Forti, Marco. *Eugenio Montale: La poesia, la prosa di fantasia e d'invenzione.* Milan, 1974.

———, ed. *Per conoscere Montale.* Milan, 1986.

Greco, Lorenzo, ed. *Montale commenta Montale.* Parma, 1980.

Grignani, Maria Antonietta. *Prologhi ed epiloghi: Sulla poesia di Eugenio Montale.* Ravenna, 1987.

Huffman, Claire de C. L. *Montale and the Occasions of Poetry.* Princeton, 1983.

Jacomuzzi, Angelo. *La poesia di Montale: Dagli "Ossi" ai "Diari."* Turin, 1978.

Letture montaliane: In occasione dell'ottantesimo compleanno del poeta. Genoa, 1977.

Luperini, Romano. *Storia di Montale.* Bari, 1986.

Manghetti, Gloria et al., eds. *Francesco Meriano: Arte e vita.* Milan, 1982. Includes correspondence between Montale and Meriano.

Mengaldo, Pier Vincenzo. *La tradizione del Novecento.* Milan, 1975.

Nascimbeni, Giulio. *Eugenio Montale.* Milan, 1975. An authorized biography.

Orelli, Giorgio. *Accertamenti montaliani.* Bologna, 1984.

Pancrazi, Pietro. "Eugenio Montale poeta fisico e metafisico," in his *Scrittori d'oggi,* vol. 3. Bari, 1946. Reprints an article from the *Corriere della Sera* (21 March 1934).

La poesia di Eugenio Montale: Atti del Convegno Internazionale tenuto a Genova, 1982. Florence, 1984.

Ramat, Silvio, ed. *Omaggio a Montale.* Milan, 1966. Reprints extracts from fifty years of criticism on the poet.

Rebay, Luciano. "Sull' 'autobiografismo' di Montale." In *Innovazioni tematiche espressive e linguistiche della letteratura italiana del Novecento.* Atti dell'VIII Congresso dell'Associazione Internazionale per gli Studi di Lingua e Letteratura Italiana. New York, 25–28 April 1973. Florence, 1976.

———. "Montale, Clizia, e l'America," *Forum Italicum* 16 (Winter 1982).

Sanguineti, Edoardo. *Tra liberty e crepuscolarismo.* Milan, 1961. Includes "Da Gozzano a Montale" and "Da D'Annunzio a Gozzano".

Singh, Ghanshyam. *Eugenio Montale: A Critical Study of his Poetry, Prose, and Criticism.* New Haven, 1973.

West, Rebecca J. *Eugenio Montale: Poet on the Edge.* Cambridge, 1981.

BIBLIOGRAPHY

Barile, Laura. *Bibliografia montaliana.* Milan, 1977.

JARED BECKER

GIUSEPPE TOMASI DI LAMPEDUSA

(1896–1957)

In this labyrinth I see a two-headed Hermes which with one face laughs and with the other weeps; it laughs with one face at the other's weeping.

—Pirandello on Sicily

BIOGRAPHY

THE ENIGMATIC PERSONALITY of the aristocratic author, the unusual composition of his late masterpiece, the tragic rejection of the book during his lifetime, and its spectacular success after his death all give an extraordinary aura to Giuseppe Tomasi di Lampedusa's *Il Gattopardo* (*The Leopard,* 1958). In this work Lampedusa grasps the present through the past and uses his own family background to make history concrete. His traditional novel has a densely textured and vividly realized nineteenth-century setting and cast of characters, but the satiric vision and the elegiac tone belong to the modern age.

The Tomasi di Lampedusa family traced their lineage back to an imperial source and claimed descent from Tiberias II, Emperor of Byzantium from 578 to 582. The family has been prominent among the grandees of Sicily for more than three centuries. In 1637 they founded an entirely new town, Palma di Montechiaro, near Agrigento, and built a lavish church and palace. Lampedusa's great-grandfather, Giulio Fabrizio, the model for the Leopard, was a distinguished mathematician and astronomer who discovered two asteroids—which he named "Palma" and "Lampedusa." He sat in the Sicilian chamber of peers in 1848, and died in Florence in 1885 during a typhus epidemic.

The novelist Giuseppe Tomasi, Prince of Lampedusa (one of the Pelagie islands, south of Sicily), was born in Palermo on 23 December 1896. He believed it was a duty to record one's memories, which would have inestimable value after three or four generations. And in "I luoghi della mia prima infanzia" ("Places of My Infancy"), written in the summer of 1955 and published in *Racconti* (*Two Stories and a Memory*) in 1961, Lampedusa evokes an only child's nostalgic vision, retrieved from the archives of memory. The memoir attempts to recapture the background, places, people, and feelings associated with his lost paradise of feudal luxury and privilege.

The earliest memories of the solitary, bookish boy—who did not learn to read until he was eight and loved the company of things more than people—were associated with the huge family mansion on the Via Lampedusa in Palermo: his father rushing in to announce the assassination of King Umberto in July 1900; the dry kiss of the aged Eugénie, ex-empress of the French, just after the turn of the century; and the reverberations of the Messina earthquake in December 1908.

Even more impressive and memorable were the summer journeys to, excursions from, and theatrical performances in the hundred-room baroque palace, Santa Margherita Belice, sixty-five miles south of Palermo, which inspired the description of Donnafugata in the novel. Lampedusa fondly describes the house (sold by his maternal uncle in 1921) as "a kind of eighteenth-century Pompeii, all miraculously preserved intact; a rare thing always, but almost unique in Sicily, which from poverty and neglect is the most destructive of countries."

Lampedusa was estranged from his shadowy father, an elegant man of the world, and subjected to scandal when his mother's sister (lady-in-waiting to the queen of Italy) was stabbed to death by her lover in a low hotel in Rome in 1911. He studied jurisprudence at the universities of Genoa and Turin during 1914–1915; and spent his early manhood as a regular artillery officer in World War I, serving on the Austrian front near Bolzano, in northeast Italy. In "Places of My Infancy" he states that he killed "a Bosnian with a pistol and who knows how many other Christians by shellfire." He was captured in battle, escaped from a prisoner-of-war camp in Hungary, and did not leave the service until 1921.

Lampedusa intended to follow a career in the diplomatic service (his uncle had been ambassador to England) but suffered a nervous breakdown in the 1920's. Between the wars, he and his mother traveled throughout Europe and lived in grand hotels in Rome, Turin, Paris, and London. In 1932 he married Alexandra Wolff-Stormersee, a Latvian whose mother was an Italian singer, and spent summers at her castle near Riga. They had no children, and Lampedusa's title was assumed by his adopted son, Gioacchino Lanza. Alexandra became a leading Freudian analyst in Palermo.

In "Lighea" ("The Professor and the Siren") the narrator says: "Then came the war, and while I was in Marmarica [the Libyan desert], rationed to half a litre of water a day 'Liberators' destroyed my home" in Palermo. On the basis of this statement, Simonetta Salvestroni unconvincingly claims that Lampedusa was called to war for the second time in 1940 and fought in Marmarica—though we know he was in Palermo and President of the Sicilian Red Cross when his house was destroyed by Allied bombs in July 1943. According to one story, he rescued his wife's furs and a painting by Bellini and carried them off on the handlebars of a bicycle.

The Ferrarese novelist Giorgio Bassani, who met the unknown Lampedusa at a literary conference in the summer of 1954 at San Pellegrino Terme, where Lampedusa's cousin Lucio Piccolo received a poetry prize, described the novelist-to-be as "a tall gentleman, corpulent, taciturn: pallid-faced, with that grayish complexion of dark-skinned southerners. . . . One would have taken him at first glance for a retired general."

Lampedusa had contemplated the novel for twenty-five years and finally wrote it during 1955 and 1956 in his favorite Café Mazzara, and in his Palermo Club, the Circolo Bellini. The book was a distillation, by an exquisitely civilized man, of a lifetime's reading in literature, history, philosophy, and science. The Sicilian novelist Elio Vittorini, who read the manuscript for Einaudi, made the biggest mistake since André Gide turned down *Du côté de chez Swann* (*Swann's Way*, 1913); he rejected *The Leopard* as "too much like an essay." Vittorini's letter of rejection was read to Lampedusa on 22 July 1957, two days before he died of lung cancer in Rome. The publisher's reader at Mondadori, who found the novel traditional in form and reactionary in thought, was also negative. For Lampedusa ignored the bleak neorealistic style of contemporary Italian fiction and created instead a lush evocation of a lost world. His view of history and politics was equally unfashionable. He suggested that Garibaldi's revolution of 1860 was a dubious gift to Sicily and that the fatalistic island was incapable of change.

Bassani was the first to recognize the merit of the manuscript, which was published by Feltrinelli in November 1958 and became an immediate international success. The French Communist poet Louis Aragon, ignoring its ideology, called *The Leopard* "one of the great books of this century, one of the great books of all time." It won the coveted Strega Prize in 1959 and was made into an intelligent film by Luchino Visconti—starring Burt Lancaster, Alain Delon, and Claudia Cardinale—which won the Golden Palm at the Cannes Film Festival in 1963. The novel had sold an astonishing 1,600,000 copies in Italy by August 1982. Like Thomas Chatterton, Emily Dickinson, Gerard Manley Hopkins, and Franz Kafka, who all wrote works that clashed with the tastes of their times, Lampedusa's literary fame is based entirely on books published after his death.

The Leopard is a historical novel that covers a period of fifty years. The first six chapters take place between May 1860 and November 1862; chapter 7 ("Death of a Prince") occurs in July 1888 and chapter 8 ("Relics") in May 1910. The novel portrays the effect on a Sicilian aristocrat and his family of the revolutionary movement (the Risorgimento) that marked the destruction of the old order by middle-class usurpers and led to the unification of Italy for the first time since the fall of the Roman empire. In May 1860 the popular general Giuseppe Garibaldi sailed from Genoa with a thousand red-shirted, nonprofessional volunteers (*I Mille*), landed at Marsala in western Sicily, and liberated the island from the reactionary rule of the king in Naples, Francis II. Garibaldi then marched up the coast, defeated the Bourbon army, and handed over southern Italy to the liberal King Victor Emmanuel, who ruled the so-called Kingdom of Sardinia in Turin and became monarch of the united country in 1861.

Prince Fabrizio, the hero of *The Leopard,* is ambivalent about these cataclysmic historical events. Aware of the revolution and too intelligent to resist the inevitable, he is too attached to the past to join the present. And he does not believe that the revolution will have a profound effect on Sicily. Fatalistic himself, he refuses to act and to prevent the destruction of his class. With a strange indifference he observes his favorite nephew, Tancredi Falconeri, join the Garibaldini, abandon the Prince's daughter Concetta (who is betrayed by both her father and lover) and, in order to retrieve a remnant of the family fortune, marry the beautiful peasant Angelica, whose father, Calogero Sedàra, has taken advantage of the revolutionary chaos to complete his theft of the prince's feudal lands.

Lampedusa insisted, in his 1959 essay on Stendhal, that "in art, the technique of execution is everything." We can best understand the profound ideas and complex artistry of *The Leopard* by placing the novel in its literary, historical, and aesthetic contexts. I will first explore the subtle symbolism, which derives from Gustave Flaubert, Charles Baudelaire, and Marcel Proust, assimilates French forms into Italian fiction, and is the primary mode of expression in the novel. I will then consider the acknowledged influence of Stendhal's *The Charterhouse of Parma* (1839), which Lampedusa adopted as a source for the hero and themes of *The Leopard*. Finally, I will examine Lampedusa's use of the visual and ideological content of the paintings of the eighteenth-century French artist Jean-Baptiste Greuze to express his skeptical and tragic sense of loss and decay.

SYMBOLISM

The Leopard is a richly symbolic novel from the first scene during the rosary to the final moment when the carcass of the dog, Bendicò, is flung out the window. There are two categories of symbols: first, a more conventional symbol that occurs only once—though such static symbols often appear in expanded moments that allow their meanings to reverberate through the novel and to foreshadow the future. Prophecy is used structurally to link the present with the future and give an air of predestined inevitability to important events. The second kind are those which emerge and disappear only to be found later in somewhat varied forms, like a pattern of dolphins leaping through the sea. These may be called recurrent symbols, and they grow to their fullest meaning toward the end of the book and through their very expansion express the theme of the novel. Through repetition and variation they also function as leitmotivs and help to achieve a structural unity. The eviscerated soldier whom Fabrizio finds in his garden, the dog Bendicò, the stars, and Sicily itself are recurrent symbols, woven like threads into the fabric and texture of Lampedusa's art.

The most successful symbols in the first category are the objets d'art that illustrate and prophesy the love of Tancredi and Angelica. Early in the work the Prince observes that the two small planets that he had discovered "would spread the fame of his family through the empty spaces between Mars and Jupiter, thus transforming the frescoes in the villa from the adulatory to the prophetic." We encounter the first of these prophetic frescoes, that of Perseus and Andromeda, in the opening scene.

Cepheus, the father of Andromeda (Angelica), chained her to a rock to be devoured. But Perseus (Tancredi) rescued the Ethiopian (Sicilian) princess from a sea serpent and married her. This fresco not only predicts Angelica's marriage to Tancredi; it also indicates her relationship to her father. His parasitism is emphasized later, when the room in which Fabrizio draws up the marriage contract with Sedàra is likened to "a Japanese print of a huge violet iris with a hairy fly hanging from a petal." When Sedàra accompanies Angelica to the ball, he is compared to "a rat escorting a flaming rose." These comparisons underline the confused and uneasy "lascivious lyricism," the attraction and repulsion that the Leopard feels for Angelica, this "rose merely fertilized by her grandfather's nickname" (Peppe 'Mmerda, "Shitty Joe"). Tancredi rescues Angelica from this heritage.

But this fresco is also filled with religious, social, and ironic connotations; for only when Father Pirrone ends his prayers and the Salina women withdraw after the rosary are the naked figures from mythology revealed. Similarly, only when Concetta withdraws from Tancredi after he tells the false and brutal anecdote of the convent rape does he turn his attention to Angelica. (Lampedusa borrowed the anecdote of the convent from a scene in part 2, chapter 6, of Tolstoy's *War and Peace* [1862–1869], in which the handsome Nevitsky tells his fellow officers that he would like to slip into the nearby convent and his friend replies, "One might at least scare the nuns a little. There are Italian girls, they say, among them. Upon my word, I'd give five years of my life for it!")

The moment that the two girls pass each other like meteors—one rising, the other sharply descending—is the most poignant in the book and registers the changes effected by "the struggle for independence." In the first scene of the novel, Christianity gives way to paganism; in the last scene, after the Jesuits have been driven from Sicily, the religious world (traditionally associated with the aristocracy) is secularized.

The dependence of the aristocracy upon the Church is symbolized when the Leopard rests his great paw on an alabaster model of St. Peter's while he talks to Chevalley, the representative of the Turin government, about the future of Sicily. But later "the tiny cross surmounting the dome was found snapped," which prophesies the decline of ecclesiastical power under the revolutionary regime that seized the Papal States for the new Italy and reduced the Church to the limits of the Vatican City when Rome became the capital in 1871. The corrupt relationship of the Church and aristocracy is revealed early in the novel when Father Pirrone reluctantly accompanies Fabrizio on a visit to his mistress in Palermo and compromises his moral role through his loyalty to the Prince.

The most lavish art object in the novel is the glorious and sensual fountain of Amphitrite at Donnafugata that emanated the Keatsian "promise of pleasure that would never turn to pain" ("Forever wilt thou love and she be fair"):

"Perched on an islet in the middle of the round basin, modelled by a crude but sensual hand, a vigorous smiling Neptune was embracing a willing Amphitrite."

According to the myth, Poseidon desired the sea goddess Amphitrite and sent a dolphin to look for her. When the dolphin brought her to Poseidon he married her and, as a reward, placed the dolphin among the constellations. The symbolic fountain, where Sedàra later spies Tancredi kissing Angelica, not only reflects the sensual nature of their love in the goddess whose wet navel gleams in the sun, but more important, reveals the role of the Prince in the marriage. He is the dolphin, associated with the constellations, who is degraded to the role of Pandar. Acting on the instructions in Tancredi's letter, he completes the loathsome marriage negotiations with Sedàra. Assuming that Sedàra would not own formal dress and not wishing to embarrass his guest, Fabrizio abandons tradition, does not change for dinner, and is shocked to see "the revolution" manifest itself as Sedàra (well prepared for the occasion) ascends the stairs wearing white tie and tails. When the Prince is on his deathbed and the illusions about Tancredi's marriage have long since been shattered, he thinks once more of the delicious fountain and fears the grotesque metamorphosis it might suffer if sold to satisfy the debased pleasures of the bourgeoisie.

Several art objects are used to reflect the love of Tancredi and Angelica and "the instincts lying dormant in the house" as these uncertain sensualists pursue each other through the ruins of Donnafugata. This "mysterious and intricate labyrinth" suggests mythological parallels: Ariadne/Angelica saves Theseus/Tancredi from the Cretan minotaur, Sedàra. The house itself represents the legacy of the decayed aristocracy to the young lovers who wander through its vastness "like the explorers of the New World," seeking to salvage something for the future. Behind the elegance and grandeur of its facade, a false front with no substance supporting it, were the empty, crumbling, forgotten rooms. Donnafugata is foreshadowed in the first section by the huge desk in the Prince's office "with dozens of drawers, recesses, hollows, and folding shelves . . . decorated like a stage set, full of unexpected, uneven surfaces, and secret drawers."

In one of its secret rooms Angelica "had hidden behind an enormous picture propped on the floor, and for a short time *Arturo Corberà at the Siege of Antioch* formed a protection for the girl's hopeful anxiety." Tancredi is named after the crusader and prince of Antioch who played an important role in the capture of the city, which was overrun by the Turks in 1094. Four years later, after an ineffectual siege of seven months, a force of 300,000 crusaders stormed the city with the help of a traitor. Once in possession, they were overtaken by disease and famine. This painting symbolizes the courtship of Tancredi, who lays siege to the alien fortress of Angelica and wins her only after the timely intervention of the Leopard, who betrays both his daughter and his class.

Tancredi, Prince of Antioch, is also one of the principal heroes of Torquato Tasso's *Gerusalemme Liberata* (completed 1575), whose subject is the First Crusade, just as Angelica is one of the main heroines of Ludovico Ariosto's *Orlando Furioso* (1532). Tasso's Tancredi has many qualities of Castiglione's *Il Cortegiano,* with his noble heart and graceful manners, his courtesy and generosity: "With majesty his noble countenance shone, / High were his thoughts, his heart was bowed in vigour." But he is best known in the poem for his agonizing passions and romantic adventures. Ariosto's Angelica, a beautiful but selfish pagan, is a strong contrast to the passionate paladin Tancredi. All men fall in love with her, but she loves no one, not even the great hero Orlando. Finally she marries a simple soldier, Medoro, whom she finds wounded on the battlefield and nurses to health.

Tasso presents a triangle of lovers: Erminia loves Tancredi, who loves Clorinda. The tender and helpless Erminia falls in love with Tancredi when he besieges Antioch, takes her prisoner, and treats her chivalrously. Completely overcome by her passion, she is unable to hide it. All this is reflected in *The Leopard,* for Concetta loves Tancredi, who loves Angelica. And Concetta, unable to contain her feelings, confides them to Father Pirrone, who then tells the prince.

The two lovers are surrounded at Donnafugata by other works of art that seem to encourage their "game full of charm and risk," their licentious desires in the decrepit rooms. Like Angelica, "a shepherdess [is seen] glancing down consenting from some obliterated fresco"; and they find on the fireplaces "delicate intricate little marble intaglios, with naked figures in paroxysms." (This too evokes the "mad pursuit," the "struggle to escape," and the "wild ecstasy" of Keats's "Ode on a Grecian Urn" [1820].) Even the accidental music of the *Carnival of Venice,* to which "they kissed in rhythm," evokes at once the festivity and sensual outbursts of the present, and the hint of Lenten austerities (their marriage, which "even erotically was no success") that must inevitably follow. Exotic Venice of fabled splendor, the most profligate of cities, the very seat of all dissoluteness, is the perfect setting for passionate abandon.

This mixture of passion and denial within a religious context leads the lovers to the climax of these scenes, the most intense and lyrical in the novel. In a secret apartment they find whips of bull's muscle, which of course are male symbols, but are afraid of themselves, leave the room immediately, and kiss as if in expiation. The following day they enter the apartment of the Saint-Duke, who, with the Blessed Corberà, foundress of the convent that Fabrizio and Tancredi visit, represents the austere religious traditions of the Salina family. This time they find another whip, used by the Saint-Duke to scourge himself and redeem the earth with his blood, for "in his holy exaltation it must have seemed that only through this expiatory baptism could the earth really become his."

But his descendant Tancredi, a different sort of man, finds his redemption through Angel-

ica's beauty and her father's money. The family's religious traditions are embodied instead in Concetta, whose ice-cold hands and denial of the flesh contrast strongly with Angelica's passion. Concetta's indifference to Tancredi's companion-in-arms, Cavriaghi, suggests that Lombardy and Sicily can never be truly united. Ironically, Concetta becomes like the nuns in Tancredi's fictive convent—virginal, isolated, and afraid.

After Angelica prostrates herself and kisses the feet of the enormous and ghastly crucified Christ in the room of the Saint-Duke, Tancredi bites her lip in a rough kiss and draws blood. Angelica assumes the traditional posture of Mary Magdalene—a fascinating mixture of sinfulness, holiness, and beauty—as if to pay for her sins before she commits them. He scourges himself by a degrading marriage to the woman he calls his whip and offers her blood, not his own, for atonement.

A few days later the lovers enter the most dangerous room with its "neat rolled-up mattress which would spread out again at a mere touch of the hand," like a Sicilian stiletto. That morning Angelica had said, "I'm your novice," offering herself for sexual rather then religious initiation. In the afternoon "already the woman had surrendered, already the male was about to overrun the man, when the church bell clanged almost straight down on their prone bodies, adding its own throb to the others" and preventing the long-desired consummation. The religious traditions have sounded their final echoes. Tancredi is neither the scourging saint nor the predatory prince, who at least takes his women when he wants them.

Symbolic paintings and allusions to literature also illuminate the character of Fabrizio and prophesy his future. When Garibaldi's general visits the Prince after the successful landing at Marsala, he exchanges the portrait of Ferdinand II, which hangs in the drawing room, for a neutral *Pool of Bethesda.* John 5:2–9 says there is at Jerusalem a pool called Bethesda, around which "lay a great multitude of impotent folk, of blind, halt, withered." Jesus found a sick man there and said, "Rise, take up thy bed, and walk," and the man was healed. The invaders picture themselves as Jesus, coming like Chevalley to cure and heal the Sicilians; and Sedàra is their grotesque John the Baptist, for "whenever he passed secret groups were formed, to prepare the way for those that were to come." The Prince, "with his sensibility to presages and symbols," knows too well that the aristocracy is blind, lame, and paralyzed.

Literature is also used symbolically, and three important references appear in *The Leopard.* On that stormy night just before Tancredi arrives with Cavriaghi, the Prince is reading Giulio Carcano's *Angiola Maria* (1839) to his family. (The critic Francesco De Sanctis condemns the sentimental novel and calls it "unbearable.") Angiola Maria loves above her class and is innocently sacrificed, as the delicacy of pure love is contrasted with harsh social conditions. Concetta obviously parallels Angiola Maria, for soon afterward she confides her pure love to Father Pirrone and finds it sacrificed by her father to political necessity. The novel provides a warning against romantic idealism. But Concetta, who fails to heed this and is unprepared for her rival Angelica, abandons the book "upside down behind an armchair."

Angiola Maria, a kind of inverted *Pamela,* also reveals the impossibility of marriage between the aristocracy and the bourgeoisie. The marriage theme serves as an ironic comment on contemporary Sicily, for Concetta paradoxically loves above her class by loving *within* it. The Prince recognizes this when he thinks, "I fear Tancredi will have to aim higher, by which of course I mean lower." Concetta is destroyed by maintaining her aristocratic rigidity against the tide of social flux.

When the Salina family receives the triumphant Angelica after her engagement, Father Pirrone, who with Bendicò and Don Ciccio Tumeo, Fabrizio's retainer and hunting companion, serves as a social conscience and moral barometer, murmurs to her, "Veni, sponsa de Libano" (Come, bride of Lebanon).

(He has to check himself to avoid other, warmer verses rising to his memory.) The context of these lines from the sensual Song of Solomon (4:11) is entirely appropriate for the luscious and beautiful Angelica: "Thy lips, O my spouse, drop as the honeycomb: honey and milk are under thy tongue; and the smell of thy garments is like the smell of Lebanon." (While hunting, Don Ciccio tells the Prince, "Her sheets must smell like Paradise.")

But this phrase is also well known to the good priest in another and very different context. In canto 30 of *Purgatorio,* "Veni, sponsa de Libano" is chanted thrice by the elder who accompanies Dante, invokes the appearance of the long-awaited Beatrice, and leads to Dante's enthralling celestial vision. When Beatrice appears, Dante experiences considerable agitation:

A lady, olive-crowned o'er veil of white,
Clothed in the colour of a living flame,
Under a mantle green, stole on my sight. . . .
But virtue invisible that went out from her
Felt old love seize me in all its mastery.
                              (lines 31–33, 38–39)

If Solomon's bride is the very essence of the earthly and carnal, Dante's Beatrice personifies the heavenly and spiritual, and comments ironically on the rapture with which the Salinas receive Tancredi's goddess.

Early in *The Leopard,* as Fabrizio leaves his mistress Mariannina, he recalls two lines from a poem by Baudelaire: "Donnez-moi la force et le courage / de contempler mon coeur et mon corps sans dégoût" (give me the strength and the courage to contemplate my heart and my body without disgust). This passage from "Un Voyage à Cythère" ("A Voyage to Cythera," 1855) describes the poet's futile quest for sensual pleasure on the island where Aphrodite was supposed to have emerged from the sea and where a famous temple was erected in her honor. His illusions are quickly destroyed when he finds a hanged man whose genitals have been torn out by birds of prey as punish-

GIUSEPPE TOMASI DI LAMPEDUSA

ment for his sexual excesses. The poet then identifies himself with the man on the gibbet and realizes that the allegory is directed toward himself. He prays, in the last lines, for the strength and courage to accept his debased sensual self.

The poem symbolizes the conflict in the Leopard between his heavenly and earthly, his spiritual and fleshly quests. (In the *Inferno*, canto 1, lines 32–42, the leopard symbolizes the sins of self-indulgence, weak will, and yielding to appetite.) His inability to dispel illusion and face reality, to reconcile the strivings of his soul and body, are the core of the Prince's weakness. Thus the lamentations and self-denunciations.

At Donnafugata, the Baudelaire poem is immediately invoked when Tancredi and Angelica are described as "two lovers embarked for Cythera on a ship made of dark and sunny rooms," and we realize at the height of their lyrical love that their hopes for happiness will be disappointed. The sunny rooms are the present, the dark ones the future.

Another static symbol associated with the fountain of Amphitrite and the two lovers is that of the foreign peaches (the first of three symbolic foods), which Fabrizio observes with Tancredi: "The graft with German cuttings, made two years ago, had succeeded perfectly; [the fruit] was big, velvety, luscious-looking; yellowish, with a faint flush of rosy pink on the cheeks." The Prince remarks, "They seem quite ripe . . . [and are] products of love, of coupling."

Unlike the Paul Neyron roses, which had been "enfeebled by the strong if languid pull of the Sicilian earth," the grafted peaches thrive and prosper. The difference is that the French roses are planted directly in the Sicilian earth that has always been (passively) hostile to alien elements, while the German peach cuttings are grafted to Sicilian stems. Like his uncle, Tancredi also has German strains in his blood, and the material fruits of his marriage to Angelica are symbolized in the grafted peaches, just as their sensual desire is reflected in the "shameless naked flesh" of the fountain.

When Tancredi steals the peaches, with their "aphrodisiac and seductive properties," from his uncle and carries them to Angelica, whom they seem to resemble, he performs a symbolical marriage ceremony. "He sidestepped a sword-waving urchin [the revolution], carefully avoided a urinating mule [Calogero], and reached the Sedàras' door." The revolution and Angelica's father are the two dangerous elements that Tancredi must accept and adjust to if the "graft" to Angelica is to take place. Tancredi recognizes this when he paradoxically says, "If we want things to stay as they are, things will have to change." But Tancredi's symbolic stroll also parallels the one Fabrizio took through the bordello district of Palermo to reach Mariannina's house. It represents yet another stage in the decline of the aristocracy—an ordeal by urine to reach the lower classes.

Here again Lampedusa's Tancredi is like Tasso's Tancredi who, in the wood enchanted by devils, boldly leaps through the flames and is unharmed. When storms and clouds follow, he ignores them and they disappear. Nevertheless Tancredi, like the crusader, is doomed to a frustrated, anxious, and unhappy love—and for the same reason. The love of both heroes is unsatisfied: the paladin loves a pagan, Falconeri loves a peasant.

Two other food symbols are introduced during the family dinner in the first section. The rum jelly "was rather threatening at first sight . . . but into its transparent and quivering flanks a spoon plunged with astounding ease. By the time the amber-colored fortress reached Francesco Paolo . . . who was served last, it consisted only of shattered walls and hunks of wobbly rubble." This symbolic jelly, the legacy of the Prince to his youngest son, represents the ruin of the aristocracy that the "last of the Salinas" is unable and unwilling to prevent. Fabrizio's second son, Giovanni, sensing the imminent disaster of his class, has already chosen the bourgeois life of a London clerk. Francesco Paolo, like his uncle who takes refuge in a British ship at the time of the invasion and leaves his house to pillagers, is blind to political realities.

The meal ends when the Leopard toasts Tancredi, who actively supports the Garibaldini, and drains his glass of Marsala in a single gulp: "The initials F. D. which had before stood out clearly on the golden color of the full glass were no longer visible." This glass was a gift from the Bourbon king (*Ferdinandus dedit*). These initials disappear when the Prince swallows the heavy and sweet Sicilian wine, just as his dynasty will disappear when the Garibaldini land at Marsala, west of Palermo, and sweep north to Naples where the "bearded Vulcan" puts his Army under the command of the new king, Victor Emmanuel II.

Two other symbolic events also have social and political significance. When Mayor Sedàra appears on the balcony of the town hall to announce the results of the fraudulent plebiscite, he is flanked by two ushers and carries a "lighted candelabra which the wind blew out at once." The light that the invaders bring to Sicily is symbolically extinguished by the dirty wind and a newborn babe, good faith, is killed at Donnafugata.

Shortly afterward, the Prince goes hunting with Don Ciccio, learns a good deal about the Sedàra family, and tells Ciccio that Tancredi will marry Angelica. Clear tradition and prophecy speak in Ciccio when he exclaims, "How foul. Excellency! It's the end of the Falconeris, and of the Salinas too." When Fabrizio locks up Ciccio in the gun room to keep him out of the way while he negotiates the final arrangements with Sedàra, he silences the voice of truth and conscience and exchanges the idealistic role of Don Quixote for that of Sancho Panza.

Lampedusa uses symbolic scenes as well as literary and aesthetic allusions to suggest both the historical pattern and the dramatic structure of the novel. The first scene portrays the dead royalist soldier who is found in the Prince's garden, "his face covered in blood and vomit, his nails dug into the soil, crawling with ants; a pile of purplish intestines had formed a puddle under his bandoleer." This awful Goyaesque image of the animal horrors of war becomes a leitmotiv of the involvement of all classes—peasant, aristocratic, and proletarian—in the bloody Sicilian revolution.

At Donnafugata, Fabrizio's tenants present him with six baby lambs, "their heads lolling pathetically above the big gash through which their lifeblood had flowed a few hours before." The Prince remembers the gutted soldier and is revolted by all the blood. The savage slaughter, typically Sicilian, of these innocents deeply wounds his humane instincts.

Fabrizio kills a rabbit while hunting with Ciccio, its "horrible wounds lacerated snout and chest. . . . The animal had died tortured by anxious hopes of salvation, imagining it could still escape when it was already caught, just like so many human beings." The rabbit is like the soldier who believed he would survive the war, the peasant who believed it would improve his lot, and the Leopard himself, who hoped to prolong the life of his class in spite of its ruined and crumbling foundation.

Finally, as Fabrizio leaves the ball, "a long open wagon came by stacked with bulls killed shortly before at the slaughterhouse, already quartered and exhibiting their intimate mechanism with the shamelessness of death." The Prince feels deep sympathy for each of these victims. He prays for the young soldier at the evening rosary, again commends his soul to God when he sees the lambs, feels compassion for the glaucous-eyed rabbit, and yearns for the faithful Venus as the bulls pass, their blood slowly dropping to the ground. These feelings constitute an almost ritualistic participation in their death. Seeing them, he longs for his own death, which has been foreshadowed in the opening words of the book: "Nunc et in hora mortis nostrae" ("Now and in the hour of our death").

Fabrizio calls the unknown person who succumbs to the Sicilian summer as he arrived at Donnafugata a "lucky person, with no worries now." When he passes someone in death agonies on the way to the ball, he gets out of the carriage and kneels in prayer on the pavement. Tancredi understands the Prince's deepest yearning when he remarks with subdued irony, "Uncle, you are courting death."

Many of the numerous death images in the novel, and not only the violent ones, converge with a powerful effect in the symphonic scene when Fabrizio gives himself to the Woman in Brown: "It was she, the creature forever yearned for, coming to fetch him. . . . When she was face to face with him she raised her veil, and there, chaste, but ready for possession, she looked lovelier than she ever had when glimpsed in stellar space. When the crashing of the sea subsided altogether," he is finally translated into her own stellar region "of perennial certitude."

Lampedusa's Woman in Brown is modeled on the death figure that for Proust took the form of a huge dark woman dressed all in black. George Painter describes how, on his deathbed, "Proust was staring at the other door, the one through which visitors came, through which, indeed, a last visitor had just entered. 'She's big, very big,' he cried, 'she's very big, very dark! She's all in black, she's ugly, she frightens me. . . . No, don't touch her, Céleste! No one must touch her! She's merciless, she's getting more horrible every moment.' "

A poor doctor is called to the Prince from the slum quarter nearby, where he had been an "important witness of a thousand wretched death agonies" such as the one Fabrizio saw on the way to the ball. The little bell with the Last Sacrament rings for him as it did for that other dying man. The Leopard scrutinizes himself in the mirror, regrets that he cannot "die with his own face on," remembers the blood-daubed soldier for the last time, and hears his own death rattle like that of parched Sicily vainly awaiting rain.

The symbolic meaning of the stars in *The Leopard* explains Fabrizio's deathwish, illustrates the major theme of change—real and illusory—and at the same time emphasizes the cyclical structure of the novel, for as the Prince is needlessly told at the ball, "fixed stars are only so in appearance." Their eternal movement, almost always within the limits of predictable laws, symbolizes the idea of permanence in transience.

The godlike Leopard feels a strong affinity for these wise bodies that are frequently named after gods, for he tells Chevalley that Sicilians are gods and are perfect and also attributes this perfection to his celestial companions. He mistakenly believes he has "lordship over both human beings and their works" and is revived by gazing at the swimming stars, which he feels are always "docile to his calculations."

The Prince constantly seeks escape from reality: in sensuality with Mariannina, in hunting with Don Ciccio, and in the stars with Father Pirrone. He calls astronomy his morphia, his path to sleep and forgetfulness; he merges into its tranquil harmony and lives the "life of the spirit in its most sublimated moments." The stars symbolize to him "the intangible, the unattainable. . . . They are the only truly disinterested, the only really trustworthy creatures." And as he dies he considers his "abstract calculations and the pursuit of the unreachable" among the few happy hours of his life. At the final "crashing of the sea" his faithful Venus leads him out of life.

Lampedusa uses the well at Donnafugata to elucidate one aspect of the more complex recurrent symbol of Sicily. On the outskirts of Donnafugata the Salina family pause at a deep well that "mutely offered its various services: as swimming pool, drinking trough, prison, or cemetery. It slaked thirst, spread typhus, guarded the kidnapped, and hid the corpses of both animals and men till they were reduced to the smoothness of anonymous skeletons." The well suggests the dual and ambiguous nature of Sicily. It sustains internal contradictions and allows decomposing corpses to lie at the bottom of the life-giving water. Death and life, corpses and prisoners, typhus and water, are wantonly and inextricably mixed, like the descendants of Byzantine, Berber, and Spanish invaders, or the culmination of violence and piety in the liturgical poison of the Communion wine.

The well is also democratic and therefore politically au courant, for it reduces all men to an egalitarian anonymity. Later in the book, Chevalley pities the Prince and the common people. "All were equal, at bottom, all were comrades in misfortune segregated in the same well." The plebiscite in which the Prince, no different from the others, has only one vote, also emphasizes this most recent political leveling. The Prince is well aware of his lineage and social position, but when he speaks to Chevalley as a Sicilian, he places himself aloft with the others and states flatly, "*We* are old. . . . *We* are gods."

Like the stars, Sicily itself embodies the theme of permanence in transience and emphasizes the cyclical structure of the novel. The cyclical pattern of Sicilian life is also stressed by the daily rosary that begins and concludes the first section; by Father Pirrone's arrangement of his niece's marriage, which repeats in a cruder way the Prince's negotiations with Sedàra; and by the final scene in the chapel, which echoes the opening rosary. Even Bendicò stresses the cyclical pattern, for he rushes into the rosary room as the novel opens and is thrown out the window as it concludes. The landscape "knows no mean between sensuous slackness and hellish drought" and oscillates eternally between these two disastrous conditions. These changes, though extreme, inevitably follow a seasonal pattern. Sicily, the scene of numerous invasions and conquests, is ultimately indifferent and unchanged. It is a constant and eternal stage upon which the transient scenes of history are performed. Sicily, like the stars, is irredeemable; "Plus ça change, plus c'est la même chose" (The more things change, the more they remain the same).

Lampedusa again stresses the timeless and static character of Sicily in a rhapsodic and lyrical passage from his story "The Professor and the Siren":

> So we spoke about eternal Sicily, nature's Sicily; about the scent of rosemary on the Nèbrodi hills, the taste of Melilli honey, the waving corn seen from Enna on a windy day in May, the solitudes around Syracuse, the gusts of scent from orange and lemon groves pouring over Palermo during some sunsets in June. We talked of the enchantment of certain summer nights within sight of Castellammare Bay, where stars are mirrored in the sleeping sea and the spirit of anyone lying back amid the lentisks is lost in a vortex of sky.

The sun, the true ruler of Sicily, is no benevolent despot or tottering Bourbon. The blinding sunlight does not enable one to see clearly, but rather prevents lucid vision. At the death of the Prince, the sun pitilessly lashes the city and the man, hastening his death. The vehemence of the light produces a voluptuous torpor, a languorous immobility, a hankering for oblivion and for the release of death. Most significant of all, it produces a sense of futility and an obsessive fatalism that causes the Leopard to watch "the ruin of his own class and his own inheritance, without ever making, still less wanting to make, any move toward saving it."

Like the stars and like Sicily itself, Bendicò symbolizes for the Prince something unchanging, constant, and faithful in a world of flux and turmoil. Rubbing the dog's big head Fabrizio says, "You, Bendicò, are a bit like them, like the stars, happily incomprehensible, incapable of producing anxiety." Bendicò, whose name is short for "good of heart," stands for unquestioned loyalty and humble compliance to the wishes of his master. Fabrizio thinks of Mariannina, who can refuse him nothing, as "a kind of Bendicò in a silk petticoat." Bendicò means the same thing to the spinster Concetta, even when he is dead and embalmed, a heap of moth-eaten fur and nest of spiderwebs, like her unused trousseau. She refuses "to detach herself from the only memory of her past which aroused no distressing sensations."

The literary model for the dead Bendicò is Loulou, the parrot of the old maid-servant Félicité in Flaubert's "A Simple Heart" (1877): "Though he was not a corpse, the worms had begun to devour the dead bird; one of his wings was broken, and the stuffing was coming out of his body. But Félicité kissed Loulou's forehead, and pressed him against her cheek. . . . When Félicité woke up, she could see him in the dawn's light, and [like Concetta] she would recall painlessly and peacefully the old days." Both Bendicò and Loulou are adored household pets whose mistresses continue to be strongly attached to them for many years after their deaths, even though they are hideously decomposed. And both works conclude with the metamorphoses of the animals into other images that reveal something important about the illusions of their owners.

Bendicò's realistic approach to things and instinctive good sense are suggested when he warns the Leopard at three crucial stages of the family's decline. The perceptive Prince merely notes these admonitions, but does not heed them. In the second scene of the novel Fabrizio watches "the desolation wrought by Bendicò in the flower beds" and remarks, "How human!" Here the dog's activity warns the fatalistic Fabrizio of the destruction and disasters of war, and the rapacity of Sedàra, who will steal the Prince's lands. Bendicò's second warning comes when the enthusiastic Salina family greets the newly engaged Angelica: "Only Bendicò, in contrast to his usual sociability, growled away in the back of his throat." Finally, when the Leopard is speaking to Chevalley, Bendicò crawls into the room and falls asleep, failing to hear the wise Northern words just as his master does. (This device is later repeated when the herbalist falls asleep while Father Pirrone is explaining the political situation to him. But Pirrone, like Chevalley, keeps on talking.)

Father Pirrone, a pastor who is compared to a sheepdog, symbolically admonishes the Salinas in much the same way on two occasions. When Tancredi is courting Angelica and kissing her hand, the priest meditates over the Biblical stories of Delilah, Judith, and Esther, three women who betrayed famous and powerful men. When Fabrizio is negotiating with Sedàra, Pirrone notices the falling barometer and predicts "bad weather ahead."

At the end of the novel the last of the Salinas' illusions are destroyed. The pathetically gullible spinster sisters have tenaciously retained their devotion to the Church, the only place where their former status appears to endure. But after the efficient priest-technician removes the relics from the family chapel, Concetta's "inner emptiness was total. . . . Even poor Bendicò was hinting at bitter memories." As the faithful dog, the last relic, is flung through the window, "his form recomposed itself for an instant; in the air one could have seen dancing a quadruped with long whiskers, and its right foreleg seemed to be raised in imprecation. Then all found peace in a little heap of livid dust."

Bendicò forms the image of the Leopard over the solid but sagging door near the deep well of Donnafugata, which "pranced in spite of legs broken off by flung stones," just as Loulou becomes an image of the Holy Ghost to the dying Félicité, who "thought she saw in the opening heavens a gigantic parrot, hovering above her head." The Prince himself had said that "the significance of a noble family lies entirely in its traditions, that is in its vital memories." Bendicò's heap of dust represents the end of all tradition, belief, and ancestral memory. At the end of *The Leopard* only the "inner emptiness" remains.

INFLUENCE OF STENDHAL

Lampedusa's "Lezioni su Stendhal," published in the Florentine *Paragone* in 1959, reveals his appreciation of the French novelist and some of the ways in which he was influenced by *The Charterhouse of Parma.*

Lampedusa writes of Fabrice, whose name he intentionally used for his own hero to draw attention to parallels in Stendhal, that his evasion of immediate experience "evokes in me only admiration for the perfect acrobat and dancer: for me, then, Fabrice is a kind of Nijinsky: a creator of beautiful postures." This evasion, necessitated by the ugliness of practical politics in the real world, allows Fabrice to glide into his own elaborately constructed ideal world, and to cause what has been called "the devaluation of reality" in *The Charterhouse.*

Fabrice, and Fabrizio in *The Leopard,* are like that "purely decorative warrior," described by Proust, "whom one sees in the most tumultuous of Mantegna's paintings, lost in dreams, leaning upon his shield, while all around him are fighting and bloodshed and death." Yet this unworldly departure from reality is no mere escape, for as Martin Turnell writes in *The Novel in France* of characters like Stendhal's Fabrice, "They made their inner life their starting point and moved outwards, examining society in the light of their own scheme of values. This attitude was in no sense an 'escape' or 'retreat' from life. Their personal systems had been worked out in opposition to society."

Two passages from *The Charterhouse* clearly illustrate this aspect of Fabrice's character. Escaping one night from the house of Priore Blanès, and in great danger, "Fabrice dashed down the staircase and emerging on the *piazza* began to run. He had scarcely arrived opposite his father's castle when the bell sounded ten times; each stroke reverberated in his bosom, where it left a singular sense of disturbance. He stopped to think, or rather to give himself up to the passionate feelings inspired in him by the contemplation of that majestic edifice." While contemplating the castle, he is suddenly surrounded by somewhat sluggish constables, and takes to his heels, stopping only to recover his breath. He "shuddered at the thought of the danger he had just escaped," though not at the danger itself, and

realized that his "mind finds pleasure in contemplating what is going to happen in ten years' time, and forgets to look out for what is actually happening beneath [his] nose." In the mad rush, and the contrast between verbs of action like "dash," "run," "fire," and "resist" and more passive and restful verbs like "stop," "think," "contemplate," and "forget," the reader also forgets the reality of the situation and is carried away into Fabrice's dreams.

Another instance of Fabrice's unreal dreaming occurs when he leaves the Church of San Petronio and gives a twenty-franc piece to the first pauper who accosts him. He is immediately surrounded by an unruly mob of beggars, all of whom demand money from him: "Fabrice increased his pace, the women following him, screaming, and a number of male paupers, running in from every street, created a sort of tumult. All this crowd, horribly dirty and energetic, cried out: *'Eccellenza!'* Fabrice had great difficulty in escaping from the rabble; the scene brought his imagination back to earth." Only the tumultuous crush and clamor of a large crowd brings Fabrice back to reality, for his imagination persistently lingers on the Seven Penitential Psalms and the Madonna of Cimabue inside the church.

Fabrice, then, could truly say with his creator, "I see that dreaming is what I have preferred to everything, even to a reputation for wit." Fabrice's reverie, his preoccupation with what is going on inside his own mind, is caused by his "boredom with life" and the fact that for him "everything which requires attention and action becomes an atrocious burden." This "strange destiny," as Fabrice explains to Clelia at the close of the novel, "obliges me to dwell in an eternal solitude, I cannot, like the majority of my brethren, taste the pleasures of an intimate society."

A second major influence on Lampedusa is Stendhal's use of astronomy in *The Charterhouse,* which is related to the theme of reverie. Stendhal introduces astronomy in the second chapter, which opens with some beautiful lines by Ronsard about how men may read their destiny in the stars and suggests the way in which the stars are used by Stendhal in the novel:

> God writes for us, in clear ways,
> The fate and the destiny of all creatures.
> For He, looking on man from on high,
> Sometimes moved to pity, shows him the road.
> By the stars of the sky, which are His signs,
> He predicts for us both good and bad.
> But men, burdened by earth and by sin,
> Scorn such writing, and do not read it.

Priore Blanès, "a man whose honesty and virtue were primitive, and a man of parts as well, spent all his nights up in his belfry," following the course of the stars. Blanès infects Fabrice with "an unbounded confidence in the signs by which the future can be foretold," in spite of his belief that "every announcement of the future is a breach of the rule, and contains this danger, that it may alter the event." Later on, in Bologna, Fabrice takes a course in astronomy, and "contemplating the stars and the immense horizon" from the Torre Farnese becomes one of his chief diversions and pleasures. For both heroes, astronomy and contemplation-reverie are closely connected.

The stars play an even more important role in *The Leopard*. Fabrizio's evasion of reality, his solitude, and his isolation from society are all synthesized in his passion for astronomy. Stendhal's description of Priore Blanès would serve equally well for Father Pirrone, who spends much of his time surrounded by telescopes and immersed in algebraic formulas, and who shares with Fabrizio the belief, with its fatalistic implications, that man's destiny is written in the stars. Returning home at dawn from the futile and depressing ball, which is the death rattle of the dying aristocracy, Fabrizio "glimpsed the sky to the west, above the sea. There was Venus, wrapped in her turban of autumn mist. She was always faithful, always awaiting Don Fabrizio on his early morning outings, at Donnafugata before a shoot,

now after a ball. Don Fabrizio sighed. When would she decide to give him an appointment less ephemeral, far from carcasses and blood?" For Fabrizio, then, the stars represent the ideal world into which he seeks to be transported. Both he and Stendhal's characters, as Lampedusa writes, seek "to blot out the memory of their actions for fear that the harmonious world they have created would fall into ruins."

The contrast between the real and the ideal in *The Leopard,* and especially in the character of Fabrizio, is revealed in three ways. First, there is Fabrizio's unfortunate evasion of responsibility by his refusal to act in the real world to save his family, his land, and his class, to oppose Sedàra, and to join the Senate in Turin. Like Fabrice, he finds action a burden; and the ball, peopled by his decrepit past mistresses, reveals that he finds no pleasure in society.

Second, there is his escape to his ideal world, symbolized by his observatory. It compensates for his boredom with life and lifts him into his own realm of "perennial certitude." For this reason E. M. Forster called *The Leopard* "one of the great *lonely* books." "From up in this observatory," Lampedusa writes, "the bluster of the one and the blood on the other merge into tranquil harmony. The real problem is how to go on living this life of the spirit in its most sublimated moments, those moments that are most like death." The stars, the distant realm of pure intellect, console the Leopard, for they represent his quest of the intangible, the unattainable, in a sublimated spiritual world. He is "accustomed to scrutinizing limitless outer space and to probing vast inner abysses," but cannot grapple with and overcome dreadful ugly realities. He realizes too well the futility of common strife with insensitive brutes like Sedàra, and his mind soars above it all. Finally, there is his inevitable wish for death, which (as we have seen) he associates with the stars.

It is clear that Lampedusa not only uses astronomy as Stendhal does, but also converts Fabrice's prison tower into Fabrizio's observatory. We are told again and again that Fabrice "let himself be charmed by the attractions of his prison" that "he had never in his life been so happy" as in his cell. When finally released, "he was in despair at being out of his prison," and realized he was "far more unhappy in this magnificent apartment, with ten flunkeys wearing his livery, than he had been in his wooden cell in the Torre Farnese, surrounded by hideous gaolers, and always in fear for his life. . . . A swarm of advantages, due to his brilliant position, produced no other effect on him than to make him ill-tempered." When he finally retires to the Charterhouse as a monk, after Clelia's death, he voluntarily "imprisons" himself again.

Fabrice, like the Leopard, despises the class struggle, the fight for money and position, and the intrigues at court. As Count Mosca realistically says of Fabrice's possibilities, "Unfortunately, a gentleman cannot become either a doctor or a barrister, and this age is made for barristers." Mosca, of course, is a perfect example of a gentleman debased by politics, for he surrenders both his principles and his self-respect for money. As the duchess discovers, "everyone here steals. . . . It means that there is nothing real, nothing that survives disgrace, save money." Since money is the only reality, Fabrice prefers his dream world, for sensitive and noble souls are debased in the real world. The Duchess is forced to trade her body for Fabrice's freedom and archbishopric; and once back in the world, he uses his ecclesiastical position only to seduce Clelia.

Both heroes deliberately remove themselves from the sphere of politics because they are fully aware of the futility of action. Both factions have, more or less, the same base principles. In *The Charterhouse,* as Turnell writes, "It is clear that a change of government would mean little more than a change of personalities. . . . The liberals pay lip-service to freedom, but it is difficult to see any difference between their policy and the ultras who are in power. . . . The official head of the Liberal Party is the governor of the Citadel; but the Citadel is full of liberals who are imprisoned in cages which are too small for them."

His conviction that action is futile (one of the major themes of *The Leopard*), combined with his Sicilian fatalism, prevents Fabrizio from becoming politically engaged. After the revolution, he says "all will be the same though all will be changed." After the surviving Bourbon police "rats" are "enrolled in the new police, this hubbub, inevitable though he realized it to be, began to seem pointless and petty." When the Leopard is forced into practical action and negotiates Tancredi's marriage, he is compelled to "swallow the toad" and, like Fabrice, debases himself. For as Georg Lukács says of *The Charterhouse* in his *Studies in European Realism,* "The fate of these characters is intended to reflect vileness, the squalid loathsomeness of the whole epoch—an epoch in which there is no longer any room for the noble minded."

Lampedusa states in his essay on Stendhal that the awful events of *The Charterhouse* (like those of *The Leopard*) have been "derived from a terrible documentary reality." "I know very well," he continues, speaking of Mosca, that "Stendhal wished to rouse the anger of the reader against such men and such methods"; and surely Lampedusa arouses our indignation against the unscrupulous Sedàra. Lampedusa also shows how Stendhal contrasts the ugliness of the real world with the beauty of his hero's imagination, and suggests how he too uses this technique: "It is through one of these personalities that the dirty and tragic world of the *Charterhouse* is shown; and the peace that perennially reigns in these singular souls comes across to the reader."

Besides the more general influences—the evasion of reality through reverie, the significance of astronomy, the meaning of the prison cell and observatory, and the futility of political strife—there is one short important scene at the beginning of *The Leopard,* Fabrizio's audience with the Bourbon King Ferdinand at Caserta, that is closely modeled on a similar scene in *The Charterhouse,* Fabrice's audience with the Prince of Parma. In both scenes the reactionary absolute monarchs are insecure, afraid of the rising threat of the powerful liberal and revolutionary forces. The older rulers assume masks and poses and unsuccessfully try to test and question the loyalty of the heroes. Both Fabrice and Fabrizio, sensing the weakness of the monarchs, remain psychologically superior, are elusive in their answers, fail to please during the interview, and are rather summarily dismissed. Both scenes are treated ironically and are used as a basis of comparison with later interviews in each novel.

Of course there are differences as well. The monarchy of King Ferdinand is in an advanced state of decay and will soon collapse entirely; Prince Ernesto, though threatened by revolutionaries, is supported by an enormous police force and manages to retain political power. Fabrizio and King Ferdinand are old friends (the King is Concetta's godfather) and have met frequently in the past; Fabrice and the Prince of Parma are meeting for the first time, and are therefore more wary of each other. Finally, though both audiences represent a mark of favor, Fabrizio is fairly secure in his position and does not need the king's protection and influence, while Fabrice's interview has been arranged by the duchess in the hope that he will gain the attention and support of Prince Ernesto.

After a few introductory words, Ernesto immediately decides to test Fabrice: " 'I shall give him a little dose of Jacobin politics; we shall see how he replies.' . . . 'Well, *Monsignore,'* he said to Fabrice, 'and the people of Naples, are they happy? Is the King loved?' " Without hesitating, Fabrice responds with a strictly aristocratic, though elusive answer: " 'I have never allowed the lower orders to speak to me about anything but the work for which I am paying them.' " The prince, annoyed by his slyness, persists in questioning him; Fabrice replies with admirable and impeccable rejoinders; and the prince "felt himself almost defied by

such correctness of manner." The prince then changes masks, and quotes the more liberal views of Fénélon, which bear little resemblance to his own "bread and butter absolutism."

In response to this new tack, Fabrice attempts to "out-Herod Herod," praises the official Parma newspaper for which the prince has just (obliquely) apologized, and states his belief in absolutist, antidemocratic views as well as in the divine right of kings. (This after the English and French revolutions!) Liberalism, says Fabrice, gives people a want of confidence in the government: " 'This fatal habit of *want of confidence* once contracted, human weakness applies it to everything, man loses confidence in the Bible, the Orders of the Church, Tradition and everything else; from that moment he is lost.' " Ernesto does not believe in Fabrice's sincerity: "Presently the Prince lost interest in his contest with this young man whose simple and serious manner had begun to irritate him. 'Good-bye, *Monsignore,'* he said to him abruptly." And as he leaves, Fabrice regretfully thinks, " 'I have quite failed to please this animal.' "

What is extraordinary and ironic, as Stendhal reveals, is that Fabrice (who reacted against his "father" and as a romantic youth ran off to fight with Napoleon), "believed practically everything that we have heard him say. . . . The desire for liberty, the fashion and cult of the *greatest good of the greatest number,* after which the nineteenth century has run mad, were nothing in his eyes but a heresy which, like other heresies, would pass away, though not until it had destroyed many souls, as the plague while it reigns unchecked in a country destroys many bodies."

This scene in *The Charterhouse* is an important one. This first meeting of Fabrice and Ernesto reveals the conflict of ideas between the two adversaries, although, ironically, they are presently in fundamental agreement, because the prince articulates the ideas that he thinks Fabrice holds in order to draw him out. This scene is a crucial point in the development of

Fabrice's political beliefs, which he will later modify. During and after prison he rises above politics (like the Leopard) and never becomes the revolutionary that Ernesto thinks he is. Immediately after this scene, the duchess arranges another interview for him, with Archbishop Landriani, "a man of superior intellect, a scholar of the first order." This second interview—with a man of so different a character, nature and understanding—provides a strong contrast to the previous one.

On the way to *his* audience, Fabrizio notices physical evidence of the decay of the Bourbon monarchy. The dirty passages and ill-kept stairs winding through revolting décor lead him through an antechamber filled with police spies, on his way to meet "the August Presence." The king, like the prince, who later finds it more adroit to address Fabrice as "young man" during the conversation rather than as "monsignore," also has his little artificial ruses and poses. He is "already standing so as not to be seen getting up," puts out his right hand "bent for the hand-kiss which he would then refuse," and sits down "waiting a second before motioning to his guest to sit down too." These mannerisms, a feeble attempt to imitate prerevolutionary kings, merely stress Ferdinand's ineptitude.

Like Ernesto, after offering some preliminary gracious courtesies, the king changes masks and asks Fabrizio an insulting question about the royalist lieutenant-general of Sicily, identical to the one Ernesto asks Fabrice about the King of Naples, " 'Tell me, Salina, what do they think of Castelcicala down in Sicily?' " Like Fabrice, the Leopard parries elusively, " 'A great gentleman, a true hero, maybe a little old for the fatigues of the lieutenant-generalcy.' " And like Ernesto, Ferdinand is dissatisfied with the response. "The King's face darkened: Salina was refusing to act the spy. So Salina was no use to him. Leaning both hands on his desk, he prepared the dismissal." Angry because Fabrizio refuses to act like the base fellows in the antechamber, upon whose information the kingdom unfortunately relies,

Ferdinand also warns Fabrizio of Tancredi's revolutionary activities, which make him question the loyalty of the Salinas. Then, just as the prince had lost interest in Fabrice, so too "the King lost patience" with the Leopard. Going back through "the sumptuously second-rate rooms," the Leopard, like Fabrice, feels discouraged and is depressed by the "plebeian cordiality" of the king. Nevertheless, he feels superior to the "plebeian" king, as Fabrice does to the "animal" prince.

This scene is vital because the unsuccessful interview inevitably makes Fabrizio think about his political principles and the future of Italy. The Leopard's principles are very like those expressed by Fabrice. For him, Garibaldi's invasion, a plague that sweeps across Italy, is symbolized by the mutilated body of the dead royalist soldier whom he finds in his garden. The values of the Church and the noble traditions of the aristocracy crumble and decay during the course of *The Leopard* and are replaced by the vile practices of the democratic and revolutionary Sedàra.

As for the future of Italy, if Victor Emmanuel succeeded Ferdinand, things would be just the same. If Mazzini governed the republic, Fabrizio would lose his title, position, and power. The Leopard then asks himself a crucial question in the novel: If all three alternatives are unsatisfactory, "what should he do? Just cling to the status quo and avoid leaps in the dark?" He decides to follow this ineffectual plan, *faute de mieux,* fully realizing its limitations, and it guides his actions for the rest of the book. In his later interviews with the base Sedàra and with the noble Chevalley, which parallel this interview with the king and must inevitably be compared with it, he is guided by the decision he first formulated after speaking to Ferdinand.

The heroes of Stendhal and Lampedusa are isolated from society by their own extraordinary gifts of intelligence and refinement. Because they are unique, their exceptional values and abilities die with them while the values they detest live on. What Lukács writes of

Stendhal applies equally to Lampedusa: "He depicts with admirable realism the inevitable catastrophe of these [lonely] types, their inevitable defeat in the struggle against the dominating forces of the age, their necessary withdrawal from life or more accurately, their necessary rejection by the world of their time."

The triumph of the forces of reaction in Parma will be historically ephemeral. Stendhal had witnessed the revolution of 1830 eight years before completing his novel, though he died six years before those of 1848, which would begin to democratize and unify the states of Europe. By 1860 the Italian revolution would transform Parma as well as Sicily. The historical process described in *The Leopard,* however, effected permanent and irrevocable changes in Italy: " 'We were the Leopards, the Lions,' says Fabrizio, 'those who'll take our place will be little jackals, hyenas.' " Fabrizio, confronted by social and political forces that he recognizes to be overwhelming, remains passive and is defeated. We admire his values and appreciate his disdain, but regret his easy surrender to the inferior standards represented by Sedàra.

A hundred years passed between Garibaldi's invasion of Sicily and the publication of Lampedusa's novel, and the political events of that century inevitably affected his attitude toward the events of the novel. His reference to "a bomb manufactured in Pittsburgh, Pennsylvania," which destroyed the ballroom in 1943, seems like an awkward intrusion by the author. But it distinctly suggests the beginning of the end of Mussolini's twenty-five-year rule in Italy, a rule which could have occurred only after the political power was shifted to the incapable hands of the democratic masses as a result of the Italian revolution.

Stendhal's strong influence on Lampedusa is benign rather than detrimental, for Lampedusa was no slavish or derivative imitator and his use of Stendhal can be compared to Milton's use of Sophocles in *Samson Agonistes.* Lampedusa is intensely aware of the tradition of the European novel. Although many literary influences find their way into *The Leopard,* Lampedusa assimilates *The Charterhouse of Parma* most completely, transforming much of Stendhal's essence into a new and noble form.

USE OF GREUZE'S PAINTING

Like Proust's *Remembrance of Things Past* (1913–1927), *The Leopard* concerns social change and the decay of values. The novel dramatizes a segment of Sicilian history to reveal the process of metamorphosis: the decline of the aristocracy, the rise of the bourgeoisie, and the efforts of the former to save itself through marriage with the latter. Just as Lampedusa's use of symbolic objets d'art is profoundly Proustian, so the Ponteleones' grand ball toward the end of the book is closely modeled on the last scene of Proust's novel, "The Princess de Guermantes Receives" in *The Past Recaptured,* which illuminates the themes of change and decay, the triumph of bourgeois values over aristocratic ones.

Before World War I, the friendship of the sensitive Charles Swann with the vulgar Odette de Crécy led to his exclusion from the fashionable Parisian salons, which would never think of admitting her. But after the war, when all the characters have become old and decayed and the traditional standards of society have been swept away by the nouveau riche, Odette enjoys a meteoric ascent and suddenly acquires great influence, prestige, and power. Similarly, in the final "Relics" chapter, Angelica, now stricken with varicose veins, organizes the celebrations that commemorate the landing of Garibaldi and offers to pull strings with the Cardinal when the family relics are reexamined.

During the Ponteleones' ball the Leopard discovers a painting in the library by Jean-Baptiste Greuze called *Death of a Just Man.* The room is decorated in the style of the 1790's, the decade of the French Revolution. (Characteristically, "the Ponteleones hadn't done it up for seventy years.") "The man was expiring on his bed, amid welters of clean linen, surrounded by afflicted grandsons and granddaughters raising arms toward the ceiling. The girls were pretty, provoking, and the disorder of their clothes suggested sex more than sorrow; they, it was obvious at once, were the real subject of the picture." The Prince is strongly attracted to this melancholy scene and identifies with the dead father because he knows that he and his class are doomed and dying. On his own deathbed he calculates that he has really lived only two or three years of his long life—the rest was pain and boredom, a kind of death in life. The bourgeois death in the Greuze painting mirrors Fabrizio's own *déclassé* death later in the novel; it predicts both the decline of his wealth and social prestige and the descent of the entire family into the middle class. The painting symbolizes the Prince's profound conviction that nothing really matters, and his fatal inability to act except when he opposes his own interests or even his own survival.

Angelica's triumph at the ball completes her conquest of Concetta and her social success ensures the defeat of the Salinas by the Sedàras, who are an old family—or soon will be. The discovery of the painting in the context of the ball, the last spasm of the moribund aristocracy and final flaring up of a dying fire, relates Sicilian to European society and shows that Palermo receives its Bourbon taste and rulers, as well as its revolutionary ideas, from France.

The painting also plays a thematic and structural role in *The Leopard.* It illustrates the two important themes of decadent taste and sexual license, and relates them both to the theme of death. The Greuze is a pictorial parody of an earlier scene, the return of the prodigal son, Tancredi; and it carefully connects "A Ball" to the last two chapters of the novel, "Death of a Prince" and "Relics," which take place many years later. In order to understand the significance of Greuze's painting in *The Leopard* (it is the only one of the numerous objets d'art that is given a specific artist and title), we must first analyze the visual and thematic content of the painting, and then show how Lampedusa's response to the interpretations of Greuze by Diderot and the brothers Goncourt explains why this particular painting is the symbolic core of the novel.

Greuze (1725–1805) painted three well-known deathbed scenes: *The Charitable Lady* (now in Lyons), *The Paralytic* (Leningrad), and *The Punished Son* (Paris). Though none of these paintings exactly matches Lampedusa's specific description, he was probably thinking of *The Punished Son* (1778), which portrays all the salient characteristics: an afflicted family, welters of clean linen, and disordered clothes that suggest sex more than sorrow. Anita Brookner writes that Greuze "seems rather to have been inspired by a wistful vision of the ideal family in which children are begotten easily, remain devoted to their parents, and are always there at the death." It is the failure of the prodigal son (who returns, alas, too late) to live up to this sentimental ideal of filial piety that is the ostensible subject of *The Punished Son.* For Greuze depicted the manners and morals of the bourgeois class in saccharine genre pictures; he aimed at high tragedy and achieved well-executed bathos.

The bad son enters stage right—bent with grief and beating his breast in remorse—frozen (like the rigid dog) at the dramatic yet anticlimactic moment, as the heavy draped canopy over the mortuary bed seems about to fall at the end of the last act. But guided by the extended arm of the mother (handkerchief in hand) and the standing daughter (holding the father's arm), our attention is directed first to the clean linen surrounding the nobly composed features of the dead father at the center of the painting, then to the distraught daughter (eyes rolled heavenward), whose grief has allowed her left breast to fall nearly out of her dress. (Is it this alarming exposure that arouses the fixed and wide-eyed stares of her siblings across the bed and that causes the kneeling lad to cover his eyes before the open Bible?) The head of the *déshabillée* daughter was inspired by the ecstatic saints of Guido Reni, for Greuze seems to have been the first artist in the eighteenth century to respond to the appeal of this master. Like Reni, Greuze was extremely successful in his own time and was even called "a second Raphael."

The critic largely responsible for establishing Greuze's Raphaelesque reputation was Denis Diderot; and the basis, and limitations, of Diderot's art criticism were analyzed by Schiller in a letter to Goethe (1797): "In his aesthetic works, I think, he still looks too much to foreign and moral aims, he does not seek these sufficiently in the subject itself and in its representation. To him the beautiful work of art must always serve some other purpose." Diderot's panegyric of *The Paralytic* in the Salon of 1763 reveals that he found in Greuze the perfect expression of moral and didactic art:

> This fellow Greuze is really my man. . . . First, I like the genre—it is moral painting. What! Haven't painters used their brushes in the service of vice and debauchery long enough, too long indeed? Shouldn't we be glad to see him at last collaborating with dramatic poetry in order to move, to educate, to inspire us and induce us to virtue? Courage, my friend Greuze, make painting moral and make it always like that!

Greuze's "collaboration with dramatic poetry" meant that works like *The Paralytic* were the equivalent in rhetorical painting of Diderot's own sentimental play *The Father of the Family* (1758), and exemplified his theory of middle tragedy, "which would have as its subject our domestic misfortunes." Diderot's high praise of Greuze suggests the artist's affinity to his contemporary English "men of feeling," Henry Mackenzie and Samuel Richardson: "Here is your painter and mine, the first among us to have the idea of making art moral and of constructing a sequence of events which could easily have been made into a novel."

Though Diderot characterized *The Punished Son* as "a lesson for fathers and children," he was also aware of Greuze's veiled (and un-

veiled) pornography, his sexual innuendo and his orgasmic women. He writes with disapproval of a pastel of Madame Greuze (a notorious spendthrift and adulteress who helped to ruin her husband), "That half-open mouth, those swimming eyes, that relaxed position, that swollen throat, that voluptuous mixture of pain and pleasure, obliges all decent women in the place to lower their eyes and blush with shame."

This Tartuffian hypocrisy of Greuze—the painter of *The Broken Eggs* and *Girl Weeping for the Death of Her Canary*, pictorial allegories of lost virginity—attracted the particular condemnation of the Goncourts in *French Painting of the Eighteenth Century* (1871), though they also attacked the influence of Diderot on Greuze and the artist's "deplorable tradition of literary painting and moralising art." To the perceptive Goncourts, Greuze's celebration of the felicities of domestic mediocrity merely masked an insidious and dangerous corruption:

> The character of the man influenced the ideas of the painter, investing all these moral narratives with the suspicion of libertinage. . . . The particular subtlety of this art is in its transformation of the simplicity and heedlessness of a young girl into something sensually inviting. . . . And white, the colour dedicated to youth, to the candour of women and the radiant modesty of their dress, becomes, in these pictures, an irritating stimulus, a delicate excitation to license, an allurement.

It is clear that Lampedusa reacts against Diderot's praise and that he employs the Goncourts' interpretation of Greuze's titillation. For the prince thinks the studied "disorder of their clothes suggested sex more than sorrow" and that the girls were obviously "the real subject of the picture."

There are two other passages in the Goncourts' influential essay that suggest important themes in *The Leopard* and illuminate the character of the dreamy prince, who "belongs to an unfortunate generation, swung between the old world and the new" and ill at ease in both. The Goncourts write of Greuze:

> He was the painter of illusion. His inspiration was the supreme example of the soaring trend towards rejuvenating affections, towards thoughts, pictures, plays, which might recover the lights of the morning for the spirit of a sinking society. He spoke directly to the sensibilities of the period, he was attached to its sentimentalities. . . . He caressed and satisfied the instincts of the time.

The Leopard concerns the hopeless attempt to maintain illusions—of class, prestige, honor, and faith—in the face of revolutionary transformations. Like Greuze, the Leopard, a famous astronomer, wants to "recover the lights of morning for the spirit of sinking society."

The aristocratic prince ironically identifies with the bourgeois banalities of Greuze, emphasized by the homely bedwarmer and kitchen utensils studiously placed on the floor of the bare room, and he never imagines a more appropriately noble and heroic death (as in the work of Jacques-Louis David) or a luxurious and exotic end (as in Eugène Delacroix). His attraction to the mediocre Greuze is the aesthetic parallel of his alliance through marriage to the rapacious Sedàras, a humiliating union that recirculates into the Prince's family some of the money stolen from him by Sedàra. Though resolutely democratic, Greuze had an aristocratic clientele (his greatest patron was the Empress Catherine II of Russia) and he was ruined by the French Revolution. The Goncourts write of Greuze, in a striking parallel with the Leopard, "Slipping into poverty, he finally vanished in oblivion. He grew old, a survival of himself, dragging along with him the heavy burden of a dead reputation."

The flattering distortion of reality and the sexual license in *The Punished Son* are appropriate to the moribund Sicilian aristocracy, and reflect the shabby grandeur and decadent taste of that reactionary and rococo class. Within this society the "aesthetic" judgments of the ignorant Angelica enable her "to acquire the reputation of a polite but inflexible art expert, which was to accompany her quite unwarrantably throughout her life." Even the Prince admires the taste, sentiments, and "affected simplicity" of the age of Greuze; his drawing room, where the rosary takes place, is decorated in the rococo style, and the palace at Donnafugata retains "an air of excited sensuality all the sharper for being carefully restrained," which it inherited from "the dying eighteenth century." He even calls his scruples concerning Angelica "Rousseauesque." Fabrizio is disgusted by the nineteenth-century novels of Dickens, George Eliot, George Sand, Flaubert, and Dumas père, which Bourbon censorship excludes from Sicily, and he attacks the latest writings of P. J. Proudhon and Karl Marx. He dislikes Verdi's tempestuous "Noi siamo zingarelli" ("We are gypsies"), which is played for him as he enters feudal Donnafugata, and dies as a barrel organ grinds out a mechanical aria by Donizetti.

By contrast, the modern Garibaldino, Tancredi, enthusiastically discusses Bellini and Verdi, whose name was used to form the patriotic acrostic Vittorio Emmanuele Re Di Italia, with the liberal Chevalley when he escorts the politician through the village. Tancredi is referred to by Fabrizio "as a kind of Mirabeau," the great French orator who attempted to reconcile the monarchy and the revolution. The noble Sicilians who own Greuzes in 1862 will soon disappear like their French predecessors, who were destroyed by the cyclical revolutions of the nineteenth century.

The sexual license of Greuze's art, thinly veiled with respectability, provides an ironic reflection of the sexual themes in *The Leopard*. The phenomenal appearance of Angelica rouses the carnal jealousy of the prince, and Tancredi's passionate yet ultimately restrained courtship of the voluptuous maiden makes the Leopard envy "the chances open to a Fabrizio Salina and Tancredi Falconeri of three centuries before, who would have rid themselves of urges to bed down with the Angelicas of their day without ever going before a priest, or giving a thought to the dowries of such local girls." Fabrizio's liaison with his mistress Mariannina is the last spark of the atavistic lust that evolved from his masochistic ancestor the Saint-Duke.

Fabrizio loves the adventurous Tancredi more than his own pallid children, and although he disapproves of Tancredi's revolutionary ardor, the Leopard gives him a roll of gold pieces when he joins Garibaldi's rebels. The moving scene of Tancredi's return from the wars with his friend Cavriaghi is influenced generally by Odysseus' return to Ithaca in book 17 of the *Odyssey* and specifically by the similar return of Nicolai Rostov and his friend Denisov from the campaigns against Napoleon in *War and Peace.* Lampedusa achieves a powerful effect by individualizing this beautifully rendered scene within the archetypal tradition of the eternal return portrayed by Homer and Tolstoy. The young warriors of both *War and Peace* and *The Leopard* are greeted with excitement by the faithful retainer at the entrance to the great house (the fictional equivalents of Odysseus' nurse, Eurycleia). They rush to the surprised and highly emotional reception of the large family circle, forget to introduce their weary companions, and search distractedly for their most beloved—Nicolai's mother and Tancredi's fiancée—who arrive after the climactic entrance. Tancredi's triumphant return, a parody of the retributive return in *The Punished Son,* is the literary embodiment of Greuze's sentimental *Filial Piety,* discussed by Diderot in the Salon of 1763.

Yet Tancredi's betrothal is also a betrayal: "It's the end of the Falconeris, and of the Salinas too." The first sentence of *The Leopard* expresses the dominant themes of the novel: aristocratic pride in a moment of decline, and the erosion and extinction of a noble fortune, fame, and family. This sense of death hangs darkly over the ruined palaces, whose inhabitants foregather to congratulate themselves on still existing. Prince Fabrizio strives to attain a sub-

limated existence that reminds him of death. Like most Sicilians he has a powerful longing for oblivion, and he reflects, "While there's death there's hope."

On the way to the ball the prince encounters the ominous figure of a priest hurrying through the crooked streets with the Last Sacrament. He senses the atmosphere of death that pervades the decaying city of Palermo, and at the ball he attempts to escape from his black gloom and the living ghosts of his past mistresses in the silent library. As soon as he sees Greuze's painting, the Leopard, who earlier in the novel prided himself on his white waistcoat, admired the nuns' purest white linen, and "saw himself as a white-haired old man walking beside herds of grandchildren," in the iconographic tradition of Greuze "asked himself if his own death would be like that; probably it would, apart from the sheets being less impeccable (he knew that the sheets of those in their *death agony* are always dirty with spittle, discharges, marks of medicine), and it was to be hoped that Concetta, Carolina, and his other womenfolk would be more decently clad. But the same, more or less. As always, the thought of his own death calmed him as much as that of others disturbed him."

Fabrizio dies a figurative and symbolic death on the very night he sees the Greuze, and this death is emphasized by the structure of *The Leopard,* for nothing in his life seems very significant after the ball, and the next chapter of the novel, "Death of a Prince," takes place twenty-one years later. For a dozen years or so he had been courting death and "feeling as if the vital fluid, the faculty of existing, life itself in fact and perhaps even the will to go on living, were ebbing out of him slowly." His *aperçu* that the sheets are too clean anticipates his own death in a seedy Palermo hotel where he reenacts, in a less sanitary and aesthetic way, the *Death of a Just Man.*

The dying Leopard is first treated by a poor doctor, "impotent witness of a thousand wretched *death agonies,*" whose description corresponds to that of the old father in Greuze's painting: "Above a torn frock coat stretched his long, haggard face stubbled with white hair, the disillusioned face of a famished intellectual." The Prince's grandson Fabrizietto sits next to him and holds his hands, and like the little boy in the painting "was staring at him with the natural curiosity of one present at his first *death agony.*" As in the Greuze, the Prince is surrounded by six figures (his grandson, nephew, three children, and the doctor), and the woman in the brown dress who arrives at the moment of death is the fictional equivalent of the punished son, who has traveled to the deathbed direct from the road and dropped his crutch at his grief-stricken entrance. Prince Fabrizio's death is a bitter parody of Greuze's sentimental idealization, for he expires far from his palace, amid the prison stench of crushed cockroaches and stale urine.

The last chapter of *The Leopard,* "Relics," which describes the final humiliation of the Salina family, is also related to the exposed daughter in *The Punished Son.* Like the Greuze, the painting of the fake Madonna in the family chapel is in bad taste and not at all what it is taken to be:

> It was a painting in the style of Cremona and represented a slim and *very attractive young woman, with eyes turned to heaven* and an abundance of brown hair scattered in *gracious disorder* on half-bare shoulders; in her right hand she was gripping a crumpled letter, with an expression of anxious expectancy not unconnected with a certain sparkle in her glistening eyes. . . . [There were] none of those symbols which usually accompany the image of Our Lady; the painter must have relied on the virginal expression as a sufficient mark of recognition [italics mine].

When the monsignor sees this painting he chastizes the family chaplain for pretending it is a holy image and saying Mass in front of a picture of a girl waiting for a rendezvous with her lover.

A few days later, the Vatican expert exposes the falsity of the numerous relics and orders a reconsecration of the family chapel. Concetta then throws out the rotting hide of Bendicò, her last link with the prerevolutionary past, and withdraws into her own closed world that "had already ceded all the impulses it could give and consisted now only of pure forms. The portrait of her father was just a few square inches of canvas, the green cases were just a few square yards of wood." Concetta had destroyed her future with Tancredi by her own imprudence and the rash Salina pride, and her bitter memories, like her father's, "left a sediment of grief which, accumulating day by day, would in the end be the real cause of [her] death."

Lampedusa uses *The Punished Son* to define the character of the Prince by placing Fabrizio in a reactionary and decadent tradition and at the same time endowing him with the capacity to recognize its falsity and sentimentality. By exploiting the biographical parallels between Greuze and the Leopard, and by emphasizing Fabrizio's old-fashioned rococo taste and his attraction to Greuze's painting, Lampedusa also maintains the necessary critical and ironic distance between himself and his eighteenth-century hero, although their class and their essential values are identical.

In *The Leopard* Lampedusa surrounds the prince with a depth and richness by evoking echoes of mythology, music, and art, of the Bible, Homer, Dante, Ariosto, Tasso, Diderot, Stendhal, Flaubert, Baudelaire, Tolstoy, and Proust. Similarly, he uses the literary interpretations of Diderot and the Goncourts to place Greuze in an aesthetic and cultural tradition; he incorporates Greuze's licentious hypocrisy, Diderot's moral self-deception, and the Goncourt's shrewd insight into the ambivalent character of Fabrizio. Lampedusa makes *The Punished Son* reflect a personal and historical crisis: the death of the Leopard, his memories, his traditions, and his class. Though Lampedusa could not admire Greuze's "pure forms," his use of Greuze's painting and the values it represents is a striking example of the great strength of *The Leopard:* Lampedusa's unusual ability to absorb and transform other works of art into his own traditional yet original masterpiece.

TWO STORIES AND A MEMORY

Lampedusa's *Racconti,* published three years after *The Leopard,* contained his nostalgic memoir "Places of My Infancy" and three stories. The slightest tale, "La gioia e la legge" (Joy and the Law), was probably omitted from the English edition because it did not, like the others, have a Sicilian setting or a connection to *The Leopard.*

This brief tale shows Lampedusa's mastery of the nineteenth-century short story form perfected by Guy de Maupassant in which a trivial episode reveals the inherent goodness and nobility of an obscure family. The poignant effect of the story is achieved chiefly by the form of narration. Girolamo, the poor accountant, is always seen through the eyes of others. Burdened with a large package and stepping on toes in a crowded bus on the way home from work, he is joyous at having been given a huge Christmas *panettone* (sweet cake) by his boss. The cake was sent to the whole office by a higher-up in the company, but the boss decides it should be given to the person whom everyone agrees deserves it most. There is something comic about the general acclamation for Girolamo, who is rather pitied by his colleagues. Girolamo's joy is short-lived, since his wife insists that they use the cake to repay an obligation to a lawyer. She buys a smaller *panettone* for the family and Girolamo has to purchase yet another one after Christmas, for his colleagues tease him and ask for their share.

The story is specifically Italian in the sense of human warmth, in the dignity of Girolamo, and in the wife's decision to sacrifice the cake. Girolamo's joy is based on anticipating his treat for the family, but it is also subject to the law: the obligation to social custom and the necessity of paying homage to the rich and the powerful. The achievement of the story is its ability to suggest the social fabric of a humble life without in any way diminishing its human value.

"Il mattino di un mezzadro" ("The Blind Kittens"), the first chapter of an uncompleted sequel to *The Leopard,* was written in March 1957. The main weakness of this fragment is that it tends to repeat rather than develop the story of the novel. According to E. M. Forster, the title refers to the ignorant and rapacious characters who "stumble blindly into a world which they cannot understand but are capable of damaging." The story concerns a Sedàra-like creature, Batassano Ibba, who by cunning, perfidy, ruthlessness, luck, defiance, and daring has gained control of almost all the land in the region. In 1901—nine years before the episode of the last chapter in *The Leopard* takes place—the agent of the Leopard's grandson, Fabrizietto, sells their land to (and is swindled by) Ibba. His methods, possessions, and wealth take on mythical qualities and arouse the passionate curiosity of the nobles in the clubs of Palermo. But these men have no real conception of their adversary and no clear idea of how to deal with him. They too are blind kittens—helpless, deluded, and destined, like the Leopard, for extinction.

The significance of the title of Lampedusa's most ambitious story, "Lighea" (the name given by a learned commentator to one of Homer's sirens), is lost in the English translation, "The Professor and the Siren." It also alludes to Ligea, the siren in Milton's "Comus" (1634) ("And fair Ligea's golden comb, / Wherewith she sits on diamond rocks / Sleeking her soft alluring locks") and to "Ligeia," the heroine of Poe's story (1838), a woman of strange beauty and great learning who dies of a wasting illness. Her husband remarries; and when Rowena, his second wife, dies and then comes back to life, he realizes that Ligeia's will to live has triumphed and that she has assumed the body of Rowena. The heroines of both Poe's and Lampedusa's stories represent wisdom, sensuality, and a powerful vitality. But whereas Poe's Ligeia symbolizes the will to live, Lampedusa's Lighea also represents a death wish, a desire for release from the pains of life and the sorrows of old age. Just as the Woman in Brown, "the creature forever yearned for," finally comes to free the prince from earthly bondage, so the sensual siren beckons the professor back to the sea.

The story concerns the relations between a young journalist, a descendant of the Leopard, and an embittered, acidulous old senator, Rosario La Ciura, the most illustrious Hellenist of his time. The two men meet in a café in Turin, discover they are both from Sicily, and develop an unusual friendship. The journalist arranges a feast of Etna wine and sea urchins, of which La Ciura is especially fond, and this leads the senator to reveal the greatest experience of his life.

When he was a handsome and innocent young Greek scholar living in a remote seaside village near Catania, an enchanting siren (with human sexual organs) climbed into his boat. She infected him with her animal joy and divine delight in existence and transported him to a superhuman plane. She said she was the daughter of Calliope, muse of epic poetry, and she spoke the Greek of the classical age. Both carnal and delicate, she devoured raw fish whose blood dripped from her chin. Yet she belonged, through her classical lineage, "to the fountainhead of all culture, of all wisdom, of all ethics." La Ciura never touched another woman after she left him at the end of that extraordinary summer.

At the conclusion of the story, the journalist hears that the senator has fallen into the sea from the deck of a ship that was taking him to a learned conference in Lisbon. Overwhelmed, apparently, by the memory of his paradisiacal youth, he could no longer bear the separation from the siren and longed to recover that elemental ecstasy. The ability of memory to recapture the lost world of the past is the great theme of "Places of My Infancy" and "The Professor and the Siren," as it is of *The Leopard.*

Selected Bibliography

EDITIONS

Il Gattopardo. Preface by Giorgio Bassani. Milan, 1958.
"Lezioni su Stendhal." *Paragone* 112:3–49 (April 1959).
Racconti. Preface by Giorgio Bassani. Milan, 1961.
Il Gattopardo (completo): Edizione conforme al manoscritto del 1957. Introduction by Gioacchino Lanza Tomasi. Milan, 1969.

TRANSLATIONS

The Leopard. Translated, with a historical note, by Archibald Colquhoun. New York, 1960.
Two Stories and a Memory. Translated, with a note on the author, by Archibald Colquhoun. Introduction by E. M. Forster. New York, 1962.

BIOGRAPHICAL AND CRITICAL STUDIES

Biasin, Gian-Paolo. "The Prince and the Siren." *Modern Language Notes* 78:31–50 (1963).
Brown, Calvin. "Parallel Incidents in Émile Zola and Tomasi di Lampedusa." *Comparative Literature* 15:193–202 (1963).
Buzzi, Giancarlo. *Invito alla lettura di Giuseppe Tomasi di Lampedusa.* Milan, 1972.
Colquhoun, Archibald. "Lampedusa in Sicily: The Lair of the Leopard." *Atlantic Monthly* 211:91–110 (February 1963).
Eskin, Stanley. "Animal Imagery in *Il Gattopardo.*" *Italica* 39:189–194 (1962).
Evans, Arthur and Catherine Evans. "*Salina e Svelto:* The Symbolism of Change in *Il Gattopardo.*" *Wisconsin Studies in Contemporary Literature* 4:298–304 (1963).
Forster, E. M. "The Prince's Tale." *Spectator* (May 13, 1960).
Gilbert, John. "The Metamorphosis of the Gods in *Il Gattopardo.*" *Modern Language Notes* 81:22–32 (1966).
Gomme, Andor. "Irony and *The Leopard.*" *Oxford Review* 6:23–35 (1967).
Heilman, Robert. "Lampedusa and Bulwer: *Sic Transit* in Different Keys." *Northwest Review* 7:21–28 (1965–1966).

Kermode, Frank. "Old Orders Changing." In *Puzzles and Epiphanies*. London, 1962.

Kirton, W. J. S. "Stendhal, Lampedusa, and the Limits of Admiration." *Trivium* 10:101–109 (1975).

Kuhns, Richard. "Modernity and Death: *The Leopard* by Giuseppe Tomasi di Lampedusa." *Contemporary Psychoanalysis* 5:95–119 (1969). See also Miltiades Zaphiropoulos, Charles Dahlberg, and Frank Hale's "Discussion" in the same issue.

Lansing, Richard. "The Structure of Meaning in Lampedusa's *Il Gattopardo.*" *PMLA* 93:409–422 (1978).

Lucente, Gregory. "Lampedusa's *Il Gattopardo:* Figure and Temporality in an Historical Novel." *Modern Language Notes* 93:82–108 (1978).

———. "*Scrivere o fare . . . o altro:* Social Commitment and Ideologies of Representation in the Debates over Lampedusa's *Il Gattopardo* and Morante's *La Storia.*" *Italica* 61:220–251 (1984).

McSweeney, Kerry. "Lampedusa and the Hour of Death." *Southern Humanities Review* 12:213–220 (1978).

Meyers, Jeffrey. "Symbol and Structure in *The Leopard.*" *Italian Quarterly* 9:50–70 (1965).

———. "The Influence of *La Chartreuse de Parme* on *Il Gattopardo.*" *Italica* 44:314–325 (1967).

———. "Greuze and Lampedusa's *Il Gattopardo.*" *Modern Language Review* 69:308–315 (1974). Reprinted in Jeffrey Meyers, *Painting and the Novel.* Manchester, 1975.

Nolan, David. "Lampedusa's *The Leopard.*" *Studies* (1966).

O'Neill, T. "Lampedusa and De Roberto." *Italica* 47:170–182 (1970).

Orlando, Francesco. *Ricordo di Lampedusa.* Milan, 1963.

Pacifici, Sergio. *The Modern Italian Novel from Pea to Moravia.* Carbondale, Ill., 1979.

Pallotta, A. "*Il Gattopardo:* A Theme-Structure Analysis." *Italica* 43:57–65 (1966).

Ragusa, Olga. "Stendhal, Tomasi di Lampedusa, and the Novel." *Comparative Literature Studies* 3:195–228 (1973).

Salvestroni, Simonetta. *Tomasi di Lampedusa.* Florence, 1973.

Samonà, Giuseppe Paolo. *Il Gattopardo, i racconti, Lampedusa.* Florence, 1974.

Wilson, Edmund. *Europe Without Baedeker.* New York, 1966.

JEFFREY MEYERS

TARJEI VESAAS

(1897–1970)

DURING THE LAST thirty years of his life, Tarjei Vesaas was generally considered the foremost Norwegian writer of his generation. His authorship spanned nearly fifty years, from the first fumbling poems and minor articles printed in provincial journals around 1920, to the twenty-three novels, handful of plays, three collections of short stories, and as many collections of poetry. Vesaas was honored with many literary prizes, including the prestigious Venice Triennale Prize for the collection of short stories *Vindane* (The Winds, 1952); the Nordic Council Literary Prize for the novel *Is-slottet* (*The Ice Palace,* 1963); and a nomination for the Nobel Prize in 1969. But perhaps equally significant is the testimony of Dag Solstad, a major Norwegian novelist who wrote in 1969:

It is with uncommon confidence we receive a new work from the hands of Vesaas. This demonstrates his special position in Norwegian literature, a position Vesaas has earned through a series of books that have left many different readers with a sense of personal liberation. I am sure there are few readers [in Norway] who would not count at least one book by Vesaas among their most important literary experiences.

The year after the author's death, the Swiss scholar Walter Baumgartner issued *Huset og fuglen* (The House and the Bird, 1971), a book of prose and poetry that had either not been published before or were out of print. As a kind of prologue, the editor included a legend about the Chinese painter Wu-Tao-Tse, originally published by Vesaas in 1926. The legend concludes with Wu-Tao-Tse, a very old man, looking back on a productive life as an artist. The emperor asks him to create a final masterpiece, and Wu-Tao-Tse paints a huge mural showing a landscape of lofty mountains. But when the emperor and his court gather to view the great work, something incredible happens: alone and silent, the master enters a cave he has painted in the landscape, and at the same moment the entire scene disappears: "The creator of dreams had redeemed his vision and took his priceless creation with him on the journey home into eternity."

The scene suggests that the artist enters through his work, as through a door, into eternity. Art is akin to vision or dream and serves the function of myth in pointing beyond itself to the universal. The legend of Wu-Tao-Tse can be read as a statement of Vesaas's aesthetic, which remains representative even for the mature author some fifty years later. There is an overall visionary, mythical quality in most of Vesaas's works, as well as specific allusions to a range of mythological motifs, some of which are of classical origin, some Nordic, others biblical. A figure of central importance is the archetypal bride and mother, the giver and nurturer of life related to the earth and seasonal cycles. In the early novels we also find a number of references to traditional beliefs and elements of Norwegian folklore.

Vesaas wrote in Nynorsk, a dialect of Norwegian that developed during the nineteenth century. Until 1814, when Norway declared itself independent, it had been under the political domination of Denmark for almost four hundred years, and the literary language and tradition identified with Norway had been gradually replaced by the Danish. For several decades after 1814 the energies of the young nation were preempted by political and economic problems, but during the 1840's, with the development of Romanticism, the course of Norwegian literature was given a new cultural foundation. Of special importance was the search for a national language based on the dialects of rural Norway and Old Norse, culminating in Ivar Aasen's *Prøver af landsmaalet* (Samples of Norwegian Landsmaal, 1853). This essentially synthetic language (after 1929 called Nynorsk, or New Norwegian, in contrast to Bokmål, or Dano-Norwegian) became the preferred idiom of a new generation of writers who had their roots in village and rural life. Their works mirrored a concern with nature, with history and local traditions, and with social conditions seen in a rural context. Some of these authors remained provincial in outlook, others achieved national and even world-wide audiences. Among the major prose writers are Arne Garborg, Olav Duun, Sjur Bygd, Kristofer Uppdal, Inge Krokann, and Tarjei Vesaas. In their novels and stories the realistic prose rhythms of a living epic tradition are employed to depict the socio-psychological and historical milieu of the authors and give it timeless significance. Among the most important lyrical poets writing in Nynorsk, Tore Ørjasæter, Olav Aukrust, Olav Nygard, Kristofer Uppdal, Tor Jonsson, Aslaug Vaa, Olav H. Hauge, Halldis Moren Vesaas, and, once again, Tarjei Vesaas, come to mind. Some of these poets use a language that is close to their own dialects. In form their poetry is rooted in traditional song and rhymed verse, conventions they helped renew or reshaped into vehicles of expressionistic modernism. Some of this poetry is visionary, reflecting elements of Christian mysticism. More often the source of inspiration is an intense experience of nature.

Vesaas contributed significantly to the acceptance of Nynorsk as a legitimate and viable literary language. Today there are two official languages in Norway, and in a sense there are two literary traditions. When Vesaas published his first novels in the 1920's, the fact that he wrote in Nynorsk determined in part the positive critical response he received in some circles. In a review of *Menneskebonn* (Children of Man, 1923) and *Grindegard. Morgonen* (The Farm at Grinde. The Morning, 1925), for example, a critic praised Vesaas's ability to utilize the "poetry, rhythm, and music of his native tongue." Some twenty years later Vesaas was hailed for being the "first all-Norwegian author writing in Nynorsk, the first who does not mean more to country people than to city people." And in eulogizing Vesaas at the time of his death, the chairman of the Nynorsk language association (Noregs Mållag), Hans Tungesvik, proclaimed that it was through Vesaas's "bountiful authorship that Nynorsk has truly become the possession of all Norwegians. . . . It was by the use of his own language that Vesaas found his identity as a person and as a writer, and by his example he helped thousands of other people find their own voice."

Vesaas's relationship to the rural environment goes beyond language, however. He was born and raised in the province of Telemark in south-central Norway, and he lived there most of his life, except for extended stays abroad, mostly in Germany during the latter half of the 1920's. Telemark has long been one of the richest cultural areas in all of Norway. Nowhere have folklorists collected a richer harvest of folktales, ballads, songs, and traditions, and nowhere have rural architecture and wood carving flowered more than in Telemark. Both of Vesaas's parents, Signe and Olav, were avid readers and interested in literature. His mother was musical and "very fond of singing"; his father's brother, Øystein Vesaas, was a well-known wood-carver and painter. As a farmer Vesaas's father spent the summer days toiling in the fields and forest, but in winter, when the evenings were long, he would gather the children and read to them "all kinds of good youth literature and huge historical novels." The family subscribed to several newspapers, books were preferred gifts at Christmas, and the children learned early to make use of the village library. As a boy, Vesaas's favorite reading included Rudyard Kipling, Knut Hamsun, Selma Lagerlöf, the contemporary Norwegian poets Aukrust, Ørjasæter, Nygard, and Olaf Bull, and the twelfth-century Persian poet and astronomer Omar Khàyyàm.

Rural writers in Norway usually received their formal education through folk high schools and teachers' colleges, and Vesaas was no exception to this rule. In 1917, at the folk high school in Voss, he met the gifted teacher Lars Eskeland, who introduced him to the poetry of Rabindranath Tagore, the Indian Nobel Prize winner (1913), whose *The Gardener* and *Gitanjali* Eskeland was translating into Nynorsk. Some fifty years later Vesaas still recalled the "marvel" of those "exotic, unrhymed Tagore poems." Some critics have argued that the escapist fascination with death found in some of the early writings of Vesaas was partly inspired by Tagore. But there is also a fundamental metaphysical affinity between the two poets that emerges with great clarity in Vesaas's mature work after he had sloughed off the sentimental tendencies of his youth.

Another major influence on Vesaas at the folk high school was the praise lavished on the life of the soil and the ancient tradition of the son following in his father's footsteps on the family farm. At the beginning of the twentieth century, the economy of Norway was mostly agricultural, and it was important for a rural school to inculcate a positive attitude toward farm-related labor and traditions among its pu-pils. For Vesaas, however, the question of what to do with his life posed a profound personal dilemma. He was born into a family that had occupied the same mountain farm—some two thousand feet above sea level—for more than ten generations. As the eldest of three sons, he was expected to take over the farm as soon as he was grown, to marry and have a son of his own, who would in turn receive his patrimony and follow his father's occupation. In keeping with this unwritten law, Vesaas began working by his father's side at an early age, and no one bothered to ask if this was what he wanted to do with his life. Although the elder Vesaas was a sociable man, he had little close communication with his son. While the boy found it easier to speak with his mother, he did not feel that he could talk about his vague intimations that he might become a writer some day. The young Vesaas became a loner who found refuge in books and in solitary wanderings in the surrounding forests and hills, "grappling with formless intuitions." It appears that during these formative years Vesaas learned to commune with nature in the special way that characterizes his works. More than setting or background, nature for him is the symbolic landscape through which the writer projects his personal insight and interpretation of universal problems.

When World War I broke out, Vesaas was seventeen. After completing his schooling at the folk high school, he did a stint in the military in Oslo from 1918 to 1919. Returning home, he expressed his isolation in sorrowful poems and small, ironic articles, which were published in local youth magazines and newspapers. The following winter, while the rest of the family spent their evenings reading, Vesaas wrote his first novel, the "tearfully tragic" *Bok um finn* (The Book About Finn). His parents and brothers ignored his writing, just as they pretended not to notice when the manuscript was rejected by the publishing house of Olaf Norli. But the same year Vesaas won a first prize in a national magazine competition for a prose poem that he wrote in the style of the admired Tagore. In 1922 he won another first prize, this time in a short story competition, but a volume of prose poems was once again rejected by Olaf Norli. Undaunted, Vesaas wrote a volume of short stories, but instead of submitting it directly he sent it to the poet Kristofer Uppdal with a request that he forward it to the publisher. Uppdal complied but recommended that Vesaas ask for the manuscript back and "write something better next time." Vesaas followed Uppdal's advice, and although his early success had been mixed, the conviction grew in him that he wanted to be a writer, no matter what his responsibilities toward the farm and family. During the winter of 1922–1923 Vesaas reshaped the collection of short stories into the loosely structured novel *Menneskebonn* (Children of Man). This manuscript was accepted for publication by Olaf Norli in April 1923, and it appeared in October of the same year. Vesaas's parents then realized that their eldest son would not take over the farm, but although they felt overworked and worn out, and Vesaas's younger brothers were not yet old enough to take his place, they did not hinder the young author. Without being asked, his father divided the daily chores so that Vesaas could sit half the day and write, and they continued this arrangement until the author was in his mid-thirties, when he bought his own home near the family farm.

In 1924 Vesaas published his next novel, *Sendemann Huskuld* (Huskuld the Herald). The book was well received and appeared in two editions within a short span of time. Later Vesaas described the novel as "unreadable," but it earned him a membership in the Norwegian Writers' Association and qualified him for government stipends and travel grants. He began studying foreign languages, including English, French, and German, and eventually spent the next nine years mostly in the big cities on the continent, especially Munich. The long sojourn abroad was of enormous importance to Vesaas's authorship. Writing during the day, he used the evenings to go to the theater and, when he could afford it, took trips to Vienna, Bratislava (Pressburg), Venice, Florence, Rome, Paris, Brussels, London, Cologne, and Berlin. In 1931 in Oslo, he met his future wife, the poet Halldis Moren, ten years younger than he. Vesaas was determined to remain a bachelor, committed only to his writing, but Halldis Moren changed his mind. He used a new travel grant to follow her to Switzerland. Three years later they were married and moved to Midtbø, a farm close to the family home in Telemark that Vesaas had bought from his uncle.

NOVELS: 1923 TO WORLD WAR II

Vesaas's works can be divided into two periods, the first twenty years or so before World War II, and the period since then until 1970, when his last volume of poems was published posthumously. His mastery of his craft developed slowly; the works that propelled him into the first rank among Scandinavian authors did not appear until after the war. But many of the fundamental characteristics of his writing, its thematic focus and certain stylistic tendencies, were present from the beginning. He was, according to his wife, from first to last "intuitive, one who knows human nature, a poet and visionary." Vesaas has stated that his writing often took its inspiration from borderline experiences between dream and awakening. He had the habit of sleeping with paper and pencil by his bedside, ready to capture a dream vision before it was pushed aside by the precise and causal grammar of reason. Not surprisingly, children, mentally abnormal individuals, and even animals play a major role in Vesaas's poetic universe. Their experience is often close to the pre-linguistic and irrational mode of perception associated with dreams. Vesaas's growth as an author can be described as the gradual development of an adequate language through which to express the inexpressible. In his early work, Vesaas frequently failed to find the adequate expression, and his language and imagery were often derivative and sentimental.

And yet he was able right from the beginning to communicate his special way of seeing. Many years later, a neighbor in Vesaas's home village wrote him a letter responding to a TV program in which the author had criticized his own early work as "romantic."

The neighbor, who was a farmer and not a learned man, wrote:

> It seems to me you don't do justice to your first books. I never felt they were so romantic that it made any difference. Rather, I discovered in them something I had never grasped before. I am thinking of "Children of Man" and the marvelously alive landscape in that book. There was a feeling about it I call the folktale feeling because it was just like the landscape in a folktale, only brighter in tone. It seemed like a landscape mirrored in a window, somehow soft and mild, a "radiant" and good place to be. At times it made me feel as if I were somewhere high up in the sky looking down on the earth. . . . I knew that I had come across something similar in other writers, in some of Hamsun's books, for example, or in the works of Olav Duun and Selma Lagerlöf. But not until I read "Children of Man" did I grow fully aware of it. When I now think of your books, three always stand out: *The Seed,* "The House in Darkness," and *The Birds.* But then my thoughts always take me back to "Children of Man."

Like all of his early novels, "Children of Man" reflects the conservative religious environment the author encountered in his home village and at the folk high school. Thematically the novel is concerned with the Christian virtues of penance and sacrifice. The story concerns a woman named Liv ("life") who is loved by two men. She, in turn, loves one of them, Torstein, but she sacrifices her love for the sake of the other, Knut. Knut is burdened by a sense of guilt because his mother died the day he was born. When he meets Liv, he stares at her face "as at a vision"; it seems to him that his mother's spirit has returned in the young woman. Liv, who accepts Knut in order to help him in his spiritual agony, later dies in a blizzard. Knut and Torstein make a wrought-iron cross, which the two men carry across the mountains to Liv's home. In raising this memorial, they are able to be reconciled to her death and find peace. In casting Liv in the role of the madonnalike woman who gives up her own life for the sake of another, the author not only reflects idealized pietistic attitudes that were quite common in the rural communities of Norway during the early twentieth century, but also continues the Romantic view of women of which we find many examples in nineteenth-century Norwegian literature; for instance, in Henrik Ibsen's *Peer Gynt,* a favorite of Vesaas. In his later work Vesaas draws a more realistic image of women, but in general they continue to play a nurturing, life-bearing role—although there are some notable examples to the contrary, such as the emotionally disturbed Jorunn in *Tårnet* (The Tower, 1948) and the nameless woman in *Brannen* (The Fire, 1961) who kills her sheep from some inner, nameless compulsion.

In Vesaas's second novel, *Sendemann Huskuld* (Huskuld the Herald, 1924), the religious theme of sacrifice and selfless love is combined with the motif of the journey or quest, a motif that has a central place in a number of Vesaas's novels. Huskuld is a simple and naive man who lives on his small, isolated farm. The birds in the woods are his only companions and he raises grain to feed them. A gypsy woman and her little son, Ingebjønn, seek shelter at the farm one winter night, and when the woman leaves the next morning, Huskuld takes care of the abandoned child. But in the spring the woman returns to claim her son, and in his grief Huskuld sets out to find someone else to love and care for. On his journey he encounters many people, sees many children, has visions, some of which are reminiscent of the revelations of Saint John the Divine, and dreams of a future when all human sorrow and pain "shall be no more." Returned home, Huskuld finds the grain the birds depend on for their survival threatened by an early frost. He tries to save the grain, covering it with blankets and even his own clothes, and becomes fatally ill from exposure. A neighbor finds Huskuld, delirious and enraptured by the vision of a "tall and fair" woman beckoning to him from paradise.

In many ways the structure of Huskuld's symbolic journey is reminiscent of what Joseph Campbell has called the "heroic monomyth." In the myth the individual is called away from his everyday life on a quest that brings about a kind of initiation, intrinsically a self-transformation by which the personality is integrated into a higher truth. Huskuld, the childlike lover of the birds, thus becomes the "herald" sought out by others who come to him to learn about life. This archetypal pattern is prevalent in a number of works by Vesaas.

In 1925 Vesaas published *Grindegard. Morgonen* and in 1926 its sequel, *Grinde-kveld eller den gode engelen* (Evening at Grinde; or, The Good Angel). The novels describe two generations of a family that takes over a deserted farm. The theme of penance still plays an important role here, but of greater importance is the struggle with various nameless anxieties and obsessions. The father and later his son, Toremun, clear land as if possessed by it. In a powerful scene the boy drowns a lamb in a pond in response to urges he neither understands nor is able to control. When Toremun's sister dies, he somehow feels responsible and yearns to atone for her death as well as for the lamb's. The underlying psychological conflicts are never made fully clear, nor are they resolved. But the two novels represent important steps in the author's growing concern with the dangers of psychological compulsions and isolation, and the linkage of these themes with nature symbolism.

Vesaas's next novel, *Dei svarte hestane* (The Black Horses, 1928), presents the theme of psychological conflict with heightened realism and a greater degree of complexity. Ambros Førnes has married for a second time, but his wife loves another man, the impoverished village poet Bjørneskinn; she has accepted Førnes only to obey her parents. There are four children, two from each marriage. Ambros escapes from his marital troubles by investing all his passion in his four black horses, takes to racing and drinking, and eventually falls into complete financial ruin. Psychologically more convincing is the portrayal of little Kjell, which foreshadows many of Vesaas's moving portraits of children who respond to conflict by escaping into fantasy and isolation. Although only six years old, Kjell is acutely aware of the strife between his parents, and when his father dies, he withdraws from his mother almost to the point of psychosis. Characteristically for Vesaas, the struggle between rejecting and needing the mother's love is resolved when the boy hears a bird calling out in the forest: thinking that it is his mother calling, he responds to it spontaneously.

Dei svarte hestane was written in Munich. After his return to Norway, Vesaas started to work on the story of Klas Dyregodt, which eventually grew into four novels, *Fars reise* (Father's Journey, 1930), *Sigrid Stallbrokk* (1931), *Dei ukjende mennene* (The Unknown Men, 1932), and *Hjarta høyrer sine heimlandstonar* (The Heart Hears Its Native Music, 1938). More than anything Vesaas had written to date, these novels reveal the impact of the author's stay abroad. There is a sense of impending catastrophe reflecting the political turmoil Vesaas had been witness to in Germany, and the threat of war hanging over Europe. The central image expressing this sense of danger is the great river running through the valley where the action takes place, a river gathered into a huge lake by an old dam that seems on the point of breaking. The rising waters can be seen as an allegorical representation of destructive forces in man as much as a blind natural force. For Aslak Dyregodt, who is the illegimate Klas's father, they become the image of his own conscience burdened to the bursting point with a sense of guilt.

The action in the four novels takes place at four different points along the river: the farm Stallbrokk at the upper end of the river where Klas's alcoholic grandmother lives; the town below the dam that runs its sawmills with the power generated by the river but is always threatened by the collapse of the old dam; the home of the cabinetmaker who raised Klas and who lives in the valley just below the dam; and the dam itself, tended by Klas's father, Aslak Dyregodt. Aslak has fathered no children in his marriage but three outside it. After Klas was born, his mother, a young girl, threw herself into the river and drowned. Aslak lives in dread not only of the possibility that the weakened dam might give way, but also that he might break under the strain of internal pressures and open the floodgates himself, bringing destruction on the valley below.

In the first volume of the tetralogy, Klas gradually recognizes the irrational forces that have destroyed the lives of his grandmother, father, and mother. He feels helpless before the fate of his family. His sense of personal doom deepens when the dam almost breaks and his father, panic-stricken, has a heart attack and dies. In the second volume, Klas goes to live with his grandmother and finds out how she fell into despair after the death of her daughter. She has no hope for herself, but wanting the family to continue through Klas, she compels him to have a child with her servant girl, Eli. In the third volume, Klas learns that Eli's child was stillborn; in despair, he tries to throw himself into the blades of the sawmill and later attempts to hang himself in one of the abandoned barns at the bottom of the reservoir. The decrepit barns, which become visible whenever water is tapped from the dam, suggest a lost connection with the soil and the vital sources of life and growth. Klas's father, too, had a deep love for the soil, but he felt separated from it. The submerged fields and barns eloquently express Aslak's sense of futility and barrenness. And Klas, in trying to end his life in one of these barns, shows his own sense of barrenness is like his father's.

If Klas finally resists the urge to self-destruct that controls the lives of his grandmother, mother, and father, it is because of the intercession of a woman and the example of the "unknown men" of the third novel's title. Såve Dyregodt, Aslak's widow, quietly urges Klas to take responsibility for his fate. And although Klas at first rejects her words, they come back to him at the moment he is about to commit suicide. In a sudden flash he sees her radiant face and hears her speaking to him, and so he turns away from death. Having accepted responsibility for his own life, Klas learns about responsibility for others from Olav and Jørgen, the two men who take over tending the dam after Aslak's death. They are workers of the soil and possess a quiet, steadying faith in life Klas has not met before. But the true meaning of responsibility is made clear when Olav, in order to stop a potentially disastrous leak in the dam, plugs the hole with his own body and is drowned. The example of Olav teaches Klas to accept his place in life, and he takes charge of the dam himself.

The fourth and last volume of the Dyregodt tetralogy was published in 1938, six years after *Dei ukjende mennene.* In the meantime Vesaas not only authored three other novels, including *Det store spelet (The Great Cycle,* 1934), which marked his real breakthrough as a major Norwegian writer, but there occurred dramatic changes in his life. The suicidal tendencies and the religious sentimentality and exaggerated nature symbolism in some of Vesaas's early works reflect his own inner struggle to free himself from the demands of a restrictive tradition that continued to burden him in spite of the fact that his family was supportive of his writing. The sense of isolation and separation from the regenerative sources of life faced by Klas and other characters in his novels parallels Vesaas's own experience; it is well known that there were times when he, too, was close to suicide. However, he was able to free himself from despair and self-destructive compulsions through his writing and in no small measure through his marriage in 1934 to Halldis Moren.

Thus, when Vesaas returned to the story of Klas Dyregodt in *Hjarta høyrer sine heimlandstoner,* he leads him beyond the mere acceptance of responsibility to a true integration of his life with that of others through love. Artistically, the final volume, which is by far the longest, is the least satisfactory of the tetralogy. The action tends to be even more repetitive and static than in the previous three volumes, and the optimistic conclusion stands in startling contrast to the earlier sense of doom and hopelessness. The mysticism of death of the earlier novels has been replaced by a mysticism of life, a vitalistic worldview based on the biological rhythms of the seasonal cycle.

In 1933 Vesaas published the remarkable novel *Sandeltreet* (The Sandalwood Tree), which, in spite of its macabre story, expresses a fundamental affirmation of life. In the account of a pregnant woman who knows that she will die when her child is born, Vesaas celebrates the mysterious and ineffable bond between life and death. The mother, able to get ready to give life while also preparing for death, stands in contrast to her husband, a writer who does not write. Heeding the wish of the mother, the father and their two half-grown children set out on a journey that ends when the child is born and the mother suffers a fatal hemorrhage. During this journey through the countryside and to the city, the family learns to see the world with new eyes. The mother is identified with the image of the sandalwood tree, fragrant, mysterious, at times unknown to them, at times protective, "drawing into itself both heaven and earth."

The theme of a journey through which the individual is initiated into an expansion of consciousness and an enhanced sense of being is made explicit in *Sendemann Huskuld* and *Sandeltreet,* but as a symbolic structure it is present in the majority of Vesaas's novels. In *The Great Cycle,* published in 1934, it is tied to the integration of the individual with the biological cycle of the soil and of animal and human life. In a letter to Halldis Moren Vesaas in the fall of 1933, Vesaas reported happily that he was working on "a great book about Mother Earth . . . and about women and fertility and life." And later he wrote, "Yes, this is a wonderful subject, all about the earth and putting down roots. I feel somehow that I am going home inside, that I know where I belong."

The Great Cycle can be said to have two main characters. On the one hand the story concerns the development of Per Bufast (the name means "settled," "rooted") from childhood until he gets married and takes over the family farm; on the other, it evokes the laws and rhythms of the earth on which the life of plants, animals, and human beings depend. Per is frightened by the demands of farm life, and he yearns to escape. But eventually he realizes that the same life-giving rhythms of the earth also pulsate through him, and in submitting to the "great cycle" in awe and responsibility, he finds his own identity.

The novel is structured in two parts, each ending with a kind of initiation. The first part climaxes in Per's confirmation at age fifteen, when he supposedly becomes an adult. However, although Per tried "with the best will in the world to feel what he should [during the ritual of confirmation], he *knew* that he did not feel what was expected of him, and that was bitter, but not unexpected." The real initiation cannot occur until Per has changed inside and become able to respond with affirmation to the unspoken question of whether he "loves the earth." Whenever Per feels connected with life, his feeling is identified with his mother and young aunt. They give birth to children and help the animals bring forth their offspring; they nourish and heal and order the rhythm of days, weeks, and seasons in a meaningful whole. Per's father, by contrast, is a threatening figure, combining explosive strength (connected with the task of slaughtering the animals each season). The father's love for the earth is passionate and blind. Whenever he talks to Per, it seems to the boy that the earth itself is opening up, "a gaping mouth that said crushing words and then shut never to speak again." Sometime after Per's confirmation, his father has a serious accident and Per must take his place working the farm, making decisions, and, most importantly, taking responsibility for the slaughter. Paradoxically, it is the latter that teaches Per that "one couldn't follow the dictates of one's own heart, that the farm decided and made strict laws." And thus when Per obeys the laws of the farm and kills an old horse that can no longer work, an incredible change comes over him, a change that amounts to a real initiation:

> At that moment something incomprehensible happened. Per thought that he sensed the earth in a way he had not done before. Wet awakening earth beneath mild, gray air. The whole meadow covered with a slight haze, a thin fog. And in front of him, on this earth, lay Goldie asleep forever. Per stood trembling and saw it all. He felt that he loved the earth. He became conscious of it. He was bound to it completely. To the earth. It seemed to him that his eyes could see and his ears hear more clearly and that his heart had become more open. He stood in front of the shot horse, filled with one thought: he loved the earth—and air and water, and the changes in the weather. It was right for him to stay here for the rest of his days.
>
> Strange that it was Goldie who made this clear to him just now. Goldie, who was lying here dead but without spreading fear around himself, and who seemed to be lying in the only place where he could rest peacefully: the place where he had worked so long.
>
> Per took in an enormous landscape: the blue line of mountains; the wooded hillsides; the river; the meadow and the field, and gray, wet air. And the big, yellow body of the dead horse.

The second of the Bufast novels, *Kvinnor ropar heim* (Women Call: Come Home), was published in 1935. It describes Per Bufast's mature years, his marriage, the birth of his children, the aging of his parents and eventually of himself. The book was written at a time when the author's wife was expecting her first child, and Vesaas confessed later that he thought the book flawed by a "kind of childbed mania" reflecting his own happiness.

With the completion of the Bufast series, Vesaas finished his long apprenticeship. He was now a successful and acknowledged author, and he had found his own voice based on an intuitive grasp of reality expressed in an elliptic, symbolic style in which nature imagery plays a central role. His subject matter was mostly the life of ordinary people in a rural setting, while thematically he was concerned with the universal problems of human alienation and isolation and with the quest for personal identity in the context of social responsibility.

NOVELS: WORLD WAR II TO 1968

The second phase of Vesaas's authorship began with a series of allegorical novels mirroring the invasion of Norway by Germany during World War II. The author discovered that the depiction of the irrationality of the war years required a modification of his style. As he stated in the preface to *Kimen* (*The Seed,* 1940), his "new way of writing" did not reflect a literary program, but resulted from "another way of reacting to things" precipitated by the catastrophe of the war. His prose of this period is even more spare and concentrated, at times surrealistic; often the boundaries between poetry and prose disappear altogether, while the structure of his novels approximates that of the drama. The change is also noticeable in Vesaas's language. Until then he had written a conservative Nynorsk that was strongly colored by dialect. By removing these dialect elements from his language and adopting the new grammatical and orthographic guidelines set down by the Language Commission in 1938, the author gave notice that henceforth his books were not to be rooted in the local milieu as they had been up to the Bufast series.

Norway was occupied in April 1940. Vesaas wrote *The Seed* the same summer, and it was published in the fall, the last of his books to appear in print until the end of the war.

The Seed deals with the problems of violence and responsibility. The instinct to kill when threatened is identified with the animal aspect in us, while the ability to accept moral and legal responsibility for our acts is what makes us essentially human. The story tells of a young man who has been mentally unbalanced by an industrial accident and comes to a quiet and idyllic island in search of rest and healing. When he witnesses a gruesome killing among animals, however, he panics and kills a young girl he happens to meet; then he himself is clubbed to death by a posse of islanders. Having satisfied their desire for revenge, the islanders must face their own consciences. They keep watch over the dead man for a night and emerge the next day ready to accept responsibility for the animal instinct that turned them into a lawless mob.

The novel is structured in two parts. The first (entitled "The Pit") demonstrates the primitive core of violence hidden in the human self below a thin layer of civilization; the second ("The Seed in the Dust") acknowledges the sources of renewal and transcendence that are also found within. The killing of the deranged man takes place before the blood-red wall of the barn where the islanders then hold their vigil over the corpse. This building, the largest on the island, is reminiscent of the whale that swallowed the biblical Jonah. Like Jonah, the islanders are swallowed by a monster and after their night journey into the depths of themselves they are spat out again, transformed. Through the small windows the men can see a great light flooding from a room in the farmhouse where the mother of the dead girl has surrounded her with many burning candles. To the sufferers in the dark barn the sight suggests a luminous mystical ship:

> When they looked out through the vents they saw something strange. From the barn with all its rooms and stalls and burdens, the shining light up at the house appeared a joyous sight that was almost unbelievable. From the window streamed a light the like of which they had never seen. A joyous, luminous ship sailing away.
> Look at the ship.
> They could see it when they just turned their heads a little. It was not for them. We are HERE. Bound hand and foot. WE are not sailing.

In many religious traditions the ship represents the transition from ignorance to knowledge, from death to rebirth, from sin to salvation. For the penitents in the barn the transition becomes possible once they accept personal responsiblity for the murder. When the sun rises the next morning, the islanders emerge from the barn. The laws of society will now claim the men, but the essential moral debt has been paid.

The Seed thus deals with the sources of violence in all human beings. Read allegorically against the background of the Nazi occupation of Norway, the book apppears pacifist in its refusal to see war as an attack provoking a justified counterattack. By contrast, in his next book, *Huset i mørkret* (*The House in the Dark*, 1945), the author clearly identifies with the resistance movement directed against totalitarian control of the country. And yet, this is not a political novel. Vesaas is less concerned with the historical situation of the Nazi invasion than he is with the perennial moral problem of justifying violence and killing for the sake of restoring freedom to the oppressed. Some of the men in the resistance choose violent and others nonviolent means of fighting evil. There are also individuals who try to evade the conflict altogether and withdraw into their private worlds. Consistent with Vesaas's ethos however, their refusal to accept responsibility excludes them from any meaningful participation in society. The author is furthermore concerned with the mentality and fate of the Nazi collaborator. Although such a betrayal is not condoned, the collaborator is seen as the product of a social structure in which individuals like him are consistently accorded low status, thus making them susceptible to the false ideals of fascism. The collaborator casts his lot with the invaders, but in secret he admires the resistance fighters. After he is rebuffed by the resistance group, he denounces their leader, who is then tortured to death by the invaders. The collaborator in turn is executed by the resistance group. Vesaas also raises the question of how those who have chosen the means of war to defeat the oppressors can build a future life based on peace. The clergyman with whom the leader of the resistance group discusses this problem many times ponders this question:

> Now it is hardness that is required. But then goodness will be needed, goodness that remains forever. It is only in this night of darkness that we must say and do things that make our hearts ache. We must, for the sake of those who come after us. But perhaps we will have become useless once this night has passed.

The House in the Dark is an abstract novel, both in setting and in characterization. As the title implies, the central image is a darkened house occupied by the invaders. Anyone resisting control from the center is forcibly brought there by a snakelike vehicle moving through corridors that are dimly lit by flaming arrows. The whole house shakes and trembles much like the dam in the Dyregodt tetralogy. The characters are types rather than individuals, referred to only by first name or occupation. Thus the collaborator is merely called "arrow polisher," the invaders are named "arrow bearers" (literally "decorated with arrows"), the clergyman is "the clergyman," and so on. But in spite of the overall tendency toward abstraction, the personal conflicts faced by the various characters are presented with complexity and depth.

Vesaas's next novel, *Bleikeplassen* (*The Bleaching Yard,* 1946), was also written during the war. Like *The Seed,* which was originally conceived as a play, *The Bleaching Yard* is dramatic in structure. The action in the former novel takes place in one location, the island, and within the span of a day and a night. *The Bleaching Yard* spans two nights and the day in between. In *The Seed* the controlling images are the darkened barn contrasting with the luminous ship and the rising sun. In *The Bleaching Yard* a parallel contrast between light and darkness is symbolized by the white washing

hanging on the clothesline at night. The story, one of Vesaas's most mysterious and unsettling, involves a man's obsession with an unspoken passion. Johan Tander has a good relationship with his wife, Elise, but he falls in love with his co-worker, Vera, a love he does not acknowledge. When another man claims Vera's attentions, however, Johan finds himself trapped by compulsive thoughts of murder. His wife resorts to the startling stratagem of writing the words "Nobody cares about Johan Tander" on a wall where everyone can see it. When Johan discovers who wrote this, the obvious falsehood of the statement jolts him out of his isolation. He talks to his wife as well as to Vera. But his rival and two companions, wanting to cow Johan, throw him into one of his own laundry tubs, and he dies from shock.

A third novel written during the war and published later is *Tårnet* (The Tower, 1948). The contrast between the harmony of a family living close to the soil on their farm and the neurosis of the family of a car-wrecker who compulsively builds a huge tower from used car parts would seem particularly relevant today. And yet *Tårnet* is not nearly as convincing as *The Bleaching Yard,* in which symbolism and realism are fused more successfully. The reaction of the car-wrecker's wife when her little child dies, possibly from a tetanus infection after he cut himself on scrap metal, seems exaggerated and unrealistic. The mother withdraws from the family, giving herself over to her grief to the point of derangement. She frantically searches for the piece of scrap on which the child may have cut himself. Eventually she stumbles upon a wasps' nest and is stung to death. In spite of powerfully evocative images, the novel lacks the structural and stylistic unity of Vesaas's best work.

In 1950 Vesaas published *Signalet* (The Signal), a book the author later characterized as a kind of "problem child." There is a sense of stagnation and hopelessness in the novel that is never resolved. The fear and irrational shame expressed are perhaps a reflection of feelings shared by many people throughout the world when the first atomic bombs were dropped over Hiroshima and Nagasaki. It is difficult to tell precisely what the author had in mind because the degree of abstraction in *Signalet* is greater than in any previous or subsequent novel by Vesaas. The story, if we can call it that, describes a trainful of passengers waiting for a departure signal that never comes, and nobody knows why. The passengers, referred to by stylized names such as Mr. Power, Mr. Top, Mrs. All-Paid, Mrs. Scrape, or by occupational titles such as "the porter," "the engineer," or "the stationmaster," are prevented from communicating with each other by their mutual indifference and self-absorption. There is a faint glimpse of hope at the conclusion of the novel, when one of the passengers suddenly announces that his wife has given birth to a child.

Vesaas was aware that *Signalet* was an obscure book, lacking the kind of immediacy of imagery characterizing his authorship as a whole. Paul la Cour, the Danish writer and a close friend of the author's, felt that in this novel Vesaas had "exceeded the limits" of symbolic expression. But Vesaas nevertheless regarded it as an important experiment: "So-called incomprehensible novels need to be written too, I believe. One must find new paths forward."

In contrast to *Signalet,* Vesaas's next novel, *Vårnatt* (*Spring Night,* 1954), was an unmitigated success. The fourteen-year-old Hallstein and his eighteen-year-old sister, Sissel, are alone at home one night when they receive unexpected visitors. A car breaks down on the road and the passengers, two married couples and a teen-age girl, seek shelter at their house. The older couple, Hjalmar and Kristine, despise each other; the wife has escaped into a kind of paralysis making it impossible for her to walk or to speak to her husband, even though she is quite capable of talking to Hallstein, for example. The younger couple, Hjalmar's son, Karl, and his wife, Grete, are equally neurotic. They are expecting a child, which is born that night. Hjalmar, who cannot drive but nevertheless tries to fix the car, accidentally causes the vehicle to crash into the house, and Kristine is killed, apparently from a heart attack.

For Sissel and especially for Hallstein, life is changed dramatically by the singular events of this spring night. They are suddenly brought out of adolescence into the world of adults. Each of the visitors confides in Hallstein, seeking understanding and help. To Hallstein the seventeen-year-old Gudrun appears to be the embodiment of a girl by the same name who had lived in his imagination. The awakening of latent sexual feelings between them is comparable to an initiation. Similarly Sissel's relation to her boyfriend, Tore, is propelled beyond the exploratory stage of teasing and bickering by her encounter with Karl.

The action of the novel, spanning only one night, is taut and concentrated. The proximity of death and birth, dream and urgent reality, instills a sense of crisis that is filled with possibilities for change and growth. The images, sounds, and fragrances of a rainy but warm spring night are fused with private symbols, such as the pair of snails representing the security and permanence of childhood Hallstein is loathe to relinquish, or the imagined serpent representing the alluring danger Hallstein encounters in an angelica glade he has planted in the woods. *Spring Night* has become a popular youth book in Norway.

In 1957 Vesaas published *Fuglane* (*The Birds*), yet another high point in his authorship. The novel has its origin in a remark Vesaas overheard as early as 1933 about stunted spruce trees growing in a bog. During the war Vesaas wrote a short story (published in revised form in 1952) in which the impoverished trees that never fully mature are associated with Mattis, a half-wit, and his sister, Hege. Mattis is incapable of doing a normal day's work, and by and large it is Hege who supports them with her knitting. But while Mattis does not function satisfactorily in the workaday world of "normal" adults, he is gifted with an unusual sensitivity to his environment, and this in fact is part of his handicap. When a man hires him to fell some birches in the woods, he experiences the forest around him with an intensity and clarity that give him great joy but also exhaust him quickly. Angered by his lack of strength and practical purpose, he chops down one of the stunted spruce trees he sees in a bog nearby, all the while sensing that the act denotes a kind of symbolic suicide.

In speaking of Mattis, Vesaas called him a "self-portrait with certain reservations"; he also referred to himself as Mattis's "father and brother." Mattis, like Vesaas, possesses the gift of vision, of an intuitive apprehension of reality; but unlike the author, Mattis is not able to give objective expression to his perceptions. For him the "unsayable" remains just that, locking him in a private world he cannot communicate to others. Mattis is thus another, and perhaps the most moving, example in all of Vesaas's works of sheer irredeemable human isolation.

In *The Birds* dreaming becomes the chief means by which Mattis compensates for his deficiency. In his dreams he is strong, witty, and sexually attractive. One day when a woodcock traces its mating track over Mattis and Hege's house, he takes it as a sign that his dream of the unattainable will be fulfilled. There are two events that spell disappointment of his dream, however, a disappointment Mattis is not able to adjust to and which thus leads to his tragic death. The first is that Mattis foolishly tells about the woodcock to one of the "normal" young men in the village, who promptly shoots the bird. In Mattis's experience the woodcock is the only one to understand who he, Mattis, is. When Mattis finds the imprints of the bird's feet and beak in the wet soil of a nearby marsh, he reads them as a graceful, dancelike message addressed to himself: "You are you," the bird had written.

Mattis is also instrumental in bringing about the second event. To keep him occupied, Hege suggests that he become a ferryman, knowing full well that normally there would not be anyone needing a ride across the lake. But one day a lumberman happens to appear on the other shore, and Mattis ferries him over and brings him to Hege. The lumberman and Hege fall in love, and just as Mattis is incapable of accepting the death of the woodcock, he cannot accept Hege's right to a life of her own. The loss of the bird and of Hege are fused together in a bewildered cry for help that is at the same time an expression of his dim understanding that the only way out lies in ending his life:

> Down at the shore Mattis had many new thoughts—about eyes under stones:
> There's lid upon lid and stone upon stone, but it can never be hidden.
> The surface of the water was white, he looked out across it. He thought in confusion:
> Help Mattis!
> Why?
> He gave a start.
> No, no, he mumbled meaninglessly and grabbed the oars.
> Lead in the wing, he thought, and stone upon stone, over the eyes.

But Mattis cannot by himself make the decision to take his own life. He leaves it to the water and the wind, that is, to nature. On a cloudless, sunny day he takes the boat out on the lake, kicks a hole in the bottom and floats on the oars. Eventually the wind rises, whipping up the waves. Desperately Mattis calls out Hege's name and then his own, his voice sounding like the "strange scream of a bird."

Vesaas's next novel, *Brannen* (The Fire, 1961), is another one among those the author called "incomprehensible" but defended as an important experiment in the antirealistic, symbolic style. The main character in this novel is a bookish young man called Jon, who lives cut off from society and in constant anxiety about the demands others may make on him. The "fire" of the title symbolizes suffering, his own and that of other people he encounters. These include a woman who tortures her sheep to death by confining them in a mountain cleft, where they cannot escape the heat reflected from the rock walls; and a man in the woods who is obsessed by his work of cutting trees into shining white disks that cover the forest floor; his little son takes Jon's hand and leads him to his father, but Jon cannot prevent the boy from eventually being buried by the disks and dying. Then he meets the owner of a meadow who burns to death in a mysterious fire. He meets a truck driver who gives him a ride in the middle of the night, only to force him to watch as he deliberately smashes his vehicle into a wooden house by the side of the road, killing the man inside. Jon joins a search party looking for a girl apparently lost in the woods; he stumbles upon her but cannot rescue her from her own desire to die. These are stations of suffering on an internal journey through which Jon comes face to face with the irrational and destructive sides of human existence.

But there are also positive experiences along the way: the repeated meetings with the woman's daughter; the lovers he overhears in a meadow; the people he watches carrying frost-chilled swallows into a barn to revive them; the brief contact with the unknown man he leans up against by the roadside one night; the marsh hen that keeps him from falling into the bottomless marsh. These experiences teach Jon about the possibility of love and concern between people and all living beings. The girl dying in the forest makes Jon promise that he will tell the others why she has chosen death: thus she will not have given up her life in vain. In assuming this responsibility, Jon finally opens himself up to life, accepting what it has to offer, both good and bad.

Jon's journey is dreamlike and abstract. Besides the fire there are several images in the novel we recognize from other works by Vesaas: the barn in which Jon holds a vigil over the dead man, the symbolic storm that makes the earth tremble, the "eye" watching Jon, mirrors reflecting aspects of himself, the serpent. And Jon, too, is a characteristic figure in many of Vesaas's writings, a "witness who feels empathy and a desire to help but is powerless." As

Halldis Moren Vesaas has put it, Jon is in many ways another self-portrait of the author, reflecting his own bewilderment in the face of the suffering he finds in human existence.

Is-slottet (*The Ice Palace*, 1963), like *Spring Night*, has a special appeal to young readers. It describes two eleven-year-old girls on the threshold of puberty. One of the girls, Unn, the daughter of an unwed mother who has recently died and a stranger in the village, cannot break through the isolation she feels imprisoning her; she dies in the "ice palace." The other girl, Siss, who comes from a secure home of loving parents, is outgoing and popular among her peers. A friendship is about to blossom between the two girls when Unn disappears, and Siss is thrown into an emotional crisis from which she only gradually recovers.

The palace of ice is both a symbolic and a tangible place. The story occurs between late winter and early spring. In a waterfall near the village the frozen water has gradually built up into a many-faceted structure of shining surfaces and luminous inner chambers. Unn knows that the frozen waterfall is dangerous, but she is fatally attracted to it.

When Unn comes to the village to live with her aunt, she is stamped an outsider because she has no parents. Siss makes contact with her, she is invited to Siss's home, and on this occasion the girls undress and together look at each other in a mirror. There is no sexual curiosity in this; rather it is an unspoken search for personal identity. Later Unn asks Siss whether she noticed anything unusual about her body when they were naked. It is not clear what she means by this, but she seems to refer to something in her past that burdens her. Siss is confused by the question and later grows frightened. Unn feels a similar ambivalence, which is the reason why she does not go to school the next day but rather walks by herself to the frozen waterfall. She finds an opening in the ice and enters without really knowing why. Entranced she moves further and further inside while growing increasingly numb with cold. The last thing she is conscious of is the huge "eye" of the winter sun filling the wall of the ice palace with its light.

The paradisiacal condition of childlike innocence and friendship described in the first of the three parts of the novel (entitled "Unn and Siss") ends abruptly with Unn's disappearance. In the second part ("Snow-covered Bridges") Siss withdraws into herself from a sense of loyalty to her missing friend. In a way she too is imprisoned in the ice palace. In the final section ("Wood Winds") Siss emerges and harmony is restored at a higher level of understanding and maturity. She is helped in accepting her friend's death as irrevocable by Unn's aunt, by the comradeship of her schoolmates, and by her growing feelings for a boy in the village. As always in Vesaas's works, personal growth is tied to suffering as well as to the concern and support the individual receives from others.

The allegorical function of images such as the ice palace notwithstanding, the plot and style of the novel are fundamentally realistic. Nevertheless there are a number of passages that have no direct bearing on the development of the story but deepen it symbolically. The most striking of these is the brief chapter describing a bird of prey swooping down again and again before the face of the frozen waterfall, perhaps because it sees the dead girl inside the translucent ice:

He was caught by his own freedom here. Could not stop. What he saw bewildered him.

He would cut himself to death in his swooping fall—hard as glass where it showed the least. The air split before it. He was bound to fall asunder.

The next novel by Vesaas, *Bruene* (*The Bridges*, 1966), also describes adolescents, two girls and a boy, all three of whom are eighteen years old. Aud and Torvil are childhood friends, and they are facing the decision whether to marry. Unexpectedly they meet Valborg, who has just given birth to an illegitimate child and has killed it in secret. Torn between the obligation to report the killing and

a desire to help the young mother, Aud and Torvil become involved with Valborg's struggle for survival. Torvil feels a growing attraction to Valborg, and in the end it is Valborg who helps the other two overcome the deepening crisis in their relationship.

In *The Bridges* Vesaas goes even further in combining a realistic plot with intermittent, abstract, prose poems in order to mirror the experience of the three young people on a symbolic level. The central image in the novel is the river, a symbol of life and of human personality. The surface of the rushing water is bright and reflects the light of the sun, but deeper down at the bottom of the river there are darkness and impenetrable layers of mud. Across this river the three protagonists build "bridges" of communication. Other important images are the wind heard when characters cross the bridge, a wind that really exists inside themselves; and the dog, an image of isolation, perhaps even of death. At times the dog appears as if from nowhere and licks the hand of someone crossing the bridge. When this happens, the wind can no longer be heard singing, and the bridge suddenly appears but a fragile span across gaping jaws.

In Vesaas's last major work of fiction, *Båten om kvelden* (*The Boat in the Evening*, 1968), the abstraction of the plot is carried to such a level that the work can hardly be regarded as a novel. Nonetheless it is organized in chapters, the first and last of which make clear references to the relationship of the author to his father and mother. Vesaas has called *The Boat in the Evening* an "inner autobiography," and his wife suggests (quoting an unnamed Danish critic) that the structure of the book can be compared to a triptych, "of which the center panel is a synthesis of adult life, while the two side panels represent childhood" and youth.

In the opening chapter the conflict between father and son is portrayed in a scene in which the boy cannot fulfill his father's demand to wash out a wound on a horse's foot with his own urine. Halldis Moren Vesaas has explained the boy's reaction:

That the boy cannot produce what according to ancient tradition is required to wash out the wound obviously has not only physical reasons. His mind protests, as does his body, against an action that would have felt like an initiation. In refusing to carry it out, he refuses to step into the role of his father and of many generations before him. He does not want it. He understands dimly that he wants something different and he conjures up—as sort of helpers—a ring of dream animals, calling them forth with such intensity that he can smell them. What may appear as impotence and failure is thus in reality the basis for a victory, a manifestation of his will to go his own way. No matter how much this whole scene borders on the unsayable, I don't believe Tarjei has ever expressed more clearly how necessary it was for him to break out of the confines of his family and find the road he was meant to take in life.

In the second chapter there occurs the initiation the boy does long for and that puts him in touch with those sources in nature from which the creativity of the poet arises. In a bog where he witnesses the mating dance of cranes, he becomes one with something much larger than himself, something "acted out in bird shape." When he touches one of the cranes, the bird strikes him with its beak, "carving a strip of fire down my face."

In the fourth chapter there occurs yet another initiation by fire. Here the fire is partly identified with the erotic, represented by a naked girl standing on the far side of the sound; partly with the sun, represented by flaming horses passing by and through the self and making it luminous, radiant, and changed.

In the eight chapters constituting the midsection of the triptych there is no overt plot. Rather these chapters amount to lyrical and highly evocative meditations on the inclusive and difficult concerns the author raises in the course of a long life and authorship: the passionate dream of a fully creative life; the fear of self-abandonment and suicide, of a life wasted in meaningless activities, of violence and war; the limitation of words in saying the "unsayable"; the despair of human isolation, the longing for fellowship and love, and the risks of openness and vulnerability; and finally, resignation and acceptance of approaching death. These themes are expressed in familiar images: the stream symbolizing both life and the many-faceted mirror of human beings; the boat representing the poet sailing on the stream, and also the boat of death sailing from the familiar shores of the human landscape toward the sea of transcendence; the threatening but alluring serpent that always "remains under the heel"; the mountain face representing the closed self, a "mouth that will not speak"; and the girl or young woman representing all that is healing and nurturing but also unattainable. The center section concludes with two short chapters evoking the most ordinary experiences that are also the most elusive, such as the fragrance of the air just before rainfall, the feel of a familiar stone on the path by the house, the sounds and smells of the morning at sunrise, or a simple daily activity, such as fetching the filled pail from the milk stop by the road.

The third panel of the triptych takes us back to the adolescence of the author. The chapter entitled "Tonen" (The Melody) focuses on the author's mother, her untiring commitment to the welfare of the family and the farm, on her love of music and sociability, and, not least, on the hidden conflict between her and the author's father, who is here described as softer and more conciliatory than in the opening chapter. The mother emerges as the individual who finds meaning by fully accepting whatever life has to offer:

> The hidden in the melody, it surrounds her. The man she is bound to. The children who have sprung from her womb. The severe law entwined in darkness with the melody to bear the burdens one has shouldered—it is all there.
>
> She stands at the center of life, with all her being.

The Boat in the Evening is framed by a prologue in the form of two poems and an epilogue. The first poem introduces central images: the dream, the river, the heart living by the shore of the stream, the serpent, the watchful eye, and the child. The second poem speaks of the "splintered image," which perhaps can be read as a reference to Vesaas's authorship in general or to the associative structure of this particular work. The poem also speaks of the heart that is split in two and the boat traveling down the river "for the sake of unanswerable riddles."

The epilogue returns to the image of the stream that now flows below the earth and makes the ground tremble. The poet has learned that more important than finding answers to the riddle is to be a part of the stream of life and to listen to its pulse: "I am listening. I am, and I hear the stream." The river has turned, it is now flowing back, toward the night and death. The final image expresses a calm and all-embracing awareness: "The night opens its clear vault, and your own eye opens its. All eyes are huge in the night, and opened wide. They are dark out to their edges."

SHORT STORIES

In subject, theme, and style, the short stories of Vesaas closely parallel his novels. The title of his first collection, *Klokka i haugen* (The Bell in the Knoll, 1929), is a reference to the world of the "invisible folk" who, according to popular belief, inhabit the hills, forests, and lakes surrounding villages. In "Signe Ton," for example, a story about a young girl who is just fully grown and ready to get married, the motif of the bell sounding in the hill is related to her anticipation that "a young man will fetch me and renew life in some stagnant house." The invisible folk "in the hill" are nature beings connected with the biological laws governing life on the soil. These are the inexorable laws Signe Ton must bow to, just as Per Bufast does in *The Great Cycle.*

Another remarkable story in Vesaas's earliest collection is "Aldri fortelle det" ("Never Tell It"), which explores the special, prerational perceptiveness of the very young. Three children find a newborn thrush that has fallen out of its nest. It is still without feathers and they can feel the heart beating against its skin. They are frightened; it seems to them that the bird "was not yet finished inside, that it was being gotten ready at that very moment." Awed, the children put the bird down and withdraw to wait. But by the time they return, ants have killed the bird and are devouring it.

By far the majority of the stories in Vesaas's four collections are studies of children, animals, rural life, and the interdependence of man and nature. In *Leiret og hjulet* (The Clay and the Wheel, 1936), several stories are closely connected with the Dyregodt and Bufast cycles the author was working on during the 1930's. They emphasize the ritualistic aspects of working the harvest and the consecrating effect of this work on both young and old.

Two of the stories in *Vindane* (The Winds, 1952) reflect the experience of the war. In "Kornet over havet" (Grain Across the Sea) the miller, through whose hands passes all the grain produced in the village, is subjected to disturbing hallucinations of emaciated strangers scraping bits of flour from the walls of his mill. And in "Naken" (Naked) a newborn child has been abandoned in the forest by its young mother, who appparently commits suicide because she is rejected by her family. Not only is the child illegitimate, but its father is a member of the German occupation forces. The focus of the story, however, is on the child. Although there is little reason to expect that it will survive, we are left with a paradoxical sense of optimism because of the innocent affirmation of life represented by the child in the conclusion:

> He is alive. The sun is a fire someplace and is there for everyone. He wakes up again in a renewed, blinding light. He did not die this night either. He is lying on his back, waiting for something he does not understand. He is seven times nameless, but still he waits. With his numb

finger he makes a numb motion. A tiny bow in the huge vault of the sky—but it was from east to west nonetheless.

Vindane also contains the story "Tusten" (The Nit-Wit), which forms the background to the novel *The Birds,* as well as the extraordinary "Den ville ridaren" (The Wild Rider). In "Tusten" dream and poetic vision are the special gift of a retarded man incapable of ordinary human relationships and social responsibilities. In "Den ville ridaren," by contrast, it is the daily routine of family commitments that drains the creative energies of a writer. But when the writer's six-year-old son suddenly becomes ill and dies, the father's sorrow is eclipsed by the certainty that he will once more be able to write. Although he feels deep shame, he accepts the death of the child as a sacrifice reviving the wellspring of inspiration in himself.

The story echoes deeply felt personal concerns of the author. The necessity to break out of the traditional mold of a farmer's life in order to become a writer for a long time saddled Vesaas with the sense of isolation and suicidal urges that nearly ended his life during the 1920's. Suicide is also briefly on the father's mind in "Den ville ridaren." He yearns for the simple tasks of the men and women he sees laboring in the fields outside his window, and for the "seething strength" of the bull he and his son pass by on the way to the hospital. The image of the wild rider in the title of the story refers to a configuration in the wood of a door in the writer's home. He had imagined his son riding on a wild stallion, a heroic figure conquering life. Instead, the child succumbs to illness. But at the moment of death, a light in the child's eyes calls up the image of the rider on the wild stallion, and the father feels an irrepressible surge of creative energy:

> Then he is alone. With the wild rider. Confused—
> Suddenly he is in the middle of something unthinkable.

No, not now! he thinks. Not here!

But it has him in its power. Bewildered and ashamed, he feels it coming. Instead of dark grief, he feels a torrent of something washing his sorrow away. Images and scenes and colors and sounds he must put into words as quickly as they well forth! Because now they are here. They have come back. He has his old ability back and important things to tell about. Instead of the empty rushing in his skull there are flashing lights that must have words—and the words are there, dancing and resounding in confusion. Not for his life can he stem the tide.

The image of the wild rider recalls the Nordic god Othin, divine horseman, master of the elements, and personification of the creative unconscious. It also recalls the ecstatic Dionysus whom Friedrich Nietzsche identified with the "madness" of poetic inspiration. In submitting to the power of creativity within himself, the father becomes the poet. One identity is sacrificed for and excludes the other. In his own life Vesaas achieved a more harmonious balance between his role of husband and father and that of the writer. And yet, as his wife says, Vesaas's creativity unfolded in an inner space where he remained essentially alone: "Basically he always lived in a ring of isolation. But we were supposed to be there, the rest of us, close by the outside of the ring."

In Vesaas's final collection, *En vakker dag* (One Fine Day, 1959), we find the most abstract of his short stories, "Det snør og snør" ("Snow"). There is no plot to speak of, but there is a series of expressionistic images cohering to a pattern of meaning. We see a house inhabited by a nameless man. Snow is falling continuously, and its weight threatens to crush the roof and walls. The only defense the man has is the music coming from within himself. There is a contrast between the man's desperate resistance and the calm submission of the river curving past the house:

> Nothing sticks up resisting or making noise. The immense flowing deep knows nothing of resistance. The snow floats down but cannot be

seen, cannot stay on the surface, is carried away in a moment by the current.

It snows and snows.

The man is cut off from contact with the outside world by the "scissors." Yet the story does not end in hopelessness. The man is incapable of calm submission like the river, but as long as there is music within, the house will not collapse: "It snows and snows down over the unbending will. . . . The house stands there and plays, cannot stop being a house."

DRAMATIC WORKS

Vesaas published three full-length stage plays, *Guds bustader* (The Dwelling Places of God, 1925), *Ultimatum* (1934), and *Morgonvinden* (The Morning Wind, 1947). His first play, "Presten" (the Pastor), premiered in Oslo in 1925 but did not appear in book form.

The best among Vesaas's stage plays is probably *Ultimatum*. Technically the piece reflects the influence of German expressionist theater of which the author saw a great deal while living in Munich during the late 1920's and early 1930's. *Ultimatum* was written as early as 1932, when Vesaas spent some time in Strasbourg on the Franco-German border and there observed the growing hostility between the two nations just a few months before Hitler rose to power in Germany. The play juxtaposes pacifist and pro-war attitudes toward the upcoming conflict.

Vesaas's early interest in drama was soon eclipsed by his more successful fiction and lyrical poetry. After World War II his experimental novels often display the structural tautness of drama and at times even approximate classical drama in respect to the unities of time and place. But the lyrical concentration of Vesaas's language and his symbolic, indirect style did not serve him well in writing for the stage.

By contrast, the author was highly successful with a series of short radio plays he composed for the Norwegian Broadcasting System during the 1950's and early 1960's. The majority of these plays overlap in subject and theme with Vesaas's novels and short stories. The disembodied voice was a medium eminently suited to Vesaas's talent for creating a lyrical atmosphere or sketching a relationship suggesting a larger problem. His approach combines understatement and restrained intimacy. The plays depict scenes from everyday life, but reveal a significance and hidden depth in an otherwise humdrum existence that cannot fail to strike a chord in the listener. No doubt Vesaas reached his largest and most devoted audience in Norway through these radio plays. Only two of them found their way into print, however, *Avskil med treet* (Farewell to the Tree, 1953) and *21 År* (21 Years, 1953).

Another measure of the dramatic potential inherent in Vesaas's fiction is the fact that a number of his novels have been adapted for the stage or made into films. The first of the novels to be filmed successfully was *Dei svarte hestane,* which premiered in 1951. Plans for a film had been discussed several years prior but foundered on the author's insistence that the dialogue had to be in Nynorsk. In 1953 a stage version of *The Bleaching Yard* premiered in Oslo and was subsequently made into a television film. A few years later a film version of *The Seed* appeared, followed in the early 1960's by *Spring Night,* which had previously been dramatized for television. The surrealistic *Brannen* was also turned into a film. But the most memorable and successful film version of a novel by Vesaas was the Polish production of *The Birds* (1968), which was directed by Witold Leszcynski (assisted by the Norwegian Håkon Sandøy). In transposing *The Birds* to the screen, Leszcynski was able to capture the most compelling dimensions of Vesaas's mature style: a tightly structured narrative surrounded by a wealth of visual and dramatic details of observation and description creating a context that is simultaneously realistic and poetic.

2053

TARJEI VESAAS

POETRY

When Vesaas published his first volume of poems in 1946, he already had two-thirds of his life's work as a novelist behind him. By contrast, between the end of World War II and the time of his death, Vesaas brought out no less than five substantial volumes of verse that established him as a leading voice among modernist poets in Scandinavia. Critics have often maintained that there is a strong lyrical element in all of Vesaas's works from the very beginning—the title of his debut volume, *Kjeldene* (The Wellsprings), perhaps points to the primacy of lyrical vision in his authorship. But it was not until the 1940's, beginning with *The Seed,* that the dramatic and lyrical dimensions in his fiction begin to manifest themselves fully, and it is at this time that Vesaas also began writing poetry in all seriousness.

In an interview printed in *Dagbladet* (Daily News) in 1964, Vesaas recalls that it was the encounter with the modernist verse of the Swedish-Finnish poet Edith Södergran that showed him the way toward a more open poetic form than he had found in traditional verse. The modernist poet turns his back on the fixed rhyme schemes and meters that in traditional verse are definitive musical elements. Also, in modernist poetry the image functions as the direct expression of thought and feeling. The poet disappears behind the image, which does not carry fixed, generalized meanings external to the poem, but rather receives its significance within a specific poetic context. On the whole the poetry of Vesaas is characterized less by musicality than by reflection and visionary perception. His poetic universe is at the same time personal and universal. Characteristically Vesaas almost never speaks through the lyrical "I" in his poems, but rather uses the terms "you," "we," "he/she," or "one," as if inviting the reader to enter the poems. The most fruitful response to Vesaas's poetry is thus not analysis and interpretation, but participation. Like his mature fiction, Vesaas's lyrical work makes considerable demands on the reader's imagination and ability to make associations.

Kjeldene is in many ways a volume that reflects Vesaas's transition to modernist poetry. The majority of the poems are quite traditional in form, some of them reminiscent of folk songs and ballads in style and idiom. Folk life and nature descriptions predominate in this collection, but there are also lyrical meditations on a variety of other subjects. The first poem in the collection, "Snø og granskog" (Snow and Spruce Woods, translated as "Snow and Fir Forests"), while not fully modernistic, shows unmistakable signs of the new technique:

> Home—
> Snow and spruce woods
> are home.
>
> From the very first hour
> they are ours.
> Before anyone has said
> that they are snow and spruce woods,
> they have become part of us—
> and then they are there
> all, all the time . . .

Here the metrically defined rhythm has been replaced by an empathic rhythm. The individual lines vary in length, and each line constitutes a unit of meaning. Thought, feeling, and rhythmic emphasis have been identified. There is no end rhyme, but certain focal images ("Snow and spruce woods," "home") are repeated throughout the poem to create a sense of rhythmic continuity. The first and last stanza consist of three lines, framing three stanzas of seven lines each, further enhancing the effect of rhythm and balance. More importantly, the imagery describes not only a scene in nature, but the perception of an internal experience. Outer and inner "landscape" are identified. The concluding image thus has a dual meaning that is specific to this poem: "innlandshjarta" can mean heart of the interior, the inland, but here it also means the human heart, the inner self. Where the two fuse and overlap, there is "home."

In his subsequent collections Vesaas's poetic style becomes completely modernistic. His language grows increasingly spare and simplified, but at the same time more fully expressive. The poet animates the phenomena he describes to convey a fundamental connectedness of human consciousness with all of life.

In Vesaas's poetry, as in his fiction, nature imagery dominates. The eternal rhythms of the earth are juxtaposed to human evil. Sun, wind, and rain are connected with life-giving, sustaining forces, while fire and storm are associated with forces that are destructive and often beyond comprehension. The river represents the dynamic process of life; the sea suggests infinity; danger is identified with bottomless lakes and bogs. Mountains and hills symbolize the security of a familiar landscape; steep rock faces, however, are also identified with isolation and failed communication. Trees most often represent growth and nurturing qualities, but a "tired tree" can also symbolize regression and death. In "Det var eingong . . ." ("Once upon a Time"), a well-known poem from Vesaas's second collection, a birch tree budding in spring becomes the image of a young girl on the threshold of womanhood:

ONCE UPON A TIME
There was this little birch tree
And they said she should have leaves
By mid-May.
She could have danced, almost,
For that promise
And because she was skinny as a child.

But first, they said, there would come
A warm wind; and he did.
He teased her, he waltzed her around, she was
dizzy and sweet and tender
In every bud.
And when the bird came
And sat on a thin twig
Singing, Now, it's Now—

She didn't understand at all,
Not at all.
But in the evening
She stood slender and gowned

In her freshness, her translucent new green,
And she was absolutely transformed.

She turned about slowly,
Loosening herself quite free of dirt.
Ho hum, she sang, very quietly, now
To sail, like a green veil, over the hill,
For ever, away for ever
—Said the little birch tree.

Among domestic animals, the horse and the cat are associated with mutual trust and interdependence with their human masters, while dogs tend to represent something threatening. Birds often symbolize freedom and the dream of the unknown, as in the poem "Fuglen" (The Bird):

The bird stood ready
by the path and waited.

The bird was a marvel.
His enormous wing span
was oblivion.
The measure of his heartbeat
was mine.

Together we sailed
into the unknown.
Without question.
Without grief.

The staring glance of the snake generally symbolizes forces that paralyze the "bird of the soul." Blind insects living underground suggest unconscious levels in the self. Fish are silent witnesses to man's existential bewilderment. In "Båten og fisken" (The Boat and the Fish) the response of the fish expresses the poet's ironic and self-mocking humor:

The boat glides out and makes
a dark shape on the thin sand.
The fish looks up at the bottom of the boat
and smiles all he can.
What is that dumb boat thinking of?
My whole life I have seen
that dumb boat coming.
That ten-times dumb boat
wanting to catch me.
I'm sick and tired of it.

The fish has a smile
in its tail.
With a few smiling strokes
he is gone.
He laughs for a long time
behind a brown stone.
(*Dikt i samling*, p. 229)

Recurrent concerns in Vesaas's poetry are the dangers of isolation, passivity, and resignation, which can be overcome through taking responsibility for fellow human beings and through the mystery of the relationship between man and woman. Vesaas is also concerned with the rootlessness of the modern individual, especially the city dweller, and with the threat of mechanization and specialization. But although he found the sources of meaning in nature, Vesaas did not reject the city; rather he felt that the "innermost wellspring of the self" flows at a place found beyond any given physical environment:

. . . But farther away than that
you must [go].
Far beyond city or country,
to your own searching stillness
where your innermost wellspring flows . . .
("Det miste" [The Lost],
in *Dikt i samling*, p. 63)

In a number of poems, Vesaas describes the demons of atomic weaponry, "the great animal / we have called / and prayed for / [and which] finally has heard our prayer." In "Napalm," a poem written during the Vietnam conflict, he explores the catastrophic effect of the fighting on a civilian child and mother:

As if it were not there—
the child's face hidden.
The mother bears it turned away,
turned away the world she meets.

No longer a face,
but turned to her.
Turned only to her.
In the dark house.

Other poems call on the reader to wake up to the ravages of military conflict and starvation in underdeveloped countries: "The fierce sky of Africa / flares in the night / while we sleep."

Yet the focus of Vesaas's poetry remains on his sense of wonder at the hidden rhythms of human existence, his preoccupation with visionary experiences and dreams, and with the meaning of life's journey. The titles of the five remaining collections reflect this focus: *Leiken og lynet* (The Game and the Lightning, 1947); *Lykka for ferdesmenn* (The Happiness of Travelers, 1949); *Løynde eldars land* (*Land of Hidden Fires*, 1953); *Ver ny, vår draum* (Be New, Our Dream, 1956); and *Liv ved straumen* (*Life by the River*, 1970).

The final volume, which was published posthumously, contains several of Vesaas's finest poems and also some of his most mystical. In "Vegen" (The Path), for example, the traveler journeys across the mountains to a ridge from where he can see the great plain that is his destination. The plain is a recurrent image both in Vesaas's poetry and his fiction, and often it is associated with dread. In this late poem, by contrast, the plain is identified with a clear-sighted and serene acceptance of death. It is overarched by the luminous, transparent vault of the sky, suggesting a reality beyond knowledge or desire. The meanings suggested here are no doubt transcendental, taking us full circle back to the legend of Wu-Tao-Tse told by the youthful Vesaas as a metaphor for the function of poetry in pointing beyond tangible, external reality to the eternal:

The footprint does not show.
It has not been stamped in soft mud
or ditch.
The step has been light.

But he who has come, knows the path.
Knows the one safe hollow
in which to set his foot.
He climbs the ridge and is happy
to see the path ahead.
Drops to rest on the ridge
and waits for company.

There they come, like friendly counselors,
they who have already received their form.
We know we can talk to them about
the most secret things,
as we sit and whittle a stick
with a little knife.

We are all gathered together. Nobody knows it,
neither will they know it.
We whittle our sticks and poke the ground
and talk about things until the sun goes down.

Later, as dusk is covering us,
we know more:
We must go into the darkness
in great falls and bends.
We don't speak another word.
If we spoke, the path would vanish.

But no one dare mention arriving.
That must happen on the wide plain
where clear arches vault
from all four directions
and stream together
in great transparent arcs,
without knowledge, without desire.
Then one has arrived
and is no more.

Selected Bibliography

EDITIONS

NOVELS

Menneskebonn (Children of Man). Christiania, 1923.

Sendemann Huskuld (Huskuld the Herald). Christiania, 1924.

Grindegard. Morgonen (The Farm at Grinde. The Morning). Oslo, 1925.

Grinde-kveld eller den gode engelen (Evening at Grinde; or, The Good Angel). Oslo, 1926.

Dei svarte hestane (The Black Horses). Oslo, 1928.

Fars reise (Father's Journey). Oslo, 1930.

Sigrid Stallbrokk. Oslo, 1931.

Dei ukjende mennene (The Unknown Men). Oslo, 1932.

Sandeltreet (The Sandalwood Tree). Oslo, 1933.

Det store spelet (The Great Cycle). Oslo, 1934.

Kvinnor ropar heim (Women Call: Come Home). Oslo, 1935.

Hjarta høyrer sine heimlandstonar (The Heart Hears Its Native Music). Oslo, 1938.

Kimen (The Seed). Oslo, 1940.

Huset i mørkret (The House in the Dark). Oslo, 1945.

Bleikeplassen (The Bleaching Yard). Oslo, 1946.

Tårnet (The Tower). Oslo, 1948.

Signalet (The Signal). Oslo, 1950.

Vårnatt (Spring Night). Oslo, 1954.

Fuglane (The Birds). Oslo, 1957.

Brannen (The Fire). Oslo, 1961.

Is-slottet (The Ice Palace). Oslo, 1963.

Bruene (The Bridges). Oslo, 1966.

Båten om kvelden (The Boat in the Evening). Oslo, 1968.

SHORT STORIES

Klokka i haugen (The Bell in the Knoll). Oslo, 1929.

Leiret og hjulet (The Clay and the Wheel). Oslo, 1936.

Vindane (The Winds). Oslo, 1952.

Noveller (Short Stories). Oslo, 1955.

Ein vakker dag (One Fine Day). Oslo, 1959.

Noveller i samling (Collected Short Stories). Oslo, 1964.

PLAYS

Guds bustader (The Dwelling Places of God). Oslo, 1925.

Ultimatum. Oslo, 1934.

Morgonvinden (The Morning Wind). Oslo, 1947.

Avskil med treet (Farewell to the Tree). Oslo, 1953.

21 År (21 Years). Oslo, 1953.

POETRY

Kjeldene (The Wellsprings). Oslo, 1946.

Leiken og lynet (The Game and the Lightning). Oslo, 1947.

Lykka for ferdesmenn (The Happiness of Travelers). Oslo, 1949.

Løynde eldars land (Land of Hidden Fires). Oslo, 1953.

Ver ny, vår draum (Be New, Our Dream). Oslo, 1956.

Liv ved straumen (Life by the River). Oslo, 1970.

Dikt i samling (Collected Poetry). Oslo, 1972.

PROSE AND POEMS

Huset og fuglen (The House and the Bird). Edited by Walter Baumgartner. Oslo, 1971.

TARJEI VESAAS

TRANSLATIONS

NOVELS

The Birds. Translated by Torbjørn Støverud and Michael Barnes. London, 1968.

The Boat in the Evening. Translated by Elizabeth Rokkan. London, 1971.

The Bleaching Yard. Translated by Elizabeth Rokkan. London, 1981.

The Bridges. Translated by Elizabeth Rokkan. London, 1969.

The Great Cycle. Translated by Elizabeth Rokkan. Madison, Wisc., 1967.

The House in the Dark. Translated by Elizabeth Rokkan. London, 1976.

The Ice Palace. Translated by Elizabeth Rokkan. London, 1966; New York, 1968 (as *The Palace of Ice*).

The Seed. British Commonwealth edition. London, 1966.

———— and *Spring Night.* Translated by Kenneth G. Chapman. New York and Oslo, 1964.

SHORT STORIES

"In the Fish's Golden Youth." Translated by Tim Schiff. *The American-Scandinavian Review* 56: 287–290 (1968).

"Never Tell It." Translated by Kenneth G. Chapman. *The American-Scandinavian Review* 47:166–171 (1959).

"Snow." Translated by Kenneth G. Chapman. *The Literary Review* 12:170–175 (1969).

"Twenty-One." Translated by Kenneth G. Chapman. *New World Writing* 14. New York, 1958.

POEMS

COLLECTIONS

Five Norwegian Poets: Tarjei Vesaas, Rolf Jacobsen, Olav H. Hauge, Gunvor Hofmo, Stein Mehren. Loanhead, Scotland, 1976.

Land of Hidden Fires. Translated and introduced by Fritz König and Jerry Crisp. Detroit, 1973.

Life by the River: Last Poems of Tarjei Vesaas. Translated by Henning K. Sehmsdorf, Crispin Elsted, and Leslie Norris, and introduced by Henning K. Sehmsdorf. Mission, Canada, forthcoming.

30 Poems. Selected and translated by Kenneth G. Chapman. Oslo, 1971.

INDIVIDUAL POEMS

"In Deep Liability." Translated by Robert Bly. *The Literary Review* 12:222 (1969).

"Once Upon a Time." Translated by Martin and Inga Allwood. In *Twentieth Century Scandinavian Poetry,* edited by M. Allwood. Oslo, 1950.

————. Translated by Henning K. Sehmsdorf and Leslie Norris. *The New Statesman* (1976), p. 12. Reprinted in Leslie Norris, *Water Voices.* London, 1980.

"One Rows and Rows." Translated by James W. Brown. *The Literary Review* 12:218–219 (1969).

"Rain in Hiroshima." Translated by James W. Brown. *The Literary Review* 12:220–221 (1969).

"Snow and Fir Forests." Translated by Martin and Inga Allwood. In *Twentieth-Century Scandinavian Poetry,* edited by M. Allwood. Oslo, 1950.

"Your Knees and Mine." Translated by James W. Brown. *The Literary Review* 12:217 (1969).

BACKGROUND AND CRITICAL STUDIES

Baumgartner, Walter. "Slik var den draumen. Om Tarjei Vesaas som visjonær." *Norsk litterær årbok* 9–32 (1970).

————. "*Det store spelet* og Blut und Boden. Mystikk og kritikk i Bufast-bøkene av Tarjei Vesaas." *Syn og Segn* 579–597 (1977).

Beyer, Edvard, et al., ed. *Tarjei Vesaas.* Oslo, 1967.

Brostrøm, Torben. "Tarjei Vesaas' symbolverden belyst ud fra hans prosaverker 1940–50." *Edda* 28–105 (1955).

Chapman, Kenneth G. *Tarjei Vesaas.* New York, 1970.

Dale, Johannes. "Tarjei Vesaas." *Nordisk Tidskrift* 185–194 (1964).

Egeland, Kjølv. "Tarjei Vesaas." In *Norges Litteraturhistorie.* 5:174–201 (1975).

Fæster, Hans. "Vår stutte tid blir her. Psykologi og budskap hos Tarjei Vesaas." *Norsk litterær årbok* 71–98 (1972).

Gimnes, Steinar. "Mattis Tust og Tarjei Vesaas." *Edda* 227–231 (1975).

Houm, Philip. "Tarjei Vesaas." In *Norsk litteraturhistorie.* 6:246–270 (1955).

Hvidt-Nielsen, Inger. "Bru til vaksenheimen. Tarjei Vesaas: 'Aldri fortelje det' og Martin A. Hansen 'Synden.' En motivisk analyse." *Norsk litterær årbok* 98–108 (1972).

Kittang, Atle. "Genre, landskap, meining. Refleksjonar kring *Båten om kvelden* av Tarjei Vesaas." *Norsk litterær årbok* 33–58 (1970).

Longum, Leif. "Forløsningens mysterium: Tarjei Vesaas." In *Et speil for oss selv.* Oslo, 1968.

Lønning, Kjell. *Vesaas.* Oslo, 1979.

Masát, András. "Verdiar og verdisyn i Tarjei Vesaas prosadiktning enda ein gong." *Norsk litterær årbok* 47–58 (1982).

Mæhle, Leif, ed. *Ei bok om Tarjei Vesaas.* Oslo, 1964.

Nordland, Odd. "Tid og ferd i Vesaas' symboldiktning." *Syn og segn* 337–349 (1957).

Næss, Harald. "Et forsøk over Vesaas' prosastil. *Edda* 148–175 (1962).

Sehmsdorf, Henning K. "Heltemyten i tre prosaverk av Tarjei Vesaas. *Det store spelet, Kimen,* og 'Den ville ridaren.'" *Norsk litterær årbok* 132–143 (1978).

———. "Tagore og Vesaas. Påvirkning eller slektskap?" *Norsk litterær årbok* 35–46 (1982).

Skrede, Ragnvald. *Tarjei Vesaas.* Oslo, 1947.

Solstad, Dag. "Myten om Vesaas (om Tarjei Vesaas' *Båten om Kvelden*)." *Vinduet* 1:41–44 (1969).

Stegane, Idar. "Lyrikaren Tarjei Vesaas." *Edda* 151–161 (1973).

———. "'Villskap må ikkje tolast!' Nazismen i diktinga til Tarjei Vesaas." In *Nazismen og norsk litteratur.* Edited by Bjarte Birkeland and Stein U. Larsen. Oslo, 1975. Pp. 122–140.

Tarjei Vesaas. 50th-anniversary *festschrift.* Oslo, 1947.

Vesaas, Halldis Moren. *I midtbøs bakkar.* Oslo, 1974.

———. *Båten om dagen.* Oslo, 1976.

Vold, Jan Erik. "Nederst i slammet: Auget i brønnen. Om *Bruene* og nye trekk ved Vesaas' prosa." In *Entusiastiske essays.* Oslo, 1975. Pp. 185–190.

———, ed. *Tarjei Vesaas.* Oslo, 1964.

HENNING K. SEHMSDORF

LOUIS ARAGON

(1897–1982)

I N THE COURSE of his remarkable career, Louis Aragon was a founder of Dada, a major surrealist poet, a hero of the French Resistance, and a militant Stalinist who became the most important intellectual of the French Communist party. He was incredibly prolific, publishing over forty books; his works included poetry, novels, essays, newspaper articles, biography, literary theory, art criticism, and virtually every genre except drama. Yet he remains one of those writers more talked about than read, and throughout his long life he was the focus of considerable controversy. He has been widely accused of falseness, of personal and political disloyalty, and of squandering his prodigious talents by debasing art to the level of propaganda. He is, however, undeniably one of the major figures of twentieth-century French culture.

Literary critics usually divide his career into two distinct parts. At first he was an immensely creative avant-garde poet, but after his break with surrealism he joined the Communist party and his style changed dramatically as he turned to socialist realism. But this is too simplistic a judgment because some of his most remarkable works—such as the elegant love poems dedicated to his wife, Elsa Triolet—were written at the height of his Stalinist period. Later, with advancing age and increasing disillusionment with Soviet policy, he experimented with new forms that combined a partial return to the surrealist aesthetics of his youth with a unique blend of prose and narrative poetry.

Aragon was brilliant, gifted, and possessed of an enviable verbal facility that overwhelmed his listeners. Even those who disliked him succumbed to his charm in spite of themselves, and he was fully conscious of this effect. As he himself rather narcissistically remarked in *Le libertinage* (*The Libertine*, 1924), "It seems I am seduction personified." He was also vacillating, weak willed, and easily led, and he apparently craved the presence of a forceful personality to give his life direction. This need was filled first by André Breton, the leader of surrealism, then by Triolet, the Russian-born writer he married, and also by the discipline of the Communist party. His peculiar upbringing could certainly have accounted for his instability, because he was an illegitimate child forced to live a lie. His birth on 3 October 1897 was considered a calamity by the respectable Andrieux family, and the surname Aragon was one arbitrarily chosen later by his natural father. So great was his grandparents' desire to conceal the circumstances of his birth that he was sent to a wet nurse in the country for the first eighteen months of his life. When he was brought back home, the family had moved and was running a pension. Everyone was led to believe that his grandmother was his mother and that his mother was his older sister, and Aragon himself learned the truth about his parentage only after he grew up. His father, a married man much older than his mother, was a diplomat and, without revealing his paternity, often visited the house and acted as tutor to his young son—but he never publicly acknowledged him.

From a very early age, Aragon exhibited a love of literature, especially of poetry, and was a very precocious reader. His family planned a medical career for him, and he studied medicine at the University of Paris after graduating from the Lycée Carnot in 1916. But to their great consternation, he rebelled by abandoning his studies just as he was to take his qualifying examinations. He had come under the influence of a brilliant circle of poets and painters with whom he founded the Dada movement in Paris. Because the dadaists scorned the idea of making a career, he broke with his family and was determined to live by his wits. In 1917 he was drafted and served at the front as a medical auxiliary. He was awarded the Croix de guerre in 1918, but he loathed the war, which was a devastating experience that affected his whole life. His hatred of war became the compelling motive for joining the Communist party—as it was for his fellow surrealists as well.

While in the army he met Breton, who exerted the most profound influence over his early career. It was Breton who introduced Aragon to Dada, an iconoclastic movement against war and militarism to which many young artists were irresistibly drawn. For both of them Dada was personified by their soldier-friend Jacques Vaché, who without even knowing of Dada, had come to the conclusion that "art is a stupidity." Vaché was in total revolt against society and was disgusted with the war, and even with life itself. His philosophy was summed up in his concept of "umour" [sic], which he defined as "the theatrical uselessness (without joy) of everything when one knows" and expressed his conviction that existence is meaningless. He committed suicide in 1919 by taking an overdose of opium, at the same time administering a fatal dose to an unsuspecting companion. But this only increased the da-

daists' admiration for him since the manner of his death was the perfect expression of contempt for the world that they rejected.

Dada, the violent and nihilistic forerunner of surrealism, reflected the despair and disillusionment felt by so many artists and intellectuals in the face of the Great War. That this pessimism was a widespread phenomenon was shown by the fact that Dada was an international movement engendered by a moral revulsion against all the traditions of European civilization. As Marcel Raymond remarked in his *From Baudelaire to Surrealism* (1950), "Those who refuse to see in the Dada movement anything but a Parisian scandal . . . will never understand the intense moral crisis of the 1920s." Although apolitical in the beginning, in reality it was born of politics because in essence it was revolt against war. As the Russian writer Ilya Ehrenburg rightly observed in his memoirs, "Dadaism had more to do with the battle of the Somme, with uprisings and putsches . . . than with what we usually consider art."

Dada began in 1916 in Zurich, where artists of all nationalities had gathered to evade the trenches, but as soon as the guns stopped firing, it spread to New York, Berlin, and Paris. The world was then treated to the spectacle of an avant-garde movement that was against not only war, patriotism, and the bourgeoisie, but was against even art itself, denying the existence of all meaning and aesthetic values and dedicated to destroying the entire cultural heritage of the West. According to Tristan Tzara, said in his "Zurich Chronicle 1915–1919" (in Robert Motherwell's anthology), the first Dada event took place in Zurich at the Cabaret Voltaire and was advertised as an evening of dance, music, theory, manifestos, poems, costumes, and masks, with all the performances going on simultaneously. The German pacifist and poet Hugo Ball recited a "phonetic poem" of meaningless sounds while wearing a cylindrical cardboard costume—which unfortunately prevented his escape from the wrath of the audience. There was "Negro music," that is, loud banging of drums; a raucous manifesto by Tzara himself, the Romanian poet who became leader of the Paris circle: "We demand the right to piss in different colors!" There was a "cubist dance"; a boxing match; and "more outcries, a big drum, piano and impotent cannon, cardboard costumes torn off by the audience . . . simultaneous poem for 4 voices and simultaneous work for three hundred hopeless idiots!"

Clearly, Dada was out to shock. If the artists had a goal, it was to show society how much they despised it, and although they were pacifists, their extreme negativism had strong implications of violence. As Tzara declared, "There is a great task of destruction and negation to be accomplished: we must sweep and clean!" His famous "recipe" for a poem was intended to destroy art by eliminating the conscious role of the creator in order to produce works totally without meaning:

> Take a newspaper. Take a pair of scissors. Choose an article the same length you want your poem to be. Cut the article out. Then carefully cut out each of the words and put them in a bag. Shake softly. Take each word out one after the other. Copy them down conscientiously in the same order that they came out of the bag. The poem will resemble you. And there you are: a writer of infinite originality and charming sensibility.
>
> ("Pour faire un poème dadaiste," in *Sept manifestes dada: Lampisteries* [1963], p. 64)

For the visual artists as well, chance replaced all aesthetic values. The German Max Ernst and the Alsatian Jean (Hans) Arp, who joined Dada before becoming surrealists, experimented with scattering pieces of cardboard on their canvases and gluing them where they fell.

In Germany some members of the group supported the Spartacist revolt and took part in the street fighting in Berlin, but most were far too pessimistic to believe in social progress. "Naturally, we cannot believe in any possibility of improving social conditions," said Breton in the May 1920 issue of the review ironically titled *Littérature*, edited by Aragon, Breton, and Philippe Soupault. Dada opposed capitalism, because it hated all bourgeois institutions, but at least in France, the artists were not consciously political. They nihilistically rejected all ideologies, as Aragon made clear in a famous protest:

> No more painters, no more writers, no more musicians, no more sculptors, no more religions, no more republicans, no more royalists, no more imperialists, no more anarchists, no more socialists, no more bolsheviks, no more aristocrats, no more armaments, no more police, no more countries, enough of all these imbecilities, no more, no more, no more, no more.
>
> ("Manifeste du mouvement dada," in *Littérature*, May 1920, p. 2)

After the war, dadaists from various countries converged on Paris, which now became the center of the movement. In addition to Arp, Ernst, and Tzara, the Cuban painter Francis Picabia and the American photographer Man Ray joined the Paris group. But another Parisian, the painter Marcel Duchamp, remained in New York and became a revered antihero for his superbly dadaist gesture of giving up his work to devote himself to chess. To celebrate Tzara's arrival *Littérature* organized a matinee on the "new art." Unaware of the intended farce, the public arrived to find Picabia supposedly lecturing on art, but in fact he was simply erasing lines on a blackboard as fast as he drew them. After announcing a manifesto, Tzara read from the telephone book, while the others rang cowbells and drowned him out. They also addressed the audience in such an insulting fashion that it caused a riot, so the evening was judged a huge success.

The provocations of the Paris circle became extremely intense as they protested against the increasing cynicism of the postwar era. They envied their German counterparts the excitement of the revolutionary ferment there, because in France it was simply business as usual. They continued to denounce war and patriotism and they jeered at the idea of heroism, for what more meaningless death could there be than to die for one's country on a battlefield? They were convinced that life was absurd, and there seemed to be only two alternatives: following nihilism to its extreme of suicide, as had Vaché, or engaging in incessant meaningless activity to express profound despair. They therefore threw themselves more and more frantically into absurd demonstrations, trying to subvert the established order through ridicule and disgust. The climax of Paris Dada was a soirée held in the dignified Salle Gaveau in 1920. Among other outrages, Soupault appeared on stage and, as he called out the names of the pope, Georges Clemenceau, and General Ferdinand Foch, balloon caricatures floated up to the ceiling. Tzara expressed his great satisfaction, saying that for the first time in the world, people not only threw rotten eggs, salads, and pennies, but beefsteaks as well. But by this time, a terrible thing began to happen: people began to enjoy these events. Even worse, from the dadaists point of view, people sympathized with them because, as Malcolm Cowley wrote in *Exile's Return* (1951), "Now it was time for a literary movement that would outdo the politicians in lunacy."

Aragon and Breton soon concluded that they had reached an impasse and that it was necessary to articulate a positive program to replace their frenetic, directionless activity. Breton proposed to hold a mock trial of the reactionary writer Maurice Barrès for "crimes against the human spirit." Breton was the judge, Aragon the counsel for the defense, the future journalist Georges Ribemont-Dessaignes was the prosecutor, and to everyone's delight, the event provoked an extremely hostile reaction from the press. But it also provoked a split in the ranks both because it was "too serious"—a cardinal sin against the spirit of Dada—and because Tzara resented Breton's assumption of leadership. Nevertheless, when Breton insisted that it was time to abandon Dada in favor of a new movement he called surrealism, most of the artists agreed to join. As Aragon later explained in *Pour un réalisme socialiste* (Toward Socialist Realism, 1934), surrealism was a desperate effort to go beyond the negation and futility of Dada to construct a new reality.

While retaining the antisocial character of Dada in many respects, the surrealists did so in the name of a new principle, revolution. At first, this meant the total liberation of mind and spirit, but later it came to mean actual political and social revolution. Breton had been greatly influenced by Freud, especially by the notion of utilizing dreams to get at the unconscious, and the group experimented with automatic writing as a way to reach the unconscious in a waking state. People had been stifled and inhibited by logic and rational thought for too long, and it was the surrealists' task, as they saw it, to liberate the mind. They wanted to teach people to rediscover the unconscious and show them how to grasp the imaginative fantasies that lay hidden even from themselves. Thus, "automatic writing"— or "psychic automism," a better term, since the concept was used in painting as well as writing—became their most important method. These young artists considered themselves scientists because they were serious explorers of a new world: the unconscious, the dream, the fantastic, or "the marvelous" (a favorite word in the surrealist vocabulary). They stressed the systematic, experimental, "scientific" character of their new method, partly in reaction to the anarchy of Dada. They were conducting "research" in the field of language, rather than merely writing poetry in the usual way. In Breton's famous definition in his *Manifeste du surréalisme* (*Manifestoes of Surrealism*, 1962), surrealism is "pure psychic automism by which it is intended to express, either verbally or in writing, the real function of thought, in the absence of any control exercised by the reason and outside of all aesthetic and moral preoccupations."

Aragon's great "discovery," the virtually unknown eccentric symbolist Lautréamont, had insisted that poetry must be made by all, not by one, and the surrealists took this very seriously. They produced collective, anonymous works while insisting that they had no talent but were merely "modest copying machines." They carefully collected and recounted dreams, attempted to produce hallucinatory states by conducting séances, and played word games such as "le cadavre exquis" (the exquisite corpse), named after the first sentence produced when they played it: "The exquisite corpse will drink the new wine." It involved writing a noun on paper, folding the paper so the word could not be seen, and passing it to the next person, who would write a verb, and so on, until complete, perfectly grammatical but nonsensical sentences were created. The conjunction of logically disparate elements was intended to produce a new kind of reality, a surreality, or a whole new way of seeing the world. Collage, which was the visual artists' counterpart of automatic writing, was given this famous definition by Max Ernst:

> A ready-made reality (a canoe), finding itself in the presence of another and hardly less absurd reality (a vacuum cleaner), in a place where both of them must feel displaced (a forest), will, by this very fact, escape into a new absolute value, true and poetic: canoe and vacuum cleaner will make love. The mechanism of collage, it seems to me, is revealed by this very simple example.
>
> (*Beyond Painting*, p. 13)

In their search for "the marvelous," the surrealists tried to obliterate the contradictions between dream and reality, and they all enthusiastically experimented with "automism." As Aragon said, "It was a time when, meeting in the evening like hunters after a day in the field, we made the day's accounting, the list of beasts we had invented, of fantastic plants, of images bagged." Although some very beautiful and haunting imagery was produced, the results were uneven, to say the least. It was the process, not the result, that was important. But one feels that Aragon was never entirely comfortable with this method of creation, since he proclaimed in *Le traité du style* (Essay on Style, 1928), "Even if you write wretched idiocies by a Surrealist method, they will still be wretched

idiocies, without excuses." Indeed, as a number of the other poets and painters confessed years later, they did not always abide by the "rules," but consciously altered their compositions for the sake of aesthetic principles.

Even in *Le mouvement perpétuel* (Perpetual Motion, 1926), a collection of poems Aragon wrote between 1920 and 1924, it is clear, according to the critic Lucille Becker, that most of the poems were the result of "conscious artistry at work," and he later revealed that this was actually the case. This is not to say that his work was ever conventional. The poem entitled "Suicide" consists solely of a recital of the alphabet, and in "Persiennes" (Venetian Blinds), he simply repeats the word *persiennes* twenty times. In true surrealist fashion, he also gratuitously insults the public by saying, "I dedicate this book to poetry and *shit* on those who read it." Another work, *Anicet ou le panorama, roman* (Anicet or the Panorama, Novel, 1921), is his first sustained prose work. Yet Becker maintains that simply putting the word *roman* (novel) in the title was an act of deliberate defiance, directed against his friends. Both dadaists and surrealists rejected the novel form because of its logical development of plot and character and its predominant place in modern European culture. *The Libertine*, the title of which is intended to shock, is a mélange of manifestos, short pieces of fiction, and poems. Love was a favorite theme for Aragon, as it was for all the surrealists, who dreamed of a great love and who idealized woman as muse. But unlike that of the Romantics, the love poetry and painting of the surrealists' is explicitly erotic. They were firm believers in complete sexual freedom, and several, including Aragon, wrote hard-core pornography that could not be legally published.

Most critics believe that Aragon's greatest literary achievement in the first phase of his career is *Le paysan de Paris* (translated as *Paris Peasant* and again as *Nightwalker*, 1926). The surrealists, however, objected to it on the grounds that it was too much like the novel form they despised and that it was the product of creative will and not of psychic automism. It is a striking prose poem about the Passage de l'Opéra, a little street that was scheduled to be razed to make way for a new boulevard. Aragon's minute descriptions of its inhabitants and its dingy shops have been compared to the *nouveau roman* (new novel) that appeared thirty years later. He also reminisces nostalgically about the nondescript Café Certa, the habitual meeting place for the surrealists. It had been chosen by them precisely because it was not an artists' café in the bohemian quarter of the Left Bank, which was a milieu they despised. Neither the street nor the café was at all picturesque, but that only made his haunting lyrical evocations all the more remarkable. As Breton said, only Aragon could have been so carried away by such intoxicating reveries about the secret life of the city.

The second part of *Paris Peasant*, "Le sentiment de la nature aux Buttes-Chaumont" ("A Feeling for Nature in the Buttes-Chaumont Park"), describes an episode in which Aragon, Breton, and a third companion break into the park at night. Aragon contrives to make even this excursion seem like a journey into "the marvelous," that special enchanted domain, the aim of all surrealist works. In the last section, "Le songe du paysan" ("The Peasant's Dream"), he speaks of love and the longed-for woman who represents the conjunction of the real and the absolute. It is an extremely idealized description of love. But earlier, in the "Le Passage de l'Opéra" section, he reveals a morbid fascination with prostitutes, and his images are violent, especially when he speaks of Landru, a famous criminal who was a modern-day bluebeard. Thus, the sexuality he expresses is, on the one hand, idealized and, on the other, explicitly cruel. During his Stalinist period, Aragon said of *Paris Peasant* that it marked the extreme point of his idealism. In *Je n'ai jamais appris à écrire ou les incipits* (I Have Never Learned to Write, or The Opening Words, 1969), he dismisses it as "the novel of what I was at that time: in which the description is reserved for places, and the story is that

of the evolution of a mind . . . leading towards a materialism which is not achieved in the final pages of the book but only *promised*."

Aragon is considered by many to have been the most brilliant and creative surrealist writer, although it was Breton, his closest friend, who worked out the theoretical ideas of the movement and who was its most dominating personality. Like Dada, surrealism was also determined to destroy traditional art by ridicule, insult, disruption, and even violence and it enthusiastically continued the Dada tradition of "scandal." The death of the famous writer Anatole France in October 1924 provided the first opportunity. France was very much a national hero, but to the surrealists he represented the hated literary establishment and bourgeois pretension, and he symbolized everything they despised. They published an insulting pamphlet entitled "Un cadavre" (A Corpse, 1924), which caused a public outcry, and Aragon's contribution, "Avez-vous déjà giflé un mort?" ("Have You Ever Slapped a Dead Man?") was the most insulting of all. He attacked "that *littérateur* saluted simultaneously today by the imbecile Maurras and by stupid Moscow," saying, "He wrote quite badly, I assure you. . . . I consider any admirer of Anatole France a degraded being," and concluding that "there are days I dream of an eraser to rub out human filth." There were several other "scandals" that year: a diatribe against Paul Claudel, the conservative Catholic poet and diplomat, and a riot that disrupted a banquet held in honor of the poet Saint-Pol-Roux. But most important, in January 1924 the group began publishing its own journal, *La révolution surréaliste*.

As yet the movement lacked a political dimension other than the vague antimilitarist, antibourgeois sentiments of the dadaists, but Aragon's remark about "stupid Moscow," which referred to the fact that the Soviet government had joined in the condolences for Anatole France, provoked a polemic with *Clarté*, an independent Marxist review that was close to the Communist party. Its editors angrily reproached Aragon for equating the Soviet Union with the reactionary writer Maurras. But he merely replied in the January 1925 issue of *La révolution surréaliste* that he had "little taste for the Bolshevik government, or for Communism in general. I have always placed the spirit of revolt far above politics. I simply shrug my shoulders at the thought of the Russian Revolution. . . . It is nothing more than a vague ministerial crisis." In later years Aragon liked to portray himself as having been fully politically conscious and a true revolutionary even in childhood, when, against his mother's wishes, he read the leading Soviet writer Maxim Gorky. But as the above comments show, this was not the case. It would be more accurate to say that at this period, like all of his friends, Aragon was an anarchist by temperament. Occasionally he wrote for *La libération*, an anarchist journal, but he was not really concerned with politics. The surrealists' attraction to anarchism was evident in the first issue of *La révolution surréaliste*, which featured a photograph of the terrorist Germaine Berton surrounded by portraits of all the surrealists, posed as though they were gazing rapturously at her. She had just assassinated the reactionary Action française leader Marius Plateau, and Aragon declared fervently that "this woman symbolizes the greatest defiance of slavery that I know." In the early days the whole group had anarchist leanings. Many articles in *La révolution surréaliste* advocated total liberty with no restraints, including freedom from military service, freedom for prisoners, freedom for mental patients, sexual freedom, and freedom from all the traditional taboos of western culture.

In 1925, however, at the instigation of Breton, surrealism took a new direction and became overtly political. The movement's first genuinely political action was to denounce the colonial war declared by France against Morocco, where a national independence group called the Riff had risen in revolt. Given the surrealists' detestation of militarism, it was logical that the outbreak of yet another war would horrify them, and they signed a French Communist manifesto entitled *Les intellectuels contre la guerre du Maroc* (Intellectuals Against the War in Morocco). They were virtually the only group outside of the party to publicly oppose the war, and because of this they began to cooperate with the editors of *Clarté*, with whom they published a joint manifesto, *La révolution d'abord et toujours* (Revolution First and Forever). In it, they denounced the Riff war and imperialism in general, and praised Lenin, demanded an end to the draft, advocated disarmament, and called for revolution. The manifesto was ideologically confused, but it was clearly a political protest, and it initiated a period of collaboration with the young Marxists of *Clarté*. The surrealists now committed themselves to the French Communist party, thinking that all that was needed on their part was some repeated expressions of goodwill.

The decision to politicize surrealism and join forces with the party was far from unanimous. In fact, it provoked another schism within the ranks that resulted in the departure or expulsion of several members, among them Antonin Artaud, who later created the theater of the absurd, and Soupault, one of the original members of the group. Nevertheless, the surrealists threw themselves enthusiastically into the study of Hegel, Marx, Lenin, and Trotsky. They insisted that properly understood, there is no philosophical contradiction between Marxist ideology and surrealist thought, that their notion of revolution in consciousness is perfectly compatible with social revolution and that, as creators of a new revolutionary form of art, they had a unique contribution to make. The surrealists and the editors of *Clarté* decided to publish a joint review to be called "La guerre civile." These plans came to nothing, but the surrealists learned much from the Clartéistes, gaining a valuable political education and staunchly affirming their belief in the necessity for social and economic revolution. In 1925 Breton wrote an important article in the December issue of *Clarté*, "La force d'attendre"

(The Strength to Wait), his first proclamation of his lifelong insistence on the essential compatibility between communism and revolutionary avant-garde literature:

> In the revolutionary sense, just as on the social and economic plane, one can honorably claim to be Marxist, in the same way on the spiritual plane, I affirm that it is always permissible to uphold Lautréamont and Rimbaud. These two strands of thought are essentially compatible. . . . I would like to believe that there is no true work of the mind that is not shaped by the desire for the *real* amelioration of the conditions of existence and of the whole world.
>
> (pp. 12–13)

He added that the famous surrealist despair, that element of pessimism and preoccupation with suicide, would cease on the threshold of the new society, and he insisted that "we belong, body and soul, to the Revolution."

Aragon, formerly denounced by the Clartéistes as a "pure anarchist," had in the space of a year apparently undergone a profound change of heart, and he wrote an article for the November 1925 issue of *Clarté*, "Le proletariat de l'esprit" (The Proletariat of the Mind), that Jean Bernier, one of the editors, described approvingly as "thoroughly Marxist." Repudiating his anarchistic past, Aragon declared flatly that "anarchy, the origin and foundation of every kind of fascism, is counter-revolutionary." He also wrote a series of two articles, "Le prix de l'esprit" (The Price of Intellect), for the October–December 1926 issue of *Clarté* that attacked intellectuals as the willing tools of the ruling class. Thought is a product for sale in that when it takes a social form, it becomes merchandise, and

> this merchandise is essentially an emanation of capitalism, the servant of capitalism, its helper. For this reason nothing is more justified than the contempt which the oppressed proletariat has for intellectuals. Intellectuals are certainly the servile enemies of the Revolution all the more be-

cause they sometimes pretend to be its defenders. I have always thought: Here is a traitor whenever I have heard one of them proclaim that he *loves the people*. . . . With the exception of a few poets outside of politics and a few theoreticians of dialectical materialism, all intellectual forces for the past hundred years have undergone a bourgeois evolution. . . . It is high time that intellectuals understood their proper role . . . [which] is to prepare for the Revolution, the worldwide Communist Revolution as it is defined by the Third International.

> (pp. 122–123)

Like an apt pupil, Aragon had absorbed the jargon and appeared to have completely accepted the point of view of his mentors at *Clarté* and *L'Humanité,* the French Communist party newspaper. Strangely, his zeal even led him to share the negative feelings of party bureaucrats toward intellectuals. But in spite of such obvious devotion to the cause, the party continued to regard Aragon and the other potential new recruits with deep suspicion.

Between 1923 and 1925 the French Communists and the International as well were undergoing a period of great change. It was the era of "bolshevization," of "going to the masses," and of "purifying" the ranks of party members in various countries. The new harsh line coincided with the failure of the last attempts at Communist uprisings in the West, the coming of Mussolini to power, the suppression of the Italian Communist party, and the Stalin-Trotsky split that ended with Trotsky's exile. Anatoli Lunacharsky, the Soviet cultural commissar, admired the surrealists and said:

> We have need of intellectuals and yet, for the most part, they are still hostile to us. . . . It is not absolutely necessary to extract a complete profession of faith from them. . . . It is not absolutely necessary to be very demanding concerning political questions. It would be unreasonable to apply the maxim "he who is not with us is against us" to problems of theory and of discipline.
> . . . No: "he who is against the bourgeoisie is

with us." This is the kind of slogan we need to found an International of Intellectuals.

(Quoted in Naville, *La révolution et les intellectuels*, p. 7)

But his position did not prevail, and he himself was shortly thereafter expelled from the Russian party as a Trotskyist, guilty of "right-wing deviation."

The surrealists published a statement in *L'Humanité* on 8 November 1925 in an earnest attempt to convince the French Communists of their sincerity.

> Only a semantic confusion has allowed the persistent misunderstanding that there was a Surrealist doctrine of Revolution. . . . There never was a Surrealist theory of Revolution. We want the Revolution, and we want revolutionary means. Of what do these means consist? Only of the Communist International and for France, of the French Communist Party, and *absolutely not of individualistic theoreticians . . . whose actions are necessarily counter-revolutionary.* When it comes to realizing the Revolution, there can be no question of a "Surrealist group" as such. . . . Their revolutionary point of view in no way differs from that of the Communist International. *They can only conceive of the Revolution in its social and economic form: the Revolution being the totality of events determining the transfer of power from the hands of the bourgeoisie to those of the proletariat and the maintenance of that power by means of the dictatorship of the proletariat* [italics in original].

(p. 2)

To say that the surrealists had always thought of revolution in strictly social and economic terms and that they had never had their own theory of revolution was stretching the truth quite a bit. But unquestionably it indicated great concessions on their part and a willingness to accommodate themselves to what they felt were the requirements of the party.

But it seemed that virtually everything the surrealists did aggravated the Communist party. They publicly criticized *L'Humanité* for its reactionary approach to literature because, among its many failings, the editors refused to publish their work. But to the Communists, the very title of their journal, *La révolution surréaliste*, was suspect, and one party official demanded to know why, if they really considered themselves Communists, they needed to be surrealists. Nevertheless, in 1927, despite a number of defections from their own ranks, Aragon, Breton, and the poets Paul Eluard, Benjamin Péret, and Pierre Unik, took the decisive step of joining the French Communist party. The rest of the group, about twenty-five artists and writers, were expected to support it as "fellow travelers." By this gesture it was hoped they would finally establish good relations with the party and earn its trust. If anything, conflicts deepened, but the surrealists continued to be very creative in their own sphere.

Aragon especially was very prolific. He published another volume of poems, *La grande gaieté* (Great Gaiety, 1929), but the title, as so often with surrealist works, stood in deliberate contradiction to the contents. The poems are sad ones that bemoan the passing of time and mourn a lost love. That lost love was Nancy Cunard of the wealthy shipping family, a radical activist with whom Aragon had a stormy affair. The end of the relationship plunged him into such a state of depression that he attempted suicide. He also published *Le traité du style* in 1928, which, despite the title, is not an analysis of literary style but rather an indictment of the great novelists of the past. He reserves his praise for surrealist "heroes" such as the rebel poet Arthur Rimbaud, the Marquis de Sade, Freud, and Einstein, and he stresses the fact that surrealism is not an aesthetic movement but a revolt outside of literature, a revolt in the "real" world. He contends that "psychic automism" is not to be the new method of art, but a way of achieving new insights that the artist will then be able to utilize in his work. He also wrote a study of the surrealist painters,

La peinture au défi (Painting as Challenge, 1930), in which he said that the painters in their search for "the marvelous" are engaged in creating a new and revolutionary realism and not—despite what their detractors said—in deliberately rejecting reality.

The most momentous event in Aragon's life was his meeting in 1928 with Elsa Triolet at La Coupole, a Left Bank restaurant that was a favorite gathering place for artists and intellectuals. Triolet, who soon became the dominant influence on his career, was born Elsa Yureyevna Kagan in 1896, the younger daughter of intellectual Russian Jews privileged to live beyond the Jewish Pale in Moscow. Swept up in the revolutionary ferment of Russia in the early years of the century, she and her older sister, Lili, became part of the Russian futurist avantgarde. The futurist leader, Vladimir Mayakovsky, much admired by the surrealists for his experimental and revolutionary poetry, was Triolet's mentor and Lili's lover.

After moving to Paris, Triolet, who had published three novels in the Soviet Union as a protegé of Maxim Gorky, began, with Aragon's encouragement, to write in French. In 1945 she became the first woman to win the Prix Goncourt, the most prestigious literary prize of France, for her volume of three novellas set in the Resistance, *Le premier accroc coûte deux cents francs* (*A Fine of Two Hundred Francs*, 1947; reissued in 1986). She was also a journalist, biographer, theater critic, and major translator of Russian prose and poetry. It was she who introduced French readers to the work of Marina Tsvetaeva, Anna Akhmatova, Osip Mandelshtam, Velimir Khlebnikov, and especially Mayakovsky. Most important, she was a novelist whose fiction was a unique blend of political commitment and fantasy. Unlike the writing of Aragon in his Stalinist period, Triolet's work reveals her love of the bizarre and owes more to Nikolai Gogol, E. T. A. Hoffmann, and Edgar Allan Poe than to the proletarian literature movement. Her fiction constitutes a new definition of socialist realism, very different from the official one. She was also an

activist decorated for her heroic role in the French Resistance and was a leader of the peace movement in the cold war era.

Aragon was genuinely devoted to her, and they remained together until her death in 1970. On the surface they appeared to have had an ideal marriage of intellectual equals. Yet much of their well-publicized happiness was probably a facade forced upon them by Communist party morality, since Aragon had homosexual leanings. He had had to suppress this aspect of his character until very late in life because the surrealists—especially Breton—in spite of their advocacy of sexual freedom, disapproved of homosexuality, and the party, with its bourgeois emphasis on marriage and family, also strongly condemned it. In 1928 Triolet, having divorced her first husband, André Triolet, was living alone in Paris and had contrived to meet Aragon because she admired *Paris Peasant*, seeing in it a close resemblance to the work of Mayakovsky. Aragon, depressed by the end of his love affair with Cunard, and Triolet, by the end of her marriage, met and soon began living together. They only married in 1939, presumably because, with the outbreak of the war, it was safer for her as a Jew and a foreigner to be Aragon's legal wife.

Triolet's convictions about literature and politics had been learned from the futurists, and at first she admired the surrealists because they too professed to be revolutionaries and were at least nominally members of the Communist party. But she had an acute grasp of political realities and soon realized that their art, with its blatant sexuality and its ludicrous games and jokes, was unacceptable to the party. She saw that the surrealists, like the futurists in the Soviet Union in the late 1920's, were becoming politically isolated. She knew of the bitter campaign waged against Mayakovsky, which grew even more virulent after his suicide in 1930, and similar attacks were being made by the French Communists against the surrealists. She also disliked Breton because of his extremely conventional attitudes toward women. Already the author of three books, she was unwilling to play the passive role of muse and inspiration that was expected. In fact, several of the women surrealist painters felt it necessary to separate themselves from the Paris circle because of the way they were treated. Male surrealists, with the exception of Aragon, found it difficult to deal with women as creators and could see them only in their idealized role as love objects. Therefore Triolet urged Aragon to abandon the movement so that together they could join the mainstream of the Left.

The surrealists continued to have a most uneasy relationship with the Communist party, which, as Triolet well understood, was shocked by their frivolous "research" on sexuality and dreams and their fascination with madness and suicide. The illustrations in *La révolution surréaliste*, especially those by Picasso, were a particular bone of contention. Breton described how he was called every month to party headquarters and forced to justify their activities, which were repeatedly denounced as petit bourgeois nonsense. Even worse, they never understood the significance of the Trotsky-Stalin split and continued to have great admiration for Trotsky. He and Aragon even called a meeting in 1929 to discuss taking action on Trotsky's expulsion from the Soviet Union. Those present could not agree on a plan of action, so the project was dropped. But in 1934, when Trotsky was refused asylum in France, the surrealists issued a manifesto, *La planète sans visa* (Planet Without a Visa), to protest his banishment, and shortly before Trotsky's assassination in 1940, Breton visited him in Mexico, and there they issued a joint manifesto calling for a new independent revolutionary art movement.

In 1930, as a conciliatory gesture to the party and to make up for past ideological errors— which included an excessive concern for the fate of Trotsky—the artists changed the title of their journal to *Le surréalisme au service de la révolution* (Surrealism at the Service of the Revolution). In every issue they reaffirmed their loyalty to the International and to the French party, but they continued to commit the unforgivable sin of washing dirty linen in public. They were openly critical of *L'Humanité* and of the new party weekly *Le Monde,* edited by the world-famous novelist Henri Barbusse, and an article by Aragon even chastised a Soviet theater for producing plays by Claudel. The same year Mayakovsky committed suicide and was the object of shameful attacks by newspapers of all political persuasions. Aragon was so angry at one right-wing journalist who had written an article insulting the Russian poet that he went to his home and assaulted him. The journalist's wife called the police and denounced Aragon as a dangerous Communist, but the man, who had cowered behind his wife when Aragon threatened him, was simply made a laughingstock, and charges were never preferred. Even worse, Mayakovsky's suicide was actually condemned in *L'Humanité* on the grounds that since no true socialist would kill himself, it meant he had revealed himself to be a bourgeois reactionary. The surrealists protested against "this miserable sort of argument in the pages of the one newspaper in France where one could expect to find a defense of Mayakovsky," but to no avail, and the protest was simply added to the list of their ideological errors.

The surrealists had also mounted a very serious campaign against proletarian literature in favor of their own art, and there were some in the party who sympathized with their position. As they were fond of pointing out, even Lenin had said that the workers have no desire to read stories about life in the factories, which they know only too well. They did not believe in the possibility of creating truly proletarian art at the present time because such a culture did not yet exist, even in the proletarian state; this was to be an achievement of the distant future. Proletarian culture would come into existence only after the transformation of the whole world, and it would take new, totally unimaginable forms. They made a definite distinction between proletarian and revolutionary art, and if their movement could not claim to be proletarian, it was certainly revolutionary. But the surrealists had much to learn about party displine. They continued to be accused of anarchism, and this particular charge was given substance by "Second manifest du surréalisme" ("The Second Manifesto of Surrealism," 1930), written by Breton and signed by the whole group. Breton had declared that "the simplest surrealist act consists of going into the street, revolver in hand, and firing into the crowd," adding that, "a man who has not had at least once, the desire to end it all in this manner, to have done with the pettiness and vileness and idiocy of the system, deserves a place in that crowd, a gun at his belly." Understandably, this statement aroused a great deal of criticism from the party, which denounced him for anarchist terrorism and bourgeois individualism. Breton explained at length that what he had really meant to advocate was spontaneity, not violence, but many in the party were not convinced.

The early 1930's were a time of expansion for communism in France. One reason was, of course, the Great Depression, but the other, especially important for intellectuals, was the growing fear of fascism. It seemed to the surrealists that their position on the Left was becoming more secure, in spite of the continuing disapproval of certain Communist bureaucrats. The party had at last recognized their usefulness, or so it appeared, for it had begun to assign them tasks for which they were well fitted, such as putting them in charge of artistic arrangements for various cultural functions. But because of the incident known as "l'affaire Aragon," which began in 1930, the inevitable conflicts came to a head and the surrealists were forced out of the party and ultimately out of all the writers' and artists' groups it sponsored. They were, in fact, condemned to the isolation Triolet had foreseen.

As a result of the affair, it became impossible for Aragon or any other surrealists who were party members to exist in the old uneasy alliance with the party. This became clear to him after he made a trip to the Soviet Union. A great deal of pressure was brought to bear by Soviet officials as well as by Triolet, and it was necessary to make a choice. Aragon decided to abandon surrealism completely to work for the revolution under the banner of communism. Triolet is always either praised or blamed, depending on one's point of view, for persuading him to become a militant Communist, and there is ample evidence that her influence was decisive. In 1930 the Soviet Union held the first meeting of the International Congress of Revolutionary Writers at Kharkov, and she used her connections with such men as Alexander Fadeyev, a leader of RAPP, the Russian Association of Proletarian Writers, to have Aragon appointed an official delegate. The surrealists were delighted to hear of this, and Aragon was instructed to make every effort to secure a favorable resolution on surrealism, but unfortunately their enemy Barbusse was the other delegate, and it was his opinion of the movement that prevailed.

The objectives of the congress were to create an international group of Communist writers who were to keep in touch with each other in order to maintain true revolutionary principles in their work. They were expected to address themselves directly to the masses, to support revolutionary movements and colonial revolts, and to encourage the development of new writers from the working class. The congress founded the International Union of Revolutionary Writers, began to publish the journal *Literature of the World Revolution,* and, most important, passed a number of resolutions defining proletarian literature. The congress declared that "only dialectical materialism can be the creative method of proletarian literature . . . and the revolutionary writers of the world look upon their art as a special form . . . of the class struggle." Middle-class writers might possibly become proletarian writers, "however, [its] fundamental and principal cadres must be drawn from the working class." Another resolution triumphantly concluded that "proletarian literature is nothing more than a weapon in the class struggle."

Even the Marxist critic and Aragon biographer Roger Garaudy called these resolutions extreme, but Aragon, carried away with enthusiasm, eagerly agreed with them. Surprisingly, the resolution on surrealism expressed guarded optimism, saying that "the passage of several members of the group to a Communist ideology . . . encourages the hope that the better part of the present group of Surrealists, by continuing its evolution toward dialectical materialism . . . and by correcting the flagrant errors contained in its 'Second Manifesto of Super-Realism' [sic], will finally find its way to the real proletarian ideology."

Aragon, who made a number of speeches, rather halfheartedly defended the movement, even though he insisted, "We are not here as surrealists but as communists." He pointed out that although he and his friends did not claim to be proletarian writers, nevertheless "we are supporters of every form having a truly proletarian class content," and "we are for the development of propaganda literature . . . everything from the pamphlet to the revolutionary poem." He also assured the congress that the surrealists favored "carrying out propaganda in harmony with the line of the Third International," and he emphasized that revolutionary literature "cannot have any other purpose than systematic preparation for the speedy establishment of the proletarian dictatorship." He then read a declaration in which he asserted that the only basis for the creation of proletarian literature was the systematic development, along the lines laid down by the International, of the *rabcors*, or working-class writers. In that era, it was believed that writers could be developed merely by encouraging workers to contribute regularly to the party press.

Aragon had, of course, no authority to make such assertions in the name of the surrealists, and his position was so extreme that it did not even win approval at Kharkov, and it was clear the delegates distrusted him. Before leaving the Soviet Union, he was prevailed upon to write a letter to the International Union of Revolutionary Writers recanting various surrealist "errors." He apologized for the surrealists' attacks on Barbusse and for the articles critical of *L'Humanité* that had appeared in *Le surréalisme au service de la révolution*. He also promised that the group would engage in no further public criticisms of the party press and ended by saying,

> We wish to make clear that we believe strictly in dialectical materialism and repudiate all idealist ideologies, notably Freudianism. We also denounce Trotskyism as a social-democratic and counter-revolutionary ideology, and we are committed to combating Trotskyism at every opportunity. Our only desire is to work in the most efficacious manner following the directives of the Party to whose discipline and control we submit our literary activity.
> (Quoted in Char et al. *Paillasse! Fin de L'affaire Aragon*, p. 6)

Breton was astounded to learn that Aragon had signed a document that was virtually a repudiation of surrealism. It certainly appears that he was a personality too easily influenced, for once back in Paris, he reversed himself and issued a manifesto, *Aux intellectuels révolutionnaires* (To Revolutionary Intellectuals, 1931), as a defense of surrealism. In an article for the December 1931 issue of *Le surréalisme au service de la révolution*, he once more vowed his fidelity and declared that the surrealists had long ago abandoned their petit bourgeois origins and wholeheartedly supported the working class. But he again reversed himself.

Aragon's transformation from surrealist poet to militant Communist was marked by the publication of the poem "Front rouge" ("Red Front") in *Literature of the World Revolution* in 1931, although at the time, he presumably still considered himself a surrealist. "This poem is his first genuinely revolutionary work," the introduction stated, but it was really less poetry than propaganda. Even Garaudy conceded that it was not a good poem. Its tone was shrill, and its theme was pure "proletcult," as these verses show:

Feu sur Léon Blum
Feu sur Boncour Froissard Déat
Feu sur les ours savants de la social-democratie
Gloire à la dialectique matérialiste
et gloire à son incarnation
l'armée
Rouge

    Shoot Léon Blum
    Shoot Boncour Froissard Déat
    Shoot the trained bears of social
       democracy
    Glory to dialectical materialism
    And glory to its incarnation
    The Red
    Army

However, the critic Peter Collier, in his "The Poetry of Protest," maintains that because of the irregular rhyme and meter, the disparate voices, and the use of slogans and slang, "Red Front" is just as avant-garde as Aragon's earlier poetry and that it is a "dazzling, outrageous tribute to one of the great moments in the twentieth century, when it seemed possible to fuse optimistic revolutionary fervor with advanced literary experiment." But to the French government, the poem was dangerously subversive. The police seized the journal, and Aragon was indicted for incitement to treason and for provoking insurrection in the army. If convicted, he could have been sent to prison for five years, but the charges were eventually dropped. The surrealists immediately launched a petition in his defense, which they persuaded hundreds of internationally known artists and writers to sign. They did this in spite of what they considered the "retrogressive" nature of the poem, which they called "poésie de circonstance" (occasional poetry), a genre they despised. The party remained unsympathetic to Aragon's plight and perhaps would have liked having a poet "martyr" in jail. He begged the signers of the petition not to concern themselves with such an insignificant affair, and clearly the surrealists' support was an embarrassment to him.

In addition to Aragon's article, the same issue of *Le surréalisme au service de la révolution* contained a scatological contribution by Salvador Dali called "Rêverie" (Dream). It described his masturbatory fantasies in great detail, and it must have shocked the party official who said disgustedly to Breton, "You stink of bourgeois rottenness!" Aragon tried to persuade the surrealists to repudiate Dali because the party demanded it, but they indignantly refused to do so. When Breton insisted on making public the party's attempt to coerce them into expelling Dali, Aragon could not dissuade him. They had a bitter argument, and it was this that brought about the final rupture. After March 1932, he never again spoke to his former friends.

Aragon's break with surrealism was not only political; it was also literary. He left his earlier style behind him to devote himself to proletarian literature, with very unfortunate results in the opinion of most literary critics. Typical of his new style was "Complainte des chômeurs" (Lament of the Strikers) published in *La Lutte anti-réligieuse et prolétarienne* in April 1932:

Chômeurs, que les flics ne vous disent plus:
    circulez!
Chômeurs, que les flics ne vous chasse plus
    de sous les ponts?
Chômeurs, qu'on ne vous fasse plus attendre
    sous la pluie?
Chômeurs, qu'on vous foute la paix sur les bancs?

Strikers, if only the cops wouldn't say: move on!
Strikers, why won't the cops let you sleep
    under bridges?
Strikers, why must they make you wait in the rain?
Strikers, why won't they damn well let you be
    on public benches?

With his propensity for going to extremes, Aragon even wrote a poem in praise of the Soviet secret police, "Prélude au temps de cerises" (Prelude to Cherry Blossom Time):

Je chante le Guépéou nécessaire de la France
Je chante les Guépéous de nulle part et de
    partout

*Je demande un Guépéou pour préparer la fin
d'un monde.*

I sing of an OGPU needed by France
I sing of OGPUs of nowhere and everywhere
I want an OGPU to make an end to this world.
(Quoted in Lecherbonnier [1976], pp. 113–114)

This sort of writing—which Aragon did not continue to do for very long—is really "agit-prop," not poetry. Garaudy summed up the situation very well when he said that the critics, if they are Communists, regard Aragon's surrealist period as youthful folly, and if they are not, they have no interest in the literary output of his Communist period. From Aragon's point of view, he had merely resolved a conflict that had troubled him for many years and one that had reached the point of a moral and political crisis. In an article titled "Pour qui écrivez-vous?" (For Whom Do You Write?) in the December 1933 issue of *Commune*, he explained the necessity for working in the proletarian literature tradition by saying that "apolitical works are militant weapons for the preservation of the regime in power."

By becoming a proletarian writer, or a socialist realist writer, to use the later term, Aragon satisfied a need for usefulness in serving the revolution. It may seem surprising that left-wing writers in the West, under no sort of compulsion, would voluntarily place themselves within the artistic constraints of socialist realism. But a writer needs a public. By this move Aragon overcame what he regarded as a great limitation: the marginal nature of surrealism, which was aggravated by the group's esoteric preoccupations. Even more important, as it was first expounded, socialist realism was a very exciting concept. Stalin's famous remark that "writers are the engineers of the soul" was inspiring and seductive. Writers and artists could now feel that they had a vital role to play in the revolution. It was not until much later that the narrow and propagandistic nature of the doctrine became apparent or that the fate of dissident Soviet artists was known.

In *Pour un réalisme socialiste*, Aragon explained, "I finally came to see that the most urgent, in fact the only thing worthy of a man and a poet, was to put his art entirely at the service of this new world, . . . to shout out the glory of the new world to come." He ended by expressing his irritation and impatience with surrealism: "Let us have done with hallucinations, the unconscious, sex, dreams, etc! [*sic*]. Enough of fantasy! I hereby proclaim the return of reality!" Socialist realism was first defined at the Soviet Writers' Congress of 1934. It differed from the previous concept of proletarian literature, being in theory somewhat less rigid, and it was now no longer necessary for the writer to come from the working class, nor even to be a Communist. However, in practice it proved to be just as conformist. Socialist realism must be realist in form, socialist in content. It should portray the working class as heroic, convey a mood of optimism, be party minded, and conform to the current political line. As a statute of the Soviet Writers' Union states, socialist realist fiction "is representative of reality not as it is, but as it ought to be"; it is not intended to reflect society but rather to depict a glowing future. Therefore, it is not identical with objective realism in the sense that the term is used to describe the nineteenth-century realist novel. Instead it is "revolutionary romanticism," as Andrei Zhdanov, the new cultural commissar, called it. Nor was it the aim of socialist realism to preserve artistic freedom. On the contrary, as Gorky had stated in his address at the first Soviet Writers' Congress, "The Revolution and the Party do not exist to ensure . . . complete liberty of expression and if a writer wants to fight hand in hand with the masses, then he must march in the ranks of these masses."

In his newly adopted style, Aragon published a volume of poems entitled *Persécuté persécuteur* (The Persecuted and the Persecutor, 1931), in which the notorious "Red Front" was reprinted. He wrote an epic poem, *Hourra l'Oural* (Hurrah for the Urals, 1934), dedicated to the antifascist workers killed in the February

1934 riots in France. The poem hails the victory of the Bolshevik Revolution and describes the beautiful new world being constructed in the Soviet Union. He also published a work of literary theory, *Pour un réalisme socialiste*, in which he elucidates the doctrine as defined by the 1934 congress. He apologizes for his surrealist past but pays tribute to Mayakovsky, "who knew how to make an arm of poetry" and who was the link that joined him to the "new world." He adds that the "art of the Communist party cannot be an art of chance, an empirical art. It is distinguished by its scientific character, by the bases for its development, just as, if I may say so, communism is distinct from utopian socialism." In a later theoretical work, *Littératures sovietiques* (Soviet Literature, 1955), he approvingly quotes a speech by the Soviet novelist Mikhail Sholokov, who said, "Each of us writes according to the dictates of our hearts, but our hearts belong to the Party." Aragon concludes triumphantly that writers must abide by the dictum, "Write the Stalinist truth!" His zeal in the matter of socialist realism has caused him to be severely criticized by those who feel that he abandoned literature for propaganda. In some of his work, this was certainly the case, but he has also extended the boundaries of socialist realism and gone beyond it to create a new kind of art.

In the early 1930's Aragon worked as an ill-paid journalist for several party organs, *L'Humanité*, *Commune*, and *Ce Soir*, but he complained that they only assigned him "les chiens écrasés" (run-over dogs) stories because they mistrusted his surrealist past. He and Triolet lived in miserable housing since it was the policy that party workers should be paid at the same rate as the average manual worker, and Triolet was forced to earn money by designing jewelry for the haute couture shops. But in 1934, in spite of these hardships, he wrote his first novel, the first of four in the cycle *Le monde réel* (The Real World). It is called *Les cloches de Bâle* (*The Bells of Basel*, 1934), and it is intended to present a panoramic view of France from the late nineteenth century through World War I. Aragon depicts society on the verge of collapse, like the old regime before 1789, or like Russia just before the Bolsheviks swept away the old order because during the depression, people on the Left were convinced that capitalism was about to be destroyed.

It was Triolet who had encouraged him to write *The Bells of Basel*, which was an important breakthrough, and his gratitude was so great that he dedicated it to her "sans qui je me serais tu" ("without whom I would be silent")— a phrase that, with the change of one letter, would read "sans qui je me serais tué" ("without whom I would have killed myself"). Aragon was apparently alluding to the fact that when they met, he was in a profound depression, and he meant to imply that he would have committed suicide had he not met Triolet. Three women are the protagonists of the book: two fictional, Diane de Nettencourt and Catherine Simonidzé; and one real, the German Communist Clara Zetkin. He employs a device in this book that he later used repeatedly: mixing actual historical figures and events with fictional ones.

Diane, immoral and parasitic, represents the woman of the past. She cares only for money, and, although she is married to a rich man, she becomes the mistress of several other rich men out of greed. Aragon makes it clear that true love is impossible in the milieu of the haute bourgeoisie, where love is nothing but a commodity to be bought and sold.

As a tribute to Triolet, the second part of the novel centers on Catherine, a young Russian woman living in France. She is modeled after a real woman of whom he had been very fond, who had lived in his family's pension. Catherine, without being consciously political, has an instinctive belief in social justice, even though she is middle class and living on an allowance from her family. Her vague sympathies become crystallized when she sees the police assaulting some demonstrators, and she comes to feel thoroughly alienated from her own class. She attempts suicide but is saved by a taxi driver, and in gratitude, she helps out when the taxi drivers go on strike. Thus the fictional Catherine becomes a participant in an actual strike that occurred in 1912. But she is unable to take the final step and fully align herself with the working class, so Aragon says sadly, interjecting himself into the novel, as he frequently does, "I can no longer speak of Catherine. Hesitating, vacillating Catherine, how slowly does she approach the light!" Clara Zetkin appears only in the epilogue and is not even a part of the plot, but she has clearly succeeded where Catherine has not, and Aragon enthusiastically describes the antiwar speech she made at the International Social Democratic Congress in Basel in 1912. He quotes from her speech and says that Zetkin is the woman of the future:

> Here for the first time in the world, there is a place for true love. Love, which is not soiled by the superiority of man over woman, by the sordid story of dresses and kisses, by the domination of the man's money over the woman, or of the woman's over the man. The woman of modern times is born and it is of her that I will sing. And it is of her that I will sing.
>
> (p. 348)

His conscious feminism, revealed in the strong heroines of his novels, owes a lot to the influence of Triolet.

The second novel of the series *Le monde réel, Les beaux quartiers* (*Residential Quarter*, 1936), is not really a continuation of *The Bells of Basel*. It can be read independently and does not require a knowledge of the previous book, although some of the same characters, such as the wealthy industrialist Wisner, reappear. Aragon dedicates this work as well to Triolet, saying, "Both what I have written here and all that I will write, I dedicate . . . to Elsa Triolet, to whom I owe everything that I am, to whom I owe having found, in the depths of my confusion, the entrance to the real world." This comment is an oblique reference to his break with the fantasy world of surrealism as well as to

the title of the quartet. The two protagonists are brothers named Armand and Edmond Barbentane. Armand first belongs to a proto-fascist organization that engages in strikebreaking, but the death of a worker in a fight with this group horrifies him and awakens his sense of social justice. He and his brother both leave the provinces for Paris, but their destinies are very different. Edmond chooses the "beaux quartiers," or upper-class milieus, and becomes the lover of a rich woman, herself a parasite on society, as was Diane in *The Bells of Basel*. Armand becomes a radical hero who after many hesitations and doubts breaks definitively with the bourgeoisie to become a trade union leader. He has been employed by an automobile factory as a scab and is very proud of himself for becoming a manual worker and living entirely on his earnings. But he comes to realize that he is doing great harm as a strikebreaker, and, just as the workers are in despair over the failure of the strike, he joins them, giving them renewed faith in their efforts. At the end, pleased with Armand's support, a worker cries out, "Comrades, you see that we must never despair!"

These books were Aragon's first sustained efforts at socialist realist fiction, and they are superior examples of the genre. But despite the impending triumph of the proletariat with which they both end, the reception of these two novels was unfavorable. The non-Communist critics largely ignored Aragon's work, as they had since he became a Communist militant. But the Communist press attacked these books, in spite of what would seem to be their "correct" slant, on the grounds that his protagonists come almost exclusively from the middle and upper classes and that his working-class characters are merely peripheral. Aragon explained that it is easier to write about the ruling classes because they have so much more time in which to live, while the workers must spend all their time working. "This is perhaps what most separates the bourgeoisie from the proletariat," he had written in *The Bells of Basel,* and he might also have said that he himself was hardly in a position to have intimate knowledge of working-class life.

It was only with World War II that he gained a national reputation as well as great stature in the party for his inspiring Resistance writings, which had tremendous appeal for French people of all classes and political persuasions. In 1939, even before the fighting began, the Communist party was banned, many of its leaders were jailed or forced into exile, and party newspapers were shut down. *Ce Soir* was outlawed as a result of an editorial Aragon wrote in which he defended the Hitler-Stalin Pact. The pact was no more popular with Communists than it was with the general public, and many quit the party because of it. But those who remained were obliged to support it, although it later proved a source of political embarrassment. When Germany invaded France, Aragon was drafted into a special punishment battalion for political unreliables, while Triolet was interrogated by the police and their apartment was repeatedly searched. Again serving as a medical auxiliary as he had done in World War I, Aragon was awarded a medal for inventing a device for opening disabled tanks from the outside in order to remove the wounded men within.

In June 1940 France surrendered and the Germans occupied the northern half of the country, leaving the southern portion, of less strategic and economic value, to the puppet government of Vichy under the elderly Marshal Pétain. Aragon was demobilized, and he and Triolet were among the many thousands who fled south to the unoccupied zone, where they stayed with various friends. Writers were in a quandary, because unless they were willing to write for the German-controlled press, they could not publish at all. The *Liste Otto*, a list (issued in September 1940) of books forbidden by the Germans during the occupation, censored books by or about Jews, Communists, or well-known antifascists, thus effectively silencing the Left. Unfortunately, there were many enthusiastic pro-Nazi writers, such as Aragon's former friend Pierre Drieu La Ro-

chelle, who denounced Triolet as a Jew and a Communist in the fascist journal *Je suis partout*. But there were others who were determined to resist. One of the most famous was Vercors, pseudonym of Jean Bruler, who wrote the first Resistance novel, *Le silence de la mer* (*Silence of the Sea*), in 1942, and he maintained that one should not even attempt to publish legally. To counteract the propaganda of the pro-German press, and to give the writers of the Resistance a forum, he founded the clandestine Editions de Minuit, which illegally published twenty-five books. These books were widely distributed, sometimes copied by hand and passed from one friend to another, and after the war it became a great mark of distinction to have been published by Vercors. Triolet's underground novella, *Les amants d'Avignon* (*The Lovers of Avignon*, 1943; included in *A Fine of Two Hundred Francs*, 1986) was published by Editions de Minuit, as was Aragon's *Le crime contre l'esprit* (*Les martyrs*) (Crimes Against the Spirit [The Martyrs], 1944) and also his *Le musée Grévin* (The Wax Museum, 1943).

By November 1942 the whole country was occupied, and Triolet and Aragon, then in Nice, were warned that they were on a list of people to be arrested, so they were forced to go underground. From then on they had false identity cards and lived in constant fear of being arrested. Each achieved an outstanding record as a writer in the "intellectual Resistance," and both were decorated after the war. Although it is common to make a distinction between writing and activism, it would be more accurate to say, as did Jean-Paul Sartre, that writing is a political act. This was never more true than during the occupation, when illegal writing was activism of the most dangerous kind, when simply being caught with underground leaflets in one's possession could mean deportation and death. They both wrote for *Les lettres françaises*, the most important underground literary journal. Founded in Paris by Jacques Decour, whose specialty, ironically, was German culture, it was to be the writers' contribution to the struggle against the Nazis. But its appearance was delayed for months because Decour, arrested with the copy for the first issue in his possession, was executed. Others took his place, and Aragon became one of the editors. After the war, *Les lettres françaises* continued publication as a cultural journal sponsored by the Communist party, with Aragon as editor in chief and Triolet as drama critic. In 1944 Triolet also edited an underground newspaper called *Le Drôme en armes*, and while in Lyons Aragon founded Les Étoiles, a movement for intellectuals in the Resistance, based on five-member cells. Les Étoiles, a movement for intellectuals in the Resistance put out a Resistance newspaper of the same name and also published fiction and poetry in its clandestine publishing house, La Bibliothèque française.

Aragon and Triolet crossed the Demarcation Line illegally many times to get to Paris for editorial meetings of *Les lettres françaises*, and on one occasion they were escorted by the young Communist Georges Dudaches. But despite his experience as a *passeur*, someone who smuggled people across the line, the three were arrested and spent several weeks in jail. Fortunately, their false papers held up and they were released. Dudaches was later deported and killed, and Aragon told the story of his tragic end in *Le crime contre l'esprit (Les martyrs)*. On another occasion, armed with false papers, Aragon and Triolet were on a train to Paris, carrying a copy of Triolet's *The Lovers of Avignon*, when a German soldier came through, searching everyone's luggage. There was no time to hide the manuscript, and they were sure they were going to be arrested; but as the soldier leafed through the pages, it became clear that he could not read French, and he simply returned the manuscript to them and left.

During the war years, despite the dangers and hardships of life in the Resistance, Aragon and Triolet were both remarkably productive, thus demonstrating the truth of Jean-Paul Sartre's paradoxical remark, "We were never more free than under the Germans." Claude Roy, a writer who worked closely with them at the time, has said that he believes that they were more free in spirit, more in accord with each other, and actually happier in the Resistance than ever before or since. With no party directives to follow, Aragon was his own man. He emerged with a reputation as the great poet of the French Resistance, and in fact this became virtually an official title. The BBC broadcast his poems in occupied France, the RAF dropped copies of them over the countryside, and the poems were translated and published in England and the United States during the war. Triolet was equally active, and because of her courageous work in the Resistance, Aragon said in a 1964 interview, "She has torn off my masculine spectacles, those male prejudices by which, under pretext of assuming all responsibility for the couple, the man confines the woman to the role of wife, and a mere reflection of her husband."

The first of Aragon's collections of verse was begun even before the defeat of France. *Le crève-coeur* (Heartbreak, 1941) speaks of his anguish at the commencement of yet another war and also of his sorrow at being separated from his beloved wife. His style changed drastically as he returned to the classical mode of the alexandrine, or twelve-syllable line. He also returned to rhyme, but with a new variation, for the meaning, and sometimes the rhyme itself, often runs over into the following line. His themes also changed, and he speaks of love, but personal love and love of country intermingle inextricably in his verse. At the same time, he evokes the grandeur of the French past, evoking the medieval era when legendary French heroes slew dragons. These works were understood by his readers to be a metaphor for the Resistance, and people became adept at reading the antifascist message concealed even in many works that were approved by the Nazi censors and legally published. In a 1941 letter to Hannah Josephson, he explained that "first we worked on the problem of language so carefully that nothing seemed worthy of it; nothing seemed worth saying. We said *nothing* magnificently and with the greatest freedom of expression. And now we have found what we had to say, more than we ever dreamed possible. Can we ever say it well enough?" At last Aragon had found his authentic voice, and there is a sense of elation discernible in his wartime works.

Les yeux d'Elsa (Elsa's Eyes, 1942) was one of many collections of poems dedicated to Triolet. Here too he mixes the personal and the political, using the image of darkness to symbolize the occupation. One of the poems, "Plus belle que les larmes" ("More Beautiful Than Tears"), was an answer to Drieu La Rochelle, who had attacked Aragon for his Resistance work and accused him (rightly) of publishing anti-German and anti-Vichy writings. The poem was read by General de Gaulle on Radio Algiers:

> *J'empêche en respirant certaines gens*
> *de vivre*
> *Je trouble leur sommeil d'on ne sait*
> *quel remords*
> *Il paraît qu'en rimant je débouche*
> *les cuivres*
> *et que ça fait un bruit à réveiller*
> *les morts*

> I keep some people from living freely
> I haunt their dreams and bring remorse
> It seems my poems are such loud trumpets
> They make a nose that wakes
> the dead

Le musée Grévin, signed with the pseudonym François La Colère (François the Angry), was a poem that paid tribute to the many women of France deported to Auschwitz for their Resistance activities, among whom were his friends Danièle Casanova, Mai Politzer, and Marie-Claude Vaillant-Couturier. He also wrote short stories, some of which were collected in the volume *Servitude et grandeur des français* (The Slavishness and Greatness of the French People, 1945). Subtitled "Scènes des années terribles" (Scenes of the Terrifying Years), these stories illustrated the grotesque as well as the heroic side of life under the occu-

pation. In *La diane française* (French Reveille, 1945), some of the poems are set in the remote past, while others are lyrical love poems of the present, and the content of Aragon's poetry was no longer sectarian, as it had been in the 1930's. In one famous poem, "La rose et le réséda" (The Rose and the Reed), he commemorates equally the execution of two Resistance heroes, one a Communist, the other a devout Catholic. There are also love poems to Triolet in *La diane française*, and one, which has been set to music, ends surprisingly with the line "There is no happy love." In the 1964 interview Aragon explained what he meant: "It was in 1943 that this poem was written, that is to say, it was at the height of the miseries of the occupation. . . . The impossibility of happiness in the midst of general misfortune is the theme expressed in this poem . . . and also in almost everything I have written." Thus, for him, individual destiny is inescapably linked to the fate of the country and to history itself.

Aragon also continued his cycle of novels, and the third volume of *Le monde réel*, completed just before the war, was published legally in 1942. It was called *Les voyageurs de l'impériale* (translated as *The Century Was Young* and again as *Passengers of Destiny*). One meaning of the word *impériale* is "double-decker bus," and he explained that this struck him as a perfect metaphor for the lives of the bourgeoisie, whom he envisions seated on the upper deck, passively viewing the sights. They are mere bystanders with no real comprehension of the world, rather than people who actively work to achieve their goals. This novel, too, draws heavily upon autobiographical elements. The protagonist, in part a portrait of Aragon's grandfather, is Pierre Mercadier, a history professor whose life is a failure both personally and professionally. He continually takes notes for a book he never writes; he plays the stock market and loses a lot of money in the Panama scandal, a stock swindle of 1889; and he is completely alienated from his family. He dies just as World War I begins in August 1914—a date that for Aragon marked the dawn of a new world. Pierre's son, Pascal, must fight in the war that Pierre and others like him were responsible for starting, and Pascal is angry and bitter toward the older generation. The study of the character of Pierre is intended to be an object lesson and a warning of the dangers of alienation, as he dies alone and forgotten. His death also serves as a symbol of the death of the old order.

The fourth and final novel of the series, generally considered the best, is *Aurélien* (1944), and the vagaries of censorship were such that it was legally published during the occupation. It was inspired by a very successful novel Triolet had just written; in fact, the only income the couple had for some time was from the royalties she had earned. Legally published in 1943, her book, *Le cheval blanc* (translated as *The White Horse*, and again as *The White Charger*), was the story of Michel, an aimless playboy who secretly longs to be a knight on a white horse doing brave deeds. In the war, he finds the cause he has been searching for and dies at the front, a hero at last. Aragon's Aurélien bears a striking resemblance to Michel. He, too, is aimless, and, having a private income, he has no need to work. But he secretly longs for something to give meaning to his life. He falls in love with Bérénice, a cousin of Edmond Barbentane, a character who first appeared in *Residential Quarter*. Bérénice, however, does not return his affection, perceiving that Aurélien is not really capable of true love, and they part. Aragon brings the novel up to the present, and Aurélien, serving in the French army in World War II, is stationed in the south of France, where he encounters Bérénice once more. She, the real hero of the novel, is very politically active. She has become the "new woman," like Clara Zetkin, and has completely broken with her class. She aids refugees from the Spanish Civil War and French refugees from the occupied zone, and she is furious because France has surrendered. She realizes that she had been right to leave Aurélien, who has no sympathy with what she stands for, and at the end, Aurélien is wounded and she

is killed by the Germans. The character of Bérénice—strong, brave, and socially conscious—is really a tribute to Triolet's wartime courage and commitment.

After the war, the Fourth Republic was founded with de Gaulle at its head. It was to be a government of social justice following the principles set forth in *La Charte de la Résistance* (Charter of the Resistance), a document signed by all the major Resistance organizations, including the Communists. But the euphoria of the liberation was short-lived, and Aragon expressed his profound disillusionment with the failure of these ideals to survive the cold war in a book of poems, *Le nouveau crève-coeur* (New Heartbreak, 1948). In it, he again calls for social change and makes an impassioned plea for an end to the petty factional strife and corruption that beset postwar France. Alarmed by the growing intensity of the cold war, Aragon and Triolet worked closely with the Communists. Having achieved renown through their achievements in the Resistance, they were certainly the most celebrated Communist couple. Those who disliked them, for either personal or political reasons, referred to them contemptuously as "the royal couple of the Communist party" because they so frequently presided over international congresses, party functions, and the like. The two also became leaders of the international peace movement. They were among the founders of the Mouvement mondial des partisans de la paix (Worldwide Movement of Partisans for Peace), and they led protest demonstrations against the atom bomb, NATO, the rearming of West Germany, the Korean War, and the execution of the Rosenbergs.

Aragon's work again became extremely sectarian, especially the multivolume *L'Homme communiste* (Communist Man) published between 1946 and 1953 but never completed. It is set in the period from February 1939, the end of the Spanish Civil War, to January 1945, the liberation of France after World War II. While Pierre Daix calls it one of the greatest military novels of Europe, most critics regard it as a propagandistic justification of Communist policies, especially of the controversial Hitler-Stalin Pact. It is virtually a hymn of praise to Maurice Thorez, the party leader whom Aragon describes as the ideal Communist, and it also glorifies the work of the Communists in the Resistance. In *L'Homme communiste* he mingles historical figures with fictional ones as he had done in *Le monde réel*, and some of the same characters reappear in this work. The novel seems less like fiction than like journalism, with its actual newspaper accounts of speeches and lengthy factual descriptions of current events. The heroes and heroines are party members, but they are not drawn with any psychological depth. The tone of the novel is humorless and didactic, and the book embodies the principles of socialist realism at their most extreme. In this work literature has been sacrificed to propaganda for the sake of a party that was increasingly persecuted and isolated by the severity of the cold war. In the early 1950's, Communists were excluded from government, forced out of their jobs, arbitrarily arrested and jailed, so inevitably the party inspired an unusually intense loyalty.

Aragon's best realist novel is probably *La semaine sainte* (*Holy Week*, 1958). The historical setting is Easter week of 1815, when Napoleon, having already been defeated, staged an attempted return to power, forcing Louis XVIII to flee ignominiously to Belgium. Again, Aragon employs the technique of having historical personages interspersed with fictional ones, but stylistically it is very different from his previous books. The hero, who is also one of the narrators, is the great Romantic painter, Théodore Géricault, who witnesses these historical events. Aragon's use of a painter as protagonist reflects his profound interest in art, a subject about which he wrote a great deal. Géricault was chosen because his famous painting of a shipwreck, *The Raft of the Medusa* (1818), was such an excellent metaphor for contemporary France and also because, according to Aragon, he was the first to paint the common people with real empathy instead of as conventional

figures dotting the landscape. In the novel Géricault's empathy is awakened by his first real contact with the people, which occurred during the dramatic events of Holy Week.

Switching to the present, Aragon, as before, interjects himself into this novel by describing the decisive event that had awakened his own feeling for the poor. In 1919 there had been strikes by miners who stopped work because of dangerous conditions in the mines. Aragon's army unit had been ordered to shoot them if they persisted in their refusal to work, but he suddenly understood that the miners were right and that their resistance was an example of "everything great and noble in life." The whole book is, in the words of Becker, a "montage," a series of flashbacks and flashforwards as the scene shifts from 1815 to 1919 and then to the 1950's and the outbreak of the Algerian war for independence. The complexity of the stream-of-consciousness style that intertwines past, present, and future time makes this book a departure from other works of his Communist period. As Becker has noted, his ideology remained the same and yet,

> Aragon has never limited his novels to a mere re-creation of the past or a description of the present. He has attempted in all of his work, especially in his novels, to express his ideas and teach his philosophy. He has failed when his vision has been too greatly affected by his political bias and has succeeded, as he did in *La Semaine Sainte*, when his political intent has not subverted his artistic genius.

He remained faithful to the party and continued to be a member of the Central Committee throughout all the vicissitudes of "de-Stalinization," enduring such humiliations as the so-called affair of the portrait. On Stalin's death in 1953, Aragon had asked Picasso for a drawing of Stalin for a special issue of *Les lettres françaises*. Picasso gladly complied but portrayed him as a dashing young man looking rather like a gypsy, instead of as the familiar father image that was so important to the cult of personality. French party leaders were scandalized, and in spite of Triolet's efforts to intervene, Aragon was forced to publish an abject apology in *L'Humanité* for allowing the portrait to appear. Triolet was apparently even more upset than he, because as a result of this incident, she wrote the novel *Le monument* (The Statue, 1957), which is a devastating satire on Communist bureaucracy and on socialist realism. She was severely criticized for this by party officials. While Aragon dutifully defended her, calling *Le monument* her masterpiece, it soon became clear that she no longer enjoyed the same favored status among the party elite as he did.

Even after Khrushchev's anti-Stalin revelations of 1956—the political move that ushered in détente—the French party remained opposed to de-Stalinization. Aragon was widely condemned for not supporting the many intellectuals on the Left who espoused a more liberal policy. But after being "wrong" in the Stalin portrait affair and having dared to defend his wife's controversial book, he seemed determined to be, in the words of one historian, "more communist than the Soviets." He aligned himself with the conservative faction of the party and remained a steadfast upholder of orthodoxy, at least until 1968.

Such were the contradictions of his character that, although supporting the Stalinist stance of his party, he proceeded to create a new kind of novel, one that was far from the socialist realism he professed. In some respects it was a return in form to his surrealist youth, but in others it was new and experimental, blurring the boundaries between prose and poetry.

La mise à mort (Put to Death, 1965) is a poetic narrative of great complexity. One of its major themes is split personality, and the principal characters are Alfred and his double, Anthoine, and Ingeborg and her double, Fougère. Aragon and Triolet also appear in the narrative under their own names, and the reader assumes that the male and female protagonists are intended to reflect aspects of their own personalities. Another theme is jealousy, and Alfred decides to kill Anthoine because of his relationship with Fougère, even though killing Anthoine means killing himself. References are made to doubles in literature, notably to Robert Louis Stevenson's *The Strange Case of Dr. Jekyll and Mr. Hyde* (1886), and also to *Othello* because it is a psychological study in jealousy. Once again, Aragon interjects himself and history into the work when he speaks of his growing disillusionment with Stalinist terror and of his good friend the Soviet journalist Mikhail Koltsev, who died in the purges. He also has Ingeborg declare that Elsa Triolet is her favorite writer, whereupon she embarks upon a discussion of Triolet's work. Another theme is the nature of the novel itself, the "mentir-vrai" (lie-truth) that is its essence. Paradoxically, fiction must illuminate reality, he says, so history itself remains the real subject in this as in all of Aragon's novels.

Blanche ou l'oubli (Blanche or Forgetfulness, 1967) is a novel that is also an analysis of the novel, and some critics regard this book as his masterpiece. In the text itself, Aragon explains his purpose. It is novels themselves that are the subject, and for Gaiffier, the hero, a novel that he imagines is being written functions as an instrument of self-discovery. Gaiffier must find out why his wife, Blanche, has left him, but to do this he must call upon his memories and gain insight into his own past. He imagines that another character, a young woman, is writing a novel about his marriage, and he answers her questions as a way of learning the truth. This work was in part inspired by Triolet's *Luna-Park* (1959), whose mysterious heroine is also named Blanche. Triolet's heroine, a test pilot lost in the Sahara, never appears. Justin, the man who is renting her house, becomes obsessed with her and tries to find out about her by reading love letters addressed to her. He reconstructs much of her life, but he never solves the puzzle of her disappearance. Aragon's Blanche was secretly writing a novel, and it was Gaiffier's jealous obsession that she was escaping from him into a fictional world that provoked the end of their relationship. This deliberately parallels Aragon's life, since he had admitted to being extremely jealous early in his marriage when he first discovered that Triolet intended to continue writing fiction. It was Aragon's belief that the novels one reads clarify one's own life and have as great an influence as do actual events. Toward the end of his life, he completely changed his attitude toward "bourgeois" literature. He conceded that the best of his work is founded on this tradition, and also that surrealism had never ceased to be a vital influence on him. *Henri Matisse, roman (Henri Matisse, A Novel*, 1971) is a "slide form," a term that describes a work that is part fiction and part autobiography, and again Aragon writes about himself as well as about the painter he greatly admired. He describes Matisse's sensuality and his religious agnosticism and discusses in detail the building of the Dominican chapel in Vence that Matisse designed. But he also provides intimate details about his own early life, including his problematic relationship with his father, and his father's agnosticism and deathbed conversion. *Théâtre-roman* (Theater-Novel, 1974), his last long work, is also a partly theoretical and partly personal meditation on art and on his own career. Its overall theme is his consciousness of old age, of his failing powers, and of his approaching death.

Triolet, his wife and colleague for more than forty years, died in 1970. Thus he lost the woman to whom he had brought a flower every day, and whom he had celebrated in so many volumes of poetry that people made a joke of it, saying, "Who ever heard of writing love poems to your wife?" It was she who bore the brunt of Aragon's adoration, since she was not only the object of the "cult of Elsa," not merely Aragon's "muse," but also a writer with her own career. In many respects her reputation suffered because of her identification with him. In all fairness, however, it should be said that Aragon, once he got over his jealousy, did sincerely try to encourage her and promote her work. On one occasion he refused to speak at a conference of writers because Triolet had not been invited,

and he was one of the few critics who seriously analyzed her fiction. He published *Elsa Triolet choisie par Aragon* (Elsa Triolet Chosen by Aragon) in 1960, which consists of selections from her novels and short stories, prefaced by a long introduction he wrote about her work. Also, on his initiative, *Les oeuvres romanesques croisées d'Elsa Triolet et de Louis Aragon* (The Crossed Works of Fiction of Elsa Triolet and Louis Aragon) appeared between 1964 and 1976. It was an undertaking that was probably unique in publishing history, a luxury edition in forty-two volumes of the fictional works of both writers. It is beautifully printed and is extensively illustrated by such artists as Marc Chagall and Henri Matisse. It includes many photographs, some of which illustrate the fiction, and translations of Triolet's first three novels, which had been written in Russian. But most significant, it includes extensive prefaces by both to their own works, and these provide a wealth of biographical information and serve to tie their respective works together. "Now, no one can separate us," Aragon declared, and it is a monument to his conception of the "couple." He also paid Triolet the compliment of drawing upon the themes of her novels for several of his own, as he did in *Aurélien* and *Blanche ou l'oubli*, and it is because of her that he became consciously feminist in his writing:

> I am the enemy of this rule of man which is not yet over. For me, woman is the future of man in the sense that Marx said that man is the future of man. I think that in order for society to progress, it must have as its basic unit the couple who are happy and in love. But all I see is a society where monogamy is legal and polygamy is general. Today, conjugal happiness seems only a utopian dream.
>
> (Quoted in Lecherbonnier [1974], p. 65)

Aragon became less politically intransigent in his later years, and it is clear that he was progressively disenchanted with the Soviet Union, although his disillusionment was with Soviet policies, not with communism as an ideal. The lifelong antiwar activist was most unhappy when the Soviets invaded Hungary in 1956, and this was indeed a decisive event for many who quit the party because of it. But Aragon remained silent and was actually identified with the most rigidly orthodox elements of the French party. He did, however, speak out in 1966 against the trial of Daniel and Sinyafsky in the Soviet Union, and also against the Soviet invasion of Prague in 1968, which indicated a profound change in his thinking. He went on to become identified with the more liberal anti-Stalinist elements of the party, publicly championing the cause of persecuted intellectuals in the Soviet Union and in other eastern European countries. Yet he did not come to the aid of his friend Garaudy, who was forced out of the party in 1970. His increasing ideological disagreement with and separation from the International and the French party became evident in his writings, and he declared that, while he does not reject communism, he does repudiate Soviet aggression. He maintained that his adherence to communism was rooted in his experiences in World War I and in his guilt over having done nothing to prevent its coming, and that he had sworn then to do whatever he could to protest any future war.

But for many his change of heart came too late. He had tried to involve himself in the student revolt of 1968, which erupted independently of the party. But the students wanted nothing to do with him. Unlike Simone de Beauvoir and Jean-Paul Sartre, who were very popular and very much involved in the student revolt, Aragon was regarded with deep hostility. He was shouted down as an apologist for the Soviet secret police and Stalinism when he tried to speak at a student meeting. He was deeply stung by the many attacks made against him by, for example, Jean Schuster, leader of the new generation of surrealists after Breton's death. Schuster called him "the chief architect of cultural terrorism" for insisting upon a rigid adherence to socialist realism, and the poet Guy Prévan devoted an entire book, *La confession d'Aragon*, to accusing Aragon of a lifetime of political lies and personal betrayals. In his last works, Aragon almost obsessively tried to explain his ideological positions in answer to his critics.

It has been said that all writing is really autobiographical, but Aragon's work represents the extreme of this truism. Having been lied to from his infancy about his true identity, he had to engage in an obsessive search for the truth about his past, like his hero Gaiffier in *Blanche ou l'oubli*. According to Daix, author of the best biography of Aragon, his search for a family and an identity was destined to fail. As a dadaist sworn to give up literature, he was devoured by a passion to create. As a surrealist opposed to bourgeois art, he was determined to write novels. As a Communist militant and theoretician of socialist realism, he was consumed by a desire to write lyric poetry and experimental fiction, and it is clear that he was never entirely content with any of the varied roles he chose to play. After spending the last few years of his life in seclusion, he died on 24 December 1982.

Selected Bibliography

EDITIONS

INDIVIDUAL WORKS

FICTION

Anicet ou le panorama, roman. Paris, 1921.
Les aventures de Télémaque. Paris, 1922.
Le libertinage. Paris, 1924.
Le paysan de Paris. Paris, 1926.
Les cloches de Bâle. Paris, 1934.
Les beaux quartiers. Paris, 1936.
Les voyageurs de l'impériale. Paris, 1942. Definitive edition, 1947.
Aurélien. Paris, 1944.
Servitude et grandeur des français. Paris, 1945.
Les communistes. 6 vols. (Vol. 5 is in 2 vols.) Paris, 1949–1951.
La semaine sainte. Paris, 1958.
La mise à mort. Paris, 1965.
Blanche ou l'oubli. Paris, 1967.
Henri Matisse, roman. Paris, 1971.
Théâtre-roman. Paris, 1974.

LOUIS ARAGON

POETRY

Le mouvement perpétuel. Paris, 1926.
La grande gaieté. Paris, 1929.
Persécuté persécuteur. Paris, 1931.
Hourra l'Oural. Paris, 1934.
Cantique à Elsa. Algiers, 1941.
Le crève-coeur. Paris, 1941.
Les yeux d'Elsa. Neuchâtel, Switzerland, 1942.
Le musée Grévin. Paris, 1943.
La diane française. Paris, 1945.
Le nouveau crève-coeur. Paris, 1948.
Les yeux et la mémoire. Paris, 1954.
Le roman inachevé. Paris, 1956.
Elsa. Paris, 1959.
Il ne m'est Paris que d'Elsa. Paris, 1964.

ESSAYS AND NONFICTION

Le traité du style. Paris, 1928.
La peinture au défi. Paris, 1930.
Pour un réalisme socialiste. Paris, 1934.
L'Homme communiste. 2 vols. Paris, 1946–1953.
Littératures sovietiques. Paris, 1955.
J'abats mon jeu. Paris, 1959.
Histoire parallèle (U.R.S.S.-U.S.A.). 4 vols. Paris, 1962. With André Maurois.
Je n'ai jamais appris à écrire ou les incipits. Geneva, 1969.

COLLECTED WORKS

Les oeuvres romanesques croisées d'Elsa Triolet et de Louis Aragon. 42 Vols. Paris, 1964–1976.

INTERVIEWS WITH ARAGON

Entretiens avec Francis Crémieux. Paris, 1964.
Aragon parle avec Dominique Arban. Paris, 1968.

TRANSLATIONS

The Adventures of Telemachus. Lincoln, Nebr., 1988.
Aragon: Poet of the French Resistance. Edited by Hannah Josephson and Malcolm Cowley. Various translators. New York, 1945.
Aurélien. Translated by Eithne Wilkins. New York, 1947.
The Bells of Basel. Translated by Haakon M. Chevalier. New York, 1936.
The Century Was Young. Translated by Hannah Josephson. New York, 1941.
Conversations on the Dresden Gallery. Translated by Francis Scarfe. New York, 1982. With Jean Cocteau.
Henri Matisse, A Novel. Translated by Jean Stewart. New York, 1972.
A History of the USSR, From Lenin to Krushchev. Translated by Patrick O'Brian. London, 1964.
Holy Week, A Novel. Translated by Haakon Chevalier. New York, 1961.
The Libertine. Translated by Jo Levy. London and New York, 1987.
Nightwalker. Translated by Frederick Brown. Englewood Cliffs, N. J., 1970.
Paris Peasant. Translated and introduced by Simon Watson Taylor. New York, 1971.
Passengers of Destiny. Translated by Hannah Josephson. London, 1947.
The Red Front. Translated by E. E. Cummings. Chapel Hill, N. C., 1933.
Residential Quarter. Translated by Haakon Chevalier. New York, 1938.

BIOGRAPHICAL AND CRITICAL WORKS

Becker, Lucille F. *Louis Aragon.* New York, 1971.
Bibrowska, Sophie. *Une mise à mort; l'itinéraire romanesque d'Aragon.* Paris, 1972.
Breton, André. *Les manifestes du surréalisme.* Paris, 1962. *Manifestoes of Surrealism.* Translated by Richard Seaver and Helen R. Lane. Ann Arbor, Mich., 1969.
Daix, Pierre. *Aragon une vie à changer.* Paris, 1975.
Fowlie, Wallace. *Age of Surrealism.* Bloomington, Ind., 1960.
Garaudy, Roger. *L'Itinéraire d'Aragon.* Paris, 1961.
Huraut, Alain. *Louis Aragon, prisonnier politique.* Paris, 1970.
Josephson, Matthew. *Life Among the Surrealists.* New York, 1962.
Juin, Herbert. *Aragon.* Paris, 1960.
Lecherbonnier, Bernard. *Aragon.* Paris, 1971.
——— . *Le cycle d'Elsa Aragon.* Paris, 1974.
——— , ed. *Les critics de notre temps et Aragon.* Paris, 1976.
Lewis, Helena. *The Politics of Surrealism.* New York, 1988. Also published as *Dada Turns Red: The Politics of Surrealism.* Edinburgh, 1989.
Lottman, Herbert. *The Left Bank: Writers, Artists and Politics from the Popular Front to the Cold War.* Boston, 1982.
Motherwell, Robert, ed. *The Dada Painters and Poets: An Anthology.* New York, 1951.

Nadeau, Maurice. *Histoire du surréalisme suivie de documents surréalistes*. Paris, 1964. Translated as *The History of Surrealism*. Translated by Richard Howard. New York, 1965; repr., 1989. Includes Aragon's "Have You Ever Slapped a Dead Man?"

Prévan, Guy. *La confession d'Aragon*. Paris, 1980.

Raymond, Marcel. *De Baudelaire au surréalisme*. Paris, 1950. Translated as *From Baudelaire to Surrealism*. Translated by G. M. New York, 1950.

Rühle, Jürgen. *Literatur und Revolution*. Köln, 1960. Translated as *Literature and Revolution*. Translated by Jean Steinberg. New York, 1969.

Sadoul, Georges. *Aragon: Présentation, choix de textes*. Paris, 1967.

Seghers, Pierre. *La résistance et ses poètes*. 2 vols. Paris, 1978.

Scott, H. G., ed. *Problems of Soviet Literature: Reports and Speeches at the First Soviet Writers' Congress*. New York, 1935.

Short, Robert. *Dada and Surrealism*. London, 1980.

Sur, Jean. *Aragon: le réalisme et l'amour*. Paris, 1966.

Timms, Edward, and Peter Collier, eds. *Visions and Blueprints: Avant-garde Culture and Radical Politics in Early Twentieth-Century Europe*. Manchester, 1988. Includes Peter Collier's "The Poetry of Protest."

Waldberg, Patrick. *Surrealism*. New York, 1978.

HELENA LEWIS

BERTOLT BRECHT

(1898–1956)

IN THE EDITION of Bertolt Brecht's works which his West German publishers issued to commemorate the seventieth anniversary of his birth (1968)—and which, for all its omissions and editorial imperfections, is likely to remain the fullest and most nearly complete corpus of Brecht's oeuvre for a very long time to come—just over three thousand pages are occupied by his dramatic output; over a thousand by his poetry; fifteen hundred by his novels and stories; and well over two thousand by his theoretical essays on aesthetics and politics. It is an impressive body of work, and one must always keep in mind that a very large proportion of it remains untranslated into English. The fact that the bulk of the translations are of plays and that only relatively few poems, essays, and stories are accessible to the English-speaking public has a distorting effect on Brecht's image in the English-speaking world. It may indeed sound heretical today, but may well be true nevertheless, that posterity might attribute greater importance to Brecht's poems and some of his short stories than to his work as a dramatist; or that of his twenty-one full-length and sixteen shorter plays, and six major adaptations, perhaps no more than half a dozen might stand the test of time. As to his theoretical writings, they have played an important part in creating Brecht's worldwide fame, for they have stimulated discussion about his plays among actors, directors, and critics and have made the study of his work

particularly attractive in academic circles. They might, however, also prove the most vulnerable element in Brecht's posthumous reputation, resting, as they do, on the fairly shaky foundations of Brecht's own peculiar view of Marxism, a very questionable conception of the psychological basis of the audience's experience in the theater, and on many passing fashions of the political and aesthetic climate of his times.

Much of Brecht's future reputation will also depend on another vital element in his artistic personality: his work as a practical man of the theater, as a teacher of actors and directors. Brecht's sudden rise to world fame in the last years of his life was, in fact, primarily due to the success of his theater, the Berliner Ensemble, which he founded after his return from exile in 1949, and which took Paris by storm on the occasion of the international festival of 1954. The Berliner Ensemble was created to test Brecht's theory of drama in performance. It is still an important theatrical company, but fears that it might deteriorate into a mere museum, exhibiting fossilized productions of Brecht's plays, have proved at least partially well grounded.

In the English-speaking world and in France Brecht's reputation has, as it were, been standing on its head: his work as a director (largely in the spheres unaffected by ignorance of the text—design, lighting, music) came first and has exercised the deepest influence; then, because it stimulated fruitful and endlessly interesting discussion, came his work as a theorist of left-wing aesthetics; and only in the third place followed his output as a dramatist, with far less convincing success. Whether in France, Britain, or America, relatively few of Brecht's plays have really achieved a decisive breakthrough and many have been signal failures. And Brecht the great poet and prose writer is virtually unknown.

Yet it is this aspect of Brecht that should come first. That many of his plays remain failures in translation is often directly attributable to the fact that in German they succeed mainly by the force of their language, their poetry, far less so as drama.

No wonder, therefore, that meaningful discussion of Brecht is very difficult in English, that a great deal of the vast literature which has grown around him and continues to proliferate has an air of irreality and is bedeviled by fierce controversy directly attributable to the widely differing basic assumptions from which different commentators start their arguments. And this situation, already complex enough, is further complicated by the highly inflammable political content of Brecht's work.

Brecht was converted to communism before he was thirty and remained a communist to the end of his life; yet much depends on the nature of his communism. It would be equally naive to regard Brecht as a mere follower of the party line at any given period or to label him a consistent deviationist; to assume that his ostensible support of, say, the Stalinist show trials also implied support for Stalinist aesthetics—or, conversely, that having been accused of being a formalist by the supporters of orthodox Stalinist aesthetics, he must also have disapproved of Stalinist policies in other fields. In fact the much-delayed publication in 1982 of his hitherto suppressed poetry showed that he had written some short poems and epigrams highly critical of Stalin, whom he dubbed "the meritorious murderer of the people."

What all this ultimately amounts to is the need to reiterate again and again the obvious, yet frequently ignored, truism that to understand Brecht one must see him against his background: the background of his language and its culture and literature, the background of the history of his times, the background of the theater against which he rebelled, the background of Marxist theory and Marxist politics.

Brecht was born at Augsburg, the chief town of the Bavarian part of Swabia, on 10 February 1898. He thus belongs to the generation that reached maturity in World War I. When the war ended in 1918 Brecht was almost twenty-one and ready to take the plunge into the whirlpool of experimentation—in life as well as in art—which was the inevitable consequence of the collapse of the hallowed—now seen to be hollow—values of respectable Wilhelmian society that, only a few years earlier, had seemed immovable and eternally stable. The feeling of liberation which the breakup and sudden disappearance of that social order produced was exhilarating, but at the same time it must also have been very frightening to be propelled directly from the straitjacket of small-town petty-bourgeois gentility into the void of almost total permissiveness. Brecht's later decision to subject himself to the new straitjacket of party discipline—and, indeed, the whole German nation's equally morbid drive to do likewise in the acceptance of the iron rule of Hitler—must be seen in the light of this experience.

The first phase of Brecht's career as a writer represents the period of that liberation into nothingness (ca. 1918–ca. 1927); it produced the plays *Baal* (1918), *Trommeln in der Nacht* (*Drums in the Night,* 1918), *Im Dickicht der Städte* (*In the Jungle of Cities,* 1923), *Leben Eduards des Zweiten von England* (Edward II, 1924), *Mann ist Mann* (*A Man's a Man,* 1926), and culminated in *Die Dreigroschenoper* (*The Threepenny Opera,* 1928) and *Aufstieg und Fall der Stadt Mahagonny* (*The Rise and Fall of the State of Mahagonny,* 1929) (the last two written after 1927 but still imbued with an afterglow of that period) and the volume of poems *Hauspostille* (*Manual of Piety,* 1927). This phase of anarchic nihilism was followed by a period of austere didacticism, a frantic search for discipline (ca. 1927–ca. 1934) which resulted in the most severely controlled, the seemingly—but only seemingly—most arid portion of Brecht's oeuvre, the *Lehrstücke* and *Schulopern* (teaching plays and school operas), *Das Badener Lehrstück vom Einverständnis* (*The Didactic Play of Baden: On Consent*, 1929), *Der Flug der Lindberghs* (*The Flight of the Lindberghs*, 1929), *Der Jasager/ Der Neinsager* (*He Who Says Yes/He Who Says No*, 1930), *Die Massnahme* (*The Measures Taken*, 1930), *Die Ausnahme und die Regel* (*The Exception and the Rule*, 1930), *Die Horatier und die Kuriatier* (*The Horatians and the Curiatians*, 1934), as well as the more "conventional" but nonetheless highly austere political plays *Die heilige Johanna der Schlachthöfe* (*Saint Joan of the Stockyards*, 1929–1930), *Die Mutter* (*The Mother*, 1932), and *Die Rundköpfe und die Spitzköpfe* (*The Roundheads and the Peakheads*, 1932). The volume of poems which represents this phase is *Lieder, Gedichte, Chöre* (Songs, Poems, Choruses, 1934), a compendium of strictly propagandist poems and songs which forms a complete contrast to the wild exuberance and parodistic anarchism of *Manual of Piety*.

In the first years of exile, particularly in the period of the Popular Front, when the Communist party sought the cooperation of all liberal and left-wing forces against the Nazi danger, the uncompromising all-or-nothing attitude of this didactic phase was clearly out of place, and it gave way to a brief period (1934–1938) of openly propagandistic writing in more conventional styles. *Dreigroschenroman* (*Threepenny Novel*, 1934) and the plays *Furcht und Elend des Dritten Reiches* (*The Private Life of the Master Race; Fear and Misery in the Third Reich*, 1935–1936) and *Die Gewehre der Frau Carrar* (*Señora Carrar's Rifles*, 1937) were the products of this period in Brecht's life as a writer.

After the threat of world war became only too obvious following the Nazi occupation of Vienna and the Munich crisis (1938), the chances of influencing the course of events by writing propaganda were clearly reduced to zero. This freed Brecht and enabled him to turn his creative energies back to more personal poetry and the composition of his most mature and greatest series of plays. In this period (ca. 1938–ca. 1947) he wrote *Leben des Galilei* (*Galileo*, 1938), *Mutter Courage und ihre Kinder* (*Mother Courage and Her Children*, 1939), *Der gute Mensch von Sezuan* (*The Good Woman of Setzuan*, 1938–1940), *Herr Puntila und sein Knecht Matti* (*Puntila and Matti, His Hired Man*, 1940–1941), *Der authaltsame Aufstieg des Arturo Ui* (*The Resistible Rise of Arturo Ui*, 1941), *Die Gesichte der Simone Machard* (*The Visions of Simone Machard*, 1943), and *Der kaukasische Kreidekreis* (*The Caucasian Chalk Circle*, 1944–1945) as well as some of his most deeply felt poetry (contained, together with some propaganda verse from the preceding phase, in the volume *Svendborger Gedichte*).

Following his return to Europe from the United States (where he lived from the summer of 1941 to the fall of 1947), Brecht concentrated on his theoretical writings and his work as artistic director of his own theater. His output as a playwright in this period (1947 to his death on 14 August 1956) is disappointing both in quantity and in quality. Apart from minor original plays (*Die Tage der Kommune* [*The Days of the Commune*, 1949], *Turandot oder Der Kongress der Weisswäscher* [*Turandot, or The Congress of Whitewashers*, 1950–1954]) his work for the theater consists largely of adaptations: *Die Antigone des Sophokles* (*The Antigone of Sophocles*, 1948), after Hölderlin's translation; *Der Hofmeister* (*The Tutor*, 1950), after J. M. R. Lenz; *Don Juan* (1952), after Molière; *Der Prozess der Jeanne d'Arc zu Rouen 1431* (*The Trial of Joan of Arc at Rouen, 1431*), after a radio play by Anna Seghers based on the record of Joan's actual trial; *Coriolan* (*Coriolanus*, 1953); and *Pauken und Trompeten* (*Trumpets and Drums*, 1956), after Farquhar's *The Recruiting Officer*. On the other hand, in this phase of relatively low creativity as a playwright, Brecht found an outlet for his emotions (of resignation at the coming of old age, of disillusionment with the philistine East German regime) in what must be regarded as his finest achievement as a lyrical poet: a body of elegantly elegiac, sadly ironical, highly economical free verse.

Brecht's career thus shows a clear pattern of development and its own dialectic: anarchic exuberance (1918–ca. 1927) abruptly turning to the opposite extreme, austere self-discipline (ca. 1927–1934); a brief interlude of openly propagandist, almost journalistic, work, undertaken to help the good cause of antifascism (1934–1938); then, as a synthesis of emotional exuberance, severe Marxist rationalism, and some elements of political special pleading, the great works of the mature phase (1938–1947); and, finally, to crown the whole, the period from Brecht's return to Europe to his death (1947–1956), when in the theater he fulfilled his theories by his practice as a great director, while, as a lyrical poet, he reached sublime heights of detached self-knowledge and melancholic self-irony. It is a pattern which bears the marks of the great career of a great man.

The anarchic exuberance of the youth and the severe rationalism of the Marxist find their common denominator, however, in the concept of rebellion: the adolescent rebelled against the narrowness of small-town life, of desiccated stiff-collared bourgeois teachers, the musty smell of respectability and sexual repression; the Marxist clung to self-discipline and Spartan abnegation of self (including its anarchic longings for freedom) only in order to accomplish effective rebellion against the social order which had produced two wars and National Socialism. The recognition that rebellion to accomplish freedom can only succeed if the rebel's own freedom is ruthlessly suppressed in the discipline of the party forms the ironical, yet tragic, leitmotiv of Brecht's oeuvre. This ambivalence—which must also be seen as a highly characteristic German quality—explains the fascination which the Hegelian dialectic held for Brecht; it is also the basis of his genius as a dramatist.

For what is a playwright if he is not an individual who can experience and express a multitude of contradictory impulses and passions with equal comprehension and empathy for each of them? Just as Shakespeare could momentarily assume the personality of Iago as well as Othello, of Shylock as well as Antonio, Brecht also was able to be at the same time Garga and Shlink, Joan Dark and Mauler, Galilei and the Grand Inquisitor, Edward II and Mortimer, MacHeath and Peachum, dumb Katrin and Mother Courage. But he went further: the tensions and contradictions often actually split Brecht's characters wide open. Anna I and Anna II in the ballet *Die sieben Todsünden der Kleinbürger* (*The Seven Deadly Sins,* 1933) express the emotional and rational components of the same girl and are the forerunners of a line of dialectical characters: Shen Te/Shui Ta in *The Good Woman of Setzuan;* Puntila, who is good when drunk and evil when sober; Azdak, who can be a good judge only because he is a rascal; Mother Courage, who is destructive in her professional capacity as a businesswoman profiting from war and a positive character in being a mother intent on keeping her children alive and well; Galilei, whose sensuality and cowardice are balanced by his heroic greatness as a scientist. At the base of this deeply ambivalent attitude toward the world there is a sense of deep disillusionment. World War I was the end not only of an epoch but of a whole system of values in Germany. And Brecht belonged to the generation which had to grow up into this moon landscape of collapse and bankruptcy. Brecht's early poetry is full of images of despair. "The blind," he says in one passage, "talk about a way out. But *I* can see." And elsewhere he speaks about an epoch when the tables of the law itself have crumbled and not even sleeping with one's own sister gives pleasure any more. There is a persistent feeling of guilt in these early poems, disgust with sex and life, and a wild strain of accusation against God, who, it is said, does not exist, but "how can *that* not exist, which can betray man so deeply?" Thus the existence of God, an evil, malevolent force, is postulated to explain the measure of suffering and corruption in the world. As to the Devil—he too has become inefficient and lazy. It is no longer worthwhile to lie; from sheer despair men speak the truth, unaware of the danger of speaking the truth. "And the Devil no longer takes his best customers."

Passages like these, which Brecht wrote in his early twenties, for all their adolescent pose of cynical world-weariness, show the background of horror which must always be kept in mind in trying to understand Brecht's later political commitment. Only the experience of the desolation caused by so total a collapse of values can explain the frantic search for a new set of values to replace those which have been discredited; only the emptiness of total isolation in a world deprived of all social ties can account for the frantic craving for a new collective consciousness, for the discipline and fellow-feeling engendered by merging into a dedicated fellowship of fighters like the Communist party. When even murder had become too strenuous for the disillusioned, then even the will to violence could appear as a positive value:

Terrible is it to kill.
But not only others, ourselves too, we must kill, if
   necessary
For this world, this killing world, can only
Be changed by violence, as
All living beings know.
As yet, we said, it is not granted to us
To be able not to kill. Only with our
Unbending will to alter the world we justified
The measure we took.

Thus do the four agitators (i.e., party activists) in Brecht's starkest tragedy, *The Measures Taken,* justify the liquidation of their young comrade who had broken the iron rules of discipline. It is the horror of the world which

justifies the horror of the measures which have to be taken to alter the world. If man's meanness to his fellowmen, his greed and brutality, are merely the product of irrational and fossilized property relations, then a rational organization of society would enable the inherent goodness of man's nature to assert itself; greed and selfishness, meanness and brutality, would disappear from the earth. This essentially Rousseauist rejection of the concept of original sin (which is indeed one of the basic assumptions of Marxism) plays an immense part in Brecht's political and also in his aesthetic thought. For Brecht's theory of drama—the epic or, later, the dialectical theater with its *Verfremdungseffekt* (wrongly translated as "alienation effect," more correctly as "strange-making effect")—ultimately stems from his conviction that Aristotle's definition of the dramatic as distinct from the epic form of poetry implied the notion of an unchanging and unchangeable human nature.

In their famous essay *Uber epische und dramatische Dichtung* (*On Epic and Dramatic Poetry,* 1797), Goethe and Schiller asserted that the "great, essential difference" between the two kinds of literature "lies in the fact that the epic poet presents the event as totally past, while the dramatic poet presents it as totally present." If the foundation of Marxism, Brecht argued, is the notion that the world can only be apprehended rationally as a dialectical, historical process, in the course of which all human values are in constant flux, ever changing, then this conception of drama was not only un-Marxist but, if accepted, a complete denial of everything that Marxism stood for. After all, if audiences could not only be brought face to face with the world of Shakespeare, Sophocles, or Goethe, but could be made to experience the events in these plays as totally present, if they could suffer with Oedipus, rage with Othello, weep with Iphigenia, then the eternally unchanging sameness of human nature would be a proven fact and Marxism would have been refuted! Had not Goethe and Schiller expressly stated in their essay that the actor, in their definition of drama,

> wants the spectators to participate exclusively in his actions and in his immediate surroundings so that they should feel the sufferings of his soul and body with him, share his embarrassments and forget their own personalities for the sake of his. . . . The listener and spectator . . . must not be allowed to rise to thoughtful contemplation; he must passionately follow the action; his imagination is completely silenced and must not be taxed; and even things that are being narrated must, as it were, be brought before the audience's eyes by the actor.

If a contemporary spectator could be made to identify himself with Oedipus or Othello to the point of actually forgetting his own personality and becoming Oedipus and Othello, how could he ever, argued Brecht, be brought to realize that Othello and Oedipus had been men determined by the social systems of their times and therefore by definition inaccessible to any such identification on the part of twentieth-century man, determined as he is by totally different social and economic conditions?

There can be little doubt that Brecht's entire theory of a truly Marxist theater springs from his angry reaction against the very essay by Goethe and Schiller we have just quoted. In Brecht's theater the action must not take place in a total present, but in a strictly defined historical past—hence the streamers with precise dates for each scene in plays like *Mother Courage;* in Brecht's theater the spectators must not be allowed to identify with the actors on stage to the extent of forgetting their own personalities—hence Brecht's striving for a multitude of *Verfremdungseffekte,* that is, devices which would prevent identification to the point of annihilating the suspension of disbelief (that is, the actors stepping out of their parts, or grotesque masks that clearly reveal them to be puppets). And, finally, the spectator in Brecht's theater must be made to rise to thoughtful contemplation, must be led to detached critical reflection on the play and its meaning. For only a detached spectator could appreciate the distance between the historical characters, determined by the social relations of their time on the one hand and contemporary man on the other. Even the familiar, argued Brecht, would yield its message only when seen with new eyes, as though it were something never before noticed. It was because Newton was capable of perceiving a falling apple as a strange and wonderful phenomenon that he had discovered the laws of gravitation. Hence Brecht asked his audience, at the end of *The Exception and the Rule:*

> You have seen the familiar, which always happens.
> But we beg you:
> What is not strange, find it disquieting!
> What is ordinary, find it inexplicable!
> What is usual, let it astonish you!
> What seems the rule, recognize it as an abuse.
> And where you have recognized abuse,
> Put things right!

Brecht's theory of "epic—i.e., nondramatic—drama" can thus be seen both as an earnest endeavor to find a Marxist aesthetic of the theater and as an angry rejection of the official, classical aesthetic codified by those twin deities of the German cultural establishment, Goethe and Schiller.

The rise of German nationhood, belatedly achieved in 1871, was intimately linked with the search for a national literature (as, indeed, the search for the great American novel sprang from the need to reassert American nationhood and the emancipation of American letters from being a mere provincial variant of British culture!). To buttress the German claim to be a great nation rather than a motley collection of barbarous tribes (whose rulers refused to use the crude vernacular and insisted on speaking French right into the middle of the eighteenth century) the need was urgent for writers of unquestioned international stature, men who could equal a Dante, a Shakespeare, a Racine, a Calderón. The two demigods of Weimar triumphantly met that need; they dominated German nineteenth-century drama by engendering a large number of feeble and insipid imitators of their style. When Germany finally achieved the status of a great power under Prussian leadership, the "classics," their immediate predecessors, and their progeny were made the pivot of the new establishment's ideal of education and became the pinnacle of *Bildung;* indeed the ability to quote Goethe's *Faust* and Schiller's *Wallenstein* was—and still is—the badge of social status in German culture.

As a result the curriculum of schools and universities effectively distorted the true situation. By the very nature of their objective, "the classics" were literary, academic, and highly respectable. Because they had been rude, uncouth, and irregular, on the other hand, the very considerable poets and dramatists of the baroque period, for example, were almost totally neglected; the immense achievement of genuine folk drama, particularly in Austria and Bavaria (a brilliant South German version of the commedia dell'arte; great writers like Nestroy or Raimund), was almost entirely ignored; and a number of dramatists who did not fit the pattern created by the classics were disregarded as freaks and eccentrics (great figures of the Sturm und Drang period like J. M. R. Lenz; drunken geniuses like C. D. Grabbe; revolutionaries like Georg Büchner).

It is against this background that Brecht's revolt must be seen. To him the ugliness and stupidity, the complacency and smugness, of the German bourgeoisie were personified by the pompous teachers at his *Gymnasium,* by the tired, routine performances of the "classics" at the Augsburg *Stadttheater.* He not only rejected the "classics" and their reactionary aesthetics, he ridiculed them by making them the target of a stream of overt and covert parody. And he went for inspiration and example to the alternative sources of a German dramatic tradition: to baroque dramatists like Andreas Gryphius (Greif); the Austro-Bavarian folk theater, whose last living exponent, the great beer-hall comedian Karl Valentin, became Brecht's mentor and friend; and above all to Büchner, a dramatist today generally acknowledged to

have been at least equal, if not superior, to Goethe or Schiller.

In Büchner's *Danton's Death* (1835) the disillusioned revolutionaries muse, before their execution, upon the futility and glory of the human condition:

> We should take off our masks, and then we would see, as in a room surrounded by mirrors, everywhere but the one age-old, innumerable, indestructible dunderhead, no more, no less. The differences aren't that big, we all are rascals and angels, idiots and geniuses, all at once: these four things find room enough in the same body, they are not as voluminous as is usually assumed. To sleep, to digest, to procreate—that's what we all do; all else is mere variation on the same theme.

In Brecht's first play, *Baal,* the same note is struck by the hero, the drunken, antisocial poet Baal, and his friend the composer Ekart:

> *Ekart:* Sleep's gone to the devil and the wind again plays the organ in the willow-stumps. Thus we are left to lean against the white breasts of philosophy; the dark and the damp until the day of our blessed demise; even to the old hags no more is left than their second sight.
> *Baal:* In this wind you need no gin, and you are still drunk. I see the world in a mild light: it is God's excrement.
> *Ekart:* God's who has sufficiently revealed his true character once and for all by combining the genital organ with the urinary tract.
> *Baal:* It is all *so* beautiful.

Büchner was not yet twenty-four years old when he died in February 1837; Brecht wrote *Baal* in 1918 when he was just twenty. Like Büchner's Danton, Brecht's Baal is a sensualist, who drifts through life, letting himself be carried by its currents, whirlpools, and eddies. There is an element of parody in Brecht's character, however: he wrote the play as an answer to a dramatized biography of the drunken playwright Grabbe by Hanns Johst, a minor expressionist who later became one of the leading Nazi poets. So Baal can also be seen as a cari-

2095

cature of the ridiculous worship of the overflowing vitality of genius in a certain type of German nationalist literature (which later became the worship of Hitler's "genius"). And yet, the lyrical passages Brecht gives to his antisocial giant of vitality have such force and beauty that we cannot but feel that there is a great deal of Brecht's own attitude in them. Thus Brecht's very first completed play already contains that characteristic tension that will dominate his entire oeuvre: the tension between a desire to drift in the glorious, passive stream of life, on the one hand, and, on the other, a yearning for rationality which rejects that oceanic feeling with its passivity and amoral yielding to sensual impulse.

In the first, anarchic phase of Brecht's career, it is the sensuous, emotional, uncontrolled, passive attitude, the yielding to impulse, which dominates, while the rational, disciplined, activist attitude merely appears in the undertone of satire, mockery, and ridicule with which the impulsive demeanor of the main character is portrayed. Kragler, the antihero of *Drums in the Night,* refuses to join the Spartacist rising because he has become totally disillusioned with fighting of any kind, having risked his hide in the war. He decides to take his bride, who is pregnant by another man, in spite of her blemish.

Irrational selfishness is driven to its utmost limit in Brecht's most enigmatic play, *In the Jungle of the Cities.* Two men are locked in a totally unmotivated fight to the death in a mythical Chicago largely derived from Upton Sinclair: Shlink, a middle-aged Malayan timber trader, and young Garga, whose family has come into the big city from the "Savannahs." They do not know why they are fighting; only at the end do they realize that their struggle was a desperate attempt to establish contact, human communication. "The infinite isolation of man makes enmity an unattainable goal," says Shlink. "Love, warmth from the contact of bodies, is our only mercy in the darkness. But the conjunction of bodies is the only possible one, it cannot bridge the division of language. . . . Yes, so great is our isolation that there cannot even be a struggle." Here then, in the blind working out of irrational impulse, society itself appears as a place of icy desolation. When Schlink is dead, Garga, left alone, decides to go on living, in society. His last words—and those of the play—are: "The chaos has been used up. It was the best time."

Emotion/Reason—Selfishness/Discipline—Chaos/Order, these three polarities sum up the dialectic of Brecht's life and work. In *A Man's a Man* the emphasis has shifted away from passivity: a mild little workman, Galy Gay, is here transformed into a highly disciplined and ferocious soldier. From a self-contained individualist who wallowed in chaos he is turned into a paragon of order, a cog in a vast collective entity—a mythical, Kiplingesque British-Indian army. In *A Man's a Man* this process is shown satirically, as a grotesque and monstrous act. But in *The Measures Taken* almost the same process, the acceptance of iron, soldierly discipline by an emotional individualist, has become a heroic act of self-abnegation cast in the great tragic mold. For here it is not the discipline of an imperialist army but that of the Communist party itself which is accepted. *Das grosse Einverständnis*—the great act of consent—has been made the leitmotiv of Brecht's thinking.

The change from the anarchic to the didactic phase of Brecht's development is clearly marked in the evolution of his language. The Büchneresque exuberance of daring metaphors strung together in chains of image-laden main clauses yields to laconic severity and sparseness of expression:

> One man has two eyes
> The Party has a thousand eyes.
> The Party sees seven nations.
> One man sees one city.
> One man has his hour
> But the Party has many hours.
> One man can be destroyed
> But the Party cannot be destroyed.
> ("Praise of the Party," from
> *The Measures Taken*)

The antimilitarist and dedicated pacifist Brecht does not seem to have noticed that he was in fact expressing the philosophy of the samurai, of the Prussian officer, in these stark lines, the harsh creed of soldiers who do and die without asking the reason why. The school opera *He Who Says Yes,* which also deals with the concept of the great act of consent, is, indeed, derived from a Japanese No play (which Brecht had come to know in Arthur Waley's translation). Here a young boy whose illness impedes the progress of a party of travelers crossing a dangerous mountain range asks to be killed in the general interest. When it was pointed out to Brecht that the moral of this self-sacrificing action was questionable, he rewrote the piece with a different ending: with the boy refusing to die and declining to abide by old, inhuman customs. This new play, *He Who Says No,* was to be performed together with the first play, which it does not replace, but complements, as an example of a dialectical tension between two attitudes.

In the great plays of his years of exile Brecht's style has lost the austerity of his didactic phase; and his characters, who had been reduced to the bare essentials (reminiscent of the highly stylized characters of French classical tragedy, who also lack all individual little human touches), again acquired a rich texture of personal idiosyncrasies. Nevertheless, these plays remain didactic in the sense that they are conceived as parables, models of human situations, cited, like the parables in the New Testament, not for their own intrinsic interest, but because of their general applicability to other human situations and problems. Galilei stands for all scientists who have submitted to the dictates of political authority (and for the atomic scientists of our time in particular); Mother Courage, for all little people who do not realize that, deriving their small profit from war or the preparation of war, they are themselves guilty of causing the death of their children and the destruction of their country (as the little people of Hitler's Germany did); Puntila—evil when sober, human when

drunk—is an emblem and exemplar of the irreconcilability between capitalistic attitudes and genuine humanity; while Shen Te, the good woman of Setzuan, demonstrates the impossibility of goodness in a world where survival depends on commercial success. The greatest of these plays, *The Caucasian Chalk Circle,* quite openly uses the parable form. It illustrates the solution of a problem which is posed in the prologue: who has the better right to a tract of land in a socialist country (a fairly mythically drawn Soviet Union), the legal owners or those who cultivate the land to the best purpose? The ancient legend of the child claimed by its natural and its foster mother is retold with a new variant to provide the answer. Solomon's judgment elicited a loving response from the natural mother and showed that it is the real mother who must also be the one who wants to spare her child pain and therefore is the one who loves it truly. In Brecht's parable it is the foster mother who really loves the child and refuses to hurt it, while the natural mother merely wants to use her abandoned child to reestablish her legal title to some property of which her son is heir. In other words, rather than to its legal proprietors, the land should belong to those who till it to the best effect and thereby show that they truly love it.

Brecht's use of the parable form expresses another aspect of his revolt against the state of German culture and the German theater in his youth. As much as he rejected the grandiloquent classicism of the followers of Goethe and Schiller (and, to a lesser extent, of the masters themselves), he also detested the naturalistic theater which had become dominant in Germany at the turn of the century. All of Brecht's dramatic work can be seen as a refutation of naturalism, the use of the stage to reproduce photographically accurate slices of life. The only plays he wrote in a realistic convention (*Señora Carrar's Rifles, Fear and Misery in the Third Reich*) were propagandist potboilers. *Drums in the Night,* which takes place in a real contemporary historical and political situation (the Spartacist uprising in Berlin in 1919), transcends any suspicion of realism by the exuberance of its language and Brecht's insistence on a nonrealistic set. At the end the romantically ominous blood-red moon that dominates the action is brought down and revealed to have been no more than a Chinese lantern.

As an anti-illusionist in the theater Brecht was logically driven toward the parable form; in the austere experimental situation of a *Lehrstück,* in the fairy-tale world of distant Setzuan or the Caucasus, it is possible to deal with real problems without having to put a realistic image of the world onto the stage. For naturalism, and indeed any attempt at a realistic convention, Brecht argued, had the drawback of overindividualization. If one showed *one* family of starving, unemployed workers in loving detail, how could one convince the audience that this was not just one individual and exceptional case and was, therefore, without general validity? To do social good the theater, Brecht felt, must be able to convince its audience that its examples were typical and of wide applicability. Hence he never shrank from openly drawing the moral from his examples, largely by the use of songs which stand outside the action, interrupt it, and underline its general conclusions, but also by pointed epilogues (*Puntila, The Good Woman of Setzuan*), projected slogans, and so forth. In the dramatic parable, distanced through the remoteness of its setting in time or space, the need for realism is greatly reduced. An audience in contemporary Germany will demand convincing realism for a play set in contemporary Germany, but will accept a highly stylized Renaissance Florence, or a picture of Germany in the Thirty Years' War, or even contemporary Finland or China. It is in these settings that the familiar can be made to appear strange so that it can be critically appraised and evaluated by an uninvolved audience.

The irony was that this doctrine of a politically efficacious left-wing theater fell afoul of the official Communist doctrine in the Soviet Union where, after 1934, socialist realism had become the orthodox doctrine. In the theater this manifested itself in a rigid insistence on the Moscow Art Theater style of meticulous naturalism as the only permissible form of "Marxist" theater. Great directors like Meyerhold and Tairov fell victim to this doctrine. Brecht wisely avoided settling in the Soviet Union after his exile from Germany; he even acted as coeditor of the German émigré literary magazine published in Moscow, *Das Wort,* from his home in Denmark. He attempted to conduct a mild polemic against the official doctrine: pointing to examples of progressive literature like Shelley's *Masque of Anarchy* or Swift's *Gulliver's Travels,* he argued that, after all, it was the political intention that mattered, not the form. But the essay on "The Range and Variety of the Realistic Style," which he wrote in 1938 for publication in *Das Wort,* did not see the light of day until almost twenty years later. Cautious as always, Brecht thought better of publishing it, which would have incurred the open wrath of the Stalinists.

Brecht, brought up on the grandiloquent cardboard heroism of the bombastic nationalist ideology of the Wilhelmian *Reich,* detested all manifestations of heroism: as Mother Courage points out, only a bad general needs brave soldiers. Mother Courage is of the same tribe as that great archetype of unheroic irony and subservient resistance, the Good Soldier Schweik as depicted in Jaroslav Hašek's immortal picaresque novel. Brecht knew and loved the book; in 1928 he had collaborated on a stage adaptation for Piscator in Berlin and during World War II he wrote a sequel to Hašek's story, the play *Schweyk im zweiten Weltkrieg* (*Schweyk in the Second World War,* 1944). But there are Schweikian characters in many of his plays and prose writings; indeed, they are among Brecht's most personal creations. The character of Mr. Keuner in the stories about Mr. Keuner, who quite clearly embodies Brecht's model of himself, the man he wanted to be, is also a close relative of Schweik. The "stories" are mostly very short, ranging from one or two sentences to about a page and a half.

And they attempt to portray an attitude of mind to life, or as Brecht himself said in a note preceding the first published batch of Keuner stories, "they constitute an experiment in making gestures quotable." The quotability of gestures is a key concept in Brecht's aesthetics. For him the essence of art, of poetry, is indeed the fact that through its perfection of form, through its concentration of thought, poetry enables truth to become transmittable, accessible to the mass of people. But a merely verbal quotation merely transmits an abstract version of the truth. The importance of drama lies precisely in its concreteness, in its ability to embody actual models of human behavior. Instead of merely hearing people quote the noble words from some play by Shakespeare or Schiller, Brecht wanted them to repeat wholesome, rational, and noble actions they might have seen on the stage. Hence his desire to create quotable gestures, in his narrative prose as well as in his plays.

Each Keuner story embodies one *gestus.* This term, which plays an important part in Brecht's theory and practice of play writing and play production, is not quite the same as a mere gesture. It denotes a basic human behavior model, an archetypal attitude. "A man who had not seen Mr. K. for a long time greeted him with the words: 'You have not changed at all.' 'Oh!' said Mr. K. and went pale." This Keuner story—quoted here in its entirety—does not embody a gesture (going pale could hardly be called that) but it does demonstrate a *gestus*—namely, Brecht's basic attitude that man, a rational, dialectical creature, must fear nothing more than lack of change. The more elegantly, the more thoroughly, such human behavior models could be encapsulated in words and stage performance, the more readily quotable, useful, and practical they would become as tools of learning for mankind.

One of the fundamental structural principles of Brecht's epic theater derives from this concept: each scene, Brecht postulated, should embody just one *Grundgestus* (basic *gestus*), no more and no less, and should be con-

structed in such a way that that basic *gestus* can be seen most clearly and to best advantage—in other words, most quotably. "The only thing Mr. Keuner had to say about style is: 'it must be quotable.' A quotation is impersonal. Who are the best sons? Those who make you forget their father." The insistence on quotability is thus a deeply anti-individualistic, antiromantic attitude. According to Brecht it is not originality which is the hallmark of the best art but, on the contrary, typicality, that is, the widest possible application and most general validity.

The writing of a play, in Brecht's view, as well as its production, would consist in evolving a sequence of scene-titles indicating the basic *gestus* of each scene (for instance, "Hamlet confronts his father's ghost" or "Three Witches foretell Macbeth's rise to the throne"), so that by simply putting these title captions together the whole story of the play (*Fabel,* or "narrative essence") emerges.

As a follower of J. B. Watson's behaviorist school, Brecht despised all psychologies based on introspection. If Stanislavsky and his followers in the techniques of "method acting" want to derive the gesture from the characters' inner life, Brecht was convinced that what comes first is the attitude which will trigger the appropriate subjective feelings.

These views had important consequences not only for the production techniques of Brecht's drama, but also for the writing of his plays, stories, and poems. Truly dramatic language is, in the last analysis, to be considered not merely in its aspect as a structure of words, form, and content, but as an action. This is the difference between ordinary and genuinely dramatic writing. Of each sentence spoken in a play it must be possible to say what function it performs as an action. For Brecht, therefore, the problem of dramatic writing came down to the development of linguistic forms which already contain the action that inevitably must accompany them. When Othello in his final speech refers to the Turk he once met in Aleppo in order to divert the attention of the bystanders from his intention to kill himself, the words "and smote him thus" cannot be spoken without the sudden suicidal stab toward which they are aimed. This, to Brecht, was ideally gestural language, words which already contain, and which compellingly impose, the *gestus,* the attitude they embody. In this Brecht was immensely successful: the gestural quality lies in the variation of pace of the writing—the alternation of quick short words and long polysyllabic ones—in the clever use of pause and caesura, which often causes the word after the caesura to come as a shock, a surprise, and many subtle devices of rhythm, contrast, and tonal color. These are the subtleties most difficult to transfer into other languages, provided the translator is even aware of them (and that often does not seem to have been the case). Basically, a text by Brecht acts itself.

Quotability of attitude is also the principal factor in Brecht's stress on the use of songs in his plays. Here the music reinforces the gestural character of the language; for the use of music doubles the possibilities for strict control of rhythm, pace, repetition of vital phrases (refrains), and the like. And music, with the added factor of melody, increases the quotability both of the words (a hit tune often cannot be got out of one's consciousness, even if one wanted to get rid of it) and of the *gestus,* the attitude embodied in it.

The actor whom Brecht admired more than any other of his time, Charlie Chaplin, also exemplifies what Brecht meant by quotable *gestus* and gestural acting. So quotable was Chaplin's characteristic grotesque walk, the way he flicked his cane, that in his heyday there was a Chaplin imitator (Brecht would have said a Chaplin quoter) at every party in the land. And these gestures which were so immensely quotable also, in a truly Brechtian sense, embodied an attitude to life—the indomitable little man's defiance of the inhuman pressures of an overly mechanized industrial society. One might formulate it in this way: as a great poet Brecht wanted to use his utmost mastery of language to force the actors appearing in his plays to act in the style of, and as brilliantly as, Chaplin.

Brecht's theory of drama, as well as his theory and practice of poetic, gestural language, ultimately amounts to a striving for simplicity and directness of structure and expression. The concentration on the clear story line (*Fabel*) in the plays and the insistence on language becoming an embodiment of simple human attitudes tend in this direction. The Truth Is Concrete was the slogan Brecht put up over his desk wherever he came to a halt in his travels of exile.

This pursuit of directness and concreteness also can be seen as a reaction against a German tradition. Much of German poetry—and therefore also of the poetic language of drama—revels in grand philosophical abstractions and flowery, nebulous concepts. Brecht not only rejected these bombastic abstractions, he also set himself against the subjectivity, the sentimental self-involvement, of the lyrical tradition. As early as 1927 Brecht rejected any purely lyrical poetry with the argument that such poems "are simply too far removed from the original *gesture* [my italics] of the communication of a thought or emotion which would also be of use to strangers." In his first published collection of poems, *Manual of Piety,* the poems are prefaced by "Directions for Use," which open with the words: "This Domestic Breviary is destined for the use of readers. It must not be senselessly gulped down." Clothing his scandalously free poetry in the outward guise of a prayer book was, for Brecht, an act of blasphemous irony, yet, at the same time, the analogy was also meant very seriously: a book of hymns or prayers is, after all, a genuine article of daily use, an instrument of mental and spiritual hygiene which has its clearly defined part to play in the life of pious folk. And this comes very close to Brecht's idea about the function of literature—and drama—in his ideal society.

Brecht's *Manual of Piety* is typical of his first exuberant, anarchic phase. The ballads it contains celebrate a kind of wild acceptance of nature and its processes of growth and decay. The great rivers that carry the corpses of the drowned down to the sea, the jungle which engulfs the conquistadors in the wilds of Central America, the pirates who roam the seas knowing full well that one day they will be swallowed up—these are typical, ever recurring images of Brecht's early poetry. There is no introspection in these poems; even the few which deal with Brecht's personal life treat him objectively, in the third person almost. There are no elaborate similes; the images are put before the reader directly, starkly, and stand by and for themselves. Formally there is still a good deal of artifice and elaboration: ballad meters, even sonnets, abound. The Bible, Rimbaud, Kipling (who may have been an imperialist but was also a pioneer in the use of vernacular speech, even broad dialect in poetry), and Wedekind—in his bitter, satirical cabaret songs—were the chief models of Brecht's early poetry; Goethe, Schiller, and the masters of the German Protestant hymn, the chief targets for his parody.

Brecht's later poetry is more cerebral, severe, and economical. Arthur Waley's translations from the Chinese became a decisive influence. Rhyme and regular rhythms were sloughed off, free verse in irregular rhythms became the norm, although for special purposes Brecht still could occasionally fall back on classical meters: he was a great believer in the hexameter as a vehicle for didactic poetry. Modeling himself on Vergil's *Georgics* and Lucretius' *De rerum natura*, he undertook, during his Hollywood exile, the gigantic task of putting the essence of Marxism into a great didactic poem in hexameters. He never finished the attempt, yet the remaining fragments are impressively powerful. But Brecht's best late poems are short, almost epigrammatic: they speak of the tribulations of exile, the sorrows of the poet's return to his ravaged homeland, aging, and death. They are among the finest poems in the German language. They reveal the real Brecht behind the facade of cheerful support for the East German regime: a wistful, disillusioned man, dreaming of the landscape of his childhood in Augsburg, praising the humble pleasures of homely food, cheese, bread, and cool beer. There even creeps into this private, late poetry a note of wry rejection of the hollow claims of the totalitarian state to which he had committed his fortunes. After the rising of 17 June 1953, when the regime reproached the people for their rebellion, Brecht, in one famous poem, simply asked why, in that case, the government did not dissolve the people and elect itself another.

At the height of his commitment to Marxism (1940) Brecht's view of the function and nature of poetry was a severely committed one: "Lyrical poetry is never mere expression. . . . The making of poetry must be regarded as a human activity, as a social practice; with all its self-contradiction, changeability, must be seen as historically conditioned and history making. The distinction lies between 'reflecting nature' and 'holding the mirror up' to it." On another, much earlier occasion—in 1927—Brecht had given a slightly wider definition of the function of poetry: "All great poems have the value of documents. They contain the manner of speaking of their author, an important human being." In other words, poetry is the memorable utterance of a memorable man.

Poetry thus holds a central position in any consideration of Brecht as a dramatist as well as a prose writer. "The poet Kin [i.e., Brecht] recognized language as a tool of action." The quotation comes from another collection of pithy short aphorisms, stories, and anecdotes, *Me-ti, Buch der Wendungen* (Me-ti, the Book of Twists and Turns, 1965), in which Brecht continued the method he adopted in the Keuner stories with the further alienation effect of a Chinese classical garb. In another passage the poet Kin (i.e., Keuner/Brecht) confesses: "How am I to write immortal works, when I am not famous? How am I to give answers, when I am not asked? Why should I lose time over writing poems, if time loses them? I write my suggestions in an enduring language, because I fear it will take a long time until they are carried out."

It is to make his suggestions for social change memorable, durable enough to remain long in currency, that Brecht had to turn to poetry. It is through the power of his language to evoke the moods of action that he becomes a great playwright; through the quality of his language as a tool for the expression of thought that he becomes a great prose writer.

In his days as a struggling young playwright—until his breakthrough into financial success with *The Threepenny Opera* in 1928—Brecht wrote numerous short stories for magazines, with the avowed aim of producing a readily salable product. He even won a short story competition run by one of Berlin's most popular illustrated papers. Nevertheless, a good many of these stories are little masterpieces of observation, irony, and, above all, style.

Some of these stories contain the germs of ideas which later blossomed into plays, some cast light on Brecht's psychology and the imagery of his mind. As in his early plays, Brecht loved to situate his action in an Anglo-American world, somewhere between a Kiplingesque India, the "savannahs" of the American West, Jack London's arctic Alaska, Upton Sinclair's Chicago of the stockyards, and a Dickensian London teeming with quaint and sinister characters. For a young German brought up in a small town of Central Europe, but avidly reading stories of adventure, this indeed was the exotic world of romance, the wide-open spaces which beckoned those who had the courage to escape from the stuffy drawing rooms of the respectable German petty bourgeoisie.

It is in the plays *A Man's a Man* (set in Anglo-India on the borders of China and Tibet), *The Threepenny Opera* (a Dickensian Victorian London with some Americanisms—the police chief is called the Sheriff), and *Mahagonny* (the brothel camp for the gold miners returning from Alaska) that the world sketched out in the short stories came to its first full fruition. Out of *The Threepenny Opera* grew Brecht's most ambitious novel, the *Threepenny Novel* (1934), a vast panorama of a pseudo-Dickensian London, brilliantly written, but marred by the extremely naive idea of capitalism which forms the basis of its argument.

A second novel, *Die Geschäftedes Herrn Julius Caesar* (*The Business Deals of Mr. Julius Caesar*, 1957), written between 1938 and 1939 in Denmark, remained unfinished. Here too Brecht attempted to show the sordid business reality behind the facade of glory of a great military hero and dictator, as an indictment of Hitler, whom he regarded, wrongly, as no more than the puppet of rich industrialists and businessmen. Here too there is much fine writing, but Brecht's decision to abandon it shows that he himself did not regard the work as a success.

Another somewhat fragmentary work, the series of dialogues entitled *Flüchtlingsgespräche* (*Refugee Conversations*), largely written between 1940 and 1941 in Finland, must be counted, however, among Brecht's masterpieces. Two men stranded in Finland, Ziffel, an intellectual (who bears many features of Brecht himself), and Kalle, a worker, try to while away the time which hangs heavily on their hands by discussing the world, the war, exile, and all the countries through which they have passed. All the bitterness of exile is in these sardonic, Schweikian dialogues: "The passport is a man's noblest part. Nor does it come into being as easily as a human being. A human being can come into being in the most thoughtless manner and without good reason, but a passport—never. That is why a passport is recognized when it is a good one, while a man can be as good as he pleases and will yet not find recognition. One can say that a man is no more than a stand on which to place a passport." The *Refugee Conversations* is probably Brecht's most openly autobiographical work, even more so than the Keuner stories, in which he deals with an ideal image rather than with a realistic assessment of his personality.

After his return from America to Europe, Brecht compiled a slim volume of stories and narrative poems which he published in 1948 under the title *Kalendergeschichten* (*Tales from the Calendar*). Clearly designed as reading matter for the common people—German peasants in rural areas in Brecht's youth probably never read anything but the moral tales inserted between the calendar pages in their almanacs—this slim volume contains some of Brecht's finest narrative prose. The eight longer stories are in the mainstream of the tradition of the German *Novelle:* they relate significant incidents from history in a sparse, objective language, eschewing all introspection or attempts at psychological subtlety, but concentrating on the actual events. Yet these stories give deep psychological insights and somehow succeed in making history come alive. In "Der Mantel des Ketzers" ("The Heretic's Coat"), for example, we see the tragedy of Giordano Bruno, the natural philosopher burned at the stake as a heretic, through the eyes of a poor tailor who had made him a coat just before he was arrested and tries to get his money for it, while the philosopher is tried and convicted.

Another story, in a quite different vein, tells of an old woman, the narrator's (and clearly Brecht's) grandmother, who, when widowed at an advanced age, shocked her village by throwing all conventions of bourgeois respectability to the winds. "Thus she might rise in summer at three in the morning and take walks in the deserted streets of the little town, which she had entirely for herself. And, it was alleged, when the priest called on her to keep the old woman company in her loneliness, she invited him to the cinema."

After two years of the joys of freedom, the old woman dies: "I have seen a photograph of her which was taken for the children and shows her laid out. What you see is a tiny little face, and a thin-lipped, wide mouth. Much that is small, but no smallness. She has savored to the full the long years of servitude and the short years of freedom and consumed the bread of life to the last crumb." Only the terse stories of Heinrich von Kleist—another great German dramatist—can rival the economy and power of these short narratives and their mastery of German prose style.

Another large-scale project for a major novel also remained a fragment—the so-called *Tui-Novel* (1965), a satire, also set in a mythical China, on the corruption of the intellectuals (*Tellekt-Uell-Ins* abbreviated into *Tuis*) in the Weimar Republic. The Tuis are people who live by selling opinions. Brecht devoted a great deal of thought to this project in the thirties; it later led to the far more successful collection of brief anecdotes and sketches, *Me-Ti,* and was finally remodeled, after Brecht's return to East Berlin in the late forties, into the material for his last play, *Turandot, or The Congress of Whitewashers.* As in the case of the *Threepenny Novel,* the partial failure of the Tui project is due to Brecht's difficulty in finding a valid satirical analogy for the vices of capitalist society. That intellectuals sell their opinions is true enough, but after half a century of Communist rule in Russia, it is difficult to maintain, as Brecht certainly wanted to, that this phenomenon is the direct result of a capitalist organization of society.

Apart from his fiction Brecht left a vast and impressive corpus of other prose writings: political articles and essays, theoretical writings on the theater, and diaries and letters. His *Arbeitsjournal* (Working Diary), covering the years of his American exile and return to East Germany until his death in 1956, was published in 1973. This tends to avoid his personal life and concentrates on his problems as a working writer. Fragments of his early diaries and autobiographical jottings, which are far more personal and revealing, were made available in 1975. An extremely selective and incomplete edition of Brecht's letters appeared in 1982. It is difficult to judge how much still remains suppressed for political reasons.

Brecht's endeavors to create a truly Marxist aesthetic of theater are brilliant and stimulating and have given rise to endless misunderstandings. Above all, it must be kept in mind that these writings do not present a unitary, finished theory, but are, themselves, the documentation of a constant process of changing and developing thought. It is very significant that many of the actual practices of Brecht's play writing and direction antedate his commitment to Marxism, so that the Marxist terminology of later writings can be seen as an attempt to find a theoretical backing for intuitions and tastes which are part of Brecht's very personal artistic approach. The same is true of much in Brecht's later theorizing: it can frequently be regarded as an ex post facto rationalization of stage inventions which emerged in rehearsal.

Indeed, in the theater Brecht was the most empirical and undoctrinaire of directors. He conducted rehearsals at the Berliner Ensemble in the most leisurely of fashions, and entirely on a trial and error basis: every actor was given the opportunity to try out as many ways of playing a scene as he could suggest; and in the end the most effective version was chosen, after ample discussion.

The most valuable part of Brecht's theoretical work therefore appears to be that part which is the most concrete—the actual descriptions he gives of the way in which his plays were acted or ought to be directed. Much of this material is contained in the model books (for *Galileo, Mother Courage, Antigone,* and *Señora Carrar's Rifles*) and in the copious notes which Brecht provided for editions of his plays.

Brecht's most ambitious theoretical—and practical—discussion of the theater is contained in the voluminous fragment entitled *Dialoge aus dem Messingkauf* (*The Messingkauf Dialogues,* 1964), which Brecht began to write in 1939 and to which he added material for the rest of his life. It was to take the form of a series of dialogues interspersed with didactic poems. The title refers to the desire of one of the participants in the dialogues (The Philosopher) to find out about the true nature of theater, and above all its usefulness for the purpose to which he wants to put it: "I feel the special nature of my interest so strongly that I see myself like a trader in brass who comes to a brass band to buy not a trumpet but merely brass." In other words, he poses the question whether the theater, in spite of its traditional shape, could ever become the raw material for a new art, "an instrument for the imitation of certain events among people to certain purposes." The four dialogues, involving, apart from the philosopher, an actor, an actress, a dramaturge (literary adviser to a theater), and an electrician, are highly stimulating and amusing; yet it is the poems, which distill the practical side of Brecht's ideas into memorable gnomic language, which prove to be the most valuable part of the unfinished edifice.

The little *Kleines Organon das Theater* (*Organon for the Theater*), a compression of the theory of epic drama into seventy-seven terse paragraphs, written in 1948, is far more dogmatic and apodictic than *The Messingkauf Dialogues,* and it has given rise to far more misunderstandings.

That Brecht evolved a body of extremely fertile ideas for the writing and staging of his type of drama is beyond doubt. What is far more questionable is the basic conception that Marxism, as a philosophy, simply must produce its own, Marxist, aesthetics. Having been brought up in a German philosophical tradition, according to which each philosopher had to produce a unitary system of thought which would provide a complete worldview comprising an epistemology, cosmology, logic, ethics, and aesthetics, Brecht thought that Marxism also should be able to provide all the answers to all the problems of the universe. Yet Marxism, in claiming to be a scientific system, also necessarily must be an open system, relying on a constant testing of its findings by experiment. Moreover, basically, Marxism is a system of political economy. Nobody ever attempted to construct aesthetics to fit Adam Smith's or John Maynard Keynes's ideas of political economy. Why, then, should it be necessary to complement Marxism with such a body of doctrine? Only at the point where Marxism ceases to be a scientific hypothesis and is turned into the pseudo-religion of a totalitarian state does it in fact acquire the need to have an aesthetic doctrine. As it happened, the "aesthetics" developed by Stalinism in the Soviet Union were diametrically opposed to Brecht's ideas about art and drama and corresponded, in fact, very closely to those of Hitler's Germany (rejection of all abstract and experimental art as degenerate). In other words, the aesthetics actually developed by Soviet Communism were not Marxist but totalitarian aesthetics, and derived not from any philosophy but from the needs of thought control in a dictatorship. Indeed, Brecht's insistence that the theater should shock its audience into critical thought made his aesthetics highly suspect in the eyes of the Stalinists and their successors.

There remains the problem about the philosophical implications of the theory of genres enunciated by Goethe and Schiller: that drama, by its insistence that what the audience sees is something which happens here and now and with which they can totally identify, presupposes that human nature is constant and unchangeable. It was this which led Brecht to reject the idea of a dramatic theater altogether and to opt for an epic theater. Yet the implications of the "Aristotelian" conception of drama as understood by Goethe and Schiller need not be quite so drastic. The declared purpose of this conception of drama might be that, human nature being always the same, the spectators ought to be made to identify with the actions of the characters on the stage. Yet, as social conditions change, in fact, the vast bulk of past drama fails to bring about any identification and becomes, indeed, unperformable. Most of the emotions portrayed in eighteenth-century larmoyant comedy, in Victorian melodrama, are incapable of arousing any echo in the minds of contemporary audiences, except perhaps ribald laughter. Only a very small proportion of the drama of past epochs still has the power of making contemporary spectators identify with the experience of characters like Oedipus, Lear, Juliet, or Othello. Yet, it could be argued, it is not with the slave-owning ancient king that audiences identify while watching Oedipus but with the man who feels guilty for having desired his own mother; not with the Moorish general but with the jealous husband; not with the Veronese aristocratic girl but with a girl kept from marrying the man she loves; not with the mythical ruler of a barbaric Britain but with an old man ousted by his daughters. In these cases the social framework behind the characters may have changed decisively, yet in their basic emotional aspects there has been little or no change. In his effort to make his actors see such characters critically, Brecht wrote "practice scenes" to be performed during rehearsals. One of these shows Romeo and Juliet being extremely heartless in their relations to their servants, to whom they deny the freedom of having high-flown emotions like their own love. Thus Brecht wanted his actors—and the audience—to be made aware that in feudal Verona only the masters could indulge in romantic love. That is a valid point, but not the point that Shakespeare wanted to make; why then should Shakespeare's play be used to yield this message rather than the one about young love, which is still valid? Likewise, husbands still tend to be as jealous as Othello. Yet, Brecht argued, they should not be made to feel that they agree with Othello. By inhibiting their tendency to identify with him, the husbands in the audience should be made to see how foolish such jealousy, based as it is on a medieval concept of ownership, must be. Yet the strong tendency toward identification in contemporary audiences exists precisely because these medieval concepts still hold sway, in spite of totally different social conditions. Once a more enlightened age has dawned, when the emancipation of women is complete and love is freed from concepts of ownership, *Othello* will automatically carry its "alienation effect," without any effort on the part of directors or theoreticians.

Conversely, in Brecht's own plays the alienation effect invariably fails in performance whenever the emotions portrayed are of such a nature that they correspond to those of the audience. Brecht wanted the audience to criticize Mother Courage for her involvement with war as a business, to condemn her for causing the death of her children. But in spite of songs, anti-illusionist staging, posters with the exact time and date, the distancing effect does not take place; the mothers in the audience—and not only they—still identify with the predicament of a loving mother who loses her children. Brecht scolded critics and audiences alike for seeing Mother Courage as a Niobe. But they did, and thereby showed clearly that the world of Oedipus and the other archetypes of Greek myth retains its power, that not only might modern audiences identify with Oedipus, but that even the most consciously Marxist conception of a character could ultimately not escape identification with a human type dating back to antiquity. And what is true of Mother Courage also applies to Puntila (whom audiences find lovable because they cannot but identify with his drunkenness); to Galilei (whose sensuousness and cowardice produce similar effects of sympathetic empathy); to Azdak and many other "alienated" Brechtian characters.

This is not to say that Brecht's technique of alienation does not produce results of supreme artistic quality. Precisely because the human tendency toward identification is so strong, the continued efforts to inhibit it produce a tension, a tug-of-war, between opposing tendencies which ultimately creates a kind of double vision, an equal stimulation of intellect and emotion, and an effect of depth, of a multitude of levels of meaning.

Hence—and this is a characteristically Brechtian paradox—those of his works which are most openly political, and therefore unidimensional, invariably turn out to be the weakest. When a play lacks human, or indeed political, truth, it invariably fails to produce identification among the spectators. They notice the author's intention and resent being manipulated.

Brecht's case is a most illuminating illustration of the problems of politically committed art. Where a ready-made political concept is dominant in his mind, even a writer of genius like Brecht cannot make it the basis of a wholly convincing work of art. The political stereotype inhibits the free play of the artist's imagination and forces him to create oversimplified characters and situations. Where, on the other hand, the political motivation is an indirect one, where it springs from the poet's experience of the injustice and suffering caused by the state of the world, and where therefore he is able to give his imagination free rein, so that the characters can develop in the three-dimensional roundness of natural growth, the result is not only a greater human impact but also, ultimately, a greater social and political effectiveness, even though that political effect may not always be the one which had been in the poet's mind.

The history of Brecht's impact on the world and the spread of his fame clearly illustrates the validity of this analysis. In vain do the followers of the totalitarian party line accuse those who make this point of trying to turn Brecht into a harmless article of aesthetic consumption and of denying him his own claim to be more, namely a revolutionary force that effectively will and can change society itself. Yet the fact remains that Brecht is as frequently and successfully performed in the Western world as in East Germany and that, indeed, his message of critical detachment has a more explosive effect in the East, where it appears anti-totalitarian, than in the West, where it can easily be taken for granted. *The Threepenny Opera* ran in New York for many years, yet it will be hard to find anyone who was converted by it to a Marxist view of politics.

That this is so makes Brecht a failure only in the eyes of those who measure the values of aesthetics according to political standards. Nobody wants to deny the enormous benefits Brecht derived artistically from his commitment to Marxism, but these benefits were of a personal nature and affected his work as a poet and playwright only indirectly. Of course a dramatist derives great advantages from having a firm philosophy of life, a clear allegiance and purpose. If one considers the wild exuberance of Brecht's early work and its undertone of despair, one realizes how dangerous it would have been for him, as an artist and as a human being, had he failed to find such a firm allegiance. The short-term political objectives of any work of art, however, are bound to be those most likely to be overtaken by events, to become obsolete and even incomprehensible. Who, today, pays any attention to the fact that a play like Shakespeare's *Richard II* was brimful of political implications to an audience who had lived through the Essex rebellion? That does not diminish the human and aesthetic values contained in the play. In the long view, therefore, the only thing that remains relevant in a work of art is its artistic value. A seventeenth-century musket may have become obsolete as a weapon, while it still remains beautiful as a work of craftsmanship. Brecht's plays might have been fashioned by him as weapons, but their aesthetic values will remain long after the conflicts to which they were relevant have been forgotten.

What does matter in a major artist, apart from his talent, is the depth and quality of his human experience: Brecht is unique among the great artists of his time in that he was more deeply involved in the experience of his epoch than almost any other poet of comparative stature. He was directly affected by World War I as well as World War II. He had firsthand experience of what will probably be the archetypal predicament of the twentieth century: political exile. He experienced vicious persecution by the Nazis, was deeply involved with the Soviet Union, lived in the United States, and became a victim of the anti-Communist witchhunt of the forties. At the end of his life, in Communist East Berlin, he took a stand against totalitarian Stalinism, which foreshadowed the renewal of Marxist thought in the Poland of the fifties and the Czechoslovakia of the late sixties. He was

equally at home in the turbulent Berlin of the dying Weimar Republic, in the Moscow of the Stalinist purges, and in the torrid climate of postwar Hollywood and New York. He saw Soviet friends, like Tretyakov, hounded to their deaths by Stalin, and Hollywood friends, like Chaplin, persecuted as subversive elements in America. He witnessed the rise and fall of Hitler, had his books burned by the Nazis, and fifteen years later stood on the ruins of Hitler's *Reichskanzlei.*

It is this experience which shines through Brecht's poetry and the best of his prose work and dramatic output. What is remarkable is that his reaction, though frequently violent and impatient, basically amounts to a grim determination to survive and to transcend all the brutality and fanaticism by an ideal of friendliness. This is a concept that owes much to a classical Chinese Confucian view of an ideal society based on mutual politeness and respect. Brecht's poetry in the last years of his life was deeply imbued with these almost quietist, Stoic values, which combine the attitudes of the Good Soldier Schweik and the serenity of Horace with the Confucian ideal.

All this is a far cry from the wild rebellion of Brecht's youth and yet is strangely consistent with the dialectics of his development from a feeling of emotional passivity and the helplessness in the face of the uncontrollable, cataclysmic forces of history, society, and man's own instincts, to a yearning for discipline, rationality, and conscious control over nature and man through science, to an ultimate synthesis of a humble recognition of man's ability to master his environment, tempered by a resolve to do his best within his modest capacity.

Brecht's oeuvre, therefore, must always be judged as a whole; the more deeply committed of his disciples have, in the past, made considerable efforts to minimize, and even to suppress, the more chaotic outpourings of the early Brecht. He himself rewrote his first play to reach the stage, *Drums in the Night,* before he included it in the collected edition of his plays in 1954. Yet gradually pressure from Western critics—and Brecht's West German publisher—induced much of the hitherto suppressed material to be published: an edition of Brecht's letters, by no means complete; his so-called *Arbeitsjournal* that covered the last twenty years of his life; some early diaries from the 1920's; some of his poems on Stalin and his early pornographic verse.

But it was only with the advent of *glasnost* that a decisive break occurred. Publication of a new, much fuller, if by no means a "variorum," edition of Brecht's works started in 1988. But what is even more surprising, this new, thirty-volume *Werke, Grosse kommentierte Berliner und Frankfurter Ausgabe* (Great Berlin and Frankfurt Edition with Commentary) is published jointly by Brecht's West German publisher, Suhrkamp, and the East German Aufbau Verlag in East Berlin, and edited by scholars from East as well as West Germany. The first six volumes that had appeared by the spring of 1989 scrupulously adhere to the first published texts and also include later versions of the plays in full if they differ substantially from the first editions. And much hitherto unpublished material is also being made available in this unprecedented all-German publishing venture, the first of its kind since Germany was divided in 1945.

The title of the new edition, with its reference to Berlin and Frankfurt, contains an obvious allusion to the great Weimar edition of Goethe. It thus finally consecrates Brecht's status as a major German "classic."

He himself would have seen the irony of this development. He always deplored the fact that once a writer had become a classic he lost his bite, his ability to disturb and shock; that he had in fact been rendered harmless as part of the cultural furniture of established power.

His publisher has revealed that, when the first attempt was made at issuing a collected edition of the plays, Brecht insisted on fairly large print and small format so that his output might be made to look more substantial on the bookshelves. He thus had a modest idea of his own oeuvre, and probably did not feel that a good deal of material posthumously published really belonged to the enduring body of his work. In the early thirties he had issued his work in progress in modest gray brochures entitled *Versuche* (experiments) and in these he had always cited a number of names beside his own, as *Mitarbeiter* (collaborators). Brecht looked at the poet's work as a craft comparable to that of medieval architects or painters who either remained anonymous or worked collectively, with a number of disciples taking part in painting one picture. He rejected the romantic ideal of the unique original genius and ridiculed the myth of divinely inspired creativity.

And yet—with the characteristic dialectical tension between opposites within his personality—he was, at the same time, aware of his importance as an artist. When, during his American period, a friend pointed out to him that he had used an Anglicism in something he had written, and that the expression concerned did not exist in German, he retorted: "Well, then, it exists from now on."

Similarly, having ridiculed the worship accorded to the "classics" of German literature in schools and universities and among the educated classes, he himself occasionally referred to himself as a classic.

And that is what, inevitably, he has become. It is Brecht's unique achievement that he has reconciled two traditions in German literature which had been kept in different compartments before him, a state of affairs which had had most unfortunate effects on the cultural life of Germany. In Brecht the rough, plebeian, popular tradition and the sophisticated, academic, refined, respectable tradition have come together. Thanks to Brecht's achievement the work of the Austro-Bavarian folk comedians and the plays of the *poètes maudits* of the eighteenth and early nineteenth centuries appear in a new light and have assumed a new importance. And, what is more, by introducing his new, rough, popular, almost dialect tone,

Brecht succeeded in forging a new German stage idiom, which is neither the highly refined, but unnatural *Bühnendeutsch* (stage German) of the one nor the broad vernacular regional speech of the other tradition. This is an achievement which has greatly eased the difficulties of the generation of young postwar dramatists and poets in Germany.

Moreover, with his preference for exotic foreign locations in his youth, with his experience of Scandinavia, the Soviet Union, and the United States in his years of exile, Brecht had done much to break down the provincialism of much of German dramatic literature. And at the same time, having achieved international success, he put Germany on the map of international drama once again. So Brecht, the outsider and rebel, has a solid claim to enduring fame.

Not that Brecht hankered after posthumous recognition. Indeed, at times he insisted that he dreaded nothing more than elevation to the status of a classic, which to him meant condemnation to ultimate innocuousness as safe reading matter for schoolchildren. He wanted his work to become an active agent for genuine change in the social and cultural condition of man. But for the fact that he had lived, the tyrants might have sat a little more securely on their thrones. That was his hope. It is, however, more than doubtful whether Hitler's fall was speeded even by a second through the exertions of Brecht and other anti-Nazi intellectuals. On the other hand, Brecht's support hardly strengthened the position of that other tyrant, Stalin, by as much as one whit. Can the exertions of writers like Brecht change the social condition of man at all? Only indirectly: by changing man's sensibility, the atmosphere, the moral climate that surrounds him. But whether Brecht's view was correct or not, his striving in its tragic irony raises the matter of the artist's importance with the impact of a major test case. And for that, as well as for the beauty and depth of his poetry, Brecht merits a place among the great writers of his time.

Selected Bibliography

EDITIONS

INDIVIDUAL WORKS

Materialien zu Brechts "Leben des Galilei." Edited by W. Hecht. Frankfurt am Main, 1963.

Materialien zu Brechts "Mutter Courage und ihre Kinder." Edited by W. Hecht. Frankfurt am Main, 1964.

Der Jasager und Der Neinsager. Vorlagen, Fassungen und Materialien. Edited by Peter Szondi. Frankfurt am Main, 1966.

Baal. Der böse Baal, der Asoziale. Edited by Dieter Schmidt. Frankfurt am Main, 1968.

Im Dickicht der Städte. Erstfassung und Materialien. Edited by Gisela E. Bahr. Frankfurt am Main, 1968.

Leben Eduards des Zweiten von England. Vorlage, Texte und Materialien. Edited by Reinhold Grimm. Frankfurt am Main, 1968.

Materialien zu Brechts "Der gute Mensch von Sezuan." Edited by W. Hecht. Frankfurt am Main, 1968.

Der Brotladen: Ein Stückfragment. Bühnenfassung und Texte aus dem Fragment. Frankfurt am Main, 1969.

Kuhle Wampe. Protokoll des Films und Materialien. Edited by W. Gersch and W. Hecht. Frankfurt am Main, 1969.

Materialien zu Bertolt Brechts "Die Mutter." Edited by W. Hecht. Frankfurt am Main, 1969.

Texte für Filme. Frankfurt am Main, 1969.

Baal. Drei Fassungen. Edited by Dieter Schmidt. Frankfurt am Main, 1970.

Die heilige Johanna der Schlachthöfe. Bühnenfassung, Fragmente, Varianten. Edited by Gisela E. Bahr. Frankfurt am Main, 1971.

Die Massnahme. Kritische Ausgabe mit einer Spielanleitung. Edited by Reiner Steinweg. Frankfurt am Main, 1972.

Arbeitsjournal. Frankfurt am Main, 1973.

Materialien zu Brechts "Schweyk im Zweiten Weltkrieg." Edited by Herbert Knust. Frankfurt am Main, 1974.

Tagebücher 1920–1922. Autobiographische Aufzeichnungen 1920–1954. Frankfurt am Main, 1975.

Brechts Modell der Lehrstücke. Zeugnisse, Diskus-

sion, Erfahrungen. Edited by Reiner Steinweg. Frankfurt am Main, 1976.

Briefe. Edited by Günter Glaeser. Frankfurt am Main, 1981.

Gedichte aus dem Nachlass. Frankfurt am Main, 1982.

COLLECTED WORKS

Gesammelte Werke. 20 vols. Frankfurt am Main, 1967.

Werke, Grosse kommnetierte Berliner und Frankfurter Ausgabe. 30 vols. Berlin and Weimar, 1988– .

TRANSLATIONS

Baal, A Man's a Man, The Elephant Calf. New York, 1964.

Brecht on Theatre. Edited and translated by John Willett. New York, 1964.

Collected Plays. Edited by John Willett and Ralph Manheim. New York. Vol. 1 (1971): *Baal; Drums in the Night; In the Jungle of Cities; The Life of Edward II of England; The Wedding; The Beggar, or the Dead Dog; He Drives Out a Devil; Lux in Tenebris; The Catch.* Vol. 2 (1977): *A Man's a Man; Rise and Fall of the State of Mahagonny; The Threepenny Opera.* Vol. 5 (1972): *Life of Galileo; The Trial of Lucullus; Mother Courage and Her Children.* Vol. 6 (1976): *The Good Person of Szechwan; Puntila and Matti, His Hired Man; The Resistible Rise of Arturo Ui; Dansen; How Much Is Your Iron?; Practice Pieces for Actors.* Vol. 7 (1974): *The Visions of Simone Machard; Schweyk in the Second World War; The Caucasian Chalk Circle; The Duchess of Malfi.* Vol. 9 (1972): *The Tutor; Coriolanus; The Trial of Joan of Arc at Rouen, 1431; Don Juan; Trumpets and Drums.*

Diaries 1920–1922. Translated by John Willett. New York, 1979.

Edward II. New York, 1966.

Galileo. New York, 1966.

Happy End. New York, 1982.

The Jewish Wife and Other Short Plays. New York, 1965.

Jungle of Cities and Other Plays. New York, 1966.

Manual of Piety (Die Hauspostille). Translated by Eric Bentley. New York, 1966.

The Messingkauf Dialogues. Translated by John Willett. London, 1965.

The Mother. New York, 1965.

Mother Courage and Her Children. New York, 1966.

Parables for the Theatre (The Good Woman of Setzuan, The Caucasian Chalk Circle). New York, 1961.

Poems, 1913–1956. Edited by John Willett and Ralph Manheim. New York, 1987.

Selected Poems. Edited by H. R. Hays. New York, 1947.

Seven Plays. Edited by Eric Bentley. New York, 1961.

Short Stories, 1921–1946. Edited by John Willett and Ralph Manheim. New York, 1983.

Tales from the Calendar. Translated by Yvonne Kapp and Michael Hamburger. London, 1961.

Threepenny Novel. Translated by Desmond I. Vesey and Christopher Isherwood. New York, 1956.

The Threepenny Opera. New York, 1964.

The Visions of Simone Machard. New York, 1965.

BIOGRAPHICAL AND CRITICAL STUDIES

Benjamin, Walter. *Understanding Brecht.* Translated by Anna Bostock. London, 1973.

Bentley, Eric. *The Brecht Commentaries.* New York, 1981.

Chiarini, P. *Bertolt Brecht.* Bari, Italy, 1959.

———. *Brecht e la dialettica del paradosso.* Milan, 1969.

Demetz, P., ed. *Brecht: A Collection of Critical Essays.* Englewood Cliffs, N.J., 1962.

Esslin, Martin. *Bertolt Brecht.* New York, 1969.

———. *Brecht: A Choice of Evils.* 4th rev. ed. London and New York, 1980.

———. *Meditations: Essays on Brecht, Beckett, and the Media.* Baton Rouge, La., 1980.

Ewen, Frederic. *Bertolt Brecht: His Life, His Art, and His Times.* New York, 1967.

Fassmann, Kurt. *Brecht: Eine Bildbiographie.* Munich, 1958.

Fuegi, John. *The Essential Brecht.* Los Angeles, 1972.

Gersch, Wolfgang. *Film bei Brecht.* Berlin, 1975.

Gray, Ronald. *Brecht the Dramatist.* Cambridge, England, 1976.

Grimm, Reinhold. *Bertolt Brecht, die Struktur seines Werks.* Nuremberg, 1959.

———. *Bertolt Brecht und die Weltliteratur.* Nuremberg, 1961.

———. *Brecht und Nietzsche.* Frankfurt am Main, 1979.

Hayman, Ronald. *Brecht: A Biography.* New York, 1983.

Hecht, W., ed. *Brecht im Gespräch. Diskussionen. Dialoge. Interviews.* Frankfurt am Main, 1975.

———, ed. *Bertolt Brecht. Sein Leben in Bildern und Texten.* Frankfurt am Main, 1978.

Hecht, W., H. Bunge, and K. Rülicke-Weiler. *Bertolt Brecht. Sein Leben und Werk.* Berlin, 1969.

Hinck, Walter. *Die Dramaturgie des späten Brecht.* Göttingen, 1959.

Hultberg, Helge. *Die ästhetischen Anschauungen Bertolt Brechts.* Copenhagen, 1962.

Ihering, Herbert. *Bertolt Brecht und das Theater.* Berlin, 1959.

Jendreiek, H. *Bertolt Brecht. Drama der Veränderung.* Düsseldorf, 1969.

Kesting, Marianne. *Bertolt Brecht in Selbstzeugnissen und Bilddokumenten.* Hamburg, 1959.

Klotz, Volker. *Bertolt Brecht, Versuch über das Werk.* Darmstadt, 1957.

Knopf, Jan. *Bertolt Brecht. Ein kritischer Forschungsbericht.* Frankfurt am Main, 1974.

Lyon, James K. *Bertolt Brecht and Rudyard Kipling.* The Hague, 1975.

———. *Bertolt Brecht in America.* Princeton, 1980.

Lyons, Charles R. *Bertolt Brecht: The Despair and the Polemic.* Carbondale, Ill., 1968.

Mann, Otto. *Mass oder Mythos: Ein kritischer Beitrag über die Schaustücke Bertolt Brechts.* Heidelberg, 1958.

Mayer, Hans. *Bertolt Brecht und die Tradition.* Pfullingen, 1961.

———. *Anmerkungen zu Brecht.* Frankfurt am Main, 1965.

———. *Brecht in der Geschichte.* Frankfurt am Main, 1971.

Mittenzwei, Werner. *Bertolt Brecht. Von der "Massnahme" zu "Leben des Galilei."* Berlin, 1962.

Müller, Klaus-Detlef. *Die Funktion der Geschichte im Werk Bertolt Brechts.* Tübingen, 1967.

Munk, Erika, ed. *Brecht.* New York, 1972.

Niessen, Carl. *Brecht auf der Bühme.* Cologne, 1959.

Pietzcker, Carl. *Die Lyrik des jungen Brecht.* Frankfurt am Main, 1974.

Reich, B. *Brecht.* Moscow, 1960.

Rischbieter, Henning. *Bertolt Brecht.* 2 vols. Velber bei Hannover, 1966.

Rosenbauer, H. *Brecht und der Behaviorismus.* Bad Homburg, 1970.

Rülicke-Weiler, Käthe. *Die Dramaturgie Brechts.* Berlin, 1966.

Schmidt, Dieter. *"Baal" und der junge Brecht.* Stuttgart, 1966.

Schuhmann, Klaus. *Der Lyriker Bertolt Brecht, 1913–1933.* Berlin, 1964.

Schumacher, Ernst. *Die dramatischen Versuche Bertolt Brechts 1918–1933.* Berlin, 1955.

———. *Der Fall Galilei. Das Drama der Wissenschaft.* Berlin, 1964.

———. *Drama und Geschichte. Bertolt Brechts "Leben des Galilei" und andere Stücke.* Berlin, 1965.

Schumacher, Ernst, and Renate Schumacher. *Leben Brechts.* Berlin, 1979.

Serreau, Genevieve. *Bertolt Brecht, dramaturge.* Paris, 1955.

Spalter, Max. *Brecht's Tradition.* Baltimore, Md., 1967.

Steinweg, Reiner. *Das Lehrstück.* Stuttgart, 1972.

Subiotto, A. *Bertolt Brecht's Adaptations for the Berliner Ensemble.* London, 1975.

Tatlow, Antony. *The Mask of Evil.* Bern, 1977.

Völker, Klaus. *Brecht Chronicle.* Translated by Fred Wieck. New York, 1975.

———. *Brecht: A Biography.* Translated by John Nowell. New York, 1978.

Wekwerth, Manfred. *Notate. Über die Arbeit des Berliner Ensembles 1956 bis 1966.* Frankfurt am Main, 1967.

———. *Schriften. Arbeit mit Brecht.* Berlin, 1973.

Willett, John. *The Theatre of Bertolt Brecht.* 4th rev. ed. London, 1977.

BIBLIOGRAPHIES

Ramthun, Herta, ed. *Bertolt Brecht Archiv/ Bestandsverzeichnis des literarischen Nachlasses.* 4 vols. Berlin and Weimar, 1969–1973.

Seidal, Gerhard, ed. *Bibliographie Bertolt Brecht.* Vol. 1. Berlin and Weimar, 1975.

MARTIN ESSLIN

MICHEL DE GHELDERODE

(1898–1962)

MICHEL DE GHELDERODE occupies a special place in the drama of the twentieth century, one that overlaps with his contemporaries and with following generations and exhales an atmosphere of bygone ages. He offers a curious and extremely personal synthesis between a nightmarish rendering of antique settings and modernist literary and theatrical techniques. Ghelderode, like his contemporary counterparts Antonin Artaud, Ramón del Valle-Inclán, and Stanisław Witkiewicz, took romanticist exploration of the dark underside of nature to its far reaches of the grotesque and scatological. Ghelderode delights in bringing corpses back to life, in sending would-be lovers on a hunt for each other that brings not love but gory death, and in rendering lewd and vile the agents of society's institutions. Each character typically embodies a vice—gluttony, avarice, lechery—and the human race is unmasked to reveal both its moral and physical decay, or masked expressly to theatrically accentuate its ugliness. Corrupt priests disport with lascivious virgins; leering dwarves, towering heresiarchs, and clownish, naïve poets—the Ghelderodian gallery runs to the picturesque and grotesque. Nonetheless, mystical overtones pervade works customarily set in an ahistorical medieval Flanders of the mind. While passively intimating a context of moral virtues overturned, few of his characters strive for good, but rather wallow in their own corruption, a corruption that is realized imagistically as physical decrepitude.

A formal innovator, Ghelderode flirted with dadaism and modernism in various forms. His masters were the Comte de Lautréamont and Alfred Jarry, August Strindberg and Maurice Maeterlinck. Yet, despite these influences, he retains a personal voice that is ill-suited to classification and a spirit that fits but awkwardly into literary groups. So although his works bear the stamp, now of symbolism, now expressionism, now modernism à la Guillaume Apollinaire or Jean Cocteau, he remains, whether revered or dismissed, uniquely, tormentingly Ghelderode. In America, Ghelderode was understood to be a writer of the sixties; his works were first translated into English at that time. In France he was a writer of the post–World War II period, since that was when his plays began to gain great popularity among Parisian theatrical troupes. The reality of the matter is otherwise. The fecund body of his upwards of sixty plays, ranging from those of several minutes to many hours in length, were largely penned between 1918 and 1937. But the common postdating has led to Ghelderode's name often being linked to the Sartrean existentialist generation or the theater of the absurd, with Eugène Ionesco, Jean Genêt, and Samuel Beckett said to be his literary contemporaries. In point of fact, he was a writer ahead of his time, one who bridged the avant-garde gap between Jarry and Maeterlinck at the beginning of the century and the absurdists in the middle.

The brief span of Ghelderode's popularity,

when compared to that of a Beckett or Ionesco, may thus be ascribed to its roots in an earlier avant-garde, one whose techniques may have felt clumsy, outmoded, or overly literary at the time of its belated efflorescence. But when one considers that the active writer Ghelderode was conducting his experiments at the same time as were the expressionists and surrealists, discovering his own version of the theater of cruelty, though ignorant of the simultaneously hatched theories of Artaud, it is possible to accurately place Ghelderode in his actual cultural milieu and begin to sense the originality and freshness of his contribution.

LIFE

The author of *Escurial* was born 3 April 1898 with the gawky first names Adémar-Adolphe and the common-as-rain Flemish last name Martens in Ixelles, a charming neighborhood of Brussels. His father, Henri-Adolphe Martens (1861–1943), originated from Waarschoot (East Flanders). Like most bourgeois or social-climbing Flemish of his generation, he insisted on bringing up his family to speak French. His mother, Jeanne-Marie Rans (1864–1944), from Louvain, defied the linguistic rules of the house by regaling her avid younger son with supernatural tales and folk ditties in her Brabant peasant dialect of Flemish (a variant of the official written and spoken Dutch). Ghelderode dated his nascent love of Flemish folklore, the Middle Ages, and the mystico-supernatural from those early influences. Never a strong child, he was forced to withdraw from school by a number of bouts with typhus. At one point the gravity of his illness obliged him to live away from his family for long spells, by the sea.

He began writing with forays into poetry and prose, including *L'Histoire comique de keizer Karel telle que la perpétuèrent jusqu'à nos jours les gens de Brabant et de Flandre* (The Comic History of Emperor Charles V as It Has Been Passed Down to Us by the People of Brabant and Flanders, 1922) and sporadically returned to the short-story form, at which he was not markedly distinguished, at those several points in his career when he was to turn his back on the stage.

The fact that a long-term quest with various genealogical archives failed to prove that he was descended from an ancient royal clan did not prevent him from assuming the fanciful, invented name of Michel de Ghelderode (which was ultimately given official sanction in 1929) in time for the presentation of his first play, *La mort regarde à la fenêtre* (*Death Looks in the Window*), in 1918. It was presented on the occasion of a conference on Edgar Allan Poe. Ghelderode often hid behind pseudonymns, among them Philostène Costenoble (Undertaker Poet) and Babylas. The former was used to sign second-rate poetry he wasn't sure would be well received and the latter for delivering savage attacks on other artists' work in literary magazines. Assuming false names was just one manifestation of his lifelong propensity for self-mystification. Ghelderode was forever trying to rise above the banality of everyday existence and to elevate his commonplace suffering to epic proportions. To this end he advertised himself as a misanthropic hermit, when he was in fact merely shy and prone to paranoid fears that conspiracies were being mounted against him. Following World War II, when his popularity was burgeoning, he had photos of himself taken in a study elaborately furnished for macabre and flamboyant effect, thus giving the false impression that he normally surrounded himself with mannequins of naked women and skulls, when in fact the study, now on display in the Central Library of Brussels, was hastily fabricated in order to immortalize a mythic vision of himself at a time when it would be given most play.

Ghelderode spoke and wrote in French, all the while harboring a nostalgic allegiance to his Flemish background. His first several forays into theater, between 1918 and 1926, were short Maeterlinckian static dramas. In each of these he presents a flat tableau of corrupt humanity—generalized characters who sense the approach of death. The final moment in each play is death's arrival and the consequent awakening of the mass-character's consciousness.

In these brief works Ghelderode established the signature for all future work by departing from his countryman Maeterlinck's models (*The Intruder, The Blind*) in accentuating the grotesque rather than the piteous nature of the life-death cycle, which results in a discordant, harsh tone. For example, in *Le cavalier bizarre* (*The Strange Rider*, 1924), the aged residents in a hospice set to dancing "spasmodically" on learning of the death of a tiny baby. The melancholy sigh that epitomized the Maeterlinckian response to the universe's indifference, in Ghelderode, changes to a harsh cackle.

Ghelderode married Jeanne-Françoise Gérard in 1924, and they remained together until Ghelderode's death. Throughout the twenties, Ghelderode belonged to Maurice Gauchez's Renaissance de l'Occident, a literary group that published many of his early plays. There he first met a number of his best friends, including Marcel Wyseur and Camille Poupeye. It was also during the early twenties that Ghelderode wrote a series of brief plays for marionettes based on biblical themes, supposedly reconstructions of classic puppet plays. By 1926 Ghelderode had come out with two full-length plays, *La mort du Docteur Faust* (*The Death of Doctor Faust*, 1925) and *Don Juan; ou, Les amants chimériques* (Don Juan; or, The Chimerical Lovers, 1926), but the cool reception by the French-speaking public and total disinterest of the French-language theaters of Brussels catapulted him toward a more welcoming Flemish troupe, Het Vlaamsche Volkstoneel (Flemish Peoples' Theater).

The frustrated quest for a sustained positive response to his idiosyncratic and off-putting dramatic work was the prime motive force throughout a career studded with moral about-faces, rejections of old friends, and radical fluctuations in political and cultural leanings. His was a personality marked by a highly unstable sense of confidence in his own creative power as a writer. Whenever Ghelderode swore off playwriting, it was due to whatever topical coolness from the public he was experiencing. And when he proclaimed the greatness or meanness of a people—whether Flemish, French, or Third-Reich German—the cause was that group's readiness or want thereof to produce and appreciate his plays.

So when, in 1926, Ghelderode loudly proclaimed his Flemish roots and announced himself a militant in the struggle for Flemish equality in the Belgian social structure, the cause may be seen in the nurturing embrace extended by the Flemish Peoples' Theater, led by Johan de Meester and Jan Boon. This group took his French-language plays, written expressly with their actors, politics, and aesthetics in mind, and made hasty translations to the Dutch. These were played throughout urban and rural Flanders. Whenever Boon and de Meester rejected one of his scripts or took too long before mounting it, Ghelderode cursed Flanders and the Flemish movement; whenever they quickly endorsed and played his works, he was once again staunchly behind the cause, bespeaking a frailty governed by personal interest that was to get him into serious trouble later on. While disdaining production of *Christophe Colomb* (*Christopher Columbus*, 1927), *Don Juan, Escurial* (1927), or *The Death of Doctor Faust*, the Flemish Peoples' Theater did mount *Images de la vie de Saint François d'Assise* (Images from the Life of Saint Francis of Assisi, 1926) and such important works as *Pantagleize* (1929) and *Barabbas* (1928). Their patronage of Ghelderode ceased only with the company's demise in 1932. From 1923 to 1939 Ghelderode was employed as an archivist by the Communal House of Schaerbeek, the neighborhood of Brussels where Ghelderode lodged. It was there, behind a stack of dusty, yellowing documents, that Ghelderode evaded his bosses and wrote his oeuvre, his chronic asthma aggravated and worsening all the while.

Ghelderode's sojourn with the Flemish Peoples' Theater permitted him to see at first hand what worked on stage and what did not. However, when recourse to that agency was no longer available, he commenced a series of works that were impressive in their scope, obsessive in the treatment of their themes, and often oblivious to the practical exigencies of the stage. During this phase he no longer limited himself to religious and political themes, as he did earlier to satisfy the Flemish Peoples' Theater, but gave free vent to his apolitical personal vision. This period saw the birth of most of his major works: *Magie rouge* (*Red Magic*, 1931), *Le siège d'Ostende* (The Siege of Ostend, 1934), *Sire Halewyn* (*Lord Halewyn*, 1934), *La balade du Grand Macabre* (The Stroll of the Great Macabre, 1934), *Mademoiselle Jaïre* (*Miss Jairus*, 1934), *Sortie de l'acteur* (The Actor's Exit, 1935), *La farce des ténébreux* (The Farce of the Shadow Cult, 1936), *Hop Signor!* (1936), *Fastes d'enfer* (*Chronicles of Hell* 1937), *L'École des bouffons* (*The School for Buffoons*, 1942), and several smaller ones.

Throughout this period Ghelderode was rarely produced. There was a short burst of popularity in the French-language theaters of Brussels in 1934 and a smattering of productions of *The Death of Doctor Faust* abroad, including one by the prestigious Parisian Théâtre d'Art et Action in 1928 and another by Anton Giulo Bragaglia's Teatro degli Indipendenti in Rome the same year. But Ghelderode's bitterness over the general neglect, together with ever-worsening health, brought his dramatic writing virtually to an end. *The School for Buffoons* was followed only by *Le soleil se couche* (The Sun Sets) in 1943 and a series of radio plays. Ghelderode looked forward to the Nazi invasion of Belgium in 1940 in the expectation that under the "new order" he would at last be appreciated and played. Although these hopes were dashed, a series of folkloric talks, *Choses et gens de chez nous* (Our Own Things and People), on German-controlled radio brought in a modicum of income, barely enough to cover certain medical expenses.

Following the war Ghelderode was prosecuted for collaboration and was stripped of both job and citizenship. A lengthy and draining series of appeals eventually led to a royal pardon and revocation of the charges. In 1949, following the pardon, he took his pension and did not return to work. Despite a deep-seated anti-Semitism and a patrician antidemocratic stance, Ghelderode's politics fluctuated radically over the course of his life; although briefly a sympathizer, he never truly converted to Nazism. His self-deluded longing for Aryan political domination grew out of a desperate personal opportunism and a false perception that National Socialism and Flemish nationalism were cut from the same cloth. He prayed that the Flemish flavor in his work would be found compatible with Teutonic culture. The postwar persecution hardened Ghelderode's resolve never again to write for the theater, although there is evidence that his creative powers had already dried up.

Ghelderode was rescued from infamy and semiobscurity by Catherine Toth and André Reybaz. The 1947 production of *Hop Signor!* by their Parisian troupe, Le Myrmidon, was followed by their production of *Chronicles of Hell* at the Théâtre de Marigny, at which the audience was so thoroughly outraged that the curtain was brought down after the fourth performance, nearly knocking out one of the actors. This *succès de scandale* shook Paris and unleashed a flood of productions through the mid-fifties. Belgium, although reluctant to recognize its native sons before a Parisian stamp of approval, then followed suit. International success came shortly thereafter, with particularly fine productions in Italy and Eastern Europe. Ghelderode was discovered in the United States in the late fifties, with a spate of productions following in the sixties, notably of *Escurial, Pantagleize* (with a most renowned production at the A.P.A. [Association of Producing Artists] Phoenix in 1967 directed by Ellis Raab), and *Les femmes au tombeau* (*The Women at the Tomb*, 1933).

Ghelderode was flattered by this attention, but his pen flowed only once more for the theater, in 1952, for the commissioned outdoor spectacle *Marie la misérable* (Marie the Miserable). Satisfaction at belated fame was further enhanced by a series of awards commemorating his accomplishments: the Prix Picard, the Prix Rubens, the Prix Triennal de Littérature, and the Prix de Concours aux Jeunes Compagnies Parisiennes. He was also under serious consideration for the Nobel Prize in literature. The body of his plays has been published in six volumes by the prestigious Editions Gallimard, although many of his plays remain either unpublished or relegated to obscure journals of the twenties. The full breadth and diversity of his work is not generally appreciated. Ghelderode died 1 April 1962 in Schaerbeek.

THE DIFFICULTY OF DYING

The one-act play *Escurial* is one of Ghelderode's most often performed works, bearing the murky stamp of symbolism, yet full of lusty histrionics. As the curtain rises to reveal a dilapidated throne room of olden times, dogs are howling outside, and the solitary King is screaming for their slaughter; they represent some terrible reminder to him. The Queen, it seems, is dying, and the entire kingdom is crouched in wait for her final breath. The King calls Folial, his jester, to while away the time until that fateful moment comes. The jester is himself gloomy and so fails to lift the King's spirits. When the King orders Folial to laugh, the raucous, uncontrolled result is actually dissimulated weeping. The King and Folial engage in sadomasochistic time-killing. Folial acts the part of a dog and then that of a king who is stripped of regality and reverts to the tattered beggar he began as. At the end of this enactment Folial is on the point of strangling the real King, when the King voluntarily adorns his jester with his own crown and scepter, ordering him to "Climb up to your throne, kinged gorilla!" The King then dons the jester's cap. In the guise of the jester, the King confides his disillusionment at his queen's infidelity and his own sense of foolishness on being cuck-

olded by her. He dances for joy at her death.

The jester evenhandedly defends the Queen from behind his guise as king and reproaches the actual king for having shut up his life-loving wife in the sepulchral, eerie castle. At this point the King intimates his suspicion that it is with Folial himself that the Queen was unfaithful to him and that he had lurked after them as they enjoyed their illicit delights. And, still in the guise of jester, he confesses to having punished the Queen with poison, for "Love does not enter this palace. It is forbidden to love in this palace." When he wants his crown back, Folial refuses to give it up, averring that he is the real king, as he had the love of the Queen. They wrestle over the crown but are interrupted when the Monk arrives to announce the death of the Queen. "May God receive her!" Folial cries, while the King mutters, "May the devil take her!" Whereupon the King has Folial peremptorily strangled. The King goes out laughing savagely as the dogs and bells that he had tried to silence now go wild with barking and chiming.

There is much in this terse tragifarce that is typical of Ghelderode: *Escurial*'s late point of attack, picking up on the action so near the end of the story, in the midst of death throes; the generic tone of laughing through gritted teeth, with a gargoyle grin forming on the actor's face; the subverted fairy-tale setting—jester and King in a desolate medieval palace of the Inquistion; the cruelty of the relations between the characters. The theatrical trappings of the piece are likewise characteristic. Ghelderode is the master of the visual statement. The two characters' inner drama is evoked by the setting of a throne perched high atop a staircase. The peripeties of their power struggle can be followed by seeing which of the two gains the high point on stage only to topple or be thrown to the lowest point.

What sets *Escurial* apart from much of his other work and accounts for the great number of productions it has been given is that the *coups de théâtres* at which Ghelderode excelled come hard upon one another. Here there is none of the excessive verbiage or superfluous inaction that renders many of his plays flaccid, and for which he has often been criticized. The transvestism and playing with identity—who is the real king, he who wears the crown or he capable of loving and being loved?; who has true power, he who can inflict murder and mortification with impunity, or he who despite physical deformities can extract joy from life?—are issues played out most piquantly in *Escurial*. It anticipates the identity play, which became the signature of Jean Genet thirty years later in *The Maids*. (This, by the way, is not an isolated instance of Ghelderode's prefiguration of Genet. The scene in *La balade du Grand Macabre* in which a masochistic husband, Videbolle, dressed as a woman, suffers a whipping from his authoritarian wife, Salivaine, puts one immediately in mind of the cruel scenes of fantasy-fulfilling, transvestite lovemaking in Mme. Irma's brothels in *The Balcony*.)

Sortie de l'acteur is set in an icy and ill-lit theater. Actors are halfheartedly rehearsing a play on the eve of its opening night. The author, Jean-Jacques, is supervising. They are waiting for the lead, Renatus, who turns up at the rehearsal's close. He seems half frozen and confides that his tardiness was on account of having attended a stranger's funeral. He suddenly drops to the floor; Jean-Jacques catches him. The two, on the actor's recovery, commiserate. Jean-Jacques laments that he thought himself "a great lyric author [but] was nothing but a big blowhard," to which Renatus seconds: "You're right. Nobody listened to you. . . . You gave what no one asked you for . . . you're hardly ever performed and then to empty houses." But for certain people, such as Renatus, Jean-Jacques's art had been totally disastrous, revealing to him his human condition. "Dear author, people die too much in your plays." He speaks of his part in the current play, in which he is beheaded in the third act. An actress, Armande, enters and agrees with Renatus, implying that Jean-Jacques is behind the latter's ill health by encouraging in the actor a certain morbidity. She and Jean-Jacques argue over their unconsummated love, exchanging recriminations that end with Armande storming out and Jean-Jacques following, leaving Renatus alone, shivering on stage. Renatus puts a dummy into his chair, covers it up, and hides under a pile of clothing. Fagot, the prompter, comes onstage in a Pierrot outfit and talks to the mannequin, taking it to be Renatus. The latter eventually reveals himself, extremely weakened. Fagot takes him home as Jean-Jacques, who then returns, knocks the head off the dummy. This practical joke and Renatus's absence give him the idea that the actor has left under his own steam.

Act 2 finds Renatus in bed the next day. Evidently the play will not be opening. Jean-Jacques has come to spell Fagot, who has stayed the night by Renatus's bedside, tending him through delirium. Fagot leaves the two alone; Jean-Jacques hears knocking, the source of which he cannot discover. A real knock follows; it is Armande, come to share Jean-Jacques's vigil. Jean-Jacques and Armande sit in the gathering darkness, turning from dispute to lovemaking, "as though engaged in a very slow, silent combat." Renatus, on the other side of the screen, relives old roles, converses with an imaginary doctor he has conjured up, whose craggy shadow is projected onto the wall, and ultimately falls from his bed, welcoming death. Fagot bursts in; the oblivious lovers fly apart and inspect the now-dead body. A group of actors appears with gifts to comfort the invalid but are held back by the solicitous Fagot: "Gentlemen, ladies . . . one moment. . . . You're all most kind. Take off your hats. You can see him in just a little while. Wait on the landing. And a bit of prayer, if you don't mind, a little scrap of prayer."

Act 3 is reset on the outskirts of town at a cafe called The Well-Being, faced by a pallid wall. Jean-Jacques enters having come from the burial of Renatus, full of remorse for his inattention to the dying man. The others who had assisted at the burial pour into the tavern, followed by Armande. She and Jean-Jacques have words, a continuation of the same vague quarrel as earlier, and she goes to join the others inside the tavern. A head appears over the wall—it is Renatus. Jean-Jacques and he converse outside the tavern. Renatus, it seems, is attempting to flee the angels who are on his trail. Jean-Jacques urges him to hide in the prompter's box, which has miraculously popped up before the tavern. An angel patrol enters and interrogates Jean-Jacques by name: Has he seen anyone of Renatus's description? When he refuses to give away his dead friend's whereabouts, the angels attack Jean-Jacques. Before they can do any damage, however, Renatus emerges from the prompter's box and gives himself up. He says his good-byes and mounts the ladder to heaven, followed by the angels.

This play, with its contemporary setting and colloquial diction, first announces itself as a Scribean well-made play, with a slight Pirandellian twist of being set on stage with actors and writer as characters. However, on examining the completed action, this first impression is overturned. The potential issues announced in the exposition—the writer's creative impotence, the male-female struggle, the notion of play and acting—finally achieve no resolution; they are intermittently toyed with and let fall. The play relegates these pseudo-themes to the status of leitmotivs in a musical structure that is laid down to adorn Renatus's primordial rite of passage from the land of the living to that of the dead. True, this major thread is intertwined with others: Armande and Jean-Jacques's murky, ambivalent, and tendentious stab at lovemaking, in which each partner holds the other in such contempt that their brief union across from Renatus's deathbed is definitively quashed by the latter's demise and their subsequent guilt at having sacrificed the purpose of their vigil to sexual pleasure. By Act 3, whatever closeness they had narrowly eked out has reverted to their habitual nastiness. Love is difficult to exchange and maintain when death's intrusion undermines the fulfillment of this life function.

Jean-Jacques, at the start of the play, evinced dissatisfaction with his own competence at his craft. He is on the point of renouncing writing, and this resolve is merely intensified over the course of the play—with the poor playing of the actors, with recognition of his plays' lack of popularity, with Renatus's collapse, then death, and most important, from his growing suspicion, reenforced by several characters, that the morbidity of his writing was the primary cause of Renatus's eclipse.

But the thematic material paradoxically seems but window dressing for the play's spectacle. As Roland Beyen, Ghelderode's principal interpreter, has noted, "the symbols are sometimes unclear, the satire peremptory, the ideas peremptory, but the images are beautiful." From the beginning of *Sortie de l'acteur*, the uncanny "otherworld" seeps into the temporal one until it fully engulfs it in Act 3. The entire play is set in greater or lesser semidarkness. The elaborate stage directions make it clear that naturalistic means are, in Ghelderode's hands, quickly dispensed with and are but stage masking for the numinous level lurking behind: characters are forever merging with shadows, seeming shadows resolve into characters, a human is spookily replaced by a mannequin, and finally, the buttresses of the temporal world are rent asunder and ghosts and angels take the stage.

Sortie de l'acteur is redolent with Ghelderode's love-hate relationship with both the theater and life itself. It was written to commemorate the death of Renaat Verheyen, principal actor with the Flemish Peoples' Theater, who had played the parts of Pantagleize and Saint Francis in *Images de la vie de Saint François d'Assise*. When the Flemish Peoples' Theater disbanded shortly after Verheyen's death, Ghelderode, who had lost his most effective production outlet, began to write only for himself, presumably forfeiting hopes of his plays' adequate presentation or reception. This play, like *Le soleil se couche* or *Le club des menteurs* (The Liars' Club, 1931), represents Ghelderode's flirtation with naturalism. But like the Frank Wedekind of *Spring's Awakening*, who also brought a character provisionally back to life in the final scene, he was too attached to the fantastic to allow himself to be long anchored to the pedestrian confines of the slice-of-life conventions.

Ghelderode's *Chronicles of Hell* is set in Lapideopolis' "decaying episcopal palace in bygone Flanders." The air is "heavy, vibrant with gnats." The wall decorations combine pagan totemic icons with Christian ones, visual signs of the heretical rule that has held sway over the archdiocese. The grotesque clerics of the realm gather one by one and gorge themselves in celebration of the death of Bishop Jan in Eremo and the conclusion of his ascetic, blasphemous rule. Their victory is uncertain, however, for the crowd outside the palace walls is humming with resentment, buzzing with angry rumors that Jan, who was a saint and savior to them, had not died a natural death, but was a victim of foul play. The auxiliary bishop, Simon Laquedeem, is last to enter. The others, who have already exposed their web of rivalries and enmities, now join together in timidly mocking the auxiliary's renowned constipation and flatulence ("Calvary of the stomach! The thorns, the nails, and the lance in it"). He, in turn, pledges to rid the diocese of what is obstructing it: the memory of the dead bishop. "I shall purge the palace of these idols—drive his shadow away, obliterate him even to the traces of his footsteps."

Sodomati, secretary for the pope's nuncio, appears and urges them to burn the idols, which have surely cast a spell over the palace, posthaste. He accuses those present of being "suspect priests of a people of possessed souls." As lightning strikes, Laquedeem and the other clerics present themselves to the people on the balcony, but are rudely booed back into the chamber. Four Swiss Guards appear and are sent to keep watch in the adjoining room over Jan's gigantic corpse, which "looks more formidable dead than living." Laquedeem relates the story of Jan in Eremo's life: Jan, as legend had it, was "born of the fornication of a monk and a mermaid," was found in the dunes, and brought up in a monastery. He set out to sea one tempest-tossed day and was given up for dead, but returned later in a boat laden with idols at a time when the city was infected with "the Plague, Famine, and Madness." In this Lapideopolis, abandoned by clergy and court, he appeared carrying a huge tar-covered cross. As people greeted him with cries of "The Antichrist!" he pitched the crucifix into a bonfire and the plague immediately evaporated. He then distributed hidden stores of food to the starving populace and won their undying loyalty. When the count and bishop returned to the city they were obliged to bow before this miracle-working impostor whom Rome ultimately accepted as legitimate bishop.

When pressured by Sodomati, Laquedeem swears that he had no part in the bishop's death. "And may a thunderbolt, if I am lying, fall in at once on our heads, may thunder . . . " at which point thunder and lightning do indeed strike. The crowd outside roars louder. The Swiss Guards, terrified, run into the room, the priests shriek, and the corpse of Jan in Eremo appears standing in the doorway! He is vainly trying to expel from his throat the poisoned host with which Laquedeem had tried to kill him. The surging people without are on the brink of rioting, demanding that the corpse be turned over the them. The priests lock Jan up, but Laquedeem's taunting draws him forth once more. Laquedeem pursues the corpse with a harquebus and then a hatchet, both of which fail. The two then engage in hand-to-hand combat. And, just as the dead Jan is about to finish Laquedeem off with an ax, an old servant woman, Veneranda, intervenes and gets Jan to cough up the poisoned host. Then, saying, "Come John, come and die," and ordering him to forgive the prelates, she leads him to his bier, where he expires a second time. "The dead man is dead!" The group then pounces on Veneranda and administers the same poisoned host to her; she dies.

A delegation of ten gigantic butchers invades the room, overturns the festive table, gathers up Jan in Eremo's mortal remains, and carries them outside the palace, where the body is greeted by a great triumphant howl from the people. Laquedeem has a gastric seizure, followed by this dialogue:

Laquedeem: Deliverance!

Krakenbus: Deliverance! The corpse is outside. . . .

Carnibos: The smell remains. Ugh! [He holds his nose.]

Laquedeem: The odor of Death!

Sodomati: Do you think so?

    [*Carnibos* disappears at the back.]

Laquedeem: True, it doesn't smell nice! . . . The odor of Death, I say! The dead stink.

Real-Tremblor: The living too.

Laquedeem: True, True . . . they stink! . . . [He gives a fat laugh.]

    [*Carnibos* comes back swinging a smoking censer.]

Laquedeem: Fine! Incense! . . . Some incense! . . . A lot of incense!

Carnibos [swinging the censer majestically]: I'm censing!

Laquedeem: Open the balcony! What d'you say, Pikkedoncker?

Dom Pikkedoncker: Dung!

    [Laughter cascades. The priests sniff each other like dogs.]

Laquedeem: Dung? Who?

Dom Pikkedoncker: Not me! Him! . . . And you, Monsignor! . . . Dung!

    [Panic laughter breaks out, and this hilarity is accompanied by digs in the ribs and monkeylike gesticulations. Seized by frantic joy, the priests jump about comically in the clouds of incense, repeating all the time, "Dung! . . . Dung!"]

Laquedeem [thundering]: The pigs! . . . They've filled their cassocks with dung!

    [He crouches—gown tucked up—his rabbinical face expressing demoniac bliss—while the curtain comes slowly down on these chronicles of Hell.]

This, arguably Ghelderode's greatest work, is typical in many ways. As in *Miss Jairus* and *Sortie de l'acteur*, it is concerned with the supernatural notion of a corpse that refuses to die. It is packed both with anticlericalism and some kind of inverted Catholic/pagan mysticism. The characters are drawn in broad, satirical, and cruel strokes; each of the clergy is physically misshapen or deviate in some way or other. Carnibos is a glutton; Krakenbus is a humpback; Dom Pikkedoncker is deaf; Duvelhond stutters; Real-Tremblor is a castrate. And Simon Laquedeem has his aforementioned gastric disorder. This flat portraiture is suitable, for the play is written, at least in part, as a physical farce, with head bangings, foot stompings, and other forms of knockabout comedy. Whether the farce elements are funny or not is another matter; rather, in the fashion of the Jonsonian comedy, the laughs are bitter and critical, the rough antics being just one further sign of human frailty and absurdity.

As in so many Ghelderode plays (*Piet Bouteille* [1918], *Red Magic, D'un diable qui prêcha merveilles* [Of a Devil Who Preached Wonders, 1942], *La balade du Grand Macabre, La farce de ténébreux, La pie sur le gibet* [*The Magpie on the Gallows*, 1938], and *Le club des menteurs*), corruption, particularly that of the church, is a recurrent theme. For while there is no atheistic rejection of the spiritual in Ghelderode, there is a blanket rejection of the church, with all its trappings and hypocrisy, and the various misuses to which religion is put. Exceptional is the Ghelderode play without at least one fat, lascivious, money-sucking monk. And in *The Chronicles of Hell* they comprise the entire cast. But fascination with a satanic, anti-Catholic, Janus-faced diabolical Christianity is very much proffered as an alternative to official religion. In this play the pagan Christianity embodied in Jan in Eremo is more potent, beloved of the people, and more mystical than the church establishment's Christianity, where hypocrisy, backbiting, and materialism reign supreme.

The great strength of *Chronicles of Hell*, as in most of Ghelderode, is its potential for powerful theatrical images that thunder down onto the stage in quick succession. From his first play, *Death Looks in the Window*, to this, one of the last, Ghelderode delighted in introducing the supernatural onstage and making death's imminence palpable. In order to propagate a sense of horror, he brought corpses back to life and confused the realm of the living with that of the dead. In *Miss Jairus* he introduces a sorcerer who conjures a dead girl back to life. However, in this reincarnated state she is more like a hollowed-out zombie than a human being. The parents who mourned at her death and rejoiced at her rebirth heave a sigh of relief when she is once more permitted to die. In *Death Looks in the Window* it is a vivid description of one tormented to death, coupled with a clamoring storm outside (or is it the dead man pounding on the window?—the same ambiguity occurs in the first act of *Sortie de l'acteur* when mysterious pounding is heard) that strikes terror in the heart. In *Le soleil se couche* the heirs to the abdicated Charles V prepare an elaborate catafalque and ceremony for the still-alive king to encourage him toward death; they will, if they have to (and they do) entomb him alive. In *Magpie on the Gallows* there is a hanging. The victim, however, proves not to be the guilty party, which leads to a comic outcome even in the jaws of death. But even when death isn't present in person, it is intimated through the sounds of chimes or dogs, in ungodly odors, in the ground "sticky like flypaper" from the blood of corpses. Along with the tooth-grinding snicker, the scream of horror is the prototypical Ghelderodian emotional reaction.

MISCAST HEROES

Têtes de bois (*Blockheads*) was written in 1924, but not performed until 1978, and then in English translation, in New York City. Its first performance in French was in Brussels in 1985. *Blockheads* has thus languished in the obscurity of a minor review, *La Flandre littéraire*, since 1924. And yet, for its tiny scale, it has extraordinary power and is a key to Ghelderode's later, more convoluted efforts. *Block-heads* shows Ghelderode in a personal key and an expressionist perspective.

There is only one speaking character, "the Poet." He bursts on stage and finds himself face to face with a series of wooden dummies representing a General, a Scholar, a Dowager, a Black Boxer, an Anarchist, and a Financier. He discourses at length, assuming or imagining the others' responses all the while. He begins by announcing his profession and assuring the dummies that they have been waiting just for him all along and somehow knew it. He tries to fathom what has impelled him toward them, since he is of a different order than they. He concludes that they might be receptive despite their grotesque appearance and recalls that he did, in fact, have a message to impart.

The Poet, little by little, confides that he came to speak of the "despair of the living God," that he has seen Him in a "blasphemous black automobile . . . [that was] carrying Him toward the shooting range." He then accuses the living God of having spied on his innermost thoughts, he who had possessed the greatest secret for humanity's salvation. At this point he notices the dummies' passivity, hurls invective at them, and slaps them up and down, ceasing abruptly on recognizing that they suffer in silence and turn the other cheek, "like the living God." He prostrates himself before them, now certain that they are his betters. Further vacillation ensues. Should he reveal his secret? What impact could it possibly have in this vast, indifferent universe? And yet, he admits, this very evening God is to be shot to death. Out of this insoluble impasse, he explodes in a feverish outburst and "throws the mask away."

It's not true. I lied! I am nothing. Or rather . . . I am an imbecile, an impostor, a sick man. I have various delusions of grandeur and persecution. And along with all that, bourgeois, filthy vices, vices. Best yet, I'm a parasite. I lived off other people, my father, my friends, women. I've stolen from the poor. And what's worse, I've lied, lied . . . at all times and in all circumstances. I've betrayed my brothers, I've soiled innocence, I have led the weak to despair. I've used words like insidious poisons. Stone me, humiliate me, insult me. Men of tomorrow, when you wish to reestablish justice, a justice which can't explain anything, but which we're all waiting for, butcher the intellectuals. Start with me. I offer myself. I'm not a poet . . . not a poet!

At this juncture, somatically sensing that the living God is now being executed, he reels, jeers at the supposedly scoffing dummies, and rushes offstage, saying, "Pardon them . . . they know not what they do."

The portrait of the poet, who comes back under different names throughout Ghelderode's oeuvre (as Pantagleize, as Jean-Jacques in *Sortie de l'acteur*, as Saint-George in *Le club des menteurs*), is evidently a self-portrait, or one of the artist in modern society. This pathetic figure, utterly contemptuous of his fellow humans, feeling himself fatally disconnected from them, either elevated to some lofty place high above them or dashed to a basement of abjection and humility, is sometimes possessed of what he feels to be the key to the universe. But through haughtiness, self-doubt, or merely from losing his train of thought, he abjures revealing this elusive truth. He compares himself to Christ under persecution. But alternately, he feels all others to be the true Christ, forced to suffer his persecuting cruelty. He never knows definitively if he is God or a Roman centurion. And if he had a secret, where has it fled?

This frustrated outcry, set in relief against the modern city, feverishly oscillating, is akin to certain canvases of the German expressionist painter, Ernst Kirchner. The Poet's companions have reality only insofar as he endows them with it; the universe is that fraught with incertitude. This purely subjective play depicts the artist projecting unsympathetic dummy-masks on those he meets. Ghelderode was rapt with admiration at the brightly colored masks in the canvases of James Ensor, a native of Ostend. He included dummies and masks in numerous plays, notably the pantomime

Masques ostendais (Ostend Masks, 1934), *Pantagleize, Le ménage de Caroline* (Caroline's Household, 1930), and *Le farce de ténébreux*. Ghelderode also had recourse to the fairground setting in several other works, including *Un soir de pitié* (*A Night of Pity*, 1929) and *Don Juan*. The fevered atmosphere of carnival is a medium for disguise and hallucination; in Ghelderode it usually turns out to be an attempt at escape from reality that only leads the protagonist smack up against it and himself. It is in *Blockheads*, this diminutive hallucination of a play, that one can see most clearly what the dummies meant to Ghelderode: untouchable humanity, now to be pitied, now scorned, but at all times beyond communication. *Blockheads* most eloquently elucidates the artist's isolation.

Ghelderode's *Don Juan* is set during carnival time. We begin in front of the Babylon Bar in the heart of a modern city, where a barker is holding forth. Don Juan (described as a gentleman of the eighteenth century, "with curly hair, thin, short, pallid, nervous," in short, the antithesis of the classic conception of Don Juan) enters. The Barker, in coaxing Don Juan to enter the bar, says "Never show your face . . . masked you are real," thus establishing one of the principal leitmotivs of the play. Three heavy fifty-year-old damsels with "prodigious thighs" preside over the establishment and attempt to seduce Don Juan. He timidly and embarrassedly demurs before their advances and begins to back out the door, but Beni-Bouftout, a stylish black man, knocks Don Juan down as he cakewalks his way into the bar. Beni-Bouftout is followed by the blind Baron Theodore, the mute Hanski, and the deaf Pamphile. Don Juan explains that he has stumbled here from a fancy-dress ball of another day and age. The Barker once more urges Don Juan to "pursue his legend . . . which begins with each hour; with each moment," and introduces Olympia, a waxen-skinned, blond Mona Lisa, perched on an altar—perhaps a real woman, perhaps one in effigy. Don Juan declares that Olympia is "HER . . . Beauty herself," she of whom he is in pursuit. Don Juan swears that he will have Olympia, all the while confusedly edging toward the door. He calls for champagne, saying that "Madame will pay." He verbally woos Olympia, who finally comes to life, losing a bit of her mannequin-like appearance, and vanishes behind a curtain. Don Juan, shaken, exclaims, "Horror! She was alive!"

Acknowledging that he cannot turn back now, since he has already tossed his hat in the ring, he follows her out. Beni-Bouftout goes out of his mind and upsets the establishment, overturning tables, roaring, and laying low each man in succession. On calming down, the assemblage sets to playing dice. Don Juan reenters, setting his clothes to rights, edging toward the exit. When no one notices him, he rejoins them, whereupon Beni-Bouftout suddenly grabs him and threatens him with a knife to the throat. Don Juan is released as, bubbling with joy at his escapade, he says, "I've just lived the most beautiful moment of my existence. . . . Drink to my glory, my legend." In the midst of his speech the Little Green Man darts across the room and out, concealing his face behind a handkerchief. Meanwhile the men have dispersed to make love with the prostitutes as Don Juan speechifies. Olympia then appears at different points in the shadows of the bar, luring Don Juan. He skittishly resists her advances, wondering if she is actually alive, and follows her off once more. Off-stage, sounds of a seduction follow in which Don Juan is heard fiercely resisting Olympia. The struggle ends with her triumphant "At last!" The supposedly blind Theodore climbs onto the bar, peeks through the curtain, and exclaims, "Look . . . look what they're doing! I see . . . oh! What they're doing!" as the curtain falls.

At the rise of Act 2, Don Juan awakens in the bar, depressed and sullen from the previous night's adventure. With tragic flourish he stabs himself with his foil, but his suicide attempt proves abortive as the weapon bends. He is about to leave the bar and the ill fortune it brings when the door swings open, knocking him down. It is Beni-Bouftout in a shepherd's costume, claiming to be the African Don Juan, exulting in "all European Don Juans' " discomfiture. It is his turn to make love to Olympia, and Don Juan gladly concedes: "You can have her." Theodore enters as a medieval knight to vie for Olympia's honor, and the set of Don Juans is complete when Pamphile and Hanski show up dressed as musketeers. "Enough of Don Juans! I've had enough of them!" cries Don Juan. Olympia appears, and the various Don Juans rush after her into the back room. Don Juan follows "to defend her honor," but is soon expelled by the other prostitutes. The various Don Juans then sheepishly emerge from the back room. "You've just discovered Beauty, it's more than enough, I do believe," gloats Don Juan. The would-be Don Juans burst into tears. "You all are truly the sons of miserable Adam!" Don Juan lectures them. They exit hangdoggedly, leaving Don Juan dejectedly alone. The Little Green Man, however, has surreptitiously entered, puts a record on, and beats time as Don Juan dances, solitary.

Act 3 opens with Don Juan having slain Olympia: "I played with you and you broke. I played too well." Three prostitutes arrive and laugh. Don Juan encourages their merriment until he realizes that their emotion is caused by a rip in his trousers; he sets to sewing up the hole as they leave. At this moment Olympia's voice is heard calling out to him, and he, overcome with horror, runs himself through with his foil. Lying on the floor, realizing that the suicide was totally ineffectual, Don Juan plays dead when Hanski (no longer dumb), Pamphile (no longer deaf), Theodore (no longer blind), and Beni-Bouftout (no longer black) enter, eulogize the "dead" Don Juan, and exit. Don Juan rises and, feeling himself reborn as his onerous Don Juan disguise is left behind him on the floor, is yet again about to exit when a second Olympia looms up before him, veiled. Who is the real Olympia? Both, says she. But the other one on the floor, whose murderer he thought he was, turns out to be a mannequin;

he had killed her effigy. For the first time, Don Juan feels himself to be truly moved with love from the depths of his being. He embraces the live Olympia warmly. She cries out and crumples to the floor in a heap. Then, the following action ensues:

> With decision he bends over and picks the woman up by her arms, lifting and placing her on a chair. Inert, Olympia drops against a table and remains still and stiff like a mummy. Dead, she seems as little human as the dismantled mannequin lying close by. The veils have come undone, uncovering her face: a furrowed, patched, cadaverous mask whose livid pigment is covered with purple spots. Her mouth is a black hole. Her eyes, in a deep socket, remain glassy and tearing. And the disjointed throat is the neck of an old plucked bird. What Don Juan is stupefiedly contemplating in the pitiless lighting is a seventy year old whom death has brought to a sudden end, and on whom death has placed its own mask. Don Juan tries to cover the mask over again with the veils when, horrors of horrors, Olympia's flamboyant hairdo rolls onto the floor. And, wig fallen off, he sees that the woman has a bald scalp.
>
> (act 3)

With much elevated apostrophe, Don Juan takes his leave of a love that was not meant to be. But his exit is yet again intercepted, this time by the Little Green Man, who challenges him to a duel in vengeance of the dead Olympia. The Little Green Man interrupts the vindication by pointing out that he too is Don Juan— an ancient one who is about to die from having had contact with Beauty. And Beauty will cause Don Juan's fall as well, he asserts; Don Juan will resemble him in the future. At this point Don Juan requests that his adversary remove the handkerchief dissembling the face that has not been visible up till now: "[He tears off the handkerchief which hides his face: A gray, spongy surface punctured by bleary eyes, no nose and a mouth which has turned into a bloody wound.]" "Is this a mask?" exclaims Don Juan. "It's my face!" shrieks The Little Green Man, whereupon Don Juan finally succeeds in fleeing from the ill-fated bar. Once

outside, however, the Little Green Man still clings to his small frantic retreating person, as Olympia, puppetlike, is seen applauding the struggle through the window of the bar. "The carnival is over," proclaims the Barker, as the curtain falls.

Don Juan turns the famous legend topsy turvy, this incarnation of it being more about man's terror before the sexual act and the oppression it exercises over him than about the hero's legendary prowess and unquenchable lust for an unending string of idealized women. The characters are ultimately revealed to be their own opposites, thus by nature ill-suited to the role they are playing. Just like Ghelderode's Doctor Faust in *The Death of Doctor Faust*, who confesses, "In truth, I am not in my proper place nor costume nor time!" his eighteenth-century Don Juan wanders into a modern harbor-dive with a fainthearted wish to fulfill his namesake's destiny. And like the later Pantagleize (or Ghelderode's Faust or his Christopher Columbus), who is thrust into a heroic destiny to which he is ill-suited (but the crest of which he must ride even to self-annihilation), this Don Juan timorously tiptoes in quest of love. But his want of virility comes in for enormous abuse from females who dare him on to conquests even as they deride his capacity to be effectual, as well as from the other males who boast of their own prodigious masculinity. The fact that this latter quality is ultimately debunked in all the male characters makes Don Juan's enforced role none the easier to play.

He fears the sexual act out of ill-defined anxieties that he will fail at it, from anticipation that he will be destroyed by it, or that, worst of all, he will destroy the ideal female "Beauty" by mere contact with her. In fact, it is his impetuous embrace at the play's denouement that transforms his Venus into a pox-ridden corpse. Female "Beauty" beckons with enigmatic but sinister allure. The character of Olympia is unreal, inhuman, and just beyond man's grasp. She evidently harbors the power to destroy the man bold enough to accept her invitation. Olympia, the embodiment of female estrangement from man (written, it goes without saying, from a male point of view), an ice-cold, castrating goddess, leaves her victims devastated and regretful; Don Juan is no match for her. However, in the hallucinatory ambience of carnival, where all unconscious urges and terrors have free reign, the Don Juan/man is laid low by venereal contact with a "Beauty" who harbored, in hindsight, all the ugliness contained in the world and infected him with it. She is a veritable Pandora's Box, and his initial hesitation before the prospect of a union with "Her" turns out to have been eminently justified as Don Juan's nightmare is realized.

The male characters are fashioned transformationally; each is equipped with a handicap that he finally abandons, as they throw off their masks once carnival is ended. Ultimately the characters have no substance, but are stuffed figures making a pretense at a chimerical virility. These male characters, all of whom emulate the Don Juans of their imagination, go through various classical charades of heroism: vying for the woman's affections, rescuing her from the grip of the enemy, laying waste the bar to give concrete emphasis to the violent potency of their manhood. But each in turn is disarmed when up against the carnal act with the woman.

Nor are these males exceptional in the Ghelderode canon. The real exception is Don Juan de Bel-Hombre in *Le siège d'Ostende,* who single-handedly takes on an entire convent of rampant nuns, an act whose grandiosity represents the wishful flip side of the man's fear of impotence. Far more common to Ghelderode are such characters as Fernand Abcaude in *La farce des ténébreux,* who as a forty-year-old virgin submits to an unsuccessful fornication cure; or the frustrated Jurreal of *Hop Signor!,* who would parade his beautiful wife before the village, but dreads to consummate his marriage with her; or Hieronymus of *Red Magic,* who keeps his wife in a state of nutritional and sexual near-starvation, preferring the company of his accumulated gold.

In the cases where Ghelderode's male characters are not afflicted with impotence, his customary vision of male-female relations is one of grotesque distancing. In *Vénus* (*Venus,* 1926), the hero, De Romeo, is prevented from making love to Venus on account of his sworn vow never to remove his diver's outfit; and Isabelle in *Le siège d'Ostende* bids the women of Flanders follow her example and eschew the sexual act by refusing to doff her eventually infested nightgown. Rare is the contact between man and woman. And when they do unite, as in *Sortie de l'acteur,* their motions are reminiscent of wrestlers locked in combat. And Armande and Jean-Jacques's guilt following that tendentious embrace curdles the experience. Love is far too tinged with danger, guilt, and contempt to be risked for very long.

The action of *Don Juan* consists literally of the title character's failed attempts to leave the bar/brothel, the scene of his obligatory romantic triumph. Farcical accidents restrain him there. He is made to play out his unwilling part to the last, when it is apparent that fate has afflicted him with syphilis, a bathetic finale indeed to a role that ought to have ended in glory.

The title character of *Pantagleize* lives in impoverished gentility in a garret, attended by a manservant, Bamboola. Ignorant of the world of fashion, he nonetheless writes articles on the subject under the pen name Ernestine. His life is both nonconformist and nourished on whimsy. "My girlfriend is a monkey at the zoo. She is called Cleopatra and has fleas, and eats half of my food every midday." Pantagleize is awakened by Bamboola one ordinary morning when Bamboola has premonitions of some unnamed apocalyptic change. Pantagleize realizes it is his fortieth birthday and wonders when his "destiny will begin, if ever. . . . I understand less and less. I have neither vanity, nor pride, nor self-respect." When Pantagleize fortuitously observes that it is a lovely day, Bamboola becomes inexplicably frantic with joy and rushes offstage, leaving Pantagleize, dumbfounded, to follow after.

The sullen bartender Innocenti and the flighty poet Blank are meanwhile starting the day in a café, tremulous with anticipation. It is the appointed date for some great event, and they await the signal that shall set it in motion. They are joined by another conspirator, Banger, and Creep, a secret-service agent who takes surreptitious notes of all the clownish, vaudeville antics that cloak revolutionary activity. Pantagleize wanders unwittingly (and coincidentally) into the bar and, equally coincidentally, says "What a lovely day." The four cabalists take this as a signal for the revolution, which is what they were in fact hatching, and the wheels start turning as each hastens to his post. "Slaves arise," proclaims Innocenti. Pantagleize, left alone in the bar, trots off to see the eclipse that is about to take place. Creep is about to radio in all his information when, as a coda to the scene, Rachel Silberschatz storms in, knocks Creep out with a barstool, and takes off.

The scene switches to a high promenade, where Pantagleize has come to witness the eclipse through a telescope. Everywhere he goes, uttering the phrase, "What a lovely day," he sends people into a frenzy that propels them to the barricades. He is, however, oblivious to the effect he is having. Two figures dressed up as medieval astronomers take their places by him on the promenade—Bamboola and Creep. As the eclipse moves in and the seething crowd beneath him snarls, Pantagleize speaks to them—and finds, to his surprise, that they respond to him.

The eclipse? To hell with it, citizens! It's all a sham. And if the sky *is* black, it's only a magic-lantern effect. Gentlemen of the proletariat, I am not a cheapjack. I won't sell you rabbit droppings. But, loving my brother, passionately, I gaze on you and admire you, grains of sand, fleas, midgets. What are you afraid of? I tell you truly, this darkness is a trick. It's a theatrical effect. The Antichrist has been dispensed with. The sun is sound at heart. It's not going to happen this time. No more can the people perish. I have written so in those pamphlets you are so fond of. And

so, comrades, let the bands play. Sing! March! . . . After all, this is your day. Beat down the lies! Boil the journalists! Enjoy yourselves. It isn't midnight yet. It's . . . never mind what time it is. It's the hour of the good man. And I declare to you what I shall not cease to declare: Long live the sun! Shame on the eclipse! It's the loveliest day there could be! In all truth, what a lovely day!

(act 1, scene 3)

As the final phrase sounds, a shot rings out, and the revolution is on. Bamboola throws Creep over the side of the promenade. Rachel Silberschatz pops up, plants a kiss on Pantagleize's mouth ("You are superman. You are great. You are wonderful!"), and drags him off.

The next scene of this cinematically structured work finds Pantagleize and Rachel alone in her room, with the revolution in full swing in the distance. They exchange passionate vows, although the apolitical Pantagleize remains oblivious to the significance of his part in the turn of events:

Rachel: . . . I love you.
Pantagleize: Really?
Rachel: Yes. And do you love me?
Pantagleize: I . . .
Rachel: Yes, you love me. We all love each other, for we are entering an epoch of love.
Pantagleize: Shall we go to bed then?
Rachel: The love of man for man, the great brotherhood of humanity. [Distant explosion.] And this love will be born of blood and ruin.

(act 2, scene 4)

This tryst is interrupted by phone calls reporting the progress of the revolution and the flight of the government. Rachel, believing Pantagleize is only continuing his naive act as an "imbecile," sends him off with a gun to sieze the national treasure. After he leaves, the gruff voice of Creep calls out her name. She turns out the lights, and a brief struggle ensues in the dark.

At the National Treasury, the incompetent, senile General MacBoom is standing watch over the national treasure, absolutely at a loss for how to face this present state of disorder. By telling each of ten sentries in succession and General MacBoom to "Go to the devil," Pantagleize gains admittance to the bank vault; having accidentally hit on the correct password, he is thus taken for some high functionary. MacBoom, greatly relieved, surrenders the national treasure to him, and Pantagleize's exit is accompanied by a series of receding exclamations to "Go to the devil." The scene ends as a telephone call apprises MacBoom of his error.

Back at the Objective Bar, the Revolutionary Committee, consisting of Innocenti, Bamboola, Banger, and Blank, is handing out ministries to each other and enjoying champagne. Pantagleize stumbles into the bar to deliver the imperial treasury. Innocenti denounces the revolution as a sham and declares it the result of a misunderstanding. But the festivities proceed undampened, although it is reported that the revolution outside has degenerated into shop-looting and the one inside into a bourgeois divvying up of the spoils. As Pantagleize speechifies, the Revolutionary Ministers are surreptitiously clobbered by secret agents in waiters' disguise and carted off. When Pantagleize discovers that his auditors have vanished and the palm tree is inhabited by Creep, he flees, taking care first to overturn the "Palm-Creep." Whistles pursue him.

Pantagleize arrives once more at Rachel's room with the crown jewels, inebriated as can be, looking forward to his reward, a night of love. He drunkenly muses over his suddenly remarkable destiny, which began with a birthday, an eclipse, and a chance phrase. But he gradually becomes aware that there is something amiss:

> I'll place the butterfly of my kiss on the flower of her brow. Like this. [He goes to her and kisses her, then draws back at once, wiping his mouth.] Bah! What a sensation! Rachel! [He wanders around.] No, no, I don't want to get panicky. Rachel, it's not nice. [He lifts his feet.] My feet are sticking to the floor. I'm walking on flypaper. [He sniffs.] Bah! There's a smell . . . a smell like a butcher's shop! What's smelling like that? What

is there in this room? I'm not afraid; but I like clear situations. [He goes to Rachel and takes hold of her.] Get up, come along, are you ill? [He lets her fall back.] My betrothed! She's had an accident. She has. [He catches sight of a paper on the table.] A note with blood on it? It's for me. [Terrified, he reads it.] "They've murdered me . . . the re . . . vo . . . lu . . . tion . . . is . . . " [He lets the note drop.] Oh! I beg your pardon. [He draws back, embarrassed, looking at his feet.] Like that, is it? Murdered? [He draws farther back.] Excuse me, Rachel. My deepest sympathy.

(act 2, scene 7)

And he flees.

Pantagleize, still fleeing, comes across a corpse on the street and lies down beside it, playing dead, as General MacBoom's mop-up squad parades through triumphantly, for the revolution has entirely dissipated. Once the squad has passed, the corpse comes to life and turns out to be the ubiquitous Creep. Introductions over, Creep gives Pantagleize a karate chop and drags the now compliant Pantagleize offstage.

> *Pantagleize*: Look at all the stars! No, the world has turned upside down. It's my diamonds that have rolled into the sky.

(act 3, scene 8)

The War Council has convened to prosecute the revolutionaries. One by one, Banger, Innocenti, Blank, and Bamboola are dragged before the tribune, found guilty, and passed out to the firing squad. The last to be tried is Pantagleize, whom the Generalissimo first takes to be a clown, asking for his dismissal. However, Creep informs the court of all of Pantagleize's wrongdoings that day. The tribune, a bunch of mannequins, finds him guilty, and the Generalissimo concludes, "Pantagleize, we think that society wouldn't lose much if it lost you." Pantagleize, ignorant of what is awaiting him, stumbles out to the firing range and there dies avowing his love for his flawed revolutionary comrades with the phrase, "What a lovely day," on his lips.

The title character of *Pantagleize* is avowedly based on Charlie Chaplin, and, like the comic, stumbles inadvertently from disaster to disaster, remaining unflappably charming throughout. This particular incarnation of the diminutive clown is the audience's guide through the societal jungle. Ghelderode, as antipolitical as his antihero, paints both institutional leaders like Creep, MacBoom, and the Generalissimo and revolutionaries like Blank, Rachel, and Bamboola in equally uncomplimentary colors.

By the time he wrote *Pantagleize*, Ghelderode had lived to see the World War I, the Russian Revolution, and the abortive German revolution. The play, indirectly drawing on these historical episodes, expresses a fatalistic view, contemptuous of the way society is arranged and pessimistic at the potential of man, as currently constituted, for making it any better. The play's action, which spans the course of a single day, is of one individual's voyage through various stations (as in German expressionist drama) or Dantesque circles of human inanity.

Ghelderode wrote another, shorter work, *La transfiguration dans le cirque* (Transfiguration in the Circus, 1927), in which six clowns in an actual circus ring mount a clown revolution against the Ringmaster. That play is replete with many classical circus *burli* and pranks. The clowns finally prove to be incompetent as revolutionaries, who get distracted from their political goal when they compete for the affections of Luna, the bareback rider. The Ringmaster, taking advantage of this Achilles heel, dynamites them all to kingdom come and celebrates the victory of the ruling class in Luna's arms.

La transfiguration dans le cirque is a microcosmic, homogeneous version of *Pantagleize*. Both plays treat of revolutionaries' incompetence through farce-business and slapstick. Rachel Silberschatz becomes Pantagleize's raison d'être, and he joins the revolutionary fold to impress her and clinch her incipient love for him, just as the clowns moon over Luna. In both cases, revolutionary zeal to unseat an unjust rule is quickly replaced by an amorous ideal. And in both works the revolutionaries' own lust for power almost immediately following the coup transforms them into the very robber barons they have overthrown.

Once again, as in *Blockheads* and *Don Juan*, Ghelderode animates a hero cast in a role for which he is entirely ill suited and so posits his extremely personal version of the modern antihero. The play, innovative in its ironic tone and panoramic structure and sudden, unexpected reversals on the endings of scenes, yet bears a trace of Ghelderodian medievalism. Even in this modernly set work, he cannot resist introducing a hint of antique alchemy in the person of the astronomers and the eclipse episode, poetically likened to the revolution. The former, like the latter, darkens the lives of its beholders for a time, inspires in them a plethora of hysterical, confused, and superstitious reactions, and finally leaves the sky clear again, as though it had never happened.

THE SOCIETAL FRESCO

Le siège d'Ostende takes place during the Spanish occupation of the Low Countries (present-day Belgium) and is based on the historical siege of 1601–1604. King Albert and Queen Isabella are in the Hall of Nobles on the "Montus Frigidus" in Brussels. The people of Ostend, it seems, are the last holdouts against Spanish domination; Isabella weighs the option of kicking them into the sea. "God wishes it, sir, since I wish it." Albert, seeing his devout wife flutter with nausea, asks if he should fetch the big bucket, for, he confides, "she has drunk too much wine at mass." They plot to raise funds to mount a siege on Ostend, subdue the renegades, and found twelve new churches, including an "Our Lady of Fine Odor." General Spinola enters with monks who belch all the while. Spinola, addressing Isabella as "your High Infanticide," urges them to order the peasants to pull up all their carrots and send them to court, where they will be sliced, their rounds serving as currency to underwrite the siege. Broer (Flemish for "brother") Kletsaf delivers a speech laced with belches and capped with a fart, asking for three new churches to be built. Isabella orders it be proclaimed throughout the land that she will not change her "chemyse" until the people of Ostend are reduced to "potatos fritos."

We next move to the workshop of Sir Jaime (modeled after the modern Belgian artist James Ensor, an acquaintance of Ghelderode's) at Ostend. He rallies the miniature devils he keeps in his cupboard against the Spaniards. He exhorts them to: "Lacerate, eviscerate, empty out viscera, pitch stinking bubbles . . . mussel scales, fish intestines. . . . " The battle cry goes up from the tiny devils.

Archduke Albert is visiting General Spinola at the front. He is searching for the royal chamber pot. When Spinola hands him his helmet, Albert makes use of that, for want of the pot. When Spinola objects, saying "Sire, that doesn't smell good!" Albert retorts that he should burn sugar. Discussing strategy, Albert counsels the general to sit out the siege quietly, that the last to flee will be the victor. But Spinola laments that conflict with the people of Ostend is not easy; they pitch salted herrings at his troops, on which the Spaniards slip and fall. The females of Ostend mount the ramparts and raise up their skirts to reveal "enormous grassy buttocks" before the eyes of the chaste Spanish. Albert advises Spinola not to take the city of Ostend at all, in order to get back at Isabella, who is depriving him of conjugal pleasures, true to her vow. He borrows some money from Spinola.

Back in Brussels, Isabella demands an explanation of General Lamoral for her army's failure to penetrate Ostend. She makes plaint that, since taking her vow, her body has become infested with tiny Belgian insects, and that despite Father Trullemans's prayers, they torment her, for they understand no Latin. Lamoral lifts her skirts and applies flea powder blessed and guaranteed by the pope. Trullemans enters and reports that the lamentable populace is in dire straits—the women exude horrible odors and the men are stiff to bursting. The priest implores Isabella to open the bordellos to alleviate the problem; Father Trullemans councils the hard-put Belgians that they ought to fornicate wearing their chemises, that besides, no prostitutes exist in Belgium, and that they'd better do their conjugal duties or find themselves cuckolded. Isabella agrees, " . . . but may I add: you shall be cuckolds and that will advance the siege of Ostend not a wit." Either they must suffer the "guilty pleasure" themselves or "belt up your females with steel of Toledo and take care not to lose the key" or "do it like the Spaniards, through a hole in a board. Go and torment me no more with these abominations." They do so, as Lamoral continues delousing Isabella with a bellows.

On the front, the Polish engineer Klabotsky visits General Don Pacheco in his field tent to suggest a scheme to him for taking the city of Ostend: not a Trojan horse, but an Ostendian fish, a boat in the form of a serpent. Pacheco, not actually wishing to win the siege at all, rewards Klabotsky with a kick that sends him flying out of the tent.

Don Juan de Bel-Hombre, of Isabella's party, is before a bordello awaiting the appearance of the Brussels prostitute Conchita. He complains that at the coastal bordellos "the whores . . . ask you for your confession receipt before authorizing you to dip your stick and sing the aspergillum." He and Conchita imagine the exotic pleasures that are to be theirs, but, following the example of "our gracious Infanta," she refuses to take off her clothes, which for him is a necessity. He slaps her, blackmails her, and takes off, at which point she relents, but it is too late. She drowns her sorrows by devouring the blood sausage that he had ordered, which "symbolizes all the lost thrills."

Generals Spinola, Mirabolar, and their troops are planting a sapling to commemorate the first anniversary of the siege of Ostend. Spinola warns them that whoever urinates against the tree will be summarily executed. Almost immediately following the dedication, Miralobar feels a urinary urgency. There is no wall for the purpose, and even though Spinola offers his own legs, Miralobar elects to urinate on the sapling, which is immediately destroyed by a bomb, whereupon Miralobar exclaims, "What I was just holding in my hand I can't find anymore!" They go off for a beer.

The next scene is set at the Convent of Saint Michael. The beguines are praying for the arrival of the marauding Spaniards and their own deflowering. Don Juan arrives at the head of his men. He counts up the beguines and Mother Superior, who counts for two, and announces he will tutor them in the use of "the shepherd's crook. . . . I am Don Juan!" At this they scream "Christmas, Christmas," each trying to get him all for herself. Offstage, the beguines are heard to remark on his prodigiousness. "We'll cut it off, impale it, and put it in the reliquary." Don Horace, witnessing the proceedings in the other room, narrates the details of "the carnage." Don Juan quickly emerges and turns his conquests over to Don Horace. The beguines insist he engage each of them seven times, "according to the tradition." When he demurs, they threaten to tie him up and hold him there till his duty is done. The subsequent entry of his men saves him from sole responsibility, and the entire retinue retires to the chapel to besport themselves.

Three Spanish doctors come on stage, each carrying a chamber pot whose contents they are attempting to analyze. They diagnose poisoned herring that the people of Ostend had pitched at the Spanish army, who dropped like flies upon ingesting the questionable fish. The doctors grab a passing soldier and proceed to do an autopsy on him. When he protests that he's not only alive but in perfect health, they set him straight: "What do you know about it? Are you the doctors or are we?" The autopsy completed and the corpse pronounced in perfect health, the doctors sit on the chamber pots and "bombard with divers sonorities." Unable to agree on a standard cure for the epidemic afflicting the Spanish army,

they prescribe pills, ointments, and injections, all together; in case of death, the last sacraments are recommended. The doctors then drink themselves into a stupor.

Meanwhile, in the tents of the Spanish troops, all are holding umbrellas as Belgian rain sweeps through the shelter. Spinola sends for the Astrologer, who had been commissioned to stop the rain. Apparently the sun is shining throughout the world, except over Ostend. The Astrologer saw Sir Jaime shaking his magic umbrella at a cloud, while the masked devils sang off key, so that the cloud took the form of a frog and split open, drenching the Spaniards. Spinola orders the useless Astrologer hung. A festival proceeds during the course of which various offenders against military law are brought in, tried, and hauled off to be hung. The last of these, a Flemish dancer, is brought in. She tells them that her mother sold mussels on rue de la Samaritaine, but that her father was Spanish. Spinola, suspicious, orders the men out of his tent. Alone with the dancer, he asks to see her identity card, whereupon she hoists her skirts up and he, fainting away, exclaims, "Caramba! It's my daughter!"

The siege has now been going on for two years. Isabella is hearing plaints: that there aren't enough umbrellas to ward off the constant Belgian rain, that the people of Ostend are pelting the Spanish army with rats, that the Ostenders have sent forth "giant fleas" which the Spaniards "scratch desperately." Isabella advises the troops to change their diet from herrings to rats. She forbids the "unworthy troop" from scratching. There has been an outbreak of homosexual activity, including the establishment of gay households.

Isabella: Do you mean to insinuate that the soldados have become ass-screwers?
Father Trullemans: That's the word all right, Highness. To say truly, I should add that those who haven't become ass-screwers have become ass-screwed.

(scene 13)

She then orders patriotic women of the nobility to the front to bring the soldiers back to the fold. They plan for the postwar period, when they will erect casinos and seafood stands on the boardwalk at Ostend.

In Ostend, a singer is brought before Lamoral and Spinola and sings a lewd ditty about Isabella's "chemyse." They send him off to be hung after having sung along with the refrain. They then receive a telegram from Albert, who is enjoying himself in the bordellos of Brussels. It says that anyone found to be singing the ditty about Isabella (penned by Sir Jaime) should be rewarded. Thus, they take the songster soldier down from the gallows.

Albert is visiting a well-known bar in Brussels (The Farting Ass, the name of an actual bar on the first floor of Ghelderode's house for a time). The mistress of the premises asks, "How's the siege going?" to which Albert replies, "Not bad, and you?" One by one he recognizes his principal generals behind their masks, as well as Broer Kletsaf and Father Trullemans. Eventually Sir Jaime enters as well and defeats them all in a brawl. A truce is declared, and Albert treats everyone to a drink.

The assembled generals at Ostend are deciding whether or not to take the city and terminate the siege when Father Trullemans hurries along to say that Isabella has ordered the siege terminated, "not being able to bear the ordeal of her chemyse one hour longer." It seems that it is flea-mating season, and her body has become a mating ground. The Spaniards finally penetrate the city to find not a soul, "not even a herring." The enemy is floating away toward Zeeland, in the Netherlands, with thumbs at their noses. The Spaniards, having lost their opponents, promenade through the deserted city and eat herring one last time.

The siege, which lasted three years and three months, is at an end. Isabella celebrates the victory in Brussels, where as usual it is raining. Albert returns, and the populace implores them to display the famed chemyse. Isabella, on doffing her chemise with the words "I offer to you, my God, my suffering, my chemyse, and all that it contains," discovers that the object has become so hardened that it must be split open with a hammer. All hold their noses at the moment it breaks open. "Little beasties" gallop through the gathering, and all scratch themselves. Fragments of Isabella's chemise are made into sacred relics, whereas those of the noblewomen are fashioned into banners. In Zeeland, Sir Jaime is royally welcomed, along with all the equally triumphant citizens of Ostend.

Le siège d'Ostende was dedicated to the Belgian experimental painter James Ensor (1860–1949), and the exuberant character of Sir Jaime is based on Ensor, who lived his whole life in the coastal Belgian city. Ensor, known for his whimsically blasphemous observations on Belgian institutions, and more for his colorful canvases of carnival masks, devils, and human caricatures, was beloved by Ghelderode, who tried to inject the debauched tone of Ensor's paintings and drawings into his "epic" play. Certain scenes, in fact, seem to take direct inspiration from particular Ensor works. The autopsy scene is taken from the 1895 etching *The Wicked Physicians*, in which several top-hatted, nasty-looking figures brandish giant hypodermics and bellows over an impaled patient as a death figure looks on. The scenes in Sir Jaime's studio are akin to the 1888 etching *Demons Teasing Me*, and the war scenes are like the 1895 etching of a battle set in an Ostend-plain landscape, *Battle of the Golden Spurs*, or like *Fight of the Demons* (1888), in which tiny diabolical creatures thrash a battalion of angels.

This is not the only play of Ghelderode's in which Ensor's influence may be felt. His pantomime *Masques ostendais* is very much like several Ensor paintings, notably *The Singular Masks* (1892), *Angry Masks* (1883), and *The Drunkards* (1883). The description of Olympia-turned-corpse at the end of *Don Juan* bears unmistakable resemblance to the decked out skeletons in Ensor's *Masks Fighting for the*

Body of a Hanged Man (1891), although the influence of another Belgian artist, Felicien Rops, can also be felt here.

Le siège d'Ostende was unpublished in Ghelderode's lifetime and only had its first performance in 1988 in Brussels, despite the fact that it is a major work and one that history may recognize as his greatest contribution. Ghelderode was initially quite proud of the play's audacity, but his early affection for it was rapidly undermined by certain friends' prudish disdain on reading a draft of it. Further, he counted on an enthusiastic response from Ensor, but the latter never wrote one word of reaction, and Ghelderode lost faith in the work; it thus languished in his drawer till long after his death.

The play is a vicious satire against the church, sexual hypocrisy, doctors, and the military. It also takes jabs at Belgium. *Le siège d'Ostende*'s historicity is that of an Aristophanes, who sends up contemporary subjects by masking them with faces and incidents of the past. And serious subjects like war, as in *Lysistrata*, whose action it resembles in part, are robbed of menace by the author's recourse to the improbable and lewd. Aside from war itself, Belgium's bilingual stew, its lethargy, and its incessant rain are all satirical butts in *Le siège d'Ostende*.

While Ghelderode pulls out all the stops in the savagery of his venomous portraiture, yet he retains a lighthearted tone from start to finish. And in contradistinction to such works as *D'un diable qui prêcha merveilles* and *Hop Signor!*, the comedy does not grow tiresome. Each of the loosely strung vignettes packs its own wallops of hilarity, and Ghelderode does not labor his comic touch. The playwright, who all too often strains a comic moment by distending it in endless speeches long past the point of engrossment, here spews forth a seemingly endless string of inventive situations, each as unexpected and mirthful as the one before.

Like Aristophanes or the Jarry of *Ubu roi*, the humor is preadolescent—running to the fecal, flatulent, and urinary. The principal, extremely concrete symbol of the siege's absurdity, Isabella's "chemyse," her example of stoic self-denial, grows more putrid and laden with excrement and insects as the play progresses. It is the folly of laying siege to subdue a people made ever more palpable. Nationalistic valor is evidenced in the rotten salted herrings with which the Ostenders pelt the Spaniards, the sour farts with which they infect them, and the giant fleas and rats they send forth; all are calculated to cripple once and for all the heroic mystification of warlike courage.

The characters are portrayed as the obverse of their historical reputations. Albert, prince of the stern Inquisition, is a whoremonger; Isabella, stuffy and puritanical, here depicted coming up with the most lascivious of pragmatic solutions to her military conundra. And all the priests, as usual, are gassy, boozing lechers. Even the "epic" structure is in itself a send-up of a patriotic cavalcade. The incidents, while improbable, are no less absurd than the nationalistic impulse or war itself.

Le siège d'Ostende is the most successful of Ghelderode's several attempts to portray societal corruption on a global scale. In *D'un diable qui prêcha merveilles* he brings an entire debased community on stage. Responding to the arrival of a celebrated preacher from Rome, each of the Flemish city's inhabitants marches dutifully and fatefully off to church, prepared to be denounced by the visiting clergyman for their panoply of unspeakable sins. They pass before the audience in an endless procession, each confessing to his transgression and quaking at the coming retribution. The mathematical regularity of their appearances becomes numbing, but is redeemed by the virtuosic sermon preached by the Devil, who finds a way to substitute for the Roman prelate in the pulpit. The already bitter play turns more acid yet at the end when the authentic evangelizing preacher bumps into the devil who had replaced him; the two get along fine and go off to

Rome arm in arm. *Le balade du Grand Macabre* portrays a society ripe for apocalypse; its action consists of the characters making ready for that catastrophe—one that ultimately never happens. And in every case in which Ghelderode employs some choric grouping—the three old ladies in *Miss Jairus*, the two leering dwarves in *Hop Signor!*, the aged and infirm in *Le cavalier bizarre* or *Les vieillards* (*The Old Men*, 1923), the townspeople in *Piet Bouteille*, (1925), or the twelve harridans in *The Women at the Tomb*—they are there to hammer home the ugliness of collective humanity and the corruption of its institutions.

MODERNITY

Ghelderode has most often been characterized as a man discontent with modern times who wishes to revive, flesh out, and inhabit ancient epochs. One may either interpret his propensity for setting plays in the Middle Ages as a distaste for the present or as a ruse by which to lambast the present by dressing it up in ancient forms and colors. In any case, the number of plays Ghelderode set in the medieval Flemish past are legion: *Chronicles of Hell, Miss Jairus, Hop Signor!, La balade du Grand Macabre, Le soleil se couche, The Magpie on the Gallows, Escurial,* and *Red Magic* among them. And he has written a number of plays wherein the past intrudes on the twentieth century or in which the present interpenetrates the past, such as *Pantagleize, Don Juan, Christopher Columbus,* and *The Death of Doctor Faust,* in which the stage is split in two simultaneous action spaces, for past and present respectively. And along with the historification technique comes a folkloric tone and the creation of a fablelike exoticism native to Flanders, which may have more grounding in artistic conception than in objective historical fact.

However, it must not be forgotten that Ghelderode had extensive exposure to the modernist trends of his time. First of all there was the quietist symbolism, the nightmarish absolutism of the German expressionists, and the apocalyptic farce of Jarry. Ghelderode's friend and sponsor, theater historian Camille Poupeye, introduced him to these figures, by report if not always by firsthand perusal. Apollinaire and Cocteau, with their typographical revolution, were all the rage, and Ghelderode often sang their praises in *La Flandre littéraire*, the journal of which he was co-editor. The Belgian dadaist poet Clément Pansaers was a friend of his during the late 1910's and early 1920's, as was Dada-modernist Paul Neuhuys. Both were tavern companions and published his early works in their respective journals, *Résurrection* and *Ça Ira.*

Three obscure short works witness Ghelderode's attraction to Dada and Apollinairian modernism (as do passages from longer works—Blank's speeches in *Pantagleize*, for instance, and Father Jairus' disjointed speeches in *Miss Jairus*): *La vie publique de Pantagleize, Venus,* and *Noyade des songes* (*Dreams Drowning*, 1928). The first play is a sketch for the later, longer *Pantagleize* and presents a somewhat different portrait of the Chaplinesque antihero. Whereas in the longer play he will-lessly stumbles into entangling situations, in the shorter version he has divorced himself from society and taken up residence in a pipe on the outskirts of a city. There he fends off incursions from the outside world—a city guard, a forensic pathologist, and finally three judges, none of whom can tolerate his nonconformity and each of whom wishes to bring him back to the societal fold. These dramatic interludes are interspersed with such Dada-like pronouncements as:

> Light me up outside, but inside as well, since I've got to find a definition for pan-pan which I used to consider a dance for the youth of Athens, which comes alive at night, when it was modestly supposed to be a philosophy, a universal vision, a science auxiliary to the powerful and magnanimous pataphysical wisdom of the future (as the omens reveal to me) and of which Western man will say its [He yawns.] necessity inevitably

makes itself felt! [He yawns.] The pan-pan is. . . . The pan.

His last word to civilization is a gigantic fart ("BANG") from inside the pipe, which sends the judges fleeing and permits him to return once more to his Walden-like serenity. While the form of this play is classical, breaking down into a series of debates and not venturing into a disintegration of form as did Pansaers in his playlet *Les saltimbanques* (The Mountebanks, 1918), the hero's attitude and the play's sympathies are dadaist.

In *Venus* the heroine is an actress who wishes to reincarnate the Venus de Milo. To this end she has stripped herself naked and is trying to rid herself of her arms. To assist her in this quest, Kapman appears. He is a German butcher who takes great joy in slicing up human beings. He gladly saws off Venus' arms, an act that sends him into a state of sexual ecstasy. Other zany characters dart on and offstage on absurd missions: Count Aspirin, a White Russian cab driver, whose arms have been removed by the "Muzhiks"; De Romeo, a deep-sea diver who has sworn not to remove his diving gear; and Curtius, an archaeologist trying to prove that the Venus de Milo's arms do exist. The entire action degenerates into bloody antics, and all the characters are finally disillusioned and abandon their quests. The play drips with a dark humor and absurdity very advanced for the time in which it was written. It forecasts the carnage that was to envelope the century and captures the combination of frantic irrationality and cruelty that were to become the century's hallmarks.

Finally there is the modernist work *Dreams Drowning*. In the prologue a salvager of sunken ships dispatches a diver to bring up treasures from the deep. The play consists of endless unpunctuated sentences uttered by an octopus, narrator of a mimed underwater spectacle. The Diver is witness to this narrated ballet, which melds actual and legendary history in an ever-accelerating maelstrom. The entire scene is ultimately reabsorbed by a whirlpool as the Octopus' phrases split off, contract, and collide. On reading *Dreams Drowning*, one is impressed by Ghelderode's experimentation with typography, his sweeping away of punctuation, and use of a verbal style that is now telegraphically terse, now unraveling in ribbons of free-floating verse.

These three works, then, show a different image of Ghelderode from the one best known and promulgated by the dramatist himself. This facet of his writing was tried on early in his career but was subsumed by the personal voice he ultimately found. In each of the plays one can still detect a yearning for the past, in that the present is depicted as being so rotten. But the forms he chose by which to express this nostalgia reveal a clear attempt to join in the latest literary ventures of his day.

A WORK MARRED BY BIGOTRY

Thorough studies of Ghelderode's work have indisputably concluded what a casual reading might lead one to suspect, that his work is dotted with ugly traces of anti-Semitism and antiblack prejudice, as well as a highly uncomplimentary view of women. He is not exceptional in these respects for a man of his time and Catholic, western European origins, but it should be remarked that these instances are not isolated or casual, but deeply felt and unfortunately widespread in his works and privately held opinions, as his lesser known prose and correspondence attest.

As previously stated, Ghelderode's world is a veritable gallery of grotesque human types, but racial barbs are reserved exclusively for Jews and blacks. Simon Laquedeem, the Jewish converted bishop in *Chronicles of Hell*, Ben Samuel, the grasping loan shark in *Le club des menteurs*, Judas' wife in *The Women at the Tomb*, Rachel Silberschatz in *Pantagleize*, and Abraham Goldenox in *D'un diable qui prêcha merveilles* all bear the typical caricatures of historical anti-Semitism. They are characterized as money-sucking, heartless, and messianically inclined. While it is an unwise policy to take any single character's words for the author's own opinion, the following sentiments uttered in *The Chronicles of Hell* seem adequately to express the author's:

> *Sodomati*: I beg your pardon, Simon Laquedeem! . . . I beg your pardon for having confused you! . . . You are not of this race. . . . I was forgetting. You are indisputably descended from kings and prophets, which I would not have believed had I not read your disclaimer of your ancestors written in Hebrew on a foreskin! . . . Burn the sodomites and the heresiarchs. In addition, burn the Jews, the filthy Jews, since this diocese is overflowing with them, Simon Laquedeem—since it is not known by what operation of unwonted charity this diocese receives them, Simon Laquedeem, to the extent of resembling a huge ghetto.

As for blacks, when depicted by Ghelderode they are little better than apes—at best violent, semiarticulate, sexually overheated barbarians. And this tendency is reenforced with each black character: Beni-Bouftout in *Don Juan*, Spiridon in *Le ménage de Caroline*, and Bamboola in *Pantagleize*.

Even more prevalent than these derogatory racial stereotypes are Ghelderode's distressing portraits of women. Despite his protestations to the contrary, one has to search high and low for a flattering characterization of a female. One such is the sweet, abused Madeleine in *Piet Bouteille*. Another is the far-seeing, sympathetic Barbara in *The Old Men*. Beyond these examples, Ghelderode's women are either harridans, bitches panting in heat for sex (the prototype of which is the lustful Margaret Harstein in *Hop Signor!*), or mean gossips. The men are forever fleeing from their inexhaustible sexual appetites or their cruel scolding. And while Ghelderode is not long on flattering portraiture of any human entity, there is a far greater variety of the male of the species than the female. And some of the men, such as Pantagleize, Charles V in *Le soleil se couche*, Lamprido in *Les aveugles* (*The Blind Men*, 1933), Jef in *Piet Bouteille*, and Christopher Columbus, are sympathetically wrought. Many others are complex, impelled by despair or insecurity, and therefore our hearts can open to them despite the ferocious grimace or eccentric mania that possesses them. Ghelderode's women have no such redeeming psychological backgrounds, and his work suffers inasmuch as it presents such a circumscribed vision.

FASHIONING RHYTHMIC SEQUENCES

While Ghelderode's thought is sometimes defective or of secondary interest, he excels at manipulating dramatic and theatrical energy, handling it as though it were palpable. For example, in his play *Lord Halewyn*, originally written for the radio, the action takes off from the following premise: Halewyn, a sorcerer of the nobility, notorious for seducing virgins and murdering them, is about to go off in quest of the last remaining virgin in the kingdom, Purmelende. The body of the play consists of an ebbing and flowing, yet constantly growing, tension, which finally culminates in the lovers' meeting. Ghelderode cheats the audience out of this carefully prepared denouement and, following a sequence of suspension in uncertainty, moves instead to the tryst's aftermath, in which the unharmed princess appears bearing the head of the savage lord, having cut it off.

Prior to this anticlimax, a panoramic series of scenes flashes by in which Purmelende, caught up in the spell Halewyn has cast on her, warmly yearns for deflowerment, alternating with scenes of dialogue rhythmically intoned by choric guards on the battlements, and yet other, equally lyrical scenes of her oblivious, serenely sleeping parents, incapable of deterring her fate. Ghelderode, by postponing Halewyn and Purmelende's meeting to an almost agonizing degree, putting it off by inserting these digressive scenes, establishes a pulsating rhythm that reflects the play's content, the passage into sexual maturity.

Another example of a play founded on such gusts of energy mounting to deferred climaxes is *The School for Buffoons*. This late work is set in a training academy for court jesters on the eve of their graduation. On receiving their diplomas they will be sent off to entertain the monarchs at all the courts of Europe. But the jesters are preparing a play within a play which, they hope, will constitute a cruel revenge on Folial, their pitiless schoolmaster, for all the humiliation he has inflicted on them during their sojourn at the academy. Again reminiscent of Genet (ironically so, for the Frenchman's better-known work was written after Ghelderode's), this time of *The Blacks*, the insubstantial thread of action is overladen with symbolic rituals, dripping with rhythmic chant and stamping feet. Scenes of menace go to the brink of explosion, but retreat just before. And the ultimate scene of conclusion in which Folial anticlimactically reveals the jester's secret to be "cru-el-ty," lets the audience, which had been implicitly prepared for a murder, down with a thud. This work of surging, primal energy, like *Lord Halewyn*, is a temporal symbol of an archetypal passage, whose trappings exceed by far its semblance of a message or conventional dramatic structure. In both plays the author deliberately plants a void where the climax would ordinarily be, violating classical rhythmic patterns of the drama and forging new formal ground.

Ghelderode's mastery of formal innovation is also frequently to be found in his surprise scene endings. Often, just as the scene moves into its natural decrescence and conclusion, Ghelderode will slip in a terse coda that will upset the audience's expectations. Examples of these dramatically superfluous, but theatrically ingenious codas may be found at the end of each of *Don Juan*'s three acts, when the Little Green Man appears for but one rhythmic beat. In the first act he simply darts mysteriously across the stage; in the second he joins Don Juan in a dance of sexual frustration; in the third he reveals his face and latches onto Don Juan, never to let go. He appears only when Don Juan is alone and susceptible to this visitation from the netherworld, when concrete grappling with life's whips and scorns have ended for the day.

Similarly, in *Pantagleize*, Ghelderode reserves endings of scenes for abrupt outbursts of violence, wherein Rachel clobbers Creep, Creep rapes Rachel, or various characters trounce, overturn, or throw Creep off cliffs, who (following the illogical logic of farce) miraculously reappears unscathed in the following scene. Dramatic rhythm, then, is Ghelderode's greatest weakness, when he labors interminable monologues in fits of self-indulgence; but when he intentionally sets to extending and cutting off suspenseful sequences or sharply shifts a dramatic sequence to a new tenor, he is matchless in skill.

Selected Bibliography

EDITIONS

INDIVIDUAL WORKS

PUBLISHED PLAYS

Têtes de bois. *La Flandre littéraire* (15 November 1924).

La mystère de la Passion de Notre Seigneur Jésus-Christ (1924). Brussels, 1925.

Piet Bouteille (1918). Brussels, 1925.

La tentation de Saint Antoine (1924). *La renaissance d'Occident* (June 1925).

Les vieillards (1923). Brussels, 1925.

Le massacre des innocents (1924). *La renaissance d'Occident* (November 1926).

Le mort du Docteur Faust (1925). Ostend-Bruges, 1926.

Vénus (1926). *La Flandre littéraire* 14 (1927).

Christophe Colomb (1927). Brussels, 1928.

Don Juan, ou les amants chimériques (1926). Brussels, 1928.

Escurial (1927). *La renaissance d'Occident* (1928).

La transfiguration dans le cirque (1927). Brussels, 1928.

Un soir de pitié (1928). Liège, 1929.

Trois acteurs, un drame (1928). Brussels, 1929.

Noyade des songes (1928). *La revue mosane* (November 1930).

Duvelor; ou, La farce du diable vieux (1924). *Le rouge et le noir* (27 May 1931).

Barabbas (1928). Brussels, 1932.

Le club des menteurs (1930). *Le rouge et* le *noir* (1932).

Arc-en-ciel (1932). Verviers, 1933.

Le chagrin d'Hamlet (1932). *Le rouge et le noir* (22 March 1933).

Les femmes au tombeau (1933). Brussels, 1934.

Pantagleize (1929). *Vers le Vrai* (1934).

Adrian et Jusemina (1933). Brussels, 1935.

La balade du Grand Macabre (1934). Brussels, 1935.

Magie rouge (1931). Brussels, 1935.

Masques ostendais (1934). Antwerp, 1935.

Le ménage de Caroline (1930). Brussels, 1935.

Les aveugles (1933). Louvain and Brussels, 1936.

Le cavalier bizarre (1924). Antwerp, 1938.

Hop Signor! (1936). Brussels, 1938.

La pie sur le gibet (1937). Verviers and Brussels, 1938.

Sire Halewyn (1934). Brussels, 1943.

La farce de la mort qui faillit trépasser (1925). Brussels, 1952.

La vie publique de Pantagleize (1926). *Audace* (January 1954).

UNPUBLISHED PLAYS

La mort regarde à la fenêtre (1918).

Le repas des fauves (1918).

Le miracle dans le faubourg (1926).

Images de la vie de Saint François d'Assise (1927).

Le roi qui danse (1928).

La nuit tombe sur la Flandre (1929).

Celui qui vendait de la corde de pendu (1930).

Godelième (1930).

La petite fille aux mains de bois (1930).

La couronne de fer-blanc (1931).

Le voleur d'étoiles (1931).

Casimir de l'académie (1932).

Généalogie (1932).

Le marchand de reliques (1932).

La nuit de mai (1932).

Paradis presque perdu (1932).

Pièce anatomique (1932).

La ronde de nuit (1932).

Le vieux soudard (1935).

UNPUBLISHED RADIO PLAYS

Le cavalier bizarre (1932).

Le coeur Révélateur (1932).

Annibal, speaker futur (1933).

Bureau ouvert de neuf à midi (1933).

Plaisir d'amour (1933).

La ronde des prisonniers (1933).

Cinq mai 1835 (1934).

Payül dans le beffroi (1934).

Payül champion (1934).

Payül lauréat (1934).

Payül au paradis (1934).

Payül reporter (1934).

L'Oiseau chocolat (1937).

Comment l'empereur Charles devint voleur des chiens (1939).

D'un fou qui se croyait empereur (1939).

Scènes de la vie d'un bohème: Franz Schubert (1941).

Il Fiammingo (1942).

PROSE

La halte catholique. Brussels, 1922.

L'Histoire comique de keizer Karel telle que la perpétuèrent jusqu'à nos jours les gens de Brabant et de Flandre. Louvain, 1922.

L'Homme sous l'uniforme. Brussels, 1923.

Kwiebe-Kwiebus. Brussels, 1926.

Chronique de Noël. Bruges, 1934.

Sortilèges. Paris and Brussels, 1941.

Choses et gens de chez nous. Liège and Paris, 1943.

L'Hôtel de ruescas. Antwerp, 1943.

Mes statues. Brussels, 1943.

La Flandre est un songe. Brussels, 1953.

POETRY

La corne d'abondance. Brussels, 1925.

Ixelles, mes amours. Ostend, 1928 (under the pseudonym Philostène Costenoble).

NONFICTION

Ultimes boutades. Liège, 1965.

COLLECTED WORKS

Théâtre Complet 1. Brussels, 1942. Contains *La farce des ténébreux, Hop Signor!, Don Juan, Mademoiselle Jaïre*.

Théâtre Complet 2. Brussels, 1942. Contains *L'École des bouffons, Magie rouge, Sortie de l'acteur,*

D'un diable qui prêcha merveilles, Le soleil se couche.

Théâtre Complet 3. Brussels, 1943. Contains *La pie sur le gibet, La balade du Grand Macabre, Les aveugles, Fastes d'enfer, Le ménage de Caroline, Pantagleize.*

Théâtre. Brussels, 1943. Contains *Sire Halewyn, Escurial, Le club des menteurs, Jeudi-Saint, Masques ostendais, Christophe Colomb.*

Théâtre d'écoute. Malines, 1951. Includes *Le singulier trépas de Messire Ulenspiegel, Le perroquet de Charles Quint, La folie d'Hugo van der Goes.*

MODERN EDITIONS

INDIVIDUAL WORKS

PLAYS

Le sommeil de la raison (1930). *Marginales* 22:119–144 (1967).

Le siège d'Ostende (1934). Brussels, 1980.

La mystère de la Passion de nôtre Seigneur Jésus-Christ (1924). Brussels, 1982.

Atlantique (1930). Brussels, 1984.

PROSE

Contes et dicts hors du temps (*La halte catholique,* 1922). Brussels, 1975.

L'Homme sous l'uniforme (1923). Brussels, 1978.

Mes statues (1943). Brussels, 1978.

COLLECTED WORKS

Théâtre. Paris, 1950–1982. The contents are as follows:

Vol. 1: *Hop Signor!, Escurial, Sire Halewyn, Magie rouge, Mademoiselle Jaïre, Fastes d'enfer.*

Vol. 2: *Le cavalier bizarre, La balade du Grand Macabre, Trois acteurs, un drame, Christophe Colomb, Les femmes au tombeau, La farce des ténébreux.*

Vol. 3: *La pie sur le gibet, Pantagleize, D'un diable qui prêcha merveilles, Sortie de l'acteur, L'École des bouffons.*

Vol. 4: *Un soir de pitié, Don Juan, ou les amants chimériques, Le club des menteurs, Les vieillards, Marie la misérable, Masques ostendais.*

Vol. 5: *Le soleil se couche, Les aveugles, Barabbas, Le ménage de Caroline, La mort du Docteur Faust, Adrian et Jusemina, Piet Bouteille.*

Vol. 6: *Le sommeil de la raison, Le perroquet de Charles Quint, Le singulier trépas de Messire Ulenspiegel, La folie d'Hugo van der Goes, La grande tentation de Saint Antoine, Noyade des songes.*

INTERVIEW

Les entretiens d'Ostende. Edited by Roger Iglésis and Alain Trutat. Paris, 1956.

CORRESPONDENCE

"Dispatches from the Prince of Ostreland." *The Drama Review* 8:24–32 (Fall 1963). Letters to George Hauger.

"Lettres à Catherine Toth et André Reybaz, René Dupuy, Roger Iglésis, Jean Le Poulain, Marcel Lupovici, Gilles Chancrin, Georges Goubert." *Revue d'histoire du théâtre* (April–June 1962): 118–156.

"Lettres mortes." *Les soirées d'Anvers* 4 (1962).

Michel de Ghelderode et Henri Vandepatte, Correspondance 1932–1934. Ostend, 1984.

"To Directors and Actors: Letters, 1948–1959." Translated by Bettina Knapp. *Tulane Drama Review* 9:41–62 (1965).

TRANSLATIONS

Escurial. An Anthology of Modern Belgian Theatre. Translated by Ingrid Strominger Gherman. Troy, N.Y., 1982.

Escurial. The Modern Theatre 5. Edited by Eric Bentley. Translated by Lionel Abel. Garden City, N.Y., 1957.

The Magpie on the Gallows. An Anthology of Modern Belgian Theatre. Translated by Nadine Dormoy-Savage. Troy, N.Y., 1982.

The School for Buffoons. Translated by Kenneth S. White. San Francisco, 1968.

Seven Plays. Translated by George Hauger. New York, 1960. Includes *The Women at the Tomb, Barabbas, Three Actors and Their Drama, Pantagleize, The Blind Men, Chronicles of Hell, Lord Halewyn.*

Seven Plays 2. Translated by George Hauger. New York, 1964. Includes *Red Magic, Hop Signor!, The Death of Doctor Faust, Christopher Columbus, A Night of Pity, Piet Bouteille, Miss Jairus.*

The Strange Rider and Seven Other Plays. Translated by Samuel Draper. New York, 1964. Includes *The Blind Men, The Women at the Tomb, The Strange Rider, Evening Lament, The Old Men, Red Magic, Christopher Columbus, Pantagleize*.

Theatrical Gestures from the Belgian Avant-Garde. Translated by David Willinger and Luc Deneulin. New York, 1987. Includes *Death Looks in the Window, Blockheads, Venus, Dreams Drowning*.

BIOGRAPHICAL AND CRITICAL STUDIES

Abel, Lionel. "Our Man in the Sixteenth Century: Michel de Ghelderode." *Tulane Drama Review* 8:62–71 (1963).

L'avant poste 3 (May–June 1938). An entire issue devoted to Ghelderode.

Beckers, Anne-Marie. *Michel de Ghelderode, un livre: Barrabas, Escurial, Une oeuvre*. Brussels, 1987.

Beyen, Roland. "Les gôuts littéraires de Michel de Ghelderode." *Les lettres romanes* 24:34–72, 132–167 (1970).

———. "Franz Hellens et Michel de Ghelderode." In *Franz Hellens*. Brussels, 1971.

———. *Michel de Ghelderode, ou la hantise du masque. Essai de biographie critique*. Brussels, 1971.

———. *Ghelderode*. Paris, 1974.

———. *Michel de Ghelderode, ou la comédie des apparences*. Brussels, 1980.

———. *Bibliographie de Michel de Ghelderode*. Brussels, 1987.

———. "Pour une nouvelle édition du *Siège d'Ostende* de Michel de Ghelderode." In *Itinéraires et plaisirs textuels: Mélanges offerts au Professeur Raymond Pouillart*. Edited by George Jacques and José Lambert. Brussels, 1987.

Blancart-Cassou, Jacqueline. *Le rire de Michel de Ghelderode*. Paris, 1987.

Bogaert, Elisabeth. "Le masque dans le théâtre de Michel de Ghelderode." *Romanica gandensia* 12:107–133 (1969).

Les cahiers de biloque 10/5 (1960). An entire issue devoted to Ghelderode.

Castro, Nadine. *Un moyen-âge contemporain: Le théâtre de Michel de Ghelderode*. Lausanne, 1979.

Corvin, Michel. "Ghelderode ou le triomphe de la mort." *Recherches et débats du C.C.I.F.* 44:142–155 (1969).

Deberdt-Malaquais, Élisabeth. *La quête de l'identité dans le théâtre de Ghelderode*. Paris, 1967.

DeBock, Paul-Aloise. "Hommages. Michel de Ghelderode, Avril 1898–Avril 1962." *Théâtre de Belgique* 15–16:39–44 (Spring–Summer 1962).

Decock, Jean. *Le théâtre de Michel de Ghelderode, une dramaturgie de l'anti-théâtre et de la cruauté*. Paris, 1969.

Draper, Samuel. "Infernal Theatre." *Commonweal* 71:279–282 (1959).

———. "Discovery of Ghelderode." *Commonweal* 73:113–115 (1960).

———. "Michel de Ghelderode, 1898–1962." *Commonweal* 76:166–168 (1962).

———. "Michel de Ghelderode: A Personal Statement." *Tulane Drama Review* 8:33–38 (1963).

Elling, Marinus. *L'oeuvre dramatique de Michel de Ghelderode*. Amsterdam, 1974.

Fox, Renée. "A Belgian Journal." *Columbia University Forum* 5:11–18 (1962).

Francis, Jean. *Michel de Ghelderode, dramaturge des pays de par-deçà*. Brussels, 1949.

———. "Michel de Ghelderode, Dramatist." *Chrysalis* 3:3–9 (1949).

———. *L'éternel aujourd'hui de Michel de Ghelderode: Spectrographie d'un auteur*. Brussels, 1968.

Gauchez, Maurice. "Michel de Ghelderode." *Le flambeau* 19:215–224 (1936).

Gérard, Michèle. "Jeu et réalité, le comédien dans l'oeuvre de Michel de Ghelderode." *Cahiers Renaud-Barrault* 61:108–127 (1967).

Gilman, Richard. "Ghelderode in America." *Commonweal* 76:259–260 (1962).

Grossvogel, David. "Plight of the Comic Author and New Departures in Contemporary Comedy." *Romanic Review* 45:259–270 (December 1954).

———. *Twentieth-Century French Drama*. New York, 1961.

Guicharnaud, Jacques. *Modern French Theatre from Giraudoux to Beckett*. New Haven, 1961.

Hauger, George. "Notes on the Plays of Michel de Ghelderode." *Tulane Drama Review* 4:19–30 (1959).

Hellens, Franz. "Michel de Ghelderode." In *Style et caractère*. Brussels, 1956.

———. *Preface à sortilèges, essais de critique intuitive*. Brussels, 1968.

Hellman, Hellen. "The Fool-Hero of Michel de Ghelderode." *Drama Survey* 4:264–271 (1965).

———. "*Splendors of Hell*: A Tragic Farce." *Renascence* 20:30–38 (1967).

———. "Hallucination and Cruelty in Artaud and Ghelderode." *French Review* 41:1–10 (1967).

Herz, Micheline. "Tragedy, Poetry, and the Burlesque in Michel de Ghelderode's Theatre." *Yale French Studies* 29:92–101 (1962).

Jans, Adrien. *La vie de Ghelderode.* Paris, 1973.

Joiret, Michel. *Recherche et connaissance de Michel de Ghelderode.* Paris, 1973.

Lepage, Albert. *Michel de Ghelderode.* Paris, 1960.

Levitt, Paul. "Ghelderode and Puppet Theatre." *French Review* 48:973–980 (1975).

Lilar, Suzanne. *The Belgian Theater Since 1890.* New York, 1958.

Luc, André. *The Contemporary Theatre in Belgium.* Brussels, 1970.

Magie Rouge Magazine 5 (1981). Issue devoted entirely to Ghelderode.

Marginales 22/112–113 (1967). An entire issue devoted to Ghelderode.

Maudit, Jean. "Michel de Ghelderode; ou, L'ange du bizarre." *Études* 265:82–88 (1950).

Michel de Ghelderode et le théâtre contemporain: Actes du Congrès International de Gênes. Brussels, 1980.

La nervie 7–8 (1932). An entire issue devoted to Ghelderode.

Poupeye, Camille. "Michel de Ghelderode, poète dramatique tourmenté et visionnaire." *Empreinte* 6:111–114 (December 1949–January 1950).

Pronko, Leonard Cabell. *Avant-Garde: The Experimental Theater in France.* Berkeley and Los Angeles, 1962.

Quaghebeur, Marc. "Balises pour l'histoire de nos lettres." *In Alphabet des lettres belges de langue française.* Brussels, 1982.

Radar, Edmond. "Le théâtre de Michel de Ghelderode." *Revue générale belge* (August 1965).

Santt, Alice. *Michel de Ghelderode.* Paris, 1970.

Stevo, Jean. *Office des ténèbres pour Michel de Ghelderode.* Brussels, 1972.

Tonelli, Franco. "Escurial de Michel de Ghelderode. Le rite et le mythe au théâtre." *French Review* 43:185–191 (1970).

———. *L'esthétique de la cruauté.* Paris, 1972.

Trousson, Raymond. "L'oeuvre et les thèmes de Michel de Ghelderode." *Le flambeau* 43:657–667 (1960).

Tulane Drama Review 8/1 (1963). An entire issue devoted to Ghelderode.

Valogne, Catherine. "Michel de Ghelderode et ses interprètes." *Revue d'histoire du théâtre* 14:113–117 (1962).

Vandegans, André. "*Le mystère de la Passion et Barabbas.*" *Revue des langues vivants* 32:547–566 (1966).

———. "Aspects d'*Escurial.*" *Marginales* 22:65–73 (1967).

———. "Les sources plastiques d'*Escurial.*" *Revue d'histoire du théâtre* 19:24–32 (1967).

———. "*Escurial* et *Hop-Frog.*" *Revue des langues vivantes* 34:616–619 (1968).

———. "Ghelderode, Andréev et la genèse de *Mademoiselle Jaïre.*" *Bulletin de L'Académie Royale de Langue et Littérature Française* 46:198–225 (1968).

———. "Reflets hugoliens dans *Escurial.*" *Revue d'histoire littéraire de la France* 69:262–268 (1969).

———. *Aux origines de Barabbas: Actus tragicus de Michel de Ghelderode.* Paris, 1978.

Vandromme, Pol. *Michel de Ghelderode.* Paris, 1963.

Van Herp, Jacques. "Michel de Ghelderode." *Ailleurs* (November 1961). Pp. 61–84.

Vermeulin, François. "Michel de Ghelderode et Bruges." *Le trait d'union* (December 1972). Pp. 39–49.

Weiss, Auréliu. *Le monde théâtral de Michel de Ghelderode.* Paris, 1966.

Wellwarth, George. "Michel de Ghelderode: The Theatre of the Grotesque." *Tulane Drama Review* 8:11–23 (1963).

———. *The Theatre of Protest and Paradox: Developments in the Avant-Garde Drama.* New York, 1964.

Willinger, David. "Michel de Ghelderode." *Encyclopedia of World Drama* 2:282–291 (1984).

DAVID WILLINGER

JOSÉ MARIA FERREIRA DE CASTRO

(1898–1974)

VERY FEW PORTUGUESE writers have gained recognition outside Portugal: Luiz Vaz de Camões, José Maria de Eça de Queirós, Fernando Pessoa, and José Maria Ferreira de Castro come to mind. Ferreira de Castro's international reputation as the greatest Portuguese novelist of the twentieth century developed very rapidly after the publication of his first two major novels, *Emigrantes* (*Emigrants,* 1928) and *A selva* (*Jungle,* 1930). Both novels have been widely translated, as have a number of his other works. *Jungle,* published in more than twenty languages, appeared on a 1973 UNESCO list of the ten most popular books in the world. Almost all of Ferreira de Castro's works attained best-seller status in Portugal, and new editions of his novels appear regularly in Portugal and Brazil.

Despite his national and international reputation, however, the critical bibliography on Ferreira de Castro is meager indeed, consisting of a few effusive homages from friends, a page or so in the standard histories of the national literature, and a scant handful of more serious studies, almost all by non-Portuguese writers and published outside Portugal. This state of affairs was understandable before the April Revolution of 1974, which overthrew the Salazar-Caetano dictatorship. Ferreira de Castro was opposed to the Salazar regime, and the harsh censorship imposed by that regime seemed a very reasonable explanation for the dearth of critical studies of the novelist's works. Nonetheless, Ferreira de Castro's ambiguous position in Portuguese letters—dutifully praised as one of the giants of the nation's literature but rarely analyzed or discussed in detail—has continued almost unchanged since 1974.

How, then, does one explain Ferreira de Castro's rapid rise to literary fame in Portugal in the 1920's and 1930's, his continued popularity among the Portuguese reading public, his remarkable international reputation, and his relative neglect by the Portuguese critical establishment? The peculiarities and ironies of Ferreira de Castro's novels and of his literary career are, in fact, inextricably bound up with the larger peculiarities and ironies of Portuguese history and society, and it is in those terms that he and his fiction must be considered.

No other western European country has endured such a roller-coaster history as Portugal. Geographically tiny, consistently underpopulated, overshadowed by larger and more powerful neighbors, Portugal nonetheless was the first nation in Europe to expand beyond the boundaries of the continent. Portuguese expansion began with the capture of the North African town of Ceuta in 1415; one hundred years later, Portuguese explorers and traders had circumnavigated Africa, dominated the Indian Ocean, and begun settling Brazil. The total population of fifteenth-century Portugal was under two million, but the Portuguese overseas empire spanned three continents and controlled portions of Africa, India, South America, the East Indies, and China. The king of Portugal was reputed to be the richest monarch in the Christian world—but little of the wealth gained from this vast empire was invested within Portugal itself.

In 1578 Portugal's young king Sebastian was killed during a foolhardy attack on North Africa. Two years later Portugal lost its independence, becoming part of Spain, and the nation was never to recover fully from the sixty years of Spanish domination the Portuguese refer to as the "Babylonian captivity." In 1640, the Portuguese managed to regain their independence, and that political independence has endured ever since.

During the six decades of Spanish rule, however, Portugal lost many of its overseas possessions, particularly in Asia. Far more important than these territorial losses and their economic consequences, however, was a general retrogression in Portuguese society as a whole. The nobility regained much of the power it had lost under the activist kings of the age of exploration, and the nation's agriculture and economy reverted to something very close to medieval feudalism.

Above all, the psychological effects of Portugal's sudden and catastrophic fall from international preeminence to subservience were intense and enduring. The speed and relative ease with which the Portuguese had built their empire in the fifteenth and early sixteenth centuries convinced many of the nation's inhabitants that they were the "new Israelites," God's chosen people in the task of discovering and Christianizing the world. Spanish domination, therefore, was not simply a loss of political independence and economic power; it was an apocalyptic fall from grace, an inexplicable divine punishment.

After the reestablishment of independence in 1640, the roller coaster of Portuguese history had a number of other shocks—most of them unpleasant—in store for the nation. Starting around 1700 the discovery of enormous reserves of gold and diamonds in the interior of

Brazil restored the wealth of Portugal—at least superficially—and appeared to many Portuguese to signal a return to divine favor. But in 1703, just as the the newfound riches of Brazil began to pour into Lisbon, the Portuguese crown signed the disastrous Methuen Treaty with Britain, agreeing, in return for British imports of Portuguese wine, to restrict its own industrialization and to open its markets to English textiles and other manufactured goods. As a result, most of the wealth from Brazil was drained from the Portuguese economy and exported to England, where it helped to finance the Industrial Revolution. When the flow of gold and diamonds came to an end, toward the end of the eighteenth century, Portugal was still an almost medieval agricultural nation.

Some of the reforms associated with the Enlightenment in other European countries did reach Portugal during the eighteenth century, but only at considerable cost. The leading proponent of political and cultural modernization in Portugal, the Marquis de Pombal, who served as minister of foreign affairs from 1750 to 1777, managed to rebuild the city of Lisbon after its virtual destruction by the great earthquake of 1755 (yet another sign of divine disfavor, in the eyes of many Portuguese). He also endeavored to reform the economy, develop a middle class, and reduce the power of the aristocracy and the church. These enlightened, progressive policies, however, were imposed upon Portugal through a ruthless and bloody dictatorship.

Pombal's police-state Enlightenment came to an abrupt end in 1777, and the royal family and the nobility dismantled most of the reforms he had attempted. Portugal vegetated quietly until Napoleon's armies invaded and occupied the nation in 1807. The royal family fled to Brazil, leaving Portugal in the hands of a regency headed by a British general, William Beresford. It is one of the paradoxes of Portuguese history that Beresford, the representative of a progressive, industrialized, Protestant nation, did everything in his power to combat economic and intellectual modernization in Portugal. Beresford persecuted Freemasons and intellectuals, and repressed dissent in the Portuguese military and among the tiny middle class.

In 1820 a liberal and nationalistic revolution forced Beresford from power, and João VI returned from Rio de Janeiro in 1821 to lead his nation. The new constitution, written in 1822, was as liberal as any produced in Europe in the nineteenth century. It sharply limited royal authority, finally halted the activities of the Inquisition, and provided for universal suffrage for literate males. The Portugal this constitution was designed to govern, however, existed only in the dreams of its framers and in their enthusiasm for foreign models. In reality, almost all the wealth of Portugal was held by a few thousand aristocrats, and only 9 percent of the population could be classified as middle class. The other Portuguese, by and large, were illiterate and superstitious peasants whose lives had not altered appreciably since 1500. The fine-sounding words of the 1822 constitution were rapidly discarded, doomed by the power of the oligarchy and the church.

João VI died in Lisbon in 1826, possibly by poisoning, without choosing a successor. His two sons, Pedro and Miguel, fought a violent and destructive civil war: Pedro had the support of the liberals and the middle class, as well as the invaluable support of the British government. Miguel was the champion of absolutism, of religious orthodoxy, and of the traditional aristocracy; much of the peasant population, particularly in northern Portugal, was convinced by landowners and clerics that Miguel was defending the nation from freemasonry and perdition.

This War of the Brothers ended in 1834 with the victory of liberalism. The new government moved quickly to attack the aristocracy's main source of power—ownership of the land. Vast properties were seized from defeated supporters of Miguel and from the church, but these lands were granted not to the peasants who had worked them for generations, but to middle-class liberals, effectively creating a new landholding aristocracy. Peasants were still tied to the land by annual feudal dues, and there is considerable evidence that their hardships were intensified by the liberals' reforms. The chaotic, almost leaderless peasant uprising of Maria da Fonte, which lasted from 1846 to 1848, was a natural response to worsening conditions on the land. This revolt of the landless and powerless so terrified middle-class liberals and conservative aristocrats alike that an uneasy truce was imposed.

From 1851 until the end of the nineteenth century, Portugal was a make-believe democracy tailored to the interests of its small upper and middle classes. Under an arrangement known as *rotativismo,* the two principal political parties alternated in power. Both parties were based upon family ties and local concerns, and it is difficult to make ideological distinctions between them. Regular parliamentary elections were held, but the results of those elections simply confirmed the rotation in power already decided upon by the two parties; the political process was so tightly restricted that it was extremely easy to control its outcome. Only about 1 percent of the population of Portugal was allowed to cast ballots, and only some 4,500 individuals were eligible to run for parliament.

This system was successful in maintaining the appearance of democracy and progress within Portugal, but it was fatally discredited in 1890 by events in Portuguese Africa. Portuguese explorers and soldiers had laid the groundwork for the union of Portugal's southwest African colony, Angola, with its dependency on the east coast of Africa, Mozambique; this union would have incorporated the area that is now Zimbabwe and allowed Portugal to control territory running across the entire continent. In 1890 Great Britain, Portugal's oldest ally, threatened to declare war unless Portugal immediately dropped these plans for union. The Portuguese government, no match for British military might, was forced to agree. This incident was widely viewed within Portugal as a national humiliation, and it dramatically increased opposition to the political status quo, particularly among the armed forces. Much of this opposition coalesced around the Republican party, founded in 1880.

As instability spread through the Portuguese political system, governments rose and fell with astonishing rapidity. In May 1907 King Carlos I decided to shut down the parliament and appoint a royal dictator to run the country. There was considerable opposition to this move, and Carlos and his eldest son were assassinated in January 1908. The new king, Manuel II, was only eighteen years old and could control neither the government nor the increasingly restive armed forces. The monarchy was overthrown on 5 October 1910, and a republic was proclaimed.

The ideology of the new regime was often inconsistent and paradoxical. Within one year after achieving power, the Republican party split into a number of factions that made it extremely difficult to develop coherent and effective policies—although there was clearly little agreement on what policies the government should pursue. The political system became increasingly polarized between fanatical adherents of radical social change and equally fanatical opponents of change. Between 1910 and 1926 as many as five thousand Portuguese may have died in the political strife—riots, bombings, assassinations—that accompanied this polarization. During this same chaotic period, Portugal was ruled by forty-five different governments.

In short, the republic brought minimal change to Portugal, and its inefficiency and infighting rapidly discredited representative government among most politically active sectors of the population. The military slowly increased its participation in government during this period, but deeply resented the civilian government's decision to enter World War I on the side of the Allies. Over four thousand Portuguese soldiers died in World War I, with

thousands more wounded. And the greed and incompetence of Republican politicians contributed to the total economic bankruptcy of the nation in 1926.

Politically and intellectually bankrupt as well, the republic was ousted by a military revolt in 1926; direct military rule quickly evolved into a right-wing dictatorship under the civilian leadership of Antonio de Oliveira Salazar, a former economics professor. Never as ambitious, egotistical, or colorful as Mussolini, Hitler, or even Franco, Salazar nonetheless managed to maintain his fascist dictatorship intact, despite the Allied victory in World War II. It survived his death in 1970 and was finally dismantled only after the Portuguese Revolution of April 1974.

This complex and fundamentally tragic national history both created and fed upon a distinctive Portuguese view of the nation's character and potential, a vision found again and again in the works of Portuguese intellectuals and creative writers. This vision was almost always deeply pessimistic; it was also self-contradictory and self-serving.

One fundamental component of this vision was an idealized view of the past, of the age of exploration and empire that had made Portugal the richest and most powerful nation on earth. Portuguese intellectuals frequently contrasted that glorious past with Portugal's present decadence. In the seventeenth and eighteenth centuries, it was theorized that some great and mysterious national sin had led God to desert and cast down his chosen people. By the nineteenth century Portuguese intellectuals were somewhat more sophisticated, but their explanations of national history retained an essential characteristic: the tendency to confuse condition and character, and to blame Portuguese decadence on its primary victims, the common people. The most general explanation largely ignored the obvious effects of bad government, of a self-serving and wasteful elite, of disastrous economic decisions and foreign adventures. Portugal was agrarian, feudal, and non-industrialized, it was asserted, because the population as a whole was Mediterranean, with a considerable admixture of Semitic and Negroid blood, and was therefore racially inferior to the Aryan populations of England, France, Germany, and other northern regions, who were genetically prepared to industrialize, modernize, and progress.

This fundamental approach to Portugal's enduring economic and social crisis was obviously comforting to the elite and to the middle classes, absolving them of any past or future responsibility. At the same time, however, particularly after 1870, at least some Portuguese intellectuals recognized the need to change Portugal, to bring the nation out of its long decadence and to strive to emulate other, more developed European nations. This desire for change was always accompanied in Portugal by an equally strong resistance to any alteration in the status quo. One of the fundamental lessons of Portuguese history appeared to be that change was inextricably linked to foreign domination or influence—the Spanish occupation, Pombal's Enlightenment dictatorship, and Beresford's British regency, for example—and that such externally imposed alterations in Portuguese society had invariably had negative effects.

It is obvious, of course, that many of those who opposed all change in Portugal had very strong and valid reasons based on their own self-interest. Nonetheless, it would be a mistake to assume that all resistance to change was so motivated. The national cult of the past, from which few educated Portuguese could escape, had managed to define as national virtues many of the characteristics that outside observers saw as symptoms of national decadence. Feudalism, subsistence agriculture, lack of industrialization, religious fanaticism, even illiteracy—all were described as fundamental traits of the Portuguese national character. Change, therefore, was vigorously opposed on patriotic grounds as an attack on the true, authentic Portugal.

Moreover, while these two political and intellectual currents—the desire for change and opposition to all change—increasingly polarized Portuguese society and politics after 1870, many intellectuals were strongly attracted to both positions; admiringly envious of other, more progressive European nations, they simultaneously feared that Portugal could not change, or that change would destroy the authenticity of Portuguese society and culture.

This contradiction was fatal for one of the greatest Portuguese poets and intellectuals of the nineteenth century, Antero de Quental (1842–1891). An apostle of radical change and one of the founders of Portuguese socialism, Quental committed suicide, in part because he concluded that the proletariat he sought to lead to freedom was unwilling, or unable, to heed his message.

Other Portuguese intellectuals finessed this contradiction with greater success than Quental, but they did not wholly escape its effects. One way to evade the dichotomy between admiration for foreign models and obeisance to the cult of Portuguese authenticity was to limit change to the superficial level of style, in life and in literature. From the nineteenth century on, Portugal's upper and middle classes were besotted with France. They read French literature, followed the latest French fashions in dress and furnishings, and visited Paris at every opportunity. The greatest Portuguese novelist of the nineteenth century, Eça de Queirós (1845–1900), was typically torn between his longing to transform Portugal into a nation as modern as France and his equally strong disgust with a Portuguese elite that mindlessly aped French fashions. Portugal, he declared, was becoming France in a bad translation. And, as Eça was bitterly aware at the end of his life, all this enthusiasm for French artifacts and styles in no way implied a desire or a commitment to make the fundamental social changes—education, industrialization, urbanization, the provision of minimal social services, a more open political system—that had created the France he and his compatriots so idolized.

A second intellectual response to the contradiction between desire for change and fear of change was the widespread rationalization that modern Portugal was so hopelessly and inherently backward that change could not and should not be attempted by mere mortals. If destiny, or divine power, had destroyed imperial Portugal in the sixteenth century, the same superhuman forces would someday return the nation to its former status. When that moment came, those characteristics that the elite had defined as central to the national soul—ignorance, feudalism, and fanaticism, for example—and that appeared, in a short view of history, to be negative traits, would again be needed, as they had been between 1415 and 1580, to power Portugal's return to international preeminence. These characteristics, then, not only could not be changed, but should not be changed, lest Portugal fail to fulfill its new mission at some future date.

During the first decades of the twentieth century, these contradictions weighed ever more heavily on Portugal's tiny literary and intellectual elite—a group overwhelmingly drawn from the traditional aristocracy and the urban upper-middle class. The poet Teixeira de Pascoaes (Joaquim Pereira Teixeira de Vasconcelos, 1877–1952), for example, led the literary movement for national cultural renewal that called itself the Portuguese Renaissance (*Renasença Portuguêsa*), but the philosophy of his movement and the focus of his verse was nostalgia—the overwhelming longing for the past that the Portuguese call *saudade.*

The most representative Portuguese intellectual of the twentieth century, Fernando Pessoa (1888–1935), is one of the greatest poets of modern European literature, but he is also a case study in personal and literary pathology. Torn apart, like so many other educated Portuguese, by contradictory and irreconcilable imperatives—to be modern and to be faithful to Portugal's past; to be European and to be patriotic; to change and to preserve—Pessoa's solution was to fragment his identity, creating his heteronyms. These were not simply pseudonyms, but multiple identities, and each possessed an ideology, a biography, and an individual style.

Pessoa's crisis of the self was a microcosm of the larger crisis of Portugal in the first decades of this century. Politically, moderate and centrist forces had been discredited by the chaos of the republic. The Left was small and disorganized, and it had not managed to develop a constituency among the nation's impoverished and illiterate rural proletariat. The forces of the Right drew upon the reactionary tendency, inherent in so much of Portuguese culture, to resist change, to fear and reject foreign influence, and to idealize and idolize the past; these forces triumphed in 1926 and dominated Portugal for almost half a century. The Salazar regime endeavored, rigidly and systematically, to protect Portugal from change, from modernization, from all the dangerous ideologies—socialism, communism, democracy, capitalism—which the nation's leader regularly denounced as threats to its identity and authenticity. Literature was tightly controlled, and writers who opposed the regime were silenced, imprisoned, and exiled. For Salazar and his followers, education was an invitation to crime and heresy; poverty and illiteracy (as late as 1974, perhaps 75 percent of Portugal's population could not read) were fundamental national virtues.

Ferreira de Castro's first novels were published just as the Salazar regime consolidated its power; his last book, *O instinto supremo* (The Supreme Instinct), appeared in 1968, the year Salazar suffered a severe stroke. For contemporary Portuguese, then, Ferreira de Castro is necessarily bound by chronology to the Salazar years. Moreover, Ferreira de Castro's biography and the themes and ideology of his novels have led many readers and critics to view him as a symbol of Portugal in the twentieth century.

It is clear that Ferreira de Castro did not begin his career with any vision of himself as a symbolic figure. Like so many of the characters in his novels, he was simply doing his best to rise out of poverty and to make his way in the world within his chosen field, literature. It is also clear, however, that once he had established himself as an important international literary figure, Ferreira de Castro sometimes saw himself in larger-than-life terms; he stressed the autobiographical nature of much of his fiction, simultaneously revising and fictionalizing the details of his life, and presented himself as an icon of change, as a symbol of intellectual opposition to the Salazar regime, and as an important link between Portuguese and Brazilian culture. And all of these visions have been considerably elaborated by his admirers.

This image does have some basis in reality. The novelist was born into an archetypically poor rural family, received very little formal education, and spent much of his youth in exile and extreme poverty. He was, therefore, an anomaly in a literary culture dominated almost entirely by the well-educated sons of the traditional aristocracy and the prosperous middle class. Ferreira de Castro was one of the first major writers to focus on the despair of Portugal's oppressed rural proletariat and on a political and economic system that encouraged tens of thousands of Portuguese to emigrate every year. Furthermore, he opposed the fascist dictatorship and served as the intellectual godfather to a younger generation of socially conscious Portuguese novelists, the neorealists.

It is also true, however, that Ferreira de Castro's life and works are often at considerable variance with his carefully constructed image. His approach to the problems of Portuguese society is considerably less authentic, forceful, and effective, in literary terms, than that found in the stories and novels of his contemporary Aquilino Ribeiro (1885–1963). Despite his humble origins, the themes and ideology found in most of Ferreira de Castro's novels are very much those of Portugal's middle class. His primary loyalty was to his readers, not to the illiterate masses from which he had come, and his works reflected the moral confusion and nostalgic pessimism of those readers. He described social problems, but declined to offer

concrete solutions, in large part because he was unable or unwilling to espouse radical and immediate change.

Ferreira de Castro did protest the Salazar regime's censorship practices by refusing to publish in Portuguese newspapers and magazines, but his novels somehow managed to escape the censors who butchered or banned the works of important neorealist novelists. And while many of his contemporaries were exiled or imprisoned for their ideas and writings, Ferreira de Castro traveled extensively, enjoyed the prosperous life-style made possible by the sales of his books, and was frequently cited by the dictatorship as one of the glories of Portugal in the twentieth century.

If the reality of Ferreira de Castro's life and works fails to measure up fully to the claims of his admirers, those admirers are not entirely in error when they view him as a symbol of modern Portugal. Many readers today find Ferreira de Castro's works profoundly disappointing, but that is only because he and his admirers have led us to expect a committed and radical champion of the silent and oppressed masses. What we find, instead, is a typical middle-class Portuguese intellectual—aware of problems but unclear about solutions; eager for change but deeply pessimistic about its viability; conscious of social injustice but highly dubious of the intellectual and moral potential of the lower classes; distrustful of imported ideologies; and convinced that peace, prosperity, and equality can be achieved only in the very distant future, when all human beings will somehow come to understand and love each other. Ferreira de Castro's dissatisfaction with the present and his vague, impractical, and rather desperate optimism about the future dovetailed neatly with the ideological confusion of his Portuguese readers; the same elements, when combined with exotic settings, were also enormously appealing to middle-class readers outside Portugal.

Ferreira de Castro was born on 24 May 1898 in the tiny farming village of Salgueiros in north-central Portugal. His family, like most

Portuguese peasants in the area, was wretchedly poor, scrabbling out a bare subsistence on tiny, rocky plots of land almost exhausted by centuries of intensive cultivation. He was the oldest of four children, and his parents managed to send him to elementary school in the nearest town, Ossela. Ferreira de Castro was one of only two children in Ossela to complete the highest level offered at the school, the equivalent of fourth grade; the other was the son of the teacher. This was the end of the novelist's formal education, for it was almost impossible for the children of poor parents to go on to secondary school; in 1911 there were only six thousand secondary-school students in all of Portugal.

Ferreira de Castro's father died around 1906, making the family's financial situation even more precarious. In January 1911, at the age of twelve, Ferreira de Castro was sent to Brazil. Several accounts of his departure appear in the novelist's autobiographical essays and in speeches and interviews; in the most common version, he claimed to have fallen in love with an older girl, who ridiculed his pretensions. "Only a real man," he wrote, "could go so far away, and Margarida would certainly pay attention to that. Had it not been for her, I never would have left. I would have never had the courage." There may be some elements of truth in this tale, but it also suggests that Ferreira de Castro always felt bitter and ashamed—not because his family was poor, but because his widowed mother, struggling with too little money and too many mouths to feed, felt she had no choice but to send her oldest child across the Atlantic alone.

The experience of emigration, along with all the details of that experience—the multiple shocks of modernity and technology in his first train ride, his first visit to a big city, his first sea voyage, the misery and nausea of three long weeks in the floating cattle car of third-class steerage on an ancient steamer—obsessed Ferreira de Castro until about 1930. He returned to it again and again in his early novels and sto-

ries, and did not finally lay its many ghosts to rest until he finished *Emigrants* and *Jungle.*

Ferreira de Castro landed in Belém do Pará, at the mouth of the Amazon River. He had a letter of introduction to a former neighbor who had immigrated earlier to Belém, but this letter was not all that helpful. It was common practice for Portuguese emigrants to greatly exaggerate their success and prosperity in letters home, and Ferreira de Castro's mother may well have believed that she was sending her son to live in relative luxury. In fact, the boy's only contact in Belém was desperately poor, resented this new responsibility, and quickly sent Ferreira de Castro hundreds of miles up the Amazon to work on the Paradise rubber plantation.

Surrounded by the mysteries and terrors of the jungle, Ferreira de Castro spent almost four years working as a secretary and bookkeeper in the plantation store. He had been saved by his fourth-grade education from the misery of the hundreds of emaciated, disease-ridden rubber collectors who were permanently enslaved by their ever-increasing debts to the plantation owner. He was paid almost nothing, but had access to the plantation's small library and quickly began to expand his education and to dream of a career in literature. He turned out puzzles and charades for almanacs, and wrote and endlessly rewrote his first novel, *Criminoso por ambição* (Ambition's Criminal, 1916).

In 1914, now sixteen years old, Ferreira de Castro wrote to his contact in Belém, begging to be allowed to leave the plantation. He received permission and reached Belém in October, but the protector in whom he placed so much faith once again abandoned him. Ferreira de Castro spent days wandering the streets of the city, scrounging for odd jobs, picking through garbage for rotted fruits and vegetables to eat. He served briefly on a coastal packet ship, but soon found himself back on the streets of Belém. This period of homelessness and utter poverty lasted for at least a year.

In 1916 Ferreira de Castro finally found the

job he had dreamed about while on the plantation: he was hired to write articles for two small newspapers published for the Portuguese colony in Belém. At the same time he found a printer willing to publish his *Criminoso por ambição* in serial form. Ferreira de Castro went from door to door to take orders for the novel and delivered copies himself to those who subscribed. The novel was a modest success, and Ferreira turned his hand to writing plays aimed directly at the Portuguese emigrant colony. The first of these was published in Belém in 1916, and a second play was performed in a bar there in 1918. Ferreira de Castro's second novel, *Rugas sociais* (Social Wrinkles), was also serialized in Belém in 1918.

These literary efforts did not bring in much money, but they did establish Ferreira de Castro's reputation in the Portuguese colony. In 1917 he and a friend founded *Portugal,* a weekly magazine aimed at that market. The venture was a considerable success, and *Portugal* was sold and read in Portuguese immigrant communities all over Brazil. Ferreira de Castro managed to travel to several Brazilian cities, sending back reports on Portuguese life there and beginning to campaign actively for better working conditions for immigrants.

In September 1919 Ferreira de Castro at last returned to Portugal. He had big plans to improve Portuguese cultural relations with Brazil, staging exhibits and importing movies, but he was almost penniless. Furthermore, despite the reputation he had established in Brazil, he was completely unknown in his native country. He traveled to his hometown, where he stayed for a few weeks, but many of his relatives and friends had died or emigrated. He felt himself a man without a country, writing in his diary that "my life in America, my years in Brazil, now seem to me but a dream, just as it used to seem that I had dreamed the first thirteen years of my life in Portugal. I feel that I live only in the present moment!"

Disillusioned by this effort to recapture his childhood, Ferreira de Castro went back to Lisbon and struggled to make a living as a journalist. He wrote for and edited a series of minor newspapers and magazines, most of which survived only a few months. His articles in favor of labor reform were heavily censored by the authorities, and he was jailed for four days in March 1919. *Mas . . .* (But . . .), a collection of literary and political essays, appeared in 1921. It received some good reviews and opened a few doors. Between 1922 and 1927 Ferreira de Castro freelanced for dozens of newspapers and magazines in Lisbon and elsewhere, often turning out more than a hundred articles, stories, and serialized novel chapters every month. The fiction Ferreira de Castro published during this period—with titles like *Sangue negro* (Black Blood, 1923) and *Carne faminta* (Hungry Flesh, 1922)—was frankly commercial, without literary pretensions, and he later refused to allow any of it to appear in his collected works.

In 1927 Ferreira de Castro began writing his first major work of fiction, *Emigrants.* He was encouraged by his lover, Maria Eugénia Haas da Costa Ramos, who wrote poetry under the name Diana de Liz. *Emigrants* was published in 1928 and rapidly became a major best-seller in Portugal and Brazil. Within two years translations began to appear in other European countries, where it was equally successful. Ferreira de Castro became famous and prosperous almost overnight, but *Emigrants* also proved that elements of his personal past—the experience of emigration and the disillusionment of returning from Brazil, in this case—could be successfully fictionalized.

In 1929 Ferreira de Castro turned to his memories of life on the rubber plantation, slowly creating *Jungle.* He tried to utilize those memories before, but "whenever I tried to write about the jungle in my first books," he later recalled, "my old terror took control of me." Published in 1930, *Jungle* was even more successful than *Emigrants;* the first Portuguese edition sold out within three months, and translations into Spanish and French (by

Blaise Cendrars) appeared quickly. The novel has since been published in twenty-one different countries.

Diana de Liz died suddenly and unexpectedly one month after *Jungle* appeared. Ferreira de Castro was devastated, and wandered alone through Europe for several months. When he returned to Lisbon, he threw himself into preparing posthumous editions of her poetry and memoirs. He became so seriously ill himself that the Lisbon newspapers prepared his obituaries for immediate publication. After his recovery he came very close to suicide. He was finally convinced to leave Lisbon for the calm and warmth of the island of Madeira, where he spent the whole of 1932.

After the painful catharsis of writing *Jungle,* Ferreira de Castro had sworn he would never write another novel. As he rested and recovered on Madeira, however, he again began to seek the same catharsis through writing fiction. *Eternidade* (Eternity), published in 1933, is at least superficially autobiographical, but it also relies heavily on the theory of "humanitarian socialism" espoused by a minor Portuguese philosopher, António Sérgio (1883–1969).

By 1933 the sales of his novels had made Ferreira de Castro a wealthy man, able to organize his life as he wished; he was also free, at long last, from the daily pressures of journalism. He was determined to write about realities that he had not experienced personally, and therefore set out to observe and to record. He spent a number of months in a small village in the far north of Portugal, and used the information he collected there as the basis for his fourth major novel, *Terra fria* (Cold Land, 1934).

After 1934 Ferreira de Castro was rarely in Portugal. Political events there alienated and depressed him, and he had serious problems with censorship. In 1936 he declared that he would not publish any more articles or fiction in Portuguese periodicals until censorship came to an end. Censorship lasted until 1974, far longer than Ferreira de Castro could possibly have imagined, but he held firm to his vow of silence.

Ferreira de Castro spent much of the period between 1934 and 1936 in Spain, where the freedom and socialist ideals of the short-lived Spanish Republic seemed to him to hold out hope that liberalism and antiauthoritarianism could be adapted to the societies of the Iberian Peninsula. In Spain he began work on a vast and ambitious project, a series of novels that would serve as a "biography of the twentieth century." The first volume, as Ferreira de Castro described it in his sketch of the project, would be entitled *As raízes* (Roots) and would study

the heritage left us by the last century—the main source of the doctrines and yearnings of our own times, for which so many men have given and are still giving their lives. We would next focus on the first world war, with the triumph of communism in Russia, continuing to chronicle this rebellious century until we die as well. Thus, in this great frieze filled with movement, we could capture the history of ideas and the story of the men—almost all of humble origins—who have struggled to rid the earth of injustice.

("Origem de *O intervalo*" [The Origins of *Intermission*], in *Os fragmentos,* p. 60)

Ferreira de Castro began with the third volume in the cycle he planned, a novel set in Spain and dealing with

the beginnings of the republican regime, since we ourselves were present for some of those early struggles. And we did not want all that we had seen and felt in those convulsive days to grow dim in our memories and cold in our hearts. The Spanish Republic came into existence at the very focal point of a worldwide crisis; it seemed to be the gateway to a new age in the western world, and all those who suffered from exploitation looked to it with hope. Many, in fact, hoped that humanity had reached the last barrier set up by a social system in its death throes, and that behind this fragile obstacle lay full economic freedom, the end of all ancient systems of oppression, and the full human solidarity of which so many men had dreamed.

("Origem de *O intervalo*," pp. 61–62)

This novel, entitled "Luta de classes" (Class Struggle), was finished in September 1936. The Spanish Civil War had begun, and the republic was no longer the triumphant dawning of a new age, but a dream threatened by what Ferreira de Castro viewed as the international forces of greed and repression. "Luta de classes" could not be published in Portugal, where the government sympathized whole-heartedly with Franco and the enemies of the Spanish Republic, and Ferreira de Castro was forced to put it away. The novel, revised and retitled *O intervalo* (Intermission), was not published until 1974. Ferreira de Castro also gave up his plans for the "biography of the twentieth century," for it seemed clear to him that the forces of freedom and social justice, whose final victory his series of novels was designed to chronicle, were in danger of destruction everywhere in the West. The lights were going out all over Europe, in Churchill's phrase, and Ferreira de Castro could only observe the spread of fascism. He visited Czechoslovakia in 1938 and witnessed the Nazi invasion, an event that confirmed all his worst fears about the future course of world history.

In 1938 Ferreira de Castro married Elena Muriel, a Spanish painter who was one of the thousands of intellectual and artistic refugees from the Spanish Civil War. He published a new novel, *A tempestade* (The Storm), in 1940. It is a psychological study of an unhappy marriage and has almost no explicit social content. It may represent one attempt by Ferreira de Castro to come to terms with the pervasive reality of censorship in Portugal, seeking to discover whether or not he could write fiction divorced from his ideals and dreams. *A tempestade* is one of his least successful novels, and seems to have taught Ferreira de Castro that psychological fiction was a dead end, at least for him. He did not publish another novel until 1947.

Ferreira de Castro's solution to censorship and to the nightmare of fascism's triumphs in Europe was to escape through travel and the production of travel narratives. He had begun serializing his *Pequenos mundos e velhas civilizações* (Little Worlds and Ancient Civilizations) in 1937, describing small countries and islands of Europe, particularly in and around the Mediterranean. Ferreira de Castro was particularly interested in lower-class life and culture in these microcosmic societies, and it is clear that he saw his travel narratives as a financially profitable end run around Portuguese censorship, enabling him to criticize political and economic injustice in his own country through the mirror of similarly rigid and insular societies elsewhere.

Pequenos mundos was extremely successful and led to an even larger project. In 1939, just as World War II was beginning, Ferreira de Castro's Portuguese and Brazilian publishers advanced him and his wife enough money to travel around the world. The product of this journey, which lasted many months, was an immense narrative entitled simply *A volta ao mundo* (Around the World). It was published in 1944 and was designed both to educate Portuguese readers about the rest of the world and to imply, once again, oblique criticism of Portugal's government and society that could not be published openly.

By the time *A volta ao mundo* appeared, Ferreira de Castro was greatly encouraged by events in Europe and confidently awaited the defeat of fascism on the continent and, more specifically, in Portugal itself. In preparation for the changes in life and literature that he felt would follow the end of the war, Ferreira de Castro began planning and researching a new novel, one that would deal openly with the oppression of Portuguese peasants. He spent many months in the Serra da Estrela mountain range, observing the lives and customs of impoverished shepherds, whose world had not changed significantly since the Middle Ages. The novel that evolved from this research, *A lã e a neve* (Wool and Snow), was published in 1947, perhaps not in the form Ferreira de Castro had originally envisioned since both the Salazar dictatorship and Portuguese censorship continued unchanged, despite the victory of democracy outside the Iberian Peninsula.

Despite these constraints, *A lã e a neve* is the best of Ferreira de Castro's nonautobiographical novels about Portugal. It is also the last of his major works to attempt to portray the reality of his own nation. The novelist spent most of the rest of his life outside Portugal; the themes and settings of his works from 1947 on are almost completely denationalized. *A curva da estrada* (The Curve in the Road, 1950) returned to his experiences in Spain during the republic, but the text is nostalgic rather than combative, resigned rather than optimistic. After 1950 Ferreira de Castro spent more and more time each year in France, and used rural France as the setting for his well-known novella *The Mission*.

After 1954 Ferreira de Castro was not only intellectually exiled from Portugal, but also seems to have largely lost faith in the novel. His energies in the late 1950's and early 1960's were devoted to the production of his massive, two-volume *As maravilhas artísticas do mundo* (Artistic Wonders of the World, 1958–1963), a text that combined his flair for describing exotic locales and his belief that the middle-class Portuguese readers who bought these large, beautifully illustrated volumes could be morally and intellectually improved by exposure to what he saw as "the creative spirit in art through the centuries."

Throughout this period Ferreira de Castro also acquired a reputation as a sort of hermit. He traveled most of the year, living most of his life after about 1955 in a few favorite hotels in Portugal and France. He was Portugal's most famous living writer, but he remained almost completely outside the Portuguese literary world. In 1958, when the Salazar government decided to experiment with the democratic election of the president (a largely ceremonial position), Ferreira de Castro was urged to run as the opposition candidate. He declined, at least in part because he was too smart, or too cynical, to believe that any opposition candidate had a ghost of a chance against the entrenched power of a government that had been in power for thirty years. Ferreira de Castro declined to run, and the opposition candidate, Humberto Delgado, was defeated overwhelmingly, if dishonestly. Delgado was murdered, almost certainly by agents of the Portuguese secret police, in 1965.

From the 1950's on Ferreira de Castro's name was frequently mentioned as a potential candidate for the Nobel Prize for literature. The social thematics and idealistic philosophy found in his works certainly embodied the values associated with the prize, but Ferreira de Castro consistently requested that his name not be considered; it seems likely that he feared that the Portuguese government he loathed would exploit such renown. Nonetheless, his reputation and readership continued to grow, in Portuguese-speaking countries and elsewhere, and a 1973 UNESCO survey found that his *Jungle* was one of the ten most popular books in the world.

During these last years of his life, depressed by the apparent immortality of Salazar and his government, Ferreira de Castro appears to have seen Brazil as the one last hope for progress and change in the Portuguese-speaking world. He visited Brazil in 1959 and was lionized by the literary world there. His books had always been extremely popular in Brazil, despite the highly negative vision of both the Amazon and São Paulo found in *Jungle* and *Emigrants,* and he used his 1959 visit to assure Brazilians that his criticisms were directed at specific forms of economic oppression that had long since come to an end.

This trip back to Brazil also encouraged Ferreira de Castro to write a new novel, his first in over a decade. *O instinto supremo* (The Supreme Instinct, 1968) is Ferreira de Castro's last novel. Like his first two major texts, *Jungle* and *Emigrants,* it is set in Brazil. The theme, however, is not the exploitation of immigrants or rubber workers; *O instinto supremo* is a fictionalized account of a real event, an expedition of the Brazilian Indian Protection Service organized by Colonel Cândido Rondon, who dedicated his life to preserving Brazil's native populations from cultural destruction and economic exploitation. This novel was extremely well received in Brazil, and when Ferreira de Castro returned in 1971, the government announced that a stretch of the Transamazonian Highway would be given his name. There is more than a little irony in this homage, since the construction of that highway has led to the forced assimilation of the Indian populations in its path, the elimination of their way of life, and massive destruction of the environment.

In April 1974 Ferreira de Castro closely followed the exciting and tumultuous series of events that led, at long last, to the end of the right-wing dictatorship that had ruled Portugal for almost fifty years, for almost all of his adult life. He was increasingly weak and suffered a stroke in early June 1974, but the April Revolution brought back all of his dreams of a new age, a new Portugal. "When we realize that our horizons are shutting down," he wrote a friend,

> one cannot set down words like these without strong feelings of sadness. I feel so much fraternal affection for my friends, an affection that is tinged, right now, with intense nostalgia. But I want to tell my friends that I am deeply comforted, as I come face to face with the idea of death, by my absolute certainty that a society of love and justice for all human beings will inevitably come to exist—and that society has been the constant and paramount aspiration of my life.

Ferreira de Castro died in Oporto on 29 June 1974.

The essence of Ferreira de Castro's life and writings is his status as an emigrant. His childhood exile to Brazil is paralleled by his virtual absence from Portugal and its literary world after 1936. His fiction is marked by an equally fundamental if less obvious movement away from his roots, experiences, and natural subject matter.

Our comprehension of this movement is clouded by the novelist's insistence, echoed and reinforced by his admirers, on the autobiographical nature of much of his fiction. This insistence is in large measure a red herring, designed to awaken our sympathy for the author and for the travails of his early life. Its stress on the uniqueness of Ferreira de Castro, as a product of rural poverty, minimal education, and the trauma of exile, makes it far more difficult to perceive that Ferreira de Castro the writer is not at all unique. He is, rather, a very typical Portuguese intellectual of the twentieth century.

Ferreira de Castro's early works, those published before *Emigrants* and excluded from his collected works, are almost impossible to obtain. What we know of those works, however, defines what might be called the original Ferreira de Castro. The essays and stories published in *Mas . . .* in 1921, seven years before *Emigrants,* are the product of a writer who is not yet in full control of the necessary literary techniques. The stories are often melodramatic, weak both in plot and characterization; the essays are poorly argued and somewhat shrill in tone. Nonetheless, the Ferreira de Castro we glimpse through the pages of *Mas . . .* is clearly a writer with an intense ideological commitment to Portugal's rural and urban proletariat and to a program of social and political change. If we look back even further, to *Criminoso por ambição* (1916), we find a quite dreadful novel, the work of a teenager who has read too much bad naturalistic fiction, which nonetheless deals directly and openly with experiences that appear in general to duplicate episodes drawn from Ferreira de Castro's life in the Amazon area.

Emigrants is quite unlike these early works, in both technique and attitude. Part of the enormous change this novel represents, when compared to the early works, is undoubtedly owing to Ferreira de Castro's despair about the prospects for rapid and radical change in Portuguese society—a reflection of the failure of the republic and the demoralization of the Portuguese Left that paved the way for the Salazar dictatorship. It also represents, however, the aspiring novelist's recognition that Portugal's tiny reading public, drawn from the elite and from the middle class, was simply not prepared to accept the ideology and approaches to national reality found in his earlier, largely unsuccessful writings.

Emigrants, then, is autobiographical only because its central character emigrates to Brazil—not to the Amazon, but to the state of São Paulo. It does not seek to idealize or even to identify with the main character. The novelist stands back from the text, with the careful impartiality of the journalist or the documentary filmmaker. It is not a call for change, finally, but a rationalization of the impossibility of change.

The main character of *Emigrants*—and both the title of the book and frequent authorial asides in the text suggest that we are to take this character as a symbol of all European immigrants to the New World—is Manuel da Bouça, an illiterate peasant from Ferreira de Castro's home area in Portugal. The first pages of the text are a lyrical evocation of the landscape there, and appear designed to suggest that Manuel da Bouça, the impoverished tiller of several unproductive strips of farm land, has a special and admirable understanding of that landscape. Within a very few pages, however, we discover that Manuel is, quite simply, a loser. He is forty-one years old, stupid, highly opinionated, filled with irrational illusions about himself and his future, and just this side of simpleminded. His decision to emigrate is not presented as the inevitable response to an archaic and intolerable social and economic system that pushed hundreds of thousands of Portuguese peasants off the land and into exile; it is, rather, the idiosyncratic product of his greed and pigheadedness. He mortgages his small holdings and deserts his wife and daughter to go to Brazil, convinced that he will return, in a matter of months, as a wealthy man.

The rest of the novel is almost without suspense; we know that Manuel da Bouça is a loser, and Ferreira de Castro simply reaffirms that conclusion with additional examples in different settings. The voice of the omniscient third-person narrator is gratingly intrusive and patronizing, mentioning the rather stereotypical virtues (such as physical strength and resilience) of Manuel and the other immigrants who have come to Brazil from all over Europe, but stressing their stupidity, provincialism, and capacity for self-delusion. Whenever the plot places Manuel da Bouça in a situation charged with real emotion—such as when he briefly falls in love with a mulatto woman, Benvinda, and shows both unexpected tenderness toward her and unexpected guilt about his infidelity, or when he learns, some years later, that his wife has died in his absence—the narrator suddenly falls silent, declining to describe the positive human feelings of his character. The only other voice we hear is that of Manuel da Bouça himself, in his conversations and in his interior monologues, and that voice is almost invariably petulant, small-minded, cowardly, and sullen.

Needless to say, Manuel da Bouça does not prosper in Brazil. Overwhelmed in turn by Oporto, Lisbon, the steamer and the ocean, Rio de Janeiro, and São Paulo, he winds up working for next to nothing on a coffee plantation in the interior of the state of São Paulo. After about a year on the land, he goes back to the city of São Paulo, where he spends some eight years as a manual laborer. He works hard but never manages to earn enough to return to Portugal.

Manuel is saved, rather melodramatically, by a short-lived and unsuccessful revolution in São Paulo. He is too stupid to understand the issues in this struggle, and only peer pressure overcomes his natural cowardice, but during his one night of action, he comes across a fresh corpse and strips it of its jewelry. The proceeds pay his passage home on a steamer crammed with other failed immigrants, "the load of weary, near-dead human flesh that America was handing back to Europe—the people no one wanted, who trailed from one hemisphere to the other, despised and rejected by their fellows."

Manuel da Bouça hires a car to return to his old village, desperately pretending even to his daughter that he has come back a rich man. He finds that many friends and neighbors have died or emigrated, but that those who remained are at least as well off as those who left. He, on the other hand, has lost his lands, his wife, his ties to his daughter and her family, his strength, and his self-respect. The show of his triumphant return has used up all of his capital, and he cannot even afford to buy the cemetery plot that holds his wife's body. At the end of the novel, Manuel secretly catches a bus to Lisbon, prepared to toil and die there in anonymity.

The moral of this depressing tale was very clear to Ferreira de Castro and to his Portuguese readers. The nation's rural poor, the novelist's family, his childhood neighbors, were poor in large measure because they deserved to be so, predestined to failure by ignorance and temperament. Emigration was not a symptom of a failed social and economic order in Portugal, but the inevitable result of the avarice and stupidity of the lower classes. Society might be unfair and unjust, not just in Portugal, but throughout the entire world, but did Manuel da Bouça and his fellows really deserve fairness, and could they comprehend justice?

Similar reactions to Ferreira de Castro's comforting conclusions help explain the success of *Emigrants* outside Portugal. His readers, after all, were not impoverished and illiterate emigrants; they were the comfortable and literate citizens of nations that exported or imported human beings and who had occasionally wondered just who the emigrants were and what the experience was really like. Ferreira de Castro answered these questions in a most comforting, nonthreatening way. Equally important, the validity of his answers was guaranteed, in every translation of the novel I have seen, by a preface or note describing the author's personal experience with emigration.

Jungle is considerably more interesting as a novel. The characters are slightly less stereotypical, and the plot contains elements of suspense impossible in the context of Manuel da Bouça's predestined failure. It again deals with a Portuguese immigrant to Brazil, this time to the Amazon area where Ferreira de Castro spent much of his youth. This character, Alberto, is a young man who works as a latex collector and bookkeeper on a rubber plantation.

While *Jungle* clearly draws upon Ferreira de Castro's memories of life on a very similar plantation, he nonetheless carefully sets himself at a distance from his narrative. As in *Emigrants,* there is a third-person narrator, and most of the text is devoted to descriptions of the setting and characters. Moreover, the central figure in the novel is very different from the Ferreira de Castro who lived and worked in the "green hell" of the Amazon. Alberto is around twenty years old, well bred and well educated (he has completed four years of law school in Portugal), and is in Brazil only because he participated in a failed monarchist revolt against the republic and was forced to flee. While some of Alberto's experiences may duplicate those of Ferreira de Castro, the young man's reactions are not those of a barely literate boy of thirteen. Rather, they represent the novelist's conclusions about the probable reactions, in the same circumstances, of the educated readers he was endeavoring to reach.

The pace of *Jungle* is very slow, meandering like some small backwater of the vast Amazon River. About the first third of the book takes Alberto from the port city of Belém to the rubber plantation in the interior. This section has almost no plot and is simply a travel narrative that describes strange and exotic landscapes. Ferreira de Castro goes to considerable lengths to present interesting details about the flora and fauna of the area. He also spends a number of pages recounting the history of rubber extraction in the Amazon and discussing the sharp decline in prices—the result of competition from British plantations in Malaya—in the years just before 1914. Furthermore, in a very typically Portuguese idealization of a more glorious past, he devotes particular attention to the heroic history of early Iberian expeditions up the Amazon and its tributaries.

The second third of the novel is equally slow-paced and documentary. Once Alberto reaches the "Paradise" plantation owned by Juca Tristão, he is sent off into the depths of the jungle to learn his new trade and environment. Through Alberto's experiences, and in almost overwhelming detail, we learn exactly how rubber is extracted and prepared for processing, how the Brazilian plantations were organized, what the debt-slave *seringueiros* (latex collectors) wore and ate and drank. We also get an insider's view of the mysteries and perils of the jungle and a carefully constructed year-long cycle of seasonal changes and activities.

On the boat that delivered him to "Paradise," Alberto did his best to distance himself from the other workers, almost all of them refugees from harsh droughts in the semiarid Brazilian state of Ceará. He generally avoided their company, and he wore his suit and tie to prove his superiority. Neither his clothes nor his pride survive his year as a *seringueiro.* He struggles to learn the complex tasks he must accomplish, and within the context of his new environment, he is an incompetent novice, very much the inferior of his only two companions in a tiny encampment surrounded by the jungle. These two *seringueiros,* both from Ceará and the products of a world of poverty, ignorance, and violence entirely outside Alberto's experience, are somewhat stereotypically designed to represent the Good Savage and the Bad Savage. Agostinho is violent and sex crazed—he copulates with the overseer's mare and lusts after a nine-year-old girl, murdering her father when he objects—but Ferreira de Castro avoids dis-

tinguishing between the effects of breeding and environment in Agostinho's case. Alberto's mentor is Firmino, a mulatto who is noble, wise, and self-sacrificing. His example breaks down Alberto's prejudices and preconceptions, and Firmino's lessons about plants, animals, and Indians make up most of this section of the text.

The actual plot of the novel is developed only in the final third of the text. Alberto, still inefficient as a *seringueiro,* is promoted to assistant bookkeeper for the plantation. His service in the owner's mansion enables him to comprehend the injustice of the whole system.

> There were the bills, showing that Juca Tristão had bought for five what he sold to the *seringueiros* for fifteen, often even for twenty. There were the receipts for the rubber, bought from the *seringueiros* for two and sold for five or six in Manaus. . . . These discoveries, these numbers and contrasts, were painful. Absolute power, whether by inheritance or other means; to serve one man, all the rest sacrificed themselves.
>
> (chap. 10)

Little more than a year before, as he began his voyage up the Amazon, Alberto had "smiled deprecatingly as he thought about the apostles of democracy, the defenders of human equality he had fought against, and by whom he had been cast into exile. . . . Only natural selection, only castes with hereditary privileges and the wealth of aristocratic families, high on the evolutionary scale—these alone could raise the masses to a higher level."

Despite, or perhaps because of, Alberto's new understanding of the evils of capitalism and oppression, he is much happier as a bookkeeper than as a *seringueiro.* He has his own room, good food, and a safe and relatively easy job. He learns that the Portuguese republic has declared amnesty for its enemies, and his mother sends him enough money to pay off his debts and buy a passage home. He still feels enough solidarity with Firmino to help the *seringueiro* escape from "Paradise," but he is terrified that Juca Tristão will discover this aid and sabotage his plans to return to Portugal. Firmino and a handful of other fugitives are recaptured, chained in a shed, and tortured by Juca Tristão, but Alberto does nothing to help his friend.

In an unexpected and highly melodramatic ending, old Tiago, a former slave and Juca Tristão's only real friend on the plantation, locks the owner inside the mansion and then sets it on fire. Tiago readily confesses to Juca's murder, but explains that he could not bear to see the *seringueiros* treated like slaves. Ferreira de Castro endeavors to imply, as the novel ends abruptly, that some fundamental change has taken place through this purification by fire, but the only evidence he provides is Alberto's decision not to serve as a prosecuting attorney once he returns to Portugal and finishes law school.

Furthermore, the novel's explicit stress on the development of human solidarity—seen in Alberto's understanding of the exploitation of the *seringueiros,* his decision to help Firmino escape, and Tiago's desire to free capitalism's new slaves—is undercut by several elements within this third section. First, Alberto's discovery of social and economic injustice is trivialized by his almost simultaneous discovery that the puzzle competitions run by Brazilian newspapers, competitions he assiduously enters, are invariably fixed. More important, the basis for much of the plot development in the third part of the text is not ideology or economics, but sex. The plantation is a world almost without women. While Ferreira de Castro carefully evades the question of homosexuality, which historical and sociological evidence suggests was widespread among *seringueiros,* he describes the effects of Alberto's sexual frustration in considerable detail, and from a decidedly naturalistic point of view. Sexual desire is the great leveler when seen in these terms, and Alberto the fastidious bookkeeper is reduced by its power to little more than an animal as he tries and fails to seduce a scrawny, ugly, and very old black maid.

The philosophy Alberto derives from his sexual frustration—"It was all filth. Even Nature itself was a big piece of filth"—runs contrary both to Ferreira de Castro's descriptions of the vast and terrifying beauty of the Amazon and to his frequent allusions to human equality and fraternity as the solutions to social injustice. In the somewhat pretentious preface to *Jungle,* he dedicates the novel to "my comrades, my brothers" in the Amazon. But while the ideological progression of the text suggests that Alberto, exposed to Firmino and the other "humbly heroic" *seringueiros,* comes to believe in the basic goodness of humanity, the hero's degradation by the power of sexual desire implies not that all men are inherently good, but that all, even well-bred Portuguese law students, are equally evil.

Implicit in this intensely negative view of human nature is a vision of society that directly contradicts Ferreira de Castro's explicit condemnation of economic oppression: men oppress themselves, men are enslaved by their own nature. And this contradiction, ironically, is perhaps the basis for the broad appeal of *Jungle.* The novel can be read, by those so disposed, as a cry for justice and solidarity; it can also be read as an exemplary tale of the dark forces within human nature, forces that must be rigidly controlled by society, government, and religion. Both viewpoints are supported by the text, whose authenticity—like that of *Emigrants*—is guaranteed by Ferreira de Castro's claims that it is based on his own experiences.

Ferreira de Castro's third major novel, *Eternidade,* is quite different from *Emigrants* and *Jungle,* but the novelist made a similar effort to validate it as an autobiographical text. It was written on the island of Madeira as Ferreira de Castro was recovering from the death of Diana de Liz and from his own serious illness; the hero—and Juvenal, unlike Manuel da Bouça and Alberto, is a real hero—goes to Madeira to recuperate after the death of his mother.

In reality, however, the autobiographical elements in *Eternidade* are rather limited. Ferreira de Castro utilized his knowledge of the landscape of Madeira. He also undoubtedly duplicated his own existential doubts during this period of his life in the weakest sections of the text, Juvenal's interminable philosophical speculations about the meaning of life, the nature of man and God, and the purpose of death. Nonetheless, the distance between novelist and text is considerable, and *Eternidade* may well owe as much to the influence of the novels of André Malraux as to autobiography.

Juvenal is a member of the Portuguese elite, a wealthy young engineer. After his mother's death he goes to Madeira and takes a job supervising the workers in a large-scale reforestation project. As in the earlier novels, the plot moves slowly, weighted down by description and, above all, by Juvenal's efforts to make some sense of his grief and by the existential impotence that arises from the sudden realization of his own mortality. He attempts to assuage this philosophical impotence through sex, but his brief and loveless contacts have no meaning for him.

The answer, Juvenal eventually realizes, is not sex; it can be found only in solidarity, in love, and in direct and united action against the forces of oppression. He encourages the workers he is supervising to protest their exploitation, and he leads their revolt. He is wounded, arrested, and finally deported to a prison colony in the Cape Verde Islands. None of this matters, in Ferreira de Castro's view, because the cause for which Juvenal sacrifices himself is worthy and because grief has led the hero to realize that, although human existence is transitory, the world as a whole inevitably improves with each generation. Elizabeth, a woman Juvenal met in London, comes to join him in Cape Verde after his imprisonment and reveals that she is carrying his child. This, for Juvenal, is the final proof that existence is not in vain. "The world will get better and better," he tells Elizabeth, "and we must teach our child to love Humanity and to have high hopes for life. He will carry our spirit onward."

Ferreira de Castro made it clear in the preface to *Eternidade* that he, like Juvenal, believed absolutely in the coming world of fraternity and intelligence, where the inequities, the useless sorrows, and the absurdities that today stain and diminish the original beauty of the world will no longer exist. I know that this world, created by human evolution, opened up by the genius of our species, will come to be; I know that we will take control of the universe, that we will learn all its secrets and its laws, that we will become the masters of life and the conquerors of death.

There is no question about the sincerity of Ferreira de Castro's belief in the coming millennium, a belief shared, even in the depths of a worldwide depression, by many intellectuals on both sides of the Atlantic. The problem is that *Eternidade,* however useful to the novelist as personal catharsis, is more travelogue, documentary, and philosophical tract than effective fiction. The problems it raises are very much part of the present—exploitation, authoritarian rule, injustice; the solutions it offers are all quite nebulous and very far in the future. It is hard indeed to argue that Juvenal's sacrifice made any difference at all. It may, in fact, have made things worse for the workers he sought to unite and save. Thus *Eternidade,* like *Jungle,* can be read both as a paean to the possibility of change and as a document that asserts the impossibility or the counterproductivity of change.

The next two novels Ferreira de Castro published, *Terra fria* and *A tempestade,* are his least successful works. He spent months in a small village in the poorest area of northern Portugal researching *Terra fria,* endeavoring in some way to recapture his roots among the rural peasantry. This effort was a failure. The famous and prosperous novelist had seemingly lost the ability to identify with characters presented as almost uniformly ignorant, illiterate, and immoral. And while the text documents the horrors of peasant life and insists upon the need for change, the one concrete symbol of change—Santiago, who immigrated to the United States and returned a wealthy man—is an utter villain, far worse than the traditional aristocrats he has replaced.

Nor, despite considerable effort, could Ferreira de Castro successfully shift from documentary and philosophical social realism to the nonideological psychological drama of an unhappy middle-class marriage, as he attempted in *A tempestade.* The characters and the plot are unconvincing, and the banality of the Lisbon setting makes it painfully obvious that the exotic locations of his early works were essential to their success.

Ferreira de Castro largely abandoned Portugal and fiction for a number of years while he published his travel narratives. He returned to the novel in 1947 with *A lã e a neve.* This text represents a considerable improvement over the earlier novels. It is less descriptive and preachy than *Eternidade* but expresses many of the same themes and ideas. One reason for the success of the novel is that Ferreira de Castro solves two troublesome technical problems. First, the workers at the woolen mill that is the focus of much of the action are already converted to the need for change, eliminating the need for pages of political oratory and philosophical exposition. Second, Ferreira de Castro recognized that the central figures of his earlier novels were flawed: Manuel da Bouça is an authentic proletarian, but is too weak to be a hero and too stupid and uneducated to present the author's ideas; Alberto and Juvenal, intelligent and educated members of the middle class, do speak for the author, but neither is a heroic representative of the common man. In *A lã e a neve,* Ferreira de Castro found a remedy by including both a lower-class hero, Horácio, as a focal figure in the action, and an intellectual spokesman, Marreta, who conveys the novel's ideological message.

Horácio, a poor shepherd, returns from military service and dreams of improving his status. He manages to move to a small city, where he works as an apprentice and then a weaver in the wool mill. He marries, has children, and slowly comes to the realization that the change from shepherd to weaver, from agriculture to industry, has in no way improved the quality of his life. Horácio is a far more sympa-

thetic character than Manuel da Bouça or the peasants in *Terra fria,* and we come to care about his problems and to sympathize with his desire to take action and force necessary changes.

Horácio's friend and mentor, Marreta, is a self-educated intellectual—Ferreira de Castro's vision, perhaps, of what he might have become had he stayed in Ossela. He is a socialist, an apostle of human dignity and labor solidarity, and he helps organize Horácio and the other weavers into a union. Marreta's passion is Esperanto, the "universal" language, and this passion symbolized his absolute belief in the equality of all men.

Horácio and the other weavers eventually go on strike. The strike fails and Marreta dies, but the impact of his sacrifice is much stronger and more concrete than that of Juvenal. The workers have learned solidarity, and they will keep on struggling until conditions improve. Moreover, while they hold to Marreta's belief in the eventual arrival of the millennium of brotherhood and progress, they are also convinced, rightly or wrongly, that the end of World War II will inevitably change their world in concrete ways.

After *A lã e a neve* Ferreira de Castro's literary emigration from Portugal became complete; he did not publish another major piece of fiction set in his native country. The war ended, the allied forces of Soviet Russia and the Western democracies defeated fascism—and Salazar's reactionary and dictatorial regime continued unchanged. Ferreira de Castro, depressed by this continuity, appears to have begun to question the noble ideals he had set forth in *Eternidade* and *A lã e a neve.* By distancing himself from events in Portugal, he sought to discover the real viability of those ideals. This new, slightly cynical attitude allowed him, for the first time in his career, to focus on fiction as a literary construct rather than as a vehicle for description and ideology.

A curva da estrada is Ferreira de Castro's account of Spanish politics in the period just before the 1936–1939 civil war. He had been in

Spain during this period, and his wife's family had important and useful connections, particularly on the Republican side. The novel displays an almost encyclopedic knowledge of the details of Spanish life and politics during this period, but all of this information is used to explain the characters and advance the plot. Ferreira de Castro manages to create real and believable characters whose philosophies and ideologies are an integral part of their personalities rather than intellectual projections of the novelist.

This is particularly evident in the case of the central character, Soriano, a weary and disillusioned middle-aged man who also happens to be a leading socialist politician. It is hard not to see a good deal of Ferreira de Castro in Soriano—an ideologue and a fighter in his youth, a man now deeply disappointed by the failure of his dreams of a better world and therefore distrustful of all ideology.

This crisis of the spirit leads Soriano to an astonishing decision: he will leave the Socialist party and join its bitter enemies, the reactionary Nationalists. Soriano's son, Enrique, and his best friend, Pepe Martínez, spend three days struggling to convince the hero that he is wrong, that socialism is still the best of a rather bad lot of options for attaining a better world and a more just society. They urge him not to turn his back on the essence of his whole existence, his political leadership of the socialists. As the three men argue, we come to know them as people, not as spokesmen for various ideological and philosophical approaches. Moreover, as the argument progresses, Soriano drifts in and out of the present, flashing back to the past as he tries to understand the path that has taken him from youthful certainty to his present disillusionment.

Equally astonishing as Soriano's decision to forsake socialism is Ferreira de Castro's subtle and ironic resolution of the conflict. Soriano cannot recover his faith in socialism, but neither is he prepared to harm the cause to which he has devoted much of his life, a cause in which his son and his friend still believe. He

had come to believe that he was at a crossroads, compelled to make a choice between past and future, Left and Right. Instead, he realizes that the past and a momentary present are all that remain for him, and he decides simply to step off the road as it slowly curves its way toward the future, to retire from politics, to leave the future to those who still care about it.

The technical and ideological sophistication and the ironic cynicism found in *A curva da estrada* are even more evident in Ferreira de Castro's short novel *The Mission*. This is by far his best work, more realistic and more convincing than any of his other fiction. The setting is a monastery in a small French town. Description is limited, but precise and carefully chosen. The main characters, a small group of Catholic missionaries, are deftly sketched. This is not a travelogue, documentary, or philosophical or political tract; it is a subtle and tightly constructed novel of character that illuminates a moral dilemma.

It is just days before the German invasion of France, and the superior of the monastery orders the caretaker to paint the word "mission" on the roof in large white letters. This was common practice at the time, since such signs were generally respected by German bombers. One of the missionaries, Father George Mournier, objects. He has noticed that the other large building in the town, a factory that employs hundreds of workers and is a natural target for the Germans, is architecturally identical to the monastery. If the German bombers come, the painted sign on the monastery roof will direct them to the factory and ensure the deaths of its workers. Thirteen men live and work in the monastery; some four hundred men work in the factory, supporting the families housed in the hovels that surround it.

The superior almost immediately understands that Mournier's objection raises issues that are extraordinarily complex and dangerous. He therefore calls a meeting of all the missionaries, asking them to debate the question and to advise him. Mournier argues in favor of human solidarity, urging his colleagues to leave the matter in the hands of the God to whom they have devoted their lives, who will decide where the bombs fall. Several other missionaries assert that their lives, as dedicated servants of God and mankind, are necessarily of more value than the lives of the factory workers. Moreover, their mission is not to save lives, but to save souls. It is clear to the superior that few of the thirteen support Father Mournier, but the debate has awakened, in his own mind, questions and fears long repressed during his rise through hierarchy of the church. He feels unable to make the decision himself, and postpones the issue by writing the provincial of the order for advice.

While the superior waits for guidance, the issues raised by Mournier slowly undermine the collective solidarity of the mission. Face to face with the inevitable human resistance to martyrdom and the natural imperative to survive, the missionaries become individuals rather than members of a disciplined order. Long-submerged personal differences begin subtly to divide them. The provincial's reply is delayed, and the members of the community become increasingly frightened and rebellious. When the reply finally arrives, ordering the painting of the roof of the monastery, the superior betrays the trust of his flock by keeping it secret as he tries to work through his own convictions and experiences and discover what is right. The terrified missionaries rebel, forcing the superior's hand, and Father Mournier, unable to accept this outcome, decides to leave the monastery and the order. But before the roof can be painted, France surrenders and the invading Germans occupy the town and commandeer the monastery as their barracks. In order to protect his troops from enemy bombers, the German captain immediately orders that the word "mission" be painted on the roof.

This summary of the plot of *The Mission* barely scratches the surface of its tightly structured complexity. The conflict it sets forth is not simplistically defined as a struggle between good and evil, between natural faith and a church grown rigid, self-seeking, and excessively comfortable. The character at the center of the text is not Father Mournier, still young, idealistic, and sure of himself. Rather, it is Ferreira de Castro's projection of his own doubts as embodied in the superior, a good man whose vocation has often isolated him from human emotions and human needs, whose privileged position has often insulated him from human suffering. The superior slowly and painfully comes to see all sides of the central dilemma as he questions his most basic assumptions, and his failure to reach a decision is owing not to cowardice but to his understanding that life itself is a dilemma incapable of resolution.

It was fourteen years before Ferreira de Castro published *O instinto supremo,* his last work of fiction and one that is far less successful as fiction than either *A curva da estrada* or *The Mission.* Set in Brazil, *O instinto supremo* is a slightly fictionalized account of a real event, a mission whose purpose was to make contact with and civilize a tribe of Indians, the Parintintins. This is the same tribe that terrorized the *seringueiros* in *Jungle*—as they undoubtedly terrified Ferreira de Castro as a boy—and Firmino mentions the mission itself to Alberto. The leader of the expedition and the hero of Ferreira de Castro's narrative, Curt Nimuendajú, is a historical figure, a German named Kurt Unkle who devoted his life to Brazil's Indians. Other members of the expedition appear to be Ferreira de Castro's own creations. The narrator presents a great deal of fascinating information about the environment, Indian life and culture, and Colonel Cândido Rondon's remarkable efforts to preserve both the land and its inhabitants. The novelist has clearly done his research. This documentary travelogue is interspersed with brief moments of exciting action and a great deal of discussion among members of the mission about the nature of progress, the value of civilization, the importance of the environment, and the need for intercultural communication and solidarity.

This last novel, then, represents a turn away

from the technical sophistication and ideological questioning of the two previous works. Like the handful of interviews and speeches Ferreira de Castro gave in the last years of his life, the novel is filled with the sort of high-minded declarations—about the future millennium of peace and justice and about the importance of brotherhood and love in attaining that goal—that weighted down earlier novels like *Eternidade*. Perhaps, as Salazar aged and his regime lost support, both inside Portugal and within the western alliance, all of Ferreira de Castro's old hopes for the future of Portugal and of humanity came back to the surface. Or perhaps he simply concluded that he could not survive psychologically without those dreams, the one constant in his many migrations and his only protection against the unanswerable questions pondered by the superior in *The Mission*.

Selected Bibliography

EDITIONS

INDIVIDUAL WORKS

PROSE NARRATIVES AND NOVELS
Criminoso por ambição. Belém, 1916.
Rugas sociais. Belém, 1918.
O êxito fácil. Lisbon, 1923.
Sangue negro. Lisbon, 1923.
A morte redimida. Oporto, 1925.
Sendas de lirismo e de amor. Lisbon, 1925.
A peregrina do mundo novo. Lisbon, 1926.
O drama da sombra. Lisbon, 1926?
A casa dos móveis dourados. Lisbon, 1927.
O voo nas trevas. Oporto, 1927.
Emigrantes. Lisbon, 1928.
A selva. Oporto, 1930.
Eternidade. Lisbon, 1933.
Terra fria. Lisbon, 1934.
A tempestade. Lisbon, 1940.
A lã e a neve. Lisbon, 1947.
A curva da estrada. Lisbon, 1950.
A missão. Lisbon, 1954.

O instinto supremo. Lisbon, 1968.
Os fragmentos. Lisbon, 1974.
O intervalo. Lisbon, 1974.

NONFICTION
Mas . . . . Lisbon, 1921.
Pequenos mundos e velhas civilizações. Lisbon, 1937.
A volta ao mundo. Lisbon, 1944.
As maravilhas artísticas do mundo. 2 vols. Lisbon, 1958–1963.

COLLECTED WORKS
Obra completa. 3 vols. Rio de Janeiro, 1958–1961.

MODERN EDITIONS

A curva da estrada. Lisbon, 1982.
Emigrantes. Lisbon, 1980.
A lã e a neve. Lisbon, 1982.
A missão. Lisbon, 1981.
A selva. Lisbon, 1984.
A tempestade. Lisbon, 1984.
Viageiro no mundo, conhecedor dos homens. Lisbon, 1980. An anthology.

TRANSLATIONS

Emigrants: A Novel. Translated by Dorothy Ball. New York, 1962.
Jungle: A Tale of the Amazon Rubber-Tappers. Translated by Charles Duff. London, 1934; New York, 1935.
The Mission. Translated by Ann Stevens. London, 1963.

BIOGRAPHICAL AND CRITICAL STUDIES

Brasil, Jaime. "Ferreira de Castro." *Books Abroad* 31:117–121 (1957).
——— . *Ferreira de Castro.* Lisbon, 1961.
Ellison, Fred P. "The Myth of the Destruction and Re-creation of the World in Ferreira de Castro's *A Selva.*" *Luso-Brazilian Review* 15 (supplementary volume): 101–109 (1978).
Franco, Georgenor. *Ferreira de Castro e a Amazônia.* Belém, 1983.

JOSÉ MARIA FERREIRA DE CASTRO

Gillespie, John C. "O conceito da fraternidade na obra de Ferreira de Castro." *Ocidente* 74:169–173 (1968).

Megenney, William. "Descriptive Sensationism in Ferreira de Castro." *Romance Notes* 13:61–66 (1971).

Moreira, Alberto. *Ferreira de Castro: Antes da glória.* Oporto, 1959.

Ornelas, José N. "Do Inferno ao Paraíso: A jornada de Juvenal em *Eternidade* de Ferreira de Castro." *Hispania* 65:180–186 (1982).

Salema, Álvaro. *Ferreira de Castro.* Lisbon, 1974.

DAVID T. HABERLY

FEDERICO GARCÍA LORCA

(1898–1936)

HE WAS LOVED by intellectuals, who endlessly interpreted his poems, and by illiterate farmers, who sang them. Even Spanish officialdom for a long time tolerated his sexual and social viewpoints. His work could be oblique and obscure, but when he was playful or indignant, he was brilliantly clear. His voice could be subtle and soft, but about suffering it rang out as loud as the fascist guns that executed him.

In the thirty-eight years of his life, he wrote ten long plays, numerous one-act plays, six major books of poetry, over a thousand other poems, a book of narrations, and critical essays. Many of his works are still hidden. All this literary activity took place while he carried on as theater director, producer, and designer. He composed and arranged music, painted, and took a graduate degree in law. He lectured all over Spain, South America, Cuba, and the United States. A literary celebrity at home, he studied a year at Columbia University and wrote his excoriating *Poeta en Nueva York* (*Poet in New York,* published in 1940), which prophesied the fall of Wall Street in 1929 and the racial revolution of the 1960's.

His many letters reveal a man whose charm was justifiably legendary. He also could be coy, cajoling, exacting, cynical, silly, and impossible. A long-overdue letter of his begins, "Late, but on time." Still, no matter what he did, said, or wrote, he never lacked humor and intelligence. No one, friend or foe, denied his endlessly varied talents.

Lorca's work brims with sex, death, nature, unnaturalness, love, mysticism, spells, and cures for which there are no known diseases. He admits being influenced by nursery rhymes, lullabies, folk songs, peasant language, Eliot, Keats, Synge, Whitman, Góngora, Cervantes, and Quevedo. He beautifies a hunchbacked painter in his essay on her work; he writes a poem to the crazed daughter of Ferdinand and Isabella, Juana, who lived with her husband's corpse.

He was a traditional, classical, modern postmodernist. He was radical yet not political. He wrote, "I am an anarchist, communist, monarchist, socialist." His religion is "Muslim-Jewish-Christian-Atheist." He seems to have been everything but bigoted.

For sheer range of work, he rivals Bernard Shaw and Robert Graves. His appreciation is worldwide. Juan Ramón Jiménez was said to have received the 1956 Nobel Prize partly on behalf of Lorca. Critical and biographical works have never ceased appearing in the fifty years since his murder. A bibliography of translations alone would fill a volume.

As a child in Granada, Lorca entertained his family with imitations of the best show in town: the Mass. He would conscript his younger brother and sisters into the production by having them perform the roles of acolytes and confessors. The maid was his costume designer. His father, a cigar-smoking, macho farmer, spent long days on horseback overseeing his vast Andalusian holdings. His mother, a former schoolteacher, spent endless hours with Federico, who needed special care because of an infantile affliction (probably poliomyelitis) that left him weak for years to come. He also had another anomaly worthy of special handling: he was a prodigy.

His mother taught him the rudiments of literature, music, and painting. Before his feet could reach the pedals, he was composing simple tunes on the family piano. The great maestro Manuel de Falla (a Granadan) later encouraged his arrangements of the local folk songs that he took seriously the rest of his life, using them as the basis of three books: *Poema del cante jondo* (*Deep Song,* 1931), *Canciones (1921–1924)* (*Songs,* 1927), and *Romancero gitano* (*Gypsy Ballads,* 1928). As for painting, his exhibitions were taken quite seriously by the important artistic communities in Barcelona and Madrid.

Lucky poet, his family was not only well heeled but well situated. Lorca grew up in Granada, a collage of Muslim-Arab-Hebraic-Christian traditions in art and thought. Every famous artist passed through. Debussy and Ravel composed there. Intellectuals from all over the world came to sit in the café and join "the circle" to discuss art and ideas. And Granada itself is in the province of Andalusia, where Seneca and Martial lived during the Roman Empire; where Moses Maimonides and Averroës later produced secular and theological masterworks of philosophy.

Thus far Lorca does not make a very interesting protagonist: his warm, uncomplicated family life, the mutual love between himself and his siblings, their gruff but interested father, and the complete lack of financial difficulties do not make for exciting dramatic action, as drawing-room plays adequately demonstrate. But one day something so melodramatically symbolic occurred that no dramatist would sink to dramatizing it. Lorca himself tells about it in one of his lectures, "Charla sobre *Romancero gitano*" (Lecture on *Gypsy Ballads*). He recalls that one day in his childhood

home of Fuente Vaqueros, where mountain-dwelling Gypsies rode down from caves, he looked up from his book to see a poor Gypsy glaring at him in his luxury. As Federico fled from the image, he heard someone calling "Amargo"—a name meaning "bitter." Amargo apparently never reappeared, but his look and the bitter taste it left stayed with Lorca. In many bristling poems later, he tried to decipher the encounter; he became obsessed with the figure, real or not, who "wanted to drown me with his hands." He began to write.

In the formative years of his creativity, he did not plunge unequivocally into poetry. His first published work, a book of his travels called *Impresiones y paisajes* (*Impressions and Landscapes*), sounds like a collection of paintings. Its publication date is 1918, when Lorca was twenty years old. The Baedekerian work is notable mainly as an attempt to exorcise the ghosts of writers past and sorrows present:

> It is frightening, a desolate orphanage with these sad and rickety children. It fills the heart with an immense weeping and a formidable yearning for equality. Maybe someday, when the children have suffered too much injustice, the meeting-house will fall on the Municipal Board and flatten them into a big omelette, the kind the poor can't have.
>
> ("Galicia")

To understand completely Lorca's development, however, one must understand Spain's cultural crisis at the beginning of our era.

BACKGROUND

Eighteen ninety-eight was a bad year for Spanish history. While the rest of Europe and America thrived, Spain had constant social, economic, and moral crises. It was rotten at its governmental core. Its colonial edges were eroding. The great Spanish Empire was a sliver of its former grandeur. When a disorganized United States Navy managed to win Cuba and the Philippines in a battle that sank the Spanish Armada, the Spanish ego went down with it. As if Spain was not in enough trouble, that year García Lorca was born.

Eighteen ninety-eight also gave birth to a movement known as the Generation of '98. This group of artists and thinkers questioned the conquistador legacy of a machismo that had founded and ruined a couple of civilizations and was about to ruin its own.

The Generation of '98 was centered mainly in Madrid. Its members were cosmopolitan, classically trained modernists who felt that the task of influencing Spain had fallen through the ages from the iron fist of the Inquisition into the hands of intellectuals and poets. Some important members were Ortega y Gasset, Unamuno, Valle-Inclán, Gómez de la Serna, Machado, Bergamín, and Jiménez. The last two were Nobel laureates.

By the time the Generation of '98 grew up it was a legitimate entity, if not assimilated, at least tolerated. It even had an innovative effect on education. The Residencia de los Estudiantes in Madrid was open to students of arts and sciences and to professionals in the experimental stages of their careers. In 1919 Lorca left his formal studies at the University of Granada to become part of the exciting body of experimentalists at the Residencia. Here a poet, a painter, a critic, or a physicist could obtain a room, domestic help, and food well served and prepared, and lead a life generally free from any cares that might detract from a busy creative day. A resident of the Residencia didn't have to worry about changing a sheet or a light bulb. He was not even required to attend a lecture, though the best minds of Spain and Europe shared their notions and theories with the eager "students."

Lorca was not one of these. He attended few lectures and fewer conferences. Instead he read the works of the most imaginative and idiosyncratic members of his generation and sought out their company in the cafés of Madrid. He began to carouse with Rafael Alberti, the openly leftist surrealist poet, and with Luis

Buñuel, the moderately leftist surrealist film director and Salvador Dali's collaborator on *Un chien andalou,* a short surrealist film. Lorca worked on the scenario with them, but to what degree we do not know. Nor do we know how close was his collaboration with Dali.

From 1919 to 1928 Lorca enjoyed the cultural favors of the Residencia, had rich and riotous friendships, took prankish tours of high and low Madrid, drank deeply of the folklore of nearby villages (and of their grape production), recited his poems, often improvising them, to the delight of modern Madrid, and managed to write half a dozen major works. All in all, one can say that the educational experiment known as the Residencia de los Estudiantes, certainly in the case of Lorca, was a success.

The Generation of '98 proselytized. They spread the word that the word was with not God but creative man. Faith in the future of Spain would be restored by its writers. Designing the background, the artists of Catalonia built monumental prophecies to cubism, abstraction, and art deco. Picasso soon began carrying messages from Toulouse-Lautrec's Paris. Gaudi's churches featured ceramic shards, factory scrap, and sea conches in architectural collages that later affected the surrealists. Freud was showing the way to the distant landscape of the unconscious. In the secular religion of art, this became known as modernism. It was in this eccentric atmosphere that Lorca was born; when Dada began to flash its weirdness within, he did not avert his adolescent eyes.

Something was being said to someone. But what to whom? Ideas were coming down from the ether of the past to the air of fin-de-siècle Spain. It was not only the turn of a hundred-year gear, though; for the newly open-minded it was a rotation of the evolutionary wheel. They wanted the wheel to revolve smoothly, to make a comfortable cultural revolution.

Valle-Inclán, the W. C. Fields of Spanish literature, wrote, "Spain is a deformation of Europe." Gómez de la Serna's book *Senos*

(Breasts, 1917), a garden of mammary delights, indicates the kind of influence the writers of the Generation of '98 had on Lorca. They wrote and translated the literary and political manifestos that appeared constantly throughout the first quarter of the century. They hawked acmeism, bizarrism, ultraism, neosymbolism, and musical impressionism. If you ran short of inspiration one week, you wrote a manifesto. There was a mass marketing of these proclamations until surrealism knocked all other "isms" out of the box.

But the most powerful manifesto was not written; it was painted on canvas. The "ism" that endured was cubism. Cubism not only affected generations of painters, it had a great influence on writing, on the fractured imagery that mirrored the breakdown of European values and systems. Lorca was born into this. Gertrude Stein said, "Cubism could only come from Spain." It traveled well though. Cubistic imagery is Eliot's "pair of claws" crossing the ocean floor. Cummings represents cubistic syntax; Joyce, cubistic linguistics.

There is a moderate modernism perceivable through the gauzy gray of Lorca's first published poems, *Libro de poemas* (Book of Poems, 1921), which stretched from actual places to where the "indecisive phantasm / of an Augustive evening / shattered the horizon," with a bitter look that shadows most of his early poems.

In "El lagarto viejo" (The Old Lizard), "The oarless gondola of idea / crosses the tenebrous waters / of your burnt-out eyes." What can remain but sinister shade "when the sun is so sugary and soluble / it melts in the cup of the mountains" and the flocks, white as they may be, "muddy the road"? So:

> Do not bother looking
> for light in the dark.
> You will have a good place
> to look at the stars
> when the worms take their time
> to eat you . . .

No one in the fields
and the mountains extinguished
and the road deserted . . .
only from time to time
the cuckoos sing to the darkness
of the poplar trees.

But darkness does not prevent this "drop of crocodile," as Lorca calls the lizard, from

> . . . meditating
> in the green cutaway coat
> of the devil's abbot
> correct in his posture
> his collar starched
> with the very sad look
> of an emeritus professor.

Even in the dark, Lorca lets us know we should watch for a wink.

In 1924 André Breton announced in the *Manifeste du surréalisme* that through surrealism's eyes one's childhood and adulthood could be reexperienced. Lorca had de-dichotomized childhood and adulthood in this 1921 book of poems. In "Los encuentros de un caracol aventurero" (Encounters of an Adventurous Snail), a snail meets a colony of ants that has imprisoned one of its drones. The prisoner tells the snail he is being punished because he saw the stars. The other ants have stripped his antennae. What are stars, they demand. The captive ant replies:

> "I saw thousands of stars
> in my own darkness. Stars
> are lights on top of our head."
> "We don't see them," the ants retort
> and the snail, in all objectivity,
> must admit he cannot see
> above the grass.

This youthful book contains other poems of mysterious if naive charm, cunningly juxtaposed with Lorca's ever-present humor. His perverse, personal religion is heard in these first poems as well:

Christ held a reason
in evil hands
multiplying
his own specter.
Projecting his heart
into the black
gazes.
Believe!
              ("Símbolo" [Symbol])

We live
beneath a big mirror.
Man is blue!
Hosanna!
("El gran espejo" [The Big Mirror])

All is fair.
Brother, open your arms.
God is the point.
              ("Rayos" [Rays])

Adam and Eve.
The serpent
split the mirror
into a thousand pieces
and the apple
was the stone.
             ("Imitación" [Imitation])

He breaks the mirror, a faded symbol that has lost its vital quicksilver and only has behind it "a dead star . . . a mummy of the source, a conch of light / closed for the night." Official symbolism is beginning to wane. Soon González Martínez will revolt against Rubén Darío, the great symbolist idol, whose swan represented Romantic image play. Martínez writes, "Strangle the swan and its conniving plumage!" What is symbolism to one culture is, after all, reality to another. Lorca's Andalusia used the moon not as a symbol but as a calendar; the sun tells what time it is, and the sea is a washtub. Use of these as images by Andalusians was personal, experienced, unsymbolic. Lorca is in the above poem recognizing symbolism as a dim, limited reflection. He intuits symbolism's etymology: half a coin waiting for the other to give it value.

His next book, *Deep Song,* takes him toward the ultimate nonduality. Eliot's Sweeney says, "What's that life is? / Life is death." Lorca says, in effect, "Love is death." Therefore he not only endures but adores Death. Death is his natural leading lady who will remain with him until the end of the show. In "Malagueña" she is in what could be the setting of an O'Neill play:

Death
enters and exits
in this tavern.
Dark horse and sinister people
pass through the deep roads of the guitar.

There is a smell of salt
and of female blood
in the burning roses
of the navy.

Death
enters and exits
exits and enters
death
in the tavern.

Death, in the corner of the bar, sits down to watch us live it up. But her presence even in this atmosphere of sexuality makes clear that Death, Love's lover, is the star. Her dancing partner is the knife, equal in efficacy and beauty to any of man's or nature's instruments. In "Puñal" (The Dagger):

The dagger enters the heart
like the blade of a plow in the fallow earth,
like the rays of the sun setting
fire to the frightening gullies.

"Sorpresa" (Surprise) presents a street-beat, scenelike variation of the theme:

Stopped off on our street, dead
with a dagger in his breast!
Nobody knew nothing.

You should have seen the lamp post
shaking! Mother!
That little street lamp shaking!

FEDERICO GARCÍA LORCA

It was dawn. Nobody
dared to see those eyes
open in the hard night air!

Yeh, death stopped off on our street
Yeh, the dagger in the breast
Yeh, nobody knew nothing.

These are done in the plaintive modality of the "deep song" of the Andalusian Gypsies.

If Spain is the death capital of the western world, Andalusia is the Hollywood of funerals. Its dirge is the deep song, a primitive musical system originating in India and sung in Spain by Gypsies, who (Lorca tells us) brought it with them when Tamerlane raided India. In Andalusia the Gypsies combined the indigenous Iberian sounds and words with their own musical imports to give deep song its wailing, obsessive use of one note, destroying ordinary metrical rhythm. Lorca tells us this and more in "El canto jondo" ("Deep Song," 1922), an essay that reminds Spanish writers of their debt to the Gypsies for

> the creation of these songs, soul of our soul. . . . These lyrical channels through which all the pain, all the rites of the race can flow . . . and cross the cemetery of time. Deep Song comes from the first sigh. It is the living, eternal enigma posed by the Oriental Sphinx of Andalusia, an awesome riddle to be solved by death. Or Oedipus! Deep Song is a frightening blue archer who never runs out of arrows.

In short, deep song is death distilled into lyric.

Lorca's essay was written at the same time he was completing his book *Deep Song.* Here is a poem, "La Lola," that the great Gypsy singer Juan Breva could have sung. It is a woman, her past and her present:

> Lola sings flamenco.
> The little bullfighters
> circle around her.
> The little barber
> from his doorway
> follows the rhythms
> with his head.

> Between the sweet basil
> and the mint, Lola sings
> flamenco, that same Lola
> who used to see herself
> often in the puddles.

And a song about the maestro himself, in the same wistful modality:

> Juan Breva had this body of a giant
> and this little tiny girl's voice.
> Nothing like his trill. It was
> that same old song of pain
> behind a smile that
> made you think of lemon trees and
> sleeping in the south of Spain.
> And in his cry was the salt of the sea,
> like Homer, singing,
> blind. His voice had
> that something of lightless ocean
> and squeezed orange.
>
> ("Juan Breva")

Suddenly the singing stops. Amargo makes a bravura appearance with his silver dagger. Death, on a horse, approaches him, offering a trade:

> *Death:* What a beautiful knife you have. But gold knives go into the heart. Silver knives only cut the throat. Rather have mine?
> *Amargo:* Don't any knives cut bread?
> *Death:* A real man tears bread with his hands.

Amargo is reluctant to yield his dagger, which perhaps too clearly symbolizes life. So Death gives him his golden knife, the hard way.

> *Death:* Come on up! Quick! We can get to Granada before the dawn breaks. Here, take this knife I give you (stabs Amargo in the heart).

Amargo's mother sings his dirge:

> They laid him out on my bedsheet,
> on my oleanders and my palm leaves.
> The twenty-seventh day of August
> with a little knife of gold.

2172

The cross! and it was all over.
He was brown and bitter.
Neighbors, give me a copper
pitcher of lemonade.

The cross. Don't cry anyone.
Amargo is on the moon.

The poetic alchemy of Lorca transforms the symbols; it blends the gold knife with the cross, blends Amargo with the moon—and all four with Death.

While Lorca still wears his symbolist cape in *Deep Song,* he also rolls up his political sleeves. A conscience stalks the book, exploding in a short ironic play about the arrest of a Gypsy. It seems to foreshadow the black New York that Lorca will later know. Brutalized, humiliated, unable to communicate adequately, a Gypsy stands before the audience, "small, with the look of a young mule casting a shadow on the officer's insignia."

Lieutenant Colonel: I'm the Lieutenant Colonel of the Civil Guard.
Sergeant: Yes.
Lieutenant Colonel: Nobody disobeys me.
Sergeant: No.
Lieutenant Colonel: I have three stars and twenty crosses.
Sergeant: Yes.
Lieutenant Colonel: The Cardinal Archbishop said "Hello" to me, in his purple tassle.
Sergeant: Yes.
Lieutenant Colonel: I'm the lieutenant, I'm the lieutenant, I'm the Lieutenant Colonel of the Civil Guard. (Indicates the manacled Gypsy.) What's that?
Sergeant: A Gypsy.
Lieutenant Colonel (to Gypsy): I am the Lieutenant Colonel of the Civil Guard.
Gypsy: Yes.
Sergeant: I found him and brung him in.
Lieutenant Colonel: Where was he?
Sergeant: The bridge of the river.
Lieutenant Colonel: What river?
Gypsy: All the rivers!

That is, the rebellion of the Gypsies lurks in all their haunts. But the nature of the rebellion is beyond the officer's understanding. The Gypsy's revolutionary crime is making revolutionary images:

Lieutenant Colonel: What were you doing there?
Gypsy: Building a cinnamon tower.
Lieutenant Colonel: Sergeant!
Sergeant: At your service, my Lieutenant Colonel of the Civil Guard.

The Gypsy's imagery keeps attacking, sabotaging. Each image is another blow:

Gypsy: I've invented wings to fly and I fly. With sulphur and roses in my mouth.

The sulphur of guns, the roses of sex, these are more than the Civil Guard can bear.

Lieutenant Colonel: Ay!
Gypsy: I really don't need wings. I fly without them. Clouds in my blood. And smoke rings.
Lieutenant Colonel: Ayyy! (The Lieutenant Colonel begins to have a heart attack.)
Gypsy: In January I have my orange blossoms.
Lieutenant Colonel: Ayyyyy!
Gypsy: And then it is *oranges in the snow.*

The rebel image is even subverting nature. It is too much for the Lieutenant Colonel, who dies. Romeo and Juliet appear:

Romeo and Juliet: We took his soul of tobacco and coffee "with" and flew it out the window—the soul of the Lieutenant Colonel of the Civil Guard.
Sergeant: Help!!

Lorca has dramatized the relationship of surrealism to revolution. What Breton, Aragon, and Picabia talked about in their manifestos, delivered successfully in Spain, he dramatizes through poetry. It is again Lorca's instinctive way of eliminating distinctions, this time between poetry, drama, and politics—a very uneasy triumvirate. But the subject and the forms

2173

here are joined as closely as lyric to song—deep song.

Death is more than subject matter for Lorca; from his developmental period onward, Death will stalk his pages until the day he joins "the southwind flame of evil skies."

> Every afternoon is Granada
> every afternoon a child is dead.
> (*Gacela* of the Dead Child)

Lorca is separated from death by "a wall of bad dreams." He writes that even the Spanish creative force, the Duende, is Death's male counterpart: "Duende serenades Death's house and doesn't arrive until he knows Death is in. The Duende loves the lip of the wound" ("Essay on Duende").

This liaison between death and the arts is possible only in Spain "because death is a national pastime." Lorca refers not only to the bullfight ("supremely civilized festival") but also to "the ice-moon heads painted by Zurbaran, the lightning yellow of El Greco, all of Goya. . . . The painting of Death with a guitar in Medina de Rioseco." These are artistic transformations of Spain's local saints' processions (where the bones play a prominent role) and the innumerable games and rites of Good Friday, "the one day the Spanish people win over Death." Elsewhere in the world death is a final curtain, elsewhere "the curtains are closed when someone dies," whereas "in Spain they open them. Most Spaniards stay home until their dying day, at which point they are taken out into the sunlight for the first time. [Spain is] a country open to death." The barren plains and surly mountains (in the second most mountainous country in Europe) allow little physical or social escape, so that "the dead are more alive in Spain than anywhere else in the world."

Each year yielded a new crop of manifestos. Lorca flitted among them like a bee with holes in its pockets. He himself never enlisted in movements of any sort. He used cubism, ab-straction, and surrealism as bridges to poetry from his early love, painting, but he could not fully be identified with any style; or any art for that matter. The poet-critic Gerardo Diego wrote of Lorca's *Canciones,* "It is hard to say whether these are poetry, painting, or music."

> Cypresses
> (stagnant water)
> poplar
> (crystal water)
> willow
> (profound water)
> Heart
> (water of the eye)
> ("Remansos"
> [Puddles])

The poem's landscape is lined with trees. The waters (in parenthetical accompaniment) irrigate the poem harmonically, then modulate into tears. The trees in sudden syncopation take on the human beat of the heart that causes tears. The abstract flow of this poem is that of a painting and a musical composition. He is a bit less abstract about the mustache of a lover—"The puddle of your mouth / under the thicket of your kisses"—or about

> . . . moon rays beating
> on the anvil of the afternoon . . .

> If you come looking
> through the highways of the air
> (night is near)
> you'll find me weeping
> under the giant aspens,
> you beautiful brunette!

And there are images lying around such as "stars of lead revolve / upon a foot," and "Bee eater in your obscure trees . . . bee eater. / Eater eater eater eater. / Bee eater"—all in different media, but with Lorca's focus and stroke: "Black bodies hide / the shore of the sea / . . . your hips of Ceres in rhetoric of marble." And there are poems etched like modern Blake, even unto the titles:

He's looking for his voice.
(The king of crickets took it.)
In a drop of water
the boy is looking for his voice.

I won't use it to speak with! (I promise not
to speak with it)
I'll only make a ring of it
for my silence to wear
on its little finger.

In a drop of water
the boy looked for his voice.

(The captive voice was very distant,
wearing the robe of the cricket.)
      ("El niño mudo" [The Dumb Boy])

I said Good afternoon.
But it was not true.
Noon was another thing
and had disappeared.
And the light shrugs its shoulders
like a virgin.

Noon? Impossible. This
noon is untrue, this noon
has half a moon of lead.
The other half won't come.
And the light, it was plain to see,
was playing statues with the boy . . .
      ("El niño loco" [The Crazy Boy])

Then the concrete and the abstract meet:

Licorice, snake, and reed.
Aroma, Trace, and Penumbra:
air, land, and solitude
(the ladder reaches the moon)
      ("Nocturno esquemático"
      [Schematic Nocturne])

Images like this unpeopled ladder standing by itself in the empty landscape wrongly relegated Lorca to the dream heap of surrealism. His talent was hospitable to any visual stimulus. He said a poet must be a professor of the five senses, "but it is sight that keeps an image in reality." Images of all sorts keep turning up in this interim period of his work. He even wel-

comes the insipid guest who tried to destroy modern painting—the Harlequin:

Red nipple of the sun.
Blue nipple of the moon.
Torso half coral.
Half silver and shadow.
      ("Arlequín")

But once he has the sad brat in his control, notice that Lorca dismembers him and transplants his parts to the sky, sea, metal, and darkness, using the scalpel of cubism.

Canciones, however, is not always all that serious. It also contains a delightful series of children's rhymes ("Through the highest corridors / comes a couple of señors,") and unrhymes:

Mama, I want to be of silver.
Son, you'll be very cold.
Mama, I want to be of water.
Son, you'll be very cold.
Mama, embroider me on your pillow.
That yes! Absolutely, this very minute!
      ("Canción tonta" [Silly Song])

Lorca understands a child's love of mystery. But who is this child making such sophisticated wishes? Or whose ear is pressed against the shell in "Caracola" (Sea Conch)?

They've brought me a seashell.
Inside, I hear the song
of an ocean of maps.
My heart fills with waters
and little fishes of shadow and silver.
They've brought me a seashell!

Who are "they"? Real children of a real mother who speaks in exaggerated wonderment? Or is it the honest amazement of a child given a seashell and hearing in it a sound he can describe only in terms of his geography book? Or is it the timeless yearning of both young and old?

Beware the small voice of these delicate poems; it calls you to a boundless space with answers to no known questions. Lorca explained the voice in an essay on Spanish nursery rhymes and lullabies (*nanas*):

> In the child-songs, the emotion of history's lasting light, without dates or facts, takes refuge. The love and breeze of our country inherent in the *nana* breathes life into dead epochs, the opposite of the stones, the bells, the people or even the language. . . . [Nursery rhyme] defines geographical character and etches a profile which time has rubbed out. . . . Its melody gives blood and palpitation and rigid erotic atmosphere to the characters in the songs.
>
> ("Essay on the Spanish Lullaby")

Canciones, like many later works, swings manic-depressively from the loving abandon of "Caracola" and "Canción tonta" to abandoned love. "Es verdad" (It's True) contains true pain:

> Why is it so much work to
> love you the way I love you?
> For love of you the air hurts me,
> my heart
> and my hat.

but humor is integrated even into this dark episode. Even the homosexuals he supported on and off the page receive an ironic verbal drubbing in "Canción del mariquita" (Song of the Sissy):

> The sissy combs his hair
> in his silken nightie . . .
> arranges his curls . . .
> sprays himself with jasmine

while the neighbors laugh and shout. But they, enviously, "spurt planets" when

> The evening disconnects itself
> from combs and entanglements.
> The scandal trembles
> striped like a zebra.
> The sissies of the South
> sing on the terraces.

What a deliciously carefree mix of abstract animal image and concrete human situation. It is in the *Canciones* that one of his most charming, disturbing poems appears. "Despedida" (Good-bye) refracts "Momento" (Moment) in *Deep Song*. In the previous volume he softly but certainly announced his burial wishes:

> When I die,
> bury me with my guitar
> beneath the sand.
> When I die,
> between the orange trees
> and the mint bushes.
> When I die,
> bury me, if you please,
> under a weather vane.
> When I die!

But by the time of "Despedida," he is not entirely certain death will affect him:

> If I die,
> leave the balcony open.
> The child is eating oranges.
> (From my balcony I see him.)
> The mower is mowing the field.
> (From my balcony I hear him.)
> If I die
> leave the balcony open.

Now it's "if" he dies, not "when." Perhaps he has received an intimation of immortality as his success has grown, and now he knows that something of him will never disappear entirely.

Death is always more than mere subject matter for Lorca; it will stalk his pages until it reaches him, as in "Canción de jinete" (Song of the Horseman), which has the brooding quality of Robert Frost:

> Cordoba.
> Far and lonely.
>
> Dark pony, big moon,
> and olives in my saddlebag.
>
> So what if I know the roads?
> I never will arrive at Cordoba.

Over the plain, through the wind
dark pony, red moon.
Death is watching me
from the towers of Cordoba.

Oh this road so long!
Oh my valiant horse
Oh to know Death awaits me
before I arrive at Cordoba.

Cordoba.
Far and lonely.

In "La imagen poética de don Luis de Góngora" (The Poetic Image of Luis de Góngora), Lorca writes:

> A poetic image is always a transference of meaning; Andalusian people call candy "Heaven's Bacon" and a cupola "Half-orange." Penetrating and sensitive imagery. I have heard a farmer in Granada say, "The rushes love to grow on the tongue of the river."

When *Gypsy Ballads* was published in 1928, it brought Lorca international acclaim. It was translated into English (by, among many others, Langston Hughes and Stephen Spender), French, Italian, German, and Esperanto. An Italian literary panel canonized it as one of the ten most important books of this century.

Spanish ballad literature from the Middle Ages is still extant. The ballad (in Spanish *romances*" is historically a miniepic, a few hundred lines of sixteen syllables divided into two equal verses, each ending feminine. Lorca used this same meter with minor variations. Generations were influenced by the ballad's dynamism, from the Golden Age of Spain through Góngora to Unamuno. The ballad is as vigorous as its heroic subjects—and as conservative. Yet this is the form Lorca found most convenient for his subversive purposes.

Lorca's use of this most traditional form in 1927 was a perverse, postmodernist slap at official modernism. (The ballads of Brecht didn't appear until after Germany had seen Lorca's ballads in an edition sponsored by Thomas Mann; Auden began writing ballads after driving an ambulance in 1936 in the Spanish Civil War.) In a letter (8 September 1928) Lorca tells of Dali's "harsh, arbitrary" criticism and of the "putrefactos" who don't understand the simplicity of his ballads, "although they say they do."

But the simplicity "died on my hands in the tenderest way. Now my poetry is on a sharper flight, more personal." Before *Gypsy Ballads* was completed, Lorca retailored this most nationalistic form to the style of the international avant-garde.

The "Romance sonámbulo" (Somnambulist Ballad) is the book's most frequently analyzed poem. The green in the line "Green I want you green" ("Verde que te quiero verde") has been taken to mean "fresh," "moonlit," "cadaverous," "lugubrious," "alive," and "dead." Take your pick of the myriad translations available. We might instead look at the more rarely translated works in the *Gypsy Ballads.* In "Reyerta" (Rumble), each line is like a camera shot in a poker scene:

> Blades beautiful with avial blood
> shine like fishes.
> Sharp gloss of playing card
> cuts through the citrus green,
> horses bucking
> and profiles on them.

Lorca's association with Luis Buñuel, the great surrealist filmmaker and his fellow student at the Residencia de los Estudiantes, bears fruit in this book. The judge surveys the bodies:

> Gentlemen of the Civil Guard,
> here it is again.
> Four Romans dead
> and five Carthaginians.

Lorca here intuits Heidegger's "destructive" principle of finding in an image the root that transcends time. He pans his camera past the local constabulary until it rests, transcending time and space, on an ancient battlefield where a similar battle was fought. Lorca often displays this instinct for mixing races and ages, an instinct not unrelated to the work of Eliot, who was being translated into Spanish at the time.

In "La casada infiel" (The Unfaithful Wife), "the starch of her petticoat / sounded in my ears / like a piece of silk / cut by ten daggers." The poem is a masterpiece of irony. A "Gypsy gentleman" makes fast love to another man's wife. It begins in the middle of a thought. Now or never!

> And so I took her down by the river
> believing she was a virgin,
> but she had a husband.

The preparatory scenes omitted, Lorca takes us to the climactic moment so quickly that the ballad becomes almost a skit. But the lines are lyrical, magical.

> The streetlights went out.
> The crickets went on.
> I touched her sleeping breasts
> and they opened to me pronto. . . .
> I scooped a little hollow in the sand
> for the bun on the back of her head.
> I took off my tie.
> She took off her dress.
> I took off my belt and revolver,
> she her four petticoats.
> Her thighs kept slipping away
> like fish caught unawares,
> one of flame, one of ice.
> That night I rode the best of all possible roads
> on a mare of mother-of-pearl. Bareback. . . .

But, being a "legitimate Gypsy gent," he gives her a sewing basket to remind her of her marital role. (It has been suggested that, to insult her, he pays her as a prostitute. What self-respecting prostitute would accept a sewing basket from a client?) His postcoital morality excuses him from falling in love with her because she was unfaithful to him when

> she had a husband
> and said she was a virgin
> when I took her to the river.

Numerical imagery generally delights Lorca; in the *Gypsy Ballads* it multiplies. The lover's wounds in "Romance Sonámbulo" are "three hundred dark red stains." In "La monja gitana" (Gypsy Nun), "five grapefruits sweeter . . . five slits in Christ . . . two riders riding" are in the sexually thwarted nun's sight and "twenty suns above" are burning into her. But the numbers soon become less arbitrary, more social.

To mine the politics embedded in these poems, they could be deconstructed into dramatic components, different voices playing lover, wife, narrator-chorus, townspeople, jury, judge, and so forth. In the three ballads to the patron saints (Raphael of Cordoba, Gabriel of Seville, and Michael of Granada), the characters in the poems help us understand Lorca's declaration that he is "Muslim-Jewish-Christian" (spoken like a devout atheist):

> St. Michael dressed in lace
> in the alcove of his tower
> shows his lovely thighs
> guided by the streetlight. . . .
> Women with hidden asses, big
> as copper planets, visit him,
> nostalgic for a yesterday of nightingales.

It is a yesterday of Arabic arithmetic elegance: "Three thousand nights old," St. Michael remains "King of worlds and odd numbers / in his Moorish finery."

By contrast, St. Raphael's numbers have cabalistic overtones: "Ten noises of Neptune." Ten, the size necessary for a synagogic congregation, where St. Raphael,

> The Jewish archangel in dark sequins
> leads the congregation of waves
> in search of sound and cradle.

The final saint, Gabriel, is decidedly Christian. A poor Gypsy virgin greets the saint of Cordoba "with three nails of joy." In a "little voice trembling with three green almonds," Gabriel promises her a son "with one mole and three wounds in his chest." Then he rises

FEDERICO GARCÍA LORCA

through the air with his "patent leather shoes and embroidered jacket" donated by the Gypsies.

In "Prendimiento de Antoñito el Camborio en el camino de Sevilla" (The Capture of Antoñito de Camborio on the Way to Seville) Antoñito wears "shoes the color of corinth / medallions of worry / and skin massaged with oil and jasmine." "Five Civil Guards" arrest him as "elegantly he strolls, curses between his eyes." His relatives accuse him of disgracing his family by not resisting arrest and not showering on the guards "five jets of blood." Instead, at "nine o' clock at night," he lets them "lock him in the calaboose" without a fight. He pays for his unmanliness in the next ballad, "Muerte de Antoñito el Camborio" (The Death of Antoñito de Camborio). His four cousins use four knives to kill him, and four angels mourn him while "two year old bulls dream / of bullfighting flowers." But suddenly, as in a group painting when Velázquez marks his presence with a self-portrait, Antoñito calls to his author:

"Ah, Federico García,
call the Civil Guard!
They've broken me in two
like a stalk of corn."
He gave three blasts of blood
and died in profile,
a living coin never to be warmed,
cushioned by a marching angel.

In "Muerto de amor" (Dead of Love), four lanterns are lit, the time is 11:00 P.M., one thousand dogs pursue a loveless lady as "seven cries, seven bloods, seven double poppies / make opaque moons break / into obscure salons."

In "The Ballad of One About To Be Executed," Amargo appears for the last time in Lorca's poetry. He must be killed again; this time the Civil Guard will do the job. The dying boy "dreams of thirteen boats of peace" as other boys unknowingly swim, like the oblivious skaters in the Nativity painting described in Auden's "Musée des Beaux Arts," or the oblivious farmer in Breughel's *Icarus* also mentioned in that poem. Lorca's imagery of the swimmers is worth noting for the originality with which he invests an old Andalusian expression: Dams, when opened, were called "bulls of the river."

The dense bulls of water
charged at the bathing boys
with their waving horns.

The horns are graphic, rather than symbolic; they are the rushing reflections of the hornlike quarter moon in the waving water. In using the plural "bulls," Lorca makes it clear that the moon appears at one time in many rivers— that all things come from one source and, like Amargo, will return to it. De-symbolizing Lorca is a deepening process.

The poem that most appealed to liberal minds helped get him killed by fascists. "Romance de la Guardia Civil española" (Ballad of the Spanish Civil Guard) is a stripped account of a moment in the life of an oppressed people. As in Germany, it was Spanish policy to persecute the Gypsies. While any comment could violate its poignancy, the poem should be discussed in order to free Lorca's reality "from the shadows that blur the outlines." The poem tells of a raid on a Gypsy village by government-sanctioned vigilantes whose "capes in the moonlight glisten with stains of ink and wax" (of the candles by which they write their dread reports). Hollow as Eliot's men of straw,

They have—which is why no tears—
skulls of lead, souls of patent leather. . . .
They order rubber silence
and fears as fine as sand.
Hunched and nocturnal,
they go where they want
and when they want.

Their minds have artillery instead of brains, says Lorca; they think in starless darkness

and hide in their heads
a vague astronomy
of unconcrete pistols.

2179

The Gypsy village with its moonlight and pumpkins is momentarily in focus:

> O city of Gypsies
> who ever saw you can forget?
> City of musk and pain
> and towers of cinnamon.

Then, raided by the Civil Guard, who "Nighten the night with their night" ("noche que noche nochera")

> The Virgin and St. Joseph
> lose their castanets
> looking for the Gypsies
> The Virgin is all dressed up
> in a mayor's-wife outfit
> of golden chocolate paper
> and a necklace of almonds.
> St. Joseph moving his arms
> under a cape of silk. . . .
> Two by two, moving
> on the city in its joy,
> a double nocturne of uniforms
> craves and advances; the sky
> is a showcase of spurs.

Even inanimate objects fear the looting of the law:

> The city multiplies its doors,
> the watches stop, and the cognac
> disguises itself as November,
> to avoid suspicion.

The town's shadowy streets become an arena of panic, as people die like saints:

> The old Gypsy women flee
> with their sleepy horses
> and their jars of coins.
> The parents of Christ
> lose faith in authority.
> St. Joseph, full of wounds,
> shrouds a lady. . . .
> The Virgin cleans the children
> with a handkerchief spat on by stars. . . .
> Rosa of the Camborio family

> sits on her stoop and mourns,
> her breasts cut off on a tray. . . .
> Young women are pursued
> by their own braids.

Nature itself capitulates to the gunfire:

> Roses of black powder
> blossom in the air.
> Then the roofs are gullies.
> Dawn shrugs its shoulders
> wearing a profile of rock
> until the Civil Guard
> in a turmoil of silence
> leave the flaming town.
> O, city of Gypsies, who
> of you has seen and forgot?
> And if you have, you are free
> to rummage through my mind—
> play of moon and sand.

"Martirio de Santa Olalla" (St. Eulalia's Martyrdom) tells of the slicing off of the breasts of Eulalia (alluded to in "Romance de la Guardia Civil española") another joining of ancient and modern. The ballad of biblical incest, "Thamar y Amnón," recounts the lubricious tale of the virgin sister who "wants snow on her belly" while the brother watches with a "groin full of spume / his nakedness bright and extended / thin and concrete." He rapes her: "warm coral paints a brook on the map / till David cuts the harp."

Finally, a gem to end the discussion: "Preciosa y el aire" (Preciosa and the Wind) is based on Preciosa the Gitanilla (little Gypsy girl) of Cervantes' eponymous novel. Cervantes adored the character enough to write a sonnet about her:

> When Preciosa touches her tambourine
> Pearls fall from her fingertips;
> Her sweet sound wounds the empty air,
> And flowers say good-bye to her lips.
> Souls are maddened and thought suspended
> By her graces so superhuman,
> So fresh, so simple, and so pure;
> Her fame reaches up and touches Heaven.

Lorca transforms this into one of the most mysterious ballads ever written. Even for him it covers vast territory, from the religious to the sexual to the political. Eventually it arrives at mythic heights, bearing as well on simple adolescent sexual fear. It is the bad dream (or, worse, reality) of a young Gypsy girl caught between a brutish god (the big wind) and the English consul, who lives off the lean of the land, protected by the Civil Guard, seducing the impoverished Gypsies with exotic luxuries, like gin. "Preciosa y el aire" speaks for itself, here in its entirety:

> Playing her parchment moon
> Preciosa is coming
> by an amphibian path
> of laurel and crystal.
> A starless silence fears
> Preciosa's simple sound
> falling into the roaring sea
> with its song of a dark
> night of fish.
> On the mountain peaks
> sleep the Civil Guard
> guarding the white towers
> where the English live.
> And the Gypsies of the water
> build, for a little fun,
> arbors of white seashells
> and branches of green pine.
>
> Playing her parchment moon
> Preciosa is coming.
> The wind who never sleeps,
> rises to take a look;
> full of starry tongues,
> peeks at the girl who plays
> a sweet, absent song.
> "My child, let me lift your dress.
> Let me see! Let me see! Let me
> open on my ancient fingers
> the blue rose of your belly."
>
> Throwing her tambourine, terrified
> Preciosa runs, can't stop.
> The god of the wind pursuing
> with his red hot sword.

> The sea muffles its roar.
> The olive tree turns pale.
> The flutes of shadow sing
> to the smooth gong of snow.
> Run, Preciosa, run,
> the green wind will get you.
> Run, Preciosa, run,
> but watch him coming closer—
> satyr of low stars
> with his glittering tongues.
>
> Preciosa, full of fear
> runs into a house,
> the high house in the pines
> where the English consul lives.
>
> Startled by her cries
> three Civil Guard arrive
> shrouded in capes of black,
> hats down over their eyes.
>
> The English give the child
> a glass of lukewarm milk,
> then a jigger of gin—
> which Preciosa does not drink.
>
> And she weeps and tells them all
> her adventure in the night
> while up on the roof the wind
> is biting at the tiles.

The gate closes behind her, but this poem is left mysteriously ajar.

Ortega y Gasset, the internationally influential philosopher, published two of Lorca's elaborate odes in his magazine *Revista de occidente*, one a turbulent prayer for spiritual peace, "Oda al Santísimo Sacramento del Altar" (Ode to the Most Holy Sacrament), and one to the man who put him in the turmoil in the first place—Salvador Dalí.

"Oda a Salvador Dalí" is rarely considered important because of Dalí's later self-advertising eccentricity, which tended to erase the dazzling talent he displayed in his early work. But there is power and control of the difficult form in the long alexandrine lines Lorca chooses for these odes.

FEDERICO GARCÍA LORCA

In a letter of 1928, Lorca wrote

for discipline I'm doing these precise *academic* things now and opening my soul before the symbol of the Sacrament. . . . "Ode to the [Most Holy] Sacrament" contains great intensity. Probably the greatest poem I've ever done. The part on which I'm working now ("Devil, second enemy of the soul") is strong. This "Devil" is really a Devil. This part is obscure, metaphysical, until the extremely cruel beauty of the enemy escapes, a wounding beauty, enemy of love. . . . It's extremely difficult. But my faith will do it. . . . The verse "The unicorn seeks what the rose forgets" I like a lot. It has the indefinable poetic enchantment of blurred conversation.

In 1929 García Lorca was invited to visit Columbia University—the crown prince of European poetry on a graduate fellowship. Morningside Heights knew nothing of his genius; he was treated as another foreign student, just another Latino. His reaction was *Poet in New York,* a violent, indignant war cry and dirge.

Like any non–New York student in his first days in a Columbia dormitory, Lorca didn't feel very secure. He felt

assassinated by Heaven
between the forms that go toward the serpent
and the forms looking for the crystal
I'm going to let my hair grow.
("Vuelta de paseo" ["Back from a Walk"])

In a blur of exile, Lorca sees shapes and forms instead of people, a serpent instead of a river. In a letter he tells of "the loneliness a Spaniard feels, especially an Andalusian! If you fall they stomp you; fall into the harbor, they will drown you in lunch bags where sailors, women, pygmies, soldiers and policemen dance on a sleepy sea, a pasture for sirens, a promenade for morning bells and buoys." He despairs at the sight of New York's "little boys who squash little squirrels with a flush of stained frenzy on the saffron hills."

It seems Central Park wasn't safe then, either. Lorca nostalgically contrasts his own childhood,

Those eyes of mine in 1910
never saw a dead man buried
never saw the weepers of the dawn feasting on garbage,
nor hearts trembling, cornered like sea horses.
Those eyes of mine in 1910
saw the white wall where the girls went to pee,
saw the muzzle of the bull, the poisonous mushrooms
and a moon that for no good reason shone on the corners
on pieces of dry lemon under the hard black of bottles.
("1910")

to growing up in New York:

cigarette butts, bits of food, and shoes without heels. On its way home from the fair, the crowd sings and vomits in groups of hundreds over the railings of the boardwalk. In groups of thousands it urinates in the corners, on abandoned boats or the monument to Garibaldi or to the Unknown Soldier.
(Charla sobre *Poeta en Nueva York* [Lecture on *Poet in New York*])

Some of his songs of the Gypsies make a safe journey from Spain to the United States: "Malagueña," for instance, with its image of death entering the tavern to the tune of a guitar, could have been set in a saloon near the Brooklyn Navy Yard, where, through mutual literary friends, Lorca met Hart Crane. Crane, surrounded by sailors all drunk on illegal beer, was in a stupor and barely knew who Lorca was. What could have been a literary moment in heaven is just another step down to a hell open twenty-four hours a night. Lorca, in raging reaction, watches sex addicts cruise for the grail of Genet, the lost and lonely of William Burroughs:

2182

Human iguanas come to eat the sleepless men,
broken hearts meet crocodiles under the tender
protest of stars.
Nobody sleeps on this earth, nobody sleeps;
the boy they buried this morning wailed so
they sent out the dogs to silence him.

The past is dead; even Calderón, who wrote *La vida es sueño (Life Is a Dream)*, is wrong:

LIFE IS NO DREAM. Watch out!
We will see another day of resurrection of
dried butterflies
and even in the landscape of gray sponges
we will see our gems brighten and roses flow
from our tongues.
But until then Watch out! Watch watch out.
You cannot ignore
that dead man with nothing on but a head and
a shoe.
You will go up against the wall [*llevaros al muro*];
no one asleep under the sky, because close one
eye, boys,
close one eye and hit 'em again, boys, hit 'em
again. . . .
No, nobody's asleep, I swear it
and by the light of the moon the fake drink
the poison and the skull of the theater.
("Ciudad sin sueño"
["The City That Never Sleeps"])

Lorca's natural ability to acquaint himself with a place, its underground, its secrets, its genius, its roots, its rot, was phenomenal. And it was this knack for locale that he displayed as no other poet during his stay in New York:

Under multiplication
there is a drop of duck blood.
Under division
there is a drop of sailor's blood.
Under addition, a river of young blood
a river that comes singing by
the dormitories and the shows,
and it is silver, cement and bronze
in the artificial dawn of New York.
The mountains exist. That I know.

I know. But I have not come to see the sky.
I come to see the oily blood
the blood that drives your car to Niagara
and your spirit to the cobra's gossip.
("New York, Oficina y denuncia"
["New York, Office and Denunciation"])

To escape his cultural isolation, Lorca often went a few blocks north for air, into Harlem. In Spain he had lived and written of the outcast Gypsies, the Andalusian dispossessed, written of them romantically, mystically. Now, he himself had been transformed into a displaced, Gypsy-like outsider in New York. Night after night he went to Lenox Avenue, walked 125th Street, visited the Apollo Theater and the clubs, and lived among the others, the blacks, Gypsies of New York. He began to see them from his underground vantage point, eye to eye, heart to heart.

He had to fashion an epic of the black race of North America, to sing the pain of the blacks in a white world, "slaves of all the white man's inventions and machines," who, as he said in his lecture on *Poet in New York,*

someday will refuse to cook for the whites, or drive their limousine, or button their stiff collar for fear of sticking a fork in their eyes. These inventions do not belong to them. The blacks live on credit, and the fathers have to maintain a strict discipline in their homes lest their women and children worship the phonograph record or eat the flat tires.

Lorca understood the spiritual roots of their politics: "The blacks long to be a nation." He notices how, in a club, an audience "black and wet as caviar, saw a naked dancer shimmying in a rain of invisible fire. But one could catch remoteness in her eyes—remoteness, reserve, the conviction that she was *not here* amid these applauding foreigners and Americans. All Harlem was like her."

Every day Lorca protested in verse. He protested to see "little black children guillotined by hard collars, suits, and violent boots as they

2183

emptied the spitoons of old men who walk like ducks." He protested to see "flesh kidnapped from Paradise" and displayed in the Cotton Club. He protested the saddest thing of all, that "the blacks did not want to be black, that they invent pomades to take away the delicious curl of their hair and powders that turn their faces gray and wither the succulent persimmon of their lips."

The "Danza de la muerte" ("Dance of Death") demonstrates his uncanny instinct for the source of suffering in others. Here he sees not only a political basis for black revenge, but a mystical one as well: the slaves were brought to America and deprived of their customs, languages, and religion when they were separated from their tribe. When a people is deprived of its gods, beware:

> Look at the mask, the mask coming
> from Africa to New York!

> Crocodile sand and fear upon New York!
> When the bank director watched the gauge
> and measured the cruel silence of coin.

The mask was heading for Wall Street; time for the crash, and then

> The mask will dance between columns of blood
> and numbers
> between hurricanes of gold and the moans of
> workers
> without work, howling in dark night at this
> lightless era
> of savage, impudent North America!

In the panic that is its revenge, the mask will go on dancing, but

> The Pope doesn't dance, nor the King,
> nor the blue tooth millionaire
> nor builders, nor emeralds, nor crazies, nor
> sodomites.
> Only the mask!

And the cobra, the recurrent image of uncoiling consciousness (cf. Eliot's *Rock*)

> . . . will hiss on the topmost penthouse
> and thorns will strike the patios and terraces
> and Wall Street will be a pyramid of moss.
> The mask, look at the mask,
> how it spits jungle poison
> into New York's unfinished anguish.

That is, New York's troubles are not over, and will not be over until we address the great cause of America's decline—racism. For though it only starts as a "black flush," the bloody revolutions will come. And they did. The famous one of the 1960's. The Harlem riot of 1943 received almost no attention until Ralph Ellison's *Invisible Man.* Lorca predicted it in 1930, in "Oda al rey de Harlem" (The King of Harlem). As the Mask represents the spirit of Africa, so the King embodies the lost dignity and power.

> Blood looking slow out of the corners of eyes,
> blood rusting the unguarded wind in its tracks,
> blood dissolving the butterflies at the
> windowpanes
> blood coming will come on the roofs and
> ceilings everywhere
> to burn the peroxide off blondes.

The white people must either understand, change, or

> escape to the corners, hide on top floors,
> because the heart of the jungle will crawl
> through the cracks
> and leave in your flesh a slimy trace of eclipse
> and a false sadness of faded love and plastic
> rose.

> In the most sapient silence
> the cooks and the waiters and those whose tongues
> clean the millionaire's wounds
> seek a king of the streets.

> Oblivion was expressed by three ink-drops on a
> monocle
> and love by a face, alone
> invisible to flowers of stone.
> Marrows and hearts of flowers under the clouds
> composed a desert of stubble, without one rose.

FEDERICO GARCÍA LORCA

The tenses have gone berserk in the frenzy.

> Black Black Black. Black.
> No serpent or zebra or mule
> even paled at death.
> No woodcutter knows
> when the thunderous tree he is cutting
> will fall . . .

But the tree does, its black anger knows when the time will be right to crash down:

> Wait in the shadow of your King
> until the hemlock and thistle and thorn
> rock the furthermost roofs.
> Only then can you dance to the doubtless end
> when flowers rise hard.

The endless clothing stores of Harlem were white owned. In them headless torsos of mannequins displayed clothes amid the music of the record stores blaring and the car horns and the wails of despair of a people whose royalty is lost in the crowds.

> Oh Harlem in disguise!
> Oh Harlem menaced by an army of suits without heads!
> Your noise has reached me
> your noise has reached me past trunks and elevators,
> past the gates of gray.

> With a spoon
> the King of Harlem
> gouged out the crocodile eyes
> and beat the monkeys on the butt
> with a spoon.

Even with so ineffectual a weapon, he must fight. Or make music with it among the smoking nightclub dwellers until dawn.

> The flame of forever lurking in the flints,
> the roaches drinking anisette
> came to the black weeper's den.
> The King was banging his spoon,
> the tanks of garbage water arriving.

Time for the white people to try to understand the fury of Harlem:

> Time to cross the bridges
> and reach that black flush
> and feel the breathing perfume
> in its hot pineapple dress
> knocking on our temples.

> Time to kill the blonde bootlegger!
> O Harlem Harlem Harlem
> there is no anguish like your bloodshot oppression,
> your blood gushing in the eclipse of darkness,
> your garnet violence deaf and dumb in the half-light,
> your great King prisoner, in janitor stripes!

But still, that night the King drummed away

> with his hardest spoon,
> gouged out the crocodile's eyes
> and beat the monkeys on the butt
> with a spoon.

> Black Harlem was weeping, confused
> beneath umbrellas and suns of gold,
> high yellow women stretched gum
> anxious for the white torso
> and the wind was dusting the mirrors
> and burst the veins of the dancers.

> Black black. Black Harlem,
> blood has no doors to your open-mouth night,
> no such furious blood beneath the skin
> alive in the spine of the knife.

> Blood that searches through a thousand highways
> dying of starch and ashes
> among the beach's abandoned objects.

> where cars float by with teeth sticking out.
> past the dead horses and petty crimes,
> past your great hopeless king
> whose beard reaches down to the sea.

Poet in New York is an epic phantasmagoria of the reality lived mostly by New York City's unknown, uptown shadows. Through Harlem's eyes Lorca looked at all of America, what it was

2185

doing to its oppressed and depressed. The years were 1929 and 1930. To the weirdly gay songs of the Depression, he wrote a series of dark chords that foretold not only the riots of the 1960's but also the rot of the 1970's and the fall of United States power and esteem, especially in the Third World. *Poet in New York* is a miracle of political poetics.

The work has been called biographical, social, prophetic, mystical, surrealist; Lorca's *Waste Land,* his *Leaves of Grass.* The truth is that from all these seeds combined grew Lorca's anthology of New World flowers of evil that has puzzled many a critic (often needlessly: *Montaña del orso,* for instance, is not "mountain of the bear," but rather the very real Bear Mountain, up the Hudson River near West Point). The bibliography on this one book occupies at least ten pages. It has been the scene of many battles of ideology and the subject of as many revisionisms as has Marx himself. During the Franco regime Spanish critics treated it, like Lorca's murder, as a subject discreetly to be avoided. In the United States during the 1940's it was considered a social excoriation in verse. During the McCarthy era, it was either detoured or approached as a surrealist spiritual breakdown brought on by too much Freudianism and an affair with Salvador Dali. But his letters at the time reveal a depression, a desperation brought on by social and spiritual conditions in the United States that made peasant Spain look comparatively fortunate.

Poet in New York is an indignant, unsurrealist work of pure suffering for the nation he is calling out to, as in his "Pequeño poema infinito" (Little Infinite Poem):

> If you take the wrong way
> you get stuck in the snow
> and stuck in the snow
> you graze twenty centuries on graveyard grass.

In 1934 Lorca devoted his energy almost entirely to writing and producing plays. But he was driven by despair to write possibly the greatest elegy of the century. It was translated, sung, recorded, and subjected to constant critical examination. Everything about Lorca was becoming hyperbolic. *Llanto por Ignacio Sánchez Mejías* (*Lament for the Death of a Bullfighter,* 1935) is a four-part invention about the death of a great bullfighter. (In Spain not even artists root for the bull.) Sánchez was also a great patron of poets. He wrote poetry himself (not great). Most of all he was a great friend. Lorca saw in his death the fall of the courage and sensitivity of Spain. He mourned it in this harmonic masterpiece.

Part 1, "La cogida y la muerte" (The Wound and the Death), begins with a tympanic beat announcing the time of his death in the ring, "five in the afternoon." The famous "a las cinco de la tarde" refrain that keeps pounding through this section is like a human nailing a coffin:

> The rest of it was death and only death
> at five in the afternoon.
> The wind blew away the bandages . . .
> at five in the afternoon.
> And a thigh with a deserted horn
> at five in the afternoon.
> The bells of arsenic and smoke
> at five in the afternoon.
> And the corners group in silence
> at five in the afternoon.
> And only the bull's heart was high
> at five in the afternoon.
> When the sweat of snow was arriving
> at five in the afternoon.
> When the stadium was covered with iodine
> at five in the afternoon.
> Death laid eggs in the wound
> at five in the afternoon.
> At five in the afternoon.
> At exactly five in the afternoon . . .
> Bones and flutes sound in his ears. . . .

In Part 2, "La sangre derramada" (The Blood Flows), Lorca refuses to look, calling on history to help:

The cow of the old world
passed her sad tongue
over a snout of bloods
spilled on the sand,
and the bulls of Guisando,
almost death and almost stone,
mooed like two centuries
tired of trodding the earth.
No.
I do not want to see it.

In Part III, "The Body Laid Out," come long lines in a solemn cadence, enormous queues of imagery slowly passing a body lying in state:

Now noble Ignacio lies on the stone.
It's over. What happened?
look at his figure
covered with pale sulphurs
Death has given him a head of dark minotaur.

It's over. It's raining in his mouth.
The air, a fool, leaves his caved-in chest,
and Love, wet with tears of snow,
dries itself on the head of the herd.

What are they saying? The silent odors repose.
We are with a body in state vanishing.

In Part IV, "The Soul Not Here," Lorca knows his friend will be forgotten by most. But those who see the secret spirit of Andalusia escaping his body will not say that he died

like the dead of the Earth,
like the dead forgotten
in a mound of extinguished dogs.

They do not know you. No. But I sing you.
I sing your profile and grace, for *them.*
The stunning maturity of your understanding,
your appetite for death and the joy of its mouth.
The sadness your valiant gaiety had.

It will be a long time, or never, before
an Andalusian so true is born, so rich in motion.
I sing his elegance with sounds that moan,
and I remember a whimpering wind in the olive
  trees.

There is an extant photo of Lorca swathed in an Arab's burnoose. In 1936 he published a book of poetry cloaked in Arabic sensibility, *Diván del Tamarit (Divan).* Some of his early poems have a transcendent, Semitic quality:

A book of poetry
is the death of Autumn.
The verses are the leaves.
Black on white earth.
      ("Prólogo" [Prologue])

But *Divan* has a fully Eastern, mystical feel

for imitating the races
beneath the ground; ignorant
of the water, I am in search
of a death of the light
that consumes me.

Divan displays Lorca's special gift for identifying with a distant poetics. It is not easy to distinguish between Lorca's original verses here and those of the Arabic poets to whom he paid the tribute of adaptation. But using Pound's "make it new" approach to translation, Lorca also made these *gacelas* very much his own, filling them with sensual surprises:

Nobody could understand the perfume
of the obscure magnolia of your belly.
Nobody knew you were martyring
a hummingbird of love between your teeth.

The following, "Gacela del mercado matutino" (Gacela of the Market in the Morning), is a lush example worth quoting in full to show how he treats a popular form.

I watch by the arch of the church of Elvira
for you to pass me by.
Then I hear them call your name
and I begin to cry.

What gray moon of the morning
sucks your blood as you pass?
Who's been reaping your seedling
that flamed in the snowy grass?

Who blew the little dart of cactus
into your heart of glass?

So go on under the arch of the church of Elvira.
I'll watch you pass me by.
I'll drink the look you do not give me
and begin to cry.

Why do you hit me on the street
with this voice of scorn?
What is a carnation like you
doing among alien thorns?
How near am I when you are gone,
how far when you and I meet!

Under the arch of the church of Elvira
I'll watch you pass me by.

But the time is 1936 and civil war approaches.

The wind is
a tulip of fear
and a very sick tulip
the dawn of Winter.

Sensing political danger, Lorca longs in these
last poems

to be far from the tumult of cemeteries,
to sleep a while, a minute, a century only,
so everyone knows I have not died.

Still he plays dangerously; his homosexuality
now politically overt, Lorca boldly states his
desire "to live with that dark boy / who wanted
to cut out his own heart at high tide." But
darker trouble is coming.

THE PLAYS

An account of Lorca's dramatic development
must consider the forces that contributed to his
complex theater aesthetic. Part of his avant-
garde legacy was left to him by Spanish experimentalists, from the baroque Góngora to the
expressionist Valle-Inclán; the rest came from
Paris, which cultivated the intellectual fads
that fed Europe's artists. Cultural France
distributed German expressionism, Russian
structuralism, and Italian futurism, to name
just three. These were eagerly assimilated into
modernist Spanish poetry, painting, and music
(Machado, Gris, and Falla are examples).

As usual, the theater resisted change. Even
the few Ibsenian modifications of the famous
Jacinto Benavente were not welcome in the
theater of rhetorical sentimentality that dominated the Spanish stage. Unfortunately, Benavente did not evolve beyond this minor realistic
innovation; he soon bored even himself. His
work degenerated into trite pleadings of honorable causes, and he received the Nobel Prize in
1922 (over Wedekind and Pirandello). Victory
for the status quo! Spanish theater strove even
harder for a new middle of mediocrity. Spanish
playwrights and reviewers conspired to keep
theatrical taste uncritically intact, managing to
halt those hordes of "isms" at the Pyrenees and
thus hold the theater in captivity. The result
was that Spanish theater had little success,
even commercially.

Lorca's first play, *El maleficio de la mari-
posa* (*The Butterfly's Evil Spell,* 1954), did not
improve the situation. Only a claque of his fellow students at the Residencia remained after
the first act for its entire run of one performance. This one-night last stand has all the lyric
bravado of a young genius. The sudden appearance of a butterfly with a wounded wing among
a colony of cockroaches alters the routine of
their grubby lives. The suspicious roach colony, though, keeps the winged lady at a
distance. She may be evil. The poetroach, an
idealist among these dung dwellers, is mesmerized by the sunlit flier's blazing aura; he
approaches her. She sings to him the wonders
of sun and sky and tree, so inspiring the poetroach that he vainly tries to flap his rudimen-
tary wings. But he cannot fly. Enamored, he
begs her to stay. But her wing heals and she
joyously flies from the soil, leaving the heart-

broken roach behind. A sad shell of his former selflessness, he is unable either to accept the sunless conditions of his existence or to fly free into the sky.

While the plot is immature, there is the free-wheeling lyric invention here that characterizes Lorca's later works. He describes the work in its prologue as:

> a kind of defeated comedy about someone who, reaching for the moon, reached only his own heartbreak. Love . . . occurs in a deep meadow of insects where life is serene and undisturbed. They are content to drink dewdrops and bring up children. They made love out of habit. . . . Ah, but one day an insect tried to go beyond this love. Perhaps he had read a book with one of those poems that begin "O Woman, unrequited, I love you" and questions why stars move in their orbits. This is very harmful to souls not yet completely formed. Needless to say, the foresaken insect dies.

In Act 1, the witchroach, the poetroach's mentor, applies to the wounded butterfly (a common symbol for the soul) warm dew and a poultice of nettle paste:

> *Witchroach:* You know the secrets of waters and
>   flowers
> How awful to see you dying in the dawn
> mourned by the prophetic nightingales.
> How lucky for us repugnant creatures
> to caress your silk-white wings
> and smell the sweetness of your dress.
>
>   (act 1, scene 2)

The poetroach approaches with antennae brazenly painted with lily pollen. He sees the wounded butterfly:

> *Poetroach:* I've never felt such deep sorrow!
> *Sylvia* (A rich roach who loves poetroach in vain):
> He doesn't love me, mother.
> *Mother:* Just who does he think he is, all gussied
> up!
> *Witchroach:* Take a moonbath and a siesta, but-

terfly, in the shade of the ancient wood. Look at her! Isn't she gorgeous?
> *Poetroach:* I can't bear what my heart is going to feel.
> *Witchroach:* My poet, your destiny hangs on the wings of this great moth! Be loathe to love her, your old teacher tells you. Night will fall on your brow, night without stars. Meditate on it.
>
>   (act 1, scene 6)

The poetroach does just that, wondering Don Juanesquely (Lorca's adverb):

> *Poetroach:* What love has the wind knit?
> The flower of my innocence gone
> and another grown.
> Who is she, come to rob my future,
> wings shining like ermine?

Two peasant roaches, one simple and one saintly, gossip about the effect the butterfly has had on the roach. It is an early indication of the sly wit lurking in Lorca's delicate verses:

> *Saintroach:* Did you see that poetroach declaiming away in the meadow?
> *Simpleroach:* That disgusts me. Singing, dreaming of not earning a living, the loafer.
> *Saintroach:* Ah, to quote the Allknowingroach in the Sky: "Dwell you not on the faults of others, for they in my kingdom who play and sing I value more than those who work all day."
> *Simpleroach:* The Allknowingroach never eats? Try telling that to the starving.
> *Saintroach:* Hunger is a demon with antennae of fire who must be driven out by—
> *Simpleroach:* Eating. Right?
> *Saintroach:* Wrong—praying!
> *Simpleroach:* The Allknowingroach in the Sky had some other life in mind. Do me a favor, dear. You're holy and wise. Tell the poetroach to get himself a job. He's going to die over that butterfly.
>
>   (act 3, scene 1)

The poetroach, passing by, is in agreement:

> *Poetroach:* A presence of transparent snow has come to my door to steal my soul away . . .

There is a Krazy Kat quality to all this.

> *Simpleroach:* The poor thing is definitely out of his mind!
> *Poetroach:* What if I die
> and there is no Allknowingroach in the Sky?
> What if I sail beyond the trees
> and find nothing in the celestial seas?
> What if I go beyond above
> and find there is no higher love?

The poetroach is having a poetic breakdown. Meanwhile, the butterfly recovers; her departure is imminent. When the poetroach plights his troth, her only answer is a silent dance, her preparation to fly off among the trees.

> *Poetroach* (to the butterfly): Where do you want to fly to?
> It's night and your wing's still broken;
> I'll heal it with kisses. Marry me
> and an immense nightingale I know
> will fly us to the dawn.
> Don't fly in the dark; dark is so subtle,
> so confusing.
> Stay here and I'll catch a cricket
> to sing you to sleep.
> I'll feed you little sips
> of dewdrops from my nipping lips.
> (He embraces her.)
> Come, you're cold, my den is warm.
> (She withdraws.)
> Heartless butterfly! You go and who
> can I tell my sorrows to?

She is healthy now, ready to fly out of reach. He begins to wail:

> If the water in summer
> is cooled by the shadows,
> if the darkness at night
> is brightened by stars,
> by the endless eyes of the skies,
> why, why can't my soul find love?
>
> (act 2, scene 7)

He curses his body:

> Who put these sightless eyes on me?
> These handless feet
> cannot touch a love I cannot comprehend

except to know that it will end my life?
> Why am I left in the darkness?
> Why can't a guy like me fly?

At which point, the Allknowingroach enters, in all his wisdom.

> *Allknowingroach:* What's happening?

This early manuscript ends here, abruptly but perhaps intentionally. It reveals all the passion of Lorca's later, less pastoral, plays, the subtleties of the poetroach lurking in its creator. There is more than promise in this patronized, patronless play. After some sixty-five years, it deserves a longer run than its last one.

The impressionistic one-act *El amor de don Perlimplín con Belisa en su jardín* (*The Love of Don Perlimplín for Belisa in His Garden,* 1938) is minimal by Anglo-American theatrical standards; the short play is to long plays as lyric poems are to epics. *Don Perlimplín,* a reworking of Lorca's own *La zapatera prodigiosa* (*The Shoemaker's Prodigious Wife,* 1938), is a transformation of the popular theme of the impotent husband and the sexy wife. Lorca's multilayered genius is never more evident than in this erotic staged poem. Absurd, touching, political, and musical, the tragic farce goes like this: Perlimplín, a rich, bookish, middle-aged nobleman, loves Belisa, who offstage sings:

> Love, love,
> between my locked-up limbs
> the sun swims like a fish.
> Warm water between the reeds,
> love, love.

But the song changes in its last lines to a warning of Perlimplín's advancing age:

> Cock of the dawn
> the night is moving on!
> Don't let it go,
> oh no!
>
> (Prologue)

Perlimplín's maid says, "Call her!" He does; she appears, seminude. Perlimplín asks for her hand. Belisa's mother enters, wearing an eighteenth-century wig full of birds and beads: "Mr. Perlimplín, you have the grace of your mother, whom I never had the luck to meet." Perlimplín thanks her. As in the absurdist plays, which had their debut a decade after Lorca's death, the characters do not talk to each other as in Ibsen, nor at each other as in Shaw, but rather through each other, addressing each other's unconscious while the outer selves ramble on, making do: business as usual. Note the nearness in tone to Wilde's *Lady Windermere's Fan,* another absurd precursor:

Maid: We have decided—
Perlimplín: We have decided—
Mother: To enter marital negotiations, isn't that so?
Perlimplín: That's so.
Belisa: And me, Mama?
Mother: And you agree, naturally. . . . Don Perlimplín has many lands; on these lands are many sheep. You take the sheep to market. In the market they give you money. Money gives you beauty. And beauty is coveted by all the other men . . . (To Perlimplín) You see her face, like a lily? (In a husky whisper) You should see what she's like on the inside! Like sugar! Forgive me. Why am I weighing you down with stuff like this, a person like you, so modern, so fantastically sophisticated . . .
Perlimplín: I don't know how to express our gratitude.
Mother: What charm! *Our* gratitude! The double thanks of your heart and your self. Not that I've had anything to do with a man for twenty years . . .
Maid: What about the wedding?
Perlimplín: Yes, the wedding . . .
Mother: Name the day . . .

In the next scene Perlimplín wonders if Belisa has the strength to strangle him; she stands on the balcony, now almost entirely naked, the stage in semidarkness. Past the balcony flies a band of black paper birds.

With the bold syncopation characteristic of Lorca's poetry, the next scene lands us immediately in a nuptial bed that takes up almost the entire stage (like the one in Harvey Fierstein's *Torch Song Trilogy* fifty years later). The sun again "swimming like a fish in her thighs" can't get him over his cold feet. He shyly tiptoes out the door (to soft guitar music), leaving Belisa alone, naked, an enormous coiffure with lace cascading down her body.

Belisa: Who looks for me with ardor will find me. My thirst is like the statues in the fountains who never get wet enough! O this music, o my God! Like the hot down of swans. God, is it me or the music?

She throws a great red velvet cape over her hot body. Suddenly five whistles are heard through five doors! Through a sixth appears Perlimplín with the good news: "I love you."

Belisa: You little gentleman you, you're supposed to.
Perlimplín: Yes?
Belisa: Yes!
Perlimplín: Why yes?
Belisa: Because yes.
Perlimplín: No . . . but when I looked through the keyhole and saw those men I felt love scalpel my throat.

(scene 1)

Five whistles again. Belisa assures Perlimplín it is the clock. Time for bed. Lights out. Five whistles, louder. Two Sprites (Duendes) appear, played by children. Puckishly, they face the audience. They chat about how nice it is to hide the characters' failures:

Sprite I: Because if things are not hidden with great care—
Sprite II: They won't be discovered. And without this hiding and finding out—
Sprite I: What would the poor audience do?
Sprite II: So there mustn't be a hole in the curtain.
Sprite I: Because the holes of today are darkness tomorrow.
Sprite II: That's the fun of fuzzy things. People look into them for secrets they already know.

2191

Here Lorca reveals the spine of the play by allowing two little ghosts to dangle the whole skeleton in front of us. Five balcony doors open, letting in men of five races, who whistle. Blackout.

The next scene, the morning after the wedding night, Perlimplín awakens. When he sits up in bed, a gorgeous rack of antlers has sprouted from his brow. The five open balcony doors have five ladders hooked over their edges, and a hat on each.

The next scene (2) is a week later. Perlimplín's dining table is set up like a distorted Last Supper. The skewed visual perspective prepares us for the juggling of time. The scene takes place shortly after the wedding night, yet there is a decade's worth of frustration in it. The maid weeps, telling Perlimplín not only of the European, Indian, African, Asiatic, and North American men who visited Belisa on her wedding night, but also that Belisa is waiting for a stranger who waves to her in her balcony. Belisa enters, fantasizing of the one whose "greeting makes my breasts tremble." A rock flies through the window; Perlimplín picks it up.

Belisa: Don't read that rock!
Perlimplín: Has he passed by today?
Belisa: Twice, but he waved as if he didn't like me.
Perlimplín: Never fear. I saw him! Never have I seen a chap in whom the virile and the delicate merged in a more harmonious manner.
Belisa: He writes me letters.
Perlimplín: Don't stand on ceremony. Tell your daddy.
Belisa: His letters are about my body.
Perlimplín (stroking her hair): Oh?
Belisa: He writes: "Who the hell wants your soul? Beautiful souls are on the brink of death living in gray hairdos and bony hands." He wants my soft, white, quivering body!
Perlimplín: What if I told you I know this beautiful young man? I am going to do for you what no one ever does for anyone. I am outside the world and its ridiculous moralities!

Don Perlimplín is about to watch his own cuckolding; he will summon the lover himself. We see the subtle satire of the voyeuristic master who cannot touch but who controls the touching, the old senator who sends the young soldier into battle. This play was, in fact, suppressed by General de Rivera, dictator and darling of the nobility.

In the final scene (3), Perlimplín instructs the maid to tell Belisa her mysterious lover will be in the garden that night:

Perlimplín: I want her to love her lover more than she loves her own body. I have no pride, no honor. No honor, no pride.

The maid quits, protesting that while he may have neither honor nor pride, a servant has hers. He begs her to wait until the night is over. What can she do? As the master moves toward his own destruction, the servant must ready him. It is a deconstructive critic's dream play, full of mystical and social puns and psychoanalytical unzippings. Consider the ending itself: the lover, his face hidden in a red cape, returns to Belisa with an emerald dagger ("Green, green, I want you green") sticking in his chest. With his last breath he tells Belisa that Perlimplín thrust the dagger there shouting triumphantly, "Belisa has a soul now!" But the soul is "the booby prize of the weak!": He suddenly reveals himself to be Don Perlimplín; he calls out to himself, "You green, impotent phony! *You* could only enjoy Belisa's soul. *I* loved her body, nothing more! That is why you killed me with your fiery sapling of rare stones!"

Perlimplín: Belisa, I am soul and you are body. (Belisa, half-naked again, embraces him.)
Belisa: Why this deception? Why pretend you were my lover?
Perlimplín: What lover? (He dies.)
Belisa: I never realized he was so complicated.

On this monumental understatement the play comes to a close.

Lorca turns this slight romantic farce into a tour de force of poetry and humor, and in musical form: four balletic conversations replete with verbal pas de deux, pas de trois, and solos. Small, deceptively delicate, it is an erotic "Halleluia" (a Spanish Valentine's card for any occasion)—lacy, flowery, three dimensional. Francis Ferguson calls Perlimplín's deception "the triumph of Lorca's imagination." He had choreographed a dance for the body and the spirit and sent it swirling toward what Cocteau called a poetry of the theater, instead of poetry in the theater.

Still, director beware: one false move and the lace hides the complications—and the laughs. Luis Buñuel ran from a production of *Don Perlimplín* that confused the sentimental with the comical. Poetic theater is a dangerous game. Postmodern poetry, like painting, thrives not on drama but on theatricality. Lorca, as far back as 1929, was experimenting in just that direction.

Tragedy deals with superhuman forces that lead to an awesome comprehension by the human protagonist. In our century, however, poetic protagonists do not have to be human. They can be: History (Pound), Belief (Eliot), Society (Williams), Language (Joyce), or Idea (Stevens). The leading character in *Boda de sangre* (*Blood Wedding*), Yerma, and *La casa de Bernarda Alba* (*The House of Bernarda Alba*) is the spirit of the harsh land in which its author was born and murdered—Andalusia. It is the line that runs throughout the trilogy.

The Andalusians have no great love of this land, which even with irrigation is mainly scrub and cactus. It is ungiving, unworkable, and not their own; from ghettolike pueblos, impoverished commuters work the fields. The men come out early and go home late to a town that is an extended family. There is unity in their love of song and verbal irony. But the most unifying factor is the code. The code says a woman must have *vergüenza,* a sense of guarding the morality of the town. A woman must embody the principles of proper womanhood. She must never talk with a man who is not a blood relative. Even being alone by herself is not desirable. Adultery, of course, is the ultimate disgrace. The violent acts of *Blood Wedding* are not melodrama; they are merely an honest representation of the sheer reality of the Andalusian code.

The early sketches and puppet plays prepared the way for the mature comedies. The poems were a rehearsal for the tragic trilogy. Belief in teaching through poetic theater inspired this tragedy of Spain, a distillation of populist and poetic tendencies. The familiar themes are love and death, but they have a political shimmer. Having no right to freedom, the frustrated heroines of the trilogy are doomed either to give death or to receive it. While their sounds are suppressed, their silence calls to all of oppressed Spain.

Blood Wedding concerns the willing seduction of a bride by her former sweetheart, Leonardo. His family has killed the bridegroom's father and brothers. Leonardo abducts her and is pursued by the bridegroom into a forest. The two men kill each other; the groom's mother mourns the inevitable death of her last son. The bride, looking for love, instead causes death in the form of traditional honor.

In Granada's newspaper there was a story of a bride who ran off with a former lover on her wedding day. Following his own method of "letting a play write itself," Lorca kept the story in the fertile dark until, directed by its author in 1933, *Blood Wedding* was a critical and popular success. The title itself is a torn and bloody curtain that opens on an old family wound. As in the newspaper account, the bride runs off with her former lover on her wedding day. This is journalism at its most dramatic. But dramatically speaking, it is journalistic. Lorca heightens the conflict by having the bride come from a family in a lifelong blood feud with the family of the groom. The poet tosses the familiar cuckoldry theme (ordinarily the province of melodrama, or its kissing cousin, farce) into the ring of tragedy, resonating with the dry wind of a landscape as arid as its rules of honor. Blood only will feed the soil that produces wine, the sensuous grapes bursting in the mouth. The blood flows on, generation to generation, grave to grave, as man after man is killed in the population-control process known as vendetta.

The bride and groom have tried to cross impossible rivers of blood; they are a kind of reverse Romeo and Juliet, their marriage grudgingly ratified by two hated and hating families. But their love is unable to quiet the blood-hate rumbling through the family's veins. The Mother of the Groom personifies this. Try as she might to start off the wedding day with a smile, she does not fully share the joy. It reminds her of her days of fulfillment with a man who lay on her "smelling of carnation and strong as a bull," a man who was killed by

> one of those little knives,
> barely fits in the palm of the hand.
> Makes you feel so grand—
> it was one of those blades
> that pierces the skin
> goes all the way in
> oh into the stream
> it goes down through the blood
> and it tickles
> the root of a scream.
>
> (act 3, scene 3)

This is the song she repeats when her dead son is carried in at the end. There is a self-fulfilling prophecy to her constantly recalling the blood images in her head, the arms flashing in the light, and her hate-lust. When, in fact, the blood spurts on the quivering air, it is as if she had been waiting to say, "I told you so!" She had lived this moment of her son's death from the day she buried her husband and put on the black costume she would never again remove. It would, she knew, come in handy all too soon in a way of life that flows with blood.

All the characters except Leonardo, the passionate, natural lover, are abstractions without personal names. They are Bride, Mother,

Groom, Death—as though their human qualities disappear into the air and sink into the land, the real villain in the piece.

Catholicism in Andalusia is fervidly joined to faith in Gypsy fertility cures. Children are a godlike proof of moral evolution, as is characteristic of the Jewish and Islamic traditions that prevail in Moorish Andalusia. In *Yerma*, the trilogy shifts to the home of a morose, childless couple. Yerma believes she is barren. She goes "in a tide of fire" to a Gypsy conjurer who assures Yerma ("May my mouth fill with ants like the mouths of the dead if I lie") that she can have a child.

Yerma thirsts for a child at her breast "even if when he grows up he will drag me through the streets by the hair! Better to live with a son who'd kill me than with this vampire husband, year after year sucking my heart dry." In the code of the infertile Andalusian plain, an empty womb is like an open grave. The land must have sons who can force the dry soil to yield, who can husband it, make it give life. The woman's joy is to feed her man's appetites, but he must repay her with a child, or she becomes the walking dead.

Yerma's husband, Juan, forever works the land, "counts money at night after a day with his sheep, then covers [Yerma] with a dutiful belly as cold as a corpse." And he doesn't want children! All that matters is what he can hold, money and land, with no children to take them from him. In the last scene she wants to know what Juan wants with her.

> *Juan:* I want you!
> *Yerma:* You mean my cleaning, my cooking, my body!
> *Juan:* I'm a man, like other men.

He forces her to the floor; she pleads with him, once and for all, to put life into her body. With his hands on her loins and his lips to her ear, he admits he is sterile.

> *Juan:* Do I have to scream in your ear to make you understand? Now just lie back peacefully.

Yerma: I should not hope for one?
Juan: No.
Yerma: Empty.
Juan: Lie back, in peace, sweetly, you and I. Hold me!

He forces himself on top of her. She looks up at his face:

Juan: In the moon you are so beautiful.
Yerma: Hunting me like a pigeon to eat!
Juan: Kiss me . . . like this. (Her hands grab his throat.)
Yerma: Never.

She chokes him to death. In the background, a passing pilgrim sings a litany to her sacrifice for the sacrament denied her.

I am alone for certain and I'll sleep with a dry body forever. I myself have killed my son, who might have announced to my blood new blood.

(act 3, scene 2)

The tomb of her womb will be empty, but not because a son has risen.

This play is not a straightforward narrative; the wild dramatic leaps, the pregnant ellipses, and the sexual images are a fertile linguistic counterpoint to the barrenness of Yerma, our lady of the wasteland.

In a letter about *The House of Bernarda Alba,* Lorca wrote "My whole style must change. This is 1936. Just reality! I have no time for hallucination. Pure reality. A simple document. See? Not a drop of poetry! A photograph!" But, as photographer Garry Winogrand noted, there is nothing as mysterious as a fact clearly described. The decorum that Bernarda Alba's household projects to the rest of the town contrasts painfully to the reality of Bernarda's five frustrated daughters. The eldest (and richest) is engaged to Pepe el Romano. Pepe is prepared to marry the unattractive, thirty-nine-year-old Angustias. The youngest, twenty-year-old Adela, is furious. Pepe has made love to her. Though another sister, Mar-

tirio, denounces Adela's outspoken affections for Pepe, they all run to the window when he passes outside.

In act 2, Martirio steals Angustias' picture of Pepe. Adela is furious to discover her sister's hypocrisy, but she also admits having "had" Pepe the night before. Before Bernarda Alba can find out, there are terrible screams in the street. A woman who has had a child out of wedlock is being punished. Bernarda tells Adela, "They ought to shove a hot poker right where she sinned." The curtain falls on Adela feeling her stomach as Bernarda shouts to the women's tormentors, "Kill her!"

In act 3, as a stallion bucks against the wall from the stable next door, desire threatens to inflame the house. Angustias' impending marriage to Pepe is discussed with frightening calm. Martirio and Adela are insanely envious of Angustias and writhing jealously. When the rest of the household is asleep, Adela tries to leave to meet Pepe. Martirio catches her and they fight. Bernarda Alba awakens. Martirio tells of Adela's affair with Pepe. Bernarda leaves the house with a rifle. A gun goes off outside. Martirio tells Adela their mother killed Pepe. Adela kills herself. But Martirio was lying; Bernarda missed and Pepe was seen on horseback carrying his sexuality off into the night—as the horse keeps bucking against the walls of the house. Bernarda says Adela will be buried as a virgin.

The barren world of *Yerma* is developed further in this, Lorca's last play (*alba* in Latin means white, the absence of all color). There is a contrast between the women locked in the house and the men outside, trying to break through the wombish walls and enter. Even the stallion is trying to kick through its stall next door—a metaphor for the unbridled passion that takes the sisters from frustration to abandon. The house's eggshell-colored walls, blanched faces, and pallid lips are all the whiter against the black of the women's dresses. Sparse furnishings emphasize the virginal emptiness, again at odds with the passion of the daughters. The occupants of the house are in the grips of a great, corroding chastity belt.

Yet the playwright tells us these "walls are barren but for a few pictures of unlikely landscapes full of nymphs and legendary kings." The "art" on the walls strokes the consciousness of the spinster daughters (and the audience); an unconscious yearning for nymphlike freedom rests its eyes on a distant painted past when rulers cared and caressed. Representing a nondimensional hope, these men in the pictures are much like the photo of the missing husband in *The Glass Menagerie.* The difference is that in *Bernarda Alba* the painted men are the only ones we ever see. When an actual photo of Pepe el Romano is lost, it is enough to cause a quiet riot among all the sisters. All, including Bernarda Alba herself, treat the image as the man himself.

This is poetry converted into dramatic action: wordless provocation of ideas, a subliminal communication of the psychological, spiritual, sexual, and sociological interplay of the characters and forces that will justify the terrifying action in the last act. In this almost Beckettian emptiness, the women live their lives to the empty accompaniment of the town bells, which toll twice for a female corpse of a virgin, and the bucking of the stallion in the stable contiguous to the house, a part of their lives.

The set and sounds are two ways Lorca builds a nonverbal case out of the echoes and shadows of poetry. Though the verse form is lacking, the moments of poetry do not stop from the opening image to Bernarda's final exhortation: "No weeping! Death must be looked at face to face. Silence. We'll drown ourselves in the mourning of the Sea." The sea, the mother of all things, the dread sea of J. M. Synge (as translated by Lorca's early master, Jiménez).

Before we leave this trilogy that gives birth to nothing but death, we should look once again at the political criticism implied in such a house, where the children are so at odds with each other that they are dominated by one they could dethrone easily, if they could but unite.

The varying factions on both the Left and Right at this time (1936) provide a link between Lorca's implicit comments on Spanish social life in the trilogy and the firing squad he faced for his efforts toward a political poetics.

Doña Rosita la soltera (*Doña Rosita, the Spinster,* 1938) has been called Lorca's Chekhovian play. There are shades of *The Cherry Orchard* and *The Three Sisters* in this pastel household's dissolution; all three acts deal with the passing of possibility as Rosita languishes over a lover who will never return. In the first act, youthful, delightful Rosita (little Rose) is happily engaged. Her fiancé, however, is needed to run his family's South American plantation. Rosita promises to wait; her lover promises to return. He never does—that is the plot, the skeleton of the play, as opposed to the story, which fleshes out the play with such details as the comically drawn aunt and uncle with whom she lives until the return of her absent lover. Her uncle discusses nothing but his roses. His favorite is Rosa Mutabile, a variety that blossoms, fades, and dies—all in one day.

> *Aunt:* Has the Rosa Mutabile blossomed yet?
> *Uncle:* Just beginning.
> *Aunt:* How long does it last?
> *Uncle:* One day. I intend to watch it all day long.
>
> (act 1)

In the first act, Rosita too is colorful in the dawn of her youth; in act 2 the empty age of thirty will blanch her skin; in act 3 the long night of her forties moves her toward despair. Others can do nothing but watch the flower of Rosita's youth decay:

> The Rosa Mutabile
> is blood red at dawn,
> coral, bursting. But
> when the afternoon faints
> the rose grows sallow
> like a cheek of salt. . . .
>
> and at the edge of darkness,
> her petals fall.
>
> (act 1)

The image is implanted in the play like a garden graft. As the plot develops, we look through a rose-colored veil, for the play is also implanted in the image. This is the dramatic imagery of a poet.

When, fifteen years after the time of act 1, Rosita receives a letter from her lover asking for her hand in marriage—by proxy—her uncle enters bearing the Rosa Mutabile "still red with the fire of its youth." But he has cut it by mistake before it has had a chance to mature. Rosita's memory is also cut; she has forgotten what her lover looks like.

The metaphor of roses is continued through act 2, but the housekeeper provides realistic comic relief when she wishes the roses were pears, cherries, or persimmons—traditionally, three sexual fruits. The aunt, mistress of the house, accuses the housekeeper of preferring food to beauty. The maid boldly replies, "I have a mouth for eating, dancing legs, and between them something else that likes to be fed." Lorca's maids are born in his political reality, unlike theater's customary wisecracking maid who seems never to have washed underwear for the household.

Lorca's humor can be satirical as well. Professor X, who speaks with the uncle, doubles as relief and chorus. The scene is set in 1900.

Professor X: What progress!! Mr. Longoria of Madrid has just bought an automobile he can drive at the fantastic speed of twenty miles per hour, and the Shah of Persia, a very pleasant man, bought a Panhard Levassor, twenty-four horsepower.
Uncle: The Paris-Madrid race was suspended because the racers all killed each other before they reached Bordeaux.
Professor X: Count Zboronsky, dead in that accident, and Marcel Renault, or Renol, such in both fashions it can be pronounced, are saints of science who will be canonized as soon as we have a progressive religion.
Uncle: You can't convert me.
Professor X: A political science professor need not argue with a rose gardener. Such mystical practices are out, believe me! Nowadays, new paths are opened by Tolstwa, or Tolstoy, since in both fashions it may be pronounced. I myself live in the *polis,* not in *natura.*
Uncle: One lives as one can.
Professor X: If Santos Durmont, instead of studying comparative meteorology had dedicated himself to watching roses, the dirigible would be still in the bosom of Brahma.
Uncle: Botany is a science.
Professor X: But an *applied* science.

(act 2)

This au courant, cosmopolitan, urbane buffoon has provided us with some laughs, but suddenly Lorca turns on a dime; the professor asks Rosita's hand in marriage. In an instant, we know what her matrimonial stock is worth: nothing.

The action of act 3 occurs ten years later. The uncle is dead, the house is sold. Aunt, Housekeeper, and Rosita are about to move. Rosita is urged to marry, but she won't abide the addlepated suitors who have appeared over the "years that fall like undergarments ripped from my body." Her lover has never again written. She is resigned, but she still speaks even of her betrayal in the pillowy murmurs of superannuated love; the maid and the aunt are more direct:

Aunt: The false heart of the man! I'd like to take a boat, pick up a whip—
Maid (interrupting): And take a sword and cut off his head and bash it with two stones and chop off that hand with its false lying letters of affection.
Aunt: Ah, yes! Make him pay with blood what has cost blood. And afterward . . .
Maid: Scatter the ashes over the sea, and
Aunt: . . . revive him and bring him to Rosita with our honor satisfied.

The aunt and the housekeeper, in adversity, speak the same class of language. Rosita appears in a dress of light rose and doll-like long curls. She has aged much. Lorca's humor, though, remains unchanged.

Rosita: What are you doing?
Maid: Criticizing a bit.

An epiphanic moment that might well have influenced Tennessee Williams then occurs: a teenage boy arrives and tells Rosita that he put on his dead mother's dress for Carnival, but it scared him. As he leaves, the wind blows up "as if to make the garden ugly and lessen the pain" of leaving the place. The housekeeper comments, "Beautiful it never was." The three women leave the house—silent but for a door banging in the wind at the final curtain.

There are traces of allegory in the potency that leaves Spain for the New World, in people playing with gardens and tools while the freshness of Spain disappears like the Rosa Mutabile that dies in the short day that is a life, a century or two of a nation.

While in New York, Lorca somehow managed to find time between *Poet in New York* and a surrealist movie script, "Trip to the Moon," to work on what he called his impossible plays. They are highly innovative and not very original. Surrealistic hijinks poorly cover the thin themes of sexual freedom and artistic integrity.

Así que pasen cinco años (*If Five Years Pass,* 1937) is a complicated play about the simple idea of trying to stop time. Time is not only the idea but the device. Clocks strike but do not move, tenses collide in one sentence. The cast is multitudinous and miraculous. A cat talks, a mannequin walks, a football player produces endless Havana cigars from his knee pads. The Young Man (all characters in the play are abstractions) awaits his Betrothed, who runs and embraces the Football Player, her "dragon" who blows smoke in her face. An Old Man says she is only fifteen years old. The young man, still trying to destroy time, says, "Why not fifteen things old? . . . or Fifteen roses old?" Lorca specialists have found virtues in this play's early attempts at expressionism.

His play *El paseo de Buster Keaton* (*Buster Keaton's Promenade,* 1928) is a slapstick, surrealist piece that works on absolutely no level except that of fun. It contains stunning images and, small as it is, shows his genius for the consequential detail, bursting with energy, full as a tick. From the ending:

> *Buster Keaton* (surprised): I wish I could be a swan. But I can't although I want to. Where would I leave my hat, my bird collar, and my tie. What bad luck!
> (A young girl, wispy and tall, enters, riding a bicycle. She has the head of a nightingale.)
> *Young Girl:* To whom do I owe the honor?
> *Buster Keaton* (with reverence): A Buster Keaton.
> (The young girl faints and falls from the bicycle. Her striped legs tremble in the grass like two dying zebras. A gramophone announces in a thousand voices, "There are no nightingales in America!")
> *Buster Keaton* (on his knees): Excuse me for what I have been! Miss! (lower) Miss! (lower still) Miss! (kisses her).
> (On the Philadelphia horizon appear the brilliant stars of a police car.)

There are other romps impossible to describe, very arbitrary and obscure; some curiously funny, some daringly dull. *Retablillo de don Cristóbal* (*In the Flame of Don Cristóbal,* 1938) is a puppet-falsetto farce, simple and cunningly contrived, as true farces must be. Cristóbal is Lorca's commedia dell'arte hero, violently in love with his wife, Rosita (no relation to the spinster). She deceives him with every other man in the play, including its Director and Author; even the man he robbed and clubbed to death returns to enjoy her favors, all three beautiful feet of her.

In the prologue, the Author-Puppet assures the audience the earthy innocence of their charmingly free language will purify the commercial vulgarity entering the audience's home. The Director threatens to deprive the Author of his crust of bread if he doesn't cease blathering about good and evil. The piece continues in this slapstick folk form which Lorca considered to be the "temperature of a country's grace."

While in New York, Lorca worked on a play that was translated only recently: *El público*

(*The Audience,* 1934), meaning either the "public" or the "audience," an intentional ambiguity. It is about the audience and the public and their attitude toward individuality in art and sex. It is too complicated to reproduce here. In fact it has proven too complicated for any theater company to produce. By 1931, gravely affected by his stay in New York, Lorca was unambiguously favoring the public rather than the audience in terms of his work. He decided to take his work and the work of the early masters he loved and place them before the deprived, the assaulted, the illiterate populace.

Lorca left his family and the literary court of Madrid and bought two busses, which he filled with actors and students, intending to travel the countryside performing plays for "the forgotten." He produced the great works of Lope, Cervantes, and Calderón—productions that, Brecht-like, teach the illiterate through theater. He rolled happily through the peasant hills with his troupe of young artists and artisans of Spain, a kind of 1960's street theater engaged in the battle he first learned existed during that year-long lesson as a Columbia student.

It would have been difficult in the Spain of the 1930's to avoid the air of social change from South America. Spain's poor were changing. They no longer thought they were predestined by God to serve the nobility. The idea of possibilities for the next generation began to grow; the avant-garde endorsed it. Diego Rivera's murals pitted Lenin and Debs against Rockefeller and the czar.

The path to economic enlightenment was a labyrinth of Marxism, Leninism, Stalinism, and social democracy. But while liberals argued ideologies, Franco's vigilantes—equipped with Spanish zeal and German weapons—struck. They were the military arm of a crusade against Freud and Marx, against Gypsies, atheists, homosexuals, and democracy.

When official education fails, the task of educating often falls to the artist. Lorca, in this activist moment, determined to educate through his group of actors, students, and professionals. His poetic guerrilla theater was

named La Barraca, after a novel by Blasco-Ibáñez about the Spanish peasants' plight. The name (The Barrack) obviously has a military connotation as well; Lorca was conscious of hermeneutics even as he was helping build sets and paint backdrops.

Lorca's La Barraca was the outcome of the bloodless revolution of April 1931 that banished Alfonso XIII from his throne and established a republic. The plan for La Barraca was presented by the Union Federal de Estudiantes Hispanicos, a students' coalition. Costs would be limited. The actors would all be students and professional friends. Lorca explained:

> La Barraca will be placed in a public park until the wandering *barraca,* the caravan theater, can go on wheels through the outskirts of Madrid on weekends and holidays. And in the summer we will tour Spain. Students in architecture will make the *barracas* and do the stage setting and assembling; students in philosophy will collaborate with the poets of the executive committee. I myself will be writing new things and helping with old ones.
>
> ("La barraca")

The new republican government approved money for the student actors and stage hands; busses were bought. La Barraca went on the road. Lorca produced his own version of Calderón's *Life Is a Dream* to celebrate the 400th anniversary of the play. He also adapted Lope de Vega's *Fuente Ovejuna (The Village of Fuente Ovejuna).* The plot: when a military commander sexually abuses the women of the town, he is flung from his palace balcony onto the prongs of the villagers' pitchforks. During the "trial" that ensues, the Inquisition tortures all the men and women of the village. They have agreed, however, not to name names. When asked who killed the commander, every citizen under oath and under the whip answers that the perpetrator was "the village of Fuente Ovejuna." The king and queen, Ferdinand and Isabella, with a wisdom Lope hints is divinely bestowed upon just rulers, decide to eliminate military rule in the town, avoiding further pollution of justice. The civilized, if not exactly civil, rule of Ferdinand and Isabella becomes abstract rather than historical in Lorca's hands. Look at production: the sets were contemporary; the medieval warlord of Lope's original became a contemporary landowner. The message was clear: peasants and bourgeoisie must never again be ruled by someone whose rape of the people is the only contact between ruler and ruled.

Following the populist footsteps of Lope (whose ars dramatica was "Damn the purists, full fun ahead!"), La Barraca presented Lope's classics on two nights—the first in the old version, the second simplified but stylized, "new as the latest experiment." Lorca charged little or no admission so that working people could attend. Lorca spattered the plays with verse set to popular melodies, like Lope, like the English Restoration ballad opera, and very much like Brecht's *Threepenny Opera*. Indeed, it seems the Brechtian commitment—already ten years on the boards—made its way across the Rhine and over the Sierras to land in Spain. Again, from "La barraca":

> The theater, in essence a part of the people, is almost dead, and the people are suffering accordingly, as they would if they had lost eyes, ears, or a sense of taste. We are going to give them back the very plays they used to love. Also, new plays in the modern manner, explained ahead of time, will be presented with the simplifications necessary to our plan.

They were in fine company. Brecht that same year turned *Richard III* into a Hitlerian Chicago gangster with *The Resistible Rise of Arturo Ui*; Lorca's Andalusian predecessor Seneca had transformed *Oedipus Tyrannus* into a moral Grand Guignol. It was "a way to educate the people of our beloved Republic, to take Good and Evil" in his bus around Spain.

La Barraca fell quickly in Spain. Conservatives in the shaky new republican government accused La Barraca of having moved politically left. They were right.

Expressionistic methods focused starkly on political implications. For instance, the lovers in Lope's *Peribáñez*, in their antisocial oblivion, reflect Unamuno's statement about Spanish intellectuals and the rise of fascism: "We never had any idea what was coming our way." So the unschooled, uncared-for audience at the dusty end of town found one place on a makeshift stage where ideas could be laughed at, applauded, and absorbed—where ideas had the floor. La Barraca toured in 1933 and 1934. While Hitler was mobilizing, Lorca's only weapon was Spain's Shakespeare, Lope.

Fifty years after Lorca's murder, it is still impossible to determine the accomplices. Several possibilities exist. In Granada a "Black Squad" of killers, whom the Civil Guard turned loose, terrorized the city. Apologists for Generalissimo Franco hoped these "uncontrollable elements" were at fault in Lorca's death. The varying factions of Spanish fascism blamed each other for the murder—and all blamed the Civil Guard. The buck was passed over Lorca's corpse writhing in an unmarked grave.

Gerald Brenan noted that the fascist journalist De Llano suggested the murder of Lorca was vengeance for the death of Benavente—a rather hysterical claim, considering Benavente lived until long after the war. A Lorchean twist.

Lorca was caught while hiding in the house of a literary Phalangist friend, Rosales. Members of the Rosales family were political and literary enemies of Ruiz Alonso, whose awful poetry had been rejected by Lorca and Rosales' magazine. It was he who turned in Lorca, according to Marcelle Auclair. Possible, Jean-Louis Schonberg suggested that the arrest was not strictly political but based on homosexual jealousy, with Ruiz Alonso again rejected by Lorca, this time personally.

Ian Gibson, after thorough research and consideration, concluded that Lorca was killed "not by any one man but by a group of ultra-Catholic members and the like-minded of *Acción Popular*, among whom Ruiz Alonso was most influential."

Of the three men who took Lorca from the Rosales' house, one, Trecastro, boasted of his part in the execution. V. S. Pritchett says we should take the words of this womanizing café hero with more than just one grain of salt, but there is no doubt Acción Popular hated Lorca for his contacts with the few liberal intellectuals in Granada. Granada was a deeply conservative city that had earlier resented the invasion of the Generation of '98. Now, with the beginnings of a peasant organization, the local establishment, traditional and intolerant since the Counter-Reformation, correctly saw liberal reform in education as a threat.

Lorca was too visible, dangerous, liberal. He was shot. Despite his literary victory over symbolism, his death had a symbolic significance; over four thousand people were shot by firing squad in Granada alone. While he had no defined political position, his death, as Pritchett noted, revealed "the ferocity which Franco awakened in a nation notoriously prone to violence."

While he was acquainted with left-wing politicians, his friends were Phalangists such as Rosales and José Antonio Primo de Rivera, the artistic dictator. What could have aroused such anger for him to be lined up one dawn in the first month of the war and machine gunned (some say through the anus)? The most significant answer comes from his betrayer, Ruiz Alonso: "He did more damage with his pen than others did with their guns."

Selected Bibliography

EDITIONS

INDIVIDUAL WORKS
Impresiones y paisajes. Granada, 1918.
Libro de poemas. Madrid, 1921.
Santa Lucía y San Lázaro. Madrid, 1927.
Primer romancero gitano. Madrid, 1928.
Poema del cante jondo. Madrid, 1931.
Llanto por Ignacio Sánchez Mejías. Madrid, 1935.
Nocturno del hueco. Madrid, 1935.
Seis poemas galegos. Santiago de Compostela, 1935.
Diván del Tamarit. New York, 1936.
Primeras canciones. Madrid, 1936.
Poeta en Nueva York. Madrid, 1940.

COLLECTED WORKS
Obras completas. Madrid, 1971. Contains bibliography.

TRANSLATIONS

Deep Song and Other Prose. Edited and translated by Christopher Maurer. New York, 1980.
Five Plays: Comedies and Tragicomedies. Translated by James Graham-Luján and Richard L. O'Connell. New York, 1965.
Impressions and Landscapes. Translated by Lawrence H. Klibbe. Hanover, N.H., 1987.
Poet in New York. Translated by Ben Bellitt. New York, 1983.
The Public and Play Without a Title. Translated by Carlos Bauer. New York, 1983.
Selected Letters. Edited and translated by David Gershator. New York, 1983.
Selected Poems. Edited by Donald Allen and Francisco García Lorca. New York, 1955.
Three Tragedies. Translated by James Graham-Luján and Richard L. O'Connell. New York, 1947.

BIOGRAPHICAL AND CRITICAL STUDIES

Adams, Mildred. *García Lorca: Playwright and Poet.* New York, 1977.
Aiken, Conrad. "Review of *The Poet in New York and Other Poems of Federico García Lorca.*" *New Republic* 103:309 (1940).
Alberti, Rafael, "García Lorca: *Poeta en Nueva York.*" *Sur* (Buenos Aires), 75:147–151 (1940).
Allen, Rupert C. *The Symbolic World of Federico García Lorca.* Albuquerque, N. Mex., 1972.
Butt, John. *Writers and Politics in Modern Spain.* New York, 1978.
Campbell, Roy. *Lorca.* New Haven, Conn., 1952.
Craige, Betty Jean. *Lorca's Poet in New York: The Fall into Consciousness.* Lexington, Kentucky, 1977.
Duran, Manuel. *Lorca: A Collection of Critical Essays.* Englewood Cliffs, N.J., 1962.
Frazier, Brenda, *La mujer en al teatro de Federico García Lorca.* Madrid, 1973.
Gabriel, Isidro. *Los mejores romances de la lengua castellana.* Buenos Aires, 1961.
Gibson, Ian. *The Death of Lorca.* Chicago, 1973.

————. *Federico García Lorca: A Life.* New York, 1989.

Gorman, John. *The Reception of Federico García Lorca in Germany.* Göppingen, 1973.

Higginbotham, Virginia. "Lorca's Apprenticeship in Surrealism." *Romanic Review* 61:109–122 (1970).

Honig, Edwin. *García Lorca.* New York, 1944.

Ilie, Paul. *The Surrealist Mode in Spanish Literature.* Ann Arbor, Mich., 1968.

Loughran, David K. *Federico García Lorca: The Poetry of Limits.* London, 1978.

Marcilly, Charles. *Ronde et fable de la solitude à New York. Prelude à Poeta en Nueva York de F. G. Lorca.* Paris, 1962.

Martínez Nadal, Rafael. *Federico García Lorca and the Public.* New York, 1974.

Ramos Gil, Carlos. *Ecos antiguos, estructuras nuevas, y mundo primario de la lírica de Lorca.* Bahía Blanca, 1967.

Rossi, Rosa. *Da Unamuno a Lorca.* Catania via Caronda, 1967.

ARNOLD WEINSTEIN

VILHELM MOBERG

(1898–1973)

IN HIS NATIVE Sweden, Vilhelm Moberg is the most widely read author of all time. His career as a published writer spanned half a century, and during this period his works were sold in some six million copies in Sweden, a staggering figure for a country that today counts only eight million inhabitants. Moberg's magnum opus, the emigrant tetralogy, has alone appeared in close to two million copies in Sweden. After August Strindberg, Selma Lagerlöf, and Pär Lagerkvist, Moberg is the most translated Swedish author; his works can be read in more than twenty languages. If we add to the number of Moberg's readers the listeners and viewers of his numerous plays presented on radio and television and the audiences around the world that have seen Jan Troell's film version of *The Emigrants,* we count vast numbers of people who have at least briefly shared Moberg's vision and been moved by his epic power.

Quantitative considerations are of course doubtful criteria of an author's true stature. Indeed, it could be argued that Moberg's great popularity, not least among people who are ordinarily immune to "good literature," has posed an obstacle to his full recognition by some established critics. Himself a lifelong critic of established institutions, a sworn foe of the four cornerstones of "the ancient kingdom" (*Det gamla riket,* the title of one of his satirical novels)—the throne, the sword, the altar, and the purse—Moberg could hardly avoid making

enemies. He gained his greatest public visibility as a towering figure in the midst of controversy, sanguine and rabulistic, of imposing physical stature with his feet planted solidly on the ground, the large hands of a farmer, a prominent jaw, and rebelliously bushy eyebrows. An author who considered it a writer's máin function to act as a salt in the body politic, he viewed official distinctions and public honors as a threat to his independence. It was largely his own fierce criticism of the Swedish Academy that deprived him of the opportunity and the satisfaction of declining admission to it, although he was qualified to occupy a seat among its eighteen members. With pride he pointed to the two most cherished "distinctions" of his career: the refusal by the chancellor of the University of Lund to accept his nomination for an honorary doctorate and the banning of all his books in Nazi Germany by Goebbels.

Moberg's unprecedented success as a writer is founded on some basic, irrefutable virtues. He is a good storyteller. His characters come alive and elicit the reader's emotional involvement. While writing the four volumes of his emigrant series, Moberg was flooded with letters from readers on both sides of the Atlantic expressing their concern for the future of the characters. Tourists have tried to locate the pioneer cemetery in Minnesota in order to place flowers on Kristina's grave or have visited the parish church in Ljuder to view the bridal crown donated by the former village whore, Ulrika, only to discover that both women are creations of Moberg's imagination.

Far from being a modernist or an experimenter with narrative techniques, Moberg subscribed to a traditional concept of realism with an unflinching respect for authentic details and unhurried elaborations of characters and events. This mode of narration lends itself to broadly epic compositions in which everyday concerns and dramatic, often drastic, events are subordinated to the flow of time, the progression of the seasons, and man's journey between birth and death, his brief sojourn on earth a link in an endless chain of generations.

Moberg's style is simple and direct; at its best it is triumphantly unobtrusive. His linguistic purism, his judicious use of dialect words for local color, and the rhythmic flow of his prose are signs of his mastery over his medium.

It is as an epic novelist that Moberg will be best remembered; as such he defends his place in Swedish literature among the major writers of this century. His most significant novels deal with the peasant society of his native province Småland, a society that remained unchanged for centuries but was rapidly transformed with the advent of the twentieth century. Moberg experienced this transformation in his own life. Born into the rural proletariat in one of Sweden's poorest provinces, he made it his task to document the former reality of a major portion of the population—farmers, crofters (tenant farmers), smallholders, and unlanded people.

Moberg's popularity in Sweden may in part be explained by the fact that his experience— and his nostalgia—were shared by great numbers of Swedes. Industrialism came late to Sweden, and the transformation from a rural-agrarian into an urban-technological society was largely completed in the 1930's, at the time Moberg emerged as a major writer. His readers had themselves participated in the internal migration from the provinces to the urban centers in the wake of the mass emigration to the United States that took place in the decades before World War I. The world Moberg re-created was the world of his readers' parents and grandparents. These readers had watched the political development in Sweden that brought about a shift of power from the few to the many with the introduction of universal suffrage, the rise to power of social democracy, and the beginnings of the welfare state. Moberg's novels enabled them to measure this progress and to evaluate both the material gains it entailed and the less tangible losses of roots and age-old values.

Moberg's themes are basic and timeless. The conflicts are clearly stated and are repeated with variations in new configurations within a work or between works. Country and city, tradition and progress, acceptance and rebellion, instinctive nature and social demands, collective conformity and individual freedom—these are a few of the opposites behind the dramatic tension in Moberg's works. The typical Moberg protagonist is a rebel motivated by dreams of social justice and individual freedom from constraints. He is an idealistic utopian without metaphysical aspirations. Recognizing this earth to be man's only home, he is acutely aware of the concrete realities around him and of his own physical being.

In most of Moberg's works we find this emphasis on physical realities. His novels abound in descriptions of hard work, depicted either as the joyful exertion of muscles pitted against recalcitrant matter, or as backbreaking toil and drudgery. There is an understated exultation of the senses, especially as they respond to the summer richness of the earth and the biological cycles in nature, the germination of the seed and its growth to fruition, and the urgings of the blood and their highest fulfillment in the sexual union of man and woman. His works constitute a celebration of the life force itself, made all the more poignant by an accompanying awareness of individual death. The robust, positive, and earthy aspects of Moberg's writing and his projection of himself as an exuberant and defiant man of the soil possessing the indomitable qualities of the Småland peasant may tend to overshadow other aspects of his work—disquieting undercurrents of pessimism and despair that add complexity to the picture of the man and his work.

THE MAKING OF AN AUTHOR

Carl Artur Vilhelm Moberg was born on 20 August 1898 in Algutsboda Parish in Småland. Algutsboda is part of the ancient region Värend, and as an ardent historian Moberg studied existing sources about the obscure tribes, the Wirds, that settled there and founded a kingdom long before Sweden became a nation. They were known to have been fiercely independent, and their society granted an unusual measure of equality to its women. Moberg was born into a way of life that had remained the same for countless generations in this remote area of deep forests and small homesteads, where people wrested a precarious living from the meager and rockbound soil and where the large families and the lack of arable land created a population surplus. During the last couple of decades of the nineteenth century a railroad was built through the region, and small glass factories were founded, drawing on the unlimited supply of firewood and cheap labor. The most traumatic event for the region, however, was mass emigration to the United States. What began as a trickle rapidly grew into an irresistible flood. Both of Moberg's parents' brothers and sisters had emigrated to America, and Moberg relates that for a long time he believed that the word "cousin" meant a refined kind of child who wore nice clothes and existed only in America.

Moberg's parents were of hardy peasant stock: his father, Carl Gottfried Moberg, lived to the age of eighty-five, and his mother, Ida Charlotta, was ninety-six years old when she died in 1960. She came from a long line of farmers and soldiers, and Moberg's father was a soldier-crofter, as his father and grandfather had been. According to the old militia system, the ranks of the standing army were made up of such soldier-crofters. In return for exemption from military service, villagers contributed to the support of an infantryman by furnishing him with a tied smallholding and some basic goods and services, and after initial training the soldier was obliged to attend month-long annual military maneuvers. Moberg senior, who was pensioned off in 1914, was the last soldier-crofter of his district, for after 1901 the old militia system was gradually phased out. In his novel *Raskens: En soldatfamiljs historia* (The Rasks: The Story of a Soldier's Family, 1927) Moberg raised a literary monument to the institution and the people whose lives were affected by it.

Vilhelm, or Carl, as he was called at home, was the fourth of seven children born in the modest crofter's cottage and the only one of the four boys to reach adulthood. Two of the brothers died in infancy, and the first-born, Hjalmar, died in 1909 at the age of eighteen. To the eleven-year-old Vilhelm, who was now the only surviving son in the family, this death appears to have been traumatic. More than fifty years later it forms the central event in the novel *Din stund på jorden* (A Time on Earth, 1962).

In an autobiographical essay, "Brodd" (Germination, 1932), Moberg views his earliest childhood with nostalgia. He depicts an idyllic world of wonders experienced in proximity to nature. The child is not burdened with a sense of poverty and deprivation, for there is no other world to compare with:

In this poor part of poor Småland there hardly existed any real economic class differences. . . .
The farmer and the farmhand were of the same stock, ate at the same table, performed side by side the same work, indulged in the same amusements in their free time and met as equals at weddings, funerals, and social events. All this gave a sense of equality, even if the farmer happened to be well off and the farmhand owned only the shirt on his back.

(p. 15)

Moberg extols the virtues of this rural order and "the people of toil and contentment." The farmer is seen as the last individualist, and the common people are described as robust men and hardy women who toiled by day and slept soundly at night, who found an outlet for excess energy in bouts of fighting and drinking, and who had no time for unhappiness, brooding, or neuroses: "They would have been of scant interest to Freud," as Moberg commented.

From the perspective of the machine age, Moberg considered these rural people enviable; their lives were freer and had more dignity. In Moberg's view, industrialism had proved to be less than a blessing to humanity. Modern man had not been content with using the machine to satisfy his most elementary needs and alleviate his lot; he had used it to create new needs, which were presented as indispensable to human happiness, but which only increased man's discontent and restless search for new satisfactions.

These views of 1932, which echo Freud's criticism in *Civilization and Its Discontents* (1930), eventually underwent certain changes. When "Brodd" was reprinted in *Berättelser ur min levnad* (Tales from My Life, 1968), he felt compelled to revise his opinion of the enviable life of his ancestors. In a postscript he admits that his earlier views had been colored by a certain romantic idealization. Having conducted more in-depth research in connection with his subsequent historical novels, he had come to realize that the history of his native region was first and foremost a history of suffering and human misery. It was dominated by pain and disease, crop failures, famine years, and endless wars through the centuries. "The more deeply I enter into the past of these people, the more I marvel at their ability to endure suffering," he wrote. "How could they survive all this want and all this misery? It seems incomprehensible to me."

His earlier mistrust of the technological age, on the other hand, had not changed, but had only been confirmed. The threat of nuclear destruction, the systematic violation of man's natural environment, the pollution of air and water, and the poisoning of the fish in lakes and streams were matters of passionate concern to the author who entitled one of his novels *Giv oss jorden!* (*The Earth Is Ours!* 1939).

In 1906 Moberg began his education in a one-room schoolhouse in the forest. Because children were expected to help with farm work, his formal schooling was restricted to four months a year for seven years, or a total of twenty-eight months. The school emphasized religion and the memorization of Luther's catechism, but the children were also taught to read and write. They were the second generation to become literate. Moberg's maternal grandmother could not read and had to rely on outside assistance for her correspondence with her six children in America.

Moberg had learned to read before he entered school, and his discovery of the magic of the written word was a revelation to him. It also marked the beginning of what he would later refer to as the greatest suffering of his childhood and early youth, his insatiable hunger for reading and the difficulty of satisfying it, especially during the long winters. His God-fearing parents looked on with approval when he read through the Bible from cover to cover at age ten, but they met his continued demands for additional reading material with incomprehension and concern, fearing that "he was not right in the head" and seeking advice from a local quack. The frustration and despair of the intellectually undernourished boy were acute. He resorted to daydreams and fantasies, but these too needed outside stimulus. He experienced temporary relief when his mother received a bunch of newspaper supplements in the village and used them to wallpaper a small room; through this "writing on the wall" he devoured most of the installments of Jules Verne's *The Secret Island.* When he discovered that it was possible to order small circulating libraries from Stockholm and to act as local librarian, he managed to get the required three crowns from his father. It was a happy moment when he picked up the box of some forty books at the train station and pulled his precious load home on a sledge. He filled the borrowing journal with fictitious names, listing old women who had never learned to read as borrowers of impressive tomes, and even added some names from the tombstones in the cemetery in order to assure the people in Stockholm that the torch of enlightenment was burning bright in the Småland forests.

The craving for books was a major force in Moberg's early life. Before he finished elementary school he began to contribute to his keep by working in a nearby glass factory, where child labor was far from uncommon. There he was exposed to politically radical ideas and became a Young Socialist. Older fellow workers loaned him literature that decisively shaped his views on social justice, made him forswear the religious faith of his parents and declare himself an atheist, and turned him into a confirmed pacifist and opponent of the monarchy. Early on he became a member of the local Good Templar lodge; the rumor of its library was a powerful incentive for Moberg to join.

When Moberg finished school, he divided his time between hard labor—in the glass factory, on a peat bog, and in the forest—and voracious reading, the latter activity viewed with increased concern by his parents. He had also begun to write. At age thirteen he had won eighteenth place (out of twenty) in a youth contest held in a weekly magazine with a highly moralistic tale about a drunkard and his dog. The disappointing reward, a mushroom chart, did not convince his parents of the profitability of his pursuits. From his seventeenth year he contributed prose sketches to the local newspaper and to the weekly magazine *Såningsmannen* (The Sower), which had a primarily rural readership.

In 1916 Moberg decided to emigrate to the United States. At his request an uncle in California sent him the ticket, but at the last moment Moberg yielded to his mother's entreaties not to go. Instead it was decided that he should

be allowed to attend the County Folk High School at Grimslöv from October to April. Moberg later referred to these months as the happiest time of his youth. The high points were the history lessons, the weekly compositions, and Moberg's enthusiastic involvement in amateur dramatics—an auspicious combination of interests for the future novelist, dramatist, and historian. Not least important, the school had a good library.

After the happy months at Grimslöv, Moberg returned to work in the forest, now with his mind set on saving enough money to continue his schooling. In January 1918 he enrolled in Katrineholms Praktiska Skola, a "crammer" in which students could force their studies toward graduation. Moberg hoped to earn the equivalent of a high school diploma and studied with desperate determination. He excelled in history and turned in compositions of such length and maturity as to arouse his teachers' suspicions at first. But his studies were brought to an abrupt end in the fall, when he contracted the dreaded Spanish influenza and nearly succumbed to it. When he was fully recovered several months later, he abandoned his hopes of acquiring a formal education.

Moberg's development is typical of a whole generation of Swedish writers who originated in the poor rural society around the turn of the century. They were deprived of the privileges of their more fortunate contemporaries, they suffered the hungers of body and mind, and eventually they amply made up for their lack of formal education by directing their reading toward the great minds of the past and the present. These brilliant autodidacts made their impact on Swedish literature in the late 1920's and 1930's with the appearance of a long line of powerful, basically autobiographical novels describing the protagonists' deprivations and struggles for political and intellectual awareness. Together, these works form an important document on the social history of Sweden in the first decades of this century. Two of these "proletarian writers," Eyvind Johnson (1900–1976) and Harry Martinson (1904–1978), shared the Nobel Prize in 1974, and another, Artur Lundkvist (1906–), became one of the most visible and active members of the Swedish Academy.

A list of Vilhelm Moberg's literary "teachers" would include a large portion of the great writers of world literature. In his partly autobiographical novel *Soldat med brutet gevär* (Soldier with a Broken Rifle, 1944), the young protagonist Valter Sträng receives powerful impulses from his reading of Leo Tolstoy, Maxim Gorky, and Peter Kropotkin, as well as Victor Hugo and the Americans Jack London and Robert Ingersoll. And there was also Strindberg, who was, Moberg said, "the Swedish writer who has taught me most over the years and whom I have loved most."

In Moberg's admiration for Strindberg there is an element of identification with the fearless rebel and social critic, the satirist, the writer of historical prose and drama, and the polemicist who in the last years of his life championed the cause of the workers. Stylistically, Strindberg's direct and forceful mode of narration undoubtedly served Moberg as a model. At age fifteen Moberg for the first time read a novel dealing entirely with the life of peasants, Strindberg's *Hemsöborna* (*The People of Hemsö*, 1887). Its earthy realism and use of words that Moberg thought were not allowed to be printed were a revelation to him. In *Berättelser ur min levnad,* however, he comments that he later felt Strindberg had not gone far enough in giving a genuine depiction of peasant life: "One had to go even further in realism and view one's subjects completely from within. At the same time it became obvious to me that for a serious writer there cannot exist any dirty or forbidden words." Unfortunately, there were readers in Sweden and America who did not share his opinion in this matter and who found certain passages in Moberg's works highly offensive. With puritanical zeal and moral outrage they started a campaign to ban Moberg's books, a controversy bordering on personal persecution that must have strengthened Moberg's feeling of affinity with Strindberg.

As a depictor of rural life Moberg had other predecessors who in varying degrees served him as models for his own work. Among these one could single out Lagerlöf, the author of *Jerusalem* (1901–1902), Sigrid Undset, the author of *Olav Audunssön* (1925–1927), and the Polish Nobel Prize winner Władisław Reymont, whose novel cycle *Chłopi* (*The Peasants,* 1902–1909) describes one year in the life of a Polish village. The Norwegian Knut Hamsun was eagerly read by Moberg. In his own prose there are occasional echoes of the almost mystical experience of nature found in Hamsun's *Pan* (1894) or of the rugged lyricism that informs his *Markens grøde* (*Growth of the Soil,* 1917), a novel about a settler in the wilderness and the blessings of life close to the soil. In the latter novel, Hamsun condemns city culture and its corrupting influence on the simple goodness of country life. In the novel *Segelfoss by* (*Segelfoss Town,* 1915) he presents a highly negative view of industrial capitalism. As an epic novelist dealing with rural life Moberg is able to hold his own, even surpassing his predecessors, not in terms of the artistry or the visionary beauty of their presentations, but in terms of his honest realism and respect for authentic details and his ability to enter into the conceptual world of his subjects.

The list of Moberg's literary mentors would not be complete without mention of Arthur Schopenhauer. He read this philosopher and prophet of pessimism as he was entering his twenties, and the experience affected him profoundly. In *The World as Will and Idea* (1819) Schopenhauer presents life as meaningless and existence as suffering, an oscillation between pain and boredom. The will expresses itself as an endless striving, as desire seeking but never attaining satisfaction. Only death offers release into a welcome nothingness. In his exemplary biography of the young Moberg, Magnus von Platen draws a portrait of a complex character in whom defiant assertiveness and obstinacy are coupled with shyness and abnormal sensitivity and moods that alternate between manic elation and depressive dejection. Clearly Schopenhauer's teaching struck responsive chords in Moberg. At the same time he realized that adopting this philosophy would have paralyzing effects. In *Soldat med brutet gevär* he makes his protagonist, Valter Sträng, formulate a remedy: "And if existence itself had no meaning, then one was driven to provide it with a meaning oneself by striving beyond this poor inadequate life. This thought helped him resist the attacks of Schopenhauer." Moberg found the best antidote against depression and "attacks of Schopenhauer" to be hard work. Throughout his life he experienced his greatest joy in the full and productive employment of his powers. His voluminous output became his justification for living, a bulwark erected against nothingness.

By Moberg's own account, his time of preparation for the writer's profession extended over fifteen years, from 1912 to 1927. In 1919 he began his career as a journalist for a number of provincial newspapers, first as an unpaid assistant with *Vadstena Läns Tidning* in the province of Östergötland, then as an assistant editor in the town of Motala in the same province, and later in the town of Arvika in the province of Värmland. In the first of these positions he had the fortune to work under the colorful editor Pälle Segerborg, who early recognized the potentials of his young assistant, offered him guidance and advice, taught him uncompromising respect for the freedom of the press, and willingly accepted Moberg's short stories for publication in his paper. He even introduced him to Margareta Törnquist, the young woman who in 1923 became Moberg's wife and lifelong companion.

In 1920 Moberg was invited back to his first newspaper, this time as Segerborg's successor. He accepted the offer and mused that at age twenty-two he was probably the youngest editor of a newspaper in Sweden. Moberg always found it difficult to take orders and to bow to superiors and authorities, and he now enjoyed his freedom and independence. The same qualities of rugged individualism and independence made him resign from his editorship in 1922 because of a disagreement with the owner of the newspaper over a matter of principle.

Along with his journalistic work Moberg continued his apprenticeship as an author and produced a seemingly endless stream of short stories, sketches, and plays. The tales— Moberg estimated that they exceeded five hundred in number—were mostly written under the pseudonym "Ville i Momåla" and were placed with various provincial newspapers. They were usually humorous pieces with a rustic setting. Although their literary importance is negligible, they were undoubtedly valuable exercises in the craft of writing fiction, in the development of plots and dialogue and the use of authentic material for realistic settings. As early as 1920 Moberg had his first novel completed, *Prinsessan på Solklinten* (The Princess at Solklinten), a romantic tale with a conventional plot—the poor farmhand who overcomes all obstacles to win the beautiful daughter of the richest and most powerful man in the parish. Moberg received many rejection slips from publishers before he finally managed to get it published in 1922. Late in life, Moberg confessed that he had not reread this first novel of his, explaining, "I don't indulge in unnecessary masochism."

In 1921 Moberg interrupted his work as an editor in Vadstena for a few months of compulsory military service in the town of Växjö in his native Småland. His experiences there resulted in his first published book, *I vapenrock och linnebyxor*, subtitled *En krigsmans intryck och upplevelser* (In Tunic and Linen Trousers: A Soldier's Impressions and Adventures, 1921). This collection of comical sketches pokes high-spirited and irreverent fun at officers and military life and its routines. Moberg, as much an avowed pacifist as he was a belligerent opponent of infringements on his personal freedom, made a poor soldier. He was subjected to a number of disciplinary actions for absences without leave and general insubordination, and he wrote most of the sketches while enjoying the leisure of six days' detention in the guardhouse. The book had considerable local success, and despite efforts by the military commander to have it suppressed, it was printed in a second edition (1921).

Moberg served his longest and most difficult stretch as a journalist in Småland. From 1922 to 1927 he was local correspondent for *Nya Växjöbladet* in Alvesta. The constant pressure to produce a set number of daily lines despite the general eventlessness of this small town and to assure payment for his contributions through solicitation of local ads was a heavy burden for the family man and aspiring author. He was dissatisfied with his life as a hack writer and was impatient for recognition and national fame. He suffered a devastating disappointment when a novel that he had submitted to a national contest did not win the first prize he had expected to get; it was not even recommended for publication.

Moberg's efforts as a playwright met with greater success. A number of his plays, facile equivalents of his stories of rustic life, were acquired by small touring companies and were performed in the provinces. More often than not, Moberg never received payment for them. One of these plays achieved some success on the Stockholm stage in 1924 (*Doktorn på nummer 18* [The Doctor at Number 18], unpublished). Another play, *Kassabrist* (Embezzlement), was turned down by eight theaters before the director of the Blanche Theater in Stockholm decided to stage it. Filled with defeatism and dreading the critical verdict of his play as his own literary "execution," Moberg traveled to Stockholm for the premier on New Year's Day 1926. But the play was a public and critical success: it had a first run of 120 performances and was soon staged in Denmark, Finland, and Norway as well. Within a few months the royalties for the play amounted to six thousand crowns, a considerable sum in those days.

At this time Moberg obtained a leave of three months from his job as local correspondent in Alvesta. He wanted to write a serious work that had occupied his mind for a long time. Some of the stories he had published in various newspapers in previous years had presented scenes from the life of a soldier-crofter, and Moberg now reworked these stories and built them into the novel *Raskens.* He must have felt confident that this novel would mark the beginning of a new phase in his life, for he resigned from his newspaper post even before the novel had been accepted for publication. Moberg's confidence was justified: Bonniers accepted the novel with enthusiasm, and it was published the following year, 1927, under the author's real name. The limited provincial notoriety of "Ville i Momåla" was now followed by the national fame of Vilhelm Moberg. His *Raskens* was judged to be the year's most promising work by a new writer. The sales were brisk, and the novel saw four new editions in as many months. Translations were commissioned in Germany and Holland, and at Christmas, Bonniers rewarded their best-selling author with a stipend of two thousand crowns and a contract for future works. Moberg's long years of apprenticeship were over.

THE NOVELIST

Moberg's change from a pseudonym to his real name was significant; it indicated a remarkable change in the quality of his writing. With *Raskens* he did in a sense "find himself," striking a vein that turned out to be the mother lode of his authorship. In his earlier writing he had mined material from his rural experience and store of memories and hearsay, but his ambition had been merely to entertain by emulating certain successful provincial writers of humorous and farcical tales from folk life. Later in life Moberg confessed that he felt ashamed of his pseudonymous writing and had come to view his literary models of the time as jesters who amused themselves and others at the expense of the common people, making them into caricatures and ridiculous figures. With *Raskens*, however, his ambition was above all to be true. This new respect for the dignity of his subjects is reflected in Moberg's narrative stance. As Magnus von Platen points out,

> In the novel the author has become one with his characters and their surroundings. As the narrator he places himself in the background. *Raskens* has no other tendency than the one the reader finds subsumed in the reality that is brought to life. The author establishes no contact with his audience over the heads of his characters and marks no distance to them; he does not look down upon them or smile at them or even pity them.
>
> (*Den unge Vilhelm Moberg,* p. 220)

It was also clear that the broadly epic format suited Moberg. As a painter of rural life, he required a large canvas for his real strength and genius to develop in full.

Raskens is the story of Gustav Karlsson, the tall and strong farmhand who is recruited as the militiaman of his village. He receives the name Rask and is commonly called Rasken. He takes over a croft and marries Ida, the dowryless maid at the Olsson farm. The novel describes their life together, a life requiring constant toil to secure the bare necessities for the growing family (nine sons are born to the couple, each birth frustrating their hopes for a daughter). Their small comforts and great disappointments are vividly shared by the readers. Who, for example, can remain unaffected by the family's joy over their first pig as it is fattened for the Christmas slaughter, the anxious and loving care bestowed upon it when it contracts an illness, and finally the grief and despair when it dies a natural death instead of filling their empty larder? The chores of everyday life, the soldier's backbreaking work to clear new ground in the hope of one day being able to buy the croft, his annual absences for the required maneuvers, and his eagerly awaited returns—these are described with supreme authority based on intimate knowledge that extends to the smallest details.

Woven into this fabric are several strands of dramatic action. There is the feud between Rasken and the farmer Oscar on the Olsson farm. Oscar, unloved and unloving, cannot forgive or forget that Gustav was selected as the district's soldier instead of one of the Olsson sons, nor that Ida had spurned his offer of marriage in favor of the penniless Rasken. The feud ends in tragedy when Axel, one of Rasken's sons, falls in love with Oscar's only daughter, Ingrid, and gets her pregnant. Ingrid gives birth to a stillborn child and shortly after suffers the same fate as her mother before her: she goes insane. Oscar takes a terrible revenge: he slays his daughter's lover and then summons Rasken to fetch his son's body before he gives himself up to the sheriff.

There is also the story of Rasken's fellow soldier Klang and his three ill-starred marriages—to the beautiful but promiscuous Nergårds-Anna, to the shrewish and deceitful candy vendor who robs him of all his possessions, and finally to the meek and timid woman whom he brutalizes and drives to suicide.

If by contrast the Raskens have a reasonably good and solid marriage, this is largely thanks to the excellent Ida, a pious and hard-working woman of quiet strength, common sense, and great integrity; Rasken made a good choice when he married her instead of Nergårds-Anna, with whom he had a wild and intoxicating affair in his youth. Rasken himself is not depicted as an idealized paragon. He is an honest provider for his family and a very good worker who earns the grudging respect of the villagers; as a soldier he is above reproach and advances to the rank of corporal, even receiving a medal. But he is hotheaded and gets into brawls, he loves a good round of drinking with his fellow soldiers, and, more serious, he is unable to remain faithful to his wife. After many years of marriage he begins to visit the still-attractive Nergårds-Anna again, and she bears him a daughter. Rasken is ashamed of himself and feels sullied by the relationship, but he keeps returning to Anna. There is a stern morality in Ida's faith in the solemnity of the marriage vows, and Moberg manages to convey a real sense of sin in Rasken's adultery. It is part of his greatness as a storyteller that the readers' sympathies are divided with equal compassion and understanding between Ida's silent hurt and Rasken's uneasy guilt. *Raskens* is not least the moving story of a marriage.

There are dark and violent strands woven into the fabric of *Raskens,* but they are never allowed to dominate. The basic tenor of the novel is positive and almost idyllic, for the soldier's optimism and Ida's sterling qualities enable them to rise above adversities.

In his next novel, however, Moberg created a work of great weight and almost classical monumentality in which the tragic elements predominate. The two-part novel about Adolf in Ulvaskog, *Långt från landsvägen* (Far from the Highway, 1929) and *De knutna händerna* (The Clenched Hands, 1930), has none of the lightness and redeeming features of *Raskens.* A brooding fatality lies over the ancestral farm of Ulvaskog and works with inexorable logic to its climactic end. The central character, Adolf Bengtsson, pits all his physical strength, his unbending will, and his self-reliance against obstacles to the fulfillment of his single-minded ambition—to acquit himself honorably of his responsibility for his forefathers' farm and to pass it on, increased and with no debts attached to it, to the next generation. But his very virtues work against him, turning into flaws that make him the chief agent of his own tragedy.

On his father's death, Adolf, as the eldest son, becomes master of the farm, Ulvaskog, which has passed from father to son for three hundred years. Adolf's first action is to mortgage the farm in order to pay his two brothers and his sister their share of the inheritance. His mother, the indomitable Lotta, remains as mistress of the farm. Adolf's sister Tilda is engaged to be married, but shortly before the wedding her fiancé drowns himself, and she remains on the farm and gives birth to a daughter.

Adolf has his eyes set on Emma, the daughter of a wealthy farmer and magistrate. They meet in secret and experience a brief period of young and tender love. Emma discovers that she is pregnant, but she is too afraid to tell her parents, and when Adolf sends a marriage broker to ask for Emma's hand, he is curtly turned down. In a society of strict social and economic hierarchies, marriages are one of the main means of preserving the status quo, and because Adolf has a mortgaged farm, he is not deemed worthy of Emma and her dowry. When her father discovers that she is with child, he turns in bitter hatred against Adolf. Emma is sent away to relatives to save the family from shame and dishonor, and her child, a boy whom she names Per-Adolf, is left in the care of a family in another province. Then, in a surprising, conciliatory gesture, Emma's father approaches Adolf and offers him his daughter on condition that the boy not be brought home as long as Emma's parents are alive. After the wedding Adolf learns that his father-in-law is bankrupt. Emma brings no dowry to Ulvaskog.

The marriage is not a happy one. Ulvaskog is an ancient farm in a remote part of the parish (people refer to it as "the end of the world"). In addition to the isolation, Emma is repelled by the old customs and superstitions that are still kept alive there. In these surroundings husband and wife cannot recapture their first love; their feelings have become hollow and tainted, and Lotta is relentlessly opposed to the new mistress. Adolf redoubles his work on the farm as if he could exorcise his troubles through the sheer force of his muscles and his will. He looks forward to the day when his and Emma's four children will be able to help on the farm. Most of all, he dreams of their first-born, the child of their love, and the day when he will be brought home to the farm. When the day arrives and Adolf decides to leave in order to fetch his son, Emma breaks down and confesses her terrible secret, which has weighed on her conscience throughout their married life; instead of leaving their son to strangers, she drowned the infant shortly after his birth. Adolf is stunned by the news and curses his wife. In the night she hangs herself.

The novels about Adolf in Ulvaskog cover

some fifty years, from the last decades of the nineteenth century through World War I. As his four children are growing up, Adolf rules over them and his farm with an iron hand. Unable to express his love for his children in any other way than through indefatigable work and a desperate grasp on his possessions, he grows into a tragic King Lear as each child in turn rebels against him. He is unable to understand their demands for new clothes, amusements, bicycles, and cash payment for their work on the farm. He blames the new times and becomes obstinate in his refusal to join the other farmers in their efforts to modernize by means of the new technology; he even sabotages their attempts to drain the swamps and to introduce electricity. The clash between the old and the new, between the ancient natural economy and the modern economy based on money, is illustrated in the fate of Adolf and his losing battle to hold onto the old.

One by one his children desert him until only Mari, his youngest daughter and his favorite, remains with him out of compassion, a Cordelia who sacrifices herself for her father. When Erik, the ne'er-do-well son, gets involved in heedless wartime speculations and goes bankrupt, the aging father is forced to take out a new mortgage on the farm. His sister Tilda's daughter has gone to Stockholm and sends reports to her proud mother of her successful life in the city; Tilda dies and is spared the truth that her daughter is a prostitute. As his physical strength fails him, Adolf becomes unable to run the farm, which is rapidly becoming dilapidated. He is viewed as a curious relic. Mari, who has been jealously watched over by her father and prevented from meeting people of her own age, begins to steal out at night to go to dances. She feels that her youth is slipping away from her and finally makes the decision to go to Stockholm. Adolf, who is sure that she will meet the same fate as Tilda's daughter, goes to her room the night before her departure and shoots her in her sleep. Throughout his life he has clenched his hands hard around his possessions in a cramped and futile attempt to

hold on to his heritage—only to see everything escape his grasp.

After his years as a journalist in Alvesta, Moberg was not to reside in Småland again, although his home province continued to be the setting for most of his novels and plays. In 1929 the family moved to Stockholm, and a few years later Moberg acquired property in the country in the vicinity of the capital for his growing family of four daughters and one son.

In the novel *A. P. Rosell, bankdirektör* (A. P. Rosell, Bank Director, 1932), the little town of Allmänninge is in large part modeled on Alvesta. One of the main characters is the local correspondent Valfrid Sterner, an aspiring author constantly on the run for news to fill his column in his efforts to support his large family. Like the journalist Arvid Falk in Strindberg's social satire *Röda rummet* (The Red Room, 1879), Sterner has ample opportunity to discover the corruption and hypocrisy in society. His news hunt takes him to the courthouse, the theater, and the charity bazaar. One strand of action is his own attempt to escape from his small-town bondage with the leading lady of a touring group; to this end he "borrows" the money he has had to collect to honor the town's foremost citizen, bank director Rosell, on his fiftieth birthday. However, the actress absconds with the money, along with the theater director. Moberg's satire triumphs in the scene in which Sterner visits the powerful bank director to confess his embezzlement, for Rosell is also an embezzler. This pillar of society is in fact a swindler who escapes discovery by forcing the board members to cover for him in order to save the bank, but he gives the threadbare journalist a moral sermon. Anxious to prevent a scandal in connection with the celebration of his birthday, he makes Sterner sign a promissory note for the missing funds.

In the courthouse, Sterner hears the paternity suit of the country girl Vendela, who tries to support herself and her baby as a seamstress. The young father of her child loses his job as a result of the cover-up of Rosell's swindle, and the girl is unable to pay her rent and the monthly installment on her sewing machine. Meanwhile, on the eve of the birthday celebrations, Sterner attends the charity bazaar arranged by Mrs. Rosell. Her marriage is childless and she is desperate in her desire for a child. After the bazaar she gives herself to Sterner, whose large family is enviable proof to her of his manhood. The town then celebrates its outstanding benefactor Rosell with adulatory speeches and with due pomp and circumstance. The occasion overshadows the news that the young unmarried mother Vendela has drowned herself and her baby in the lake. Nine months later the newspaper carries the proud announcement of the birth of a son to the bank director. Thus, Moberg skillfully gathers the different threads of action and brings them to an effective climax.

In *A. P. Rosell, bankdirektör* Moberg proves his ability to deal with contemporary urban reality. The satirical thrust of the novel is directed at the reckless speculations and swindles of the late 1920's and early 1930's, the time of roller-coaster economies preceding the Great Depression. With exemplary clarity Moberg reveals the economic mechanisms and shows how the little people become the ultimate victims of the unconscionable transactions of the powerful in society.

With his next novel, *Mans kvinna* (*Fulfillment*, 1933), Moberg returns to his rural Värend and presents a work of great beauty in its balladlike lyricism. It is also a significant contribution to a subgenre in Swedish literature of the early 1930's that arose from the so-called primitivist movement, which can be seen as a reaction against the threatening mechanization of an emerging technological society by idealizing the vital, regenerative forces of sex and basic instincts. This sexual romanticism was in part inspired by such writers as D. H. Lawrence and Sherwood Anderson and can ultimately be traced back to Freudian psychology and its warnings against undue repression of the sexual instinct. In *Fulfillment* the irresistible attraction between a man and a woman is played out against social taboos and moral proscriptions within a closely knit village collective in the 1790's. The unmarried farmer Håkan Ingelson conceives an ardent passion for Märit, the young wife of his kind and helpful neighbor Påvel Gertson. Håkan prevails over her vacillating resistance. In his embraces all her dormant sensuality awakens, and they abandon themselves completely to their joy in each other. The knowledge of the inhuman punishments meted out to adulterous women in those days adds an element of great danger to their clandestine meetings. Both Håkan and Märit are upright and honorable people; he is filled with revulsion over his abuse of Påvel's trust and would like to have a clean confrontation with the husband, and she suffers from her own deceptions. When she discovers that she is pregnant, she brings about a miscarriage in her despair over not knowing which of the two men in her life is the father.

The theme of freedom from constraints, embodied in the vision of sexual individualism in response to the instincts, is contrasted with the thralldom of possessions. Påvel is a man of the earth, deriving his sense of security from his land, his cattle, and other possessions. He is an upholder of the established social order. Håkan, by contrast, feels that he is in bondage to his farm, a slave to the exorbitant rents and taxes that make his labor seem meaningless. He is one in a long line of Moberg protagonists who nourish a dream of freedom and escape. To him the deep and endless forest, the traditional sanctuary for outlaws and misfits, holds the promise of such freedom, and he pleads with Märit to join him in a life outside of society. Without regret, he relinquishes his livestock and other possessions and prepares to leave the farm to his creditors. But Märit is torn between her deep-rooted need for material security and the urgings of her blood. It is not until Påvel discovers her unfaithfulness and makes her realize that she is no more to him than another possession and that his main concern is to preserve the outward signs of respectability that she gets the strength to tear herself from her material fetters and join her lover.

Readers are not allowed to follow Håkan and Märit into their lawless "freedom." Moberg convincingly describes the chain of events that makes their escape seem inevitable, and the ending of the novel is not an example of romantic escapism. Whether unwittingly or deliberately, Moberg suggests a deeper form of human bondage, the biological necessity that Schopenhauer saw as the sweetest and therefore the most cruel of illusions. As a proponent of a life-promoting "primitivism," in *Fulfillment* Moberg was probably reluctant to subscribe to his philosophical mentor's views in this regard.

The theme of escape in Moberg's novels stems from the protagonists' revolt against the present. Their restlessness and discontent express a frustrated desire for wholeness and fulfillment, which is projected either into the future in the form of longing for freedom and the realization of idealistic goals, or into the past in the form of nostalgic memory.

The two movements, the impulse to break away and the impulse to return, are strikingly illustrated in Moberg's trilogy about Knut Toring, *Sänkt sedebetyg* (*Memory of Youth,* 1935), *Sömnlös* (*Sleepless Nights,* 1937), and *The Earth Is Ours!* The reader encounters Knut Toring at a time of crisis in his life. To all appearances he has succeeded and has come a long way from his beginnings on the parental farm Lidalycke in Småland. He has a well-paid job as editor of a weekly magazine in Stockholm and a good and attractive wife and two children. But with middle age approaching, his life seems devoid of meaning. His work consists in reading banal and stereotypical stories submitted to the magazine, and he feels that he is prostituting himself in catering to the public's demand for cheap entertainment. His marriage has stagnated, and he seems to be drifting away from his wife. The city, with its crowded streets, its noise and rush, and mechanical routines, oppresses him like a prison.

He suffers from insomnia and feels as though his body and soul were atrophying.

The simple and artless letters from his parents make him return in his thoughts to his youth in the village, and through his recollections he attempts to come to terms with his present situation. The first part of the trilogy is the recreation of his childhood and youth. The novels about Knut Toring are to some extent autobiographical, and Moberg clearly draws on his own memories in the descriptions of sun-drenched adventures close to nature, of the school in the forest and the protagonist's conflict with his teacher that brings down on him the shame of a lowered conduct mark. Like Moberg himself, Knut Toring had also experienced the constraints and limitations imposed upon his intellectual development, the insatiable hunger for books, and the longing to break away. But the novels are basically fictionalized accounts and are autobiographical only insofar as they attempt to analyze a fundamental dividedness in the author, a dividedness Moberg termed constitutional. With some oversimplification, this conflict could be reduced to such oppositions as country versus city, instinct versus civilization, soul versus intellect. The novels about Knut Toring describe attempts to reconcile these opposites.

Knut Toring does not idealize his life in the village, but certain memories stand out untarnished and sensuously vivid, such as the moments of ecstatic contemplation before the vegetative fullness of summer and the intense satisfaction of physical exertion when he manages for the first time to carry a sack of grain up the ladder to the loft or to mow a field of oats in a single day. Most vividly of all, he remembers his first experience of physical love. Set against his present life in the city, these memories are powerful epiphanies and moments of fulfillment.

In the second volume, Toring's doubts and self-examinations continue and result in his decision to break with his wife, resign from his job, and return to his native village. He leases a small croft and again works close to the soil. He regains his physical strength and sleeps well at night, but his return is not what he had hoped. Things have changed in the village, and he himself is viewed with suspicion and as a failure. His parents are dismayed over his separation from his wife and children. Their own marriage has not been based on love or even great affection, but it has lasted because of their common material interests in the farm. Knut is critical of this emphasis on possessions and sees it as an enslavement and a hindrance to real growth and development.

In the last volume of the trilogy the perspective widens as Knut Toring's personal problems are more and more relegated to the background, or rather they are seen as problems of national and ultimately of international scope. Knut realizes that the old peasant self-sufficiency must yield to greater cooperation and widened participation in culture, and he joins in the efforts of a young and progressive woman, Betty, who runs her father's farm rationally and efficiently and is passionately concerned about keeping the young from leaving the country for the cities. She has started a little library and dreams of a community center to be built as a joint enterprise to which everybody will donate time and materials. This project is in keeping with Toring's own ideas concerning breaking up the old self-centered individualism of the farmers; he feels that they should join together to possess the earth as free men instead of being possessed by it. He is working on a book in which he develops these ideas, called "The Kingdom of the Earth Is Ours." The work on reforming the old village life along these idealistic lines is accompanied by news from the outside world. It is 1938, the year of the Munich Crisis, and the danger signals from Nazi Germany and the universal war preparations pose a threat to the realization of Toring's utopian vision. They also force him to reconsider his earlier pacifism and antimilitarism and to conclude that the violations perpetrated by a gang of criminals must be resisted. He proceeds to formulate the principles

he holds more dear than his own life, principles that he would be willing to die for and to kill for:

> It is the right to dispose of myself, body and soul. It is the right of my children to live free lives in their native land. . . . It is, finally, the freedom of the spirit on this earth, my faith in the sovereignty and inviolability of the mind—all that I have poured into my beautiful dream of an earthly realm really possessed by man.
>
> (*The Earth Is Ours! p. 667*)

These principles are tested in Moberg's next novel, *Rid i natt! (Ride This Night!* 1941). The novel is set in a Värend village in 1650 during the reign of Queen Christina. The independent farmers are threatened with the loss of their right to dispose of themselves—their minds and bodies and especially their right to work for themselves. In return for services rendered during the Thirty Years' War, the queen has granted Swedish and even some foreign noblemen the right to levy taxes on the farmers. The village of Brändebol is obliged to pay taxes to the German Bartold Klewen on his nearby estate. After two successive years of crop failures the farmers are unable to pay their dues and are instead summoned to work on the estate. The Swedish peasantry had never known the feudal system, and the farmers are outraged over this infringement on their age-old independence. The village council meets to discuss this threat and the possibility that force may be used to make them comply. Certain compromise measures are discussed but are rejected after an impassioned speech by the young farmer Svedje. The farmers swear to stand united and resist any attempts to force them to work on the estate. But Klewen's sheriff arrives with armed men and first visits the alderman, Stånge, and succeeds in persuading him to save his village from unnecessary bloodshed and suffering by peacefully submitting to Klewen's demands. Thus, village unity breaks down from the very beginning, and the farmers begin their humiliating servitude. Only the farmer Svedje offers active resistance and later manages to escape into the forest, preferring to live as an outlaw rather than bow to Klewen's demands. His farm is confiscated and his betrothed, the alderman's daughter, is promised to the "collaborator" Mats Elling.

The farmers grumble under their new yoke, and their discontent is directed at the alderman, while Svedje becomes a symbol of the spirit of resistance. Under Klas Bock a resistance group is formed and a fiery cross is sent out to summon the people to revolt. When the message reaches the alderman, he swears to pass it on, but instead he fearfully buries the token. A posse is formed to track down Svedje in the forest. He is found and suffers the ancient punishment of being buried alive. The fiery cross that had also been "buried alive" is miraculously unearthed, and the message "Ride this night, this night!" is relayed through the region.

Ride This Night! is a novel set in the seventeenth century, for which Moberg had begun his research a few years earlier. The story contains a number of elements close to the author's heart: the re-creation of an ancient form of democratic village life, the love of freedom and independence, and the spirit of resistance to oppression from authorities. With the outbreak of World War II and Germany's subsequent occupation of a number of independent nations, the story suddenly gained special actuality and significance. Moberg seized the opportunity to develop the contemporary parallels and to make his novel into an impassioned appeal for resistance. Moberg was a vociferous critic of Sweden's policy of neutrality and of the coalition government's concessions to Nazi Germany and its attempts to censor news and silence opposition in order to preserve this state of neutrality. Moberg sent out the novel as his own fiery cross in 1941, in the darkest hour of the war. Its message was not lost on the readers or the viewers of the subsequent dramatized versions for stage and movie screen.

In his next novel, the massive *Soldat med brutet gevär* (partially translated under the title *When I Was a Child*) Karl Artur Vilhelm Moberg describes the early years and development of Karl Artur Valter Sträng. As the names indicate, there is similarity but not identity between the novel's protagonist and its author. In no other novel has Moberg re-created so closely the outer framework of the first couple of decades of his own life, leading his protagonist through the different stations of his own development up to the moment of his literary breakthrough. Readers familiar with Moberg's biography will recognize the descriptions of Valter's childhood in the soldier's croft, the adolescent's work in the glass factory, on the peat bog, and in the forest, his attendance at a folk high school and at a "crammer," his close scrape with death from the Spanish flu, and finally his years as a journalist for provincial newspapers. However, Magnus von Platen has examined the autobiographical elements in the novel and has shown many points of difference between the fictional Valter Sträng and the author, delineating the process of elimination and addition and of shifting emphases through which Moberg presents what Philip Holmes terms the "memoirs of an idealist."

In his excellent study on Moberg and his work, Holmes discusses the novel as autobiography, as a typical *Bildungsroman,* as a historical novel, and as a political novel. Moberg originally intended the title of his novel to be "Upptäckt" (Discovery), and as a novel of development the story of Valter Sträng is indeed the story of the young protagonist's discovery of fundamental truths and falsehoods. In accordance with the conventions of the *Bildungsroman* genre, the protagonist comes under the influence of different "mentors," each of whom shape or test his views. The earliest one is Valter's father, with whom he has an excellent relationship. There is also the pious village carpenter, whose religious views Valter rejects in favor of a self-reliant atheism (Philip Holmes correctly points out that Moberg's own settling of accounts with his parents' faith was a more painful process accompanied by doubts; this process is more accurately described in the novels about Knut Toring). In the glass factory, Valter is won over to a socialist view of the world expounded by two fellow workers, one advocating an extreme leftist radicalism, the other a more moderate social democracy. During his time at the "crammer," a teacher introduces Valter Sträng to the philosophy of Schopenhauer.

At the publisher's suggestion, the novel about Valter Sträng was given the title *Soldat med brutet gevär,* a reference to the emblem of a broken rifle worn by the protagonist (as well as the adolescent Moberg) to indicate his radical pacifism. The young idealist is also actively involved in the temperance movement. The novel shows the importance of this and other idealistic popular movements in engaging young people of the working class.

One major aspect of the novel is that it traces the history of the Social Democratic party during the first two decades of this century—its growth and ultimate rise to power. Valter Sträng is a passionate observer and participant, fired by the great promises in the party program and inspired by the early leaders of the movement. One of these is Per Albin Hansson, who in 1932 became Sweden's prime minister and remained in this position throughout World War II. Moberg held the opinion that the Social Democratic party in its ascendency to power had compromised and betrayed its high ideals of the early years, and in the late 1920's he forswore allegiance to any political party. However, he remained an outspoken critic of the policies of the different parties, not least of the party for which he had fought in his youth. Through his protagonist, Valter Sträng, Moberg invited his readers of the 1940's to contrast the fearlessly idealistic pioneers with the cautiously pragmatic members of the majority party in wartime Sweden. Valter Sträng's ardent admiration for the young Per Albin Hansson's defense of free speech becomes bitterly ironic in view of the prime minister's measures during the war to introduce censorship of the press and even to confiscate newspapers in the interest of national security. In his previous

novel, *Ride This Night!* Moberg had in part used Per Albin Hansson as the model for the village alderman Stånge, the leader who breaks his oath and buries the fiery cross with its urgent message.

As a fighter in the class struggle, Valter Sträng begins to question some of his earlier beliefs and his tendency to blame the social order for the lies and injustices around him. He realizes that it is man himself who needs to be changed along with society. As a journalist, he begins to write a novel entitled "The Soldier's Croft," in which he wants to draw on his own background and experiences. In so doing, he makes one of the last "discoveries" in the novel and a very important one, the discovery of his true calling in life. A soldier with a broken rifle, he decides to fight the class struggle with his pen and to become the chronicler of the people that history (and to a large extent also literature) has forgotten—the "clog people," his people.

The novel about Valter Sträng is firmly rooted in historical time and in Moberg's personal experience. Through his protagonist's eyes, Moberg views the social development and the political history of Sweden during the first decades of this century. With his next novel he transcends the limitations of a single individual awareness and establishes a perspective that extends from the present back to prehistoric pagan times. *Brudarnas källa* (The Brides' Spring, 1946) is a lyrical meditation on some timeless themes—love, fertility, and death. Each of the four sections of the book has its own first-person narrator, a musician who plays at the midsummer celebration on a meadow in Värend close to a spring reputed to have healing powers. On the contemporary level, the narrator is a fiddler who has been forced to step down and yield his place to an accordion player due to the demands of modern times. The other three narrators are his eighteenth-century counterpart, a sixteenth century piper, and finally a prehistoric buckhorn-blower. Each musician finds his death in the spring, which is also seen as a mother symbol, a giver of life. The meadow on which the young people dance and make love is the site of an old plague cemetery, a coincidence illustrating the close connection between procreation and death. Part of the novel's suggestive poetry lies in the contrast between the static unchangeability of the place, with its perennially clear spring, cyclical return of the same wildflowers under the same summer solstice, and the brief appearance of each generation of human occupants. With each story the midsummer celebration is moved back in time, all the way to its origin in pagan fertility rites with the sacrifice of a young maiden. *Brudarnas källa* is Moberg's most experimental novel and one of his most inspired works.

In 1947 Moberg embarked upon the most extensive writing project of his career, the story of the early emigration from his home region to North America. The work absorbed his energies for the next twelve years and resulted in the monumental emigrant tetralogy.

THE EMIGRANT NOVELS

Vilhelm Moberg's four novels about a group of Småland people who in 1850 uprooted themselves from their meager native soil to sink roots in the fertile soil of Minnesota mark the crowning achievement of the author's career. The tetralogy includes *Utvandrarna* (*The Emigrants,* 1949), *Invandrarna* (*Unto a Good Land,* 1952), *Nybyggarna* (*The Settlers,* 1956), and *Sista brevet till Sverige* (*The Last Letter Home,* 1959). (In translation, the last two parts were condensed into one sadly mutilated volume entitled *The Last Letter Home.* However, the two works can now be read in Gustav Lannestock's unabridged translations of 1978.) The tetralogy records what has been called the most important event in modern times, the mass migration from the Old World to the New World. The novels belong to the history of both.

The publication in Sweden of Moberg's novel cycle gave a tremendous boost to serious research in migration history. Moberg's own research, conducted on both sides of the Atlantic, resulted in massive documentation collected from letters, diaries, photos, personal interviews, and every kind of printed material. Moberg donated this voluminous source material to the Emigrant Museum in Växjö as the foundation of its extensive archives and library. Moberg's own tetralogy has been the subject of a large number of dissertations and studies in which the work is viewed both as history and as literature.

Moberg's epic vision and his talent as a storyteller saves the work from becoming merely a textbook illustration of a historical event. The author admirably strikes a balance between fantasy and reality, the fabulation of fiction and the facts of history, the representational and the individualized. He succeeds in his aim of presenting a work of fiction that in no essentials violates historical truth. His painstaking naturalism is an attempt to strip his characters of an aura of myth and heroism; at the same time the very structure of the story of migration is that of a timeless quest myth in which the seemingly incidental is often raised to the level of the archetypal. The story of the Småland peasants' dream of a better life with freedom and human dignity on another continent is the millenarian dream of the golden future, the search for utopia and the earthly paradise. The theme of escape in Moberg's fiction, expressed as a Promethean impulse to rebel and break away or as a longing to return to a paradise lost, is ultimately a striving for transcendence beyond the human condition itself. The two movements are simply and movingly illustrated in the characters of the two central figures, Karl Oskar, bent on using all his strength and will to build a new future for himself and his family, and his wife, Kristina, forever returning in her thoughts to the land they left and gradually directing her longing to a home beyond this earthly existence.

The land they left is represented by Ljuder Parish. Moberg establishes his narrative authority and his respect for facts and figures from the very beginning: his introduction pre-

2219

sents a factual description of the parish, its inhabitants, and the social and economic conditions prevailing in 1846. This narrative authority naturally carries over into the fictional part of the novel, binding credibility to the events.

The sixteen people who eventually make the momentous decision to emigrate to North America form a tiny vanguard in the swelling flood that in the subsequent decades was to carry away one fourth of Sweden's population. As Moberg points out, "The new land had soil without tillers and called for tillers without soil." One such tiller is Karl Oskar Nilsson. As the eldest son he takes over the family homestead, Korpamoen, which has been reduced to a sixteenth of its original size through successive divisions resulting from deaths. He has been named after two Swedish kings, but the kingdom he inherits is only seven acres of stony soil. His father is prematurely broken and made an invalid after an uneven struggle with one massive stone, but Karl Oskar continues the battle with his considerable physical strength and stubborn determination. By his side is his wife, his beloved Kristina, from the village of Duvemåla in the neighboring parish Algutsboda. But his efforts are of little avail. As his family grows, the returns for his labors decrease; every year he goes deeper into debt to pay interest on the mortgage. Potato rot, excessive rains in one year and parching droughts in another severely test both Karl Oskar's belief in his own powers and Kristina's faith in God.

Karl Oskar's younger brother, Robert, is one of the parish's 274 farm servants. A dreamer and a misfit, he tries to run away from his service with the brutish and miserly farmer Aron at Nybacken, but he is caught and receives a box on the ear that causes permanent injury. The teenager seeks an escape from the harsh realities around him—the endless drudgery, the miserable food, and the narrow-minded cruelty of the farm people—by fantasizing about a life without bondage. Daydreaming by the stream in the forest, he follows in his mind the running water on its course to the sea, to an unbounded freedom away from all masters and authorities. It is in his fertile brain that the dream of America is first born. His schoolteacher gives him a couple of books in which he reads about the wonders of the world and finds descriptions of North America. In the vermin-infested quarters he shares with his fellow servant Arvid, he reads and embellishes the accounts of the land where rice porridge is plentiful and rancid herring is forbidden as food; where it would have been impossible for David to kill Goliath because no stone even the size of a pebble could be found; where there is no need to bow or curtsy because there is no one to bow or curtsy to; where many black slaves have better care and work conditions than most of England's factory workers or the peasants of Europe, even being allowed to have their own chickens and pigs and their own piece of land. Robert and Arvid decide that America is a land for them. Arvid suggests that the best one can do on arrival in America would be to sell oneself as a slave; here in Sweden he would never be able to acquire chickens and pigs and his own patch of land. Robert explains that it is forbidden for white-skinned people to sell themselves as slaves and Arvid is disappointed: "Arvid thought that probably there was a difference between people in America after all, if the whites did not have the same rights as the blacks to become slaves and have their own land with chickens and pigs."

In the village of Kärragärde the relatively prosperous farmer Danjel Andreasson, Kristina's uncle, has received the calling to revive the old Åkianism, a religious sect patterned on the communism of the early Christians. Among the poor and despised who have joined the sect and are living with Danjel are the former parish whore Ulrika, the Glad One, and her illegitimate daughter, Elin. Ulrika, one of Moberg's most memorable characters, was the early victim of a cruel social order according to which an orphan would be auctioned off to the bidder willing to provide for the child with the least strain on the communal coffer. The farmer who was awarded the care of young Ulrika started her on her career by raping her when she was fourteen. Through the Åkians, Ulrika has been accepted into a new community where she is allowed to partake of the sacraments that the official church denies her; she receives Christ's body and sheds her own sinful one. But her fiery temper, her outspokenness, and her indignation over social hypocrisy and injustice remain unchanged. They are put to magnificent use when a nocturnal communion service in Danjel's home is interrupted by the dean, the sheriff, and the church warden, the representatives of divine and secular authority, who have come in the name of the law to prohibit private worship outside the fold of the established church. Flaming with righteous anger, Ulrika gives the intruders a piece of her mind, tells the dean her honest opinion of the clergy, and singles out the church warden as one of her former customers.

As the nineteenth century approaches its midpoint, conditions become worse. The Åkians are punished for their refusal to bow to the church and are fined two hundred dalers in silver for transgressing the sacrament law and the ordinance pertaining to unlawful meetings. Most of the members, unable to pay the sum, receive prison sentences and serve twenty-eight days on bread and water.

At Korpamoen, Karl Oskar fights a hopeless struggle against continued years of crop failure. He is haunted by a picture he has seen in a newspaper depicting a wheat field in North America and has begun to discuss with Kristina the possibility of their leaving for America. But she is violently opposed to the idea. She counters Karl Oskar's claims that they owe their children a better future with the argument that they have no right to expose them to the dangers and uncertainties of such a drastic move. Then comes the hardest winter of all: famine stares everybody in the face, and hordes of starving children are sent begging by their parents. Kristina gives birth to a boy. For the christening she has saved some precious barley, even some sugar and butter, and she

prepares a bowl of porridge for the guests and sets it in the cellar to cool. Their daughter Anna steals down to look at the delicious food; at first she only wants to smell it, then to taste it just a little. But once she has started tasting it, she cannot stop; she almost finishes the bowl and then is too afraid to leave the cellar. When she is finally found, she is in violent pain from overeating and is filled with remorse for her disobedience. Early in the morning the child dies in terrible agony. The tragedy makes Kristina change her mind:

> A month had passed since Anna's funeral when Kristina one evening said to Karl Oskar: After what had happened, she had now changed her mind, she was not averse to their emigration to North America. Before she had thought she would be lacking in responsibility if she endangered her children's lives on the ocean. Now she had learned that God could take her little ones even on dry land, in spite of her great care. . . . And so—if he thought it would be best for them and their children to emigrate, she would comply.
>
> (*The Emigrants,* p. 108)

With Robert, too, the resolution to emigrate has ripened. After an unusually harsh beating from his master, he has run away and taken refuge at his brother's. He is sought by the sheriff for having broken his servant's contract. When he approaches Karl Oskar to ask for his share of his inheritance in order to emigrate to America, he learns to his astonishment and joy that Karl Oskar has made the same decision. Shortly thereafter, Danjel Andreasson comes to Korpamoen and announces that the Lord has ordered him, as he once ordered Abraham, to leave his country. With him he is taking his wife and four children, as well as Ulrika and her daughter and the farmhand Arvid, who is now in his employment. The farmer Jonas Petter, the inveterate teller of ribald stories, also decides to join the group. To him the emigration provides an escape from twenty years of daily quarrels with a woman he should never have married.

There are sixteen of them leaving Ljuder Parish in early April 1850. At Korpamoen the hired flat-wagon is loaded with the peasants' possessions, and as they prepare to leave, "the sons shook hands with their parents, a bit awkwardly, perhaps shamefacedly, almost like little boys who had been disobedient but were embarrassed to ask forgiveness." There is reproach in the parents' silence as they stand on the stoop watching the departure. It is not only their sons and grandchildren who are leaving; untold unborn generations are leaving the country with them. Karl Oskar catches a last glimpse of his parents, who

> seemed to him as still and immobile as dead, earth-bound things, as a pair of high stones in the field or a couple of tree trunks in the forest, deeply rooted in the ground. It was as if they had assumed that position once and for all and intended to hold it forever. And as he saw them in the half-mist, this early morning, so they were forever to return to his mind.
>
> (*The Emigrants,* pp. 175–176)

By the time the Ljuder emigrants reach the little Baltic port of Karlshamn to board the old brig *Charlotta* for their voyage to the unknown, readers have been given a very authentic picture of conditions in Sweden and most of rural Europe in the past century and have been shown a broad spectrum of "push-and-pull factors" behind the emigration. They have also become irresistibly involved in the lives and fates of Moberg's Småland peasants. Moberg himself did not have a definite plan for the future of his characters. During the twelve years he worked on his emigrant epic he repeatedly pointed out that his characters assumed a high degree of independence and that he felt compelled to write in order to find out what was going to happen to them. At times they took their author by surprise, especially Ulrika, who proved to be the most self-willed, intractable, and independent of them all.

The first volume ends when the *Charlotta* anchors at the pier in New York at midsummer after ten weeks at sea. It has been a hazardous voyage, and the seventy-eight passengers have suffered from seasickness, cramped quarters, poor food, scurvy, and lice. Eight people have died during the crossing, among them Danjel Andreasson's wife.

The following three volumes, with almost two thousand pages, cover the events of the next four decades in the New World. The people from Ljuder continue together their journey to Minnesota's St. Croix Valley. The narrative increasingly focuses on the Nilsson family—Karl Oskar, Kristina, and Robert—and to a large extent also Ulrika, who become the main characters in the unfolding story about the immigrants, their ability to adjust to the new conditions, and the ways in which they change the new country and it in turn changes them. Each character depicts a variation on the theme of freedom and fulfillment.

Karl Oskar's is the story of the hard work, stubborn determination, and self-reliance through which the wilderness is transformed into cultivated land and material prosperity. He never regrets his decision to emigrate, and only wishes he had not wasted so many precious years of his youth in the hopeless struggle against the stones in Småland. A few weeks after his arrival in New York he is already staking his claim to land by Lake Khi-Chi-Saga and erecting a temporary shanty while he works on their first log cabin. This in turn shelters his growing family while he builds their two-story frame house. Karl Oskar is the almost mythical figure of the provider, the patriarch, the builder of a family, a community, a nation. He refuses to bow to any authority, secular or divine, that threatens his independence and his right to forge his own destiny in honest exertion of all his powers. In America he finds a society that grants him this right, and in return he becomes a loyal citizen. Although a pacifist by conviction, he volunteers his services as a soldier during the Civil War, but an old leg injury prevents him from actively defending the system he believes in.

His relations with the Almighty are less harmonious. The reader gets the impression that Karl Oskar would have liked the Lord to learn a thing or two from Franklin and Jefferson about human freedom and dignity. Back in Småland during the drought he had flung the pitiful wisp of hay on his rake up into the air and shouted heavenward: "As you have taken the rest of the hay you might as well have this too!" When lightning set fire to their barn shortly after this incident, Kristina was sure this was God's punishment for Karl Oskar's blasphemy, but he cannot reconcile himself to the thought of a God who is so petty and vindictive. To his dying day Karl Oskar cannot forgive God that he let Kristina die after only twelve years in the new country. She is told by the doctor that another childbirth will endanger her life; placing all her trust in God, she allows herself to get pregnant again, a trust that costs her her life.

In the portrait of Kristina, Moberg shows his remarkable ability to enter into the mind of a deeply religious person, an ability already demonstrated in his descriptions of Rasken's Ida and Knut Toring's mother. Although an atheist, Moberg deals with the faith of these women with great understanding, even tenderness. Kristina never wanted to leave Sweden, and she cannot think of the new place by Lake Khi-Chi-Saga as "home"; she exemplifies the loneliness and isolation of many immigrant women. Whereas the language of most of the settlers undergoes a gradual change under the influence of the American language around them—an aspect of the novels that by necessity gets lost in the translation—Kristina's Swedish remains unaffected. Yet she changes in other ways, as is illustrated by her evolving attitude toward Ulrika. At first Ulrika fills her with the outrage and loathing of the good and respectable housewife, culminating in the unforgettable scene on board the *Charlotta* when she discovers to her horror that she has lice and bursts out in shrill accusations directed at Ulrika. Later, during the ride by the "steam-wagon" from Albany to Buffalo, Kristina is cut-

ting her last loaf of bread to feed her family. At the same time she is acutely aware of the fact that Ulrika and her daughter have no food left, although they proudly pretend not to be concerned. Moberg lets the reader follow Kristina's battle with herself as she sits with the bread knife resting on her knee:

> Kristina's heart beat faster, so greatly was she perturbed. Should she cut the last loaf—or should she save it? She had a vague feeling that what she did now would be of great importance to all of them. She had a foreboding that fundamental changes awaited them in this new land, everything seemed different from home, they were forced to act in new and unaccustomed ways.
>
> (*Unto a Good Land*, p. 78)

She thinks of her three hungry children and of the fourth, "the free passenger" that she is carrying. But here in the New World they are all poor, wretched creatures; the creator had made the Glad One too, and from the beginning considered her as worthy as others. "She took out the last loaf, cut generous slices, and handed them to Ulrika of Västergöhl and her daughter. Wouldn't they please share her bread? It was old and dry, but she had scraped off the mildew as best she could."

Kristina loyally fulfills her tasks as wife and mother and member of the settlement, but her heart is in the Old World. She gradually accepts her lot in silent submission, and her sense of alienation and her homesickness become metaphysical expressions of the longings of her soul. As a girl and even as a young wife, Kristina loved to ride a swing. The image of the swing and its motion is used by Moberg as a leitmotiv and as an ambivalent symbol that is connected with Kristina throughout the novels. Kristina's fondness for riding a swing expresses her reluctance to leave her childhood; she is always being pulled back by the past. (During the stormy crossing in the *Charlotta* the ship gives her a terrifying variation on the motions of the swing.) In a more general sense, the to-and-fro of the swing is a perfect simile for the vacillations of her divided self, the push-and-pull factors that both attract and repel her in the two worlds, in neither of which she finds a lasting home. It is a sign of Moberg's mastery and artistic sophistication that he is able to bring in the motif of the swing in a perfectly natural and seemingly unlabored manner toward the very end of the last volume, where it forms a dying echo of the powerful oscillations of the tetralogy. Kristina has been dead for twenty-five years, and Karl Oskar makes one of his frequent visits to her grave by the lake. It is a calm and beautiful day:

> Around him the world was silent. There was a faint sighing in the branches above Kristina's grave, like calm, quiet breathing. The blades of grass bent gently in the soft wind, rose as gently again. Down the lake, below the cliffs, a flock of ducklings rode the waves which broke against the cliffs. The water moved easily back and forth, as it had done since the beginning of time.
>
> (*The Last Letter Home*, p. 377)

And later he watches the waves ebb and flow in their play against the cliffs: "And this motion without ending was to Karl Oskar like generations growing up and dying. What was the purpose of this repetition—coming and going, living and dying?"

It would be a mistake to view Robert as simply an effective contrast to his elder brother Karl Oskar—the dreamer versus the realist, the adventurer versus the tiller of the soil—in yet another variation on the old fable about the industrious ant and the profligate grasshopper. On one level Robert is an obvious illustration of the immigrant who did not make it in the New World, the escapist unwilling to face reality and to seize the opportunities close at hand, who instead reaches for the rainbow and ends up with two empty hands. On a deeper level on which the novels about the emigrants are ultimately about the human condition itself, its bondage and its freedom, Robert is a tragic figure. He is more complex than his brother and closer to Moberg's own heart than

Karl Oskar, who remains unchanging and monolithic in his excellence. Robert is forever seeking a freedom away from masters; he is the dreamer, the poet, the romantic for whom reality will never live up to the image he has made of it in his mind. The throbbing ache in his ear, the result of the blow he received from Aron at Nybacken, is a constant reminder of the conditions the emigrants left behind. On an existential level, however, it becomes the symbol of human bondage, of Schopenhauer's prison of suffering in which the soul is trapped and from which death offers the ultimate liberation. Upon arrival in New York he catches a glimpse of the *Angelica*, a ship ready to set sail for the gold fields in California, a vision of beauty and irresponsible freedom in sharpest contrast to the homely *Charlotta*, with her dirty brown sails that resemble potato sacks. After a few months' work on the settlement in Minnesota, Robert and his friend Arvid take off to join the hundreds of thousands of goldseekers on the California Trail. Four years later Robert returns alone, broken in body and spirit.

A series of flashbacks relate his nightmarish experiences on the California Trail, culminating in Arvid's death in the desert. Half-crazed with thirst the two friends come upon a watering hole, and Arvid tries to quench his thirst without heeding the warning that the water is poisoned. Robert himself is restored to life with the fresh water from the gourd of Mario Vallejos, whom he joins and whose gold he receives when Vallejos dies from yellow fever. But the gold means little to Robert now: something happened to him by that poisoned water hole. Without ever having heard of Schopenhauer, Robert has had a vision of the philosopher's world as blind will and illusion; behind the veneer of reality he has confronted the grinning face of death and nothingness. From this point on he is spiritually dead. A smart compatriot lures the gold from him in exchange for worthless "wildcat" money. Robert's will to live is gone, but the thought of handing over the money to Karl Oskar keeps him going. In one of the most painful scenes in the tetralogy, Karl Oskar finds out that Robert's money "ain't worth a plugged nickel," and in his anger and frustration he hits his brother, whom he has always regarded as a liar. Robert explains to Kristina that he has become "unreachable." A few days after his return he is found dead by a stream in the woods very similar to the one he had often dreamed by in the home parish. He has been released from his last master, the excruciating pain in his ear. While he has been gone, Karl Oskar and his neighbors in the growing community have chosen a site for a cemetery. Robert, at age twenty-two, becomes its first occupant.

In Robert's story Moberg skillfully works with a complex of symbols centered on the contrast between water and gold—the yellow sand, the yellow gold, and the yellow fever versus the restless water of Robert's childhood stream, the ocean, the poisoned water in the desert, and Robert's return to the beginning by the stream in the Minnesota forest. Just as Robert is associated with water, Karl Oskar's element is the earth, and Kristina's the air, the medium of her swinging and of the aspirations of her soul.

The fourth principal character, Ulrika, left Sweden, which she refers to as "that hellhole," without regrets, and with it she abandoned her old identity and reputation. In her new surroundings all her best qualities are allowed to develop and blossom—her indestructible spirit, her sense of fairness, and her innate warmth and generosity. There is both social and poetic justice when she becomes the wife of the kind and admirable Baptist minister Henry O. Jackson and proceeds to become a pillar of the church and the community. Her dream that her son will one day become a minister in the church would make her apotheosis complete, but there is a limit even to Ulrika's success in the New World. The boy shows no inclination for the priesthood, and much to his mother's annoyance he runs away with a circus. In her old age Ulrika lifts the curse she had pronounced on her homeland, and as a token of her reconciliation with her past she donates a bridal crown to the parish church in Ljuder.

One by one the main characters complete their destinies, each one closing the circle that took the emigrants from their Småland parish to the other side of the world. After Kristina's death Karl Oskar continues his labors to improve and expand, but he becomes more and more withdrawn. When an oak tree falls over him and injures his back (just as the big stone had incapacitated his father), Karl Oskar leaves the farm to his eldest son. His children are leaving home, and he remains alone in the last house he built for his family. He is now Charles O. Nelson, one of the survivors of the original group of settlers, an old man whose way of speaking English is a bit of an embarrassment to his children and grandchildren. From his window he can look out over fertile fields and the flourishing community that he has helped to build. He walks with difficulty, and his back causes him constant pain, but as long as he can do so, he makes his visits to Kristina's grave. In his last years his most cherished possession is a map of Ljuder Parish that his son-in-law has given him. For hours he studies the map, follows with his finger the familiar roads and reads the familiar names, and in his mind he relives his courtship with Kristina. When he dies in 1890 none of his children is able to communicate the news to his sister in Sweden; an old Swedish neighbor is asked to write this last letter to Sweden.

Most of the emigrant epic was written in California. Moberg took an immediate liking to the West Coast, and he experienced long stretches of almost intoxicating creativity during his stays in Carmel and Laguna Beach. He gave much credit to the beneficial influence of the Pacific Ocean, claiming that his daily swims restored his body and revived his spirits. With the completion of the last volume he did not experience the expected sense of relief and liberation; instead he was plunged into a deep and paralyzing depression and periods of dreaded unproductivity. He moved restlessly around, sojourning in California, Switzerland,

Italy, the French Riviera, and England. These moves were in part an attempt to escape from growing demands on his time and person and to find undisturbed work conditions, but they were also indicative of a sense of homelessness.

The novel *A Time on Earth* grew out of this emotional frame of mind; the story of the aging Albert Carlson can be seen as a contemporary sequel to the emigrant epic in the form of a melancholy coda. From his native Småland Albert has emigrated to the United States. Living in a small hotel apartment in Laguna Beach between a freeway and the Pacific Ocean, between the temporal and temporary and the eternal, he looks back over a life that did not fulfill his expectations. His past life as a businessman seems meaningless to him; it only placed him in a suffocating middle-class confinement. His two marriages were failures, and he has little contact with his two sons. The precariousness of his existence is emphasized by the geographic conditions—frequent minor earthquakes—and by the political situation of the Cuban Crisis and the more distant threat of destruction by the hydrogen bomb. The novel is informed by a deep and disturbing pessimism about civilization, against which Albert Carlson's reminiscences make his childhood world appear as a paradise lost. He knows that it cannot be regained; his visits to his native country have made it very clear that he no longer belongs there either. A major part of the novel is filled with Albert Carlson's childhood memories of his elder brother Sigfrid, whose life was cut short when he was only nineteen. The protagonist's own life of missed opportunities and unfulfilled promises—he would have liked to be a historian, for instance—is effectively juxtaposed with the memories of his gifted brother. In the course of the novel the painful circumstances surrounding Sigfrid's death are gradually unfolded. We are reminded of the profound impact his elder brother's death had on Vilhelm Moberg as a child as well as the author's ambitions to be a historian. *A*

Time on Earth is one of Moberg's most personal novels, a meditation on man as an immigrant in life and on the great ocean that erases his footsteps in the sand.

THE DRAMATIST

Throughout his writing career Moberg remained faithful to his early love, the theater. In his production, novels and plays alternate with great regularity, the two genres often dealing with the same problems and occasionally offering different solutions. In addition to the plays written directly for the stage or for the radio, Moberg dramatized a number of his own novels, producing such dramas as *De knutna händerna* (The Clenched Hands, 1939), *Mans kvinna* (Man's Woman, 1953), *Rid i natt!* (Ride This Night! 1942), and *Din stund på jorden* (A Time on Earth, 1967). Among adaptations for the screen the most notable ones are Gustaf Molander's film *Rid i natt!* and Jan Troell's two films about the emigrants. More recently, special adaptations for television have been made of *Raskens* and *Soldat med brutet gevär*.

Although a prolific playwright, with some forty plays to his credit, Moberg made his most lasting contribution to Swedish literature as an epic novelist. As a dramatist he is a good craftsman with a sure sense of plot, dialogue, and dramatic effects, but he is not a renewer of the genre. Despite his great admiration for August Strindberg, he remained unaffected by the innovations and experimentations of the master, whereas his Småland compatriot Pär Lagerkvist from the very beginning of his dramatic career received fruitful impulses from Strindberg's later works. Moberg builds on a more conventional tradition and brings this tradition to a high level of perfection, which at the same time marks a terminus. This is particularly true of his early folk dramas and rural comedies. Among the former is the suspenseful *Hustrun* (The Wife, 1929) and among the latter are such gems as the one-act comedies *Marknadsafton* (Market Eve, 1920) and *Änkeman Jarl* (Widower Jarl, 1940).

In a number of plays Moberg discusses relations between man and woman and the institution of marriage. *Våld* (Violence, 1933) offers a critical view of marriage that is reminiscent of Strindberg's. The play critiques three marriages within the same family; it exposes a sham of loveless cohabitation in the case of the middle-aged parents and, in the case of their elder daughter, a humiliating comedy of infidelity and spying. The action takes place on the wedding day of the younger daughter, who has been too cowardly to accept her lover's ideal of a "free" union and has violated his deepest convictions by compelling him to marry her. In *En löskekarl* (A Vagabond, 1941) a young farmer's wife experiences the same dilemma as Märit in *Fulfillment.* Married to an older and very decent man, she is torn between her sense of duty to her husband and her love for the young man who has sought shelter on the farm and is given employment there. Unlike Märit, the wife does not obey the urgings of her blood; when she discovers that she is expecting her husband's child, she renounces her hopes for happiness through love and faces up to her responsibility as a wife. *Vår ofödde son* (Our Unborn Son, 1945) is Moberg's eloquent contribution to the abortion debate. The play is about a schoolteacher in a remote country school who becomes pregnant. Her boyfriend will have to sacrifice his chances to get ahead in life if he marries her. Here Moberg shows great sympathy with the woman's plight: caught between her fears of social condemnation and her concern for her boyfriend's future, she violates her conscience and her strongest instincts and obtains an abortion. The operation leaves her barren and emotionally traumatized for life. *Kvinnas man* (Woman's Man, 1965) is about a doomed relationship between a young and gifted man and a warm, witty, and wealthy woman who is old enough to be his mother. They try in vain to challenge estab-lished conventions, gossip, sensationalism, and family disapproval.

Moberg frequently used the theater as a forum for his ideas and views on ongoing debates in Sweden. In the comedy *Jungfrukammare* (The Maid's Room, 1938), for example, the satirical edge is directed at the literary establishment and the contemporary critics who had been vociferous in condemning Agnes von Krusenstjerna's novels as offensive, even pornographic. In *Domaren* (The Judge, 1957) Moberg continues his much-publicized battle against the corruption among Swedish officials; the characters of the judge who embezzles the fortune of his legal charge and of the newspaper editor and the prosecuting attorney are thinly disguised portraits of the players in the real-life drama. *Sagoprinsen* (The Fairytale Prince, 1962) is also based on an actual scandal involving a member of the royal family who was alleged to have lent his name and prestige to some highly questionable financial transactions.

More general in scope are Moberg's two dramas *Gudens hustru* (Wife of the God, 1954) and *Lea och Rakel* (Leah and Rachel, 1954). The former is a "pagan cult comedy," in spirit close to Moberg's novel *Brudarnas källa.* The latter is a dramatized version of the Old Testament story of Jacob and Laban's two daughters. It reflects Moberg's great admiration for the Bible as literature and as a source of inspiration for his own work. The play *Nattkyparen* (The Night Waiter, 1961) is Moberg's deeply personal statement about getting old. The protagonist is an artist, a painter who contemplates suicide when he feels that his creative powers are failing him and that the future offers only progressive deterioration and humiliation through the aging process.

THE FIGHTER FOR FREEDOMS

Vilhelm Moberg's sense of justice was unfailing, his personal integrity above reproach, and his capacity for indignation and anger formidable. With great moral courage and a sanguine eagerness to do battle he espoused a number of causes during his career and fought for them with all the means at his disposal, presenting his views through the press, in satires, in pamphlets, and in personal appearances at public meetings.

From very early in life Moberg was a confirmed pacifist and antimilitarist. However, the political events in Europe in the 1930's forced him to revise his views. Like Knut Toring in *The Earth Is Ours!* he recognized the necessity of actively resisting evil, and he formulated the principles for which he was willing to kill and to die. Thus, he vocally resisted Swedish neutrality in World War II. In a book in which Swedish authors and artists expressed their solidarity with the democratic cause during the Spanish Civil War, Moberg symptomatically entitled his contribution "Vi är inte neutrala!" (We Are Not Neutral!), published in the anthology *Till Madrid från svenska författare* (To Madrid from Swedish Writers, 1937). When Russia attacked Finland in November 1939, a number of writers with Moberg, Eyvind Johnson, and Harry Martinson in the vanguard pleaded for assistance to Finland. Following the German occupation of Denmark and Norway in April 1940, Moberg intensified his efforts to rally the Swedes to resistance, but he found it increasingly difficult to make himself heard because of restrictions officially imposed on the press in the interest of Sweden's neutrality; Torgny Segerstedt, the fearless editor of the repeatedly confiscated newspaper *Göteborgs Handels- och Sjöfartstidning*, was one of the few who welcomed Moberg's contributions. In 1941 Moberg wrote a pamphlet entitled *Svensk strävan* (The Swedish Struggle) in which he gave eloquent reasons why Sweden should be defended. The pamphlet was distributed to all Swedish recruits. In the same year Moberg repeated the message in fictional form in the novel *Ride This Night!* Exercising what he claimed to be "a Swedish citizen's ancient right freely to give his opinion in matters that concern him personally," he published the pamphlet *Sanningen kryper fram* (The Truth Emerges, 1943) in which he exposed the full extent of the government's concessions to Nazi Germany.

Moberg continued to follow international events after the war. He was an outspoken critic of the Communist takeover in Czechoslovakia in 1948 and the Soviet intervention in Prague in 1968. His lifelong admiration for the United States and the American brand of democracy made his condemnation of the American involvement in Vietnam particularly bitter.

Concurrently with the writing of the emigrant tetralogy in the 1950's, Moberg turned his attention to investigating a number of scandals in public life in Sweden and to uncovering corrupt practices and misuses of authority. In each case he looked into, he found that the civil rights of individuals had been violated in order to protect officials in high positions. One such case even involved King Gustav V. As he had done during the war when newspapers were unwilling to accept his articles, Moberg published a number of pamphlets or turned directly to the citizens in large public meetings. One of his pamphlets was entitled *Att övervaka överheten* (On Being Vigilant of the Authorities, 1953) and another, *Komplotterna* (The Conspiracies, 1956). In order to obtain proof of wrongdoings Moberg once made himself guilty of a criminal offense when he smuggled documents from the Justice Department and had them photocopied. He cheerfully paid the fine out of his own pocket and donated the money collected nationally to defray the cost of the fine to the Association for the Protection of Legal Rights. As a part of his efforts to expose corruption in public life, Moberg published the already-mentioned plays *Domaren* and *Sagoprinsen* and also a novel, *Det gamla riket* (The Ancient Kingdom, 1953). The similarity of the latter title to Strindberg's biting satire *Det nya riket* (The New Kingdom, 1882) is not accidental. In his depiction of the kingdom of Idyllia as seen through the eyes of the young and somewhat uncritical Swedish visitor Secretessius, Moberg gives free rein to his considerable satirical gift in order to castigate conditions in the Sweden of the 1950's.

The last decade of Moberg's life was marked by restless moves and growing fears of failing creative powers. The great emptiness he had felt ever since completing the emigrant tetralogy he intended to fill by embarking on another gigantic project, even larger in scope than his emigrant cycle, namely a history of Sweden written according to his own particular concept of history. This concept differed from traditional historiography's emphasis on rulers, military leaders, and decisive battles; Moberg wanted to write a history from the perspective of the common people. Out of his extensive research for this undertaking grew the novel *Förrädarland* (Land of Traitors, 1967), in which Moberg returns to Värend, this time the Värend of the sixteenth century, when the Danish-Swedish border cut a more or less arbitrary line through the region. The peasants of this region were bound together by innumerable ties across the border—through intermarriage, shared pastures, and peaceful commerce. Thus they refused to take part in the wars fought by kings and crowns in the interest of some abstract concept of nationalism; instead they made their own peasant peace treaties and thus became "traitors" in the eyes of the rulers. Moberg's novel invites contemporary analogies. Moberg views the peace-loving peasants as freedom fighters whose example ought to be followed in those parts of the world where unnatural borders separate people, whether in Berlin or Ireland, Korea or Vietnam.

Moberg's work on Swedish history resulted in two volumes published in 1970 and 1971: *Min svenska historia. Berättad för folket* (*A History of the Swedish People*), I, *Från Oden till Engelbrekt* (*From Odin to Engelbrekt*), and II, *Från Engelbrekt till och med Dacke* (*From Engelbrekt to Dacke*). As his research progressed, Moberg encountered source material that kept accumulating beyond his ability to manage it.

In the first volume of the emigrant cycle, Karl Oskar's father faces defeat when he becomes crippled by a particularly recalcitrant stone. In the last volume, Karl Oskar himself is forced to capitulate when an oak tree he is felling lands on his back. Similarly, Moberg was forced to bow before the insurmountable task before him.

As early as 1939 Moberg made his protagonist Knut Toring formulate a few absolute principles he was willing to defend with his life. First among them was "the right to dispose over myself, over mind and body." It seems entirely in character that Moberg, the man who had always been fiercely independent and who had refused to bow to any authority threatening his sense of freedom, should refuse to accept the ultimate authority, death, on its own terms. As a final exercise of personal freedom Vilhelm Moberg took his own life on the morning of 8 August 1973, only a few days before his seventy-fifth birthday.

Selected Bibliography

EDITIONS

INDIVIDUAL WORKS

FICTION

(All published in Stockholm, except as noted)
I vapenrock och linnebyxor. En krigsmans intryck och upplevelser. Växjö, 1921 (under the pseudonym Ville i Momåla).
Prinsessan på Solklinten. Göteborg, 1922 (under the pseudonym Ville i Momåla).
Raskens: En soldatfamiljs historia. 1927.
Långt från landsvägen. 1929.
De knutna händerna. 1930.
A. P. Rosell, bankdirektör. 1932.
Mans kvinna. 1933.
Sänkt sedebetyg. 1935.

VILHELM MOBERG

Sömnlös. 1937.
Giv oss jorden! 1939.
Rid i natt! 1941.
Soldat med brutet gevär. 1944.
Brudarnas källa. 1946.
Utvandrarna. 1949.
Invandrarna. 1952.
Det gamla riket. 1953.
Nybyggarna. 1956.
Sista brevet till Sverige. 1959.
Din stund på jorden. 1962.
Förrädarland. 1967.

PLAYS
(All Published In Stockholm)
Hustrun. 1929.
Marknadsafton. 1930.
Bönder emellan. 1933.
Våld. 1933.
Kyskhet. 1937.
Jungfrukammare. 1938.
Kassabrist. 1939.
De knutna händerna. 1939.
Änkeman Jarl. 1940.
En löskekarl. 1941.
Rid i natt! 1942.
Vår ofödde son. 1945.
Mans kvinna. 1953.
Gudens hustru. 1954.
Jungfru Maria på fattiggårn. 1954.
Lea och Rakel. 1954.
Domaren. 1957.
Nattkyparen. 1961.
Sagoprinsen. 1962.
Kvinnas man. 1965.
Din stund på jorden. 1967.

NONFICTION
(All Published In Stockholm)
Svensk strävan. 1941.
Sanningen kryper fram. 1943.
Segerstedtstriden. 1945.
Den okända släktenk 1950.
Fallet Krukmakaregatan. 1951.
Att övervaka överheten. 1953.
Därför är jag republikan. 1955.
Komplotterna. 1956.
Bondeåret. 1966.
Berättelser ur min levnad. 1968. Includes the essay "Brodd."

Min svenska historia. Berättad för folket. Första delen. Från Oden till Engelbrekt. 1970.
Min svenska historia. Berättad för folket. Andra delen. Från Engelbrekt till och med Dacke. 1971.
Otrons artiklar. 1973.
I egen sak. Edited by Otto von Friesen, 1984.

TRANSLATIONS

The Earth Is Ours! Translated by E. Björkman. New York, 1940.
The Emigrants. Translated by G. Lannestock. New York, 1951.
Fulfillment. Translated by M. Heron. London, 1953.
A History of the Swedish People. Part I. From Odin to Engelbrekt. Translated by Paul Britten Austin. New York, 1972.
A History of the Swedish People. Part II. From Engelbrekt to Dacke. Translated by Paul Britten Austin. New York, 1974.
The Last Letter Home. Translated by G. Lannestock. New York, 1961. Abridged version of Nybyggarna and Sista brevet till Sverige.
The Last Letter Home. Translated by G. Lannestock. New York, 1978. This is the unabridged version. Together with The Settlers it restores the tetralogy to the length it has in the original.
Memory of Youth. Translated by E. Björkman. New York, 1937.
Ride This Night! Translated by H. Alexander. New York, 1943.
The Settlers. Translated by G. Lannestock. New York, 1978.
A Time on Earth. Translated by Naomi Walford. New York, 1965.
Unto A Good Land. Translated by G. Lannestock. New York, 1954.
When I Was a Child. Translated by G. Lannestock. New York, 1956.

BIOGRAPHICAL AND CRITICAL STUDIES

Alexis, Gerhard T. "Sweden to Minnesota: Vilhelm Moberg's Fictional Reconstruction." American Quarterly 18:81–94 (1966).
Eidevall, Gunnar. Vilhelm Mobergs emigrantepos: Studier i verkets tillkomsthistoria, dokumentära bakgrund och konstnärliga gestaltning. Stockholm, 1974.

————. *Berättaren Vilhelm Moberg.* Stockholm, 1976.

Holmes, Philip. *Vilhelm Moberg.* Boston, 1980.

Lagerroth, Erland, and Ulla-Britta Lagerroth eds. *Perspektiv på Utvandrarromanen.* Stockholm, 1971.

Lundkvist, Artur. "Epikern Vilhelm Moberg." In *Vilhelm Moberg—en vänbok.* Stockholm, 1973: 110–146.

Mårtensson, Sigvard. *Vilhelm Moberg: En biografi.* Stockholm, 1956.

Von Platen, Magnus, ed. *Emigrationer. En bok till Vilhelm Moberg 20.8 1968.* Stockholm, 1968.

————. *Den unge Vilhelm Moberg.* Stockholm, 1978.

LARS G. WARME

YURI OLESHA

(1899–1960)

LIFE

YURI KARLOVICH OLESHA was born on 3 March 1899 (new style) in the southwestern Russian town of Elizavetgrad (today Kirovograd). His parents were impoverished Polish gentry. Karl Antonovich, the writer's father, formerly a landowner and nobleman and later a government inspector of spirits, appears in his son's reminiscences as weak, given to gambling and to drink. Olesha does not seem to have been very close to him or to his mother, who scarcely appears in Olesha's stories of his childhood. His grandmother, on the other hand, supervised the boy's early education and was probably closer to him. The family's Polish descent and Catholic upbringing perhaps helped to give Olesha a Western outlook.

When Olesha was three, his family moved to Odessa, the great port city on the Black Sea. Compared to other Russian cities, Odessa was the most Mediterranean in its culture and in certain respects the most cosmopolitan and Western. The city is renowned for the large number of writers and artists it has given the world. Besides Olesha, the writers Valentin Kataev, Eduard Bagritski, and Ilya Ilf came from Odessa; all three were companions of Olesha in his youth, and Kataev remained his friend throughout his life.

Olesha was an exceptionally apt pupil and repeatedly gained honors in school. He showed considerable talent for science, but literature was his favorite subject, and he had already begun writing by 1916. After graduating from the *gimnaziza* (high school) in 1917, he enrolled the same year in the Novorossiiski University in Odessa as a student of law. In 1919 the civil war interrupted his studies, and he volunteered for service in the Red Army, serving as a telephone operator in a Black Sea artillery battery. He also wrote newspaper articles and propaganda materials, including short plays, for the cause of the revolution.

Olesha's identification with the revolution estranged him from his family, who fled to Poland and remained there until their deaths. After World War II, when it was possible for Soviet citizens to visit Poland, friends brought Olesha news of meetings with them, but he showed little interest. He never saw his parents again, although he did undertake to support his mother after his father died.

In this early period Olesha composed verses; he was active, together with Kataev and Bagritski, in a literary circle of young people formed in Odessa called "The Green Lamp." Moving to Kharkov in 1921, Olesha continued to write propaganda materials; at the same time he published his first story, "Angel" ("The Angel"), which appeared in a Kharkov newspaper in 1922. The same year he moved to Moscow, where he joined the staff of the widely read railway workers' journal, *Gudok* (The Whistle). His first job on the periodical consisted of nothing more serious than stuffing and stamping envelopes. But soon, taking the pen name of "Zubilo" (the chisel), Olesha began to write humorous and satirical verses that became a repeated and memorable feature of the magazine. Much of Olesha's satire was directed at the bureaucracy, graft, and inefficiency of the state railroad system. Two collections of these verses were subsequently published in 1924 and 1927, but their popularity was a phenomenon of the times, and they cannot be said to read very well today. Still, the verses did serve the young writer as exercises in literary style and wit. More and more Olesha turned, however, to the writing of prose fiction and drama. Two of his most-read works, *Zavist'* (*Envy*, 1927) and *Tri tolstyaka* (*The Three Fat Men*, 1928) were written in this period, the early and mid 1920's. He continued his work on *Gudok* through the early 1930's, some years after he had become an established writer.

Olesha emerged in the public eye with the publication of his novel *Envy* in 1927. Its popularity brought about the publication of a whole series of subsequent works, including a fairy-tale romance about the socialist revolution, *The Three Fat Men*, which Olesha had written in 1924 and published in 1928; a series of stories; a dramatization of *Envy* for the Moscow Vakhtangov Theater entitled *Zagovor chuvstv* (*The Conspiracy of Feelings*) in 1929; and an original stage play, *Spisok blagodeyanii* (*A List of Assets*) in 1931. Olesha also rewrote *The Three Fat Men* as a play for Konstantin Stanislavski's theater, and eventually the story was produced as an opera, a ballet, and even a radio play, becoming something of a Soviet classic.

This period appears in retrospect as Olesha's time of mature greatness, which he sought vainly to recover in later years. Although his writings no doubt show some hesitation in his acceptance of the revolution and the building of socialism in the Soviet Union, and although they ultimately tend toward an aestheticism totally at variance with the world around him, throughout the 1920's Olesha

could still claim to be a child of the revolution, one who sought only the fulfillment of the socialist dream.

In the 1930's, however, such a posture became more difficult for him to maintain. In the still relatively utopia-directed Soviet atmosphere of the 1920's, it was possible for young writers such as Olesha, Kataev, or Kaverin to dream of utopian art, of an ideal art in an ideal society. But the art and literature Stalin and his cohorts demanded, beginning in 1933, were rigidly aligned with the new order and ethically and aesthetically philistine.

The first sign of Olesha's discontent was voiced in 1934, at the First Congress of Soviet Writers, the union Stalin had created as a straitjacket for the new literature. Indeed, his speech at the congress was perhaps the most noteworthy and certainly the most poignant thing said there. Olesha conceives the idea of writing a story about his own youth, about himself as a beggar, a man whose life is bitter, deprived, vulgar, and insignificant:

> I wanted to write a story like that. I thought about it. I drew conclusions and I understand that my chief aim was to keep my right to the colors of youth, my chief aim was to keep the right to youth, to protect my freshness from any assertion that it might not be needed, that freshness is vulgarity, worthlessness.
>
> I am not to blame that my youth passed in circumstances when the world around us was a terrifying one. . . . While I was planning my story about the beggar . . . our country was building factories. It was the First Five Year Plan for the creation of socialist industry. But that was not my subject. I could travel to the site, live in the factory with the workers, write a sketch about them, or even a novel, but that was no subject for me; it was not a subject that came out of my circulatory system, from my breathing. Such a subject would not make me a true artist. I would have lied and invented; I would have had no inspiration. I have difficulty understanding the social type of the worker, the social type of the revolutionary hero. I cannot be that kind of a writer.
>
> (*Povesti i rasskazy*, pp. 427–428)

Olesha's fall from grace in official Soviet eyes was marked somewhat earlier, in 1931, by his publication of a bitter fragment, "Koe-chto iz sekretnykh zapisey poputchika Zanda" ("From the Secret Notebook of Fellow Traveler Zand"). Zand is a writer—obviously Olesha himself—who hides himself behind a mirror that reflects reality and who cannot "merge with the masses." But the fragment, as well as a play, "The Death of Zand," was never completed.

The 1930's and 1940's represented a period of continual difficulties for Olesha, during which he managed to live the public life of a writer but succeeded in publishing almost nothing. He turned to the writing of film scenarios at this time. One film, *Strogi yunosha* (The Strict Youth) was finally completed in 1942, but it has never been released. Although apparently he worked on many films in the decades that preceded his death, it is very difficult to point to any concrete evidence of his accomplishments.

After the Germans invaded the Soviet Union in 1941, Olesha was evacuated to Ashkabad, the capital of Turkmenistan in Central Asia. There he was assigned to duties as a political agitator in addition to his work as a scenarist, and he gave frequent talks on the radio. In 1946 he and his wife, Olga Suok, returned to Moscow, but his apparent failure to obtain a residence permit caused the couple great difficulties, and they kept moving from one friend's apartment to another's. (This suggests that Olesha had no official permission to reside in Moscow, and that, in effect, his status as a writer was no longer officially acknowledged.) The apartment crisis was solved only in 1954, when he was granted permanent residence in Moscow. Thus commenced the final period of his life, one that was relatively more peaceful and secure and at the same time somewhat more productive from a literary point of view. At this time he commenced serious work on a collection of memoirs and literary reflections, which he entitled *Ni dnya bez strochki* (No Day

Without a Line, 1961). With the publication of such a work he intended, no doubt, to fill up the long void of silence that marked his last decades. The work was never actually completed, but after Olesha's death in 1960 his widow and his friend, the writer Viktor Shklovski, labored to bring the materials Olesha had left into order, and it was finally published in 1961.

During the mid 1950's Olesha worked on the preparation of a one-volume edition of his writings, which appeared as *Izbrannye sochineniia* (Selected Works) in 1956. From 1955 to 1958 he also worked on a stage adaptation of Feodor Dostoevski's novel *Idiot* (The Idiot, 1868) for the Vakhtangov Theater in Moscow, and the play was produced in 1958 with considerable success. On 10 May 1960 Olesha died of heart failure.

FICTION

Envy

While it is difficult to date the beginnings of Olesha's work on his short novel *Envy*, it is possible that he began writing it as far back as 1921 and the time of his first publication of stories and verses. The novel cost him immense labor, and he tells us that he wrote nearly three hundred versions of its opening. Olesha probably worked on it more or less continuously through the 1920's, until in 1927 it was published in *Krasnaya nov'* (Red Virgin Soil), the leading literary journal of the leftist or proletarian writers and critics. The following year the novel appeared in book form.

Envy is no doubt Olesha's masterpiece. At the same time it is a major work of literature to the extent that, had he written virtually nothing else, he would still stand in the first rank of Soviet writers. Late in life the author regarded it as a unique work on which his fame would rest, a masterpiece that he would no longer be able to duplicate. At the same time critics in the West have sometimes spoken of *Envy* as the greatest Soviet (or anti-Soviet) novel.

Especially memorable for the fresh, striking quality of its style and imagery, *Envy* proved popular with its Soviet readership from the very first, and even today the novel remains an early Soviet classic from a period whose writers have generally fallen into disfavor or neglect. Abroad, too, *Envy* has been popular. It was published in English as early as 1936 and has since gone through a number of English-language editions.

The theme of the novel, as of much of Olesha's writing, is the conflict between vitalism and mechanism, a theme that seems to derive in large measure from the philosophy of Henri Bergson. Western European literature of the day, vitalist, cubist, and impressionist, also had its influence on Olesha. The young Jean Giraudoux and his novel, *L'École des indifférents* (The School for Indifference, 1911), a work popular in the Soviet Union in the 1920's, was one channel of this influence. The preeminence of an aesthetic view of reality—a transformation or stylization of observed or experienced reality in a work of art—not only in literature but in the life and attitudes of these writers' protagonists and fictional observers, is one similarity between Olesha's works and his European contemporaries'. But the main source of literary (as opposed to ideological) influence was unquestionably the poet Vladimir Mayakovsky, whom Olesha literally adored. Mayakovsky's fascination with images as central to the literary process and with the extended metaphor or conceit is taken over by Olesha as probably his favorite literary device. No doubt this notion was a common article of literary trade in Russian writing of the 1920's: Venyamin Kaverin, Konstantin Fedin, Shklovski, and Ilya Ehrenburg—all Olesha's immediate contemporaries—were also preoccupied with the central role of the image in fiction.

Envy contrasts the forces of an old and a new order within the Soviet world. The old order, full of a nostalgia for the prerevolutionary past, is represented by Nikolay Kavalerov, a young man with an irregular life-style who composes verses to be sung in taverns, and by Ivan Babichev, a Chaplinesque buffoon who presumes to be the leader of an antiestablishment "conspiracy of feelings," a conspiracy that will give back feeling to an overly rationalistic new order. Kavalerov's name derives from the word for "knight" or "cavalier" and thus suggests an air of romanticism appropriate to nostalgia for a bygone order; but the word in Russian has more vulgar connotations as well, and in everyday parlance means "swain" or "boyfriend." Hence Kavalerov's seemingly romantic impulses turn out to be a mere bathetic pose, and like so many other heroes of Russian literature he is to be regarded as a *poshlyak* (a vulgarian or philistine), as, indeed, is Ivan Babichev as well.

Ivan's conspiracy seems to be directed primarily toward socially negative feelings that romanticism may value, such as honor, vengeance, or unrequited love. Primarily, Ivan feels envy, and Kavalerov, whom Ivan adopts as a willing pupil, is obsessed by this feeling, which he directs against the more positive forces of the new order.

These forces are exemplified by Andrey Babichev, Ivan's younger brother, the commissar of the Soviet food trust and the patron of Volodya Makarov, a young soccer player. Volodya, who lives with Andrey, is in love with a girl student, Valya, Ivan Babichev's daughter. Andrey, a former revolutionary who is dissatisfied with his personality, filled as it is with vestiges of bourgeois attitudes and bourgeois culture, has taken Volodya in to live with him, partly because he has no family and partly out of respect for the forward-looking younger generation. When Volodya goes off to visit his parents in Murom, Andrey takes in Kavalerov, whom he finds lying in the street, the victim of a drunken brawl, and gives him Volodya's sofa to sleep on. The realization that Volodya, the hero of the future, is the permanent possessor of the sofa and the permanent protegée is what inspires the sentiment of envy in Kavalerov.

Kavalerov, too, is in love with Valya. Meeting

her father by accident on the street, he joins the conspiracy of feelings, which he seeks to use to wreak vengeance against Andrey and Volodya. His own role will be the murder of Andrey. But the conspiracy turns out to be nothing more than a sham, and Ivan Babichev a fraud. In the end the two conspirators are forced to take refuge with the widow in whose apartment Kavalerov had formerly lodged. She, a figure of repulsive feminine sexuality, offers them the dubious consolation of physical satisfaction and comfort. Sitting on her bed, they drink to absolute indifference and the abandonment of their conspiracy.

Envy is difficult to summarize because its essence lies not so much in story action as in the imagery associated with that action. Its opening is most memorable, as Andrey Babichev sings lustily in the toilet. His aggressively physical characterization is further developed with the observation that on the stairs his breasts shake in time with his stride. He does a whole series of gymnastic exercises in the morning in Kavalerov's room, as if for his benefit.

> Mornings he sings in the toilet. You can't imagine what a cheerful, healthy man he is. The urge to sing wells up in him like a reflex. His singing, which has no melody or words, is just a kind of "ta-ra-ra," sounded in various keys, which you might interpret as follows:
> "How much I enjoy life . . . tara! tara! My bowels are firm . . . ratatatarari. My juices are circulating properly . . . ratatadutata . . . tighten up, you bowels, tighten up . . . trambababum!"
> (*Povesti i rasskazy*, p. 19)

Later we are treated to a loving description of a new sausage that Andrey has created, intended to win honors abroad and to revolutionize Soviet food production.

At the climax of his novel Olesha inserts a description of a soccer match between the Soviet team and the Germans. This, one of the first and most notable descriptions of sports in a major work of Soviet literature, serves several functions in the novel. First, it gives Volodya a heroic role, one entirely independent of his mentor Andrey. It also suggests that the communal spirit of the Soviet team will triumph over the competitive one of the Germans (and hence over a romantic conspiracy of feelings as well). But the game also serves as an anticlimax: Kavalerov has announced that at the soccer game he will kill Andrey, but nothing happens, and Kavalerov retreats in shame and disgust, a shame and disgust that are subsequently confirmed by his reception at the widow's. In this substitution of anticlimax and inaction for action, Olesha makes it clear that the story is not really told in the actions of the characters so much as in their characterizations, postures, and stances (a fact that gave the author enormous difficulty several years later when he undertook to dramatize *Envy*).

In this light Olesha uses dreams, memories, fantasies, and lies (Ivan Babichev is a chronic liar) and intermingles them with reality to the degree that the reader can hardly separate the various commingled elements. Such a scene is the imaginary one in which Ivan Babichev resolutely stands in the middle of the street and stops his brother's official car—a scene heroic in terms of attitude, posture, and gesture, but that in fact, we are told later, never takes place.

> And it seemed his brother Ivan ran out of the crowd into the street, the very man, the famous one. Catching sight of his brother riding past, he stepped into the path of the car, spreading wide his arms the way a scarecrow does, or a man seeking to frighten a bolting horse to make it stop. The driver just had time to slow down. He signaled and continued to roll along slowly, but the scarecrow did not quit the street.
> "Stop!" the man cried full volume. "Stop, commissar. Stop, abductor of other men's children. . . . Brother," the man spoke. "Why do you ride in a car, while I go on foot? Open the door, make room, let me in. It's not right for me to walk, either. You're a leader, but I too am a leader."
> (*Povesti i rasskazy*, p. 78)

The upshot of this episode is that Andrey calls

the political police, who take Ivan in and interrogate him concerning his "conspiracy of feelings." But the entire scene is imagined and goes nowhere in the story that follows. Its unfactual quality suggests that Ivan and Kavalerov are antiheroes; the roles they conceive for themselves are heroic, but they do not fulfill them.

A similar case is that of the entire sequence connected with Ivan Babichev's invention of a fantastic machine, to which he gives the name Ophelia. Ivan's machine can counterfeit life: she can sing the faded romances and gather the withered flowers of the past age. But she can also kill, by impaling her victim on a metal proboscis, and thus she is designated as the instrument of Ivan and Kavalerov's revenge. In a fantasy scene presented as real, Ophelia destroys the "Quarter" (a new restaurant where Soviet citizens can eat cheaply and in cleanliness and comfort) and impales Andrey on her metallic proboscis. Thus the novel's climax, put off from the bungled murder attempt of the soccer game, emerges here. But of course this is not a real climax either, and it is followed again by an anticlimax in the final scene where Ivan and Kavalerov drink to indifference. For the forces of the new order there is no climax either, unless Volodya's playing in the soccer match is to be taken as such.

The machine Ophelia no doubt owes its inspiration to Olesha's love for such writers as H. G. Wells and Karel Čapek (especially Čapek's robots). Indeed, the ability of the machine to counterfeit life seems to have fascinated Olesha, and he refers to the subject several times, especially in his later story "Al'debaran" ("Aldebaran," 1931) in which a planetarium serves two lovers as a counterfeit substitute for the blue sky and the open air at night. But in "Aldebaran" the machine substitute is effective; in *Envy* it is not. As a machine Ophelia serves only as a kind of blasphemy of the Soviet cult of the machine and of a machine order. Ophelia's presumed human qualities (to sing songs and pick flowers) suggest only that

here the machine is a caricature of life: the songs are from the past and the flowers are withered. Ophelia is an expressionistic symbol of the machine's threat to life and plays a crucial role in the development of the novel's theme of vitalism versus machanism. The possession of a proboscis that impales and kills seems to symbolize castration by a female (Ophelia); the Russian word for "machine" is also feminine in gender; and there is other evidence of castration by a female in *Envy*, especially in Kavalerov's repulsive landlady. It is not certain wheter the symbol of castration can be entirely related to that of vitalism versus mechanism or to that of the conspiracy of feelings, but it may be that it is an expressionistic symbol of the true nature of Ivan's conspiracy of feelings.

After the first wave of popularity that greeted *Envy*, its critics quickly came to find fault with the novel. The figures embodying the world of the future (Andrey, Volodya, Valya) seemed increasingly inadequate or negative: Andrey was little more than a "sausage maker" (the epithet Kavalerov hurls at him); Volodya merely the "soccer player," a comparable epithet; and Valya a creature of mere dreams and fantasy—in one scene of the novel she even floats through the air (an example of one of Olesha's extended metaphors). True, the figures of the past world are no better, but in some ways their impotent buffoonery commands our affection more. This same line was soon taken up by critics outside the Soviet Union, though with an inverse implication of praise rather than blame, and thus Olesha's novel gained a reputation as an anti-Soviet classic. This reputation compromised Olesha's own career and almost destroyed it, but it has stuck with Olesha among critics and readers abroad.

The impression that *Envy* is an anti-Soviet novel is not totally wrong, of course. But it is important to point out that to some extent this impression results from misreading and neglecting certain aspects of the work. There can be no doubt that both Kavalerov and Ivan Babichev are conceived as negative figures in Soviet society, warped by the unhappy legacy of the past. Both are vagabonds, able to survive in the dubious moral climate of the Soviet New Economic Policy of the mid 1920's. Does it then follow that their antagonists are heroic? That expectation is not borne out, but still we can find certain elements of heroism in them. Andrey Babichev has his faults, but these are rooted in the same bourgeois past that produced Kavalerov and Ivan. Andrey seriously intends a revolution in the Soviet food production system: if his sausage is a caricature, his plan for the "Quarter," a restaurant where Soviet families can eat at modest prices, is not. It is true, of course, that the image is somewhat philistine, and it is also true that the social habit of eating out may weaken the links binding the Soviet family together, as Ivan suggests. But this is only one of a series of uncontrollable contradictions that the new order brings with it, as part of the price that must be paid to achieve it.

Volodya, the "soccer player," seems rude and barbaric, an unworthy suitor for Valya. But Volodya's heroic playing wins the soccer game for the Soviets. Olesha played soccer as a boy and, judging from his other fiction, seems genuinely to have idolized sports and sports figures. Thus Volodya's rudeness may well represent a normal characteristic for Soviet youth of the 1920's, caught up in a cultural revolution directed in large part at their elders and superiors and the life-style the latter followed and imposed upon their juniors.

Finally Valya, the shadowy heroine, corresponds precisely to Olesha's image of an ideal woman as described in *No Day Without a Line*. For Olesha, it is her feminine nature to lack substance and reality; she flies through the air in a realized simile of a woman in love. She is not precisely one of the forces of the future; she is rather the prize to be awarded to the hero of the future, presumably Volodya Makarov. Last of all, it is important to note that she is the exact opposite of the repulsive widow: she is unreal, while the widow is triumphant physicality incarnate. In this respect we should also note that Valya is ultimately a sexless figure while the widow is extremely sexual, for all her repulsive nature.

What Olesha seems to be saying in *Envy*, then, is that we cannot escape the past without loss while the future is where we must go, even though we are naturally apprehensive about it. Such a reading, though it may seem to trivialize *Envy* as such thematic reductions often do, can be confirmed by comparing the novel with Olesha's early stories, in particular with "Vishnyovaya kostochka" ("The Cherry Stone," 1929). It can also be confirmed by the role the young Olesha had himself played in the revolution.

Olesha admitted several times that there was a link between himself and his hero Kavalerov, the narrator of the first part of *Envy*. We may guess that in fact envy was an appropriate sentiment for the young intellectual and writer, especially as it was directed against false heroes of the new order; the commissars who enjoyed privilege and the young leaders of the cultural revolution might have inspired the sentiment among those less fortunate or less brash than they.

Envy dramatizes a number of thematic oppositions beside its basic one of vitalism versus materialism. Perhaps the most significant of these is individualism versus collectivism, an opposition developed in the soccer game between the Germans and the Soviets. Kavalerov, Ivan Babichev, and the widow are undoubted individuals, but in their cases individualism exacts its own price and offers few if any advantages. Ivan's conspiracy of feelings seeks to foster individualism in others but gives little to help them sustain it. Of the two young people, Volodya resolves to turn himself into a machine, a collectivist goal parodied in mechanist terms. Andrey seems ambivalent, for he comes out of an individualist order, and, although it is his task to help create a collectivized one, he has reservations. The novel's opposition between collectivism and individualism is never resolved.

The role of the family in Soviet society is an

evident theme of *Envy*. The family had been a major subject of the nineteenth-century Russian novel. Although Aleksandr Pushkin's Onegin and the heroes of Ivan Turgenev fail to become linked in stable family relationships, still the family obviously constitutes a social norm by which their failures are to be judged. Leo Tolstoy's novels, *Voina i mir* (*War and Peace*, 1862–1869) and *Anna Karenina* (1873–1876), have done more than those of any other writer to make this theme canonical for classical Russian literature.

In the 1920's marriage and the family had ceased to possess the traditional sentimental value that nineteenth-century novels had placed on them. The heroes of the Russian revolutionary novels, beginning with Nikolay Chernyshevski's *Chto delat'?* (*What Is to Be Done?*, 1863), embrace an ascetic life in which marriage has no place. This was the fashion of the Soviet proletarian novel of the 1920's. During this period, both marriage and divorce had become legally very easy to accomplish, and for these reasons Olesha's references to the stability of the family verge on being comic. It is against this background, literary as well as social and ideological, that Andrey Babichev's bachelorhood must be viewed, and it may seem somewhat pretentious of Andrey to claim for himself and Volodya the status of a family. What he apparently means by this assertion is that the rewards and privileges of family life should be open even to those embracing the new communist life-style. But since these rewards and privileges are hardly sacrosanct, his claim only further undercuts them and their seriousness.

Friedrich Engels and, in Soviet Russia, Anatoli Lunacharsky had argued that the revolution should liberate women from servitude and domestic toil so that they might participate freely and creatively in the building of socialism. This is the goal of Andrey's experimental family restaurant, "The Quarter." The family of the future will eat out in order that wives and mothers may be liberated.

Thus in *Envy* Olesha seems to embrace a proletarian view of the family and its ideological needs. But in fact he undercuts those same ideological values in a parody of family values. The question must be asked whether the novel is not in fact a parody as a whole, aiming its satirical thrust at the vision of the world of the future and the rewards it brings to those who build it.

Early Stories

Olesha's early stories are deeply philosophical, in certain cases even more so than the novel *Envy*. One major cycle or group of stories is concerned with problems of epistemology and metaphysics. Another group is directed, however, toward the writer's past; this group includes "Chelovecheski material" ("Human Material," 1928), "Ya smotryu v proshloe" ("I Look into the Past," 1928), "Cep'" ("The Chain," 1929), as well as the later tales "V mire" ("In the World," 1937), "My v tsentre goroda" ("We're in the Center of Town," 1937), "V tsirke" ("At the Circus," 1938), and several others.

Olesha was always preoccupied with reminiscence and its artistic fruits, and these stories prepare the way for his final major work of reminiscence, *No Day Without a Line*; indeed, the editors of that volume drew on several of the stories for material in the compilation of the later volume. Some of theses stories are fragmentary reminiscences and seem to have been intended for incorporation in a larger context.

Most of these stories are actually sketches with a free form that permits the narrator to cut in and out at will, to go backward and forward in time. (The sketch has always been a popular form in Russian letters, partly because it allows the author so much liberty.) The first one, "Human Material," tells how the boy's father, himself a failure in life, introduces the boy to a certain Mr. Kovalevski, evidently an official, who is obviously intended to serve as a role model for him, partly because the father cannot. The boy reflects that in certain respects he is already a "Mr. Kovalevski"—he and Mr. Kovalevski both wear uniforms, for instance (Russian schoolboys wear uniforms to school). In other respects, say beards, they are different. But the goal held up by his father—that of making him into an engineer—is out of the question, for the adult writer knows that the boy will grow up to be a writer. He is a failure, it would seem, but in fact, a writer can serve as an engineer of human material. This formulation, intended by Olesha as humorous, recalls Stalin's later definition of writers as "engineers of human souls."

The urbaneness of these sketches proceeds partly from the contrast between the author's cheerful style of narration and the deeper pain and frustration of adolescence he feels within him. In this respect the next sketch, "I Look into the Past," is less concise and more lyrical as the author grants the reader glimpses of the pain and conflict deep within him. The boy makes his way into his father's bookcase and begins to read; his father approves of this and encourages him. But the family continues to be obsessed with suspicion that the boy is playing with himself under his blanket, and the father continues to demand that boy become an engineer. The boy's reading brings him to the conclusion that a relation to his father is precisely what he needs, but he realizes that, as their relationship stands, he only resents his father and is in fact utterly alone.

"The Chain" relates an incident taken from this childhood of frustration and loneliness. The boy borrows the bicycle of a student who is courting his sister, but while riding he loses the bicycle's chain. He imagines the scene of his return home with bitterness. But he fantasizes that he is rescued by Odessa's record-breaking bicyclist, Utochkin. An athlete, champion, and master of machinery, Utochkin is the boy's hero. Utochkin takes him home and admonishes the student not to mistreat him. The story ends with an apotheosis of the writer's

youth, the time when "Bleriot had flown the Channel," a fine time even if it was before the revolution. And he, the writer Olesha, is no longer worthy of it:

> Now I've fallen behind, look, how far I'm behind, I'm puffing along—a fat man on short legs. . . . Look how hard it is for me to run, but run I do, though I'm out of breath, though my legs get stuck—I run after the roaring storm of the century!
>
> (*Povesti i rasskazy*, p. 252)

Also based in part on reminiscence, but more a series of exercises in a writer's fantasy, is "In the World." This story develops the image of a beggar—a Russian peasant—an image that apparently haunted Olesha and one to which he refers elsewhere, but an image that he never fully developed. It is difficult to believe that he was obsessed with the figure of a beggar for purely social or psychological reasons, since this sort of thinking is not very characteristic for him, but it is of course possible that the beggar could have been another emotional and expressive symbol of Kavalerov's envy in the novel of that name.

"In the World" also develops Olesha's fondness for optical distortion, frequently observed by the critics and referred to in *Envy* and in the story "Lyubov'" ("Love," 1929). He cites with approval Edgar Allan Poe's story "The Gold Bug" (1843), in which a monstrous apparition visible on a nearby hillside turns out to be nothing more than a tiny insect crawling up a windowpane.

"We're at the Center of Town" is a lively guided tour through a city zoo, made all the more lively for its display of Olesha's virtuoso imagery.

Finally, "We're at the Circus" is a lament for the passing of old-fashioned circuses, which Olesha vividly recalled from his childhood; new circuses seem to him to substitute timorous performance for true heroism. Although not a word is said about socialism or the new era, this is perhaps the clearest single instance of a reproach made by Olesha to the new socialist order: collectivism has deprived him of the emotions of boyhood, and the passage of time will never bring them back.

A second group of tales focuses on questions of epistemology and metaphysics. These include, among the early stories, "Liompa" ("Liompa," 1928), "The Cherry Stone," "Love," and "Aldebaran," and among the later stories, "Natasha" (1936). Several of them are strongly influenced by the philosophy of Bergson, to which Olesha was attracted by his vitalist interests and sympathies. Vitalism links these stories to the novel *Envy,* as does the fact that the stories are constructed in terms of a number of antitheses: not only vitalism versus mechanism but also idealism versus materialism, romanticism versus realism, traditionalism versus futurism. Antitheses imply a dialectic and a resolution in synthesis, but resolution is lacking in *Envy,* where there is no reconciliation of the adherents of the past with those of the future. In this respect there are pronounced differences between the stories and *Envy;* the stories do achieve such a reconciliation, at least in "The Cherry Stone," and thus they transcend *Envy.* The point of view imperfectly represented by Volodya Makarov and Valya in *Envy* comes to full expression in the young people of "The Cherry Stone," "Love," and "Aldebaran": they seek to find love as well as the utopia of the future, and they insist on their right to be happy. This was not a traditional theme in Soviet literature of the 1920's, for the communist hero was supposed to abjure love and happiness for the sake of the victory of the revolution.

Love for Olesha is the highest manifestation of the vital and organic, and it is above material existence; love is the irrational antithesis of rational geometry and technology. Yet a reconciliation of vitalism and mechanism can be found, at least in fun. In "Aldebaran" the lovers can watch the stars (and make love) as effectively at the planetarium as in the open air. They outwit an older man who, enamored of the girl, holds her to her promise to meet him one evening if it rains, in which case she and her lover will have no starry sky to meet under. But the young people evade the dilemma by taking refuge on the rainy evening in the technological world of the planetarium that the new order has provided for them.

Similarly, in "Natasha" a girl who practices parachute jumping tries to conceal the dangerous pastime from her father, telling him that she is spending her time with a friend named Stein. When the father discovers that she is lying, he jumps to the conclusion that there is no such friend, that the story of a friend was only an invention to conceal the truth. But in fact the friend not only exists but is also a parachute jumper; there was no lie and no contradiction, but only an overlapping of two apparently opposed orders of truth.

It is the story "Love" that expresses this contradiction in perfect form, and that, along with the story "Liompa," has come to be regarded as Olesha's masterpiece. A young Marxist, Shuvalov, is in love with a girl named Lola. He waits for her to meet him in the park, but she is late. While waiting for her, his imagination engages in "scientific" observation: he classifies the trees and grasses and uses the flight of birds and insects to organize his perceptions into a kind of visual architecture constructed in the air. This last activity suggests that his scientific perception can also be aesthetic.

Shuvalov comes upon a colorblind observer in the park. Olesha uses colorblindness as a metaphor for a materialist perception that is cold, rational, and systematic, whereas color itself is a metaphor for irrational emotion and spontaneity. The colorblind man perceives everything quite correctly and precisely, but without that which gives things their true quality and intangible nature, their feel and their texture. The colorblind man laments that he must eat blue pears, to which Shuvalov replies coldly that "blue pears are inedible."

Later Shuvalov meets Lola, and they go home and make love. Ecstatic, Shuvalov flies through the air, propelled by the transports of love, and hears someone say from a window as he flies past, "He's soaring on the wings of love." This realized metaphor or conceit is carried even further when Sir Isaac Newton turns up to defend the law of gravitation that Shuvalov has violated in his flight. Thus the transports of love, symbolized by flight, are contrasted to science (Newtonian physics). But more broadly, the very arbitrariness and inappropriateness of the scientific point of view (geometric, architectural, botanical, physical) suggests that nature actually evades the categories of materialist science, just as Shuvalov's love seems to defy the law of gravity.

Shuvalov eventually wakes from his dream of Newton to find himself again confronted by the colorblind man, who reminds Shuvalov of his proper duty. He warns the young Marxist of the dangers inherent in his new idealistic view of life, colored and deformed by the experience of love:

> "I'm living in paradise," the young Marxist Shuvalov said in a turgid voice.
> "Are you a Marxist?" the question sounded from quite close at hand.
> "Yes, I'm a Marxist," said Shuvalov.
> "Then you may not live in paradise."
> (*Povesti i rasskazy*, pp. 273–274)

But now Shuvalov is possessed of a new truth besides the Marxist one, and the roles of the two men are reversed. The colorblind man begs Shuvalov to give him his love, but Shuvalov answers him scornfully, "Go and eat blue pears!" Fruits in Olesha's writings are universal symbols of love: Lola comes into the park eating apricots and trickling their juice, and Sir Isaac Newton refers to his apples. The "blue pears" seen by the colorblind man are no expressionist or surreal fantasy, but rather an imperfect substitute for the sensual apprehension of reality; they represent reality distorted by the systematic viewpoint of scientific perception.

"The Cherry Stone" operates with similar thematic material, but it resolves the antithe-

ses of vital versus mechanical. A young writer, Fedya, loves a girl named Natasha, but his love is unrequited; she loves the young Communist hero Boris Mikhailovich. One day the three of them eat cherries and spit out the stones, but Fedya carries away one cherry stone in his mouth and ultimately plants it in the ground as a symbol of his unrequited love. Later he learns that according to the Five Year Plan a building is to be erected on the very spot where he had planted the stone. He cannot bear the idea that his suffering should be fruitless, but in the end he discovers that the plan has provided the building with a garden, and in this garden his cherry tree will grow and bear fruit. This possibility of synthesizing vitalism and materialism presents the possibility of creating a third world, neither old nor new but their synthesis:

> So what, then? So then, in spite of all, in spite of order and society, have I really succeeded in creating a world not subject to any laws save the illusory laws of my own perception? What does that mean? There are two worlds, the old and the new, but what world is this? A third world? There are two ways, but what sort of way can this be?
> (*Povesti i rasskazy*, pp. 254–255)

It is the world of the future, not only new, but new and transcendent, and in it a miraculous synthesis of technology and life will be possible. It is the world of the cherry tree germinating from the stone, at once a symbol of barrenness and of fruition.

"The Cherry Stone" contains another theme, that of observation and art. Fedya is a writer, and hence he translates his experience of unrequited love into the domain of art. He calls this domain the "invisible land" and walks there arm in arm with two sisters, Observation and Imagination. Though dialectically opposed, both are fundamental to the artistic process; in the final analysis, however, Observation must be sacrificed to Imagination.

Finally, "The Cherry Stone" makes a comment on language: language, as a mediator for reality, is suspect; reality itself is superior. On the country stroll Fedya, Natasha, and Boris take, Fedya inquires vainly whether a certain bird is actually a "thrush," but he receives no reply for the lovers are entwined in a kiss. The name is meaningless, for it is powerless to control reality, which is itself nameless.

Bergson had actually taken a rather different view of language: in his view, it can liberate man from material reality and free the operation of the mind. In *L'Évolution creatrice* (*Creative Evolution,* 1907) he writes: "Without language, intelligence would probably have remained riveted to the material objects which it was interested in considering. . . . Language has greatly contributed to its liberation." This Bergsonian view of language is developed by Olesha in the story "Liompa." "Liompa" contrasts the world of a dying man, for whom only meaningless names are left but no living contact with reality, to that of a child, who as yet knows no names but for whom the world of reality is brilliantly alive. The child himself has no name, but is only called the "rubber boy," perhaps to emphasize his spontaneity and flexibility. The child is in close contact with reality, but although he exploits it insofar as he is capable, he cannot manipulate it except through physical contact. On the other hand, the old man lying on his deathbed, Ponomarev, has lost both the power and the will to control reality. We require a mediator between these two extremes, a figure capable of using language to manipulate objects conceptually, one who would construct civilization for us. And in fact there is such a third personage in the story, the boy Alexander, who builds model airplanes.

Tormented by a noisy rat that he cannot see, Ponomarev tries desperately to come up with the name of the beast, although he knows quite well that this effort is meaningless. Finally resolving that the name will occur to him at the moment of his death, he utters the name "Liompa!" which is in fact a meaningless collection of syllables. He does not die quite yet, but with his meaningless cry he does perform the operation of semiotically destroying language—and giving birth to a kind of poetry. The dying man crawls through the communal kitchen of the apartment, seeking objects to take with him on his journey. The last thing he sees is Alexander's model plane flying towards him. He does not take it, for unlike his wild cry, it is a product of civilization.

"Liompa" is not merely a parable about language; it is also a parable about art. Alexander's activity symbolizes that of the artist creator, which cannot function in a purely aesthetic world but only in one that contains purpose, names, and definitions as well. The flight of the model plane is at once a symbol of unconstrained imagination and of the consequence of knowing scientific law. The rubber boy's rude contact with reality, made without benefit of language, may be more purely poetic, but without language it can have no aesthetic structure.

At the story's end a coffin is brought for the dead man and is carried through the narrow passage with enormous difficulty. The rubber boy runs along the corridor shouting, "Grandpa! Grandpa! They've brought you a coffin!" With the acquisition of the coffin's name, the rubber boy makes a first stride toward civilized knowledge. And he brings to art the spontaneity of his crude contact with reality, as well as his observation.

DRAMA

The Conspiracy of Feelings

Olesha wrote two dramas, not counting his dramatization of *The Three Fat Men* for Stanislavski's Moscow Art Theater or his dramatization of Dostoevsky's novel *The Idiot* for the Vakhtangov Theater, which he wrote in the last years of his life.

The first of these is a dramatization of his novel *Envy,* retitled *The Conspiracy of Feelings.* The play is worthy of special mention because of its points of departure from the novel that inspired it. It was staged by the Vakhtangov Theater in 1929, two years after the novel had appeared, and the task of transferring the work to the stage gave Olesha great difficulty. The year 1929 saw a much greater degree of political control over literature than did the year 1927, for the institution of the First Five Year Plan implied that all literature should serve the purposes of the plan. The result was Olesha's unilateral realignment of ideological oppositions in the novel, with the forces of the "new order" now clearly winning out. The protagonist of the play is not Kavalerov, but Andrey Babichev, and it is probably for this reason that the romantic interest in the novel shifts to him: Valya is in love with him and not with Volodya. He hesitates, reflecting on the fate of Shakespeare's Othello, but finally decides to declare his love to her. Thus he becomes the rival of Kavalerov for the affection of his own niece.

Olesha was poorly prepared by his experience with fiction for writing drama. His fiction is lyric rather than dramatic: it contains relatively little dialogue, and he shows a special fondness for short speeches that go unanswered. At almost no point does the dialogue in his novel form the usual structure of give and take, of true exchange. This lack is striking, if mannered, in fiction, but it is almost an impossible handicap on the stage. Consequently, Olesha was forced to follow his strong concise speeches with rather meaningless, bathetic replies.

The dramatic opposition between Andrey and Kavalerov is much sharpened, and the now unnecessary Volodya almost drops out of the play. On the stage Valya becomes a somewhat more lifelike character since she is now forced to speak and since she is physically represented by an actress. And for somewhat similar reasons, Kavalerov becomes more sympathetic: rather than being a focus for the sentiment of envy, in the play he is depicted as an ambivalent, weak man in conflict with himself. His ambivalence is used to develop a radically new ending for the play in which, urged on by Ivan to kill Andrey, he ends up by turning against Ivan and cutting his throat with a razor.

Ivan Babichev is much the same in the play, perhaps because in the novel many of his speeches are quoted and his physical presence is strongly marked. His ideological role is heightened in the play: he is the villain who represents the old order and opposes the new. Kavalerov is no more than his follower, whom he incites to kill Andrey. Ivan has ample opportunity for dramatic expression: a fat, Chaplinesque figure in a bowler hat, he comes alive on the stage. The preaching of his conspiracy of feelings to the masses is actually represented on stage, whereas in the novel it was merely reported.

It is difficult to say how much of this change was motivated by ideological reasons and how much by the needs and restrictions of the stage. But the play is hardly as vital as the novel from which it was taken, nor has it survived as well.

A List of Assets

Olesha's only completely original play, *A List of Assets,* was written for Vsevolod Meyerhold's theater and was first performed under Meyerhold's direction in 1931. This is Olesha's most ideological work: it is built on a contrast of values between Soviet and western culture that cannot be resolved in any compromise but only in assertion of Soviet values.

Olesha had accumulated a plethora of dramatic material for his play, which helps to sustain it, but often the playwright fails properly to use or develop the material. Another fault is that his play is divided into eight scenes of unequal length, while the whole play is rather short. This construction frustrates proper development of the shorter scenes and prevents the dramatic line from cresting as it should.

A Soviet actress, Lola Goncharova, is torn by her love for both Soviet and western cultural values. She has obtained permission to travel to the West and swears that she will return to the Soviet Union, although obviously she is thinking of remaining abroad as so many of her countrymen have done. In Paris she dreams of attending the International Actors' Ball and of wearing a beautiful gown that she cannot afford. Such temptations lure her to remain abroad; at the same time they serve to compromise her in the eyes of the Soviet officials who are observing her movements. She attempts to stage a performance of excerpts from *Hamlet,* but finds that the local impresario is only interested in involving her in an indecent sex show. Penniless and with nowhere to turn, she falls into the clutches of an older émigré, editor of the local Russian-language newspaper who, it is hinted, may be her father. Shocked by her experiences, Lola now resolves to go back to the Soviet Union, even if she must walk the whole way and even if she must stand trial when she arrives there. But ironically she becomes involved in a workers' demonstration against the government and sacrifices herself by stopping a bullet intended for the chief of the demonstrators. Lola's last request, that the people drape her dead body with a red flag, is ignored because the crowd needs the flag for its demonstration.

Olesha has loaded his play with enough antiwestern material to leave no real doubt of its ideological intent, and the play seems to justify the Soviet Union's contemporary isolationist policy in reaction to an anti-Soviet conspiracy of western capitalist forces. Lola Goncharova is a martyr to socialism, and the real point of Olesha's play is that it is not the Party hacks who are the true patriots, but rather those who, recognizing the faults of the Soviet Union, nonetheless love the country.

This last point is made through a calculus of "assets and liabilities" that Lola keeps, which plays an important role in the plot and from which the play's title derives. This list represents the fundamental ambiguity of her loyalty, since the Russian émigré forces who compromise her suppress the list she has made of the Soviet Union's assets and publish only the liabilities. The true patriot will recognize both assets and liabilities, the author seems to say.

Two other typical subjects are incorporated in the play. The first is that of *Hamlet,* a play that Goncharova performed with great success in the Soviet Union just before her departure for the West. She questions whether she will ever be permitted to play the role of Hamlet again in the Soviet Union, not foreseeing that it is in the West that she will be barred from playing it, where she is to turn it into a lewd spectacle. It is true that, a woman, she insists on playing the part of Hamlet—a male part—herself; this notion seems to derive from Olesha's conception of the stage and of the power of technique and acting to create an illusion independent of reality.

The second reference Olesha has incorporated into this play is that of Charlie Chaplin. Chaplin was a favorite actor of Olesha's, and the figure of Ivan Babichev with his bowler hat is to some extent modeled on Chaplin. Olesha seems to be implying that Chaplin, a universal artist, could appeal to both East and West and that artistic appreciation could thus transcend political boundaries. No doubt Olesha was aware that Chaplin himself was a leftist in politics. Chaplin does not actually appear in the play, but his presence is strongly felt: he is mentioned several times, and the fifth scene of the play ends with a comic interlude in which a Chaplinesque figure appears, eating splinters of wood with relish and pretending it is soup.

ROMANCE FOR CHILDREN: THE THREE FAT MEN

As with *Envy,* Olesha's work on this fairy-tale romance seems to have begun in the early 1920's. Apparently the work was finished as early as 1924, but it was published only in 1928, after the success of *Envy* had gained Olesha fame with the reading public.

It would be easy to pass off this work as mere children's literature, but *The Three Fat Men* has achieved the sure status of a classic in

Soviet literature. It has been adapted in two stage versions (the first of which was made by Olesha with Stanislavski), a ballet, an opera, a radio play, and two film versions, one live and one animated. It has gained success in many translated versions. Finally, although it is unquestionably a work of children's literature, *The Three Fat Men,* like many such works, has gained the status of a classic with adult readers as well. It is noteworthy that Soviet critics invariably bring it up in any discussion of Olesha's work, however brief, perhaps because they once felt a tie to it as children or perhaps because it has achieved a unique status as a work of fiction that portrays the revolution for children.

The Three Fat Men represents an attempt to allegorize the Russian Revolution in fairy-tale form. This was an original conception, no doubt, and one that ran considerable risk. One risk was the obvious danger of ideological heresy, which Olesha tried to avoid by largely avoiding ideology itself. Another was the danger of trivializing the revolution, a danger the author did not entirely escape. Ultimately the charm and whimsy of the work made *The Three Fat Men* appealing, but literalistic Soviet critics did not hesitate to attack it and try to show its ideological shortcomings—for instance, only one of the many revolutionaries in Olesha's fairy tale is of proletarian origin.

The generic classification of Olesha's work has caused much trouble, and there has been no proper resolution. In Russian the work is commonly called a *skazka,* a word usually translated as "fairy tale" despite the fact that Russian folktales do not contain fairies in the western European sense of the term. The work is also sometimes called a "magic tale" (in Russian, *volshebnaya skazka*), but Olesha's novel contains no magic either, except for a doll that grows but whose growth is apparently due to scientific causes.

Opening his fairy tale, Olesha writes: "The time of enchanters is past. In all probability they never existed, in fact. All that is fabrica-

tions and fairy tales for the tiniest of children. It's just that some tricksters were clever and could outwit the idlers; those tricksters were taken for magicians and enchanters." Just as Olesha undercuts the role of the hero in *Envy,* so he writes a "fairy tale" in which the role of enchanter is undercut. For magic he substitutes science and technology: Dr. Gaspar Arneri is his chief scientist, a figure worthy of E. T. A. Hoffmann except that he practices no magic. He is aided by a series of circus performers—Olesha was a passionate circus devotee—but their presence in the story is also motivated by their devotion to technical skill. On the whole, we are presented with a typical Oleshan realized metaphor: magic represents a high degree of technical skill.

Olesha's fairy-tale world is ruled by clearly symbolic figures—three fat men, monopolistic capitalists who control all the grain, coal, and iron. Although they rule, they never act or decide anything, and their collective rule as a triumvirate is also intended to make them comic, no doubt. Their fatness is certainly symbolic, and we can associate it with the fatness of the two Babichev brothers in *Envy:* fatness was a common symbol of capitalism in Soviet literary and film typology of the 1920's.

The revolutionary poor of the land have rebelled, led by the smith Prospero and the tightrope walker Tibul, but their uprising is premature and is quickly crushed. Prospero is taken prisoner, but Tibul escapes. Dr. Arnari finds him and transforms him with an ointment into a black man. The dancer Suok (this was the family name of Olesha's wife) is persuaded to play the role of the magic doll of Prince Tutti, the Fat Men's adopted heir; thus gaining admission to the palace, she is able to free the imprisoned Prospero. The forces of the revolution have now gained sufficient strength, the army is won over, the Fat Men are apprehended, and the people celebrate their new freedom. In the epilogue, set a year later on the anniversary of liberation, it is revealed that Suok and Prince Tutti are actually brother and sister. Thus, in a metaphorical analogy, just as Suok had taken the place of a mechanical doll, so Prince Tutti has been transformed through the revolution from a self-centered, selfish, and capricious child into a free human spirit.

The Three Fat Men is ultimately a failure, for it fails to coalesce as a unified fairy tale. Granted, it has some success as a new, "modern" fairy tale, and its author deserves credit for his brashness in winning the status of a classic for his innovative work, written in the difficult times of early postrevolutionary controversy as to what Marxist literature should be and what it should accomplish. (We have seen that a strictly Marxist view would, on balance, have to deal rather harshly with Olesha's story.) But a more conventional approach would hardly give it a much higher appraisal. Although his work is very much in the same genre, Olesha largely fails to create imaginative symbols that capture the reader's fancy, such as Hoffmann's animated doll Coppélia or Maurice Maeterlinck's Blue Bird.

Why then has *The Three Fat Men* been so popular, and why has it succeeded in capturing attention in so many artistic forms? The tale itself is notable for its style—precise and relatively concise, elegant, and well turned if rarely eloquent or very expressive. Its real heroes are children and thus attract the fancy of a young audience. The use of circus performers was also fresh in a time when the art of the circus was taken seriously by symbolist and futurist poets. Circus performers lend strength to the stage and film adaptations of the tale, for even when they are not performing, their movements still express their artistic training and discipline. Finally, successful modern fairy tales are rare, and if Olesha failed to create a totally integrated modern specimen of the genre, he did demonstrate the correct quality of fantasy and whimsy required by the form. Furthermore, in substituting science for traditional magic (according to Sir James Frazer's well-known evolutionary formula), he was apparently trying to create a modern myth.

LATE AND UNFINISHED WRITINGS

After 1931 both the quality and frequency of Olesha's publication decreased rapidly. In this period he turned to writing film scripts, and he seems to have been involved in this work almost continuously from the early 1930's until his death in 1960. Curiously, little or nothing of his film work seems to have survived for the public, and the question must be asked whether he was not kept working largely as a form of philanthropic support, a practice not unknown in Soviet society for those who had protection. His most important film, entitled *Strogi yunosha* (*A Strict Youth*), depicts a disciplined young Communist's conflict between party morale and the sentiment of love. The film was completed in 1936, but it was never released, probably because ideologically it deals with problems of the 1920's that were simply suppressed under the new family-centered morality of the Stalinist 1930's.

During the early 1930's Olesha worked on a major dramatic project, a play entitled "The Death of Zand," and although it may have been completed by the author, only several fragments have been published. The character of Zand, a "fellow traveler," seems to have been an alter ego of Olesha himself. (Fellow travelers, as Leon Trotsky nicknamed them in 1923, were writers who sympathized with the goals of the revolution and with socialism, but who were not party members and hence were not subject to party discipline. Zand is, like Olesha, a typical intellectual whose actions are often tentative, constrained by cultural and intellectual considerations. Zand envies the great writers of the past but realizes that such envy is futile. Confronted with the writer's futility within a totalitarian order, he wavers between suicide and killing someone else; at the same time he projects a play about murder. (We should note that both Olesha's published plays involve murder.)

Olesha's later reminiscences have been mentioned above. Besides these, only a small cycle of war-time sketches from his late period is worthy of mention. Olesha's later writing is stylistically as strong as ever, dominated as it is by an exceptional precision and clarity. But it lacks the artifice of the younger writer's style as well as the brilliant imagery, and if it is free from mannerisms it is also largely without excitement.

"Turkmen" ("The Turkoman," 1948) is the sole legacy of Olesha's war-time stay in Turkmenistan. It describes how the news of a young soldier's death in the war arrives at his collective farm, and the effect it has on the soldier's mother and brother. "Ivolga" ("The Oriole," 1947) tells of the death of a young partisan among his comrades, who are joined by a young girl and an old man. The soldier dies recognizing the call of the oriole, a bird that the young girl could not identify (this motif links the story to Olesha's earlier "Cherry Stone"). "Vospominanie" ("A Recollection," 1947) describes how a trainful of passengers celebrate the news of victory in the war as they cross the steppes of Central Asia. A little girl and her sleeping mother, who do not realize what is going on, are the center of the narrative. This device represents a kind of *ostranenie* (defamiliarization) of the event, a literary strategy advocated by Olesha's friend, the theoretician Viktor Shklovski.

All these stories focus on children and a child's point of view, as if Olesha was trying to find a fresh approach to the depiction of the world around him. Unfortunately, however, he did not go far enough in this new and creative literary bent.

MEMOIRS: NO DAY WITHOUT A LINE

I have chosen the word "memoirs" as the least misleading term for this final, remarkable work by Olesha, but it is only partly appropriate. The book is a series of short, extremely concise pieces, many of which are short essays; others are examples of literary and artistic criticism.

Olesha conceived of such a collection as early as 1934. The title translates the Latin maxim of Pliny, "Nulla dies sine linea." His intention, no doubt, was to prod his flagging spirit, but in retrospect the title seems more an ironic self-reproach for the wasted years of his long final period. At this time Olesha was reacting to the hard critical line that was being imposed on him, and even more, one must suppose, to a sense that the years had bypassed him. A creature of the proletarian revolution and the New Economic Policy of the 1920's, Olesha could hardly adjust to the new, reactionary era of Stalin's Russia that began in the 1930's. His impassioned self-defense at the First Congress of Soviet Writers in 1934 could only be turned against him and read as a clear statement of his opposition to the Stalinist wave. The wonder is that he survived the time of the purges (one explanation is the fact that his few writings of this final period contain obsequious and flattering statements about the party and the government).

Not until Olesha's rehabilitation in the 1950's did he occupy himself seriously with work on the projected collection. Apparently he left assorted variants of some passages, and the entire mass of material was uncompleted at his death in 1960. Accounts differ: either there was no plan for the completed work or there were too many plans. The task of organizing the material fell to the writer's widow, Olga Suok, and to his friend Shklovski, the critic and literary theoretician, who worked with several younger literary scholars to develop a plan for the final work. In general the principle of chronological order was followed by the editors, at least for the major sections of the work. *No Day Without a Line* was published posthumously in 1961.

The work reveals two decidedly new and striking aspects in Olesha's writing: a pronounced aestheticism that controls decisions concerning what to include or not include in the work; and a lack of a political or social point of view, despite the fact that such a point of view was almost compulsory in the Soviet Union.

Aestheticism as such is no doubt new, but it had always seemed to be threatening to break out in Olesha's writing; in stories such as "The Cherry Stone," "Love," and "Aldebaran," and in *The Three Fat Men* the aesthetic principle is very strong. His fascination with the circus was clearly aesthetic, and his love for sports is of the same sort: sport embodies human movement without practical purpose, but movement controlled by form. Finally, through repeated comparisons of his own work to that of Marcel Proust, he seems to have arrived at the notion that the past recollected in tranquility would produce an aesthetic effect.

It is the last principle that yields the best results in Olesha's book, in the recollections of his childhood. These are fresh, still vivid, and frequently poignant. Olesha plays on the contrasts between the child's naive view and the adult narrator's sophisticated one. For example the child, still unable to read, is presented with a volume of Pushkin. The child can describe the volume given him, but what it contains—"a poet, verses, a work of literature, a writer, a duel, death"—the child does not know; nor could he understand if he did.

The absence of the political and social point of view becomes obvious as the child grows up and grows into history. World War I, the revolution, and the civil war are mentioned without any of the customary Soviet political glosses. Even the mutiny on the battleship *Potemkin*, which occurred in the harbor of Odessa, Olesha's hometown, is mentioned without political comment.

As time moves on and the boy grows up, the burden of aestheticism passes from recollection to the cult of art, and Olesha the writer turns into Olesha the reviewer. At this point the reader may have an uneasy sense that the writer has disappeared, and indeed to read through the book is to experience a tragedy of personal loss; a creative spirit seems to have vanished from the stage. Still, Olesha's artistic career is not the only larger context into which

these materials can be fitted. We must remember that Olesha had been one of the most Western-oriented writers of Soviet Russia. The isolation of Stalinist Russia created a situation in which very few individuals were left who could serve their compatriots as cultural missionaries, and Olesha was one of those few. Together with Ilya Ehrenburg's memoirs, *People and Life* (1960–1961), Olesha's played a great role in bringing an awareness of western literature and art to Soviet readers of the postwar period.

In *No Day Without a Line* Olesha has left us an apology for his life, as well as a commentary on his art and the art of many others and an apology for those tormented years of silence under Stalin. We must be grateful that the discipline implied in his title never wholly deserted him.

CONCLUSION

What is Olesha's place in world literature? To answer this question we must first consider his place in Soviet literature. In Soviet literature, as we have noted, Olesha is one of the most western-oriented of writers. This is not so much a question of ideology in his case, for in that he shows considerable vacillation and ambivalence. It is rather a question of literary style, ambience, and texture.

The 1920's were an ambivalent period in this respect in Soviet literature. To the strongly Russian influences of Tolstoy, Dostoevsky, or Gorky, marked by a rather heavy if powerful style, strong emotionality, and vivid characterization, certain writers and critics of the 1920's opposed a variety of western influences; viewed in hindsight they now seem to have been engaged in a systematic westernization of Russian literature. Isaac Babel''s Cossack stories had a typically "Russian" manner and "Russian" characters, but the style was something new, recalling the precise, concise, understated manner of Guy de Maupassant. The Russian formalist critic, Shklovski, an admirer of Lawrence Sterne, sought to make fiction not a vehicle for ideological expression as it had typically been for Soviet readers, but a game in which ideas and characters were no more sacrosanct than images or other devices. Shklovski was a member of the Serapion Brotherhood, a group of writers to whom Olesha was very close, although he came on the Moscow scene too late to join them. The Serapions had preached freedom and variety in literature, slogans that under the conditions of the times, were virtually code words for western influence. The Russian futurist poets, influenced by Marinetti and Italian futurism, promoted another brand of westernism. All this experimentation flourished under the aegis of internationalism; the idea that the revolution was somehow strictly a Russian or even a Russian-led phenomenon had yet to come.

When it finally did come under Stalin during the first Five Year Plan and in the 1930's, it was to play havoc, of course, with freedom of experimentation and western influence. Olesha's play *A List of Assets,* in which an interesting ideological problem is posed but resolved in an uninteresting and stereotypical "Russian" way, is one effect of this change.

Yet Shklovski's influence had one important effect on Olesha's writing: more than any other Russian writer of the 1920's, Olesha gave embodiment to Shklovski's leading concept of "making strange," or "defamiliarization" (*ostranenie*), as it has come to be called in English. Shklovski argued that literature is essentially a set of devices, a kind of strategic attack on imagery through the medium of language. Literature deforms reality, which it depicts, but that very deformed reality becomes interesting to us and attracts our attention precisely because it is deformed. Were it merely everyday reality, to which we have become immune because of everyday contact, we could ignore it. In its distorted, deformed aspect, reality is presented with a new face by literature. Shklovski likened such literature to a traveler who perceives a landscape through colored spectacles; these lend reality a new appeal to which we can re-

spond with a new, fresh vision. Defamiliarization is indeed a prime principle in Olesha's use of imagery. Shuvalov's revived view of the world in the story "Love" is a case in point, as is the "rubber boy's" fresh, wordless contact with reality. And surprisingly, these fresh, spontaneous images of Olesha's have survived until now without any diminution of their brilliance.

The literary experiments of the 1920's yielded, however, to the hack Stalinist writing of the 1930's, a stagnant time that persisted some twenty-five years. When the thaw came in Soviet literature after Stalin's death in 1953, Russians sought to reestablish a new literary culture based on pre-Stalinist writing. For this project the 1920's proved the most fruitful point of departure, and Babel' and Olesha perhaps the two most productive sources of inspiration. The modernism of the West was too far advanced, no doubt, and the Russians had too far to catch up in their lag; besides, it was desirable to find a stalk that was "Russian," not western, on which to graft the new writing. From our point of view we may consider Soviet writing of the 1920's, and in particular such writers as Zamyatin, Babel', or Olesha, a special Russian brand of modernism. And this is the way Russians today consider them.

These and other facts may well lead many readers to the conclusion that Olesha is predominantly a writer of manner, not of matter. Yet in *Envy,* his first book, he achieved a balance, if a precarious one, between the two. In that work, as in "The Cherry Stone," he ventured to seize the utopian theme, one of the great themes of literature. True, he had tinged it, as have so many writers, with its opposite, dystopian hue: utopia was not to constitute an unmixed blessing for the human species.

What seems certain is that the writing of Zamyatin, Babel', and Olesha, along with other writers of the 1920's, is powerfully rooted in the principle of undercutting: whatever these writers may *seem* to be (both Babel' and Olesha seem superficially to be Soviet writers supporting Soviet reality and Soviet progress), they are anti-ideological. This does not mean that they oppose Soviet society or Soviet socialism—the major mistake in interpretation that has been made in the West. It means that they do not consider literature to tell a truth that must be interpreted as *ideological* truth. In this respect it must be noted that they are both anti-psychological writers, although the Russian reading public normally regarded literature as a vehicle of psychological expression. In the same way they do not claim or wish to be purveyors of social or political truth.

Olesha's private mythology seems to have focused very largely on a new kind of heroism: that of aviators, circus performers, and sports heroes. These are heroes of deeds, it is clear; the heroism of words is no true heroism for Olesha, and he consistently undercuts it in his writing. For example, Kavalerov's vow to kill Andrey Babichev is meaningless, while Lola Goncharova's resolve to return to the Soviet Union is likewise false and is made true largely in irony. Similarly, Volodya Makarov's resolve to turn himself into a machine is pure rhetoric and therefore comic, but his soccer playing is heroic.

This preoccupation with circus and sports heroes was something new in Soviet literature, and something that could obviously be regarded as modern, as part of a twentieth-century world. It took its inspiration from the futurist poetry of Marinetti and Mayakovski; it found parallels in artistic expressionism, and in the ballets of Stravinski and Eric Satie. But Olesha seems to have believed rather naively that it would be a simple thing to transfer to the printed page the excitement he felt as a spectator of the circus or the sports arena. Nor was the analogy of heroism necessarily true: it did not follow that Volodya Makarov was a hero in the construction of socialism (in which he does nothing, in fact) merely because he played well in the soccer game against the Germans. Even the proposition that his playing with the Soviet team is a new, collective form of play is not quite true, since Volodya is a goalkeeper, a particularly independent position. Similarly, Tibul and the other members of the circus are not heroic revolutionaries by virtue of the fact that they are heroic circus performers.

When we look back at Olesha's characters, it is the negative ones, of course, that we remember, and even with some affection. For them Olesha found a very special device, the verbal pose, the lie. This is the counterfeit of heroism and is used to buy time for them; ultimately it must be exposed, of course, and then the character is deflated like a balloon. But to an extent the illusion is renewable, as with Ivan Babichev, who has told lies his whole lifetime and yet has never quite ceased to be the menace his words threaten to make him. Kavalerov is less successful in maintaining his pose, perhaps because he is more like a flesh-and-blood human, perhaps because he has his roots as a literary character in Dostoevsky's Underground Man, and we therefore soon perceive that he is self-denying and self-contradictory.

The stories also give us characters of another type who, since they are less epic and more lyrical, need not be compared to real life figures. Shuvalov in "Love" is a rare, perhaps unique, example of a synthesis of the ideological hero with the hero of language, and he is triumphant at the end of the story. And Fedya, the writer of "The Cherry Stone," is a rare example of a negative hero who achieves a positive goal: he is true to himself as an artist. These two stories, along with "Liompa," are the pinnacle of Olesha's art.

But there is another group of stories, those that reach back in memory and retrieve the past. These stories, together with *No Day Without a Line,* have probably been underrated, perhaps because in them Olesha achieved only brief and fragmentary views of the past—incisive ones, no doubt, but lacking narrative structure. But it is not inconceivable that Olesha's future reputation, at least for his Soviet readers, will depend chiefly on the sense of nostalgia that he imparts for the prerevolutionary period.

For us, however, Olesha's greatest strength remains his fresh, crisp use of imagery, embodied in his laconic, forthright, almost brusque but still flowing style. No other writer could imitate it, it would seem, and certainly none has. It is the immutable trademark of a truly revolutionary artist.

Selected Bibliography

EDITIONS

FIRST EDITIONS

Zavist'. Krasnaya nov' 7:64–101 (1927); 8:3–46 (1927).

Tri tolstyaka. Moscow-Leningrad, 1928.

Lyubov'. Moscow, 1929.

Zagovor chuvstv. Oktyabr' 1:33–50 (1929).

Spisok blagodeyanii. Berlin-Charlottenburg, 1931.

Zapiski pisatelya. Moscow, 1931.

Ni dnya bez strochki. Oktyabr' 7:147–169 (1961); 8:135–156 (1961).

COLLECTED EDITIONS

Izbrannye sochineniia. Introduction by V. Pertsov. Moscow, 1956.

Povesti i rasskazy. Introduction by B. Galanev. Moscow, 1965.

P'esy. Introduction by P. Markev. Moscow, 1968.

TRANSLATIONS

The Complete Plays. Edited and translated by Michael Greer and Jerome Katsell. Ann Arbor, Mich., 1983.

Complete Short Stories and The Three Fat Men. Translated by Aimee Anderson. Ann Arbor, Mich., 1979.

Envy. Translated by Anthony Wolfe. London, 1936.

Envy. Translated by P. Ross. London, 1947.

Envy and Other Works. Translated by Andrew R. MacAndrew. New York and London, 1967.

"A List of Benefits." Translated by Andrew R. MacAndrew. In *Twentieth Century Russian Drama.* New York, 1963.

Love and Other Stories. Translated by Robert Payne. New York, 1967.

No Day Without a Line. Translated with an introduction by Judson Rosengrant. Ann Arbor, Mich., 1979.

BIOGRAPHICAL AND CRITICAL STUDIES

Beaujour, Elizabeth. *The Invisible Land: A Study of the Artistic Imagination of Iurii Olesha.* New York and London, 1970.

Chudakova, M. *Masterstvo Yuriya Oleshi.* Moscow, 1972.

Harkins, William E. "The Philosophical Tales of Jurij Oleša." In *Orbis Scriptus: Dmitrij Tschiževskij zum 70. Geburtstag.* Edited by Dietrich Gerhardt et al. Munich, 1966.

———. "The Theme of Sterility in Olesha's *Envy.*" In *Major Soviet Writers: Essays in Criticism.* Edited by Edward J. Brown. London, Oxford, and New York, 1973.

———. "*No Day Without a Line:* The World of Iurii Olesha." In *Russian Literature and American Critics.* Edited by Kenneth N. Brostrom. Ann Arbor, Mich., 1984.

Ingdahl, Kazimiera. *The Artist and the Creative Act. Acta Universitatis Stockholmiensis: Stockholm Studies in Russian Literature* 17 (1984).

Nilsson, Nils Ake. "Through the Wrong End of Binoculars." In *Major Soviet Writers: Essays in Criticism.* Edited by Edward J. Brown. London, 1973.

Pertsov, V. *My zhivem vpervye: O tvorchestve Yuriya Oleshi.* Moscow, 1976.

Vospominaniya o Yurii Oleshe. Suok-Olesha, O., and E. Pel'sen, eds. Moscow, 1975.

"Yuri Karlevich Olesha." *Sovetskie pisateli: autobiografii.* Vol. 3. Moscow, 1966.

WILLIAM E. HARKINS